EVIDENCE LAW AND PRACTICE
Fifth Edition

LEXISNEXIS LAW SCHOOL ADVISORY BOARD

William Araiza
Professor of Law
Brooklyn Law School

Ruth Colker
Distinguished University Professor & Heck-Faust Memorial Chair in Constitutional Law
Ohio State University, Moritz College of Law

Olympia Duhart
Associate Professor of Law
Nova Southeastern University, Shepard Broad Law School

Samuel Estreicher
Dwight D. Opperman Professor of Law
Director, Center for Labor and Employment Law
NYU School of Law

David Gamage
Assistant Professor of Law
UC Berkeley School of Law

Joan Heminway
College of Law Distinguished Professor of Law
University of Tennessee College of Law

Edward Imwinkelried
Edward L. Barrett, Jr. Professor of Law
UC Davis School of Law

Paul Marcus
Haynes Professor of Law
William and Mary Law School

Melissa Weresh
Director of Legal Writing and Professor of Law
Drake University Law School

EVIDENCE LAW AND PRACTICE

Fifth Edition

Steven I. Friedland
Professor of Law
Elon University School of Law

Paul Bergman
Professor of Law Emeritus
U.C.L.A. School of Law

Andrew E. Taslitz
Professor of Law
Howard University School of Law

ISBN: 978-0-7698-4900-3 (casebook)
ISBN: 978-0-7698-4901-0 (looseleaf)

Library of Congress Cataloging-in-Publication Data

Friedland, Steven I.
  Evidence law and practice / Steven I. Friedland, Paul Bergman, Andrew E. Taslitz. -- 5th ed.
    p. cm.
  Includes index.
  ISBN 978-0-7698-4900-3
  1. Evidence (Law)--United States. 2. Evidence (Law)--United States--Problems, exercises, etc. I. Bergman, Paul, 1943- II. Taslitz, Andrew E., 1956- III. Title.
    KF8935.Z9F747 2012
    347.73'6--dc23

2012017112

This publication is designed to provide authoritative information in regard to the subject matter covered. It is sold with the understanding that the publisher is not engaged in rendering legal, accounting, or other professional services. If legal advice or other expert assistance is required, the services of a competent professional should be sought.

LexisNexis and the Knowledge Burst logo are registered trademarks of Reed Elsevier Properties Inc., used under license. Matthew Bender and the Matthew Bender Flame Design are registered trademarks of Matthew Bender Properties Inc.

Copyright © 2012 Matthew Bender & Company, Inc., a member of LexisNexis. All Rights Reserved.

No copyright is claimed by LexisNexis or Matthew Bender & Company, Inc., in the text of statutes, regulations, and excerpts from court opinions quoted within this work. Permission to copy material may be licensed for a fee from the Copyright Clearance Center, 222 Rosewood Drive, Danvers, Mass. 01923, telephone (978) 750-8400.

NOTE TO USERS

To ensure that you are using the latest materials available in this area, please be sure to periodically check the LexisNexis Law School web site for downloadable updates and supplements at www.lexisnexis.com/lawschool.

Editorial Offices
121 Chanlon Rd., New Providence, NJ 07974 (908) 464-6800
201 Mission St., San Francisco, CA 94105-1831 (415) 908-3200
www.lexisnexis.com

MATTHEW♦BENDER

PREFACE

The Fifth Edition of Evidence Law and Practice was prompted in large part by the restyling of the Federal Rules of Evidence. The stylistic changes, which went into effect on December 1st, 2011, were intended to simplify the rules and improve their form without changing their substance. Time of course will tell whether the rules are indeed more user-friendly -- although we can declare right now we will not miss the use of the word "admissions," for example, to describe the admissibility of party-opponent statements in Article VIII, Hearsay. Whether the revisions work or not, it was imperative to incorporate these newer rules into the book.

In our continuing effort to produce a book that satisfies the teaching and learning needs of both instructors and students, we also used this opportunity to update and tweak the entire text to enhance its transparency. We updated and added problems, both to provide additional classroom options and to maintain currency with existing law. Some of the changes we made were in response to feedback we have received from instructor and student users of the book. We encourage all who use our book to continue to suggest any means of improving it.

This new edition incorporates the most recent United States Supreme Court Confrontation Clause decisions since the publication of the Fourth Edition, including *Michigan v. Bryant*, __ U.S. __ (2011). Confrontation Clause doctrine continues to unfold and we plan to use the publisher's website devoted to this textbook to keep users apprised of subsequent developments.

Also, we have been able to follow-up on prior rule changes, such as the amendment to Rule 804(b)(3) and the addition of Rule 502. The privileges chapter has been amended to reflect the complexities of amended Rule 501.

Last but not least, thank you to our readers, law faculty and students alike. Our goal as always is to produce a text that facilitates learning and stimulates interest in the topic of evidence by examining the rules from both scholarly and practical perspectives.

Paul Bergman thanks his wife Andrea for her emotional support and constructive feedback and the UCLA School of Law Dean's Fund for providing financial support. Steve and Andy, and Leslie Levin at Lexis, thanks for your positive attitudes and cooperative spirits, it's been my great pleasure to work with you. Jeanne Fontenot and Claire Schwartz, thank you for helping with photo still permissions. A belated thank you to Mozart for providing the music I often listened to while working on the book.

Steve Friedland thanks his wife, Jennifer Sadock, for her perspective and good energy, and children, Adin and Tylie, for making him laugh. He thanks research assistants Hasina Lewis and Susanna Guffy for their consistent willingness to help out and their quality work. Last, but not least, he extends his appreciation to coauthors Paul Bergman and Andy Taslitz, who provided the spark, enthusiasm and internal combustion to make this project both fun and productive.

Professor Taslitz thanks his wife, Patricia V. Sun, Esq., and Professor Robert P. Mosteller for their helpful feedback on drafts of several of this book's chapters. He also thanks his research assistants, Carla Bedrosian and Sylvia Irvin, for their outstanding efforts; Mrs. Delphyne Bruner, Mrs. Allison Green, Ms. Carolyn Minor, and Ms. Chantell Randall for their superb secretarial help; and the Howard University School of Law for its financial

PREFACE

support of this project. A special thanks to Howard "Jerry McGuire" Katz, who knows why. Most of all, Professor Taslitz thanks his co-authors for the opportunity to grow together as teachers, while exchanging new ideas and perspectives and building two new friendships. This project has been an awful lot of fun.

Finally, in a book of this nature, meant primarily for classroom use in teaching, and facing the need to limit space, it is impossible for the authors to thank and cite all of the many evidence scholars whose insights on law and teaching helped to inform our efforts here. To all those unnamed colleagues whose work has helped us, and, in particular, to Professors David Faigman, Edward J. Imwinkelried, David Leonard, Roger Park, and Christopher Slobogin, all three authors of this work say "thank you."

Table of Contents

Chapter 1	**INTRODUCTION TO EVIDENCE**	1
§ 1.01	CHAPTER CHECKLIST	1
§ 1.02	RELEVANT FEDERAL RULES OF EVIDENCE	1
§ 1.03	LAWSUITS AND RULES OF EVIDENCE	1
§ 1.04	THE DIFFERENT MEANINGS OF "EVIDENCE"	3
	Problem 1-1: Prove It	4
	Problem 1-2: Inspector Clousseau	5
§ 1.05	CATEGORIES OF EVIDENCE: REAL; REPRESENTATIVE; AND TESTIMONIAL EVIDENCE	6
	Problem 1-3: Clousseau Revisited	6
§ 1.06	ANOTHER HELPFUL DISTINCTION — DIRECT OR CIRCUMSTANTIAL EVIDENCE	6
	Problem 1-4: Drawing Inferences in the Sand	7
§ 1.07	EVIDENCE IN THE TRIAL COURTS	7
	United States v. Wayne Gillis	8
§ 1.08	A JURY OF HER PEERS	12
	Problem 1-5: A Jury of Her Peers	12
§ 1.09	CHAPTER REVIEW PROBLEMS	27
	Review Problem 1-A	27
	Review Problem 1-B	28
Chapter 2	**THE ROLES OF JUDGES, JURIES, AND ATTORNEYS AT TRIAL**	29
§ 2.01	CHAPTER CHECKLIST	29
§ 2.02	RELEVANT FEDERAL RULES OF EVIDENCE	29
§ 2.03	INTRODUCTION	30
§ 2.04	THE TRIAL JUDGE'S ROLE	30
[A]	Questions of Admissibility	32
	Problem 2-1: Alimony Al	34
[B]	Appellate Judges: The Standard of Review on Appeal	36
	Problem 2-2: "Justice was Done, so Appeal Immediately"	36
§ 2.05	THE JURY'S ROLE	37
§ 2.06	THE ATTORNEY'S ROLE	38
	Problem 2-3: My Cousin, the Lawyer, Vinnie	41
§ 2.07	SUMMARY AND REVIEW	42
§ 2.08	CHAPTER REVIEW PROBLEMS	42
	Review Problem 2-A	42
	Review Problem 2-B	42

TABLE OF CONTENTS

	Review Problem 2-C	43
Chapter 3	**RELEVANCE**	**45**
§ 3.01	CHAPTER CHECKLIST	45
§ 3.02	RELEVANT FEDERAL RULES OF EVIDENCE	45
§ 3.03	THE IMPORTANCE OF RELEVANCE	46
§ 3.04	DEFINING RELEVANCE	46
	Problem 3-1: Judge Judy	50
	Problem 3-2: Bermuda Love Triangle	50
	Problem 3-3: Missing	51
	Problem 3-4: Eddie From Boston	51
	Problem 3-5: The Reel Thing	52
	Problem 3-6: "Beam Me Up . . ."	52
	Problem 3-7: Fire! (a.k.a. Burning Down the House)	52
	Problem 3-8: I Wuz Robbed!	53
	Problem 3-9: Benny and Jets	53
	Problem 3-10: Ahnald	53
	Problem 3-11: Ahnald's Younger Brother	54
	Problem 3-12: Sexual Battery	54
	Problem 3-13: The Commuter	54
	Problem 3-14: A Bottle of Red	56
	Problem 3-15: "Name Your Price"	56
	Problem 3-16: Too Rough Justice	56
	Problem 3-17: "Lions and Tigers and . . ."	56
	Problem 3-18: Evidence, Politics, and Race	57
	Problem 3-19: Exploding Tire	58
	Problem 3-20: Parnell v. Asbestos, Inc.	58
	Problem 3-21: Blowing Smoke	58
§ 3.05	CONDITIONAL RELEVANCE	58
	Problem 3-22: On a Cloudy Day	60
	Problem 3-23: Stone Crabs	60
	Problem 3-24: Defective Paint	60
	Problem 3-25: An Accident?	60
	Problem 3-26: Joe C. Boss	62
§ 3.06	COMPARING RULES	62
§ 3.07	SUMMARY AND REVIEW	62
§ 3.08	CHAPTER REVIEW PROBLEMS	63
	Review Problem 3-A: The Swallower	63
	Review Problem 3-B	63
	Review Problem 3-C	64
§ 3.09	CASE LIBRARY — KNAPP V. STATE	64

TABLE OF CONTENTS

    Knapp v. State 64

Chapter 4	**RELEVANT BUT INADMISSIBLE — UNFAIRLY PREJUDICIAL EVIDENCE** **67**
§ 4.01	CHAPTER CHECKLIST 67
§ 4.02	RELEVANT FEDERAL RULES OF EVIDENCE 67
§ 4.03	INTRODUCTION 68
	Problem 4-1: "One Drink Too Many" 70
	Problem 4-2: A Day in the Life of Susan White 70
	Problem 4-3: In a New York State of Mind 71
§ 4.04	PROBABILITY EVIDENCE OF IDENTITY IN A CRIMINAL CASE .. 72
	Problem 4-4: Chances Are 72
§ 4.05	EVIDENCE OF EXCESSIVE VIOLENCE 72
	Problem 4-5: Lose Your Lunch 72
	Problem 4-6: Legs 73
§ 4.06	SCIENTIFIC EVIDENCE 73
	Problem 4-7: Videotape Replay 76
	Problem 4-8: To Tell the Truth 76
§ 4.07	SIMILAR OCCURENCES, HAPPENINGS, AND EVENTS 76
	Problem 4-9: Slipped Up 78
	Problem 4-10: Spoiled Shrimp 78
	Problem 4-11: Double Decker 78
	Problem 4-12: Sugar or Sweetener? 78
	Problem 4-13: Harassment 78
	Problem 4-14: Unfair Prejudice 79
	Problem 4-15: People v. Penny 79
§ 4.08	SUMMARY AND REVIEW 80
§ 4.09	CHAPTER REVIEW PROBLEMS 80
	Review Problem 4-A 80
	Review Problem 4-B 81
	Review Problem 4-C 81
	Review Problem 4-D 81
§ 4.10	CASE LIBRARY 82
	People v. Collins 82
	Old Chief v. United States 87

Chapter 5	**CHARACTER AND HABIT EVIDENCE** **91**
§ 5.01	CHAPTER CHECKLIST 91
§ 5.02	RELEVANT FEDERAL RULES OF EVIDENCE 92
§ 5.03	CHARACTER EVIDENCE BASICS 97
[A]	Defining "Character Evidence" 97

TABLE OF CONTENTS

	Problem 5-1: The Ogler	101
	Problem 5-2: At the Movies: Insane Anatomy of a Murder	102
[B]	Act Versus Mental Propensity Evidence: The General Rules: Rules 404(a) and 405(b)	102
	Problem 5-3: The Negligent Driver	107
	Problem 5-4: Seduced No More	108
	Problem 5-5: Entrapped!	109
	Problem 5-6: At the Movies: Custody Fight	109
	Problem 5-7: Creativity	110
§ 5.04	FORMS OF CHARACTER EVIDENCE	110
[A]	Admissibility of Reputation, Opinion, and Specific Acts Evidence: Rule 404(b), 1st Sentence, Rule 405(a)–(b)	110
[B]	Problems on the Form of Character Evidence	114
	Problem 5-8: The Warden Cross-Examined	114
	Problem 5-9: Group Therapy	114
	Problem 5-10: The Violent Victim	114
	Problem 5-11: United States v. Lorean	114
	Problem 5-12: Rambo II	115
§ 5.05	LAYING THE FOUNDATION FOR CHARACTER EVIDENCE	115
[A]	Reputation	115
[B]	Opinion	116
	Problem 5-13: Ogling Again	117
	Problem 5-14: More Creativity	117
	Problem 5-15: Negligently Entrusting Redux	117
	Problem 5-16: More United States v. Lorean	117
§ 5.06	EXCEPTIONS TO THE RULE 404(a) PROPENSITY BAN	117
[A]	Admissible Instances of Propensity Evidence	117
[B]	Character of the Accused: Rule 404(a)(2)(A)	118
	Problem 5-17: The Tortious Criminal Assailant	120
	Problem 5-18: The Escaping Hostage	120
	Problem 5-19: Suicidal Homicide	121
	Problem 5-20: At the Movies: Treason	121
[C]	Character of the Victim in Cases Other Than Homicide and Sexual Misconduct: Rule 404(a)(2)(B)	121
	Problem 5-21: Urban War Syndrome	122
	Problem 5-22: The Scarlet Letter	122
	Problem 5-23: False Pretenses	123
[D]	Prosecutor Attack on the Criminal Defendant's Same Character Trait Permitted Once the Defense Has Attacked the Victim on that Trait	123
	Problem 5-26: More Urban War Syndrome	124
	Problem 5-27: What Goes Around Comes Around	124

TABLE OF CONTENTS

	[E]	Character of the Victim in Homicide Cases: Rule 404(a)(2)(C)	125
		Problem 5-24: The Green-Eyed Monster	126
		Problem 5-25: Knife Fights	127
§ 5.07		SEXUAL OFFENSES AND SEXUAL MISCONDUCT: CRIMINAL AND CIVIL	128
	[A]	The Rape Shield Law: Exception to an Exception: Rule 412	128
	[1]	The General Rule: Rule 412(a)	128
		Problem 5-28: At the Movies: Pre-Shield	130
		Problem 5-29: On the Tube: Liar	130
		Problem 5-30: At the Movies: At the Bar	130
		Problem 5-31: At the Movies: Quick Re-Marriage	131
		Problem 5-32: Rhonda's Outrage	131
		Problem 5-33: Stained Reputations	131
		Problem 5-34: Romantic Dreams	131
	[2]	Exceptions in Criminal Cases: Rule 412(b)(1)	132
		Problem 5-35: Satanic Rites	133
		Problem 5-36: Fantasies	133
		Problem 5-37: Toby Wyatt: Adulterer or Rapist?	133
		Problem 5-38: Homage to "To Kill a Mockingbird"	134
	[3]	Exception in Civil Cases: Rule 412(b)(2)	135
		Problem 5-39: Romantic Dreams Redux	137
		Problem 5-40: Sexual Harassment	137
	[4]	Procedure to Determine Admissibility: Rule 412(c)	138
		Problem 5-41	139
	[B]	Character of the Defendant in a Criminal or Civil Sexual Assault or Child Molestation Case: Rule 413, 414, 415	139
		Problem 5-42: Not-Quite Pinched Buttocks	142
		Problem 5-43: S & M	142
§ 5.08		IMPEACHMENT: RULES 404(a)(3), 608, AND 609	142
	[A]	Distinction between Impeachment and Substantive Evidence	142
	[B]	Rule 608 — Impeachment Generally	146
	[1]	Opinion and Reputation: Rule 608(a)	146
		Problem 5-44: Johnny Larsen's Divorce	149
		Problem 5-45: Married Robbers	149
		Problem 5-46: Married Robbers Revisited	149
	[2]	Specific Acts: Rule 608(b)	150
		Problem 5-47: Johnny Larsen's Return	155
		Problem 5-48: The Harassing Politician	155
	[C]	Rule 609-Impeachment by Prior Convictions	156
	[1]	Felony Convictions: Rule 609(a)(1)	156
	[2]	Misdemeanor and *Crimen Falsi* Convictions: Rule 609(a)(2)	159
	[3]	Special Qualifications to Rule 609	162

TABLE OF CONTENTS

	[4]	Extrinsic Evidence	163
	[5]	Eliciting Details of Prior Convictions	163
		Problem 5-49: The Matasow Corporation	163
		Problem 5-50: Johnny Winter's Lament	164
		Problem 5-51: At the Movies: Snitch Attack	165
		Problem 5-52: Forging a Defense	165
§ 5.09		MID-CHAPTER REVIEW	166
	[A]	Schematic	166
	[B]	Synthesizing the Rules Studied Thus Far: The Diagrammatic Approach	171
	[1]	Categorizing Character	171
	[2]	Mini-Review Problems	172
		Problem 5-53: O.J. Mimpson Defamed	172
		Problem 5-54: Wherefore Art Thou, Romeo?	173
		Problem 5-55: The Drunken Suspect	174
§ 5.10		NON-PROPENSITY USES OF CHARACTER EVIDENCE: RULES 401, 404(a), 405(b)	175
		Problem 5-56: The Violent Drunk	176
§ 5.11		THINGS THAT LOOK LIKE ACT PROPENSITY EVIDENCE BUT ARE NOT	177
	[A]	Rule 404(b)-Specific Acts Offered for Non-Character Uses or Mental Propensity Uses	177
	[1]	General Principles and Problems	177
	[a]	Purposes Other Than Character	177
	[b]	Proof of Specific Acts	179
	[c]	Rule 403 Balancing	180
	[d]	Problems	182
		Problem 5-57: Fearing the Navy Seal	182
		Problem 5-58: O.J. Accused	182
	[2]	Motive	182
		Problem 5-59: Illegitimate Prescriptions	186
		Problem 5-60: The Pokemon Gang	186
		Problem 5-61: Infidelity	186
		Problem 5-62: Cocaine and Concealed Currency	186
		Problem 5-63: Attempted Murder, She Wrote	187
	[3]	Opportunity	187
		Problem 5-64: High-Tech Terrorism	187
		Problem 5-65: Oprah Wanafree	187
	[4]	Identity	188
		Problem 5-66: Count Dracula	188
		Problem 5-67: Gambling for Drugs	189
		Problem 5-68: Drug Courier Profile	189

TABLE OF CONTENTS

	[5]	Intent or Knowledge	190
		Problem 5-69: The Mysterious Crib Death	193
		Problem 5-70: The Malicious Prisoner	193
		Problem 5-71: The Confused Bookkeeper	193
		Problem 5-72: Brass Knuckles	193
		Problem 5-73: Duress	193
		Problem 5-74: People v. Chambers	194
	[6]	Common Plan, Scheme, or Design	199
		Problem 5-75: The Comic Book Thief	200
		Problem 5-76: Inheriting by Murder	201
		Problem 5-77: Government Kickbacks	201
		Problem 5-78: Drug Dealers	201
[B]		Habit	201
		Problem 5-79: Stolen Sneakers	205
		Problem 5-80: "The Hurrieder I Go, The Behinder I Get" ..	205
		Problem 5-81: Chivas	205
		Problem 5-82: Don't Do Me Like That	205
§ 5.12		CHARACTER EVIDENCE REVIEW PROBLEMS	205
		Problem 5-83: Orwellian Defamation	205
		Problem 5-84: Perjuring Clergy	206
		Problem 5-85: Perjuring Clergy Revisited	206
		Problem 5-86: Maxwell's Silver Tongue	207
		Problem 5-87: False Cries	207
		Problem 5-88: Reasonable Belief?	207
		Problem 5-89: Mistaken Identification	208
		Problem 5-90: Simply Assaulting	208
		Problem 5-91: Tax Fraud	208
§ 5.13		CASE LIBRARY	209
		Michelson v. United States	209

Chapter 6	**OTHER EXCLUSIONS OF RELEVANT EVIDENCE: THE QUASI-PRIVILEGES** **225**

§ 6.01		CHAPTER CHECKLIST	225
§ 6.02		RELEVANT FEDERAL RULES OF EVIDENCE	226
§ 6.03		OVERVIEW	228
§ 6.04		SUBSEQUENT REMEDIAL MEASURES: RULE 407	228
		Problem 6-1: The Ruptured Bulldozer	231
		Problem 6-2: The Painful Beach Party	232
		Problem 6-3: Rotund University	232
§ 6.05		OFFERS TO COMPROMISE: RULES 408 AND 410	232
[A]		Importance of Compromise in Civil and Criminal Cases	232

TABLE OF CONTENTS

	[B]	Evidence of Civil Settlement Agreements and Negotiations: Rule 408	233
		Problem 6-4: The Car Crash	240
		Problem 6-5: The Non-Settling Defendant	240
		Problem 6-6: The Recalcitrant Health Insurer	240
		Problem 6-7	242
	[C]	Plea Bargains and Related Statements in Criminal Cases: Rule 410	243
		Problem 6-7: Rodney Ransom	247
		Problem 6-8: Turning on Mr. Big	248
		Problem 6-9: Waiving Rule 410	248
§ 6.06		PAYMENT OF MEDICAL AND SIMILAR EXPENSES	249
		Problem 6-10: Med X	250
		Problem 6-11: Kommander Condominium Club	250
§ 6.07		LIABILITY INSURANCE: RULE 411	251
		Problem 6-12: "I Forgot"	252
		Problem 6-13: Go Ahead and Jump	253
		Problem 6-14: Columbo	253
		Problem 6-15: Statutory Interpretation Exercise	253
§ 6.08		REVIEW PROBLEMS: SYNTHESIZING THE QUASI-PRIVILEGES	254
		Problem 6-16: Let's Make a Deal	254
		Problem 6-17: Engulf and Devour	254
		Problem 6-18: Battery	254
		Problem 6-19: Gorkey Park	255
		Problem 6-20: Did I Say That?	255
		Problem 6-21: The Singing Sparrow	256
		Problem 6-22: Rosetta's Orwellian Plight	256
		Problem 6-23: Maxwell's Comeuppance	256
§ 6.09		CASE LIBRARY	257
		United States v. Mezzanatto	257
Chapter 7		**THE EXAMINATION AND IMPEACHMENT OF WITNESSES**	**271**
§ 7.01		CHAPTER CHECKLIST	271
§ 7.02		RELEVANT FEDERAL RULES OF EVIDENCE	271
§ 7.03		EXAMINATION OF WITNESSES	274
	[A]	Overview	274
	[B]	Competency: Who May Testify	275
		Problem 7-1: The Habitual Drug Addict	277
		Problem 7-2: Say What?	277
		Problem 7-3: Dead Again and Again	278
		Problem 7-4: Hypnotized	278
	[C]	Requirement of Personal Knowledge	278

TABLE OF CONTENTS

	Problem 7-5: Robbin the Hood	279
[D]	Competency of Judges and Attorneys as Witnesses (Rule 605)	279
	Problem 7-6: Anyone But You	280
	Problem 7-7: The Deal	280
[E]	Competency of Jurors as Witnesses (Rule 606)	281
	Problem 7-8: At the Movies	283
	Problem 7-9: Stop the Reading!	283
[F]	Sequential Order and Objections to Witness Testimony	284
[G]	Witness Strategy	285
[1]	General Principles	285
[2]	Direct Examination	286
	Problem 7-10: Returning to Form Objections	287
	Problem 7-11: More Form	288
[3]	Cross-Examination	289
	Problem 7-12: Scope	290
	Problem 7-13: Succa Mucca Rucca	291
§ 7.04	IMPEACHMENT OF WITNESSES	291
[A]	Introduction	292
[B]	Comparing Intrinsic and Extrinsic Impeachment	292
[C]	Common Types of Impeachment	293
[1]	Overview	293
	Problem 7-14: Cross My Heart: An Overview	295
[2]	Contradiction	296
	Problem 7-15: Cross.com	296
[3]	Bias	296
	Problem 7-16: The Right Direct-Ion	297
	Problem 7-17: Just Friends	297
	Problem 7-18: Losing Religion	297
[4]	Convictions of Crime	298
[a]	Crimes of Dishonesty or False Statement	298
[b]	Felony Convictions	299
	Problem 7-19: Forgery, Fake, Fraud	300
	Problem 7-20: Medical Mal	300
	Problem 7-21: One Bad Apple	300
[5]	Prior Untruthful Acts	301
	Problem 7-22: Liar, Liar	302
[6]	Testimonial Capacities	303
	Problem 7-23: Psychotic Chips	303
[7]	Prior Inconsistent Statements	304
[8]	Poor Character For Truthfulness — Extrinsic Impeachment Only . . .	305
	Problem 7-24: Truth-o-Meter	306

TABLE OF CONTENTS

		Problem 7-25: Cavalier and Convicted	306
[D]		Two-Way Admissibility of Some Prior Inconsistent Statements	306
		Problem 7-26: Yeah, Right	307
[E]		More Impeachment Problems	307
		Problem 7-27: "You Took the Tag Off of Your Mattress?!"	307
		Problem 7-28: Defamation Redux	308
		Problem 7-29: The Young Freud	308
		Problem 7-30: Extrinsically Yours	309
		Problem 7-31: More Perjury	310
		Problem 7-32: Bigfoot	310
		Problem 7-33: Buddies Revisited	311
		Problem 7-34: Edna to Rachel to Frank	311
		Problem 7-35: Mortgage	311
		Problem 7-36: Interregnum	311
[F]		Rehabilitation of Witnesses	312
		Problem 7-37: Rehab	312
[G]		Refreshing the Witness's Memory	313
		Problem 7-38: "Sammy Says"	313
[H]		Impeachment Statutes	314
§ 7.05		SUMMARY AND REVIEW	315
§ 7.06		CHAPTER REVIEW PROBLEMS	316
		Review Problem 7-A	316
		Review Problem 7-B	316
		Review Problem 7-C	317
		Review Problem 7-D	317
Chapter 8		**LAY OPINION EVIDENCE**	**319**
§ 8.01		CHAPTER CHECKLIST	319
§ 8.02		RELEVANT FEDERAL RULES OF EVIDENCE	319
§ 8.03		DISTINGUISHING BETWEEN LAY AND EXPERT TESTIMONY	319
[A]		The Distinction	319
[B]		Connection to Conditional Relevance	320
[C]		When Laypersons Can Offer Opinions	321
[1]		Rationally Based on Perceptions of Witness	321
[2]		Collective Facts	322
[3]		Skilled Lay Observers	323
[4]		Some Caveats	324
§ 8.04		PROBLEMS	325
		Problem 8-1: High on Marijuana	325
		Problem 8-2: More My Cousin Vinnie and Tire Marks	325
		Problem 8-3: The Stolen Ring	326

TABLE OF CONTENTS

    Problem 8-4: The Wound 327
    Problem 8-5: The Insanity Defense 328
    Problem 8-6: The Plane Crash 328
    Problem 8-7: The Wink 329

Chapter 9		**EXPERT OPINION EVIDENCE** 331
§ 9.01		CHAPTER CHECKLIST 331
§ 9.02		RELEVANT FEDERAL RULES OF EVIDENCE 332
§ 9.03		NATURE OF EXPERT TESTIMONY 334
	[A]	Why Experts Are Needed 334
	[B]	The Syllogistic Nature of Expert Reasoning 335
		Comment: 335
		Problem 9-1: Radioactive Taggants 337
		Problem 9-2: Rape Trauma Syndrome 337
	[C]	Why Special Expert Admissibility Rules Are Needed 338
		Problem 9-3: Taggants Revisited 338
		Problem 9-4: Rape Trauma Syndrome Revisited 338
§ 9.04		PRESENTATION OF EXPERT TESTIMONY 339
	[A]	Rule 702 — Helpfulness of Expert Opinion and Qualifications of Expert 339
		Comment: 342
		Comment: 342
		Problem 9-5: Bomb-Blast Terrorism 345
		Problem 9-6: Rape and Consent 345
		Problem 9-7: The Inaccurate Eyewitness 345
		Problem 9-8: Dr. Borg 346
	[B]	Direct Examination of Experts 346
	[1]	The Hypothetical Question and the Four Data Sources 346
		Problem 9-9: Bomb-Blast Terrorism Continued 349
		Problem 9-10: Rape and Consent Continued 349
	[2]	Liberalization Under the Federal Rules of Evidence 349
	[a]	Rule 703 349
	[b]	Rule 705 352
		Problem 9-11: The Gullible Personality 355
		Problem 9-12: The Negligent Radiologist 356
		Problem 9-13: Monopolies and Economists 357
	[3]	"Or Otherwise" 357
		Problem 9-14: The Radiologist and Psychologist Meet 358
	[4]	The Ultimate Issue Rule 358
		Problem 9-15: Gullibility Revisited 360
		Problem 9-16: The Insanity Defense Revisited 361

TABLE OF CONTENTS

[5]	Reasonable Degree of Professional Certainty	361
[6]	The Opinion Rule and Out-of-Court Statements	361
[C]	Cross-Examination: Scope and Manner	363
	Problem 9-17: My Cousin Vinnie Cross-Examined	364
	Problem 9-18: Or Was It the Accurate Eyewitness?	364
	Problem 9-19: Trial Transcript Exercise on the Scope and Manner of Examining Experts	364
	Problem 9-20: Black Rage	367
§ 9.05	THE MAJOR PREMISES: RELEVANCE AND RELIABILITY OF GENERAL PRINCIPLES AND METHODS	368
[A]	Defining Terms	368
	Comment:	369
	Problem 9-21: Principled Methods	370
[B]	Scientific Evidence	371
[1]	The *Frye* Test	371
[a]	The Test Stated	371
[b]	Validity v. Reliability	372
	Comment:	372
[c]	Defining the Relevant Field	373
	Comment:	373
	Comment:	374
[d]	Developmental Stages of Forensic Evidence	374
	Problem 9-22: The Battered Child	375
	Problem 9-23: "Fresh" Fingerprints	378
	Problem 9-24: Fortune Cookie	379
[2]	The *Daubert* Test	380
[a]	Holding and Rationale: Interpreting the Federal Rules of Evidence	380
[b]	The *Daubert* Factors	381
[i]	The Factors Stated	381
[ii]	Defining "Testability"	383
[iii]	The Gatekeeping Function	384
	Caution:	385
	Problem 9-25: Linguistic Rage	385
	Problem 9-26: The Horizontal Gaze Nystagmus Test	386
	Problem 9-27: My Brand New Miata	387
	Problem 9-28: Harassment!	387
	Problem 9-29: Probably Guilty	388
[iv]	Procedural Concerns	389
	Problem 9-30: Reversal of Rage	391
	Problem 9-31: Concluding Methods	391
	Problem 9-32: HGN and Daubert Hearings	392

TABLE OF CONTENTS

[C]	Evidence Based on Technical or Other Specialized Knowledge, Including Social Science	392
	Problem 9-33: Raging Against Daubert	396
	Problem 9-34: Fred Fraud Fred	396
	Problem 9-35: Baseball	396
	Problem 9-36. The Best Defense	397
§ 9.06	THE MINOR PREMISES	397
	Problem 9-37: Probabilities Revisited	403
	Problem 9-38: The Crime Scene Investigator	403
	Problem 9-39: Psychologists' Hearsay	404
§ 9.07	EXPERT EVIDENCE REVIEW PROBLEMS	404
	Problem 9-40: Physician, Heal Thyself	404
	Problem 9-41: Coercive Indoctrination	404
	Problem 9-42: Experts Not	405

Chapter 10	**PROTECTING THE ADVERSARY SYSTEM: THE HEARSAY RULE AND THE CONFRONTATION CLAUSE**	**407**
§ 10.01	CHAPTER CHECKLIST	407
§ 10.02	RELEVANT FEDERAL RULES OF EVIDENCE	408
§ 10.03	INTRODUCTION	408
§ 10.04	HEARSAY DEFINED	410
§ 10.05	THE HEARSAY RULE AND THE ADVERSARY SYSTEM	412
[A]	Hearsay Rule Protects the Right to Cross-Examine	412
[B]	The "Hearsay Dangers"	413
[C]	Why Not Admit Hearsay "For What It's Worth?"	418
[D]	"Hearsay Policy" Problems	420
	Problem 10-1: The Telephone Game	420
	Problem 10-2: Beyond Question?	420
	Problem 10-3: What's the Use?	420
	Problem 10-4: Hearsay Expert	420
§ 10.06	WHO ARE "DECLARANTS?"	421
[A]	Definitions and Examples	421
[B]	"Declarant" Problems	422
	Problem 10-5: Where's the Declarant?	422
	Problem 10-6: Bloody Glove	422
	Problem 10-7: Polly Wants a Conviction	422
	Problem 10-8: News to Me	423
	Problem 10-9: Photo Finish	423
	Problem 10-10: Print — Out?	423
	Problem 10-11: My Better Side	424

TABLE OF CONTENTS

	Problem 10-12: Just the Ticket	424
§ 10.07	WAS THE STATEMENT MADE "OUT-OF COURT?"	424
[A]	General Rule	424
[B]	"Out-of-Court" Problems	425
	Problem 10-13: On My Word	425
	Problem 10-14: On My Word Again	425
	Problem 10-15: Big Mouth	425
	Problem 10-16: Same Ol', Same Ol'	425
§ 10.08	WHAT IS A "STATEMENT?"	426
[A]	Definition and Examples	426
[B]	Hidden Statements	427
[1]	Sub-Assertions	427
[2]	Linked Assertions	428
[3]	Invisible Assertions	428
[4]	Vicarious Assertions	430
[5]	Assertive Conduct	430
[6]	Implied Assertions	432
[C]	"Statement" Problems	435
	Problem 10-17: Flight	435
	Problem 10-18: Knock Knock	435
	Problem 10-19: Hard Landing I	436
	Problem 10-20: Hard Landing II	436
	Problem 10-21: Hard Landing III	436
	Problem 10-22: Help!	436
	Problem 10-23: Take Notes	436
	Problem 10-24: Raise a Glass	437
	Problem 10-25: Cell Phone	437
	Problem 10-26: Loot Lips	437
	Problem 10-27: Slippery Slope I	437
	Problem 10-28: Slippery Slope II	438
	Problem 10-29: Slippery Slope III	438
	Problem 10-30: Slippery Slope IV	438
	Problem 10-31: Beersay	439
	Problem 10-32: Eye Message	439
	Problem 10-33: A Civil Action	440
	Problem 10-34: Need Moe Money	440
	Problem 10-35: A Ticket, Attack It	440
	Problem 10-36: Brief Case I	441
	Problem 10-37: Brief Case II	441
	Problem 10-38: Alibi-Bye	441
	Problem 10-39: At the Movies: Take Dictation	441

TABLE OF CONTENTS

§ 10.09	COMMON HEARSAY MISCONCEPTIONS	441
[A]	"It's Not Hearsay If You Paraphrase"	442
[B]	"It's Not Hearsay If the Witness Is Also the Declarant"	442
[C]	"The Statement Isn't Hearsay If It's Circumstantial Evidence"	443
[D]	"It's Not Hearsay If The Statement Was Made in a Police Officer's Presence"	444
§ 10.10	HEARSAY REVIEW PROBLEMS	444
	Problem 10-40: Carded	444
	Problem 10-41: Loretta	444
	Problem 10-42: Stat!	445
	Problem 10-43: No Parking	445
	Problem 10-44: Instant Replay	446
	Problem 10-45: Bettor Beware	446
§ 10.11	HEARSAY AND THE CONFRONTATION CLAUSE	447
	Problem 10-46: Scarred	451
	Problem 10-47: One and Done	451
	Problem 10-48: Tender Years	451
	Problem 10-49: Tipping Point	452
	Problem 10-50: It's Not What You Say, It's Where You Say It	452
	Problem 10-51: There Goes the Neighbor, Hood	452
	Problem 10-52: Brothers in Lawlessness	453
	Problem 10-53: About Time	454
	Problem 10-54: Potpourri	454
§ 10.12	CHAPTER REVIEW PROBLEMS	456
	Review Problem 10-A	456
	Review Problem 10-B	457
	Review Problem 10-C	457
	Review Problem 10-D	457
§ 10.13	CASE LIBRARY	458
	United States v. Zenni	458
	Crawford v. Washington	461
	Davis v. Washington	469
	Melendez-Diaz v. Massachusetts	477
	Michigan v. Bryant	485
	Bullcoming v. New Mexico	497
Chapter 11	**NON-HEARSAY PURPOSES FOR OUT-OF-COURT STATEMENTS**	**507**
§ 11.01	CHAPTER CHECKLIST	507
§ 11.02	RELEVANT FEDERAL RULES OF EVIDENCE	507
§ 11.03	INTRODUCTION	507

TABLE OF CONTENTS

§ 11.04	STEP TWO OF THE HEARSAY MATRIX: IDENTIFYING AN ASSERTION'S NON-HEARSAY PURPOSE	508
§ 11.05	STEP THREE OF THE HEARSAY MATRIX: DETERMINING THE RELEVANCE OF A CLAIMED "NON-HEARSAY USE"	511
§ 11.06	PROBATIVE VALUE VERSUS UNFAIR PREJUDICE	513
§ 11.07	COMMON NON-HEARSAY USES	515
[A]	Overview	515
[B]	Assertion Relevant to Declarant's State of Mind	515
	Problem 11-1: Up the Creek I	518
	Problem 11-2: Up the Creek II	518
	Problem 11-3: Mother and Child	518
	Problem 11-4: Mine!	518
	Problem 11-5: Backache	518
	Problem 11-6: At the Movies: The Boyfriend	518
	Problem 11-7: At the Movies: Motive for Murder	519
[C]	Assertion Relevant to Listener's State of Mind	519
	Problem 11-8: Bagged	520
	Problem 11-9: Medical Mal	520
	Problem 11-10: Hold the Dressing	521
[D]	Assertion Offered as a "Verbal Act" (aka "Words of Independent Legal Significance" or "Legally Operative Conduct")	523
	Problem 11-11: Death and .	524
	Problem 11-12: Payback Time	525
	Problem 11-13: Cellar Dweller	525
	Problem 11-14: Protection	525
	Problem 11-15: Mea Culpa	525
	Problem 11-16: Up in Arms	525
[E]	Assertion Offered to Contradict (Impeach) Testimony ("Prior Inconsistent Statement")	525
	Problem 11-17: Speed Test 1	526
	Problem 11-18: Speed Test 2	527
[F]	Assertions Offered to Provide Context and Meaning	527
§ 11.08	CHAPTER REVIEW PROBLEMS	528
	Problem 11-19: Summation	528
	Problem 11-20: My Case is Shot	529
	Problem 11-21: Policy Argument	529
	Problem 11-22: Bad Heir Day 1	529
	Problem 11-23: Bad Heir Day 2	530
	Problem 11-24: Bad Heir Day 3	530
	Problem 11-25: Affordable Hearsay	531
	Problem 11-26: Honeymoon Over	531
	Problem 11-27: Mind the Gap	531

TABLE OF CONTENTS

	Problem 11-28: Garden Variety Hearsay 1	531
	Problem 11-29: Garden Variety Hearsay 2	532
	Problem 11-30: Garden Variety Hearsay 3	532
	Problem 11-31: Garden Variety Hearsay 4	532
	Problem 11-32: Alternate Defenses	533
	Problem 11-33: Security Alert (Role Play)	533
	Problem 11-34: Zoo Suit	534
	Problem 11-35: Last Words (Role Play)	534
	Problem 11-36: Under Cover	535
	Problem 11-37: Rite to Trial	535
	Problem 11-38: Pre-School	535
	Problem 11-39: Self Service	536
	Problem 11-40: Parole Evidence	537
	Problem 11-41: 2-B or Not 2-B	537
	Problem 11-42: At the Movies: Self-Defense	537
	Problem 11-43: At the Movies: Addiction	538
	Problem 11-44: Bad Call	538
	Problem 11-45: Sold!	538
	Problem 11-46: At the Movies: The Shout	538
	Problem 11-47: Probable Claus	539
	Problem 11-48: Transcript Analysis	539
§ 11.09	MULTIPLE-CHOICE REVIEW PROBLEMS	542
	Review Problem 11-A	542
	Review Problem 11-B	543
	Review Problem 11-C	543
	Review Problem 11-D	544
	Review Problem 11-E	544

Chapter 12	**THE ADMISSIBILITY OF TESTIFYING WITNESSES' HEARSAY STATEMENTS**	**545**
§ 12.01	CHAPTER CHECKLIST	545
§ 12.02	RELEVANT FEDERAL RULES OF EVIDENCE	545
§ 12.03	INTRODUCTION	546
§ 12.04	WHY DISTINGUISH EXEMPTIONS FROM EXCEPTIONS?	547
§ 12.05	LAYING FOUNDATIONS FOR HEARSAY ADMISSIBILITY THROUGH "MINI-TRIALS"	548
§ 12.06	TESTIFYING WITNESSES' PRIOR STATEMENTS	552
[A]	Three Categories of Exempt Statements	552
[B]	Prior Inconsistent Statements (Rule 801(d)(1)(A))	552
	Problem 12-1: Try to Remember	556
	Problem 12-2: Blame Worthy	558

TABLE OF CONTENTS

	Problem 12-3: Bar Exam 1	559
	Problem 12-4: Bar Exam 2	559
	Problem 12-5: Computer Caper	559
	Problem 12-6: Baby Ruth	560
	Problem 12-7: Ask the Expert	561
	Problem 12-8: Excuse Me	562
	Problem 12-9: The Woodshed	562
	Problem 12-10: Gimme Shelter	563
[C]	Prior Consistent Statements (Rule 801(d)(1)(B))	563
	Problem 12-11: The Howling	565
	Problem 12-12: Sun Burned	566
	Problem 12-13: Park Place	566
	Problem 12-14: Just One More Thing	567
	Problem 12-15: Emot ("Tome" Reversed)	568
[D]	Pretrial Identifications (Rule 801(d)(1)(C))	568
	Problem 12-16: Bagged	570
	Problem 12-17: Hitting a Brick Wall	570
	Problem 12-18: Lengthy Rivalry	571
	Problem 12-19: The Lineup	571
	Problem 12-20: At the Movies: Turncoat	574
	Problem 12-21: At the Movies: Better Late Than Never	574
	Problem 12-22: Statutory Interpretation Process	574
	Problem 12-23: Transcript Exercise	575
§ 12.07	MULTIPLE-CHOICE REVIEW PROBLEMS	579
	Review Problem 12-A	579
	Review Problem 12-B	579
	Review Problem 12-C	580
	Review Problem 12-D	580
§ 12.08	CASE LIBRARY	581
	Tome v. United States	581
	United States v. Owens	590

Chapter 13	**THE ADMISSIBILITY OF OPPOSING PARTIES' HEARSAY STATEMENTS**	**593**
§ 13.01	CHAPTER CHECKLIST	593
§ 13.02	RELEVANT FEDERAL RULES OF EVIDENCE	593
§ 13.03	INTRODUCTION	594
§ 13.04	OPPOSING PARTIES' STATEMENTS AND THE ADVERSARY SYSTEM	596
§ 13.05	DECLARANT IS THE OPPOSING PARTY (RULE 801(d)(2)(A))	597
	Problem 13-1: Multiple Choys	598

TABLE OF CONTENTS

	Problem 13-2: Who's a Party?	598
	Problem 13-3: Oh Canida	599
	Problem 13-4: Wrenching an Admission	602
	Problem 13-5: Pleading Ticket	603
	Problem 13-6: Brag Art	603
	Problem 13-7: Nocturnal Admission?	603
§ 13.06	ADOPTIVE STATEMENTS (RULE 801(d)(2)(B))	603
	Problem 13-8: On the Tube: "Barb-Accuse"	605
	Problem 13-9: I Wanna Hold Your Hand (of Cards)	605
	Problem 13-10: Silent Right	607
	Problem 13-11: Car Jack	607
	Problem 13-12: Keeping Up Appearances	607
§ 13.07	AUTHORIZED STATEMENTS (RULE 801(d)(2)(C))	608
	Problem 13-13: Lawyer Lee	609
	Problem 13-14: Scoop	609
	Problem 13-15: Gilligan's Island	610
	Problem 13-16: Way Out	610
§ 13.08	EMPLOYEE STATEMENTS (RULE 801(d)(2)(D))	611
	Problem 13-17: Late for Class	613
	Problem 13-18: Pickup Line	613
	Problem 13-19: No Brakes	614
	Problem 13-20: Acid Remark	614
	Problem 13-21: Rumor Mill	614
§ 13.09	CO-CONSPIRATOR STATEMENTS (RULE 801(d)(2)(E))	615
	Problem 13-22: Et tu Ilona?	616
	Problem 13-23: Loot Out	617
	Problem 13-24: Handoff	618
	Problem 13-25: The Latecomer	619
	Problem 13-26: At the Movies: Change of Emphasis	619
	Problem 13-27: Unfilled Offer	619
	Problem 13-28: Transcript Exercise	620
§ 13.10	MULTIPLE-CHOICE REVIEW QUESTIONS	624
	Review Problem 13-A	624
	Review Problem 13-B	625
	Review Problem 13-C	625
	Review Problem 13-D	625
§ 13.11	CASE LIBRARY	626
	Bourjaily v. United States	626

TABLE OF CONTENTS

Chapter 14 THE ADMISSIBILITY OF HEARSAY STATEMENTS UNDER RULE 803 629

§ 14.01	CHAPTER CHECKLIST 629
§ 14.02	RELEVANT FEDERAL RULES OF EVIDENCE 630
§ 14.03	INTRODUCTION 632
§ 14.04	TRUSTWORTHINESS 634
	Problem 14-1: Redraft 635
§ 14.05	CONTEMPORANEOUS AND EXCITED UTTERANCES (RULES 803(1) AND (2)) 636
	Problem 14-2: Red or Blue 638
	Problem 14-3: Excited Acceptance 639
	Problem 14-4: Stepdaddy 640
	Problem 14-5: Mach Trial 1 640
	Problem 14-6: Mach Trial 2 642
	Problem 14-7: Nine One Mum 644
	Problem 14-8: Eek Mail 645
	Problem 14-9: Mind the Gap 645
	Problem 14-10: Second Opinion 645
	Problem 14-11: When the Bough Breaks 645
	Problem 14-12: First Words 645
§ 14.06	STATEMENT OF PRESENTLY-EXISTING STATE OF MIND, FEELING OR BELIEF (RULE 803(3)) 646
	Problem 14-13: Before and After 651
	Problem 14-14: Driver's Ed 651
	Problem 14-15: At the Movies: Last Page 652
	Problem 14-16: Fearsay 1 652
	Problem 14-17: Fearsay 2 652
	Problem 14-18: Fearsay 3 653
	Problem 14-19: Proof Possibles 653
	Problem 14-20: Tea Party 653
	Problem 14-21: Chat Room 654
	Problem 14-22: Pheaster 1 656
	Problem 14-23: Pheaster 2 656
	Problem 14-24: Pheaster 3 656
§ 14.07	STATEMENTS MADE FOR PURPOSES OF MEDICAL DIAGNOSIS OR TREATMENT (RULE 803(4)) 656
	Problem 14-25: Blue Skye 658
	Problem 14-26: Child Abuse Expert 659
	Problem 14-27: Bitten 659
	Problem 14-28: At the Movies: Sister 659
	Problem 14-29: Back Talk 660
	Problem 14-30: Friendly Advice 660

TABLE OF CONTENTS

	Problem 14-31: Medi-Cal	661
§ 14.08	PAST RECOLLECTION RECORDED (RULE 803(5)); REFRESHING RECOLLECTION (RULE 612)	662
	Problem 14-32: Forget It	666
	Problem 14-33: Forget Me Not	668
	Problem 14-34: Lasting Freshness	669
	Problem 14-35: Preppie-ration	669
§ 14.09	BUSINESS RECORDS (RULES 803(6), (7))	670
	Problem 14-36: Floor-ida	676
	Problem 14-37: On the Tube: Dear Diary	676
	Problem 14-38: Hotel California Alibi	677
	Problem 14-39: Track Record 1	677
	Problem 14-40: Track Record 2	677
	Problem 14-41: Building the Foundation	678
	Problem 14-42: Truss-worthiness	678
	Problem 14-43: Report In?	678
	Problem 14-44: Nail File	679
	Problem 14-45: Safety Record	679
	Problem 14-46: Testimonial Custodian?	679
	Problem 14-47: Lay A Foundation	680
§ 14.10	PUBLIC RECORDS (RULE 803(8))	680
	Problem 14-48: Reporting for Duty	683
	Problem 14-49: Weather Report	683
	Problem 14-50: Bad Breath	684
	Problem 14-51: Confrontation	684
	Problem 14-52: Guarded Remarks	684
§ 14.11	OTHER RULE 803 HEARSAY EXCEPTIONS	688
[A]	Records of Vital Statistics (Rules 803(9), (11))	688
[B]	Family Records (Rule 803(13))	688
[C]	Statements in Dispositive Documents (Rule 803(15))	689
[D]	Statements in Ancient Documents (Rule 803(16))	689
[E]	Market Reports and Commercial Publications (Rule 803(17))	689
§ 14.12	MULTIPLE-CHOICE REVIEW QUESTIONS	689
	Review Problem 14-A	689
	Review Problem 14-B	690
	Review Problem 14-C	690
	Review Problem 14-D	691
	Review Problem 14-E	691
§ 14.13	CASE LIBRARY	692
	Mutual Life Insurance Company v. Hillmon	692
	United States v. Pheaster	695
	United States v. Tome	699

TABLE OF CONTENTS

    Palmer v. Hoffman 702

    Beech Aircraft Corporation v. Rainey 704

Chapter 15   **ADMISSIBILITY OF HEARSAY STATEMENTS UNDER RULES 804 AND 807** **709**

§ 15.01   CHAPTER CHECKLIST 709
§ 15.02   RELEVANT FEDERAL RULES OF EVIDENCE 710
§ 15.03   INTRODUCTION 712
§ 15.04   UNAVAILABILITY 712
    Problem 15-1: Fair-Weather Friend 719
    Problem 15-2: Wherefore Art Thou, Waldo? 719
    Problem 15-3: Doctor's Orders 720
    Problem 15-4: Try to Remember 720
    Problem 15-5: Fear of Testifying 720
    Problem 15-6: Building a Foundation 721
§ 15.05   FORMER TESTIMONY (RULE 804(b)(1)) 722
    Problem 15-7: You Go First 729
    Problem 15-8: Play It Against Sam 729
    Problem 15-9: Blazing Objections 729
    Problem 15-10: Bus Stop 730
    Problem 15-11: Fire Escape Clause 730
    Problem 15-12: No Questions Asked 1 731
    Problem 15-13: No Questions Asked 2 732
§ 15.06   DYING DECLARATIONS (RULE 804(b)(2)) 733
    Problem 15-14: Famous's Last Words 734
    Problem 15-15: Safe Passage 735
    Problem 15-16: Jesse and Billy 735
    Problem 15-17: Capital Letter 735
    Problem 15-18: On the Tube: Tight Squeeze 736
    Problem 15-19: Dying Declaration Mini-Trial 736
§ 15.07   STATEMENTS AGAINST INTEREST (RULE 804(b)(3)) 737
    Problem 15-20: Spoke Too Soon 740
    Problem 15-21: Deep-Pocket Defendant 741
    Problem 15-22: I Owe You? 741
    Problem 15-23: Stool Pigeon 1 742
    Problem 15-24: Stool Pigeon 2 742
    Problem 15-25: Defense Pigeon 1 742
    Problem 15-26: Defense Pigeon 2 743
    Problem 15-27: At the Movies: Cell Talk 743
    Problem 15-28: Fishing Expedition 744
§ 15.08   FORFEITURE BY WRONGDOING (RULE 804(b)(6)) 745

TABLE OF CONTENTS

	Problem 15-29: Owens' Flip Side	747
	Problem 15-30: Five-feiture	747
§ 15.09	RESIDUAL HEARSAY (RULE 807)	749
	Problem 15-31: Hospital Hearsay	754
	Problem 15-32: Home Work	755
	Problem 15-33: Cartune	755
	Problem 15-34: Fireside Chat	756
	Problem 15-35: Voicemail	757
	Problem 15-36: Building a Foundation	757
	Problem 15-37: Transcript Analysis I	758
	Problem 15-38: Transcript Analysis II	763
§ 15.10	MULTIPLE-CHOICE REVIEW PROBLEMS	768
	Review Problem 15-A	768
	Review Problem 15-B	769
	Review Problem 15-C	769
	Review Problem 15-D	770
	Review Problem 15-E	770
	Review Problem 15-F	771
	Review Problem 15-G	771
	Review Problem 15-H	772
§ 15.11	CASE LIBRARY	772
	Williamson v. United States	772
	Giles v. California	779

Chapter 16	**SHAPING OUTCOMES: BURDENS OF PROOF, PRESUMPTIONS, AND JUDICIAL NOTICE**	**793**
§ 16.01	CHAPTER CHECKLIST	793
§ 16.02	RELEVANT FEDERAL RULES OF EVIDENCE	793
§ 16.03	INTRODUCTION	794
[A]	Burdens of Proof	795
[B]	Presumptions (Rule 301)	795
[C]	Judicial Notice (Rule 201)	796
§ 16.04	BURDENS OF PROOF	796
	Problem 16-1: Allocating Burdens	799
	Problem 16-2: Into the Breach	799
	Problem 16-3: Don't Believe It	800
	Problem 16-4: Got the Blues	801
	Problem 16-5: High Witness Testimony	801
	Problem 16-6: Note Worthy?	802
	Problem 16-7: Cold Case	802
§ 16.05	PRESUMPTIONS IN CIVIL CASES (RULE 301)	803

TABLE OF CONTENTS

	Problem 16-8: Party Smarty	810
	Problem 16-9: Pick Your Own	810
	Problem 16-10: Make-Up Case	810
	Problem 16-11: The Classifieds	811
	Problem 16-12: Donna For	811
	Problem 16-13: Basic Training	812
	Problem 16-14: Donna Speaks	813
	Problem 16-15: Dueling Wills	813
	Problem 16-16: Conclusive Presumption	814
	Problem 16-17: A Night at the Opera	814
	Problem 16-18: Dueling Presumptions	815
§ 16.06	PRESUMPTIONS IN CRIMINAL CASES	815
	Problem 16-19: Pet(ty) Offense	817
	Problem 16-20: Fire Escape	817
§ 16.07	JUDICIAL NOTICE (RULE 201)	818
	Problem 16-21: The Knowledgeable Judge	821
	Problem 16-22: The Expert Judge	821
	Problem 16-23: Consider the Source	821
	Problem 16-24: Source Spot	822
	Problem 16-25: Read My Clips	822
	Problem 16-26: Hear No Evil	822
	Problem 16-27: Power Play	823
	Problem 16-28: Attorney's Fees	823
	Problem 16-29: Fellin Down	823
	Problem 16-30: Pane and Simple	824
	Problem 16-31: Dicta	825
	Problem 16-32: Transcript Analysis	825
§ 16.08	MULTIPLE-CHOICE REVIEW PROBLEMS	829
	Review Problem 16-A	829
	Review Problem 16-B	829
	Review Problem 16-C	830
	Review Problem 16-D	830
§ 16.09	CASE LIBRARY	831
	County Court of Ulster County v. Allen	831
Chapter 17	**PRIVILEGES**	**837**
§ 17.01	CHAPTER CHECKLIST	837
§ 17.02	RELEVANT FEDERAL RULES OF EVIDENCE AND PROPOSED (BUT REJECTED) RULES	837
§ 17.03	INTRODUCTION TO PRIVILEGES	844
[A]	The Definition of Privileged Evidence	844

TABLE OF CONTENTS

[B]	Federal and State Privileges	845
[C]	Sources of Privilege	845
[D]	The Operation of Privileges	847
[E]	Confidential Communication Privileges Generally	847
[F]	Public Policy-Based Privileges Generally	848
§ 17.04	THE FEDERAL RULES OF EVIDENCE APPROACH TO PRIVILEGE	848
§ 17.05	SOME SPECIFIC PRIVILEGES	850
[A]	The Husband-Wife Privileges — Adverse Spousal Testimony and Confidential Communications	850
[1]	The Adverse Spousal Testimony Privilege	850
[2]	The Husband-Wife Confidential Communications Privilege	851
[3]	Problems	851
	Problem 17-1: Bonnie and Clyde — Scenarios	851
[B]	The Attorney-Client Privilege	852
[1]	Elements of Privilege	852
	Problem 17-2: Free Toaster Oven	852
	Problem 17-3: No Name	853
	Problem 17-4: Waiver?	854
[2]	The Attorney-Client Privilege and the Corporate Client	854
	Problem 17-5: I.B.S.	855
	Problem 17-6: L.A. Cooke	855
[C]	Other Privileges	855
[1]	"Work Product" Privilege	855
	Problem 17-7: The Union	856
[2]	Psychotherapist-Patient Privilege	856
	Problem 17-8: Crazy for You	857
	Problem 17-9: Bundy	857
	Problem 17-10: Still Crazy, After All These	857
[3]	The Physician-Patient Privilege	857
	Problem 17-11: Booth	858
	Problem 17-12: Booth II	858
[4]	The Fifth Amendment Privilege Against Self-Incrimination	858
	Problem 17-13: Lowering the Bar	858
	Problem 17-14: Illegal Gambling	859
[D]	Additional Privilege Problems	859
	Problem 17-15: Father and Son	859
	Problem 17-16: Deep Throat	859
	Problem 17-17: Confession	859
	Problem 17-18: Accidental Discovery Disclosure	860
§ 17.06	EXAMPLES OF STATE LAW PRIVILEGES	860
§ 17.07	SUMMARY AND REVIEW	861

TABLE OF CONTENTS

§ 17.08	CHAPTER REVIEW PROBLEMS	862
	Problem 17-A	862
	Problem 17-B	862
	Problem 17-C	863
	Problem 17-D	863
§ 17.09	CASE LIBRARY	864
	Upjohn Co. v. United States	864
	Nix v. Whiteside	867
	Jaffee v. Redmond	870

Chapter 18	**AUTHENTICATION, IDENTIFICATION, AND THE "BEST EVIDENCE" RULE**	**873**
§ 18.01	CHAPTER CHECKLIST	873
§ 18.02	RELEVANT FEDERAL RULES OF EVIDENCE	873
	ARTICLE IX. AUTHENTICATION AND IDENTIFICATION	873
	ARTICLE X. CONTENTS OF WRITINGS, RECORDINGS, AND PHOTOGRAPHS	876
§ 18.03	AUTHENTICATION AND IDENTIFICATION	878
[A]	Requirement of Authentication	878
[B]	Procedures for Authentication	879
	Problem 18-1: Yeah, That's the Ticket	881
	Problem 18-2: Authenticate This	881
	Problem 18-3: Not So Sweet	881
	Problem 18-4: Making Money the Old-Fashioned Way	882
§ 18.04	THE BEST EVIDENCE RULE	883
[A]	The Production of Original Documents	883
[B]	Exceptions to the Requirement of an Original	885
	Problem 18-5: Hagar	887
	Problem 18-6: Sweet Suit	887
	Problem 18-7: More Breach	887
	Problem 18-8: Meet the Jetsons	888
	Problem 18-9: Elroy Was Here	888
	Problem 18-10: All Business	888
	Problem 18-11: I Confess!	888
	Problem 18-12: Dat's Da Guy	888
	Problem 18-13: Roll the Videotape, Please	889
	Problem 18-14: Damages	889
§ 18.05	SUMMARY AND REVIEW	889
§ 18.06	CHAPTER REVIEW PROBLEMS	890
	Problem 18-A	890
	Problem 18-B	890

TABLE OF CONTENTS

	Problem 18-C	890
	Problem 18-D	891
§ 18.07	CASE LIBRARY	891
	Seiler v. Lucasfilm, Ltd.	891

Chapter 19	**REVIEW PROBLEMS**	**897**
§ 19.01	PROBLEMS	897
	Problem 19-1: United States v. O'Ruben	897
	Problem 19-2: Crash Davis	902
	Problem 19-3: Benni and Hannah	902
	Problem 19-4: United States v. Bowie	902
	Problem 19-5: Not Again!	903
	Problem 19-6: One Tough Hombre	903
	Problem 19-7: Transcript	905
	Problem 19-8: "The Sheriff"	907
	Problem 19-9	907
	Problem 19-10	908
	Problem 19-11	908
	Problem 19-12	908
	Problem 19-13	908
	Problem 19-14	908
	Problem 19-15	908
	Problem 19-16	909
	Problem 19-17	909
	Problem 19-18	909
	Problem 19-19	909
	Problem 19-20	909
	Problem 19-21	909
	Problem 19-22	910
	Problem 19-23	910
	Problem 19-24	910
	Problem 19-25	910
	Problem 19-26	910
	Problem 19-27	910
	Problem 19-28	910
	Problem 19-29	911
	Problem 19-30	911
	Problem 19-31	911
	Problem 19-32	911
	Problem 19-33	911
	Problem 19-34	911

TABLE OF CONTENTS

Problem 19-35 911
Problem 19-36 912
Problem 19-37 912
Problem 19-38 912
Problem 19-39 912
Problem 19-40 912
Problem 19-41 912
Problem 19-42 912
Problem 19-43 912
Problem 19-44 913
Problem 19-45 913
Problem 19-46 913
Problem 19-47 913
Problem 19-48 913
Problem 19-49 913
Problem 19-50 914
Problem 19-51 914
Problem 19-52 914
Problem 19-53 914
Problem 19-54 914
Problem 19-55 915
Problem 19-56 915
Problem 19-57 915
Problem 19-58 915
Problem 19-59 915
Problem 19-60 915
Problem 19-61 916
Problem 19-62 916
Problem 19-63 916
Problem 19-64 917
Problem 19-65 917
Problem 19-66 917
Problem 19-67 917
Problem 19-68 917
Problem 19-69 917
Problem 19-70 917
Problem 19-71 918
Problem 19-72 918
Problem 19-73 918
Problem 19-74 918
Problem 19-75 918

TABLE OF CONTENTS

	Problem 19-76	918
	Problem 19-77	918
	Problem 19-78	918
	Problem 19-79	919
	Problem 19-80	919
	Problem 19-81: The Breckenridge Bandit	919
	Problem 19-82: Megan's Law	919
§ 19.02	ANSWERS	920
	Problem 19-9	920
	Problem 19-10	920
	Problem 19-11	920
	Problem 19-12	920
	Problem 19-13	920
	Problem 19-14	920
	Problem 19-15	921
	Problem 19-16	921
	Problem 19-17	921
	Problem 19-18	921
	Problem 19-19	921
	Problem 19-20	921
	Problem 19-21	921
	Problem 19-22	922
	Problem 19-23	922
	Problem 19-24	922
	Problem 19-25	922
	Problem 19-26	922
	Problem 19-27	922
	Problem 19-28	922
	Problem 19-29	922
	Problem 19-30	922
	Problem 19-31	923
	Problem 19-32	923
	Problem 19-33	923
	Problem 19-34	923
	Problem 19-35	923
	Problem 19-36	923
	Problem 19-37	923
	Problem 19-38	923
	Problem 19-39	923
	Problem 19-40	923
	Problem 19-41	924

TABLE OF CONTENTS

Problem 19-42 924
Problem 19-43 924
Problem 19-44 924
Problem 19-45 924
Problem 19-46 924
Problem 19-47 924
Problem 19-48 925
Problem 19-49 925
Problem 19-50 925
Problem 19-51 925
Problem 19-52 925
Problem 19-53 925
Problem 19-54 925
Problem 19-55 925
Problem 19-56 926
Problem 19-57 926
Problem 19-58 926
Problem 19-59 926
Problem 19-60 926
Problem 19-61 926
Problem 19-62 926
Problem 19-63 927
Problem 19-64 927
Problem 19-65 927
Problem 19-66 927
Problem 19-67 927
Problem 19-68 927
Problem 19-69 927
Problem 19-70 927
Problem 19-71 927
Problem 19-72 928
Problem 19-73 928
Problem 19-74 928
Problem 19-75 928
Problem 19-76 928
Problem 19-77 928
Problem 19-78 928
Problem 19-79 928
Problem 19-80 928

TABLE OF CONTENTS

Appendix	**EXISTING AND PROPOSED FEDERAL RULES OF EVIDENCE**	**929**
Table of Cases		**TC-1**
Index		**I-1**

Chapter 1

INTRODUCTION TO EVIDENCE

§ 1.01 CHAPTER CHECKLIST

1. How do the rules of evidence affect the conduct of a lawsuit?
2. What role does evidence law play at trial?
3. What are several well-established meanings of the term "evidence"?

§ 1.02 RELEVANT FEDERAL RULES OF EVIDENCE

Rule 101. Scope

These rules govern proceedings in the courts of the United States and before the United States bankruptcy judges and United States magistrate judges, to the extent and with the exceptions stated in Rule 1101.

Rule 102. Purpose and Construction

These rules shall be construed to secure fairness in administration, elimination of unjustifiable expense and delay, and promotion of growth and development of the law of evidence to the end that the truth may be ascertained and proceedings justly determined.

Rule 106. Remainder of or Related Writings or Recorded Statements

When a writing or recorded statement or part thereof is introduced by a party, an adverse party may require the introduction at that time of any other part or any other writing or recorded statement which ought in fairness to be considered contemporaneously with it.

§ 1.03 LAWSUITS AND RULES OF EVIDENCE

The rules of evidence are best understood in context, operating as a part of a larger process, a lawsuit. Despite notorious claims of "justice denied" (such as wrongful convictions, wrongful acquittals, and massive damage awards for coffee burns), lawsuits play an important role in the United States. Institutionally, lawsuits serve as a nonviolent method of dispute resolution and offer an accepted method of fact-finding. The evidentiary rules are critical to the smooth operation of lawsuits.

The Federal Rules of Evidence, the focus of this book, govern court proceedings in the federal court system. These rules superseded the common-law evidence rules upon their adoption in 1975. The Federal Rules of Evidence were designed with lofty goals, reminiscent of a document imbued with equally broad ambitions in 1776. The new evidence rules were intended to "secure fairness . . . to the end that the truth may be ascertained . . . ." Rule 102. From a practical perspective, the evidentiary rules were created to promote an even playing field and to provide advance notice of the rules of the adversarial process. In this respect, the evidentiary rules help the trial to proceed in a routine and predictable manner, acting as a stabilizing backbone of the trial.

The rules of evidence apply in both civil and criminal cases. While the application of the rules is generally uniform, at times they are specifically tailored to assist the differing functions of the criminal and civil justice systems. (For example, a criminal defendant is given several special dispensations because of the great significance of a conviction. *See, e.g.*, Rules 404(a), 609.)

In addition to supplying rules at trial, the rules of evidence reach some pre-and post-trial matters, such as formal interviews under oath of persons with relevant information, called depositions, the discovery of relevant information, some pre-trial motions, and post-trial proceedings.[1] However, the rules primarily apply to the trial stage of a lawsuit.

The rules can be sorted according to function. There are "traffic" rules concerning the smooth operation of the trial, such as Rule 611, on the order and development of testimony. There are "accuracy" rules promoting truthful verdicts, such as Rule 403, which excludes unfairly prejudicial evidence. There are "policy" rules advancing external policies larger than the individual lawsuit, such as Rule 501 on privileges.

Each rule can be viewed as advancing one or more of these functions. For example, Federal Rule of Evidence 106, known as the rule of completeness, offers an illustration of an accuracy rule. It provides an opposing party with the opportunity to introduce the remainder of a writing or recording in the interest of fairness. Accuracy is further preserved by the interpretation of the rule, which limits proffered remainders to that which is relevant to the case. The goal in allowing filtered remainders as evidence is to minimize the prejudicial impact on the jury.

A major purpose of the Federal Rules of Evidence is to provide a coherent and fair structure for the resolution of legal disputes. The biggest challenge for many law students is to synthesize the rules into a usable and unified framework. All too often, the Rules seem to spin in their own individual orbits, rather than in concert with each other.

While both state and federal courts currently rely on codified evidentiary rules, vestiges of the earlier common-law system still remain. The Federal Rules of Evidence still rely on the earlier common law in certain instances, such as in the

---

[1] *See, e.g., United States v. Davis*, 170 F.3d 617, 622 (6th Cir. 1999), in which the court held that hearsay is admissible in a sentencing hearing.

domain of privileges.[2]

The creation of the Federal Rules of Evidence was an interesting exercise in statutory construction. A decade in the making, the Rules were originally composed in 1965 by an Advisory Committee appointed by then Chief Justice Earl Warren. The Advisory Committee's proposal was revised prior to being finally approved by the Supreme Court. The Court then forwarded the rules to Congress for review and revision. Congress disagreed with several provisions so they enacted the rules with modifications. The Federal Rules of Evidence went into effect on July 1, 1975.

Since that time, the rules have been periodically revised on an individual basis. Revisions have been proposed for different reasons. Some rules needed more clarity. Other rules needed upgrades in functionality. Currently, there is a sweeping proposal to clarify the language of all of the rules en masse without changing their substantive effect. The proposals are included in this book and will go into effect, if adopted, after the publication of this Fourth Edition.

§ 1.04 THE DIFFERENT MEANINGS OF "EVIDENCE"

One of the initial points of confusion in an Evidence course is the different uses of the term "evidence." There are at least three commonly used definitions of "evidence," especially at trial. The definitions include: (1) *proof* of a cause of action, claim, or defense; (2) the *rules* governing the admissibility and exclusion of proof at trial; and (3) what is *in evidence*, that is, the *things* that jurors can take back with them to the jury room for the process of deliberations.

(1) *Proof* refers to what is offered by the parties at trial to meet the legal requirements for showing the elements of a claim, cause of action, or defense. Despite the rush to judgment that often occurs in celebrated trials, the American system focuses on the proof admitted in the case and not the innuendo, rumors, and inadmissible allegations that might be swirling around the lawsuit. Lawsuits are generally won or lost through the admissible proof offered by the parties.

Proof takes a variety of forms, from the testimony of witnesses to tangible material marked as exhibits to intangible information or data. Because proof is so important to the effective functioning of the legal system, certain prerequisites or foundations must be met prior to offering it at trial.

(2) *The rules* governing the admissibility of proof not only provide the focus of a law school course but also guide how a judge conducts a trial. These rules can be found in the Federal Rules of Evidence or state codifications, as well as in the common law. Significantly, the rules contain numerous evidentiary elements that are prerequisites to the admissibility of evidence at trial. Thus, much like a tort or a crime that has elements that must be proven to win, evidence law has elements that must be shown before evidence can be admitted and considered by the trier of fact. Lawyers and law students struggle to understand and apply these foundations, which are critical to the proper introduction of evidence. Those attorneys who can best negotiate these foundations maximize their chances for success at trial. (One

---

[2] Rule 501 refers to the pertinent federal common law to determine what privileges apply in federal courts.

pointed example to the contrary can be found in the film, *The Verdict*, starring Paul Newman as a plaintiff's attorney. In the film, the court excluded crucial evidence provided by a nurse about the medical negligence of several defendant physicians. Despite the exclusion, the jury obviously considered the evidence in a stunning finding for the plaintiff.)

(3) The third common use of the term "evidence" refers to the items of proof that were admitted *into evidence*. Such evidence has met the requirements of the rules and may be taken back to the jury room by the jury and considered during deliberations. This type of evidence, which includes a large portion of tangible proof under meaning (1) above, is distinguished from mere demonstrative evidence, which is used only to illustrate a point, usually during testimony. Demonstrative evidence is generally not subject to the same rigorous admissions requirements as other evidence and is not permitted to be taken by the jury back to the jury room. Once proposed exhibits are admitted in evidence, they no longer are controlled by the parties, but become a part of the official case file and are under the control of the court.

Example

Dr. Amy Millsap, a general surgeon, is sued by her patient, Lenny Ferona, for medical malpractice. Surgeon Millsap allegedly performed an important operating procedure with the incorrect scalpel. At trial, the plaintiff introduced the scalpel that Dr. Millsap is believed to have used during the operation. *Does the scalpel constitute evidence?*

Answer: The scalpel used by Dr. Millsap touches on all three uses of the term "evidence." The scalpel may be relevant to proving malpractice and thus might be admitted as the "stuff" or physical evidence offered by a party at trial. The scalpel also must satisfy the rules governing admissibility, including being properly authenticated and shown to be relevant to the case.[3] If the scalpel is admitted *in evidence* as an exhibit, and not merely as a demonstrative aid to assist the testimony of a witness, the scalpel and may be brought to the jury room for the jury's deliberations.

Problem 1-1: Prove It

Mr. Rick Turkish, owner and President of Turkish Advertising, Inc., created an advertising campaign for Bill's Furniture Store. Rick had negotiated the advertising deal for Bill's with one of Bill's employees, Sarina, who agreed to a fee of $40,000 for Rick's services. Sarina told Rick to send her the bill. After completing the work, Rick dropped it off at Bill's, along with an invoice for $40,000, the only written confirmation of the job. Eleven months later, Rick still had not been paid by Bill's Furniture Store, so he filed suit to collect his fee.

What are the legal grounds for recovery? What should Rick allege in his complaint? Why? Write a brief complaint.

Suppose Rick testified at trial on his own behalf.

---

[3] If it was not *the* scalpel in question, but rather a different scalpel, it may not be admitted.

§ 1.04 THE DIFFERENT MEANINGS OF "EVIDENCE" 5

Excerpt of Rick's Direct Examination

PLAINTIFF'S ATTORNEY: Rick, would you please state your name for the record and spell it for the court reporter.

A: Rick Turkish, that's R-i-c-k. T-u-r-k-i-s-h.

PLAINTIFF'S ATTORNEY: What do you do for a living, Mr. Turkish?

A: I own a small advertising firm.

PLAINTIFF'S ATTORNEY: What is your family status?

A: I have been married for 17 years and have three children.

PLAINTIFF'S ATTORNEY: Please describe what happened on the afternoon of October 1st.

A: I spoke to Sarina Johnson, of Bill's Furniture Store, about doing an advertising campaign for the store. I agreed during the conversation to design and set up several advertisements in the local newspapers for Bill's Fall Sale.

PLAINTIFF'S ATTORNEY: What happened after you agreed to do the work?

A: I created and designed the advertising campaign and gave the ad campaign to the store — all of the materials, master copies and the like. I dropped them off at Bill's with one of his employees, Jimmy, along with an invoice for the work.

PLAINTIFF'S ATTORNEY: Who's Jimmy?

A: He used to work at Bill's. I gave the ad campaign to him because Sarina and Bill were not in the office that day.

PLAINTIFF'S ATTORNEY: What happened after that?

A: Nothing. I didn't hear from Bill's. And I would like to get paid for the work I did for them.

What additional questions would you want to ask Rick? (Keeping in mind that proof is required in this contract action and all other actions at trial.) What are your goals in asking these questions?

If you represented Bill's, how would you cross-examine Rick? What would be your objectives?

Problem 1-2: Inspector Clousseau

Inspector Clousseau investigates the scene of a gruesome murder. He finds, among other things:

1. A blueprint of the building in which the murder occurred.

2. One of the victim's earrings, lying on the ground near the victim's body.

3. A paint brush spattered with blood.

4. A photograph of the scene without the body in it.

5. A "Saturday Night Special" handgun, lying under a nearby bed.

The Inspector then interviews three people who are standing in the area. One of the three, a neighbor, knew the murder victim. The neighbor, Bill, tells Clousseau that the victim was Jane Duplane and that she was having a torrid affair with Bill's best friend. During the interview, Clousseau observes the maid furtively placing an object in her pocket, and a young man running away with what appeared to be an earring in his hand.

Which of Clousseau's findings or interviews constitutes proof of the crime? What rules of evidence might apply to that proof? What proof might the jury be allowed to take back with them to the jury room? Why?

§ 1.05 CATEGORIES OF EVIDENCE: REAL; REPRESENTATIVE; AND TESTIMONIAL EVIDENCE

Another useful tool is to classify evidence as (a) real, (b) representative, or (c) testimonial. (a) Real evidence is physical, tangible evidence, the thing itself. It is the gun used in an armed robbery, the fender from a car in an auto accident or the original contract in a breach of contract action. (b) Representative evidence is evidence that represents another thing: a diagram, chart, photograph, x-ray, etc. (c) Testimonial evidence comes from witnesses "viva voce," meaning by voice. An example is the eyewitness testifying to what she observed at the pertinent time. These three forms of evidence have differing requirements for admissibility, particularly in the area of authentication, which is covered in Chapter 18.

Problem 1-3: Clousseau Revisited

In Problem 1-2, above, which of the evidence would qualify as real evidence? Representative evidence? Testimonial evidence? Explain.

§ 1.06 ANOTHER HELPFUL DISTINCTION — DIRECT OR CIRCUMSTANTIAL EVIDENCE

Evidence also can be categorized as either direct or circumstantial in nature. Circumstantial evidence requires an inference to be drawn for the evidence to be relevant. To illustrate, a reasonable inference from observing people walking in the streets all bundled up in hats, scarves, and heavy jackets is that it is cold outside. Thus, circumstantial evidence is used indirectly through inferences. Direct evidence does not require an inference to be drawn from it to be relevant. Instead, it proves a fact — generally a material fact — without requiring any deductions. For example, an eyewitness to a murder who testifies "I saw the defendant fire the gun, killing the victim," provides direct evidence of the killer's identity. A bloody knife found at the scene of the crime, on the other hand, provides indirect or circumstantial evidence of the murder, as does the fact that a suspect fled the scene after the killing. The bloody knife and running suspect both require inferences to prove the material fact, in this case that the suspect committed a murder.

Example

Julie Janson, a school teacher of modest means, allegedly stole her neighbor's priceless Picasso painting in October. One month later, in

November, Julie purchased a million dollar yacht. *Is the purchase of the yacht direct or circumstantial evidence of the larceny?*

Answer: The newly purchased yacht would be circumstantial evidence of the larceny. It can be inferred from Julie's recent purchase of the yacht that she suddenly obtained a significant amount of money and that the windfall was consistent with the theft and sale of a priceless Picasso painting. Direct evidence of the larceny would be an eyewitness who actually observed Julie take the painting.

Problem 1-4: Drawing Inferences in the Sand

Which of the following are examples of circumstantial evidence? Which are examples of direct evidence? Explain.

1. To show that a letter was received, evidence is offered that the letter was properly postmarked, addressed, and mailed.

2. On the issue of whether it was raining on March 14th, Ellie testified, "I looked out my window and saw rain falling."

3. On the issue of whether it was raining on March 14th, Paul testified, "When people came into the office on that day, they were wearing raincoats and shaking water from their umbrellas."

4. On the issue of whether the elephant that escaped from the circus had crossed Alexandra's backyard, Alexandra testified, "I looked into my backyard and saw huge elephant footprints."

5. On the issue of whether Betty robbed the bank, an employee of the police department testified that the handgun the perpetrator had dropped at the bank was registered in Betty's name.

6. On the issue of whether Larry robbed Sandra, a bystander testified, "I saw Larry rob Sandra."

7. On the issue of whether Barney attended the hockey game, Sheila's statement, "Ed told me he saw Barney walking towards the arena where the hockey game was played."

§ 1.07 EVIDENCE IN THE TRIAL COURTS

While appellate courts rule on a wide variety of evidentiary issues, the primary locus of evidentiary rulings lies in the trial courts. Evidentiary issues arise throughout a trial and the numerous evidentiary rulings by trial courts are seldom appealed, let alone reversed on appeal. For example, an improper leading question will rarely be considered by a court on appeal or constitute a ground for reversal because the question likely does not impact the outcome of the case. Competent trial lawyers must know how to negotiate the evidence rules to successfully advance their cases.

Transactional lawyers who may never set foot in a courtroom (as per their desire) still must have great familiarity with evidence rules. While transactional attorneys provide advice to businesses on how to avoid legal problems, the attorneys must prepare clients for the possibility of a lawsuit. Transactional attorneys must know how to maintain records, analyze the evidentiary significance of documents and other business-related materials and otherwise protect clients under the rules of evidence if litigation should arise.

One way to better understand how the rules work is to situate them in the broader environment of a lawsuit. The lawsuit includes far more than the evidentiary rules, extending to: (1) the pleadings that initiate the case and propel it forward, either to trial or to an alternative disposition, such as a plea or settlement; (2) lawyering strategies and arguments; and (3) jury selection and deliberation.

UNITED STATES v. WAYNE GILLIS

The following excerpt from a narcotics prosecution is based on a real case that occurred in Washington, D.C. Many similar cases are brought on a daily basis throughout the United States. The inclusion of this case is intended to provide useful background information; it offers an opportunity to observe how evidence exists within the context of a lawsuit.

A. The Facts of the Case

The basic facts of the case are in dispute. The facts according to the prosecutor and defense follow.

1. The Facts According to the Prosecutor

On August 24th, at approximately 2:15 p.m., W-1 (Officer Friday), a Park Police officer, was traveling north on Rock Creek Parkway in Washington, D.C. As he passed by Parking Lot # 6, he observed a 1990 Green Volvo without a front tag. The officer drove up to the car, approached the driver's window, and motioned for the driver to open it. The driver, later identified as the defendant, rolled down the window several inches.

W-1 smelled marijuana. W-1 then asked the defendant to get out of the car.

The defendant showed W-1 his license and registration for the car. Defendant's license and registration were from the State of Alabama. W-1 asked the defendant whether there was any marijuana inside the car. Defendant went back into the car, pulled out the front ashtray, and brought it outside to W-1.

W-1 then asked the co-defendant, a male who was sitting in the front passenger seat, to get out of the car. W-1 discovered rolling papers and a package of white powder under the right front mat. W-1 then conducted a complete search of the car. When W-1 removed the thick seat mats off the front seat, he observed a .22 caliber Smith & Wesson pistol wedged in the crack separating the back of the driver's seat and the driver's seat itself.

W-1 then searched defendant and co-defendant. Nothing was discovered on the defendant. A large quantity of greenish brown weed in a plastic bag was found on the passenger.

W-1 seized all of the evidence and field-tested the powder and weed. The greenish brown weed discovered on the co-defendant tested positive for marijuana. The package of white powder tested positive for cocaine.

Defendant did not appear to be under the influence of narcotics, but the co-defendant did. Both were extremely cooperative.

The defendant and co-defendant were read their rights. During the reading, the defendant spontaneously said, "That stuff you found was not mine, but a friend's! I'm not going to say anything more without a lawyer."

2. The Facts According to the Defense

The defendant, Wayne Gillis, is 34 years old. Wayne is not married, but resides part of the time with his girlfriend, with whom he has two children: Samantha (age three) and Chase (age five). Wayne is employed as a long-distance trucker by Amalgamated Trucking, Inc., and is consequently out-of-town for long periods of time.

On August 24th, Wayne had driven to Rock Creek Park to relax after a five-day trip to Nebraska for Amalgamated. He was accompanied by his good friend, Bob, who was sitting in the passenger's seat. Wayne routinely lets friends borrow the car while he is out-of-town and had let his friend Jim use it during this past trip.

At the park, Wayne and Bob were chatting in the car, minding their own business, when a police officer approached Wayne and tapped loudly on the window. The officer rudely asked Wayne what he was doing and then ordered him out of the car. The officer searched them and the car without permission. When the officer confronted Wayne, claiming to have found a gun and drugs in the car, Wayne told the officer that he (Wayne) knew nothing about it. Later, Wayne informed me (his attorney) that the stuff was either planted by the police or left there by his friend, Jim, who had used the car a couple of times in the preceding month because his car was in the shop.

Wayne did not have Jim's address or last name; Jim was a friend from the neighborhood. Wayne also noted there were others in the neighborhood that could verify that Jim lived and hung out there, although Jim had not been seen lately.

Wayne states that he had been convicted of the possession of marijuana eight years ago and disorderly conduct seven years ago. Five years ago, he was charged with conspiracy to distribute cocaine and weapons possession, but all of the charges were dropped. Wayne also thought he should mention that 15 years ago, when he was in middle school, he had been caught taking a teacher's car for a joyride with a classmate. As a result, the boys were sent to a juvenile home for a few months.

B. The Criminal Case File

Excerpts from a case file constructed by the prosecutor follow. *When reviewing these excerpts: (1) identify the possible evidence in the case; and (2) arrange the evidence in a persuasive manner, first for the prosecution and then for the defense.*

1. The Information

[The following is the prosecutor's charging document, called the "Information."]

United States v. Wayne Gillis

Misdemeanor # 468459-98 Washington, D.C.

CRIMINAL DIVISION

The United States Attorney for the District of Columbia informs the Court that within the District of Columbia:

DEFENDANT'S NAME   Wayne   Gillis   (PDID)
(FIRST)   (LAST)

DEFENDANT'S ADDRESS
1204 P Street N.W.,
Washington, D.C.

Defendant did on or about <u>August 24, 1998</u> commit the crime or crimes indicated herein and identified by an X-mark or X-marks.

POSSESSION OF A CONTROLLED SUBSTANCE — in that he unlawfully, knowingly, and intentionally had in his possession a controlled substance consisting of <u>Cocaine</u> in violation of 33 **District of Columbia Code, Section 541(c)**.

POSSESSION OF A CONTROLLED SUBSTANCE — in that he unlawfully, knowingly, and intentionally had in his possession a controlled substance consisting of <u>Cannabis</u>, in violation of 33 **District of Columbia Code, Section 541(c)**.

DISTRIBUTION OF A SCHEDULE V CONTROLLED SUBSTANCE — in that he unlawfully, knowingly, and intentionally did distribute a quantity of <u>Cannabis</u>, a Schedule V controlled substance, in violation of 33 **District of Columbia Code, Section 541(a)(1)**.

POSSESSION WITH INTENT TO DISTRIBUTE A SCHEDULE V CONTROLLED SUBSTANCE — in that he unlawfully, knowingly, and intentionally did possess with intent to distribute a quantity of <u>Cannabis</u>, a Schedule V controlled substance, in violation of 33 **District of Columbia Code, Section 541(a)(1)**.

CARRYING PISTOL WITHOUT A LICENSE — in that he carried openly and concealed on and about his person, a <u>Pistol</u> without a license therefor issued as provided by **Section 22-3206, District of Columbia Code**, in violation of Section 22-3204, District of Columbia.

UNITED STATES ATTORNEY FOR THE DISTRICT OF COLUMBIA BY ASSISTANT UNITED STATES ATTORNEY FOR THE DISTRICT OF COLUMBIA

BY: Janet Parker
DATE: 9/3/98
OFFICER: Friday
DISTRICT: Rock Creek Park, Washington, D.C.

2. The Prosecutor's Notes

Summary of Case

8/24/98-2:15 p.m.
6th Parking Lot, Rock Creek Park, N.W.

Charges: Possession of Cocaine, Possession of Marijuana, Carrying a Pistol Without a License

Witnesses	
Witness #1	Arresting Officer/Chain of custody
Witness #2	Assisting Officer
Witness #3	Crime Scene Search Officer — Took fingerprints
Witness #4	Transporting Officer

Evidence	Who and Where Found
1 .22 Caliber Pistol	Witness # 1: wedged in the front seat.
1 Bag of Marijuana	Witness # 1: in possession of passenger.
3 Marijuana Cigarettes	Witness # 1: front ashtray.
2 Packets of Cocaine	Witness # 1: under front passenger's mat.
1 Package of Rolling Paper	Witness # 1: under front passenger's mat.
1 Hemostat	Witness # 1: under front driver's mat.

3. Transcript of Deposition of Eyewitness, Ronald Samoa

[taken on September 14, 1998, in the office of the defense counsel]

DEFENSE COUNSEL: Would you please state your name for the record?

A: Ronald T. Samoa

DEFENSE COUNSEL: Where do you live, Mr. Samoa?

A: I live at 1405 Cleveland Park Circle, N.W., Washington, D.C.

DEFENSE COUNSEL: Where were you on August 24, 1998, at approximately 2:15 p.m.?

A: I was in Rock Creek Park, taking a walk.

DEFENSE COUNSEL: What did you see at that time, if anything?

A: I saw a police officer go over to a parked car and animatedly say something through a rolled up window. The driver rolled down the window a crack and I saw what looked like smoke come out of it.

DEFENSE COUNSEL: Then what happened?

A: The driver then got out of the car, put his hands up in front of him, and seemed to tell the officer to take it easy. The passenger got out at the same time. Then the officer practically dove into the car and emerged with some stuff in his hands.

DEFENSE COUNSEL: Where did the stuff in his hands come from?

A: I could not see.

DEFENSE COUNSEL: When the officer went into the car, can you describe what he was doing with his hands?

A: The officer's right hand was balled up, like a fist, but I couldn't see if he was holding anything in it; I just am not sure.

DEFENSE COUNSEL: Thank you.

How would you approach the case as the prosecutor? As the defense counsel? Explain your strategy for each side.

What would you include in an opening statement to the jury in this case? Note that the opening statements by counsel are not evidence. Instead, they can be thought of as the "road maps" of what the evidence will show. They offer a peek at all of the pieces in the puzzle, presented whole before the evidentiary component of the trial begins, much like the table of contents for a book. Note that when evidence is finally presented at trial, the organization and clarity of the opening statement is often torn apart by necessity. Sometimes a single witness can testify only about pieces of several events and several witnesses often are required to explain a part of the overall narrative. The opening statement is not an opening argument about the other side's evidence. While attorneys construct their openings subject to personal preference, common features include: (1) a one-line theme for the case, much like the title of a book or film; (2) a story about what happened (that is, what the evidence will show); and (3) a request for a favorable verdict based on the evidence.

§ 1.08 A JURY OF HER PEERS

Problem 1-5: A Jury of Her Peers

Susan Glaspell's classic short story, A Jury of Her Peers, *is below. In reading the story, identify what types of evidence the women rely upon: Character? Opinion (lay or expert)? Eyewitness? Circumstantial versus direct? Physical evidence? Hearsay? How probative (how persuasive) is each item of evidence? Do the men and the women assign different probative value to the same kinds of evidence? Do they discover and focus attention upon different kinds of evidence? Do they interpret the evidence differently? What do the answers to these questions suggest to you about whom you would want on a criminal jury trying the wife if you were defense counsel? If you were the prosecution? What sorts of opening and closing arguments should each side make? What story will each side want to tell? Which story is more persuasive and why?*

A JURY OF HER PEERS — 1917

When Martha Hale opened the storm-door and got the north wind, she ran back for her big woolen scarf. As she hurriedly wound that round her head her eye made a scandalized sweep of her kitchen. It was no ordinary thing that called her away — it was probably farther from ordinary than anything that had ever happened in Dickson County. But her kitchen was in no shape for leaving: bread ready for mixing, half the flour sifted and half unsifted.

She hated to see things half done; but she had been at that when they stopped to get Mr. Hale, and the sheriff came in to say his wife wished Mrs. Hale would come too — adding, with a grin, that he guessed she was getting scared and wanted another woman along. So she had dropped everything right where it was.

"Martha!" now came her husband's impatient voice. "Don't keep folks waiting out here in the cold."

She joined the three men and the one woman waiting for her in the sheriff's car.

After she had the robes tucked in she took another look at the woman beside her. She had met Mrs. Peters the year before, at the county fair, and the thing she remembered about her was that she didn't seem like a sheriff's wife. She was small and thin and didn't have a strong voice. Mrs. Gorman, the sheriff's wife before Gorman went out and Peters came in, had a voice that seemed to be backing up the law with every word. But if Mrs. Peters didn't look like a sheriff's wife, Peters made it up in looking like a sheriff — a heavy man with a big voice who was particularly genial with the law-abiding, as if to make it plain that he knew the difference between criminals and non-criminals. And right there it came into Mrs. Hale's mind that this man who was so lively with all of them was going to the Wrights' now as a sheriff.

"The country's not very pleasant this time of year," Mrs. Peters at last ventured.

Mrs. Hale scarcely finished her reply, for they had gone up a little hill and could see the Wright place, and seeing it did not make her feel like talking. It looked very lonely this cold March morning. It had always been a lonesome-looking place. It was down in a hollow, and the poplar trees around it were lonely-looking trees. The men were looking at it and talking about what had happened. The county attorney was bending to one side, scrutinizing the place as they drew up to it.

"I'm glad you came with me," Mrs. Peters said nervously, as the two women were about to follow the men in through the kitchen door.

Even after she had her foot on the doorstep, Martha Hale had a moment of feeling she could not cross this threshold. And the reason it seemed she couldn't cross it now was because she hadn't crossed it before. Time and time again it had been in her mind, "I ought to go over and see Minnie Foster" — she still thought of her as Minnie Foster, though for twenty years she had been Mrs. Wright. And then there was always something to do and Minnie Foster would go from her mind. But now she could come.

The men went over to the stove. The women stood close together by the door. Young Henderson, the county attorney, turned around and said, "Come up to the fire, ladies."

Mrs. Peters took a step forward, then stopped. "I'm not-cold," she said. And so the two women stood by the door, at first not even so much as looking around the kitchen.

The men talked about what a good thing it was the sheriff had sent his deputy out that morning to make a fire for them, and then Sheriff Peters stepped back from the stove, unbuttoned his outer coat, and leaned his hands on the kitchen table in a way that seemed to mark the beginning of official business. "Now, Mr. Hale," he said in a sort of semi-official voice, "before we move things about, you tell Mr. Henderson just what it was you saw when you came here yesterday morning."

The county attorney was looking around the kitchen.

"By the way," he asked, "has anything been moved?" He turned to the sheriff. "Are things just as you left them yesterday?"

Peters looked from cupboard to sink; to a small worn rocker a little to one side of the kitchen table.

"It's just the same."

"Well, Mr. Hale," said the county attorney, "tell just what happened when you came here yesterday morning."

Mrs. Hale, still leaning against the door, had that sinking feeling of the mother whose child is about to speak a piece. Lewis often wandered along and got things mixed up in a story. She hoped he would tell this straight and plain, and not say unnecessary things that would make it harder for Minnie Foster. He didn't begin at once, and she noticed that he looked queer, as if thinking of what he had seen here yesterday.

"Yes, Mr. Hale?" the county attorney reminded.

"Harry and I had started to town with a load of wood," Mrs. Hale's husband began.

Harry was Mrs. Hale's oldest boy. He wasn't with them now, for the wood never got to town yesterday and he was taking it this morning, so he hadn't been home when the sheriff stopped to say he wanted Mr. Hale to come over to the Wright place and tell the county attorney his story there, where he could point it all out. With all Mrs. Hale's other emotions came the fear Harry wasn't dressed warm enough — they hadn't any of them realized how that north wind did bite.

"We come along this road," Hale was going on, "and as we got in sight of the house I says to Harry, 'I'm goin' to see if I can't get John Wright to take a telephone.' You see," he explained to Henderson, "unless I can get somebody to go in with me they won't come out this branch road except for a price I can't pay. I'd spoke to Wright about it before; but he put me off, saying folks talked too much anyway, and all he asked was peace and quiet — guess you know about how much he talked himself. But I thought maybe if I went to the house and talked about it before his wife, and said all the women-folks liked the telephones, and — that in this lonesome stretch of road it would be a good thing — well, I said to Harry that

that was what I was going to say — though I said at the same time that I didn't know as what his wife wanted made much difference to John — — "

Now, there he was! — saying things he didn't need to say. Mrs. Hale tried to catch her husband's eye, but fortunately the county attorney interrupted with:

"Let's talk about that a little later, Mr. Hale. I do want to talk about that, but I'm anxious now to know just what happened when you got here."

When he began this time, it was deliberately, as if he knew it were important.

"I didn't see or hear anything. I knocked at the door. And still it was all quiet inside. I knew they must be up — it was past eight o'clock. So I knocked again, louder, and I thought I heard somebody say, 'Come in.' I wasn't sure — I'm not sure yet. But I opened the door — this door," jerking a hand toward the door by which the two women stood, "and there, in that rocker" — pointing to it — "sat Mrs. Wright."

Everyone in the kitchen looked at the rocker. It came into Mrs. Hale's mind that this chair didn't look in the least like Minnie Foster — the Minnie Foster of twenty years before. It was a dingy red, with wooden rungs up the back, and the middle rung gone; the chair sagged to one side.

"How did she — look?" the county attorney was inquiring.

"Well," said Hale, "she looked — queer."

"How do you mean — queer?"

He took out note-book and pencil. Mrs. Hale did not like the sight of that pencil. She kept her eye on her husband, as if to keep him from saying unnecessary things that would go into the book and make trouble. Hale spoke guardedly: "Well, as if she didn't know what she was going to do next. And kind of — done up." "How did she seem to feel about your coming?" "Why, I don't think she minded — one way or other. She didn't pay much attention. I said, 'Ho' do, Mrs. Wright. It's cold, ain't it?' And she said, 'Is it?' — and went on pleatin' of her apron." "Well, I was surprised. She didn't ask me to come up to the stove, but just set there, not even lookin' at me. And so I said, 'I want to see John.' And then she-laughed. I guess you would call it a laugh." "I thought of Harry and the team outside, so I said, a little sharp, 'Can I see John?' 'No,' says she — kind of dull like. 'Ain't he home?' says I. Then she looked at me. 'Yes,' says she, 'he's home.' 'Then why can't I see him?' I asked her out of patience with her now. 'Cause he's dead.' Says she just as quiet and dull and fell to pleatin' her apron. 'Dead?' says I, like you do when you can't take in what you've heard." "She just nodded her head, not getting a bit excited, but rockin' back and forth."

"'Why — where is he?' says I, not knowing *what* to say."

"She just pointed upstairs — like this — pointing to the room above."

"I got up, with the idea of going up there myself. By this time I — didn't know what to do. I walked from there to here, then I says, 'Why, what did he die of?'"

"'He died of a rope around his neck.' Says she; and just went on pleatin' at her apron."

Hale stopped speaking, staring at the rocker. Nobody spoke; it was as if all were seeing the woman who had sat there the morning before.

"And what did you do then?" the attorney asked.

"I went out and called Harry. I thought I might — need help. I got Harry in, and we went upstairs." His voice fell almost to a whisper. "There he was — lying over the — "

"I think I'd rather have you go into that upstairs," the county attorney interrupted, "where you can point it all out. Just go on now with the rest of the story."

"Well, my first thought was to get that rope off. It looked — "

He stopped; he did not say how it looked.

"But Harry, he went up to him and he said, 'No, he's dead all right, and we'd better not touch anything. So we went downstairs.'"

"She was still sitting that same way. 'Has anybody been notified?' I asked. 'No' says she, unconcerned."

" 'Who did this, Mrs. Wright?' said Harry. He said it business-like, she stopped pleatin' at her apron. 'I don't know,' she says. 'You don't *know*?' says Harry. 'Weren't you sleepin' in the bed with him?' 'Yes,' says she, 'but I was on the inside.' 'Somebody slipped a rope around his neck and strangled him, and you didn't wake up?' says Harry. 'I didn't wake up,' she said after him."

"We may have looked as if we didn't see how that could be, for after a minute she said, 'I sleep sound.' "

"Harry was going to ask her more questions, but I said maybe that weren't our business; maybe we ought to let her tell her story first to the coroner or the sheriff. So Harry went fast as he could over to High Road — the Rivers' place, where there's a telephone."

"And what did she do when she knew you had gone for the coroner?"

"She moved from that chair to this one over here, and just sat there with her hands held together and looking down. I got a feeling that I ought to make some conversation, so I said I had come in to see if John wanted to put in a telephone; and at that she started to laugh, and then she stopped and looked at me — scared."

At sound of a moving pencil the man who was telling the story looked up.

"I dunno — maybe it wasn't scared; I wouldn't like to say it was. Soon Harry got back, and then Dr. Lloyd came, and you, Mr. Peters, and so I guess that's all I know that you don't."

He said this with relief, moved as if relaxing. The county attorney walked to the stair door.

"I guess we'll go upstairs first — then out to the barn and around there."

He paused and looked around the kitchen.

"You're convinced there was nothing important here?" he asked the sheriff. "Nothing that would — point to any motive?"

The sheriff too looked all around. "Nothing here but kitchen things," he said, with the insignificance of kitchen things.

The county attorney was looking at the cupboard. He opened the upper part and looked in. After a moment he drew his hand away sticky.

"Here's a nice mess," he said resentfully.

The two women had drawn nearer, and now the sheriff's wife spoke.

"Oh — her fruit," She said, looking to Mrs. Hale for understanding. "She worried about that when it turned so cold last night. She said the fire would go out and her jars might burst."

Mrs. Peters' husband broke into a laugh.

"Well, can you beat the women! Held for murder, and worrying about her preserves!"

The young attorney set his lips.

"I guess before we're through with her she may have something more serious than preserves to worry about."

"Oh, well," said Mrs. Hale's husband, with good-natured superiority, "women are used to worrying over trifles."

The two women moved closer together. Neither of them spoke. The county attorney seemed to remember his manners — and think of his future.

"And yet," said he, with the gallantry of a young politician, "for all their worries, what would we do without the ladies?"

The women did not speak. He went to the sink to wash his hands, turned to wipe them on the roller towel, pulled it for a cleaner place.

"Dirty towels! Not much of a house-keeper, would you say, ladies?" He kicked his foot against some dirty pans under the sink.

"There's a great deal of work to be done on a farm," said Mrs. Hale stiffly.

"To be sure. And yet" — with a little bow to her — "I know there are some Dickson County farm-houses that do not have such roller towels."

"Those towels get dirty awful quick. Men's hands aren't always as clean as they might be."

"Ah, loyal to your sex, I see," he laughed. He gave her a keen look. "But you and Mrs. Wright were neighbors. I suppose you were friends too."

Martha Hale shook her head.

"I've seen little enough of her of late years. I've not been in this house — it's more than a year."

"And why was that? You didn't like her?"

"I liked her well enough," she replied with spirit. "Farmers' wives have their hands full, Mr. Henderson. And then — "She looked around the kitchen.

"Yes?" he encouraged.

"It never seemed a very cheerful place," said she, more to herself than to him.

"No," he agreed; "I don't think anyone would call it cheerful. I shouldn't say she had the home-making instinct."

"Well, I don't know as Wright had either," she muttered.

"You mean they didn't get on very well?"

"I suppose anything Mrs. Peters does 'll be all right?" the sheriff inquired. "She was to take in some clothes for her, you know — and a few little things. We left in such a hurry yesterday."

The county attorney looked at the two women they were leaving alone among the kitchen things.

"Yes — Mrs. Peters," he said, his glance resting on the woman who was not Mrs. Peters, the big farmer woman who stood behind the sheriff's wife. "Of course Mrs. Peters is one of us," he added in a manner of entrusting responsibility. "And keep your eye out, Mrs. Peters, for anything that might be of use. No telling; you women might come upon a clue to the motive — and that's the thing we need."

Mr. Hale rubbed his face in the fashion of a slow man getting ready for a pleasantry. "But would the women know a clue if they did come upon it?" he said. Having delivered himself of this, he followed the others through the stair door.

The women stood motionless, listening to the footsteps, first upon the stairs, then in the room above them.

Then, as if releasing herself from something too strange, Mrs. Hale began to arrange the dirty pans under the sink, which the county attorney's disdainful push of the foot had upset.

"I'd hate to have men coming into my kitchen, snoopin' round and criticizing."

"Of course it's no more than their duty," said the sheriff's wife, in her timid manner.

"Duty's all right, but I guess that deputy sheriff that come out to make the fire might have got a little of this on." She gave the roller towel a pull. "Wish I'd thought of that sooner! Seems mean to talk about her for not having things slicked up, when she had to come away in such a hurry."

She looked around the kitchen. Certainly it was not "slicked up." Her eye was held by a bucket of sugar on a low shelf. The cover was off the wooden bucket, and beside it was a paper bag — half full.

Mrs. Hale moved towards it.

"She was putting this in there," she said to herself — slowly.

She thought of the flour in her kitchen at home — half sifted, half not sifted. She had been interrupted, and had left things half done. What had interrupted Minnie Foster? Why had that work been left half done? She made a move as if to finish it — unfinished things always bothered her, and then she saw that Mrs. Peters was watching her, and she didn't want Mrs. Peters to get that feeling she had of work begun and then — for some reason — not finished.

"It's a shame about her fruit," she said, going to the cupboard. "I wonder if it's all gone."

"Here's one that's all right." she said at last. She held it towards the light. "This is cherries, too." She looked again. "I declare I believe that's the only one."

"She'll feel bad, after all her hard work in the hot weather. I remember the afternoon I put up my cherries last summer."

She put the bottle on the table, and was about to sit down in the rocker. But something kept her from sitting in that chair. She stood looking at it, seeing the woman who had sat there "pleatin' at her apron."

The thin voice of the sheriff's wife broke in upon her: "I must be getting those things from the front room closet." She opened the door into the other room, started in, stepped back. "You coming with me, Mrs. Hale?" She asked nervously. "You — you could help me get them."

They were soon back. "My!" said Mrs. Peters, dropping the things on the table and hurrying to the stove.

Mrs. Hale stood examining the clothes the woman who was being detained in town had said she wanted.

"Wright was close!" she exclaimed, holding up a shabby black skirt that bore the marks of much making over. "I think maybe that's why she kept so much to herself. I s'pose she felt she couldn't do her part; and then, you don't enjoy things when you feel shabby. She used to wear pretty clothes and be lively — when she was Minnie Foster, one of the town girls, singing in the choir. But that — oh, that was twenty years ago."

With a carefulness in which there was something tender, she folded the shabby clothes and piled them at one corner of the table. She looked up at Mrs. Peters, and there was something in the other woman's look that irritated her.

"She don't care," she said to herself. "Much difference it makes to her whether Minnie Foster had pretty clothes when she was a girl."

Then she looked again, and she wasn't so sure; in fact she hadn't at any time been sure about Mrs. Peters. She had that shrinking manner, and yet her eyes looked as if they could see a long way into things.

"This all you was to take in?" asked Mrs. Hale.

"No," said the sheriff's wife; "she said she wanted an apron. Funny thing to want," she ventured in her nervous way, "for there's not much to get you dirty in jail, goodness knows. But I suppose just to make her feel more natural. She said they were in the bottom drawer of this cupboard. Yes — here they are. And then her little shawl that always hung on the stair door."

She took the small grey shawl from behind the door leading upstairs.

Suddenly Mrs. Hale took a quick step towards the other woman.

"Mrs. Peters!"

"Yes, Mrs. Hale?"

"Do you think she — did it?" Mrs. Peters looked frightened, "Oh I don't know," she said, in a voice that seemed to shrink from the subject.

"Well, I don't think she did," affirmed Mrs. Hale. "Asking for an apron, and her little shawl. Worryin' about her fruit."

"Mr. Peters says — " Footsteps were heard in the room above; she stopped, looked up, then went on in a lowered voice: "Mr. Peters says — it looks bad for her. Mr. Henderson is awful sarcastic in a speech, and he's going to make fun of her saying she didn't wake up."

For a moment Mrs. Hale had no answer. Then, "Well, I guess John Wright didn't wake up — when they was slippin' that rope under his neck," she muttered.

"No, it's *strange*," breathed Mrs. Peters. "They think it was such a — funny way to kill a man."

"That's just what Mr. Hale said," said Mrs. Hale, in a resolutely natural voice. "There was a gun in the house. He says that's what he can't understand."

"Mr. Henderson said, coming out, that what was needed for the case was a motive. Something to show anger — or sudden feeling."

"Well, I don't see any signs of anger around here," said Mrs. Hale. "I don't — " She stopped. Her eye was caught by a dish-towel in the middle of the kitchen table. Slowly she moved towards the table. One half of it was wiped clean, the other half untidy. Her eyes made a slow, almost unwilling turn to the bucket of sugar and the half-empty bag besides it. Things began — and not finished. She stepped back. "Wonder how they're finding things upstairs? I hope she had it in better shape up there. Seems kind of *sneaky* locking her up in town and coming out here to get her own house to turn against her!"

"But, Mrs. Hale," said the sheriff's wife, "the law is the law."

"I s'pose it is," answered Mrs. Hale shortly.

She turned to the stove, saying something about that fire not being much to brag of. "The law is the law — and a bad stove is a bad stove. How'd you like to work on this?" with the poker pointing to the broken lining. She opened the oven door. The thought of Minnie Foster trying to back in that oven — and the thought of her never going over to see Minnie Foster —. She was startled by hearing Mrs. Peters say, "A person gets discouraged — and loses heart." The sheriff's wife had looked from the stove to the sink — the pail of water which had been carried in from outside. The two women stood there silent, above them the footsteps of the men who were looking for evidence against the woman who had worked in that kitchen. That look of seeing into things, of seeing through a thing to something else, was in the eyes of the sheriff's wife now. When Mrs. Hale next spoke to her, it was gently.

"Better loosen up your things, Mrs. Peters. We'll not feel them when we go out."

Mrs. Peters went to the back of the room to hang up the fur tippet she was wearing. "Why, she was piecing a quilt," she exclaimed, and held up a large sewing basket piled high with quilt pieces.

Mrs. Hale spread some of the blocks on the table.

"It's log-cabin pattern," she said, putting several of them together. "Pretty, isn't it?"

They were so engaged with the quilt that they did not hear the footsteps on the stairs. As the stair door opened Mrs. Hale was saying, "do you suppose she was going to quilt it, or just knot it?"

The sheriff threw up his hands.

"They wonder whether she was going to quilt it, or just knot it!"

There was a laugh for the ways of women; a warming of hands over the stove, and then the county attorney said briskly, "Well, let's go right out to the barn and get that cleared up."

"I don't see as there's anything so strange," Mrs. Hale said resentfully, after the outside door had closed on the three men — "our taking up our time with little things while we're waiting for them to get the evidence. I don't see as it's anything to laugh about."

"Of course they've got awful important things on their minds," said the sheriff's wife apologetically.

They returned to an inspection of the blocks for the quilt. Mrs. Hale was looking at the fine, even sewing, preoccupied with thoughts of the woman who had done that sewing, when she heard the sheriff's wife say, in a startled tone, "Why, look at this one."

"The sewing," said Mrs. Peters, in a troubled way. "All the rest of them have been so nice and even — but — this one. Why, it looks as if she didn't know what she was about!"

Their eyes met — something flashed to life, passed between them; then, as if with an effort, they seemed to pull away from each other. A moment Mrs. Hale sat there, her fingers upon those stitches so unlike the rest of the sewing. Then she had pulled a knot and drawn the threads.

"Oh, what are you doing Mrs. Hale?" asked the sheriff's wife.

"Just pulling out a stitch or two that's not sewed very good," said Mrs. Hale mildly.

"I don't think we ought to touch things." Mrs. Peters said.

"I'll finish up this end," answered Mrs. Hale.

She threaded the needle and started to replace bad sewing with good. Then in that thin, timid voice, she heard: "Mrs. Hale!"

"Yes, Mrs. Peters?"

"What do you suppose she was so — nervous about?"

"Oh, I don't know," said Mrs. Hale, as if dismissing a thing not important enough to spend much time on. "I don't know as she was — nervous. I sew awful queer sometimes when I'm just tired."

"Well, I must get these clothes wrapped. They may be through sooner than we think. I wonder where I could find a piece of paper — and string."

"In that cupboard, maybe," suggested Mrs. Hale.

One piece of the crazy sewing remained unripped. Mrs. Peter's back turned, Martha Hale scrutinized that piece, compared it with the dainty, accurate stitches of the other blocks. The difference was startling. Holding this block it was hard to remain quiet, as if the distracted thoughts of the woman who had perhaps turned to it to try and quiet herself were communicating themselves to her.

"Here's a bird cage," Mrs. Peters said. "Did she have a bird, Mrs. Hale?"

"Why, I don't know whether she did or not." She turned to look at the cage Mrs. Peters was holding up. "I've not been here in so long." She signed. "There was a man round last year selling canaries cheap — but I don't know as she took one. Maybe she did. She used to sing real pretty herself."

"Seems kind of funny to think of a bird here. But she must have had one — or why would she have a cage? I wonder what happened to it."

"I suppose maybe the cat got it," suggested Mrs. Hale, resuming her sewing.

"No; she didn't have a cat. She's got that feeling some people have about cats — being afraid of them. When they brought her to our house yesterday, my cat got in the room, and she was real upset and asked me to take it out."

"My sister Bessie was like that," laughed Mrs. Hale.

The sheriff's wife did not reply. The silence made Mrs. Hale turn. Mrs. Peters was examining the bird cage.

"Look at this door," she said slowly. "It's broke. One hinge has been pulled apart."

Mrs. Hale came nearer.

"Looks as if someone must have been — rough with it."

Again their eyes met — startled, questioning, apprehensive. For a moment neither spoke nor stirred. Then Mrs. Hale, turning away, said brusquely, "If they're going to find any evidence, I wish they'd be about it. I don't like this place."

"But I'm awful glad you came with me, Mrs. Hale." Mrs. Peters put the birdcage on the table and sat down. "It would be lonesome for me — sitting here alone."

"Yes, it would, wouldn't it?" agreed Mrs. Hale. She had picked up the sewing, but now it dropped to her lap, and she murmured: "But I tell you what I *do* wish, Mrs. Peters. I wish I had come over sometimes when she was here. I wish — I had."

"But of course you were awful busy, Mrs. Hale. Your house — and your children."

"I could've come. I stayed away because it wasn't cheerful — and that's why I ought to have come. I" — she looked around — "I've never liked this place. Maybe because it's down in a hollow and you don't see the road. I don't know what it is, but it's a lonesome place, and always was. I wish I had come over to see Minnie Foster sometimes. I can see now."

"Well, you mustn't reproach yourself. Somehow we just don't see how it is with other folks till — something comes up."

"Not having children makes less work," mussed Mrs. Hale, "but it makes a quiet house. And Wright out to work all day — and no company when he did come in. Did you know John Wright, Mrs. Peters?"

"Not to know him. I've seen him in town. They say he was a good man."

"Yes — good," conceded John Wright's neighbor grimly. "He didn't drink, and kept his word as well as most, I guess, and paid his debts. But he was a hard man, Mrs. Peters. Just to pass the time of day with him — " She shivered. "Like a raw wind that gets to the bone." Her eye fell upon the cage on the table before her, and she added, "I should think she would've wanted a bird!"

Suddenly she leaned forward, looking intently at the cage. "But what do you s'pose went wrong with it?"

"I don't know," returned Mrs. Peters; "unless it got sick and died."

But after she said this she reached over and swung the broken door. Both women watched it.

"You don't know — her?" Mrs. Hale asked.

"Not till they brought her yesterday," said the sheriff's wife.

"She — come to think of it, she was kind of like a bird herself. Real sweet and pretty, but kind of timid and — flutterly. How — she — did — change."

Finally, as if struck with a happy thought and relieved to get back to everyday things: "Tell you what, Mrs. Peters, why don't you take the quilt in with you? It might take up your mind."

"Why, I think that's a real nice idea, Mrs. Hale. There couldn't possibly be any objection to that, could there? Now, just what will I take? I wonder if her patches are in here?" They turned to the sewing basket.

"Here's some red," said Mrs. Hale, bringing out a roll of cloth. Underneath this was a box. "Here, maybe her scissors are in here — and her things." She held it up. "What a pretty box! I'll warrant that was something she had a long time ago — when she was a girl."

She held it in her hand a moment; then, with a little sigh, opened it.

Instantly her hand went to her nose. "Why!"

Mrs. Peters drew nearer — then turned away.

"There's something wrapped up in this piece of silk," faltered Mrs. Hale.

"This isn't her scissors," said Mrs. Peters, in a shrinking voice.

Mrs. Hale raised the piece of silk. "Oh, Mrs. Peters!" she cried. "It's — "

Mrs. Peters bent closer.

"It's the bird," she whispered.

"But, Mrs. Peters!" cried Mrs. Hale, "*Look* at it! Its *neck* — look at its neck! It's all — other side *to.*"

The sheriff's wife again bent closer.

"Somebody wrung its neck," said she, in a voice that was slow and deep. The eyes of the two women met — this time clung together in a look of dawning comprehension, of growing horror. Mrs. Peters looked from the dead bird to the broken door of the cage. Again their eyes met. And just then there was a sound at the outside door.

Mrs. Hale slipped the box under the quilt pieces in the basket. The county attorney and sheriff came in.

"Well, ladies," said the attorney, as one turning from serious things to little pleasantries, "have you decided whether she was going to quilt it or knot it?"

"We think," said the sheriff's wife hastily, "that she was going to knot it."

"Well, that's very interesting, I'm sure." He caught sight of the cage. "Has the bird flown?"

"We think the cat got it," said Mrs. Hale in a prosaic voice.

He was walking up and down, as if thinking something out.

"Is there a cat?" he asked absently.

Mrs. Hale shot a look up at the sheriff's wife.

"Well, not *now*," said Mrs. Peters. "They're superstitious, you know; they leave."

The county attorney did not heed her. "No sign at all of anyone having coming in from the outside," he said to Peters, continuing an interrupted conversation. "Their own rope. Now let's go upstairs again and go over it, piece by piece. It would have to have been someone who knew just the — "

The stair door closed behind them and their voices were lost.

The two women sat motionless, not looking at each other, but as if peering into something and at the same time holding back. When they spoke now it was as if they were afraid of what they were saying, but could not help saying it.

"She liked the bird," said Martha Hale. "She was going to bury it in that pretty box."

"When I was a girl," said Mrs. Peters, under her breath, "my kitten — there was a boy took a hatchet, and before my eyes — before I could get there — " She covered her face an instant. "If they hadn't held me back I would have" — she caught herself, and finished weakly — "hurt him." Then they sat without speaking or moving. "I wonder how it would seem," Mrs. Hale began, as if feeling her way over strange ground — "never to have had any children around." Her eyes made a sweep of the kitchen. "No, Wright wouldn't like the bird — a thing that sang. She used to sing. He killed that too."

Mrs. Peters moved. "Of course we don't know who killed the bird."

"I knew John Wright," was the answer.

"It was an awful thing was done in this house that night, Mrs. Hale," said the sheriff's wife. "Killing a man while he slept — slipping a thing round his neck that choked the life out of him."

Mrs. Hale's hand went to the bird-cage. "His neck. Choked the life out of him."

"We don't *know* who killed him," whispered Mrs. Peters wildly. "We don't *know*."

Mrs. Hale had not moved. "If there had been years and years of nothing, then a bird to sing to you, it would be awful — still, after the bird was still."

"I know what stillness is," whispered Mrs. Peters. "When we homesteaded in Dakota, and my first baby died — after he was two years old — and me with no other then — "

Mrs. Hale stirred. "How soon do you suppose they'll be through looking for the evidence?"

"I know what stillness is," repeated Mrs. Peters. Then she too pulled back. "The law has got to punish crime, Mrs. Hale."

"I wish you'd seen Minnie Foster when she wore a white dress with blue ribbons, and stood up there in the choir and sang."

The picture of that girl, the thought that she had lived neighbor to her for twenty years, and had let her die for lack of life, was suddenly more than the woman could bear.

"Oh, I *wish* I'd come over here once in a while!" she cried. "That was a crime! That was a crime! Who's going to punish *that*?"

"We mustn't — take on," said Mrs. Peters, with a frightened look towards the stairs.

"I might 'a *known* she needed help! I tell you, it's *queer*, Mrs. Peters. We live close together, and we live far apart. We all go through the same things — it's all just a different kind of the same thing! If it weren't — why do you and I *know* — what we know this minute?"

Seeing the jar of fruit on the table, she reached for it. "If I was you I wouldn't *tell* her her fruit was gone! Tell her it *ain't*. Tell her it's all right — all of it. Here — take this in to prove to her! She — she may never know whether it was broke or not."

Mrs. Peters took the bottle of fruit as if glad to take it — as if touching a familiar thing, having something to do, could keep her from something else. She looked about for something to wrap the fruit in, took a petticoat from the pile of clothes she had brought from the front room, nervously started wading that round the bottle.

"My!" she began, in a high voice, "it's a good thing that men couldn't hear us! Getting all stirred up over a little thing like a — dead canary. As if that could have anything to do with — with — My, wouldn't they *laugh*?"

There were footsteps on the stairs.

"Maybe they would," muttered Mrs. Hale — "maybe they wouldn't." "No, Peters," said the county attorney, "it's all perfectly clear, except the reason for doing it. But you know juries when it comes to women. If there was some definite thing — something to *show*. Something to make a story about. A thing that would connect up with this clumsy way of doing it."

Mrs. Hale looked at Mrs. Peters. Mrs. Peters was looking at her. Quickly they looked away from one another. The outer door opened and Mr. Hale came in.

"I've nailed back that board we ripped off," he said.

"Much obliged, Mr. Hale," said the sheriff. "We'll be getting along now."

"I'm going to stay here awhile by myself," the county attorney suddenly announced. "You can send Frank out for me, can't you?" he asked the sheriff. "I want to go over everything. I'm not satisfied we can't do better."

Again, for one brief moment the women's eyes met.

The sheriff came up to the table.

"Did you want to see what Mrs. Peters was going to take in?"

The county attorney picked up the apron. He laughed.

"Oh, I guess they're not very dangerous things the ladies have picked out."

Mrs. Hale's hand was on the sewing basket in which the box was concealed. She felt that she ought to take her hand off the basket. She did not seem able to. She picked up one of the quilt blocks she had piled on to cover the box. She had a fear that if he took up the basket she would snatch it from him.

But he did not take it. With another laugh he turned away, saying, "No, Mrs. Peters doesn't need supervising. For that matter, a sheriff's wife is married to the law. Ever think of it that way, Mrs. Peters?"

Mrs. Peters had turned her face away. "Not — just that way," she said.

"Married to the law!" chuckled Mrs. Peters' husband. He moved towards the door into the front room, and said to the county attorney, "I just want you to come here a minute, George. We ought to take a look at these windows."

"Oh — windows!" scoffed the county attorney.

"We'll be leaving in a second, Mr. Hale," Mr. Peters told the farmer, as he followed the county attorney into the other room.

"Can't be leavin' too soon to suit me," muttered Hale, and went out.

Again, for one final moment, the two women were alone in the kitchen.

Martha Hale sprang up, her hands tight together, looking at the other woman, with whom it rested. At first she could not see her eyes, for the sheriff's wife had not turned back since she turned away at that suggestion of being married to the law. Slowly, unwillingly, Mrs. Peters turned her head until her eyes met the eyes of the other woman. There was a moment when they held each other in a steady, burning look in which there was no evasion or flinching. Then Martha Hale's eyes pointed the way to the basket in which was hidden the thing that would convict the third woman — that woman who was not there, and yet who had been there with them through that hour.

For a moment, Mrs. Peters did not move. And then she did it. Threw back the quilt pieces, got the box, tried to put it in her hand-bag. It was too big. Desperately she opened it, started to take the bird out. But there she broke — she could not touch the bird. She stood there helpless, foolish.

There was a sound at the door. Martha Hale snatched the box from the sheriff's wife and got it in the pocket of her big coat just as the sheriff and the county attorney came back into the kitchen.

"Well, Henry," said the county attorney, facetiously, "at least we found out that she was not going to quilt it. She was going to — what is it you call it, ladies?'

Mrs. Hale's hand was against the pocket of her coat.

"We call it — knot it," was her answer.

§ 1.09 CHAPTER REVIEW PROBLEMS

Review Problem 1-A

A famous movie star is arrested for shoplifting three expensive dresses from the Durn's Department Store. The star asserts her innocence and claims, "It was all a huge misunderstanding. I just wanted to show my personal assistant the cute buttons on the front of the dresses and she happened to be standing outside the store." At trial, the star offers the fact that she already was the owner of similar dresses, which she often wore to fancy dinner parties. The star testified, "Why would I need additional similar dresses? My own dresses are fabulous."

Which of the following is the most accurate statement about the star's own dresses?

1. The fact that the star owned similar dresses is relevant because it is direct evidence of her attendance at numerous dinner parties.

2. The similar dresses constitute representative evidence of the dresses allegedly shoplifted by the star.

3. The similar dresses require no evidentiary foundation from the star's attorney because they "speak for themselves."

4. The similar dresses constitute relevant circumstantial evidence in the case.

Review Problem 1-B

Arturo Montejo is charged with the murder of Sandy Mitrani. At trial, the prosecutor, Ms. Parnell, offers Sandy's statement as she lay dying from a bullet wound to the abdomen. The defense counsel, Ms. Sarno, objected and the Judge called both attorneys to the bench to discuss the question of admissibility.

JUDGE: Ms. Parnell, please proffer what the statement Sandy allegedly made was?

MS. PARNELL: The statement Sandy made that we would like to introduce is: "I can't believe this! I left myself open for being shot, and by that $%@#%@# ^ Montejo!" The statement is a dying declaration, Your Honor.

MS. SARNO: Your Honor, a dying declaration requires that the maker of the statement be unavailable to testify, that the statement be about the circumstances of the maker's death, that the person believe death was imminent at the time of the statement, and that the statement be made in a homicide or civil case. The pertinent rule is Federal Rule of Evidence 804(b)(2) and pursuant to that rule, Sandy's statement was not a dying declaration.

Which of the following propositions is most accurate regarding the admissibility of Sandy's statement?

1. The statement is direct evidence of Sandy's death.

2. The prosecutor, Ms. Parnell, has an affirmative obligation to offer some evidence that Sandy knew death was imminent prior to the judge admitting it into evidence.

3. Since the jury must decide whether Sandy believed her death was imminent, the prosecutor, Ms. Parnell, need not lay any foundation concerning that point.

4. The prosecutor, Ms. Parnell, must show that Sandy died from the gun shot wound or was otherwise unavailable to testify beyond a reasonable doubt.

Chapter 2

THE ROLES OF JUDGES, JURIES, AND ATTORNEYS AT TRIAL

§ 2.01 CHAPTER CHECKLIST

1. How is the judge the "gatekeeper" of the evidence admitted at trial?
2. How can attorneys satisfy their dual roles of representing their clients zealously and serving as officers of the court?
3. How can attorneys represent their clients zealously at trial and preserve the record for a potential appeal at the same time?
4. Why is the jury described as the "judge of the facts"?
5. Is it important for jurors to evaluate the credibility of evidence?

§ 2.02 RELEVANT FEDERAL RULES OF EVIDENCE

Rule 103. Rulings on Evidence

(a) **Effect of erroneous ruling.** Error may not be predicated upon a ruling which admits or excludes evidence unless a substantial right of the party is affected, and

   (1) **Objection.** In case the ruling is one admitting evidence, a timely objection or motion to strike appears of record, stating the specific ground of objection, if the specific ground was not apparent from the context; or

   (2) **Offer of proof.** In case the ruling is one excluding evidence, the substance of the evidence was made known to the court by offer or was apparent from the context within which questions were asked.

   Once the court makes a definitive ruling on the record admitting or excluding evidence, either at or before trial, a party need not renew an objection or offer of proof to preserve a claim of error for appeal.

(b) **Record of offer and ruling.** The court may add any other or further statement which shows the character of the evidence, the form in which it was offered, the objection made, and the ruling thereon. It may direct the making of an offer in question and answer form.

(c) **Hearing of jury.** In jury cases, proceedings shall be conducted, to the extent practicable, so as to prevent inadmissible evidence from being suggested to the jury by any means, such as making statements or offers of proof or asking questions in the hearing of the jury.

(d) **Plain error.** Nothing in this rule precludes taking notice of plain errors affecting substantial rights although they were not brought to the attention of the court.

Rule 104. Preliminary Questions

(a) **Questions of admissibility generally.** Preliminary questions concerning the qualification of a person to be a witness, the existence of a privilege, or the admissibility of evidence shall be determined by the court, subject to the provisions of subdivision (b). In making its determination it is not bound by the rules of evidence except those with respect to privileges.

(b) **Relevancy conditioned on fact.** When the relevancy of evidence depends upon the fulfillment of a condition of fact, the court shall admit it upon, or subject to, the introduction of evidence sufficient to support a finding of the fulfillment of the condition.

(c) **Hearing of jury.** Hearings on the admissibility of confessions shall in all cases be conducted out of the hearing of the jury. Hearings on other preliminary matters shall be so conducted when the interests of justice require, or when an accused is a witness and so requests.

(d) **Testimony by accused.** The accused does not, by testifying upon a preliminary matter, become subject to cross-examination as to other issues in the case.

(e) **Weight and credibility.** This rule does not limit the right of a party to introduce before the jury evidence relevant to weight or credibility.

§ 2.03 INTRODUCTION

Judges, juries, and attorneys have different responsibilities at trial, including the gathering, offering, and admission of evidence. While evidence rules play a significant role in the division of these duties, general rules of trial procedure and standards of professional conduct have a large impact as well.

§ 2.04 THE TRIAL JUDGE'S ROLE

Judges are responsible for the overall management of trials. As the trial's "chief operating officer," the judge is at once an umpire of disputes and an air traffic controller. The judge must ensure that the case progresses in an orderly and predictable fashion (*see* Rule 611). As part of this general responsibility, it is the judge's job to rule on evidentiary objections and on the admissibility of evidence. The Federal Rules give judges discretion in making evidentiary rulings and constrain judges' power. For example, while judges can call witnesses (*see* Rule 614) and may even comment on the evidence, they must exclude both irrelevant evidence (*see* Rule 402) and improper lay opinion testimony (*see* Rule 701). Further, a federal judge's ability to comment on the evidence is limited to the extent that it must not interfere with the jury's fact-finding function.

A judge makes admissibility determinations about whether evidence is hearsay, whether a witness is properly qualified to testify, whether a sufficient foundation has been laid for an exhibit, and whether a privilege applies to certain evidence. In making these and other admissibility determinations, a judge has wide latitude to consider many types of evidence. In the interest of accurate rulings, the judge is even permitted to consider inadmissible evidence, including hearsay. Nevertheless, the rules prohibit judges from considering privileged information when making admissibility determinations (*see* Rule 104(a)). Privileged information is consequently unique; judges cannot consider it when deciding whether evidence is admissible and a trier of fact cannot consider it when determining the facts of the case.

Example

At 2:00 a.m. on January 6th, two cars collided on Interstate 95. One of the cars was going the wrong way. After the crash, the cars were turned and entangled in such a manner that it was difficult to determine which driver was at fault.

At a civil trial between the drivers of the two cars, both of whom survived with serious injuries, the plaintiff offered in evidence a piece of metal located approximately 40 feet away from the crash, claiming that it was part of the defendant's car. The plaintiff offered the piece of metal because its location supported the plaintiff's theory that the defendant's car was the one traveling in the wrong direction.

At an earlier part of the trial, an expert from the Ford Motor Company had testified that this piece of metal "looked like" the kind that came from a 1994 Ford Galaxy, the defendant's car. An eyewitness had testified that he had seen the accident and that the impact had spewed pieces of metal everywhere, even as much as 60 feet away.

From the judge's perspective, the eyewitness was not very credible, and evidence suggested that the expert witness had made several mistakes in the past. Further, an affidavit from a passenger of another car, who attempted to describe the accident, was filled with statements made by other bystanders. The affidavit generally supported the plaintiff's claim about the piece of metal, however. Despite all of these deficiencies, the judge admitted the piece of metal on the basis that a reasonable juror could decide that the piece of metal was indeed a part of the defendant's car.

The judge also believed the jury could reasonably discredit the evidence of the eyewitness and the expert, and find that the metal was not part of the defendant's car. However, that possibility was not a reason under the rules to exclude the metal. The basic fact-finding function belongs to the jury and not the judge. It was simply the judge's job to screen out "bad" evidence, meaning evidence whose relevance was not supported by evidence sufficient to support a finding of fact pursuant to Rule 104(b).

[A] Questions of Admissibility

Perhaps the best-known job of the judge is the duty to rule on questions of admissibility. Judges must decide whether to sustain (uphold) or overrule (deny) a party's objections to evidence. If the attorneys fail to object to evidence or make a proffer, judges generally bite their tongues and remain silent, as it is the prerogative of the attorneys to try their own cases.

When a judge is asked to rule on a question of relevancy, the judge bases the ruling on reason and experience and the supporting evidence presented. (*See, e.g.*, Advisory Committee Note to Rule 401.) When a judge is asked to rule on other evidentiary areas, the judge may need to apply additional legal rules and principles. In areas like hearsay and privilege, the judge must determine whether evidentiary prerequisites have been met. Since admissibility rulings often involve the particular facts of a case, each ruling may pose new and challenging considerations that permit a judge to use her discretion. (*See* Rules 104(a), 104(b).) (Some admissibility questions, like those involving judicial notice, are not intended to promote diverse results from case to case or judge to judge. *See* Rule 201, which is discussed in Chapter 16.)

Rule foundation admissibility questions, meaning whether the requirements of the Rules are met, are governed by Rule 104(a). These questions depend on fact as well as law, such as whether a proposed "excited utterance" hearsay statement was made under the stress of excitement or whether an expert is relying on data or information of the type reasonably relied on in the expert's field. Thus, the judge alone decides if an out-of-court statement meets the criteria for an excited utterance or whether an expert is basing her testimony on information "reasonably relied on in the field," but it is the jury that decides whether to give that excited utterance or expert any credit or weight.

The burden of supplying supporting evidence in *rule foundation* admissibility matters is generally on the party offering the evidence and requires a preponderance of proof. The Advisory Committee observes that for fact determinations, "the judge will of necessity receive evidence pro and con on the issue." Advisory Committee Note 104(a). Significantly, the supporting evidence is not limited by the Rules, meaning a judge can even consider inadmissible evidence in making the admissibility decision, except a judge is not permitted to consider evidence that qualifies as privileged in making the admissibility determination. (*See* Rule 104(a).)

The preponderance of proof includes witness credibility questions. This means that a judge must resolve credibility questions should they arise. For example, if two witnesses contradict each other on the existence of a foundational fact, the judge must decide which witness to believe. Of course, the judge's *preliminary* determination of fact is not dispositive; the jury may disregard the evidence if it chooses.

Conditional relevance admissibility determinations are governed by Rule 104(b) and have a different standard of admissibility. These questions, as discussed further in the section on conditional relevance in the Relevance chapter, involve the facts surrounding the claimed event. Conditional relevance, also called relevance conditioned on fact, asks whether there is enough evidence to support a party's claims about what the facts are. For example, what actually happened at a meeting, an auto accident or homicide may all depend on a supporting fact or facts. Under the minimal threshold of Rule 104(b), the judge simply must ask whether sufficient evidence has been introduced for a reasonable jury to find that the fact exists. If the judge concludes a reasonable jury *could* find — not necessarily *would* find — that the fact exists, the judge will admit the evidence for the jury's consideration.

Unlike preliminary competency determinations pursuant to Rule 104(a), the judge does not resolve credibility questions in finding conditionally relevant foundational facts. That is, the judge generally assumes the truthfulness of the proponent's foundational witnesses. These standards of proof are not recited in either Rule 104(a)'s or 104(b)'s text, but result from a "judicial gloss" on the rules. This is not the only area where holes in the rules are filled by "judicial gloss", but it is one of the more important ones. *See Huddleston v. United States*, 485 U.S. 681 (1988) (104(b) conditional relevancy standard); *Bourjaily v. United States*, 483 U.S. 171 (1987) (104(a) competency standard).

Example

In a breach of contract action brought by a fencing manufacturer against its primary supplier, the plaintiff manufacturer offers the testimony of a witness to the agreement. The testimony includes the following:

DEFENDANT'S ATTORNEY: Objection, Your Honor, the witness' answer will be riddled with inadmissible hearsay. May we approach the bench?

JUDGE: Certainly. (at sidebar) Plaintiff's counsel, please proffer what Sheila will say if she is allowed to answer the question.

PLAINTIFF'S ATTORNEY: Of course, Your Honor. She will testify she heard the defendant's brother say to the defendant, "You realize the agreement does not allow us to supply the manufacturer with materials from our usual supplier in Maine and that it's going to cost us a heap more to get supplies elsewhere?" and that the defendant just stared back at his brother prior to signing the agreement.

JUDGE: Why is this objectionable, counsel?

DEFENDANT'S ATTORNEY: It is inadmissible hearsay, Your Honor.

JUDGE: I rule that the evidence is admissible, constituting an adoptive admission by a party opponent by silence. The defendant acquiesced in the statement and it is offered against him, as Rule 801(d)(2) provides. I am satisfied, based on the entire record in this case, that the evidence is relevant to the breach of contract issue and is not hearsay because it qualifies as an admission by a party opponent.

Problem 2-1: Alimony Al

Al sues his ex-wife, Anne, for increased alimony payments. Anne seeks to introduce at trial a journal that Al regularly kept of his expenses. Al objects, claiming that the book is a fake. Al submits a letter from a person who claims to have written the journal in exchange for a $4000 payment from Anne.

1. Can the judge consider the letter from the purported author of the journal in determining whether to admit the book? Why?

2. Anne calls Al's new wife, Kristine, to the witness stand. Al objects, relying on the marital communications privilege. What standard of admissibility applies in determining whether the privilege exists? How does the standard compare to general relevancy determinations?

Exercise: The Judge's Role

A judge often rules on evidence objections in seconds. The speed at which a judge must react is like the speed cars travel on the interstate — fast, to say the least. Thus, judges must become adept at saying "overruled" (the question or evidence will be permitted), or "sustained" (the question or evidence will be excluded), after objections are lodged by counsel. In addition, judges often ask for a response by opposing counsel prior to ruling.

The exercise below is intended to provide students with the opportunity to experience the judge's role at trial. If possible, students should stay in role during the entire exercise.

***

Exercise

For a statement to be admitted under the hearsay exception commonly referred to as "dying declarations," Rule 804(b)(2), the attorney must lay a foundation showing that the statement was made "by a [currently unavailable] declarant while believing that the declarant's death was imminent, concerning the cause or circumstances of what the declarant believed to be impending death." Thus, the attorney has several evidentiary foundations to meet prior to a judge finding the statement admissible. The attorney must show the unavailable declarant not only made a statement about his death, but he believed he was about to die at the time of the statement. (Note that the rule does not require the declarant to die, just for the declarant to believe she was about to die.)

Assume that a trial has commenced concerning the following fact pattern: Joan Jacobs was shot in an aborted robbery attempt outside a shopping mall in broad daylight on a very hot July day. As she slumped against her sports utility vehicle in the parking lot, she started rambling to the security guard, Sharon Stanley, who had come to help her, and the crowd of bystanders that had gathered. Jacobs muttered, "Get me a priest . . . and a last glass of water . . . I am bleeding everywhere. I am in big trouble. Does anyone else have the chills? It is cold here. If I ever see that guy who shot me again, I would recognize him anywhere! He looks just like Tom Cruise, only taller, about six feet tall. And oh yeah, he had a beard and a scar across his right cheek. I better not talk now, I am really hurting and may not make it. Tell my husband I love him . . . oh, I really want to hug my dog. Get Dr. Smaltz over here to help me; he's the best."

Joan subsequently dies. You are the prosecutor in the murder trial. James Jackson is accused of the murder. At trial, you first called Sharon Stanley to the witness stand to lay the appropriate foundations for the dying declaration.

After Sharon Stanley has testified, you call another witness who was a bystander in the crowd surrounding the deceased. The bystander, Bobby Barnwell, will testify that as he was leaving the shopping mall, he was attracted by a small crowd around a woman, who he later learned was named Joan Jacobs. Barnwell will state:

"I saw a man walking quickly in the other direction look back over his shoulder several times — as if he was hiding something. I think, but can't be sure, it was the defendant here. The guy slyly dropped something into a garbage can, but I couldn't see what it was." (The garbage can was later searched and discovered to contain a handgun with one of the defendant's fingerprints on it.)

Barnwell is currently unemployed and has been arrested four times for disorderly conduct.

Place Mr. Barnwell on the witness stand and ask him questions on direct examination to elicit information about the man he saw walking in the other direction. In addition, be prepared to ask the questions listed below.

Because you are just starting your journey of learning the rules of evidence, for the purposes of this exercise, the opposing counsel should object to those questions believed to be impermissible with the following phrase, "Objection, Your Honor; that was improper." (In actual trials, lawyers must identify the precise bases of their objections. "C'mon, Your Honor, she can't ask that" may be good enough for TV lawyers, but not for real ones.) The judge can ask the prosecution for a brief response, stating why the form or substance of the question is appropriate (pointing out, for example, that the response will help to prove the case or that the response is not unfairly prejudicial). The judge must then rule, either overruling the objection or sustaining the objection.

Some of the questions in the list below are clearly admissible or inadmissible. Many of the questions, however, are borderline, depending on the judge and the factual context of the questioning for their propriety. A student playing the examining attorney should ask the questions, and a student playing a witness should answer the questions. Also, a student playing opposing counsel should object to those questions believed to be improper and, after brief advocacy from each counsel, one or more students playing judges should rule.

The questions that counsel should ask the witness ought to include the following:

1. How did Ms. Jacobs appear when you first saw her?

2. What was the man doing when he walked in the other direction?

3. What did you have for breakfast that morning, Mr. Barnwell?

4. Why were you at the shopping mall?

5. Were you arrested for disorderly conduct recently?

6. Explain.

7. Did you think Ms. Jacobs was dying?

8. How long have you been unemployed?

9. Where do you live?

10. Describe the parking lot in the area where Ms. Jacobs was lying.

11. What did you hear Ms. Jacobs say about Tom Cruise?

[B] Appellate Judges: The Standard of Review on Appeal

An appellate judge usually does not retry a case on appeal. This means that the judge must take the record made below "as is," including the facts. The standard of review, meaning the test the appellate judges apply in considering the issues on appeal, can vary, depending on the nature of the issue. Variables include the type of error alleged (e.g., Did the error involve a constitutional right? Was the error made by the jury, prosecutor, judge, or other person?) and whether the error occurred in a criminal or civil case.

Standards of review include: abuse of discretion, de novo, and plain error. *Abuse of discretion* means a rule afforded discretion to a trial judge and the judge's evidentiary ruling exceeded the boundaries of that discretion. *De novo* review occurs when the issue is a question of law and the appellate court starts with a clean slate for its review. *Plain error* is an evidentiary error that concerns important evidence and is so apparent from the record that an appellate court is likely to consider it, even though a party failed to object. It is, in effect, the appellate court saying, "I know it when I see it." Reversible error generally cannot be found in an evidentiary ruling unless the error caused harm that rendered the trial proceedings unfair. The Federal Rules of Evidence require that an error affect a "substantial right" of the parties to amount to reversible error. (*See* Rule 103(d).)

Problem 2-2: "Justice was Done, so Appeal Immediately"

Rebecca is tried on charges of robbing a grocery store. In her defense, Rebecca offers to testify that she exchanged blows with the grocery store's manager more than one year prior to the alleged robbery and had not been in the store since that time. The prosecution objects, claiming the evidence is irrelevant. The trial judge improperly sustains the objection, ruling that no mention of the altercation would be allowed. Rebecca is convicted. She appeals the conviction, claiming the exclusion of the evidence was in error. *What is the appropriate standard of review by the appellate court?*

§ 2.05 THE JURY'S ROLE

The jury is commonly called the "judge of the facts." As fact-finder, the jury weighs the admissible evidence according to the applicable standard of proof (e.g., preponderance of the evidence or beyond a reasonable doubt). On a different level, the jury's role transcends the individual case. In a jury-based legal system, the jury arguably becomes an integral part of democratic governance, particularly in criminal cases, where an accused is entitled to a jury selected from a cross-section of society. (*See* U.S. Const. amend. VI.)

Especially in criminal cases, the jury becomes the conscience of the community. As the community's moral conscience, a jury has considerable power, including the power to nullify the law and return a verdict of "not guilty," no matter how rationally compelling the prosecutor's evidence. This law-shaping power is not expressly communicated to the jury at a trial, but to a certain extent is accepted as implied. *See, e.g.*, M.P. Harrington, *The Law-Finding Function of the American Jury*, 1999 Wis. L. Rev. 377 ("Most [judges] recognized that juries might ignore their instructions, and bring in a verdict contrary to the law stated in the charge."). The law-finding function makes sense if one views the jury as having important constitutional and democratic dimensions, drawn from the community at large and acting on its behalf.

The jury's role differs from that of the judge. While the judge oversees the trial process and can make preliminary factual determinations, the jury comprises the basic trial machinery, acting as the final arbiter of the facts as they relate to guilt, liability, and other weighty matters.

The determination of the facts is perhaps the jury's most important responsibility. The jury's job is to weigh the evidence, decide how events took place, and apply the law to the facts. For example, a jury must decide in a breach of contract action whether there was a contract and then whether it was breached. Of course, the jury's role is interdependent with the attorneys, who must offer admissible evidence for the jury's consideration.

Fact determination is complex. This is attributable in large part to the nature of human behavior. Studies have shown that even though a juror's "common sense" may indeed be common, it does not always make sense. These studies indicate that people tend to forget information much more rapidly immediately after an event than later on (a phenomenon called "the forgetting curve"), and that the confidence of eyewitnesses in their identifications often does not correlate with the accuracy of their identifications. While jurors are supposed to use common sense when evaluating witness' credibility, their common sense may not include awareness of these studies.

The rules of evidence intrude on the jury's fact-finding role when there are special kinds of proof problems. On rare occasions in civil cases, for example, when facts are beyond dispute, the court will instruct juries to accept certain facts as true. (*See* Rule 201.) This judicial declaration of fact is called judicial notice. On some occasions an opposite problem may exist, a lack of proof that threatens to deny justice. In this situation, the rules of evidence permit the creation of a presumption, which shifts at least some of the burden of proving the case to the opposing party in order to flush out evidence and promote fairness. (*See* Rule 301.) (Judicial notice and presumptions are discussed in Chapter 16.)

The judge and jury actually share some fact-finding responsibilities under the rules, with the judge making preliminary fact-finding decisions in several contexts. In one context, judges often must make preliminary determinations of fact in ruling on the competency of evidence, determining whether the evidence meets the admissibility standards set forth in the Federal Rules of Evidence. In another context, judges determine questions of *conditional relevance*, meaning whether facts exist to sufficiently connect evidence to the case.

§ 2.06 THE ATTORNEY'S ROLE

An attorney must juggle two different roles at trial. Counsel must keep one eye on strategy in an attempt to win the case at hand and the other eye on creating a record for a potential appeal. Further, an attorney is both an officer of the court with a responsibility to the judicial system and a zealous representative of the client. These sometimes conflicting responsibilities increase the difficulty of the attorney's role.

A successful case depends not only on what evidence is offered by counsel but also on how the evidence is marshaled in support of counsel's theory of the case. An unsuccessful case generally permits an appeal, but only if the attorney creates an adequate record. The duty to create an appellate record translates into several requirements for the competent attorney. These include objecting to the admission of evidence and making a proffer ("offer of proof") for the record when the court has excluded an attorney's evidence or an answer to a question. More specifically:

1. *Objection.* If an adversary offers improper evidence, a lawyer must object, setting forth the specific basis for the objection. (*See* Rule 103(a)(1).) A general objection of "irrelevant, incompetent and immaterial" is rarely sufficient.

2. *Proffer.* If a judge excludes evidence and it is not apparent from the record what the excluded evidence consisted of, the offering lawyer must make an offer of proof, called a proffer, identifying the substance of the excluded evidence. (*See* Rule 103(a)(2).)

3. *Plain Error.* If the attorney fails to object or make a proffer, the point is generally foreclosed on appeal. However, one major exception to the proffer requirement exists. An appellate court can consider plain error, even though there was no objection or proffer (*See* Rule 103(d).) Attorneys should not rely on the plain error rule to save them from objection omissions, but rather should use it only as a last resort.

Practice Tip — Ask it twice:

If an objection to a question is overruled, a new trial attorney often follows up by instructing the witness to answer the question. Instead, counsel should ask the question again, just in case the jury missed it during the objection interplay. Even if the witness starts to answer before the question can be reasserted, control the witness with a quick hand "stop sign" motion, so that you can re-ask the question prior to eliciting the answer.

Trial attorneys must juggle another duality in roles. Attorneys are considered officers of the court and, as such, have a duty to act ethically and maintain the integrity of the judicial system. Lawyers also serve as representatives of their clients. In this capacity, attorneys must act competently and zealously on their clients' behalf. Sometimes these roles yield underlying tensions and even outright conflict, such as when a client informs counsel she intends to testify falsely (or has already done so).

The dual roles of the trial attorney seem to unite in one of the attorney's most important tasks — laying foundations for the admissibility of evidence. Laying foundations for evidence cannot be underestimated as a lawyering responsibility. This task means being able to demonstrate the prerequisites to admissibility as required by the rules of evidence. These evidentiary prerequisites are better thought of as affirmative admissibility ingredients, rather than as negative prohibitions. If the right foundational ingredients are shown, the evidence is admitted. With the notable exception of irrelevant evidence, most evidence can be offered for some purpose, either to prove an element of the case or to impeach a witness.

Attorneys' arguments to the judge about evidence issues typically focus on the sufficiency of foundations, not on "what the rules ought to be." Foundations can be viewed as the organizational center of evidence law; they serve as the primary intersection of evidence law in a classroom and evidence law in the courtroom. That is why this textbook emphasizes the laying of foundations.

Exercise: The Attorney's Role in Laying Evidentiary Foundations

Remember that for a hearsay statement to be admitted under the hearsay exception commonly referred to as "dying declarations," Rule 804(b)(2), the attorney must lay a foundation showing the statement was made "by a declarant while believing that the declarant's death was imminent, concerning the cause or circumstances of what the declarant believed to be impending death."

Assume the same facts as "The Dying Declaration" problem in the Judge's Role section, above. [In brief, Joan Jacobs had been shot in an aborted robbery attempt outside a shopping mall in broad daylight on a very hot July day. As she slumped against her sports utility vehicle in the parking lot, she started rambling to the security guard, Sharon Stanley, who had come to help her, and the crowd of bystanders that had gathered. Jacobs muttered, "Get me a priest . . . and a last glass of water . . . I am bleeding everywhere. I am in big trouble. Does anyone else have the chills? It is cold here. If I ever see that guy who shot me again, I would recognize him anywhere! He looks just like Tom Cruise, only taller, about six feet tall. And oh yeah, he had a beard and a scar across his right cheek. I better not talk now, I am really hurting and may not make it. Tell my husband I love him . . . oh, I really want to hug my dog. Get Dr. Smaltz over here to help me; he's the best. Joan subsequently dies.]

You are the prosecutor in the subsequent murder trial of James Jackson. At trial, you call the security guard, Sharon Stanley, to the witness stand to lay the appropriate foundations for the dying declaration.

You want to ask Stanley six questions in order to lay the foundation about Joan's belief of impending death. Your questions are to be asked after the following testimony. (Please write out the six questions.)

PROSECUTOR: Good morning, Ms. Stanley.

STANLEY: Good morning.

PROSECUTOR: Please state your name for the court reporter and spell your last name if you would.

STANLEY: Sure. Sharon Stanley. S-t-a-n-l-e-y.

PROSECUTOR: Ms. Stanley, why are you testifying in court today?

STANLEY: I was one of the first people to respond to the parking lot, aisle 21, of the Town and Country Mall on January 14th, where Joan Jacobs lay dying.

PROSECUTOR: [*begin your questions*]

Practice Tip:

Listening to your witness is an important trial skill. You may certainly refer to notes during a trial, but you need to pay complete attention to witnesses while they answer your questions. Resist the temptation to look down and review your notes while a witness is testifying.

If you do that, the jury may be left with a wrong impression that everything has been scripted or that you do not care what a witness says and you might miss something significant in the witness' answer.

The jury deliberates a murder defendant's fate in *12 Angry Men*.*

Problem 2-3: My Cousin, the Lawyer, Vinnie

Vinnie, a new member of the bar, was conducting his first trial, a murder defense of his cousin in a small, conservative Southern town. In its case-in-chief (initial presentation of evidence), the prosecution offered evidence that the defendant had committed adultery on several occasions and had made contributions to animal rights groups. Vinnie objects to the evidence, saying "No way those things are admissible, Judge! The evidence is incompetent, immaterial, and irrelevant, and I object." The defendant was convicted and he appealed. *Should the appellate court consider these objections? Explain.*

Practice Tip — Never let the others in the courtroom see you perspire:

You may need a bit of seasoning before you feel comfortable speaking in public as a trial attorney. One way to deal with those inevitable moments of "brain freeze," when you start perspiring even though the courtroom is ice cold, is to ask the judge for a brief chance to consult your notes or co-counsel, if there is one. Say in a cool, calm, and collected voice, "May I

---

* *12 Angry Men* copyright © 1957 The Estate of Henry Fonda and Defender Productions, Inc.

have a moment, Your Honor?" While you may feel lost, you do not appear so to the court or the jury.

§ 2.07 SUMMARY AND REVIEW

1. Can the judge, *sua sponte* (i.e., on his or her own motion), offer strategy suggestions to a party?

2. What are the two different types of admissibility determinations made by judges?

3. How do those admissibility determinations differ?

4. What are the ethical limitations on attorneys at trial?

5. Why should attorneys state the specific grounds of an objection?

6. Who decides how much weight to give evidence?

7. What are evidentiary foundations?

8. What is an offer of proof?

§ 2.08 CHAPTER REVIEW PROBLEMS

Review Problem 2-A

In a case involving the murder of a convenience store clerk late at night in a store located right off the interstate highway, the prosecution offers the confession of the defendant, a 19-year-old youth. Over objection, the judge admitted the confession into evidence, ruling that it was voluntarily made in conformity with the Due Process Clause of the Constitution. At trial, the defendant offers evidence of coercion, noting the proximity of the officers asking the questions from the defendant, the length of the interrogation, the location of the confrontation and other such factors. The prosecutor objects to these questions. *How should the judge rule on the objection?*

1. Overrule the objection, since the defense in a criminal case can revisit the legal issue of whether a confession was voluntarily made.

2. Overrule the objection, if the questions go to the weight and credibility of the confession.

3. Sustain the objection, because once the evidence is admitted, the facts relating to the ruling are off-limits.

4. Sustain the objection, because Constitutional questions are within the province of the court and the court alone.

Review Problem 2-B

In a breach of contract action between the plaintiff, Ralph's Remodeling Company (Company), and Marsha Johnson, the defendant, the Company alleges nonpayment after remodeling Marsha's kitchen. In her defense, Marsha claims that the job was not completed and that the work done was entirely inadequate.

At trial, the Company calls one of its project supervisors, Alberto Martin, who testifies about the work performed. The judge, Martha Pelos, had a gut feeling that Martin was misstating the facts and was somewhat unbelievable, although she recognized that reasonable people might find Martin reliable. *What should the judge do after Martin testifies?*

1. Inform the jury that Martin's testimony is being struck from the record because the judge found it to be questionable.

2. Strike the testimony from the record if the judge believes the jury would discredit it.

3. Allow the testimony if the judge concludes that the jurors could rationally believe Martin's testimony.

4. Allow the testimony if Martin's testimony is important to the defense.

Review Problem 2-C

In a diversity action alleging strict products liability arising from the rollover of a sports utility vehicle, the plaintiff's expert explained how the vehicle's defects contributed to the rollover. The cross-examination eroded the witness' credibility, undermining her opinion that the defect caused the rollover. The jury, however, found for the plaintiff and awarded considerable damages. *Upon the return of the verdict, what action should the judge take?*

1. The judge should accept the verdict because the jury's verdict is final no matter what the jury considered in reaching its determination, even if it drew straws.

2. The judge should accept the verdict because it is within the province of the jury to weigh the evidence, including the credibility of experts, even if the judge disagrees with the jury's assessment.

3. The judge should order a new trial if the jury's consideration of the expert's testimony gave the expert somewhat excessive credibility.

4. The judge should order a new trial if the jury's consideration of the expert's testimony would not be in accord with a preponderance of jurors.

Chapter 3

RELEVANCE

§ 3.01 CHAPTER CHECKLIST

1. Why is it important to ask, "To what is the evidence relevant?" and not just, "Is the evidence relevant?"

2. What do inferences have to do with relevance?

3. What do relationships have to do with relevance?

4. What does *probative* mean in the definition of relevance?

5. What does *fact of consequence* mean in the definition of relevance?

6. How does the *probative* prong of the relevance test relate to the *fact of consequence* prong?

7. How difficult is it for evidence to meet the threshold test of relevance?

8. Why is some evidence *conditionally relevant?*

9. At what point in time during a party's case can proof of a conditionally relevant fact be offered during the trial?

10. How does *Knapp v. State*, 79 N.E. 1076 (Ind. 1907) (found in the case library at the end of this chapter), shed light on the concept of relevance?

§ 3.02 RELEVANT FEDERAL RULES OF EVIDENCE

Rule 401. Definition of "Relevant Evidence"

"Relevant evidence" means evidence having any tendency to make the existence of any fact that is of consequence to the determination of the action more probable or less probable than it would be without the evidence.

The Advisory Committee Note to Rule 401 states, "Relevancy is not an inherent characteristic of any item of evidence but exists only as a relation between an item of evidence and a matter properly provable in the case."

Rule 402. Relevant Evidence Generally Admissible; Irrelevant Evidence Inadmissible

All relevant evidence is admissible, except as otherwise provided by the Constitution of the United States, by Act of Congress, by these rules, or by other rules prescribed by the Supreme Court pursuant to statutory authority. Evidence which is not relevant is not admissible.

Rule 104. Preliminary Questions

(a) Questions of admissibility generally. Preliminary questions concerning the qualification of a person to be a witness, the existence of a privilege, or the admissibility of evidence shall be determined by the court, subject to the provisions of subdivision (b). In making its determination it is not bound by the rules of evidence except those with respect to privileges.

(b) Relevancy conditioned on fact. When the relevancy of evidence depends upon the fulfillment of a condition of fact, the court shall admit it upon, or subject to, the introduction of evidence sufficient to support a finding of the fulfillment of the condition.

§ 3.03 THE IMPORTANCE OF RELEVANCE

Why is relevance an important concept? The answer lies partly in its primacy; relevance is the first hurdle to admissibility. Just as the judge is the gatekeeper of admissibility determinations, relevance is the threshold through which evidence must pass. Significantly, all evidence must be relevant to be admissible. *See* Rule 402. Serving as the first in a long line of evidentiary requirements is significant enough, but relevance also plays a recurring role on the "evidence highway." It is a factor in assessing the admissibility of hearsay, impeachment, and other forms of evidence as well.

Relevance determinations also help with sorting evidence. For example, it dictates whether evidence applies to proving the elements of the case, impeaching a witness, or both. While relevance decisions depend flexibly on several factors, including everyday human experience, science, and the facts of the case, the relevance rules offer at least one bright line: irrelevant evidence is inadmissible. *See* Rule 402. Irrelevant evidence is distracting, unhelpful, and counterproductive to judicial economy.

Of course, the fact that evidence is relevant does not mean that it will be admitted. (If that were the case, a course in Evidence Law might be extraordinarily short.) Not all relevant evidence is admissible. Relevant evidence still must overcome other exclusionary obstacles to qualify for admission, such as those concerning character, hearsay, privilege, and improper impeachment, among others. Thus, rather than acting as the sole hurdle to admissibility, relevancy only serves as one of many prerequisites.

§ 3.04 DEFINING RELEVANCE

The definition of relevance is often divided into two distinct parts. Evidence is relevant pursuant to Rule 401 if it is (1) probative of (2) a fact of consequence to the determination of the action.

The term "probative" essentially means to make something else more or less likely. Evidence is probative of a fact at issue in the case if it makes such a fact more or less likely. This means that a "chain of inferences" can be constructed connecting the evidence to the case. The fact that the evidence also yields inference chains that do not relate to the case is of no significance; all that is needed is one inference chain that bears on the case at hand. Further, evidence satisfies this standard even if it only makes the pertinent fact a tiny bit more or less likely. As the Advisory Committee observed, "[a]ny more stringent requirement is unworkable and unreasonable." Advisory Committee Note, Rule 401.

Example 1

The accused, Joey, was charged with the robbery of a clothing store, The Glow. At trial, the prosecutor, Jenna, offers evidence that Joey was in the store the day before the robbery, and that he walked around the aisles without purchasing anything before he left. *Is this evidence probative of whether Joey robbed the store?*

Answer: On the one hand, inferences may be drawn from Joey's presence in the store that are not probative of whether he committed the crime, such as: (1) Joey likes that Glow store; (2) Joey likes to shop for clothes; (3) Joey does not buy clothes often; or (4) Joey knows what kind of merchandise is sold at Glow stores. On the other hand, the fact that Joey was in the store the day before the robbery is probative in two different ways. If Joey was in the store the day before and was just looking around, it makes it more likely he was the robber because it appears that he was "casing the store" in preparation for the robbery. From the defense perspective, if Joey was in the store the day before the robbery, it makes it less likely that he was the robber, because a person would be afraid of being recognized if he were going to rob the store the very next day.

A "fact of consequence to the determination of the action" is a fact helpful to resolving the suit, also sometimes described as a fact "properly provable" in the case. Facts of consequence include: (1) an element of the cause of action, claim, or defense; (2) the credibility of the witnesses; and (3) background facts (e.g., helpful facts filling in gaps in the evidence). The term "material fact," commonly used prior to the Federal Rules of Evidence, was abandoned by the Advisory Committee in favor of "fact of consequence." As the Advisory Committee noted in its Comment on Rule 401, the word "material" was "loosely used and ambiguous." Advisory Committee Note, Rule 401.

It is worth noting that the relevance definition does not exclude evidence simply because the evidence concerns a fact of consequence not in dispute. To the contrary, many parties offer evidence about facts of consequence that are not in dispute; the parties want to bolster their cases on relevant matters. If objections are lodged to this evidence the judge can still exclude it, but only because the evidence was unfairly prejudicial (perhaps as a waste of time or cumulative) not because it concerned an undisputed fact of consequence.

Example 2

Balou sued Rodriguez for breach of contract regarding a deck that Rodriguez had agreed to build in Balou's backyard. Balou claimed that the deck was incomplete; Rodriguez had left woodwork unfinished and excess garbage everywhere. Rodriguez responded by claiming the deck was finished and the contract completed. At trial, Balou testified that a similar agreement between the same parties for a different deck on the side of Balou's house included the purchase and application of a wood sealer and the removal of garbage. Rodriguez objected to this evidence, claiming it was irrelevant. Later, on cross-examination of Balou, Balou was asked whether he had been convicted of grand theft auto, a felony, five years earlier. Balou objected to this evidence as well. *How should the judge rule on these objections?*

Answer: Both objections should be overruled. The prior agreement clarifies a fact of consequence in the case, namely the intent of the parties as it relates to their current agreement, and makes it more likely that Balou's claim will succeed. The impeachment of Balou with a felony conviction also makes a fact of consequence, Balou's believability, less likely, and therefore makes it less likely that Balou's claim will succeed. While the facts of consequence differ, both the intent of the parties and the believability of the witnesses are important to resolving the suit.

The key to understanding relevance is that it describes how one thing *relates to* another thing, if at all. (*See* Advisory Committee Note, Rule 401.) A relationship indicates that there is some connection between the evidence and something else. Relevance indicates that the evidence is connected through a process of inferences to the case at hand. A single piece of evidence can give rise to a wide variety of inferences, all based on logic, science, and experience.

Because there is usually some uncertainty about what may be inferred from particular evidence, relevance is oriented around probabilities. That is to say, if we want to know whether it was raining at the time of an accident, evidence that pedestrians were wearing raincoats makes it more probable that it was raining than it was before the evidence was introduced. For that matter, the reconstruction of prior events, what fact-finding really constitutes at trial, is hardly ever based on certainty. Instead, most facts are really probabilities, no matter how sure we are of their existence. Even scientific evidence, which some say is "certain," is subject to differing opinions, exceptions, revisions, and new discoveries. (Consider, for example, the debates about the origins of the universe, "nature versus nurture," and other continuing scientific disagreements.)

The drawing of inferences in the relevance enterprise differs from general forms of logic. One judge has noted that relevance analysis is unlike the process of deduction, where major and minor premises are supplied. Instead, "[i]nferential processes . . . generally proceed from one proven premise to a conclusion. The one drawing the inference supplies the missing premise, typically from a reservoir of experience." *United States v. Hannigan*, 27 F.3d 890, 898 n.3 (3d Cir. 1994) (Becker, J., concurring). Thus, relevance determinations are rooted in a combination of science and experience. *See* Advisory Committee Note, Rule 401.

Judge Becker offered an illustration of relevance in *Hannigan*, stating that an eyewitness who hears gunfire can only assume that the gunshot hit the victim who was standing nearby. If a bullet in fact was fired from the gun and struck a victim, it was traveling much too fast for the witness to actually see it go by. Yet, logic and experience dictate that if one observes a person aim a gun at another person and pull the trigger (with the gun making a loud retort), and the person in the line of fire falls down covered with blood, then a bullet must have been fired from the gun and must have struck the victim. This kind of probabilistic reasoning occurs routinely and, generally, unconsciously. With relevance, however, a more conscious approach is favored. *See United States v. Hannigan*, 27 F.3d 890, 898 n.3 (3d Cir. 1994) (Becker, J., concurring).

In relevance analysis, numerous helpful inferences may be drawn from a single fact. To illustrate, in a case involving the attempted robbery of a person in a shopping mall parking lot, eyeglasses found on the ground at the scene of the crime could relate to several pertinent conclusions. For example, the found glasses could indicate the alleged victim struggled to prevent the robbery (if it is shown the glasses belonged to the alleged victim), or that the alleged victim wore glasses and needed them to perceive the alleged perpetrator (which relates to the witness's credibility), or that the alleged perpetrator wore glasses (which relates to identification). On the other hand, the pair of eyeglasses found at the scene may relate to a variety of irrelevant facts as well. The glasses might belong to a person not involved in the incident. Even if they did belong to a participant, the glasses could still indicate irrelevancies, such as which brand of eyeglasses the wearer prefers, whether the glasses are designed for athletic usage, or whether the glasses are made with special shock-resistant glass.

This "eyeglasses" example illustrates how a single piece of evidence can relate to a wide variety of facts. The example also demonstrates that relevancy is not an inherent characteristic of a piece of evidence, but depends on the facts of the case. *See, e.g.*, Advisory Committee Note, Rule 401. For example, if a banana peel is found on the floorboard beneath the passenger seat of an automobile, it may be probative of many facts, including: the driver eats in the car; the driver is messy; the driver carries groceries in the car; the driver has a pet monkey; there was a passenger in the car; the passenger eats in the car; the passenger is messy; and so on. Thus, the relevance of the banana peel depends on the specific issues in the case.

With such a wide variety of inferences that can be drawn from a single piece of evidence, the task for the attorney is to find a connection between the evidence and the substantive issues at trial, the credibility of witnesses, the background facts, or a combination of these things. Whether the evidence can be linked to the case requires an answer to the question: "Relevant to what?" Stated differently, the operative question to answer in resolving relevance issues becomes, "What is the evidence being offered to prove?"

Example 3

One evening, Bruce was killed in a one-car accident. The only issue in a subsequent lawsuit was whether Bruce's death was an accident or a suicide.

Bruce's close friend, Natasha, said that on the day of the crash, Bruce appeared to be "very sad." *Is this evidence relevant?*

Answer: The evidence that Bruce appeared to be very sad prior to the accident is relevant to something, but to what? This fact may be relevant to the case if Bruce's sadness is probative of (makes more likely) a fact in issue (the reason Bruce died). The sadness is probative of suicide because sadness tends to make it more likely that Bruce was depressed, which in turn could provide a motive for suicide. While there may be many other explanations for Bruce's sadness, the alternative inference chains probably would be irrelevant to the case. As long as one inference chain can be connected to the case, making it even a little bit more (or less) likely that Bruce died as a result of a suicide, the evidence will be considered relevant.

Appellate courts typically review trial courts' relevance determinations under an "abuse of discretion" standard. This standard reflects the factual and contextual nature of relevance rulings and that, particularly with such a low threshold for relevancy requirements, appellate courts should avoid second-guessing trial judges' relevance determinations.

The following problems provide the opportunity for you to apply the relevance rules by constructing inference chains that link various types of evidence to the case. In drawing these inference chains, it becomes clear that the application of the doctrine of relevance can be quite complex.

Problem 3-1: Judge Judy

Judge Judy was asked to decide a most difficult question: which of two women claiming to be the mother of an infant child was indeed the biological mother? Each woman claimed that the child was hers. Judge Judy told the women that there was an easy solution — she was going to cut the child in half. At this pronouncement, one of the women began to cry. She shouted, "No! I can't stand it; don't do it!" The other woman was ashen-faced, but silent.

1. Are the women's reactions to Judge Judy's decision relevant? To what issue is their reaction relevant?

2. What assistance do the Advisory Committee Notes provide in resolving the relevancy issues in this problem?

3. If the parable instead involved two men who both claimed to be the father of the child, would their reactions be similarly relevant or irrelevant? Compare the relevancy of the reactions of the alleged mothers to the reactions of the alleged fathers.

Problem 3-2: Bermuda Love Triangle

Freddy Krueger is accused of killing his friend, Jason, with a single blow to the head. At trial, the prosecution wishes to introduce love letters written by Freddy to Jason's wife only months before Jason's death. The defense objects to the introduction of the letters.

If Freddy did write the letters, are the letters relevant? To what are they relevant? Write out the chain of inferences that makes the letters relevant.

Problem 3-3: Missing

Joan accidentally left her purse on the snack bar after purchasing popcorn at the local movie theater. Joan remembers seeing other patrons in the area, but cannot describe any of the people, even in the most general of terms because she was in a hurry to catch the beginning of the feature film. In her purse were four new $50 bills. The purse was recovered after the movie. All of the money was missing from the purse.

Which of the following evidence is relevant in determining who took the money? Explain your answers by describing the inferences you drew from the evidence.

1. Bob, another patron, paid for popcorn right before the movie started with a new $50 bill.

2. Patrons Susan and Jamie left the movie theater halfway through the film.

3. Harvey, another patron, was convicted of the possession of marijuana in 1990.

4. The purse was found in the restroom. (Does it matter whether the purse was recovered in the women's room or the men's room? Why? If the purse was recovered in the women's room, what impact, if any, is there on the relevance of the evidence in parts 1, 2, and 3, above?)

Problem 3-4: Eddie From Boston

Eddie from Boston was accused of robbing the First City Bank of Massachusetts. Eddie is alleged to have used a "Saturday Night Special" revolver during the robbery.

Which of the following items of evidence would be relevant to the prosecution's case? Explain, using inference chains.

1. Eddie withdrew money at the same bank the day prior to the robbery after having a friendly ten-minute conversation with the teller (no one else was in line).

2. Eddie had an eight-year-old bank robbery conviction in a different state, Maryland.

3. Eddie was fired from his previous job as a clerk in a convenience store as a result of an unproven allegation that he stole money from the cash register.

4. Eddie had participated in two barroom brawls the week before the bank robbery.

5. Eddie was divorced and delinquent in his payments of $400 per month in child support.

6. Eddie was virtually broke. His only asset was a $49 savings account at a different bank.

7. Eddie owned a rifle.

8. Eddie has two children, ages two and seven.

9. Eddie has been convicted of marijuana possession on two separate occasions in the past four years.

10. Eddie prefers "rock" to Bach and gin without tonic.

Problem 3-5: The Reel Thing

Wanda brought suit against three insurance companies, all of which had insured the life of her husband, Harry. She claimed that the body recently found in Pond Apple Creek was Harry's and that, as the beneficiary, she should be paid the million dollars from the insurance policies on Harry's life. Wanda offers in evidence an authenticated letter from Harry's fishing buddy, Al. Al wrote to Harry saying, "I look forward to fishing with you at the Pond Apple Creek at the end of September." Harry has been missing since September 30th.

Is this letter relevant? If yes, relevant to what? Write out the inference chain that justifies your conclusion.

Problem 3-6: "Beam Me Up . . ."

Scotty was a driver for the Letrek Company. While driving a Letrek truck, Scotty collided with a car driven by Kirk. Kirk sued the Letrek Company for damages in tort based on the theory of *respondeat superior*. The parties reached a written stipulation on most of the facts. The only issue at trial was whether Scotty was acting within the scope of his employment at the time of the accident or whether he was on a "fun and frolic" detour. Plaintiff Kirk offers evidence that "at the time of the accident, Scotty was not looking where he was going. In fact, he was falling asleep."

Is this evidence relevant? If so, relevant to what?

Problem 3-7: Fire! (a.k.a. Burning Down the House)

Hal was driving in his car when he turned on the radio and heard that his own house had burst into flames. Hal was subsequently charged with burning down the house to obtain the insurance proceeds. At trial, the prosecutor intended to offer evidence that Hal took out additional fire insurance seven months before the fire.

The following exchange occurred at trial:

PROSECUTOR: Wanda, as the insurance agent for the defendant, Hal, could you please describe the insurance that Hal had on the house, especially within the past year of its destruction?

DEFENSE COUNSEL: Objection, your honor. Irrelevant.

JUDGE: Counsel, please approach the bench.

How would you argue this objection if you were the prosecutor? How would you argue the objection if you were the defense counsel? What ruling would you make if you were the judge?

Problem 3-8: I Wuz Robbed!

John and Johanna are being prosecuted for robbing a bank on June 4th at 9:00 a.m. Their defense is mistaken identity. At trial, Tommy, the bank teller who was robbed, testified about the robbery.

PROSECUTOR: Tommy, directing your attention to 8:55 a.m. on June 4th, where were you?

DEFENSE ATTORNEY: Objection! Where the teller was at that particular time is irrelevant.

1. Is the question necessarily irrelevant? What answer would make the question relevant?

PROSECUTOR: How did you feel, Tommy, as the robbers handed you the note that read "your money or your life"?

A: I felt-

DEFENSE ATTORNEY: Objection! Irrelevant. How the teller felt is irrelevant to whether a robbery occurred.

2. You are the prosecutor; how would you respond?

3. How should the judge rule and why?

Problem 3-9: Benny and Jets

The defendant, Benny, is charged with the *distribution* of cocaine. The prosecution calls Benny's friend, Jets, to the witness stand to testify that he, Jets, had *used* cocaine with the defendant three months prior to the defendant's arrest.

PROSECUTOR: Jets, please tell the ladies and gentlemen of the jury where you were on March 6th, at approximately 3:00 p.m.?

A: I was at the Giants football game with my friend, Benny.

PROSECUTOR: Describe what happened between you and Benny at the game.

DEFENSE COUNSEL: Objection. Irrelevant.

Is this evidence relevant to the charge of distribution? Explain.

Problem 3-10: Ahnald

The defendant, Franz, is prosecuted for assault and battery on Ahnald. Franz claims self-defense. Franz testified that immediately before the altercation with Ahnald, Franz was told by a third party that Ahnald, a weight lifter, was out to get him.

1. Is this testimony relevant? Relevant to what?

2. Does it matter whether Ahnald was in fact "out to get" Franz?

3. If Franz cannot recall who told him that Ahnald was out to get him, is the evidence still relevant?

Problem 3-11: Ahnald's Younger Brother

Ahnald's younger brother, Sly, was stopped by the police late one Saturday night while driving on the interstate. He was glassy-eyed and appeared to be intoxicated. When he refused to cooperate with the detaining officer, the officer called for backup. Before the backup arrived, the officer mistakenly thought that Sly was reaching for a gun, and shot him dead. In a civil rights action brought by the survivors of Sly, the officer testified as follows:

OFFICER TOOJAY: I saw Mr. Sly move his hand toward the pocket of his jacket, like he was reaching for a gun. I thought he was going to shoot at me, so I took the safety off of my weapon and shot him.

The plaintiff wishes to offer in evidence that in a search of the victim after the shooting, no weapon was found. *Is this evidence admissible? Explain.*

Problem 3-12: Sexual Battery

Joe is charged with sexual battery. To prove the victim's age, which is relevant to the elements of the offense, the government offers evidence that Joe generally dates women between the ages of 15 and 18.

If you were the judge, would you find that this evidence is relevant to this case? Why? See Francis v. State, 512 So. 2d 280 (Fla. Dist. Ct. App. 1987).

Problem 3-13: The Commuter

Sean was approached by four youths while riding on a nearly empty commuter train one weekend morning. The youths stood on both sides of Sean, two to a side. One of them said, "Give me five dollars." Sean, fearing an attack that would result in serious bodily harm, took out a revolver and shot the four youths, injuring each of them seriously. *In a subsequent prosecution for attempted murder, which of the following facts is relevant?*

1. Sean (or any of the four youths) is female or male.

2. Sean (or any of the four youths) is of color or Caucasian.

3. Sean (or any of the four youths) is younger or older than 21.

4. Sean (or any of the four youths) is of high, average, or low socioeconomic status.

5. Sean (or any of the four youths) is gay, lesbian, or straight.

6. Any of the four youths has a prior criminal record.

7. The train is in a subway or above ground.

8. The train is located in a rural area, the suburbs of a city, or an inner city.

9. The incident occurred at night or during the day. Or during the summer or the winter.

10. Sean had been mugged once before, but not on a train.

Explain your conclusions.

"The Commuter" is based on the so-called "subway vigilante" case, *People v. Goetz*, 73 N.Y.2d 751, 532 N.E.2d 1273 (1988). The defendant, Bernhard Goetz, was found not guilty by a jury on charges of attempted murder. Goetz shot and injured four youths on December 22, 1984, in a New York City subway train after the youths flanked him and one of the youths asked Goetz to give him five dollars. Goetz successfully claimed that he acted in self-defense. The following is an excerpt from the jury instructions given by Justice Stephen Crane of the Supreme Court of New York (the trial court) in *People v. Goetz*.

Justice Crane's jury instruction stated:

> Please note that before he can be justified in using deadly physical force in defense of the person, the defendant must have reasonably believed that he was being threatened with deadly physical force.
>
> What then is a reasonable belief? A determination of reasonableness must be based upon the circumstances facing the defendant or his situation in terms encompassing more than the physical movements of the potential assailant or assailants. These terms include any relevant knowledge the defendant had about that person or persons; they also necessarily bring in the physical attributes of a person's involvement, including the defendant.
>
> Furthermore, the defendant's circumstances encompass any prior experiences he had, which would provide a reasonable basis for belief that another person's intentions were to injure him or that the use of deadly force was necessary under the circumstances.
>
> A person may be said to reasonably believe that deadly physical force is about to be used against him, if a reasonable person in his shoes, that is, in the same circumstances and situation that he faced, would so believe. In other words, in this case you must scrutinize the reasonableness of any belief the defendant claims to have had by reference to a hypothetical reasonable person who was transported into the subway car on December 22, 1984, and who faced the exact situation which confronted the defendant.[1]

1. How is the *Goetz* jury asked to deal with the particular circumstances of the shooting?

2. How does the jury instruction define the scope of relevant evidence in the case?

3. In light of the jury instructions, how broad is the permissible scope of relevant evidence?

4. How is the scope of relevant evidence affected by whether the self-defense instruction is "objective" or "subjective"?

---

[1] Charge to Jury, Justice Stephen Crane, Supreme Court of the State of New York, County of New York, Criminal Term: Part 81. *The People of the State of New York v. Bernhard H. Goetz.*

Problem 3-14: A Bottle of Red

Billy was observed purchasing a bottle of red wine at a liquor store at 2:00 p.m. on Tuesday. At 7:00 p.m. on the same day, he was arrested for driving while intoxicated on the local highway. The prosecution offers evidence about Billy's wine purchase in Billy's subsequent trial for driving while intoxicated. The defense objects.

1. Should the judge admit the evidence? Why?

2. Would it be relevant if Billy was seen carrying an empty, rather than a full, bottle of wine at 2:00 p.m.?

3. Would it be relevant if Billy was seem carrying a half-empty wine bottle at 2:00 p.m.?

4. Would the 2:00 p.m. purchase of wine be relevant, if, at the time Billy was arrested, he smelled of beer? Explain.

Problem 3-15: "Name Your Price"

The defendant offers the testimony of Price in a workers' compensation action. Price states, "The plaintiff tried to bribe me to testify in his favor."

Is this testimony relevant? If so, relevant to what? Explain.

Problem 3-16: Too Rough Justice

Centuries ago, in the days of yore, Judge Martin presided over the judicial system. The primary test used at that time to determine guilt or innocence in criminal cases was the "jump" test. An accused was told to jump off of a 50-foot cliff into the trees and jagged rocks below. It was widely believed that an innocent person would survive the fall without serious injury.

Haynes is charged with battery after biting his former friend, Jockey. Judge Martin tells Haynes, "Jump thou, Sirrah!" Haynes refuses, saying, "Hearest thou me well, thou dost not appreciate my situation if thou thinkest I would go over yon cliff."

1. Is Haynes's refusal to jump relevant? To what?

2. Is it relevant if Haynes, prior to being told to jump, attempted to escape while in custody? Why?

Problem 3-17: "Lions and Tigers and . . ."

The defendant, Bear, is charged with extortion. Bear allegedly threatened to shoot the local butcher if the butcher did not pay for "protection." At trial, the government offers evidence that the defendant kept several guns in his bedroom.

Tony Lawrence (Paul Newman) prepares to conduct an experiment while examining haughty butler George Archibald (Richard Deacon) in *The Young Philadelphians*.*

Is this evidence relevant? Explain. See United States v. Gilley, 836 F.2d 1206 (9th Cir. 1988).

Problem 3-18: Evidence, Politics, and Race

Mike Espy was indicted for taking gifts while serving as Secretary of Agriculture. Espy, an African-American, claimed that some of the charges were outright lies and that others were misinterpreted. Espy did not deny that he took some of the things that might be described as gifts, but argued that he did not have wrongful intent in doing so. He further stated that some of his failures to comply with the law were mistakes or oversights, given the extreme pressures he faced in his job.

Richard Douglas, a deputy agriculture secretary under Espy, was called to testify by the prosecution. On cross-examination by the defense, Douglas admitted that Espy made major changes at the Department by promoting women and minorities. Douglas referred to the Department as "the last plantation" and said, "You have people working there that in their mind cannot fathom the thought of someone who would be Black that could possibly [be] in a decision-making position" and "[the fact] that Espy changed the complexion of the Secretary's office, all the top people, rubbed a lot of people the wrong way."

---

* *The Young Philadelphians* copyright © 1959 Warner Bros. Pictures Inc. All Rights Reserved.

The prosecutor objected to Douglas' testimony. *Should the objection be sustained?*

Problem 3-19: Exploding Tire

The plaintiff, Petra, was injured by an exploding tire at the Fox's Used Tire Superstore. At trial, one of the defendants, Uniyear Treads, called several experts to testify that the RH5 design of the tire was entirely safe. On cross-examination, Petra wished to ask the defendant's experts about other accidents involving the RH5 design to test the witnesses' credibility.

Can *she ask the witnesses about the other tire accidents? See, e.g., Cooper v. Firestone Tire and Rubber* Co., 945 F.2d 1103 (9th Cir. 1991).

Problem 3-20: *Parnell v. Asbestos, Inc.*

The plaintiff, Parnell, sued the defendant, Asbestos, Inc., for injuries relating to alleged long-term exposure to asbestos. The plaintiff offered several premises showing causation. The first premise was that all forms of asbestos cause cancer. The second premise was that Parnell had been exposed to the asbestos products of several different manufacturers, including the defendant's asbestos. Therefore, according to the plaintiff, the defendant's products had at least in part caused the asbestosis. In rebuttal, the defendant wishes to call an expert witness to testify that one form of asbestos, chrysolite asbestos, does not cause cancer at all.

What is this evidence offered to show? Is it relevant? To what? Should it be admitted?

Problem 3-21: Blowing Smoke

Morris Philip is charged with the murder of Chester Fields. Philip offers evidence of an alibi. To strengthen his defense, Philip seeks to offer evidence that Marley Burroughs, Fields's former partner in an insurance business, had a motive to kill Fields. The motive evidence consists of testimony that after finding out that Fields had embezzled more than a hundred thousand dollars from the business and caused it to go bankrupt, Burroughs swore, "I'll get back at Fields for this outrage if it's the last thing I do." *Is the motive evidence relevant?*

§ 3.05 CONDITIONAL RELEVANCE

When the relevance of evidence depends on the existence of a fact, the evidence is considered to be "conditionally relevant." Rule 104(b) of the Federal Rules of Evidence codifies conditional relevance. Rule 104(b) gives judges the discretion to conditionally admit evidence so long as the missing link in that evidence will be connected up by proof of the missing fact. For example, if a gun is offered in a murder case, its admissibility depends on a fact of whether it was the gun used in the murder or has some other connection to the crime. Likewise, when a person claims another person was present at a meeting, that claim is predicated on a meeting occurring.

Judges can admit this evidence upon a subsequent showing that the gun was used in the crime and that a meeting took place, respectively. Conditionally relevant evidence will be admitted by the judge if a reasonable jury *could* find by a preponderance of the evidence that the fact exists. The judge does not actually determine whether the fact really exists; the judge's role is simply to exclude the evidence if no reasonable jury *could* find that the fact exists. Thus, a judge acts to screen facts when making these relevance determinations.

Given the way conditional relevance distinguishes between the judge's prefatory fact-finding role and the jury's primary fact-finding responsibility, it can be viewed as more about the division of fact-finding responsibilities at trial than about relevance. The procedural orientation of Rule 104(b) is further illuminated by the fact that a judge can admit this type of evidence "subject to" the later introduction of the missing fact. Thus, the Rule also can be viewed as a timing mechanism.

Conditional relevance also can be considered an example of foundational evidence, since it serves as a prerequisite to admissibility. There are many other types of foundations, from authenticating exhibits to meeting the requirements of hearsay exceptions to establishing a claim of privilege. In another sense, conditional relevance poses a type of competency requirement, because it demands that evidence have a minimum level of connection to the facts in the case. Without a sufficient showing of a connection, the evidence is incompetent and ineligible for consideration by a jury.

From another perspective, conditionally relevant evidence is like a chain with one or more of its links missing. The missing link signifies the omitted but necessary separate fact. When evidence is conditionally admitted, this means that counsel promises to supply the missing fact or facts at a later time. If the missing link is not provided, the evidence will be subject to exclusion.

Conditional relevance situations arise for a variety of reasons. A single witness may not be able to lay the entire foundation required for a piece of evidence, in which case the party must use additional evidence or witnesses. Further, even if a party is able to offer its evidence chronologically, so as to avoid gaps, the party may choose to rearrange its order of presentation for strategic purposes. Thus, a party may rely on several witnesses to lay the foundation for a single piece of evidence, such as a gun or a computer printout, even though a fragmented approach is not necessary.

The admissibility of conditionally relevant evidence provides needed flexibility to attorneys in presenting their case. It allows the attorneys to control what evidence to present and in what order. While a counsel's ordering of witnesses may be confusing to the jury, the opening statement and closing arguments can offer clarity and guidance.

Example

Jorge was charged with the shooting death of his girlfriend, Lourdes. A gun was found outside of the house where Lourdes was killed. *Is the gun relevant evidence?*

Answer: The gun may be conditionally relevant to the shooting death of Lourdes if additional evidence shows that it was the particular gun used in the shooting (and not a gun unconnected to the incident). The gun may be admitted in evidence pending a later showing, through ballistics tests or otherwise, that this was the gun in question.

Problem 3-22: On a Cloudy Day

With wispy white clouds drifting lazily overhead one hot and sunny May day, Gilligan was severely injured while cutting the hedges. He claimed that he was injured when the rotary hedge cutter he was using suddenly exploded. At trial, Gilligan offers a piece of steel blade found 10 yards away from the accident site.

1. The defendant objects to this evidence. What is the basis for this objection?

2. How is this evidence conditionally relevant?

3. Does adding visual language to the problem, such as "[w]ith wispy white clouds drifting lazily overhead one hot and sunny May day," affect the way this problem is considered? How would this visual language be received by a jury?

Problem 3-23: Stone Crabs

Alice is accused of breaking into Jim's Stone Crab Restaurant through a rear window and stealing eighty stone crab claws and two tins of mustard sauce. No fingerprints were discovered. At trial, the prosecution offers in evidence a pair of thin black kitchen gloves found near the perpetrator's point of entry. The defendant objects to this evidence.

1. Are these gloves conditionally relevant? Why?

2. What must be shown for the gloves to be admitted?

Problem 3-24: Defective Paint

Assume that a painting contractor buys five large drums of white paint from the Power Paint Company. Four months later, the contractor buys five drums of yellow paint from the same company. After buying the yellow paint, the contractor starts using the white paint and realizes that it is defective. The contractor then refuses to pay for the yellow paint, and sends it back unopened. The contractor is sued.

The judge rules, "It is irrelevant that the white paint was defective. There's no connection between white paint and yellow paint manufactured four months later."

What foundational evidence might you offer to show a connection between the two sets of paint drums?

Problem 3-25: An Accident?

Vanessa De La Beckworth and Daniel Jimenez lived together for thirteen months as girlfriend and boyfriend. One night, they had a fight in the kitchen over who was to feed their dog, a pit bull. Vanessa called 911 and stated, "Help! I've been cut by my boyfriend, Daniel! I need a doctor. Fast!" Police and an ambulance arrived shortly after the call, and found that she had been cut and bruised.

Three weeks later, Daniel was charged with two counts of aggravated domestic violence. The prosecutor requested an interview with Vanessa, and during the interview she stated that the bruise and cut had been of her own doing. She explained that she blamed it on Daniel because she was angry with him. She also told the prosecutor that, while she knew Daniel had faults, she loved Daniel and would not testify against him or do anything to hurt him.

The prosecution intends to go forward with the case. The prosecutor subpoenas Vanessa to testify, knowing that she will deny that her injuries are Daniel's fault and that the prosecution will have to rely on what she said to the 911 operator. The prosecution wishes to call Eric Mendleson, PhD, to testify about Battered Woman's Syndrome. The prosecutor proffers the following will be Mendleson's testimony if it is permitted:

PROSECUTOR: Dr. Mendleson, tell us what happens to battered women when they are confronted about their injuries at the hands of their significant other.

A: At first, in their agitated and injured state, they often blurt out the truth about what caused their injuries. Only later do they often recant. In fact, one study showed that 80% of women will recant after an assault. Further, many women assaulted by their boyfriends exhibit the Stockholm Syndrome — which is where some hostages view their attackers as essentially a good person who is just misunderstood.

If the defense attorney objects based on relevance, what should defense counsel argue in support of the objection? Why?

How is this evidence only conditionally relevant?

The trial court admitted the testimony subject to a limiting instruction by the judge pursuant to Federal Rule of Evidence 105.

If you were the judge, how would you craft the limiting instruction?

On appeal, what would you argue was improper about giving a limiting instruction? Why? See People v. Gomez, 72 Cal. App. 4th 405, 85 Cal. Rptr. 2d 101 (1999).

Exercise: Relevance Foundations

Johnny Blutone is prosecuted for battery on Patrick Houston after a fight in a local bar; the defense is self-defense. Johnny and Patrick knew of each other from living in the same town, but had never met until the bar fight. At trial, Johnny wished to testify that Johnny heard that Patrick had started a previous bar fight with another person, brutalizing that person and sending him to the hospital with severe injuries. The prosecutor objected to the evidence and the judge ruled at the bench the evidence was inadmissible unless the defense offers additional information making the prior bar fight conditionally relevant. Specifically, the judge stated that in order to be admissible, the defendant must show he, Johnny, knew about the prior fight before the one in question had occurred. Johnny thereupon offered a new witness, Fariq Abdul, a friend, to testify that Abdul told Johnny about the attack about a week prior to the bar fight in question, while they were sitting at lunch at the Quarterdeck restaurant.

1. You represent the defendant, Johnny. Lay the foundation for the prior bar fight evidence as the judge instructed. In other words, question Fariq Abdul about what he told Johnny. Include: (1) Fariq's name and brief background (personalize him), (2) the setting (describe where they were), and (3) the action (what was said in the conversation).

2. A student should play Fariq and testify, staying in role while on the witness stand. Another student or students can role-play opposing counsel. At the end of the examination, a person acting as judge should rule whether a foundation has been created to make the prior bar fight relevant pursuant to Rule 104(b).

Problem 3-26: Joe C. Boss

Joe Celebrity Boss admitted various improper romantic office affairs with employees in a lawsuit brought by one of the women involved. In the subsequent lawsuit brought by another former female employee alleging a similar affair with Boss, the plaintiff wished to use the prior statement by Joe that he "had various improper affairs with women employed by me at the same company."

(a) Is Joe's statement in the prior suit a binding judicial admission?

(b) Is Joe's statement in the prior suit relevant in the later suit?

§ 3.06 COMPARING RULES

Compare Federal Rule of Evidence 401 with a different approach, formerly used in Texas:

Test of Relevancy

(a) "Materiality" inquires whether there is any rational relationship or pertinence of the offered evidence to any provable or controlling fact issue in dispute.

(b) "Relevancy" inquires whether the offered evidence has probative value tending to establish the presence or absence, truth or falsity, of a fact.

(c) Test: Is it material? If not, exclude. If yes, and only in that event, is it relevant? If not, exclude. If yes, admit.

Which is the clearer rule, the Texas rule or the Federal Rule of Evidence? Why?

§ 3.07 SUMMARY AND REVIEW

1. Why is the application of the relevance rules dependent on the particular case?

2. What is the definition of relevance under the Federal Rules of Evidence?

3. Compare the concept of "probativeness" with the concept of "fact of consequence."

4. Define conditional relevance.

5. Specify whether each of the following statements is True or False:

   a. Only certain select forms of irrelevant evidence are admissible at trial.

   b. If evidence is relevant, it will be admitted at trial.

   c. Evidence requiring more than 15 links to connect it with the issues in the case will be excluded.

   d. Circumstantial evidence is more likely to be relevant than direct evidence.

   e. Conditionally admitted evidence is admitted for a limited purpose.

   f. Relevance objections are almost always sustained.

§ 3.08 CHAPTER REVIEW PROBLEMS

Review Problem 3-A: The Swallower

The defendant, Alan Onano, is charged with knowingly possessing heroin with the intent to distribute it in violation of 21 U.S.C. § 841(a). On March 14th, Onano was a passenger on Nigerian Airlines Flight 859, traveling from Nigeria to Kennedy Airport in New York. He was arrested at the airport after acting suspiciously. Several days later, following a bowel movement, he was found to have swallowed 83 condoms containing heroin. At trial, the defendant did not deny swallowing the condoms, but claimed that he believed he was swallowing diamonds, not drugs. The defendant offered an expert witness, Dr. Elliot Berns, a gemologist and a professor at the Fashion Institute of Technology. Dr. Berns was expected to testify on two points: the feasibility of smuggling diamonds by ingesting condoms, and the value of the smuggling venture if diamonds had been placed in the 83 condoms.

1. Is Dr. Berns's testimony relevant? Explain.

2. If Dr. Berns is allowed to testify, is his testimony conditionally relevant? Why?

3. How would you question Dr. Berns on direct examination? How would you question him on cross-examination? Prepare both examinations.

Review Problem 3-B

JK Lassiter is accused of forgery, allegedly writing several false checks in his employer's name and then cashing them. When the prosecutor asks the defendant to submit handwriting exemplars to further identify the forged handwriting, he refuses. The prosecutor wishes to offer evidence of the refusal at the subsequent trial, and the defense objects. *Which of the following is the most accurate statement about the defendant's refusal?*

1. The evidence is irrelevant because the defendant's pre-trial refusal to do something is not related to a fact of consequence in the case.

2. The evidence is irrelevant because the defendant's pre-trial refusal is not probative of his frame of mind at a previous time.

3. The evidence might be excluded, but not because of its lack of relationship to the case.

4. The evidence should be excluded because it violates the false hearsay document rule, unless its substantive value outweighs its probative nature.

Review Problem 3-C

Which of the following examples will most likely be excluded as irrelevant?

1. In a prosecution for the destruction of property, when the defendant was arrested, he used a false name. The prosecutor wants to offer the fact that the defendant offered a false name as evidence of guilt.

2. In a prosecution for defacing government property, a protester allegedly had thrown ashes and mud at the Pentagon walls. In his defense, the protester wants to introduce evidence about the vagaries of United States policy toward nuclear weapons control.

3. In a tort action for strict products liability after a tire exploded, the defendant used a substantially similar tire to test whether the same type of tire was defective.

4. In a prosecution for securities fraud, the fact that just before the defendant was arrested, the defendant deleted many of the files on his computer.

§ 3.09 CASE LIBRARY — KNAPP V. STATE

KNAPP v. STATE
Supreme Court of Indiana
168 Ind. 153, 79 N.E. 1076 (1907)

GILLET, J.:

Appellant appeals from a judgment in the above-entitled cause, under which he stands convicted of murder in the first degree. Error is assigned on the overruling of a motion for a new trial.

Appellant, as a witness in his own behalf, offered testimony tending to show a killing in self-defense. He afterwards testified, presumably for the purpose of showing that he had reason to fear the deceased, that before the killing he had heard that the deceased, who was the Marshall of Hagerstown, had clubbed and seriously injured an old man in arresting him, and that he died a short time afterwards. On appellant being asked, he answered: "Some people around Hagerstown there. I can't say as to who it was now." The state was permitted, on rebuttal, to prove by a physician, over the objection and exception of the defense, that the old man died of senility and alcoholism, and that there were no bruises or marks on his person. Counsel for appellant contend that it was error to admit this testimony; that the question was as to whether he had, in fact, heard the story, and not as to its truth or falsity.

While it is laid down in the books that there must be an open and visible connection between the fact under inquiry and the evidence by which it is sought to be established, yet the connection this required is in the logical processes only, for to require an actual connection between two facts would be to exclude all presumptive evidence . . . . Within settled rules, the competency of testimony depends largely upon its tendency to persuade the judgment . . . .

We are of the opinion that the testimony referred to was competent. While appellant's counsel are correct in their assertion that the question was whether appellant had heard a story to the effect that the deceased had offered serious violence to the old man, yet it does not follow that the testimony complained of did not tend to negative the claim of appellant as to what he had heard. One of the first principles of human nature is the impulse to speak the truth. "This principle . . . has a powerful operation, even in the greatest liars; for where they lie once they speak the truth 100 times." Truth-speaking preponderating, it follows that to show that there was no basis in fact for the statement appellant claims to have heard had a tendency to make it less probable that his testimony on this point was true. Indeed, since this court has not, in cases where self-defense is asserted as a justification for homicide, confined the evidence concerning the deceased to character evidence, we do not perceive how, without the possibility of a gross perversion of right, the state could be denied the opportunity to meet in the manner indicated the evidence of the defendant as to what he had heard, where he, cunningly perhaps, denies that he can remember who gave him the information. The fact proved by the state tended to discredit appellant, since it showed that somewhere between the fact and the testimony there was a person who was not a truth speaker, and, appellant being unable to point to his informant, it must at least be said that the testimony complained of had a tendency to render his claim as to what he had heard less probable.

Judgment affirmed

Chapter 4

RELEVANT BUT INADMISSIBLE — UNFAIRLY PREJUDICIAL EVIDENCE

§ 4.01 CHAPTER CHECKLIST

1. Compare prejudicial evidence to unfairly prejudicial evidence.

2. What is the test to determine if unfair prejudice exists?

3. How many steps are there in analyzing whether unfairly prejudicial evidence exists?

4. What are the two main types of unfairly prejudicial evidence that are excluded by Rule 403?

5. What do certain types of probability evidence in criminal cases, excessively violent evidence, similar acts or occurrences, and scientific tests have in common?

6. What is the significance of a limiting instruction?

§ 4.02 RELEVANT FEDERAL RULES OF EVIDENCE

Rule 402. Relevant Evidence Generally Admissible; Irrelevant Evidence Inadmissible

> All relevant evidence is admissible, except as otherwise provided by the Constitution of the United States, by Act of Congress, by these rules, or by other rules prescribed by the Supreme Court pursuant to statutory authority. Evidence which is not relevant is not admissible.

Rule 403. Exclusion of Relevant Evidence on Grounds of Prejudice, Confusion or Waste of Time

> Although relevant, evidence may be excluded if its probative value is substantially outweighed by the danger of unfair prejudice, confusion of the issues, or misleading the jury, or by considerations of undue delay, waste of time, or needless presentation of cumulative evidence.

The Advisory Committee Note to Rule 403 states in part, "These circumstances [in which relevant evidence is excluded] entail risks which range all the way from inducing decision on a purely emotional basis, at one extreme, to nothing more harmful than merely wasting time, at the other extreme."

§ 4.03 INTRODUCTION

Not all relevant evidence is admissible. As Rule 402 provides, relevant evidence may be made inadmissible by the "Constitution of the United States, by Act of Congress, by these rules, or by other rules prescribed by the Supreme Court pursuant to statutory authority." The reasons for excluding relevant evidence may vary, from violation of a criminal defendant's constitutional rights to violation of the hearsay rule.

Pursuant to Rule 403, trial courts have the authority to exclude relevant evidence if it poses a significant risk of unfair prejudice, misleads the fact finder, confuses the issues, or simply wastes time. In effect, there are two types of unfairly prejudicial evidence — one that misleads the jury and one that wastes its time. "Dangerous unfair prejudice" does not simply mean that the evidence strongly influences the jury. Evidence is usually offered by a party for the very purpose of persuading jurors to decide in that party's favor. That is, evidence is offered by parties to "prejudice" the jury in a party's favor. Most evidence in fact will cause jurors to form immediate initial impressions or judgments — effectively triggering some prejudging — based on the jurors' own experiences and natures. According to the Advisory Committee, evidence creates "unfair prejudice" when it has "an undue tendency to suggest a decision on an improper basis, commonly, though not necessarily, an emotional one." *See* Advisory Committee Note to Rule 403. Thus, the risk of "unfair prejudice" is the risk that the jury may not be able to assess or evaluate the evidence properly. This risk arises when admission of the evidence would be perceived as unfair or when the evidence would adversely affect the fairness of the trial process.

Not all evidence posing a danger of unfair prejudice is excluded under Rule 403. Instead, the court must administer a weighted balancing test and decide whether the probative value of the evidence is *substantially* outweighed by one or more of these prejudice factors.

Some evidence that is highly prejudicial is also highly probative of a fact in issue. Prior acts of a party offered to show a party's propensity to act in a certain manner, for example, can be both highly probative and highly prejudicial at the same time. Thus, in a robbery case, the fact that the defendant stole a car the day before the event to use in the robbery makes it more likely that the defendant was indeed the robber — but also carries the inference that the defendant has a propensity toward criminal behavior (i.e., that he is a one-man crime gang). Under the Federal Rules of Evidence, the need for relevant evidence often is considered greater than the potential harm that could result from the admission of at least some prejudicial evidence. Thus, evidence that poses a danger of unfair prejudice is excluded only if the danger of unfair prejudice "substantially outweighs" the probative value of the evidence. This weighted balancing test favors admissibility by exhibiting a preference for relevant evidence, even if the relevant evidence presents a risk of prejudice. However, the application of the balancing test is firmly committed to the judge's sound discretion, and rulings under Rule 403 are rarely reversed on appeal.

As the Advisory Committee Note to Federal Rule of Evidence 403 points out, excluding evidence because it is unfairly prejudicial should be a last resort. Exclusion should occur only after the judge has determined that a limiting instruction to the jury will not be sufficient to offset any prejudice. A limiting instruction is a directive by the judge to the jury to use the evidence only for a legitimate purpose. For example, if a judge in the robbery case admits evidence at trial showing that the defendant stole a car on the day preceding the robbery, the judge may instruct the jury to use the evidence only as it pertains to the robber's common scheme or plan and not as it relates to the defendant's propensity to violate the law.

One case that traces the intricacies of the unfair prejudice balancing test is *Old Chief v. United States*, 519 U.S. 172 (1997). (*See* Case Library.) In *Old Chief*, the accused was charged with possessing a firearm as a previously convicted felon. The accused offered to stipulate to the fact that he was a prior felon, but the prosecution refused to accept the stipulation. Instead, the prosecution wished to offer evidence at trial of the prior crime, which was one of violence. The district court and the court of appeals both sided with the prosecution, allowing the government to prove its own case. The Supreme Court reversed.

While the Court found that the type of conviction was relevant to the current charge, and observed that the prosecution usually has the option of proving its own case as it sees fit (even on matters that are not in dispute), the Court found that the evidence still should have been excluded as unfairly prejudicial. In defining "unfair prejudice," the Court turned to the Advisory Committee Note to Rule 403, which defined "unfair prejudice" as "an undue tendency to suggest decision on an improper basis, commonly, though not necessarily, an emotional one." Justice Souter concluded that unfair prejudice of this sort had occurred in the case of Johnny Lynn Old Chief. Said Justice Souter's majority opinion:[1]

> Such improper grounds certainly include the one that Old Chief points to here: generalizing a defendant's earlier bad act into bad character and taking that as raising the odds that he did the later bad act now charged (or, worse, as calling for preventive conviction even if he should happen to be innocent momentarily).

Justice Souter went on to discuss the analytical method that courts should employ in balancing probative value against the risk of unfair prejudice under Rule 403. He observed that a court's decision on admissibility might require a review of evidentiary alternatives as well as the evidence in question: "what counts as the Rule 403 'probative value' of an item of evidence, as distinct from its Rule 401 'relevance,' may be calculated by comparing evidentiary alternatives." These alternatives might include revealing only the general nature of the offense to the jury or some other method of minimizing prejudice.

Example

Susan alleges that she was raped by an acquaintance, John. At the criminal trial, John introduces a photograph of Susan dancing with him one year prior to the alleged rape. The photograph shows Susan wearing a strapless gown. Does the photograph present a risk of unfair prejudice?

Answer. The photograph may have some probative value, such as

---

[1] 519 U.S. at 181–182.

showing that Susan and John were acquainted with each other prior to the incident in question. However, the danger of unfair prejudice would be substantial.

If Susan's manner of dress on an earlier occasion would lead some jurors to consider punishing her through a verdict, the jury would be influenced to decide the issue based on emotion and not on the requirements of the law. The photograph consequently would obfuscate the relevant facts and hinder the jury in fulfilling its duty to find the truth. If Susan claimed she did not know John, and the photograph is the only evidence that the two were acquainted, then the photograph would have stronger probative value, yielding a much greater chance of admissibility.

Problem 4-1: "One Drink Too Many"

On a dark, moonless night in late November, a truck and passenger car collided on a remote section of the interstate. The driver of the car, Albert, was killed. Albert's estate filed a negligence suit against the driver of the truck, Tina, and her company, Studio 53, Inc. At trial, the defendants called Dr. Robert Orsky, a hematologist at the Regional Crime Laboratory, to discuss blood tests performed on Albert after the accident that showed the presence of intoxicants in his blood, indicating that he was drunk. The plaintiff objected and called for a sidebar, at which time the following discussion occurred.

JUDGE: What is the basis for your objection, counsel?

PLAINTIFF'S ATTORNEY: The blood test done by Dr. Orsky is not reliable, Your Honor, and should be excluded on grounds of unfair prejudice. We proffer the testimony of Nurse Wilma Jones, who, only minutes before the horrible accident, had assisted in taking the stitches out of Albert's hand at the nearby medical office. Nurse Jones will testify that she came within 18 inches of Albert's face and that Albert in no way, shape, or form smelled of alcohol.

JUDGE: Defense Counsel, any reply?

How should the defense counsel reply to the plaintiff's assertions?

JUDGE: In this case, because I find the nurse's testimony believable and the blood test of questionable value, I find that admitting the results of the blood test would unfairly prejudice the plaintiff's case. The blood test evidence will be excluded.

Did the judge rule correctly? Explain. See Ballou v. Henri Studios, Inc., 656 F.2d 1147 (5th Cir. 1981).

Problem 4-2: A Day in the Life of Susan White

Susan White, a crane operator at a major road construction site, was severely injured in a crane accident. Susan brought suit against the crane manufacturer based on a theory of strict products liability. To show damages, Susan offered a film depicting an average day in her life subsequent to the accident, including how she eats, gets out of bed, bathes, and travels on the city streets with other pedestrians.

Is such a "day in the life" film unfairly prejudicial?

Problem 4-3: In a New York State of Mind

[The following problem is based on an actual incident that occurred in New York City in the fall of 1992. The facts apply not only to the groups mentioned, but to all stereotypes that can enter into jurors' interpretive assumptions relating to an event. Professor Claude Steele, who later became the Provost of Columbia University, describes the phenomenon of "stereotype threat." This occurs when individuals live up — or down — to stereotypes of themselves by others. In essence, a person is sometimes treated by others based on their "social identity," which includes group membership in categories such as age, gender, race, and ethnicity. Everyone is subject to such threats, not simply minorities. *See, e.g.,* C. Steele, A Threat in the Air: How Stereotypes Shape the Intellectual Identities and Performance of Women and African-Americans, 52 Am. Psychologist 613 (1997).]

Dora and Bart, a white female and white male, respectively, were transit police officers in New York City. One day, while on an anti-crime detail, they came upon two young black males in the subway who they believed to be robbing a woman subway rider. The black males were holding handguns. Dora and Bart quickly opened fire, wounding one of the apparent assailants. It turned out that the apparent assailants, Johnny Patton and George Diamond, were undercover police officers from a different district who were in the process of arresting a suspect. Officer Patton was injured.

Assume for the purposes of this problem that Dora and Bart are charged with aggravated assault for the injuries caused to Officer Patton. Dora and Bart wish to argue that their conduct was not culpable.

1. What is the relevance, if any, of perceptions, stereotypes, and statistical data about race?

2. What is the relevance of the fact that the apparent assailants were male and relatively youthful in appearance?

3. Are generalizations about a group always an improper use of stereotypes and, therefore, unfairly prejudicial?

A plethora of evidence may be labeled "unfairly prejudicial," but certain kinds of evidence are particularly susceptible to exclusion on this basis. Consequently, the rest of this chapter will focus on recurring types of evidence often believed to present a special danger of unfair prejudice: (1) probability evidence about identity in criminal cases (specifically, the likelihood of another person with the same characteristics committing the crime charged), (2) evidence depicting violence in a manner that is physically revolting, (3) novel scientific evidence, and (4) similar events, happenings or occurrences.

§ 4.04 PROBABILITY EVIDENCE OF IDENTITY IN A CRIMINAL CASE

Statistical evidence is routinely admitted at trial to assist the trier of fact. One type of statistical evidence, however, is particularly misleading and is generally excluded. This type of evidence, denoted here as "probability evidence of identity," is specifically offered to show the unlikelihood of another person with the same characteristics as the defendant committing the crime charged. Such evidence suffers from a variety of defects, not the least of which is its power to exert extreme influence over a jury. A problem will illustrate this concept.

Problem 4-4: Chances Are . . .

The defendant, Lester, is charged with first-degree murder in Walhalla, South Carolina, a rural town of 4,000 people. At trial, the prosecution introduced evidence showing that the defendant had the same general physical description, the same type of accent, and the same brand of sneakers (Nike) as the person linked to the crime by various witnesses. The defendant claims mistaken identity. In rebuttal, the prosecution offers a professor of statistics, Dr. Egbert Einstein. Dr. Einstein intends to testify there is an extreme improbability, one in 12 million, of these characteristics belonging to a second person in Walhalla.

(a) What flaws, if any, can you find in Professor Einstein's evidence? (b) Should his testimony be admitted? (c) Why? See, e.g., People v. Collins, 68 Cal. 2d 319, 66 Cal. Rptr. 497, 438 P. 2d 33 (1968), which is reprinted in the Case Library at the end of this chapter.

§ 4.05 EVIDENCE OF EXCESSIVE VIOLENCE

Evidence showing the results of violence is a routine part of many trials, particularly in criminal homicide cases. Homicide requires proof of an unlawful killing of another human being. In a murder case, for example, the prosecutor must prove that a person died. The death may have been horrific. While evidence of the death is permitted in order to prove the case, Rule 403 imposes some limitations. Specifically, it is improper to offer evidence that so blinds a jury to the facts of the case that the jury makes an emotional determination. A shorthand description of this limit is that the evidence cannot be so violent in appearance that a reasonable jury will "lose its lunch" as a result of viewing it.

Problem 4-5: Lose Your Lunch

Ernest and Samantha, the leaders of a radical political party, were found shot to death in their living room. The scene was gruesome, and the stench of death was everywhere. Franklyn, a known contract killer, was charged with the murders. At trial, the government offers testimony of a crime scene search officer, Jan, who testified that she visited the scene immediately following the murders and took color photographs of the bodies. The prosecutor then attempted to introduce in evidence the glossy 8 × 10 photographs taken by Jan. Franklyn's attorney objected.

1. How should a judge rule on the objection?

2. Should the prosecutor agree to stipulate to the fact that Ernest and Samantha were killed by gunshots?

3. Should the judge approve the stipulation if both parties agree to it?

Problem 4-6: Legs

Ned Carlyle lost both of his legs to amputation after an automobile accident. After being fitted with prosthetics, he learned to walk again. Ned sued the driver of the other car for damages. At trial, Ned testified about the accident.

PLAINTIFF'S ATTORNEY: Ned, please describe the injuries you received from the accident.

A: My legs were crushed from the knees down. The "jaws of life" were used to extract me from the car. Here's what happened —

DEFENDANT'S ATTORNEY: Objection. This evidence is unnecessary and unfairly prejudicial.

JUDGE: *What ruling and why?*

PLAINTIFF'S ATTORNEY: Can you show the ladies and gentlemen of the jury what your legs look like today?

A: Certainly. (Ned begins to remove his prosthetics to show the jury his stumps, intending to point to where his legs once were.)

DEFENDANT'S ATTORNEY: Objection. Your Honor, the witness' actions are unfairly prejudicial.

JUDGE: *What ruling and why?*

If the judge rules in favor of the defendant, but the plaintiff already has engaged in the forbidden behavior, does the defense counsel have any recourse?

What can the defense counsel do?

§ 4.06 SCIENTIFIC EVIDENCE

Scientific experiments that seek to replicate or simulate the events on which a lawsuit is based have the potential to be both highly probative and highly misleading. Consequently, experimental scientific evidence will likely be excluded as unfairly prejudicial, unless it is "substantially similar" to what it intends to recreate.

While any form of novel scientific evidence, whether based on experiment, observation, or other formulation, also may be unfairly prejudicial, courts have placed the analysis of most scientific evidence questions squarely within the expert testimony rules, Rule 702 et seq. *See* Chapter 9 for extensive discussion of the admissibility of scientific evidence through expert testimony.

Example

Al Wiley is prosecuted for white-collar fraud after allegedly bilking several large health care companies of millions of dollars. At trial, the prosecutors offer the testimony of Dr. Ziggy Topstein, an expert in polygraphy. Dr. Topstein intends to testify that he has administered "lie detector" tests for 20 years and has an advanced degree specializing in interpreting the physiological data from such tests. He administered a "lie detector" test to the defendant, Wiley, immediately after the allegations against him. The test was conducted at Wiley's request, but the results indicated that Wiley was evasive and likely untruthful about the events in question. The defendant objected to the testimony. *How should the judge rule?*

Answer: Despite claims about the accuracy of polygraph tests, the judge should exclude the evidence as both unfairly prejudicial and insufficiently reliable to meet the standards for reliable scientific evidence under Rule 702. Jurors may tend to overvalue such evidence, and may forsake their own independent review of the defendant's credibility. Moreover, the testimony does not yet have a sufficiently reliable scientific basis. Many experts find that the human interpretation of polygraph tests is subjective, to the extent that the results are subjective and solely within the "eye of the beholder." Further, there may be disputes about replicating such tests in a laboratory setting.

A brief preview of how courts have approached novel scientific evidence follows. (This area will receive in-depth coverage in Chapter 9.)

Frye vs. Daubert

Courts have been struggling with the admissibility of novel scientific evidence for decades. From 1923 until fairly recently, the federal courts mostly applied the singular test of whether the evidence was "sufficiently established to have gained general acceptance in the particular field in which it belongs." *Frye v. United States*, 293 F. 1013, 1014 (D.C. Cir. 1923). In 1993, however, the Supreme Court held that the *Frye* test had been superseded by the adoption of the Federal Rules of Evidence. Under the Federal Rules, the appropriate test allows trial courts to consider multiple factors. These factors include the following: (1) whether the subject matter was "scientific knowledge," (2) whether the theory or technique can be or has been tested, (3) whether the theory or technique has been subjected to peer review and publication, (4) whether the technique has a known or potential rate of error, (5) whether standards controlling the technique's operation exist and are maintained, and (6) finally, but not exclusively, the *Frye* test of general acceptance in the particular field. *See Daubert v. Merrell Dow Pharmaceuticals, Inc.*, 509 U.S. 579, 593–594 (1993). Justice Blackmun stated:

> Faced with a proffer of expert scientific testimony, then, the trial judge must determine at the outset, pursuant to Rule 104(a), whether the expert is proposing to testify to (1) scientific knowledge that (2) will assist the trier of fact to understand or determine a fact in issue. This entails a preliminary assessment of whether the reasoning or methodology underlying the testimony is scientifically valid and of whether that reasoning or methodology properly can be applied to the facts in issue.[2]

---

[2] 509 U.S. at 592–593.

The meaning of the multiple-factor test of *Daubert* is still unfolding. Courts are being asked to admit novel scientific evidence in a wide variety of cases, many dealing with illness and injury allegedly caused by faulty products or pharmaceuticals. The Supreme Court has decided subsequent cases in an effort to clarify the meaning of *Daubert*.

Amanda Bonner (Katherine Hepburn) examines Beryl Caighn (Jean Hagen) in *Adam's Rib*.*

In *Kumho Tire Co., Ltd. v. Carmichael*, 526 U.S. 137 (1999), for example, a suit resulting from an automobile accident allegedly caused by a defective tire, the Supreme Court attempted to further delineate the scope of the *Daubert* test. The Court considered whether the *Daubert* reliability test should be used for a non-scientific expert, in this case an expert in tire failure analysis. The Court held that the *Daubert* test also must be applied to testimony by "technical" or other non-scientific experts, such as engineers, but emphasized that the *Daubert* reliability test was a flexible one. The Court referred to its prior decision in *General Electric Co. v. Joiner*, 522 U.S. 136 (1997), where it held that courts of appeals must use an "abuse of discretion" standard when reviewing reliability findings by the district courts. *Id.* at 143. (In *Joiner*, the Supreme Court reviewed the exclusion of an expert witness' opinion on whether a type of chemical, PCBs (polychlorinated biphenyls), caused the plaintiff's cancer.) The chapter on expert testimony delves into these cases and the rules governing experts in great detail. The problem that follows illustrates the role Rule 403 still plays with some scientific evidence.

---

* *Adam's Rib* copyright © 1949 Turner Entertainment Co. A Warner Bros. Entertainment Company. All Rights Reserved.

Problem 4-7: Videotape Replay

A tractor-trailer truck collided with a Buick Riatta automobile. The driver of the Buick brought suit against the tractor-trailer driver and his insurance company. At the time of the accident, 1:00 p.m., the pavement was dry and the weather was clear.

At trial, the plaintiff offered in evidence the results of an experiment between a tractor-trailer truck similar to the one involved in the accident and an identical Buick automobile to show that the defendant must have been driving the tractor-trailer at an excessive speed at the time of the accident. The plaintiff could not obtain the actual truck that collided with the car because it had been too badly damaged in the crash. The only differences between the experiment and the actual crash were that the experimental truck was approximately 115 pounds heavier than the truck involved in the accident and the experiment occurred on a slight incline, not on flat land like the actual accident.

1. Are the results of the experiment unfairly prejudicial? Why?

2. Would it be reversible error if the experiment results were improperly admitted? Why?

Problem 4-8: To Tell the Truth

After a series of rapes committed by a masked rapist, the police apprehended a suspect. There was no positive eyewitness identification of the defendant as the perpetrator of the crime. Instead, the prosecution relied on:

(a) DNA testing, which revealed that the semen found on the clothes of two of the victims was that of the defendant; and (b) a witness who claimed after hypnosis that she remembered observing the defendant at the scene of a rape immediately prior to their occurrences.

1. Is either the DNA or hypnosis evidence relevant? Why?

2. Is either the DNA or hypnosis evidence unfairly prejudicial? Why?

3. What is the relevance of *Daubert v. Dow Pharmaceuticals, Inc.*, *Kumho Tire Co., Ltd. v. Carmichael*, or *Frye v. United States*?

4. Which of the following types of evidence would most likely be excluded:

(a) polygraph evidence, (b) handwriting analysis (graphology) evidence, (c) voice spectrography identification evidence, or (d) blood alcohol testing? Why? Discuss.

§ 4.07 SIMILAR OCCURENCES, HAPPENINGS, AND EVENTS

Evidence of similar occurrences, happenings, or events is generally offered to corroborate or bolster a party's theory of the case. Often, there is an insufficient quantity of direct evidence about an incident or event to explain it adequately. For example, there may be inadequate information about the cause of a person's slip and fall on a dimly lit sidewalk or why a person became ill an hour after eating at a particular restaurant. When there is a lack of information, comparisons to other events or occurrences are especially useful. In a broad sense, the history of an event may be instructive as to its cause, its significance, or its meaning.

This type of evidence has great potential for unfair prejudice, however, leading to the general rule, "*res inter alios acta*," meaning things between others are inadmissible. Prior events, happenings, or occurrences often occur under widely disparate circumstances. Dissimilarities in the circumstances between the other events and the event in question diminish the net worth of the evidence. In addition, jurors may be misled or distracted by other events, to the extent that they are led to focusing on the nuances of other events instead of the event at issue. Further, no matter how similar or helpful to the jury the other occurrences are, the prior events are nevertheless collateral to the specific facts to be decided. For all of these reasons, evidence of similar occurrences, happenings, and events is often excluded at trial.

Exceptions to the general exclusion of similar occurrences exist. Sometimes, the evidence overcomes the specter of unfair prejudice, in part because of substantial similarities. Similar events evidence has been admitted in the following contexts: (1) to show causation (such as that of an illness or injury); (2) to show a dangerous condition existed (such as a bump or hole in the road); (3) to show the mental state of a party when it is at issue (such as in a suit claiming discrimination); (4) to rebut a party's claim of impossibility (such as subsequent similar events the defendant claimed could not occur); (5) to show the sales of other real property (to prove value); (6) to show the meaning of a contract, contract provision, or document (by offering prior dealings between the parties); and (7) to show the meaning of a contract, contract provision, or document (by the custom or usage in the industry). These exceptions are limited, however, and do not swallow up the general rule of exclusion.

A lack of similar occurrences, sometimes offered to show a lack of culpability, fault, or responsibility, is even more prejudicial than the existence of similar events and is generally excluded. The fact that an injury occurred for the very first time at the hands of an experienced taxi driver, surgeon, waiter, or store manager does not accurately portray whether negligence, fault, or responsibility on the part of the defendant existed. This evidence misleads a jury because a first-time accident could very well be the result of negligence or fault, there may have been reporting problems about prior similar events, and the prior experience may not have been under similar circumstances (e.g., the surgeon removed gall bladders for years and this was her first removal of an appendix).

Example

Josephine's house was condemned by the state after a new highway was designated to run through her kitchen. The only issue at trial was what constituted just compensation for her house. Josephine introduced the sale price of other homes in her neighborhood. *Are the prices of these other sales admissible?*

Answer. The other sale prices are relevant and not unfairly prejudicial, provided that the other houses being used for comparison are comparable to Josephine's. If the other houses are not sufficiently similar, and can be distinguished based on differences in size, features, location, etc., the admission of the sale prices of other homes probably would be unfairly prejudicial.

Problem 4-9: Slipped Up

Wally Witness testifies for the plaintiff in a "slip and fall" personal injury case. The plaintiff contends that the defendant negligently permitted puddles of water to accumulate on the defendant's walkway where the plaintiff fell.

Can Wally testify that he had observed puddles regularly form on the walkway during the three weeks prior to the plaintiff's fall? Can Wally testify that he had seen three people other than the plaintiff fall on the same walkway that week? Why?

Problem 4-10: Spoiled Shrimp

Memphis Frozen Foods, Inc., shipped three tons of frozen shrimp with Benner Shipping. The shrimp spoiled en route, and Memphis Frozen Foods brought suit against Benner Shipping for damages. The key issue was how to interpret the requirements of the contract. Benner Shipping attempted to introduce in evidence prior contracts between the parties concerning the sale of scallops and clams. Memphis Frozen Foods objected, claiming that the prior contracts were irrelevant because they did not deal with shrimp.

How should a judge rule on this objection? Why?

Problem 4-11: Double Decker

Suzanne was injured when she was thrown from a ride at the State Fair called the "Double Decker." Suzanne sued the ride's owner and its manufacturer. At trial, the defendants attempted to introduce evidence that no one had been injured in 5,000 previous rides on the Double Decker.

How is this problem different from other offers of similar acts, occurrences, or happenings evidence? Is this evidence unfairly prejudicial?

Problem 4-12: Sugar or Sweetener?

Polly, an employee in an artificial sweetener factory, was severely injured when a "No-Sweet" machine exploded. Polly sued the manufacturer of the machine. At trial, Polly attempted to introduce evidence concerning other "No-Sweet" machine explosions.

Should such evidence be considered unfairly prejudicial? Why? See generally Ponder v. Warren Tool Corp., 834 F.2d 1553 (10th Cir. 1987).

Problem 4-13: Harassment

The plaintiff, Janet Fife, brought suit in 1995 against her boss and former employer (Ace Barnes and Ace Hardware, Inc., respectively), claiming sexual harassment and unlawful retaliation. The plaintiff testified at trial.

PLAINTIFF'S ATTORNEY:	Do you know if you are the only person to make allegations of this kind against the defendant?
DEFENDANT'S ATTORNEY:	Objection. This question calls for an irrelevant and unfairly prejudicial answer.
JUDGE:	*How should the judge rule on this objection? [Assume the objection was overruled.]*
A:	Actually there were three other complaints — one by Barnes's former secretary in 1988, one by his store clerk in 1997, and one by his truck driver in 1999.
PLAINTIFF'S ATTORNEY:	What were the outcomes of those other complaints?
DEFENDANT'S ATTORNEY:	Objection, Your Honor. This question calls for an irrelevant and unfairly prejudicial response.
JUDGE:	Counsel, please approach the bench.

How should the judge rule on this objection if the answer to the question were as follows:

A:	One of the complaints, the one by the truck driver, was dismissed. The other two complaints were found to have merit by the administrative body that reviewed the complaints, and damages were awarded.

Problem 4-14: Unfair Prejudice

The accused in a bank fraud prosecution, Serena Ortuno, had worked for the bank for seven years and allegedly defrauded the bank for five of those seven years. You are the defendant's attorney. In the course of the direct examination of Serena, you attempt to elicit the following information: (1) the various jobs held by the defendant in the bank; (2) the number and names of the defendant's siblings; (3) that the bank recovered its entire corpus of funds; (4) that the defendant sometimes suffered from impaired judgment; (5) that the defendant took and passed a lie detector test given by her attorney in front of three neutral observers (not associated with the prosecution); (6) that the bank changed its procedures for accounting for $50 bills, the ones allegedly stolen, after the defendant's arrest; (7) that the defendant would offer a computerized reenactment of how the defendant usually walked through the vault; and (8) that the defendant received a Girl Scouts award for honesty, years before.

With a student role-playing Serena, ask her about the eight items above. Other students can be given the role of opposing counsel and asked to object, based on either irrelevance or unfair prejudice. A different student can role-play a judge and rule on the admissibility of these items.

Problem 4-15: People v. Penny

Jimmy Penny was prosecuted for molesting a six-year-old girl. At trial, the prosecution offered the following evidence. Which evidence is unfairly prejudicial?

(a) Pornographic magazines of young children that police officers found in Penny's home when executing a valid search warrant.

(b) Pornographic magazines depicting only adults that the police found in Penny's home when executing the same search warrant.

(c) Non-pornographic pre-teen and teen magazines depicting children in stylish clothing that the police found in Penny's home when executing the same search warrant.

§ 4.08 SUMMARY AND REVIEW

1. Should a judge exclude evidence that is more prejudicial than probative upon a proper objection?

2. What is the difference between unfairly prejudicial evidence and prejudicial evidence?

3. Why do the Rules use a weighted balancing test for excluding unfairly prejudicial evidence?

4. Why is most statistical evidence allowed even though courts usually exclude probability evidence about the likelihood of a person other than the accused committing the alleged crime?

5. What are the dangers of other similar acts evidence?

6. Why admit gruesome evidence of a murder scene?

7. Should scientific test or experiment evidence always be admitted when performed by a qualified scientist?

8. Does the Supreme Court's approach to the admissibility of scientific evidence make sense? Why or why not?

§ 4.09 CHAPTER REVIEW PROBLEMS

Review Problem 4-A

Arlen Spanos was prosecuted for securities fraud after skimming from several mutual funds he managed. At trial, the defendant offered a psychiatrist who testified that Spanos had "impaired judgment" during the relevant time period. When the prosecutor confronted the psychiatrist on cross-examination, she admitted that the condition did not rise to the level of insanity. The prosecution then objected to the testimony and requested that it be struck from the record. *How should the judge rule?*

1. The testimony should be excluded because it was an irrelevant opinion about the defendant's state of mind.

2. The testimony should be excluded because while it was relevant to the defendant's state of mind, it would mislead jurors into thinking the defendant was insane during the relevant period.

3. The testimony should be allowed, because it was relevant to a crucial aspect of fraud, the defendant's state of mind.

4. The testimony should be allowed, unless the jury would be influenced by the psychiatrist's status as an expert in the field of "impaired judgment."

Review Problem 4-B

Alou was charged with conspiracy to distribute cocaine. At trial, the judge overruled an objection by the defense to evidence that Alou participated previously in a similar operation involving the distribution of cocaine. The court ruled the evidence was not unfairly prejudicial. *If Alou was convicted and appealed the trial court's ruling, how should the appellate court rule?*

1. Uphold the trial judge's decision, unless other trial courts have excluded similar evidence under identical circumstances.

2. Uphold the trial judge's decision, because of the great deference by appellate courts to trial judges, in large part because the appellate court must decide based only on a "cold" record.

3. Reverse the trial judge's decision if it fails the litmus test of being a reliable decision more likely than not.

4. Reverse the trial judge's decision if the ruling affected a substantial right of the defendant.

Review Problem 4-C

Ali Staton, the manager of a successful coffee shop, was charged with embezzling funds from the business. At trial, the prosecutor offered evidence that Staton earned an annual salary of $45,000 from the coffee shop, with yearly bonuses of up to $10,000. The prosecutor then offered a new witness to testify that in the months leading up to the arrest, Staton was seen leasing a Porsche Boxster and traveling to Hawaii in the first-class section of the airplane. *If the defense objects to this evidence, how should the judge rule?*

1. Admit the evidence, providing the defense has an opportunity to rebut it under the "rule of completeness," permitting opposing parties to submit remainders.

2. Admit the evidence, but only if its prejudicial impact is not very high.

3. Exclude the evidence, but not if the probative value and danger of unfair prejudice of the evidence are both considerable.

4. Exclude the evidence because it is not relevant to whether the defendant embezzled as charged.

Review Problem 4-D

Rasheed went to the Lotus Room one Friday night for a dinner of Chinese food. Later that evening, he became very ill and attributed it to food poisoning. After being out of work for several weeks and still feeling unable to work at a competent level, he sued the restaurant for damages. At trial, Rasheed wished to offer the fact that in the month before Rasheed's dinner there, eight other people, all in separate parties, had become ill after eating at the Lotus Room for dinner. *If the defendant objects to this evidence, how should the judge rule?*

1. The judge should admit the evidence, because it is relevant to how Rasheed became ill.

2. The judge should admit the evidence, because everyone else became ill after eating dinner, just like the plaintiff.

3. The judge should exclude the evidence, because it is hearsay and irrelevant.

4. The judge should exclude the evidence, unless additional evidence is offered showing a much greater similarity between the other events and the dinner in question.

§ 4.10 CASE LIBRARY

PEOPLE v. COLLINS
Supreme Court of California
68 Cal. 2d 319, 66 Cal. Rptr. 497, 438 P.2d 33 (1968)

SULLIVAN, JUSTICE:

We deal here with the novel question whether evidence of mathematical probability has been properly introduced and used by the prosecution in a criminal case. While we discern no inherent incompatibility between the disciplines of law and mathematics and intend no general disapproval or disparagement of the latter as an auxiliary of the fact-finding processes of the former, we cannot uphold the technique employed in the instant case. As we explain in detail, *infra*, the testimony as to mathematical probability infected the case with fatal error and distorted the jury's traditional role of determining guilt or innocence according to long-settled rules. Mathematics, a veritable sorcerer in our computerized society, while assisting the trier of fact in the search for truth, must not cast a spell over him. We conclude that on the record before us defendant should not have had his guilt determined by the odds and that he is entitled to a new trial. We reverse the judgment.

. . . .

On June 18th, 1964, at about 11:30 a.m., Mrs. Juanita Brooks, who had been shopping, was walking home along an alley in the San Pedro area of the City of Los Angeles . . . . As she stooped down to pick up an empty carton, she was suddenly pushed to the ground by a person whom she neither saw nor heard approach . . . . She managed to look up and saw a young woman running from the scene. According to Mrs. Brooks the latter appeared to weigh about 145 pounds, was wearing "something dark," and had hair "between a dark blond and a light blond," but lighter than the color of the defendant Janet Collins' hair as it appeared at trial. Immediately after the incident, Mrs. Brooks discovered that her purse, containing between $35 and $40, was missing.

§ 4.10   CASE LIBRARY   83

About the same time as the robbery, John Bass, who lived on the street at the end of the alley, was in front of his house watering his lawn . . . . [H]e saw a woman run out of the alley and enter a yellow automobile parked across the street from him . . . . The latter then saw that it was being driven by a male Negro, wearing a mustache and beard. At the trial Bass identified defendant as the driver of the yellow automobile. . . .

. . . .

At the seven-day trial the prosecution experienced difficulty in establishing the identities of the perpetrator of the crime. The victim could not identify Janet and had never seen the defendant. The identification by the witness Bass, who observed the girl run out of the alley and get into the automobile, was incomplete as to Janet and may have been weakened as to the defendant. . . .

In an apparent attempt to bolster the identifications, the prosecutor called an instructor of mathematics at a state college. Through this witness he sought to establish that, assuming the robbery was committed by a Caucasian woman with a blond ponytail who left the scene accompanied by a Negro with a beard and mustache, there was an overwhelming probability that the crime was committed by any couple answering such distinctive characteristics. The witness testified, in substance, to the "product rule," which states that the probability of the joint occurrence of a number of mutually independent events is equal to the product of the individual probabilities that each of the events will occur. Without presenting any statistical evidence whatsoever in support of the probabilities for the factors selected, the prosecutor then proceeded to have the witness assume probability factors for the various characteristics which he deemed to be shared by the guilty couple and all other couples answering to such distinctive characteristics.[3]

Applying the product rule to his own factors the prosecutor arrived at a

---

[3] (Court's original footnote 10.) Although the prosecutor insisted that the factors he used were only for illustrative purposes — to demonstrate how the probability of the occurrence of mutually independent factors affected the probability that they would occur together — he nevertheless attempted to use factors which he personally related to the distinctive characteristics of the defendants. In his argument to the jury he invited the jurors to apply their own factors, and asked defense counsel to suggest what the latter would deem reasonable. The prosecutor himself proposed the individual probabilities set out in the table below. Although the transcript of the examination of the mathematics instructor and the information volunteered by the prosecutor at that time create some uncertainty as to precisely which of the characteristics the prosecutor assigned to the individual probabilities, he restated in his argument to the jury that they should be as follows:

Characteristic	*Individual Probability*
A. Partly yellow automobile	1/10
B. Man with moustache	1/4
C. Girl with ponytail	1/10
D. Girl with blond hair	1/3
E. Negro man with beard	1/10
F. Interracial couple in car	1/1000

In his brief on appeal the defendant agrees that the foregoing appeared on a table presented in the trial court.

probability that there was but one chance in 12 million that any couple possessed the distinctive characteristics of the defendants. Accordingly, under this theory, it was to be inferred that there could be but one chance in 12 million that defendants were innocent and that another equally distinctive couple actually committed the robbery. Expanding on what he had thus purported to suggest as a hypothesis, the prosecutor offered the completely unfounded and improper testimonial assertion that, in his opinion, the factors he had assigned were "conservative estimates" and that, in reality "the chances of anyone else besides these defendants being there, . . . having every similarity, . . . is somewhat like one in a billion."

Objections were timely made to the mathematician's testimony on the grounds that it was immaterial, that it invaded the province of the jury, and that it was based on unfounded assumptions. The objections were "temporarily overruled" and the evidence admitted subject to a motion to strike. When that motion was made at the conclusion of the direct examination, the court denied it, stating that the testimony had been received only for the "purpose of illustrating the mathematical probabilities of various matters, the possibilities for them occurring or re-occurring."

. . . .

As we shall explain, the prosecution's introduction and use of mathematical probability statistics injected two fundamental prejudicial errors into the case:

(1) The testimony itself lacked an adequate foundation both in evidence and in statistical theory; and (2) the testimony and the manner in which the prosecution used it distracted the jury from its proper and requisite function of weighing the evidence on the issue of guilt, encouraged the jurors to rely upon an engaging but logically irrelevant expert demonstration, foreclosed the possibility of an effective defense by an attorney apparently unschooled in mathematical refinements, and placed the jurors and defense counsel at a disadvantage in sifting relevant fact from inapplicable theory.

We initially consider the defects in the testimony itself. As we have indicated, the specific technique presented through the mathematician's testimony and advanced by the prosecutor to measure the probabilities in question suffered from two basic and pervasive defects — an inadequate evidentiary foundation and an inadequate proof of statistical independence. First, as to the foundation requirement, we find the record devoid of any evidence relating to any of the six individual probability factors used by the prosecutor and ascribed by him to the six characteristics as we have set them out in footnote 10, *ante*. To put it another way, the prosecution produced no evidence whatsoever showing, or from which it could be in any way inferred, that only one out of every ten cars which might have been at the scene of the robbery was partly yellow, that only one out of every four men who might have been there wore a mustache, that only one out of every ten girls who might have been there wore a ponytail, or that any of the other individual probability factors listed were even roughly accurate. . . .

We can hardly conceive of a more fatal gap in the prosecution's scheme of proof. A foundation for the admissibility of the witness' testimony was never even attempted to be laid, let alone established. His testimony was neither made to rest on his own testimonial knowledge nor presented by proper hypothetical questions based upon valid data in the record. . . .

But, as we have indicated, there was another glaring defect in the prosecution's technique, namely an inadequate proof of the statistical independence of the six factors. No proof was presented that the characteristics selected were mutually independent, even though the witness himself acknowledged that such condition was essential to the proper application of the "product rule" or "multiplication rule." . . . To the extent that the traits or characteristics were not mutually independent (e.g., Negroes with beards and men with mustaches obviously represent overlapping categories . . .), the "product rule" would inevitably yield a wholly erroneous and exaggerated result even if all of the individual components had been determined with precision. . . .

In the instant case, therefore, because of the aforementioned two defects — the inadequate evidentiary foundations and the inadequate proof of statistical independence — the technique employed by the prosecutor could only lead to wild conjecture without demonstrated relevancy to the issues presented. It acquired no redeeming quality from the prosecutor's statement that it was being used only "for illustrative purposes" since, as we shall point out, the prosecutor's subsequent utilization of the mathematical testimony was not confined within such limits.

We now turn to the second fundamental error caused by the probability testimony. Quite apart from our foregoing objections to the specific technique employed by the prosecution to estimate the probability in question, we think that the entire enterprise upon which the prosecution embarked, and which was directed to the objective of measuring the likelihood of a random couple possessing the characteristics allegedly distinguishing the robbers, was gravely misguided. At best, it might yield an estimate as to how infrequently bearded Negroes drive yellow cars in the company of blonde females with ponytails.

The prosecution's approach, however, could furnish the jury with absolutely no guidance on the crucial issue: *Of the admittedly few such couples, which one, if any, was guilty of committing this robbery?* Probability theory necessarily remains silent on that question, since no mathematical equation can prove beyond a reasonable doubt (1) that the guilty couple *in fact* possessed the characteristics described by the People's witnesses, or even (2) that only *one* couple possessing those distinctive characteristics could be found in the entire Los Angeles area.

As to the first inherent failing we observe that the prosecution's theory of probability rested on the assumption that the witnesses called by the People had conclusively established that the guilty couple possessed the precise characteristics relied upon by the prosecution. But no mathematical formula could ever establish beyond a reasonable doubt that the prosecution's witnesses correctly observed and accurately described the distinctive features which were employed to link defendants to the crime . . . . Conceivably, for example, the guilty couple might have included a light-skinned [African-American] with bleached hair rather than a Caucasian blonde; or the driver of the car might have been wearing a false beard as a disguise; or the prosecution's witnesses might simply have been unreliable. (Footnote omitted.)

The foregoing risks of error permeate the prosecution's circumstantial case.

Traditionally, the jury weighs such risks in evaluating the credibility and probative value of trial testimony, but the likelihood of human error or of falsification obviously cannot be quantified; that likelihood must therefore be excluded from any effort to assign a *number* to the probability of guilt or innocence. Confronted with an equation which purports to yield a numerical index of probable guilt, few juries could resist the temptation to accord disproportionate weight to that index; only an exceptional juror, and indeed only a defense attorney schooled in mathematics, could successfully keep in mind the fact that the probability computed by the prosecution can represent, *at best*, the likelihood that a random couple would share the characteristics testified to by the People's witnesses — *not necessarily the characteristics of the actually guilty couple.*

As to the second inherent failing in the prosecution's approach, even assuming that the first failing could be discounted, the most a mathematical computation could *ever* yield would be a measure of the probability that a random couple would possess the distinctive features in question. In the present case, for example, the prosecution attempted to compute the probability that a random couple would include a bearded Negro, a blonde girl with a ponytail, and a partly yellow car; the prosecution urged that this probability was no more than one in 12 million. Even accepting this conclusion as arithmetically accurate, however, one still could not conclude that the Collinses were probably *the* guilty couple. On the contrary, as we explain in the Appendix, the prosecution's figures actually imply a likelihood of over 40 percent that the Collinses could be "duplicated" by at least *one other couple who might equally have committed the San Pedro robbery.* Urging that the Collinses be convicted on the basis of evidence which logically establishes no more than this seems as indefensible as arguing for the conviction of X on the ground that a witness saw either X or X's twin commit the crime.

Again, few defense attorneys, and certainly few jurors, could be expected to comprehend this basic flaw in the prosecution's analysis. Conceivably even the prosecutor erroneously believed that his equation established a high probability that *no* other bearded Negro in the Los Angeles area drove a yellow car accompanied by a ponytailed blonde. In any event, although his technique could demonstrate no such thing, he solemnly told the jury that he had supplied mathematical proof of guilt.

Sensing the novelty of that notion, the prosecutor told the jurors that the traditional idea of proof beyond a reasonable doubt represented "the most hackneyed, stereotyped, trite, misunderstood concept in criminal law." He sought to reconcile the jury to the risk that, under his "new math" approach to criminal jurisprudence, "on some rare occasion . . . an innocent person may be convicted." "Without taking that risk," the prosecution continued, "life would be intolerable . . . because . . . there would be immunity for the Collinses, for people who chose not to be employed to go down and push old ladies down and take their money and be immune because how could we ever be sure they are the ones who did it?"

In essence this argument of the prosecutor was calculated to persuade the jury to convict defendants whether or not they were convinced of their guilt to a moral certainty and beyond a reasonable doubt . . . . Undoubtedly the jurors were unduly impressed by the mystique of the mathematical demonstration but were unable to assess its relevancy or value. Although we make no appraisal of the proper applications of mathematical techniques in the proof of facts, . . . we have strong feelings that such applications, particularly in a criminal case, must be critically examined in view of the substantial unfairness to a defendant which may result from ill conceived techniques with which the trier of fact is not technically equipped to cope . . . . We feel that the technique employed in the case before us falls into the latter category.

We conclude that the court erred in admitting over defendant's objection the evidence pertaining to the mathematical theory of probability and in denying defendant's motion to strike such evidence . . . . The judgment against defendant must therefore be reversed.

. . . .

Appendix

. . . .

Hence, even if we should accept the prosecution's figures without question, we would derive a probability of over 40 percent that the couple observed by the witnesses could be "duplicated" by at least one other equally distinctive interracial couple in the area, including a Negro with a beard and mustache, driving a partly yellow car in the company of a blonde with a ponytail. Thus the prosecution's computations, far from establishing beyond a reasonable doubt that the Collinses were the couple described by the prosecution's witnesses, imply a very substantial likelihood that the area contained *more than one* such couple, and that a couple *other* than the Collinses was the one observed at the scene of the robbery. . . .

OLD CHIEF v. UNITED STATES
United States Supreme Court
519 U.S. 172, 117 S. Ct. 644, 136 L. Ed. 2d 574 (1997)

SOUTER, J., delivered the opinion of the Court, in which STEVENS, KENNEDY, GINSBURG, AND BREYER, JJ., joined. O'CONNOR, J. filed a dissenting opinion, in which REHNQUIST, C.J., and SCALIA and THOMAS, JJ., joined.

Subject to certain limitations, **18 U.S.C. Section 922(g)(1)** prohibits possession of a firearm by anyone with a prior felony conviction, which the Government can prove by introducing a record of judgment or similar evidence identifying the previous offense. Fearing prejudice if the jury learns the nature of the earlier crime, defendants sometimes seek to avoid such an informative disclosure by offering to concede the fact of the prior conviction. The issue here is whether a district court abuses its discretion if it spurns such an offer and admits the full record of a prior judgment, when the name or nature of the prior offense raises the risk of a verdict tainted by improper considerations, and when the purpose of the evidence is solely to prove the element of prior conviction. We hold that it does.

In 1993, petitioner, Old Chief, was arrested after a fracas involving at least one gunshot. The ensuing federal charges included [possession of a firearm by a convicted felon.] . . . . The earlier crime charged in the indictment against Old Chief was assault causing serious bodily injury. Before trial, he moved for an order requiring the Government "to refrain from mentioning . . . the prior criminal convictions of the Defendant, except to state that the Defendant has been convicted of a crime punishable by imprisonment exceeding one (1) year." The Assistant United States Attorney refused to join in a stipulation, insisting on his right to prove his case his own way, and the District Court agreed. . . .

We granted Old Chief's petition for writ of certiorari . . . because the Courts of Appeals have divided sharply . . . . As a threshold matter, [the nature of the prior conviction is relevant.] A documentary record of the conviction for that named offense was thus relevant evidence in making Old Chief's Section 922(g)(1) status more probable than it would have been without the evidence.

. . . .

The principal issue is the scope of a trial judge's discretion under Rule 403, ... The term "unfair prejudice," as to a criminal defendant, speaks to . . . "an undue tendency to suggest decisions on an improper basis . . . . Advisory Committee's Notes on Fed. Rule Evid. 403.

Such improper grounds certainly include the one that Old Chief points to here: generalizing a defendant's earlier bad act into bad character and taking that as raising the odds that he did the later bad act now charged . . . . There is, accordingly, no question that propensity would be an "improper basis" for conviction . . . . [W]hen a court considers "whether to exclude on grounds of unfair prejudice," the "availability of other means of proof may . . . be an appropriate factor." Advisory Committee's Notes on Fed. Rule Evid. 403 . . . .

. . . Where a prior conviction was for a gun crime or one similar to other charges in a pending case, the risk of unfair prejudice would be especially obvious, and Old Chief sensibly worried that the prejudicial effect of his prior assault conviction, significant enough with respect to the current gun charges alone, would take on added weight from the related assault charge against him.

. . . In arguing that the stipulation or admission would not have carried equivalent value, the Government invokes the familiar, standard rule that the prosecution is entitled to prove its case by evidence of its own choice, or, more exactly, that a criminal defendant may not stipulate or admit his way out of the full evidentiary force of the case as the government chooses to present it . . . .

This is unquestionably true as a general matter. The "fair and legitimate weight" of conventional evidence showing individual thoughts and acts amounting to a crime reflect the fact that making a case with testimony and tangible things not only satisfies the formal definition of an offense, but tells a colorful story with descriptive richness. . . .

This recognition that the prosecution with its burden of persuasion needs evidentiary depth to tell a continuous story has, however, virtually no application when the point at issue is a defendant's legal status, dependent on some judgment rendered wholly independently of the concrete events of later criminal behavior charged against him. . . .

. . . In this case, . . . the only reasonable conclusion was that the risk of unfair prejudice did substantially outweigh the discounted probative value of the record of conviction, and it was an abuse of discretion to admit the record when an admission was available.

. . . .

The judgment is reversed, and the case is remanded to the Ninth Circuit for further proceedings consistent with this opinion.

Chapter 5

CHARACTER AND HABIT EVIDENCE

§ 5.01 CHAPTER CHECKLIST

1. Is the testimony being offered "character" evidence?

2. If yes, what is the purpose for which evidence of a person's character is being offered?

    a. Is the person's character itself a material fact, that is, an essential element of a crime, claim, or defense?

    b. Is the person's character offered to prove "action in conformity therewith," that is, how the person behaved on a specified occasion ("act propensity")?

    c. Is the person's character offered to prove that person's mental state ("mental propensity")?

    d. Is the person's character offered to prove or disprove the person's credibility as a witness? If so, is "intrinsic" or "extrinsic" evidence of character being offered, and what is the difference?

3. Do any of the exceptions to the general bar on act propensity evidence apply?

4. Is this a homicide or sexual assault case, to which special character evidence rules apply?

5. What type of evidence of a person's character is being offered?

    a. The person's reputation?

    b. The opinion of a witness who knows the person?

    c. Specific acts in which the person has previously engaged?

6. Is evidence that looks like character evidence but is not — such as some uses of prior bad acts — being offered and, if so, for what purposes?

7. What distinguishes "character" evidence from "habit" evidence?

8. What distinguishes "character" evidence from "motive" evidence?

9. Why does the Case Library to this chapter present *Michelson v. United States*?

§ 5.02 RELEVANT FEDERAL RULES OF EVIDENCE

Rule 404. Character Evidence; Crimes or Other Acts

(a) **Character Evidence.**

  (1) *Prohibited Uses.* Evidence of a person's character or character trait is not admissible to prove that on a particular occasion the person acted in accordance with the character or trait.

  (2) *Exceptions for a Defendant or Victim in a Criminal Case.* The following exceptions apply in a criminal case:

   (A) a defendant may offer evidence of the defendant's pertinent trait, and if the evidence is admitted, the prosecutor may offer evidence to rebut it;

   (B) subject to the limitations in Rule 412, a defendant may offer evidence of an alleged victim's pertinent trait, and if the evidence is admitted, the prosecutor may:

     (i) offer evidence to rebut it; and

     (ii) offer evidence of the defendant's same trait; and

   (C) in a homicide case, the prosecutor may offer evidence of the alleged victim's trait of peacefulness to rebut evidence that the victim was the first aggressor.

  (3) *Exceptions for a Witness.* Evidence of a witness's character may be admitted under Rules 607, 608, and 609.

(b) **Crimes, Wrongs, or Other Acts.**

  (1) *Prohibited Uses.* Evidence of a crime, wrong, or other act is not admissible to prove a person's character in order to show that on a particular occasion the person acted in accordance with the character.

  (2) *Permitted Uses; Notice in a Criminal Case.* This evidence may be admissible for another purpose, such as proving motive, opportunity, intent, preparation, plan, knowledge, identity, absence of mistake, or lack of accident. On request by a defendant in a criminal case, the prosecutor must:

   (A) provide reasonable notice of the general nature of any such evidence that the prosecutor intends to offer at trial; and

   (B) do so before trial — or during trial if the court, for good cause, excuses lack of pretrial notice.

Rule 405. Methods of Proving Character

(a) **By Reputation or Opinion.** When evidence of a person's character or character trait is admissible, it may be proved by testimony about the person's reputation or by testimony in the form of an opinion. On cross-examination of the character witness, the court may allow an inquiry into relevant specific instances of the person's conduct.

(b) **By Specific Instances of Conduct.** When a person's character or character trait is an essential element of a charge, claim, or defense, the character or trait may also be proved by relevant specific instances of the person's conduct.

(c) **Rule 406. Habit; Routine Practice**

Evidence of a person's habit or an organization's routine practice may be admitted to prove that on a particular occasion the person or organization acted in accordance with the habit or routine practice. The court may admit this evidence regardless of whether it is corroborated or whether there was an eyewitness.

Rule 412. Sex-Offense Cases: The Victim's Sexual Behavior or Predisposition

(a) **Prohibited Uses.** The following evidence is not admissible in a civil or criminal proceeding involving alleged sexual misconduct:

(1) evidence offered to prove that a victim engaged in other sexual behavior; or

(2) evidence offered to prove a victim's sexual predisposition.

(b) **Exceptions.**

(1) *Criminal Cases.* The court may admit the following evidence in a criminal case:

(A) evidence of specific instances of a victim's sexual behavior, if offered to prove that someone other than the defendant was the source of semen, injury, or other physical evidence;

(B) evidence of specific instances of a victim's sexual behavior with respect to the person accused of the sexual misconduct, if offered by the defendant to prove consent or if offered by the prosecutor; and

(C) evidence whose exclusion would violate the defendant's constitutional rights.

(2) *Civil Cases.* In a civil case, the court may admit evidence offered to prove a victim's sexual behavior or sexual predisposition if its probative value substantially outweighs the danger of harm to any victim and of unfair prejudice to any party. The court may admit evidence of a victim's reputation only if the victim has placed it in controversy.

(c) **Procedure to Determine Admissibility.**

(1) *Motion.* If a party intends to offer evidence under Rule 412(b), the party must:

(A) file a motion that specifically describes the evidence and states the purpose for which it is to be offered;

- (B) do so at least 14 days before trial unless the court, for good cause, sets a different time;
- (C) serve the motion on all parties; and
- (D) notify the victim or, when appropriate, the victim's guardian or representative.

(2) *Hearing.* Before admitting evidence under this rule, the court must conduct an in camera hearing and give the victim and parties a right to attend and be heard. Unless the court orders otherwise, the motion, related materials, and the record of the hearing must be and remain sealed.

(d) **Definition of "Victim."** In this rule, "victim" includes an alleged victim.

Rule 413. Similar Crimes in Sexual-Assault Cases

(a) **Permitted Uses.** In a criminal case in which a defendant is accused of a sexual assault, the court may admit evidence that the defendant committed any other sexual assault. The evidence may be considered on any matter to which it is relevant.

(b) **Disclosure to the Defendant.** If the prosecutor intends to offer this evidence, the prosecutor must disclose it to the defendant, including witnesses' statements or a summary of the expected testimony. The prosecutor must do so at least 15 days before trial or at a later time that the court allows for good cause.

(c) **Effect on Other Rules.** This rule does not limit the admission or consideration of evidence under any other rule.

(d) **Definition of "Sexual Assault."** In this rule and Rule 415, "sexual assault" means a crime under federal law or under state law (as "state" is defined in 18 U.S.C. § 513) involving:

(1) any conduct prohibited by 18 U.S.C. chapter 109A;

(2) contact, without consent, between any part of the defendant's body — or an object — and another person's genitals or anus;

(3) contact, without consent, between the defendant's genitals or anus and any part of another person's body;

(4) deriving sexual pleasure or gratification from inflicting death, bodily injury, or physical pain on another person; or

(5) an attempt or conspiracy to engage in conduct described in subparagraphs (1)–(4).

Rule 414. Similar Crimes in Child-Molestation Cases

(a) **Permitted Uses.** In a criminal case in which a defendant is accused of child molestation, the court may admit evidence that the defendant committed any other child molestation. The evidence may be considered on any matter to which it is relevant.

(b) **Disclosure to the Defendant.** If the prosecutor intends to offer this evidence, the prosecutor must disclose it to the defendant, including witnesses' statements or a summary of the expected testimony. The prosecutor must do so at least 15 days before trial or at a later time that the court allows for good cause.

(c) **Effect on Other Rules.** This rule does not limit the admission or consideration of evidence under any other rule.

(d) **Definition of "Child" and "Child Molestation."** In this rule and Rule 415:

(1) "child" means a person below the age of 14; and

(2) "child molestation" means a crime under federal law or under state law (as "state" is defined in 18 U.S.C. § 513) involving:

(A) any conduct prohibited by 18 U.S.C. chapter 109A and committed with a child;

(B) any conduct prohibited by 18 U.S.C. chapter 110;

Rule 415. Similar Acts in Civil Cases Involving Sexual Assault or Child Molestation

(a) **Permitted Uses.** In a civil case involving a claim for relief based on a party's alleged sexual assault or child molestation, the court may admit evidence that the party committed any other sexual assault or child molestation. The evidence may be considered as provided in Rules 413 and 414.

(b) **Disclosure to the Opponent.** If a party intends to offer this evidence, the party must disclose it to the party against whom it will be offered, including witnesses' statements or a summary of the expected testimony. The party must do so at least 15 days before trial or at a later time that the court allows for good cause.

(c) **Effect on Other Rules.** This rule does not limit the admission or consideration of evidence under any other rule.

Rule 608. A Witness's Character for Truthfulness or Untruthfulness

(a) **Reputation or Opinion Evidence.** A witness's credibility may be attacked or supported by testimony about the witness's reputation for having a character for truthfulness or untruthfulness, or by testimony in the form of an opinion about that character. But evidence of truthful character is admissible only after the witness's character for truthfulness has been attacked.

(b) **Specific Instances of Conduct.** Except for a criminal conviction under Rule 609, extrinsic evidence is not admissible to prove specific instances of a witness's conduct in order to attack or support the witness's character for truthfulness. But the court may, on cross-examination, allow them to be inquired into if they are probative of the character for truthfulness or untruthfulness of:

(1) the witness; or

(2) another witness whose character the witness being cross-examined has testified about. By testifying on another matter, a witness does not waive any privilege against self-incrimination for testimony that relates only to the witness's character for truthfulness.

Rule 609. Impeachment by Evidence of a Criminal Conviction

(a) **In General.** The following rules apply to attacking a witness's character for truthfulness by evidence of a criminal conviction:

(1) for a crime that, in the convicting jurisdiction, was punishable by death or by imprisonment for more than one year, the evidence:

(A) must be admitted, subject to Rule 403, in a civil case or in a criminal case in which the witness is not a defendant; and

(B) must be admitted in a criminal case in which the witness is a defendant, if the probative value of the evidence outweighs its prejudicial effect to that defendant; and

(2) for any crime regardless of the punishment, the evidence must be admitted if the court can readily determine that establishing the elements of the crime required proving — or the witness's admitting — a dishonest act or false statement.

(b) **Limit on Using the Evidence After 10 Years.**

This subdivision (b) applies if more than 10 years have passed since the witness's conviction or release from confinement for it, whichever is later. Evidence of the conviction is admissible only if:

(1) its probative value, supported by specific facts and circumstances, substantially outweighs its prejudicial effect; and

(2) the proponent gives an adverse party reasonable written notice of the intent to use it so that the party has a fair opportunity to contest its use.

(c) **Effect of a Pardon, Annulment, or Certificate of Rehabilitation.** Evidence of a conviction is not admissible if:

(1) the conviction has been the subject of a pardon, annulment, certificate of rehabilitation, or other equivalent procedure based on a finding that the person has been rehabilitated, and the person has not been convicted of a later crime punishable by death or by imprisonment for more than one year; or

(2) the conviction has been the subject of a pardon, annulment, or other equivalent procedure based on a finding of innocence.

(d) **Juvenile Adjudications.** Evidence of a juvenile adjudication is admissible under this rule only if:

(1) it is offered in a criminal case;

(2) the adjudication was of a witness other than the defendant;

(3) an adult's conviction for that offense would be admissible to attack the adult's credibility; and

(4) admitting the evidence is necessary to fairly determine guilt or innocence.

(e) **Pendency of an Appeal.** A conviction that satisfies this rule is admissible even if an appeal is pending. Evidence of the pendency is also admissible.

§ 5.03 CHARACTER EVIDENCE BASICS

[A] Defining "Character Evidence"

Rule 404(a), the general rule concerning character evidence reads as follows:

"Evidence of a person's character or character trait is not admissible to prove that on a particular occasion the person acted in accordance with the character or trait, " though there are exceptions. Understanding even this single sentence requires understanding just what "character" is, as distinguished from other sorts of evidence, and what it means to use character to prove an act as an element, rather than to prove some other element, of a crime, civil claim, or defense, for the rule prohibits only proving *action* via character. Nor, however, can this single sentence be understood in complete isolation from the other character rules. Before we can examine those other rules in detail, therefore, an overview is needed both of the concept of character and its various relevant uses in litigation and of the general scheme for handling character that is embodied in the federal character evidence rules taken as a whole. This section provides that overview.

This section introduces you to the study of character evidence by first defining the term. The term's meaning is only understood, however, by exploring the distinction between "act propensity" and "mental propensity" evidence, including the Federal Evidence Rules' apparent special distrust of the former.

"Character," in common sense terms, refers to the "kind of person" someone is: kind or cruel, peaceful or violent, careful or sloppy. "Character" is often used broadly to describe much of a person's nature. For example, to say "Johnny is an honest man" is to describe him as an overall good person, who would neither steal nor lie nor mislead another. The term "character trait" is used more narrowly to refer to a particular aspect of our character, perhaps as punctual, quick-tempered, or fastidious. Most people judge others quite readily based on their confident assessments of others' characters. We believe that honest people won't lie, punctual people won't be late, and fastidious people won't leave dirty dishes.

At trial, these beliefs can distort a jury's ability to find the truth for several reasons:

1. Most people are willing to make quick, confident judgments about another person's character based on very little evidence. For example, we might label someone a liar whom we once catch in a significant lie when that untruth may have been an aberration.

2. Character is not very predictive of how people will react in particular situations. Character describes average behavior only. A "nasty-tempered person" may be grumpy more often than most other people. Nevertheless, he or she may still often, perhaps even usually, be friendly and kind. (Remember Vito Corleone in *The Godfather*, gently playing with his grandchildren one minute, then ordering killings of "business" associates the next!) The more broadly defined and "cross-situational" the character trait, the less its predictive power. Thus we might expect a person we label as "tardy" to be late for all or most appointments. In fact, such persons may be often tardy for social events but punctual at their job.

3. Character evidence has moral overtones. Jurors may dislike someone they perceive as dishonest. Jurors may, therefore, feel that defendants "deserve" punishment, convicting them more for who they are than for what the evidence has shown that they have done.

4. Character can change over time, often in subtle but important ways that jurors might ignore in light of dramatic evidence of earlier positive or negative character traits. Even violent persons can have a religious experience that leads them to peace.

The Advisory Committee summarized these concerns this way:[1]

"Character evidence is of slight probative value and may be very prejudicial. It tends to distract the trier of fact from the main question of what actually happened on a particular occasion. It subtly permits the trier of fact to reward the good man and to punish the bad man because of their respective characters despite what the evidence in the case shows actually happened."

Consider the following set of circumstances:

Example 1

Ronald Meldman is charged with armed robbery. Meldman is a 28-year-old postal clerk caught by police officers running near the scene of the crime and arguably fitting the offender's description. Meldman, in handcuffs and surrounded by four police officers, is brought before the victim and told, "We found this guy running from the scene, and he seems to fit the description." The victim responded, "Well, he does sort of look like the guy." There were no other eyewitnesses. Meldman told the police he was running to catch the bus to work when they grabbed him.

At trial, the prosecution offers evidence in its case-in-chief that Meldman was convicted nine years earlier of robbery. If this evidence is admitted, there is a grave danger that the jury will simply assume, "He robbed

---

[1] Rule 404, Advisory Committee Note (quoting California Law Revision Committee).

before, so, of course, he did it again. Those people never change." The jury might ignore the nine years in which Meldman earned an honest living, suggesting he has indeed changed. Or the jury might ignore the unique circumstance that he committed the armed robbery when he was homeless and starving, a situation that has now changed. Most important, the jury might ignore the weak evidence that Meldman committed the current crime — the tenuous identification, the lack of corroborating evidence, and the plausible explanation for his alleged "flight." If the prior conviction caused the jurors to ignore all these things, they would be convicting him simply because they think he is a bad man. For reasons like these, evidence of Meldman's prior crime will in fact be inadmissible to prove that he committed the current one. Nevertheless, these concerns about the misuse of character evidence are not equally strong for all situations. Accordingly, the admissibility rules vary based on the category of character evidence and the purposes for which the proponent offers it, that is, what the proponent seeks to prove.

Example 2

Suppose that in the example above the prosecution did not mention Meldman's earlier conviction in its case-in-chief. However, Meldman takes the stand at the start of the defense case-in-chief and denies committing the crime with which he is now charged. The prosecution now asks him whether he was convicted previously of felony armed robbery. The prosecution argues that this evidence is not being offered to prove that, because Meldman robbed in the past, he probably robbed again. Rather, this evidence is offered because convicted felons should not be believed, so the jury should consider Meldman a liar. Whether you think that this makes sense or not, the Rule accepts this logic and would admit this evidence if the trial judge believes that its probative value outweighs its prejudicial effect to the accused. The same evidence inadmissible in the earlier example when offered for one purpose (proving that a robber, like Meldman, probably robbed again) may be admissible for another purpose (proving that a robber, like Meldman, probably lied on the stand).

There are two broad purposes for which character evidence may be offered at trial, each purpose divisible into sub-purposes:

1. Propensity uses: arguing that, because someone acted or thought a certain way in the past, they have a character that makes it likely that they acted or thought that way again.

2. Non-propensity uses: offering character evidence or similar evidence for any other reason.

In analyzing these uses below, remember that we are initially addressing only whether some form of character evidence is admissible. Even where character is admissible, it may be limited to certain forms or kinds. (*See* Rules 404(b), 405.) There are three kinds of character evidence: reputation (what people in the relevant community say about you), opinion (what knowledgeable people think of you), and specific acts (what you have done). These kinds of evidence will be defined in more detail shortly.

Generally (subject to details provided below), if character evidence is offered to prove that a person acted in a certain way, the person's character may be shown only by reputation or opinion evidence, not by evidence of specific acts. For example, a defendant in an assault case might prove his peaceful nature by calling neighbors to say that his reputation in the community is as a peaceful man, or by calling his best friend to say that in his opinion the defendant is nonviolent. Since he is a nonviolent person, the defendant argues, it is not likely that he would commit the violent assault with which he is charged. But the defendant may not call witnesses to recount *specific occasions* where they say they saw others trying to pick a fight with the defendant but failing because he found peaceful ways to resolve the dispute.

Compare Rule 405(a) ("When evidence of a person's character or character trait is admissible, it may be proved by testimony about the person's reputation or by testimony in the form of an opinion") with Rule 404(b)(1) ("[But] [e]vidence of a crime, wrong, or other act is not admissible to prove a person's character in order to show that on a particular occasion the person acted in accordance with the character.").

There are, however, some circumstances where character can be proved by specific acts. Thus, if character is offered to prove that a person thought, rather than acted, a certain way on a particular occasion, the general rules on character evidence probably do not apply. Character may then be proven by specific acts. *See* Rule 404(b)(2) ("This evidence may be admissible for another purpose [than proving act propensity], such as proving motive, opportunity, intent, preparation, plan, knowledge, identity, absence of mistake or lack of accident. . . ."). (Note: Rule 404(b)(2) refers to both non-character evidence and character evidence used to prove mental state, a matter discussed in depth later in this chapter.) Similarly, the usual prohibitions are not triggered when character matters in and of itself, and character evidence is not offered to prove any propensity to think or act a certain way. Thus if a statute increases the sentence for a felony conviction where the person convicted is a "habitual criminal," the character trait of being a "habitual criminal" would be an element of the crime. That trait could therefore be proven by showing repeated specific prior acts of criminality. (*See* Rule 405(b) ("When a person's character or character trait is an essential element of a crime, claim, or defense, the character or trait may also be proved by relevant specific instances of conduct.").) (Note: When the rules refer to character mattering in itself, that is, that there is no other logical way to prove an element but by proving character, the rules say that "character is an essential element of a crime, claim, or defense.").

Additionally, some evidence looks like character evidence but is not. Thus specific prior bad acts might be offered to prove a "motive" to commit a crime, because "motive" is not evidence of "character." As an example, a man accused of killing his wife might be shown to have committed numerous acts of adultery. Fearing that his wealthy wife would find him out and leave him penniless, the prosecution argues, the accused killed his wife preemptively to inherit her money. The specific acts of adultery are permissible "motive" evidence, not impermissible "character" evidence. *See* Rule 404(b)(2) ("This evidence may be admissible for another purpose, such as proving motive, opportunity, intent, preparation, plan, knowledge, identity, absence of mistake, or lack of accident".).

At the risk of some repetition (hopefully, necessary repetition), greater detail on the forms of proof, including special rules for certain classes of cases (such as sexual assaults) and for using character evidence to impeach a witness' credibility, is offered below. For now, it is sufficient that you be aware of these general principles and have at least some sense of their significance as you work through the problems below. If you would like a more detailed introduction now to the forms of proof, read section 5.04 now, although you should be able to complete the problems below simply by first doing a careful reading of Rules 404 and 405.

It is important to stress here the close connection between Rules 404 and 405. The two easily could have been written as one rule. Rule 404(a), subject to certain exceptions, forbids using character — *no matter in what form* (reputation, opinion, or specific acts) — to prove actions in conformity therewith. If a 404(a) exception applies, however, then you know only that *some form* of character evidence is admissible. But it is then necessary to go to Rules 405(a) and 404(b)(1) to determine *what form* of proof is admissible (usually only reputation or opinion are allowable, as Rule 405(a) explains), *not* specific acts (see Rule 404(b) ("Evidence of a crime, wrong, or other act is not admissible to prove a person's character in order to show that on a particular occasion the person acted in accordance with the character."), with the understanding that special rules govern some evidence in sexual assault cases (*see* Rules 412–415) and some evidence for impeaching witnesses (*see* Rules 608 and 609)). When character is offered *to prove mental state*, or when non-character evidence is offered to prove an action *or* a mental state, or when character is itself an element of the crime, claim, or defense, then Rule 404(a) does not bar the evidence in the first place, so there is no reason to consider 404(a)'s exceptions. Indeed Rules 404(b)(2) and 405(b) permit such evidence *in any form*. So the two rules — 404 and 405 — address both substance and form, and one cannot be read independently from the other, as we will see in greater detail soon.

Problem 5-1: The Ogler

Every time that Ronald Moland passes a woman on the street whom he finds attractive, he ogles her and makes lascivious comments in a loud voice. He is a defendant in a sexual harassment civil law suit brought against his employer by a female employee. The employee alleges that Moland, her boss, fondled her on the job on numerous occasions despite her continuing protests. She further alleges that Moland repeatedly looked at her on the job in a lascivious way, despite her continuing requests that he stop eyeing her "like a piece of meat." The employee is not, however, someone whom Moland has ever ogled on the street. Except where otherwise stated, answer questions 1 to 8 below by consulting only Rules 401 and 402.

1. Would evidence of Moland's behavior in repeatedly ogling numerous women on the street concern his "character" — as defined in everyday usage — or something else? Why?

2. If the evidence does concern "character," what character trait or traits is the plaintiff likely trying to prove, or is Moland's "general character" at issue?

3. For what purpose or purposes might the plaintiff want to offer this evidence of Moland's behavior in her case-in-chief at trial? Why?

4. What if Moland took the stand and denied that he committed the acts on which the plaintiff bases her sexual harassment claim? Would that change the purposes for which the evidence might be offered by the plaintiff in cross-examining Moland or on rebuttal? How? What if he testified simply that he has "never harassed a woman in his life"?

5. **If a "character" trait is involved, what sort of evidence might the plaintiff want to use to prove that character in addition to the acts of ogling noted above? What witnesses should the plaintiff call to the stand?**

6. What is the likely impact of each of these sorts of evidence on the jury, and is that impact "unfair?" Even if there were no character evidence rules (no Rules 404, 405, 412–415, 608, 609), might the defense argue for exclusion of any or all of these sorts or forms of evidence under Rule 403? How?

7. As a matter of good policy, should any of this evidence be admissible if Moland were charged with assault arising out of his punching a male co-worker in the face instead of sexual harassment? Would any of the evidence be relevant in such a trial? Why?

8. Do you need any additional information to answer any of the above questions? Why? How and why might that additional information alter your answers to the above questions?

9. Would the evidence in questions 1, 3, and 5 be admissible if we now consider the character rules?

Problem 5-2: At the Movies: Insane Anatomy of a Murder

In the film *Anatomy of a Murder*, Lt. Manion is charged with murdering Barney Quill. Manion admits that he killed Quill, but claims that he did so as a result of "irresistible impulse," a form of temporary insanity resulting from finding out that Quill had raped and beaten Manion's wife, Laura. The prosecution theory is that Quill and Laura were lovers, and that Manion killed Quill after learning of the affair. Cross-examining Manion, the prosecutor asks Manion how many enemy soldiers he has killed in combat. The prosecutor argues that Manion's wartime experience may have conditioned him to killing. The defense objects, claiming that evidence of wartime combat killing is irrelevant and an improper attempt to show that Manion has a propensity to be violent. *How should the judge rule on the objection?*

[B] Act Versus Mental Propensity Evidence: The General Rules: Rules 404(a) and 405(b)

Rule 404(a)(1) reads as follows:

Rule 404 (a) Character evidence.

(1) **Prohibited Uses.** Evidence of a person's character or character trait is not admissible to prove that on a particular occasion the person acted in accordance with the character or trait [subject to exceptions discussed below]."

This rule creates a general prohibition against character evidence only if used by its proponent for the purpose of proving that someone acted consistently with that character in a particular case. Our shorthand term for this prohibition is "act propensity" evidence.

Example 1

A prosecutor in a murder case calls a witness to testify that the defendant has a reputation for being a violent man. That evidence is offered to prove that the defendant was therefore violent on this occasion, so the jury is asked to believe that he, and not someone else, committed the crime. The defense objection under Rule 404(a) will be sustained.

Note the reasoning process involved in this example:

1. Evidence of the defendant's reputation for violence is offered.

2. The jury is asked to infer from this evidence that he indeed has a violent character.

3. The jury is further expected to infer that a violent man is more likely than a peaceful one to commit this particular murder, that is, to commit this act of unlawful killing.

This three-step reasoning process raises all the strongest concerns about character evidence. Reputation is an elusive thing and may vary with the eye of the beholder. Even if the defendant has this reputation, it may be undeserved. His tough demeanor or hoodlum friends may lead his neighbors to see him as violent when he is not. Even if he is violent, he may display physical force, for example, only toward rival gang members, a group that does not include the murder victim. Finally, jurors are likely to dislike such a man and to convict him for who he is rather than what he has done.

But these concerns may not apply with equal force if character is offered for other purposes than "act propensity." For example, Rule 405(b) declares:

Rule 405(b). By Specific Instances of Conduct. When a person's character or character trait is an essential element of a charge, claim, or defense, the character or trait may also be proved by relevant specific instances of the person's conduct.

The "also" links Rule 405(b) to Rule 405(a). The latter rule allows proof of character by reputation or opinion whenever character evidence is admissible. The former allows specific acts when character is an essential element of a crime, claim, or defense and is thus not being offered to prove act propensity.

Example 2

The *Washington Post* prints a story accusing William Jefferson Clinton of being a promiscuous man. Clinton files a defamation suit against the *Post*. Because truth is a defense to defamation, the *Post*'s defense is that Clinton actually is a promiscuous man. Thus, the character trait of "promiscuity" is an essential element of the *Post*'s defense. There is no way for the *Post* to prove its defense without showing that Clinton has sexual intercourse with many women. Therefore, the court will overrule Clinton's objections to neighbors' testimony about his reputation for having diverse sexual partners, about his friends' opinions on that same subject, and about observers' recounting numerous specific instances of his infidelity.

This direct evidence of Clinton's character does not raise all the same concerns as did the circumstantial evidence of violence offered to prove that a defendant committed the act of murder in the earlier example. In the Clinton hypothetical, only a two-step reasoning process is involved:

1. Evidence of Clinton's reputation for promiscuity, informed opinions about his promiscuous nature, and specific sexual acts showing promiscuity are offered.

2. The jury is asked to infer from this evidence that Clinton indeed has a promiscuous nature, a specific type of character trait.

The reputation, opinion, and specific acts witnesses may be wrong in their assessments. Moreover, reputation, for example, may be poor evidence of whether Clinton truly has a wandering eye. Nevertheless, if the jury believes that Clinton is a satyr, their task is done. They are not asked to infer that Clinton slept with a particular woman on a particular occasion, consistently with his character. While one inferential danger is missing, however, the need for the evidence is great: without it, the *Washington Post* has no defense. Thus, Rule 405 admits it.

Direct evidence of character as an element of a crime, claim, or defense is an example of a non-propensity use of character evidence. But there are other non-propensity uses of character evidence too, which we will discuss later in this chapter.

It is also important, however, to be alert to one sort of inferential chain that cannot be categorized as either "act propensity" or "non-propensity." Instead, this reasoning chain constitutes "mental propensity" — a use of character evidence that is *not* barred by Rule 404(a).

Example 3

George Harrison is arrested in possession of a large quantity of cocaine. Harrison is charged with possessing narcotics with the intention of selling them. There is no serious question whether he committed the "act" of possession. The only issue is whether there is evidence to prove beyond a reasonable doubt that he did so with the intention to sell rather than for personal use. The prosecution seeks to offer evidence of Harrison's long history as a seller of cocaine.

This sort of character evidence is sometimes called "mental propensity" evidence to distinguish it from "act propensity" evidence. The prosecution is using Harrison's character not to prove conduct but to prove mental state. But, in the view of some commentators, the same three-step reasoning process, and thus the same analytical dangers, are involved with both sorts of propensity reasoning. Thus:

1. Evidence of Harrison's prior acts of drug-selling are offered.

2. The jury is asked to infer from this evidence that he indeed is the kind of person who sells narcotics.

3. The jury is further expected to infer that a narcotics-seller is more likely than a mere user or an honest man to have possessed cocaine with the intent to sell it in this particular instance.

The inferential dangers involved seem similar to those of act propensity evidence. It may be doubtful whether the alleged prior unconvicted acts of drug-selling in fact happened. Even if Harrison is proven to have sold narcotics in the past, we need more information, for he may since then have found an honest way to make a living. Moreover, even if he is still the kind of person who would sell narcotics, that does not necessarily mean that he did so on this occasion. He may merely have held the drugs for his own use. Yet juries may easily assume that he meant to sell the drugs in his possession here, overweighing the character evidence and convicting him for being a bad man, though there may be little other evidence of his wrongful intentions in the case at hand. Accordingly, some commentators suggest that Rule 404 either does or should prohibit both act and mental propensity evidence. *See, e.g.*, McCormick on Evidence §§ 188, 190 (4th ed. 1992) ("[E]vidence of character in any form — reputation, opinion from observation, or specific acts — generally will not be received to prove that a person engaged in conduct or did so with a particular intent on a specific occasion.").

There are several problems with this reasoning, however. First, "mental propensity" and "act propensity" evidence have different weight in creating an inference of conforming behavior. We often think or feel a certain way without acting on our thoughts or emotions.

Example 4

Adam is "quick-tempered," in the sense that he screams, gets red-faced, and utters cruel obscenities when anyone frustrates him or disagrees with him. At such times, Adam feels anger and hatred toward the source of his ire. But Adam has never resorted to physical violence.

It makes sense to argue that Adam is therefore more likely to feel anger on a specific occasion. However, to argue that he is therefore also more likely to act on that anger by assaulting others requires a more significant inferential leap.

Second, many of the uses of specific acts evidence permitted by Rule 404(b) involve proving mental states. Some of these uses do not involve character evidence at all. We will soon see, however, that some of these uses are "mental propensity" character evidence in disguise, without fitting into any exceptions to the propensity bar. To classify "mental propensity" evidence as barred by Rule 404(a) but permitted by Rule 404(b) would render the rules incoherent.

Third, the literal language of Rule 404 bars evidence of character or a trait of character to prove that on a particular occasion he "acted" in accordance with that character. The word "acted" suggests that only physical acts — that is, act propensity uses — are barred by the rule.

To recap: Rule 404(a) generally bars, subject to certain exceptions, "act propensity evidence," which is a shorthand term for the circumstantial use of character evidence to prove action in conformity therewith on a particular occasion. But the Rule does not prohibit non-propensity uses, such as the direct use of character evidence when character is an essential element of a charge, crime, claim, or defense. There is a dispute, however, over whether Rule 404(a) also bars "mental propensity" evidence, which is character evidence offered to prove that a person experienced a mental state in conformity therewith on a particular occasion. The sounder view — and the one overwhelmingly held by courts and commentators — is that it does not. *A cautionary note:* Some courts and commentators use the term "propensity evidence" as a shorthand for "act" propensity evidence. Do not be confused by this usage. Analytical clarity requires maintaining the "act" versus "mental" propensity distinction.

This analytical clarity is required even though neither the term "act propensity" nor the term "mental propensity" appears in Rule 404(a). Indeed, the word "propensity" does not appear either, yet most courts and commentators use it. These terms are all shorthand phrases to express concepts implicit in the Rule — concepts created by Rule 404(a)'s words and structure and relationship to other portions of the character evidence rules. Using the loose term "propensity" without distinguishing between the different kinds of character propensity evidence — act and mental propensity — can lead you to results in particular cases contrary to what the rules in fact demand.

Practice Tip:

Do not immediately assume that reputation, opinion, or especially specific acts evidence is "character" evidence. As you will see later in this chapter, many times evidence *looks like* character evidence but is not (the motive example above being one of many such instances). Instead, start by asking yourself whether the evidence meets the definitions of "character" or a "character trait" as just discussed (i.e., is it referring to "on-average" thoughts or behavior relative to others, thus having the relatively low probative value of character, or is it referring to something with greater probative value?). Even if evidence is "character" evidence, do not assume that it is being offered for "act propensity purposes," for the character prohibition applies solely to act propensity. Indeed, sometimes it is debatable whether evidence is "character" at all or whether, if it is character, it is proffered for act propensity purposes. Counsel opposing admissibility will latch onto the character act propensity arguments, while counsel favoring admissibility will embrace the very opposite position.

Hint: It is important that your analysis proceed in the following order: *first,* determine whether you are dealing with character evidence and, only if you are, *then* determine why it is relevant. This order of analysis is necessary because a tendency to act or think in a certain way can be relevant to proving how you respectively thought or acted on a specific occasion even if that tendency is proven by evidence that is *not character.* Rule 404(a) bars using evidence to prove act propensity *only* if the evidence constitutes proof of "character" or a "trait of character." Other propensity uses are outside the Rule 404(a) bar.

On Civil Versus Criminal Cases: Students sometimes make the error of reading Rule 404(a)'s character act propensity bar as applying only in criminal cases. No such limitation is contained in the Rule's text. Indeed, in 2006, the Rule was amended to clarify that two of its three exceptions apply only in criminal cases (*see* Rule 404(a)(1)–(2)), the point being to emphasize that the general prohibition therefore applies in *both* civil and criminal litigation, though some of the exceptions may be limited to one of those domains. (The third exception — for impeaching witnesses — applies in both civil and criminal litigation, and there is a fourth collection of exceptions not stated in the rule but created by a separate set of rules governing sexual assault and related offenses.) (*See* Rules 413–415; Rule 413 applies to criminal cases involving an offense of sexual assault; Rule 414 applies to criminal cases involving child molestation; Rule 415 applies to civil cases involving either sort of evidence.) The Advisory Committee explained its rationale for the Rule 404(a) revisions:

> The rule has been amended to clarify that in a civil case evidence of a person's character is never admissible to prove that the person acted in conformity with the character trait. The amendment resolves the dispute in the case law over whether the exceptions in subdivisions (a)(1) and (a)(2) permit the circumstantial use of character evidence in civil cases. . . . The amendment is consistent with the original intent of the Rule, which was to prohibit the circumstantial use of character evidence in civil cases, even where closely related to criminal charges.

Problem 5-3: The Negligent Driver

Jane Lambada loans her car to 17-year-old Murray Straub, who gets into an accident on a freeway while speeding. Murray is killed. Murray's parents bring a civil suit against Jane for negligently entrusting a motor vehicle to a teenager with a well-known record of numerous car accidents and reckless driving.

1. At trial, Murray's parents offer evidence of Murray's reputation as a reckless driver. Admissible or not? Why?

2. Would it make any difference if Murray's parents instead offered evidence of specific acts of Murray's negligent driving?

3. Would it make any difference if no evidence is offered that Jane was aware of Murray's reputation or of his prior instances of negligent driving?

4. Assume instead that Murray survives the accident but the driver of a car that Murray hit was killed instantly. Now Murray is criminally charged with vehicular manslaughter, which is defined as recklessly causing another's death while driving a motor vehicle. The indictment alleges that Murray was reckless because he drove 20 m.p.h. over the speed limit. The prosecutor offers evidence in her case-in-chief of (a) Murray's reputation as a reckless driver; (b) Murray's reputation as a speeder; (c) specific instances of Murray's tailgating other drivers; (d) specific instances of Murray's speeding. Will any or all of this evidence be admissible? As a policy matter, should it be?

5. At his criminal trial, Murray takes the stand and testifies that he was not aware that he was speeding — though he concedes that physical evidence suggests that he exceeded the legal limit — because his speedometer was broken. "Recklessness" is defined as conscious awareness of a substantial and unjustifiable risk of harm. Although the prosecutor was originally barred from offering the evidence mentioned in question 4 above, she now again attempts to offer that same evidence in rebuttal. Should defense objections be sustained under the Federal Rules of Evidence? As a policy matter, should this evidence be admissible? For what purposes? How, if at all, would you amend the Federal Rules to increase the likelihood that these objections will be sustained?

Problem 5-4: Seduced No More

Warren Beetney is charged with the crime of seduction, which has among its elements having sexual intercourse with a previously chaste, then-unmarried female. It turns out that the female was under the age of consent in this state, so Beetney is also charged with statutory rape. Because the same conduct is the basis for both alleged crimes, Beetney is tried on both charges at a single trial. The defense, in its case-in-chief, offers evidence of the victim's reputation as a promiscuous woman. The prosecution objects. Assume that you are in a jurisdiction that in most respects follows the Federal Rules of Evidence but has never enacted Rules 412 through 415. *Select the best answer:*

1. The objection will likely be sustained.

2. The objection will likely be overruled.

3. The trial judge probably has discretion to admit the evidence but only if he or she: (a) instructs the jury that it may consider it as to the seduction charge only but not as to the statutory rape charge; and (b) reasonably believes that the jury will be able to follow that instruction.

4. The trial judge probably has discretion to admit the evidence but only if he or she: (a) instructs the jury that it may consider it as to the statutory rape charge only but not as to the seduction charge; and (b) reasonably believes that the jury will be able to follow that instruction.

5. None of the above.

Why did you select the answer that you did, and why did you not select the other answers?

Problem 5-5: Entrapped!

Mark Dairy, the well-known mayor of a major city, is caught on videotape in a hotel room using crack cocaine. The sound portion of the video reveals Wanda Clagley, an undercover police officer, offering the cocaine to Dairy. He at first refuses repeatedly. But when Clagley intimates that she is put in an amorous mood when she shares cocaine with a potential sexual partner, Dairy relents and smokes the crack. Dairy raises an entrapment defense at his trial for possessing crack cocaine. This jurisdiction follows a subjective theory of entrapment, which it defines as agents of the state inducing a crime by one who is not predisposed to do so. Dairy takes the stand at trial and testifies in his defense. *In the colloquy below, specify and explain one or more bases for each of the prosecutor's objections, state how the judge should rule and why.*

DEFENSE COUNSEL: Mr. Dairy, have you ever been convicted of possessing crack cocaine?

PROSECUTOR: Objection! *What basis?*

JUDGE: *What ruling?*

DEFENSE COUNSEL: What is your reputation in the community regarding whether you are known as a consumer of illegal drugs?

PROSECUTOR: Objection! *What basis?*

JUDGE: Overruled. *Correct ruling?*

DEFENSE COUNSEL: Do you consider yourself to be an honest man?

PROSECUTOR: Objection! *What basis?*

JUDGE: Sustained. *Correct ruling?*

DEFENSE COUNSEL: Are you generally a law-abiding person?

PROSECUTOR: Objection! *What basis?*

JUDGE: Sustained. *Correct ruling?*

DEFENSE COUNSEL: Have you ever smoked crack cocaine?

PROSECUTOR: Objection! *What basis?*

JUDGE: Overruled. *Correct ruling?*

Are there other questions that the defense counsel should have asked to increase the chances of prevailing on the entrapment defense? What questions? Other witnesses who should have been called in addition to, or instead of, Dairy? Why?

Can the prosecution on cross-examination offer evidence that: (a) 15 years ago Dairy was arrested for selling marijuana? (b) 10 years ago Dairy was arrested for assault?

Problem 5-6: At the Movies: Custody Fight

The film *Kramer vs. Kramer* focuses on a child custody dispute. Resolution of that dispute turns on what the "best interests of the child" require. Joanna had left her husband Ted and their six-year-old son. About a year and a half later she returns and goes to court to gain custody of the son. Cross-examining Ted, Joanna's attorney elicits evidence that Ted's inattentiveness resulted in the son's falling from a park climbing apparatus, resulting in a permanent scar. Moreover, after Joanna left, Ted lost his job because of inattention to a number of important accounts. Ted had to take a new job at a much lower salary. Finally, Joanna's attorney asks Ted whether he has a bad temper. *If Ted's attorney were to object to these questions as improper character evidence, should the objections be sustained?*

Problem 5-7: Creativity

Create three new examples of propensity evidence other than the examples discussed above in text or suggested by the preceding problems. Draw on your other courses, such as contracts, torts, and property, in crafting a response.

§ 5.04 FORMS OF CHARACTER EVIDENCE

[A] Admissibility of Reputation, Opinion, and Specific Acts Evidence: Rule 404(b), 1st Sentence, Rule 405(a)–(b)

Although these matters have been touched on above, here we examine in more detail the forms of character evidence. If the situation is one in which character evidence is admissible, which form or forms of character evidence may be used?

Character evidence comes in these three forms:

1. *Reputation:* what people in a relevant community say about a particular person's character.

2. *Opinion:* what an individual who knows another person well thinks of that other person's character (as opposed to what the individual has heard other people say about that character).

3. *Specific acts:* specific instances of a person's behavior that reveal something about his or her character.

In general, whenever character evidence is admissible to prove act propensity, character may be proven by reputation or opinion but not by specific acts, as the first sentence of Rule 405(a) explains:

Rule 405. Methods of Proving Character

(a) By Reputation or Opinion. When evidence of a person's character or character trait is admissible, it may be proved by testimony about the person's reputation or by testimony in the form of an opinion. [second sentence deleted]

Rule 404(b)(1) completes the rule:

Rule 404. Character Evidence; Crimes or Other Acts

(b) Crimes, Wrongs, or Other Acts.

(1) Prohibited Uses. Evidence of a crime, wrong, or other act is not admissible to prove a person's character in order to show that on a particular occasion the person acted in accordance with the character.

Although specific acts are arguably more probative of character than either reputation or opinion evidence, the latter forms of character evidence are less time-consuming and less likely to lead to confusing collateral issues. For these reasons, therefore, the Federal Rules of Evidence generally prefer these latter two forms of proof.

Example 1

In a criminal perjury trial, the defense calls a witness to testify to specific instances in which most people would lie (for example, because an honest answer would have cost defendant his job) but the defendant nevertheless told the truth. This evidence is offered by the accused to prove the "pertinent" trait of truthfulness to show that he was unlikely to lie on the stand, that is, to commit perjury in this particular case. Under Rule 404(a)(2)(A), he may offer some form of character evidence. But under Rules 404(b)(1) and 405(a), he is prohibited from proving character by the specific instances of conduct he proffers.

Example 2

Same case as Example 1, but instead of proffering specific instances of truthful conduct, the defendant offers a witness to testify to the defendant's reputation in his community as a truthful person. Objection overruled. If this witness is properly qualified, this form of character evidence (reputation) is specifically sanctioned by Rule 405(a).

Example 3

Same case as Example 1, but the witness testifies that he has been the defendant's best friend for 25 years and, in his opinion, the defendant is a truthful person. Objection overruled.

In cases in which a person's character is directly in issue as an essential element of a charge, claim, or defense, the parties may introduce specific instances of conduct as proof of character. Thus, specific acts are admissible when character evidence is offered as direct evidence of an element of a charge, crime, claim, or defense, instead of as circumstantial proof of propensity. This rule is set forth in Rule 405(b):

Rule 405.

(b) By Specific Instances of Conduct. When a person's character or character trait is an essential element of a charge, claim, or defense, the character or trait may also be proved by relevant specific instances of the person's conduct.

Note the use of the word "also." Rule 405(a), which permits reputation and opinion as forms of character testimony, applies not only to propensity evidence but to all cases ("when[ever]") in which evidence of a person's character or character trait is admissible. Thus, reputation and opinion evidence are appropriate forms of proof when character evidence is being used directly, to prove elements, not merely for propensity uses. But Rule 405(b) makes clear that, when direct proof of elements is involved, proof may "also" be in the form of specific acts, a form of proof that is prohibited with propensity evidence.

Example 4

In the earlier defamation case filed by William Jefferson Clinton against *The Post* for calling Clinton "promiscuous," *The Post* can, in seeking to establish its defense of truth, try to prove that Clinton indeed had a promiscuous character. Because this is direct proof of character as an essential element of a defense, *The Post* may do so by reputation, opinion, or specific acts testimony revealing Clinton's wandering eye. Contrast this example with the criminal perjury trial example where the defendant offered evidence of his truthful character to show his "propensity" not to lie in the specific charged case, thus tending to prove that he did not commit perjury. Under the "mercy rule" of Rule 404(a)(2)(A), the defendant was allowed to offer some form of character evidence. But that character evidence could only be in the forms of reputation or opinion, not specific acts.

Even a character witness who is limited to reputation or opinion testimony, however, may be impeached on cross-examination by questions about specific acts. Such questions test the judgment of an opinion witness and the adequacy of a reputation witness' knowledge. In other words, they are forms of impeachment rather than of substantive evidence. The last sentence of Rule 405(a) says it this way: "On cross-examination of the character witness, the court may allow inquiry into relevant specific instances of the person's conduct."

Example 5

Benjamin Rodegard is charged with murder. The defense calls Benjamin's next door neighbor, Rabbi Joseph Gold, to testify that Benjamin has a reputation in his community as a peaceful person. On cross-examination, the prosecution may ask the rabbi whether he had heard that Rodegard had stabbed two other neighbors in a bar brawl that he started earlier that year. If the rabbi says "no," that suggests he really does not know much about critical relevant aspects of Rodegard's reputation. If he says "yes," the rabbi's judgment is suspect: How can someone with a reputation as a stabbing bar brawler be described as a person known to be "peaceful"?

Example 6

Same facts as previous example, but this time the rabbi did not testify to Rodegard's reputation as peaceful but rather to the rabbi's personal opinion that Rodegard is a peaceful person. Inquiry into specific acts is still permissible on cross-examination of the character witness (the rabbi). In cross-examining an opinion witness, the question would probably be phrased, "Didn't you know that Rodegard stabbed two neighbors in a bar brawl?" rather than "Hadn't you heard that Rodegard stabbed two neighbors in a bar brawl?" This is because opinion turns on the witness' personal knowledge of the person's behavior rather than on what the witness heard others say about the person's behavior. However, while traditional character evidence rules were often meticulous about the "Have you heard" versus "Do you know" distinction, the drafters of the Federal Rules of Evidence viewed the words as formulaic mantras. The Rules permit cross-examining character witnesses about specific instances of conduct regardless of the precise form of the words used.

The cross-examiner must, however, have a good-faith basis to believe that the specific acts happened. Those acts must also be relevant and must survive weighing under Rule 403. Furthermore, and related to these points, the acts must be of a type likely to be known by the witness or the community. Arguably private acts, such as Rodegard's beating his children in his sound-proofed basement, would not fit the bill. Additionally, the cross-examiner must take the witness' answer. In other words, if during cross-examination the witness denies knowledge of the specific acts, the questioner may not offer extrinsic evidence (evidence from another witness rather than from the cross-examined witness's own mouth while on the stand) that those acts in fact took place. Even if the witness does concede knowledge of the acts, however, the jury should be instructed *not to use the answers as proof that the acts happened*. Instead, the answers may be used only to test the witness' standard for forming an opinion about, or for evaluating the reputation of, the person about whose character the witness testifies.

Cross-examining about specific acts within the character witness' awareness as a way of testing the witness' knowledge and judgment of *another's* character must be distinguished from impeaching the character witness by attacking that witness's *own* character. If the prosecutor in example 2 immediately above called a witness to testify that the rabbi witness himself had a reputation as a liar, that impeachment technique would be governed by Rule 608 concerning character used to impeach witnesses. Under Rule 608, specific acts may sometimes be used to impeach or support a witness' character respectively for truthfulness or untruthfulness and, under Rule 609, prior convictions may be used for a similar purpose, as is explored further in § 5.08.

Specific acts may also be inquired into when offered for a non-character purpose, or to prove mental propensity, as is discussed shortly in more detail in §§ 5.10, 5.11.

In addition to these general rules on form, there are more specific rules, to be discussed shortly for sexual assault cases (*see* § 5.07). Thus, in a civil or criminal case involving sexual assault or child molestation, the prosecutor or plaintiff may offer specific acts evidence of the defendant's commission of another offense or offenses of sexual assault — for its bearing on *any* relevant matter, presumably including proof of propensity. Furthermore, under the rape shield statute, reputation or opinion evidence as to other sexual behavior by, or the alleged sexual predisposition of, the victim of sexual misconduct is flatly inadmissible in a criminal case (unless admission is required by the constitution). In a civil case, reputation evidence is admissible only if first placed in controversy by the alleged sexual assault victim. However, specific acts are admissible in a criminal case to show that a third party was the source of semen, physical injury, or other physical evidence. Specific acts of prior consensual sex with the charged defendant are also admissible to show consent on the occasion in question. In a civil case, opinion and specific act

[B] Problems on the Form of Character Evidence

Problem 5-8: The Warden Cross-Examined

John Quinn, a prison inmate, is charged with assaulting another inmate. The prison warden, Warden Jamison, was permitted to testify on the defendant's behalf that, in his opinion, Quinn is a peaceful person, and Quinn has a reputation in the prison community as a peaceful person. Should the prosecution be permitted, despite defense objections, to ask the following questions on cross-examination?

1. Wasn't Quinn written up twice for starting fights in the mess hall?

2. Didn't Quinn severely beat his cell mate when first admitted to the prison five years ago?

3. Doesn't Quinn have a reputation as a vicious man whom other inmates feared?

4. Doesn't Quinn have a reputation for involvement in failed prison escapes, though there was never enough evidence to prosecute him?

Problem 5-9: Group Therapy

The psychiatrist who has been treating a prison inmate, Johnny Berro, who is now charged with assault is called to the stand by the defense to testify that Berro is peaceful. *Can the prosecution properly ask the psychiatrist on cross, "Didn't Mr. Berro assault another patient in a group therapy session under your care?"*

Problem 5-10: The Violent Victim

A defendant is charged with attempted homicide on a victim named Margie O'Laris. The defendant claims self-defense, arguing that O'Laris was the first aggressor. To support this claim, the defense offered evidence that the victim was a violent person. *Can the prosecution offer evidence that the victim, Margie O'Laris,:*

1. Had a reputation among students in her night-time GED program as a peaceful woman?

2. Was, in the opinion of her co-workers at McDonald's, a peaceful woman?

3. Despite being punched three times in the face by a neighbor, had never defended herself or retaliated with violence?

Problem 5-11: United States v. Lorean

The defendant, Lorean, is charged with possession with intent to distribute cocaine after a government "sting" operation. Lorean admits to possessing the cocaine, but claims that he was entrapped by an undercover police officer. The jurisdiction uses a subjective test of entrapment, which asks (1) whether the police induced or created the crime and (2) whether the defendant was predisposed to committing the crime charged.

Which, if any, of the following evidence offered by Lorean is admissible?

1. Testimony by Lorean's father stating that his son would never violate any criminal laws whatsoever. To the father's knowledge, his son had violated the law only once, when he stole a ball at the local five-and-dime store. Admissible?

2. Lorean's brother testifies that, in his opinion, Lorean is an extremely honest person. Admissible?

3. Can the prosecution offer evidence that Lorean was arrested for the possession of marijuana 15 years prior to trial?

Problem 5-12: Rambo II

Jim Rambo was known around town as a "one-man terrorist gang." He had burned down the town hall, shot three different people in the leg, and participated in 24 separate bar fights. One hot and dusty June day, Perry, the owner of Perry's grocery, hired Rambo to serve as the security guard for the store. Perry gave Rambo a low-caliber pistol to carry while on duty. During his fifth day on the job, Rambo got into a fight with one of the customers and shot him. The customer brought suit against Perry, claiming negligent hiring.

Plaintiff's first witness is the mayor of the town. The mayor will testify that, in his opinion, Rambo is extremely dangerous, if not lethal. He will also recount all the prior incidents involving Rambo's harmful behavior. *Which parts of the mayor's testimony, if any, are admissible?*

§ 5.05 LAYING THE FOUNDATION FOR CHARACTER EVIDENCE

Once we have determined that a particular form of character evidence is admissible, we must be able to lay the required foundation for that particular form of evidence. These foundational requirements are dictated more by general rules of logical and pragmatic relevancy (respectively, Rules 401 and 403) than by any specific language in the character evidence rules.

[A] Reputation

A reputation witness must be shown to be familiar with the subject's reputation in the relevant community. The courts split on what "communities" are "relevant." Some common-law cases limit the term to the neighborhood in which the subject lives. Other cases also include the subject's workplace, and still others include any group of persons likely to be familiar with the pertinent character trait involved. The broadest view seems to make the most sense, because in the modern world a person may have closer acquaintances among workmates or church members than neighbors. The Federal Rules seem to take a broad view, by creating a hearsay exception for reputation of a person's character "among associates" or "in the community" (Rule 803(21)).

A streamlined sample foundation in the Rodegard murder case in § 5.04 might look like this:

DEFENSE COUNSEL: Do you know other people who know Benjamin Rodegard?

A: Yes, I do.

DEFENSE COUNSEL: How many such people?

A: Scores. Benjamin is very well-known in our area.

DEFENSE COUNSEL: What area is that?

A: Benjamin and I both live in the Town Heights area, only two blocks from each other.

DEFENSE COUNSEL: Have you ever heard these people discuss Rodegard's reputation as a peaceful man?

A: Yes, on many occasions.

DEFENSE COUNSEL: What is that reputation?

A: Excellent. A regular Gandhi or Martin Luther King Jr.

[B] Opinion

With opinion evidence, the question is whether the witness personally knew, from his or her own observations and not merely from the views of others, data sufficient to allow the witness to make a judgment about the subject's character. A streamlined sample opinion foundation in the Rodegard case might look like this:

DEFENSE COUNSEL: Do you know Benjamin Rodegard?

A: Yes.

DEFENSE COUNSEL: Is he in court today?

A: Yes.

DEFENSE COUNSEL: Please point him out. (pause while this happens) Thank you. Let the record reflect that the witness pointed to the defendant, Benjamin Rodegard.

DEFENSE COUNSEL: How long have you known Benjamin?

A: Twenty years.

DEFENSE COUNSEL: How did you come to know him?

A: I am his father's best friend, and I am Benjamin's godfather. I live across the street from Benjamin now, as I have for the last six years.

DEFENSE COUNSEL: During that six years, how often have you seen him?

A: We play tennis twice a week, we play cards with some other guys every other week, and I'm often over his house on weekends watching ballgames or playing with his kids.

DEFENSE COUNSEL: Do you know Benjamin Rodegard well enough to form an opinion on his character for peacefulness?

A: Yes.

DEFENSE COUNSEL: What is that opinion?

A: He is a very peaceful man.

Our discussion of the foundation for proving specific acts will await our analysis of specific acts offered for non-character purposes, to be reached shortly, in § 5.10.

Problem 5-13: Ogling Again

In Problem 5-1, draft the foundational questions for presenting the evidence noted in parts 1 through 4 of that problem. If you think that the streamlined foundations in the text above are in any way inadequate models, add questions that you deem appropriate, and be ready to explain why you chose them.

Problem 5-14: More Creativity

Draft the foundational questions for the character witness examples you created in response to Problem 5-7. If you think that the streamlined foundations in the text above are inadequate models, add questions that you might deem appropriate, and be ready to explain why you chose them.

Problem 5-15: Negligently Entrusting Redux

Draft the foundational questions for parts 1 through 5 of Problem 5-3. If you think that the streamlined foundations in the text above are inadequate models, add questions that you deem appropriate, and be ready to explain why you chose them. Address the differences, if any, between the criminal and civil trials.

Problem 5-16: More United States v. Lorean

Draft the foundational questions for items 1, 2, and 3 in Problem 5-12. If you think that the streamlined foundations in the text above are in any way inadequate models, add questions that you deem appropriate, and be ready to explain why you chose them.

§ 5.06 EXCEPTIONS TO THE RULE 404(a) PROPENSITY BAN

[A] Admissible Instances of Propensity Evidence

Even though "propensity" evidence is generally prohibited under Rule 404, there are several exceptions to that prohibition. In these situations, limited forms of character evidence are admissible to prove a person's propensity to act in conformity with that character trait. These types of admissible propensity evidence are briefly summarized as follows:

1. Character evidence offered by the accused.

2. Character of the victim in cases other than homicide or sexual misconduct.

3. Character trait of peacefulness of the victim at a homicide trial.

4. Character of the accused offered by the prosecution where there has first been an attack made on the *victim's* character by the accused.

5. Character of the defendant in a criminal or civil case involving sexual assault or child molestation.

6. Character impeachment of a witness.

The first four of these exceptions are addressed below, with sexual assault and child molestation cases and impeachment addressed later in this chapter.

[B] Character of the Accused: Rule 404(a)(2)(A)

Rule 404(a)(2)(A) creates, among other things, one particularly important exception to the propensity bar. That provision, in relevant part, applies the exception in the following circumstances:

Rule 404. Character Evidence; Crimes or Other Act

(a) Character Evidence.

(2) Exceptions for a Defendant or Victim in a Criminal Case. The following exceptions apply in a criminal case:

(A) a defendant may offer evidence of the defendant's pertinent trait, and if the evidence is admitted, the prosecutor may offer evidence to rebut it.

This exception is sometimes called the "mercy rule."

Example

Chunah Rubenstein is charged with assault. After the prosecution rests (its sole testimony being from the alleged victim), the defense calls a rabbi and a priest to the stand, both of whom testify that in their opinion Rubenstein is a peaceful man. In rebuttal, the prosecution calls Rubenstein's ex-wife, who opines that Rubenstein is a violent man. All this testimony is propensity evidence; the rabbi and priest suggest that such a peaceful man is unlikely to commit a violent crime, and the ex-wife suggests the opposite. Yet none of the testimony is barred, because all of it fits within the Rule 404(a)(2)(A) exception. "Peacefulness" and "violence" are character traits "pertinent" to an assault charge; thus, evidence of the former may be offered by the accused, and evidence of the latter may be offered in rebuttal by the prosecutor.

The requirement that the character trait be "pertinent" has been explained this way:[2]

Not all aspects of the accused's character are open to scrutiny under this exception. The prevailing view is that only pertinent traits — those involved

---

[2] McCormick on Evidence, § 191, at 347 (4th ed. 1992).

in the offense charged — are provable. One charged with theft might offer evidence of honesty, while someone accused of murder might show that he is peaceable, but not vice versa.

Other sources, however, have defined "pertinent" as synonymous with "relevant," as it is defined in Rule 401: evidence having *any* tendency to make the existence of any fact that is of consequence to the determination of the action more probable or less probable than it would be without the evidence. Arguably, an honest person is at least marginally less likely than a dishonest one to commit any crime, thus less likely to commit murder (rephrased, honesty may be associated with "law-abidingness"). Under this very broad view, therefore, the trait of "honesty" is "pertinent" to both a theft case and a murder trial. Even under such a reading of "pertinent," however, an argument for exclusion might be made under Rule 403 that the minimal probative value of honesty evidence in a murder trial is substantially out-weighed by the risk of unfair prejudice. In practice, therefore, the differing approaches might rarely (though perhaps sometimes) lead to different results. Thus, most courts agree that a character for "truthfulness" is pertinent to theft, robbery, burglary, and perjury but not to aggravated or simple assault, kidnapping, false imprisonment, or carrying concealed weapons.

Note, too, that the rule refers to a specific "trait" of character and not to character generally. This suggests that testimony that an accused is truthful might be admissible but that he or she has a "good character" would not.

The justification for the rule is unclear. The rule may reflect the idea that good character evidence is less worrisome than bad in a system that presumes innocence. Alternatively, the rule may simply be an act of mercy toward a defendant who has generally led a good life. In any event, the rule is a well-established one with deep roots in evidentiary history.

An accused taking advantage of the rule must be cautious, however. Introducing character evidence on one's own behalf opens the door to prosecution rebuttal. Thus, if a defense character witness opines that the defendant is kind, the prosecution might call a witness to testify that, to the contrary, the defendant is cruel. The prosecutor would not have been permitted to offer that evidence if there had been no defense character witness.

A Civil Versus Criminal Case Caution: It is important to emphasize that the "mercy rule" exception applies only in a criminal case, not a civil one. Thus if a defendant in a civil case seeks to offer evidence of his good character to show that he had a propensity not to perform certain bad acts, therefore making it less likely that he did the bad acts alleged in the current suit, that evidence will still be inadmissible. It is excluded by Rule 404(a)(1)'s broad general bar on admitting act propensity evidence. The Advisory Committee Note to the 2006 amendments to Rule 404 explained the rationale for excluding such evidence in civil cases but admitting it, when offered by the accused as to a pertinent trait, in criminal cases:

> The circumstantial use of character evidence is generally discouraged because it carries serious risks of prejudice, confusion and delay. . . . In criminal cases, the so-called "mercy rule" permits a criminal defendant to introduce evidence of pertinent character traits of the defendant and the

victim. But that is because the accused, whose liberty is at stake, may need "a counterweight against the strong investigative and prosecutorial resources of the government." C. Mueller & L. Kirkpatrick, *Evidence: Practice Under the Rules*, pp. 264–5 (2d ed. 1999). *See also* Richard Uviller, *Evidence of Character to Prove Conduct: Illusion, Illogic, and Injustice in the Courtroom*, 130 U. Pa. L. Rev. 845, 855 (1982) (the rule prohibiting circumstantial use of character evidence "was relaxed to allow the criminal defendant with so much at stake and so little available in the way of conventional proof to have special dispensation to tell the factfinder just what sort of person he really is"). Those concerns do not apply to parties in civil cases.

Problem 5-17: The Tortious Criminal Assailant

Charlton Hestown has been civilly sued for intentional tortious assault. In this jurisdiction, that cause of action has the same elements as criminal assault, that is, attempting to cause or purposely, knowingly, or recklessly causing bodily injury to another person.

1. Hestown calls his priest to the stand, who testifies that Hestown has a reputation as a "good, kind man." Admissible? Why or why not?

2. Assume instead that the priest testifies that Hestown's reputation is that of a "law-abiding man." Does this change the result?

3. What if, instead, the priest opines that Hestown is a "peaceful person"? What result, and why?

4. What if the priest also says that Hestown is an "honest man"?

5. The prosecution now calls Hestown's former best friend to testify that Hestown in fact has a reputation as a drug dealer. Will the likelihood of this testimony's being admissible vary if

   a. the priest first testified that Hestown was a "kind, caring man"?

   b. he instead said Hestown is law-abiding?

   c. he instead said Hestown is peaceful?

   d. he instead said that Hestown is honest?

6. Do your answers to any of the questions change if Hestown is prosecuted criminally, instead of sued civilly? Why?

Problem 5-18: The Escaping Hostage

Quinn Maton is charged with escaping from a federal prison. In his defense, Quinn testified that he never "escaped" at all. Instead, he was dragged outside his cell block by a mass of angry, fleeing inmates who planned to use him (a well-known former politician) as a hostage. Quinn calls the warden, Robert Jamison, to the stand. Jamison plans to testify that Quinn had a good work record and was making great progress toward rehabilitation. *Should the prosecutor's objection be sustained?*

Problem 5-19: Suicidal Homicide

Yogi Berro has been charged with assaulting a federal officer. The officer testified that when he arrived at Berro's home to arrest him on another charge, Berro pointed a gun at the officer and threatened to shoot. Berro testified that he in fact pointed the gun at himself, planning to commit suicide. Berro calls a psychiatrist who testifies that Berro has a self-destructive personality, making it far more likely that he would try to hurt himself than someone else.

1. Should the prosecutor's objection be sustained? Why or why not?

2. If the prosecutor's objection is overruled, should the prosecutor be free on rebuttal to call Berro's ex-wife to testify that Berro has a reputation as a violent man?

3. Would your answers to the above two questions change if the officer had sued Berro for damages in tort for assault rather than proceeding by way of a criminal trial?

Problem 5-20: At the Movies: Treason

In the film *Bananas*, Fielding Mellish is charged with treason under bizarre circumstances that only Woody Allen, the film's writer, director, and star, could imagine. A prosecution witness surprisingly testifies that Mellish is "a warm, wonderful human being." *Is the witness' testimony admissible under the so-called "mercy rule" Rule 404? Would your answer change if the suit was a civil one for damages for revealing state secrets rather than a criminal one for treason?*

[C] Character of the Victim in Cases Other Than Homicide and Sexual Misconduct: Rule 404(a)(2)(B)

Rule 404(a)(B) and (C) create additional exceptions to the act propensity bar. Rule 404(a)(2)(B) provides as follows:

> subject to the limitations imposed in Rule 412, a defendant may offer evidence of an alleged victim's pertinent trait, and if the evidence is admitted, the prosecutor may:
>
> (i) offer evidence to rebut it; and
>
> (ii) offer evidence of the defendant's same trait.

The word "pertinent" here apparently has the same meaning as under Rule 404(a)(2)(A) (*see* [B], above).

Example

Patricia Fun is charged with assaulting Renee Schlager. Fun, in the defense's case-in-chief, calls Marci Wilt, a neighbor of Schlager's, to the stand to testify that Schlager has a reputation in the community as a violent person. Fun claims self-defense, arguing that Schlager was the first aggressor. The prosecution's objection will be overruled, as this testimony fits within the exception to the propensity rule created by Rule 404(a)(2)(B). The victim's violent nature is "pertinent" to the defendant's claim of self-defense. However, the prosecution would then be entitled to call a character witness to the stand who will testify, in rebuttal, that Schlager's true reputation in the community is as a very gentle and kind individual.

Note the difference between this example and the Chunah Rubenstein example in [B], above. Chunah, the defendant, was permitted under the mercy rule to offer evidence of his own good character under Rule 404(a)(1)(A). But, in this current example, Fun offers evidence not of her own character concerning violence but rather of her alleged victim's character for violence under Rule 404(a)(2)(B)(i). Likewise, the prosecution's rebuttal evidence concerns the victim's character, not the defendant's.

On the other hand, Rule 404(a)(2)(B)(ii) does permit the prosecutor, if she so chose, also to offer evidence of the defendant's character on the same trait as the defendant attacked the victim's character, as we will see in more detail below.

Problem 5-21: Urban War Syndrome

Harry Howdeen claims self-defense at his assault trial. The defense makes the following offer of proof: Leonard Jesperson, a psychiatrist who has examined the victim, Margie O'Laris, will testify in the defense case-in-chief that O'Laris suffered from Urban War Syndrome. This behavioral syndrome results in unpredictably violent behavior among its sufferers, poor inner-city dwellers who have been surrounded by violence. *Should the prosecution objection be sustained? What sort of foundation, if any, would improve the chances of admitting Jesperson's testimony? If the objection is overruled, will the prosecution succeed in rebuttal in admitting evidence that Margie O'Laris had been cured?*

Problem 5-22: The Scarlet Letter

Donovan Leisure calls to the stand at his rape trial Loudon Foster, a neighbor of the alleged victim, Marci Lorraine. Foster begins to recount his opinion that Loraine is a "slut," but the prosecution objects. Leisure's defense is consent. This is a jurisdiction that has never enacted Rules 412 through 415 (which generally prohibit evidence of a sexual assault victim's prior sexual conduct to prove her consent, while sometimes permitting evidence of the assailant's prior sexual assaults to prove that he committed the current one) or analogous statutes or rules. *Should the trial court sustain or overrule the objection? Why? If the objection is overruled, will the prosecution succeed in admitting evidence that:*

1. Leisure has sexually assaulted three other women?

2. Lorraine is studying to be a nun?

3. Lorraine has a reputation among other high school students (of which she is one) as "an iceberg with guys"?

4. Lorraine has a reputation among high school teachers as a scrupulously honest student?

Problem 5-23: False Pretenses

Marty Cunningham's defense at his trial for the crime of false pretenses is that his alleged victim, Hollis Holloway, is well-known as a skeptical, distrustful man. The trial judge sustains the prosecution's objection and instructs the jury to disregard the witness' testimony to this effect. False pretenses requires proof of (1) a false representation of a material present or past fact, (2) which causes the victim (3) to pass title to his property (4) to the wrongdoer, (5) who (a) knows his representation to be false and (b) intends thereby to defraud the victim. *Do you agree with the trial judge's ruling? Why or why not?*

[D] Prosecutor Attack on the Criminal Defendant's Same Character Trait Permitted Once the Defense Has Attacked the Victim on that Trait

Remember that under Rule 404(a)(2)(B), the defendant in a criminal case can offer evidence of a pertinent trait of character of the alleged victim. Rule 404(a)(2)(B)(i), however, permits the prosecutor to respond by defending the victim's character on that same trait. But Rule 404(a)(2)(B)(ii) also permits the prosecutor then to attack the defendant's character on that same trait. Restated, once the defense attacks a pertinent trait of the victim's character in a criminal case, the prosecutor can not only defend the victim's character on that trait but can also attack the defendant's character on that same trait. A defendant choosing to attack a victim's character thus opens the door to an attack on the defendant's own character by the prosecution that would otherwise be barred. That can be a risky gamble.

Remember too that when Rule 404(a)(2) exceptions to the act propensity bar apply, those exceptions permit proving character only by reputation or opinion, not by evidence of specific acts. *Once again, this exception applies only in criminal, not civil, cases.*

Example

In an earlier example, Patricia Fun, a criminal defendant in an assault case, offered evidence of the violent character of her alleged victim to show that the victim was the first aggressor. Under the original law, the prosecution could under Rule 404(a)(2) respond only with evidence of the victim's peaceful nature. Old Rule 404(a)(1) barred any attack on the *accused's* character because she did not first offer evidence of her own good character. Under the amendment, however, the result is different. Now when the defense offers evidence about the victim's violent character, the prosecution becomes free also to present evidence of *defendant Fun's* violent nature to prove that she, not the victim, was indeed the first aggressor.

The Advisory Committee Note, relied upon by the Judicial Conference, explained that, without this amendment, unfairness and distortion would result when the defendant offers evidence, for example, of the victim's violent character:

If the government has evidence that the defendant has a violent character, but is not allowed to offer this evidence as part of its rebuttal, the jury has only part of the information it needs for an informed assessment of the probabilities as to who was the initial aggressor. This may be the case even if evidence of the accused's prior violent acts is admitted under Rule 404(b), because such evidence can be admitted only for limited purposes and not to show action in conformity with the accused's character on a specific occasion. Thus, the amendment is designed to permit a more balanced presentation of character evidence when an accused chooses to attack the character of the alleged victim.

The Committee recommended placing the proposed amendment in Rule 404 to limit the evidence to proof of character by way of reputation or opinion only. Furthermore, that placement makes it clear that the amendment governs only character attacks on the victim for substantive purposes and not attacks on the victim's truthfulness as a witness, which is still governed by Rules 607, 608, and 609. The amendment also does not affect the special standards for proof of character by evidence of other sexual behavior or sexual offenses under Rules 412 through 415, as discussed later in this chapter.

Problem 5-26: More Urban War Syndrome

Return to the facts of Problem 5-21. Still assume that the prosecutor's objection to testimony that the assault victim suffered from urban war syndrome was overruled. In rebuttal, the prosecutor offers evidence that defendant Harry Howdeen has a reputation as an extremely violent man. *Would this testimony be admissible under the old Rule 404(a)(2)? Under the amended Rule 404(a)(1)? Why? Would your answers change if this were a civil rather than a criminal case?*

Problem 5-27: What Goes Around Comes Around

Return to the facts of Problem 5-22. Assume that the prosecution's objection is overruled. Again, assume that this jurisdiction is one that has not enacted rules equivalent to Rules 412–415. *Under the amended rule 404(a)(1), does your opinion change regarding whether the prosecutor may offer evidence that Leisure has sexually assaulted three other women?* Would your answer change if this were a civil rather than a criminal case?

Caution:

We will see later in this chapter that special rules govern the use of evidence of the victim's character in a proceeding involving alleged sexual misconduct. *See* Rule 412. Indeed, that is why the Rule 404(a)(2) exception declares that it is "subject to the limitations imposed by Rule 412." Similarly, as the immediately following section of this chapter will explain, special rules govern evidence of a homicide victim's character. *See* Rule 404(a)(2)(C).

Civil Versus Criminal Case Caution: Again, as with Rule 404(a)(2)(A), this Rule 404(a)(2)(B) exception applies only in criminal cases. In civil cases, no Rule 404(a)(2)(B) exception will apply, and the same evidence admissible in a criminal case will now be inadmissible in a civil one.

[E] Character of the Victim in Homicide Cases: Rule 404(a)(2)(C)

Rule 404(a)(2)(C) creates another exception to the act propensity rule. This exception is limited, however, to criminal homicide cases and authorizes the admission of act propensity evidence in such cases only under the following circumstances:

> (C). In a homicide case, the prosecutor may offer evidence of the alleged victim's trait of peacefulness to rebut evidence that the victim was the first aggressor.

Civil Versus Criminal Versus Criminal Homicide Caution: This exception, it must be remembered, applies only in criminal cases, and, even then, only in one kind of criminal case: homicide. The exception does not, therefore, even apply to attempted homicide. Rather, it applies only to the completed, successful crime of homicide, meaning that the victim must die. The exception does not apply to civil cases, thus rendering inadmissible evidence of the alleged victim's peaceful character to rebut evidence that the victim was the first aggressor in a civil assault or civil wrongful death suit.

Example

> This example takes place after the events chronicled in the example in [C], above. Schlager developed a grudge against Marci Wilt, because Wilt testified against Schlager when Schlager charged Patricia Fun with assault. Schlager broke into Wilt's home and shot Wilt dead. After the prosecution rests at Schlager's homicide trial, Schlager calls a purported eyewitness, Lance Medallion, to the stand. Medallion testifies that he saw Wilt pull a gun out first, and that Schlager simply shot to save her own life. On rebuttal, the prosecution, over the defense's overruled objection, calls Wilt's husband, Mung Ciao, who testifies that Wilt was always a peaceful person, the kind who would never hurt a fly. The trial court's ruling will be upheld on appeal under Rule 404(a)(2)(C). Because Medallion's testimony suggested that Wilt was the first aggressor, the prosecution properly responded with evidence of Wilt's peaceful nature under this subsection. Pay close attention to the important difference between the prosecutor's role here and in the preceding two exceptions. In Rule 404(a)(2)(A) and (B), the prosecutor could offer character evidence only after the defense first did so. But here, the prosecutor is entitled to offer character evidence even though the defense has not. Instead, the defense merely called an alleged eyewitness to the disputed events themselves. Nevertheless, Rule 404(a)(2)(C) permits the prosecutor to use one narrow sort of character evidence (evidence of the peacefulness of the victim in a homicide prosecution) to rebut any "evidence that the victim was the first aggressor." Presumably, such evidence can include eyewitness testimony or character testimony claiming that the victim started the attack.

Problem 5-24: The Green-Eyed Monster

Homicide defendant Randy Maestro asserts self-defense. His counsel, Vicky Lea, cross-examined an eyewitness, Hedda Gebler, concerning the victim, Mr. Maestro's wife:

DEFENSE COUNSEL: You have been friends with the Maestros for more than 20 years?

A: Yes. Good friends.

DEFENSE COUNSEL: And you lived next door to them for that entire time?

A: Yes.

DEFENSE COUNSEL: You are active in community activities in which they participated during that time?

A: Of course.

DEFENSE COUNSEL: And you have, I take it, talked to other persons in the neighborhood on numerous occasions about the kind of people the Maestros are?

PROSECUTOR: Objection. Vague and insufficient foundation.

JUDGE: Overruled. You may answer the question.

A: Yes, I have talked to other persons in the neighborhood on many occasions about the kind of people the Maestros are.

DEFENSE COUNSEL: And my client, Mr. Maestro, had a reputation, as well, as a philanderer?

A: (after hesitation) Yes.

DEFENSE COUNSEL: While Mrs. Maestro's reputation in the neighborhood was as a very jealous wife?

A: (sounding resigned) Yes.

DEFENSE COUNSEL: No more questions.

The prosecution next calls, still in its case-in-chief, Maestro's spiritual advisor. On defense request, the prosecution gives the following offer of proof: "The advisor will testify that he has known Mrs. Maestro for 20 years and, in his opinion, she was a peaceful woman." The defense objects. *As trial judge, would you sustain or overrule the objection? Why? What if instead of being asked his opinion, the spiritual advisor were asked whether Mrs. Maestro had a reputation for peacefulness? Would defense counsel's having elicited any additional information change your mind, and why? What sorts of information? Would any of your decisions change if Ms. Gebler were called by the defense on direct examination in its case-in-chief rather than, as here, on cross during the prosecution's case? Would any of your answers change if this were a civil wrongful death suit rather than a criminal homicide charge?*

Problem 5-25: Knife Fights

In the same homicide case as in Problem 5-24, assume instead that the defense never cross-examined Hedda Gebler. However, defense counsel did cross-examine the local jail physician, Quincy Klugman:

DEFENSE COUNSEL: You were the physician on duty on January 1st of this year at the Cross County Jail when my client, Mr. Maestro, first became an inmate there on a charge of murdering his wife?

A: Correct.

DEFENSE COUNSEL: Did you conduct a physical examination of Mr. Maestro that night?

A: Yes.

DEFENSE COUNSEL: Didn't that exam reveal that he had a triangular-shaped knife wound in his belly?

A: Yes.

DEFENSE COUNSEL: And you were worried about this because such wounds bleed profusely and often do not heal on their own, is that correct?

A: Quite right.

DEFENSE COUNSEL: Such knives are very hard to get, requiring much planning to do so?

A: Yes.

DEFENSE COUNSEL: What sort of planning?

A: Getting a permit to carry it, raising money, as it is quite expensive, and getting training on how to use it.

The prosecutor calls as its final witness in its case-in-chief Monty Hill to testify that Mrs. Maestro's reputation was as a peaceful woman. *Should the defense objection be sustained? Why? Would it change your decision if Hill testified to Mrs. Maestro's law-abidingness rather than her peacefulness? Would your answers to these questions change if this victim lived, that is, if this were an attempted homicide charge? Again, would your answers to these questions change if this were a civil wrongful death suit rather than a criminal homicide charge?*

§ 5.07 SEXUAL OFFENSES AND SEXUAL MISCONDUCT: CRIMINAL AND CIVIL

[A] The Rape Shield Law: Exception to an Exception: Rule 412

[1] The General Rule: Rule 412(a)

We have now finished reviewing the major exceptions to the prohibition against act propensity evidence. Here we consider an exception to one of those exceptions, that is, a reinstitution of the bar on act propensity evidence for one class of persons: victims of rape and similar offenses. The federal "rape shield" statute accomplishes this re-institution, and we address it here because you should now be ready to understand its complexities and assess its policy wisdom.

The exception to Rule 404(a)(2) that permits propensity attacks on pertinent traits of a victim's character, discussed in [C], above, is politically charged. Whether a trait is "pertinent" very much depends on the lawmakers' worldview. For many years, under common-law analogues to Rule 404(a)(2)(B), and for several years under Rule 404(a)(2)(B) itself, evidence of a rape victim's promiscuous character was considered "pertinent" to whether she consented to sexual intercourse. Moreover, judges were rarely willing to exclude such evidence as unfairly prejudicial under a 403-like analysis. Testimony that a victim had a reputation as a "slut," that "everyone knew she slept around," and of the specific nitty-gritty alleged incidents of the victim's sex life became standard fare.

The federal rape shield statute, Rule 412, seeks to reduce dramatically, without completely eliminating, the use of such victim character evidence at criminal trials for rape and other sexual offenses, and at civil trials raising similar issues. Rule 412, in its original form, became law several years after the Federal Rules of Evidence were adopted. The current version of Rule 412, substantially amended from the original version, was adopted in 1994, amended for stylistic reasons in 2011. Subsection (a) states a general ban on victim character evidence:

Rule 412. Sex-Offense Cases: The Victim's Sexual Behavior or Predisposition

> (a) **Prohibited Uses.** The following evidence is not admissible in a civil or criminal proceeding involving alleged sexual misconduct:
>
> > (1) evidence offered to prove that a victim engaged in other sexual behavior; or
> >
> > (2) evidence offered to prove a victim's sexual predisposition.

Rule 412, subsection (a), thus carves out a general exception to the exception from the act propensity rule established by Rule 404(a)(2)(B). Rephrased, Rule 412, subsection (a), reinstates the propensity bar for one category of crime victims (as well as reaffirming the bar in similar civil cases): victims of alleged sexual misconduct, such as rape.

The Advisory Committee did not justify this general prohibition on victim propensity evidence on grounds of its irrelevance. Rather, the Committee viewed the new rule as creating incentives to identify accurately and prosecute such misconduct while protecting victim privacy:

> The rule aims to safeguard the alleged victim against the invasion of privacy, potential embarrassment and sexual stereotyping that is associated with public disclosure of intimate sexual details and the infusion of sexual innuendo into the fact-finding process. By affording victims protection in most instances, the rule also encourages victims of sexual misconduct to institute and to participate in legal proceedings against alleged offenders.

While the Committee did not consider victim character irrelevant in a Rule 401 sense, the Note makes clear that Rule 403-like concerns about unfair prejudice also underlay the new rule. The rule also reaches beyond substantive propensity uses to bar impeachment uses, except in certain designated circumstances discussed under the topic of Rule 412(a) exceptions below.

Example 1

An alleged rape victim has finished her direct testimony at trial. The defense concedes sexual intercourse but argues consent. The defense offers evidence of the victim's sexual trysts with numerous third parties on other occasions. The defense argues that this evidence is offered to impeach, because promiscuous women are usually liars. This sort of inference, and thus the proffered evidence, is barred by Rule 412(a).

Rule 412 does not bar evidence that the victim made numerous allegedly false prior claims of others' sexual misconduct. Such evidence can be viewed as propensity impeachment evidence; Rules 404 and 608 govern instead.

Rule 412's broad general prohibition against any evidence of "sexual predisposition" extends beyond reputation or opinion evidence of a victim's promiscuous nature and specific instances of sexual conduct. The word "behavior" is here meant to include "activities of the mind, such as fantasies or dreams," as well as any activity that implies sexual contact, such as using contraceptives or having a venereal disease. Furthermore, concludes the Advisory Committee, the prohibition is "designed to exclude evidence that does not directly refer to sexual activities or thoughts but that the proponent believes may have a sexual connotation for the fact finder." Illustrations might include evidence relating to the victim's mode of dress, speech, or lifestyle, if not fitting within a subsection (b) exception.

Example 2

The defendant in a rape case offers evidence that the victim wore a short, tight dress, with a deep "V" neck, to prove that she consented to sexual intercourse with the defendant. This evidence will ordinarily be barred by Rule 412(a).

Note that "consent" can be understood as a mental state of the victim, in which case the 412(a) bar is extending to *mental* propensity, as well as act propensity by prohibiting the argument that women wearing short dresses are more likely to consent to sex generally and thus are more likely to have consented in this case. Moreover, whether or not "consent" is a mental state or an act, the language of Rule 412(a) simply prohibits evidence of sexual predisposition or other sexual behavior without (in contrast to Rule 404(a)) limiting that prohibition to certain particular uses of that evidence, that is, without requiring that it be offered only for certain particular purposes. Thus Rule 412(a)'s express language seems to prohibit *any* use of sexual predisposition or other sexual behavior evidence, whether offered to prove act propensity or mental propensity or something else, and whether offered to prove a substantive element of a crime, claim, or defense or to impeach.

Civil Versus Criminal Cases: The rule extends to all criminal and civil cases because the social policies involved may matter in any case where sexual misconduct is alleged, not just rape prosecutions. For example, the rule would apply in a kidnapping charge where evidence of the defendant's sexually assaulting the victim is offered to prove motive or as background for the kidnapping. As we will soon see, however, different exceptions apply to the rule in criminal versus civil cases. Do not worry about these exceptions yet in doing the problems immediately below.

Problem 5-28: At the Movies: Pre-Shield

In the film *Town Without Pity*, four U.S. soldiers stationed in Germany are charged with raping a young German woman. Their defense is that she consented to sexual intercourse. To prove that the sexual conduct was consensual, defense attorney Maj. Garrett aggressively cross-examines the young woman and elicits evidence that she often exercised naked in front of her window, with the blinds pulled up. Moreover, she often allowed her boyfriend to see her naked. *Would this evidence be admissible under Rule 412?*

Problem 5-29: On the Tube: Liar

In the made-for-TV film *Defense of Edward Brannigan*, successful lawyer Brannigan is charged with raping his law clerk. Brannigan's defense is that his clerk consented to engage in sexual intercourse. To attack the law clerk's credibility, the defense seeks to offer evidence that some years earlier, the clerk had had a child out of wedlock and falsified the father's identity on the hospital birth record. The prosecutor objects that the evidence is inadmissible under the rape shield law, because it would reveal the law clerk's prior sexual behavior. *Should the judge sustain the prosecutor's objection?*

Problem 5-30: At the Movies: At the Bar

In the film *The Accused*, the defendant is charged with raping Sarah Tobias. The defendant claims that Sarah consented to sexual intercourse. The defendant seeks to testify that he met Sarah for the first time on the night of the rape, in a bar. Sarah was inebriated, and dressed in a low-cut mini-dress. Prior to their having sex, Sarah had danced provocatively with the defendant, with other men in the bar, and alone in the middle of the dance floor. They left the bar together and had sex in his truck; he then dropped her off at home. *What part, if any, of this testimony would be admissible under Rule 412?*

Problem 5-31: At the Movies: Quick Re-Marriage

In the film *Anatomy of a Murder*, Lt. Manion is charged with murdering Barney Quill. Manion admits that he killed Quill, but claims that he did so as a result of "irresistible impulse," a form of temporary insanity resulting from finding out that Quill had raped and beaten Manion's wife, Laura. The prosecution theory is that Quill and Laura were lovers, and that Manion killed Quill after learning of the affair. Cross-examining Laura, the prosecutor elicits testimony that she had married Manion only three days after divorcing her first husband. *Does the evidence of the quick re-marriage constitute evidence of "other sexual behavior" within the meaning of Rule 412? If so, does Rule 412 render the evidence inadmissible?*

Problem 5-32: Rhonda's Outrage

In a criminal rape case, the victim, Rhonda Sun, angrily responds as follows to cross-examination by the defense suggesting that she consented to sexual intercourse: "Sir, I am devoutly religious and unmarried. My religion prohibits premarital sexual intercourse. I have not had, and until I am married will not have, sex with any man, much less that beast." In response, the defense seeks to offer evidence that Rhonda had consensual sexual intercourse with at least three men during her lifetime. The prosecution objects, citing Rule 412(a). *Ruling? Cf. State v. Williams*, 477 N.E. 2d 221 (Ohio Ct. App. 1984), *aff'd*, 487 N.E. 2d 560 (Ohio 1986).

Problem 5-33: Stained Reputations

Now the defense in Problem 5-32 offers evidence that Rhonda filed false rape charges against three other men in other cities — all of whom were acquitted — under very similar circumstances to the charges made here. The prosecutor objects. *What ruling? What additional information, if any, would help to guide your decision? Does it matter that Rhonda stands ready to testify that the other charges were true and that the prosecutor has evidence that both the assaults and the acquittals were motivated by prejudice against practitioners of Rhonda's religion?*

Problem 5-34: Romantic Dreams

In a civil sexual harassment case filed by Betty Nomad against her employer, Kirk McCoy, McCoy plans to argue that Betty both invited and welcomed his caresses of her breasts and buttocks. To support this claim, he calls to the stand one of Betty's co-workers, who begins to recount a conversation that she had with Betty in which Betty said that on many nights she had had dreams of intimate sexual contact with Mr. McCoy. Betty's counsel objects. *Ruling?*

To further support his argument, McCoy offers evidence, over Betty's counsel's objection, that Betty routinely wore low-cut dresses to the office covered by a shawl. But she removed the shawl whenever Mr. McCoy entered the room and did so near the time of the alleged harassing conduct. *Did the trial judge rule correctly?*

[2] Exceptions in Criminal Cases: Rule 412(b)(1)

Rule 412(b)(1) creates exceptions, however, to this reinstated propensity bar as to victims of alleged sexual misconduct in criminal cases:

(b) Exceptions.

(1) *Criminal Cases.* The court may admit the following evidence in a criminal case:

(A) evidence of specific instances of a victim's sexual behavior, if offered to prove that someone other than the defendant was the source of semen, injury, or other physical evidence;

(B) evidence of specific instances of a victim's sexual behavior with respect to the person accused of the sexual misconduct, if offered by the defendant to prove consent or if offered by the prosecutor; and

(C) evidence whose exclusion would violate the defendant's constitutional rights.

The effect of these exceptions is to retain a flat bar on reputation or opinion evidence of a victim's sexual behavior in criminal cases but to permit evidence of specific instances of a victim's sexual conduct in two very narrowly defined circumstances and in the rare situation in which the constitution demands admissibility. In theory, of course, there may be circumstances under which the constitution would also mandate admissibility of reputation or opinion evidence. This text focuses largely on the Federal Rules of Evidence, so we will focus only tangentially on the constitutional issues in the examples below.

Example 1

Hope Elkhoond alleges that she was raped by Monty Mountebank. Monty, however, claims that Hope's mother found evidence that Hope was having sexual intercourse with her father. To divert evidence from her dad, Hope claimed that she had been raped by Monty, against whom she already had a variety of grudges anyway. Hope's mom rushed her to the hospital, where tests were run and semen found. At his rape trial, Monty seeks to introduce evidence of specific instances when Hope had sexual intercourse with her father to prove that the abusive father, not Monty, was the source of the semen. This testimony will likely be admissible under Rule 412(b)(1)(A).

Example 2

Same case as example 1, but this time Monty concedes that the semen was his but argues that Hope consented. To prove his point, he offers evidence that he and Hope had consensual sexual intercourse on five prior occasions during the month before the alleged rape. The prosecutor's objections are overruled by the trial judge.

Although Rule 403 is not expressly mentioned in Rule 412, it may be relied on as a ground for excluding evidence that would otherwise be admissible under Rule 412(b)(1).

Example 3

A 10-year-old rape victim's injuries demonstrated that her assailant used force. The defense offers evidence that a third person, Mosby, sexually abused the same victim on one occasion five years earlier, causing her no physical injuries. The prosecution's objection to this stale evidence involving very different conduct will likely be sustained under Rule 403.

The Rule 412(b)(1)(B) exception, as the Advisory Committee has noted, extends beyond prior instances of sexual activities between the alleged victim and the accused to include "statements in which the alleged victim expressed an intent to engage in sexual intercourse with the accused, or voiced sexual fantasies involving the specific accused." *See* [1], above.

Problem 5-35: Satanic Rites

Rape defendant Harry Harlan, in support of his consent defense, offers evidence that the victim, Cheryl Browner, had engaged in group consensual sexual activity with Harlan and a series of other men on three prior occasions, one five years ago, one a year ago, and one the month before this incident. All three incidents were part of Satanic prayer rites, Ms. Browner being a Satanist. *Should the prosecution's objection be sustained? Cf. People v. Keith*, 118 Cal. App. 3d 973, 173 Cal. Rptr. 704 (1981); *Eyes Wide Shut* (the Stanley Kubrick film starring Tom Cruise and Nicole Kidman).

Would your ruling change if Harlan tried to prove that the rape occurred during such a group Satanic rite, and that Ms. Browner made clear that she no longer wanted to participate? What if Harlan says that he backed off, but others in the group would not do so, despite his efforts to stop them? In the hubbub, he argues, Browner mistook him for one of the rapists.

Problem 5-36: Fantasies

In the same prosecution as in Problem 5-35, Harlan offers evidence that Ms. Browner often told co-workers that she frequently fantasized about Harlan making love to her. *Should this evidence be admissible? How, if at all, does this problem differ from the fantasies of Betty Nomad in Problem 5-34?*

Harlan also offers evidence that Ms. Browner has a reputation of being "loose" with other members of her coven, of which Harlan was one. *Is this evidence admissible under Rule 412? Would your view change if the coven's Master Warlock offered his opinion that Ms. Browner was promiscuous with her coven "brethren"?*

Problem 5-37: Toby Wyatt: Adulterer or Rapist?

Toby Wyatt, a well known basketball star with a previously squeaky-clean image, has been accused by 19-year-old Noe I. Dentity of felony sexual assault. Wyatt does not deny that intercourse took place but claims that it was consensual. At a preliminary hearing to determine whether the prosecution has enough evidence to take the case to trial, the defense team plans to present the following evidence:

a) The accuser's medical records, including a possible attempted suicide;

b) The accuser's academic records, showing that she was a poor student;

c) The accuser's psychiatric records, showing that she has frequently been treated for depression and paranoia;

d) Notes of the accuser's conversations with her rape counselor.

1. Why might the defense want to present such evidence?

2. Is the evidence in a through d admissible? Why or why not?

3. If not, are there facts or circumstances not stated above that, if true, would make such evidence more likely to be admitted?

4. At the preliminary hearing in the Toby Wyatt rape case, the defense, on cross-examination, asks the doctor who examined the alleged victim whether her injuries would be consistent with those of a woman who had had sex with three different men within three days. The defense presents no evidence to support the inference that the alleged victim in fact had sexual contact around the time of the incident with anyone other than the accused.

As the attorney for the prosecution, on what basis could you possibly object if a similar question is asked at trial? Would your answer change if the defense had evidence of the three prior instances? How much evidence would be needed, that is, is this a 104(a) or 104(b) foundational evidence question? Assume alternatively that the prosecution argues that vaginal abrasions show that the intercourse with Wyatt was non-consensual. The defense argues that the abrasions instead stemmed from the alleged victim's having had consensual intercourse with three different men in three different days. *Would that change your answer? What if the three prior instances were non-consensual? Would your answer change if, instead of consent, Wyatt's defense was misidentification, that is, that someone else was the rapist?*

5. In the same preliminary hearing, the defense presents DNA evidence of semen that did not belong to the accused found on the alleged victim's underwear to suggest that she may have had sex with another man between the time that she claimed Wyatt raped her and the next day, when she reported the incident and was examined by a doctor.

Is such evidence admissible? Why or why not?

Assume in answering all the above questions that the Federal Rules of Evidence apply at the preliminary hearing.

Problem 5-38: Homage to "To Kill a Mockingbird"

Tom Robinson, an African American, is on trial for raping Mayella Ewell, a white woman; his defense is consent. They both reside in a small Southern town that maintains many of the cultural vestiges of the Old South, including the social unacceptability of sexual relationships between blacks and whites. Robinson offers evidence that on previous occasions Mayella had been intimate with three other African Americans. *Admissible?*

[3] Exception in Civil Cases: Rule 412(b)(2)

In civil cases, Rule 412(b)(2) creates a very different set of exceptions than Rule 412(b)(1) recognizes in criminal cases:

> **(2) *Civil Cases.*** In a civil case, the court may admit evidence offered to prove a victim's sexual behavior or sexual predisposition if its probative value substantially outweighs the danger of harm to any victim and of unfair prejudice to any party. The court may admit evidence of a victim's reputation only if the victim has placed it in controversy.

Subdivision (b)(2), governing only civil cases, employs a balancing test rather than listing specific exceptions like those recognized in criminal cases under subdivision (b)(1). According to the Rule 412 Advisory Committee Note, the rule adopted this approach "in recognition of the difficulty of foreseeing future developments in the law." "Greater flexibility is needed to accommodate resolving causes of action such as claims for sexual harassment." Moreover,

> [T]his test for admitting evidence offered to prove sexual behavior or sexual propensity in civil cases differs in three respects from the general rule governing admissibility set forth in Rule 403. First, it reverses the usual procedure spelled out in Rule 403 by shifting the burden to the proponent to demonstrate admissibility rather than making the opponent justify exclusion of the evidence. Second, the standard expressed in subdivision (b)(2) is more stringent than the original rule; it raises the threshold for admission by requiring that the probative value of the evidence substantially outweigh the specified dangers. Finally, the Rule 412 test puts "harm to the victim" on the scale in addition to prejudice to the parties.

Evidence of an alleged victim's reputation may be received in a civil case, but only if the alleged victim has "put his or her reputation into controversy."

> *Example 1*
>
> Renee Wilt has brought a Title VII sexual harassment suit against her employer, the local fire department, for creating a "hostile environment" by permitting the posting of pornography throughout the fire station. The fire department seeks to offer evidence of Renee's reputation as a longtime producer and consumer of pornography to show that there was nothing personally intimidating to her in the fire station environment. Her objection under Rule 412(b)(2) will likely be sustained, as it is hard to argue that her allegations of improper conduct by the department put her reputation at issue.

> *Example 2*
>
> Same case as Example 1, but instead of offering reputation evidence, the fire department offers evidence of specific recent instances in which Renee both collected pornography for her own use and jokingly posted it in the fire station. A trial judge would likely be well within her discretion to overrule any objection, by finding that the probative value of the evidence substantially outweighs the danger of harm to Renee, the alleged victim, and of any unfair prejudice to any party.

Example 3

Same case as Example 1, but Renee testifies at trial that the men in the fire station put a photo of Renee's face on the head of a nude woman in each of the pornographic photos and spread rumors throughout the department and the neighborhood that Renee was a "well-known slut." She seeks damages for the harm to her reputation. Now the department offers evidence that Renee had a reputation as a slut long before her co-workers spread any rumors to that effect. This evidence arguably would be admissible, because Renee placed her reputation "in controversy," and the probative value of the evidence may under the circumstances be deemed high relative to unfair prejudice.

The chart on the next page summarizes the rape shield law analysis and is followed by several problems intended further to clarify the analysis:

SPECIAL RULES FOR CASES INVOLVING ALLEGED SEXUAL MISCONDUCT: RAPE SHIELD

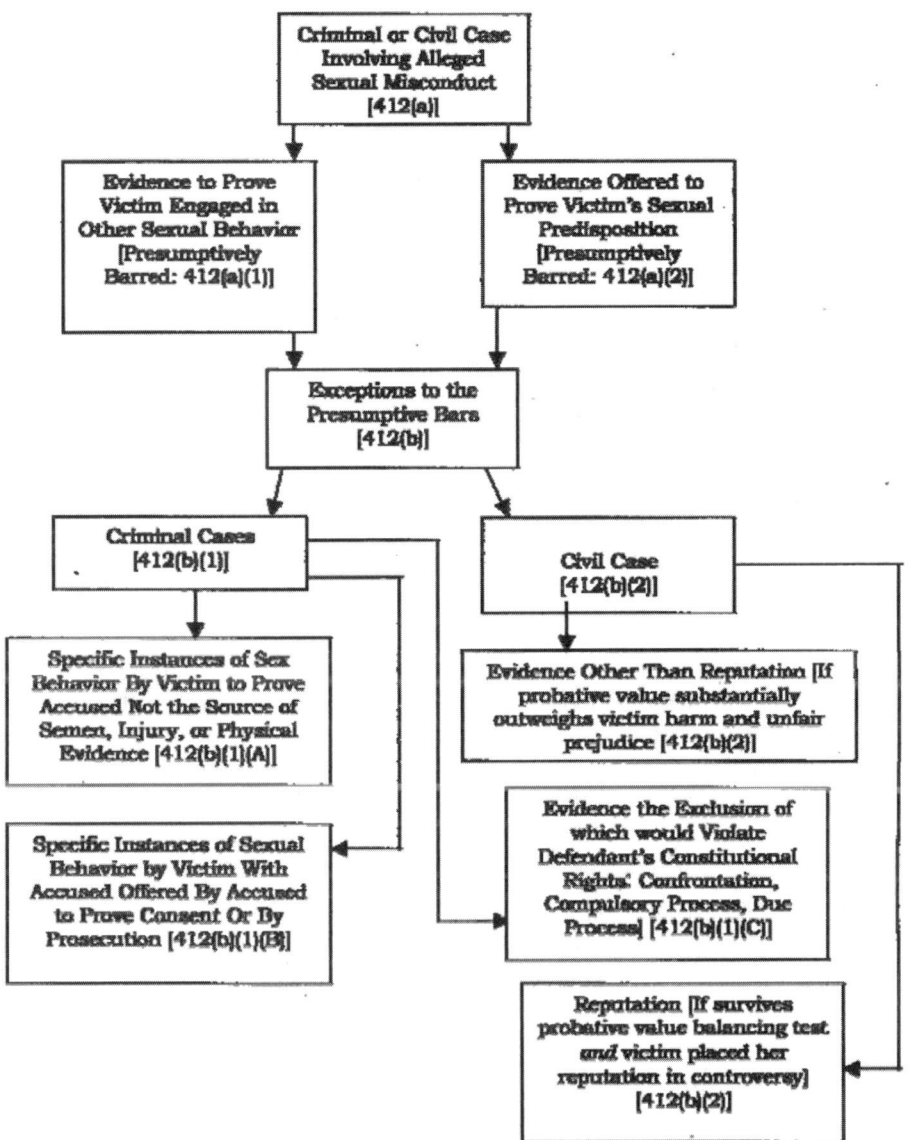

Problem 5-39: Romantic Dreams Redux

Does Rule 412(b)(2) change any of your responses to problem 5-34? Why?

Problem 5-40: Sexual Harassment

Lilah Falew has filed a civil sexual harassment suit against her employer, a well-known insurance company, Mandebell Insurance. Falew was a very successful insurance agent. She claims that her fellow agents, all male, subjected her to repeated sexually tinged verbal abuse. For example, one agent might smile when Falew wore a short skirt to work, saying, "Now I know why you get so many clients." Another agent might say, "Oh, baby, you can insure me any time!" Falew also alleged that male agents openly commented on the attractiveness of various parts of her body. All the comments were severe and pervasive in creating a hostile working environment, and they continued despite her objections. Falew testified about each of these incidents at the civil trial. *Answer the following questions.*

1. May Mandebell's lawyer call rebuttal witnesses to say that, "Lilah had quite a reputation for sleeping with her clients. You know, she slept her way to the top"? What if they instead testified that she generally had a "promiscuous reputation"? Would your answer to either question change if Lilah blurted out on direct examination, "I was so upset by these comments. I'm single, and a very religious woman, and I pride myself on my reputation for chastity. They were killing my reputation"?

2. May Mandebell's lawyer call Lilah's former best friend, a female co-worker in the claims department, to say, "In my opinion, Lilah loved these comments. She loved the attention, and she loved men. She wore those short skirts because she wanted to elicit their comments. And if she liked one of the guys, she might just take his comment as a clue to, shall we say, try to get more intimate"?

3. Now Mandebell's lawyer calls witnesses to testify to specific and repeated instances in which Lilah herself made sexual comments, smilingly, about the anatomy of various male agents. Furthermore, they recite instances in which the men indeed made sexually suggestive comments, and Lilah responded with her own, often cruder suggestions. Moreover, these comments continued over a course of years. Lilah did not file this lawsuit until shortly after her boss told her that her sales were slipping and that she would have to shape up or ship out. Should any or all of this testimony be admissible?

4. Finally, Mandebell calls a secretary who said that she overheard Lilah telling a friend during a phone conversation, "I just love when the men make these dirty comments. It makes coming to work so much fun." Admissible or not? Why or why not?

[4] Procedure to Determine Admissibility: Rule 412(c)

Under any of the Rule 412 exceptions, the following procedures must be followed:

(c) Procedure to Determine Admissibility.

(1) *Motion.* If a party intends to offer evidence under Rule 412(b), the party must:

(A) file a motion that specifically describes the evidence and states the purpose for which it is to be offered;

(B) do so at least 14 days before trial unless the court, for good cause, sets a different time;

(C) serve the motion on all parties; and

(D) notify the victim or, when appropriate, the victim's guardian or representative.

(2) *Hearing.* Before admitting evidence under this rule, the court must conduct an in camera hearing and give the victim and parties a right to attend and be heard. Unless the court orders otherwise, the motion, related materials, and the record of the hearing must be and remain sealed.

Example

In the Renee Wilt sexual harassment case (*see* [3], above), the department files in court, and serves on Renee, 13 days before trial, a motion stating its intention "to offer evidence of plaintiff's sexual obsessions to disprove her claims of perceived intimidation and her damages." The motion should be summarily denied, both because it is untimely without stating good cause for the delay and it is so vague that it fails "specifically" to describe the evidence and state the purpose for which it is offered.

Problem 5-41

In Problem 5-40, assume that Mandebell did not file written notice of its intention to use any of the evidence until five days before trial. Mandebell maintains that no witnesses were willing to come forward before that time despite Mandebell's best efforts. The notice finally filed said, "Mandebell will call witnesses to establish that the plaintiff invited and enjoyed the sorts of comments about which she now complains and now says merit awarding her damages. These witnesses will testify to specific acts by the plaintiff, as well as to her reputation, showing how she sought out, participated in, and often initiated what she now says were lewd comments." *Should the trial judge excuse the late filing of this notice, and is the notice adequate?*

[B] Character of the Defendant in a Criminal or Civil Sexual Assault or Child Molestation Case: Rule 413, 414, 415

Rule 404 generally bars use of propensity evidence subject to the few exceptions noted in that rule. However, Rules 413, 414, and 415 create additional exceptions for criminal or civil cases involving, or predicated on, offenses of sexual assault or child molestation. Rules 413, 414, and 415 are identical in all but one respect. Rule 413 governs criminal sexual assault cases only, Rule 414 governs criminal child molestation cases only, and Rule 415 governs civil sexual assault or child molestation cases. Jointly read, therefore, these three rules apply roughly the same standards to criminal and civil sexual assault or child molestation cases.

Rule 413(a) is thus representative of all three rules and states the core standard:

Rule 413. Similar Crimes in Sexual Assault Cases

    (a) Permitted Uses. In a criminal case in which a defendant is accused of a sexual assault, the court may admit evidence that the defendant committed any other sexual assault. The evidence may be considered on any matter to which it is relevant.

Notice that Rule 413 limits the prior offense evidence to offenses of the same type as the one charged. Thus, in a current case charging rape, which is an offense of sexual assault, the rule permits evidence of other rapes or other sorts of sexual assaults but not of child molestation. Similarly, Rule 414 requires that current child molestation cases permit use of prior offenses of child molestation but not of adult rape. While Rule 415 is less clear, it is probably best read similarly as permitting in civil cases based on sexual assault, for example, the use of character evidence only of a prior sexual assault.

Rule 413(d) defines "sexual assault" broadly, including: "contact, without consent, between any part of the defendant's body — or an object — and another person's genitals or anus," "contact, without consent, between the defendant's genitals or anus and any part of another person's body," "deriving sexual pleasure or gratification from inflicting death, bodily injury, or physical pain on another person," and any attempt or conspiracy to engage in any of this conduct. This definition obviously includes rape, some indecent assaults, and other common sexual offenses. Importantly, there is case law holding that the Rule's reference to an offense of "sexual assault" requires only proof that the specified conduct happened but not that it resulted in an arrest, charge, or conviction.

Rule 414 defines "offense of child molestation" in a fashion similar to Rule 413's definition of "offense of sexual assault," but with a child, whose consent is irrelevant.

Example 1

Wealthy socialite Wilhelm Cannady Smythe is charged with raping Cathy Bator while on a date. Smythe concedes that he engaged in sexual intercourse with Bator but maintains that it was consensual, though this theory has so far become clear only on cross-examination of the state's witnesses, as its case-in-chief is still proceeding. Near the end of that case, the state calls three women to the stand to testify that each of them were raped by Smythe while on dates with him during the past year under circumstances similar to those described by Bator. None of them originally reported the crimes because of their fear of mistreatment by the judicial system. Their testimony will likely be admissible under Rule 413 for "any matter to which it is relevant." Thus, it may, based on a propensity inference, tend to show that Smythe acted "forcibly" (an element of the rape statute in this jurisdiction), as well as that Bator did not consent and that Smythe knew so (whether these mental state inferences involve "propensity" was discussed earlier in this chapter).

Example 2

Same facts as in example 1, but Smythe denies ever engaging in sexual intercourse with Bator. The evidence of Smythe's prior sexual assaults is now offered to prove that he committed the current act of intercourse, that is, "act propensity" evidence is offered. The evidence will still likely be admissible under Rule 413.

Because the exceptions in Rules 413–415 permit use of prior offenses for any relevant purpose, they create another set of exceptions to the rule against act propensity evidence. The exceptions are apparently justified by the difficulty of proof in sexual assault cases, especially consent defense cases, where there rarely is a third-party witness or corroborating physical evidence of force. Other justifications can also be articulated, rooted in jurors' biased preconceptions about sexuality that may cloud their ability fairly to consider a rape victim's tale. *See* Andrew E. Taslitz, Rape and the Culture of the Courtroom (1999); *see also* Steven Friedland, *Date Rape and the Culture of Acceptance*, 43 Fla. L. Rev. 487 (1991). Nevertheless, the recently enacted exceptions are controversial ones, arguably representing a sea change in our thinking about character evidence. To the critics of Rules 413–415, the same character dangers apply in sexual assault cases as in robbery cases. Accordingly, they see no justification for carving out a special exception for one class of cases but not the other.

One other troubling aspect of original Rule 413 was whether it was limited by Rule 403. Original Rule 413 flatly said that evidence of other sexual assault offenses "is admissible," rather than "may be" admissible, making no reference to Rule 403 whatsoever (original Rules 414 and 415 contained similar language). Yet Rule 403 presumptively applies to all evidence questions, unless another rule expressly states otherwise (as, for example, portions of Rule 609 do). Moreover, the rule said that the evidence "may" be considered for its bearing on any relevant matter, not that it "must" be considered, in apparent contradiction to the rule's earlier "is admissible" language and opening the door to a Rule 403 analysis. The Floor Statement of the principal House Sponsor, Representative Susan Molinari, also says:

> In other respects, the general standards of the rules of evidence will continue to apply, including the restrictions on hearsay evidence and the Court's authority under Evidence Rule 403 to exclude evidence whose probative value is substantially outweighed by its prejudicial effect.

Molinari's view had generally been adopted by the courts, resulting in substantially different outcomes compared to a contrary interpretation that ignores Rule 403. The 2011 stylistic amendments to the Federal Rules of Evidence eliminated any ambiguity on this point, replacing the "is" admissible language with "may" be admissible language, a phrasing much more consistent with Rule 403 balancing still being available as a ground for exclusion of evidence otherwise admissible under Rule 413.

Example 3

Assume instead that the three women who testify against Smythe all recount events that occurred 20 years earlier, while he was a teenager. At that time, he had squeezed their buttocks and fondled their hips through their clothing without their permission but stopped immediately when each slapped him and said, "No!" These are circumstances very different from those testified to by Bator. If Rule 403 applies, a trial judge might exclude this evidence as stale and of low probative value in proving rape, given the less serious nature of the earlier offenses and the very different circumstances under which they took place.

Rule 413(b) also imposes a notice requirement when the prosecution expects to use Rule 413(a) evidence at trial. The attorney for the government "must" disclose the evidence to the defendant at least 15 days before the scheduled trial or at such later time as the court may for good cause allow. That disclosure must include statements of witnesses or a summary of the substance of any testimony that is expected to be offered. Rules 414(b) and 415(b) contain similar notice requirements.

Problem 5-42: Not-Quite Pinched Buttocks

At Thornell Hamhurst's trial on charges of rape, the prosecution calls several female witnesses to testify that Hamhurst tried to pinch each of their buttocks, while making lascivious comments about their bodies, at a variety of fraternity parties during the past two years. In each case, however, one of the women or an onlooker spotted Hamhurst and stopped him when he was but inches away from completing his pinch. The defense objects. *Ruling? Would your ruling change if Hamhurst had instead sought to grab each of these women's breasts? To grab each of the women between their legs? If he succeeded in completing any of these acts?*

Problem 5-43: S & M

Refer to the previous problem, but assume instead that Thornell Hamhurst is charged with indecent assault, which is defined in this jurisdiction as a nonconsensual touching of the defendant's genitals to any part of another person's body but not involving sexual intercourse. Hamhurst's defense is mistaken identity: someone near Hamhurst on a crowded subway had apparently pressed his crotch against a female passenger, and the passenger mistook Hamhurst for the culprit. The prosecutor offers evidence in its case-in-chief that Hamhurst was convicted of aggravated assault for whipping a prostitute severely as part of a sadomasochistic ritual. No notice of the prosecutor's intention to offer this evidence had been given because, said the prosecutor, he had never imagined that Hamhurst would have the gall to raise a mistaken identity defense when there were so many eyewitnesses in the brightly lit train. The defense objects. *Ruling? Would your ruling change if the prosecutor instead offers evidence that the earlier aggravated assault took place when Hamburst had been tried for, but acquitted of, that offense? Why or why not?*

§ 5.08 IMPEACHMENT: RULES 404(a)(3), 608, AND 609

[A] Distinction between Impeachment and Substantive Evidence

Rule 404(a)(3) excepts from the act propensity rule, "Evidence of a witness's character," which "may be admitted under Rules 607, 608, and 609." Thus, the special standards recited in Rules 607, 608, and 609 apply when character evidence is used to impeach a witness. A witness, for these purposes, may be someone who is now testifying under oath at the current trial or a hearsay declarant whose out-of-court statement has been received in evidence. *See* Rule 806 ("When a hearsay statement, or a statement defined in Rule 801(d)(2)(C), (D), or (E), has been admitted in evidence, the credibility of the declarant may be attacked, and if attacked may be supported, by any evidence which would be admissible for those purposes if declarant had testified as a witness."). Thus, for example, a defendant in a criminal case is not a witness if he never takes the stand at his trial. Indeed, given the constitutional privilege against self-incrimination, and the fact that the state bears the burden of persuasion as to all elements of the crime beyond a reasonable doubt, criminal defendants ("accuseds") usually do not in fact testify at their trials. When they do not testify, the 404(a)(3) exception to the propensity bar (which incorporates Rules 608 and 609) will not apply.

However, if the accused nevertheless chooses to take the stand and testify, he now becomes a witness, and Rules 608 and 609 can be used to impeach him. Because these rules authorize impeachment uses of act propensity evidence, it is, therefore, important to learn to distinguish between act propensity evidence used to impeach (governed primarily by Rules 608 and 609) and other act propensity evidence — often referred to as "substantive" character evidence (governed primarily by Rules 404 and 405, and, in special cases, by Rules 412 to 415). Both substantive and impeachment uses of character rely on act propensity inferences — character used to prove conduct on a particular occasion. But, with impeachment, the "act" to be proven is not necessarily that of a plaintiff, defendant, or crime victim done out of court or at an earlier trial but rather of a witness in the current case. That witness's act is the giving of untruthful or inaccurate testimony on the stand at the current trial. Of course, a plaintiff, defendant, or crime victim may become a witness, but it is their role as witness, not as a party or victim, that triggers application of Rules 608 and 609.

Rephrased, substantive evidence is relevant to establish facts in issue while impeachment evidence affects the weight to be given substantive evidence, weight that may, for example, be diminished if the witness is lying, confused, or mistaken. If the party with the relevant burden fails to offer a witness to testify to evidence supporting the existence of an element of a crime, claim, or defense, that party's burden has not been met. (For ease of illustration, we are for now ignoring complications raised by the distinction between the burden of production — roughly speaking, the burden of offering "some evidence" — and the burden of persuasion, that is, of convincing the factfinder, complications addressed in a later chapter, though we will use those terms here where necessary). Accordingly, judgment will be entered in his opponent's favor. On the other hand, if evidence *is* offered by the party with the relevant burden as to every element on which he has that burden, then the case will get to the jury if the trial judge concludes that a reasonable jury could find the existence of the element by the relevant standard, for example, by a preponderance of the evidence in most civil cases. But whether the jury in fact finds that standard met will turn in part on whom they believe.

Impeachment evidence may, therefore, be offered to suggest that that party's witness is just wrong — either lying or mistaken. If the jury agrees that the impeaching evidence shows that the witness is indeed lying or mistaken, and if there is no evidence of the existence of the relevant element other than this witness's testimony, then the jury will give the testimony no weight, treating it as if it never existed. Consequently, the jury will find that the party's burden of persuasion has not been met and will instead find in favor of his opponent. There are many forms of substantive and impeachment evidence, character being but one form, but it is that form that is the focus of this portion of this chapter.

Substantive evidence, it must be noted, can also be offered by the opposing party — defined here as the party who does not bear the relevant burden as to an element. Because the opposing party has no such burden, he may choose *not* to offer any evidence on the point yet still have a chance to prevail. But if he nevertheless concludes that, as a matter of sound trial tactics in a particular case, offering evidence will encourage the jury to find that the party with the burden has not met it, then the opposing party may indeed make the tactical choice to offer evidence in his favor. He will thus seek to *disprove* the existence of the relevant element. In this situation as well, however, the party with the burden may respond with impeachment evidence suggesting that the opposing party's witnesses are lying or mistaken.

Example 1

The defendant in a homicide case calls witness X to the stand. X testifies that, in his opinion, the defendant is a peaceful person. Furthermore, under Rule 404(a)(2)(A), the "mercy rule," this evidence is offered to prove that the defendant, as a peaceful person, has less of a propensity to commit an act of violence, such as killing, making it less likely that he in fact committed the act of killing in this case. That is substantive evidence that, if believed, helps to disprove an element of the crime of homicide, namely that it was this defendant, and not someone else, who struck the deadly blow. The defendant makes the tactical choice to offer this evidence even though he has no obligation to do so, for the burdens of production ("some evidence") and persuasion (beyond a reasonable doubt) as to who did the crime rest entirely with the prosecution. However, the prosecutor might then respond with evidence that witness X has been convicted twice for perjury. That is impeachment evidence offered to suggest that because X has lied under oath in the past, he is more likely to be doing so now on the stand. If the jurors in fact conclude that X is now lying, they will discount his testimony entirely, and, if there are no other character witnesses testifying in defendant's favor, will act as if no evidence of defendant's peaceful character has been offered. They will thus rely on other evidence in deciding whether the state has met its burden of persuading the jury beyond a reasonable doubt that the defendant did this crime. Impeachment can generally be accomplished either by cross-examining the witness in an effort to get him to admit to the impeaching facts or by offering other witnesses to impeach on rebuttal. (This general point, however, has exceptions, for example, as we will see under Rule 608, impeachment by specific acts relevant to the witness's character for truthfulness or untruthfulness under that Rule's subdivision (b) can sometimes be limited to the method of cross-examination.)

Example 2

In *Example 1* just above, the prosecutor might have asked witness X on cross to admit to having been twice convicted of perjury. If that strategy fails — X denies the convictions — then the prosecutor will await rebuttal (after the defense "rests," that is, finishes offering witnesses in its case-in-chief). On rebuttal, the prosecutor might, for example, submit records of the perjury convictions and call the court reporters from those cases to the stand to identify witness X as the person so convicted.

Another way to distinguish between substantive and impeachment uses of character evidence is to outline the inferential chain relied upon, much in the way we have earlier in this chapter, as these examples illustrate.

Example 3

Defense counsel in the homicide case above now calls the defendant himself to the stand as a witness. The defendant testifies that he is ensnared in a case of mistaken identity. Someone else committed the crime, the defendant insists. The prosecutor, on cross-examination, asks the defendant, "Isn't it true that you have twice been convicted of perjury in just the past two years?" The question seeks to impeach the defendant — to suggest that he lied in testifying that he did not commit the crime. The inference chain runs like this:

1. Evidence is offered that the defendant has committed perjury, an untruthful act in an earlier case.

2. The jury is asked to infer from this evidence that the defendant has the character trait of being a liar.

3. The jury is further expected to infer that a liar — the kind of person who lies — is more likely than someone else to have just lied on the stand in the current trial.

Example 4

Alternatively, now suppose that the defendant is charged with criminal fraud, intentionally lying about some material fact to get the listener to rely on the misrepresentation. The prosecutor again offers evidence of the defendant's prior perjury convictions. But the defendant never testifies in the case. Because he never testifies, there is no testimony to impeach. The character evidence offered is thus substantive evidence that he committed the currently charged fraud. The inference chain runs like this:

1. Evidence is offered that the defendant has committed perjury, an untruthful act in an earlier case.

2. The jury is asked to infer from this evidence that the defendant has the character trait of being a liar.

3. The jury is further expected to infer that a liar is more likely than someone else to have committed the lie that is the basis for the currently charged substantive crime.

In *Example 3*, above, the evidence was offered to show that the defendant-witness lied on the stand; this use of the evidence for impeachment activated Rule 609, dealing with impeachment by prior convictions and to be discussed in depth shortly. In *Example 4*, however, the testimony is offered to show that the defendant committed the currently charged offense. Thus, this testimony involves the use of substantive, rather than impeaching, character evidence, and the evidence of the perjury convictions is inadmissible under Rule 404.

Rule 609, as just mentioned, is a special rule governing the impeachment use of a particular sort of impeaching character evidence: conviction of a crime. Before reaching that rule, however, it is helpful first to examine Rule 608, which governs all other sorts of character evidence used to impeach.

[B] Rule 608 — Impeachment Generally

Rule 608 creates different rules based on the form of the character impeachment evidence — one rule, in paragraph (a), for proof of character by opinion and reputation, another rule, in paragraph (b), for proof of character by specific acts:

Rule 608. A Witness's Character for Truthfulness or Untruthfulness

(a) **Reputation or Opinion Evidence.** A witness's credibility may be attacked or supported by testimony about the witness's reputation for having a character for truthfulness or untruthfulness, or by testimony in the form of an opinion about that character. But evidence of truthful character is admissible only after the witness's character for truthfulness has been attacked.

(b) **Specific Instances of Conduct.** Except for a criminal conviction under Rule 609, extrinsic evidence is not admissible to prove specific instances of a witness's conduct in order to attack or support the witness's character for truthfulness.

But the court may, on cross-examination, allow them to be inquired into if they are probative of the character for truthfulness or untruthfulness of:

(1) the witness; or

(2) another witness whose character the witness being cross-examined has testified about. By testifying on another matter, a witness does not waive any privilege against self-incrimination for testimony that relates only to the witness's character for truthfulness.

[1] Opinion and Reputation: Rule 608(a)

Rule 608(a) declares that the "a witness's credibility may be attacked or supported by testimony about the witness's reputation . . . or by testimony in the form of an opinion. . . ." However, under Rule 608(a), a credibility attack must involve evidence that refers *only* to "character for . . . untruthfulness." Other types of character traits may not, therefore, be used as the basis for impeachment.

Example 1

Jolly Jamison is an alibi witness for his friend, Bart Timpson, at Timpson's robbery trial. The prosecutor seeks to call two witnesses to the stand to impeach Jamison: first, Jamison's next-door-neighbor, who will testify that Jamison has a reputation in his neighborhood as an untruthful man; second, Jamison's ex-wife, who will testify to her opinion that Jamison is a thief and a violently abusive man. The next-door neighbor's testimony concerns witness Jamison's character for untruthfulness and therefore should be admitted. But the ex-wife's testimony concerns character traits (thievery and violence) that have nothing to do with truthfulness or its opposite and should thus be beyond the scope of what is authorized by this Rule.

Under Rule 608(a), evidence of truthful character may not be admitted, however, unless that particular character trait and no other has first been attacked. The current restyled version of the rule does not expressly state the form of evidence to be used to constitute an attack on character for truthfulness. However, an earlier version of the rule permitted the attacks to be by reputation or opinion evidence "or otherwise," as well as by convictions admitted under Rule 609 (discussed in more detail shortly). Because the restyling project was designed to bring the Rules closer to plain language without altering their substance, presumably the new language does not change the meaning intended by the old language. For example, evidence of prior convictions (see Rule 609(b)) or a showing of corruption would constitute an attack on "character for truthfulness"; such impeachment would permit responsive testimony to show that the witness does indeed have a truthful character. This showing can be made by cross-examination or by the testimony of other witnesses.

Impeachment by a prior inconsistent statement is not an "or otherwise" attack (using the language of the older version of the rule) on the witness's character if the inconsistency merely suggests a flawed memory or a mistake. But an inconsistency raising an inference of untruthful nature may meet what was previously called the "or otherwise" requirement. However, it is generally held that mere contradicting evidence offered by an opponent, or even showings of interest, bias, or coercion, do not constitute sufficient attacks on character to trigger the right to response by evidence of reputation for, or opinion of, truthful character. But the Rule 608 Advisory Committee Note considers the question whether contradiction is a sufficient attack on character to depend on the circumstances. In the language of the restyled rules, sometimes, though rarely, impeachment by prior inconsistent statements or contradiction will constitute an "attack" on character for truthfulness, permitted a response with evidence of the witness's truthful character.

The bottom line: merely suggesting that a witness is lying or mistaken is not the same thing as suggesting that the falsehood or error stemmed from an untruthful character. For example, the witness may simply have been momentarily confused, or this conduct may be aberrational. Only a suggestion of untruthful character permits a truthful character counter-strike. Whether an impeachment technique not overtly involving character (such as by prior inconsistent statements, contradiction, bias, interest, or coercion) in fact constitutes an attack on *character* for truthfulness is a case-specific question guided by the circumstances and may turn, for example, on the egregiousness and nature of the inconsistency, that is, on whether it is so extreme or made under such circumstances that it would not be expected to be uttered from the lips of someone whose general character — their nature or on-average behavior relative to most other people — is other than that of a liar, the kind of person who lies. Whether such a showing has been made will often be the subject of heated debate at trial and is subject to no simple or easy litmus test.

Example 2

Morris Manor is accused of committing a robbery that occurred two months ago. Manor offers an alibi defense, taking the stand and testifying that he was at home with his mother watching T.V. on the date of the robbery and that he even remembers what they were watching: the hit television show *24*. If the defense next calls Manor's mother to the stand to testify that she was indeed home with him at the time of the crime, but she admits on cross that they were watching the opera, not *24*, that inconsistency with her son's testimony may easily be explained as his memory simply failing him on a relatively minor matter, particularly if he was not arrested until many weeks later so that nothing unusual happened to give him any reason accurately to remember what was on T.V. Accordingly, his mother's cross-examination testimony would not likely constitute an attack on his "character" for truthfulness, so he could not offer evidence of his truthful character in response. On the other hand, if he did not call his mom to the stand but rather the prosecution did, and if she testified that he was not home with her that night because it was his birthday, and he always goes out with his friend, George, on his birthday for a big celebration at a special restaurant, and if George next testifies that for the first time in 10 years he and the defendant did not see each other on the defendant's birthday, that might arguably constitute an attack on Manor's "character for truthfulness." Manor would debatably be highly likely to remember where he was on his birthday, especially because he makes such a big deal out of it and it was only two months ago, and he follows a regular birthday celebration routine. Moreover, his inconsistency is one so easily caught — the prosecution could simply call his mother to the stand, as they did. Under these circumstances, a trial judge might easily conclude that this inconsistency was so likely a lie under such outrageous circumstances as to suggest to the jury that the defendant is a liar, that is, that he has a *character* for untruthfulness. Accordingly, the trial judge might permit the defendant to respond with evidence that he in fact has a truthful, not an untruthful, character. (Note: This example involves the mother simply assuming that her son was not home with her on his birthday because he must have been out with his friend, as is his birthday routine. If the evidence instead was that the son specifically lied to his mom — falsely telling her that he was going out with George to celebrate his birthday, that might constitute a specific act of lying suggesting an untruthful character, under Rule 608(b), which we analyze below. In that circumstance, the attack would be a direct one on character for truthfulness under Rule 608 rather than a more debatable "or otherwise" attack as that term was defined under the earlier version of Rule 608(a).

Problem 5-44: Johnny Larsen's Divorce

Johnny Larsen, a well-known television personality, is accused of adultery in a divorce action. *Which of the following items of evidence are relevant: (a) substantive character evidence, (b) impeachment character evidence, (c) neither?*

1. Larsen's attorney, in cross-examining his wife, Joanna, seeks to prove that she too is an adulteress.

2. Larsen offers evidence that Joanna has a reputation as a violent woman, to prove that she physically abused him.

3. Larsen seeks to prove that Joanna was convicted of larceny; Joanna has not testified at the trial.

4. The same evidence as in #3 above, but Joanna has testified at the trial.

5. Larsen seeks to prove that Joanna falsely claimed that her first husband (a very wealthy man) was an adulterer, in a blatant effort to get most of his money in a divorce settlement; Joanna has not testified at the trial.

6. The same evidence as in #5 above, but Joanna has testified at the trial.

Which rules govern each of these six items of evidence? Are these items admissible?

Problem 5-45: Married Robbers

Derrick Lowell testifies at his trial on a robbery charge involving a crime that took place in New York City. Lowell swears that he was in San Francisco visiting a friend on the date of the crime. The prosecutor calls Lowell's ex-wife to the stand, who tearfully recounts that Lowell was indeed in New York City on the relevant date, a date she cannot forget because it is the date that she and Lowell married. In rebuttal, Lowell calls a priest to testify that Lowell is a kind, truthful man. The prosecutor objects. *Should the objection be sustained or overruled? Why?*

Problem 5-46: Married Robbers Revisited

At the same trial of Derrick Lowell summarized in Problem 5-45, which of the following would trigger Lowell's right to call a witness to testify to Lowell's truthful character:

1. Lowell admits on cross-examination that he has been convicted of a previous gunpoint robbery.

2. Lowell admits on cross-examination that he was convicted of burgling a television set from his neighbor's home while the neighbor was at church.

3. Lowell admits that he absconded with $3,000 he obtained from the parents of a terminal eight-year-old cancer patient. Lowell had falsely told them that the money would fund a novel but effective cancer treatment that Lowell had invented. No such treatment existed.

4. The prosecution calls Lowell's best man to the stand to testify that he saw Lowell at Lowell's wedding on the date of the alleged crime.

5. The prosecutor calls Lowell's former roommate to the stand. Lowell and the roommate lived together before Lowell married and at the time of the crime. Lowell had testified that he never owned or wore a red running suit, which was what the robber wore. The roommate testifies, however, that Lowell indeed owned such a suit at the time of the crime, and the roommate saw Lowell wear the suit on many occasions.

6. The prosecution calls the same roommate to testify that Lowell had said, on several occasions before the crime, that he knew and despised the robbery victim because Lowell believed that the soon-to-be victim was having an affair with Lowell's fiancée.

[2] Specific Acts: Rule 608(b)

Rule 608(b) declares that, "[e]xcept for a criminal conviction under Rule 609, extrinsic evidence is not admissible to prove specific instances of a witness's conduct in order to attack or support the witness's character for truthfulness." The rule continues:

> But the court may, on cross-examination, allow them to be inquired into if they are probative of the character for truthfulness or untruthfulness of (1) the witness; or
>
> (2) another witness whose character the witness being cross-examined has testified about. ...

Remember that the general rules governing the substantive use of character evidence, Rules 404 and 405, permit proof in most cases only by reputation or opinion evidence but not by evidence of specific acts. Rule 608(b) changes this rule for character evidence used to impeach. Specific acts may be used to impeach character, but only if those acts are elicited "intrinsically," meaning from the mouth of the witness whose character is being challenged, *if* extrinsic evidence would be relevant only to prove the witness's character for truthfulness or untruthfulness. If the witness being cross-examined denies committing the alleged wrongful acts, the cross-examiner is thus not permitted to call another witness (one whose testimony is "extrinsic" to the witness being cross-examined) to prove the contrary *unless* that testimony has some relevance additional to that of proving the witness's untruthful character. The cross-examiner is stuck with the challenged witness' false denial.

Example 1

Robert Deck is a witness who testifies for the defense in a "date" rape trial. Deck testifies that he was at the fraternity party where the rape allegedly happened and saw the victim being the sexual aggressor. The prosecutor asks Deck whether he once committed perjury by lying about the size of his assets when testifying at his recent divorce trial. Deck denies that he lied at that earlier trial. Deck has never been convicted of perjury, or even charged with it. The prosecutor seeks to call witnesses to establish: (1) the amount of money Deck testified to having in the bank in his divorce case, and (2) the much greater amount of money Deck in fact had in the bank at that time. A defense objection to these witnesses' testimony should be sustained if the sole purpose of this testimony is to prove Deck's character for untruthfulness. Their testimony would be extrinsic evidence of Deck's act of lying under oath at his divorce trial, an act that Deck has just denied in his testimony at the rape trial.

Important reminder: Note that Rule 608(b) refers to "specific instances of a witness's conduct," *not* "specific instances of conviction." If a witness is being cross-examined about prior *convictions* of crime to impeach his character for truthfulness, then Rule 609 (discussed below) applies. But if the evidence concerns only the fact that the relevant act happened, even if the defendant was never even tried much less convicted of that act — indeed, even if the act is not itself a crime but does go to character for truthfulness or untruthfulness — then Rule 608(b) applies. That is why Deck could be asked whether he *committed* perjury, there being no evidence that he was *convicted* of such a crime.

The original rule prohibited using extrinsic proof of specific acts to attack or support a witness' "credibility." The rule was amended to replace the word "credibility" with the phrase "character for truthfulness." The point of this change was to "clarify that the absolute prohibition on extrinsic evidence applies only when the *sole reason* for proffering that evidence is to attack or support the witness' character for truthfulness." *See* Advisory Committee Note, amended Rule 608(b):

> The "Rule 608(b) extrinsic evidence prohibition does not apply when it is offered for a purpose other than proving the witness' character for veracity." *Id.* Thus, if extrinsic evidence is offered to impeach on grounds other than character — such as by contradiction or a showing of bias — Rules 402 and 403 control.

Although this change was meant to "clarify" the Rule, it arguably instead creates ambiguity. Thus, in the Deck example above, how do we determine whether an attack on character for truthfulness is the "sole" purpose of the extrinsic evidence? The extrinsic evidence bar would seem to be most commonly involved when a witness such as Deck denies committing the prior act of lying. If he admits the act, there is no need for extrinsic proof. If he denies the act, extrinsic proof would have to be in the form of contradiction or a prior inconsistent statement to show that the lie in fact happened. But that would mean that most extrinsic proof will also be offered for impeachment purposes other than just proving character itself. Nor would it seem that a Rule 403 analysis must focus on whether the jury might wrongly use the extrinsic proof as evidence of untruthful character, since only the form of (extrinsic rather than intrinsic), not the character inference itself, is prohibited.

The primary rationale for barring extrinsic proof of acts going to truthful or untruthful character is that it wastes time. The trial court becomes bogged down in a series of mini-trials over whether events relatively peripheral to the current case ever happened. Perhaps the intended effect of the amended Rule is to prohibit initial use of extrinsic proof of character in the hope that the witness will admit his lies (given the risk of perjury prosecution), thus avoiding a mini-trial. But this happy outcome may often not come to pass, requiring mini-trials, unless a Rule 403 "waste of time" argument prevails.

Note, moreover, that even efforts to prove a witness' specific acts "intrinsically" may be made only if the acts are probative of the witness' character for truthfulness or untruthfulness. Like proof of opinion or reputation under Rule 608(a), questions about specific instances of conduct under Rule 608(b) may not address other character traits (ones unconnected to truthfulness or its opposite) or attack the witness' credibility on some basis other than character. Furthermore, the court has discretion whether to permit intrinsic proof at all, making a case-specific judgment that balances the act's probative value against other concerns. That is why the Rule declares that the relevant acts "may," . . . be inquired into on cross-examination if probative of character for truthfulness or untruthfulness.

Example 2

Now assume that witness Deck's alleged perjury at his divorce trial took place 10 years ago (Deck is an older student, returning to college). A trial judge might consider the event so remote as to have little probative value regarding Deck's current character for truthfulness. The judge might, therefore, exercise discretion to bar the prosecutor from questioning Deck about the perjury.

Example 3

Now the prosecutor asks Deck whether he assaulted his girlfriend two days ago. The defense objection will be sustained, as the answer would not concern Deck's character for truthfulness or untruthfulness.

It is important to emphasize again that the bar on extrinsic evidence of a witness' character for truthfulness or untruthfulness also applies only when the "*sole reason* for proffering that [extrinsic] evidence is to attack or support the witness's character for truthfulness." Accordingly, Rule 608(b) does not automatically bar extrinsic evidence about specific acts concerning a witness' character for truthfulness or untruthfulness if those acts are also relevant to impeaching by showing bias, limited competence, contradiction, prior inconsistent statements, or mental incapacity. The use of these other impeachment techniques is governed primarily by Rules 401, 402, and 403, though Rule 613 and analogy to the common law "collateral matter rule" (discussed in this text's chapter on impeachment techniques) may also be relevant. Confusion about this point — whether 608(b) barred extrinsic evidence of specific acts offered for dual purposes — was so great under an earlier version of the Rule that Congress amended the rule.

Example 4

Deck, having just testified that he saw many of the relevant events and that the victim was the sexual aggressor, is now asked on cross-examination by the prosecutor, "Didn't you run downstairs at the time this happened and tell your friend John, 'Oh, my God, the defendant is upstairs raping Ginnie!' " Deck responded, "I never said any such thing." The prosecutor next asked, "Didn't you tell the police, when they interviewed you about these events the day after the party, 'Ginnie wanted it. She was the aggressor?' " To this Deck replied, "Yes." "And," continued the prosecutor, "didn't you change the true story — the one you told John — to the lie that you told to the police because the defendant threatened to hurt you badly if you ever told the police what really happened?" Again Deck responded, "No. Of course not."

The prosecutor seeks to call Deck's friend John in rebuttal to testify to two things: first, Deck did indeed frantically tell John at the party that the defendant was upstairs raping Ginnie; second, John was present when, shortly before Deck was to be interviewed by the police, the defendant (unaware that John was close enough to hear this conversation) threatened to hurt Deck if Deck told the police the truth. The trial judge permits John to so testify, over defense objection.

John will be testifying to extrinsic evidence of a specific act of Deck's lying (telling a false story to the police) that arguably suggests Deck has an untruthful character. But that evidence, when put in the context of Deck's very different story told to John, also suggests that Deck had a strong motive to lie today on the stand.

Furthermore, John's testimony impeaches Deck with a prior inconsistent statement (Deck's expressed fear to John that Ginnie was being raped is inconsistent with his claim on the stand that "she wanted it") and by contradiction (directly opposing Deck's denial that he had been threatened by the defendant). These are both matters of independent relevance in, and important to, the resolution of the case.

Additionally, as you will see in later chapters, Deck's statement to John that Ginnie was being raped might be admissible as substantive evidence — for the truth of what it asserts — under the excited utterance exception to the rule barring admission of hearsay. The trial judge's ruling was thus likely well within his discretion because the proffered "extrinsic evidence" had multiple purposes beyond proving the witness' character as an untruthful man.

On a different point, the Advisory Committee further declares: "It should be noted that the extrinsic evidence prohibition of Rule 608(b) bars any reference to the consequences that a witness might have suffered as a result of an alleged bad act." The Advisory Committee explained the point thus:

> For example, Rule 608(b) prohibits counsel from mentioning that a witness was suspended or disciplined for the conduct that is the subject of impeachment, when that conduct is offered only to prove the character of the witness. *See United States v. Davis*, 183 F. 3d 231, 257 n. 12 (3d Cir. 1999) (emphasizing that in attacking the defendant's character for truthfulness "the government cannot make reference to Davis's forty-four day suspension or that Internal Affairs found that he lied about" an incident because "[s]uch evidence would not only be hearsay to the extent that it contains assertion of fact, it would be inadmissible extrinsic evidence under Rule (608(b))." *See also* Stephen A. Saltzburg, *Impeaching the Witness: Prior Bad Acts and Extrinsic Evidence*, 7 Crim. Just. 28, 31 (Winter 1993) ("counsel should not be permitted to circumvent the no-extrinsic-evidence provision by tucking a third person's opinion about prior acts into a question asked of the witness who has denied the act.").

So far, we've discussed the application of Rule 608(b) when challenging the credibility of the testifying witness. It also applies to "another witness whose character the witness being cross-examined has testified about." In other words, on cross-examining a witness who has testified about the character of another witness, the witness being cross-examined may be questioned about acts relating to that other witness' character for truthfulness or untruthfulness.

Example 5

Now assume that Deck and the defendant both testified at the rape trial. The defendant claimed that the alleged victim consented. In rebuttal, the prosecution called Norman, a well-qualified witness who testified that the defendant has a reputation in his neighborhood as a liar. Deck testified in response for the defendant that, in his opinion, the defendant has the character of a very truthful man. The prosecutor cross-examines Deck as follows: "Weren't you present when the defendant purchased liquor from The Brewery Pub using a false identification card, incorrectly representing his age as 21 at a time when he was in fact only 16 and thus well below the legal age for drinking?"

This question fits within the scope of Rule 608(b). Deck has just testified that another witness (the defendant) has a truthful character. It is therefore within the trial judge's discretion to permit a question to challenge Deck's claim about the other witness by suggesting (via specific acts) that the other witness in fact has an untruthful nature.

Note an important difference between this rule and Rule 405(a), last sentence. Both rules concern impeachment only where a character witness has first testified to *another person's* character on those traits. Rule 405(a), last sentence, however, concerns *any* relevant character trait. Furthermore, the person about whose character the character witness vouches need not have been a witness for Rule 405(a), last sentence, to apply. By contrast, Rule 608(b) governs only where a character witness has first testified to another *witness's* character. Additionally, Rule 608(b) is limited to authorizing questioning about *only one relevant character trait:* a character for truthfulness or untruthfulness. But both rules are similar in one important way: they both permit proof of prior acts only by *intrinsic*, not extrinsic, evidence.

Example 6

Now assume that Deck has testified at the rape trial but the defendant has not. Assume further that Deck's testimony on direct was that the defendant had a reputation for peacefulness, and the trial court admits this testimony as relevant to proving that a peaceful man was less likely than most men to commit rape, an act of violence. On cross-examination, the prosecutor asks, "Had you heard that just one week before this rape, the defendant beat his next-door neighbor, Johnny Crenshaw, to a pulp, hospitalizing Crenshaw?" This question is not objectionable under the character evidence rules because it fits within the terms of Rule 405(a), last sentence: "On cross-examination, inquiry is allowable into relevant specific instances of conduct." Here, unlike example 5, Rule 608(b) does not govern for two reasons: first, character witness Deck has testified about a character trait other than truthfulness or untruthfulness (and Rule 608 applies only to those truth-related character traits); second, the defendant (for whose character Deck vouches) has not been a witness at the trial. Like Rule 608(b), however, Rule 405(a) prohibits *extrinsic impeachment* because inquiry is allowable *only* on cross-examination. Thus, if Deck denies hearing about the defendant's beating of Crenshaw, no other witness may be called to contradict Deck's testimony.

Problem 5-47: Johnny Larsen's Return

In Problem 5-44, involving Johnny Larsen, would evidence items 1, 2, 3, 4, and 5 be admissible under Rule 608(b)? Assume for purposes of the current problem that there is evidence that Joanna committed the larceny mentioned in item 3, but she has not in fact ever been arrested, much less convicted, of that charge.

Problem 5-48: The Harassing Politician

William Fenton has been charged with sexual harassment. Fenton is a well-known political figure. Fenton's accuser, Paula Lorbin Cones, was employed by Fenton when he was governor of a small southern state. Cones alleges that Fenton repeatedly exposed himself to her and asked her to perform oral sex on him if she wanted to keep her job. She repeatedly refused and was subsequently fired. The case proceeds to trial. Fenton testifies that none of the alleged acts happened and that he fired Fenton because she was not doing a good job. *Answer the following questions:*

1. On cross-examination, plaintiff's counsel asks Fenton: "Didn't you expose yourself repeatedly to another employee, Lilly Lantree, every day for six weeks before you turned your attentions to Ms. Cones?" Should the defense's objection to this question be sustained under Rule 608(b) (ignore other admissibility theories for the purposes of this question)? Why or why not?

2. Fenton is next asked on cross-examination by plaintiff's counsel: "Isn't it true that, while governor, you stole $200,000 in state money to line your own pockets, cooking the books to get away with it?" Should the defense's objection to this question be sustained or overruled under Rule 608(b)? Why or why not?

3. Assume that question 2 above is permitted and Fenton's answer is "No, I did not steal any money." Can the plaintiff now call to the stand on rebuttal Fenton's accountant while Fenton was governor, who allegedly was an eyewitness who saw Fenton taking the funds? Should the defense's objection to this witness' testifying be sustained? Why or why not?

4. Fenton is next asked on cross-examination: "You had a consensual sexual affair with a Veronica Mawinsky for two years, ending just last month, and you repeatedly lied about that affair to your wife and to the press, didn't you?" Should the defense's objection to this question be sustained? Why or why not?

5. If the trial judge permits question 4 and Fenton answers, "I neither lied to the press nor to my wife because I never had an affair with Ms. Mawinsky," can the plaintiff call Ms. Mawinsky to the stand on rebuttal to testify that she indeed did have a long-standing sexual affair with Mr. Fenton? Why or why not?

6. Fenton is now asked on cross-examination whether he beat his wife on five specifically identified (by time, place, and context) recent occasions. Should the defense objection to this question be sustained? Why or why not?

7. Mack O'Hanrahan, Fenton's lifelong friend, takes the stand after Fenton steps down and testifies that, in his opinion, Fenton never lies. If O'Hanrahan is asked on cross-examination any of the questions originally posed to Fenton in questions 1–6, will that testimony be admissible? Why or why not? Would the phrasing of the questions need to be different in any way? In answering this question, consider what differences and similarities exist between Rule 608(b) and the last sentence of Rule 405(a). Is there any overlap in the application of these two rules? In their logic?

[C] Rule 609-Impeachment by Prior Convictions

Rule 609 divides criminal convictions that can be used to impeach a witness into two categories: (a) crimes involving dishonesty or false statement, regardless of whether they are felonies, misdemeanors, or summary offenses; and (b) felonies (crimes punishable by death or imprisonment over one year), regardless of whether they did or did not involve false statement. The latter sort of convictions are addressed below first. Although a record of conviction is a form of hearsay, it falls under an exception to the hearsay rule found in Rule 803(22).

[1] Felony Convictions: Rule 609(a)(1)

Rule 609(a)(1) reads as follows:

Rule 609. Impeachment by Evidence of a Criminal Conviction

> **(a) In General.** The following rules apply to attacking a witness's character for truthfulness by evidence of a criminal conviction: **(1)** for a crime that, in the convicting jurisdiction, was punishable by death or by imprisonment for more than one year, the evidence:
>
> **(A)** must be admitted, subject to Rule 403, in a civil case or in a criminal case in which the witness is not a defendant; and
>
> **(B)** must be admitted in a criminal case in which the witness is a defendant, if the probative value of the evidence outweighs its prejudicial effect to that defendant.

We use the term "felony" as a shorthand for crimes "punishable by death or by imprisonment for more than one year," though a particular criminal code might not necessarily classify such a crime as a felony. Some jurists long considered any such crimes as probative of credibility. The theory was that anyone who would maim, kill, or steal large amounts will worry little about lying under oath. Other jurists considered only crimes involving falsehood to be probative of credibility. Rule 609(a)(1) takes a compromise position: some felonies are significantly probative of falsehood, some are not. The admissibility determination is a case-specific judgment requiring the trial judge to balance unfair prejudice against probative value.

Rule 609(a)(1) sets up two different balancing tests, depending on the nature of the witness being impeached: one test for a witness who is a criminal accused, another test for all other witnesses. For most witnesses, Rule 609(a)(1)(A) applies the usual Rule 403 balancing test. Rule 403 admits relevant evidence unless the "probative value of the evidence outweighs" its unfairly prejudicial impact or other countervailing concerns. For a witness who is also a criminal accused, the court may admit the evidence under Rule 609(a)(1)(B) only if it determines that the "probative value of the evidence outweighs its prejudicial effect to that defendant." This latter test places the burden of admitting the evidence on the proponent, and is thus more protective of the accused than the test of Rule 403, which places the burden of excluding the evidence on the opponent. In other words, Rule 403 favors admissibility while the special Rule 609(a)(1)(B) test for the criminal accused favors exclusion.

Neither Rule 609 nor its commentary explains what should guide a court's discretion in applying the special balancing test for a criminal accused. However, the following factors have been identified by commentators as helpful in gauging the degree of prejudice to the criminal accused:[3]

1. *The degree to which the crime reflects on credibility. For example, a sex crime may not reflect on credibility as much as a robbery conviction.*

2. The nearness or remoteness of the prior conviction. A person who has led a blameless life for years after a conviction is entitled to more consideration than one who was recently convicted. . . .

3. The similarity of the prior offense to the offense charged. This is a factor that weighs against admissibility when the only theory of admission is impeachment of the accused as a witness. The reason is that the jury may use the evidence not for its bearing upon the credibility of the witness, but for the inference that "because she did it before she probably did it again" — or, even worse, decide to re-punish the accused for the prior crime whether or not the current one was committed. Thus, a stronger case can be made for receiving a prior auto theft conviction in a bank robbery case than in an auto theft case. Of course, if the two auto thefts were so similar that the first one was admissible under Rule 404(b) to show plan, intent, modus operandi, or the like, then the evidence should not be excluded on this ground. But when the only basis for receiving it is to impeach credibility, similarity between the two crimes is a factor disfavoring admission.

4. The extent to which defendant's testimony is needed for fair adjudication of the trial. If defendant's testimony is crucial for his defense, this fact weighs against the admissibility of the prior convictions, because if the evidence will be admissible, it is less likely that the defendant will testify.

5. Whether the defendant's credibility is central to the case. Some courts will consider whether the witness' credibility can be explored adequately without using evidence of the witness' prior conviction. If the witness can be

---

[3] Roger C. Park et al., Evidence Law: A Student's Guide to the Law of Evidence as Applied in American Trials § 9.09, at 455 (1998).

impeached convincingly using other means (e.g., bias, prior inconsistent statement) the existence of such alternative impeachment methods is a factor weighing against allowing use of the prior conviction.

Example 1

Tony Leduca is charged with simple assault. Leduca takes the stand and claims self-defense. The prosecutor seeks to impeach Leduca with evidence that he was convicted nine years ago of felony assault, a crime punishable by up to 20 years in prison, for an incident that occurred on his eighteenth birthday. That offense involved Leduca smashing his girlfriend's suspected lover on the head with a metal pipe, an act of jealous revenge. The current simple assault charge arises out of Leduca's punching a co-worker who insulted Leduca based on Leduca's ethnicity. There were no eyewitnesses to the current simple assault case: it is Leduca's word against his co-worker's. However, Leduca's brother is a reluctant witness to whom, says the prosecution, Leduca admitted starting the fight in the current case with very little provocation for doing so. A trial court would be well within its discretion to exclude the prior conviction because assault, a crime entirely of violence, reflects little on credibility; the conviction is stale; the two offenses are quite similar; the defendant's testimony is essential to his defense given the lack of eyewitnesses; the defendant's credibility is central to the case; and there are other adequate means for challenging that credibility, namely the testimony of Leduca's brother.

Note Concerning Grounds for Appeal: In *Luce v. United States*, the United States Supreme Court held that a trial court's *in limine* (generally meaning before trial) ruling to permit impeachment of the accused with a prior felony conviction under what is now Rule 609(a)(1)(B) is preserved for review only if the accused testifies at his trial. If he chooses not to testify for fear of being cross-examined about his prior felony conviction, he thus loses his right to object to the 609(a)(1)(B) admissibility ruling on appeal. The Court reasoned that an appellate court would otherwise have to speculate whether the impeachment in fact would have happened since *in limine* rulings are subject to change during trial and the prosecution might have tactical reasons for ultimately foregoing that type of impeachment. Additionally, it is speculative to assume that the sole reason a defendant did not testify was because of an adverse 609(a)(1)(B) ruling. Furthermore, the details of the defendant's testimony are necessary for a reviewing court to judge the weighing of prejudice against probative value that Rule 609(a)(1)(B) requires. *See also Ohler v. United States*, 529 U.S. 753 (2000) (reaffirming the Court's willingness to follow and extend *Luce*).

Example 2

Assume in *Example 1* above that the trial court ruled *in limine* that Leduca's assault conviction would be admissible to impeach him if he testified at trial. Leduca is convicted in the current case and, on appeal, seeks to claim that he chose not to testify because of this incorrect Rule 609(a)(1)(B) ruling. As *Example 1* explained, Leduca had a good argument for excluding this impeachment evidence. Nevertheless, because he chose not to testify at trial, he has waived his right to complain on appeal about the 609(a)(1)(B) decision, as the *Luce* rule requires. It must be stressed that Rule 609 does not apply at all if a conviction is offered to impeach a witness (challenge his credibility) on grounds other than that the conviction suggests that the witness has a poor character for truthfulness. Indeed, the phrase "character for truthfulness" was inserted by a 2006 amendment to replace the word "credibility" to emphasize Rule 609's limited scope. As the 2006 Advisory Committee Note put it:

> The amendment also substitutes the term "character for truthfulness" for the term "credibility" in the first sentence of the Rule. The limitations of Rule 609 are not applicable if a conviction is admitted for a purpose other than to prove the witness's character for untruthfulness. *See, e.g., United States v. Lopez*, 979 F.2d 1024 (5th Cir. 1992) (Rule 609 was not applicable where the conviction was offered for purposes of contradiction). The use of the term "credibility" in subsection (d) is retained, however, as that subdivision is intended to govern the use of a juvenile adjudication for any type of impeachment.

[2] Misdemeanor and *Crimen Falsi* Convictions: Rule 609(a)(2)

Under Rule 609(a)(2), evidence that a witness has been convicted of a crime involving a dishonest act or false statement "must be admitted." The trial judge has no discretion to weigh prejudice against probative value. Nevertheless, exclusion is still possible if one of the limitations stated in Rule 609(b), (c), or (d) applies. These limitations are addressed below, under the heading "Special Qualifications to Rule 609."

Crimes of dishonesty or false statement (i.e., "*crimen falsi*") are probably admissible under Rule 609(a)(2) whether they are felonies or misdemeanors. (*Caution:* A misdemeanor — here meaning a crime punishable by one year or less imprisonment — that is not *crimen falsi* is not admissible under Rule 609 at all because it is neither a 609(a)(1) felony nor a 609(a)(2) crime of "dishonest act[s] or false statement.") The difficult question in applying Rule 609(a)(2) is determining what constitutes a crime of dishonesty or false statement. The Advisory Committee Note to the 1990 amendments to Rule 609 listed some offenses clearly meeting the test:

> Congress extensively debated the rule, and the Report of the House and Senate Conference Committee states that '[b]y the phrase dishonesty and false statement, the Conference means crimes such as perjury, false statement, criminal fraud, embezzlement, or false pretense, or any other offense in the nature of *crimen falsi*, commission of which involves some element of deceit, untruthfulness, or falsification bearing on the accused's propensity to testify truthfully.'

The 1990 Advisory Committee went on, however, to disapprove of "some decisions that take an unduly broad view of 'dishonesty,' admitting convictions such as bank robbery or bank larceny." The comment suggests an intention to exclude stealing as a crime of dishonesty. Some courts have complied with this apparent intention of the Advisory Committee to exclude theft crimes from the *crimen falsi* category. But other courts have considered theft crimes, such as armed robbery, to fit within the common-sense understanding of "dishonesty." Still other courts look beyond the definition of the elements of the crime to the particular facts of the witness's offense, in a search for deceit. However, this approach has been criticized by some commentators as raising collateral issues and wasting time, and, as is discussed below, the Advisory Committee consequently later saw fit to weigh in further on this debate.[4]

Example

A plaintiff had earlier been convicted of the misdemeanor offense of tampering with electric meters, a kind of theft of electricity. Some courts, following the Advisory Committee's lead, would not consider meter-tampering to be a *crimen falsi* crime, thus barring use of the conviction for impeachment. Others would consider the offense one of "dishonesty" and allow its use for impeachment. Still other courts would inquire whether the method used to steal the electricity in the particular case involved deceit, and would admit the conviction for impeachment only if the method involved dishonesty or false statement.

This example illustrates the difficulty courts have had in deciding whether a crime is *crimen falsi*, especially when the crime's elements might not on their face suggest that the crime is always of that nature but, in the particular case, acts of dishonesty or false statement may have been involved in the course of committing the crime. In part to clarify this confusion, Rule 609(a)(2) was amended in 2006 to declare that "evidence that any witness has been convicted of a crime shall be admitted regardless of the punishment," but only "if it readily can be determined that establishing the elements of the crime required proof or admission of an act of dishonesty or false statement by the witness." Note the presence of the word "required" to emphasize that the acts of dishonesty had to be *necessary* to proving the crime's elements, even if the statutory elements on their face did not expressly refer to deceit. Here is how the Advisory Committee explained this necessity requirement:

> The amendment provides that Rule 609(a)(2) mandates the admission of evidence of a conviction only when the conviction required proof of (or in the case of a guilty plea, the admission of) an act of dishonesty or false statement. Evidence of all other convictions is inadmissible under this section, irrespective of whether the witness exhibited dishonesty or made a false statement in the process of the commission of the crime of conviction. Thus, evidence that a witness was convicted of a crime of violence, such as murder, is not admissible under Rule 609(a)(2), even if the witness acted deceitfully in the course of committing the crime.

The Advisory Committee went on in its note concerning the 2006 amendment to emphasize how truly narrow its definition of "dishonesty or false statement" was:

---

[4] *See* Roger C. Park et al., Evidence Law: A Student's Guide to the Law of Evidence as Applied in American Trials § 9.09, at 455 (1998).

This amendment is meant to give effect to the legislative intent to limit the convictions that are to be automatically admitted under subsection (a)(2). The Conference Committee provided that by 'dishonesty or false statement' it meant 'crimes such as perjury, subornation of perjury, false statement, criminal fraud, embezzlement, or false pretense, or any other offense in the nature of *crimen falsi*, the commission of which involves some element of deceit, untruthfulness, or falsification bearing on the [witness's] propensity to testify truthfully." Historically, offenses classified as *crimen falsi* have included *only those crimes in which the ultimate criminal act was itself an act of deceit* (emphasis added).

In another sense, however, this definition of crimes of "dishonesty or false statement" is not as narrow as it could have been because, as noted above, it still can include some crimes not expressly mentioning deceit in the defining statute. "For example, evidence that a witness was convicted of making a false claim to a federal agent is admissible under this subsection regardless of whether the crime was charged under a section that expressly references deceit (e.g., **18 U.S.C. sec. 1001**, Material Misrepresentation to the Federal Government) or a section that does not (e.g., **18 U.SC. sec. 1503**, Obstruction of Justice)." *See* 2006 Advisory Committee Note.

In arguing that a crime is *crimen falsi*, a party may thus go beyond the text of the statute, inquiring into its logic as to what proof it necessarily requires, and may go even further by arguing that, *in this specific case*, the ultimate criminal act was one of deceit. However, this does not entitle the proponent to a wide-ranging evidentiary issue on this question. The evidence offered must be relevant to the relatively narrow definition of "dishonesty or false statement." Perhaps more importantly, only a narrow range of evidence may be consulted by the trial court in answering the *crimen falsi* question, for Rule 609(a)(2)'s current 2011 version now expressly declares that convictions fall within its terms only if " the court can readily determine that establishing the elements of the crime required proving — or the witness's admitting — a dishonest act or false statement." What does it mean to say that these things can "readily be determine[d]"? The Advisory Committee Note to the 2006 amendment answered this question thus:

> The amendment requires that the proponent have ready proof that the conviction required the factfinder to find, or the defendant to admit, an act of dishonesty or false statement. Ordinarily, the statutory elements of the crime will indicate whether it is one of dishonesty or false statement. Where the deceitful nature of the statute is not apparent from the statute and the face of the judgment — as, for example, where the conviction simply records a finding of guilt for a statutory offense that does not reference deceit expressly — a proponent may offer information such as an indictment, a statement of admitted facts, or jury instructions to show that the factfinder had to find, or the defendant had to admit, an act of dishonesty or false statement in order for the witness to have been convicted . . . . But the amendment does not contemplate a 'mini-trial' in which the court plumbs the record of the previous proceeding to determine whether the crime was in the nature of *crimen falsi*.

[3] Special Qualifications to Rule 609

Under Rule 609(b), evidence of a conviction that is more than 10 years old is not admissible[5] unless the court determines, in the interests of justice, that "its probative value, supported by specific facts and circumstances, substantially outweighs its prejudicial effect" and that the proponent has given the adverse party sufficient advance written notice of the intent to use such evidence to give the adverse party a fair opportunity to contest admissibility. The time period is computed from the date of the conviction or the date of release from confinement imposed for that conviction, whichever is later. Unlike the test under Rule 403, the balancing test here strongly favors exclusion, since the burden is placed on the proponent to show by "specific facts and circumstances" that, despite the age of the conviction, its probative value substantially outweighs the risk of prejudice.

Crimes that have been pardoned and juvenile adjudications are also usually inadmissible. However, impeachment by a pardoned conviction will be permitted if the pardon was not based on a finding of innocence and the offender was convicted of a subsequent felony. Additionally, juvenile adjudications may be used to impeach witnesses other than the accused if the trial court finds impeachment necessary for a fair determination of guilt or innocence.

The pendency of an appeal does not render evidence of a conviction inadmissible, but evidence of the pendency of the appeal is admissible.

Example

Paulo Victor has testified at his embezzlement trial, denying any wrongdoing. The prosecutor seeks to impeach Paulo with a conviction for felony robbery, which is punishable by up to 20 years in prison. Paulo was convicted 12 years ago and served five years in prison, being released upon a pardon based on a finding that he had been rehabilitated. Unfortunately, Paulo was arrested one year later for committing a felony assault, of which he was also convicted but for which he served only two years. The prosecutor also seeks to impeach Paulo with a juvenile rape adjudication received 20 years ago, for which Paulo served two years in confinement at a juvenile home. The special qualifications in Rule 609(b), (c), and (d) will not bar impeaching Paulo with the adult robbery conviction. Because he was released from prison seven years ago, the conviction is not more than 10 years old in the terms of Rule 609(b), although the date of conviction was 12 years ago. While he was ultimately pardoned of that crime, that pardon was not based on a finding of innocence. Thus, the fact that he was convicted of a subsequent crime punishable by more than one year in prison means that Rule 609(c) does not bar the impeachment. However, Rule 609(d) prevents the prosecutor from impeaching Paulo with the juvenile adjudication, because he is the criminal accused. Even were this not true, the prosecution would have a heavy burden to show great probative value under Rule 609(b), because the adjudication was well over 10 years old.

---

[5] Rule 609(c), (d).

[4] Extrinsic Evidence

Rule 608(b) bars the use of extrinsic evidence to impeach a witness by proof of specific acts concerning the witness' character for truthfulness or untruthfulness that did not result in a conviction (*see* [B] [2], above). Under Rule 609, on the other hand, impeachment by a prior conviction may be done by intrinsic or extrinsic evidence. Thus, the cross-examiner need not accept a witness's denial that he or she was previously convicted of the impeaching crime. The conviction may be proven by a public record.

[5] Eliciting Details of Prior Convictions

How much detail about a prior conviction may be elicited before the jury? There is no single approach followed by all courts. Under one view, the impeacher may ask only about the existence and name of the crime and when the conviction occurred. Under another view, the impeacher may also inquire about the length of the punishment imposed. It is also commonly held that details of the crime itself may be elicited if the witness impeached tried to explain the conviction away, for example, by claiming that he pled guilty to protect a loved one or that he was drunk at the time of the crime. Before all judges, however, an impeacher may seek to inquire into details by finding a substantive character theory to rely on instead of an impeachment theory, a substantive theory requiring further detail.

Example

At Harding's trial for felony cocaine distribution, the prosecutor seeks to impeach Harding's testimony with evidence of Harding's felony conviction for possession of marijuana with intent to sell. Although the trial court permits impeachment by noting the name, existence, and date of the marijuana conviction, and even by further noting the punishment imposed, he excludes further details. Specifically, the prosecutor had sought to show that the earlier crime involved 80 pounds of marijuana found in the defendant's home and that the marijuana was actually in the defendant's home at the time of his arrest on the cocaine charge. The trial court thought that these details unduly stressed the similarity between the two crimes, with the risk that the marijuana offense would become evidence of substantive guilt rather than of a lack of credibility. If, however, the current charge was selling cocaine laced with marijuana, evidence of the details of prior offenses of possessing, with the intent to sell, large quantities of marijuana at the same location (the defendant's home) where the cocaine was found might, depending on further details, be admissible on the Rule 404(b) substantive theory of a common plan, scheme, or design.

Problem 5-49: The Matasow Corporation

Ronald Matasow's corporation, in which he is the sole shareholder, has been civilly sued for sexual harassment. The basis for the suit by his ex-secretary, Mary Beckett, is her allegation that Matasow repeatedly fondled Ms. Beckett's breasts against her will, despite her protests. She finally quit, she says, because she could no longer handle his advances. Matasow testifies at the trial that he never fondled Ms. Beckett and that she resigned because she knew that she would otherwise soon be fired for incompetence. Matasow is cross-examined by Beckett's counsel. *In connection with that cross-examination, consider the following:*

1. Matasow is asked whether he was convicted nine years ago of a felony rape of his then-secretary, Mary Baldwin. Should defense counsel's objection be sustained? Why or why not? Would deleting any details — and, if so, which — from the question improve the chances of the objection's being overruled? Why or why not?

2. If the objection in question 1 is overruled but Matasow denies the conviction, what options, if any, does Beckett's counsel have for proving that Matasow was in fact convicted? What documents, if any, would be required, and what witnesses, if any, should be called to the stand and when? What questions would you ask the witness or witnesses? What details should you elicit?

3. Would your answer to question 1 change if the rape conviction happened 11 years ago and resulted in probation? If it happened 11 years ago, resulting in a prison sentence of five years? If Matasow only served three years when he was pardoned based upon a finding of his innocence of the crime? If the rape conviction is still tied up in the courts, going through a ponderous process of appeals?

4. Would your answer to question 1 change if, instead of a civil harassment trial, the trial were a criminal misdemeanor sexual assault trial naming Matasow as the defendant? A criminal rape trial against Matasow?

5. Suppose at the civil harassment trial Matasow is now asked, "Weren't you recently convicted of a bank robbery that occurred two years ago?" Should the defense objection be sustained? Why or why not? Would your answer change if this question is asked of Matasow at his criminal misdemeanor sexual assault trial? His criminal felony rape trial? Why or why not? Could you elicit any of the following details, whether at one of the criminal trials or at the civil harassment trial:

   a. Matasow wore a convincing disguise at the time of the bank robbery, gaining entrance to the bank after banking hours by presenting a phony identification card naming him as the newly hired manager of the bank to replace the acting manager?

   b. Matasow was sentenced to 10 years imprisonment for the bank robbery?

6. Would your answers to question 5 change if the bank robbery conviction involved a 15-year-old juvenile adjudication?

Problem 5-50: Johnny Winter's Lament

Johnny Winter has been charged with burglary. He testifies at the trial that he broke into the victim's home because he was cold and homeless, not because he planned to commit any crime inside. His story, if believed, will reduce his crime from burglary to criminal trespass. The prosecutor, over defense objection, elicits on cross-examination an admission by Winter that he had previously been convicted of a burglary. Unasked, Winter adds, "But I didn't do it. I pled guilty to save my mother the agony of attending my trial, rest her soul. She died recently." The prosecutor now seeks to ask questions about the details of the earlier burglary, designed to show that: (1) Winter was the mastermind, supervising a gang of thieves in pulling off a massive theft of goods from a furniture warehouse; and (2)

Winter's mother was in fact a member of the gang. *Should these details be admitted into evidence? Why or why not?*

Problem 5-51: At the Movies: Snitch Attack

In the film *Anatomy of a Murder*, Lt. Manion is charged with murdering Barney Quill. Manion admits that he killed Quill, but claims that he did so as a result of "irresistible impulse," a form of temporary insanity resulting from finding out that Quill had raped and beaten Manion's wife. Laura. Miller, incarcerated in the same cell as Manion, testifies on the prosecution's behalf that Manion told him during the trial that "I'm pulling the wool over the eyes of my lawyer and the jury, and will take care of Laura after I get out of here." On cross-examination, defense lawyer Paul Biegler elicits testimony that Miller had previously been convicted of three felonies: arson, assault with a deadly weapon, and larceny. Moreover, Miller had been arrested for indecent exposure, peeping into windows, perjury, and disorderly conduct. *What, if any, of this evidence would be admissible under Rules 608 and 609? Would it matter if the convictions were for misdemeanors rather than for felonies?*

Problem 5-52: Forging a Defense

a. George Parker is charged with homicide. Parker testifies that he acted in self-defense. The prosecutor seeks to impeach Parker by eliciting on cross-examination Parker's misdemeanor forgery conviction five years ago, for which he received probation. *Should the defense objection be sustained? Why or why not?*

b. Assume instead that Parker has a previous murder conviction. The circumstances of the murder were as follows. Parker was angry at his next-door neighbor's eight-year-old son for repeatedly knocking over Parker's garbage cans and ruining his flower bed. The son was diagnosed with cancer. Parker pretended to be an "herbal oncologist," giving the son herbs that, said Parker, were guaranteed to cure the cancer but only if the child stayed away from more traditional medical treatments. Parker insisted that he treated many children this way, with a 100% cure rate. The parents believed him, and the child died of the cancer, just the result that Parker intended. He was convicted of wilful, deliberate, and premeditated first-degree murder precisely five years before the start of his current homicide trial arising from an entirely different and recent incident.

At his current homicide trial, after Parker testified that he acted in self-defense, the prosecution first sought to impeach Parker with the earlier conviction of homicide in the eight-year-old's death under Rule 609(a)(1). The trial judge expressed an inclination, however, to sustain the defense objection on grounds of the probative value of the evidence not outweighing its unfairly prejudicial effect. The unfair prejudice arose, said the judge, from the danger that the jury, rather than using the conviction to assess Parker's character for truthfulness, would instead use it as substantive act propensity evidence, reasoning that if he murdered once before, then he must now have done so again. The prosecutor then makes the back-up argument that the murder conviction, on these facts, involved "dishonesty or false statement" so that it "shall" be admitted without any balancing of probative value against unfair prejudice. *Will the prosecutor succeed on this argument? What evidence, if any, may he rely upon to support his admissibility argument? In concrete terms, what must that evidence specifically show in this case if he is to prevail, or will he lose no matter what the evidence shows?*

§ 5.09 MID-CHAPTER REVIEW

[A] Schematic

Below are two schemes for analyzing character evidence problems — one a short version of "Five Simple Rules," one a longer version. These schemes should help you to review and organize the material studied thus far.

FIVE SIMPLE RULES FOR UNDERSTANDING CHARACTER EVIDENCE

All that we have studied so far on character evidence can be simplified into five broad, generally true rules, subject to the various details and qualifications that we have studied or will study shortly:

1. If evidence concerns "character" and is offered to prove act propensity, then the evidence is presumptively inadmissible (Rule 404(a)(1)).

2. But the evidence can nevertheless be rendered admissible if it fits within a 404(a) (2), or (3) exceptions or into the exceptions embodied in Rules 413–415. (Remember that 404(a)(3) directs you to Rules 608 and 609.)

3. If evidence is not "character," or if it is "character" but is offered for a purpose other than proving act propensity (*e.g*, to prove mental propensity or because character is itself an essential element of a crime, claim, or defense), then the evidence is not barred by the character evidence rules in the first place and is therefore admissible in any form (reputation, opinion, or prior acts) so long as it is not barred by some rule other than the character rules (*e.g.*, Rule 403).

4. If character evidence is admissible for any reason (either because it fits an exception to the act propensity rule or because it is offered for a purpose other than act propensity), then it may generally be proven by reputation or opinion; it can also be proved by prior acts *if* the evidence is offered for a non-act-propensity purpose or is not character at all. (Rules 404(b)(2); 405(a),(b)).

5. If the rape shield law applies, then a whole special set of rules governs (*see* Rule 412).

Below is a more detailed review of what we have studied so far in the form of a series of questions to guide you through any character evidence problem. These questions and corresponding comments are really just an elaboration of the "Five Simple Rules for Understanding Character Evidence" presented above.

SCHEME FOR ANALYZING CHARACTER EVIDENCE PROBLEMS:

THE LONG VERSION (WARNING: READ EACH RULE CITED BELOW CAREFULLY AS YOU SEE THE RULE CITED.)

Ask yourself the following questions:

1. Does the evidence being offered consist of someone's reputation, or an opinion about that person, or prior acts committed by that person?

2. If "yes," what is the evidence being offered to prove, that is, what is its relevance as will likely be claimed by the proponent (the person who wants the evidence admitted)? If the answer to this question is, "to prove a person's character or a trait of character," then the evidence is character evidence.

Caution:

A character trait is a general tendency to think or act a certain way in a certain set of situations, for example, being a "tardy" person means being someone who is late for business and social engagements more often than is true of most people, or at least more often than someone who is never or very rarely late. Yet, frequently, courts accept a single act as evidence of character when one bad act may instead arguably simply be an aberration. Thus, a single prior act of a defendant's killing, then mutilating, someone is thought to be so extreme as to suggest that the defendant is a violent man, that is, that he has a violent character. That may seem unobjectionable, but what about one prior act of lying to prove that you are a liar, especially if it was a little lie, such as lying to your spouse about how much you paid for a recent purchase? Logically, a single, minor lie would not seem to suggest that your character is that of a liar, someone who lies more than most people likely do, or at least more than someone who never lies. And you might raise a 403 objection on those grounds.

> Nevertheless, because a character trait's "relevance" is such a low standard, judges often accept the idea that even proving one act of lying makes it some tiny amount more likely than without that proof that you are the sort of person who lies: a liar. Even if you are not a liar in the sense of lying more often than most people (what most people do is called the "base rate"), one act of lying at least suggests that you are not always honest and, therefore, may be more subject to lying than someone who has never lied in his life. That courts may permit a single act to be used as relevant to proving "character" — a general tendency — counters common sense and makes it hard to see an act as being "character" evidence, and thus sometimes confuses students, but that is nevertheless how the courts approach the matter.

3. If the evidence is character evidence, is the evidence relevant because we only need to prove character itself and are not arguing for drawing any inferences from that person's character? In other words, is the evidence offered to prove character because character is an essential element of a crime, claim, or defense? (An essential element is one that

must be proven in a particular case in order for the party to prevail.) Here are examples of two common instances in which character is an essential element:

a. *Character expressly stated to be an essential element of an offense:* Subjective entrapment as a defense in a criminal case has only three elements: (1) the government (ii) induced (iii) someone not predisposed to do so to commit the crime. Element (iii) is a trait of "character": the accused is the kind of person who would not ordinarily commit this kind of crime. Usually, entrapment is raised when a defendant admits both that he did the criminal act (perhaps smoking cocaine) and did it with the necessary mental state (he knew that it was cocaine) but should still be not guilty because, in a sense, the government "made him do it," that is, entrapped him. The character trait of not being predisposed to commit the crime is therefore not used to prove an act (act propensity) because the act is admitted and not to prove a mental state (because the mental state is admitted) but rather simply to prove the character trait itself and nothing more, for proving the trait itself proves an element of the defense of entrapment.

b. *Character Not Mentioned in the Statute But an Essential Element Under the Particular Facts:* Assume defamation has these elements: (i) a material (ii) misrepresentation (iii) of fact (iv) published to others (v) causing damage to the plaintiff. One primary defense is that the statement was true, not a "misrepresentation." But if the statement concerned a person's character, then showing the nonexistence of the element of "misrepresentation" can only be done by proving that the plaintiff in fact does have the character trait that the author of the published statement alleged. Nowhere does the defamation statute expressly mention character, but under this particular set of facts defamation can be disproved only by proving character; therefore, character is an "essential element" of a crime, claim, or defense.

If the evidence is relevant to prove character in and of itself, that is, as an "essential element" of a crime, claim, or defense, then the evidence is admissible, unless it violates some other evidence rule than the character rules (e.g., unfair prejudice under Rule 403).

4. If the answer to question 3 above is "no," that is, the character evidence is not relevant in itself — is not an essential element of a crime, claim, or defense — then is it offered to prove "mental propensity," that is, for example, to prove a party's mental state, the argument being that someone with a violent character is more likely to want to hurt another than to do so accidentally in an assault case, or that someone who is a thief is more likely to know that the property that he possesses is stolen in a trial for receiving stolen property, or that a drug addict is more likely to know that the powder in his possession is cocaine? If yes, that is, if it is mental propensity evidence, it is not barred by Rule 404(a)(1), which excludes "act propensity" character evidence. But Rule 402 says all relevant evidence must be admitted unless excluded by

another rule. Because Rule 404(a) bars act propensity only, Rule 402 renders relevant mental propensity evidence admissible, unless some other rule (such as 403) than the character evidence rules bars the evidence.

5. If the answer to question 4 is "no," that is, it is not mental propensity, then is it act propensity? If yes, it is presumptively inadmissible under 404(a)(1) unless an exception applies.

6. If the answer to question 5 is yes, that is, it is indeed act propensity evidence, what act is it relevant to and offered to prove: (i) an act that is an element of, or relevant to proving an element of, a crime, claim, or defense — an act committed outside the current courtroom at the current trial — thus being substantive character evidence — or is it instead (ii) the act of lying on the stand at the current trial? If the act is lying now on the stand, Rule 404(a)(3)'s exception applies because the character is relevant to the person's role as a witness, and Rule 404(a)(3) directs you to Rules 608 and 609. If instead the act concerns an element, then you must investigate Rule 404(a)(2) in a criminal case not involving sexual assault, Rules 413–414 in a criminal sexual assault case, and 415 in a civil sexual assault case. We won't repeat the details of the Rules 404 and 413 exceptions here.

7. If "character" evidence is admissible under any of the above situations (as an essential element, as mental propensity, or as an exception to the act propensity bar), that only means that *some form* of character evidence is admissible. But now you must ask, "What form?"

    a. If substantive act propensity evidence fitting into an exception to the usual act propensity bar: Rule 404(b)(1) prohibits proving act propensity by specific acts. Rule 405(a), however, permits doing so by reputation or opinion.

    b. If impeachment act propensity evidence, i.e., if you are attacking or supporting the character of a witness — someone currently testifying on the stand under oath or a hearsay declarant: all three forms are permitted but only if the character trait involved concerns character for truthfulness or untruthfulness and the other limitations stated in Rule 608 are met. Rule 608(a) permits reputation or opinion concerning character for truthfulness, and Rule 608(b) concerns prior acts relevant to character for truthfulness. One key question for debate is whether a particular act indeed concerns truthfulness or instead some other character trait. If the person committing the impeaching prior act was convicted, then Rule 609 controls, prior convictions of acts that are *crimen falsi* generally being admissible and other convictions, if felonies only (i.e., subject to imprisonment of more than one year) being admissible if they survive a balancing test (usually the Rule 403 balancing test, but sometimes instead a special test governing when impeaching the "accused.")

c. If mental propensity evidence: then all three forms may be permitted. This is so because Rule 404(a)(1) bars only act propensity, and Rule 404(b)(1), when read together with Rule 405(a), limits the forms of proving act propensity (when permitted by an exception) to reputation or opinion (unless the character involves a witness, in which case Rules 608 and 609 apply). But neither Rule 404 nor any other rule bars *mental propensity evidence*, and thus certainly does not bar any particular form of that evidence. Thus, all three forms may be acceptable. However, prior acts are thought to have the most probative value. Rule 404(b)(2) states that prior acts may be used for any relevant purpose other than act propensity as a way of underscoring that not all substantive act evidence is barred but rather only act evidence involving act propensity. Thus prior acts going to mental propensity are one sort of prior act not barred. Rule 404(b)(2) lists a number of examples, most (but not all) of which are mental propensity uses of prior acts.

8. How may the evidence be elicited, that is, may it only be elicited from the mouth of the witness on the stand ("intrinsic" evidence, one form of which is "cross-examination," the other form of which is "direct examination"), or, if the witness denies what the questioner suggests, can "extrinsic" contradicting evidence (evidence from a witness other than the one currently on the stand) be offered? The usual answer is that both ways to, or sources for, eliciting character evidence are generally acceptable because, again under Rule 402, if no specific rule bars one procedure and the witness's answers would be relevant, then the procedure is acceptable.

So far, we have studied only two character rules limiting which procedure may be used: (1) Rule 608(b), which permits questioning a witness ("intrinsic" evidence) about specific acts that show his character for truthfulness or its opposite but *prohibits* calling other witnesses if this witness denies the accusation ("extrinsic evidence") (an example: the witness on the stand denies having lied to his mom last week about whether he took out the garbage; the mom cannot be called to the stand to testify to the contrary, that he did indeed then lie to her); and (2) Rule 405(a), last sentence, which permits impeaching a character witness by showing that he knows little about the character of the person for whom he has vouched or attacked or has bad judgment about that other person's character by offering specific acts; these specific acts are not character evidence because they do not go to a party's or the witness's character but just show that the witness is mistaken in his judgment; this may only be done on cross, not on direct and not extrinsically (example: witness A says the defendant has a peaceful character and so is not the kind of person to commit the assault with which he is charged; the prosecutor can ask witness A on cross, "Didn't you know that the defendant beat his own mother to a bloody pulp last week?" If the witness says "no," then he doesn't know important things about the defendant's character; if the witness says "yes," he seems to have poor judgment in considering such a cruel person to be "peaceful.") (*Reminder:* Our impeachment chapter discussed two impeachment techniques that have nothing to do with character, but for which this "intrinsic"/"extrinsic" evidence distinction is also important, those two techniques being impeachment by prior inconsistent statements and impeachment by specific contradiction).

[B] Synthesizing the Rules Studied Thus Far: The Diagrammatic Approach

For those of you who are more visually oriented, below are two diagrammatic versions of the schemes set forth above. Again, one diagram is a short one, giving you the lay of the land, while the other fills in the details.

[1] Categorizing Character

CATEGORIZING CHARACTER

Applying the character evidence rules correctly requires identifying the category of evidence before you. Once you locate the correct category, the rules guide you along a particular path necessary to making the admissibility decision. The approach is much like having a series of labeled boxes or folders, and you must sort the evidence in question into the correct box. Here is a first cut at a simple way to conceive of the set of character-evidence-related boxes.

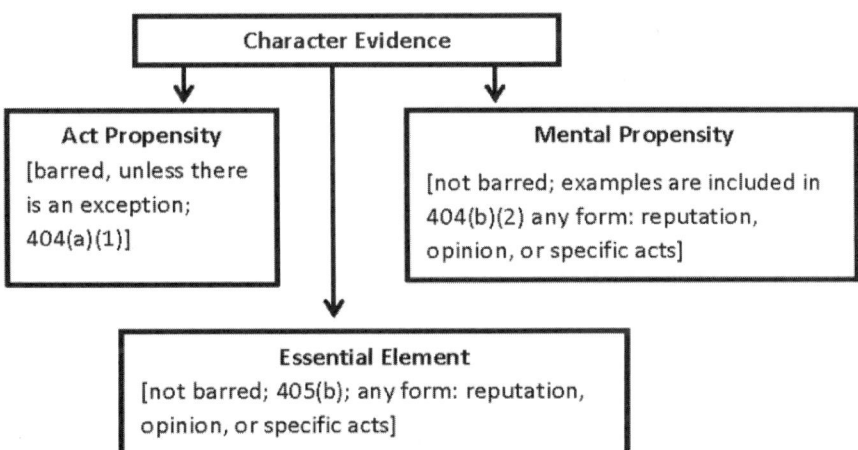

Here is a cut at a more complex version that incorporates the exceptions:

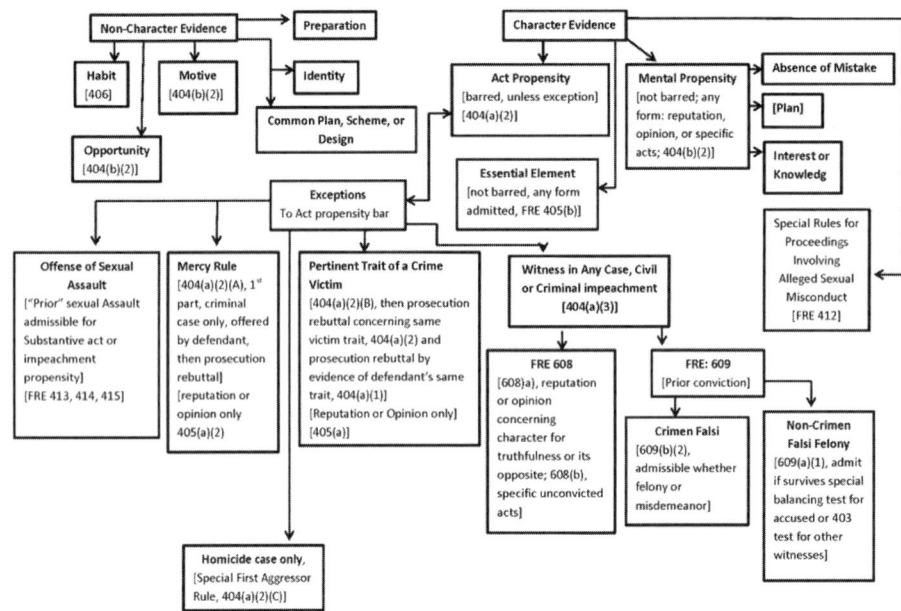

[2] Mini-Review Problems

In doing the problems below, first determine whether character evidence is admissible at all, then, if it is, in what form.

Problem 5-53: O.J. Mimpson Defamed

O.J. Mimpson, a well-known actor and former football star, has civilly sued Fred Moldman for defamation that occurred earlier this year. Moldman has said in newspaper interviews that "Mimpson is a wife-beater, and he finally killed his ex-wife and my son too, because he got in the way." The story concerned the stabbing-murder of Mimpson's ex-wife, Mikel Mimpson, and her friend, Bob Moldman, by a thus far unidentified assailant just four months ago. Mimpson is also being criminally prosecuted for murdering Mikel Mimpson and Bob Moldman.

1. Mimpson, in his civil case-in-chief, calls a well-qualified witness, Roland Butler, to testify that Mimpson has a reputation as a kind, peaceful man. Should Moldman's objection to this testimony be sustained? Would your answer differ if this were a criminal trial in which defendant Mimpson called this same witness in his case-in-chief?

2. If Butler were permitted to testify, could Moldman's counsel on cross ask Butler:

   a. Did you know that 12 years ago defendant Mimpson was observed by police standing shirtless in his driveway, his then-wife Mikel in bra and panties crying nearby, while Mimpson held a baseball bat that he had just used to smash his car's windshield?

b. Have you heard that in seven years ago Mimpson hit Mikel on her forehead, then repeatedly slapped her, bruising her face and resulting in his no-contest plea to assault?

c. Didn't Mr. Mimpson three years ago kick in his now ex-wife Mikel's double French doors, breaking the glass and threatening to kill Mikel?

Does your answer depend on whether this happens in plaintiff Mimpson's case-in-chief in the civil defamation suit or in defendant Mimpson's case-in-chief in the criminal case?

3. Assume instead that Mimpson never called Butler to the stand. However, Mimpson himself offers this brief testimony: "I did not stab or kill my wife." Can Moldman's counsel successfully make any of the inquiries of Mimpson that were made of Butler in question 2a-c above?

4. Assume now that Mimpson's objections in question 3 above were sustained. Can Moldman succeed in admitting evidence from any of the following witnesses:

a. Harry Hamlin, to testify in the civil case that Mimpson has a reputation as a wife-beater? That Mimpson has a reputation as a violent man? Does your answer change if Hamlin were called by the prosecution in its case-in-chief in the criminal case?

b. Rosy O'Gear, to testify in the civil case that he has been Mimpson's friend for 30 years, and, unfortunately, it is his opinion that Mimpson is a wife-beater? A violent man? Does your answer change if O'Gear were called by the prosecution in its case-in-chief in the criminal case?

c. Various witnesses in the civil case, to testify from their personal knowledge to the incidents recounted in question 2a-c above? Does your answer change if the witnesses were called by the prosecution in its case-in-chief in the criminal case?

5. Could Mimpson successfully have a leading expert on battered women's syndrome (a set of behaviors often displayed by battered women) testify that, based on reviewing Mikel's medical records and interviewing her family and friends, she did not suffer from battered women's syndrome? Does it matter whether this testimony is offered in plaintiff Mimpson's case-in-chief in the civil case or in defendant Mimpson's case-in-chief in the criminal case?

What if Mimpson called an expert on battered women's syndrome in either the civil or criminal case to testify that Mimpson does not display the traits of a typical battering spouse? Admissible? Would your answer change if the prosecution in the criminal case instead offered this same expert to testify that Mimpson does have the traits of a typical batterer?

Problem 5-54: Wherefore Art Thou, Romeo?

Ronald Speiser shot Victor Romeo, paralyzing him from the waist down. Speiser's defense was that he was trying to protect his brother, Randy, from attack by Romeo and two other angry men. Randy testified in part as follows:

DEFENSE COUNSEL: Randy, were you present in this courthouse yesterday, the first day of this trial?

A: I was.

DEFENSE COUNSEL: Where precisely were you in the courthouse at about 2 p.m.?

A: I was in the hallway outside this courtroom, waiting for the lunch break to end.

DEFENSE COUNSEL: What, if anything, happened at that time?

A: Victor Romeo . . .

PROSECUTOR: Objection, Your Honor! Irrelevant. I'd ask for an offer of proof.

JUDGE: Counselor?

DEFENSE COUNSEL: (at side bar) Your Honor, this witness will testify that Romeo slammed the witness against the wall, smacked him in the face, and said, "This time your brother won't be able to protect you."

PROSECUTOR: I renew my irrelevance objection, and object as well on character evidence and hearsay grounds.

What ruling? Why? Would your ruling change if Randy instead just testified, "Every one knows Victor Romeo, and he is a nasty, violent guy you want to stay clear of." What if Randy had never met or heard of Romeo, but a local merchant had done both for 10 years and the merchant, not Randy, offers this same testimony?

Problem 5-55: The Drunken Suspect

Gonzo Ravel is facing trial for burglarizing a supermarket; he stole meat, beer, and money by drilling a hole in the roof. Ravel's counsel calls Leonard Rundy to the stand to testify to Ravel's reputation as an honest, law-abiding citizen. The following exchange took place:

DEFENSE COUNSEL: Mr. Rundy, do you know others in your community who know Mr. Ravel?

A: Yes, practically everybody in the building. I am the janitor of 24 units and practically everybody in the units knows him because he does favors for them occasionally.

DEFENSE COUNSEL: Have you heard others in your community discuss . . . . ?

PROSECUTOR: Your Honor, may we approach the bench?

PROSECUTOR: (at the bench) Fair warning, Mr. [Counsel]. He has got 20 public drunkenness arrests, two of which resulted in convictions. Once you put his character in evidence, I can ask this man about each and every one of them.

DEFENSE COUNSEL: Whose character, the defendant or the witness?

PROSECUTOR: You are starting to put the defendant's character in evidence, aren't you?

DEFENSE COUNSEL: What does Your Honor have to comment about this argument?

JUDGE: I am afraid it is correct.

DEFENSE COUNSEL: Well, I disagree and so note it for the record, but I will withdraw the question.

JUDGE: All right.

Should the trial court's ruling be reversed on appeal? Why or why not?

§ 5.10 NON-PROPENSITY USES OF CHARACTER EVIDENCE: RULES 401, 404(a), 405(b)

This chapter has repeatedly stressed that there are two sorts of propensity uses of character — "act" and "mental" propensity — and that only the former is generally viewed as fitting within Rule 404(a)'s character evidence bar and exceptions. But sometimes character is used to prove something other than a propensity to think or act in a certain way on a specific occasion. Where that is so, Rule 404(a) serves as no bar to admission; on the other hand, Rule 402 declares that all relevant evidence is admissible unless excluded by another rule. Since no other character rule excludes such evidence (the only general bar on character evidence, at least outside of sexual offense cases, is the bar on act propensity evidence), these non-act propensity uses of character will be admissible and admissible in any form. For some of these non-act propensity uses, there is additional specific language in the rules (as we will soon see) while for others there is not.

We have already discussed one such "non-propensity" use of character: character as an "essential element" of a crime, claim, or defense. *See* Rule 405(b) ("When a person's character or character trait is an essential element of a charge, claim, or defense, the character or trait may also be proved by relevant specific instances of the person's conduct."). Character is an essential element when the substantive law requires proof of a particular character trait. As one example, we saw that the defense of truth to a defamation charge based on a newspaper article calling President Clinton a "gigolo" would require the paper to prove that Clinton was sexually promiscuous. As another example, we considered a statute imposing a greater sentence on anyone committing a felony who is a "habitual criminal." This statute requires proof that the defendant is a repeat offender. However, "essential element" character evidence is to be contrasted with cases in which character evidence is used to create an inference of other facts that are themselves at issue. Thus, in neither example are we asked to infer from Clinton's promiscuity or the felon's habitual criminality some further fact, such as that Clinton or the felon thought or acted a certain way on a specific occasion.

Another common non-propensity use of character evidence is to establish that someone *other than* the person whose character we are discussing reasonably held a particular thought. This use arises whenever it is argued that someone's knowledge of another's character led that person to perceive events in a special light. It is, therefore, not so much character as belief about character that is involved, a matter addressed not by the character evidence rules but rather by those of ordinary relevance.

Example

John Marcy claims self-defense in a murder prosecution. Marcy offers evidence that, before the incident, he had learned that his victim, Killer Kong, a pro-wrestler, had ruthlessly beaten five other men to the extent that they needed hospitalization. Each of those men, Marcy discovered, had dated Killer's sister, just as Marcy himself was doing. When Marcy saw an angry-looking Killer approaching, Marcy believed that he was about to become Killer's latest victim. Consequently, Marcy shot Killer dead. However, numerous prosecution witnesses suggest that Killer in fact approved of Marcy's relationship with Killer's sister and simply wanted to welcome Marcy into the family. Nevertheless, Marcy offers the evidence of his awareness of Killer's prior assaults to prove that he (Marcy) reasonably believed that he faced an imminent deadly attack by Killer. Marcy is not using evidence of Killer's violent character to prove Killer's propensity to behave violently in the case at hand, that is, Marcy is not trying to prove that Killer was in fact the first aggressor. Rather, Marcy is arguing only that, because of what he knew about Killer's character, Marcy was in imminent fear of serious bodily injury — one of the elements of the self-defense claim. Because this state of mind is an element of a claim of self-defense, evidence altering the probabilities that Marcy had that state of mind in this case is still relevant under Rule 401. Accordingly, this evidence is not prohibited by Rule 404(a) yet may be admissible (provided that no other rules, such as 403, keep it out) as relevant evidence.

Problem 5-56: The Violent Drunk

Jason Benra smashed his car into a parked car, staggered to his home one block away, and fell asleep. The owner of the parked car called the police, who rang Mr. Benra's doorbell. In his subsequent federal civil rights suit, Benra testified that three police officers grabbed him as soon as he opened the door and threw him over some bushes, breaking his arm. The officers' testimony is that they smelled alcohol on his breath, and he started flailing his arms and mouthing obscenities. They immediately tried to restrain him out of fear that they would otherwise imminently suffer bodily injury. They seek to testify further that their fear arose from six prior domestic violence calls involving Benra. In each of these calls, he was drunk, verbally abusive, and violent toward the officers. Benra broke one of the officers' jaws in one incident, tried to stab a second officer in another incident, and whacked a third officer on the head with a hammer in a third incident. The officers also seek to testify that Benra has three drunk driving misdemeanor convictions, to suggest that he left the scene of the accident to avoid a fourth conviction, which would have resulted in jail time and the loss of his license. *Should the officers' testimony about Benra's prior violence be admissible? Should the officer's testimony about Benra's prior drunk driving convictions be admissible? Why or why not? See Senra v. Cunningham, 9 F.3d 168 (1st Cir. 1993).* In the next section, we examine two related issues: (1) evidence that looks like character evidence but is in fact not character evidence at all, and (2) evidence that may involve character but, if it does involve character, sloppy thinking may lead to treating it like act propensity evidence when the real purpose of the evidence is to prove mental propensity. The purpose of the next section, therefore, is to guard you against being deceived by a Trojan horse that looks like act propensity, but is not.

§ 5.11 THINGS THAT LOOK LIKE ACT PROPENSITY EVIDENCE BUT ARE NOT

[A] Rule 404(b)-Specific Acts Offered for Non-Character Uses or Mental Propensity Uses

[1] General Principles and Problems

[a] Purposes Other Than Character

Rule 404(b) reads as follows:

(b) Crimes, Wrongs, or Other Acts.

(1) *Prohibited Uses.* Evidence of a crime, wrong, or other act is not admissible to prove a person's character in order to show that on a particular occasion the person acted in accordance with the character.

(2) *Permitted Uses; Notice in a Criminal Case.*

This evidence may be admissible for another purpose, such as proving motive, opportunity, intent, preparation, plan, knowledge, identity, absence of mistake, or lack of accident. On request by a defendant in a criminal case, the prosecutor must:

(A) provide reasonable notice of the general nature of any such evidence that the prosecutor intends to offer at trial; and

(B) do so before trial — or during trial if the court, for good cause, excuses lack of pretrial notice.

Most commentators describe Rule 404(b) as permitting use of specific acts when offered for a purpose other than character. One group of commentators explained it this way: "The theory of admission is that the evidence is not offered to show character, but to show something else, either a trait of personality that is too narrow to be called character, or something that is not a trait of personality at all. The Federal Rules of Evidence provide for admission under the formula in Rule 404(b)."[6]

The problem, however, is that there are few clear guidelines, if any, for determining when specific acts evidence is character evidence and when not. Specific acts often look like character evidence. Certainly, a jury upon hearing, for

---

[6] Roger C. Park, et al., Evidence Law: A Student's Guide to the Law of Evidence as Applied in American Trials 158 (1998).

example, that a defendant in a robbery case committed a prior robbery, may be likely to use such evidence for act propensity purposes no matter what "non-character" theory is offered. The discussion below of specific categories of Rule 404(b)(2) character evidence will seek to add a little more clarity to the law's ambiguity in this area by suggesting the following principles:

First, several of the categories of specific acts evidence admitted under Rule 404(b)(2) may at least arguably be understood as involving propensity inferences. However, even where that is so, these inferences often involve mental, rather than act, propensity. Because the overwhelming consensus is that Rule 404(a)'s general prohibition on character evidence extends only to *act propensity* uses, mental propensity uses are not prohibited by that rule and are indeed affirmatively sanctioned by Rule 404(b)(2).

Second, while some other specific acts evidence under Rule 404(b) does indeed involve using the prior acts in an "act" propensity fashion — that is, the prior actions are used to prove current conduct — the prior acts may be so situationally specific that they have more predictive value than do more general "character" traits. In other words, there is a continuum of situational specificity: *general character* describes our likely behavior across many different sorts of situations; *character traits* describe our behavior in a more narrow set of circumstances; and "non-character" *specific acts under Rule 404(b)(2)* describe our behavior in a still more narrow set of circumstances. There is a fourth category, "habit," covered by Rule 406, that extends to a still more narrow set of circumstances. The more situationally specific the evidence, the greater its predictive power, and the less like "character" it should be considered.

While situational specificity is thus a helpful guideline, however, "The ultimate question presented (when is specific past human conduct a reliable predictor of present actions?) is so difficult, so susceptible to differences of opinion, and so dependent upon the peculiar facts of the individual case, that it is unlikely that any set of hard-and-fast rules will provide exact answers."[7] Nevertheless, the rules require that an answer be found. A propensity use is deemed "non-character" when showing the prior act helps to prove the current conduct without making the intermediate inference that the act shows a person's "character." In other words, the prior act itself, and not any character trait, tends to prove an aspect of the current case on trial.

Practice Tip 1:

It is often advantageous for a party to get prior *bad acts* by the opposing party into evidence, if for no other reason than that the concrete specificity of acts helps to build a powerful narrative that holds the jury's attention. Often it is unclear whether acts will be used by the jury for prohibited act propensity inferences or permissible alternative inferences. It is therefore helpful for an advocate to search for plausible arguments supporting a good-faith contention that prior acts are being offered for permissible Rule 404(b)(2) purposes rather than impermissible Rule 404(a) or 404(b)(1) act

---

[7] Roger C. Park et al., Evidence Law: A Student's Guide to the Law of Evidence as Applied in American Trials 160 (1998).

propensity purposes. Jury instructions can be suggested as a way to limit jurors to the proper uses of prior bad acts evidence.

Practice Tip 2:

It is important to remember that Rule 404(b) governs both civil and criminal cases. There may be reasons in either sort of case making specific acts relevant for purposes other than proving character to show act propensity. Once relevant specific acts are outside the character act propensity bar of Rules 404(a) and 404(b)(1), they fall under Rule 404(b)(2). This point will be illustrated in examples and problems below.

[b] Proof of Specific Acts

The most common use of Rule 404(b)(2) is as justification for introducing a criminal defendant's prior misconduct to prove matters such as intent, knowledge, or identity. However, Rule 404(b)(2) authorizes the use of specific acts evidence in both civil and criminal cases. In fact, *any* specific act can be offered under Rule 404(b)(2) for a purpose other than showing act-propensity. The list of approved specific act uses in Rule 404(b)(2) is illustrative and not exhaustive.

While we often, for shorthand, speak of "*prior*" specific acts, acts occurring *after* the events at issue (e.g., after the charged offense) can also sometimes be relevant. Additionally, while we generally speak of prior "misconduct," good acts may sometimes be offered under Rule 404(b)(2) to show lack of guilt or responsibility for the current behavior on trial.

Under Rule 404(b)(2) the specific act must be shown by evidence sufficient to enable a reasonable jury to conclude by a preponderance of the evidence that the prior acts occurred and that the defendant or other relevant actor committed them. *See Huddleston v. United States*, 485 U.S. 681, 689, 108 S. Ct. 1496, 99 L. Ed. 2d 771 (1988). For example, the mere fact of arrest is not sufficient to meet this burden; there must be evidence that the defendant actually committed the prior crime. *See, e.g., United States v. Robinson*, 978 F.2d 1554, 1559 (10th Cir. 1992). Convictions constitute sufficient proof of specific acts of misconduct, but Rule 404(b) also applies to "uncharged misconduct," misconduct that has not resulted in an arrest or formal charge. Indeed, misconduct can include criminal charges that resulted *in an acquittal*, provided that the occurrence of the earlier crime is shown by the appropriate standard of proof required for that jurisdiction. This conclusion follows from the differing standards of proof for conviction of a crime and for admission of Rule 404(b)(2) evidence. An acquittal establishes only that the state could not prove guilt beyond a reasonable doubt; it does not prove the accused innocent. Thus, a prosecutor could offer sufficient evidence to enable a reasonable jury to find guilt by a preponderance of the evidence under Rule 404(b)(2) even though another jury has entered an acquittal.

Dowling v. United States, 493 U.S. 342, 110 S. Ct. 668, 107 L. Ed. 2d 708 (1990), supports this conclusion. Dowling had been charged with a bank robbery in which the perpetrator wore a ski mask and carried a handgun. At trial, a prosecution witness testified, over defense objection, that she had been assaulted in her home two weeks after the robbery by two men who entered without her permission, one of whom wore a ski mask and carried a handgun. She was able to identify that man as Dowling, because she pulled off his ski mask while struggling with him. She also identified a man named Christian as the other assailant. Dowling was charged with burglarizing and robbing her but was acquitted. At Dowling's trial for the bank robbery, the prosecutor nevertheless offered this woman's testimony to strengthen its identification of Dowling and to link him to Christian, who drove the getaway car in the charged bank robbery. The Third Circuit held that this was error, albeit harmless, because Rule 404(b) did not sanction admission of other crimes evidence that resulted in acquittal. On further appeal to the Supreme Court, the other crimes evidence was challenged under the collateral estoppel component of the Double Jeopardy Clause (not under Rule 404(b)). The Court rejected this challenge, partly because of the different standards of proof concerning criminal guilt and Rule 404(b) evidence: "Because a jury might reasonably conclude by a preponderance of the evidence that Dowling was the masked man who entered Henry's home, even if it did not believe beyond a reasonable doubt that Dowling committed the crimes charged at the first trial, the collateral estoppel component of the Double Jeopardy Clause is inapposite."

While the Rule 404(b) question was not before the Court, the *Dowling* rationale suggests that bad acts may be admissible under Rule 404(b)(2) even though the defendant has been acquitted of those acts. We say "may," however, because a defendant remains free to argue in a particular case that the act has minimal probative value in light of the acquittal. As the Supreme Court has said elsewhere, "the strength of the evidence establishing the similar act is one of the factors the court may consider when conducting the Rule 403 balancing."

Finally, Rule 404(b) (2)(A)–(B) contains a "reasonable notice" requirement. No specific form of notice is required. Only a general notice is required, one that need not even be as specific as would be allegations in an indictment or information. Nor must the notice disclose the names and addresses of witnesses. The notice requirement does not even apply to evidence of acts "intrinsic" to the charged offense (Advisory Committee Note). However, notice must be given whether the evidence will be used in the prosecution's case-in-chief, for impeachment, or for possible rebuttal. Furthermore, the notice requirement is a "condition precedent" to admissibility, that is, the court has no discretion to admit the evidence if the court finds that any aspect of the notice requirement has not been met.

[c] Rule 403 Balancing

While "non-character" evidence is not barred by Rule 404(a)(1), Rule 403 may still provide grounds for exclusion. Factors relevant to the 403 balancing test will include the wrongful act's capacity to arouse horror or sympathy; its remoteness in time from the current offense; whether the fact sought to be proved by it is really in dispute; and whether, if so, there is other, less prejudicial evidence with which to prove it. *Old Chief v. United States*, 519 U.S. 172, 117 S. Ct. 644, 136 L. Ed. 2d 574 (1997), clarifies the Court's approach to Rule 403 balancing when deciding whether character evidence should be admitted. While not involving Rule 404(b), *Old Chief* sheds useful light on the connection between Rule 404(b) and Rule 403. (*Old Chief* is in the Chapter 4 Case Library).

Old Chief was charged with violating a federal statute that makes it a crime for anyone convicted of a felony to possess any firearm. Old Chief offered to stipulate to his prior felony conviction. He argued that this offer to stipulate "rendered evidence of the name and nature of the offense [assault causing serious bodily injury] inadmissible" because of the risk of unfair prejudice. The prosecutor refused to stipulate, and the trial court denied Old Chief's motion to limit any testimony about his prior conviction to the information offered in his stipulation. The name of the prior offense and the punishment imposed for it were revealed at trial, and a jury convicted Old Chief on all counts. The Ninth Circuit, on appeal, found no abuse of the trial court's discretion.

The Supreme Court disagreed, reversing the judgment of the Ninth Circuit. In general, the Court upheld the prosecution's right to prove its case by evidence of its own choice, free from any right of the defendant to block evidence by stipulating to the element it is offered to prove. But sometimes Rule 403 requires a contrary result, at least where witness testimony is needed to provide the "evidentiary richness" that a stipulation does not. The Court explained its concept of "evidentiary richness" as follows:[8]

> [M]aking a case with testimony and tangible things not only satisfies the formal definition of an offense, but tells a colorful story with descriptive richness. Unlike an abstract premise, whose force depends on going precisely to a particular step in a course of reasoning, a piece of evidence may address any number of separate elements, striking hard just because it shows so much at once; the account of a shooting that establishes capacity and causation may tell just as much about the triggerman's motive and intent. Evidence thus has force beyond any linear scheme of reasoning, and as its pieces come together a narrative gains momentum, with power not only to support conclusions but to sustain the willingness of jurors to draw the inferences, whatever they may be, necessary to reach an honest verdict. This persuasive power of the concrete and the particular is often essential to the capacity of jurors to satisfy the obligations that the law places on them.

The Court went on to explain that jurors may find it difficult to either send another human being to prison or hold out for acquittal:[9]

> When a juror's duty does seem hard, the evidentiary account of what a defendant has thought and done can accomplish what no set of abstract statements ever could, not just to prove a fact but to establish its human significance and so to implicate the law's moral underpinnings and a juror's obligation to sit in judgment.

Moreover, the Court concluded that jurors' expectations of receiving certain evidence, and in a certain form, might be violated by a stipulation. Failed expectations create the impression that the prosecutor is "cloaking something" when he is not. "A syllogism is not a story," said the Court, "and a naked proposition

---

[8] 519 U.S. at 187.

[9] *Id.* at 187–188.

in the courtroom may be no match for the robust evidence that would be used to prove it. Jurors hearing a story interrupted by 'gaps of abstraction' will be puzzled by 'missing chapters.' An assurance that the missing chapters are there is never more than second-best."[10]

In this case, however, the prior conviction was necessary only to prove the defendant's status as a felon. Thus, the actual nature of the prior conviction was unnecessary, and added no "evidentiary richness" to the prosecution's case. In light of the danger that a jury would misuse the prior assault conviction as inappropriate character evidence, the risk of unfair prejudice substantially outweighed its probative value, and the nature of the conviction should have been excluded under Federal Rule of Evidence 403.

[d]   Problems

Problem 5-57: Fearing the Navy Seal

Henry Mancini, a homicide defendant asserting self-defense, offers evidence that he had heard that his alleged victim, Jesse Rentura, was an evil, cruel man. He had also heard that Rentura, a former Navy Seal, had been trained to kill and had the inclination to do so. Overwhelming evidence presented by the prosecution suggests that this view was wrong and that Rentura's reputation was profoundly undeserved. Perhaps it arose from societal stereotypes about the violent nature of large bald men like Rentura. Nevertheless, Mancini argues, over prosecution objection, that the proffered evidence is still relevant non-character (in the sense of non-propensity) testimony and is, therefore, admissible.

The judge admits the defendant's testimony. *Is the judge's ruling right? Why or why not? Any change in your ruling if, instead of reputation evidence, Mancini offered: (1) an opinion witness, testifying that he shared with Mancini his view that Rentura had a violent nature? (2) a series of witnesses who told Mancini that they had observed Rentura's violent nature? (3) a series of witnesses testifying to their personal observation of Rentura's violent acts?*

Problem 5-58: O.J. Accused

Assume that O.J. Mimpson in Problem 5-53 is facing criminal homicide charges. The prosecution seeks to admit the evidence noted in part 2 a-c of that problem in its case-in-chief. The defense objects on the grounds that the evidence is inadmissible character propensity evidence. *How should the prosecutor respond? What additional details might you want to know that would aid the prosecutor?*

[2]   Motive

Rule 404(b)(2) states that evidence of specific acts may be admissible to prove motive. There is sometimes a fine line between "motive" and "character" evidence, a distinction that is not clarified by the rules, their drafting history, or most commentators. One useful definition of motive is this: "motive is the reason *why* a

---

[10] *Id.* at 189.

specific offender acted with a mental state required by the definition of a charge, crime, claim, or defense."

Example 1

Harry Osterling, a thirty-something accountant, shows up at a Jewish daycare center, shoots three five-year-old children, and flees. Assuming that he is sane, it is clear from the nature of his acts that he meant to cause serious bodily injury or death to these children. But *why* would such a man want to hurt innocent children? Investigation reveals that he is a neo-Nazi who was personally insulted by the daycare center's rabbi, who called Osterling a "hateful, powerless barbarian" the day before the shooting. Osterling's status as a neo-Nazi is proven by evidence of instances of his wearing swastikas and giving racist speeches. Osterling's *purpose* was to harm the children, but his motive was revenge against the rabbi for the insult.

The "motive" in this example is narrow and case-specific: it turns on knowledge of prior interactions between this specific offender and a symbolic representative (the rabbi) of the offender's victims. Therefore, it is not character evidence. A "character" propensity argument, by contrast, would rely on more general claims having nothing to do with the specific parties. Using evidence that Osterling is a violent man, for example, the prosecution would argue that he expressed his violent character by acting violently here, apart from whether he had ever met his victims before. Precisely because motive frequently turns on specific interactions rather than generalizations about a defendant's "good" or "evil" nature, motive may be seen as having more probative value and less danger of unfair prejudice than character evidence.

But there are arguably close cases:

Example 2

Same example as above, but Osterling was never insulted by the rabbi. Rather, Osterling simply shot the children because they were Jewish, and he hates all Jews. Is evidence of Osterling's embrace of neo-Nazi anti-Semitism and racism "character" or "motive" evidence? Many courts might view this evidence as concerning "motive" because his ideology is the reason why he wanted to and did shoot the Jewish children. But Osterling in this revised example has had no specific interaction with the kids or their rabbi. He is simply a Jew-hating, racist man, who, for that reason, is more likely to hurt any specific Jew or racial or ethnic minority member simply because of their religion, race, or ethnicity. This general claim about his nature, offered to prove actions based on that nature, sounds much like "character" propensity evidence.

Criminal law scholars sometimes object to defining crimes to include motive as an element, given "that motive analysis borders on an inquiry into character because it requires detailed information about the actor and an in-depth examination of his psychological nature." Andrew E. Taslitz, *Condemning the Racist Personality: Why the Critics of Hate Crimes Legislation Are Wrong*, 40 B.C.L. Rev. 739 (1999) (summarizing, but ultimately rejecting, aspects of these critics' views). Even many substantive criminal law scholars who favor including motive as an element of certain crimes conclude, "We look to motives not to punish them as thoughts alone but as evidence of the ultimate character of the person being punished." Jeffrie G. Murphy, *Bias Crimes: What Do Haters Deserve?*. 11 Crim. J. Ethics 23 (1992). For example, hate crimes legislation might increase the penalties for Osterling's assault or murder conviction in the two examples above if the "motive" for his actions was religious or ethnic hatred. But many scholars view racial hatred as meriting greater punishment because such hatred is evidence of an evil character. Of course, motive usually is not an element of a crime but is offered to prove some non-motive element. Nevertheless, these scholars' insight remains: understanding a person's motive requires understanding their nature, and that borders on character evidence.

The difficulty in distinguishing "motive" from character is further highlighted by the fact that motive can be used to prove act propensity.

To Kill a Mockingbird (1962)
Directed by Robert Mulligan
Shown in foreground, from left: Paul Fix (as Judge Taylor), Brock Peters (as Tom Robinson), Gregory Peck (as Atticus Finch)
Credit: Universal Pictures/Photofest © Universal Pictures

Example 3

Assume we know that *someone* shot the children at the Jewish daycare center, but we do not yet know who. Investigation reveals circumstantial evidence that Osterling was in the vicinity of the daycare center shortly before the shooting and that he is a skilled marksman. To bolster its murder charge against Osterling, the prosecution offers evidence of his neo-Nazi affiliations. This "motive" evidence is offered to prove that Osterling, and not someone else, committed the "act" of shooting the

Jewish children. If this is indeed "motive" evidence, it may be admissible, subject to Rule 403 balancing. If it is "character" evidence, it is inadmissible under Rule 404(a)(1). Even if it is "motive" evidence, the danger that jurors will use it as "character" evidence may require exclusion under Rule 403.

Despite this difficulty in distinguishing "motive" from "character" evidence, the rules adopt this dichotomy. Accordingly, there is a need for workable guidelines for separating admissible motive evidence from inadmissible character propensity evidence. Judicial opinions usually do not state explicit guidelines by which the courts make this distinction. Nevertheless, the following two guidelines are implicit in the logic of the rules and the writings of some courts and commentators; they should prove useful:

First, a guideline that helps distinguish between act propensity and mental propensity: if the reason why a suspect acted is offered to prove that the action was done with a particular mental state, not to prove that the suspect committed the criminal act in the first place, the evidence addresses mental propensity and should be considered evidence of "motive."

Example 4

Numerous credible eyewitnesses saw Osterling shoot the children at the daycare center, so his identity as the criminal actor is clear. But evidence of his racism is offered to increase the likelihood that he intended to kill and that he acted "deliberately" and with "premeditation." Proof of these qualities would demonstrate the kind of "hardness of heart" or "cold-bloodedness: required to establish first-degree murder, rather than mere second-degree murder. Here, the evidence concerns Osterling's propensity to *think* a certain way rather than to act a certain way. If Rule 404(a)'s prohibition of character evidence extends only to "act propensity," but not to "mental propensity," this evidence should be admissible and can safely be labeled "motive."

Second, a guideline that addresses the admissibility of evidence offered to show "act propensity": the risk of unfair prejudice varies inversely with the specificity of the evidence. Thus, the more specific the evidence is to the relationship between the defendant and the victim, the less severe is the Rule 403 danger that the jury will use the evidence for generalized character inferences, and the more willing we should be to accept the "motive" label.

Example 5

There is no evidence that Osterling is a racist or neo-Nazi at all. The only evidence offered is of Osterling's loud argument with the rabbi the day before the shooting. There is some danger that jurors will label Osterling as the "kind of person" who is disrespectful to rabbis and quick to anger, and thus is of a sort more likely to shoot Jews (character propensity evidence). But the more likely inference will be that Osterling experienced and acted in anger over a *specific disagreement* with the rabbi. While, as the commentators discussed above have noted, this sort of inference contains implicit character judgments, jury deliberations are more likely to concern the specific dispute than generalities. The Rule 403 dangers of abusing generalized character propensity inferences and of convicting a person for his evil nature rather than his evil deed are small. Labeling this evidence "motive" seems wise.

Problem 5-59: Illegitimate Prescriptions

Physician Dr. Stephen Kamar is charged with prescribing controlled substances "not in the usual course of professional practice" and "not for a legitimate medical purpose." In litigating a motion *in limine*, the prosecution called five witnesses, each of whom was a woman who testified roughly as follows:

When she asked Kamar to prescribe Quaaludes, he responded by asking her to perform fellatio. After each woman completed this act, Dr. Kamar wrote her the requested prescription. *Should the court grant the prosecution's motion for a pretrial ruling that this testimony is admissible? Why or why not?*

Problem 5-60: The Pokemon Gang

Ronald Goldblum is on trial for possessing controlled substances with the intent to distribute them. The prosecution seeks to offer evidence that every day he wears the colors of the Pokemon gang. Goldblum's defense will be that he possessed the illegal substances solely for his personal use. But the prosecution also proffers the testimony of a police expert on gang culture, who will testify about the code of the Pokemon gang. Under that code, no member may personally use any illegal or narcotic drug or alcohol. Instead, every member must sell addictive illegal substances in inner-city African-American communities. The Pokemon gang is a secret arm of the American Purist Party, which is bent on "purifying" America of its non-white minorities. The gang punishes any infraction of its rules with torture, followed by death. *Should this testimony be admissible? Why or why not?*

Problem 5-61: Infidelity

Montana Redwood is on trial for homicide. In cross-examining prosecution witnesses, defense counsel revealed the defense theory, that Redwood killed Molly Ringwater because Ringwater was attacking Redwood's wife. The prosecutor offered evidence that Redwood had had sexual relations with at least 20 other women during the year before the killing. *Admissible? Why or why not? Should the ruling change if the prosecution also offers evidence that Ringwater had told Redwood's wife of Redwood's infidelity in a conversation that took place shortly before Ringwater's demise?*

Problem 5-62: Cocaine and Concealed Currency

Maggie Arturo allegedly failed to report her transportation of certain foreign currency into the United States, contrary to a federal statute. The prosecutor proffers evidence that Maggie was involved in an international cocaine distribution conspiracy. *Admissible? Why or why not?*

Problem 5-63: Attempted Murder, She Wrote

The defendant, Agnes, has AIDS. After biting an FBI agent, she is charged with attempted murder. The prosecution wants to offer evidence that the FBI agent had arrested the defendant on three prior occasions. *Should these prior acts be allowed in evidence?*

[3] Opportunity

Rule 404(b)(2) states that evidence of specific acts may be admissible to prove opportunity. "Opportunity," as used in Rule 404(b)(2), means access to or presence at the scene of a crime, or having distinctive or unusual skills or abilities employed in the commission of the crime charged.

Example

Robin Macduff is accused of burglarizing a local mansion. While items were missing, there were no signs of forced entry, and all windows were protected by bars. The prosecutor offers evidence, however, that Macduff is a contortionist, and that she was observed on several occasions entering similarly barred homes by squeezing her body between the bars. This special ability demonstrates the kind of "unusual skill" that might offer her the opportunity to commit a crime that others could not.

Problem 5-64: High-Tech Terrorism

Lteef Ulima was arrested for the bombing of a federal office building after police viewed a videotape that showed Ulima hurriedly leaving the building moments before the explosion. Forensic analysis revealed that the explosion was caused by an experimental explosive device, one that was part of a governmental research project contracted to a private entity. The State offers evidence that three weeks before the explosion, Ulima burglarized a warehouse of Regotech Corporation, the private contractor working on the experimental explosive device. *Admissible or not? Why?*

Problem 5-65: Oprah Wanafree

Purported medium Oprah Wanafree is charged with fraudulently accepting money for putting clients "in touch" with their dead relatives. Wanafree would hold seances during which the "dead" would talk to the living. The prosecution proffers evidence of Wanafree's involvement in three scams in which she would mimic other person's voices and appearance to gain access to that person's bank accounts, stock trading accounts, and pension funds. The prosecution also proffers evidence that Wanafree had a reputation as the "Crooked Female Frank Gorshen," referring to the well-known celebrity impersonator. The defense objects to both proffers. *What should be the ruling on each proffer, and why?*

[4] Identity

Rule 404(b)(2) states that evidence of specific acts may be admissible to prove identity. "Identity" is the ultimate purpose for which much Rule 404(b) evidence is offered. *See, e.g.*, motive discussion in [B], above. However, case law and commentary often read the term "identity" narrowly. They limit its meaning to one specific method of proving who did the crime: *"modus operandi."* *"Modus operandi"* means the criminal's method of operating. It proves identity by relying on the argument that the pattern and characteristics of the crimes are so unusual and distinctive as to be like a signature.

A *modus operandi* argument does not arise simply because crimes are of the same general type. It is improper to argue, for example, that merely because the accused burgled a home thrice before, the jury should believe that he burgled again. That sort of inference is the classic character propensity inference: "He is a burglar — the kind of person who burgles — so he probably committed this burglary too." Instead, the two crimes must involve some sufficiently unusual pattern or tool to have high probative value in suggesting that the same person committed both crimes. Some courts even speak of the "uniqueness" of the method or pattern, though it is doubtful that uniqueness (being one of a kind) is literally required. But the signature trait concept is nevertheless often stringently applied. In fact, similar stringency is generally employed by the courts for any use of misconduct to prove identity rather than the perpetrator's state of mind. Furthermore, the similarity between or among the unusual crimes must be high.

Example

Five men are found murdered in Beverly Hills at different times and places over the course of a year. In each of the five killings, the deadly deed was done by stabbing the victim in the heart with a three-sided knife — one that promotes rapid bleeding and prevents healing. Moreover, in each case, such a knife was used to carve a different zodiac sign on the victim's body. Ronny Wood has been linked to the first four killings because his fingerprints were found at the crime scenes. But no physical evidence linked him to the fifth killing. At Wood's trial on the fifth killing, the prosecutor will likely succeed, over defense objection, in admitting evidence of the occurrence and manner of the first four killings, and of Wood's connection to them, as "signatures" showing that Wood, by using the distinctive knife and by his zodiacal signing, effectively identified himself as the perpetrator of the fifth killing.

Problem 5-66: Count Dracula

On October 31 (Halloween), at midnight, a man wearing a ski mask and a "Count Dracula-like cape" held up a taxicab driver at gunpoint. No one saw the offender's face, but Richard Harrington has been charged with the crime. The prosecution's case consisted entirely of witnesses who linked Harrington to each of four prior cabbie robberies. Each of these robberies took place one year apart, each happening at midnight on Halloween for each of the four years preceding the current robbery. In the first three robberies, eyewitnesses saw Harrington's face when he removed his mask and fled. Harrington was tried but acquitted of all three offenses. In the next case, eyewitnesses saw a caped, ski mask-wearing man flee into Harrington's apartment building. Subsequent police searches with warrants uncovered a cape but no mask. Harrington fled and was thus never arrested. *Should any or all of these witnesses be permitted to testify? Why or why not?*

Problem 5-67: Gambling for Drugs

On March 31 of last year, two local detectives saw Willie Wonka accepting money from passersby, then immediately handing each of them a brown paper bag that he plucked from the wheel well of a pick-up truck. After each transaction, Wonka crossed the street and handed something to Dr. Moriss Dolittle, who stood in front of his store, Dolittle's Video. As it turned out, Dolittle owned the pickup truck. On that date, one of the detectives purchased what appeared to be cocaine and marijuana from Wonka via this procedure. When the detectives later legally searched the pickup truck and Dolittle's Video, they found illegal lottery betting slips in both locations. However, Dolittle was not then charged with illegal bookmaking.

Five months later, officers executed a search warrant at 555 Co-op City Avenue, based on an informant's report of drug dealing at that address. They found crack cocaine, a triple-beam scale, a digital scale, small bags of the kind used to package cocaine, and $12,000 cash in a suitcase, as well as illegal lottery numbers and lists of bets written on them.

At Dolittle's trial for possessing the cocaine found at 555 Co-op City Avenue, the prosecution seeks to offer evidence of (1) the Willie Wonka investigation of last year and the betting slips uncovered during that investigation, (2) Dolittle's conviction five years ago for running an illegal lottery, and (3) the lists of bets found during the Co-op City Avenue search. The prosecution argued that these items are admissible to prove Dolittle's identity as the owner of the Co-op City apartment. *How should the trial judge rule and why?*

Problem 5-68: Drug Courier Profile

Jason Mellwood is on trial for possession of cocaine with intent to distribute it. The prosecution called a police expert on drug courier profiles to testify that Mellwood fit most of the elements of the following drug courier profile:

Flight arrival from or departure to an identified source city, such as Miami.

Arrival carrying little or no baggage, or large quantities of empty suitcases.

Unusual itinerary, such as rapid turnaround time for a lengthy airplane trip.

Use of an alias.

Carrying unusually large amounts of currency (many thousands of dollars), usually on the person, in briefcases, or in bags.

Purchasing airline tickets with a large amount of currency in small denominations.

Unusual nervousness, beyond that ordinarily exhibited by airplane passengers.

The almost exclusive use of public transportation, particularly taxicabs in departing from the airport.

Making a telephone call immediately after deplaning.

Leaving a false or fictitious call-back telephone number with the airline.

Excessively frequent travel to source or destination cities.

Mellwood was observed engaging in the same profile-like behavior on five separate occasions over the course of the three months preceding his arrest. Only on the fifth occasion did officers arrest him as he picked up a bag from the luggage carousel, a bag they later found to have cocaine stored in hidden pockets. The state's proffer includes these officers' testimony.

Mellwood's defense is that he simply picked up the wrong baggage at the luggage pickup area, since the bag containing the cocaine had no tags identifying its owner. Defense counsel objects to the profile testimony as relying on a prohibited propensity evidence. The prosecutor responds that the evidence is offered to prove both *modus operandi* and that Mellwood did not merely possess the cocaine for his own use. Rather, he was a "drug courier," i.e., a person who acted with the intention of aiding in the distribution and sale of cocaine to ultimate buyers. *What ruling and why?*

[5] Intent or Knowledge

Rule 404(b)(2) states that evidence of specific acts may be admissible to prove intent or knowledge. In other words, evidence of other similar acts may help to establish that a defendant did not act mistakenly or accidentally but rather with the intent or knowledge required by the elements of the applicable tort or crime.

Example

John Connor is charged with raping Janine Francis on a date. Connor insisted that he believed that she consented, as he was told by her brother that she likes to "play coy" but her "no really means yes." The prosecution offers evidence that Connor committed five other date rapes and, in each case, when confronted with a rape allegation, he told authorities that he believed the woman had consented because the woman's brother, friend, or the like told Connor that the victim merely feigns resistance but "always wants it bad." It defies common sense to believe that the defendant could so often be mistaken about his victim's consent on the same grounds, and never have learned from all those alleged errors. Thus, the evidence is admissible to prove that Connor acted with full awareness in the case at hand of Janine's lack of consent.

This is an application of the doctrine of "objective chances" to mental state. The doctrine of objective chances expresses the idea that the repeated occurrence of certain unusual events is so unlikely as to render improbable the claim that any one of those events happened mistakenly or accidentally. In other words, the "objective chances" of mistake or accident are slim. Thus, it is simply not credible that a man can be innocently mistaken time after time about whether a woman consented. Of course, this same evidence might be admissible under Rule 413 as well.

Note in this example that there is a grave danger that the jury will use the prior date rapes as character propensity evidence. As a result, the jury might either assume Connor's guilty mental state or convict him for who he is rather than for what he has thought and done in this instance. Indeed, it might be argued that the doctrine of "objective chances" is but a kind of character propensity evidence in disguise, albeit mental propensity. When we discuss "objective chances," we are really just saying that Connor is a rapist — the kind of man who rapes. Because he is such a man, he must have acted in this case with the same wrongful mental state of knowing Janine did not consent (the act of intercourse was never in doubt). This point is no problem, however, if we continue to interpret Rule 404(a)(1)'s general character prohibition to bar only "act" and not "mental" propensity evidence. Moreover, Rule 413 would permit use of even act propensity evidence in rape cases.

If we do so interpret Rule 404(a)(1), it is important that in this example Connor admits to the act of sexual intercourse. If he denied the act entirely, we would be using the doctrine of objective chances to prove conduct, which would arguably involve "act propensity" evidence. On the other hand, if the events are sufficiently similar to have high probative value, a court might view this as proper "identity" evidence rather than improper "character act propensity evidence," as discussed in [4], *above*.

Huddleston v. United States, 485 U.S. 681, 108 S. Ct. 1496, 99 L. Ed. 2d 771 (1988), further illustrates using other acts to prove identity or knowledge. There, Huddleston allegedly sold 5,000 stolen blank videocassette tapes. He was charged with selling stolen goods in interstate commerce and possessing stolen property in interstate commerce. The only issue at trial was whether Huddleston knew that the tapes were stolen. To prove such knowledge, the government successfully used similar acts testimony from two witnesses: first, the owner of a record store testified that, about three months before the current incident, Huddleston offered to sell him thousands of new television sets for only $28 each; and, second, an undercover FBI agent testified that Huddleston, posing as a buyer for an appliance store, offered to sell the agent many refrigerators and icemakers. Huddleston himself testified that he got the tapes, televisions, and appliances from a third party, who assured him that the items were legitimate. The trial court instructed the jury that the "similar acts" evidence was to be considered only in determining Huddleston's knowledge that the items he sold were stolen, and could not be considered to prove his character. The jury convicted Huddleston on the stolen property charge.

The Sixth Circuit initially reversed, because the state had not proven by "clear and convincing" evidence that the televisions were indeed stolen (one of the two "similar acts"). After a rehearing, however, the court affirmed the convictions, concluding that proof by a preponderance of the evidence was sufficient and that the evidence concerning the televisions was admitted for a proper purpose not outweighed by its potential prejudicial effect.

The Supreme Court accepted *certiorari*. "The threshold inquiry," said the Court, "before admitting similar acts evidence under Rule 404(b) is whether that evidence is probative of a material issue other than character." (485 U.S. at 686.) Rule 404's text itself "contains no intimation that any preliminary showing is necessary before such evidence may be introduced for a proper purpose." Accordingly, "the evidence is subject only to general strictures limiting admissibility such as Rules 402 and 403." (485 U.S. at 687–688.) Indeed, the Advisory Committee Note expressly rejected any "mechanical solution" to the admission of evidence under Rule 404(b). Rather, said the Advisory Committee, a trial court must decide "whether the danger of undue prejudice outweighs the probative value of the evidence in view of the availability of other means of proof and other factors appropriate for making decisions of this kind under Rule 403."

The relevance of the similar acts evidence turned on whether the acts occurred and whether Huddleston committed them. When the relevance of an item of evidence turns on proof of preliminary facts, the problem is one of "conditional relevance," which is controlled by Rule 104(b). The Court noted that Rule 401 defines relevance as whether evidence has any tendency to make a fact of consequence more or less probable. In light of this low threshold, the Court concluded that the appropriate standard for proving conditional relevance is this: whether a reasonable jury could find the preliminary foundational facts (here, the occurrence of the similar acts and defendant's involvement in them) by a preponderance of the evidence. The trial court need not itself be convinced that these acts occurred. On the introduction of sufficient evidence, the issue is to be resolved by the jury (or court in a bench trial). The similar acts in question — and they were similar — would be probative of a material issue other than character, namely, whether Huddleston had the necessary state of mind. The evidence was important in this case, because the only means available in the case for proving mental state were inferences drawn from conduct.

As to Huddleston's argument that the low standard for conditional relevancy would allow the admission of other acts evidence that might be unduly prejudicial, the Court explained:

> We share petitioner's concern that unduly prejudicial evidence might be introduced under Rule 404(b). We think, however, that the protection against such unfair prejudice emanates not from a requirement of a preliminary finding by the trial court, but rather from four other sources: first, from the requirement of Rule 404(b) that the evidence be offered for a proper purpose; second, from the relevancy requirement of Rule 402 as enforced through Rule 104(b); third, from the assessment the trial court must make under Rule 403 to determine whether the probative value of the similar acts evidence is substantially outweighed by the potential for unfair prejudice, . . . ; and fourth, from Federal Rule of Evidence 105, which provides that the trial court shall, upon request, instruct the jury that the similar acts evidence is to be considered only for the proper purpose for which it was admitted.

Problem 5-69: The Mysterious Crib Death

Lolly Faludi's three-month-old baby recently died, in what she claimed was an instance of crib death. Crib death is a sudden and unexpected cessation of breathing or an inability to take in sufficient oxygen. In effect, babies "drown" in a sea of air. This is Faludi's fourth child to die of apparent crib death, and she has been charged with homicide. *Will the prosecution succeed in admitting evidence of the three prior crib deaths at Faludi's homicide trial? Why or why not? What additional information, if any, will help you decide?*

Problem 5-70: The Malicious Prisoner

Quentin Kress is charged with malicious assault of a fellow prisoner. "Malicious assault" in this jurisdiction is defined as assault done with "malice," which is a "a purpose to cause intense physical pain or psychological humiliation." The prosecutor seeks to offer evidence of Kress' subsequent acts of cruelty toward the same victim. *Will the prosecutor succeed in admitting this evidence? Why or why not? What additional information, if any, will help you in making this decision?*

Problem 5-71: The Confused Bookkeeper

Dalton Rumbo admits that he made a serious error in bookkeeping but told his employer that this was an unknowing mistake. An auditor uncovers 10 similar such mistakes by Rumbo during the past year. *Should evidence of these 10 earlier mistakes be admitted at Rumbo's embezzlement trial based on his most recent bookkeeping error? Why or why not?*

Problem 5-72: Brass Knuckles

Bluto Olive claims self-defense at his trial for aggravated assault. Over defense objection, the trial court admits evidence that, shortly before the assault, Olive purchased brass knuckles and put them into his pants pocket. Possession of brass knuckles constitutes the crime of "possessing an instrument of crime." *Did the trial judge rule correctly? Why or why not?*

Problem 5-73: Duress

The defendant, Carla Shinoy, is charged with bank robbery. She asserted the defense of duress. The defendant claimed that a couple, William and Emily Potter, coerced her into committing the robbery. The prosecution offers evidence at trial of other criminal activity in which the defendant had participated.

About a month before the bank robbery, officers tried to apprehend William for alleged shoplifting. Shinoy fired a rifle, which permitted William to escape.

On another occasion, William and Emily kidnapped a third party. Shinoy was present but did not attempt to assist the victim or to escape herself, even though she had an apparent opportunity to do so.

The court's law clerk researched the question of duress. The clerk found that duress exists when "[a] defendant who, without opportunity to escape, has a well grounded fear of imminent death or serious injury unless he complies with his captor's wrongful commands." *United States v. Hearst*, 563 F.2d 1331, 1335 n.1 (9th Cir. 1977).

Should these two other acts described above be admitted at trial?

Problem 5-74: People v. Chambers

The following transcript is an excerpt from the so-called "preppy murder" case: *People v. Chambers*, 512 N.Y.S. 2d 631 (Sup. Ct. 1987). The defendant, Robert Chambers, was charged with the strangulation death of a woman named Jennifer Levin. He claimed that the death was accidental, that it occurred during consensual "rough sex." At trial, Chambers was found guilty. This excerpt reveals how other acts issues apply in the context of an actual murder case.

SUPREME COURT OF THE STATE OF NEW YORK, COUNTY OF NEW YORK

THE PEOPLE OF THE STATE OF NEW YORK, against ROBERT M. CHAMBERS Defendant	6394/86 Charge: Murder 2nd Degree

AFTERNOON SESSION

(Whereupon the following was taken in the jury room outside the presence of the general public:)

MR. KENDRIS [the prosecutor]: Judge, so we can illuminate what we are talking about for the Court, for the record, there is evidence that money, that Jennifer was in possession of some money on the night she was at Dorian's Bar. I think the Court is aware there will be testimony from people perhaps on both sides of this case who were at Dorian's with the defendant and Jennifer Levin that night.

There is also evidence that Jennifer Levin was wearing earrings, very specifically earrings that looked like diamond earrings.

As to the earrings, the state of the evidence I think is that there will be some testimonial evidence that she had earrings on and there also photographs taken at the bar that evening. I don't know whether the Court has seen them at any stage in this case so far and there are several photographs of Jennifer Levin and at least one, maybe more, I don't recall very clear shots of the earrings, that she is wearing at the bar, sometime after midnight that night, maybe even later than that, or earlier in the morning than that.

At the crime scene, Judge, no money is found on her person, only a torn dollar bill and at the crime scene, no earrings are found either at the scene around her body, anywhere in Central Park, no earrings are recovered and there are no earrings in her ears. These are diamond stud earrings. They are not actually diamond that will be probably also be part of the proof, but the fact is they were missing.

THE COURT: What type of earrings, ones that screw?

MR. KENDRIS: Screw on, studs.

She leaves with the defendant and as she leaves she sees a good friend and she doesn't give the earrings to that friend.

Now, we have the video tape which your Honor has also seen in addition to the two photographs.

The defendant says he leaves with her, walks to Central Park with her, kills her accidentally as he described. He says he watches the scene until the police arrive.

Mentions nothing about anyone else taking earrings or her money.

He mentions nothing about Jennifer Levin taking her earrings off at anytime.

When Jennifer Levin's body is found while the defendant is watching, no earrings are found on her and no earrings are found in the surrounding area, not the backs, not the jewel itself.

Judge, the conclusion is inescapably that the defendant took those earrings.

It's circumstantial evidence, but it's compelling.

It goes directly to what this defendant's defense is as he puts it out on a video tape, whether or not he's being truthful on that video tape.

THE COURT: I am concerned right now and you probably answered part of it as to what value is this to your case, that is the elements that you have to prove, that's what I'm concerned with. You see, if it's not necessary with respect to the elements and you have to prove the elements of the case before you even get to the jury.

MR. KENDRIS: I'll address it.

THE COURT: That's it.

If it's not necessary, that's a different story.

MR. KENDRIS: Judge, we think this evidence is very probative in this case.

This defendant's state of mind before and after the crime, the murder or the accident, whichever the jury is going to decide this was, is what's this case is about.

That's what we have to prove. Whether he intended to kill her; whether he acted intentionally at all that night or whether he acted with depraved indifference to human life and there might be lesser included charges like recklessness involved or intent to cause physical injury.

The defendant in his videotaped statement claims that a certain fact transpired before the incident and then he claims after the incident he was in shock, he was in a daze, he couldn't believe he wasn't moving. He walked over and sat on a wall and was in a daze.

If this jury finds, Judge, that he took those earrings and her money and the conclusion is inescapable that he did, there's no one else who could have taken them and there's no other reasonable argument as to what happened to them.

If this jury concludes that he took them, that goes to whether or not he's in a daze, goes to his state of mind.

It goes to whether or not he tried to help her after she was accidentally killed, and that goes to whether or not he showed a depraved indifference to human life.

It goes to whether or not this is an accident or intentional act, whether or not he was thinking clearly or whether or not he was in a daze and didn't know what was going on.

It goes to motive, because if he did take the earrings and the money pursuant to this crime, then he might have a motive to kill her or to hurt her in the course of that.

So those are the reasons why it's highly probative, Judge.

Now, I'm — I'll get back to that in a second.

I would like to discuss some other things that I think are important.

Very briefly, Judge, if the jury doesn't draw the inference that the defendant took the earrings and money, if they say, "Hey, I don't buy that — this, I don't think he did, maybe she did take them off on the walk to Central Park and tossed them into the street," that's what they think, then it is evidence — this evidence is not prejudicial.

This isn't a case where the jury will hear evidence about a prior distinct crime with different victims who were traumatized, where a juror can say, "I don't think they proved to me that he committed that prior crime," but because they heard the evidence about the prior crime they are now themselves inflamed, their passions are aroused because they heard about prior rape — they don't think the defendant did it, but they heard about another rape and now they want to convict him for this rape because they heard about the other one, even though they have not decided that the defendant committed that other one.

This isn't the case.

This isn't, Judge, a prior distinct crime.

Therefore, there is not possibility of that type of prejudice occurring here.

Either it's probative or it's not.

That's all I have to say about it, Judge.

THE COURT: All right.

You want to be heard? Mr. Litman?

MR. LITMAN [defense counsel]: Your Honor, I deny what the prosecutor says about what he claims the facts are, other than at a time very close to 12:00 o'clock midnight, this photograph was taken (indicating), which shows at sometime around midnight or 12:15 or so in the morning, there is an earring in Jennifer Levin's right ear. That's what this photograph shows in terms of the earring.

And when this photograph was taken (indicating), your Honor, which was at approximately 9:00 o'clock or 8:30 in the morning, some eight hours or eight-and-a-half hours later, from a view of this photograph, there is no earring in the right ear.

I will admit that this photograph was taken at around 12:30 in the morning and that there was an earring in the right ear, and some eight hours later this photograph was taken and there is no earring in the right ear (indicating).

There is no credible witness who would testify at a hearing, and you have heard none of their supposed offer of proof, that they claim they saw Jennifer Levin leave the bar with an earring.

Nobody says that.

He tried to draw that conclusion by saying that she didn't give them to anybody else.

I don't have to tell you that there are — I won't even speculate — that there are plenty of other ways that the earrings could have been gotten rid of other than handing them to someone.

She could have taken them off. People take off jewelry. Kids take off jewelry. I have the — a kid . . . who takes them on and off faster than you can whistle it.

Again, your Honor, remember some other facts.

Please remember that the person that they claim stole this on this quote offer of proof, was sitting on the wall in the full view of the police while the police came to the scene.

So they want to believe, and they call this speculation what I am about to say, that he took the stuff and sat on the wall in full view of the police, with scratches all over his face, with this quote incriminating stuff on him.

They ask you to buy that.

He is sitting on a wall with this stuff, according to them, while the police are all over the place.

It's not irrational to say that she could have taken it off or that it came off during the struggle, someone looked at it. There is a whole variety of possibilities.

Your Honor asked what this has to do with the case. They don't even know what it has to do with the case.

They say it proves that it happened beforehand, but then say that it happened afterhand.

You can't allow a prosecutor, Judge, in a case like this to get up before a jury and say he had candidly admitted yesterday, and today, "I don't really know if it happened before or after, but either way, Ladies and Gentlemen, it ain't good for the defendant."

That's not the way you should do things in producing proof of prior crimes.

And what probative value does it have here?

But I will get to what I think is the determinative issue, which is the prejudice, which is so overwhelming.

MR. STAVIS: Can I have one minute? I am usually a man of few words.

THE COURTS: Yes.

MR. STAVIS: If your Honor had a case before you where a defendant is charged with a robbery or larceny by the D.A.'s office, and at twelve o'clock somebody has a piece of property and six-and-a-half hours later they don't have the piece of property, and within the six-and-a-half hours the defendant is with the victim, would that case go to a jury, your Honor? I don't think that it would.

I don't think in this case that there is any proof that Robert Chambers took the earrings. That's number one.

Then number two, Mr. Kendris said if the jury finds that he took the earrings, it would go to whether or not he had depraved indifference or intent to kill, it would go to whether or not he murdered her. To have said that and to then say that there is no possibility of prejudice here, is just to ignore the realities.

If this robbery business comes in, it would blow the case out of the water.

The defendant is on trial for murder, your Honor. Let him be tried for murder.

How would you have ruled on this other acts evidence if you were the judge?

How should the Court in People v. Chambers *instruct the jury about other acts evidence?*

Is the following jury instruction appropriate? Would the prosecutor request this instruction? Would the defense counsel request it?

Ninth Circuit Pattern Jury Instructions: 4.04 — Similar Acts of Defendant

You have heard evidence that the defendant committed acts similar to the crime charged here. You may consider such evidence, not to prove that the defendant did the acts charged here, but only to prove defendant's state of mind, that is, that the defendant acted with the necessary intent and not through accident or mistake.

Therefore, if you find:

that the government has proved beyond a reasonable doubt that defendant committed the acts charged in the indictment; and

that the defendant committed similar acts at other times,

then you may consider these similar acts as evidence that the defendant committed the acts here deliberately and not through accident or mistake.

Contrast Federal Rule of Evidence 404(a) with the following California rule. Which is the preferable rule?

California § 1103. Evidence of character of victim of crime.

In a criminal action, evidence of the character or a trait of character (in the form of an opinion, evidence of reputation, or evidence of specific instances of conduct) of the victim or the crime for which the defendant is being prosecuted is not made inadmissible by Section 1101 if the evidence is:

Offered by the defendant to prove conduct of the victim in conformity with the character or trait of character.

Offered by the prosecution to rebut evidence adduced by the defendant under paragraph (1).

[6] Common Plan, Scheme, or Design

One common non-propensity use of other acts evidence under Rule 404(b)(2) is:[11]

---

[11] McCormick on Evidence 315 (Kenneth S. Broun ed., 6th ed. 2006).

To prove the existence of a larger plan, scheme, or conspiracy, of which the crime on trial is a part . . . . Each crime should be an integral part of an over-arching plan explicitly conceived and executed by the defendant or his confederates. This will be relevant as showing motive, and hence the doing of the criminal act, the identity of the actor, or his intention.

Example

Timothy McWeigh is a member of a terrorist group that needs billions of dollars to raise an army devoted to the violent overthrow of the U.S. government. To further this goal, McWeigh and his cohorts rob numerous banks nationwide. McWeigh is charged with the sixth robbery. The prosecution will likely succeed in admitting evidence of McWeigh's involvement in the first five robberies to prove a common scheme. This would help demonstrate McWeigh's motive and would also help prove his identity as a person who was involved in the sixth robbery.

Note that acts committed pursuant to a common scheme can also become admissible if the charging instrument includes them in the charged offenses, e.g., by charging a conspiracy. In many jurisdictions, each co-conspirator is liable for all acts done by other co-conspirators during the course of, and in furtherance of, the conspiracy. Even in jurisdictions where there is no joint liability for co-conspirators, a similar rule generally governs accomplice liability. Moreover, especially in a conspiracy case, the defendant may be tried on all charges stemming from the criminal agreement in a single trial. Thus, numerous criminal acts may be provable at the same trial to prove the elements of the crimes charged, even though the acts might otherwise be admissible under Rule 404(b)(2) to show a "common plan, scheme, or design."

Problem 5-75: The Comic Book Thief

Morris Morrison is charged with burglarizing Mary Johnson's home and stealing her valuable collection of rare Marvel comic books. The only evidence against Morrison is that the stolen comic book collection was found in his apartment when it was searched pursuant to a valid search warrant. Morrison's counsel plans to argue that this argument supports a conviction for the lesser offense of receiving stolen property but does not establish burglary. The prosecutor offers evidence via eyewitnesses that Morrison engaged in the follow prior uncharged acts: (1) one year ago, he used his building superintendent's passkey to enter a neighbor's home and steal her collection of DC comic books; (2) he used a hatchet five years ago to break into a local comic book store, where he stole the entire collection; and (3) two years ago he bribed a salesperson in a comic book store to sell him rare comic books at below their fair market value.

The defense objects. *Should the objection be sustained? Why or why not? Would your answer change if the evidence of each prior act involved the stealing or purchase of (via bribery) Spider-Man comic books, with the result that Morrison, after the Johnson burglary, had a copy of every Spider-Man comic ever published? What if, in addition, all these prior acts took place within two weeks of the Johnson burglary?*

Problem 5-76: Inheriting by Murder

Eight persons are found murdered over the course of one year. All are murdered in very different and bizarre ways: (1) stabbed with a three-sided knife, (2) thrown out a window, (3) run over by a car, (4) poisoned, (5) killed by an exploding car bomb, (6) died because heart medication had been stolen, (7) bludgeoned with a hammer, and (8) shot in the heart. There is circumstantial evidence linking Fenton Armstrong to the first seven killings but not to the eighth. He is charged with the eighth killing and goes to trial. At the trial, the prosecutor seeks to offer evidence of Armstrong's involvement in the first seven killings as a way to prove that he committed the eighth. The prosecutor also has evidence that each of the murder victims was in line to inherit a fortune from Armstrong's uncle, Michael O'Malley. With all eight victims dead, however, Armstrong will inherit the money. The defense objects to all the proffered evidence. *Should the defense objections be sustained or overruled? Why or why not? Would any additional information aid your inquiry? What information?*

Problem 5-77: Government Kickbacks

George Felberg is in charge of hiring construction firms on various government projects. He is charged with hiring overly expensive firms that do shoddy work because they paid him kickbacks. At his trial for taking one such kickback, the prosecutor offers evidence of 10 other kickbacks he received from similarly incompetent but expensive construction companies over the past year. *Should this evidence be admissible?*

Problem 5-78: Drug Dealers

Mary Marfoon is charged with dealing cocaine. Prosecutors seek at her trial to offer evidence of 40 other cocaine sales she made that year, all to well-known city government officials. Prosecutors further seek to offer evidence of a form letter sent by the defendant to all the cocaine purchasers four days after the purchase being prosecuted (or, alternatively, sent to each buyer four days after that person bought cocaine from her; would it make any difference?). The form letter said, "If you'd rather not have the press aware of your chemical recreational habit, you'll deliver $40,000 to the address below within 10 days of receiving this letter." *Should any of the proffered evidence be admitted? Why or why not?*

[B] Habit

A proper understanding of Rule 404(b) specific acts evidence requires distinguishing it from habit. "Habit," unlike character, evidence is routinely admissible:

> **Rule 406. Habit; Routine Practice**
>
> Evidence of a person's habit or an organization's routine practice may be admitted to prove that on a particular occasion the person or organization acted in accordance with the habit or routine practice. The court may admit this evidence regardless of whether it is corroborated or whether there was an eyewitness.

The starting place for gauging the distinction between character and habit is the Rule 406 Advisory Committee Note:

> Character is a generalized description of one's disposition, or of one's disposition in respect to a general trait, such as honesty, temperance, or peacefulness. Habit in modern usage, both lay and psychological, is more specific. It describes one's regular response to a repeated specific situation. If we speak of character for care, we think of the person's tendency to act prudently in all the varying situations of life, in business, in family life, in handling automobiles, and in walking across the street. A habit, on the other hand, is the person's regular practice of meeting a particular kind of situation with a specific type of conduct, such as the habit of going down a particular stairway two stairs at a time, or of giving the hand-signal for a left turn, or of alighting from railway cars while they are moving. The doing of the habitual acts may become semi-automatic.
>
> Equivalent behavior on the part of a group is designated 'routine practice of an organization' in the rule.
>
> There is general agreement that habit evidence is highly persuasive as proof of conduct on a particular occasion. Again quoting McCormick § 152, p. 341:
>
> Character may be thought of as the sum of one's habits though doubtless it is more than this. But unquestionably the uniformity of one's response to habit is far greater than the consistency with which one's conduct conforms to character or disposition. Even though character comes in only exceptionally as evidence of an act, surely any sensible man in investigating whether X did a particular act would be greatly helped in this inquiry by evidence as to whether he was in the habit of doing it.

This excerpted portion of the Advisory Committee Note sets forth what Professor Thomas Mengler has called the "probability theory" of habit.[12] Under this theory, the probability of someone reacting in a specific, predictable way to a narrow, specific situation is quite high. The person always or nearly always reacts as expected.

Example 1

Joanie Mirez showers immediately upon awakening each morning. She will not eat, play with her kids, or read the newspaper until she showers. Her husband of 20 years remembers only one exception to this rule: the day he thought he was having a heart attack, and she had to rush him to the hospital.

Example 2

Andrew Paslitz watches the television science fiction show *Sliders* every Thursday night at 8:00 p.m., even when it is in reruns. He turns down professional and social invitations rather than miss this show.

---

[12] *See* Thomas Mengler, *The Theory of Discretion in the Federal Rules of Evidence*, 74 Iowa L. Rev. 413, 417 (1989).

Fully understanding the probability theory of habit requires exploring some social science. The legal concept of "character" is analogous to the psychologists' concept of "personality." But empirical research reveals that global personality traits — ones displayed in many circumstances — do not exist. Personality traits tend to be more situationally specific.

Example 3

Reginald usually arrives at faculty meetings precisely on time. He is certainly far more punctual than his colleagues, most of whom have developed the custom of arriving "fashionably late." There is rarely a quorum until at least 15 minutes after the official meeting time. For these reasons, Reginald's colleagues often joke that he is "compulsive about time." In fact, however, Reginald is a good 10 minutes late about three times per year, and is the last to arrive once each year. A hot sports game on the radio, an offer from a prestigious law journal, or an occasional fit of pique will slow Reginald down. But most faculty members, who arrive even later than he, don't notice his 10-minute tardiness and view his one exceptional lateness each year as aberrational. However, as there are only 10 faculty meetings each year, "Punctual Reggie" is actually late 40% of the time!

Reggie's 40% tardy rate makes it hard to predict with a high degree of confidence that Reggie will be on time for any particular faculty meeting. But Reggie has never, since his fourth birthday, failed to brush his teeth upon wakening. We can be almost 100% confident on any given, randomly selected morning that Reggie will brush his teeth. The "habit" of Reggie's "brushing-teeth-upon-wakening" therefore has a much higher probative value than Reggie's "character" trait of being "punctual at work."

However, the meaning of "habit" is not limited to a definition based on the "probability theory." An alternative definition has been based on the "psychological theory."[13] Under this theory, not only is "habit" limited to a frequently repeated, specific behavioral response to a narrow set of circumstances. In addition, the conduct must be "unconsciously mechanical — Pavlovian."[14] Surprisingly, the Advisory Committee Note also adopts this theory:

> In *Levin v. United States*, 338 F.2d 265, 119 U.S. App. D.C. 156 (1964), testimony as to the religious "habits" of the accused, offered as tending to prove that he was at home observing the Sabbath rather than out obtaining money through larceny by trick, was properly excluded:
>
> It seems apparent to us that an individual's religious practices would not be the type of activities which would lend themselves to the characterization of "invariable regularity." [1 Wigmore 5201. Certainly the very volitional basis of the activity raises serious questions as to its invariable nature, and hence its probative value.

---

[13] *See* Thomas Mengler, *The Theory of Discretion in the Federal Rules of Evidence*, 74 Iowa L. Rev. 413, 417 (1989).

[14] *Id.*

One modern court has similarly defined "habit," as have many lower courts, as "semi-automatic, almost involuntary and invariably specific responses to fairly specific stimuli."[15] The idea is that if the behavior is barely, if at all, under your conscious control, you are highly unlikely to vary it, both because you are not really aware of it and because changing it may even be beyond your control.

Example 4

Doug Lars is a chain smoker. When he finishes one cigarette, he lights another. Even if he promises a host at a party not to smoke, shortly thereafter he is lighting up. When the hostess complains, Doug responds with genuine surprise, "I'm so sorry! I didn't even realize that I was doing that."

The Advisory Committee Note states both the probability and psychological theories of habit but does not choose between them. Yet choice is necessary. Thus, in the earlier example in which Paslitz watches the *Sliders* television show every Thursday night, the behavior is specific, oft-repeated, and regular, but probably not semi-automatic. The behavior would be habit under the probability theory but not under the psychological theory. Mengler argues that the Advisory Committee intended for the courts to resolve the dispute. Indeed, given the rules' general preference for trial court discretion and distrust of appellate review, Mengler concludes that trial courts were meant to resolve the question on a case-by-case basis. This would permit different definitions of habit to prevail in different cases, as the needs of the case dictated.

One important use of habit in modern trials is its manifestation as the "routine practice of an organization." In busy, often large, corporate or government entities, overworked staff may often forget the details of specific transactions. But businesses set up procedures that they rely on to maintain profit, efficiency, and effectiveness that function much like habits.

Example 5

The chair of a large law firm's litigation department is being deposed. He cannot remember whether he attended a particular department meeting on January 3, 2004, which was a Monday. However, further questioning reveals that the written firm policy manual mandates a litigation department meeting every Monday to be attended by all department members and presided over by the department chair. The Manual further requires written notice from any attorney who cannot attend any meeting, and requires the notice to be kept in the attorney's personnel file. No such note from this department chair is in his personnel file. Furthermore, the chair concedes that the firm has always rigidly enforced the terms of its policy manual. This evidence of the routine practice of the law firm strongly suggests that the chair was indeed present at the January 3 meeting.

---

[15] *Washington St. Physicians Ins. v. Fisons Corp.*, 122 Wash. 2d 299, 858 P.2d 1054, 1068 (1993).

Problem 5-79: Stolen Sneakers

The defendant was accused of stealing sneakers from My Left Foot, a sporting goods store. The defendant claimed at trial that he purchased the goods but was not given a sales receipt. The prosecution then attempted to introduce evidence showing that it was the custom of the store to give sales receipts with every purchase.

Is the evidence admissible? Why?

Must specific examples of the store's practice regarding receipts be provided prior to the admission of evidence showing the habit of a person or a routine business practice?

Problem 5-80: "The Hurrieder I Go, The Behinder I Get"

A fiery crash occurred between cars driven by plaintiff and defendant. Plaintiff claimed that defendant negligently caused the accident.

At trial, plaintiff attempted to introduce evidence that defendant "is always in a rush." *Admissible? Why?*

Plaintiff testifies that she "regularly uses turn signals." *Is this permissible habit evidence? Why?*

Problem 5-81: Chivas

The defendant, Rob, is prosecuted for driving while intoxicated at 1:00 p.m. on a Tuesday. The state introduced evidence at trial that the defendant always drank a shot of Chivas Regal liquor promptly at noon every day.

Is the evidence admissible? Why?

Would it be admissible habit evidence if the state offered to show that Rob was in a habit of getting drunk every day around noon?

Problem 5-82: Don't Do Me Like That

The plaintiff claims he was fired from the police force because he exercised his First Amendment right to freedom of speech. The plaintiff offers evidence at trial that the police department habitually fired individuals who exercised their First Amendment rights, evidence that the department fired several different people for speaking out. *Is this evidence admissible? Why? See McWhorter v. City of Birmingham,* 906 F.2d 674 (11th Cir. 1990).

§ 5.12 CHARACTER EVIDENCE REVIEW PROBLEMS

Problem 5-83: Orwellian Defamation

Maxwell has civilly sued George Orwell for defamation. Maxwell's first Witness, Blue True, at trial testified that he overheard Orwell tell a local newspaper, *The Daily Globe:* "John Maxwell is a well-known liar; he raped my daughter, Rosetta, and now he's trying to lie his way out of it; just like he always does." *The Globe* printed this quote in a story about Rosetta's rape. When Maxwell calls his second witness, Father O'Reilly (Maxwell's next-door neighbor and parish priest for the past 23 years), to testify that Maxwell has a reputation for truthfulness in the community in which they both live, Orwell objects. *Orwell's objection should be:*

1. Overruled because O'Reilly's testimony is admissible under both Rule 405(b) and Rule 608(a).

2. Overruled because O'Reilly's testimony is admissible under Rule 405(b) only.

3. Sustained because O'Reilly's testimony is an act propensity use of character evidence.

4. Sustained because the mercy rule does not apply.

Problem 5-84: Perjuring Clergy

On cross-examining Father O'Reilly, Orwell's counsel asks the following question: "Isn't it true that you perjured yourself 11 years ago, lying to a grand juror about whether your brother ran an illegal gambling operation?" *Maxwell's objection to this question should be:*

1. Sustained under Rule 609 because the perjury occurred more than 10 years ago.

2. Overruled under Rule 609 if Orwell gave sufficient written notice to Maxwell of the intent to ask the question, offered a fair opportunity to contest its admissibility, and provided specific facts and circumstances demonstrating that the evidence's probative value substantially outweighs it prejudicial effect.

3. Admissible under Rule 608(b) in the discretion of the court.

4. Inadmissible under Rule 608.

Problem 5-85: Perjuring Clergy Revisited

Assume that the trial judge permits the question in multiple-choice Problem 5-84 above to be asked, and in response, Father O'Reilly denies the perjury. Orwell's counsel later seeks in the defense case to call O'Reilly's brother to testify that he, the brother, had indeed been an illegal gambler, and had told O'Reilly about the gambling, and heard O'Reilly admit to lying about that knowledge to a grand jury. Maxwell's objection to this testimony should be:

1. Sustained because it is extrinsic evidence offered solely to prove character for truthfulness or untruthfulness.

2. Overruled because prior crimes used to impeach a witness may be proved by extrinsic evidence.

3. Overruled because, although it is extrinsic evidence that may prove character for truthfulness or untruthfulness, it is also relevant as proper impeachment by specific contradiction, provided it survives Rule 403 balancing.

4. Sustained because it is hearsay not fitting within a recognized exception.

Problem 5-86: Maxwell's Silver Tongue

Assume now that O'Reilly was permitted to testify and, on cross-examination is asked, "You have heard that John Maxwell lied by falsely claiming in an employment application last year that he had a Ph. D. in Economics?" Any objection to this question should be:

1. Sustained because act propensity character evidence may not generally be proven by specific acts.

2. Sustained because the answer would be prejudicial to Maxwell under Rule 403.

3. Overruled because the evidence would be admissible under both Rule 405 and Rule 608.

4. Overruled because the evidence would be admissible under Rule 405(a) alone.

Problem 5-87: False Cries

Assume now that, instead of being at a civil defamation trial, Maxwell is the defendant in a criminal trial on charges that he raped Rosetta, and Rosetta has testified in the prosecution's case. The defense seeks to cross-examine Rosetta as a means of offering evidence that she falsely cried rape on three earlier occasions involving three men (one man per occasion) other than Maxwell. This evidence should be:

1. Inadmissible under Rule 412.

2. Admissible under Rule 412.

3. Admissible under Rule 413.

4. Admissible under Rule 608(b).

Problem 5-88: Reasonable Belief?

Maxwell's defense at his rape trial is that he reasonably believed that Rosetta had consented. The prosecution proffers evidence that on three prior occasions Maxwell had sexual intercourse with three other women who charged Maxwell with rape, though each dropped the charges before the trial because they feared that the wealthy Maxwell would besmirch their names in the press. The proffered evidence is:

1. Inadmissible act propensity evidence.

2. Admissible act propensity evidence.

3. Admissible, if the trial court concludes that a reasonable jury could by the preponderance of the evidence believe that the three earlier incidents happened and involved the defendant as the three women described.

4. Admissible, if the trial court concludes that she is personally convinced by a preponderance of the evidence that the three earlier incidents happened and involved the defendant as the women described.

Problem 5-89: Mistaken Identification

Assume instead that Maxwell's defense at his criminal rape trial is mistaken identification. The prosecution offers evidence of 10 instances in the last year in which Maxwell gently fondled the breasts of various women against their will.

Upon a proper objection, the evidence is:

1. Admissible evidence of an offense of sexual assault, to be used for any relevant purpose.

2. Admissible evidence of an offense of sexual assault, so long as it is used for purposes other than act propensity.

3. Inadmissible because prior offenses of sexual assault are logically irrelevant to proving rape.

4. Inadmissible act propensity evidence.

Problem 5-90: Simply Assaulting

Maxwell takes the stand at his criminal rape trial and raises an alibi defense. On cross-examination, the prosecutor asks Maxwell to admit that he was convicted of misdemeanor simple assault one year ago. Defense counsel's objection should be:

1. Sustained because simple assault is not a felony.

2. Overruled because simple assault is *crimen falsi*.

3. Sustained under both Rule 609 and Rule 404(a).

4. Sustained only under Rule 403.

5. Her prior identification is admissible if it is part of a signed statement made under oath.

Problem 5-91: Tax Fraud

Defendant Ozzie Harriet takes the stand as part of his defense. On cross-examination, the prosecutor asks Harriet whether he was convicted two years ago for tax fraud. The question is:

1. Proper to show Harriet is inclined to lie.

2. Proper to show that Harriet is inclined to steal.

3. Improper because the conviction has insufficient similarity to the crime charged.

4. Improper because the probative value of the evidence is outweighed by the danger of unfair prejudice.

§ 5.13 CASE LIBRARY

MICHELSON v. UNITED STATES
Supreme Court of the United States
335 U.S. 469, 69 S. Ct. 213, 93 L. Ed. 168 (1948)

MR. JUSTICE JACKSON delivered the opinion of the Court.

In 1947 petitioner Michelson was convicted of bribing a federal revenue agent.[16] The Government proved a large payment by accused to the agent for the purpose of influencing his official action. The defendant, as a witness on his own behalf, admitted passing the money but claimed it was done in response to the agent's demands, threats, solicitations, and inducements that amounted to entrapment. It is enough for our purposes to say that determination of the issue turned on whether the jury should believe the agent or the accused.[17]

On direct examination of defendant, his own counsel brought out that, in 1927, he had been convicted of a misdemeanor having to do with trading in counterfeit watch

---

[16] (Court's original footnote 1.) The first count charged petitioner with bribing in violation of **18 U.S.C. § 91** (now **18 U.S.C. § 201**), and the affirmance of his conviction on this count by the Court of Appeals, 2 Cir., 165 F.2d 732, is the judgment here under review. The second count charged "offering" the bribe as a violation of the same statute but his conviction on this count was reversed by the Court of Appeals and is not here involved.

[17] (Court's original footnote 2.) Details appear in the Court of Appeals opinion, 2 Cir., 165 F.2d 732.

dials. On cross-examination it appeared that in 1930, in executing an application for a license to deal in second-hand jewelry, he answered "No" to the question whether he had theretofore been arrested or summoned for any offense.

Defendant called five witnesses to prove that he enjoyed a good reputation. Two of them testified that their acquaintance with him extended over a period of about thirty years and the others said they had known him at least half that long. A typical examination in chief was as follows:

Q: Do you know the defendant Michelson?

A: Yes.

Q: How long do you know Mr. Michelson?

A: About 30 years.

Q: Do you know other people who know him?

A: Yes.

Q: Have you had occasion to discuss his reputation for honesty and truthfulness and for being a law-abiding citizen?

A: It is very good.

Q: You have talked to others?

A: Yes.

Q: And what is his reputation?

A: Very good.'

These are representative of answers by three witnesses; two others replied, in substance, that they never had heard anything against Michelson.

On cross-examination, four of the witnesses were asked, in substance, this question: "Did you ever hear that Mr. Michelson on March 4, 1927, was convicted of a violation of the trademark law in New York City in regard to watches?" This referred to the twenty-year-old conviction about which defendant himself had testified on direct examination. Two of them had heard of it and two had not.

To four of these witnesses the prosecution also addressed the question the allowance of which, over defendant's objection, is claimed to be reversible error:

Did you ever hear that on October 11th, 1920, the defendant, Solomon Michelson, was arrested for receiving stolen goods?

None of the witnesses appears to have heard of this.

The trial court asked counsel for the prosecution, out of presence of the jury, "Is it a fact according to the best information in your possession that Michelson was arrested for receiving stolen goods?" Counsel replied that it was, and to support his good faith exhibited a paper record which defendant's counsel did not challenge.

The judge also on three occasions warned the jury, in terms that are not criticized, of the limited purpose for which this evidence was received.[18]

Defendant-petitioner challenges the right of the prosecution so to cross-examine his character witnesses. The Court of Appeals held that it was permissible. The opinion, however, points out that the practice has been severely criticized and invites us, in one respect, to change the rule.[19] Serious and responsible criticism has been aimed, however, not alone at the detail now questioned by the Court of Appeals but at common-law doctrine on the whole subject of proof of reputation or

---

[18] (Court's original footnote 3.) In ruling on the objection when the question was first asked, the Court said:

> " . . . I instruct the jury that what is happening now is this: the defendant has called character witnesses, and the basis for the evidence given by those character witnesses is the reputation of the defendant in the community, and since the defendant tenders the issue of his reputation the prosecution may ask the witness if she has heard of various incidents in his career. I say to you that regardless of her answer you are not to assume that the incidents asked about actually took place. All that is happening is that this witness' standard of opinion of the reputation of the defendant is being tested. Is that clear?"

In overruling the second objection to the question the Court said:

> "Again I say to the jury there is no proof that Mr. Michelson was arrested for receiving stolen goods in 1920, there isn't any such proof. All this witness has been asked is whether he had heard of that. There is nothing before you on that issue. Now would you base your decision on the case fairly in spite of the fact that that question has been asked? You would? All right." The charge included the following: "In connection with the character evidence in the case I permitted a question whether or not the witness knew that in 1920 this defendant ha been arrested for receiving stolen goods. I tried to give you the instruction then that that question was permitted only to test the standards of character evidence that these character witnesses seemed to have. There isn't any proof in the case that could be produced before you legally within the rules of evidence that this defendant was arrested in 1920 for receiving stolen goods, and that fact you are not to hold against him; nor are you to assume what the consequences of that arrest were. You just drive it from your mind so far as he is concerned, and take it into consideration only in weighing the evidence of the character witnesses."

[19] (Court's original footnote 4.) Footnote 8 to that court's opinion reads as follows [165 F.2d 735]:

> "Wigmore, Evidence (3d ed. 1940) § 988, after noting that 'such inquiries are almost universally admitted,' not as impeachment by extrinsic testimony of particular acts of misconduct,' but as means of testing the character 'witness' grounds of knowledge,' continues with these comments: "But the serious objection to them is that practically the above distinction-between rumors of such conduct, as affecting reputation, and the fact of it as violating the rule against particular facts- cannot be maintained in the mind of the jury. The rumor the misconduct, when admitted, goes far, in spite of all theory and of the judge's charge, towards fixing the misconduct as a fact upon the other person, and thus does three improper things, -(1) it violates the fundamental rule of fairness that prohibits the use of such facts, (2) it gets at them by hearsay only, and not by trustworthy testimony, and (3) it leaves the other person no means of defending himself by denial or explanation, such as he would other-wise have had if the rule had allowed that conduct to be made the subject of an issue. Moreover, these are not occurrences of possibility, but of daily practice. This method of inquiry or cross-examination is frequently resorted to by counsel for the very purpose of injuring by indirection a character which they are forbid-den directly to attack in that way; they rely upon the mere putting of the question (not caring that it is answered negatively) to convey their covert insinuation. The value of the inquiry for testing purposes is often so small and the opportunities of its abuse by underhanded ways are so great that the practice may amount to little more than a mere subterfuge, and should be strictly supervised by forbidding it to counsel who do not use it in good faith."

> "Because, as Wigmore says, the jury almost surely cannot comprehend the judge's limiting instruction, the writer of this opinion wishes that the United States Supreme Court would tell us to follow what appears to be the Illinois rule, i.e., that such questions are improper unless they relate to offenses similar to those for which the defendant is on trial. See *Aiken v. People*, 183 Ill. 215, 55 N.E. 695; cf. People v. Hannon, 381 Ill. 206, 44 N.E.2d 923."

character.[20] It would not be possible to appraise the usefulness and propriety of this cross-examination without consideration of the unique practice concerning character testimony, of which such cross-examination is a minor part.[21]

Courts that follow the common-law tradition almost unanimously have come to disallow resort by the prosecution to any kind of evidence of a defendant's evil character to establish a probability of his guilt.[22] Not that the law invests the defendant with a presumption of good character, *Greer v. United States*, 245 U.S. 559, 38 S.Ct. 209, 62 L.Ed. 469, but it simply closes the whole matter of character, disposition and reputation on the prosecution's case-in-chief. The State may not show defendant's prior trouble with the law, specific criminal acts, or ill name among his neighbors, even though such facts might logically be persuasive that he is by propensity a probable perpetrator of the crime.[23]

The inquiry is not rejected because character is irrelevant;[24] on the contrary, it is said to weigh too much with the jury and to so overpersuade them as to prejudge one with a bad general record and deny him a fair opportunity to defend against a particular charge. The overriding policy of excluding such evidence, despite its admitted probative value, is the practical experience that its disallowance tends to prevent confusion of issues, unfair surprise and undue prejudice.[25]

---

[20] (Court's original footnote 5.) A judge of trial and appellate experience has uttered a warning which, in the opinion of the writer, we might well have heeded in determining whether to grant certiorari here:

> . . . evidence of good character is to be used like any other, once it gets before the jury, and the less they are told about the grounds for its admission, or what they shall do with it, the more likely they are to use it sensibly. The subject seems to gather mist which discussion serves only to thicken, and which we can scarcely hope to dissipate by anything further we can add." L. Hand in *Nash v. United States*, *2 Cir., 54 F.2d 1006, 1007.*

In opening its cyclopedic review of authorities from many jurisdictions, Corpus Juris Secundum summarizes that the rules regulating proof of character "have been criticized as illogical, unscientific, and anomalous, explain-able only as archaic survivals of compurgation or of states of legal development when the jury personally knew the facts on which their verdict was based." 32 C.J.S., Evidence, § 433.

[21] (Court's original footnote 6.) *See Maguire, Evidence: Common Sense and Common Law* (1947). Compare pp. 203–209 and pp. 74–76.

[22] (Court's original footnote 7.) *Greer v. United States*, 245 U.S. 559, 38 S. Ct. 209, 62 L. Ed. 469; 1 Wigmore, *Evidence* (3d ed., 1940) § 57; 1 Wharton, *Criminal Evidence* (11th ed., 1935) § 330. This was not the earlier rule in English common law and is not now the rule in some civil law countries. 1 Wigmore, *Evidence* (3d ed., § 1940) § 193.

[23] (Court's original footnote 8.) This would be subject to some qualification, as when a prior crime is an element of the later offense; for example, at a trial for being an habitual criminal. There are also well-established exceptions where evidence as to other transactions or a course of fraudulent conduct is admitted to establish fraudulent intent as an element of the crime charged. See, e.g., *Fall v. United States, 49 F.2d 506, 60 App. D.C. 124, certiorari denied, 283 U.S. 867, 51 S. Ct. 657, 75 L. Ed. 1471; Hatem v. United States, 4 Cir., 42 F.2d 40, certiorari denied, 282 U.S. 887, 51 S.Ct. 103, 75 L. Ed. 782; Williamson v. United States, 207 U.S. 425, 28 S. Ct. 163, 52 L. Ed. 278; Allis v. United States, 155 U.S. 117, 15 S. Ct. 36, 39 L. Ed. 91; Wood v. United States, 10 L. Ed. 987, 16 Pet. 342.*

[24] (Court's original footnote 9.) As long ago as 1865, Chief Justice Cockburn said, "The truth is, this part of our law is an anomaly. Although, logically speaking, it is quite clear that an antecedent bad character would form quite as reasonable a ground for the presumption and probability of guilt as previous good character lays the foundation of innocence, yet you cannot, on the part of the prosecution, go into evidence as to character." Reg v. Rowton, 10 Cox's Criminal Cases 25, 29–30. And see 1 Wigmore, Evidence (3d ed., 1940) § 55.

[25] (Court's original footnote 10.) 1 Wigmore, Evidence (3d ed., 1940) § 57.

But this line of inquiry firmly denied to the State is opened to the defendant because character is relevant in resolving probabilities of guilt.[26] He may introduce affirmative testimony that the general estimate of his character is so favorable that the jury may infer that he would not be likely to commit the offense charged. This privilege is sometimes valuable to a defendant for this Court has held that such testimony alone, in some circumstances, may be enough to raise a reasonable doubt of guilt and that in the federal courts a jury in a proper case should be so instructed. *Edgington v. United States*, 164 U.S. 361, 17 S.Ct. 72, 41 L.Ed. 467.

When the defendant elects to initiate a character inquiry, another anomalous rule comes into play. Not only is he permitted to call witnesses to testify from hearsay, but indeed such a witness is not allowed to base his testimony on anything but hearsay.[27] What commonly is called "character evidence" is only such when "character" is employed as a synonym for "reputation." The witness may not testify about defendant's specific acts or courses of conduct or his possession of a particular disposition or of benign mental and moral traits; nor can he testify that his own acquaintance, observation, and know edge of defendant leads to his own independent opinion that defendant possesses a good general or specific character, inconsistent with commission of acts charged. The witness is, however, allowed to summarize what he has heard in the community, although much of it may have been said by persons less qualified to judge than himself. The evidence which the law permits is not as to the personality of defendant but only as to the shadow his daily life has cast in his neighborhood. This has been well described in a different connection as "the slow growth of months and years, the resultant picture of forgotten incidents, passing events, habitual and daily conduct, presumably honest because disinterested, and safer to be trusted because prone to suspect . . . . It is for that reason that such general repute is permitted to be proven. It sums up a multitude of trivial details. It compacts into the brief phrase of a verdict the teaching of many incidents and the conduct of years. It is the average intelligence drawing its conclusion." Finch J., in *Badger v. Badger*, 88 N.Y. 546, 552, 42 Am. Rep. 263.

While courts have recognized logical grounds for criticism of this type of opinion-based-on-hearsay testimony, it is said to be justified by "overwhelming considerations of practical convenience" in avoiding innumerable collateral issues which, if it were attempted to prove character by direct testimony, would complicate and confuse the trial, distract the minds of jurymen and befog the chief issues in the litigation. *People v. Van Gaasbeck*, 189 N.Y. 408, 418, 82 N.E. 718, 22 L.R.A.,N.S., 650, 12 Ann.Cas. 745. Another paradox in this branch of the law of evidence is that the delicate and responsible task of compacting reputation hearsay into the "brief phrase of a verdict" is one of the few instances in which conclusions are accepted from a witness on a subject in which he is not an expert. However, the witness must qualify to give an opinion by showing such acquaintance with the defendant, the community in which he has lived and the circles in which he has moved, as to speak

---

[26] (Court's original footnote 11.) 1 Wigmore, Evidence (3d ed., 1940) § 56; Underhill, Criminal Evidence (4th ed., 1935) § 165; 1 Wharton, Criminal Evidence (11th ed., 1935) §§ 330, 336.

[27] (Court's original footnote 12.) 5 Wigmore, Evidence (3d ed., 1940) § 1609; Underhill, Criminal Evidence (4th ed., 1935) § 170; 1 Wharton, Criminal Evidence (11th ed., 1935) § 333.

with authority of the terms in which generally he is regarded. To require affirmative knowledge of the reputation may seem inconsistent with the latitude given to the witness to testify when all he can say of the reputation is that he has "heard nothing against defendant." This is permitted upon assumption that, if no ill is reported of one, his reputation must be good.[28] But this answer is accepted only from a witness whose knowledge of defendant's habitat and surroundings is intimate enough so that his failure to hear of any relevant ill repute is an assurance that no ugly rumors were about.[29]

Thus the law extends helpful but illogical options to a defendant. Experience taught a necessity that they be counterweighted with equally illogical conditions to keep the advantage from becoming an unfair and unreasonable one. The price a defendant must pay for attempting to prove his good name is to throw open the entire subject which the law has kept closed for his benefit and to make himself vulnerable where the law otherwise shields him. The prosecution may pursue the inquiry with contradictory witnesses[30] to show that damaging rumors, whether or not well-grounded, were afloat-for it is not the man that he is, but the name that he has which is put in issue. Another hazard is that his own witness is subject to cross-examination as to the contents and extent of the hearsay on which he bases his conclusions, and he may be required to disclose rumors and reports that are current even if they do not affect his own conclusion.[31] It may test the sufficiency of his knowledge by asking what stories were circulating concerning events, such as one's arrest, about which people normally comment and speculate. Thus, while the law gives defendant the option to show as a fact that his reputation reflects a life and habit incompatible with commission of the offense charged, it subjects his proof to tests of credibility designed to prevent him from profiting by a mere parade of partisans.

To thus digress from evidence as to the offense to hear a contest as to the standing of the accused, at its best opens a tricky line of inquiry as to a shapeless and elusive subject matter. At its worst it opens a veritable Pandora's box of irresponsible gossip, innuendo and smear. In the frontier phase of our law's development, calling friends to vouch for defendant's good character, and its counterpart-calling the rivals and enemies of a witness to impeach him by testifying

---

[28] (Court's original footnote 13.) *People v. Van Gaasbeck*, 189 N.Y. 408, 420, 82 N.E. 718, 22 L.R.A., N.S., 650, 12 Ann. Cas. 745. The law apparently ignores the existence of such human ciphers as Kipling's Tomlinson, of whom no ill is reported but no good can be recalled. They win seats with the righteous for character evidence purposes, however hard their lot in literature.

[29] (Court's original footnote 14.) *Id.*; 5 Wigmore, *Evidence* (2d ed., 1940) § 1614; Underhill, *Criminal Evidence* (4th ed., 1935) § 171; 1 Wharton, *Criminal Evidence* (11th ed., 1935) § 33.

[30] (Court's original footnote 15.) 1 Wigmore, Evidence (3d ed., 1940) § 58; Underhill, Criminal Evidence (4th ed., 1935) § 167; 1 Wharton, Criminal Evidence (11th ed., 1935) § 330.

[31] (Court's original footnote 16.) A classic example in the books is a character witness in a trial for murder. She testified she grew up with defendant, knew his reputation for peace and quiet, and that it was good. On cross-examination she was asked if she had heard that the defendant had shot anybody and, if so, how many. She answered, "Three or four," and gave the names of two but could not recall the names of the others. She still insisted, however, that he was of "good character." The jury seems to have valued her information more highly than her judgment, and on appeal from conviction the cross-examination was held proper. People v. Laudiero, 192 N.Y. 304, 309, 85 N.E. 132. See also People v. Elliott, 163 N.Y. 11, 57 N.E. 103.

that his reputation for veracity was so bad that he was unworthy of belief on his oath-were favorite and frequent ways of converting an individual litigation into a community contest and a trial into a spectacle. Growth of urban conditions, where one may never know or hear the name of his next-door neighbor, have tended to limit the use of these techniques and to deprive them of weight with juries. The popularity of both procedures has subsided, but courts of last resort have sought to overcome danger that the true issues will be obscured and confused by investing the trial court with discretion to limit the number of such witnesses and to control cross-examination. Both propriety and abuse of hearsay reputation testimony, on both sides, depend on numerous and subtle considerations, difficult to detect or appraise from a cold record, and therefore rarely and only on clear showing of prejudicial abuse of discretion will Courts of Appeals disturb rulings of trial courts on this subject.[32]

Wide discretion is accompanied by heavy responsibility on trial courts to protect the practice from any misuse. The trial judge was scrupulous to so guard it in the case before us. He took pains to ascertain, out of presence of the jury, that the target of the question was an actual event, which would probably result in some comment among acquaintances if not injury to defendant's reputation. He satisfied himself that counsel was not merely taking a random shot at a reputation imprudently exposed or asking a groundless question to waft an unwarranted innuendo into the jury box.[33]

The question permitted by the trial court, however, involves several features that may be worthy of comment. Its form invited hearsay; it asked about an arrest, not a conviction, and for an offense not closely similar to the one on trial; and it concerned an occurrence many years past.

Since the whole inquiry, as we have pointed out, is calculated to ascertain the

---

[32] (Court's original footnote 17.) *See, e.g., Mannix v. United States*, 4 Cir., 140 F.2d 250. It has been held that the question may not be hypothetical nor assume unproven facts and ask if they would affect the conclusion, *Little v. United States*, 8 Cir., 93 F.2d 401; *Pittman v. United States*, 8 Cir., 42 F.2d 793; *Filippelli v. United States*, 9 Cir., 6 F.2d 121; and that it may not be so asked as to detail evidence or circumstances of a crime of which defendant was accused. *People v. Marendi*, 213 N.Y. 600, 107 N.E. 1058. It has been held error to use the question to get before the jury a particular derogatory newspaper article. *Sloan v. United States*, 8 Cir., 31 F.2d 902. The proof has been confined to general reputation and that among a limited group such as fellow employees in a particular building held inadmissible. *Williams v. United States*, 168 U.S. 382, 18 S. Ct. 92, 42 L. Ed. 509.

[33] (Court's original footnote 18.) This procedure was recommended by Wigmore. But analysis of his innovation emphasizes the way in which law on this subject has evolved from pragmatic considerations rather than from theoretical consistency. The relevant information that it is permissible to lay before the jury is talk or conversation about the defendant's being arrested. That is admissible whether or not an actual arrest had taken place; it might even be more significant of repute if his neighbors were ready to arrest him in rumor when the authorities were not in fact. But before this relevant and proper inquiry can be made, counsel must demonstrate privately to the court an irrelevant and possibly unprovable fact-the reality of arrest. From this permissible inquiry about reports of arrest, the jury is pretty certain to infer that defendant had in fact been rested and to draw its own conclusions as to character from that fact. The Wigmore suggestion thus limits legally relevant inquiries to those based on legally relevant facts in order that the legally irrelevant conclusion which the jury probably will draw from the relevant questions will not be based on unsupported or untrue innuendo. It illustrates Judge Hand's suggestion that the system may work best when explained least. Yet, despite its theoretical paradoxes and deficiencies, we approve the procedure as calculated in practice to hold the inquiry within decent bounds.

general talk of people about defendant, rather than the witness' own knowledge of him, the form of inquiry, "Have you heard?" has general approval, and "Do you know?" is not allowed.[34]

A character witness may be cross-examined as to an arrest whether or not it culminated in a conviction, according to the overwhelming weight of authority.[35] This rule is sometimes confused with that which prohibits cross-examination to credibility by asking a witness whether he himself has been arrested.

Arrest without more does not, in law any more than in reason, impeach the integrity or impair the credibility of a witness. It happens to the innocent as well as the guilty. Only a conviction, therefore, may be inquired about to undermine the trustworthiness of a witness.

Arrest without more may nevertheless impair or cloud one's reputation. False arrest may do that. Even to be acquitted may damage one's good name if the community receives the verdict with a wink and chooses to remember defendant as one who ought to have been convicted. A conviction, on the other hand, may be accepted as a misfortune or an injustice, and even enhance the standing of one who mends his ways and lives it down. Reputation is the net balance of so many debits and credits that the law does not attach the finality to a conviction, when the issue is reputation, that is given to it when the issue is the credibility of the convict.

The inquiry as to an arrest is permissible also because the prosecution has a right to test the qualifications of the witness to bespeak the community opinion. If one never heard the speculations and rumors in which even one's friends indulge upon his arrest, the jury may doubt whether he is capable of giving any very reliable conclusions as to his reputation.

In this case the crime inquired about was receiving stolen goods; the trial was for bribery. The Court of Appeals thought this dissimilarity of offenses too great to sustain the inquiry in logic, though conceding that it is authorized by preponderance of authority. It asks us to substitute the Illinois rule which allows inquiry about arrest, but only for very closely similar if not identical charges, in place of the rule more generally adhered to in this country and in England.[36] We think the facts of this case show the proposal to be inexpedient.

The good character which the defendant had sought to establish was broader than the crime charged and included the traits of "honesty and truthfulness" and "being a law-abiding citizen." Possession of these characteristics would seem as incompatible with offering a bribe to a revenue agent as with receiving stolen goods. The crimes may be unlike, but both alike proceed from the same defects of

---

[34] (Court's original footnote 19.) *See Stewart v. United States, 104 F.2d 234, 70 App. D.C. 101; Little v. United States, 8 Cir., 93 F.2d 401; Filippelli v. United States, 9 Cir., 6 F.2d 121.*

[35] (Court's original footnote 20.) *See Mannix v. United States, 4 Cir., 140 F.2d 250; Josey v. United States, 135 F.2d 809, 77 U.S. App. D.C. 321; Spalitto v. United States, 8 Cir., 39 F.2d 782, and authorities there cited.*

[36] (Court's original footnote 21.) The Supreme Court of Illinois, in considering its own rule which we are urged to adopt, recognized that "the rule adhered to in this State is not consistent with the great weight of authority in this country and in England." *People v. Hannon*, 381 Ill. 206, 209, 44 N.E.2d 923, 924. Authorities in all states are collected in *State v. Shull*, 131 Or. 224, 282 P. 237, 71 A.L.R. 1504.

character which the witnesses said this defendant was reputed not to exhibit. It is not only by comparison with the crime on trial but by comparison with the reputation asserted that a court may judge whether the prior arrest should be made subject of inquiry. By this test the inquiry was permissible. It was proper cross-examination because reports of his arrest for receiving stolen goods, if admitted, would tend to weaken the assertion that he was known as an honest and law-abiding citizen. The cross-examination may take in as much ground as the testimony it is designed to verify. To hold otherwise would give defendant the benefit of testimony that he was honest and law-abiding in reputation when such might not be the fact; the refutation was founded on convictions equally persuasive though not for crimes exactly repeated in the present charge.

The inquiry here concerned an arrest twenty-seven years before the trial. Events a generation old are likely to be lived down and dropped from the present thought and talk of the community and to be absent from the knowledge of younger or more recent acquaintances. The court in its discretion may well exclude inquiry about rumors of an event so remote, unless recent misconduct revived them. But two of these witnesses dated their acquaintance with defendant as commencing thirty years before the trial. Defendant, on direct examination, voluntarily called attention to his conviction twenty years before. While the jury might conclude that a matter so old and indecisive as a 1920 arrest would shed little light on the present reputation and hence propensities of the defendant, we cannot say that, in the context of this evidence and in the absence of objection on this specific ground, its admission was an abuse of discretion.

We do not overlook or minimize the consideration that "the jury almost surely cannot comprehend the Judge's limiting instructions," which disturbed the Court of Appeals. The refinements of the evidentiary rules on this subject are such that even lawyers and judges, after study and reflection, often are confused, and surely jurors in the hurried and unfamiliar movement of a trial must find them almost unintelligible. However, limiting instructions on this subject are no more difficult to comprehend or apply than those upon various other subjects; for example, instructions that admissions of a co-defendant are to be limited to the question of his guilt and are not to be considered as evidence against other defendants, and instructions as to other problems in the trial of conspiracy charges. A defendant in such a case is powerless to prevent his cause from being irretrievably obscured and confused; but, in cases such as the one before us, the law foreclosed this whole confounding line of inquiry, unless defendant thought the net advantage from opening it up would be with him. Given this option, we think defendants in general and this defendant in particular have no valid complaint at the latitude which existing law allows to the prosecution to meet by cross-examination an issue voluntarily tendered by the defense. See *Greer v. United States*, 245 U.S. 559, 38 S.Ct. 209, 62 L.Ed. 469.

We end, as we began, with the observation that the law regulating the offering and testing of character testimony may merit many criticisms. England and some states have overhauled the practice by statute.[37] But the task of modernizing the long-standing rules on the subject is one of magnitude and difficulty which even

---

[37] (Court's original footnote 22.) Criminal Evidence Act, 61 & 62, Vict. c. 36. See also 51 L.Q. Rev. 443,

those dedicated to law reform do not lightly undertake.[38]

The law of evidence relating to proof of reputation in criminal cases has developed almost entirely at the hands of state courts of last resort, which have such questions frequently before them. This Court, on the other hand, has contributed little to this or to any phase of the law of evidence, for the reason, among others, that it has had extremely rare occasion to decide such issues, as the paucity of citations in this opinion to our own writings attests. It is obvious that a court which can make only infrequent sallies into the field cannot recast the body of case law on this subject in many, many years, even if it were clear what the rules should be.

We concur in the general opinion of courts, textwriters and the profession that much of this law is archaic, paradoxical and full of compromises and compensations by which an irrational advantage to one side is offset by a poorly reasoned counter-privilege to the other. But somehow it has proved a workable even if clumsy system when moderated by discretionary controls in the hands of a wise and strong trial court. To pull one misshapen stone out of the grotesque structure is more likely simply to upset its present balance between adverse interests than to establish a rational edifice.

The present suggestion is that we adopt for all federal courts a new rule as to cross-examination about prior arrest, adhered to by the courts of only one state and rejected elsewhere.[39] The confusion and error it would engender would seem too heavy a price to pay for an almost imperceptible logical improvement, if any, in a system which is justified, if at all, by accumulated judicial experience rather than abstract logic.[40]

The judgment is

Affirmed.

MR. JUSTICE FRANKFURTER, concurring.

Despite the fact that my feelings run in the general direction of the views expressed by Mr. Justice RUTLEDGE In his dissent, I join the Court's opinion. I

---

for discussion of right to cross-examine about prior arrests. For review of English and State legislation, see 1 Wigmore, *Evidence* (3d ed., 1940) § 194, et seq. The Pennsylvania statute, Act of March 15, 1911, P.L. 20, § 1, discussed by Wigmore has been amended, Act of July 3, 1947, P.L. 1239, § 1, **19 P.S. § 711**. The current statute and Pennsylvania practice were considered recently by the Superior Court of that state. *Commonwealth v. Court*, 163 Pa. Super. 232, 60 A.2d 828.

[38] (Court's original footnote 23.) The American Law Institute, in promulgating its "Model Code of Evidence," includes the comment, "Character, whenever used in these Rules, means disposition not reputation. It denotes what a person is, not what he is reputed to be. No rules are laid down as to proof of reputation, when reputation is a fact to be proved. When reputation is a material matter, it is proved in the same manner as is any other disputed fact." Rule 304. The latter sentence may seem an oversimplification in view of the decisions we have reviewed.

[39] (Court's original footnote 24.) See note 21.

[40] (Court's original footnote 25.) It must not be overlooked that abuse of cross-examination to test credibility carries its own corrective. Authorities on practice caution the bar of the imprudence as well as the unprofessional nature of attacks on witnesses or defendants which are likely to be resented by the jury. Wellman, *Art of Cross Examination* (1927) p. 167 et seq.

do so because I believe it to be unprofitable, on balance, for appellate courts to formulate rigid rules for the exclusion of evidence in courts of law that outside them would not be regarded as clearly irrelevant in the determination of issues. For well-understood reasons this Court's occasional ventures in formulating such rules hardly encourage confidence in denying to the federal trial courts a power of control over the allowable scope of cross-examination possessed by trial judges in practically all State courts. After all, such uniformity of rule in the conduct of trials is the crystallization of experience even when due allowance is made for the force of imitation. To reject such an impressive body of experience would imply a more dependable wisdom in a matter of this sort than I can claim.

To leave the District Courts of the United States the discretion given to them by this decision presupposes a high standard of professional competence, good sense, fairness and courage on the part of the federal district judges. If the United States District Courts are not manned by judges of such qualities, appellate review, no matter how stringent, can do very little to make up for the lack of them.

Mr. Justice Rutledge, with whom Mr. Justice Murphy joins, dissenting.

The Court's opinion candidly and interestingly points out the anomalous features characterizing the exclusion and admission of so-called character evidence in criminal cases. It also for the first time puts the stamp of the Court's approval upon the most anomalous and, what is more important, the most unfair stage in this evidentiary sequence.

There are three stages. The first denies the prosecution the right to attack the defendant's reputation as part of its case in chief, either by proof of bad general reputation or by proof of specific derogatory incidents disconnected from the one charged as the crime. The second permits the defendant, at his option, to prove by qualified witnesses that he bears a good general reputation or at least one not tarnished by ill repute. The witness is forbidden, however, to go into particular incidents or details of the defendant's life and conduct. The witness, once qualified, can state only the general conclusions of the community concerning the defendant's character as the witness knows that reputation. The third stage comprehends the prosecution's rebuttal, and particularly the latitude of cross-examination to be allowed.

I do not agree that this whole body of law is anomalous, unless indeed all the law of evidence with its numerous rules of exclusion and exceptions to them is to be so regarded. Anomalies there are, no doubt with much room for improvement. But here, if anywhere, the law is more largely the result of experience, of considerations of fairness and practicability developed through the centuries, than of any effort to construct a nicely logical, wholly consistent pattern of things. Imperfect and variable as the scheme has become in the application of specific rules, on the whole it represents the result of centuries of common-law growth in the seeking of English-speaking peoples for fair play in the trial of crime and other causes.

Moreover, I cannot agree that, in the sequence of the three stages relating to character evidence, the anomalous quality is equally present in each. In my judgment there is a vast difference in this respect between the rulings summarizing our experience in the first two stages and those affecting the third.

Regardless of all considerations of mere logical consistency, I should suppose there would be few now, whether lawyers or laymen, who would advocate change in the prevailing rules governing the first two stages of the sequence. In criminal causes especially, there are sound reasons basic to our system of criminal justice which justify initially excluding the Government from showing the defendant's bad general character or reputation.

The common law has not grown in the tradition of convicting a man and sending him to prison because he is generally a bad man or generally regarded as one. General bad character, much less general bad reputation, has not yet become a criminal offense in our scheme. Our whole tradition is that a man can be punished by criminal sanctions only for specific acts defined beforehand to be criminal, not for general misconduct or bearing a reputation for such misconduct.

That tradition lies at the heart of our criminal process. And it is the foundation of the rule of evidence which denies to the prosecution the right to show generally or by specific details that a defendant bears a bad general estimate in his community. In the light of our fundamental conceptions of crime and of the criminal process, there is nothing anomalous in this exclusion. It is designed to restrain proof to the limits of the charge and to prevent conviction for one offense because perhaps others, or misconduct not amounting to crime at all, have been perpetrated or are reputed generally to lie at the defendant's door.

The rule which allows the defendant to prove his good standing by general reputation is, of course, a kind of exception to the hearsay rule of exclusion, though one may inquire how else could reputation be proved than by hearsay if it is to be proved at all. This indeed presents the substantial question. Apart from its long acceptance, *Edgington v. United States*, 164 U.S. 361, 17 S.Ct. 72, 41 L.Ed. 467, the rule allowing the evidence to come in rests on very different considerations from the one which forbids the Government to bring in proof of bad public character as part of its case in chief. The defendant's proof comes as rebuttal. It is subject to none of the dangers involving the possibility of conviction for generally bad conduct or general repute for it which would characterize permitting the prosecution initially to show bad general reputation. The basic reason for excluding the latter does not apply to the defendant's tender of proof.

On the positive side the rule is justified by the ancient law which pronounces that a good name is rather to be chosen than great riches. True, men of good general repute may not deserve it. Or they may slip and fall in particular situations. But by common experience this is more often the exception than the rule. Moreover, most often in close cases, where the proof leaves one in doubt, the evidence of general regard by one's fellows may be the weight which turns the scales of justice. It may indeed be sufficient to create a clear conviction of innocence or to show that reasonable doubt which our law requires to be overcome in all criminal cases before the verdict of guilty can be returned.

The apparent anomaly which excludes the prosecution's proof of bad character in the beginning but lets in the defendant's proof of good character is thus only apparent. It is part and parcel of our scheme which forbid: conviction for other than specific acts criminal in character and which, in their trial, casts over the defendant the presumption of innocence until he is proved guilty beyond all reasonable doubt. To take away his right to bring in any substantial and pertinent proof bearing upon the existence of reasonable doubt is, so far, to nullify the rule requiring removal of that doubt. I reject the Court's intimation that these considerations have to some extent become obsolete or without substantial effects because we now live in cities more generally than formerly. They are basic parts of our plan, perhaps the more important to be observed because so much of our life now is urban.

But, for a variety of reasons, the law allows the defendant to prove no more than his general reputation, by witnesses qualified to report concerning it. He cannot show particular acts of virtue to offset the proof of his specific criminality on any theory that "By their fruits ye shall know them." Whether this be because such proof is irrelevant, it is too distracting and time-consuming, is summarized in the general report of good character, or perhaps for all of these reasons, the rule is settled, and I think rightly, which restricts the proof to general repute. Thus far, whatever the differences in logic, differences which as usual inhere in the premises from which thinking starts, there is no general disagreement or dissatisfaction in the results. All of the states and the federal judicial system as well, approve them. No one would open the doors initially to the prosecution. No one would close them to the defense.

But the situation is different when we come to the third stage, that of the prosecution's rebuttal. Obviously rebuttal there should be, when the defendant has opened a line of inquiry closed to the prosecution and has sought to gain advantage by proof which it has had no chance to counteract. But the question of how the rebuttal shall be made presents the difficult problem.

There can be no sound objection, of course, to calling witnesses who will qualify as the witnesses for the defense are required to do, but who also will contradict their testimony. And the prosecution may inquire concerning the qualifications of the witnesses for the defense to speak concerning the defendant's general reputation. Thus far there is nothing to exceed the bounds of rebuttal or take the case out of the issues as made.

But these have not been the limits of proof and cross-examination. For, in the guise of testing the standards of the witness' when he speaks to reputation, the door has been thrown wide open to trying the defendant's whole life, both in general reputation and in specific incident. What is worse, this is without opportunity for the defendant to rebut either the fact or the innuendo for which the evidence is tendered more generally than otherwise. Hardly any incident, however remote or derogatory, but can be drawn out by asking the witness who testifies to the defendant's good character, "Have you heard this" or "Have you heard that." And many incidents, wholly innocent in quality, can be turned by the prosecutor, through an inflection or tone, to cast aspersion upon the defendant by the mere asking of the question, without hope of affirmative response from the witness.

The dangers, the potential damage and prejudice to the defendant and his cause, have not been more clearly summarized than in the excerpt from Wigmore's classic treatise, quoted in note 4 of the Court's opinion. 335 U.S. 473, 69 S.Ct. 217. His summary of the consequences produced by the rule bears repetition and greater emphasis. He said:

"The rumor of the misconduct, when admitted, goes far, in spite of all theory and of the judge's charge, towards fixing the misconduct as a fact upon the other person, and thus does three improper things, — (1) it violates the fundamental rule of fairness which prohibits the use of such and not by trustworthy testimony, and (3) facts, (2) it gets at them by hearsay only, it leaves the other person no means of defending himself by denial or explanation, such as he would otherwise have had if the rule had allowed that conduct to be made the subject of an issue." Wigmore, *Evidence* (3d ed., 1940) § 988.

These consequences are not denied. But it is said two modes of protection are available to the accused. One is to refrain from opening the inquiry into his reputation. That answer would have weight if the rebuttal were limited to inquiry concerning the witness' opportunity for knowing the accused and his reputation and to producing contrary evidence by other witnesses of the same general sort as that which is refuted. But if the rule is sound which allows the accused to show his good repute and restricts him to that showing, it not only is anomalous, it is highly unjust, to exact, as the price for his doing so, throwing open to the prosecution the opportunity not only to rebut his proof but to call in question almost any specific act of his life or to insinuate without proving that he has committed other acts, leaving him no chance to reply. A fair rule either would afford this chance or would restrict the prosecution's counterproof in the same way his own is limited. The prevailing rule changes the whole character of the case, in a manner the rules applying to the two earlier stages seek to avoid.

Nor is it enough, in my judgment, to trust to the sound discretion of trial judges to protect the defendant against excesses of the prosecution. To do this effectively they need standards. None are provided under the Court's ruling; indeed it would be difficult to provide them except for each case and question as they might arise.

The facts in this case, it seems to me, show the inadequacy of any such general and largely unrestricted delegation. They demonstrate how far and how unfairly the prosecution may be allowed to go in bringing extraneous and immaterial matters to the jury's attention, with however a probable effect of prejudice. Petitioner himself had made a clean breast of his twenty-year-old conviction for violating the New York trademark laws. That fact of course was of some use for testing his character witnesses' standards for speaking to his general repute, although the conviction was so old that conceivably it could have but little weight on the accused's reputation in 1947.

Then the prosecution went back seven. years further and inquired whether the witnesses had heard that petitioner was arrested "on October 11th, 1920" for receiving stolen goods. None of the witnesses had heard of this fact. The court solemnly instructed the jury that they were not to consider that the incident took place, that all that was happening was that the prosecutor was testing the witness' standard of opinion of the accused's reputation. This, after the court out of the jury's presence had required the prosecutor to make pro(satisfactory to the court that the incident had taken place.

The very form of the question was itself notice of the fact to the jury. They well might assume, as men of common sense, that the court would not allow the question if the fact were only fiction. And why "on October 11th, 1920," rather than merely "in 1920" or "Have you ever heard of the defendant's being arrested, other than for the trademark violation?" Why also "for receiving stolen goods"? In my opinion the only answers to these questions are, not that the prosecution was "testing the witness' standard of opinion of reputation," but that it was telling the jury what it could not prove directly and what the petitioner had no chance to deny, namely, that he had been so arrested; and thereby either insinuating that he had been convicted of the crime or leaving to the jury to guess that this had been the outcome. The question was a typical abuse arising from allowing this type of inquiry. It should have been excluded. There is no way to tell how much prejudice it produced.

Moreover, I do not think the mere question of knowledge of a prior arrest is one proper to be asked, even if inquiry as to clearly derogatory acts is to be permitted. Of course men take such an inquiry as reflecting upon the person arrested. But, for use in a criminal prosecution, I do not think they should be allowed to do so. The mere fact of a single arrest twenty-seven years before trial, without further showing of criminal proceedings or their outcome, whether acquittal or conviction, seldom could have substantial bearing upon one's present general reputation; indeed it is not per se a derogatory fact. But it is put in generally, and I think was put in evidence in this case, not to call in question the witness' standard of opinion but, by the very question, to give room for play of the jury's unguarded conjecture and prejudice. This is neither fair play nor due process. It is a perversion of the criminal process as we know it. For it permits what the rule applied in the first stage forbids, trial of the accused not only for general bad conduct or reputation but also for conjecture, gossip, innuendo and insinuation.

Accordingly, I think this judgment should be reversed. I also think the prevailing practice should be changed. One judge of the Court of Appeals has suggested we do this by adopting the Illinois rule,[41] namely, by limiting inquiry concerning specific incidents to questions relating to prior offenses similar to that for which the defendant is on trial. Logically that rule is subject to the same objections as the generally prevailing one. But it has the practical merit of greatly reducing the scope and volume of allowable questions concerning specific acts, rumors, etc., with comparable reduction of innuendo, insinuation and gossip. My own preference and,

I think, the only fair rule would be to foreclose the entire line of inquiry concerning specific incidents in the defendant's past, both on cross-examination and

---

[41] (Court's original footnote 1.) See *People v. Hannon*, 381 Ill. 206, 211, 44 N.E.2d 923, for the most recent statement of the rule established by *Aiken v. People*, 183 Ill. 215, 55 N.E. 695; cf. People v. Page, 365 Ill. 524, 6 N.E.2d 845. In North Carolina a character witness may be asked on cross- examination about the "general reputation of the defendant as to particular vices or virtues," but not about rumors of specific acts of misconduct. *State v. Shepherd*, 220 N.C. 377, 379, 17 S.E.2d 469, 470; *State v. Holly*, 155 N.C. 485, 492, 71 S.E. 450. The Arizona Supreme Court, which once followed the rule adopted by the Court today, *Smith v. State*, 22 Ariz. 229, 196 P. 420, more recently, in reversing a judgment because a character witness was cross-examined as to his know-edge of specific acts of misconduct, stated that cross-examination should be limited to questions concerning the source of the witness' knowledge of the accused's reputation and should not include questions concerning specific acts of misconduct. *Viliborghi v. State*, 45 Ariz. 275, 285, 43 P. 2d 210.

on new evidence in rebuttal. This would leave room for proper rebuttal without turning the defendant's trial for a specific offense into one for all his previous misconduct, criminal or other, and would put the prosecution on the same plane with the defendant in relation to the use of character evidence. This, it seems to me, is the only fair way to handle the matter.

Chapter 6

OTHER EXCLUSIONS OF RELEVANT EVIDENCE: THE QUASI-PRIVILEGES

§ 6.01 CHAPTER CHECKLIST

1a. Is evidence of "subsequent remedial measures" being offered, that is, of measures taken after an injury or harm occurs that make its reoccurrence less likely? *See* Rule 407.

1b. If yes, is the evidence offered to prove negligence, culpable conduct, a defect in a product's design, or a need for a warning or instruction, in which case it is not admissible, or is it instead offered for some other purpose, such as proving ownership, control, or feasibility of precautionary measures, in which case it may be admissible? *See* Rule 407.

2a. Is evidence being offered of (1) furnishing or offering or promising to furnish, or (2) accepting or offering, or promising to accept a valuable consideration to compromise or attempt to compromise a claim that is disputed as to either validity or amount, or of (3) conduct or statements made in compromise negotiations? *See* Rule 408.

2b. If yes, is the evidence offered to prove liability for or invalidity of a claim or its amount, in which case it is — with one exception — inadmissible, or is it instead offered for some other purpose, such as proving bias or prejudice of a witness, negating a contention of undue delay, or proving an effort to obstruct a criminal investigation, in which case it may be admissible? *See* Rule 408.

2c. Even if the evidence is offered to prove liability for or invalidity of a claim or its amount, which would ordinarily make it inadmissible, does the evidence consist of conduct or statements made in compromise negotiations in a criminal case in which the negotiations related to the claim of a public office or agency in the exercise of regulatory, investigative, or enforcement authority? If yes, contrary to the usual rule, the evidence is admissible.

3a. Is evidence being offered of furnishing or offering or promising to pay medical, hospital, or similar expenses occasioned by an injury? *See* Rule 409.

3b. If yes, is it offered to prove liability for injury, in which case it is inadmissible? *See* Rule 409.

4a. Is evidence being offered in any civil or criminal proceeding of (see Rule 410):

    (1) a plea of guilty later withdrawn?

    (2) a plea of *nolo contendere* (that is, "no contest," meaning that the defendant neither admits nor denies the crime but nevertheless agrees to be sentenced for it)?

    (3) any statement made in the course of any proceedings under Rule 11 of the Federal Rules of Criminal Procedure or comparable state procedure regarding either of the foregoing pleas?

    (4) any statement made in the course of plea discussions with an attorney for the prosecuting authority which does not result in a plea of guilty or which results in a plea of guilty later withdrawn?

4b. If yes, is the statement offered in any proceeding wherein another statement made in the course of the same plea or plea discussions has been introduced and the statement ought in fairness to be considered contemporaneously with it, or in a criminal proceeding for perjury or false statement if the statement was made by the defendant under oath, on the record, and in the presence of counsel? *See* Rule 410.

4c. If yes to 4b, the evidence may be admissible, but, if no, is the evidence offered against the defendant who made the plea or was a participant in the plea discussions, in which case it is inadmissible? *See* Rule 410.

5a. Is evidence offered that a person was or was not insured against liability? *See* Rule 411.

5b. If yes, is it offered on the issue whether the person acted negligently or otherwise wrongfully, in which case it is not admissible, or is it instead offered for another purpose, such as proof of agency, ownership, or control, or bias or prejudice of a witness in which case it may be admissible?

See Rule 411.

§ 6.02 RELEVANT FEDERAL RULES OF EVIDENCE

Rule 407. Subsequent Remedial Measures

When measures are taken that would have made an earlier injury or harm less likely to occur, evidence of the subsequent measures is not admissible to prove:

- negligence;
- culpable conduct;
- a defect in a product or its design; or
- a need for a warning or instruction.

But the court may admit this evidence for another purpose, such as impeachment or — if disputed — proving ownership, control, or the feasibility of precautionary measures.

Rule 408. Compromise Offers and Negotiations

(a) PROHIBITED USES. Evidence of the following is not admissible — on behalf of any party — either to prove or disprove the validity or amount of a disputed claim or to impeach by a prior inconsistent statement or a contradiction:

(1) furnishing, promising, or offering — or accepting, promising to accept, or offering to accept — a valuable consideration in compromising or attempting to compromise the claim; and (2) conduct or a statement made during compromise negotiations about the claim — except when offered in a criminal case and when the negotiations related to a claim by a public office in the exercise of its regulatory, investigative, or enforcement authority.

(b) EXCEPTIONS. The court may admit this evidence for another purpose, such as proving a witness's bias or prejudice, negating a contention of undue delay, or proving an effort to obstruct a criminal investigation or prosecution.

Rule 409. Offers to Pay Medical and Similar Expenses

Evidence of furnishing, promising to pay, or offering to pay medical, hospital, or similar expenses resulting from an injury is not admissible to prove liability for the injury.

Rule 410. Pleas, Plea Discussions, and Related Statements

(a) PROHIBITED USES. In a civil or criminal case, evidence of the following is not admissible against the defendant who made the plea or participated in the plea discussions:

(1) a guilty plea that was later withdrawn;

(2) a nolo contendere plea;

(3) a statement made during a proceeding on either of those pleas under Federal Rule of Criminal Procedure 11 or a comparable state procedure; or

(4) a statement made during plea discussions with an attorney for the prosecuting authority if the discussions did not result in a guilty plea or they resulted in a later-withdrawn guilty plea.

(b) EXCEPTIONS. The court may admit a statement described in Rule 410(a)(3) or (4):

(1) in any proceeding in which another statement made during the same plea or plea discussions has been introduced, if in fairness the statements ought to be considered together; or

(2) in a criminal proceeding for perjury or false statement, if the defendant made the statement under oath, on the record, and with counsel present.

Rule 411. Liability Insurance

Evidence that a person was or was not insured against liability is not admissible to prove whether the person acted negligently or otherwise wrongfully. But the court may admit this evidence for another purpose, such as proving a witness's bias or prejudice or proving agency, ownership, or control.

§ 6.03 OVERVIEW

Exclusionary evidence rules are most often justified in one of two ways:

1. The evidence, if admitted, will mislead the jury or otherwise impede an accurate and efficient search for the truth.

2. Exclusion of the evidence will promote some public policy that has little to do with the "truth" in a specific case. For example, excluding illegally seized but highly probative evidence (a matter beyond the scope of this course) is often thought to encourage police to respect individuals' Fourth Amendment right to be free from unreasonable searches and seizures.

Evidence rules seen as primarily serving the second of these two goals are often called "privileges." There is no common term for rules that primarily serve the first goal, but that category would include most evidence rules other than privileges. Thus, the hearsay rule, the exclusion of most forms of character evidence, and the court's power to exclude unfairly prejudicial evidence with low probative value are often justified as aiding the search for the truth at trial. "Quasi-privileges" are rules justified as serving *both* the determination of truth and external public policies. Recent scholarship suggests, however, that *all* evidence rules at least partly serve goals unconnected with "truth" and that "truth" itself may be a notion imbued with value judgments. But we avoid entering that debate here. *See, e.g.*, Robert P. Burns, A Theory of the Trial (1999); Andrew E. Taslitz, *What Feminism Has to Offer Evidence Law*, 28 Sw. U. L. Rev. 171 (1999). Moreover, while some scholars prefer alternative phraseology, we find the term "quasi-privileges" a useful shorthand.

The major quasi-privileges are: (1) Rule 407's exclusion of much evidence of subsequent remedial measures; (2) Rules 408 and 410, which exclude much evidence of compromise negotiations; (3) Rule 409's bar on admitting evidence of offers to furnish, or payment of, a person's medical expenses to prove the offeror's liability for the injury; and (4) Rule 411's bar on admitting much evidence that a person was insured against liability.

§ 6.04 SUBSEQUENT REMEDIAL MEASURES: RULE 407

After an incident that causes an injury, persons or organizations that are potentially responsible for the harm may take measures to prevent its recurrence. But if those persons or entities are later sued by the injured parties, those parties might offer evidence that the defendants took such "subsequent remedial measures." There are many reasons that evidence of subsequent remedial measures might be offered. Among the most problematic of such reasons is proving that the remediator was at fault for not fixing the problem sooner.

Example 1

John Smith drove a Volvo truck whose rear end was at the height of the heads of the drivers of most ordinary cars. One day, Smith suddenly changed lanes without signaling and was hit from behind. He was hit by a GM car driven by Ronald Patterson, who was instantly decapitated. Volvo immediately recalled all its trucks of the model involved in the accident to install "safety bars" that effectively lowered the rear of the trucks in a way that should avoid future decapitations in accidents like Patterson's. Patterson's estate sued Volvo, both for negligence in designing its truck and for defectively designing the truck, a theory of strict products liability. The estate sought at trial to offer evidence of the trucks' recall and of the installation of the safety bars (1) to prove Volvo's negligence in not earlier installing such bars on all trucks of this model, and (2) to show that the model's design was defective. This evidence seemed to be relevant under Rule 401 to show both Volvo's negligence and the defective design of the truck. However, were the evidence to be admitted at trial, Volvo might be reluctant to take corrective measures after future accidents revealing other defects, because Volvo would fear that evidence of such measures would be used against it at trial.

Partly to encourage such remedial measures, Rule 407 requires the exclusion of evidence like that immediately above against Volvo:

Rule 407. Subsequent Remedial Measures

When measures are taken that would have made an earlier injury or harm less likely to occur, evidence of the subsequent measures is not admissible to prove:

- negligence;
- culpable conduct;
- a defect in a product or its design; or
- a need for a warning or instruction.

But the court may admit this evidence for another purpose, such as impeachment or — if disputed — proving ownership, control, or the feasibility of precautionary measures.

The Advisory Committee considered the "social policy of encouraging people to take, or at least not discouraging them from taking, steps in furtherance of added safety" to be the "more impressive ground" for exclusion. Advisory Committee Note, Rule 407. The Committee noted that courts had applied this principle to exclude evidence of "subsequent repairs, installation of safety devices, changes in company rules, and discharge of employees" and that "the language of the present rule is broad enough to encompass all of them." While conceding that subsequent remedial measures might in a particular case have *some* relevance (*some* probative value) for each of the prohibited purposes, the Committee saw the probative value as minimal, thus further justifying the rule:

> The conduct is not in fact an admission, since the conduct is equally consistent with injury by mere accident or through contributory negligence. Or, as Baron Bramwell put it, the rule rejects the notion that "because the world gets wiser as it gets older therefore it was foolish before."

Some commentators describe Rule 407 as an "inclusionary rule," because the last sentence makes clear that subsequent remedial measures are admissible under Rule 407 (though they may be excluded by other rules) for any other purpose than the prohibited ones listed in the Rule's first sentence. The specific admissible purposes noted in the last sentence are, therefore, really just *non-exhaustive* examples of admissible purposes. Nevertheless, to avoid speculative claims that evidence is offered for an admissible purpose, given the dangers that jurors will use it for an inadmissible one, the last sentence requires that there be a real controversy about one of the listed issues to justify admissibility.

Example 2

Jana Fallahy, attending a party, slips on highly polished kitchen tile and severely injures her back. Reginald Melbourne, who gave the party, later replaces the tile with slip-resistant carpet. Jana sues Reginald for negligence in inviting partygoers into a home with slippery tile and offers evidence that the defendant replaced the tile with carpet. The defendant objects.

If the evidence is offered to prove Reginald's negligence in not earlier installing the carpet, the defense objection should be sustained. Suppose Jana's counsel argues that the evidence is really offered simply to show that Reginald owned the home in which the accident took place, which would render him responsible for its condition. For the evidence to be admissible for that purpose, the issue of ownership must be "controverted." If Reginald admitted ownership in his answer to the complaint, ownership is conceded, and the objection should be sustained. If, on the other hand, Reginald's answer denied ownership (perhaps claiming that he was just house-sitting and is at least not solely responsible for the injuries), then ownership is in dispute, and the objection should probably be overruled.

A careful lawyer must also be sensitive to this timing issue: to what event must the remedial measure be "subsequent"? Again, the 1997 Advisory Committee Note answers this question:

> [Under] the [1997] amendment to Rule 407 . . . , the words "an injury or harm allegedly caused by" were added to clarify that the rule applies only to changes made after the occurrence that produced the damages giving rise to the action. Evidence of measures taken by the defendant prior to the "event" do not fall within the exclusionary scope of Rule 407 even if they occurred after the manufacture or design of the product.

Example 3

Assume that in the first example in this chapter, Volvo realized that its trucks created a decapitation danger because numerous Volvo trucks had been involved in similar accidents before Ronald Patterson's accident. All but one of the trucks — the one that killed Patterson — had the new "safety bars" added by the time Patterson was killed. Patterson offered, over defense objection, evidence of the recall and safety bar installation concerning all the other trucks to prove Volvo's negligence in the Patterson case. The objection should be overruled because the remedial measures, while "subsequent" to the "manufacture or design of the product," were not "subsequent" to the "occurrence that produced the damages giving rise to the action."

Problem 6-1: The Ruptured Bulldozer

John Faro was injured while operating a Ford F4 bulldozer. The injury occurred when a hydraulic hose ruptured; it sprayed him and the engine with a flammable liquid, which ignited on contact. Forty-eight percent of Faro's body was burned. Faro, who had been injured in New York State, sued Ford, a Michigan corporation, in federal court, on theories of negligent design and strict products liability. Specifically, Faro argued that a protective shield should have enclosed the driver, protecting him from being sprayed if any hose ruptured. Faro sought to call a witness who would testify that Ford in fact installed such shields on its F5 earth-moving scraper, three weeks after Faro's injury. But, upon Ford's objection, the trial court excluded this evidence.

At the motion *in limine* on whether to exclude this evidence, Faro's expert had testified that the F5 moving scraper's design was not different from the F4 bulldozer's design in any significant way that would prevent installing such deflection shields on the bulldozer too. Prior to this motion *in limine*, however, Faro had succeeded in admitting all of the following evidence to support the proposition that deflecting shields could have been installed on the F4 bulldozer: an instructional aid on mechanical engineering, an engineering code of ethics, an alleged shielding standard published by the International Standards Organization, internal Ford memoranda, magazine articles, and service letters regarding the effects of possible ruptures in the F4 hoses.

1. Did the trial judge rule correctly? Would any additional information help you to answer this question? Should the trial judge's ruling be reversed on appeal?

2. Would your answer to question 1 change if Ford had offered an expert at the motion *in limine* who testified that F5 wheeled-earth moving scrapers, which scrape rocky roads flat, are of a radically different design from, and serve different functions than, the F4 bulldozer, which moves large amounts of earth and dirt? What if he further testified that installing a shield on the F4 bulldozer would have raised its cost by $10,000? That it was not yet scientifically feasible to install an effective deflecting shield on bulldozers?

3. Assume that, after excluding the evidence about the F5, and after plaintiff Faro rested, defendant Ford called an expert to the stand. Would your answer to

question 1 above change if the expert testified:

a. That it is not scientifically feasible yet to install deflecting shields on bulldozers?

b. That it is feasible but is prohibitively expensive?

c. That it is not feasible on any construction equipment?

d. That it is prohibitively expensive on any construction equipment?

Problem 6-2: The Painful Beach Party

John Patrick rented a beach house from Maurice Applebaum. One day, when Patrick threw a beach party at the house, a guest slipped in the outdoor shower and sustained serious back and neck injuries. Applebaum, hearing about the incident, came by one day and installed non-slip rubber mats on the shower floor. The guest sued both Patrick and Applebaum for the injuries suffered as a result of the slip in the shower. At trial, the plaintiff seeks to offer evidence of Applebaum's installing the non-slip mats. *Will this evidence be admissible against one or both of the defendants?*

Problem 6-3: Rotund University

A Rotund University School of Law student was recently raped while studying late at night in one of the study carrels in the stacks. The University hired an outside consulting firm to prepare a report on what steps, if any, the school could take to avoid future such incidents. The consultant recommended that the library be locked during night hours; that only students, faculty, and staff have keys; that locks be changed each semester; and that video cameras and emergency alarm buttons be installed on every floor. However, none of these changes has yet been implemented. The rape victim sues the University for damages and seeks to offer the report into evidence. *Ignoring hearsay issues, should the University's objection be sustained or overruled?*

§ 6.05 OFFERS TO COMPROMISE: RULES 408 AND 410

[A] Importance of Compromise in Civil and Criminal Cases

High percentages of both civil and criminal cases are resolved by compromise, generally by settlement agreements (civil cases) or plea bargains (criminal cases). Our legal system generally seeks to encourage compromises as fair and efficient ways to settle disputes, thus reducing the otherwise unmanageable burden on trial courts. At the same time, some claims are settled to avoid the costs and risk of a trial, rather than as an admission of responsibility or guilt, thus suggesting that compromises are of limited probative value in proving fault or guilt at trial. The Rules, in recognizing these policy concerns, often exclude evidence of compromises reached or statements made during compromise negotiations, though negotiations arising in the civil versus the criminal context are treated somewhat differently.

[B] Evidence of Civil Settlement Agreements and Negotiations: Rule 408

Rule 408 addresses use of evidence of civil settlement agreements and negotiations in trials arising in the same or other cases than the one in which the negotiations took place:

Rule 408. Compromise Offers and Negotiations

> (a) PROHIBITED USES. Evidence of the following is not admissible — on behalf of any party — either to prove or disprove the validity or amount of a disputed claim or to impeach by a prior inconsistent statement or a contradiction:
>
> (1) furnishing, promising, or offering — or accepting, promising to accept, or offering to accept — a valuable consideration in compromising or attempting to compromise the claim; and (2) conduct or a statement made during compromise negotiations about the claim — except when offered in a criminal case and when the negotiations related to a claim by a public office in the exercise of its regulatory, investigative, or enforcement authority.
>
> (b) EXCEPTIONS. The court may admit this evidence for another purpose, such as proving a witness's bias or prejudice, negating a contention of undue delay, or proving an effort to obstruct a criminal investigation or prosecution.

The Advisory Committee explained that it based Rule 408 (compromises and offers to compromise) on essentially the same two grounds as support Rule 407 (subsequent remedial measures):[1]

> As with evidence of subsequent remedial measures, dealt with in Rule 407, exclusion [under Rule 408] may be based on two grounds: (1) The evidence is irrelevant, since the offer may be motivated by a desire for peace rather than from any concession of weakness of position. The validity of this position will vary as the amount of the offer varies in relation to the size of the claims and may also be influenced by other circumstances. (2) A more consistently impressive ground is promotion of the public policy favoring the compromise and settlement of disputes.

The Advisory Committee worried, however, that these purposes were not well served by the traditional approach, which excluded only the compromise itself, but admitted evidence of both negotiations leading up to a compromise and offers to compromise:[2]

> The practical value of the common law rule has been greatly diminished by its inapplicability to admissions of fact, even though made in the course of compromise negotiations, unless hypothetical, stated to be "without"

---

[1] Advisory Committee Note, Rule 408.

[2] *Id.*

prejudice, or so connected with the offer as to be inseparable from it. McCormick § 251, pp. 540–541. An inevitable effect is to inhibit freedom of communication with respect to compromise, even among lawyers. Another effect is the generation of controversy over whether a given statement falls within or without the protected area. These considerations account for the expansion of the rule herewith to include evidence of conduct or statements made in compromise negotiations, as well as the offer or completed compromise itself.

Example 1

Matt Wrightley is dying from lung cancer, allegedly caused by his 50 years of chain-smoking Winston-Salem cigarettes. He sues Winston-Salem, the manufacturer of the cigarettes, for failing to warn consumers adequately of the dangers of smoking, as these dangers were known to the cigarette manufacturers long before they were known to the federal government. During the course of settlement negotiations, the attorney for Winston-Salem concedes that a single study conducted by the company itself 40 years ago concluded that cigarettes could cause lung cancer but denies that this lone study constituted "knowledge" of a cancer danger. Winston-Salem did not at any point in the litigation produce such a report during discovery despite the plaintiff's requests. The company's attorney offered $1,000,000 to settle the suit. The plaintiff, declaring the offer obscenely low, walked out of the settlement negotiations, and the case proceeded to trial. Rule 408 prohibits introduction of either the $1,000,000 offer or the Winston-Salem lawyer's admission about the company's report concerning cancer danger if offered to prove either: (1) that Winston-Salem is liable for failing to convey early adequate warnings of cancer dangers to its customers, or (2) that Winston-Salem caused the plaintiff to suffer at least $1,000,000 in damages.

Example 2

Same example as above, but the case was indeed settled for $1,000,000. A new plaintiff sues Winston-Salem on the same theory as did Matt Wrightley, seeking at trial to offer evidence of the Wrightley settlement as an admission of liability generally for negligently failing to make early and adequate warnings of the cancer dangers of its product. Winston-Salem's objection to this evidence will be sustained.

Rule 408 bars admitting evidence of accepting a compromise to settle a claim disputed as to validity or amount *at any future civil or criminal trial* to prove liability for the claim. An earlier version of the Rule declared that the Rule "does not require the exclusion of any evidence otherwise discoverable merely because it is presented in the course of compromise negotiations." This language was deleted by a 2006 amendment but, according to the Advisory Committee, this deletion was not done to effect any change in meaning but because the language was "superfluous." Although the "intent of the sentence was to prevent a party from immunizing admissible information, such as a pre-existing document, through the pretense of disclosing it during compromise negotiations," explained the Advisory Committee, "even without the sentence, the Rule cannot be read to protect pre-existing information simply because it was presented to the adversary in compromise negotiations."

Example 3

In the first Winston-Salem hypothetical above, assume that Winston-Salem does indeed admit in response to interrogatories that it has copies of its damaging internal cancer report in its possession. It refuses to produce the report, however, and later moves *in limine* to bar its introduction at trial, because the report was discussed during the failed settlement negotiations. While the *mention* of the report during settlement negotiations is inadmissible to prove liability or damages at trial, Rule 408 does not bar admission of the *report itself* for the same purposes. The Rule was never intended as a shield for otherwise discoverable documents.

Furthermore, because the report is likely admissible at trial, under rules consistent with the Federal Rules of Civil Procedure, Winston-Salem cannot withhold the report during discovery on the ground that the report is either inadmissible or unlikely to lead to admissible evidence.

Importantly, the Rule applies only to compromise offers concerning a claim that is "disputed as to either validity or amount." Rule 408. The Advisory Committee explains: "The policy considerations which underlie the rule do not come into play when the effort is to induce a creditor to settle an admittedly due amount for a lesser sum."

Example 4

The Classic Books Club sends one of its customers, Martha Evans, a letter threatening to sue her for $5,000 she owes them for books ordered and received at her request. She calls Classic Books, admits that she owes them the full $5,000, but says that it will cost her little to contest that fact and represent herself in any lawsuit. She therefore offers to pay $3,000, but not one penny more, arguing that it is in the company's interest to accept the settlement rather than face the litigation costs of suit. The company rejects her offer, files a complaint, and seeks to use her $3,000 settlement offer and admission of $5,000 liability against her at trial. Her objection under Rule 408 will be overruled because the negotiation statements concerned a matter not seriously disputed as to either "validity or amount."

Like Rule 407, Rule 408 is arguably an inclusionary rule because civil settlements, offers, and statements during compromise negotiations are not excluded by Rule 408 if offered for *any* purpose *other than* proving the validity or liability of the claim then in dispute. In particular, the Rule expressly declares that the use of compromise evidence for "proving bias or prejudice of a witness, negating a contention of undue delay, or proving an effort to obstruct a criminal investigation or prosecution" does "not require exclusion." To say that Rule 408 does not require exclusion does not mean, however, that some other rule might nevertheless exclude the evidence if a proper objection under another rule is made.

Example 5

Carter, Guttman, Inc., has been civilly sued for wrongful termination by its former employee, Harold Carswell. Carswell is also the star witness against Carter, Guttman, Inc., executives in a criminal bribery prosecution. The Chief Executive Officer of Carter, Guttman, Inc., offers to pay Carswell $2,000,000 to settle his civil suit for wrongful termination ($1,000,000 more than he asked for in that suit) if Carswell will leave the country before he can be subpoenaed in the criminal case and not return until the criminal case is resolved. Carswell refuses and reports the Carter, Guttman, Inc., proposal to the local prosecutor. The company's CEO is indicted for attempted obstruction of justice. In the criminal prosecution, the CEO objects under Rule 408 to evidence of his offer to settle the civil wrongful termination suit and of his related statements during settlement negotiations. This objection will be overruled. The evidence is not offered to prove that the company is liable for the civil claim but rather to prove the CEO's effort, in an unrelated case, "to obstruct a criminal investigation or prosecution."

Example 6

The Federal Railroad Administration ("FRA") has assessed a substantial civil fine against the Kay-Cee Railroad Company for violation of federal railroad safety regulations. Kay-Cee disputes both whether it has engaged in any violations in the first place and the size of the fines. The attorney for the FRA enters into negotiations over this matter with Kay-Cee. During those negotiations, Kay-Cee's President admits to knowing that certain safety violations had caused a railroad engineer's death yet ordered that the violations not be corrected because it would be cheaper just to pay the fine. As a result, as the company President further admits, a second engineer died, so the President finally ordered those violations corrected. The company and the FRA do ultimately agree to settle their fine dispute for approximately half the amount that FRA originally sought.

Subsequently, the U.S. Attorney files negligent homicide charges against Kay-Cee. At trial, the government seeks to offer testimony about the above statements made by Kay-Cee's President during the civil dispute. Kay-Cee objects under Rule 408 on the grounds that these were statements made during compromise negotiations. Although ordinarily such statements would be barred by the rule, the objection should be overruled because the statements fit within the exception for statements made during compromise negotiations relating to a civil claim "*by a public office or agency in the exercise of regulatory, investigative, or enforcement authority.*" Note that this exception applies only to the statements made during the civil negotiations, *not* to the furnishing or offering or accepting of consideration. As the Advisory Committee Note to the 2006 amendment that created this exception explains:

> The amendment distinguishes statements and conduct (such as a direct admission of fault) made in compromise negotiations of a civil claim by a government agency from an offer or acceptance of a compromise of such a claim. An offer or acceptance of a compromise of any civil claim is excluded under the Rule if offered against the

defendant as an admission of fault. In that case, the predicate for the evidence would be that the defendant, by compromising with the government agency, has admitted the validity and amount of the civil claim, and that this admission has sufficient probative value to be considered as evidence of [criminal] guilt. But unlike a direct statement of fault, an offer or acceptance of a compromise is not very probative of the defendant's guilt. Moreover, admitting such an offer or acceptance could deter a defendant from settling a civil regulatory action, for fear of evidentiary use in a subsequent criminal action.

Remember too that the exception is only to Rule 408, not to other rules. Thus the statements by Kay-Cee's President still might be excluded under Rule 403 under appropriate circumstances. As the Advisory Committee Note again explains:

> Statements made in compromise negotiations of a claim by a government agency may be excluded in criminal cases where the circumstances so warrant under Rule 403. For example, if an individual was unrepresented at the time the statement was made in a civil enforcement proceeding, its probative value in a subsequent criminal case may be minimal. But there is no absolute exclusion imposed by Rule 408.

Example 7

Assume instead that the family of the second engineer killed as a result of the Kay-Cee Railroad Company's safety violations mentioned in Example 6 has brought a civil suit for wrongful death against the railroad. The FRA has not yet assessed civil penalties or begun any negotiations with the company. However, during negotiations between the company and the engineer's family in the wrongful death suit, Kay-Cee's President admits that he knew that these violations had already caused one other death, that he did not order them corrected because of the expense of doing so, and that his failure contributed to this second engineer's death. No settlement agreement can be reached, however, so the case is scheduled for trial. Meanwhile, the local prosecutor's office brings criminal charges against Kay-Cee for negligent homicide. At the criminal trial, Kay-Cee objects under Rule 408 when the engineer's family member present at the civil negotiations is called to testify to the President's statements made during those negotiations. This objection will be sustained. Rule 408 generally bars admission of offers to settle, settlements, or statements made during civil settlement negotiations to prove fault or guilt respectively at *any* later civil or criminal trial *other than where the later criminal trial involves offering statements made during civil negotiations with a government regulatory, investigative, or enforcement agency.*

Why does the Rule prohibit offering civil compromise negotiation statements made in negotiations *between private parties* to prove guilt at a criminal trial but *not* prohibit them if the civil negotiations were with a government regulatory, investigative, or enforcement agency? Here is the Advisory Committee's justification for the general prohibition on using civil settlement negotiation statements at later criminal trials to prove guilt:

[S]tatements made during compromise negotiations of other disputed claims [that is, *other than* those claims involving the government] are not admissible in subsequent criminal litigation, when offered to prove liability for, invalidity of, or amount of those claims. When private parties enter into compromise negotiations they cannot protect against the subsequent use of statements in criminal cases by way of private ordering. The inability to guarantee protection against subsequent use could lead to parties refusing to admit fault, even if by doing so they could favorably settle the private matter. Such a chill on settlement negotiations would be contrary to the policy of Rule 408.

By contrast, the Advisory Committee believed that it was fair to admit such statements where negotiations were with the government rather than with private parties. There were two reasons for this conclusion: first, the parties should expect that statements made to one governmental entity might be reported to another one; and, second, governmental negotiators may be able to gain concessions from, or at times bind, other governmental actors (specifically prosecutors) where that is necessary to obtaining a civil settlement. In other words, the civil parties can by contract negotiate prohibitions against use of civil compromise negotiations in a later criminal trial — prohibitions not created by Rule 408. The underlying theory seems to be that the default position should be admissibility because that empowers governmental negotiators. However, those negotiators can move away from that default where it is in the public interest to do so. It will be in the public interest to do so where the state sees it as worthwhile to forego using the civil settlement negotiation statements as evidence in a criminal case where that is the only way to get the other side to agree to settle the civil matter. The other side, correspondingly, sees it as not worth settling the civil case if it risks criminal conviction in a serious matter. In the Advisory Committee's words:

> [T]he [2006] amendment provides that Rule 408 does not prohibit the introduction in a criminal case of statements or conduct during compromise negotiations regarding a civil dispute by a government regulatory, investigative, or enforcement agency. *See, e.g., United States v. Prewitt*, 34 F.3d 436, 439 (7th Cir. 1994) (admissions of fault made in compromise of a civil securities enforcement action were admissible against the accused in a subsequent criminal action for mail fraud). Where an individual makes a statement in the presence of government agents, its subsequent admission in a criminal case should not be unexpected. The individual can seek to protect against subsequent disclosure through negotiation and agreement with the civil regulator or an attorney for the government.

Example 8

Jason Dunkin is involved in a car crash in which he hits another car at high speed, seriously injuring the other car's driver. That driver has sued Jason for damages caused by Jason's negligent driving. The whole suit turns on whether Jason ran a red light. During settlement negotiations, Jason admits that he ran the red light, but no settlement is reached because the two parties cannot agree on damages. The case goes to trial, and Jason takes the stand, this time testifying that the light facing him was green, not red, when he entered the intersection. Plaintiff's counsel seeks to cross-examine Jason with reference to his admission during settlement negotiations that the light facing him was in fact red, not green, at the time of the accident. Plaintiff's counsel's theory for admission is that the statement is simply being offered to impeach by a prior inconsistent statement, not to prove validity or invalidity of the claim or amount. Jason's lawyer objects. His objection should be sustained, for Rule 408, as amended in 2006, expressly states that when the requirements set forth in parts (1) or (2) of the rule are otherwise met, the rule bars using settlement offers or statements made during them to impeach if the impeachment method is by contradiction or use of a prior inconsistent statement. Here is the 2006 Advisory Committee Note's justification for this position:

> The amendment prohibits the use of statements made during settlement negotiations when offered to impeach by prior inconsistent statement or through contradiction. Such broad impeachment would tend to swallow the exclusionary rule and would impair the public policy of promoting settlements. *See* McCormick on Evidence at 186 (5th ed. 1999) ("Use of statements made in compromise negotiations to impeach the testimony of a party, which is not specifically treated in [original] Rule 408, is fraught with danger of misuse of the statements to prove liability, threatens frank interchange of information during negotiations, and generally should not be permitted."). *See also EEOC v. Gear Petroleum, Inc.*, 948 F.2d 1542 (10th Cir. 1991) (letter sent as part of settlement negotiation cannot be used to impeach defense witness by way of contradiction or prior inconsistent statement; such broad impeachment would undermine the policy of encouraging uninhibited settlement negotiations).

Example 9

Assume that during the negotiations in the immediately preceding example, Jason Dunkin had also said, "I never went one mile per hour past the speed limit" and that the plaintiff alleged that Jason was negligent both in running a red light and in speeding. No settlement is reached, and the case goes to trial. At trial, Jason seeks to offer his own statement made during the negotiations denying speeding as substantive evidence that he in fact was not speeding at the time. The plaintiff objects. The objection will be sustained. According to the Advisory Committee, again in its 2006 Note:

> The amendment makes clear that Rule 408 excludes compromise evidence even when a party seeks to admit its own settlement offer or statements made in settlement negotiations. If a party were to reveal its own statement or offer, this could reveal the fact that the adversary entered into settlement negotiations. The protections of Rule 408 cannot be waived unilaterally because the Rule, by definition, protects both parties from having the fact of negotiation disclosed to the jury. Moreover, proof of statements and offers made in settlement would

often have to be made through the testimony of attorneys, leading to the risks and costs of disqualification. *See generally Pierce v. Tripler & Co.*, 955 F.2d 820, 828 (2nd Cir. 1992) (settlement offers are excluded under Rule 408 even if it is the offeror who seeks to admit them; noting that the "widespread admissibility of the substance of settlement offers could bring with it a rash of motions for disqualification of a party's chosen counsel who would likely become a witness at trial.").

Problem 6-4: The Car Crash

Two cars collide. One driver, Harry Marsden, said to the other driver, Julian Cort, "Look, let's not hassle this; will you take $1,000, and let's forget the whole thing?" Cort subsequently files a civil complaint against Marsden, seeking damages caused by Marsden's negligence. *Will any or all of Marsden's statements be admissible at the subsequent trial on this complaint? Why or why not?*

What if, instead, Marsden said, "I screwed up; I wasn't paying attention. How about taking $1,000 to forget the whole thing?" *Will any or all of these statements be admissible? Why or why not?*

Problem 6-5: The Non-Settling Defendant

Plaintiff Robert Belton filed a diversity action against Pittsburgh Corning and 15 other defendants, alleging that exposure to their asbestos-containing products caused him to develop various diseases. Immediately before trial, the 15 defendants other than Corning settled with plaintiff Belton. Corning, in its opening statement to the jury, stated that it would prove that plaintiff had been exposed to asbestos-containing products manufactured by 15 other companies, identifying them by name. Those companies were the settling defendants, though the jury did not yet know this. Thus, Corning argued, plaintiff could not prove that any of his injuries were caused by Corning's products. Over Corning's objection, however, plaintiff presented evidence in the liability phase of the trial that each of the 15 other defendants had settled immediately before trial, though the amounts of the settlements were not revealed. The jury entered a verdict in favor of the plaintiff, and the case proceeded to the damages phase.

At the damages phase, again over defense objection, the plaintiff presented evidence of the precise amount of the settlement agreements. The jury returned a massive verdict against Corning. *Were either or both of the trial judge's rulings in error? Why?*

Problem 6-6: The Recalcitrant Health Insurer

Dallas Park's health insurer was Aetna Life Insurance Company. Park obtained "immuno-augmentative" anti-cancer treatment at the Immunology Center (IC) in Freeport, Bahamas, when more traditional treatments had failed. Aetna refused to reimburse Park for the cost of these treatments on the ground that the treatments were not broadly accepted in the medical profession and were not necessary to treat her cancer.

1. At trial, Park offers evidence that another Aetna insured who had been treated with the same sort of anti-cancer therapy at the IC was reimbursed in full by Aetna without any dispute. Aetna objects. If you were the trial judge, how would you rule and why?

2. Assume the same facts, but with one variation: Aetna had, by letter, expressed a concern to the earlier insured about the efficacy and necessity of these treatments. That insured asked to have an Aetna representative meet with the insured and her physician. Mid-way during that meeting, the Aetna representative said, "Well, you've convinced me. These really are effective treatments in cases like yours, and we will be happy to cover them." Again, if you were the trial judge in *Park v. Aetna*, how would you rule, and why?

3. Now assume that, in the present case of *Park v. Aetna*, the parties met to try to negotiate a settlement. This time, the Aetna representative says, during the negotiations, "This really is an effective, promising treatment in many cases, but the amount you are requesting to settle the claim is ridiculously large." At trial, another Aetna representative, much higher in the company hierarchy, testified, "We long ago concluded that these treatments are worthless in fighting Mr. Park's sort of cancer, and all our representatives are trained to understand this conclusion." Plaintiffs counsel asks this latter Aetna representative, "Didn't Mr. McAuliffe [the first Aetna representative] meet with my client and admit that this treatment is effective? Didn't he contest only the amount of the claim?" Aetna objects. How should the trial judge rule?

4. Returning to the facts of Problem 6-5, assume that plaintiff Belton calls each of the settling co-defendants to the stand to testify during the liability phase that each of them manufactured a type of asbestos different from the unique type made only by Corning. They so testify to lay the groundwork for plaintiff's experts to testify that the asbestos particles found in plaintiff's lungs were of the unique type made by Corning. Assume further in this variation that the trial judge has not told the jury of Belton's settlements with the 15 co-defendants and has no intention of doing so. Corning's counsel on cross-examination asks each co-defendant, "Isn't it true that you were originally named as a co-defendant in this lawsuit and that you settled with the plaintiff immediately before this trial? And isn't it further true that a condition of this settlement was that you would testify as you now have at his trial?" Objections to both questions were sustained as to each witness. Did the trial judge rule correctly?

5. What if, in part 2 above, Aetna offered to settle the claim for $50,000? At trial, an Aetna representative testifies that the medical treatment is worthless in fighting cancer. Can plaintiff's counsel impeach the representative with the $50,000 settlement offer, arguing that it shows that Aetna did, contrary to the representative's testimony, recognize that the treatment indeed had value?

6. Assume the facts of part 2 above. At trial, Park seeks to have his physician testify about the same medical research presented during the part 3 settlement negotiations that enabled Park to get Aetna tentatively to concede the value of the treatment. Aetna objects on the ground that the jury would be exposed to "evidence of conduct or statements made in compromise negotiations." How should the trial judge rule?

Problem 6-7

Marc Wayne is the CEO of Megatech, Inc, a corporation involved in agribusiness. Megatech has allegedly failed to obey Environmental Protection Agency ("EPA") regulations governing the disposal of animal waste on its farms. Small family-run corn farmers on adjacent land maintain that the run-off of animal waste from Megatech farms is killing nearby corn crops. The small farmers jointly bring a class action suit against Megatech for damages for negligence and for an injunction in abatement of a nuisance. The farmers also report the matter to the EPA, which begins an investigation. As a result of that investigation, the EPA concludes that there have been serious violations of its regulations, and they seek civil penalties as well as strict future compliance with the law, threatening to sue Megatech if their demands are not promptly met. Megatech meets with the farmers to discuss settlement of their suit. During that meeting, CEO Wayne says, "I've known for years that our run-off was draining into your farms, but I had no idea that animal waste run-off could be dangerous to corn crops, I don't see how I could have known, and we just aren't responsible for any damages." After much haggling, the suit is settled for $1,000,000. The EPA thereafter meets with Megatech, insisting that the settlement is a paltry sum and does not prevent future harms. The EPA still seeks civil penalties and wants an agreement to changes in farming practices that will minimize future run-off. During this negotiation with EPA, CEO Wayne says, "Look, my employees have been telling me for at least two years that animal waste run-off could harm the adjacent corn crops, but they never showed me any scientific evidence to support it, and I wasn't going to kill our profits by putting big bucks into alleviating the problem if it didn't really hurt anyone." EPA refuses to settle and files a civil action against Megatech. Simultaneously, the United States Attorney files federal criminal charges against Megatech for violating federal criminal environmental law statutes.

1. At the criminal trial, the prosecution seeks to offer into evidence CEO Wayne's statement from Megatech's negotiation with the small farmers, "I've known for years that our run-off was draining into your farms." Megatech objects. Sustained or overruled?

2. Suppose that the objection in question 1 is sustained. Now Megatech, in its case-in-chief, seeks to offer into evidence the statement of its CEO made during settlement negotiations with the small farmers that he "had no idea that animal waste run-off could be dangerous to corn crops, I don't see how I could have known, and we just aren't responsible for any damages." The CEO has not taken the stand, but other Megatech employees present at the negotiation are available to testify to CEO Wayne's statements. The prosecution objects. How should the judge rule?

3. Assume now that CEO Wayne takes the stand at Megatech's criminal trial and denies ever having been aware, until the farmers complained to him, that any Megatech animal waste was running onto adjacent farmers' land. On cross-examination, the prosecution seeks to have Wayne admit to his statement during his civil negotiation with the small farmers that he had "known for years that our run-off was draining onto your farms." Megatech objects to the question. Sustained or overruled?

4. The prosecution seeks to offer into evidence the fact that Megatech settled with the farmers for $1,000,000, arguing that that settlement constituted an admission of guilt. Megatech objects. How should the trial judge rule?

5. The prosecution next seeks to offer in its case in chief at the criminal trial the statement that CEO Wayne made to the EPA: "Look, my employees have been telling me for at least two years that animal waste run-off could harm adjacent corn crops." Megatech objects. How should the trial judge rule?

6. Assume that the objection in question 5 is sustained. CEO Wayne later takes the stand in Megatech's case in chief, testifying that no one had ever warned him before he met with the farmers that animal waste run-off could kill corn crops. The prosecution seeks on cross to have Wayne admit to his statement to the EPA that "my employees have been telling me for at least two years that animal waste run-off could harm adjacent corn crops." Megatech objects. Sustained or overruled?

7. Wayne is still on the stand. Prosecutors seek on cross to have him admit to his statement to the EPA that he "wasn't going to kill our profits by putting big bucks into alleviating the problem [of run-off harming corn crops]." Megatech objects. Sustained or overruled? Does your answer depend upon whether the objection to question 6 was sustained or overruled?

8. Megatech seeks in its case-in-chief to offer evidence of Wayne's statement during Megatech's negotiations with the small farmers that he had "no idea that animal waste run-off could be dangerous to corn crops" and he "didn't see how [he] could have known," and Megatech just is not "responsible for any damages. The prosecution objects. How should the trial judge rule?

9. Could Megatech's attorney have reduced the risk of evidence of Wayne's statements made during civil negotiations with the EPA being admitted in evidence against Megatech at a potential later criminal trial? How?

10. Would your answers to any of the above questions change if CEO Wayne himself, and not Megatech, was being criminally tried?

11. Would your answers to any of the above questions change if, instead of CEO Wayne making the statements noted above, Megatech's lawyer had made the statements, that is, for example, the lawyer admitted that Wayne knew about the run-off for years? (Assume that Wayne was not even present at the negotiations).

12. Would your answers to any of the above questions change if the evidence noted were sought to be offered at the trial of the civil suit brought by the EPA rather than at a criminal trial?

[C] Plea Bargains and Related Statements in Criminal Cases: Rule 410

Rule 410 addresses the use of evidence in any proceeding, civil or criminal, of guilty plea negotiations arising from a criminal case. Rule 410's general prohibition on using such evidence reads as follows:

Rule 410. Pleas, Plea Discussions, and Related Statements

(a) PROHIBITED USES. In a civil or criminal case, evidence of the following is not admissible against the defendant who made the plea or participated in the plea discussions:

(1) a guilty plea that was later withdrawn;

(2) a nolo contendere plea;

(3) a statement made during a proceeding on either of those pleas under Federal Rule of Criminal Procedure 11 or a comparable state procedure; or

(4) a statement made during plea discussions with an attorney for the prosecuting authority if the discussions did not result in a guilty plea or they resulted in a later-withdrawn guilty plea.

(b) EXCEPTIONS. The court may admit a statement described in Rule 410(a)(3) or (4):

(1) in any proceeding in which another statement made during the same plea or plea discussions has been introduced, if in fairness the statements ought to be considered together; or

(2) in a criminal proceeding for perjury or false statement, if the defendant made the statement under oath, on the record, and with counsel present.

The purpose of this rule is to encourage plea negotiations between the prosecution and the defense, by assuring defendants that, if the negotiations fail, the defendants' statements will not be used against them at trial. If the prosecution and defense reach a plea agreement, that agreement must be approved by the trial judge. The trial judge conducts a "colloquy" in open court in which the defendant is questioned under oath to ensure that his or her decision to plead guilty was knowingly, intelligently, and voluntarily made. The defendants will thus be informed of the content and implications of the rights being waived by entering the guilty plea (such as the right to a jury trial); of the potential penalties that may result from pleading guilty; and of the limited grounds for appealing or withdrawing a guilty plea. Additionally, the prosecutor usually reads a summary of the facts to which the defendant admits.

Once a plea is entered, it may be withdrawn only for a very few, narrow reasons such as that the plea was involuntary or that defense counsel was ineffective in advising the defendant to plead guilty. Even then, proving these grounds can be hard, since the plea would not have been accepted until after a detailed colloquy in which the defendant, for example, denied that he or she was pressured in any way to enter into the plea. Nevertheless, if the court does permit the plea to be withdrawn and the case proceeds to trial, subsection (1) prohibits using the fact of the plea against the defendant at that trial or in any other civil or criminal proceeding. Subsection (2) extends similar protection to statements made during the colloquy, which is the procedure described in subsection (3) as a "proceeding on either of those pleas under Federal Rule of Criminal Procedure 11 or comparable state procedure. . . ." The prohibition against using colloquy statements applies in any future civil or criminal proceeding, even if the resulting guilty plea is not withdrawn.

A *"nolo contendere"* or "no contest" plea is, in common sense terms, a statement by the defendant that, "I will neither admit nor deny that I am guilty, but I will not contest the charge, and I therefore agree to allow the state to sentence me as if I were guilty." A defendant entering a no contest plea faces the same criminal penalties as one entering a guilty plea. However, there is one huge advantage in entering a *nolo* plea: the plea may not usually (though there are some exceptions beyond the scope of this course) be used against a defendant as an admission of guilt in a subsequent civil case. A colloquy is also required, though a defendant may be asked only to concede that the state can prove an agreed-upon summary of facts rather than admitting (as he would with a guilty plea) that those facts actually happened.

Subsections (2) and (3) of Rule 410 extend the same evidentiary protections to a no contest plea as they extend to a guilty plea later withdrawn, including protection of statements made during the colloquy. Subsection (4) further extends protection to any statements made between the defendant or defense counsel and the prosecutor while attempting to negotiate a guilty plea, even if no plea ever results or a plea does result but is later withdrawn. In this respect, Rule 410 differs from the analogous Rule 408 for civil settlement negotiations. Under Rule 408, statements made during negotiations with any person involved in the case are protected (for example, with an insurance company agent trying to settle a civil claim before suit is brought). Under Rule 410, however, negotiations are protected only if they are made *with the prosecutor*. Statements to the police are outside Rule 410's scope. Thus, statements made during purported negotiations between a defendant and interrogating police officers are not barred by this rule (unless, of course, the officers are acting as agents for the prosecutor for these purposes — in which case the statements made to the police would be protected by Rule 410 because they would in effect really be statements to the prosecutor). Although statements made to police officers during purported settlement negotiations where the officers are not acting on behalf of the prosecutors are not protected by Rule 410, they may under certain circumstances be barred by other rules, such as the constitutional prohibition against involuntary confessions.

Rule 410 provides broader protection than Rule 408 in at least one respect, however: evidence of a guilty plea later withdrawn or a *nolo* plea may not be admitted to show bias or for any other purpose unconnected to criminal liability for the offense charged. Unlike Rule 408, under which civil settlement offers or agreements are excluded from trial only if offered for the purpose of proving liability for or invalidity of the claim or its amount, Rule 410 excludes withdrawn pleas or offers to plead for *any purpose whatsoever*, other than two narrow exceptions discussed below. The same is true for statements made in the course of plea discussions with the prosecuting authority. These discussions must, however, involve an attempted *quid pro quo*, thus involving a "plea" and not simply an admission. *Compare United States v. Leon Guerrero*, 847 F. 2d 1363, 1367 (9th Cir. 1988) (making this determination by inquiring whether the offender had an actual and reasonable expectation that he was negotiating a plea), *with State v. Fox*, 760 P. 2d 670, 674–675 (Haw. 1988) (Rule's language requires only a subjective inquiry into the offender's state of mind).

Importantly, however, Rule 410 does not extend protection against using a guilty plea against the declarant in another civil or criminal case if the plea is never withdrawn and becomes the basis for a conviction. A guilty plea in a criminal case is therefore often admissible as a party admission in a civil case. *See* Chapter 13.

Rule 410 continues with the following provisions creating exceptions to the general rules outlined above:

> EXCEPTIONS. The court may admit a statement described in Rule 410(a)(3) or (4):
>
> (1) in any proceeding in which another statement made during the same plea or plea discussions has been introduced, if in fairness the statements ought to be considered together; or
>
> (2) in a criminal proceeding for perjury or false statement, if the defendant made the statement under oath, on the record, and with counsel present.

The rationale for the first exception (concerning statements that ought in fairness be considered together) has been explained by the Rules of Criminal Procedure Advisory Committee Note to Rule 11(e)(6) of the Federal Rules of Criminal Procedure, which Rule corresponds to Rule 410, thus:

> This change is necessary so that, when evidence of statements made in the course of or as a consequence of a certain plea or plea discussion are introduced under circumstances not prohibited by this rule (e.g., not "against" the person who made the plea), other statements relating to the same plea or plea discussions may also be admitted when relevant to the matter at issue. For example, if a defendant upon a motion to dismiss a prosecution on some ground were able to admit certain statements made in aborted plea discussions in his favor, then other relevant statements made in the same plea discussions should be admissible against the defendant in the interest of determining the truth of the matter at issue.

The second exception permits, for example, a perjury prosecution based on the defendant's lies under oath in a guilty plea colloquy. The colloquy statements may be used against the defendant at a perjury trial.

The United States Supreme Court has read a third exception into the Rule as implied by its nature and the nature of the adversary system: a defendant may waive the right to the rule's protection if the prosecutor insists on such a waiver as a precondition to the plea negotiations.

The Court recognized this waiver rule in *United States v. Mezzanatto*, 513 U.S. 196, 115 S. Ct. 797, 130 L. Ed. 2d 697 (1995). (*See* Case Library.) There, a defendant charged with possessing methamphetamine with intent to distribute it sought to negotiate a plea with the prosecutor. The prosecutor agreed to do so only if the defendant first agreed — which he did — that any statements made during the negotiation could be used to impeach him should the case go to trial. During the negotiations, however, the defendant sought to shift primary responsibility to another individual, a Mr. Shuster. The prosecutor thus cut short the negotiations, believing that the defendant had lied. At trial, the prosecutor, over defense objection, impeached the defendant with prior inconsistent statements that he had made during the plea bargaining. The jury convicted him, and he appealed, arguing that he had been impeached in violation of Rule 410 of the Federal Rules of Evidence. The Ninth Circuit reversed the defendant's conviction, holding that, because neither Rule 410 nor its two narrowly drafted exceptions said anything about waiver, Congress must have meant to preclude it.

The United Stated Supreme Court, however, reversed the Ninth Circuit, reinstating the conviction. First, the Court was unconvinced that the Rule's silence about waiver mattered, given the routine trial practice of granting waivers for tactical purposes. Second, the Court believed that the waiver agreements before it would enhance truth-seeking by discouraging lies. Third, said the Court, the Rule's reference to making certain statements inadmissible "against" the defendant, and its exception where a defendant has first offered such statements in his favor, contemplates the tactical freedom of a defendant to agree to the use of such statements where he believes that the result may work in his favor. Fourth, and most importantly, the Court rejected the argument that permitting waivers would defeat the Rule's purpose of encouraging plea bargains:[3]

> To use the Ninth Circuit's metaphor, if the prosecutor is interested in "buying" the reliability assurance that accompanies a waiver agreement, then precluding waiver can only stifle the market for plea bargains. A defendant can "maximize" what he has to "sell" only if he is permitted to offer what the prosecutor is most interested in buying. And while it is certainly true that prosecutors often need help from the small fish in a conspiracy in order to catch the big ones, that is no reason to preclude waiver altogether. If prosecutors decide that certain crucial information will be gained only by preserving the inadmissibility of plea statements, they will agree to leave intact the exclusionary provisions of the plea-statement rules.

Justice Souter dissented on a number of grounds, most importantly rejecting the conclusion that Congress meant to leave waiver to the mercy of market forces. Souter believed that waivers would diminish the "zone of unrestrained candor" because a defendant must pause to think whether the guilty plea negotiations are worth the risk, thus undermining the Rule's pro-plea-negotiation purpose.[4]

Problem 6-7: Rodney Ransom

Rodney Ransom is the driver of a car that was involved in an accident with a car driven by Myron Cohen. A police officer who arrived on the scene gave Ransom a ticket for reckless driving. Cohen civilly sues Ransom on a negligence theory. When Ransom meets with his newly retained defense lawyer, Lola Brandon, Ransom says, "I'll just go down to traffic court and plead guilty, so at least that will be over with, and we can concentrate on the silly civil suit. OK?" *What advice should Ransom's lawyer give him in response to this question? Why?*

---

[3] 513 U.S. at 208.

[4] *Id.* at 214–215.

Problem 6-8: Turning on Mr. Big

Morris Mumford is arrested on a charge of distributing cocaine. Detective Jacob Marlee tells Mumford, "Look, I know you're just a little guy. If you turn in Mr. Big, the prosecutor has promised me you'll get probation." Mumford then recounted the complete details of his involvement in the cocaine distribution scheme, and this confession was admitted against him at trial, over Mumford's objection. *Did the trial judge rule correctly? Does it matter, in reaching this decision, whether Marlee told Mumford the truth?*

Problem 6-9: Waiving Rule 410

Assume that in Problem 6-8 above, the prosecutor joins Marlee's discussions with Mumford, but the prosecutor agrees to discuss a plea with Mumford only if he first waives his right to exclude his statements from trial under Rule 410. At first, Mumford refuses, saying he does not understand what Rule 410 is and does not want to give up something without knowing its importance. The prosecutor leaves the room to make a phone call. While he is gone, Marlee tells Mumford, "Trust me, if you don't agree to this waiver thing, you're going away for at least 20 years." When the prosecutor returns, Mumford agrees to the waiver and confesses everything. The prosecutor believes that Mumford is lying about some details and refuses to agree to a plea. At Mumford's trial, the prosecutor calls Marlee to the stand to recount Mumford's confession. The defense objects. *How should the trial judge rule? Are there any additional facts that would help you in answering this question? What facts?*

1. What if, on this same set of facts, Mumford and the prosecutor do reach an agreement. Mumford recounts the details of the crime during the plea colloquy, and a plea is entered. Subsequently, the prosecutor obtains evidence that some of what Mumford said during the colloquy was false. May the colloquy statements be admitted against Mumford at his later perjury trial?

2. Suppose in a civil case against Mumford for the wrongful death of a teenager who died from an overdose of drugs sold to him by Mumford, Mumford takes the stand and denies any involvement in a drug distribution scheme.

    a. Under the original set of facts here, in which no plea agreement is reached, may Mumford's statements made during plea negotiations be used to impeach him at his civil trial?

    b. Under variation 1, may the fact of his plea be used to impeach him at the civil trial?

    c. Under variation 1, assume that Mumford successfully withdraws his guilty plea. Before that criminal case proceeds to trial, he testifies in the civil case, denying involvement in the drug scheme. May his colloquy statements be used to impeach him at the civil trial?

§ 6.06 PAYMENT OF MEDICAL AND SIMILAR EXPENSES

Rule 409 reads as follows:

Rule 409. Offers to Pay Medical and Similar Expenses

> Evidence of furnishing, promising to pay, or offering to pay medical, hospital, or similar expenses resulting from an injury is not admissible to prove liability for the injury.

Example 1

Layla DePaul rear-ends a car driven by Lindsey Lee. Lindsey exits the car, able to speak but complaining of back pain. Layla says, "Don't worry. We'll get you immediate medical care, and if your insurance company won't pay for it, I will." Layla's statement will be excluded from evidence, upon Layla's objection, at any trial in which Lindsey or someone acting on her behalf seeks to recover damages from Layla.

The Advisory Committee Note explains the rationale for the rule:[5]

> [G]enerally, evidence of payment of medical, hospital, or similar expenses of an injured party by the opposing party, is not admissible, the reason often given being that such payment or offer is usually made from humane impulses and not from an admission of liability, and that to hold otherwise would tend to discourage assistance to the injured person.

Rule 409 differs from Rules 408 and 410 in that Rule 409 does not extend to "conduct or statements not a part of the act of furnishing or offering or promising to pay." Advisory Committee Note. The Advisory Committee explains that this difference arises "from a fundamental difference in nature. Communication is essential if compromises are to be effected, and consequently broad protection of statements is needed. This is not so in cases of payments or offers or promises to pay medical expenses, where factual statements may be expected to be incidental in nature."

Example 2

In Layla's accident with Lindsey above, assume that Layla really said, "Don't worry. I'm so sorry. It's all my fault. I shouldn't have tailgated you. We'll get you immediate medical attention, and if your insurance company won't pay for it, I will." In a subsequent suit by Lindsey against Layla, Rule 409 will result in the exclusion of the offer to pay medical expenses. But Rule 409 will not apply to exclude the statements clearly admitting fault, such as, "It's all my fault. I shouldn't have tailgated you." It also would not exclude the apology ("I'm so sorry"), which could be viewed as an admission of fault on the theory that people do not apologize unless they have done some wrong calling for an apology. Of course, a judge has discretion to exclude an apology like "I'm sorry" under Rule 403.

---

[5] Advisory Committee Note, quoting Annot. 20 A.L.R.2d 291, 293.

No dispute is necessary for Rule 409 to apply. Moreover, the offer need not have been made directly to the injured party; it can be made to anyone who can accept payment. Importantly, the Rule's prohibition is only against using the evidence to "prove liability for the injury." But furnishing, offering, or promising to pay medical expenses can be used for any other purpose, such as showing control or identity.

Example 3

In Layla's accident with Lindsey above, assume that Layla and Linda were in the car that hit Lindsey. Layla said to Lindsey, "We'll get you to a hospital. Don't worry about the money. If your insurance company won't pay the cost, I will." Lindsey did not, however, see who drove the car that hit her, and there were no eyewitnesses outside the cars. Moreover, Linda died before her deposition could be taken. Lindsey offers into evidence Layla's offer to pay Lindsey's medical expenses. This offer is made not to prove Layla's fault but merely to show that Layla had control over the car, that is, that Layla was the driver.

The argument would be that the driver is the one most likely to feel responsible enough (in the sense of having some active involvement in the events, even if not "at fault") to offer to pay medical expenses. Of course, other inferences are possible (maybe Layla was the passenger but just a nice person), but Layla's being the driver is at least a relevant plausible inference. Rule 409 would not bar this evidence. However, a trial court might nevertheless fear that a jury would make the prohibited fault inference and that a limiting instruction would not cure the problem. Accordingly, the trial judge still might exclude the evidence under Rule 403.

Problem 6-10: Med X

After a frustrating business meeting, Jan hurried away, lost in thought. Jan crashed her car into Arsenio, knocking him over. As Arsenio writhed in pain on the ground, Jan stated, "I'm really sorry; I was preoccupied, and this mess was all my fault. If you don't bring suit, I'll be more than happy to pay for all of your medical expenses. Hey, I'll even pay for your ripped pants and for any embarrassment this incident may have caused you. What do you say?" Arsenio said, "No," and filed suit. *Are any of Jan's statements admissible at trial?*

Problem 6-11: Kommander Condominium Club

One crisp fall day at the Kommander Condominium Club, Rob Arbuckle was late for his 10:30 a.m. tennis appointment. He left the elevator while looking at his watch and bowled over 86-year-old Alfred Macumber. A distraught Rob exclaimed, "Oh Mac! I hope you're okay. Why don't you go to the Mellon Hospital, and I'll pay for the check-up?" Later that night, Mac's attorney called Rob and told him that Mac was thinking of bringing suit because of his fairly severe injuries. Rob responded, "Look, I don't want any trouble. I admit I was not looking when I ran into Mac; I was in a hurry. If I gave Mac $1,000, would this whole thing go away?" The attorney refused Rob's proposal. Prior to the civil trial, Rob was prosecuted for battery on Mr. Macumber. He sought a plea bargain in which he would admit guilt if he received a suspended sentence. The prosecutor rejected Rob's offer. *Which, if any, of Rob's statements are admissible against him in the civil trial?*

Plaintiff's attorney Jed Ward (Gene Hackman) and defense co-counsel Michael Grazier (Colin Friels) and Maggie Ward (Mary Elizabeth Mastrantonio) battle over the admissibility of a safety report in *Class Action*.*

§ 6.07 LIABILITY INSURANCE: RULE 411

Rule 411 reads as follows:

Rule 411. Liability Insurance

> Evidence that a person was or was not insured against liability is not admissible to prove whether the person acted negligently or otherwise wrongfully. But the court may admit this evidence for another purpose, such as proving a witness's bias or prejudice or proving agency, ownership, or control.

> *Example 1*

> Assume the facts, set forth in § 6.06, about Lindsey's suit against Layla, which arises out of an automobile accident. At trial, Lindsey offers evidence that Layla was insured to prove Layla's own awareness of her poor driving skills and thus her effort, by obtaining insurance, to protect herself against the consequences of her own carelessness. Layla's objection will be sustained.

---

* Class Action copyright © 1991 Twentieth Century Fox. All Rights Reserved.

The Advisory Committee Note sets forth two justifications for the rule: (1) "(at best the inference of fault from the fact of insurance coverage is a tenuous one, as is its converse)"; and (2) "the feeling that knowledge of the presence or absence of liability insurance would induce juries to decide cases on improper grounds." Commentators have also described the rule as encouraging people (and companies) to obtain insurance by limiting the risk that the insurance contract will create an inference of their carelessness.

The rule is not limited to evidence that the *defendant* was insured against liability; it was broadly drafted "so as to include contributory negligence or other fault of a plaintiff as well as fault of a defendant."

Note that the Rule does not prohibit using the evidence for purposes other than proving negligence or wrongful conduct.

Example 2

Layla, in varying our continuing example above, had been driving a truck with the phrase, "Acme Trucking Company," emblazoned on its side. Part of Lindsey's claim is that the truck's owner was negligent for not maintaining its brakes in tip-top shape. Lindsey's suit is only against Layla. Layla, in her answer to the complaint, denies owning the truck. She denies being responsible for its maintenance, and alleges that the maintenance responsibility belongs to the Acme Trucking Company. Lindsey introduces evidence at trial that the truck was insured in Layla's name, to prove that Layla was the truck's true owner and therefore was obligated to keep it well-maintained. Layla's objection under Rule 411 will probably be overruled, because the evidence is offered to prove ownership, not to prove Layla's negligence or otherwise wrongful conduct. However, the evidence may be excluded if the trial judge is not convinced that jurors will comply with a limiting instruction directing them to use the evidence of insurance only for the permitted purpose.

Problem 6-12: "I Forgot"

Defendant is sued for injuries resulting from an automobile accident. The defendant did not have automobile liability insurance; he "forgot to buy some." At trial, the defendant testified on direct examination.

DEFENDANT'S ATTORNEY: How careful a driver are you?

PLAINTIFF'S ATTORNEY: Objection. This evidence is irrelevant and unfairly prejudicial.

JUDGE: *(How should the judge rule? Why?)*

DEFENDANT'S ATTORNEY: What is your motive to be careful while driving?

PLAINTIFF'S ATTORNEY: Objection.

DEFENDANT'S ATTORNEY: (at the bench) I will proffer, Your Honor, that the defendant will say that "I'm a careful driver in large part because I forgot to take out car

§ 6.07   LIABILITY INSURANCE: RULE 411   253

insurance; I knew that I could be held personally liable if I was in an automobile accident."

PLAINTIFF'S ATTORNEY: Objection.

JUDGE: *(How should the judge rule? Why?)*

Is this evidence admissible if it is offered to rebut the implicit assumption that, because many people have automobile insurance, the defendant likely has automobile insurance as well?

Problem 6-13: Go Ahead and Jump

Plaintiff, Laurie, brought suit against a bungee-jumping facility in Michigan. Plaintiff jumped and was injured when the rope broke. Plaintiff offered evidence at trial that the defendant was insured, to corroborate her claim that the defendant operated the business with a lackadaisical attitude. The facility's unofficial motto was: "Why worry? Be happy." *Is this evidence admissible?*

Problem 6-14: Columbo

Defense witness, Samantha, testified about the position of two cars involved in an automobile accident at a busy intersection. On cross-examination, she was asked by an apparently bumbling attorney named Columbo whether she was employed by the defendant's insurer. The defendant objected to the question and the court sustained the objection. *Should the lower court's ruling be affirmed on appeal?*

Problem 6-15: Statutory Interpretation Exercise

Read *United States v. Mezzanatto*, 513 U.S. 196 (1995) (*see* Case Library), and answer the following questions:

1. *Text and Silence:* What role did text play in the majority's analysis? The dissent's? How much weight did each opinion give to text? What audience was assumed to assign the text meaning? What was the relative weight given to text versus silence, that is, what the text failed to say? Why?

2. *Truth:* What respective weight did the majority and dissenting opinions give to truth-finding as a value? Why did each opinion give truth its respective weight?

3. *The Free Market:* What significance did each opinion give to the importance of a free versus a regulated market in plea bargains? Why? What was the source of each opinion's view of the relevance meaning, an importance of this market? What narrative did each opinion craft, and what was the role of the free market in that narrative?

4. *Congressional Intent Versus Congressional Purpose and Its Alternatives:* Did any of the opinions relay on "actual" congressional intent on "actual" congressional purpose? What intent or purpose would Congress have had, had it thought specifically about the matter before the Court? What sources did each opinion rely on for these real or imagined designations of legislative intent? What was the relative role of the Advisory Committee and the Supreme Court in determining legislative intent or purpose, real or imagined? What weight did intent

or purpose receive relative to other data sources on which each opinion relied?

5. *Candor:* Is there a difference between what each opinion claims to be doing in its approach to statutory interpretation and what it is in fact doing?

§ 6.08 REVIEW PROBLEMS: SYNTHESIZING THE QUASI-PRIVILEGES

Problem 6-16: Let's Make a Deal

Barbara owed Alice $500. When Barbara saw Alice hanging out in front of the local convenience store, Barbara asked Alice, "If I give you $350 and a ticket to the Harry Connick Jr. concert, would that be an adequate settlement? I don't have the full $500 I owe you, and I just won't have it by the agreed date. I'm very short on cash at the moment." *If Alice does not accept Barbara's offer, can Alice introduce Barbara's statements in a later trial for payment of the $500?*

Problem 6-17: Engulf and Devour

Johann is sued by a business partner, Domino. Domino claimed that Johan understated profits by $1 million over a period of five years and clandestinely siphoned off partnership money for personal use. During negotiations with Domino, Johann admitted to taking some money because he needed to pay off gambling losses. Johann claimed, however, that he did not owe Domino anything because Domino had swindled him at the time they had formed the partnership, and, therefore, the money he took was rightfully his.

Can Domino offer Johann's statements at trial?

If Johann, hoping to get a more favorable settlement by showing his meager current assets, had produced during the negotiations all of the tax forms relating to the years in question and the betting slips verifying his losses, could these documents still be offered at trial?

If Johann had agreed that he owed Domino the $1 million as Domino claimed, but offered during negotiations to pay "500 grand" to have the lawsuit dropped, are any factual admissions made in conjunction with Johann's offer to pay admissible?

If subsequent criminal proceedings are initiated against Johann for his failure to pay income taxes on the monies in question, would the statements he made during the previous settlement negotiations be admissible in the subsequent criminal case?

Problem 6-18: Battery

Jessel is sued by Cohan for damages resulting from an alleged battery outside of a local nightclub, Crickett Place. Cohan and Jessel engaged in a series of discussions about settling the suit before trial. During one discussion, Cohan stated, "The only reason I hit you from behind was because you were doing a song and dance with my girlfriend inside the club." Negotiations were unsuccessful. At trial, Cohan takes the stand and states, "I was in the club until after Jessel left; I didn't learn about him getting hurt until I heard the sirens and ran outside to see what had happened."

Jessel seeks to impeach Cohan with the admissions he made during settlement negotiations. Is this permissible?

Problem 6-19: Gorkey Park

McGillicuddy is charged with two counts of breaking and entering the kitchen of a local restaurant, Sim's Place. A day after the charges were filed, McGillicuddy visited a local police officer, Officer Gorkey. McGillicuddy and Gorkey were social acquaintances. McGillicuddy proposed to Gorkey that "if you ditch these charges against me, I can help you catch some big-time crooks. I admit I broke into Sim's, but I was hungry and wanted some food; you can understand that, right?"

At McGillicuddy's trial for breaking and entering, can the prosecution offer McGillicuddy's statements to Officer Gorkey?

Assume that McGillicuddy's friend, Bobby, also is charged with breaking and entering as an aider and abetter. But the real mastermind of the operation, says Bobby, was McGillicuddy, who planned everything. Bobby agrees to testify against McGillicuddy, provided that the prosecution drops the charges against Bobby. *Can statements made by Bobby while entering a plea of guilty be used by McGillicuddy to impeach Bobby on cross-examination (e.g., a statement in which Bobby describes his own planning activity in a way suggesting that he, not McGillicuddy, was the mastermind, so McGillicuddy could show that he was just Bobby's innocent dupe)?*

McGillicuddy unsuccessfully attempted to negotiate a plea directly with the prosecutor. At trial, McGillicuddy introduces some of his own statements made during plea discussions with the prosecutor. These are statements suggesting that McGillicuddy thought he had permission to enter the kitchen. *What can the prosecutor do in response to McGillicuddy's evidence, if anything?*

After reading Rule 410 of the Federal Rules of Evidence, McGillicuddy concluded that the Rule is designed to protect the accused during plea bargaining. Consequently, McGillicuddy offered the statements made by the prosecutor during their unsuccessful plea negotiations. *Are the prosecutor's statements admissible?*

Problem 6-20: Did I Say That?

Leslie is sued by her neighbor, Murray, for breaking a very expensive mirror in Murray's house. During settlement negotiations, Leslie admitted she had been smoking marijuana at Murray's at the time the mirror broke. She denied, however, actually breaking the heirloom. The following month, Leslie is prosecuted for the possession of marijuana at her neighbor's house.

Can the prosecution offer the admission about marijuana use that Leslie made during the earlier settlement negotiations?

If Leslie had pled guilty to using marijuana at her neighbor's house, and then was sued in a civil action by her neighbor for breaking the mirror, could the guilty plea be used against her in the later civil trial?

Problem 6-21: The Singing Sparrow

The defendant, Sparrow, is charged with murdering Goodot. During a plea negotiation with the prosecutor, the defendant blurts out, "You guys don't know who you're up against! You think I killed Goodot, but you really should ask me about the unsolved murder of Blaine in the next county. I have personal knowledge about that one, and you coppers are way off base in your investigation!"

Sparrow is subsequently charged with Blaine's murder. *At that trial, can the prosecutor offer Sparrow's inculpatory statements made during the Goodot plea negotiations?*

Problem 6-22: Rosetta's Orwellian Plight

Rosetta sues Maxwell civilly for injuries growing out of Maxwell's alleged sexual assault. Rosetta seeks to testify to the following: "I called an ambulance right after the rape and was rushed to the Center City Hospital Emergency Room. Maxwell was waiting there and said to me: "I'm sorry that I hurt you. I just couldn't control myself. I promise to pay all your medical expenses if you promise not to tell the cops what happened, even if they ask you, and not to sue me." *This testimony, in the face of a proper objection, should be:*

(a) Admissible if there is a limiting instruction prohibiting the jurors from using the words, "I promise to pay all your medical expenses" as showing Maxwell's consciousness of guilt for in fact raping Rosetta.

(b) Inadmissible under Rule 408.

(c) Inadmissible under Rule 409.

(d) Inadmissible under both Rules 408 and 409.

Problem 6-23: Maxwell's Comeuppance

Just before the criminal trial arising from the situation mentioned in the immediately preceding multiple-choice question, defense counsel approaches the prosecutor to begin plea discussions. The prosecutor refuses to negotiate unless the defendant responds personally to the prosecutor's question during the negotiation and further waives his right to raise any Rule 410 objections at any future trial. Additionally, the prosecutor promises to seek the highest possible sentence if the defendant is convicted of the rape charge if the defendant does not immediately agree to the Rule 410 waiver. Reluctantly, the defendant and his counsel agree to the prosecutor's terms. During the negotiation, defendant Maxwell admits that he raped Rosetta, and the prosecutor immediately cuts off negotiations and proceeds to trial. Defendant Maxwell testifies at his rape trial that he did not rape Rosetta but, rather, that she consented. The prosecutor seeks to cross-examine Maxwell with this statement made during the plea negotiations and later files perjury charges against Maxwell for lying under oath at his rape trial. *Select the best answer:*

(a) Maxwell's statement made during the plea negotiations is admissible at both the rape trial and the perjury trial.

(b) Maxwell's statement made during the plea negotiations is inadmissible at the rape trial but admissible at the perjury trial, so long as the trial court concludes by a preponderance of the evidence that the waiver was not voluntary.

(c) Maxwell's statement made during the plea negotiations is not admissible at either the rape trial or the perjury trial.

(d) Maxwell's statement made during the plea negotiations is admissible at the rape trial but not the perjury trial.

§ 6.09 CASE LIBRARY

UNITED STATES v. MEZZANATTO
Supreme Court of the United States
513 U.S. 196, 115 S. Ct. 797, 130 L. Ed. 2d 697 (1995)

Argued Nov. 2, 1994.

Decided Jan. 18, 1995.

JUSTICE THOMAS delivered the opinion of the Court.

Federal Rule of Evidence 410 and Federal Rule of Criminal Procedure 11(e)(6) provide that statements made in the course of plea discussions between a criminal defendant and a prosecutor are inadmissible against the defendant. The court below held that these exclusionary provisions may not be waived by the defendant. We granted certiorari to resolve a conflict among the Courts of Appeals, and we now reverse.

I

On August 1, 1991, San Diego Narcotics Task Force agents arrested Gordon Shuster after discovering a methamphetamine laboratory at his residence in Rainbow, California. Shuster agreed to cooperate with the agents, and a few hours after his arrest he placed a call to respondent's pager. When respondent returned the call, Shuster told him that a friend wanted to purchase a pound of methamphetamine for $13,000. Shuster arranged to meet respondent later that day.

At their meeting, Shuster introduced an undercover officer as his "friend." The officer asked respondent if he had "brought the stuff with him," and respondent told the officer it was in his car. The two proceeded to the car, where respondent produced a brown paper package containing approximately one pound of methamphetamine. Respondent then presented a glass pipe (later found to contain methamphetamine residue) and asked the officer if he wanted to take a "hit." The officer indicated that he would first get respondent the money; as the officer left the car, he gave a prearranged arrest signal. Respondent was arrested and charged with possession of methamphetamine with intent to distribute, in violation of 84

Stat. 1260, as amended, **21 U.S.C. § 841(a)(1)**.

On October 17, 1991, respondent and his attorney asked to meet with the prosecutor to discuss the possibility of cooperating with the Government. The prosecutor agreed to meet later that day. At the beginning of the meeting, the prosecutor informed respondent that he had no obligation to talk, but that if he wanted to cooperate he would have to be completely truthful. As a condition to proceeding with the discussion, the prosecutor indicated that respondent would have to agree that any statements he made during the meeting could be used to impeach any contradictory testimony he might give at trial if the case proceeded that far. Respondent conferred with his counsel and agreed to proceed under the prosecutor's terms.

Respondent then admitted knowing that the package he had attempted to sell to the undercover police officer contained methamphetamine, but insisted that he had dealt only in "ounce" quantities of methamphetamine prior to his arrest. Initially, respondent also claimed that he was acting merely as a broker for Shuster and did not know that Shuster was manufacturing methamphetamine at his residence, but he later conceded that he knew about Shuster's laboratory. Respondent attempted to minimize his role in Shuster's operation by claiming that he had not visited Shuster's residence for at least a week before his arrest. At this point, the Government confronted respondent with surveillance evidence showing that his car was on Shuster's property the day before the arrest, and terminated the meeting on the basis of respondent's failure to provide completely truthful information.

Respondent eventually was tried on the methamphetamine charge and took the stand in his own defense. He maintained that he was not involved in methamphetamine trafficking and that he had thought Shuster used his home laboratory to manufacture plastic explosives for the CIA. He also denied knowing that the package he delivered to the undercover officer contained methamphetamine. Over defense counsel's objection, the prosecutor cross-examined respondent about the inconsistent statements he had made during the October 17 meeting. Respondent denied having made certain statements, and the prosecutor called one of the agents who had attended the meeting to recount the prior statements. The jury found respondent guilty, and the District Court sentenced him to 170 months in prison.

A panel of the Ninth Circuit reversed, over the dissent of Chief Judge Wallace. The Ninth Circuit held that respondent's agreement to allow admission of his plea statements for purposes of impeachment was unenforceable and that the District Court therefore erred in admitting the statements for that purpose. We granted certiorari because the Ninth Circuit's decision conflicts with the Seventh Circuit's decision in *United States v. Dortch*, 5 F.3d 1056, 1067–1068 (1993).

II

Federal Rule of Evidence 410 and Federal Rule of Criminal Procedure 11(e)(6) (Rules or plea-statement Rules) are substantively identical. Rule 410 provides:

> Except as otherwise provided in this rule, evidence of the following is not, in any civil or criminal proceeding, admissible against the defendant who . . . was a participant in the plea discussions: . . . (4) any statement made

in the course of plea discussions with an attorney for the prosecuting authority which do not result in a plea of guilty. . . .

The Ninth Circuit noted that these Rules are subject to only two express exceptions,[6] neither of which says anything about waiver, and thus concluded that Congress must have meant to preclude waiver agreements such as respondent's. 998 F.2d, at 1454–1456. In light of the "precision with which these rules are generally phrased," the Ninth Circuit declined to "write in a waiver in a waiverless rule." *Id.*, at 1456.[7]

The Ninth Circuit's analysis is directly contrary to the approach we have taken in the context of a broad array of constitutional and statutory provisions. Rather than deeming waiver presumptively unavailable absent some sort of express enabling clause, we instead have adhered to the opposite presumption. *See Shutte v. Thompson*, 21 L. Ed. 123, 15 Wall. 151, 159 (1873) ("A party may waive any provision, either of a contract or of a statute, intended for his benefit"); *Peretz v. United States*, 501 U.S. 923, 936, 111 S. Ct. 2661, 2669, 115 L. Ed. 2d 808 (1991) ("The most basic rights of criminal defendants are . . . subject to waiver"). A criminal defendant may knowingly and voluntarily waive many of the most fundamental protections afforded by the Constitution. *See, e.g., Ricketts v. Adamson*, 483 U.S. 1, 10, 107 S. Ct. 2680, 2685–2686, 97 L. Ed. 2d 1 (1987) (double jeopardy defense waivable by pretrial agreement); *Boykin v. Alabama*, 395 U.S. 238, 243, 89 S. Ct. 1709, 1712, 23 L. Ed. 2d 274 (1969) (knowing and voluntary guilty plea waives privilege against compulsory self-incrimination, right to jury trial, and right to confront one's accusers); *Johnson v. Zerbst*, 304 U.S. 458, 465, 58 S. Ct. 1019, 1023, 82 L. Ed. 1461 (1938) (Sixth Amendment right to counsel may be waived). Likewise, absent some affirmative indication of Congress' intent to preclude waiver, we have presumed that statutory provisions are subject to waiver by voluntary agreement of the parties. *See, e.g., Evans v. Jeff D.*, 475 U.S. 717, 730–732, 106 S. Ct. 1531, 1538–1540, 89 L. Ed. 2d 747 (1986) (prevailing party in civil-rights action may waive its statutory eligibility for attorney's fees).

Our cases interpreting the Federal Rules of Criminal Procedure are consistent with this approach. The provisions of those Rules are presumptively waivable, though an express waiver clause may suggest that Congress intended to occupy the field and to preclude waiver under other, unstated circumstances. *See Crosby v. United States*, 506 U.S. 255, 113 S. Ct. 748, 122 L. Ed. 2d 25 (1993); *Smith v. United States* 360 U.S. 1, 79 S. Ct. 991, 3 L. Ed. 2d 1041 (1959). In *Crosby*, for example, we held that a defendant's failure to appear for any part of his trial did not constitute

---

[6] A statement made by a criminal defendant in the course of plea discussions is "admissible (i) in any proceeding wherein another statement made in the course of the same . . . plea discussions has been introduced and the statement ought in fairness be considered contemporaneously with it, or (ii) in a criminal proceeding for perjury or false statement if the statement was made by the defendant under oath, on the record and in the presence of counsel." Fed.Rule Evid. 410. Accord, Fed.Rule Crim.Proc. 11(e)(6).

[7] Respondent also goes to great lengths to establish a proposition that is not at issue in this case: that the plea-statement Rules do not contain a blanket "impeachment" exception. We certainly agree that the Rules give a defendant the right not to be impeached by statements made during plea discussions, but that conclusion says nothing about whether the defendant may relinquish that right by voluntary agreement.

a valid waiver of his right to be present under Federal Rule of Criminal Procedure 43. We noted that the specific right codified in Rule 43 "was considered unwaivable in felony cases" at common law, and that Rule 43 expressly recognized only one exception to the common-law rule. 506 U.S., at 259, 113 S. Ct. at 751. In light of the specific common-law history behind Rule 43 and the express waiver provision in the Rule, we declined to conclude that "the drafters intended the Rule to go further." *Id.*, at 260, 113 S. Ct. at 752). Our decision in *Smith* followed a similar line of reasoning. It held that waiver of the indictment requirement embodied in Federal Rule of Criminal Procedure 7(a) is confined to the specific circumstances outlined in the Rule's text: "Rule 7(a) recognizes that this safeguard may be waived, but only in those proceedings which are noncapital." 360 U.S., at 9, 79 S. Ct. at 997. Unlike Rules 43 and 7(a), however, the plea-statement Rules make no mention of waiver, and so *Crosby* and *Smith* provide no basis for setting aside the usual presumption.

The presumption of waivability has found specific application in the context of evidentiary rules. Absent some "overriding procedural consideration that prevents enforcement of the contract," courts have held that agreements to waive evidentiary rules are generally enforceable even over a party's subsequent objections. 21 C. Wright & K. Graham, Federal Practice and Procedure § 5039, pp. 207–208 (1977) (hereinafter Wright & Graham). Courts have "liberally enforced" agreements to waive various exclusionary rules of evidence. Note, Contracts to Alter the Rules of Evidence, 46 Harv. L.Rev. 138, 139–140 (1933). Thus, at the time of the adoption of the Federal Rules of Evidence, agreements as to the admissibility of documentary evidence were routinely enforced and held to preclude subsequent objections as to authenticity. *See, e.g., Tupman Thurlow Co. v. S.S. Cap Castillo*, 490 F.2d 302, 309 (CA2 1974); *United States v. Wing*, 450 F.2d 806, 811 (CA9 1971). And although hearsay is inadmissible except under certain specific exceptions, we have held that agreements to waive hearsay objections are enforceable. *See Sac and Fox Indians of Miss. in Iowa v. Sac and Fox Indians of Miss. in Okl.*, 220 U.S. 481, 488–489, 31 S. Ct. 473, 476–477, 55 L. Ed. 552 (1911); *see also United States v. Bonnett*, 877 F.2d 1450, 1458–1459 (CA10 1989) *(party's stipulation to admissibility of document precluded hearsay objection at trial).*

Indeed, evidentiary stipulations are a valuable and integral part of everyday trial practice. Prior to trial, parties often agree in writing to the admission of otherwise objectionable evidence, either in exchange for stipulations from opposing counsel or for other strategic purposes. Both the Federal Rules of Civil Procedure and the Federal Rules of Criminal Procedure appear to contemplate that the parties will enter into evidentiary agreements during a pretrial conference. *See* Fed. Rule Civ. Proc. 16(c)(3); Fed. Rule Crim. Proc. 17.1. During the course of trial, parties frequently decide to waive evidentiary objections, and such tactics are routinely honored by trial judges. *See* 21 Wright & Graham § 5032, at 161 ("It is left to the parties, in the first instance, to decide whether or not the rules are to be enforced . . . . It is only in rare cases that the trial judge will . . . exclude evidence they are content to see admitted"); *see also United States v. Coonan*, 938 F.2d 1553, 1561 (CA2 1991) (criminal defendant not entitled "to evade the consequences of an unsuccessful tactical decision" made in welcoming admission of otherwise inadmissible evidence).[8]

III

Because the plea-statement Rules were enacted against a background presumption that legal rights generally, and evidentiary provisions specifically, are subject to waiver by voluntary agreement of the parties, we will not interpret Congress' silence as an implicit rejection of waivability. Respondent bears the responsibility of identifying some affirmative basis for concluding that the plea-statement Rules depart from the presumption of waivability.

Respondent offers three potential bases for concluding that the Rules should be placed beyond the control of the parties. We find none of them persuasive.

A

Respondent first suggests that the plea-statement Rules establish a "guarantee [to] fair procedure" that cannot be waived. Brief for Respondent 12. We agree with respondent's basic premise: There may be some evidentiary provisions that are so fundamental to the reliability of the fact-finding process that they may never be waived without irreparably "discredit[ing] the federal courts." *See* 21 Wright & Graham § 5039, at 207–208; *see also Wheat v. United States*, 486 U.S. 153, 162, 108 S. Ct. 1692, 1698–1699, 100 L. Ed. 2d 140 (1988) (court may decline a defendant's waiver of his right to conflict-free counsel); *United States v. Josefik*, 753 F.2d 585, 588 (CA7 1985) ("No doubt there are limits to waiver; if the parties stipulated to trial by 12 orangutans the defendant's conviction would be invalid notwithstanding his consent, because some minimum of civilized procedure is required by community feeling regardless of what the defendant wants or is willing to accept"). But enforcement of agreements like respondent's plainly will not have that effect. The admission of plea statements for impeachment purposes *enhances* the truth-seeking function of trials and will result in more accurate verdicts. Cf. *Jenkins v. Anderson*, 447 U.S. 231, 238, 100 S. Ct. 2124, 2129, 65 L. Ed. 2d 86 (1980) (once a defendant decides to testify, he may be required to face impeachment on cross-examination, which furthers the " 'function of the courts of justice to ascertain the truth' ") (quoting *Brown v. United States*, 356 U.S. 148, 156, 78 S. Ct. 622, 627, 2 L. Ed. 2d 589 (1958)); Note, 46 Harv. L. Rev., at 142–143 ("[A] contract to deprive the court of relevant testimony . . . stands on a different ground than one admitting evidence that would otherwise have been barred by an exclusionary rule. One contract is an impediment to ascertaining the facts, the other aids in the final determination of the true situation") (footnote omitted). Under any view of the evidence, the defendant has made a false statement, either to the prosecutor during

---

[8] Respondent contends that a pretrial agreement to waive the exclusionary provisions of the plea-statement Rules is unlike a typical stipulation, which is entered into while the case is in progress, and is more like an extrajudicial agreement made outside the context of litigation. Brief for Respondent 39. While it may be true that extrajudicial contracts made prior to litigation trigger closer judicial scrutiny than stipulations made within the context of litigation, see 21 Wright & Graham § 5039, at 206, there is nothing extrajudicial about the waiver agreement at issue here. The agreement was made in the course of a plea discussion aimed at resolving the specific criminal case that was "in progress" against respondent.

the plea discussion or to the jury at trial; making the jury aware of the inconsistency will tend to increase the reliability of the verdict without risking institutional harm to the federal courts.

Respondent nevertheless urges that the plea-statement Rules are analogous to Federal Rule of Criminal Procedure 24(c), which provides that "[a]n alternate juror who does not replace a regular juror shall be discharged after the jury retires to consider its verdict." Justice Kennedy's concurrence in *United States v. Olano*, 507 U.S. 725, 741, 113 S. Ct. 1770, 1781, 123 L. Ed. 2d 508 (1993), suggested that the guarantees of Rule 24(c) may never be waived by an agreement to permit alternate jurors to sit in on jury deliberations, and respondent asks us to extend that logic to the plea-statement Rules. But even if we assume that the requirements of Rule 24(c) are "the product of a judgment that our jury system should be given a stable and constant structure, one that cannot be varied by a court with or without the consent of the parties," *id.*, at 742, 113 S. Ct. at 1782, the plea-statement Rules plainly do not satisfy this standard. Rules 410 and 11(e)(6) "creat[e], in effect, a privilege of the defendant," 2 J. Weinstein & M. Berger, Weinstein's Evidence ¶ 410[05], p. 410–43 (1994), and, like other evidentiary privileges, this one may be waived or varied at the defendant's request. The Rules provide that statements made in the course of plea discussions are inadmissible "against" the defendant, and thus leave open the possibility that a defendant may offer such statements into evidence for his own tactical advantage. Indeed, the Rules contemplate this result in permitting admission of statements made "in any proceeding wherein another statement made in the course of the same . . . plea discussions *has been introduced* and the statement ought in fairness be considered contemporaneously with it." Fed. Rule Evid. 410(i) (emphasis added); accord, Fed. Rule Crim. Proc. 11(e)(6)(i). Thus, the plea-statement Rules expressly contemplate a degree of party control that is consonant with the background presumption of waivability.[9]

B

Respondent also contends that waiver is fundamentally inconsistent with the Rules' goal of encouraging voluntary settlement. *See* Advisory Committee's Notes on Fed. Rule Evid. 410 (purpose of Rule is "promotion of disposition of criminal cases by compromise"). Because the prospect of waiver may make defendants "think twice" before entering into any plea negotiation, respondent suggests that enforcement of waiver agreements acts "as a brake, not as a facilitator, to the plea-bargain process." Brief for Respondent 23, n. 17. The Ninth Circuit expressed similar concerns, noting that Rules 410 and 11(e)(6) "aid in obtaining th[e] cooperation" that is often necessary to identify and prosecute the leaders of a criminal conspiracy and that waiver of the protections of the Rules "could easily

---

[9] The Ninth Circuit relied on *Brooklyn Savings Bank v. O'Neil*, 324 U.S. 697, 65 S.Ct. 895, 89 L.Ed. 1296 (1945), but that case is easily distinguishable in this regard. *Brooklyn Savings Bank* held that certain statutory entitlements guaranteed to employees by the Fair Labor Standards Act of 1938 were unwaivable because the structure and legislative history of the Act evinced a specific "legislative policy" of "prevent[ing] private contracts" on such matters. *Id.*, at 706, 65 S. Ct. at 902. Respondent has identified nothing in the structure or history of the plea-statement Rules that suggests that they were aimed at preventing private bargaining; in fact, the above discussion suggests that the Rules adopt a contrary view.

have a chilling effect on the entire plea bargaining process." 998 F.2d at 1455. According to the Ninth Circuit, the plea-statement Rules "permit the plea bargainer to maximize what he has 'to sell' " by preserving "the ability to withdraw from the bargain proposed by the prosecutor without being harmed by any of his statements made in the course of an aborted plea bargaining session." *Ibid.*

We need not decide whether and under what circumstances substantial "public policy" interests may permit the inference that Congress intended to override the presumption of waivability, for in this case there is no basis for concluding that waiver will interfere with the Rules' goal of encouraging plea bargaining. The court below focused entirely on the *defendant's* incentives and completely ignored the other essential party to the transaction: the prosecutor. Thus, although the availability of waiver may discourage some defendants from negotiating, it is also true that prosecutors may be unwilling to proceed without it.

Prosecutors may be especially reluctant to negotiate without a waiver agreement during the early stages of a criminal investigation, when prosecutors are searching for leads and suspects may be willing to offer information in exchange for some form of immunity or leniency in sentencing. In this "cooperation" context, prosecutors face "painfully delicate" choices as to "whether to proceed and prosecute those suspects against whom the already produced evidence makes a case or whether to extend leniency or full immunity to some suspects in order to procure testimony against other, more dangerous suspects against whom existing evidence is flimsy or nonexistent." Hughes, Agreements for Cooperation in Criminal Cases, 45 Vand. L. Rev. 1, 15 (1992). Because prosecutors have limited resources and must be able to answer "sensitive questions about the credibility of the testimony" they receive before entering into any sort of cooperation agreement, *id.*, at 10, prosecutors may condition cooperation discussions on an agreement that the testimony provided may be used for impeachment purposes. *See* Thompson & Sumner, Structuring Informal Immunity, 8 Crim. Just. 16, 19 (spring 1993). If prosecutors were precluded from securing such agreements, they might well decline to enter into cooperation discussions in the first place and might never take this potential first step toward a plea bargain.[10]

Indeed, as a logical matter, it simply makes no sense to conclude that mutual settlement will be encouraged by precluding negotiation over an issue that may be particularly important to one of the parties to the transaction. A sounder way to encourage settlement is to permit the interested parties to enter into knowing and voluntary negotiations without any arbitrary limits on their bargaining chips. To use

---

[10] We cannot agree with the dissent's conclusion that the policies expressed in the Advisory Committee's Notes to the plea-statement Rules indicate congressional animosity toward waivability. The Advisory Committee's Notes *always* provide some policy justification for the exclusionary provisions in the Rules, yet those policies merely justify the default rule of exclusion; they do not mean that the parties can never waive the default rule. Indeed, the dissent is unwilling to accept the logical result of its approach, which would require a wholesale rejection of the background presumption of party control over evidentiary provisions. Hearsay, for example, is generally excluded because it tends to lack "trustworthiness," *see* Advisory Committees Notes on Article VIII of the Fed. Rules of Evid., 28 U.S.C.App., p. 770, yet even the dissent concedes that the hearsay rules are "waivable beyond any question," *post*, at 807. Thus, the mere existence of a policy justification for the plea-statement Rules cannot provide a sound basis for rejecting the background presumption of waivability

the Ninth Circuit's metaphor, if the prosecutor is interested in "buying" the reliability assurance that accompanies a waiver agreement, then precluding waiver can only stifle the market for plea bargains. A defendant can "maximize" what he has to "sell" only if he is permitted to offer what the prosecutor is most interested in buying. And while it is certainly true that prosecutors often need help from the small fish in a conspiracy in order to catch the big ones, that is no reason to preclude waiver altogether. If prosecutors decide that certain crucial information will be gained only by preserving the inadmissibility of plea statements, they will agree to leave intact the exclusionary provisions of the plea-statement Rules.

In sum, there is no reason to believe that allowing negotiation as to waiver of the plea-statement Rules will bring plea bargaining to a grinding halt; it may well have the opposite effect.[11] Respondent's unfounded policy argument thus provides no basis for concluding that Congress intended to prevent criminal defendants from offering to waive the plea-statement Rules during plea negotiation.

C

Finally, respondent contends that waiver agreements should be forbidden because they invite prosecutorial overreaching and abuse. Respondent asserts that there is a "gross disparity" in the relative bargaining power of the parties to a plea agreement and suggests that a waiver agreement is "inherently unfair and coercive." Brief for Respondent 26. Because the prosecutor retains the discretion to "reward defendants for their substantial assistance" under the Sentencing Guidelines, respondent argues that defendants face an " 'incredible dilemma' " when they are asked to accept waiver as the price of entering plea discussions. *Ibid.* (quoting *Green v. United States*, 355 U.S. 184, 193, 78 S. Ct. 221, 226, 2 L. Ed. 2d 199 (1957)).

The dilemma flagged by respondent is indistinguishable from any of a number of difficult choices that criminal defendants face every day. The plea bargaining process necessarily exerts pressure on defendants to plead guilty and to abandon a series of fundamental rights, but we have repeatedly held that the government "may encourage a guilty plea by offering substantial benefits in return for the plea." *Corbitt v. New Jersey*, 439 U.S. 212, 219, 99 S. Ct. 492, 497–498, 58 L. Ed. 2d 466 (1978). "While confronting a defendant with the risk of more severe punishment clearly may have a 'discouraging effect on the defendant's assertion of his trial rights, the imposition of these difficult choices [is] an inevitable' — and permissible — 'attribute of any legitimate system which tolerates and encourages the negotiation of pleas.' " *Bordenkircher v. Hayes*, 434 U.S. 357, 364, 98 S. Ct. 663, 668–669,

---

[11] Respondent has failed to offer any empirical support for his apocalyptic predictions, and data compiled by the Administrative Office of the United States Courts appear to contradict them. Prior to the Ninth Circuit's decision in this case (when, according to the Solicitor General, federal prosecutors in that Circuit used waiver agreements like the one invalidated by the court below, see Pet. for Cert. 10–11), approximately 92.2% of the convictions in the Ninth Circuit were secured through pleas of guilty or *nolo contendere*. Annual Report of the Director, Administrative Office of the United States Courts, Judicial Business of the United States Courts 278 (1992) (Table D-7). During that same period, about 88.8% of the convictions in all federal courts were secured by voluntary pleas. *Id.*, at 276.

54 L. Ed. 2d 604 (1978) (quoting *Chaffin v. Stynchcombe*, 412 U.S. 17, 31, 93 S. Ct. 1977, 1985, 36 L. Ed. 2d 714 (1973)).

The mere potential for abuse of prosecutorial bargaining power is an insufficient basis for foreclosing negotiation altogether. "Rather, tradition and experience justify our belief that the great majority of prosecutors will be faithful to their duty." *Newton v. Rumery*, 480 U.S. 386, 397, 107 S. Ct. 1187, 1194, 94 L. Ed. 2d 405 (1987) (plurality opinion); *see also United States v. Chemical Foundation, Inc.*, 272 U.S. 1, 14–15, 47 S. Ct. 1, 6, 71 L. Ed. 131 (1926) ("[I]n the absence of clear evidence to the contrary, courts presume that [public officers] have properly discharged their official duties"). Thus, although some waiver agreements "may not be the product of an informed and voluntary decision," this possibility "does not justify invalidating *all* such agreements." *Newton, supra,* 480 U.S. at 393, 107 S. Ct. at 1192 (majority opinion). Instead, the appropriate response to respondent's predictions of abuse is to permit case-by-case inquiries into whether waiver agreements are the product of fraud or coercion. We hold that absent some affirmative indication that the agreement was entered into unknowingly or involuntarily, an agreement to waive the exclusionary provisions of the plea-statement Rules is valid and enforceable.

IV

Respondent conferred with his lawyer after the prosecutor proposed waiver as a condition of proceeding with the plea discussion, and he has never complained that he entered into the waiver agreement at issue unknowingly or involuntarily. The Ninth Circuit's decision was based on its *per se* rejection of waiver of the plea-statement Rules. Accordingly, the judgment of the Court of Appeals is reversed.

It is so ordered.

JUSTICE GINSBURG, with whom JUSTICE O'CONNOR and JUSTICE BREYER join, concurring.

The Court holds that a waiver allowing the Government to impeach with statements made during plea negotiations is compatible with Congress' intent to promote plea bargaining. It may be, however, that a waiver to use such statements in the case in chief would more severely undermine a defendant's incentive to negotiate, and thereby inhibit plea bargaining. As the Government has not sought such a waiver, we do not here explore this question.

JUSTICE SOUTER, with whom JUSTICE STEVENS joins, dissenting.

This case poses only one question: did Congress intend to create a personal right subject to waiver by its individual beneficiaries when it adopted Rule 410 of the Federal Rules of Evidence and Rule 11(e)(6) of the Federal Rules of Criminal Procedure, each Rule providing that statements made during plea discussions are inadmissible against the defendant except in two carefully described circumstances? The case raises no issue of policy to be settled by the courts, and if the generally applicable (and generally sound) judicial policy of respecting waivers of rights and privileges should conflict with a reading of the Rules as reasonably construed to accord with the intent of Congress, there is no doubt that congressional intent should prevail. Because the majority ruling is at odds with the intent of Congress and will render the Rules largely dead letters, I respectfully dissent.

At first glance, the question of waivability may seem short on substance, given the unconditional language of the two virtually identical Rules, unsoftened by any provision for waiver or allusion to that possibility:

> Except as otherwise provided in this rule, evidence . . . is not . . . admissible against the defendant who . . . was a participant in . . . plea discussions [of]
>
> . . . .
>
> any statement made in the course of plea discussions with an attorney for the prosecuting authority which do not result in a plea of guilty . . . [subject to two stated exceptions]. Fed. Rule Evid. 410.

Believers in plain meaning might be excused for thinking that the text answers the question. But history may have something to say about what is plain, and here history is not silent. If the Rules are assumed to create only a personal right of a defendant, the right arguably finds itself in the company of other personal rights, including constitutional ones, that have been accepted time out of mind as being freely waivable. *See, e.g., Johnson v. Zerbst*, 304 U.S. 458, 465, 58 S. Ct. 1019, 1023, 82 L. Ed. 1461 (1938) (Sixth Amendment right to counsel may be waived). The possibility that the Rules in question here do create such a personal right must, indeed, be taken seriously if for no other reason than that the Rules of Evidence contain other bars to admissibility equally uncompromising on their face but nonetheless waivable beyond any question. *See* Fed. Rule Evid. 802 (hearsay); Fed.Rule Evid. 1002 (best evidence).

The majority comes down on the side of waivability through reliance on the general presumption in favor of recognizing waivers of rights, including evidentiary rights. To be sure, the majority recognizes that the presumption does not necessarily resolve the issue before us, and the majority opinion describes some counterexamples of rights that are insulated against waiver, at least when waiver is expressly prohibited or limited in terms that speak of waiver expressly. *See Crosby v. United States*, 506 U.S. 255, 113 S. Ct. 748, 122 L. Ed. 2d 25 (1993); *Smith v. United States*, 360 U.S. 1, 79 S. Ct. 991, 3 L. Ed. 2d 1041 (1959). Still, the majority seems to assume that the express-waiver cases describe the only circumstances in which the recognition of waiver is foreclosed, and since the Rules in question here say nothing about "waiver" as such, the majority finds that fact really to be the end of the matter.

If there were nothing more to go on here, I, too, would join the majority in relying on the fallback rule of permissible waiver. But there is more to go on. There is, indeed, good reason to believe that Congress rejected the general rule of waivability when it passed the Rules in issue here, and once the evidence of such congressional intent is squarely faced, we have no business but to respect it (or deflect it by applying some constitutionally mandated requirement of clear statement). There is, of course, no claim in this case that Congress should be hobbled by any clear statement rule, and the result is that we are bound to respect the intent that the Advisory Committee's Notes to the congressionally enacted Rules reveal. *See Williamson v. United States*, 512 U.S. 594, 614–615, 114 S. Ct. 2431, 2442, 129 L. Ed. 2d 476 (1994) (Kennedy, J., concurring in judgment) (citing cases in which Advisory Committee's Notes are taken as authoritative evidence of intent).

The fact underlying those Notes, and the fact of which all congressional and judicial action must take account in dealing with the possible evidentiary significance of plea discussions, is that the federal judicial system could not possibly litigate every civil and criminal case filed in the courts. The consequence of this is that plea bargaining is an accepted feature of the criminal justice system, and, "[p]roperly administered, it is to be encouraged." *Santo-bello v. New York*, 404 U.S. 257, 260, 92 S. Ct. 495, 498, 30 L. Ed. 2d 427 (1971). Thus the Advisory Committee's Notes on Rule 410 explained that "[e]xclusion of offers to plead guilty or *nolo* has as its purpose the promotion of disposition of criminal cases by compromise." 28 U.S.C. App., p. 750. "As with compromise offers generally, . . . free communication is needed, and security against having an offer of compromise or related statement admitted in evidence effectively encourages it." *Ibid.* The Advisory Committee's Notes on Rule 11(e)(6) drew the same conclusion about the purpose of that Rule and summed up the object of both Rules as being "to permit the unrestrained candor which produces effective plea discussions between the attorney for the government and the attorney for the defendant or the defendant when acting pro se." 18 U.S.C. App., p. 745 (1979 Amendment) (internal quotation marks omitted).

These explanations show with reasonable clarity that Congress probably made two assumptions when it adopted the Rules: pleas and plea discussions are to be encouraged, and conditions of unrestrained candor are the most effective means of encouragement. The provisions protecting a defendant against use of statements made in his plea bargaining are thus meant to create something more than a personal right shielding an individual from his imprudence. Rather, the Rules are meant to serve the interest of the federal judicial system (whose resources are controlled by Congress), by creating the conditions understood by Congress to be effective in promoting reasonable plea agreements. Whether Congress was right or wrong that unrestrained candor is necessary to promote a reasonable number of plea agreements, Congress assumed that there was such a need and meant to satisfy it by these Rules. Since the zone of unrestrained candor is diminished whenever a defendant has to stop to think about the amount of trouble his openness may cause him if the plea negotiations fall through, Congress must have understood that the judicial system's interest in candid plea discussions would be threatened by recognizing waivers under Rules 410 and 11(e)(6). *See* ABA Standards for Criminal Justice 14-3.4, commentary (2d ed. 1980) (a rule contrary to the one adopted by Congress "would discourage plea negotiations and agreements, for defendants would have to be constantly concerned whether, in light of their plea negotiation activities, they could successfully defend on the merits if a plea ultimately was not entered"). There is, indeed, no indication that Congress intended merely a regime of such limited openness as might happen to survive market forces sufficient to supplant a default rule of inadmissibility. Nor may Congress be presumed to have intended to permit waivers that would undermine the stated policy of its own Rules.

Brooklyn Savings Bank v. O'Neil, 324 U.S. 697, 704, 65 S. Ct. 895, 900, 89 L. Ed. 1296 (1945) ("Where a private right is granted in the public interest to effectuate a legislative policy, waiver of a right so charged or colored with the public interest will not be allowed where it would thwart the legislative policy which it was designed to effectuate").

It bears emphasizing that I would not suggest that there is only one reasonable balance possible between society's interest in encouraging compromise (which Congress thought to be served most effectively by refusing to recognize waivers of rights under these Rules) and society's interest in providing a vigorous adversary system when cases are tried (which may be served by recognizing waivers). The majority may be right that a better balance could have been struck than the one Congress intended. The majority may also be correct as a matter of policy that enough pleas will result even if parties are allowed to make their own rule of admissibility by agreement, with prosecutors refusing to talk without a defendant's waiver (unless such refusal overloads the system beyond its capacity for trials) and defendants refusing to waive (unless they are desperate enough to forgo their option to be tried without fear of compromising statements if the plea negotiations fail). But whether the majority is right or wrong on either score is beside the point; the policy it endorses is not the policy that Congress intended when it enacted the Rules. *See Touche Ross & Co. v. Redington*, 442 U.S. 560, 578, 99 S. Ct. 2479, 2490, 61 L. Ed. 2d 82 (1979) ("The ultimate question is one of congressional intent, not one of whether this Court thinks that it can improve upon the statutory scheme that Congress enacted into law").

The unlikelihood that Congress intended the modest default rule that the majority sees in Rules 11(e)(6) and 410 looms all the larger when the consequences of the majority position are pursued. The first consequence is that the Rules will probably not even function as default rules, for there is little chance that they will be applied at all. Already, standard forms indicate that many federal prosecutors routinely require waiver of Rules 410 and 11(e)(6) rights before a prosecutor is willing to enter into plea discussions. Pet. for Cert. 10–11. *See also United States v. Stevens*, 935 F.2d 1380, 1396 (CA3 1991) ("Plea agreements . . . commonly contain a provision stating that proffer information that is disclosed during the course of plea negotiations is . . . admissible for purposes of impeachment"). As the Government conceded during oral argument, defendants are generally in no position to challenge demands for these waivers, and the use of waiver provisions as contracts of adhesion has become accepted practice.[12] Today's decision can only speed the heretofore illegitimate process by which the exception has been swallowing the Rules. *See, e.g., Guidry v. Sheet Metal Workers Nat. Pension Fund*, 493 U.S. 365, 377, 110 S. Ct. 680, 687–688, 107 L. Ed. 2d 782 (1990) (no exception should be made by Court because it would be too difficult to "carve out an exception that

---

[12] The argument that the plea-bargaining system still works even though waiver has become the accepted practice does not answer the question whether Congress intended to permit a waiver rule. The Court's obligation is to interpret criminal procedure and evidentiary rules according to congressional intent. If the Government believes that the better rule is different from what is currently the law, the Government can petition Congress to change it. *See TVA v. Hill*, 437 U.S. 153, 194, 98 S. Ct. 2279, 2301–2302, 57 L. Ed. 2d 117 (1978) ("Our individual appraisal of the wisdom or unwisdom of a particular course consciously selected by the Congress is to be put aside in the process of interpreting a statute").

would not swallow the rule"); *United States v. Powell*, 469 U.S. 57, 68, 105 S. Ct. 471, 478–479, 83 L. Ed. 2d 461 (1984) (respondent's suggested exception to the *Dunn* rule "threatens to swallow the rule"). *See also* 23 C. Wright & K. Graham, Federal Practice and Procedure 121–122, n. 7.3 (1994 Supp.) ("It would seem strange if the prosecutor could undermine the judicial policy, now endorsed by Congress, of encouraging plea bargaining by announcing a policy that his office will only plea bargain with defendants who 'waive' the benefits of Rule 410"). Accordingly, it is probably only a matter of time until the Rules are dead letters.

The second consequence likely to emerge from today's decision is the practical certainty that the waiver demanded will in time come to function as a waiver of trial itself. It is true that many (if not all) of the waiver forms now employed go only to admissibility for impeachment.[13] But although the erosion of the Rules has begun with this trickle, the majority's reasoning will provide no principled limit to it. The Rules draw no distinction between use of a statement for impeachment and use in the Government's case in chief. If objection can be waived for impeachment use, it can be waived for use as affirmative evidence, and if the Government can effectively demand waiver in the former instance, there is no reason to believe it will not do so just as successfully in the latter. When it does, there is nothing this Court will legitimately be able to do about it. The Court is construing a congressional Rule on the theory that Congress meant to permit its waiver. Once that point is passed, as it is today, there is no legitimate limit on admissibility of a defendant's plea negotiation statements beyond what the Constitution may independently impose or the traffic may bear. Just what the traffic may bear is an open question, but what cannot be denied is that the majority opinion sanctions a demand for waiver of such scope that a defendant who gives it will be unable even to acknowledge his desire to negotiate a guilty plea without furnishing admissible evidence against himself then and there. In such cases, the possibility of trial if no agreement is reached will be reduced to fantasy. The only defendant who will not damage himself by even the most restrained candor will be the one so desperate that he might as well walk into court and enter a naked guilty plea. It defies reason to think that Congress intended to invite such a result, when it adopted a Rule said to promote candid discussion in the interest of encouraging compromise.

---

[13] Waiver for impeachment use, however, has been applied broadly. For example, plea statements have been used to impeach a defendant's witnesses even where the defendant has chosen not to testify. *See United States v. Dortch*, 5 F.3d 1056, 1069 (CA7 1993) ("[J]ust as the defendant must choose whether to protect the proffer statements by not taking the stand, the defendant must choose whether to protect the proffer by carefully determining which lines of questioning to pursue with different witnesses"), cert. pending *sub nom. Suess v. United States*, No. 93-7218.

Chapter 7

THE EXAMINATION AND IMPEACHMENT OF WITNESSES

§ 7.01 CHAPTER CHECKLIST

1. Is a witness testifying at a hearing, proceeding, or trial?
2. Is the witness under oath and subject to cross-examination?
3. Is the witness offering evidence going to the background of the case, an element of a claim, defense, or cause of action, or the impeachment of another witness?
3. Is the witness on direct, cross, redirect, or recross examination?
5. If this is the proponent's witness, what objections to the witness' testimony can be anticipated?
6. If the witness is being impeached, is the impeachment intrinsic (from the witness' mouth) or extrinsic (by offering other evidence or another witness)?
7. If the impeachment is intrinsic, is it in a permissible form?
8. If the impeachment is extrinsic, does it satisfy the collateral issue rule?

§ 7.02 RELEVANT FEDERAL RULES OF EVIDENCE

Rule 601. General Rule of Competency

Every person is competent to be a witness except as otherwise provided in these rules. However, in civil actions and proceedings, with respect to an element of a claim or defense as to which State law supplies the rule of decision, the competency of a witness shall be determined in accordance with State law.

Rule 602. Lack of Personal Knowledge

A witness may not testify to a matter unless evidence is introduced sufficient to support a finding that the witness has personal knowledge of the matter. Evidence to prove personal knowledge may, but need not, consist of the witness' own testimony. This rule is subject to the provisions of Rule 703, relating to opinion testimony by expert witnesses.

Rule 603. Oath or Affirmation

Before testifying, every witness shall be required to declare that the witness will testify truthfully, by oath or affirmation administered in a form calculated to awaken the witness' conscience and impress the witness' mind with the duty to do so.

Rule 604. Interpreters

An interpreter is subject to the provisions of these rules relating to qualification as an expert and the administration of an oath or affirmation to make a true translation.

Rule 605. Competency of Judge as Witness

The judge presiding at the trial may not testify in that trial as a witness. No objection need be made in order to preserve the point.

Rule 606. Competency of Juror as Witness

(a) **At the trial.** A member of the jury may not testify as a witness before that jury in the trial of the case in which the juror is sitting. If the juror is called so to testify, the opposing party shall be afforded an opportunity to object out of the presence of the jury.

(b) **Inquiry into validity of verdict or indictment.** Upon an inquiry into the validity of a verdict or indictment, a juror may not testify as to any matter or statement occurring during the course of the jury's deliberations or to the effect of anything upon that or any other juror's mind or emotions as influencing the juror to assent to or dissent from the verdict or indictment or concerning the juror's mental processes in connection therewith. But a juror may testify about (1) whether extraneous prejudicial information was improperly brought to the jury's attention, (2) whether any outside influence was improperly brought to bear upon any juror. . . .

Rule 607. Who May Impeach

The credibility of a witness may be attacked by any party, including the party calling the witness.

Rule 608. Evidence of Character and Conduct of Witness

(a) **Opinion and reputation evidence of character.** The credibility of a witness may be attacked or supported by evidence in the form of opinion or reputation, but subject to these limitations: (1) the evidence may refer only to character for truthfulness or untruthfulness . . . .

(b) **Specific instances of conduct.** Specific instances of the conduct of a witness, for the purpose of attacking or supporting the witness' character for truthfulness, other than conviction of crime as provided in Rule 609, may not be proved by extrinsic evidence. They may, however, in the discretion of the court, if probative of truthfulness or untruthfulness, be inquired into on cross-examination of the witness (1) concerning the witness' character for truthfulness or untruthfulness, or (2) concerning the character for truthfulness or untruthfulness of another witness as to which character the witness being cross-examined has testified.

(c) The giving of testimony, whether by an accused or by any other witness, does not operate as a waiver of the accused's or the witness' privilege against self-incrimination when examined with respect to matters that relate only to character for truthfulness.

Rule 609. Impeachment by Evidence of Conviction of Crime

(a) **General rule.** For the purpose of attacking the character for truthfulness of a witness, (1) evidence that a witness other than an accused has been convicted of a crime shall be admitted, subject to Rule 403, if the crime was punishable by death or imprisonment in excess of one year under the law under which the witness was convicted, and evidence that an accused has been convicted of such a crime shall be admitted if the court determines that the probative value of admitting this evidence outweighs its prejudicial effect to the accused; and (2) evidence that any witness has been convicted of a crime shall be admitted regardless of the punishment, if it readily can be determined that establishing the elements of the crime required proof or admission of an act of dishonesty or false statement by the witness.

. . . .

Rule 610. Religious Beliefs or Opinions

Evidence of the beliefs or opinions of a witness on matters of religion is not admissible for the purpose of showing that by reason of their nature the witness' credibility is impaired or enhanced.

Rule 611. Mode and Order of Interrogation and Presentation

(a) **Control by court.** The court shall exercise reasonable control over the mode and order of interrogating witnesses and presenting evidence . . . .

(b) **(b) Scope of cross-examination.** Cross-examination should be limited to the subject matter of the direct examination and matters affecting the credibility of the witness. . . .

(c) **(c) Leading questions.** Leading questions should not be used on the direct examination of a witness except as may be necessary to develop the witness' testimony. Ordinarily leading questions should be permitted on cross-examination. . . .

Rule 612. Writing Used to Refresh Memory

Except as otherwise provided in criminal proceedings by **Section 3500 of Title 18, United States Code**, if a witness uses a writing to refresh memory for the purpose of testifying, either

(1) while testifying, or

(2) before testifying, if the court in its discretion determines it is necessary in the interests of justice,

an adverse party is entitled to have the writing produced at the hearing, to inspect it, to cross-examine the witness thereon, and to introduce in evidence those portions which relate to the testimony of the witness. . . .

Rule 613. Prior Statements of Witnesses

(a) **Examining witness concerning prior statement.** In examining a witness concerning a prior statement made by the witness, whether written or not, the statement need not be shown nor its contents disclosed to the witness at that time, but on request the same shall be shown or disclosed to opposing counsel.

. . . .

Rule 614. Calling and Interrogation of Witnesses by Court

(a) **Calling by court.** The court may, on its own motion or at the suggestion of a party, call witnesses, and all parties are entitled to cross-examine witnesses thus called.

(b) **(b) Interrogation by court.** The court may interrogate witnesses, whether called by itself or by a party.

(c) **Objections.** Objections to the calling of witnesses by the court or to interrogation by it may be made at the time or at the next available opportunity when the jury is not present.

Rule 615. Exclusion of Witnesses.

At the request of a party the court shall order witnesses excluded so that they cannot hear the testimony of other witnesses, and it may make the order of its own motion. This rule does not authorize exclusion of (1) a party who is a natural person, or (2) an officer or employee of a party which is not a natural person designated as its representative by its attorney, or (3) a person whose presence is shown by a party to be essential to the presentation of the party's cause, or (4) a person authorized by statute to be present.

§ 7.03 EXAMINATION OF WITNESSES

[A] Overview

Witness testimony, sometimes referred to as *viva voce*, or "by voice," is one of the most common types of evidence at trial. Witnesses produce potentially powerful evidence; witness examination sometimes becomes a "trial within a trial," much like the individual battles within a war. Because of the significance of witness testimony, special rules have been adopted to govern it. Many trials are won or lost on the nature and impact of witness testimony and how the attorneys negotiate the rules governing the admissibility of that testimony.

The Rules place the examination of witnesses squarely within the control of the judge. Under Rule 611, the judge has the discretion to decide whether to allow witness testimony and if so, in what form and at what time. For example, the judge has the authority to govern the use of leading questions on direct examination, to restrict the length of time for cross-examination, and to limit the scope of cross-examination. *See* Rule 611. Of course, the Federal Rules of Evidence provide the judge with guidance and impose a variety of prohibitions, including the subject matter of the questions. For example, questions must concern a relevant matter under Rules 401 and 402 and not elicit privileged information under Rule 501.

The Federal Rules of Evidence impose several different types of limits on witness testimony. These limits range from who may testify (i.e., witness competency), to the substance of the testimony, to the form of the questions asked. Competency restrictions, such as those imposed on judge and jurors as provided in Rules 605 and 606, help to maintain the fundamental fairness of the trial process. Substantive limits are utilized to deter suspect evidence, such as hearsay, propensity character evidence, and settlement offers. Form limits also are intended to foster fairness and efficiency in the stylized "dance" that constitutes a trial.

[B] Competency: Who May Testify

The competency of witnesses to testify in federal court is generally determined by Federal Rule of Evidence 601. While it may seem obvious that federal law should govern in federal courts, there exists one glaring exception in the area of witness competency. Rule 601 directs that state laws govern the competency of witnesses in a federal civil action or proceeding when the state law provides the rule of decision. In this manner, Rule 601 becomes a choice-of-law rule. The use of state law in federal court is not restricted solely to competency matters. State law sometimes may be used in federal court when determining whether evidence is privileged. *See* Rule 501. Privileges are discussed in Chapter 17. *See also* Presumptions, Rule 302.

Under the Federal Rules of Evidence, all witnesses are presumptively competent to testify. *See* Rule 601. Rule 601 reverses the common law practice, which for many years excluded from the witness stand various categories of persons, such as those convicted of certain crimes, persons having an interest in the action (such as a party or a party's spouse), and persons without religious beliefs. These grounds of incompetency have largely disappeared from both federal and state courts, with the one remaining vestige in some state courts often called "Dead Man's Statutes." These statutes essentially prohibit interested parties from testifying about an oral transaction or communication against a deceased or incompetent person essentially because such a person would not be able to rebut that testimony. Under the federal rules, all of the aforementioned persons are permitted to testify, although some prior conduct, such as convictions of crime, may be the subject of impeachment. An example of a "Dead Man's Statute" follows.

Idaho Code § 9-202. Who may not testify [Dead Man's Statute]

The following persons cannot be witnesses:

3. Parties or assignors of parties to an action or proceeding, or persons in whose behalf an action or proceeding is prosecuted against an executor or administrator, upon a claim or demand against the estate of a deceased person, as to any communication or agreement, not in writing, occurring before the death of such deceased person.

The presumption of competency under Rule 601 is not a free pass to testify. The presumptive witness must meet the foundational requirement of understanding what it means to tell the truth, must possess some relevant information, and must bypass several carefully delineated prohibitions involving testimony by the judge and jurors.

The primary foundational requirement for witness competency is that the witness must be able to understand what it means to be truthful. This prerequisite has no bright-line litmus test, perhaps because imposing a bright-line standard would be difficult, if not impossible. As the Advisory Committee Note to Rule 601 aptly stated, "No mental or moral qualifications for testifying as a witness are specified. Standards of mental capacity have proved elusive in actual application." Consequently, it is assumed in the Rules that the overwhelming majority of witnesses understand their obligation to testify truthfully. This assumption extends even to convicted perjurers (who will be given an opportunity to incur yet another perjury conviction). There is one category of witness for which the "meaning of truthfulness" requirement is regularly tested, however, and that is the child witness. An attorney must carefully lay a foundation with child witnesses to establish their understanding of the difference between truth and falsehood.

Example

ATTORNEY: Hi, Rebecca. How are you?

C: Fine.

ATTORNEY: Good. I am going to ask you a few questions, Okay?

C: Okay.

ATTORNEY: May I call you Becca?

C: My Mommy and Daddy do.

ATTORNEY: Becca, how old are you?

C: Four. Last week!

ATTORNEY: Did you have a party on your birthday?

C: Yes. With cake.

ATTORNEY: With whom do you live, Becca?

C: My Mommy and Daddy and Emma.

ATTORNEY: Who is Emma?

C: My sister.

ATTORNEY: Becca, do you know what it means to tell the truth?

C: Yes.

ATTORNEY:	What happens when you don't tell the truth?
C:	Mommy sends me to time-out.
ATTORNEY:	What is that?
C:	It is when I am in trouble.
ATTORNEY:	What happens during time-out?
C:	I stand in a corner. I'm not allowed to talk.
ATTORNEY:	Is it fun?
C:	Noooo.
ATTORNEY:	What happens if you tell the truth?
C:	Nothing.
ATTORNEY:	No time-out?
C:	No.
ATTORNEY:	Are you going to tell the truth here today?
C:	Yes. (nodding her head up and down)
ATTORNEY:	If I told you that I was wearing a green tie, would that be the truth or a lie?
C:	That's silly. That would be a lie.
ATTORNEY:	And if I told you that Santa Claus and the Easter Bunny were phony merchandising creations of a capitalist economy . . . please don't cry Becca, I withdraw the question.
ATTORNEY:	Now, remember when there was a fire at your house?
A:	Yes.
ATTORNEY:	Who was home at the time?

Problem 7-1: The Habitual Drug Addict

Paul observed an armed robbery in Pacific Heights one foggy Sunday morning. When Paul was called to testify for the prosecution, the defense objected. In an earlier deposition, Paul admitted that he was a heroin addict, and had been one for more than a decade. *Should Paul's testimony be permitted?* Explain.

Problem 7-2: Say What?

Archie Oakley, age 102, was on his front porch when he observed a purse snatching approximately 20 yards away. While Archie could not positively identify the assailant, he was called to testify by the prosecution to provide other relevant information. Archie concedes that he is deaf in one ear, needs a hearing aid in the other, and has very poor vision. The defendant objects to Archie's testimony, claiming it is extremely unreliable. *Is Archie competent to testify?*

Problem 7-3: Dead Again and Again

Josie agreed in writing to sell Bernard her boat, pending an inspection. The inspection occurred and it was a complete success. Before the completion of the sale, however, Josie died. Bernard then brought suit against Josie's estate based on diversity of citizenship. Bernard sought specific performance of the contract. At trial, Bernard took the witness stand to testify about the terms of the contract. *Will Bernard be allowed to testify about the agreement if a "Dead Man's Statute" applies? Explain.*

Problem 7-4: Hypnotized

Lil, the victim of an armed robbery at gunpoint, could not remember what happened during the robbery, no matter how hard she tried to recall the events, with the exception of the general time and place. After she made numerous unsuccessful attempts to recall the crime, a certified police neuropsychologist hypnotized her. After the hypnosis, Lil was able to recall what had occurred during the robbery and even remembered the identity of the perpetrator. *Will Lil be allowed to testify at trial?* Explain.

[C] Requirement of Personal Knowledge

Federal Rule of Evidence 602 requires almost all lay witnesses to possess personal knowledge in order to testify. Without personal knowledge, a layperson likely violates the Rules in at least two ways: (1) the testimony is probably based on hearsay, in which case the hearsay declarants would be the preferable witnesses; and (2) the testimony is probably speculation, which would distract the jury from drawing its own inferences from the admitted evidence.

Rule 602 permits some witnesses to testify without personal knowledge. The most significant example of testimony without personal knowledge involves expert witnesses, who routinely testify based on facts supplied to them either before or during their testimony. *See* Rule 703. Similarly, out-of-court admissions of party opponents (generally offered through the testimony of in-court witnesses) are admissible in evidence, even if they were not based on the party's personal knowledge. *See* Rule 801(d)(2). These exceptions are discussed at length in Chapters 9 and 13, respectively.

Rule 602 can be viewed in conjunction with Federal Rule of Evidence 701, which describes when laypersons may offer opinions. As Rule 701 explains, a lay witness may offer opinions or inferences if the opinions "are (a) rationally based on the perception of the witness and (b) helpful to a clear understanding of the witness' testimony or the determination of a fact in issue." Thus, the personal knowledge requirement leaves some room for lay witnesses to offer opinions and inferences, but only within narrow guidelines.

Example

Peter brings suit against his neighbor, Stanley, for civil assault, trespass, and conversion. At trial, Peter calls another neighbor, Howard, to testify. The following exchange occurs on direct examination:

PLAINTIFF'S ATTORNEY: Now, Howard, what happened at 6:45 p.m. on January 4th?

A: Stanley walked across the path between his and Peter's house. He was carrying a disgusting dead animal and —

DEFENDANT'S ATTORNEY: Objection. Lack of personal knowledge, Your Honor.

JUDGE: Please approach the bench, counsel.

PLAINTIFF'S ATTORNEY: Your Honor, Howard had seen Stanley walk across that path innumerable times on prior occasions and was told by Elma, who always is a reliable source of information for what happens in that part of the neighborhood, that Stanley walked across the path on this occasion with the dead animal.

JUDGE: I am going to sustain the objection. Even if Howard had observed Stanley traverse the path many times before, he cannot opine that Stanley did so on this occasion. If anyone should testify about Stanley's alleged trip with the dead animal, it ought to be Elma. Instead, Howard's testimony is hearsay when he offers Elma's statement as his own. There is a preference for putting Elma on the witness stand to hear about her observations directly. Please continue with the examination. Again, the objection is sustained.

Problem 7-5: Robbin the Hood

Robbin the Hood is prosecuted for bank robbery. At trial, Robbin's wife, Gayle, testifies for the defense. She states that before Robbin robbed the bank to give to the poor, he was despondent about the state of affairs in this country. The prosecution objects to this testimony, claiming that Gayle lacks personal knowledge about Robbin's state of mind. *What ruling and why?*

[D] Competency of Judges and Attorneys as Witnesses (Rule 605)

Rule 605 sensibly disqualifies judges from testifying in trials over which they preside. Serious doubts about objectivity would arise if a judge were called to testify at the behest of a party. In practice, a situation in which a party seeks to have a judge testify to case-related information is unlikely to arise. If judges have personal knowledge about events giving rise to litigation they are supposed to preserve both the reality and the appearance of impartiality by recusing themselves, regardless of whether they are likely to be called as witnesses.[1] In the unlikely event a party does call a presiding judge to testify, Rule 605 provides that the adversary need not object to preserve the impropriety for appeal. The

---

[1] For an analysis of whether judges must disqualify themselves from presiding over cases in which they have personal knowledge of case-related matters regardless of whether any party intends to call the judge as a witness, *see* Glen Weissenberger & James Duane, *Federal Rules of Evidence: Rules, Legislative History, Commentary and Authority* 253–256 (LexisNexis Pub. Co. 2005).

automatic objection protects a party from having to directly challenge a judge's competency in open court.

The Federal Rules of Evidence do not have a rule barring attorneys from testifying in cases in which they appear as counsel. Again, the situation rarely arises because ethical rules generally bar lawyers from appearing as counsel in trial if they are likely to be called as witnesses.[2] However, the lack of a rule flatly rendering attorneys incompetent as witnesses means that judges sometimes do allow attorneys to testify to uncontested and formalistic matters. For example, a judge may allow an attorney of record to testify to efforts to locate an unavailable witness for the purposes of establishing a hearsay declarant's unavailability under Rule 804(a).

Problem 7-6: Anyone But You

Judge Liz Wilber lived in a suburban neighborhood outside of Chicago. One cold Saturday morning, while she was walking her dog, Pudge, the Judge witnessed two of her neighbors engaged in a fistfight. The fight ended when one neighbor took out a knife and stabbed the other, causing a serious wound. Judge Wilber coincidentally drew the case and presided over the trial.

The defense calls Judge Wilber as a "necessary" witness.

1. Can she testify if she states from the bench that testifying will not impede her impartiality?

2. If no objection is lodged by the opposing counsel, can Judge Wilber then testify?

3. Can the bailiff, who also lives in the neighborhood, testify?

4. Can the court reporter, who is a friend of the defendant, testify as a character witness?

5. Can the defendant's best friend, who was convicted of murder twice and perjury once, testify for the defendant on a minor question of fact?

6. Suppose Judge Wilber had recessed the case for the day and was heading to her car. As she did so, she overheard a witness who had just testified say, "My testimony today really pulled the wool over their eyes; I can't believe they bought that garbage!" What should the judge do?

7. Suppose that instead of Judge Wilber overhearing the witness, it was the opposing counsel. What should the opposing counsel do?

Problem 7-7: The Deal

Enos, Nasty, and Usta are members of a radical environmental group that allegedly fire-bombed the office of the Sierra Club, killing two people. Only Nasty and Usta are charged with the bombing. Enos is called to testify for the

---

[2] *See, e.g.,* Rule 3.7(a) of the Model Rules of Professional Conduct. If the need for an attorney's testimony arises only after the attorney-client relationship is underway, the attorney should withdraw as counsel unless doing so would cause "substantial hardship." *Id.*

prosecution. The defense counsel believes that Enos has been offered a deal by the prosecution in exchange for his testimony, but that he would refuse to acknowledge such a deal at trial. The defense counsel wants to call in rebuttal the assistant prosecutor who negotiated with Enos. *Can the assistant prosecutor be asked to testify? See United States v. Newman*, 476 F.2d 733 (3d Cir. 1973).

Practice Tip: Competency to testify — why attorneys use investigators:

Often lawyers interview the adverse witnesses in a case either formally, in depositions, or informally. When lawyers cross-examine the opposing witnesses after such interviews, they are "locked in" to their stories based on the interviews.

Sometimes, witnesses deny having made the prior statements, especially those made during the informal interviews. This situation could create a significant dilemma. Counsel is not about to testify in order to extrinsically impeach the witness, but still does not want to let the witness' credibility remain whole. The answer lies in the use of investigators. If an investigator had been employed, the investigator could be called to testify about what was said, consequently impeaching the witness and letting the attorney play the sole role at trial for which she prepared — lawyer, not witness.

[E] Competency of Jurors as Witnesses (Rule 606)

Rule 606(a) closely resembles Rule 605, in that it bans jurors from testifying in cases where they are sitting as jurors. The primary difference, should the unlikely scenario of a juror being called as a witness occur, is that an adversary has to object to preserve the point for appeal. The rule allows the adverse party to object out of the jury's presence, reducing the risk that the objection will prejudice the remaining jurors. A mistrial likely would result should a party seek to call a juror to testify. Removing the juror from the jury and continuing with the trial in front of the remaining jurors (perhaps with the addition of an alternate) is unlikely to be a satisfactory solution, since the ability of the remaining jurors to evaluate the credibility of their ex-colleague's impartiality would be in question.

It might be unimaginable that judges and jurors would testify in actions in which they are professionally involved. However, Rules 605 and 606(a) sit at the polar extreme from trial procedures as they initially evolved in England. Hundreds of years ago, judges and jurors had firsthand knowledge of the parties and their disputes. Rather than listening to evidence, they reviewed what they knew and rendered judgments accordingly. Implicit in Rules 605 and 606(a), by contrast, is the policy that judges and jurors should not be personally acquainted with parties or their disputes.

Unlike Rules 605 and 606(a), Rule 606(b) applies to scenarios that arise often. After a verdict is rendered and a jury is discharged, the losing party may talk to jurors and uncover deliberative improprieties that the party thinks justify setting aside the verdict. There are numerous possible improprieties. A party may find out that, despite an out-of-court statement being admitted only for a limited, non-hearsay purpose, the jurors in fact violated the hearsay rule by using it for its truth. Similarly, jurors might have used evidence admitted for a non-character use as evidence that a defendant was a bad person and therefore deserved to be convicted despite doubts over whether the defendant committed the charged crime. Perhaps the jurors speculated about inadmissible evidence or agreed they had no idea what the phrase "malice aforethought" meant, but were too embarrassed to ask the judge for clarification. In addition, some jurors might have changed their votes because they wanted to conclude the deliberations quickly.

Rule 606(b)'s response to such problems is consistent with the aphorism widely attributed to Otto Von Bismarck, "If you like laws and sausages, you should never watch either one being made." That is, while such happenings hardly symbolize the jury system's finest moments, Rule 606(b) keeps the deliberations largely hidden from view by forbidding jurors from testifying about them: "Upon an inquiry into the validity of a verdict . . . a juror may not testify as to any matter or statement occurring during the course of the jury's deliberations or the effect of anything upon that or any other juror's mind or emotions as influencing the juror to assent to or dissent from the verdict . . . or concerning the juror's mental processes in connection therewith. . . ." The rule rests in part on a judgment that perfection in the trial process is impossible to achieve and the need for finality means that improprieties in the jury process generally must be tolerated. In addition, underlying Rule 606(b) is a fear that a general policy admitting evidence about jury deliberations would chill jurors' abilities to speak openly and would encourage losing parties to hound jurors who suffered from "buyer's remorse" into describing improprieties that might not have occurred.

Example 1

Tanner was convicted of mail fraud. Following his conviction, in an effort to obtain a new trial, Tanner submitted affidavits from two of the jurors describing events that had taken place during the trial and the deliberations. The affidavits claimed that a number of the jurors smoked marijuana regularly during the trial, and others had snorted cocaine. In addition, one juror sold marijuana to another during the trial, and a number of jurors fell asleep. Further, jurors consumed beer and wine during lunch breaks and at recesses. Despite these apparent events, the United States Supreme Court still upheld the verdict, concluding that Rule 606(b) barred the use of the affidavits. *See Tanner v. United States*, 483 U.S. 107 (1987).

Rule 606(b) does not turn a completely blind eye to jury improprieties. The rule's exceptions permit jurors to "testify on the question whether extraneous prejudicial information was improperly brought to the jury's attention or whether any outside influence was improperly brought to bear upon any juror." Even if a judge considers such evidence, jurors are nevertheless not allowed to testify to the impact of the improper influence on their reasoning processes. Rather, a judge decides what the impact would have been on a "reasonable juror," and either upholds a verdict or sets it aside accordingly.

Example 2

Assume that a juror in *Tanner* had submitted an affidavit stating that while the bailiff was escorting the jurors to lunch, the bailiff had told the juror, "This wasn't allowed in evidence, but you all should know that Tanner is a really bad guy. He has a string of convictions for mail fraud a mile long." The juror's affidavit also states: "I never would have voted to convict Tanner if the bailiff hadn't said that." The judge can consider the juror's affidavit when deciding whether the bailiff's statement was sufficiently prejudicial to justify setting aside the guilty verdict. However, the juror's assertion as to the effect of the impropriety on the juror's vote is inadmissible.

Rule 606(b) governs inquiries "into the validity of a verdict." Often, serious problems in the jury process become evident prior to the time a jury arrives at a verdict. Rule 606(b) does not bar jurors from testifying to improprieties that arise prior to the time of verdict.

Problem 7-8: At the Movies

In the film *12 Angry Men*,[3] jurors debate whether a young Puerto Rican defendant is guilty of stabbing his father to death with a knife. During the deliberations, the following incidents take place:

1. The prosecution claims that the knife found lying next to the victim and owned by the defendant was an extremely unusual one. During the deliberations, Juror # 8 counters the prosecutor's claim by producing an almost exact replica of the knife. Juror # 8 tells the other jurors that he bought it the night before in a shop while walking in the defendant's neighborhood.

2. An elderly prosecution witness who walks with a limp testified that he lives directly underneath the victim's apartment. On the night of the victim's death, the witness heard a violent argument coming from the victim's apartment and heard the door slam and someone run out of the apartment. The witness walked from his bedroom to his front door, in time to see the defendant run past. In the jury room in front of all the jurors, Juror # 8 conducts an experiment in which he walks with a limp over the distance from the witness' apartment to his front door. The experiment suggests that the witness could not have gotten to his front door in time to see the defendant run past.

3. Juror # 10 argues that the defendant is guilty because "We all know that these kind of people are violent and that human life doesn't mean the same to them as it does to us," the jurors.

Following the verdict, which, if any, of these incidents would jurors be competent to testify about under Rule 606(b)?

Problem 7-9: Stop the Reading!

1. Maryann Twonnette is on trial for murder. While the jury is deliberating, a group of jurors seeks to inform the judge that one of the jurors refuses to deliberate. Instead, the juror continuously sits in a corner and reads a book, and tells the other jurors, "Tell me when you're done deliberating, then I'll vote not guilty and we can get out of here."

---

[3] United Artists (1957).

Can the judge consider this information? If so, how, if at all, might the judge be able to respond?

2. The jury convicts Maryann Twonnette of first-degree murder. One of the jurors later informs Twonnette's attorney that during the deliberations, another juror had violated the judge's order to ignore media reports about the case by bringing into the jury room a newspaper article detailing Twonnette's lengthy prior criminal history. Some, but not all, of the information in the article had been introduced into evidence at trial. The juror also tells the defense attorney that a few of the jurors changed their votes from "not guilty" to "guilty" after reading the article. The defense attorney submits a motion for a new trial, attaching as exhibits the newspaper article and an affidavit from the juror swearing to the above information.

What, if any, information can the judge consider in ruling on the motion for a new trial?

[F] Sequential Order and Objections to Witness Testimony

Witness examination usually unfolds in a ritualistic order. The proponent of the witness first calls the witness to testify on direct examination. After direct examination, the opposing party has the opportunity to conduct cross-examination. Rule 611(b) provides that cross-examination "should be limited to the subject matter of the direct examination and matters affecting the credibility of the witness." Following the cross-examination, the proponent may conduct a redirect examination. As its name implies, a "redirect" examination is a variant of direct examination and is governed by rules similar to the initial direct examination, particularly with respect to the rule prohibiting leading questions. Redirect examination allows a rebuttal or exploration of points raised on cross-examination.

Testimony:
1. Direct Examination
2. Cross-Examination
3. Redirect Examination
4. Recross Examination

A wide variety of objections can be raised concerning a witness' testimony, particularly objections to the form of the examiners' questions. Some of the more common objections and their definitions are offered below:

1. Leading questions: questions that suggest an answer. Questions calling for a yes or no response are often leading. Primary examples of leading questions are questions beginning with words such as Was, Were, Did, Does, Have, or Had.

2. Asked and answered questions: questions that have already been asked of the witness and answered.

3. Compound questions: questions that actually incorporate two or more questions in a single sentence.

4. Questions assuming facts not in evidence: questions that assume the existence of facts not yet testified to by a witness or otherwise introduced into evidence.

5. Argumentative questions: questions that are phrased in such a way that they don't seek information but rather they merely engage the witness in improper argument.

6. Questions calling for speculation: questions asking for information beyond the witness' personal knowledge or questions asking the witness to provide an inadmissible opinion. *See* Rule 701 and Chapter 8. In such cases, the witness has either no knowledge or insufficient information about the subject matter of the testimony.

7. Non-responsive answers: answers by witnesses that do not respond to the examiner's question.

8. Narrative answers: answers by witnesses that exceed the scope of the questions put to them. A party may object to a vague or overbroad question that would likely result in an objectionable answer; in that case, the objection would be phrased as "Calls for a Narrative Answer."

[G] Witness Strategy

[1] General Principles

An attorney may follow various strategies with witness testimony, particularly when it is recognized that effective testimony "paints a picture," or "tells a story," and there are many ways to paint a single picture or tell a story. Trial practice strategies include the tone of voice attorneys adopt with witnesses, where attorneys stand when examining witnesses, in which direction attorneys face, or how they frame particular questions. Much of what a jury receives from testimony lies in the nonverbal subtext and not in the words themselves. Some attorneys hire jury consultants, who assist with jury selection or suggest how to approach the witnesses at trial in the most persuasive manner.

One strategy commonly followed by trial lawyers is embodied in Rule 615. This rule permits attorneys (or the judge, *sua sponte*) to request that prospective witnesses be excluded from the courtroom when other witnesses are testifying. This rule is commonly known among trial attorneys as "The Rule on Witnesses." Attorneys sometimes use verbal shorthand, asking the judge "to invoke the rule." Despite invocation of the rule, certain witnesses must be permitted to remain in the courtroom: the parties, certain experts, and persons whose presence might be authorized by statute, such as the victims of crimes.

[2] Direct Examination

The function of direct examination is to elicit information that is relevant to the cause of action, claim, or defense. The testimony of a witness on direct examination can be viewed as consisting of three parts: background, scene, and action. The "background" component establishes the witness as a three-dimensional person and not merely as a blank conduit of information. Juries and judges can identify more with a whole person than with an empty name with nothing behind it. The background also helps lay a foundation of authenticity (a showing that this witness is who she says she is) and of credibility (that this witness is believable). Common background questions address the witness' age, employment, education, and family status.

The "scene" component of testimony is usually the locus or place in which the action occurs. If the case is a prosecution for bank robbery, the scene is the bank. If the case is a domestic family dispute, the scene is the family house. The scene component, while very important, often is given short shrift. Many attorneys jump right into the action part of the testimony instead.

The "action" component is usually the focal point of the testimony and is readily identifiable. In a bank robbery, the action is the robbery itself. In a family dispute, the action is the actual dispute.

The prohibition against leading questions on direct examination has several rationales. One reason for the rule is to allow the jury to hear the testimony directly from the witness and not from the attorney. If leading questions were permitted, an attorney could present the entire factual story through leading questions, with the witness serving as nothing more than a stage prop. A second reason is witnesses are assumed to be aligned with the party who called them to the witness stand. Consequently, there is no need for the attorney to lead the witness through the testimony.

The assumption about witness alignment, however, is not always accurate. Sometimes a party must call a hostile witness, i.e., a person who is biased in favor of the opposing side or is otherwise aligned with an opposing party. For example, an eyewitness with important information may be a family member or neighbor of the opposing party. If the witness is considered to be hostile to the examiner, the examiner may seek the judge's permission to ask leading questions on direct examination, or simply, "to lead the witness."

The rule prohibiting the use of leading questions on direct examination is subject to several exceptions in addition to the one for hostile witnesses. The usual non-leading questions may be inappropriate with a witness who is aged, infirm, or a child. Thus, Rule 611(c) provides that leading questions are allowed on direct examination if the court decides they are necessary to develop the witness' testimony.

Example

PROSECUTOR: (on direct examination) Wally, where do you live?

DEFENSE COUNSEL: Objection! Leading.

JUDGE: Objection overruled.

[The judge most likely ruled in this manner because the question was not leading. Like most "where," "why," "when," or "how" questions, this question does not suggest an answer. Further, the question properly elicits background information.]

A: I live on the corner of 4th and Overland Street.

PROSECUTOR: What happened on July 10th, at 7:00 p.m.?

A: I saw Johnny B. Badd shoot and kill Louie Ratatooie.

PROSECUTOR: Did Johnny shoot Louie with a revolver?

DEFENSE COUNSEL: Objection. Leading.

JUDGE: Objection sustained.

[The judge concluded that the question suggests an answer — that Johnny shot Louie with a revolver. There is no reason to lead the witness during this portion of the direct examination pursuant to Federal Rules of Evidence 611.]

PROSECUTOR: So Johnny shot Louie dead? And after the shooting, in which direction did Johnny drive away and where did he hide the gun?

DEFENSE COUNSEL: Objection on three grounds, Your Honor, asked and answered, compound question, and assuming facts not in evidence.

[If the judge permits an explanation, probably at a sidebar, the defense counsel might elaborate as follows. "First, the question of whether Johnny shot Louie dead has been asked and answered. Second, the question asked by the prosecutor about the events after the shooting is objectionable because it is really two separate questions posed in compound form. The witness was asked where did Johnny drive and where did Johnny hide the gun. Finally, the question is objectionable because it assumes facts not in evidence — that Johnny drove away (he may have walked, taken a boat, or even remained at the scene) and that he hid the gun (he may not have hidden it at all)."]

Problem 7-10: Returning to Form Objections

Plaintiff sues Defendant for breach of contract. Plaintiff is questioned at trial on direct examination.

PLAINTIFF'S ATTORNEY: Would you state your name for the record?

A: Alfreida Cohen.

PLAINTIFF'S ATTORNEY: You live in San Francisco, right?

DEFENDANT'S ATTORNEY: Objection! (*On what grounds?*)

JUDGE: (*How should the judge rule? Why?*)

PLAINTIFF'S ATTORNEY: Do you live in San Francisco, or somewhere else?

DEFENDANT'S ATTORNEY: Objection! (*On what grounds?*)

JUDGE: (*How should the judge rule? Why?*)

PLAINTIFF'S ATTORNEY: Where were you on the night of June 1st, at 9:00 p.m.?

DEFENDANT'S ATTORNEY: Objection! (*On what grounds?*)

JUDGE: (*How should the judge rule? Why?*)

A: I was at the Burger King, having a candlelight dinner.

PLAINTIFF'S ATTORNEY: What did you see and hear at that time?

DEFENDANT'S ATTORNEY: Objection! (*On what grounds?*)

JUDGE: (*How should the judge rule? Why?*)

A: I saw the defendant selling goods to my competitor.

PLAINTIFF'S ATTORNEY: So you saw the defendant selling goods to someone else?

DEFENDANT'S ATTORNEY: Objection! (*On what grounds?*)

JUDGE: (*How should the judge rule? Why?*)

PLAINTIFF'S ATTORNEY: After you saw the defendant with your competitor, what happened next?

A: They left and I went to my office. Later that week I saw the defendant's sister. Now she's in business with the defendant and —

DEFENDANT'S ATTORNEY: Objection! (*On what grounds?*)

JUDGE: (*How should the judge rule? Why?*)

Problem 7-11: More Form

At a trial in a civil conversion case, the plaintiff testifies on direct examination as follows:

PLAINTIFF'S ATTORNEY: When you saw the defendant walk by your house at 3:30 p.m., on July 5th, what did you do?

DEFENDANT'S ATTORNEY: Objection! (*On what grounds?*)

JUDGE: (*How should the judge rule? Why?*)

PLAINTIFF'S ATTORNEY: What happened at 3:30 p.m. on July 5th?

DEFENDANT'S ATTORNEY: Objection! (*On what grounds?*)

JUDGE: (*How should the judge rule? Why?*)

PLAINTIFF'S ATTORNEY: Did the defendant have anything in his hands when, as you say, he walked by your house at 3:30 p.m.?

DEFENDANT'S ATTORNEY: Objection! (*On what grounds?*)

JUDGE: (*How should the judge rule? Why?*)

A: Yes, he held what appeared to be a glass statue.

PLAINTIFF'S ATTORNEY: Do you think the defendant looked suspicious or shifty?

§ 7.03　　　　　　EXAMINATION OF WITNESSES　　　　　　289

DEFENDANT'S ATTORNEY:　Objection! (*On what grounds?*)

JUDGE:　(*How should the judge rule? Why?*)

A:　(if objection overruled) Yes, definitely.

PLAINTIFF'S ATTORNEY:　So where were you when you saw the defendant?

A:　At first, I was still in front of my house. Then I went inside to telephone the police. I was steaming! By 4:00 p.m., the police came and I had calmed down some. It took until 5:00 p.m. before I was fully relaxed. I did drink a beer at 4:50 p.m., but then I was itching to —

DEFENDANT'S ATTORNEY:　Objection! (*On what grounds?*)

JUDGE:　(*How should the judge rule? Why?*)

[3] Cross-Examination

> ### *Practice Tips*
>
> On cross-examination, it is generally a good practice to ask short, clear questions, the answers to which are known by the questioner.

Cross-examination is the part of the trial approached by some attorneys with unrestrained exuberance. Novices in particular often labor under the mistaken belief that a good cross-examination always crushes a witness into tiny pieces. Nothing could be further from the truth. Cross-examination of a witness should depend on what can be achieved in the context of the case. The witness might have helpful information as well as hurtful evidence, and even the hurtful information may not hurt that much. Belligerent cross-examination of an unimportant witness, especially one who happens to be sympathetic in the jury's eyes, can be much more harmful to the case than not cross-examining the witness at all.

Leading questions are permitted on cross-examination, and many effective cross-examinations consist almost entirely of them. In fact, leading questions are the preferred type. When a cross-examiner uses a series of well-framed leading questions, it almost seems as if the attorney is testifying, and not the witness.

It is an oft-stated maxim that examiners should not ask a question to which they do not know the answer. A question such as, "Why did you do that?" invites a new and possibly harmful response by the witness, one that could surprise the examiner and greatly damage the case. For example, the question, "So if you did not observe the defendant stab the victim, how can you testify he did it?" could result in the extremely unfortunate answer, "I saw the videotape of the knifing" or "I saw everything up to the point of impact." In addition, a non-leading question permits the witness to explain, bolster, or augment the testimony previously given on direct examination.

Arguing with witnesses about major points of the witness' testimony is usually a vain attempt to get the witness to recant what the witness stated on direct examination. Instead, it is more useful to make smaller points, especially those about which the attorney already knows the answer. The attorney can argue the salient central questions (such as guilt or liability), using inferences and logic in the closing argument to the jury. It is the rare case, indeed, where a witness collapses on the stand with bowed head, saying, "Yes, you're right. I will finally, after all of these years, admit I did it. I am the culprit who committed the evil deed!"

Example

An eyewitness to an automobile accident, Lucy Lubner, has testified on direct examination about how the accident occurred. She is now on cross-examination. This cross-examination suggests inferences that can be argued and aggregated for the jury during closing argument.

DEFENDANT'S ATTORNEY: Now, Lucy, you say the accident occurred at approximately 5:00 p.m.?

A: Yes, about that time.

DEFENDANT'S ATTORNEY: You were on your way home after working a six-hour shift in the town mill?

A: Yes, I work from 10:00 a.m. to 5:00 p.m. on Fridays.

DEFENDANT'S ATTORNEY: Is it fair to say that your work requires you to stand over a moving machine for most of the day?

A: Yes, that's right.

DEFENDANT'S ATTORNEY: While you are standing over that machine, you are also operating it, right?

A: Yes.

DEFENDANT'S ATTORNEY: Now this accident occurred on December 18th, true?

A: Yes.

DEFENDANT'S ATTORNEY: The sun was setting at that time, right?

A: Yes.

DEFENDANT'S ATTORNEY: Some of the cars around you had their headlights on.

A: Yes.

Problem 7-12: Scope

Bam was employed as a truck-driver for a mouthwash company. After detouring from his usual delivery route to visit his friend, Barney, Bam was involved in an accident with a pedestrian, Fred. Fred sued Bam and Bam's employer. The only issue at trial was whether Bam was acting outside of the scope of his employment at the time of the accident. At trial, Bam was called to testify by the plaintiff, Fred. Bam was asked only four questions that elicited whether he was working at the time of the accident. On cross-examination, Bam was asked several additional questions:

DEFENDANT'S ATTORNEY: Bam, were you distracted at the time of the crash by your friend, Pebbles, yelling at you from the sidewalk?

PLAINTIFF'S ATTORNEY: Objection! (*On what grounds?*)

JUDGE: (*How should the judge rule? Why?*)

DEFENDANT'S ATTORNEY: Had you been drinking any alcoholic beverages immediately prior to the crash?

PLAINTIFF'S ATTORNEY: Objection! (*On what grounds?*)

JUDGE: (*How should the judge rule? Why?*)

DEFENDANT'S ATTORNEY: Describe what you saw immediately after the crash occurred.

PLAINTIFF'S ATTORNEY: Objection! (*On what grounds?*)

JUDGE: (*How should the judge rule? Why?*)

Problem 7-13: Succa Mucca Rucca . . .

Arsenic, a prominent local banker, sues Lacey, the mayor of the town, for slander. Lacey called Arsenic a "succa mucca rucca cheat whose business deals are all criminal in nature." At trial, plaintiff Arsenic calls his business partner, Sharon, to testify. Sharon testifies that Arsenic is an honest businessman whose truthfulness, in her opinion, is beyond reproach. Sharon is asked the following questions on cross-examination:

DEFENDANT'S ATTORNEY: Sharon, didn't Arsenic take 20 legal pads owned by the bank for his own personal use two years ago?

PLAINTIFF'S ATTORNEY: Objection! The question is irrelevant.

JUDGE: (*How should the judge rule? Why?*)

DEFENDANT'S ATTORNEY: Sharon, is it true that you cheated on your civil service examination last year?

PLAINTIFF'S ATTORNEY: Objection! The question is beyond the scope of the direct examination, your honor.

JUDGE: (*How should the judge rule? Why?*)

§ 7.04 IMPEACHMENT OF WITNESSES

> Key Words: Attack — Witness — Truth (or Accuracy)

[A] Introduction

"To impeach a witness," means to attack the witness' believability, often called *credibility*. A witness' credibility may be undermined by showing that the testimony is either untrue or inaccurate. Even a well-intentioned witness may have low credibility, if only because the person needs eyeglasses or has a poor memory.

Thus, impeachment is not simply about whether a witness is lying or deceitful. An examiner generally impeaches a witness to undermine the weight that will be accorded the witness' testimony by the trier of fact. It bears emphasizing that the impeachment of a witness can be viewed almost as a trial within a trial, since it is distinct from the admissibility of the witness' initial evidence.

Under the common-law "voucher rule," parties were presumed to vouch for the credibility of their own witnesses. Consequently, parties were forbidden to impeach their own witnesses unless the witnesses were shown to be hostile or adverse. The Federal Rules of Evidence and the evidence codes of many states have abandoned the voucher limitation. *See* Rule 607. The modern rules recognize that parties often do not have a real choice in selecting their own witnesses. Consequently, parties should be able to impeach those witnesses when appropriate. Further, parties may seek to impeach their own witness for strategic purposes. The proponent of the witness may wish to "lessen the sting" or "soften the blow" of harmful impeachment evidence by offering the evidence on direct examination. The disclosure makes it appear that the party has not attempted to hide damaging testimony.

Two of the primary considerations in understanding the impeachment rules are the type of impeachment, e.g., proof of bias or prior convictions, and whether the impeaching evidence is considered *intrinsic* or *extrinsic*. The intrinsic-extrinsic distinction is the first important analytic step in determining the admissibility of evidence offered to impeach a witness. Essentially, intrinsic and extrinsic impeachment methods are governed by different parameters.

[B] Comparing Intrinsic and Extrinsic Impeachment

Whether impeachment will be permitted will first depend on whether it is intrinsic or extrinsic in nature. The most common impeachment is intrinsic.

Definition of Intrinsic Impeachment

Intrinsic impeachment means that an attack on truthfulness essentially depends on answers given by the witness being impeached. It is impeachment from the witness' "own mouth." Intrinsic impeachment questions include: "Didn't you cheat on your driver's license exam?", "Didn't you tell a different story last month compared to what you are saying today on the witness stand?", "Don't you owe the defendant, on behalf of whom you are now testifying, $20,000?"

Extrinsic evidence impeachment, on the other hand, depends either on a new witness, one other than the witness to be impeached, or on the introduction of new evidence, such as a document. Thus, confronting a witness during cross-examination with inconsistent testimony that the witness had previously given in a deposition is a form of intrinsic evidence impeachment, whereas introducing the inconsistent portion of the deposition itself into evidence constitutes a form of extrinsic evidence impeachment.

Most types of impeachment, notably: (1) *contradiction*, (2) *bias*, (3) *convictions of certain crimes*, (4) *prior acts relating to a witness' truthfulness*, (5) *testimonial capacities*, and (6) *prior inconsistent statements* are permissible forms of intrinsic evidence impeachment. Extrinsic evidence impeachment, on the other hand, is more restricted because it has greater potential for wasting time and distracting the jury.

The rule governing when a witness may be impeached through extrinsic evidence is popularly called the "collateral issue" rule. This rule prohibits the use of extrinsic evidence to impeach a witness on a collateral matter. Correspondingly, it permits extrinsic evidence impeachment only for non-collateral (i.e., important) matters. The non-collateral or important matters that are properly the subject of extrinsic impeachment are: (1) *bias*, (2) *impeachment relating to a fact at issue*, (3) *the witness' testimonial capacities*, (4) *convictions of a crime*, and (5) *reputation or opinion evidence about the truthfulness or veracity of another witness*.

Under the collateral issue rule, therefore, extrinsic evidence may not be used to impeach a witness when: (1) contradicting the witness on a collateral (unimportant) fact, (2) showing a witness' prior inconsistent statement on a collateral fact, or (3) offering a prior "bad" act relating to the witness' truthfulness. To ensure that judges do not admit extrinsic evidence of prior untruthful act impeachment, Rule 608(b) includes an express prohibition of such evidence.

[C] Common Types of Impeachment

[1] Overview

Most types of impeachment are implicitly accepted by tradition and case law, rather than expressly described in the Federal Rules of Evidence. Types of impeachment commonly employed at trial include the following:

- Contradiction (*see* [2], *below*).
- Bias (*see* [3], *below*).
- Criminal convictions (*see* [4], *below*).
- Prior untruthful acts (*see* [5], *below*).
- Testimonial capacities (*see* [6], *below*).
- Prior inconsistent statements (*see* [7], *below*).
- Poor character for truthfulness (*see* [8], *below*).

Example

The witness, Amy Sue, testified on direct examination that she observed the defendant rob the Charley's Chicken restaurant on 9th Street and escape through the side door. The following occurred on cross-examination of Amy Sue.

This is an example of impeachment by contradiction:

DEFENSE COUNSEL: Now, Amy Sue, the Charley's Chicken restaurant that was robbed is actually located at 3200 S.W. 9th Street, not 3400 S.W. 9th Street, as you just testified, right?

A: Actually, you're correct, come to think of it.

This is an example of impeachment by showing bias:

DEFENSE COUNSEL: Amy Sue, you hate people who are charged with violent crime, isn't that right?

A: Well, that's true, but this defendant is the person who I saw rob Charley's.

This is an example of impeachment by prior, untruthful acts:

DEFENSE COUNSEL: Please just answer the question asked. Last March, you committed mail fraud against the United States Postal Service, did you not?

A: So? What about it?

This is an example of impeachment by prior felony conviction:

DEFENSE COUNSEL: You were convicted nine years ago of attempted murder, right?

A: Yes, but that so-called conviction was a colossal mistake. I was framed!

This is an example of impeachment by showing defects in the witness' testimonial capacities:

DEFENSE COUNSEL: You were not wearing your prescription eyeglasses at the time you say you observed the alleged robber, were you?

A: No, I was not wearing my glasses.

This is an example of impeachment by prior inconsistent statement:

DEFENSE COUNSEL: So it is your testimony here in court that the robber was about 5 feet, 10 inches tall and had brown hair?

A: Yes.

DEFENSE COUNSEL: Didn't you say to your mother after the incident that "the robber was about 6 foot 2 and had blonde hair"?

A: Yes, I did say that to my mother.

[Note: Most attorneys probably would not be able to squeeze in all six forms of intrinsic impeachment with a single witness unless the witness is Attila the Hun or otherwise thoroughly discreditable.]

Problem 7-14: Cross My Heart: An Overview

Jim Stone is sued by his neighbor for the conversion of his neighbor's very expensive Cannondale bicycle, which disappeared at around 11:45 a.m. At trial, Jim testifies on his own behalf, claiming misidentification. Jim offered an alibi. He asserted that he was at work several miles away from 9:00 a.m. to noon, including the time when the alleged theft occurred. On direct examination, Jim stated, "If someone took that fancy bicycle of yours, I'm really sorry. But I can tell you this, I was at work several miles away from 9:00 a.m. until noon on that day." On cross-examination, Jim is questioned as follows:

PLAINTIFF'S ATTORNEY: Isn't it true that on the day in question, you worked in the morning from 9:00 a.m. to 11:25 a.m., and not to noon as you just testified?

DEFENDANT'S ATTORNEY: Objection! Irrelevant!

JUDGE: *(How should the judge rule? Why?)*

PLAINTIFF'S ATTORNEY: Are you going to lose your job if you are found liable in this case?

DEFENDANT'S ATTORNEY: Objection! *(On what grounds? What type of impeachment is occurring? Explain.)*

JUDGE: *(How should the judge rule? Why?)*

PLAINTIFF'S ATTORNEY: Weren't you convicted of a felony, the distribution of marijuana, three years ago?

DEFENDANT'S ATTORNEY: Objection! *(On what grounds? What type of impeachment is occurring? Explain.)*

JUDGE: *(How should the judge rule? Why?)*

PLAINTIFF'S ATTORNEY: You cheated on your Law School Admission Test last year, didn't you?

DEFENDANT'S ATTORNEY: Objection! *(On what grounds? What type of impeachment is occurring? Explain.)*

JUDGE: *(How should the judge rule? Why?)*

PLAINTIFF'S ATTORNEY: You have intermittent amnesia, Mr. Stone, don't you?

DEFENDANT'S ATTORNEY: Objection! *(On what grounds? What type of impeachment is occurring? Explain.)*

JUDGE: *(How should the judge rule? Why?)*

PLAINTIFF'S ATTORNEY: Didn't you say in your deposition on June 5th that you drove to work via the Parkway, not U.S. 1, as you just testified?

DEFENDANT'S ATTORNEY: Objection! *(On what grounds? What type of impeachment is occurring? Explain.)*

JUDGE: *(How should the judge rule? Why?)*

[2] Contradiction

Contradiction occurs when the examining attorney disputes the witness' testimony about a fact (e.g., "Ms. Witness, you said on direct examination that the house at Greentree Place has no garage, when in fact it has a two-car garage, isn't that right?"). On cross-examination, a witness may be impeached by contradiction concerning facts that need not be dispositive or even important to the outcome of the case. The theory of impeachment by contradiction is that if a witness is inaccurate about one fact, she is more likely to be inaccurate about other facts as well.

Extrinsic Contradiction Impeachment: Permitted Only if Important to the Case.

If the witness denies the asserted contradicting facts, however, the cross-examiner will not be allowed to prove them by extrinsic evidence, unless the subject fact is important to the case. For example, the color of the traffic light as the defendant's car proceeded through the light's intersection in a negligence action would be a fact important to the case and a proper basis for extrinsic impeachment.

Problem 7-15: Cross.com

Carolyn testified in a commercial litigation action. *Which of the following questions are permissible during the cross-examination of Carolyn? Explain.*

1. "You used your personal computer to make notes of the meeting with the opposing party only two days after the meeting occurred, not immediately thereafter as you testified on direct examination, isn't that right?"

2. "You have a Macintosh computer, not a Dell as you just testified on direct, isn't that correct?"

3. "You left your office last Wednesday at 5:30 p.m., not 7:30 p.m. as you testified on direct examination, right?"

4. "Your boss, Ms. Sanders, was wrong when she testified that she deposited the March proceeds on March 4th, wasn't she?"

5. "Isn't it true that you are one big liar?"

[3] Bias

Bias is a form of impeachment in which a witness is shown (usually on cross-examination or through extrinsic evidence) to be influenced, prejudiced, or predisposed toward or against a party. Bias may exist because the witness is hostile, interested in the outcome, or otherwise non-neutral (e.g., "Mr. Witness, is it true that you owe the plaintiff money, that you hate the plaintiff because he's now married to your ex-wife, and that you were promised a job by the plaintiff's brother if the plaintiff wins this case?").

Extrinsic Bias Impeachment: Permitted

Extrinsic impeachment of bias is routinely permitted because bias is considered non-collateral to the case. Extrinsic bias impeachment generally follows failed intrinsic bias impeachment, where the witness has denied the allegation of bias. Watch for extrinsic evidence of specific acts used to show bias. This extrinsic evidence is generally permitted, despite being confused with prior untruthful acts, which cannot be used extrinsically.

Problem 7-16: The Right Direct-Ion

Shawn is prosecuted for allegedly battering Bobbi on a Colorado ski slope. The only eyewitness is Shawn's sister, Tya. The prosecutor calls Tya as a witness. On direct examination, the prosecutor questions Tya.

PROSECUTOR: Tya, you are the sister of the defendant, Shawn, correct?

DEFENSE COUNSEL: Objection. The question is leading and therefore improper.

JUDGE: *(How should the judge rule? Why?) If this is proper impeachment, can it occur on direct examination? Why?*

PROSECUTOR: Tya, are you currently facing a criminal charge of attempted murder?

DEFENSE COUNSEL: Objection. This question is improper impeachment on several grounds. *(What are the grounds for this objection?)*

JUDGE: *(How should the judge rule? Why?)*

PROSECUTOR: Have any deals been made in return for your testimony?

DEFENSE COUNSEL: Objection! *(What are the grounds for this objection?)*

JUDGE: *(How should the judge rule? Why?)*

Problem 7-17: Just Friends

The defendant, Alexander, is charged with the unlawful possession of a firearm by a felon. At trial, the defendant's friend, Preston, testifies for the defense. Preston states that the gun in question, found on the ground near Alexander, was really Preston's. On cross-examination, the prosecutor asks Preston whether he and Alexander are both members of the same gang, "Red 'N Blue Violins."

Is this evidence permissible impeachment? Explain.

Problem 7-18: Losing Religion

Shawana is prosecuted for the distribution of cocaine. Father O'Malley testifies for the prosecution as an eyewitness to the crime. On cross-examination he is asked by defense counsel, "Father, isn't it true that Shawana was at one time a member of the church where you are the priest, but she quit the church after having an argument with you?"

Is this question permissible? Explain.

[4] Convictions of Crime

The underlying theory of impeachment by conviction is that a witness who has been convicted of certain types of crime is less believable. According to Federal Rule of Evidence 609, two types of crimes affect a witness' credibility and can be used to impeach the witness: (1) crimes of dishonesty or false statement involving deception or fraud, regardless of the potential length of incarceration; and (2) felonies punishable by more than one year in prison. Other crimes, such as misdemeanor crimes of violence or drug possession, are not permitted to impeach, although state rules often vary from jurisdiction to jurisdiction. Likewise, Rule 609 generally excludes juvenile adjudications and "stale" convictions, which are less probative of truthfulness. Convictions are stale if more than 10 years have elapsed since the date of the conviction or of the witness' release from incarceration, whichever is later. Under Rule 609, for example, a witness could not be impeached with an 11-year-old felony conviction for which the sentence was probation and a fine.

[a]   Crimes of Dishonesty or False Statement

What qualifies as a crime of "dishonesty or false statement" is not always clear from the face of the crime. In *United States v. Brackeen*, 969 F.2d 827 (9th Cir. 1992) (*per curiam*), the defendant was indicted on one count of aiding and abetting an armed bank robbery and two counts of unarmed robbery. The defendant pled guilty to both counts of unarmed robbery and was tried and convicted of aiding and abetting the armed bank robbery. At the trial of the aiding and abetting charge, the court permitted the defendant to be impeached with the robbery convictions under Federal Rule of Evidence 609(a)(2), as crimes of dishonesty or false statement. On appeal, the Ninth Circuit, *en banc*, reversed. The court held that the unarmed robberies were not crimes of dishonesty or false statement for purposes of Rule 609. The phrase "dishonesty or false statement" could have been intended to refer either to crimes broadly evidencing a lack of integrity or those more narrowly indicating a breach of trust, such as deceit or fraud. The Court chose the narrower construction, stating that Congress, in enacting the rules, intended the narrower view. The phrase is limited to crimes that are "crimen falsi," i.e., crimes that are bad in and of themselves and have some relationship to deceit and lying. It does not include "those crimes which, bad though they are, do not carry with them a tinge of falsification." *Id.* at 831 (quoting *U.S. v. Glenn*, 667 F.2d 1269 (9th Cir. 1982)). The Court proceeded to cite with approval similar constructions from other circuits.

If a crime does not require proof of fraud or deception on its face, such as obstruction of justice, it still can qualify as a crime of dishonesty or false statement under some circumstances. As an amendment to the original text of Rule 609 clarifies: if the prosecutor had to prove dishonesty or false statement to obtain a conviction, the crime qualifies as a permissible conviction under Rule 609.

Unfair Prejudice

Crimes of dishonesty or false statement are directly probative of the truthfulness of a witness and generally are not subject to the Rule 403 balancing test. Appellate courts also view the use of limiting instructions given by the trial court to the jury as an extra safeguard against the risk of unfair prejudice.

[b] Felony Convictions

Prior felony convictions are not automatically permitted for the purpose of impeaching a witness. Under Rule 609, the use of felony convictions first must satisfy the unfair prejudice test of Rule 403 for all witnesses, with the exception of a testifying criminal defendant, a situation that warrants a special balancing test. The exclusion of some felonies reflects the belief that a felony conviction is less likely to bear on a witness' truthfulness than a crime of dishonesty or false statement. (For the situation preceding the rule change, see *Green v. Bock Laundry Machine Co.*, 490 U.S. 504, 109 S. Ct. 1981, 104 L. Ed. 2d 557 (1989).) Rule 609 provides greater protection to criminal defendants who choose to testify on their own behalf. The rationale for this special treatment is to prevent felony convictions offered to impeach the accused from being used by the trier of fact as substantive evidence of guilt. Under a special balancing test, felony convictions will be permitted to impeach the testifying accused only if their probative value outweighs the prejudicial effect to the accused. This balancing test reverses Rule 403's built-in presumption in favor of admissibility and favors the accused.

Courts may consider a variety of factors in determining whether a defendant's felony conviction will be unfairly prejudicial when offered as impeachment evidence. One important factor is the similarity between the impeachment felony and the crime charged. The greater the similarity, the greater the likelihood that the impeachment will be misused by the jurors as evidence that "if the defendant did it before, it is more likely the defendant did it again" (e.g., "Once a criminal, always a criminal"). Other factors that might be considered include the importance of the defendant's credibility to the case, the nature and date of the impeachment crime, and the significance of the defendant's testimony to the case overall. *See, e.g., United States v. Sloman*, 909 F.2d 176, 180–181 (6th Cir. 1990).

The admissibility of a crime offered to impeach a testifying accused is not tied to the use of that crime in other ways, such as its use as an "other act" under Rule 404(b). A conviction may be used to impeach even if the underlying crime has been offered. and rejected by the trial court — as an "other act" pursuant to Rule 404. In essence, the fact that evidence is impermissible for one purpose does not mean it is impermissible for another purpose. *See, e.g., United States v. Haslip*, 160 F.3d 649, 653–654 (10th Cir. 1998). Of course, with evidence admitted for one purpose and not another, a limiting instruction accompanying the evidence may be appropriate. *Id.* at 655.

What constitutes a "conviction" for impeachment purposes can be perplexing, especially to a layperson. A conviction can result from a jury or court verdict or a guilty plea. Having been indicted, arrested, or otherwise charged with a crime is insufficient to qualify as a conviction under the rules. Further, contrary to a popular misconception, a conviction is fodder for impeachment regardless of whether the accused received a sentence of incarceration, probation, or no penalty at all. A person who has been given probation and has never stepped foot in a jail cell can still have multiple felony convictions. Like other types of impeachment (*see*

Rule 607), a witness' criminal convictions may be offered on either direct or cross-examination. Parties may offer evidence during direct examination of a favorable witness that the witness has been convicted of a crime to "soften the blow" of the ensuing cross-examination and demonstrate to the jury that counsel is not hiding anything.

Extrinsic Conviction Impeachment: Permitted

If a witness denies a conviction on cross-examination, it may be proved by extrinsic evidence. The form of the extrinsic evidence is limited, though, usually to a certified copy of the conviction. Thus, the judge or the members of the jury that convicted a witness cannot be called to testify to the conviction.

Problem 7-19: Forgery, Fake, Fraud

Sylvia is prosecuted for forging signatures on applications for food stamps. The prosecution, in its case-in-chief, offers a witness, Wally, who will testify that Sylvia (1) has been convicted of forgery on three prior occasions, and (2) was charged with embezzlement on a fourth prior occasion.

Are these convictions and the criminal charge admissible? Why?

If it had been Wally, and not Sylvia, who was convicted of forgery and charged with embezzlement, would the convictions and charge be admissible?

Problem 7-20: Medical Mal

Mal brought suit against Dr. Sloan for failing to diagnose Mal's prostate cancer. At trial, the plaintiff's expert, Dr. Inos, testified. On cross-examination, the defendant wished to question the doctor about his misdemeanor conviction for willfully failing to file a federal income tax return.

Is this impeachment permissible? See Cree v. Hatcher, 969 F.2d 34 (3d Cir. 1992).

May Dr. Inos be asked about a pending suspension of his medical license by the State of Iowa if he is testifying in an Arkansas federal court? Explain.

Problem 7-21: One Bad Apple

Johnny Apple was prosecuted for attempted murder. Johnny testified at trial and denied committing the crime charged. On cross-examination, the prosecution attempted to impeach Johnny with the following crimes. *Can any of the crimes be used to impeach Johnny? In addition, what test applies in determining whether impermissible prejudice would result?*

1. A 15-year-old conviction for attempted murder.

2. A seven-year-old conviction for assault, punishable by six months in jail and a fine of $1,000.

3. A 19-year-old juvenile adjudication for murder.

4. A 10-year-old conviction for aggravated battery, punishable by a maximum of three years in prison, for which the defendant was sentenced to two months incarceration, sentence suspended.

5. A six-year-old conviction for grand theft, for which the defendant was sentenced to six months incarceration.

[5] Prior Untruthful Acts

Impeachment by prior acts under Rule 608(b) is limited to specific prior acts of the witness that reflect on the witness' capacity for truthfulness or veracity. These acts are the functional equivalent of the acts underlying the dishonesty or false statement convictions under Rule 609. Prior untruthful acts impeachment, as it is sometimes called, is still distinguishable from impeachment by conviction, because no conviction is required for bad acts impeachment. In fact, the act may not have been the subject of a criminal charge at all or might even have been the subject of a criminal charge resulting in an acquittal.

Describing this conduct as "bad acts" is a misnomer of sorts, because there is a limit on the type and nature of the prior acts that fall in this category. The acts that may be used for impeachment are limited to those involving truthfulness or veracity, such as fraud, obtaining property under false pretenses, or perjury. Acts of violence, such as disorderly conduct, battery, or even murder, do not constitute "bad" acts relating to truthfulness and generally cannot be used to impeach. Acts such as drug use, driving at excessive speed, failing to return a library book on time, and filing for bankruptcy also fail to be sufficiently related to witness truthfulness to be admissible untruthful act impeachment.

Sometimes, a judge will probe beneath the surface of a crime that does not on its face appear to involve dishonesty to determine if the manner in which the crime was committed was deceitful. For example, if a larceny was directly intertwined with deceit, it might meet the requirements of Rule 608(b) impeachment. *See, e.g., United States v. Payton*, 159 F.3d 49 (2d Cir. 1998).

If impeachment by a prior act is proper, the witness may be asked only about the underlying act itself and not about an arrest, charge, indictment, suspension, or expulsion relating to the act. The witness' truthfulness does not hinge on the arrest, indictment, etc., but rather on commission of the act itself. Thus, it is permissible to ask, "You defrauded your insurance company, didn't you?" but not, "You were indicted for defrauding your insurance company, weren't you?"

The original language of Rule 608(b) was clarified by an amendment that deleted the bracketed words and added the italicized words:

> (b) Specific instances of the conduct of a witness, for the purpose of attacking or supporting the witness' [credibility] *character for truthfulness*, other than conviction of crime as provided in Rule 609, may not be proved by extrinsic evidence. They may, however, in the discretion of the court, if probative of truthfulness or untruthfulness, be inquired into on cross-examination of the witness (1) concerning the witness' character for truthfulness or untruthfulness, or (2) concerning the character for truth-

fulness or untruthfulness of another witness as to which character the witness being cross-examined has testified.

The giving of testimony, whether by an accused or by any other witness, does not operate as a waiver of the accused's or the witness' privilege against self-incrimination when examined with respect to matters [which] *that* relate only to [credibility] *character for truthfulness.*

The rationale behind substituting the phrase "character for truthfulness," for the word "credibility," might not be immediately apparent. The answer lies in the fact that the term "credibility" can have broader connotations than the phrase "character for truthfulness." As the Committee Note explaining the change observes, "The rule has been amended to clarify that the absolute prohibition on extrinsic evidence applies only when the sole reason for proffering that evidence is to attack or support the witness' character for truthfulness." Advisory Committee Note to Rule 608(b). What the amendment emphasizes is that the prohibition of extrinsic evidence is limited to prior acts impeachment under Rule 608(b); other forms of impeachment are governed separately. As the Committee Note elaborates, "By limiting the application of the Rule to proof of a witness' character for truthfulness, the amendment leaves the admissibility of extrinsic evidence offered for other grounds of impeachment (such as contradiction, prior inconsistent statement, bias and mental capacity) to Rules 402 and 403," (citations omitted).

Extrinsic Untruthful Act Impeachment: Disallowed

Permissible prior untruthful act impeachment cannot be proven by extrinsic evidence. If the witness denies the act, the questioner generally must take the witness' answer without any further follow-up. *See* Rule 608(b). Otherwise, a mini-trial would result and the jury would be distracted.

Problem 7-22: Liar, Liar

Janet is prosecuted for committing perjury during her testimony before the grand jury. At trial, she testifies on her own behalf and is asked the following questions on cross-examination:

PROSECUTOR: You were arrested for lying on your income tax statement last year, weren't you?

DEFENSE COUNSEL: Objection. Improper impeachment.

JUDGE: (*How should the judge rule? Why?*)

PROSECUTOR: You deceived your boss three weeks ago, didn't you, when you claimed you missed an important meeting because your train was late?

DEFENSE COUNSEL: Objection. Improper impeachment.

JUDGE: (*How should the judge rule? Why?*)

[6] Testimonial Capacities

The term "testimonial capacities" refers to aspects of a witness' testimony that are important for accuracy: (1) perception — what the witness saw, heard, smelled, or touched at the time in question; (2) memory — the ability of the witness to recall the prior occurrence, happening, or event; (3) narration — the ability of the witness to communicate this perception and memory to others; and sometimes (4) sincerity (which is often viewed as a combination of the other three capacities) — a measurement indicating a lack of prevarication. Sincerity is distinct from accuracy, because a witness can be sincere but still inaccurate.

Attacking a witness' testimonial capacities is accomplished by presenting intrinsic or extrinsic evidence revealing defects in any one or more of these capacities. By revealing these defects, the jury is shown the limits of a witness' ability to provide an accurate recounting of prior events. For example, many witnesses have limited and inaccurate memories, particularly with the passage of time. Additionally, the opponent is allowed to present extrinsic evidence (*see* [C], *below*) of a witness' reputation for untruthfulness or offer a qualified witness' opinion of another witness' untruthfulness under Rule 608(a).

Defects in testimonial capacities often extend beyond common deficiencies to encompass physiological defects that result in problems of perception, memory, or narration. These problems are more severe than those reflected by statements such as "I forgot" or "I could not hear something so far away," which happen to everyone. Instead, these defects concern some physical or psychological condition, such as bad eyesight, amnesia, hearing loss, or schizophrenia. Physiological defects are particularly injurious to a witness' ability to be accurate.

Extrinsic Testimonial Capacities Impeachment: Permitted

Testimonial capacities impeachment is considered important in a case and is routinely permitted. It generally follows a failed attempt on cross-examination to impeach a witness' testimonial capacities intrinsically.

Problem 7-23: Psychotic Chips

In a tort action for false imprisonment, Don Geo is about to testify as an eyewitness for the defense. As he takes the witness stand, he yells to the jury, "Would you like some of my fantastic psychotic chips?" referring to a bag of potato chips he is carrying. Don adds, "They're mind-altering."

1. On cross-examination, the plaintiff's attorney questions Don about two previous hospital stays for undifferentiated schizophrenia. *Are such questions permissible? Why?*

2. Don is also questioned on cross-examination about whether his psychotic chips contain any mind-altering substances. *Admissible?*

3. May Don be asked on cross-examination whether he was under the influence of alcohol or other drugs at the time he observed the alleged false imprisonment? May he be asked whether he is currently under the influence of a mind-altering substance at the time of trial? Why?

[7] Prior Inconsistent Statements

Impeachment by a prior inconsistent statement pursuant to Rule 613 is actually a specialized form of impeachment by contradiction, namely self-contradiction. Two statements by the witness are necessary for this type of impeachment. One of the statements usually occurs during the witness' testimony at trial and the second statement generally occurs prior to the testimony. The two statements must, on the whole, be inconsistent. The statements can be in the form of oral, written, or assertive conduct and need not be sworn.

If the witness at trial forgets facts while testifying and says, "I don't remember" in response to a question or fails to make a certain statement at trial, there is no trial statement. If there is then only the one statement prior to trial, impeachment with that prior statement is generally forbidden. If the witness is acting in bad faith by intentionally "forgetting" the facts at trial, however, an exception is made to this requirement of two statements and the prior statement may be used to impeach.

Federal Rule of Evidence 613 drops the common-law requirement of *The Queen's Case*, 2 Br. & B. 284, 129 Eng. Rep. 976 (1820). That case created a "fairness" rule by requiring the examining counsel to give a witness the opportunity to deny or explain the witness' own prior written statement before being impeached on it. However, Rule 613 imports its own version of fairness by requiring the contents of a prior statement to be shown or disclosed to opposing counsel on request.

Extrinsic Prior Inconsistent Statement Impeachment: Permitted Only if the Subject Matter is Important to the Case

Many parties who attempt to impeach a witness through a prior inconsistent statement will have to take the witness' answer if it involves a question unimportant to the issues in the case. The relative importance to the issues of the case raises a relevance inquiry for the judge, who will make the admissibility decision. For this category, the analysis is similar to that of contradiction impeachment: no extrinsic evidence of a prior inconsistent statement is allowed, unless the subject matter is non-collateral. The judge must exercise some discretion in determining what is non-collateral.

Example

Jean sues Ted for allegedly breaching a commercial lease extension for Ted's Tender Chicken, a fast food restaurant located in Jean's shopping center. Ted's defense is that no extension occurred. An important issue at trial concerned a meeting at Ted's restaurant on June 24th. An eyewitness to the meeting, Sophia, testified that on the day in question at the restaurant, both Jean and Ted met, discussed the lease, appeared to agree on an extension, and signed several documents. On cross-examination, Sophia was impeached by a prior inconsistent statement.

DEFENDANT'S ATTORNEY: Now, Sophia, you have just testified on direct examination that Jean and Ted signed several documents during the meeting on the day in question?

A: That is correct.

DEFENDANT'S ATTORNEY: You discussed what happened at this meeting with me before, didn't you?

A: Yes, I believe so.

DEFENDANT'S ATTORNEY: It was during your deposition, way back in May, right?

A: Yes, I think it was in May.

DEFENDANT'S ATTORNEY: The meeting occurred only five months or so prior to the deposition, true?

A: Yes.

DEFENDANT'S ATTORNEY: At the deposition, you were under oath?

A: True.

DEFENDANT'S ATTORNEY: You swore to tell the truth?

A: Definitely. Yes.

DEFENDANT'S ATTORNEY: The whole truth and nothing but the truth?

A: Sure.

DEFENDANT'S ATTORNEY: Referring opposing counsel to the witness' deposition, page eight, line nine, I asked you during the deposition: "How many documents did Jean and Ted sign?" You answered: "They signed only one document." Isn't that correct?

A: Yes, that is what you asked and I answered.

[8] Poor Character For Truthfulness — Extrinsic Impeachment Only

Poor character for truthfulness is a type of extrinsic impeachment expressly permitted under Rule 608(a). Under Rule 608(a), a witness can have his or her truthfulness attacked by another witness in the form of reputation or opinion testimony only. Extrinsic evidence of specific acts of that prior witness is not permitted. *See* Rule 608(b). When opinion or reputation evidence is offered, counsel must lay a foundation showing that the character witness has an adequate basis for forming an opinion about the impeached witness' character or for having heard about the impeached witness' reputation.

A critical intersection that often arises is between character evidence offered to impeach and character evidence offered to prove an issue in the case. Reputation or opinion-type testimony offered to impeach a witness is only about the witness and the witness' truthfulness. Reputation or opinion-type testimony offered as character evidence concerns a party or victim and is generally circumstantial character evidence about a party's guilt, fault, or liability.

Problem 7-24: Truth-o-Meter

The prosecutor called Paula as a witness in a DUI manslaughter case. When Paula testified, she stated that she saw the defendant's car swerve in front of her car and that the driver of her car, Sadie, yelled, "That driver is going at least 90 mph!" Because Sadie had already testified for the prosecution and been impeached by Defendant, Paula was asked, "Do you have an opinion as to Sadie's truthfulness?" Paula responded, "If Sadie said the guy was doing 90, I, for one, would certainly believe her."

If Defendant objected to Paula's statement about Sadie's truthfulness, what ruling and why?

Problem 7-25: Cavalier and Convicted

Joe Cavalier was convicted of receiving stolen property nine and a half years prior to his trial for mail fraud and conspiracy to commit mail fraud. Cavalier testified in his own defense, and the prosecution offered evidence of the prior conviction in order to impeach him. The defense objected. *What ruling and why?*

[D] Two-Way Admissibility of Some Prior Inconsistent Statements

Significantly, some prior inconsistent statements are admissible for two purposes — for their truth as well as to impeach a witness. To determine whether this "two-way" admissibility situation exists, the nature of the prior inconsistent statement matters. As discussed further in Chapter 12, on Rule 801, if a prior inconsistent statement of a witness has certain qualifying features (e.g., it was made under oath in a prior proceeding, like those in a deposition), it will be admitted not only for its impeachment value, but also for the truth of the matter asserted. This means that in the example above, if the deposition statement by the witness, Sophia, qualifies under Rule 801, it can be considered by the jury. The jury can consider not only the effect of the apparent inconsistency on Sophia's believability, but also for the truth of the matter asserted — what was actually signed at the meeting and by whom.

Special significance also accrues to prior statements of testifying parties offered against them. These statements may qualify as admissions of a party opponent under Rule 801(d)(2) and would be admitted for their truth as well as for impeachment purposes.

Sometimes, a witness confronted with a prior inconsistent statement denies making the statement, even if the statement was taken down by a court reporter as part of a deposition. If this occurs, the witness may be impeached by extrinsic evidence of the statement (such as a writing or a witness) but only if the inconsistency is about a matter at issue in the case. If extrinsic impeachment is permitted, a foundation must be laid for the extrinsic evidence. To promote efficiency, it is worth attempting to use the witness to be impeached to help lay the foundation. If a new witness is required, and the witness to be impeached may be needed at a later time, it is important not to excuse the witness, but rather to explain to the court the intended additional use of the witness.

Problem 7-26: Yeah, Right

Ted, the primary witness for the defense in a tort action, states on direct examination that he was not aware that a lawsuit had been filed until four days prior to trial. On cross-examination, Ted is asked whether he told a good friend eight months earlier, right after the suit had been brought, "I heard that good old Plaintiff filed suit this week." *Is this question permissible impeachment?*

[E] More Impeachment Problems

Problem 7-27: "You Took the Tag Off of Your Mattress?!"

Cheryl is prosecuted for shoplifting from the "We R Toys" store. The store clerk, Laurie, testifies for the prosecution. On cross-examination, the clerk is asked the following questions:

DEFENSE COUNSEL: Isn't it true that the "We R Toys" store has only four parking spaces out front and not five, as you testified?

PROSECUTOR: Objection. (*On what grounds?*)

JUDGE: (*How should the judge rule? Why?*)

DEFENSE COUNSEL: You've been arrested for child abuse, haven't you?

PROSECUTOR: Objection. (*On what grounds?*)

JUDGE: (*How should the judge rule? Why?*)

DEFENSE COUNSEL: Laurie, you faked a workers' compensation injury last year to collect benefits, didn't you?

PROSECUTOR: Objection. (*On what grounds?*)

JUDGE: (*How should the judge rule? Why?*)

DEFENSE COUNSEL: You were told by your boss that you'd get an extra vacation day if you testified today, isn't that correct?

PROSECUTOR: Objection. (*On what grounds?*)

JUDGE: (*How should the judge rule? Why?*)

DEFENSE COUNSEL: Laurie, you were convicted last year of shoplifting at a "Toys R Not U" store, isn't that right?

PROSECUTOR: Objection. (*On what grounds?*)

JUDGE: (*How should the judge rule? Why?*)

DEFENSE COUNSEL: You took the tag that says "Do Not Remove" off of your mattress, didn't you?

PROSECUTOR: Objection. (*On what grounds?*)

JUDGE: (*How should the judge rule? Why?*)

Problem 7-28: Defamation Redux

Sue is called an "inept, tabloid-loving, dimwit surgeon" in the local newspaper. She sues for libel. At trial, her brother, Bob, also a surgeon, testifies on her behalf as a character witness about Sue's professional competence. Bob is cross-examined by counsel for the defendant newspaper.

DEFENDANT'S ATTORNEY: So, Bob, isn't it true that you punched the defendant newspaper editor in the nose outside of Rosie O'Sady's restaurant last week?

PLAINTIFF'S ATTORNEY: Objection. Improper impeachment.

JUDGE: (*How should the judge rule? Why?*)

DEFENDANT'S ATTORNEY: Bob, you are aware that there were two incidents in which your sister was cited by the hospital for cutting into the wrong location, correct?

PLAINTIFF'S ATTORNEY: Objection! Improper impeachment.

JUDGE: (*How should the judge rule? Why?*)

DEFENDANT'S ATTORNEY: You said on direct examination that your sister has participated in at least 800 operations. Yet, in your deposition on October 5th, at page three, line four, you were asked, "In how many operations did your sister participate?" and you answered, "Oh, I don't know, maybe 400."

PLAINTIFF'S ATTORNEY: Objection! Improper impeachment.

JUDGE: (*How should the judge rule? Why?*)

DEFENDANT'S ATTORNEY: Bob, didn't you misrepresent your college class rank on your medical school application?

PLAINTIFF'S ATTORNEY: Objection. Improper impeachment.

JUDGE: (*How should the judge rule? Why?*)

Problem 7-29: The Young Freud

The young Dr. Von Freud testified about the cause of death in a prosecution for homicide.

1. Dr. Von Freud is asked on cross-examination whether his opinion is consistent with *Gray's Anatomy*, which is considered to be an authoritative medical treatise in the field. *Admissible? Why?*

2. He also is asked on cross-examination whether he has been convicted of child abuse. *Permitted?*

3. Dr. Von Freud is questioned on cross-examination about whether he had been fired from his previous employment because he had forged medical records. *Admissible? Why?*

Extrinsic Impeachment Example

Harold testified for the plaintiff, Maude, in a breach-of-contract action. On cross-examination, Harold was asked if: (1) he was dating Maude, (2) Maude had agreed to enter into the contract without qualification, (3) he had been convicted of mayhem 10 years earlier, and (4) he had lied on his bar application four years earlier. Harold answered "no" to all four questions. On rebuttal, can the defendant offer a new witness to testify: (1) Harold was dating Maude, and (2) Maude had agreed to the contract offer without qualification? Can the defense also offer: (3) a certified copy of Harold's prior conviction for mayhem, and (4) a copy of his bar application with the allegedly untruthful statement?

Answer: The collateral issue rule permits the defendant to impeach Harold extrinsically in three of the four instances because in those instances the impeachment is considered important or non-collateral. The new witness may testify about: (1) whether Harold and Maude were dating, because it shows bias, which is never collateral; and (2) the dispute about Maude's responses to the contract offer, because it involves a fact in issue. The certified copy of Harold's conviction for mayhem is admissible, because convictions of crime are considered to be non-collateral matters as well. However, the prior bad act, the alleged lie on the bar application, cannot be the subject of extrinsic impeachment, because prior bad acts are considered collateral. Even if Harold is lying anew with respect to the bar application, the questioner must take the witness' answer.

Problem 7-30: Extrinsically Yours

Xavier testifies for the defense in an action involving the sale of real property. Xavier was an eyewitness to the alleged contract to sell the property.

1. During cross-examination by the plaintiff, Xavier is asked whether he had been convicted of attempted robbery 10 years earlier. *Is this question permissible?*

2. Xavier denied having been convicted of attempted robbery. ("Preposterous!" he exclaimed). *Can the opposing counsel offer in evidence a certified copy of the attempted robbery conviction? Why?*

3. On cross-examination, Xavier is asked whether he was wearing his hearing aid at the time of the alleged sale. Xavier responded by saying that he was indeed using his hearing aid. *May the opposing counsel call a different witness, Alec, to testify that Xavier was not wearing a hearing aid at the time of the alleged sale?*

4. On cross-examination, Xavier is asked whether he had worn white sneakers on the day in question, not red ones as he had testified on direct. Xavier answered the question by denying that he had worn white sneakers. *May the opposing counsel call a different witness in rebuttal to testify that Xavier was wearing white sneakers at the meeting about the sale?*

5. Xavier also is asked whether he had said in a deposition two months before trial, "I was the first one there for the meeting about the sale," when on direct he testified that he "was only the third or fourth person there." *If Xavier claims he made no such prior statement, may a rebuttal witness who was present at the deposition testify that Xavier made the statement?*

6. *If Xavier is asked on cross-examination whether he owes the defendant a large sum of money and he denies it, may the plaintiff call a different witness in rebuttal to confirm this fact?*

Problem 7-31: More Perjury

Clark is being prosecuted for perjury. He calls his best friend, Lenny, with whom he went to grade school, to testify on his behalf.

DEFENSE COUNSEL: What is Clark's reputation for truthfulness?

A: Clark's reputation in the community is one of complete honesty; he would never lie.

PROSECUTOR: (on cross-examination) Have you heard, Lenny, that Clark was expelled from night school for cheating on an examination two years ago?

(Does this question relate to impeachment, to character evidence, or to both?)

DEFENSE COUNSEL: Objection. *(On what grounds?)*

JUDGE: *(How should the judge rule? Why?)*

Lenny finishes testifying, and the prosecutor calls Sheila, a rebuttal witness, who testifies as follows:

A: In my opinion, Lenny is a liar. Furthermore, everyone in this community says that Clark is about as truthful as that television character, Bart Simpson; basically, Clark has a reputation for having no veracity at all.

DEFENSE COUNSEL: Objection. *(On what grounds?)*

JUDGE: *(How should the judge rule? Why?)*

Sheila finishes testifying, and the defense calls Sheila's estranged husband, George, to testify on behalf of Clark. On direct examination, after being asked about Sheila's and Lenny's reputations, George declares:

A: In my opinion, Sheila is a liar. In any event, Lenny's reputation in the community is one of unimpeachable honesty.

PROSECUTOR: Objection. *(On what grounds?)*

JUDGE: *(How should the judge rule? Why?)*

Problem 7-32: Bigfoot

Bernie is charged with conspiracy to import heroin. At the time of his arrest, which occurred one week after the alleged conspiracy concluded, Bernie was apprehended with alleged heroin in his shoe. At trial, Bernie testified in his own defense and denied being a part of a conspiracy.

1. On cross-examination, the prosecution asked Bernie if he had heroin in his shoe at the time he was apprehended. Is the question permissible?

2. If the question is permitted, and Bernie denies having had heroin in his shoe, may the prosecutor then call the arresting officer to the witness stand to testify to that fact?

Problem 7-33: Buddies Revisited

Alexander is prosecuted for a felony. At trial, Alexander's fellow gang member, Preston, testifies on the defendant's behalf. On cross-examination, Preston is asked whether he belongs to the same gang as the defendant. Preston says no. On rebuttal, the prosecution calls a police officer specializing in gangs to testify that both Preston and Alexander belong to the gang, "R U Blud." The officer further testifies that the gang is known for lying to protect fellow members. Alexander is convicted, and he appeals, claiming that both the cross-examination of Preston and the police officer's extrinsic testimony should have been excluded.

What ruling and why? See United States v. Martinez, 962 F.2d 1161 (5th Cir. 1992).

Problem 7-34: Edna to Rachel to Frank

In a civil assault-and-battery action, the defense calls an eyewitness, Edna. She testifies that the defendant was not the first aggressor, but was merely defending himself.

1. In rebuttal, the plaintiff calls Rachel, who testifies that, in her opinion, Edna is not a very truthful person. *Allowed?*

2. In surrebuttal (the reply to the rebuttal), the defendant calls a new witness, Frank, who testifies that Edna has a stellar reputation for truthfulness in the community. *Permitted?*

Problem 7-35: Mortgage

The defendant, Adin, was charged with the unlawful possession of a firearm.

1. The central prosecution witness, Tylie, testified in the prosecution's case-in-chief. On cross-examination, she was asked whether she had made a false statement on her recent mortgage application. Is the question permissible?

2. After Tylie denied making any false statements, the judge permitted the prosecutor to offer the mortgage application in evidence. *Was this error?*

Problem 7-36: Interregnum

In a slip-and-fall negligence action, the defendant, Belinda, testified about the fall. Belinda stated that she observed boxes flying all around the plaintiff, Irving, as he fell. On cross-examination, plaintiff's counsel asked Belinda about her deposition, which was taken one month prior to trial.

1. The plaintiff's counsel questioned Belinda about her failure to mention flying boxes when she was asked during the deposition to describe the incident. *Is this question permissible impeachment?*

2. Plaintiff's counsel also asked Belinda whether Irving had ever fired her from a job. Belinda responded, "No!" *Can plaintiff offer Belinda's former co-worker to testify that Belinda had been fired by Irving? Why?*

[F] Rehabilitation of Witnesses

> Steps: (1) Impeachment; then (2) Rehabilitation

A witness' character for truthfulness can be rehabilitated only after his or her veracity has been directly attacked. A direct attack on a witness' character includes prior convictions, prior untruthful bad acts, and reputation or opinion evidence of untruthfulness. As noted earlier, preemptive rehabilitation, which occurs in anticipation of impeachment, is not permitted. Rehabilitation can occur either through questions on redirect examination or through a separate reputation or opinion witness testifying about the impeached witness' good character for truthfulness or veracity.

Note that rehabilitation generally occurs on redirect examination. This new direct examination permits the witness to explain his or her answers on cross-examination, if appropriate. The explanations, however, are still limited by Rule 403 and unfair prejudice.

A significant form of rehabilitation occurs under Rule 608(a). After a witness' character for truthfulness has been directly attacked, the proponent of the witness can then offer opinion or reputation evidence bolstering the witness' veracity. This form of rehabilitation involves calling a new witness whose primary purpose is to rebut the attacks on the other witness' character.

Problem 7-37: Rehab

Maryanne was the star defense witness in a forfeiture action. The government claimed that a considerable amount of marijuana was found in the back seat of the defendant's car, justifying the car's forfeiture. Anticipating a ferocious cross-examination of Maryanne, the defense first called Maryanne's partner, Marcy, to testify that, in her opinion, Maryanne has an unimpeachable character for truthfulness and veracity.

The prosecution objects to Marcy's testimony. *What ruling and why?*

After Maryanne testified on direct examination, the prosecution zealously cross-examined her, suggesting that Maryanne recently fabricated her testimony to assist the defendant's case. On redirect examination, the following occurred:

DEFENSE COUNSEL: When did you first learn of this incident?

A: Almost immediately after the forfeiture occurred.

DEFENSE COUNSEL: What did you do upon hearing about it?

§ 7.04　　　　　　　IMPEACHMENT OF WITNESSES　　　　　　313

A:　　　　　　I immediately told my friend Julian the same exact thing that I just testified to on direct, that the hitchhiker had unloaded and then repacked his bag in the back seat before leaving the car.

PROSECUTOR:　　Objection! (*What is the basis for the prosecutor's objection?*)

JUDGE:　　　　(*How should the judge rule? Why?*)

[G]　Refreshing the Witness's Memory

Stuck somewhat incongruously in the middle of the impeachment rules, Rule 612 pertains to refreshing a witness' memory. The Rule appears misplaced in several ways. Refreshing a witness' memory most often occurs during the direct examination of the proponent's own witness and is generally performed to bolster the witness' credibility by facilitating an accurate memory of events or occurrences. Thus, it effectively accredits the witness, instead of impeaching the witness' credibility. A witness who has forgotten events that happened long ago often appears more believable than one who remembers prior events with crystal clarity.

Another incongruity is that impeachment is a form of evidence to be considered by the jury, while refreshing a witness' recollection is not. Because the items used to refresh memory are not being offered into evidence, but rather are being used as memory aids, whatever an attorney may employ to refresh a witness' memory is not subject to the rules of authentication or put to the usual test of admissibility. This means that inadmissible hearsay or even inadmissible real evidence may be used to refresh a witness' memory. While this may sound like a "free ride," a way to sneak in evidence under the guise of refreshing memory, it is not; the items must be disclosed to the opposing counsel and may be used to impeach the witness as well.

The process of refreshing memory comes closest to impeachment when it is being employed during cross-examination, where a witness' forgetfulness may be highlighted by an examiner to show duplicity or inaccuracy, particularly if a prior written statement made by the witness exists. (The hearsay exemption for certain kinds of witnesses' prior inconsistent statements is addressed in Chapter 13.)

Judges retain discretion to refuse to permit some writings to be used for refreshing the recollection of witnesses. If a writing is to be used as the actual basis for testimony and not merely to refresh a witness' memory, it may be excluded by the court.

Problem 7-38: "Sammy Says"

Sammy testifies for the plaintiff in a complex commercial litigation action. He is asked on direct examination about a particular business meeting the previous year and he answers, "Hmmmm, I really don't remember it." Counsel then shows Sammy the notes Sammy took during the meeting.

1. May plaintiff's counsel give Sammy his own meeting notes to refresh his memory? What is the proper procedure by which to refresh recollection? May Sammy read the notes to the jury?

2. Do the notes have to be authenticated?

3. Does it matter if the notes were not written by Sammy, but by someone else at the meeting? May Sammy still rely on the notes to refresh his memory about the meeting? May Sammy read the notes to the jury?

4. If Sammy reviews his notes during the direct examination, may he be questioned about the notes on cross-examination?

5. If Sammy carefully took the notes immediately after the meeting when the events were fresh in his mind, but he has no current recollection about the meeting, may the notes be admitted in evidence at trial? See Rule 803(5).

[H] Impeachment Statutes

Compare the current form of Federal Rule of Evidence 609(a) with various preliminary draft proposals.

House Subcommittee Draft (1973)

> For the purpose of attacking credibility of a witness, evidence that he has been convicted of a crime is admissible if, but only if (1) the crime involved dishonesty or false statement, or (2) the crime was punishable by death or imprisonment in excess of one year under the law under which he was convicted, unless the judge determines that the danger of unfair prejudice outweighs the probative value of the evidence of conviction.

House Bill H.R. 5463 (February 1974)

> For the purpose of attacking the credibility of a witness, evidence that he has been convicted of a crime is admissible only if the crime involved dishonesty or false statement.

Senate Judiciary Committee Draft (October 1974)

> For the purpose of attacking the credibility of a witness, evidence that he has been convicted of a crime may be elicited from him or established by public record during cross-examination but only if the crime (1) involved dishonesty or false statement or (2) in the case of witnesses other than the accused, was punishable by death or imprisonment in excess of one year under the law under which he was convicted, but only if the court determines that the probative value of admitting this evidence outweighs its prejudicial effect.

Current Version

> For the purpose of attacking the credibility of a witness, (1) evidence that a witness other than an accused has been convicted of a crime shall be admitted subject to Rule 403, if the crime was punishable by death or imprisonment in excess of one year under the law under which the witness was convicted, and evidence that an accused has been convicted of such a crime shall be admitted if the court determines that the probative value of admitting this evidence outweighs its prejudicial effect to the accused; and (2) evidence that any witness has been convicted of a crime shall be

admitted if it involved dishonesty or false statement, regardless of the punishment.

Compare the current Federal Evidence Rule 609(a) with the following state rules:

Alaska 609(a)

(a) General rule. For the purpose of attacking the credibility of a witness, evidence that he has been convicted of a crime is only admissible if the crime involved dishonesty or false statement.

Montana 609

For the purpose of attacking the credibility of a witness, evidence that the witness has been convicted of a crime is not admissible.

Compare the Federal Rules of Evidence with the following state laws on impeachment:

N.Y. CPLR § 4514

In addition to impeachment in the manner permitted by common law, any party may introduce proof that any witness has made a prior statement inconsistent with his testimony if the statement was made in a writing subscribed by him or was made under oath.

Indiana Code Chapter 34-45-4-2

When a witness, whether a party to the record or not, is cross examined to lay the foundation for his impeachment by proof of an act or statement inconsistent with his testimony, and is asked if he did not do the act or make the statement, and he answers that he does not recollect having done the act or made the statement, the party thus laying the foundation for impeachment shall have the right to introduce evidence of the act or statement in the same manner as if the witness had answered that he had not done the act or made the statement.

Hawaii Chapter 626, Rule 609.1

(a) General rule. The credibility of a witness may be attacked by evidence of bias, interest, or motive.

(b) Extrinsic evidence of bias, interest, or motive. Extrinsic evidence of a witness' bias, interest, or motive is not admissible unless, on cross-examination, the matter is brought to the attention of the witness and the witness is afforded an opportunity to explain or deny the matter.

§ 7.05 SUMMARY AND REVIEW

1. Compare impeachment evidence and character evidence. What are the major differences? What are the major similarities?

2. How are prior inconsistent statements a form of contradiction?

3. Why is extrinsic impeachment more restrictive than intrinsic impeachment?

4. Define "bias."

5. What types of crimes may be used to impeach a witness?

6. Why are the permissible forms of impeachment by conviction limited to felonies and crimes of dishonesty or false statement?

7. Why did the Federal Rules of Evidence adopt a special "prejudice" balancing test for the use of felony convictions to impeach a criminal defendant?

8. What types of acts are permissible in "prior bad acts" impeachment? Why?

9. What is impeachment by omission?

10. What are the permissible ways to refresh a witness' memory?

§ 7.06 CHAPTER REVIEW PROBLEMS

Review Problem 7-A

Accountant Zakkiah Jones was arrested for driving under the influence of alcohol one dark night on the main road of her Pennsylvania town. Jones testified in a subsequent trial, stating she made a left turn onto Main Street from 3rd Avenue prior to being stopped. The prosecutor did not ask her any questions on cross-examination about how she ended up on Main Street, but called Officer Lemke in rebuttal. Lemke testified, "After she was stopped, Ms. Jones told me she turned onto Main Street from 4th Avenue." *Which of the following statements about the Officer's testimony is the most accurate?*

1. It is admissible as prior inconsistent statement impeachment, so long as the two statements were inconsistent.

2. It is admissible as prior inconsistent statement impeachment if the prior statement had been made under oath.

3. It is not admissible as prior inconsistent statement impeachment because the statement's probative value is substantially outweighed by its danger of unfair prejudice.

4. It is not admissible as prior inconsistent statement impeachment because it is offered by Officer Lemke.

Review Problem 7-B

In a negligence action arising from an automobile accident, the plaintiff called an eyewitness, Sheila Scranton, to testify about what she observed on the pertinent morning at approximately 8 a.m. The witness testified that after leaving the International House of Pancakes, where she had breakfast, she almost immediately observed the accident. On cross-examination, Sheila is asked, "Isn't it true that you were eating that morning at the Original Pancake House and not at the International House of Pancakes?" *If there is an objection to this question, how should the judge rule?*

1. Allow the question because it is permissible impeachment by prior inconsistent statement.

2. Allow the question because it contradicts Sheila's testimony.

3. Disallow the question because it is collateral to the issues in the case.

4. Disallow the question because it is confusing and unfairly prejudicial.

Review Problem 7-C

Allan Jackson is charged with larceny. At trial, he takes the witness stand to deny committing the crime. On cross-examination, the prosecutor wishes to ask him about a nine-year-old conviction for robbery, for which the defendant received probation. *Can the prosecutor use the conviction to impeach Jackson?*

1. Yes, since the conviction is less than 10 years old.

2. Yes, if the prejudicial impact does not substantially outweigh the conviction's probative value.

3. No, because the defendant did not serve any jail time on the conviction.

4. No, unless the judge determines that the probative value of the conviction outweighs its prejudicial impact on the defendant.

Review Problem 7-D

In a murder trial, a critical witness for the defense is the cashier at the convenience store where the killing took place. The cashier will testify that the police never asked him whether the defendant looked like the perpetrator and ignored his protests about arresting the defendant. In the prosecution's case-in-chief, a police officer is called to testify that he had previously arrested the cashier and at the time the cashier kept saying, "I hate cops; I hate cops." This testimony is:

1. Admissible to impeach the cashier based on bias.

2. Admissible to impeach the cashier based on prior bad untruthful acts.

3. Inadmissible to impeach the cashier because it occurred in the prosecution's case-in-chief.

4. Inadmissible to impeach the cashier because the impeachment is extrinsic, not intrinsic.

Chapter 8

LAY OPINION EVIDENCE

§ 8.01 CHAPTER CHECKLIST

1. Is the testimony sought "lay" or "expert"?
2. If the testimony involves "lay opinion," is the opinion:
   a. "rationally based" on the perception of the witness, and
   b. helpful to a clear understanding of the witness' testimony or the determination of a fact in issue?
   c. Does it express a "collective fact" or a "skilled lay observer's" opinion?

§ 8.02 RELEVANT FEDERAL RULES OF EVIDENCE

Rule 701. Opinion Testimony by Lay Witnesses

Rule 701. Opinion Testimony by Lay Witnesses

If a witness is not testifying as an expert, testimony in the form of an opinion is limited to one that is:

(a) rationally based on the witness's perception;

(b) helpful to clearly understanding the witness's testimony or to determining a fact in issue; and

(c) not based on scientific, technical, or other specialized knowledge within the scope of Rule 702.

§ 8.03 DISTINGUISHING BETWEEN LAY AND EXPERT TESTIMONY

[A] The Distinction

Expert testimony can serve many functions, but its distinctive quality is that it often involves opinions. For example, a physician might testify thus: "In my opinion, the plaintiff will never walk again." At least at common law, laypersons were generally prohibited from testifying to opinions. This prohibition flowed in part from an idea similar to that expressed in Rule 602 which, you may recall, bars a witness from testifying to a matter "unless evidence is introduced sufficient to support a finding that the witness has personal knowledge of the matter." "Personal knowledge" means that the witness obtained the information by using one of his or her senses: hearing, seeing, smelling, tasting, or feeling the object or event. Inferences or conclusions, a category that includes opinion, are, however, derived by the human power of reason rather than by observation. The role of witnesses is ordinarily to convey their observations, the jury's job to draw appropriate inferences therefrom.

Example

The following is a section of testimony in a rape case:

PROSECUTOR: What did you observe that night?

A: I saw George looking at Martha with lust in his eyes.

DEFENSE COUNSEL: Objection, improper lay opinion. The witness can know and recount only what he saw, heard, etc. He can't read minds, and he shouldn't be allowed to speculate on what my client was thinking or feeling that night.

JUDGE: Sustained.

The witness, let us say a neighbor, may have seen George using obscene gestures or heard George expressing sexual desire for Martha. Such observations might support the inference that George felt lust. But this section of questioning reveals no foundation showing an adequate basis of personal knowledge. Recounting the observations was seen, at least at common law, as the witness' role; drawing the inferences from those observations was the jury's role.

In the case of experts, however, common-law courts were less concerned about the witness' personal knowledge and about the proper division of responsibilities between witness and jury. The common law saw experts as having the ability to engage in the analysis of underlying data necessary to rendering opinions. The Federal Rules of Evidence retain the lay/expert distinction, but are more skeptical about drawing a sharp line between "fact" and "opinion." The rules also exhibit less concern than the common law about the division of labor between witness and factfinder. However, the approach of the Federal Rules to lay opinions has not radically changed modern practice. Thus, examination of common-law practice is still helpful. Nevertheless, the Rules are more receptive to lay opinion than was earlier law.

Before the Federal Rules approach is examined here in detail, however, it is still helpful to further clarify the meaning of the "personal knowledge" requirement of Rule 602 as an aspect of "conditional relevancy."

[B] Connection to Conditional Relevance

The Rule 602 requirement that evidence be "sufficient to support a finding" of personal knowledge is, according to that Rule's Advisory Committee Note, "in fact a specialized application of the provision of Rule 104(b) on conditional relevancy." Lay testimony is not considered relevant within the meaning of Rule 401, and is thus inadmissible under Rule 402, unless the proponent first offers a foundation showing of sufficient evidence for a reasonable jury to find by a preponderance of the evidence that the witness had personal knowledge of the events he or she relates. The *Huddleston* case, which is discussed in Chapter 5, imposes this preponderance standard of proof on all Rule 104(b) conditional relevancy questions.

Example

Q: (the first question posed to this witness) What happened at 2 p.m. on June 26, 2000, at Maple and Pine, Philadelphia, Pennsylvania?

OPPOSING COUNSEL: Objection, no foundation as to personal knowledge under Rule 602.

At this point, we do not even know whether the witness was at the intersection of Maple and Pine at 2 p.m. Consequently, we certainly don't know whether he was close enough to the relevant events (for example, an automobile accident) to see them. Perhaps he only heard about the accident from a friend, or perhaps he read about it in a newspaper or perhaps he was actually at the scene but did not arrive until after the accident, seeing only the wreckage. If he heard or read about the accident, he has personal knowledge only of what others said (which would raise hearsay problems); he has no personal knowledge of the accident itself. The witness' testimony is not admissible unless and until the proponent offers sufficient evidence of personal knowledge.

[C] When Laypersons Can Offer Opinions

[1] Rationally Based on Perceptions of Witness

Nevertheless, even laypersons are sometimes permitted to offer opinions. Rule 701 thus declares that a witness "not testifying as an expert" (i.e., a layperson) may testify in the form of opinions or inferences if, and only if, they are limited to those opinions or inferences that are "(a) rationally based on the witness's perception; [and] (b) helpful to clearly understanding the witness's testimony or to determining a fact in issue . . . ." This rule is generally understood as expressing a preference for more specific over more general description. It vests substantial discretion in the trial judge. Thus, lay opinions may be challenged as "unhelpful" when they are too general to be of use to the jury. Lay opinions may also be excluded when they are superfluous, because the inferences to be drawn are obvious from the witness' detailed testimony about the underlying perceptions. Thus, in the rape case example opening this chapter, it might be argued that a specific description of what George said about Martha or what he did in her presence is more helpful than the conclusory opinion that he "lusted" after her. But once his words and actions are concretely described, his lust or its absence should be clear, and there is no need for an opinion on that question.

The Advisory Committee Note to subdivision (a) of Rule 701 says that it merely expresses the "familiar requirement of first-hand knowledge or observation." That is, the opinion must be based on firsthand, personal knowledge, though the opinion itself is by definition an inference that goes beyond such knowledge. The word "rationally," however, can be interpreted as requiring the judge to decide whether the witness' firsthand knowledge is adequate to support the opinion.

Example

A witness has testified that he was 200 feet away from the scene of an auto accident, facing in the opposite direction. He heard squealing brakes and a loud crash. From these observations alone, he testifies that the defendant's car was traveling at 65 mph on a residential street when it entered the intersection. Absent any special training, the witness cannot so precisely determine the defendant car's speed merely from the sound of the crash, especially when the witness was then 200 feet away.

[2] Collective Facts

Subsection (b) of Rule 701 merely states a general rule that the lay opinion must be helpful to the factfinder. The trial judge must give that rule meaning in specific cases and has substantial discretion in making this judgment. The idea of helpfulness includes situations in which "you had to be there," that is, cases in which this witness' recounting of details alone cannot fully capture the reality of what happened. Only an opinion can help to convey the scene effectively. Opinions may also be helpful because they aid clear expression. Thus a witness' opinion that the defendant was "smiling" more clearly conveys what the witness saw than does the statement, "The left corner of his mouth upturned one-eighth of an inch." These sorts of concerns underlay the "collective facts doctrine." This doctrine arose at common law and is now used under the Federal Rules as one way to help guide the judge's discretion.

A "collective fact" is really a shorthand rendition of what the witness perceived. The event observed may involve so many details that what registers in the witness' mind is an overall impression more than specifics. That impression must be the sort of inference that laypersons commonly and reasonably draw. If expert testimony is instead needed to support the inference, the layperson may not draw it.

Example 1

PROSECUTOR: What, if anything, did you observe about the defendant's demeanor that night?

A: He was very drunk.

Many, probably most, judges would permit this answer as a collective fact. Laypersons describe others as drunk in ordinary life all the time, and we generally know and trust what they mean. However, some judges will push the lawyer to probe first whether the witness can instead describe the specific observations underlying the inference of drunkenness — that the defendant's breath smelled of alcohol, his eyes were red, his gait wobbly, etc. — on the theory that there is then no need for the opinion. If so, the witness can convey enough details and forbear from giving overall impressions. Other judges will insist that, without the details, there is no way for a jury to judge the accuracy of the witness' inference. They will, therefore, exclude the opinion if the witness cannot recount the details. Another group of judges favor, where possible, admitting both the details and the opinion on the theory that both are necessary to conveying an overall accurate impression. Similar disagreements and case-specific judgments will be found in all applications of the collective facts concept. In any event, the witness must, of course, have sufficient knowledge of supporting details to meet the requirement that the opinion be "rationally based on the perception of the witness." A fleeting glimpse of a person is not sufficient to support the opinion, "He was drunk."

Example 2

PROSECUTOR: From the odor you smelled on the defendant's breath, could you tell how many beers he had consumed that night?

DEFENSE COUNSEL: Objection; perhaps a specially trained expert can draw such a conclusion, but this witness cannot do so.

JUDGE: Sustained

[3] Skilled Lay Observers

Another useful concept, suggested by Professor Edward J. Imwinkelried, is that of the "skilled lay observer." The admissibility of a skilled lay observer's testimony turns not on whether most laypersons commonly could reasonably draw the inference. Rather, the question is whether this layperson has prior experience that enables laypersons with such experience reasonably to draw the proffered conclusion.

Example

John has seen George sign his name on checks on many hundreds of occasions. John may be qualified to testify that the signature on a particular check is George's, even though John did not personally see George sign that check. But a similar witness who had never seen George sign a check, or who had seen him do so only once, would not be able to opine that this particular signature was George's.

Skilled lay observer opinion lies in the borderland between lay and expert testimony, and courts may sometimes have to draw a fine line. But that line must be drawn, because an expert opinion must jump through more admissibility hoops than a lay opinion. Some counsel try to avoid those hoops by "the simple expedient of proffering an expert in lay witness clothing" (Rule 701 amendment, Advisory Committee Note). To obviate this "end run" around the expert witness rules, Rule 701 was amended by the addition of subsection (c). Subsection (c) provides that lay opinion testimony may not be "based on scientific, technical, or other specialized knowledge within the scope of Rule 702." The point of this amendment is to ensure that the admissibility of expert testimony is determined under the expert evidence rules — especially Rule 702 (which governs "scientific, technical, or other specialized knowledge") — and not the less stringent rules governing lay opinion.

Not all commentators embrace Professor Imwinkelried's "skilled lay observer" terminology (and the term does not itself appear in Rule 701). Nevertheless, it is clear that some lay opinion is permitted when the lay witness has experience or information not common to all laypersons but falling short of the "specialized knowledge" required of experts. Drawing the sometimes fine line between an informed layperson and a true "expert" is ultimately a policy question, even if this point is not always clearly made by the courts. If there is substantial reason to worry that an opinion may not be trustworthy, and if its flaws may not be readily recognizable by a jury, it may make sense to subject that testimony to the heightened scrutiny of the expert evidence rules.

[4] Some Caveats

A few caveats are in order. First, many common-law courts permitted lay opinion only when "necessary" to an understanding of the witness' testimony. The Rule 701 "helpfulness" test is more flexible and discretionary than the "necessity" concept.

Second, "fact" and "opinion" are not always clearly divisible; sometimes the distinction is a matter of degree. Ordinary folks speak all the time with less than absolute certainty, but neither in everyday life nor in the courtroom does that hesitation render their testimony opinion. For a witness to say, "I think the car was red," is to testify from personal knowledge rather than to offer an opinion.

Third, the common law flatly banned opinions on "ultimate issues," such as whether the crane operator was negligent or whether the killer acted in the heat of passion. Rule 704(a) abolishes this prohibition for both lay and expert testimony, except for a subcategory of expert opinion to be discussed in the next chapter. However, ultimate issue opinions may still be excluded if unhelpful under Rule 701 (lay opinions) or of no assistance to the factfinder under Rule 702 (expert opinions), or if prejudice and related concerns substantially outweigh their probative value under Rule 403.

Fourth, as our discussion above of the recent amendment to Rule 701 noted, the lay/expert opinion distinction has important consequences. To be more precise, the proper distinction is between lay and expert testimony, not between "laypersons" and "experts." The same witness might offer both lay observations based on personal knowledge and expert opinions. Thus, if a doctor explains that her patient's nose bled profusely, his eyelids were swollen, and he coughed repeatedly, the doctor is simply conveying observations based on her personal knowledge. Those observations could have been made by any layperson. But if the doctor says, "The patient had the flu," that is an expert opinion, not a lay opinion or a personal observation.

Some expert "observations," however, fuse personal knowledge and opinion. A doctor who describes a bone fracture based upon touch or diagnoses a bruise that is several days old by its appearance is applying expert knowledge to firsthand observation. The greater the extent to which an "observation" in fact involves an inference, the more likely that the observation will be labeled an opinion. Moreover, the greater the degree of specialized knowledge, skill, or experience required to have some confidence in an opinion, the more likely that the opinion will be viewed as an "expert" one. Whether someone offers a lay or an expert opinion is thus to some extent a case-by-case judgment. That judgment should be guided by the policy concerns underlying the expert evidence rules, to which we will turn in more detail in the next chapter. For now, it is useful simply to remember that courts often worry that juries will be confused by expert testimony, or that jurors will defer to the expert's authority without critically examining the bases of his or her opinions, or that they will be so in awe of the expert as to give the opinions more weight the they deserve. For these reasons, special evidence rules make it harder to admit expert opinions than lay opinions.

§ 8.04 PROBLEMS

Problem 8-1: High on Marijuana

Two automobiles collided at the corner of Third and Elm Streets, seriously injuring one of the drivers, Ronald Patterson. Patterson has sued the other driver, Gerald Rabinowitz, alleging that he caused the accident by negligently running a red light. Patterson's passenger, Jose Ramirez, testifies at trial that, immediately after the accident, Ramirez and Rabinowitz both left their cars and chatted. You are Patterson's attorney and want to call Ramirez to the stand to testify that Rabinowitz was obviously very high on marijuana at the time of the accident. You know from pre-trial discovery that Rabinowitz' defense will be that the light facing him was in fact green, and it was Patterson who ran the red light.

1. What is your theory of the relevance of Ramirez's testimony?

2. Is any portion of his testimony opinion, or does it all involve personal observation?

3. If any portion is opinion:

a. Is it lay or expert?

b. What questions would you ask to establish the foundation for admissibility of the opinion? Why?

c. What cross-examination questions on voir dire do you anticipate from opposing counsel? Why?

Problem 8-2: More My Cousin Vinnie and Tire Marks

Vinnie Barbarino is a recent law school graduate. His cousin, Johnny Barbarino, allegedly shot and killed the cashier at a 7-Eleven during the course of a robbery. An eyewitness has testified that he saw Johnny and his cohort, Merv Griffin, fleeing from the robbery in a 1967 green Camaro. Johnny was in fact stopped while driving such a car 10 minutes after the killing. At that time he admitted to the police that he had purchased something at the 7-Eleven 10 to 15 minutes before being stopped. The police examination at the 7-Eleven shows tire tracks leaving the scene. The prosecution expert has testified that these tracks were consistent with those that would be left by the sorts of tires that can be used on 1967 Camaros. Vinnie calls to the stand his girlfriend, Fran Chabowski, to offer the opinion that the tire impressions in the police photographs at the 7-Eleven could not have been made by a 1967 Camaro, both because the impressions left were more like those of a heavier car and because the tire marks had unusual curlicues found only on tires used exclusively on 1967 Buick Le Sabres. Vinnie seeks as follows to qualify Ms. Chabowski to offer this opinion:

DEFENSE COUNSEL: Ms. Chabowski, what do you do for a living?

A: I am a hairdresser.

DEFENSE COUNSEL: And what do your father and brother do for a living?

PROSECUTOR: Objection, Your Honor. Irrelevant.

DEFENSE COUNSEL: Your Honor, the relevance will soon be clear.

JUDGE: It had better be, Mr. Barbarino. Proceed.

DEFENSE COUNSEL: So what do your father and brother do for a living?

A: They run their own car repair business.

DEFENSE COUNSEL: Have you ever been involved in that business?

A: Yes, I worked there for twelve years.

DEFENSE COUNSEL: I am handing you a photograph marked P-1. Could those tire marks in the photo have been made by a 1967 Camaro?

PROSECUTOR: Objection, inadequate foundation.

JUDGE: Objection sustained.

1. Was the opinion that Vinnie sought to elicit "lay" or "expert"? Would your answer change if Ms. Chabowski had never worked for an auto repair shop but instead was simply a car buff, who read extensively on auto design and repair and spent all her free time for the past decade repairing and restoring classic cars, including 1967 Camaros and LeSabres?

2. Was the prosecution's objection precise enough? How could you have more precisely and convincingly stated that objection?

3. What questions should Vinnie have asked to improve the chances that the foundation laid would be found adequate to justify admitting the opinion? Why?

4. If, instead of sustaining the objection, the trial judge first permitted cross-examination by the prosecutor on voir dire, what questions should the prosecution ask? Why?

5. Should the questions in 3 and 4 above be asked within, or outside of, the jury's hearing? Why?

Problem 8-3: The Stolen Ring

Drew Gavel is charged with felony theft of a diamond ring from a jeweler. For the offense to be a felony, rather than a mere misdemeanor, the fair market value of the ring must be more than $5,000. Officer John Kelly is called to the stand by the prosecution to testify that the ring stolen by Gavel has a fair market value of at least $7,000. The bases for Officer Kelly's opinion are that: (1) he had recently comparison-shopped at more than 20 jewelry stores for an engagement ring for his fianc'ee; (2) he had also for the last three months read extensively on the quality and pricing of diamond rings, relying largely on Internet searches for information; and (3) he had purchased, during the very week of the theft, an engagement ring identical to the one stolen by Gavel for $7,000 — which was the lowest price he could find anywhere for that kind of ring. The defense objects.

1. What ruling and why?

2. Would another sort of witness have been a better choice? Who? Why?

3. What if the fair market value of a single-family home had instead been at issue? Of recently released Rolling Stones CDs? Of grocery store items? Which, if any, of these items are suitable for lay opinion testimony? Expert opinion? Who would you call to the stand? What foundation would you lay?

Problem 8-4: The Wound

Dr. Richard Speck has been sued for negligently treating Arnold Paslitz's ankle wound, by prescribing only an antiseptic and a Band-Aid. The wound turned out to be the bite of a poisonous brown recluse spider. It developed an infection common in such bites but left so long untreated that permanent physical damage was done to the ankle. Paslitz maintains that he delayed seeking treatment solely because of Speck's advice that there was nothing to worry about that a Band-Aid and a little Bactine couldn't cure. Paslitz calls his wife, Patricia, to testify about her observations of the wound that ultimately led her to urge her husband to go to the emergency room. She is a securities lawyer with no medical training. The following exchange took place at trial as she was being questioned by Paslitz's counsel:

PLAINTIFF'S ATTORNEY: Please describe the wound, as you observed it on that day.

A: Its appearance was very unusual. There was a round two-inch hole on Arnold's ankle. Green pus oozed out of the hole. A half-inch ring of what looked like charred black flesh surrounded the hole. A bright red, swollen, tender-looking circle, about two inches in thickness and elevated, like a little volcano, surrounded the charred-looking area. Every part of the wound was sensitive to touch, causing great pain. The wound was hot to the touch, as was Arnold's whole ankle and foot. The foot was itself a bright red, hugely swollen, and sensitive to touch.

DEFENDANT'S ATTORNEY: Objection. Move to strike.

[In a real trial, the objection likely would have preceded the answer, at which point Paslitz's counsel may have made an offer of proof outside the jury's hearing (perhaps at sidebar), to aid the trial judge in her ruling.]

1. What ruling? Why?

2. Are some parts of the answer more objectionable than others? Which portions of the answer should be deleted to increase the likelihood of the testimony's being admitted without sacrificing too much tactical gain for Paslitz? How should the witness be prepared to articulate her answer most effectively given the

requirements of the rules of evidence? To deal with objections that are sustained?

3. What if the witness' answer had simply been, "The wound was the grossest I've ever seen — sore, swollen, oozing pus, green, and ugly. Arnold was in pain and scared." *Does any or all of this answer in any way alter your analysis? What portions, if any, of this answer are opinion? Could the witness be prepared to answer in a way that seems more like a recitation of fact than opinion?*

Problem 8-5: The Insanity Defense

Wolin Yerguson boarded a Long Island Railroad rush hour train and pulled out a gun, screaming, "You evil haters must die and save us all!" He then indiscriminately shot 20 passengers, one by one, killing five of them and seriously wounding the rest. He mumbled throughout this episode; the other passengers were able to make out only a word or phrase here and there. His bloodshot eyes kept whirling in circles, never making contact with his victim's eyes. As he fired his last bullet, he screamed, "This will appease the dragon."

1. One of the passengers was asked by Yerguson's lawyer on cross-examination at trial, "Did he appear sane during this incident?" The prosecution objects. What ruling? Why?

2. Would your answer change if Yerguson's brother, with whom Yerguson is quite close, were asked that same question about his observations of Yerguson at the police station one-half hour after the crime? The two brothers had spent an hour together at the police station before Yerguson was questioned by the police. Why?

Problem 8-6: The Plane Crash

A small plane crashed onto a busy highway, injuring the passengers of the plane and the occupants of two cars. Anna was an eyewitness. At trial, Anna testified on direct examination.

PLAINTIFF'S ATTORNEY: Anna, in your opinion, how fast was the car traveling when it was hit by the plane?

DEFENDANT'S ATTORNEY: Objection.

JUDGE: (*How should the judge rule? Why?*)

The examination continues:

PLAINTIFF'S ATTORNEY: Anna, how fast was the plane traveling just before it collided with the car?

DEFENDANT'S ATTORNEY: Objection.

JUDGE: (*How should the judge rule? Why?*)

The examination switches gears:

PLAINTIFF'S ATTORNEY: After the plane touched down, you testified that the pilot wobbled out of the craft. Can you describe the pilot?

A: (1) First, I saw him stumble.

A: (2) It smelled like he had been drinking some sort of alcohol.

A: (3) I'd estimate he was about six feet, two inches tall, and 195 pounds.

A: (4) He looked like he'd been without sleep for a while; he appeared disoriented.

A: (5) By the way he carried himself, it also appeared as if he had a very large ego; I can usually tell these things right off the bat.

Which of the above five statements, if any, are proper lay opinions? Explain your conclusions.

Problem 8-7: The Wink

Detective Kim Gorel was testifying in a homicide trial about her interview with the defendant, Ken. The defense had claimed mistaken identity in its opening statement.

PROSECUTOR: What happened when you were talking with the defendant?

A: The defendant said, "It's a shame that a person was killed," and then he winked at me.

DEFENSE COUNSEL: Objection! Improper opinion.

JUDGE: (*How should the judge rule? Why?*)

The questioning continues

PROSECUTOR: What do you mean by, "he winked"?

A: He raised his left eyebrow and then quickly closed and opened that same eye.

PROSECUTOR: What did you take that to mean?

DEFENSE COUNSEL: Objection. Calls for speculation.

JUDGE: (*How should the judge rule? Why?*)

The prosecution calls a second witness, Al, to testify. It had already been established that a bottle of Kouros cologne was found in the knapsack the defendant was carrying at the time he was arrested.

PROSECUTOR: What did you observe at 9:40 p.m. in the alley adjacent to John's street?

A: I saw a man raise up a knife and stab another person. Then he ran quickly by me.

PROSECUTOR: What did you observe when he ran by you?

A: Actually, I was so startled and the shadows were so thick, I did not see his face. But I can tell you this, the guy was wearing Kouros cologne.

DEFENSE COUNSEL: Objection! Improper opinion.

How would you rule on this objection if you were the judge and why? How could the prosecutor have done a better job?

Chapter 9

EXPERT OPINION EVIDENCE

§ 9.01 CHAPTER CHECKLIST

1. What are the major and minor premises of the "expert syllogism"?

2. To what relevant issues does any proffered expert testimony relate?

3. If the opinion testimony is "expert," is the expert "qualified" by knowledge, skill, experience, training, or education to testify in the form of an opinion or otherwise?

4. If the expert is so qualified, does the expert's testimony involve: (a) scientific knowledge; (b) technical knowledge; or (c) other specialized knowledge? Does this matter?

5. Is the expert basing an opinion on:

    a. a hypothetical question?

    b. observations personally made by the expert in the courtroom?

    c. observations personally made by the expert outside of the courtroom?

    d. information provided to the expert prior to trial?

6. Does the expert offer his or her opinion to a "reasonable degree of professional certainty?" Does this matter?

7. What is the likely impact of the expert's opinion on the jury? For example, will the testimony "overawe" the jury or otherwise lead it to be unfairly prejudiced, misled, or likely to give the testimony undue weight?

8. Has the expert testified to an "ultimate issue" by stating an opinion or inference as to whether a criminal defendant did or did not have a mental state or condition constituting an element of a charged crime or defense?

9. As to the major premises of the expert syllogism, have the principles and methods (techniques) used by the expert been shown to be both relevant and "reliable," with reliability shown by weighing a wide range of pertinent factors, including:

    a. Whether the principles and techniques are testable and have been tested (that is, has a hypothesis been generated, and have adequate efforts been made to falsify that hypothesis, with no such falsification yet having been achieved)?

    b. Have the theory and technique been subjected to:

(1) peer review?

(2) publication?

c. What is the technique's known or potential error rate?

d. Has the principle or technique attained "widespread acceptance"?

e. Are there standards controlling the technique's operation?

10. As to the minor premises of the expert-syllogism:

a. Has the witness reliably applied the general principles and methods to the facts of the specific case?

b. If the expert has based any portion of an opinion on otherwise inadmissible facts or data, are those facts or data of the type "reasonably relied upon" by other experts in the field?

11. Has cross-examination of the expert inquired into such matters as:

a. The non-existence of any particular basis on which the expert relied that might, if shown, alter the opinion?

b. The existence of contrary or additional bases that would alter the expert's opinion?

c. The materials the expert reviewed or failed to review?

d. The tests or other investigations the expert conducted or failed to conduct?

e. Any financial compensation the witness received for giving advice and testimony?

f. The contradiction between his assertions and those by others in "learned treatises"? exception to the hearsay rule?

§ 9.02 RELEVANT FEDERAL RULES OF EVIDENCE

Rule 702. Testimony by Expert Witnesses

A witness who is qualified as an expert by knowledge, skill, experience, training, or education may testify in the form of an opinion or otherwise if:

(a) the expert's scientific, technical, or other specialized knowledge will help the trier of fact to understand the evidence or to determine a fact in issue;

(b) the testimony is based on sufficient facts or data;

(c) the testimony is the product of reliable principles and methods; and

(d) the expert has reliably applied the principles and methods to the facts of the case.

Rule 703. Bases of an Expert's Opinion Testimony

An expert may base an opinion on facts or data in the case that the expert has been made aware of or personally observed. If experts in the particular field would reasonably rely on those kinds of facts or data in forming an opinion on the subject, they need not be admissible for the opinion to be admitted. But if the facts or data would otherwise be inadmissible, the proponent of the opinion may disclose them to the jury only if their probative value in helping the jury evaluate the opinion substantially outweighs their prejudicial effect.

Rule 704. Opinion on an Ultimate Issue

(a) IN GENERAL — NOT AUTOMATICALLY OBJECTIONABLE. An opinion is not objectionable just because it embraces an ultimate issue.

(b) EXCEPTION. In a criminal case, an expert witness must not state an opinion about whether the defendant did or did not have a mental state or condition that constitutes an element of the crime charged or of a defense. Those matters are for the trier of fact alone.

Rule 705. Disclosing the Facts or Data Underlying an Expert's Opinion

Unless the court orders otherwise, an expert may state an opinion — and give the reasons for it — without first testifying to the underlying facts or data. But the expert may be required to disclose those facts or data on cross-examination.

Rule 706. Court-Appointed Expert Witnesses

(a) APPOINTMENT PROCESS. On a party's motion or on its own, the court may order the parties to show cause why expert witnesses should not be appointed and may ask the parties to submit nominations. The court may appoint any expert that the parties agree on and any of its own choosing. But the court may only appoint someone who consents to act.

(b) EXPERT'S ROLE. The court must inform the expert of the expert's duties. The court may do so in writing and have a copy filed with the clerk or may do so orally at a conference in which the parties have an opportunity to participate. The expert:

(1) must advise the parties of any findings the expert makes;

(2) may be deposed by any party;

(3) may be called to testify by the court or any party; and

(4) may be cross-examined by any party, including the party that called the expert.

(c) COMPENSATION. The expert is entitled to a reasonable compensation, as set by the court. The compensation is payable as follows:

(1) in a criminal case or in a civil case involving just compensation under the Fifth Amendment, from any funds that are provided by law; and

(2) in any other civil case, by the parties in the proportion and at the time that the court directs — and the compensation is then charged like other costs.

(d) DISCLOSING THE APPOINTMENT TO THE JURY. The court may authorize disclosure to the jury that the court appointed the expert.

(e) PARTIES' CHOICE OF THEIR OWN EXPERTS. This rule does not limit a party in calling its own experts.

§ 9.03 NATURE OF EXPERT TESTIMONY

[A] Why Experts Are Needed

Experts play an increasingly important role in both civil and criminal trials. In a medical malpractice case, for example, a professor specializing in heart surgery might testify that a defendant doctor botched a surgical procedure. In a civil antitrust case, an expert might opine that Microsoft has attained overwhelming domination of the market for computer operating systems. In a criminal case, an expert might discuss his view that O.J. Simpson's blood and the blood at the crime scene of his ex-wife's murderer show matching DNA. In each instance, a party maintains that a full, fair, and informed jury decision requires expert guidance. Without such guidance, the proponents of the expert testimony argue, the jury cannot understand why the surgeon fell short, Microsoft rules, and O.J. murdered.

Inferences necessary to courtroom arguments are based on generalizations. For example, a prosecutor argues in a homicide trial that a married woman's male lover killed the woman's husband in a jealous rage. This argument is based on the generalizations that: (1) men in love with married women are jealous of the women's husbands, and (2) jealous men are more likely than other men to kill the person who inspires the jealousy. Generalizations like these are within factfinders' common experience, so no supporting expert testimony is needed. But some generalizations are beyond everyday experience. Thus the generalization "Women suffering from battered women's syndrome may see danger in their husband or lover's behavior that is not apparent to most other observers" is not one that can be drawn from common events. The expert provides the experience that the lay factfinders lack.

We have, however, up until now spoken in each case of *an* expert but, in fact, many experts are sometimes needed to make a fairly specific point, as will shortly become clear. Furthermore, in addition to offering opinions, an expert may testify to the expert's own observations that underlie the opinions. For example, a psychiatrist might testify that the defendant emitted a wolf-like howl, or a physical therapist might testify about seeing the injured plaintiff's pained grimace. Similarly, experts might recount observations that they made in court, such as a linguist noting aspects of a defendant's speech while the defendant was testifying at trial, then matching that speech to an obscene phone caller's tape-recorded voice.

[B] The Syllogistic Nature of Expert Reasoning

To understand who may qualify as an expert, how they may testify, and what they might say, it is helpful to examine the syllogistic nature of expert testimony. *See* Edward J. Imwinkelried, *The Educational Significance of the Syllogistic Structure of Expert Testimony*, 87 Nw.U. L. Rev. 1148 (1993). A syllogism is a form of argument consisting of a major premise (a general statement), a minor premise (a more specific statement), and a conclusion that must necessarily be true if the premises are true. For example:

Major Premise: All dogs have teeth.

Minor Premise: Lassie is a dog.

Conclusion: Therefore, Lassie has teeth.

The major premise in this example involves a broad generalization: that all dogs have teeth. The minor premise involves an observation about one particular creature, Lassie, namely, that Lassie is a dog. If both premises are true, that is, if all dogs do indeed have teeth and if Lassie is a dog, then Lassie necessarily must have teeth. But we might easily disprove the major premise, perhaps by observing at least one dog who has no teeth — an observation easy to make in a kennel of geriatric canines. If all we can then say is that some dogs have teeth, then it does not necessarily follow that Lassie, a dog, has teeth (though it may nevertheless turn out that she does). Similarly, even if it were correct that all dogs have teeth, the minor premise might be proven false: Lassie might be a wolf instead of a dog. That assertion may itself require a separate expert opinion distinguishing between dogs and wolves. Expert testimony can be analyzed in a similar fashion.

Example

In the infamous criminal trial of O.J. Simpson for murdering his ex-wife, Nicole Brown Simpson, and her friend, Ronald Goldman, the prosecution argued that blood found at the crime scene was O.J.'s blood, thus making it highly likely that he was the killer. DNA testing revealed a match between O.J.'s blood and the blood of someone other than the two victims found at the crime scene. This evidence was used to support the claim that O.J.'s blood was at the scene. The implicit syllogism was as follows:

Major Premise 1: Each human has unique DNA.

Major Premise 2: DNA tests can accurately identify a match between a known person's DNA and that of an unknown offender at a crime scene.

Minor Premise: O.J.'s DNA matches that found in blood at the crime scene.

Conclusion: Therefore, O.J. was the killer.

Comment:

Note that this example uses two major premises, that is, two general statements. For the practical purposes of trial, there is no need to explore the technicalities of formal logic further. You should simply be aware that real arguments may have several general statements and several more specific ones. It is less important that you be able to label premises accurately as "major" or "minor" than that you understand that the argument must proceed from the most general statement to increasingly more specific ones.[1]

The syllogistic model of the form illustrated above greatly oversimplifies the true nature of the arguments involved. A DNA expert does not in fact testify that O.J.'s blood and crime scene blood are the same. Rather, the expert testifies that there is a certain "probability" of a match, which is a much more cautious statement than the flat assertion that there is indeed a match. Nevertheless, juries may use expert testimony in syllogistic fashion. Perhaps more importantly, the syllogistic model, while not 100% accurate, helpfully focuses our attention and trial planning on what a proponent must prove to prevail. Thus the probative value of DNA evidence requires the prosecution to prove something close to the general statements in major premises 1 and 2 above: that each human has unique DNA and that it is identifiable by testing. These are assertions that apply to any DNA. In addition, the prosecution must prove something close to the minor premise statement specific to *this case* before *this jury:* that O.J.'s unique DNA matches that in blood found at the crime scene. Moreover, the simplistic syllogism offered here can be expanded, or syllogisms can be placed within syllogisms, or other sorts of reasoning processes combined with the overall syllogism to improve its usefulness. For example, two other premises might be:

Major Premise: Any DNA testing must involve steps A through D done in a specified manner, to produce a high degree of confidence in the claimed existence of a match.

Minor Premise: The DNA testing of O.J. indeed involved steps A through D, done in the properly specified manner.

---

[1] The use of more than one major or minor premise might arguably violate certain principles of formal logic. *See* Ruggero J. Aldisert, Logic for Lawyers: A Guide to Clear Legal Thinking 146 (1989). That problem can be avoided by breaking up what is presented here in the form of a single syllogism into multiple shorter syllogisms involving only one major and one minor premise each. *Id.* Nevertheless, this quicker and more informal way of proceeding, using multiple major and minor premises in a single "syllogism," is useful for the practical purposes of trial preparation; more closely mimics the implicit reasoning processes of practicing lawyers; and has proven itself to be a valuable educational tool. *See, e.g.* T.R. van Geel, Understanding Supreme Court Opinions 44 (1991) (effectively using a similar method as a way to teach students to analyze United States Supreme Court opinions on constitutional law). Furthermore, some leading evidence scholars, without using the "syllogism" terminology, have used essentially the same method: a series of premises, moving from the most general to the most specific, that must be true to support an expert's conclusion. *See* David L. Faigman, et al., Modern Scientific Evidence: The Law and Science of Expert Testimony § 1-3.3.1, at 24–25 (1997). The "syllogism" terminology is used here for ease of reference and to emphasize the importance of identifying premises *and identifying proof* that each premise is true, since these concepts are well-illustrated in the language of syllogisms. It is the practical value of this approach as a teaching and trial preparation tool that matters more for the purpose at hand than do the complexities of formal logic, for this approach is unlikely to lead a student or practitioner into logical error. Furthermore, while there are ways to conceptualize the expert rules other than in terms of a syllogism, the syllogism offers clarity (without distortion) to what often seems, especially to students, like chaos. *See* Edward J. Imwinkelried, *Educational Significance of the Syllogistic Structure of Expert Testimony*, 87 Nw. U. L. Rev. 1148 (1993).

Conclusion: Therefore, we can have a high degree of confidence in the claimed match between the crime scene blood and O.J.'s blood. In the real case, the defense, of course, argued in part that the DNA testing concerning the blood in this case was flawed: steps were missing or were done in an improper manner, so there could be little confidence in the claimed match.

Problem 9-1: Radioactive Taggants

A federal office building was bombed in downtown Chicago, killing many, injuring many more, and reducing the building to rubble. The bomb used was apparently a homemade one, combining some fertilizer ingredients with fuel oil. But the detonating device contained commercially-produced materials, including a fuse. The fuse contained a radioactive taggant. A "taggant" is a radioactive molecule placed into the fuse as a tracking device. Its presence is designed to enable law enforcement to track the precise lot of fuses involved and thus to locate the store where this particular fuse was sold. That store's customer list then enables the FBI to link the fuse to a purchaser, who becomes a criminal suspect. Somewhat different taggants are used in each lot so that each lot of fuses has its own distinctive taggant "signature." However, sometimes one lot's taggants touch and thus "contaminate" another lot. This problem can arise at the retail level, where one lot sitting on a shelf may leave a residue that then affects another lot stored in the same location. Lab-testing errors also occasionally result in the misidentification of a particular taggant and thus of a particular lot. Moreover, undue exposure to direct sunlight sometimes causes a chemical reaction that skews lab results. Furthermore, although they are rare, the same radioactive isotopes used in these taggants sometimes appear in other natural or man-made substances in everyday use.

1. Richard McDear is on trial for planning the explosion. Write out the expert syllogism that must be proven if the prosecution seeks to introduce expert testimony linking McDear to the explosion as a purchaser of a fuse from a lot marked with a taggant found in fuse remnants at the bomb site.

2. What witnesses should the prosecution call to prove each of the major and minor premises? What sorts of questions should be asked of each witness?

3. What sorts of questions will the defense ask of each of these witnesses to challenge admissibility? What information might the defense seek in discovery and from whom?

Problem 9-2: Rape Trauma Syndrome

The term "rape trauma syndrome" (RTS) has many meanings, but is being used in Ethan Dogard's rape trial to mean a collection of post-rape symptoms often experienced by rape victims. These symptoms include depression, fear of men or of being alone, "flashbacks," difficulty concentrating, and a generalized sense of anxiety and guilt. Not all rape victims display these symptoms, and some victims display some symptoms but not others. Some victims exhibit behaviors not listed in the RTS criteria or show no unusual symptoms of any kind. Moreover, some women who have not been raped may also display some or all the RTS symptoms.

Dogard's defense is consent. He calls an expert psychologist to the stand who, pursuant to court order, examined Dogard's alleged victim. The psychologist will opine that the victim displayed none of the symptoms of RTS. Dogard's lawyer will argue that this conclusion shows that the victim engaged in consensual, unforced sexual intercourse and was, therefore, not raped.

1. Write out the expert syllogism that Dogard's counsel must prove to get this psychologist's opinion admitted into evidence at trial.

2. What witnesses should the defense call to the stand to prove each of the major and minor premises? What sorts of questions should be asked of each witness?

3. What course of action should the prosecution take to combat the admission of the expert's testimony and why?

[C] Why Special Expert Admissibility Rules Are Needed

Courts and legislators have long feared jurors' reactions to expert testimony. Juries are thought to be so "overawed" by experts that they will defer to the expert's opinions and abandon their obligation as jurors independently to judge the strength and credibility of the evidence for themselves. Alternatively, courts and scholars have feared the "battle of the experts" in which two experts, one representing each side in a dispute, offer diametrically opposite opinions. In such cases, argue critics, unsophisticated jurors will simply accept the word of the clearer, flashier, more likable expert rather than the one with the soundest bases for the opinion. The concern is that these aspects of trial theater, rather than reason, will lead jurors to follow a misleading or baseless opinion. Accordingly, the rules of evidence have long required expert opinions to pass special admissibility tests — tests raising higher hurdles than those facing lay witnesses. While the Federal Rules of Evidence liberalized, that is, relaxed, some of these tests, the tests for experts were always, and still are, more stringent than those facing lay witnesses. Moreover, media stories of enormous civil verdicts based on "junk science" (alleged science with few adequate bases) have led to court interpretations of existing expert evidence rules, or legislative modification of those rules, in the direction of greater stringency.

Problem 9-3: Taggants Revisited

Review the facts of *Problem 9-1*. *Is expert testimony in that problem likely to raise any of the policy concerns that justify more stringent admissibility rules for admitting expert testimony as compared to lay testimony? Are there ways to address these concerns other than excluding the testimony?*

Problem 9-4: Rape Trauma Syndrome Revisited

Review the facts of *Problem 9-2*. *Is expert testimony in that problem likely to raise any of the policy concerns that justify more stringent admissibility rules for admitting expert testimony as compared to lay testimony? Are there ways to address these concerns other than excluding the testimony? Is the case for admissibility of RTS stronger or weaker than the case for admitting expert taggants evidence in Problem 9-1?*

§ 9.04 PRESENTATION OF EXPERT TESTIMONY

[A] Rule 702 — Helpfulness of Expert Opinion and Qualifications of Expert

Expert testimony is addressed specifically by Federal Rules of Evidence 702, 703, 704, and 705. The first of these rules that we will explore is Rule 702, which originally read as follows:

Rule 702. Testimony by Experts

> If scientific, technical, or other specialized knowledge will assist the trier of fact to understand the evidence or to determine a fact in issue, a witness qualified as an expert by knowledge, skill, experience, training, or education may testify thereto in the form of an opinion or otherwise.

Rule 702 was later amended to add the following proviso to the end of the rule:

> provided that (1) the testimony is based upon sufficient facts or data, (2) the testimony is the product of reliable principles and methods, and (3) the witness has applied the principles and methods reliably to the facts of the case.

The reasons for this addition to Rule 702 will be explored later in this chapter. For now, the interesting point is that the modification had the effect of more clearly codifying the syllogistic approach to expert evidence questions outlined here. Provision (2)'s reference to "reliable principles and methods" concerns the major premises, for example, that each human being has unique fingerprints and that a method exists for accurately identifying those unique fingerprints. Provision (3) concerns the minor premises, e.g., that fingerprints were properly taken from a specific suspect and crime scene and that the method for accurately matching that suspect's prints to those at the scene was properly applied in the case before the court. Provision (1) is ambiguous; it may apply to both the major and minor premises or instead only to the latter, a matter we will address shortly. We pay significant attention to this amendment because it helps to clarify many issues of expert evidence. Having established that special admissibility rules are needed for expert testimony, we now examine in greater detail what those rules are and what they mean. This section looks at when it is appropriate to admit expert testimony, when an expert is qualified to offer expert evidence, and the proper manner for presenting expert testimony. These subjects lay the groundwork for the rest of the chapter, which examines when a qualified expert's opinion should be seen as based on solid general principles properly applied to the case at hand.

The current version of Rule 702 is substantively identical to these earlier versions but was amended to read in a fashion closer to "plain language." The current version of the Rule in its entirety reads as follows:

Rule 702. Testimony by Expert Witnesses

A witness who is qualified as an expert by knowledge, skill, experience, training, or education may testify in the form of an opinion or otherwise if:

(a) the expert's scientific, technical, or other specialized knowledge will help the trier of fact to understand the evidence or to determine a fact in issue;

(b) the testimony is based on sufficient facts or data;

(c) the testimony is the product of reliable principles and methods; and

(d) the expert has reliably applied the principles and methods to the facts of the case.

We earlier discussed the distinction between "lay" and "expert" testimony. We must return to that distinction here because an expert must be qualified to offer an opinion on the particular subject concerning which the expert's opinion is being sought. A person who is an expert on some things may be a mere layperson on others. Expert opinion should be limited to those matters about which the witness has adequate *expert* qualifications.

Example 1

Dr. Joseph Lewis, a skilled heart surgeon, is called to testify in a medical malpractice trial that another heart surgeon, Dr. Jesse Smith, improperly performed an angioplasty (insertion of a small tube to open up a blocked artery feeding the heart). Dr. Lewis would arguably be qualified to offer such an expert opinion. Suppose, however, that, instead of testifying about heart surgery, Dr. Lewis were called to testify in a dental malpractice trial that Dr. Bright, a dentist, had offered inadequate dental care. In that case, Dr. Lewis' opinion, as a heart surgeon, would be little more informed about dental care than a layperson's; it would be inadmissible.

What if Dr. Shine, a renowned dentist, were called to the stand at Dr. Bright's trial for dental malpractice, to opine that Bright's patient, Harvey Bateson, was in great pain for many days after being treated by Dr. Bright? Is Shine any more qualified than Bateson himself, or perhaps Bateson's wife or employer, to offer the opinion that Bateson was in pain?

The answer to this last question shows a close link between what *qualifications* are required for a person to be eligible to testify as an expert and what *topics of inquiry* are appropriate for an expert opinion. Some common-law cases have said that the only proper topics of inquiry of an expert are those "beyond the ken of laypersons." However, this means that experts must have *qualifications* enabling them to offer opinions on matters that laypersons (including jurors drawing their own inferences) could not. Of course, on the question of dental patient pain, it might be argued that no opinion is necessary at all, lay or expert. Any witness-observer might describe Bateson's grimaces, tears, and screams, from which jurors could infer that Bateson was in pain. Moreover, if some opinion is needed, it should be "within the ken" of laypersons to offer and understand it.

If, however, Dr. Shine wanted to testify that he could tell the difference between faked and real pain, based on training unavailable to laypersons, that would indeed be a subject "beyond the ken" of laypersons. But Shine would have a hard time showing that he was specially qualified by "knowledge, skill, experience, training, or education" to offer such an opinion. Dentists, unlike polygraphers (lie detector technicians), do not get any special training on how to spot their patients' lies. (Of course, close examination of the underlying empirical research would be necessary to determine whether polygraphers' special training actually makes them any better than dentists at lie identification.) The Federal Rules of Evidence relax the common law "beyond the ken" requirement. All that is necessary is that the testimony will be helpful, that is, will "assist the trier of fact to understand the evidence or to determine a fact in issue." Under this standard, experts may testify about topics that concern matters within the general knowledge of jurors, if they have special qualifications such that their opinion will nevertheless aid the jury. The Advisory Committee Note explained the topics-of-inquiry (helpfulness) link to expert qualifications this way:[2]

> There is no more certain test for determining when experts may be used than the common sense inquiry whether the untrained layman would be qualified to determine intelligently and to the best possible degree the particular issue without enlightenment from those having a specialized understanding of the subject involved in the dispute.

Note that the Advisory Committee Note expressly links "when experts may be used" (What are the proper *topics* of expert testimony?) with whether the expert is one of "those having a specialized understanding of the subject involved in the dispute" (Is the expert "qualified"?). Furthermore, the Note stresses that qualifications and topic-appropriateness must be measured as to "the particular issue" about which the expert will testify. The expert need not, however, refer only to matters "beyond the layman's ken" but rather may address any topic that enables the jury to determine an issue to "the best possible degree" by hearing from the expert. Perhaps the existence of dental pain is within lay experience. But an expert's opinion that a particular patient was in more pain than the vast majority of other patients whom the expert dentist treated in his long career might nevertheless allow the jury to make a more accurate and informed judgment.

Example 2

Jolinda offers the testimony of an expert on battered women's syndrome, who will testify that: (a) some battered women display a fear of great harm from their abusers in situations where danger may not be apparent to non-battered third parties; (b) these women see no safe way to escape when others might; and (c) Jolinda suffered from BWS, and was fearful that her husband would kill her.

---

[2] Rule 702, Advisory Committee Note, quoting Ladd, *Expert Testimony*, 5 Vand. L. Rev. 414, 418 (1952).

Comment:

A common-law court might hold that fear of assault and inter-spousal disagreements are within the "ken" of ordinary laypersons. Under the Federal Rules of Evidence, by contrast, a court might concede that fact but nevertheless admit the evidence after concluding that it would be helpful for jurors to learn of the experiences and behaviors of other battered women. With that information, they could more effectively judge Jolinda's credibility and, if finding her truthful, better see the world through her eyes.

The syllogistic nature of expert testimony must also be kept in mind in judging an expert's qualifications, as in the following example.

Example 3

John O'Barr, the President of a major university, is being charged with making obscene phone calls. One of his victims has tape-recorded all his phone calls. Pursuant to a court order, O'Barr has tape-recorded himself reciting a specified script. The prosecution wants to offer a voice-print analysis to prove that the voice on the tape of the obscene phone caller matches O'Barr's voice. The term "voice-print" is commonly used to refer to a spectrogram, which is a visual representation of a human voice's qualities.

The prosecution calls Ronald Nelson, a police officer spectrogram technician, to the stand as the prosecution's sole expert witness. Nelson has a high school degree and has attended five training sessions on how to administer spectrograms. He has administered more than 50 voice spectrograms over the course of 10 years; in each case he testified as a voice spectrogram expert at a criminal trial. O'Barr's counsel objects on the ground that Nelson is not adequately qualified to establish the foundation necessary for his expert opinion.

The trial court should sustain the objection. The implicit syllogism is as follows:

Major Premise 1: Each human has a unique voice.

Major Premise 2: The voice spectrogram analyzer is a device that accurately records each person's voice's features and correctly represents those features in a written diagram.

Major Premise 3: Voice spectrogram analyzer accuracy depends on the technician's following certain specified procedures.

Minor Premise: Those procedures were accurately followed in matching O'Barr's voice tape to the obscene phone caller's voice tape.

Conclusion: O'Barr made the obscene phone calls.

Comment:

Police Officer Nelson is definitely qualified to testify concerning the minor premise, that is, to describe what procedures he followed in doing spectrographic analysis. He is probably qualified to testify as to Major Premise 3, that is, to explain what are the proper procedures. But he is not qualified to testify concerning the first two major premises. Only a scientist, preferably an academic who has done research in, or is at least familiar with, voice spectrographic analysis or voice identification more generally would be qualified to testify that each human voice is unique and that the principles and methods involved in the voice spectrograph make it a reliable way of identifying otherwise unknown speakers. Thus, the prosecution can cure Nelson's qualification problem by limiting his testimony to Major Premise 3 and the Minor Premise and calling an unbiased but well-credentialed scientist to the stand to testify concerning the first two major premises.

Some commentators have suggested that, in addition to an expert on general principles and methods (here, the scientist) and one on the proper application of those methods in a particular case (here, Officer Nelson), we also need an expert on how to interpret the results of that application. Thus, Nelson might arguably be qualified to testify that he followed proper procedures but lacks the combination of theoretical training and practical experience to interpret the resulting spectrograms, that is, to say, "Yes, these are from the same person." Three separate experts are not always necessary. A single witness, such as a voice identification scientific researcher with ample practical experience administering and interpreting spectrograms, might serve all three expert roles: as theorist, technician, and interpreter.

A lawyer seeking to establish, or to challenge, an expert's qualifications must explore issues such as the following: (1) the expert's formal education and degrees received, (2) the expert's specialized training in his or her field of expertise, (3) the time the expert has spent practicing in that field, (4) the expert's professional licenses, teaching experience, publications, and membership in professional organizations, and (4) previous testimony given by the expert. Pretrial discovery may well arm an advocate with knowledge about these aspects of the expert's qualifications, especially in civil cases, where depositions are more likely to be available.

Example 4

A portion of a sample voir dire qualifying an expert witness follows. This voir dire (as used here, the term means the questioning done to establish the foundation for admitting expert testimony as qualified) arises at a hearing to determine the competency of a criminal defendant to stand trial. The prosecution calls Dr. Susan Trautman Borg to the stand as an expert in the psychiatric diagnosis and treatment of mental illness.

PROSECUTOR: Good morning, Dr. Borg. Please state your full name for the record and spell it for the court reporter.

A: Susan Trautman Borg, M.D.

PROSECUTOR: What is your educational background?

A: I received my B.A. and M.D. degrees from Case Western Reserve University. After graduating, I did my internship and residency at Jackson Memorial Hospital in Miami. I had a post-doctoral fellowship in psychiatry at the National Institute of Mental Health in Washington, DC.

PROSECUTOR: Are you employed?

A: Yes, at the South Allenton State Psychiatric Facility.

PROSECUTOR: What is your job at South Allenton State?

A: I am the Director of Psychiatric Services.

PROSECUTOR: How long have you worked there?

A: I have been the Director for seven years. I began at South Allenton as the head resident, spent two years in that position, and then served as Associate Director for three years.

PROSECUTOR: How many patients have you treated for psychiatric illness in those seven years?

A: Based on the Diagnostic and Statistical Manual III-R, which is generally used by psychiatrists and psychologists, I'd say quite a few. Probably several hundred.

PROSECUTOR: What are your job responsibilities?

A: I currently handle a reduced caseload of approximately 10 to 15 patients along with my administrative duties. These duties involve overseeing a department of 20 psychologists, 10 social workers, and 75 other staff members.

PROSECUTOR: What does Board-certified in psychiatry mean?

A: Board certification exists in various medical specialties. In psychiatry, it means that the psychiatrist has passed an examination designed to ensure an advanced degree of knowledge in the field of psychiatry and has been approved by the American Board of Medical Specialties. To become Board-certified, a person must first become Board-eligible, which requires successfully completing several prerequisites, including an examination. Only a small percentage of psychiatrists are Board-certified.

PROSECUTOR: What is your board status, Doctor?

A: I am Board-certified.

PROSECUTOR: Doctor, to which, if any, professional organizations do you belong?

A: I belong to the American Psychiatric Association, where I am the immediate past president.

PROSECUTOR: Have you published any writings in your field?

A: I published the paper "Psychotropic Drugs: the Good, the Bad, and the Ugly," in the journal Nature in 1991, and have co-authored approximately 50 other pieces in a wide variety of journals. Co-authoring is the general practice of scholars in my medical specialty.

PROSECUTOR: Have you ever testified as an expert in psychiatry?

A: About 150 times, mostly for the prosecution, but sometimes for the defense.

PROSECUTOR: Have you continued your education in psychiatry?

A: Yes. I take three continuing education courses in psychiatry each year, as required, and teach at Allenton University as an adjunct. I also participate in as many educational colloquia as time permits.

PROSECUTOR: Your Honor, I now offer Dr. Borg as an expert in the diagnosis and treatment of mental illness.

To recap: (1) There is a close connection between what topics of inquiry are appropriate for expert advice and what qualifications must be demanded of the expert. Accordingly, a good lawyer first carefully specifies the precise opinions the expert will offer, why those opinions will help the jury, and why the expert has the qualifications to offer the specific opinion requested. (2) A good lawyer also understands the syllogistic nature of expert testimony. With this understanding, the lawyer is able to determine all the premises involved in proposed expert testimony and which experts are qualified to testify about the various premises in the syllogism-specifically, in the roles of theorist (educator), technician, and interpreter.

Problem 9-5: Bomb-Blast Terrorism

Assume the facts stated in Problem 9-1:

1. Who would you, as the prosecutor, call to the stand as an expert in the *McDear* case? Would you need more than one expert? Remember the roles of educator, technician, and interpreter and the syllogistic nature of expert testimony.

2. What questions would you ask the expert (or experts) to qualify him (her, or them)? Be ready to conduct the qualifying examination in class.

Problem 9-6: Rape and Consent

Assume the facts stated in Problem 9-2:

1. Who would you, as the defense counsel, call to the stand as an expert? Would you need more than one expert? Remember the roles of educator, technician, and interpreter and the syllogistic nature of expert testimony.

2. What questions would you ask the expert (or experts) to qualify him (her, or them)? Be ready to conduct the qualifying examination in class.

Problem 9-7: The Inaccurate Eyewitness

Dr. John La Rue is an academic psychologist specializing in the areas of the accuracy of human perception and memory. Jonathan Brill was robbed at gunpoint at an ATM machine at 10 p.m. during October. Mr. Brill gave a description of his assailant to the police that night. Approximately 72 hours later, Brill picked the defendant, Horace Weatherwax, out of a lineup, saying, "I'm certain that's the man. I'd never forget that face." The defense calls Dr. La Rue to the stand at Weatherwax's trial to discuss the factors that affect the accuracy of eyewitness identifications generally, what factors were present in this particular case and their significance, and to opine that Brill's identification of Weatherwax was not trustworthy.

Which of the following are relevant to qualifying (or disqualifying) Dr. La Rue as a witness:

1. He has published 17 articles on the impact of various traumas (war wounds, child abuse, and spousal abuse) on human perception and memory.

2. His Ph. D was in clinical psychology rather than experimental psychology.

3. He has never specifically done research on the accuracy of eyewitness identification.

4. He teaches, and has for the past 10 years taught, an undergraduate course on the accuracy of eyewitness identification.

5. He has extensively read the literature on eyewitness identification accuracy.

6. He published an article in *Psychology Today* on the accuracy of bystander eyewitness testimony, as distinguished from testimony by the victim.

7. He has testified concerning eyewitness accuracy in 50 cases, each time testifying for the defense.

8. He has provided psychotherapeutic counseling to Mick Jagger, Tom Cruise, and other well-known musicians and actors.

9. He received his degree from a little-known small-town night school.

10. He is president of the American Society of Forensic Psychologists.

If Dr. La Rue is offered as an expert witness and the prosecution asks to voir dire the witness, will the judge allow it? If so, what kinds of questions should the prosecution ask Dr. La Rue?

Problem 9-8: Dr. Borg

Review the illustrative voir dire of Dr. Borg in Example 4, *above. Even after this voir dire, are there plausible grounds for objection to her qualifications to offer an opinion regarding whether the criminal defendant (asserting an insanity defense) suffered from a particular mental disease or defect at the time of the crime and to explain the significance of that disease or defect? What sorts of additional questions on the voir dire by the prosecution could have reduced the chances of such objections? Why did the prosecutor ask each of the question that she did?*

[B] Direct Examination of Experts

[1] The Hypothetical Question and the Four Data Sources

There are four potential sources of data on which an expert may base an opinion:

1. Firsthand observations made by the expert out of court. For example, a dermatologist testifies about the color, shape, feel, and smell of a rash that

she observed on a patient's arm.

2. Information provided to an expert in the courtroom that the expert is asked to assume is accurate.

3. An expert's observation of in-court testimony by one or several witnesses.

Example 1

The issue in a negligent driving case in which the driver's passenger was seriously injured is whether the driver exceeded the 55 mph speed limit. A police officer who arrived on the scene shortly after the accident describes his observation of the length of skid marks and the extent and nature of the damage to the defendant's car. The emergency room physician describes the plaintiff's injuries. A physicist who has listened to the officer's and the physician's testimony is later asked whether, assuming the truth of that testimony, the physicist has an opinion about what speed the defendant's car was traveling at the time of the accident.

4. Facts or data made known to the expert out of court, such as a forensic internist opining about the reasons for a diagnosis, which include X-ray reports and lab tests done by other doctors and technicians that the expert examined prior to trial.

Traditionally, courts often required experts to base their opinions on facts or data that were already admitted into evidence, or at least facts that were admissible. Thus, data source category 4 (facts or data presented to the expert out of court) could not, in the strictest versions of the traditional rule, be the basis for expert opinion unless those facts or data were separately admitted into evidence. Usually (but courts differed on this point), they would have to be admitted *before* the experts could recite their opinions for the jury. For example, the X-ray report and results would first have to be admitted into evidence before the emergency room physician in the last example above could offer the patient's diagnosis. In less restrictive versions of the traditional rule, the X-ray and lab results would, if not already admitted, have at least to be admissible.

These traditional rules were not especially troublesome for data sources 1 and 3 (firsthand observations made by the expert either in or outside of court) because such observations are usually admissible (unless unduly prejudicial under Rule 403). In addition, observations can often be easily and concisely stated by the expert, who in this capacity serves more as an eyewitness (*e.g.* "He moaned in pain, had bruises across much of his calf, etc.," as recounted by an emergency-room physician treating an automobile accident victim). But data sources 2 and 4, we will soon see, more often require the expert to rely on evidence whose admissibility is questionable. Trial courts needed to police expert opinions as being based on evidence that had been admitted (or at least was admissible) in evidence. To ensure that an expert revealed the bases of an opinion before offering it, courts traditionally often required that the opinions be elicited by a hypothetical question — a question asking the expert to assume certain listed facts to be true and to offer an opinion based upon that assumption. Courts sometimes failed to distinguish among the four data sources, and required hypothetical questions involving any of the four sources.

The most common sort of hypothetical question expressly stated, often in list-like form, every fact that the expert was asked to assume to be true:

Example 2

Dr. Johnson, a well-known physician, is called as a knee injury expert in a case in which the plaintiff/accident-victim's knee was treated in an emergency room. Dr. Johnson did not himself observe the plaintiff's injuries, nor has he ever treated the plaintiff. The direct examination includes this hypothetical question:

PLAINTIFF'S ATTORNEY: Dr. Johnson, please assume the following facts are true: One, Johnny Bender [the plaintiff] groaned when trying to bend his right knee. Two, he bent that knee slowly, never achieving more than a 20-degree angle. Three, the knee was swollen, red, and puffy. Four, the knee was bleeding profusely. Doctor, given these assumptions, do you have an opinion, to a reasonable degree of medical certainty, as to the nature of Mr. Bender's knee injury?

For Dr. Johnson to be allowed to offer this opinion, another witness would have had to testify (or plaintiff would have had to promise to produce such a witness) that he or she observed the plaintiff's bloody, swollen, stiff knee as well as groans in the emergency room. The emergency-room physician or, if present, the plaintiff's spouse, might be able to offer such testimony. Of course, the emergency-room physician, rather than the high-priced Dr. Johnson, could also be queried about his diagnosis of the plaintiff. Many judges traditionally would have encouraged such queries also to be done in the form of a hypothetical question. Nevertheless, the plaintiff may still want to call the better-credentialed Dr. Johnson to the stand to buttress the emergency-room physician's opinion about the extent of the plaintiff's injuries.

An alternative form of the hypothetical question, rather than reciting every fact to be assumed by the expert, simply asks the expert to assume the truth of the previous testimony of a witness or witnesses that the expert has heard testify in court:

PLAINTIFF'S ATTORNEY: Dr. Johnson, assuming the truth of the observations testified to today by Mr. Bender's spouse and the emergency room physician, do you have an opinion regarding when, if ever, Mr. Johnson will recover full use of his knee?

Such an approach may be misleading or confusing, however, if the testimony is conflicting or complex. In such a case, a court might require use of the more detailed, specific version of the hypothetical question.

Problem 9-9: Bomb-Blast Terrorism Continued

Review Problem 9-1 again. List all the facts that you think would be important to an expert opinion linking the defendant to the bomb blast via the taggants. You may need to speculate about the sorts of facts the experts might recount. Use that list to craft a detailed version of a hypothetical question.

Problem 9-10: Rape and Consent Continued

Review Problem 9-2 again. List all the facts that you think would be important to an opinion that the alleged victim did not suffer from RTS. You may need to speculate about the sorts of facts the experts might recount. Use that list to craft a detailed version of a hypothetical question.

[2] Liberalization Under the Federal Rules of Evidence

[a] Rule 703

The hypothetical question was often strategically advantageous to counsel. Attorneys were able to use a hypothetical question as a mini-summation during the trial. Furthermore, credibility might be lent to an advocate's case by asking a well-respected expert to assume the truth of the advocate's witnesses.

But the hypothetical question had down sides as well. Some such questions had to be quite lengthy, which made them boring and lengthened the trial. Hypothetical questions could construct a misleading, one-sided hypothesis. And much courtroom time was consumed by attorneys arguing for and against the inclusion of various details in hypotheticals.

Moreover, they opened the door to reversals on appeal if an appellate court later concluded that some of the assumed facts were not supported by other evidence in the trial. Additionally, reciting the bases for an opinion before hearing the opinion itself may have left the jury confused, uncertain of why the data presented in the hypothetical was important.

For reasons like these, the Federal Rules of Evidence rejected the requirements that: (1) expert opinions must be based only on admitted, or at least admissible, evidence; (2) the data underlying the opinion must be revealed before presenting the opinion itself; and (3) the hypothetical question is the preferred mode of inquiry. Lawyers remain free, however, to adhere to traditional approaches where they believe it is strategically wise to do so.

The first of these three changes to traditional rules is contained in the beginning two sentences of Rule 703 as originally drafted:

> The facts or data upon which an expert bases an opinion or inference may be those received by, or made known to, an expert at or before the hearing. If of a type reasonably relied upon by experts in the particular field in forming opinions or inferences upon the subject, the facts or data need not be admissible in evidence in order for the opinion or inference to be admitted.

The provision that inadmissible evidence may be the basis for an opinion only if "reasonably relied upon" by experts in the particular field retains a hint of the traditional rules. First, some opinions still may not be based on inadmissible evidence, if the evidence is not "reasonably relied upon." Second, if an advocate is concerned about this limitation, it may be avoided by seeking opinions based only on admissible evidence. Thus, counsel may in close cases have an incentive to adhere to more traditional rules.

Why retain these shades of the traditional rules? The implicit answer: because these remnants help prevent misleading end runs around the purpose of the rules of evidence, which is "to secure fairness in administration . . . to the end that truth may be ascertained and proceedings justly determined." (Rule 102.) While not expressly relying on Rule 102, the Advisory Committee Note to Rule 703 gives this example of how 703's limitations promote truth-seeking: "The language [of reasonable reliance] would not warrant admitting in evidence the opinion of an 'accidentologist' as to the point of impact in an automobile collision based on statements of bystanders, because this requirement is not satisfied." If the bystanders do not testify and cannot, therefore, be cross-examined, and if no exception to the hearsay rules justifies admitting their statements as reliable ones, then the expert's opinion is based on data whose adequacy will never be challenged before the jury and that lacks other guarantees of trustworthiness. Presumably, evidence relied upon by an expert that is independently admissible has survived the gauntlet of the other evidence rules, thus creating some minimal guarantee of trustworthiness. But nothing in an "accidentologist's" training increases the accuracy of bystander statements otherwise barred by the hearsay rules. Before we can have confidence in the expert's opinion being based on worthy data, we therefore at least require that the data either be admissible or be "reasonably relied upon" by experts in the field. We will explore what "reasonable reliance" means in more depth later in this chapter. Briefly, it is reasonable to rely on data that most experts in a given field would rely upon (say some courts) or data that the trial judge independently considers trustworthy (say other courts).

Even if an expert "reasonably relies upon" inadmissible data, does that mean that the expert may reveal that data to the jury? If the answer is yes, again an end run might be possible around other rules of evidence. Thus an advocate might intentionally ask the expert to interview persons who will not be at trial to enable the advocate indirectly to reveal (via the expert) those persons' otherwise inadmissible hearsay statements. Yet some commentators have concluded that a new hearsay exception should be established for the data underlying an expert opinion that complies with Rule 703's reasonable reliance requirement. *See, e.g.*, Paul Rice, *Inadmissible Evidence as a Basis for Expert Opinion Testimony: A Response to Professor Carlson*, 40 Vand. L. Rev. 583 (1987). Other courts and commentators permit revelation of the reasonably relied upon but otherwise inadmissible bases of expert testimony only on a non-hearsay rationale. The jury is instructed that it may not consider these bases for the truth of what they assert. Rather, the jury is told that the bases are offered only so that the jurors know on what the expert relies, thus enabling jurors to judge the credibility of the expert's opinion. If the jury sees no reason to believe that such bases in fact exist, or concludes that there were other ignored bases that the expert should have considered, the jury may choose not to credit the expert's opinion. Juries will often, however, use the recited bases precisely for the prohibited purpose — to prove the truth of what they assert — despite a court's instructions to the contrary.

Example

A physician testifies, based partly upon lab test results, that a patient suffered from a certain type of infection. Assume that the lab report is inadmissible, perhaps because the records were not kept in the way expected in the ordinary course of business (which would violate hearsay rules to be studied later). May the physician nevertheless reveal the content of the lab report to the jury, so long as the lab report contains a "type" of fact or datum "reasonably relied upon by experts in the field"? The proponent of such disclosure will argue that jurors cannot evaluate the worth of the physician's opinion without knowing the contents of the lab report on which he relied. The jury can simply be instructed that it may not use the statements in the lab report for the truth of what they assert, only to assess the credibility of the expert's opinion. For example, was there thorough investigation by the expert? Does evidence other than the statements themselves suggest that they were right? The opponent of such revelation will argue that the jury will improperly use the lab report for the truth of what it asserts, and that such use would both violate hearsay rules and unfairly prejudice the opponent under Rule 403.

To reduce the incentive for attorneys to use experts as conduits for inadmissible hearsay, Rule 703 was amended and the following language added to the end:

Facts or data that are otherwise inadmissible shall not be disclosed to the jury by the proponent of the opinion or inference unless the court determines that their probative value in assisting the jury to evaluate the expert's opinion substantially outweighs their prejudicial effect.

This amendment emphasizes that the purpose of Rule 703 is to specify circumstances when an expert *opinion* or inference is admissible. It does not render the otherwise inadmissible bases for that expert opinion freely admissible as substantive evidence. Thus, Rule 703 does *not* create an exception to the hearsay rule. *See* Advisory Committee Note to 2000 amendment. Underlying bases may be revealed under the specified conditions, but "the trial judge must give a limiting instruction upon request, informing the jury that the underlying information must not be used for substantive purposes." *Id.* That is, the information is admitted only so that the jury can know the opinion's basis and thus better assess its credibility. But the amendment provides a "presumption against disclosure to the jury." *Id.* A significant burden is thus placed on the proponent to overcome that presumption. This balancing test should be contrasted with the test under Rule 403, which favors admissibility of relevant evidence by excluding it only if its probative value is substantially outweighed by unfair prejudice and related concerns. Rule 703 takes quite the opposite approach; it presumes that the inadmissible bases for expert opinion are unfairly prejudicial, but will admit those bases if their probative value in assisting the jury to evaluate the expert's opinion substantially outweighs their prejudicial effect. In engaging in this balancing process, the trial judge must consider the probable effectiveness or lack thereof of a limiting instruction. *Id.*

The amendment to Rule 703 applies only to evidence of the underlying bases when offered by the *proponent* of the expert. It does not restrict "the presentation of underlying expert facts or data when offered by an adverse party." *Id.* Thus, it does not prevent the presentation of underlying facts or data on cross-examination of the expert by an adverse party. Importantly, an adversary's attack on an expert's basis on cross might open the door to an opponent's rebuttal with information that was reasonably relied upon by the expert but not initially discloseable under the balancing test. *Id.* However, in a multi-party case, even if only one party proffers the evidence, each party for whom evidence is beneficial is considered a "proponent." *Id.* Finally, amended Rule 702, not amended Rule 703, governs an opinion's reliability, regardless of whether the opinion is based on admissible or inadmissible evidence, a point that will be made clearer when we return to it later.

Rule 703 is closely related to Rule 705, so we will examine the latter before analyzing problems involving both rules.

The current version of Rule 703 was amended for stylistic purposes only, changing none of the substance just discussed. The current rule reads as follows:

Rule 703. Bases of an Expert's Opinion Testimony

> An expert may base an opinion on facts or data in the case that the expert has been made aware of or personally observed. If experts in the particular field would reasonably rely on those kinds of facts or data in forming an opinion on the subject, they need not be admissible for the opinion to be admitted. But if the facts or data would otherwise be inadmissible, the proponent of the opinion may disclose them to the jury only if their probative value in helping the jury evaluate the opinion substantially outweighs their prejudicial effect.

[b] Rule 705

Rule 705 embodies two changes from the traditional rules. It permits an opinion to be stated before its bases are revealed (or not to reveal the bases on direct examination at all). The rule also provides that hypothetical questions are no longer required:

Rule 705. Disclosing the Facts or Data Underlying an Expert's Opinion

> Unless the court orders otherwise, an expert may state an opinion — and give the reasons for it — without first testifying to the underlying facts or data. But the expert may be required to disclose those facts or data on cross-examination.

The Advisory Committee Note makes clear that eliminating the frequent requirement of presentation by a hypothetical question was one major goal of Rule 705. Although it is no longer required, the direct examiner might choose, for strategic reasons, nevertheless to proceed via hypothetical. *See also* Rule 702, Advisory Committee Note ("The language 'facts or data' is broad enough to allow an expert to rely on hypothetical facts that are supported by the evidence."). If the hypothetical is short, clear, and punchy, it offers the proponent the traditional advantage of a mini-summing up midtrial. Regardless of whether a hypothetical question is used, Rule 705 gives the advocate the flexibility to determine *when*, if at all, to reveal the bases for an expert opinion at trial. Many advocates find it effective to elicit the opinion first, then its bases, enabling jurors to understand why the bases matter, to give them a road map:

Example

Dr. Reginald Gobert, a renowned psychiatrist, takes the stand at defendant Johannes Brahms' criminal trial in support of his insanity defense. Defense counsel, after eliciting Dr. Gobert's credentials, proceeds on direct examination as follows.

DEFENSE COUNSEL: Did you personally examine Mr. Brahms to assess his mental capacities at the time of the crime?

A: Yes, I examined him on at least four occasions, for a total of 10 hours of observation.

DEFENSE COUNSEL: Of what did your examination consist?

A: I interviewed him extensively about his background and his current thoughts and feelings; I observed his demeanor, the clarity and responsiveness of his speech, whether he made eye contact; and I administered a variety of written tests. [Gobert then explains what these tests and other observations involved and why they mattered].

DEFENSE COUNSEL: Did you engage in any other investigations besides meeting with the defendant to form an opinion about Mr. Brahm's mental state at the time of the alleged crime?

A: Yes. I read all the police reports; reviewed his school and employment records and his physician's files; and interviewed his family, friends, teachers, and current co-workers.

DEFENSE COUNSEL: Based upon these investigations, did you form an opinion to a reasonable degree of professional certainty whether Mr. Brahms suffered from a mental disease or defect at the time of the crime?

A: Yes.

DEFENSE COUNSEL: What is that opinion?

A: He did then, and still does, suffer from the mental disease of paranoid schizophrenia.

DEFENSE COUNSEL: What is paranoid schizophrenia?

A: [Here Dr. Gobert explains the symptoms of the disease]

DEFENSE COUNSEL: What are your reasons for reaching that conclusion?

A: He repeatedly insisted that he is really Napoleon Bonaparte reborn, making this point not just to me but to all his family and friends for at least two years before this incident. Moreover, [here Dr. Gobert recites the bases for the opinion in detail and then explains why each is significant, that is, why it supports his conclusion].

Defense counsel's manner of proceeding here — eliciting the opinion before asking for recitation of its bases — was traditionally unacceptable but is perfectly appropriate under Rule 705. Indeed, under Rule 705, defense counsel need not have begun, as he did in the above example, by reciting the general sorts of investigations he undertook (that is, for example, noting that he interviewed the defendant without then recounting what the defendant said). Rather, defense counsel could have simply proceeded this way:

DEFENSE COUNSEL: Do you have an opinion to a reasonable degree of professional certainty whether Mr. Brahms suffered from a mental disease or defect at the time of the crime?

A: Yes.

DEFENSE COUNSEL: What is that opinion?

A: He did then, and still does, suffer from paranoid schizophrenia.

DEFENSE COUNSEL: What is paranoid schizophrenia?

A: [Here Dr. Gobert explains].

DEFENSE COUNSEL: What investigations did you do to help you reach your opinion?

A: [Here Dr. Gobert notes that he interviewed the defendant and his family and friends, etc.]

Q: What were the results of those investigations, that is, the bases for your opinion?

A: [Here Dr. Gobert recites what the defendant and his family and friends actually said during the interviews, what the test results were, etc.]

The order of examination is thus generally in the advocate's control. However, there are other problems with the manner in which Dr. Gobert's opinion was elicited, as we will soon see in examining the ultimate issue rule.

Some have objected to Rule 705's liberalization of traditional rules because the new Rule allows a direct examiner to choose not to elicit any bases at all. That would place the cross-examiner in the perhaps awkward position of eliciting bases for the first time, possibly thereby inadvertently injuring his own case. Such concerns are overblown. Significant pretrial discovery of expert opinions and their bases is now standard procedure, especially in civil cases. A cross-examiner should, therefore, be well aware of the nature and bases of opinions to be expressed by the opponent's expert. Cross-examiners can thus elicit what they believe will help their client and harm the opposition. Moreover, where this is not the case (that is, in jurisdictions following Rule 705 but with limited discovery), the trial court has discretion under the rule to require disclosure of bases on direct, for example, where necessary to prevent unfair surprise. Finally, sound strategic reasons encourage proponents to reveal the bases for expert opinions on direct. Juries are simply not likely to credit raw opinions unsupported by convincing facts or data, especially if an opposing expert offers a well-supported opinion. An advocate might withhold some bases on direct in the hope that they will be more powerful if elicited by the opponent on cross. But that scenario is likely only if the opponent did inadequate investigation or if the trial is set in a jurisdiction with very limited expert discovery; otherwise, there would be no prospect of the opponent's being surprised by the witness' answers.

Problem 9-11: The Gullible Personality

Ms. B was charged with knowingly possessing nine stolen welfare checks. The prosecution's undisputed evidence showed that six checks, made out to different payees, were given to Ms. B by her boyfriend's good friend, Scott. Ms. B deposited the checks, which supposedly had been endorsed to Scott, into her account. One check was returned unpaid, and her account was charged accordingly, but Scott made good her loss. He subsequently gave her three more checks to deposit. The prosecution's theory is that Ms. B "must have known" that the checks were stolen, but Ms. B testified that she did not in fact believe that the checks were stolen; she believed Scott's story that the checks had been given to him in payment for a debt, and he needed her assistance because he had no bank account of his own.

Ms. B calls a psychologist to the stand at trial to testify that Ms. B's personality is characterized by an unusually high degree of gullibility and dependency. To reach this conclusion, the psychiatrist, Dr. P, administered various psychological tests, interviewed Ms. B, and interviewed: (1) her parents, who described numerous instances in which Ms. B, as a child, believed clear lies told her daily by her brother; (2) Ms. B's ex-husband, who admitted to cheating on Ms. B with other women, then telling ridiculous lies (all believed by Ms. B) to cover his deception; (3) Charlene, Ms. B's lifelong close friend, who said that she and Ms. B had frequently used hallucinogenic drugs for 10 years; and (4) Ms. B's childhood teachers, who described numerous violent assaults by Ms. B on other children. All those interviewed are outside the subpoena power of the court, and none of their statements fit within any hearsay exception or exclusion. Moreover, the results of some of the psychological tests administered by Dr. P, such as the Rorschach test and the Thematic Apperception Test, are inadmissible because they have been held by the state's appellate court to be unreliable. However, some of the other tests, such as the Myers-Briggs Personality Test, have been held to be reliable. Furthermore, the trial court ruled that Dr. P's opinion meets the *Daubert* test (discussed later in this chapter), requiring an expert opinion to be "relevant and reliable" as to its major premises, and the court ruled that the expert is well-qualified.

1. May Dr. P testify to his opinion that Ms. B has an unusually gullible personality?

2. If yes, should the trial judge permit Dr. P to reveal all of the bases for the opinion to the jury? Only some of those bases? Which ones and why? As a strategic matter, how many of Dr. P's bases will Ms. B want to elicit?

3. What questions would you use to elicit Dr. P's opinion in a form other than a hypothetical question and why?

4. Strategically, should Ms. B's counsel use a hypothetical question or some other sort of question to elicit Dr. P's opinion? Craft an appropriate hypothetical question.

5. What questions would you, as Ms. B's counsel, ask to elicit whatever bases you desire from Dr. P?

6. What questions should the prosecutor ask of Dr. P on cross-examination, and does Ms. B's counsel have any plausible grounds to object to those questions?

7. Are there any rules other than the expert evidence rules (Rules 702 through 706) that may be plausible grounds for objecting to any portions of Dr. P's testimony, whether on direct or cross? Why?

Problem 9-12: The Negligent Radiologist

John MacKinnon brings a wrongful death suit against Dr. Reginald Robinson for failing to diagnose Mr. MacKinnon's wife's breast cancer at an early stage. Dr. Joseph DePaul, a renowned radiologist, is called to testify as an expert regarding whether Dr. Robinson failed to exercise the expected degree of care in his field.

PLAINTIFF'S ATTORNEY: Dr. DePaul, do you have an opinion regarding when a competent radiologist would first have spotted Ms. MacKinnon's breast cancer?

A: Yes.

PLAINTIFF'S ATTORNEY: What is that opinion?

DEFENDANT'S ATTORNEY: Objection! Dr. DePaul has not provided the bases for his conclusions before offering them.

1. Is defense counsel correct? Why or why not?

PLAINTIFF'S ATTORNEY: Doctor, assuming that the mass was observable on the mammogram taken on October 1 but Ms. MacKinnon was not advised by Dr. Robinson or anyone else of that fact until the following March 1, what impact did that have on Ms. MacKinnon's survival chances?

DEFENDANT'S ATTORNEY: Objection! Calls for speculation!

2. How should plaintiff's counsel respond to this objection?

PLAINTIFF'S ATTORNEY: What do you rely on for your conclusion that Ms. MacKinnon would have had a very significantly greater chance of surviving her cancer had it been diagnosed in October?

A: Well, the lab report dated February 25 said. . . .

DEFENDANT'S ATTORNEY: Objection! Hearsay.

3. How should plaintiff's counsel respond to this objection?

The trial judge now gets into the act:

JUDGE: Doctor, what is the basis of your conclusion that as of October 1 the mass had not spread beyond its borders?

4. Is the court permitted to ask such a question?

Problem 9-13: Monopolies and Economists

The United States government has filed an antitrust suit against Microsoft. As part of the government's case, it must prove that Microsoft effectively monopolized the market for computer operating systems. The government called to the stand Dr. Peter Kostick, a leading economist, who opined that Microsoft had indeed monopolized the noted market. That opinion was partly based on the report of an independent consumer rights organization, which had placed undercover "moles" in the employ of Microsoft. The report declared that "Microsoft controls 90% of the operating system market and sets unduly low prices, at a severe financial loss, where necessary to drive competitors out of business."

Can the economist testify if the report statement is inadmissible hearsay? If yes, can he reveal the content of the report to the jury?

[3] "Or Otherwise"

Rule 702 includes this phrase: "may testify in the form of an opinion or otherwise." The "or otherwise" language is meant to permit expert witnesses to recount information clearly within the scope of their expertise but merely as background, without offering any opinion about any aspect of the case before the court. The jury then is free to apply that background to the facts of the specific case. The original Advisory Committee Note explains:

> Most of the literature assumes that experts testify only in the form of opinions. The assumption is logically unfounded. The rule accordingly recognizes that an expert on the stand may give a dissertation or exposition of scientific or other principles relevant to the case, leaving the trier of fact to apply them to the facts. Because much of the criticism of expert testimony has centered upon the hypothetical question, it seems wise to recognize that opinions are not indispensable and to encourage the use of expert testimony in nonopinion form when counsel believes the trier can itself draw the requisite inference. The use of opinions is not abolished by the rule, however. It will continue to be permissible for the expert to take the further step of suggesting the inference which should be drawn from applying the specialized knowledge to the facts.

Example

Problem 9-7 involved an expert psychologist testifying that a victim witness' identification of the defendant as the victim's assailant was suspect. But under Rule 702, the expert need not go that far. She could simply explain the circumstances under which witness identifications are and are not reliable, leaving it to the jury to apply those principles to decide whether the identification in the case before them was reliable.

The Advisory Committee Note to Rule 702 gives further guidance for assessing the value of such "generalized testimony." For such testimony, the rule requires that: "(1) the expert be qualified; (2) the testimony address a subject matter on which the factfinder can be assisted by an expert; (3) the testimony be reliable; and (4) the testimony 'fit' the facts of the case."

To recap: An expert can thus testify in at least three capacities:

1. *As an observer*, akin to an ordinary lay witness describing perceived events. E.g., "The wound was red, oozing a slimy green substance," or, using some expertise in the description, "The wound was red, oozing a slimy green pus."

2. *As an opinion-articulator* about the facts of the specific case. E.g. "This defendant suffers from paranoid schizophrenia."

3. *As an "or otherwise" testifier*, educating the jury about background principles helpful in understanding a particular case but not including an opinion about the specific case. E.g., "Paranoid schizophrenics are often so out of touch with reality that they often lose much of the ability to tell right from wrong," offering no opinion about whether this defendant — who happens to be a paranoid schizophrenic — can tell right from wrong.

Problem 9-14: The Radiologist and Psychologist Meet

1. In Problem 9-12, in which capacity would the expert testify if permitted to respond to the various questions posed? Why?

2. In Problem 9-11, what sorts of questions should be asked of the psychiatrist, Dr. P, to avoid his giving an "opinion," thus limiting him instead to "or otherwise" background?

[4] The Ultimate Issue Rule

Traditionally, evidence law prohibited any witness, lay or expert, from offering an opinion on the "ultimate issue" in the case.

Example

A car owner brings a negligence action against a mechanic, alleging that faulty repair of the car's brakes caused an accident in which the car owner was severely injured. The plaintiff calls an expert mechanic to the stand. The following exchange occurs after the mechanic testifies that he examined the following: (1) the automobile brakes, (2) the extent of the damage to the car, (3) the police reports, and (4) the depositions of the plaintiff and the defendant.

PLAINTIFF'S ATTORNEY: Do you have an opinion to a reasonable degree of professional certainty whether defendant Joseph Roscoe negligently repaired the brakes on plaintiff John Roten's car?

A: Yes, I do.

PLAINTIFF'S ATTORNEY: What is that opinion?

DEFENDANT'S ATTORNEY: Objection, calls for an opinion on an ultimate issue.

JUDGE: Objection sustained.

The reason given for the ultimate issue bar was that opinion testimony about an ultimate issue "usurps the function" or "invades the province" of the jury. These vague phrases express the concern that jurors will too readily defer to an expert's views on the ultimate question. But the rule proved problematic for three reasons:

1. It often made it unreasonably difficult for advocates to present their cases, forcing the witnesses into verbal contortions to avoid the disfavored "magic phrasing."

2. Doubts grew about the ultimate issue rule's assumption that juries would be so gullible and irresponsible as to ignore weighing the reasons for an expert's opinion.

3. It was often difficult to distinguish "ultimate" from "non-ultimate" issues. The above example is clear. But what if the expert mechanic had instead been asked, "Did the defendant fail to exercise the same sort of care as other mechanics ordinarily do in repairing brakes?" Or instead: "What procedures do mechanics customarily follow in brake repairs of this kind?" "Why do they do so?" "Did the defendant fail in any way to follow such procedures?" "How?" "What impact did this have on the brakes' safety?" The sometimes substantial differences in the phrasing of these questions show that it can be hard to draw a line between "ultimate" and "penultimate" issues. Even this latter set of questions, which seems to be on the "right" side of the line, raise another question: "Do these questions really accomplish the task of fairly conveying the necessary information better than do the other options, combined with their own follow up questions?"

For similar reasons, a majority of jurisdictions have abandoned the ultimate issue rule. The Federal Rules of Evidence followed suit for most kinds of cases in Rule 704(a):

> IN GENERAL — NOT AUTOMATICALLY OBJECTIONABLE. An opinion is not objectionable just because it embraces an ultimate issue.

The abolition of the ultimate issue rule does not mean that opinions on ultimate issues are always permitted. Rules 701 and 702 respectively require that opinions be helpful to the trier of fact. Rule 403 similarly gives the trial court discretion to exclude unfairly prejudicial or time-wasting opinions. The Advisory Committee Note to Rule 704 offers clarification:

> These provisions [Rules 403, 701, and 702] afford ample assurances against the admission of opinions which would merely tell the jury what result to reach, somewhat in the manner of the oath-helpers of an earlier day. They also stand ready to exclude opinions phrased in terms of inadequately explored legal criteria. Thus the question, "Did T have capacity to make a will?" would be excluded, while the question, "Did T have sufficient mental

capacity to know the nature and extent of his property and the natural objects of his bounty and to formulate a rational scheme of distribution [the legal test for testamentary capacity]?" would be allowed.

Congress added Rule 704(b) in 1984 to reinstitute the ultimate issue rule for one class of cases. Rule 704(b), as recently further amended in 2011 for stylistic purposes, declares that:

> EXCEPTION. In a criminal case, an expert witness must not state an opinion about whether the defendant did or did not have a mental state or condition that constitutes an element of the crime charged or of a defense. Those matters are for the trier of fact alone.

The Senate Judiciary Committee Report concerning the amendment cites with approval an American Psychiatric Association statement as expressing the Rule's intentions:

> Psychiatrists, of course, must be permitted to testify fully about the defendant's diagnosis, mental state and motivation (in clinical and common sense terms) at the time of the alleged act so as to permit the jury or judge to reach the ultimate conclusion about which they and only they are expert.

Despite this guidance, Rule 704(b) reintroduces all the same uncertainties that have always accompanied the ultimate issue rule. For example, the Committee Report declares that a psychiatrist would be permitted to testify that a patient suffered from a "mental disease or defect." Yet whether a patient suffered from a mental disease or defect is an element of the insanity defense and thus presumably logically involves an "ultimate issue." On the other hand, many commentators agree that Rule 704(b)'s ultimate issue rule would bar an opinion that a defendant could not appreciate the distinction between right and wrong, which is another element of the insanity defense. The most plausible way to distinguish these facially similar situations is to view the underlying policy concern as limiting experts to opinions on subjects that they commonly address in their fields and disallowing opinions about standards that the legal system creates. The term "mental disease or defect" is arguably close enough to the sorts of medical terminology used by psychiatrists every day (though even this point is debatable) so that the legal standard and professional terminology overlap. Consequently, no "ultimate issue" is involved. But whether a patient can appreciate the distinction between right and wrong seems farther afield from traditional psychiatric terms, and it involves moral judgments better made by a jury than an expert. This distinction is one of degree more than a dichotomy — that is, the term "mental disease or defect" may also involve moral judgments, but to a lesser degree than determining someone's ability to tell right from wrong. The distinction thus, again without providing bright lines, may nevertheless be helpful in resolving close cases.

Problem 9-15: Gullibility Revisited

Review Problem 9-11 concerning Ms. B's alleged gullibility. *Would the expert's opining that Ms. B was "unusually gullible" be objectionable under Rule 704? What if the expert were instead asked: "In your opinion, did Ms. B know that the checks that she cashed were stolen?" What if she were asked, "In your opinion, was*

Ms. B capable of knowing that the checks were stolen?" Finally, what if he were asked to (a) describe the indicators of an unusually gullible personality and (b) opine on whether Ms. B displayed any or all of those indicators, identifying which ones he found to be present?

Problem 9-16: The Insanity Defense Revisited

Assume the facts of Problem 9-5. *At trial, an expert psychiatrist is called to the stand and asked, "Was Mr. Yerguson incapable, because of a mental disease or defect, of telling right from wrong?" Which of the following possibilities best characterizes this question?*

1. Objectionable under both traditional law and Rule 704.

2. Unobjectionable under Rule 704, which permits inquiries into ultimate issues.

3. Unobjectionable under either traditional law or Rule 704. because no ultimate issue is involved.

4. A debatably close one concerning whether it deals with an ultimate issue and is therefore objectionable.

Would your answer change if the psychiatrist were instead asked: "What if your diagnosis concerning whether Mr. Yerguson suffered from any mental abnormality at the time of the crime"? Why?

[5] Reasonable Degree of Professional Certainty

Some jurisdictions insist that experts may testify only if they describe their opinions as "reasonably certain" or, in other jurisdictions, as "reasonably probable." The idea is that they must have formed their opinions to "a reasonable medical or scientific certainty." Other jurisdictions abandon these formalities, and require simply that an opinion be helpful to the factfinder. This latter approach is shared by the Federal Rules of Evidence. Under this approach, there is thus no categorical rule prohibiting opinions stated to be "mere possibilities." However, such opinions might be vulnerable to attack under Rule 702 as unlikely to assist the trier of fact or under Rule 403 as more prejudicial than probative.

[6] The Opinion Rule and Out-of-Court Statements

We will examine hearsay in Chapters 10 though 15. But it is worth alerting you here to another problem at the intersection of the rules on hearsay and expert testimony: Assume that a hearsay document is admitted, for example, under the business records exception to the hearsay rule. If the document contains opinions, including expert ones, must the opinion be admitted only if it complies with the opinion rules, like Rules 701 through 705, that would apply were a live witness to state the opinion on the stand? Many courts say "yes," although common sense suggests that the rules should be more liberally applied in the hearsay setting.

Example 1

A report written by an infectious disease specialist, after describing the patient's symptoms, says: "Diagnosis: Patient suffers from cellulitis [fat cell infections], probably caused by brown recluse spider bite. The infections have spread significantly, due to the late start of treatment." The report is offered into evidence by the plaintiff at a medical malpractice trial charging the plaintiff's family doctor with recommending hospitalization at a later point than sound professional judgment required.

The report is hearsay — an out-of-court statement offered for the truth of what it asserts. But the report probably fits within the business records exception to the hearsay rule. However, the report contains opinions, and many courts would read the business records exception as including opinions only if the requirements of Rules 701 through 705 are met. Because this opinion is offered by a highly qualified infectious disease specialist, it may be relatively easy for most or all of the excerpted statements to fulfill the opinion rules. But had those statements instead been made by the emergency-room technician (who knows far less about infectious diseases than does the specialist), the admissibility of some or all of the stated opinions would be in much greater doubt.

Furthermore, the opinion rule has long been held not to apply to statements admitted under the exclusion or exception to the hearsay rule for party admissions. The rationale for this exclusion partly involves adversarial rather than reliability concerns. In other words, parties should fairly expect to be bound by their own words when they bring or defend a lawsuit (see Chapter 13 for details). Moreover, parties are likely to have both the incentive and the resources to challenge any misleading or false statements purportedly their own. This rationale applies to opinions as much as to "facts."

Example 2

Plaintiff sued Ford Motor Company for personal injuries after his Ford Pinto exploded into flames when hit from behind at 5 m.p.h. The plaintiff seeks to admit into evidence this portion of a memorandum written by Ford's Chief Automotive Engineer within the scope of his employment: "The Pinto gas tank is poorly placed and may too easily spark fires in low impact collisions. Production should be postponed to address this problem." Is it admissible?

The quoted statement is offered by the plaintiff for the truth of what it asserts and is thus hearsay. However, the statement arguably fits within the party admissions exemption from the hearsay rule. Moreover (unlike the approach of many courts to the business records exception), the party admissions exemption overcomes both hearsay and opinion rule objections. Thus, no independent showing need be made that the opinion meets the requirements of Rules 701 through 705.

Broadening the opinion rule exception to documents other than those containing admissions is a trend apparently now under way in many jurisdictions. If the opinion rule is modernly thought of as a preference, where possible, for specific over general testimony, this makes sense. When documents contain otherwise admissible hearsay, the documents cannot be "prompted" in the way that a live witness could to rephrase an opinion in more specific terms.

[C] Cross-Examination: Scope and Manner

Many of the restrictions on the direct examination of experts do not apply on cross-examination. Thus, even under traditional rules, hypothetical questions are generally not required, as the cross-examiner's function is typically to challenge, rather than to elicit, an opinion. For similar reasons, traditional rules requiring bases to be revealed before opinions are elicited and requiring other admitted or admissible evidence being available to support those bases are of no concern.

Under Rule 705, if an expert has not revealed any or all the facts, data, and opinions underlying his in-court opinion, the opponent may elicit those matters on cross-examination. Available methods for impeaching the expert include the following:

- Exploring how the non-existence of any particular basis on which the expert relied would alter his or her opinion.

- Exploring how the existence of contrary or additional bases (presumably to be supported by evidence from the cross-examiner at a later stage) would alter the expert's opinion.

- Determining which materials the expert reviewed or failed to review in preparing to offer the opinion.

- Determining which tests or other investigations the expert conducted (or failed to conduct) and how they were done.

- Exploring the financial compensation received by the expert for the advice and testimony.

- Revealing contradictions between the expert's assertions and those made by other experts in published works, provided those works comply with the learned treatise exception to the hearsay rule, Rule 803(18).

- Posing a hypothetical question based upon an alternative set of assumptions.

- Exploring what prior expert testimony the expert has given, for whom, and its content.

Practice Tip: Retaining Qualified Forensic Experts.

Litigators have a variety of methods of locating properly qualified forensic experts. Many litigators are themselves specialists in the fields in which they litigate and may personally know other experts who offer forensic services. Even if they are not themselves specialists in a field, many litigators limit their practices to particular types of litigation and so become familiar with numerous experts. Litigators may belong to professional lawyer groups whose members provide referrals to effective experts. In addition, the Internet, that ubiquitous source of information, is a ready source of experts. For example, a search for "expert witnesses" will produce scads of web sites listing forensic experts by specialty who are available for hire. Thus, when preparing this edition, the authors visited the web site http://expertpages.com/experts/accidentreconstruction.htm and found lists of accident reconstruction experts listed by state (province in Canada) and sub-specialty. One expert's listing included the following information: "45 years experience in construction & safety; 160+ trials; Time 50% Expert & 50% practicing. 50%/50% — Plaintiff & Defense." *Assuming the expert is otherwise qualified, how would this information help you decide whether to retain this particular expert?*

Problem 9-17: My Cousin Vinnie Cross-Examined

Assume the facts in the My Cousin Vinnie case, Problem 8-2, and draft a set of cross-examination questions for the expert.

Problem 9-18: Or Was It the Accurate Eyewitness?

Assume the facts in Problem 9-7 and draft a set of cross-examination questions for the expert psychologist.

Problem 9-19: Trial Transcript Exercise on the Scope and Manner of Examining Experts

The Federal Military Institute ("FMI") is an all-male, government-funded school for training "citizen-soldiers." This school uses the "adversative method" of training. In this method, upperclassmen bully, abuse, taunt, physically challenge, and otherwise harass freshmen "grunts," who are expected not to resist. The method is thought to build physical and emotional strength, discipline, teamwork, subordination of individual ego to the greater good, obedience, acceptance of hierarchy, and adaptability.

Several women have brought a civil lawsuit challenging the male-only admissions policy of FMI. FMI's response was to create a small all-female school, the Federal Women's Military Institute ("FWMI") as an alternative. That school does not use the adversative method, on the theory that women better learn leadership in a more nurturing environment. FMI calls feminist historian Barbara Randall to the stand. Excerpts from her direct examination follow:

DEFENDANT'S ATTORNEY: Dr. Randall, what is your educational background?

A: I received my Ph.D in history from Yale University in 1979, specializing in twentieth-century women's history. I did post-graduate work at Princeton's Women's Studies Programs.

DEFENDANT'S ATTORNEY: And where are you now employed?

A: I am a Full Professor holding the Elizabeth Shelbourne Chair in Women's History in the History Department of Harvard University, a post I have held since completing my post-graduate work. I also simultaneously hold a post as a tenured professor in Harvard's Women's Studies Program.

DEFENDANT'S ATTORNEY: What is your area of research specialization?

A: I study gendered differences in the ways that women and men learn in many settings. Twentieth-century history is replete with examples of both mythological and real such differences.

DEFENDANT'S ATTORNEY: Do you rely entirely on historical research in your work?

A: I read widely in many disciplines — social science, philosophy, politics, literary criticism, feminist studies, all of which inform my work.

DEFENDANT'S ATTORNEY: Dr. Randall, are you familiar with FMI and FWMI?

A: Yes. I have extensively studied both institutions. I have interviewed all current students, faculty, and administrators at both schools, as and have sat in classes and reviewed their curricula.

DEFENDANT'S ATTORNEY: Have you formed any opinion about whether FMI would be an institutionally effective institute for training women as citizen-soldiers?

A: Yes.

DEFENDANT'S ATTORNEY: What is that opinion?

A: FMI would be a terrible place to educate women to be any sort of soldier or leader. Few women, if any, could thrive there, and even those who might succeed would very likely do better elsewhere.

DEFENDANT'S ATTORNEY: Why is that?

A: Because women do not learn well in an adversative model.

DEFENDANT'S ATTORNEY: And do you have an opinion about whether FWMI would be more effective than FMI at training citizen-soldiers?

A: Yes.

DEFENDANT'S ATTORNEY: What is that opinion?

A: FWMI is very effective in an absolute sense, and far more effective certainly than FMI, in training women as citizen-soldiers.

DEFENDANT'S ATTORNEY: Why is that?

A: The overwhelming scholarly evidence from history and in all fields of gender studies is that, by college, young women have far less confidence in themselves than do young men. They need a chance to see females succeeding in leadership roles and to take those roles themselves to restore self-confidence. Moreover, women learn and develop best in close relationships with other women. A caring, nurturing environment — support from fellow students, from teachers, from teammates — gives them the strength and skill to be tough with opponents and to learn more effectively. FWMI provides exactly this sort of environment for young women.

DEFENDANT'S ATTORNEY: What is your opinion, if any, on whether FMI discriminates against women by FMI's males-only admissions policy.

A: FMI does not so discriminate. It does treat men and women differently, but not all differences in treatment are discriminatory. These differences are in fact necessary to equality. FMI sends the applications of all women whom FMI rejects to FWMI so that women learn to be peer soldiers with the male graduates of FMI. And, correspondingly, it is only at FMI that men learn to be the best soldiers they can be. These separate institutions are the only way to have male-female equality in the military.

DEFENDANT'S ATTORNEY: On what do you base the opinions that you have shared with us today, Dr. Randall?

A: On my observations at both institutions and my knowledge of history from my own research and on my wide multi-disciplinary reading in feminist studies.

DEFENDANT'S ATTORNEY: No more questions, Thank you.

If this testimony were presented before the jury, should objections have been made at any point by the plaintiffs' counsel to any of the questions? Why? What would be the basis for such objections? How likely would the objections be to succeed? If this testimony were instead an offer of proof before the trial judge, would you permit this expert to testify before the jury? Why or why not? Consider all the bases for objection thus far reviewed in this chapter.

Another impeachment technique is to cross-examine the expert with a learned treatise whose position contradicts that of the expert on the stand. At common law, cross-examination by learned treatises was permissible only to impeach the witness, e.g., by showing the witness' unfamiliarity with a respected work or by implying the weakness of the witness' opinion because it was contrary to such a well-respected piece of scholarship. But the treatise could not be used as substantive evidence, that is, as proof of the truth of what the treatise asserts. The common law feared that substantive use of learned treatises would confuse the jury with technical information and statements taken out of context or that statements from treatises would be unreliable because of the rapid change in the state of scientific knowledge.

The Federal Rules of Evidence reject this approach. Instead, they created a new hearsay exception for learned treatises under these circumstances. Under Rule 803(18), the following statements are not excluded by the hearsay rule:

(18) *Statements in Learned Treatises, Periodicals, or Pamphlets.* A statement contained in a treatise, periodical, or pamphlet if:

(A) the statement is called to the attention of an expert witness on cross-examination or relied on by the expert on direct examination; and

(B) the publication is established as a reliable authority by the expert's admission or testimony, by another expert's testimony, or by judicial notice.

If admitted, the statement may be read into evidence but not received as an exhibit.

The drafters of Rule 803(18) believed that the requirement that the expert must be questioned about the treatise would help prevent jurors from misunderstanding or misapplying statements from a treatise. On the other hand, the expert being challenged cannot simply block questioning by denying the authoritative nature of the treatise. Another expert or, in appropriate cases, judicial notice, may establish that the treatise has the necessary authority. Authors of treatises and other scholarly works (any scholarly work will do) have an incentive to produce reliable work to avoid criticism by professional peers so, without the hearsay exception, the jury might be deprived of valuable information. But a restriction is still imposed on "receiving" the treatise as an exhibit, that is, it may not be taken into the jury room because of the residual fear that the jury may there misapply the treatise without the expert's guidance.

Problem 9-20: Black Rage

Dr. John LeFlew is a defense expert in a homicide trial in which the defendant claims imperfect self-defense as a ground for mitigating his crime from murder to manslaughter. LeFlew testifies on direct examination that the defendant suffers from "black rage syndrome," a psychological disorder that results in an intense fear of white males by some African Americans, and the defendant's victim was indeed a white male. Cross-examination of Dr. LeFlew by the prosecution proceeded as follows:

PROSECUTOR: Dr. LeFlew, you are of course familiar with Mellon Dondakait's book, Black Rage: A Non-Existent Malady, published in 1996?

A: Yes, I am familiar with it.

PROSECUTOR: And it is widely recognized among the professional psychological community as the leading, authoritative work on whether "black rage syndrome" is a valid concept, that is, in laymen's terms, on whether such a syndrome in fact exists?

A: I do not so consider it. I think it is a flawed work based on weak research.

PROSECUTOR: That was not my question. My question was whether others in the professional psychological research community widely recognize it as authoritative?

DEFENSE COUNSEL: Objection. Asked and answered.

JUDGE: Overruled. You may answer the question, Dr. LeFlew.

A: Yes, a majority of the research community so recognize it.

PROSECUTOR: I ask that this book, *Black Rage: A Non-Existent Malady*, be marked, for purposes of identification only, as P-24. Dr., have you read this book, marked as Exhibit P-24?

A: Yes, I have.

PROSECUTOR: I direct your attention to page 207. Doesn't the book there state that . . .

DEFENSE COUNSEL: Objection! Your Honor, this is hearsay, and Dr. LeFlew does not recognize this book as a learned treatise.

JUDGE: Overruled. Please finish your question, Mr. Prosecutor.

PROSECUTOR: Dr. LeFlew, doesn't this book state at page 207 the following: "In sum, there is simply no scientifically trustworthy evidence to support the existence of the so-called 'black rage syndrome'?"

A: Yes, it does so state that.

DEFENSE COUNSEL: Objection, Your Honor! No foundation has been established for the learned treatise exception.

JUDGE: P-24 is admitted as an exhibit.

Which, if any, of the trial judge's three rulings are correct, and which not? Why? What additional grounds for objection, if any, should defense counsel have raised to maximize the chance of altering the judge's third ruling? Why?

§ 9.05 THE MAJOR PREMISES: RELEVANCE AND RELIABILITY OF GENERAL PRINCIPLES AND METHODS

[A] Defining Terms

It is helpful, in understanding how courts treat the admissibility of testimony concerning the major premises of the expert witness syllogism, to distinguish "principles" from "methods." The distinction is important because it is often made in case law, scholarly commentary, and codified evidence rules. Nevertheless, rarely do courts, advisory committees, or legislatures clearly define the terms. Moreover, different cases or code commentaries may suggest different meanings. Yet authorities are increasingly fond of saying that expert testimony must be the product of both reliable "principles" and "methods." One by-no-means sharp, but still helpful, definition of these terms may be to say that they refer to differing levels of generality, but both are still best thought of as major premises in the expert syllogism. The "principle" is the most general statement, the "method" somewhat less general, but both are still broad assertions not yet applied to the facts of the specific case. Often "method" is seen as a means for applying a "principle" to a specific case. Using alternative terminology, a "method" is a *technique* for applying principles in specific instances. Therefore, if either the principle or the method is flawed, even their perfect application to a particular situation cannot be said to reach a trustworthy result. For example, two "principles" may be that DNA exists and is unique for each person, and a "method" may be that DNA testing can accurately identify each person's unique DNA. The Advisory Committee Note to the amendments to Rule 702 (those amendments are recited earlier in this chapter) offered this example:

When a law enforcement agent testifies regarding the use of code words in a drug transaction, the principle used by the agent is that participants in such transactions regularly use code words to conceal the nature of their activities. The method used by the agent is the application of extensive experience to analyze the meaning of the conversations.

If it is untrue that participants in drug transactions regularly use code words, then testimony that a particular suspect was using "common" drug-dealer code words is unhelpful. Similarly, the helpfulness of the agent's expert testimony is suspect if the principle of the use of code words is true but it has not been shown that drug agents are generally capable of identifying when code words are being used and what they mean. Even if we rephrase this last point to say that we need only show that *this agent* can reliably interpret drug-dealer code, we again must be confident that the agent can generally do so before we will allow him or her to interpret a particular suspect's conversation as containing such code.

While principles and methods can, therefore, be distinguished, they are also related. Thus drug agents may base the principle that drug dealers regularly use code on their repeated experiences of hearing and identifying them doing so. Similarly, while the existence of DNA may be proposed as a theory, empirical support for the theory's accuracy may be derived from repeated experimental identification of DNA via DNA testing. Nevertheless, to say that the two concepts of "principles" and "methods" are related does not mean that the distinction is useless.

Example

Dr. Eugene Smart, a psychologist, testifies that there is a dramatically increased likelihood of recidivism by a violent criminal offender if certain factors are present. He further testifies that he is effective at identifying, from a clinical interview with a patient, whether those factors are present in that patient's case. The expert's ultimate goal is to testify that Joey Small, who was recently convicted of first-degree murder, displays the necessary traits and is thus likely to re-offend. His testimony is relevant to issues being considered by a jury in determining whether to recommend the death penalty.

Comment:

Even if Dr. Smart is right that the presence of the specified factors leads to an increased probability of future violence, it does not necessarily follow that he can generally determine their presence in individual patients based solely upon a clinical interview. It may be the case, for example, that a combination of written psychological tests, interviews with family members and friends, and extended observation of the patient's behavior by a team of properly trained psychologists who reach consensus are necessary in order to accurately identify the presence of the relevant factors, and that a simple clinical interview is insufficient. Absent proof by the proponent of the trustworthiness of Dr. Smart's method for *applying* the general principle of violence-identifying-factors to individual suspects, Smart's testimony should, upon objection, be excluded.

One of the Advisory Committee Notes to Rule 702 also addresses the requirement that "the testimony is based upon sufficient facts or data." The Note initially declares that this requirement "calls for a quantitative rather than a qualitative analysis." But the Note does not define "facts" or "data" other than to say that the "term 'data' is intended to encompass the *reliable* opinions of other experts" (emphasis added). The Note's point might be that the way in which either a "principle" or a "method" is derived must be trustworthy. For a magician to say that he had a dream that something called DNA (which he describes) exists and is unique for each human being (other than identical twins) would not be a sufficient "datum" upon which an expert can base an opinion. But reliance on careful, repeated laboratory studies on the same question by well-respected chemists and biologists using sound scientific procedures would be sufficient. This interpretation is further supported by the Note's declaration that "an analysis of the sufficiency of the expert's basis cannot be divorced from the ultimate reliability of the expert's opinion."

This example reveals the slipperiness of terminology. What we think of as the "scientific *method*" seems to be one sort of reliable set of "facts or data" within the meaning of the Advisory Committee's terminology. For example, the failure of repeated experiments to disprove the hypothesis that a certain vaccine wards off the flu may be given great weight if the experiments were well-designed, including adequate controls ruling out other factors (e.g., the content of clear drinking water was the same for all subjects, thus ruling out the influence of contaminants). When the Advisory Committee refers to a "method," however, it is apparently referring to the means for applying a principle to a specific case rather than to the soundness of the procedures for deriving the principle in the first place. Scientists and many legal commentators, as well as many laymen, may thus find the Advisory Committee's terminology confusing. Furthermore, the Committee's use of "facts or data" can alternatively be read to refer to case-specific bases — minor premises, instead of the procedures for deriving major premises — as some commentators urge. Or, still other commentators suggest, "facts" may refer to case-specific bases, and "data" to the soundness of procedures for deriving principles. Complete agreement on terminology among all interested persons is unlikely, and it is the distinctions underlying the terms — and whether those distinctions are useful (which we and the Advisory Committee believe they are) — that matters most, even if we may disagree about which word best labels which concept.

Problem 9-21: Principled Methods

In the problems listed below, identify the major and minor premises. Then, for each of the problems, identify the "principles and methods"/techniques involved in the major premises and the "facts or data" supporting the bases for all the listed premises.

1. Problem 9-1.
2. Problem 9-2.
3. Problem 9-7.
4. Problem 9-8.

5. Problem 9-9.

6. Problem 9-10.

Vinny Gambini (Joe Pesci) displays an unusual method of concluding the testimony of expert witness Mona Lisa Vito (Marisa Tomei) in front of a surprised Judge Haller (Fred Gwynne) in *My Cousin Vinny*.*

[B] Scientific Evidence

[1] The *Frye* Test

[a] The Test Stated

Many courts had long carved out for special treatment one sort of expert testimony: that concerning "novel" "scientific" evidence. The reasons for requiring additional admissibility tests, or more stringent application of existing admissibility tests, to scientific evidence have not always been made clear in the cases. Clarification of that justification was thus often made in the first instance by commentators. Furthermore, the courts generally provided little guidance for distinguishing "scientific" from "non-scientific" evidence. The distinction was not one founded in the philosophy of science or the experience of scientists themselves. Rather, the courts seemed, sometimes implicitly, sometimes explicitly, to deem "scientific" any evidence for which the justifications for special admissibility hurdles applied.

---

* *My Cousin Vinny* copyright © 1992 Twentieth Century Fox. All Rights Reserved.

Among the justifications for these special hurdles were that: (1) an "aura of infallibility" surrounded the evidence so that a jury was unlikely to evaluate independently, or to be skeptical of, its worth; (2) scientific evidence relies on such arcane information that it will be very difficult for jurors to evaluate its worth, even if they are not "overawed" by any view of science as infallible; therefore, jurors just won't try, it being easier simply to take the expert's word; (3) the evidence is so unfamiliar to the courts that judges will have difficulty guiding juries on how fairly to evaluate it; and (4) the evidence "invades the province of the jury" in a particularly powerful way, such as lie-detector test results determining for the jury who speaks "truth" and who does not.

Courts were particularly concerned about "novel" scientific evidence because it presented more of the above dangers to a greater degree than scientific evidence with a longer pedigree of testing in the courts. The classic test for the admissibility of novel scientific evidence was articulated in *Frye v. United States*, 293 F. 1013, 1014 (D.C. Cir. 1923), which barred the use of polygraph evidence:

> Just when a scientific principle or discovery crosses the line between the experimental or demonstrable stages is difficult to define. Somewhere in this twilight zone the evidential force of the principle must be recognized, or while courts will go a long way in admitting expert testimony deduced from a well-recognized scientific principle or discovery, the thing from which the deduction is made must be sufficiently established to have gained general acceptance in the particular field in which it belongs.

[b]   Validity v. Reliability

The *Frye* test raised numerous questions. Notably, what precisely was the "thing" that had to be generally accepted? One influential answer to this question is that both the "validity" and "reliability" of a scientific principle must be shown by sound empirical data. "Validity," as used by a scientist, asks, "Is this test accurate; does it measure what it is supposed to measure?" "Reliability" asks, "Does this test consistently yield the same results upon repeated challenge?"

Example

An expert seeks to testify that: (1) cocaine has a unique scent; and (2) a new "sniffer" machine (such a machine is indeed being tested as we write this text) can detect that unique scent.

Comment:

If there is indeed a unique scent for cocaine, a sniffer's reaction (say, by ringing a bell or flashing a red light) might validly detect what it purports to detect — cocaine. However, sometimes the sniffer might fail to react when cocaine scent is present, or might react when the scent is not present. If so, the sniffer test would not be "reliable" because it does not reach consistent results. Validity and reliability can, of course, be connected. Thus, if a sniffer is unreliable, that is, highly inconsistent in when it reacts to cocaine, then it is hard to tell when its reaction is "valid," when the bells and lights indeed reflect what they purport to reflect: the presence of cocaine. On the other hand, a test can be "reliable" but invalid. If the sniffer consistently reacted when substance X, believed to be cocaine, was placed near the sniffer, it would be reliable. However, if substance X is in fact sugar, then the sniffer is invalid; it does not measure what it purports to measure, the presence of cocaine.

[c] Defining the Relevant Field

Another problem with the *Frye* test was determining what was the relevant "scientific" field in which the technique must be accepted.

Example 1

An expert is called by the prosecution in a murder case to testify about his use of a "dog scent lineup" to identify the defendant as the killer. In a dog scent lineup, a dog sniffs an item taken from the offender, such as a hat dropped by a killer while fleeing. The dog sniffs the hat and then sniffs each of the six to eight persons placed in a line. If the pooch barks at number 7, that is the equivalent of the dog's saying, "Number 7's scent matches the scent on the hat." Such testimony would support the inference that number 7 is the killer.

Comment:

Though not often recognized by the courts, several premises contribute to the value of this testimony. Its validity turns on proving that: (1) each human has a unique scent; (2) that scent remains on items of clothing for a significant period of time after they are worn; and (3) properly trained dogs can reliably match the unique scent on an item of clothing to its human source. Does the "relevant field" that must "generally accept" each of these propositions consist of biologists specializing in scenting, canine anatomy specialists, experimental dog psychologists, policemen trained in the use of dog-scent identification techniques, the scientist who invented the dog-scent lineup technique, or some combination of any or all these fields? This question highlights the difficulties in determining the relevant field. It also raises a qualifications question. Some courts would prohibit persons who made their living from inventing or applying a technique from testifying about its value or that of its underlying principles, on the theory that such persons are hopelessly biased.

Courts applying *Frye* also often reached inconsistent and seemingly random results as to what techniques were "novel" or not, "scientific" or not.

Example 2

Many courts began admitting evidence of battered woman's syndrome (a set of behaviors displayed by many women abused by their male spouses or lovers) to establish self-defense on the theory that such women see grave danger where others do not. The samples in the studies on which the syndrome was based consisted entirely of white heterosexual women. A defense attorney now offers battered women's syndrome evidence in support of an insanity defense raised by an African-American lesbian charged with killing her lover. The prosecution objects on the ground that the *Frye* test has not been met.

Comment:

The defense might respond that battered women's syndrome evidence is not "novel," as its use has frequently been upheld by the courts. Such an argument is questionable, however, asserts the prosecutor, because the concept of battered women's syndrome was developed using white heterosexual women as the sample. It may be that different behaviors would be seen in battered African-American women, or battered lesbians, or especially battered African-American lesbians, given these groups' different social circumstances. Some prosecutors have gone beyond this "external validity" argument (that you can't easily generalize from one set of conditions to a very different set) to make the racist and homophobic arguments that African-American and lesbian women are "too tough" to display the vulnerabilities of BWS "victims." The prosecutor might argue, on more solid ground, that while the existence of BWS might alter a woman's perception of danger (relevant to self-defense), that does not mean BWS is relevant to the defendant's ability to tell right from wrong or the other aspects of legal insanity.

Defense counsel might now, however, take another tack, arguing that a psychologist's testimony about BWS is not "scientific." Jurors are naturally skeptical about social science evidence, and it is relatively easy for them to understand, so no special admissibility hurdle is required. The prosecution's response would be to argue the contrary: that social science evidence is more complex than jurors realize, and precisely because jurors see it as easy to understand, they may miss many of its weaknesses and be too accepting of testimony consistent with the juror's own pre-existing prejudices and assumptions.

[d] Developmental Stages of Forensic Evidence

Among the supposed advantages of *Frye* was its ease of application, at least in the sense that it purportedly freed trial judges from the difficult task of understanding and evaluating scientific evidence. The judge's job would simply be to "count noses" to ensure general acceptance in the relevant field (how many noses constitute "general" acceptance is, of course, another question *Frye* did not answer). But in practice, careful judges had to determine what the relevant field was, whether "validity" and "reliability" were both generally accepted, and who was properly qualified to testify about general acceptance. All of these matters required the trial court to learn a good deal of the science.

Professor Andre Moenssens helped trial courts to determine whether "general acceptance" has been achieved concerning particular scientific evidence by offering the following description of the stages in the development of forensic science:

Stage 1: A theory is postulated.

Stage 2: Experiments are designed to verify the validity of the theory.

Stage 3: If the theory's validity is not disproved after a searching inquiry and empirical testing, it is "proven" valid and a court then appropriately may take judicial notice of the theory. This result is unlikely to occur at this stage, however, because no vehicle exists for translating the theory into relevant evidence in a lawsuit.

Stage 4: A technique is devised, or an instrument is designed and built, that will permit the theory to be applied practically in a forensic setting.

Stage 5: After a methodology has been devised, further tests must demonstrate a positive correlation between the results and the underlying theory. This stage is necessary to prove that the effects observed are not the result of some unidentified cause.

Stage 6: After the test has been shown to yield reliable results that are relevant to disputed issues in a law suit, a court may admit these results properly into evidence, and a qualified expert may interpret the results before the jury.

Moenssens's six stages, while helpful in guiding judges, underscore the inability of judges under *Frye* to escape careful study of the underlying science. Courts' involvement in such science led many to doubt not only *Frye's* supposed simplicity but also its wisdom: why exclude a technique that may in fact be trustworthy simply because, due to its very newness, it was not yet generally accepted? On the other hand, growing fears of "junk science" led others to ask, "why admit weak science just because it is foolishly accepted among some professional groups?" The growing chorus of criticism led to experimentation with a variety of options, ultimately leading to the growing dominance of a new test, articulated by the Supreme Court in *Daubert v. Merrell Dow Pharmaceuticals*, which will be discussed shortly. But *Frye* continues to be the test in many states, and the *Frye* "test" now survives as one factor to be weighed among many others under *Daubert*, so mastering the ambiguities of *Frye* remains important.

Problem 9-22: The Battered Child

Sixteen-year-old Johnny Appletree and his seven-year-old sister, Kristen, had endured years of physical and psychological brutality at their mother's hands, largely occurring, and being at its worst, when the mother was drunk. One day, Johnny, who was soon to be a defendant on a murder charge, sensed trouble brewing and tried to arrange for him and his little sister to be any place but home that night. He failed. Fearing what might happen, he took all his savings and purchased a bow and arrow, which he hid under his mattress. He locked his door and had his sister sleep with him that night. Suddenly, his mom, in a rage, started beating on the door of his room. She kept up the pounding for hours and threatened repeatedly to beat him silly. Finally, the pounding stopped. Johnny gingerly opened the door and saw his mother on the floor asleep and snoring, a bottle of vodka in her hands. He pushed her over with his foot, but she did not wake. He then got his bow and arrow, and shot her in the heart and eyes with many arrows, until she lay dead.

At his trial, Johnny's lawyer sought to prove self-defense. To this end, counsel offered expert evidence about battered child syndrome, which consists of two major symptoms: hypervigilance ("being acutely aware of his or her environment and remaining always on alert for any signs of danger, events to which the unabused child might not attend") and learned helplessness ("believing that no one can help them and there is no means of escape, though nonabused children might see such means"). At a motion in limine outside the hearing of the jury, the prosecutor cross-examines the defense psychologist, Martin Rosenkranz, as follows:

PROSECUTOR: Dr. Rosenkranz, you say your theory of hypervigilance is based on just two case studies?

A: Yes.

PROSECUTOR: In the first of these, Drs. Martin and Beezley observed 50 children, ranging in age from two and 13 years, correct?

A: Yes.

PROSECUTOR: And all 50 children were in psychiatric confinement because of severe behavioral problems — problems of long standing that extended to teachers, classmates, and many sorts of relationships other than just the parent-child relationship?

A: Yes.

PROSECUTOR: You and a colleague of yours conducted the second study, which observed mother-and-child interactions, correct?

A: Yes.

PROSECUTOR: In neither study was there a control group — that is, a group of nonabused children observed to watch for the same sorts of behaviors?

A: Correct.

PROSECUTOR: And the populations involved in both studies consisted entirely of white children, of European ancestry, from low-income families?

A: Yes.

PROSECUTOR: The defendant and his mother were Asian-American, correct?

A: Yes.

PROSECUTOR: And they were quite well off financially?

A: Yes.

PROSECUTOR: Paper-and-pencil psychological tests of personality traits have never been done regarding the claim of hypervigilance?

A: That's right.

PROSECUTOR: Nor have any methods of investigation been done other than clinical studies?

A: That's right.

PROSECUTOR: And you lecture widely on the "battered child syndrome" and the role of hypervigilance?

A: Yes.

PROSECUTOR: And you are paid substantial fees for these lectures?

A: Yes.

PROSECUTOR: As for the role of learned helplessness, all the studies done have simply found a high rate of severe depression among abused children but have never separately studied directly whether such children feel "helpless" when nonabused children would not?

A: Right again.

PROSECUTOR: Indeed, you simply assume that a sense of helplessness is a corollary of depression?

A: A methodologically correct assumption, but you are right.

PROSECUTOR: Your Honor, I renew my objection that this testimony concerns a novel scientific technique not generally accepted in the relevant scientific community under our state's version of the *Frye* test.

DEFENSE COUNSEL: Your Honor, may I ask just a few questions on redirect before you rule?

JUDGE: You may.

DEFENSE COUNSEL: The Battered Women's Syndrome has long been widely accepted among the academic psychological research community as valid and as reliably applied?

A: Yes.

DEFENSE COUNSEL: And you see the research in the area of the battered child syndrome as merely an extension, another manifestation, if you will, of BWS to battered children?

A: Of course.

DEFENSE COUNSEL: Hypervigilance is also one of the possible, albeit not necessary, symptoms of Post Traumatic Stress Disorder, PTSD, is it not?

A: Yes.

DEFENSE COUNSEL: And PTSD is recognized as an official diagnosis in the Diagnostic and Statistical Manual — the latest version — which all mental health workers use in making diagnoses?

A: Yes.

DEFENSE COUNSEL: And you consider battered child syndrome to be a specialized form of PTSD?

A: Yes.

DEFENSE COUNSEL: There is also a National Association of Battered Child Syndrome Researchers?

A: Yes.

DEFENSE COUNSEL: This association has more than 100 members, all of whom are leaders in the field of child psychology research?

A: Yes.

DEFENSE COUNSEL: And you have been President of that association since its founding six years ago?

A: Yes.

DEFENSE COUNSEL: Has any member of that association ever written an article or given a speech of which you are aware challenging your findings?

A: No.

DEFENSE COUNSEL: And all your research on battered child-syndrome has been published in prestigious psychological research journals?

A: Yes.

DEFENSE COUNSEL: Has anyone ever challenged, in any of those publications, any of your findings?

A: No.

1. How should the trial judge rule? Why?

2. Should the prosecutor or the defense counsel have asked any additional questions to buttress their respective cases? Why or why not?

3. By way of review, were any of the questions asked objectionable as to form? Why? How would you have better framed the questions?

Problem 9-23: "Fresh" Fingerprints

George LoStanza is charged with rape. The only evidence linking him to the crime scene is fingerprints that match his that were found on the victim's car, which was parked in her driveway. No fingerprints of his were found inside the house. LoStanza lived in the same neighborhood as his victim and occasionally did chores for her, such as carrying groceries to the car. He argued at trial that he could have left his prints during any of these chores. The prosecution's expert, Morrie Signfield, responded that the prints, taken one hour after the crime, were then "fresh." Courts have long recognized fingerprint comparison as involving valid and reliable scientific principles and methods/techniques. The defense objects, however, under *Frye*, and, with the trial court's permission, engages in the following voir dire of the expert:

DEFENSE COUNSEL: What is a "fresh" print?

A: One no more than a few hours old.

DEFENSE COUNSEL: How can you identify a print as fresh?

A: It grabs the fingerprint powder readily, and it is an extremely clear print.

DEFENSE COUNSEL: How did you learn this technique for determining when a print is "fresh?"

A: I studied it in a fingerprinting course at the police academy.

DEFENSE COUNSEL: Did they teach you at the academy of any experiments done to support the validity or reliability of these criteria in identifying a print as "fresh?"

A: No.

DEFENSE COUNSEL: Do you know of any such experiments?

A: Yes.

DEFENSE COUNSEL: How many such experiments do you know of?

A: One.

DEFENSE COUNSEL: Who did the experiment?

A: I did.

DEFENSE COUNSEL: What did you do?

A: I took two beer cans, put my hands on some greasy fried chicken, then put my left thumb on a can, later my left index finger, etc., doing all my fingers at different times. The only prints that quickly absorbed powder and were instantly clear were those put on the cans two hours before I dusted for the prints. I had left all the cans outdoors, in my backyard, with the time span between placing a print and dusting for it ranging between two hours and two weeks.

DEFENSE COUNSEL: I renew my objection. Any reference to the "freshness" of the prints runs afoul of *Frye*.

What ruling and why? See James E. Starrs, *Judicial Control over Scientific Supermen: Fingerprint Experts and Others Who Exceed the Bounds*, 35 Crim. L. Bull. 234 (1999).

Problem 9-24: Fortune Cookie

Dr. Alice Barton-Smith, M.D. is a psychiatrist specializing in patients who malinger and fake symptoms. In a personal injury case, she is called to testify by the defendant insurance company. Dr. Barton-Smith will testify that, based on her 15 years of experience in studying malingering, her specific observations of the plaintiff totaling one hour, and her evaluation of the records in this case, the plaintiff was not truthful in her testimony about her whiplash injury. Instead, plaintiff was malingering. *Is this an adequate foundation to survive Frye?*

[2] The *Daubert* Test

[a] Holding and Rationale: Interpreting the Federal Rules of Evidence

In *Daubert v. Merrell Dow Pharmaceuticals, Inc.*, 509 U.S. 579, 113 S. Ct. 2786, 125 L. Ed. 2d 469 (1993), the Court squarely considered whether the 1923 *Frye* test survived adoption of the Federal Rules of Evidence. The plaintiff, Joyce Daubert, gave birth to a deformed child after taking Bendectin, an anti-nausea drug, during her pregnancy. She sued Merrell Dow Pharmaceuticals, Inc., the manufacturer of Bendectin. The trial court granted the defendant's motion for summary judgment on the ground that the Dauberts could not prove that Bendectin caused the birth defect. In doing so, the trial court gave no weight to affidavits of the plaintiffs' experts that addressed the issue of causation, concluding that those experts' opinions were not based on generally accepted scientific theories. The Court of Appeals for the Ninth Circuit affirmed on similar grounds, squarely questioning whether *Frye* survived the Federal Rules. The Supreme Court held that *Frye* did not survive adoption of the Federal Rules, and that in its stead the Rules established a "relevancy and reliability" test. *Daubert* vacated the lower court's decision and remanded the case for determination of the admissibility of the plaintiffs' expert opinions under the newly announced test.[3]

The Court's analysis was straightforward and largely textual. Rule 702 governed, and nowhere did it mention "general acceptance." Moreover, there was no legislative history suggesting that Congress intended to incorporate the general acceptance tests into the rules. To the contrary, the drafting history made no mention of *Frye*. The "austere" *Frye* standard, which made it difficult to admit scientific evidence, would be contrary to the "liberal thrust" of the Rules, which took the "general approach of relaxing the traditional barriers," like *Frye*, "to 'opinion' testimony."

What replaced *Frye*, said the Court, was a new "relevancy and reliability" standard. That new test, said the Court, is rooted in Rule 702, which in relevant part says that a qualified expert may offer an opinion "[i]f *scientific*, technical, or other specialized knowledge will assist the trier of fact to understand the evidence or to determine a fact in issue" (emphasis added). The Court sought to give meat to that test by accepting the parties' assumption that the evidence before the Court was "scientific," rather than "technical, or other specialized knowledge," and that that assumption had evidentiary significance. The purported "scientific" evidence consisted of proffered expert testimony (summarized in affidavits) claimed to support the proposition that Bendectin had caused Joyce Daubert to give birth to a deformed child.

Rule 702's "clear contemplation" of regulation of expert testimony was thus obvious, said the Court, from the Rules' reference to "scientific knowledge." 'Scientific' implies a grounding in the methods and procedures of science. Similarly, the word 'knowledge' connotes more than subjective belief or unsupported

---

[3] On remand, the Ninth Circuit Court of Appeals concluded that plaintiffs' experts' opinions were not reliable and dismissed the case. *Daubert v. Merrell Dow*, 43 F.3d 1311 (9th Cir. 1995).

speculation." The something "more" that defined knowledge was, according to Webster's, "any body of known facts or . . . any body of ideas inferred from such facts or accepted as truths on good grounds." "Scientists, however, viewed themselves as dealing with the 'scientific method,'" which is a process, not a guarantee of certainty. "Scientific knowledge" was therefore derived from the scientific method and based on "good grounds." Significantly, concluded the Court, the requirement of "good grounds" was a clear standard of "evidentiary reliability."

But the then-Rule 702 requirement that the evidence offered would "assist the trier of fact to understand the evidence or to determine a fact in issue" (today the word "assist" is replaced by the word "help") also mattered, said the Court. The Court viewed this requirement as going primarily to relevance, for evidence that is not relevant cannot be helpful to the jury. One aspect of relevance stressed by the Court is "fit," the notion that scientific validity for one purpose is not necessarily validity for other, unrelated purposes. Thus, knowledge of the phases of the moon, noted the Court, might be relevant to how dark it was on a particular night, but not to how likely it was that a particular individual behaved irrationally.

The Court also found that Rules 701, 703, and 602 embodied the relevancy and reliability requirements. Rule 701 bars lay witnesses from giving opinions unless "rationally based on the perception of the witness." This restates the "familiar requirement of first-hand knowledge or observation." Unlike lay witnesses, however, experts have wide latitude to offer opinions not based on firsthand knowledge. Under Rule 703, for example, experts may opine based on hearsay if it would be "reasonably relied upon by experts in the particular field." As the Advisory Committee Note to Rule 602 noted, the requirement of firsthand knowledge reflects a "pervasive manifestation" of the common-law insistence on the "most reliable sources of information." Thus, the Court stated, the Rules must have eliminated the firsthand knowledge requirement for experts only because it was assumed that the knowledge and experience of their disciplines provided a reliable basis for the opinion.

[b] The *Daubert* Factors

[i] The Factors Stated

Next, drawing on a wide array of sources (from philosophers of science to practicing scientists), the *Daubert* Court crafted a series of factors to guide the trial court in its decision on evidentiary reliability:

1. Are the theory (the underlying scientific principle) and the technique applying that theory (what the proposed Rule 702 amendment refers to as "methods") testable and have they been tested? By "tested," the Court apparently meant, "Has a hypothesis been generated, and have adequate efforts been made to falsify that hypothesis, with no such falsification yet having been achieved?"

2. Have the theory and technique been subjected to peer review and publication?

3. What is the known or potential error rate of the technique?

4. Are there standards controlling the technique's operation, that is, an authoritative statement of the circumstances under which the technique's application to a particular case will be considered trustworthy?

5. Has the principle or technique attained "widespread acceptance" (something undefined but arguably less than general acceptance, though later cases seem to treat the two terms as equivalent)?

There is no need for a "yes" answer to every question for evidence to be admissible. These questions merely help to guide the trial judge's policy judgments. Moreover, these factors are not exclusive. "Many factors will bear on the inquiry," said the Court, "and we do not presume to set out a definitive checklist or test." Rather, the trial court's inquiry is to be a "flexible one." In a footnote, the Court cited several authorities that listed overlapping guiding factors. One such citation was to Judge Jack Weinstein and Professor Margaret Berger's treatise, which listed these factors:[4]

1. The technique's general acceptance in the field.
2. The expert's qualifications and stature.
3. The use to which the new technique has been applied.
4. The technique's potential rate of error.
5. The existence of specialized literature concerning the technique.
6. The novelty of the new invention.
7. The extent to which the technique relies on the subjective interpretation of the expert.

Another of the Court's citations was to Justice Mark McCormick's suggestion of 11 factors:[5]

1. The potential error rate in using the technique.
2. The existence and maintenance of standards governing its use.
3. The presence of safeguards in the characteristics of the technique.
4. Analogy to other scientific techniques whose results are admissible.
5. The extent to which the technique has been accepted by scientists in the field involved.
6. The nature and breadth of the inference adduced.
7. The clarity and simplicity with which the technique can be described and its results explained.
8. The extent to which the basic data are verifiable by the court and the jury.
9. The availability of other experts to test and evaluate the technique.

---

[4] 3 J. Weinstein & M. Berger, Weinstein's Evidence 702[03] (1988).

[5] Mark McCormick, *Scientific Evidence: Defining a New Approach to Admissibility*, 67 Iowa L. Rev. 879 (1982).

10. The probative significance of the evidence in the circumstances of the case.

11. The care with which the technique was employed in the case.

The five factors articulated by the *Daubert* Court, and the additional factors noted in the treatise and article cited by the Court, mostly seem readily understandable, though their application to particular cases may be difficult. But one factor — whether a theory or technique is testable and has been tested — deserves special explanation.

[ii] Defining "Testability"

While it is unlikely, contrary to the views of some commentators, that the Court adopted wholesale the views of any particular philosopher of science, the Court's use of the "testability" factor has links to a philosopher of science named Karl Popper, whom the Court quoted. Popper made the important point that if we look for confirmation of our hypotheses, we will likely find it everywhere, ignoring the contradicting evidence. The true test of a science, Popper suggested, is whether our theory enables us to make predictions that can be proven wrong. So long as our predictions come true, our theory has not been "falsified." But our acceptance of the theory must be provisional, for some future prediction may indeed prove false, requiring us to reject or revise the theory.

Two commentators have explained the point thus:[6]

> Psychoanalysts, for example, could "explain" any clinical observation in terms of their theories, sometimes without even seeing the patient. And "[a] Marxist could not open a newspaper without finding on every page confirming evidence for his interpretation of history; not only in the news, but also in its presentation — which revealed the class bias of the paper." By contrast, Einstein's theory of relativity — which was also a matter of great popular interest at the time — made specific predictions about the world, any one of which could demolish the theory if not borne out. Psychoanalysis and Marxism were not falsifiable, Popper concluded. Relativity was.

> To be scientific, Popper argued, a theory must make predictions concrete enough to be proved wrong if the claim is not in fact true. The more the theory excludes (at least in principle), the better it is. Thus, Popper's criterion was intended to separate empirical science from other domains of human knowledge. But it also helped to distinguish good science from bad. A theory, even though it may be scientific in its basic thrust, is not a very good theory at all if it is so loosely phrased that it cannot be proved wrong — if it is in fact wrong.

These same two commentators offered this example:[7]

---

[6] Kenneth R. Foster & Peter W. Huber, Judging Science: Scientific Knowledge and the Federal Courts 39 (1997).

[7] *Id.* at 39–40.

In 1980 the conservative economist Julian Simon made a wager with Paul Ehrlich, a liberal ecologist well known for his dire predictions that the world is running out of natural resources. If Ehrlich is right, basic commodities of every kind should grow increasingly scarce, and their prices should rise. Simon predicts that commodities will become increasingly abundant as improvements in technology make it possible to extract more resources from the environment. Simon bet Ehrlich that the price of a basket of five metals — any five that Ehrlich cared to choose — would fall between 1980 and 1990. Ehrlich took the bet. Ten years later he lost it, decisively. He sent Simon a check.

Many might disagree that economics is a science, and many more writers have subjected Karl Popper's theories to withering criticism. Nevertheless, those theories do help to shed light on what the Court meant by its "testability" criterion. The Court also noted that, in applying this and other factors, the trial court's search is for "*evidentiary* reliability," which is shown by "*scientific* validity." Thus scientific evidence is evidentiarily "reliable" if it measures or supports what it purports to measure or support — which is the very definition of scientific "validity" given above. This does not mean, however, that scientific "reliability" (i.e., consistency) is irrelevant to the *Daubert* inquiry. As noted earlier, it is hard to gauge scientific validity if the results of experiments are inconsistent and thus unreliable.

[iii] The Gatekeeping Function

Finally, although the Court rejected the "austere" *Frye* approach, the *Daubert* opinion makes clear that easy admission of scientific evidence is not the Court's suggested alternative. Rather, the trial court must exercise a "gatekeeping" function in reviewing the quality of scientific evidence before it reaches the jury. "We are confident," declared the Court, "that federal judges possess the capacity to undertake this review." At the same time, however, the Court recognized that its flexible test might admit some evidence that *Frye* would exclude. To this point, the Court summarily noted that rules other than 702 — such as 703 and 403 — might sometimes justify excluding scientific evidence. More importantly, the Court, arguably directing its comments to trial judges, urged faith in the adversarial jury system, rejecting fears that

> abandonment of "general acceptance" as the exclusive requirement for admission will result in a "free-for-all" in which befuddled juries are confounded by absurd and irrational pseudoscientific assertions. In this regard respondent seems to us overly pessimistic about the capabilities of the jury, and of the adversary system generally. Vigorous cross-examination, presentation of contrary evidence, and careful instruction on the burden of proof are the traditional and appropriate means of attacking shaky but admissible evidence.

Caution:

Remember that, while the *Frye* inquiry is no longer determinative, a *Frye*-like analysis may be one of the factors considered by the trial court in its flexible weighing process under *Daubert*.

Problem 9-25: Linguistic Rage

John Cheng is a graduate student in philosophy who killed the members of his doctoral thesis committee. Cheng claims that he was insane, or at least extremely emotionally disturbed, at the time of the crime.

Cheng emigrated from Hong Kong a few years ago. He came from an upper-middle-class family there, but his family severed all ties when Cheng refused to join the family business. Cheng had been an outstanding and privileged student in Hong Kong, but in the United States, he met one disappointment after another. For years, he was unable to get a teaching assistantship ("TA") or office job, finding work only as a busboy in a Chinese restaurant. When he finally did get a TA position, he got such poor teaching evaluations that his contract was not renewed. His grades were barely passing. He blamed all this on discrimination based on his accent and race, for he was confident that he otherwise had a strong command of English and a talented mind. The rejection of his dissertation was the final straw, and he reacted with violence.

His defense attorney raised a novel defense: linguistic rage. Linguistic rage is rooted in sociolinguistic studies of accent. The studies show that accent is not physically a bar to understanding, but that it is part of a social categorization process by which outsider groups are subordinated. "People in power are perceived as speaking normal, unaccented English. Any speech that is different from that constructed norm is called an accent."

The defense plans to call a linguist to the stand who will testify that this ideology of linguistic subordination is widespread. Accent discrimination thus systematically excludes talented workers from jobs, promotions, and other kinds of recognition for achievement. Yet, after childhood, many adults are physiologically incapable of losing their accents. Moreover, accents are generally not a bar to understanding by those willing to listen. Furthermore, our ways of speaking are central to our social and individual identities, so failed efforts to lose our accents and the resulting ridicule cause great emotional pain. Additionally, accent and race discrimination are linked. While some Asian Americans have now achieved visible success in American society, Asian accents activate the worst stereotypes about Asians. In short, "accent, when it acts in part as a marker for race, takes on special significance."

The linguist, Rosini Pfund, has published articles concerning her theories on accent discrimination in numerous prestigious professional journals, mostly ones specializing in linguistic ethnography. An ethnographic study involves careful recording and description of an individual case. For example, the speech of selected immigrants with ostensible "accents" might be recorded in their various interactions with different communities — at work, in the subject's neighborhood, at church, and at home. Information may then be gathered as well from documentation, from interviews with subjects concerning their experiences — for example, losing a job, not getting a promotion, being shunned by neighbors — and concerning others' stated perceptions (under a promise of anonymity) of the subjects. Alternatively, others' perceptions may be inferred from indirect questions; their answers to questions such as, "Did you understand what Mr. Sun just said?" or "Do you think he would make a good supervisor?" might be taken as reflecting deeper but not explicitly stated views about the connections among his accent, personality, and intelligence.

Dr. Pfund relied for most of her testimony on the following sources of information:

- Ethnographic studies conducted by linguists.

- Linguistic histories of various ethnic groups who have emigrated to the United States, especially Asian-Americans, and how they have fared here.

- Writings by philosophers of language on its nature and its role in human reasoning and social organization.

- Writings by political activists in the Hispanic-American and Asian-American communities.

The defense also plans to call a psychologist who will testify that, as a result of accent discrimination, Cheng suffered from a mental disease or defect. The psychologist will also testify that Cheng suffered an extreme emotional disturbance that would justify the mitigation of murder to manslaughter.

1. How would Ms. Pfund's testimony fare under each of the *Daubert* reliability factors? Why or why not?

2. Is Ms. Pfund's testimony "relevant" under *Daubert's* "relevancy and reliability" test? Why?

3. What cross-examination questions should the prosecution ask Ms. Pfund? Why?

4. Would Ms. Pfund's testimony more likely be admitted under *Daubert* or under *Frye*? Why?

Problem 9-26: The Horizontal Gaze Nystagmus Test

Patricia Kurland is on trial for drunk driving. Officer Butch Leibel testifies that he stopped her car because it was weaving slightly. To test her for drunkenness, he administered the horizontal gaze nystagmus test (HGN). HGN is based on the theory that alcohol consumption affects eye movement. Thus, an officer might, as Officer Leibel did, ask a suspect to focus on and follow a moving pen held by the officer 12 inches from the suspect's eyes. The officer seeks to observe: (1) whether the onset of nystagmus (eye jerking) occurred when the pen was at an angle of less than 45 degrees from the center of the suspect's face; (2) whether nystagmus was moderate or distinct when the suspect's eyes have been moved as far as possible in one direction or the other; and (3) whether the suspect's eyes moved smoothly in tracking the pen. Based on the HGN results, Officer Leibel testified that Kurland: (a) was then under the influence of alcohol and (b) that she had operated her car at a blood alcohol level of more than .10, the legal limit in this state. Officer Leibel testified that he was trained to test for horizontal gaze nystagmus at the police academy and that he has since administered hundreds of HGN tests. He testified that he had tested Kurland following the Drug Evaluation and Classification Program standards that had been developed during the 1980s and 1990s by the Los Angeles Police Department to guide its officers in the correct procedures for administering HGN. Franklin Eyeworth, a well-respected local optometrist, also took the stand. He testified that optometrists routinely look for nystagmus and generally accept the principle that it is measurably affected by alcohol consumption.

1. Should any or all of the officer's and the optometrist's testimony be excluded under *Daubert*? Why or why not?

2. Would it change your opinion to learn that the National Highway Traffic Safety Administration (NHTSA) had conducted both laboratory studies and field tests of HGN accuracy using the L.A. Police Department standards? NHTSA issued a report concluding that: (1) in laboratory studies, officers using HGN were 90% accurate in identifying persons who had recently consumed alcohol and 70% accurate in identifying who had a blood alcohol level higher than .10; and (2) in field studies (observing officers using HGN on real suspects on the street, then measuring the suspects' blood alcohol level using blood tests), the officers were 70% accurate in identifying who had recently consumed alcohol and 40% accurate in identifying who had a blood alcohol level higher than .10?

Problem 9-27: My Brand New Miata

Two brand new Miata automobiles collided at the intersection of Fourth and Vine. At trial in a personal injury action arising from the collision, the plaintiff is expected to offer a police officer as an expert in accident reconstruction. Several eyewitnesses are also expected to testify at the trial about the accident. You, as defense counsel, are about to take the deposition of the officer. *What questions should you ask him specifically to help you determine whether to file a motion in limine to exclude his testimony at trial as violative of* Daubert? *What do you think his answers are likely to be? Do you think it likely that his testimony will ultimately be admitted? Why?*

Problem 9-28: Harassment!

In a sexual harassment action, the plaintiff offered the testimony of Dr. Lucy Barnes, an expert psychologist, to describe the profile of a sexual harasser. Dr. Barnes will testify that a sexual harasser is typically married, is the victim's supervisor, and has known the victim for at least six months. Dr. Barnes bases this conclusion on surveys done of men who either voluntarily sought treatment once their alleged harassment was revealed or were ordered to do so by their employers as a condition of continued employment. *Is this testimony admissible?*

Problem 9-29: Probably Guilty

Ms. Juanita Brooks was robbed by a blonde woman wearing a ponytail who fled in a partly yellow automobile, driven by a mustached and bearded African-American man, which immediately drove away from the scene at high speed. The defendants, Robert Mollins and Sandy Travolta, were stopped by the police 10 minutes after the crime in the general vicinity of the robbery, and they fit the victim's description of the thieves, though the victim made only a tentative identification at trial of Travolta as the robber and Mollins as the lookout and getaway driver.

To bolster its case, the prosecution called an instructor of mathematics at a state college. The prosecutor asked the mathematician, Randall Numerology, the following:

PROSECUTOR: Dr., please assume the following probabilities:

Characteristic	*Individual Probability*
A. Partly yellow automobile	1/10
B. Man with moustache	1/4
C. Girl with ponytail	1/10
D. Girl with blond hair	1/3
E. Negro man with beard	1/10
F. Interracial couple in car	1/1000

What is the probability that the crime was committed by any single couple with such distinctive characteristics?

A: One in 12,000,000.

PROSECUTOR: How did you come up with that figure?

A: By using the product rule, which states that the probability of the joint occurrence of a number of mutually independent events is equal to the product of the individual probabilities that each of the events will occur.

PROSECUTOR: So you multiplied these probabilities?

A: Yes.

PROSECUTOR: What does it mean to say that events are "mutually independent"?

A: It means that the probability of one event's happening does not alter the probability of another event's happening. For example, the probability of rolling a "2" with one die is 1/6, as is the probability of rolling a "3." If you now roll a "2," that does not make it any more or less likely that your next die throw will be a "3." That probability was 1/6 before the "2" was rolled and is still 1/6 after.

Should defense counsel have objected under Daubert? *Why or why not?*

[iv] Procedural Concerns

Several procedural concerns further illuminate the meaning of the *Daubert* test. First, the Court declared the reliability inquiry to be a competency question under Rule 104(a). Accordingly, the proponent of the evidence has the burden of proving that a scientific principle or technique is reliable to the trial judge's personal satisfaction by a preponderance of the evidence. This may require a pretrial or mid-trial hearing at which the trial court will hear and resolve conflicting evidence on both sides of the reliability question. In making this judgment, the trial judge may need to resolve credibility disputes between experts. The trial court must keep in mind, however, that her focus is to "be solely on principles and methodology, not on the conclusions that they generate." While the meaning of this phrase is ambiguous, it should not mean that evaluating the reliability of a scientific theory or technique (method) must be done without considering the conclusions drawn from the data gathering or the selection of research strategies:[8]

> When scientists conduct research, they generally do not draw sharp distinctions between the research methodology chosen and the conclusions drawn from that research. Some conclusions are permitted by a particular methodology and some are not. Thus, when studying the toxic effects of drugs, use of animals rather than humans as subjects restricts the conclusions that might be drawn from the data. The decision to use multiple regression analysis affects what conclusions are within contemplation. Research on the carcinogenic character of second-hand smoke conducted on white rats, by subjecting them to the equivalent of ten packs-a-day, might employ exactly the right methodology and reasoning for concluding that such smoke causes cancer in white rats; but if the researcher is interested in generalizing the study to humans, then we must evaluate the methodology and reasoning in light of that purpose. Scientific conclusions are inextricably connected to the methodologies used to reach them.

What the Court seems to be saying, therefore, in delegating to the trial judge the task of evaluating the reliability of "principles and methodology" but not of conclusions, is that the trial court's admissibility decision is not to be swayed by the expert's final conclusion when applying the general principles and methods (techniques) to the specific case. In other words, the trial court's evaluation of the reliability of the major premises in the expert syllogism is not to be affected by the expert's view of the accuracy of the minor premises or the resulting conclusion. Professor Faigman and his colleagues, using slightly different language, explain the matter this way:[9]

> There is, however, another way to understand Justice Blackmun's [the author of the *Daubert* majority opinion] distinction between methodology/reasoning and conclusions that appeals to both legal and scientific mindsets. Most science comes to the courtroom as part of a four-tiered system

---

[8] David L. Faigman et al., Modern Scientific Evidence: The Law and Science of Expert Testimony § 1-3.3.1[21], at 22 (1997). *See also* Advisory Committee Note to amended Rule 702 amendment (making similar point).

[9] *Id.* at 24–25.

of knowledge acquisition. The most general or abstract might be termed "general theory," the next most abstract is "general application," the third might be termed "general technology," and the fourth, and most concrete for legal purposes, might be termed "individual application." An example will illustrate these tiers. DNA profiling is perhaps the most powerful and, thus, the most troubling forensic technology ever to be used in a court of law. But in the courtroom, DNA evidence is a product of a complex web of science and technology. First, at the level of "general theory," is the biological theory of the DNA molecule. Second, at the level of "general application," the general theory has been studied in respect to various populations. In doing so, scientists have hypothesized and analyzed data about the complexion and distribution of DNA characteristics in populations of more or less homogeneity. Third, at the level of "general technology," scientists and technicians have devised various techniques for "profiling" DNA, including the two best known of Restriction Fragment Length Polymorphisms (RFLP) and Polymerase Chain Reaction (PCR), the latter used to amplify DNA found in small forensic samples. Finally, and most obviously pertinent to the law, at the level of "individual application," lab technicians take this general technology and apply it to individual cases to determine whether a match has been found between a forensic sample and a known sample.

. . . .

This understanding of the division of science into levels of abstraction offers the best interpretation of Justice Blackmun's distinction between methodology/reasoning and conclusions. Specifically, the first three levels of science, "general theory," "general application," and "general technology," are all aspects of science that transcend individual cases and for which the judge is more likely, over time, to be the better evaluator of scientific merit. These three "general" levels are contemplated by Justice Blackmun's "methodology and reasoning" category. [The fourth level of individual application is, however, not the judge's concern].

Under the amendment to Rule 702, however, the judge has a role to play at the level of individual application, namely ensuring that the principles and methods have been reliably applied to the individual case. *See* Advisory Committee Note to Rule 702. But if there is a dispute about the underlying facts to which the principles and methods are applied, under the proposed amendment, the trial court should not exclude the expert's testimony because the court believes one version of the facts and not the other. *Id.* Moreover, at any level of abstraction, two experts might each rely on competing principles or methods that are both found by the court to be reliable. *Id.*

The second procedural concern arises because, in *General Electric Co. v. Joiner*, 522 U.S. 136, 138–139, 118 S. Ct. 512, 139 L. Ed. 2d 508 (1997), the Court held that a trial court's decision concerning the *Daubert* reliability requirement is subject to appellate review only for an abuse of discretion. Thereafter, in *Kumho Tire Co. v. Carmichael*, 526 U.S. 137, 119 S. Ct. 1167, 143 L. Ed. 2d 238 (1999), the Court held that trial judge discretion extends to two other decisions as well: (1) what factors are to be used in making the reliability judgment concerning a particular principle or technique in a particular case (in the Court's words, "whether *Daubert's* specific factors are, or are not, reasonable measures of reliability in a particular case is a matter that the law grants the trial judge broad latitude to determine"); and (2) whether it is necessary to hold a "*Daubert* hearing" in the first place, that is, whether the reliability inquiry can instead be resolved by judicial notice or by other procedures that do not require taking testimony. This enormous discretion vested in the trial court limits appellate courts' role in achieving consistency in the treatment of scientific evidence and implementation of *Daubert's* dictates. Indeed, even before *Kumho Tire*, many trial courts have started to show increasingly close scrutiny of various forms of scientific evidence, despite the *Daubert* Court's language about the "liberal thrust" of the federal expert evidence rules. Accordingly, in practice it is unlikely that *Daubert* will necessarily prove to be a more lenient standard than *Frye*. *But see* Advisory Committee Note to Rule 702 ("A review of the case law after *Daubert* shows that the rejection of expert testimony is the exception rather than the rule".).

Problem 9-30: Reversal of Rage

Assume the facts of Problem 9-25 on linguistic rage:

1. Which of the original *Daubert* factors, if any, would you as trial judge apply in conducting your *Daubert* analysis? Why?

2. What additional factors, if any, would you decide are relevant to the *Daubert* inquiry if you sat as the trial judge? Why?

3. If a trial judge ruled that all the original *Daubert* factors — and no others — not only had to be considered but had to be met so that the failure of any one factor would result in exclusion in this case, would that ruling likely be reversed on appeal? Why?

Problem 9-31: Concluding Methods

Is it relevant, in assessing the reliability of principles and methods under Daubert:

1. That a psychologist concludes that a murder suspect was 100% incapable of committing a violent act, when all treatises in the field explain that, according to the empirical data, there are no circumstances under which psychologists can confidently make such claims?

2. That a polygrapher concludes that the subject was telling the truth when every one of the indicators on the polygraph test are the kind that standard training texts describe as indicating a lie?

3. That a handwriting examiner declares that the signature on a forged check matches the defendant's signature when scholars are split on whether handwriting examiners can make any such judgments with a high degree of confidence?

4. That a biologist testifies that an anti-nausea drug causes cancer in humans when studies on its carcinogenic effects have all involved white rats?

Problem 9-32: HGN and Daubert Hearings

Two experts disagree over whether the horizontal gaze nystagmus test mentioned in Problem 9-26 can identify persons whose blood alcohol level is more than .10. *Which of the following should the trial judge do?*

1. Not hold a *Daubert* hearing but summarily exclude HGN testimony.

2. Admit the testimony to avoid invading the province of the jury to decide credibility questions.

3. Hold a *Daubert* hearing, decide who is credible, and find the facts necessary to deciding the *Daubert* question by a preponderance of the evidence.

[C] Evidence Based on Technical or Other Specialized Knowledge, Including Social Science

The *Daubert* factors, we have seen, were crafted in the context of determining when to admit "scientific" evidence. Furthermore, *Daubert* itself involved the natural, not the social, sciences. Three questions thus arose: (1) Does the *Daubert* test apply to non-scientific expert testimony, that is, to "technical or other specialized knowledge?" (2) If yes, how, if at all, should the *Daubert* test be modified to accommodate these other sorts of knowledge? (3) Is social science "science," and, whatever the answer to that question, how, if at all, should *Daubert* be applied differently to this sort of knowledge as compared to natural scientific knowledge?

The Court answered the first two of these questions in *Kumho Tire Co. v. Carmichael*, 526 U.S. 137, 119 S. Ct. 1167, 143 L. Ed. 2d 238 (1999). Before *Kumho Tire*, some courts admitted some evidence that would likely be excludable under a careful application of the *Daubert* factors, arguing that a more lenient standard applied because the particular principle or technique involved was not "scientific" evidence. *Kumho Tire* held otherwise, concluding that all expert testimony, including "technical and other specialized knowledge," is governed by *Daubert's* "relevancy and reliability" standard. *Kumho Tire* involved an engineer's testimony. The Court explained:[10]

> [I]t would prove difficult, if not impossible, for judges to administer evidentiary rules under which a gatekeeping obligation depended upon a distinction between "scientific" knowledge and "technical" or "other specialized" knowledge. There is no clear line that divides the one from the others. Disciplines such as engineering rest upon scientific knowledge. Pure scientific theory itself may depend for its development upon observation and properly engineered machinery. And conceptual efforts to distinguish the two are unlikely to produce clear legal lines capable of application in particular cases.

Rule 702, noted the Court, articulated a single standard for admitting expert testimony, regardless of its type. Furthermore, the reason the Federal Rules of

---

[10] *Kumho Tire Co. v. Carmichael*, 526 U.S. 137, 119 S. Ct. 1167, 1174, 143 L. Ed. 2d 238 (1999).

Evidence grant experts more latitude than other witnesses, the Court concluded, is the assumption that all expert testimony has a reliable basis. All expert testimony must therefore be relevant and reliable. The opinion suggested, although this question was not specifically before the Court, that social science is governed by this same standard, whether we consider that discipline "scientific" or not.

Reliability does not necessarily have to be judged, however, by the same five factors articulated in *Daubert:*

> We can neither rule out, nor rule in, for all cases and for all time the applicability of the factors mentioned in *Daubert*, nor can we now do so for subsets of cases categorized by category or expert or by kind of evidence. . . .
>
> *Daubert* itself is not to the contrary. It made clear that its list of factors was meant to be helpful, not definitive. Indeed, those factors do not all necessarily apply even in every instance in which the reliability of scientific testimony is challenged. It might not be surprising in a particular case, for example, that a claim made by a scientific witness has never been the subject of peer review, for the particular application at issue may never previously have interested any scientist. Nor, on the other hand, does the presence of *Daubert's* general acceptance factor help to show that an expert's testimony is reliable where the discipline itself lacks reliability, as, for example, do theories grounded in any so-called generally accepted principles of astrology or necromancy.

After *Kumho Tire*, trial courts will be faced with the perhaps daunting task of coming up with helpful factors to guide the admissibility decision in a wide range of very different expert disciplines. The Court has not, therefore, entirely erased the distinction between "scientific" and "non-scientific" testimony because, for example, the reliability of a physicist's opinion necessarily requires understanding what are the standards of "good physics," a natural science. But that does not correspondingly mean that, on the other hand, Freudian psychology is to be judged by the standards of "good Freudian psychology," for *Kumho Tire* requires a court to determine whether an entire discipline is reliable. Some commentators have argued that Freudian psychology, unlike some other sorts of psychology, is so subjective that there is no objective way to gauge its reliability. Thus, a Freudian psychologist might interpret a particular dream to mean that a patient was obsessively attached to his mother, while another Freudian psychologist might offer a completely different interpretation of the same dream. How would we devise a "test" to determine who is right? On the other hand, some aspects of Freudian psychology are testable but yet have not been sufficiently tested. We could thus devise tests, as some indeed have, to determine whether Freudian talking therapy alleviates depression. Some commentators would therefore insist that all Freudian psychology — indeed all social science — be judged by the same sorts of factors as were involved in *Daubert* itself, with special emphasis on "testability and testing." Where this is found wanting, the testimony should be excluded.

Much social science can and should indeed be done using procedures similar to, or at least analogous to, those in the natural sciences. But even social science that cannot, or has not, yet met such standards of pseudo-natural-scientific testing can still sometimes be useful to a jury. This can be so even if the social scientist, while drawing on general principles, uses techniques and reaches conclusions in some ways unique to the particular case. Under *Kumho Tire*, therefore, there may be certain types of expert testimony using methods significantly different than those in the natural sciences that are nevertheless arguably still reliable. *Cf.* Advisory Committee Note to Rule 702 ("In certain fields experience is the predominant, if not sole, basis for a great deal of reliable testimony."). Here are three illustrations:

Example 1: The Acute Observer

Forensic linguists study conversations that are relevant to issues at trial, to interpret to the jury meanings that might not be evident on their face. One such linguist testified for the defense in a case in which the defendant, a chemical manufacturer, was charged with conspiring to find a pill press to aid a drug dealer. The suspect's defense was that he became so uncomfortable when he finally realized what the other party had proposed, that he sought only to get out of the conversation. His audiotaped statements did not, therefore, reveal his agreement to anything.

The linguist was able to explain why the other party's early offers were ambiguous (thus explaining why the listener would participate for so long), and to point out why the rules of social politeness would make it hard for the listener to extricate himself from the conversation. Similarly, the linguist noted that the listener-defendant brought up only 15 percent of the words used, and spoke in much shorter sentences than did the primary speaker. Furthermore, most of the listener's turns at talk were one-word utterances, largely feedback markers, "uh-huh," "yeah," "hmmm," "oh," "okay," and "man." These tactics were arguably efforts of the listener to distance himself from the conversation without alienating the primary speaker, instead of actual acceptance of the speaker's proposal.

The only direct statement of agreement by the listener was in offering to "check around," which was an indirect response to the speaker's asking where he could get a pill press. But eight days later, in a second conversation, the listener simply reports, "I haven't had any luck." This lack of specificity about where and how he looked, about his prior experiences with or contacts in locating pill presses, and his lack of enthusiasm or elaboration, are the kind of hollow offers that people often use to end uncomfortable exchanges quickly, like "Let's get together for lunch sometime."

Henry Drummond (Spencer Tracy) examines Biblical expert Matthew Harrison Brady (Fredric March) in *Inherit the Wind.**

This combination of close observation of the defendant's speech with background information on the sociodynamics of ordinary conversation arguably offered a plausible alternative to the prosecution's conspiracy theory.

Example 2: Overcoming Cognitive Blinders

A prosecution expert in a rape case involving an African-American victim testifies about empirical research showing that most people, including jurors, are likely to be more skeptical of the testimony of African-American victims than white victims. Similarly, they are more willing to believe that an African-American woman consented to the defendant's behavior than that a white woman did. The defense objects that the testimony is irrelevant and only concerns generalizations, thus offering no reliable guidance concerning whether this alleged victim is telling the truth.

The prosecution responds that the testimony alerts the jurors to an unconscious racist bias that may hamper their ability to decide fairly. The testimony enhances jurors' rationality by alerting them to their own prejudices, the "cognitive blinders" that can bar them from seeing the truth. *Cf.* Advisory Committee Note to Rule 702 ("it might also be important in some cases for an expert to educate the factfinder about

---

* *Inherit the Wind* copyright© 1960 Metro-Goldwyn-Mayer Studios Inc. All Rights Reserved.

general principles, without ever attempting to apply these principles to the specific facts of the case").

Example 3: Valuing Interpretive Social Science

A sociologist testifies at a sexual harassment trial in support of a hostile environment claim. A state sexual harassment statute extends gender-based harassment to include non-sexual but systematic forms of gender disparagement, exclusion, and hostility. The sociologist recounts her ethnographic study of legal practice, which revealed a discriminatory emotional division of labor. Thus, male lawyers turned social events into competitions over who could drink the most beer, routinely mistook female associates for secretaries, and considered those associates shrill if they behaved aggressively but thought them weak if they took a more relational approach. Yet male associates were praised for their "hardball" tactics. Males also laughed at women lawyers who told tales of their aggressive behavior, which put women in a one-down position. As a consequence, women lawyers generally had a lower social and professional status than male lawyers in the study. The sociologist similarly interpreted the behavior she observed in visiting the law firm involved in the current sexual harassment suit, relying on her earlier ethnographic study in evaluating the current defendant's conduct. This testimony relies on interpretive social science, which assigns meaning to human action rather than, for example, doing experiments.

Problem 9-33: Raging Against Daubert

Return again to *Problem 9-25* on linguistic rage. *After* Kumho Tire, *can you articulate arguments that* Daubert's *"testimony" and error rate factors should not apply (or at least not apply in the same way as with the natural sciences) to the linguistic rage inquiry? What other factors should apply?*

Problem 9-34: Fred Fraud Fred

The defendants, brothers named Fred, were charged with mail fraud, securities fraud, and conspiracy. At trial, the prosecution called a well-known securities analyst to testify about the defendants' conduct. The witness, Rex Limbart, testified that, in his opinion, the actions by the defendants Fred constituted a "clear scheme to defraud others." *Is Mr. Limbart's testimony admissible? Why?*

Problem 9-35: Baseball

James Bell, a promising outfielder for the New Haven Hawks baseball team, signed a multi-year contract with a Japanese major league team. His then-existing New Haven contract allowed both sides to be excused from the contract if "good faith negotiations did not produce an extended agreement." The Hawks sued, claiming Bell did not act in good faith. At trial, James called his brother, an expert in negotiations, to testify that "In my opinion, James definitely acted in good faith." *Is this testimony admissible? Why?*

Problem 9-36. The Best Defense

Plaintiff filed a civil rights action for damages against the Sheriff's Office, alleging that the Sheriff conducted warrantless searches of his home and office. The plaintiff called famous attorney Matlock Mason to the stand to testify as an expert. Matlock states that the officers' conduct qualifies as a "search" and that the plaintiffs had not legally "consented" to the search. *Is Matlock's opinion admissible?*

§ 9.06 THE MINOR PREMISES

Once an expert has testified that underlying scientific principles and the techniques applying them are sound (the major premises), those principles and techniques must be applied to the facts in the specific case (the minor premises). There has been some dispute about which rule should be central to the questions of admissibility of minor premises testimony: Rule 702, which requires helpfulness to the trier of fact, or Rule 703, which requires experts to "reasonably rely" on data not otherwise admissible. There has also been some disagreement about whether something like *Daubert's* analysis governed the application of Rule 703. Courts often evade the question simply by applying both Rule 702 and Rule 703 and using similar analyses under each. Whichever approach is adopted, the clear trend is to subject minor premises, not merely major premises, to a searching reliability inquiry. Here we adopt the analytical scheme of Rule 702. Under that scheme, Rule 702 governs both major and minor premises, and both must be reliable. Thus, the last clause requires that "the witness has applied the principles and methods reliably to the facts of the case." Principles and methods may be misapplied in innumerable ways, most obviously including the failure to follow prescribed procedures and the failure to collect all necessary information.

Example 1

Several researchers have proposed that properly trained dogs can accurately sniff the scent on an item dropped by a fleeing criminal offender and match it to the scent of a person in a line of suspects (a "dog-scent lineup"). The researchers specify, however, that confidence in such a lineup is possible only where the dog has been: (1) specially trained in the technique; (2) "calibrated," that is, repeatedly and recently tested in controlled experiments for proof that the individual dog can do these lineups accurately; (3) placed in a room with the suspects hidden behind a screen and the handler outside the room so that no one can give the dog "minimal cues," subtle subconscious gestures that might prod the dog to identify a particular suspect; and (4) allowed to sniff suspects who are all wearing similar, recently washed clothing. The principle that each person has a unique scent and the method/technique that properly trained dogs can accurately identify and match that scent have been proven to the trial judge by a preponderance of the evidence, thus meeting the *Daubert* test.

John Van Jones, a police dog handler with 10 years of experience tracking fleeing suspects with dogs, testifies concerning the results of a scent lineup in which his dog, Flea-Bit, identified the defendant, George

Harrison, as a killer. Defense counsel objects that Jones failed on direct to establish a foundation of reliable application of the principles and methods of scent lineups to Harrison's case. The trial judge, rather than immediately sustaining the objection, permits Cory Little, defense counsel, to question Jones on voir dire. That questioning reveals that: (1) Flea-Bit was trained to track suspects fleeing the crime scene but never trained in dog-scent lineups; (2) Flea-Bit has not been calibrated; (3) Jones was in the room with Flea-Bit when he identified Harrison; (4) Jones did not arrange for the lineup participants to wear similar, recently cleaned clothing; and (5) this was Jones' first lineup. Little renews his objection that the case-specific application of lineup principles and methods was not reliably done and asks the court to reconsider its earlier ruling that Jones was qualified to testify, objecting to those qualifications. The trial judge granted the reconsideration motion and sustained both objections.

Example 2

Jenny Jones is charged with fraudulently cashing bad checks. She testifies at trial that she was given the checks by her boyfriend, who assured her that they were good but said he was too busy to cash them. Douglas Lee, a psychologist, then testified that he had interviewed Ms. Jones and concluded that she was an abnormally gullible woman, unable to believe that someone she loved would lie to her. The following exchange takes place between the prosecutor and Dr. Lee on cross-examination.

PROSECUTOR: Dr. Lee, you received your degree in forensic psychology from the University of Utah, is that correct?

A: Yes.

PROSECUTOR: And the course you studied there on how to do character assessments of patients was done under the eminent Dr. Wilfred Daily?

A: Yes.

PROSECUTOR: "Gullibility" is a character trait, I take it?

A: Yes.

PROSECUTOR: In judging whether a patient displays a character trait, you were taught to begin with a clinical interview, were you not?

A: Yes.

PROSECUTOR: And you did such an interview here?

A: Yes.

PROSECUTOR: But you were also taught to interview the patients' family, friends, teachers, and co-workers?

A: Yes.

PROSECUTOR: But you didn't interview any of Ms. Jones' family, did you?

A: No.

PROSECUTOR: Nor did you interview her friends?

A: No.

PROSECUTOR: You never once spoke to any of her co-workers, correct?

A: Yes.

PROSECUTOR: Nor did you talk to her teachers?

A: No, I did not.

PROSECUTOR: Indeed, you never even asked Ms. Jones the names of any of her family, friends, teachers, or co-workers?

A: Correct.

PROSECUTOR: You interviewed no one other than Ms. Jones in reaching your assessment that she was "abnormally gullible?"

A: Yes.

PROSECUTOR: And you assumed, without checking for corroborating evidence from anyone else, that all that she told you in your clinical interview was true?

A: Yes.

PROSECUTOR: I ask the court to reconsider its ruling that Dr. Lee may testify and move to strike his testimony as not based on the reliable application of relevant psychological principles and methods to this case.

JUDGE: Motion granted.

There is an ambiguity in Rule 702. The Rule requires that "the testimony [be] based upon sufficient facts or data," next requires that the "testimony [be] the product of reliable principles and methods," and concludes that "the expert has applied the principles and methods reliably to the facts of the case." The placement of the initial reference to "facts or data" immediately before "principles and methods" suggests that "facts or data" refers to sound information and procedures being used to establish the reliability of the major premises, that is, to the "principles and methods." Furthermore, the focus of the Advisory Committee Note on *Daubert* — which addressed principles and methods — supports this interpretation. Moreover, only the last clause of Rule 702 mentions "the facts of the case," suggesting that the first two clauses (the first one including the phrase "facts or data") concern non-case-specific inquiries, that is, major premises.

However, the Advisory Committee Note to Rule 702, in the context of defining the term "data," refers to the Advisory Committee Note to Rule 703. The Rule 703 Note declares that the "facts or data" upon which an expert opinion may be based may be derived from three possible sources: (1) the expert's firsthand observations, (2) a hypothetical question, and (3) data presented to the expert outside of court other than by the expert's own perception. This Note, some commentators have argued, clearly considers "facts or data" to refer to the case-specific (minor premise) basis for an expert opinion. If that is so, then Rule 702's use of that same term arguably also refers solely to the minor premises.

If "facts or data" in Rule 702 refers only to the minor premises, however, why does the Rule apparently require that all expert testimony be "based upon sufficient" facts or data but also require that the principles and methods be "applied . . . reliably" to the facts of the case? The reference to case-specific application would seem redundant if the early "facts or data" reference includes both major and minor premises but even more redundant if it refers only to minor (case-specific) premises. The redundancy can be avoided if "facts or data" instead refers only to the major premise. The Advisory Committee Note does not clear up the confusion.

One argument that the "facts or data" phrase should nevertheless be read as including both the major and minor premises turns on distinguishing between two sorts of minor premise error:

Example 3

An oncologist (cancer specialist) testifies that X-rays of the plaintiff showed what could be a malignant lung tumor. Accordingly, he had advised the plaintiff to have a painful biopsy, but the biopsy revealed no tumor at all, malignant or otherwise. The source of this error turns out to be twofold: first, the oncologist misread the X-ray; second, the radiologist took the X-ray poorly, creating avoidable shadows that made it hard to read.

Because of the radiologist's error, the oncologist's case-specific opinion — that *this patient* needed a biopsy to examine a potentially cancerous tumor — was based on flawed X-rays, that is, case-specific facts or data that were not reliable. But, even given the flawed X-rays, the oncologist compounded the problem by misreading what could be clearly seen, thus "misapplying" the principles and methods for sound X-ray interpretation. The "facts or data" phrase in Rule 702 could easily be read to include the former sort of minor premises problem, while the Rule's reference to reliable application of principles and methods can easily be read as referring to the latter sort of minor premises issue.

For the reasons we noted earlier, we do not think that the rule's text supports the argument that "facts or data" as there used refers solely to the minor premises. The phrase most likely refers to the sources of information justifying belief in the trustworthiness of both the major and minor premises. Whatever "facts or data" means, however, the X-ray example illustrates two different sorts of case-specific errors that can arise, whatever we call them.

If it is true that Rule 702 governs both major and minor premises, would there still be a minor premise role for Rule 703? The answer is "yes." Rule 702 would govern whether an opinion is based on sufficiently reliable information and whether that information has been sufficiently reliably applied to the specific case to merit admission. But some of that information might, under other evidence rules, be inadmissible, or making it admissible might require costly subpoenaing of witnesses. The original Advisory Committee Note to Rule 703 explains as follows:

Thus a physician in his own practice bases his diagnosis on information from numerous sources and of considerable variety, including statements by patients and relatives, reports and opinions from nurses, technicians and other doctors, hospital records, and X rays. Most of them are admissible in evidence, but only with the expenditure of substantial time in producing and examining various authenticating witnesses. The physician makes life or death decisions in reliance upon them. His validation, expertly performed and subject to cross-examination, ought to suffice for judicial purposes.

As amended, Rule 702 thus first determines whether minor premises are reliable, but Rule 703 controls whether, if some of the bases of the reliable minor premises are inadmissible under other rules, the expert's opinion should nevertheless be admitted. The Advisory Committee Note to Rule 702 puts it this way:

> There has been some confusion over the relationship between Rules 702 and 703. The amendment makes clear that the sufficiency of the basis of an expert's testimony is to be decided under Rule 702. Rule 702 sets forth the overarching requirement of reliability, and an analysis of the sufficiency of the expert's basis cannot be divorced from the ultimate reliability of the expert's opinion. In contrast, the "reasonable reliance" requirement of Rule 703 is a relatively narrow inquiry. When an expert relies on inadmissible information, Rule 703 requires the trial court to determine whether that information is of a type reasonably relied upon by other experts in the field. If so, the expert can rely on the information in reaching an opinion. However, the question of whether the expert is relying on a *sufficient* basis of information-whether admissible information or not — is governed by the reliability requirements of Rule 702.

The Advisory Committee Note to Rule 702 also goes on to articulate a connection between underlying information and conclusions, at least in the minor premise (case-specific) context, though suggesting a similar point for the major premise context:

> The Court in *Daubert* declared that the "focus, of course, must be solely on principles and methodology, not on the conclusions they generate." 509 U.S. at 505. Yet, as the Court later recognized, "conclusions and methodology are not entirely distinct from one another." *General Elec. Co. v. Joiner*, 522 U.S. at 146. Under the amendment, as under *Daubert*, when an expert purports to apply principles and methods consistent with professional standards, and yet reaches a conclusion that other experts in the field would not reach, the trial court may fairly suspect that the principles and methods have not been faithfully applied. *See Lust v. Merrell Dow Pharmaceuticals, Inc.*, 89 F. 3d 594, 598 (9th Cir. 1996). The amendment specifically provides that the trial court must scrutinize not only the principles and methods used by the expert, but also whether those principles and methods have been properly applied to the facts of the case.

One final question remains: If a case-specific minor premise inquiry survives Rule 702 reliability analysis but the minor premise is based on inadmissible data, when may an expert "reasonably rely" on such data in forming an opinion? No consensus has emerged, but the courts have suggested some approaches. The liberal school equates "reasonable" reliance with "regular" or "customary" reliance. The judge's task is to determine whether it is the customary practice of other experts in the relevant specialty to use a particular data source in their reasoning. A more restrictive school considers "reasonable" reliance to be a matter for independent determination by the trial judge, who must conduct a searching inquiry to determine the wisdom of an expert's relying on a particular data source. The trial judge need not defer to customary practice, although that may be a relevant factor. A middle approach regards customary reliance on a data source by experts in a field as strong evidence of reasonableness, perhaps even creating a rebuttable presumption of reasonableness.

There is also a dispute over to what information the "reasonable reliance" standard must apply. Rule 703 refers to facts or data being "*of a type*" reasonably relied upon by experts in the field. Some courts conclude, therefore, that the trial judge's narrow inquiry should be whether the expert properly relied on the particular "type" or category of information, rather than whether it was reasonable to rely on the *specific* facts or data of that type in this case. A contrary view reads Rule 703 as empowering the trial judge to question the expert's wisdom in relying on *particular* facts or data, not simply determining whether those relied upon were of the general sort to which experts would reasonably look.

Finally, there is a dispute over whether the phrase "facts or data" in Rule 703 referred only to the case-specific minor premise bases of an expert opinion or whether it also referred to the bases for the major premise. Professor Imwinkelried has forcefully argued that the only way to avoid unnecessary overlap between Rules 702 and 703, and otherwise to make sense of those two rules, is to interpret the latter as limited to the minor premises and the former to the major premises. But we saw early in this chapter that Rules 702 and 703 seem to treat the term "facts or data" as applying to both major *and* minor premises ("facts" probably referring to major, and "data" to minor, premises). Rules 702 and 703 thus probably regulate all premises, with Rule 702 testing whether those premises are reliable and Rule 703 determining whether, even if the premises are reliable, the opinions are permissible when based on otherwise inadmissible evidence. But even before Rules 702 and 703 were amended, many courts and commentators treated the phrase "facts or data" — which originally appeared only in Rule 703 — as including all premises in the expert syllogism. This interpretation creates room for confusion concerning the respective roles of the two rules.

Example 4

Remember that in *Daubert* plaintiffs argued that the anti-nausea drug, Bendectin, caused a child to be born with birth defects. Among the types of expert evidence used by the plaintiffs was epidemiological analysis. Plaintiffs conceded that the published epidemiological analyses did not show a statistical correlation between the use of Bendectin and congenital birth defects. But plaintiff's expert contended that after pooling the data on which the earlier studies relied (a technique known as "meta-analysis"), the epidemiological data did yield a statistically significant, and therefore potentially causal, relationship. Under this approach to the current rules, Rule 702 (as interpreted in *Daubert*) addresses whether the meta-analysis of epidemiological data is a reliable scientific technique (a major premise question). Rule 703, on the other hand, would determine this other major premise question: Was it reasonable for the expert to rely on the data in these earlier studies in doing a meta-analysis? Rule 703 would also govern case-specific questions, such as whether an adequate basis existed for the experts to assume that Mrs. Daubert ingested Bendectin (as opposed to another product) and that her son suffered from the specific types of defects that Bendectin is capable of causing.

An alternative view of the current rules would addresses all major premise questions under Rule 702 (the reliability of meta-analysis and the wisdom of relying on the data in the earlier studies to do a meta-analysis) and minor premises questions (what Mrs. Daubert ingested and what were Jason's symptoms) under Rule 703.

Problem 9-37: Probabilities Revisited

In Problem 9-29, assume that the prosecutor offered no proof concerning the probabilities he noted of the "independent events." Rather, he simply asked the mathematician to assume those probabilities. In his closing argument, the prosecutor told the jury that they were free to apply whatever probabilities they believed were adequate, understanding that they had to apply the product rule to whatever probabilities they chose.

1. What grounds, if any, should the defense have raised in objecting to the mathematician's testimony beyond those already discussed in Problem 9-29?

2. What additional proof could the prosecution have offered, if any, to fend off such an objection?

Problem 9-38: The Crime Scene Investigator

A well-known former professional football player is charged with stabbing his ex-wife to death. According to police DNA forensic scientists, blood found at the crime scene matched the defendant's blood. But the defense argues that the crime scene investigation was so poorly done as to risk contamination and tampering. The defense calls Michael Straub, an experienced murder forensic investigator, to opine that the investigation did indeed raise these risks. His analysis relied on his interviews with the lead detectives on the case, the lab representatives at the crime scene, and the lab technicians who did the testing. Straub testifies that each of the officers and technicians he interviewed recounted myriad details contrary to what is required by the National Guidelines for Death Investigations. However, according to the prosecutor, each of the officers and technicians denies telling Straub what he claims they said. Straub is unquestionably well-qualified. The police officers' and technicians' out-of-court statements to Straub as he recounts them are all inadmissible hearsay.

1. Should Straub be permitted to recount his opinion to the jury? Why or why not?

2. If yes, should he be allowed to relate the bases for his opinion to the jury? Why or why not?

Problem 9-39: Psychologists' Hearsay

In the linguistic rage problem, Problem 9-25, the psychologist bases his testimony that linguistic rage rendered Cheng incapable of telling right from wrong on: (1) his interviews of Cheng, Cheng's parents, friends, and employers, all of which statements are inadmissible hearsay; and (2) the opinion of the linguist that Cheng's history and behavior fit the prototypical description of linguistic rage, again a hearsay statement not fitting within any exceptions.

1. Is the psychologist's opinion admissible? Why or why not?

2. If yes, may the bases for his testimony be revealed to the jury?

§ 9.07 EXPERT EVIDENCE REVIEW PROBLEMS

Problem 9-40: Physician, Heal Thyself

Robert Allen is injured in an automobile accident. He brings a civil suit against the other car's driver. At trial, plaintiff calls a physician to the stand, hired solely for purposes of this litigation, to testify that, in his opinion, the accident compressed a previously healthy nerve in plaintiff's neck, a compression likely to cause plaintiff a lifetime of pain. In reaching his opinion, the physician relied on the treating radiologist's report, the emergency-room physician's medical records, an interview with the plaintiff, and interviews with the plaintiff's family members. *Select the best answer.*

1. The physician's opinion is inadmissible.

2. The physician's opinion is admissible if the proponent establishes that all its bases are of the type reasonably relied upon by other experts in the relevant field, but those bases are presumptively inadmissible.

3. Both the physician's opinion and all its bases are admissible, absent a showing of unfair prejudice to one of the parties.

4. The physician's opinion is admissible, but its bases may never be revealed to a jury on direct examination.

Problem 9-41: Coercive Indoctrination

John Dalvo is charged with murder and conspiracy to murder. John's defense is that "coercive indoctrination," (colloquially known as brainwashing) by John's older, more charismatic co-conspirator, rendered John temporarily insane. John calls a psychologist to the stand who will testify that in his opinion, John was indeed indoctrinated into his crime by his co-conspirator. *Select the best answer.*

1. The physician's opinion's admissibility will turn on whether it is the product of reliable principles or methods reliably applicable to the facts of the case and based upon sufficient facts or data.

2. The *Daubert* test does not apply to "soft" sciences like psychology.

3. The *Daubert* test does apply, but the opinion is admissible if it is generally accepted in the field of psychology.

4. The *Daubert* test applies only if the study of coercive indoctrination is based on novel principles using novel methods.

Problem 9-42: Experts Not

Which of the following statements is NOT true concerning an expert witness?

1. An expert witness may base her opinion on irrelevant information as long as it is made available to the opposing side prior to trial.

2. A person testifying as an expert witness may qualify as an expert even if she does not possess a college degree.

3. An expert witness may base her opinion on double hearsay.

4. An expert witness may not testify in a criminal case for the defendant on an ultimate mental state issue.

Chapter 10

PROTECTING THE ADVERSARY SYSTEM: THE HEARSAY RULE AND THE CONFRONTATION CLAUSE

§ 10.01 CHAPTER CHECKLIST

1. What are the two types of arguments supporting the admissibility of out-of-court statements?

2. What is the Five-Step Hearsay Matrix?

3. How does the hearsay rule protect the right to cross-examination?

4. What are the four hearsay dangers?

5. Can animals and machines be hearsay declarants?

6. What is a statement for purposes of the hearsay rule?

    a. What are implied assertions?

    b. What are sub-assertions?

    c. What are invisible assertions?

    d. What are attributed assertions?

7. Can I avoid the hearsay rule by asking witnesses to paraphrase out-of-court statements?

8. Can witnesses' own out-of-court statements constitute hearsay?

9. What is the status of hearsay statements prior to trial?

10. What are *testimonial* hearsay assertions?

11. What is the link between *testimonial* hearsay assertions and the Confrontation Clause of the Sixth Amendment?

12. Case Library:

United States v. Zenni
Crawford v. Washington
Davis v. Washington
Melendez-Diaz v. Massachusetts
Michigan v. Bryant
Bullcoming v. New Mexico

§ 10.02 RELEVANT FEDERAL RULES OF EVIDENCE

Rule 801. Definitions That Apply to This Article; Exclusions from Hearsay

(a) Statement. "Statement" means a person's oral assertion, written assertion, or nonverbal conduct, if the person intended it as an assertion.

(b) Declarant. "Declarant" means the person who made the statement.

(c) Hearsay. "Hearsay" means a statement that:

(1) the declarant does not make while testifying at the current trial or hearing; and

(2) a party offers in evidence to prove the truth of the matter asserted in the statement.

Rule 802. The Rule Against Hearsay

Hearsay is not admissible unless any of the following provides otherwise:

- a federal statute;
- these rules; or
- other rules proscribed by the Supreme Court.

United States Constitution. Sixth Amendment: "In all criminal proceedings, the accused shall enjoy the right . . . to be confronted with the witnesses against him."

§ 10.03 INTRODUCTION

While some evidentiary rules are narrow and technical, others (such as those limiting the admissibility of character evidence) embody the U.S. conception of a fair trial. The hearsay rule, the basic principles of which are the focus of this chapter, is at the core of this conception. Reinforced in criminal cases by the U.S. Constitution's Sixth Amendment (the Confrontation Clause), the hearsay rule is virtually synonymous with the adversary system of trial because it protects parties' rights to cross examine adverse witnesses.

The hearsay rule reflects a centuries-old distrust of secondhand information. For example, early in the sixteenth century, famed Swiss alchemist Paracelsus wrote that he was not the creator of the Philosopher's Stone, and so could speak of it only from hearsay.[1] And a few years later, soon after Queen Anne Boleyn's beheading in 1536, palace governess Lady Bryan wrote a letter stating that she didn't know the current whereabouts of the Queen's daughter Elizabeth "except by hearsay."[2] The long-standing suspicious attitude toward hearsay underlies Rule 802, which sets forth the general rule that hearsay is not admissible in evidence.

Under Rule 801, a hearsay statement is one made orally or in writing at a time or place other than on the witness stand during the trial or hearing in which the

---

[1] M. Pachter, Paracelsus: Magic Into Science 133 (1951).

[2] Joan Glasheen, *The Secret People of the Palaces* 40 (B.T. Batsford, 1998).

statement is offered into evidence. Judges and lawyers often reduce this definition to the shorthand term, "out-of-court statement." For example, Bob would be offering Joan's out-of-court statement into evidence in the following situations:

- Bob testifies that "Soon after the accident, Joan told me that she saw the car that collided with mine run a red light."

- Bob seeks to read into the trial record Joan's deposition testimony that "I saw the car that collided with Bob's run a red light."

- Bob offers into evidence an affidavit signed under oath by Joan during pre-trial discovery proceedings stating that "I saw the car that collided with Bob's run a red light."

- Bob offers into evidence a portion of the transcript from an earlier trial in which Joan testified under oath that "I saw the car that collided with Bob's run a red light."

Each excerpt of Bob's testimony refers to an out-of-court statement by Joan, because Joan made each statement other than "while testifying at the trial or hearing" in which Bob offered Joan's statement into evidence.

Any hearsay that you picked up about the hearsay rule before enrolling in the Evidence course may be more confusing than helpful. For one thing, not all out-of-court statements constitute hearsay. Under Rule 801, an out-of-court statement constitutes hearsay only if it is offered in evidence "to prove the truth of the matter asserted in the statement." Thus, a statement that is offered for a legitimate "non-hearsay purpose" (a purpose that does not depend on an out-of-court statement's accuracy) is not barred by Rule 802.

Second, even if a party does offer an out-of-court statement into evidence for the truth of what it asserts, it may well be admissible under one or more of the gaggle of exemptions and exceptions identified by Rules 801, 803, 804, and 807. Thus, a conclusion that an out-of-court assertion constitutes hearsay does not necessarily mean that the evidence is inadmissible at trial.

Finally, even if a hearsay statement is admissible under an exemption or exception, the Confrontation Clause might bar a prosecutor from offering it into evidence against a criminal defendant.

This chapter begins hearsay analysis by focusing on Rule 801's definition of hearsay, and on the reason that the hearsay status of out-of-court statements depends on the purpose for which parties offer them into evidence. To keep your eyes on the forest of admissibility as you go through the individual definitional trees, keep the following "Five-Step Hearsay Matrix" in mind. The questions set forth in the matrix provide a helpful approach for analyzing hearsay issues.

Five-Step Hearsay Matrix

Step One: Does evidence constitute an out-of-court statement?

Step Two: If so, for what purpose does the offering (or "proferring") party offer the out-of-court statement?

Step Three: If the offering party offers an out-of-court statement for a non-hearsay purpose (that is, for a purpose that does not depend on the statement's accuracy), is that purpose relevant and, if so, is its probative value substantially outweighed by the risk of unfair prejudice or the other factors set forth in Rule 403?

Step Four: If the offering party offers an out-of-court statement for its truth, can the party satisfy the foundational requirements of any of the numerous exemptions or exceptions to the hearsay rule?

Step Five (necessary only when prosecutors offer hearsay statements into evidence against criminal defendants): Even if an out-of-court statement is admissible for purposes of the hearsay rule, does the Confrontation Clause require its exclusion? This chapter concludes with an analysis of Confrontation Clause issues.

§ 10.04 HEARSAY DEFINED

Under Rule 801 (c), an out-of-court statement is hearsay when:

- A "declarant;"
- makes an out-of-court oral or written assertion; or
- engages in non-verbal conduct that is intended as an assertion; that is
- offered to prove the truth of the matter asserted.

"The truth of the matter asserted" is the definitional element that most commonly determines whether out-of-court statements are hearsay. A party offers an out-of-court statement for its truth if the statement must be accurate to be relevant. If the purpose for which a party offers a statement makes the statement relevant without regard to its accuracy, the statement is non-hearsay. Thus, *the very same statement can be either hearsay or non-hearsay, depending on the point that the offering party attempts to prove.*

Example 1

Jean is present when Melissa tells her friend Joe that "The bank where I work has decided to substitute blanks for real bullets in its guards' guns." If Jean were asked to testify to Melissa's statement in a trial, the testimony might be hearsay. Melissa is a declarant, and her statement to Joe was made out-of-court. But whether the statement is hearsay depends on what it's offered to prove. Melissa's statement would be:

Hearsay if Joe were injured in a robbery that took place in the bank where Melissa works and sues the bank for not adequately protecting its customers, and if Joe's attorney offers Melissa's out-of-court statement as evidence that the banks' guards were armed only with blanks. Joe's attorney would then be offering Melissa's statement "for its truth," because Melissa's statement would be relevant to prove that the guards' guns were filled with blanks only if it were accurate.

Non-hearsay if Joe is charged with robbing the bank, and the prosecution offers Melissa's statement to prove that a motive for the robbery was that Joe didn't fear being shot by the guards. Melissa's statement would now be relevant even if it were inaccurate — that is, even if the guards were in fact armed with real bullets.

Hearing Melissa's statement could have led Joe to *believe* that the guards only had blanks. Joe's belief permits an inference that Joe would not be fearful of being shot during a robbery attempt, which strengthens an inference that Joe robbed the bank.

As you'll see in Chapter 11, finding a non-hearsay use for out-of-court statements is not an automatic ticket to admissibility. The admissibility of an out-of-court statement as non-hearsay depends on its relationship to the material facts in dispute and the factual contentions of the parties. As suggested by Step Three of the Hearsay Matrix, judges may exclude out-of-court statements if their claimed non-hearsay use is irrelevant, or if the danger that jurors will improperly accept an out-of-court statement for its truth substantially outweighs the probative value of the statement's legitimate non-hearsay use (Rule 403).

Example 2

Joe is charged with robbing the bank in which Melissa works. Joe's defense is mistaken identity. The prosecutor's direct examination of Melissa proceeds as follows:

PROSECUTOR: Melissa, do you know a teller in your bank by the name of Jean?

A: Sure. Jean often works at the window next to mine.

PROSECUTOR: Do you recall Jean talking to you about bank robberies a day before this robbery took place?

A: I do.

PROSECUTOR: And what did Jean tell you in this conversation?

A: Jean told me that most bank robbers are professionals who will go on committing bank robberies until they're apprehended.

DEFENDANT'S ATTORNEY: Objection and move to strike, hearsay.

[In practice, the defense attorney should object after the question and before the answer.]

JUDGE: Prosecutor, any response?

PROSECUTOR: I'm not offering Jean's statement for its truth, Your Honor. I'm offering it for the limited purpose of showing that at the time the robbery took place, a day after Jean spoke to Melissa, Melissa had a motive to focus especially closely on the person who robbed her. Hearing Jean's statement made Melissa especially anxious to make sure that the robber was caught.

JUDGE: Defense counsel, response?

DEFENDANT'S ATTORNEY: Yes, I object to the non-hearsay use under Rules 402 and 403. The claimed non-hearsay use is irrelevant because any bank teller has a desire to see a bank robber apprehended. And a substantial danger exists that despite any limiting instruction Your Honor may give, the jury will use the statement as evidence that my client is a professional bank robber.

[This colloquy would in all likelihood take place at sidebar, out of the jurors' hearing.]

JUDGE: Objection sustained. I strike the witness' last answer under Rule 403 and instruct the jurors to disregard it.

The next section explains the policies underlying the hearsay rule and describes why offering out-of-court statements for a "non-hearsay purpose" obviates the concerns giving rise to the rule.

§ 10.05 THE HEARSAY RULE AND THE ADVERSARY SYSTEM

[A] Hearsay Rule Protects the Right to Cross-Examine

The primary reason that out-of-court statements are hearsay only when parties offer them for "the truth of the matter asserted" is the close connection between the hearsay rule and the adversary system of justice. The adversary system relies heavily on cross-examination as a method of ferreting out truth, and the hearsay rule protects a party's right to cross-examine adverse witnesses. In other words, the hearsay rule's primary purpose is to protect a party from the use of evidence from speakers (hearsay declarants) who the party cannot cross-examine. In the words of the great evidence scholar John Wigmore, "The hearsay rule . . . signifies *a rule rejecting assertions . . . which have not been in some way subjected to the test of cross-examination.*[3] Thus, the hearsay rule is the legal equivalent of the common expression, "Tell it to the judge (or jury)." The rule reflects a belief that in an adversarial system of justice, witnesses ought to tell their stories in court, where judges and jurors can observe and evaluate them and adverse parties can cross-examine them.

If the purpose of the hearsay rule is to allow cross-examination of speakers whose out-of-court statements are offered into evidence, why aren't all out-of-court statements treated equally? Why does the bar of the hearsay rule disappear when out-of-court assertions are offered for "non-hearsay purposes"? The answer is that when an out-of-court statement is offered for a non-hearsay use, the declarant's presence on the witness stand is not necessary for meaningful cross-examination to occur. When a statement is offered as non-hearsay, the credibility issue concerns the in-court witness who serves as the "conduit" of the out-of-court statement, not the declarant. And, of course, the adversary can cross-examine and test the credibility of the in-court witness.

By contrast, when an out-of-court statement is offered for its truth, the important credibility issues generally revolve around the *hearsay declarant*, not the "conduit" witness. That is why a hearsay declarant's presence at trial is almost always necessary for an opportunity for meaningful cross-examination to occur.

---

[3] Vol. 5, Wigmore on Evidence — Chadbourn Revision § 1362 (1974) (emphasis in original).

To understand why the admission of hearsay from non-testifying speakers typically precludes adversaries from testing its credibility, recognize that accepting the accuracy of hearsay gives rise to four "hearsay dangers." Depriving parties of the opportunity to cross-examine hearsay declarants prevents them from demonstrating that the presence of one or more of these dangers renders hearsay inaccurate or incomplete. The subsection below explains the four hearsay dangers and then illustrates how the opportunity for meaningful cross-examination depends on whether a statement is offered for its truth or for a non-hearsay purpose.

[B] The "Hearsay Dangers"

The factors that cross-examiners are unable to probe when hearsay substitutes for in-court testimony are as follows:

Sincerity. Does a hearsay declarant's out-of-court statement actually reflect the declarant's belief? For example, was Graham intending to be accurate when he told his neighbor, Beverly, the day after a collision that "the Beemer ran a red light?" Beverly's testifying to Graham's out-of-court statement at trial is likely to foreclose a cross-examiner from probing Graham's sincerity and perhaps showing that Graham had a motive to make an intentionally false statement. Common motives that cross-examiners pursue at trial include a witness' financial stake in a trial's outcome, close personal relationship with the adversary, or bad feelings toward the cross-examiner's client. Or, a cross-examiner might be able to show that Graham's demeanor and manner of answering questions under oath (e.g., shifty eyes, sweaty palms) demonstrate that he is insincere.

Perception. Even if a hearsay declarant was sincere, did the declarant have an adequate opportunity to observe the events to which the hearsay statement refers? For example, how well could Graham observe the Beemer that he said ran the red light? Beverly's testifying to Graham's out-of-court statement at trial is likely to foreclose a cross-examiner from probing Graham's perception and perhaps showing that Graham was too far away to observe accurately, or that the intersection was badly lit, or that Graham was preoccupied and therefore not paying close attention to the Beemer.

Memory. Even if a hearsay declarant was sincere and had an adequate opportunity to observe events, how well did the declarant recall those events at the time the hearsay statement was made? For example, how well did Graham recall the color of the light and the Beemer's location at the time he said that the car ran the light? Beverly's testifying to Graham's out-of-court statement at trial is likely to foreclose a cross-examiner from probing Graham's memory and perhaps showing that Graham is unable to recall other important details, or that he has given conflicting accounts of the event.

Communication Difficulties. Even if a hearsay declarant was sincere, had an adequate opportunity to observe events, and adequately recalled those events, how accurately does a declarant's choice of words describe those events? For example, did Graham misspeak? Beverly's testifying to Graham's out-of-court statement at trial is likely to foreclose a cross-examiner from probing Graham's use of language at trial and perhaps showing that Graham meant to say that a Toyota ran the red light. In addition, admission of Graham's hearsay is likely to prevent a cross-examiner from showing that Graham uses language in an idiosyncratic way. For example, perhaps the cross-examiner could show by questioning Graham that he is especially cautious and considers any driver whose car is in an intersection when a light turns red to have "run a red light."

Practice Tip.

"ROTC" is a military mnemonic that may help you to remember the hearsay dangers. Cross-examination tests a witness' ability to R emember; O bserve; T ell the Truth; and C ommunicate.

The following samples of testimony illustrate the linkage between the hearsay rule and cross-examination. The first testimonial excerpt demonstrates how the admission of hearsay is likely to negate the opportunity for meaningful cross-examination. Assume that Melinda is a defendant in an auto accident case. Dave, the plaintiff, claims that Melinda negligently drove her Ford automobile through a red light and ran into Dave's car. To prove that Melinda was negligent, Dave is allowed to testify that, "About 10 minutes after the collision, a bystander came up to me and said, 'I saw what happened. The driver of the Ford that ran into your car ran a red light.'" Because Dave has not produced the bystander (the hearsay declarant) as a witness, Melinda's attorney has to try to undermine the bystander's credibility by cross-examining Dave. A portion of the cross-examination might go as follows:

DEFENDANT'S ATTORNEY: A bystander told you that the Ford ran the red light?

A: That's correct.

DEFENDANT'S ATTORNEY: Do you know whether the bystander was acquainted with my client? (sincerity question)

A: No, I don't.

DEFENDANT'S ATTORNEY: Do you know whether the bystander had ever made negative statements about people who drive Ford automobiles? (sincerity question)

A: No, I'd never met or talked to the bystander before the collision.

DEFENDANT'S ATTORNEY: Do you know whether the bystander would be squirming uncomfortably if the bystander had to respond to my questions in court, under oath? (sincerity question)

A: Sorry, haven't a clue.

DEFENDANT'S ATTORNEY: What was the bystander's physical location at the time that the bystander claims to have seen the Ford run the red light? (perception question)

A: I don't know.

DEFENDANT'S ATTORNEY: Do you know whether the bystander was facing toward or away from the sun at the time the bystander claims to have seen the Ford run the red light? (perception question)

A: No, I don't know.

DEFENDANT'S ATTORNEY: Do you know whether the bystander was concentrating on work or family problems at the time the bystander claims to have seen the Ford run the red light? (perception question)

A: I don't know. Look, why are you asking me all these questions? All I know is what the bystander told me after the collision.

DEFENDANT'S ATTORNEY: I understand. But I suspect that this cross-examination is going to be used as an example in an Evidence textbook, so I need to show readers how use of the bystander's assertion for its truth really frustrates my opportunity to conduct meaningful cross-examination. Does the bystander now recall how fast the Ford was going when it allegedly ran the red light? (memory question)

A: I don't know.

DEFENDANT'S ATTORNEY: Well, can the bystander recall how fast your car was going when it collided with my client's car? (memory question)

A: How the heck would I know?

DEFENDANT'S ATTORNEY: Can the bystander tell us what the weather was like at the time of the collision? (memory question)

A: I have no idea.

DEFENDANT'S ATTORNEY: Has the bystander given a conflicting account of what happened to anyone else? (memory question)

A: I don't know.

DEFENDANT'S ATTORNEY: Do you know whether the bystander can accurately distinguish a Ford automobile from other makes of car? (ambiguity question)

A: I don't know.

DEFENDANT'S ATTORNEY: Do you know whether the bystander meant that the light turned red before or during the time the Ford was in the intersection? (ambiguity question)

A: I don't know.

As you can see, the admissibility of hearsay largely negates the defense attorney's opportunity for meaningful cross-examination. The bystander's out-of-court statement might be subject to any of the four dangers, but the substitution of the hearsay assertion for the bystander's in-court testimony prevents the attorney from exploring them.

If the distinction between hearsay and non-hearsay makes any sense, then an opportunity for meaningful cross-examination should be available when a party offers an out-of-court statement for a non-hearsay purpose. To test this, consider a second sample of testimony from a revised version of the previous case. As in the previous example, Melinda is a defendant in an auto accident case. And, as before, Dave, the plaintiff, claims that Melinda negligently drove her Ford automobile through a red light and ran into Dave's car. In this version, to counter Melinda's affirmative defense that Dave and not she ran the red light, Dave testifies that moments before the collision, Chuck, a passenger in Dave's car, told Dave, "Be careful at this intersection. Cops are always around and people get tickets for running red lights here all the time." Chuck's statement, Dave testifies, made him especially wary and careful not to go through a red light.

In this example, Dave offers Chuck's statement for a non-hearsay use. Even if what Chuck said about cops ticketing motorists is inaccurate, the statement is relevant because Dave claims that Chuck's remark affected how Dave drove as he approached the intersection where the collision occurred. Thus, if the hearsay/non-hearsay distinction makes sense, Melinda's attorney should have a reasonable chance to cross-examine Dave:

DEFENDANT'S ATTORNEY: You say that moments before the collision, Chuck told you that cops often ticket motorists for running red lights at that intersection, right?

A: That's correct.

DEFENDANT'S ATTORNEY: We only have your word for this and not Chuck's, right? (sincerity question)

A: That's true.

DEFENDANT'S ATTORNEY: Do you recall anything else that Chuck said to you during the five minutes prior to the collision? (memory question)

A: No.

DEFENDANT'S ATTORNEY: Do you recall what if anything you and Chuck had been discussing when Chuck made this statement to you? (memory question)

A: No.

DEFENDANT'S ATTORNEY: Has Chuck previously been a passenger in your car?

A: Yes, often.

DEFENDANT'S ATTORNEY: On any prior occasion, has Chuck ever given you a warning about the presence of police officers? (memory/sincerity question)

A: Not that I can remember.

DEFENDANT'S ATTORNEY:	You didn't personally see any police officers at the intersection, did you? (perception question)
A:	No.
DEFENDANT'S ATTORNEY:	Have you driven through that intersection previously? (memory question)
A:	Sure.
DEFENDANT'S ATTORNEY:	Can you estimate for us how many times in the six months prior to the events giving rise to this lawsuit that you drove through that intersection? (memory question)
A:	Oh, I can't be sure. Let's say 15–20 times.
DEFENDANT'S ATTORNEY:	And you'd never been stopped by a police officer for any reason connected to that intersection, isn't that true? (memory/ sincerity question)
A:	I guess that's right.
DEFENDANT'S ATTORNEY:	You talked to Police Officer Jones about what happened about 15–20 minutes after the accident, is that right?
A:	That's about right.
DEFENDANT'S ATTORNEY:	And you didn't mention to Officer Jones that Chuck had made this statement to you, did you? (sincerity/memory question)
A:	No.
DEFENDANT'S ATTORNEY:	Before approaching the intersection where the collision took place, you had been driving with Chuck in your car for about 15 minutes, right?
A:	That's true.
DEFENDANT'S ATTORNEY:	And Chuck might have made this statement earlier in the drive, isn't that right? (perception question)
A:	I'm pretty sure that he said it right before the accident.
DEFENDANT'S ATTORNEY:	How much time elapsed between the time Chuck said this to you and the collision took place? (memory question)
A:	I'm not exactly sure. A few seconds, I'd say.
DEFENDANT'S ATTORNEY:	And did you ask him how he knew that cops often ticketed drivers in that area? (sincerity question)
A:	No.
DEFENDANT'S ATTORNEY:	Yet you immediately slowed down after hearing Chuck say this?

A: Yes.

DEFENDANT'S ATTORNEY: At the time you claim that Chuck made this statement to you, you were talking on your mobile phone to your sales manager about an important customer you were going to see later in the day, isn't that right? (memory/perception question)

A: Yes.

DEFENDANT'S ATTORNEY: So you weren't paying close attention to what Chuck might have said to you, isn't that right? (sincerity/perception question)

A: I could do both things.

As may be apparent, Dave's offering Chuck's statement for a non-hearsay use allows Melinda's attorney to conduct meaningful cross-examination. What is relevant to the case is whether Chuck made the statement, whether Dave heard it, and, if so, how the statement might have affected Dave's driving. These non-hearsay uses provide Melinda's attorney with a fair opportunity to test Dave's sincerity, memory and perception.

Practice Tip: Identifying non-hearsay uses.

Out-of-court statements do not come neatly packaged with tags listing "possible non-hearsay uses" attached. If you become a litigator, your pre-trial preparation is often likely to include developing arguments supporting non-hearsay uses for helpful out-of-court statements that you cannot offer under a hearsay exemption or exception. Anticipating potential objections, you will also commonly develop arguments that the non-hearsay purposes you have identified are relevant and that the statements' probative value outweighs the risk that jurors will improperly consider them for their truth. For more on non-hearsay uses, see Chapter 11.

[C] Why Not Admit Hearsay "For What It's Worth?"

You might concede that the admission of hearsay is apt to frustrate cross-examination, yet argue that Rule 802's general policy of excluding hearsay is unwarranted. After all, if it accomplishes nothing else, the first cross-examination above should serve as a warning to a sensible judge or juror that the accuracy of the bystander's hearsay assertion is untested. You could support your argument with the results of empirical evidence, admittedly based on simulated jury studies, suggesting that jurors are wary of untested hearsay.[4]

If this is so, why not routinely admit hearsay (at least in "small cap" cases) and rely on judges and jurors to discount its weight according to the circumstances? If we trust them to evaluate the probative worth of other evidence, shouldn't we also trust them to evaluate the probative worth of hearsay? Moreover, trial judges

---

[4] *See, e.g.*, Margaret Kovera, Roger Park & Steven Penrod, *Jurors' Perceptions of Eyewitness and Hearsay Evidence*, 76 Minn. L. Rev. 703 (1992).

would retain the power under Rule 403 to exclude hearsay when particular circumstances wouldn't allow for a reasonable assessment of hearsay's probative value; in such situations, the hearsay's probative value might be substantially outweighed by the likelihood of confusion or undue consumption of time. In addition, a rule of general admissibility would be much more coherent and easier for judges and lawyers to apply in the heat of battle than a rule of exclusion accompanied by a bewildering array of non-hearsay uses and hearsay exemptions and exceptions. And the resultant time that students would save in the Evidence course could be profitably devoted to the study of oil and gas leases.

If this is your attitude, you're not alone. In fact, you can point to the support of an entire country — England's adversary system very much resembles our own, yet in the Civil Evidence Act of 1968 the English Parliament largely abolished the hearsay rule in civil cases. However, American rule-makers have thus far been unwilling to reverse the general policy of excluding hearsay. They would probably respond to an "admit hearsay for what it's worth" argument as follows:

- In many circumstances, judges and especially jurors are unable to rationally assess hearsay's probative value. They'd be guessing, based on unarticulated and untested assumptions, and in general would probably be inclined to accord hearsay assertions more weight than they are "really" worth.

- If hearsay were generally admissible, crafty lawyers would "witness-shop," producing impressive witnesses who could repeat the hearsay assertions of percipient witnesses of questionable demeanor or background.

- The hearsay rule as presently constituted enables lawyers to predict with at least a fair amount of accuracy whether an out-of-court assertion will be admitted into evidence. This predictability helps lawyers plan trial strategies, and may also foster pretrial settlements.

- The hearsay rule protects cross-examination, a fundamental trial right that is too important to be left to the uncertain whims of judges and jurors with varying degrees of judgment, experience and common sense.

- The current format of the hearsay rule is flexible enough to satisfy those who think that hearsay ought to be generally admissible. First, rule-makers can craft new exceptions as they deem warranted, and have done so.

Example: Many states have in recent years enacted a "tender years" hearsay exception for young children's out-of-court assertions of abuse.

Example: In response to the exclusion of prosecution evidence in the famous 1995 murder trial of O.J. Simpson, California enacted a new hearsay exception (**Cal. Evid. Code Sec. 1370**) for statements describing physical injuries made by victims who are unavailable to testify at trial.

Second, Rule 807's residual ("catch-all") exception allows judges to admit hearsay that they deem reliable even if it doesn't fall into one of the preexisting exceptions. If these changes don't go as far as some would like, they perhaps relieve the pressure for a general change of hearsay policy.

[D] "Hearsay Policy" Problems

Problem 10-1: The Telephone Game

True or False: The primary risk that the hearsay rule is designed to prevent is exemplified by "The Telephone Game," in which a message tends to change as it's whispered from one person to the next. That is, the hearsay rule exists because of worry that witnesses will inaccurately report out-of-court assertions.

Problem 10-2: Beyond Question?

Slip-and-Fall Case. To prove that she slipped on a wet spot in a restaurant, Lynn Oleum offers into evidence signed and sworn affidavits from three community religious leaders who happened to be dining in the restaurant that night. Each affidavit declares under oath that the affiant saw Lynn's foot slip on a wet spot on the floor. The restaurant objects that the affidavits are hearsay. Lynn argues that the affidavits are not barred by Rule 802 because like in-court testimony they were made under oath and because the stature and number of the declarants renders the hearsay dangers negligible. *Ruling?*

Problem 10-3: What's the Use?

Bart Harbour is charged with illegally poaching seals on Seal Rock in Acadia Cove. Bart's defense is that he was unaware that it was against the law to capture seals. (Assume that this is a legitimate defense to the charge.) The prosecution calls Davy Jones and elicits testimony that he is Acadia's Covemaster. The examination continues as follows:

PROSECUTOR: Are you familiar with a location known as Seal Rock?

A: I am. Seal Rock is in Acadia Cove, about 50 yards offshore. It's a large oval-shaped rock about 25 yards in length and about 10 yards across where seals breed and are commonly present. PROSECUTOR: Are there any notices posted on Seal Rock?

A: Yes indeed. There are two signs on the rock with large, dark letters at the top saying "Illegal to Hunt or Harm Seals" and indicating that both federal and state laws forbid human contact with seals.

DEFENDANT'S ATTORNEY: Objection, hearsay, move to strike the last answer. The notices are out-of-court statements offered for their truth.

PROSECUTOR: *How will you respond to the objection?*

Problem 10-4: Hearsay Expert

You are speaking to the Hearsay Rule Sub-Committee of the Congressional Federal Rules of Evidence Oversight Committee. They have asked for your views on a proposal that the Rule 801 definition of hearsay be retained, but that Rule 802 be amended to provide that "The admissibility of hearsay is committed to the discretion of the trial judge, and trial judges' rulings shall be final except for manifestly unjust rulings that are likely to have affected a verdict. Existing hearsay exceptions shall serve only as factors that trial judges may take into account when making their rulings." *What advice will you give the Sub-Committee as to the wisdom of this proposal?*

§ 10.06 WHO ARE "DECLARANTS?"

[A] Definitions and Examples

Now that you've been introduced to the concept of "the truth of the matter asserted," consider next the three additional elements of Rule 801's definition of hearsay. Begin with the term "declarant," the maker of an out-of-court statement. The typical hearsay situation involves two people: the declarant (the speaker who makes the statement) and the witness (who testifies to the statement in court).

Example 1

PLAINTIFF'S ATTORNEY: What happened after the defendant's car collided with yours?

A: A bystander walked over to me and said that the car that hit mine ran the red light.

Here, the declarant is the bystander; the driver is the witness.

The hearsay definition limits declarants to "persons." Pity the animals; not only are most all of them barred from restaurants, but also they can't be declarants. Likewise, the output of mechanical devices like thermometers and speedometers is not hearsay.

Example 2

A prosecution witness in a murder case testifies as follows:

PROSECUTOR: What time did you hear the gunshots?

A: It was 3:00 p.m.

PROSECUTOR: And how do you know that the shots were fired at 3:00 p.m.?

A: Because I looked at my watch as soon as I heard the gunshots, and according to my watch it was 3:00.

No hearsay declarant exists. The watch is a mechanical device and cannot "assert" that the time was 3:00.

Example 3

A landlord in an eviction case testifies as follows:

PLAINTIFF'S ATTORNEY: And what is it that wakes you up every morning?

A: I hear roosters crowing in the tenant's backyard.

No hearsay declarant exists; roosters are not declarants. (The cross-examination justification for the hearsay rule suggests that this aspect of the rule makes good sense, preventing attorneys from making demands such as, "Get those roosters into this courtroom so I can cross-examine the living daylights out of them.")

[B] "Declarant" Problems

Problem 10-5: Where's the Declarant?

Are there hearsay declarants in these scenarios?

1. As evidence that a statement was made by a computer store employee, the plaintiff seeks to testify that "I phoned the number that was listed for the computer store on its website."

2. To prove the magnitude of her damages in a personal injury case, professional basketball player Shirley Knott offers into evidence the "Statistics" section from the daily newspaper, showing that she was leading the league in blocked shots on the day of her injury.

3. To prove that the Fizzy Cola Co. owned and operated a truck that was involved in an accident, a bystander seeks to testify that painted on the side of the truck was a logo that read, "Fizzy Cola — The Healthy Cola."

4. Yon is called as a witness and testifies that "My name is Yon Yonsin, I come from Wisconsin."

Problem 10-6: Bloody Glove

Lerna Hand is charged with murder. To prove Lerna's identity as the murderer, the prosecution calls Police Officer Tracy, who testifies as follows:

PROSECUTOR: What led you to arrest Lerna?

A: I held the bloody glove that I found at the murder scene up to the nose of Cinders, the police bloodhound I've personally trained. Cinders sniffed the glove for a few moments and followed a scent directly to Lerna.

DEFENDANT'S ATTORNEY: Objection, hearsay. Cinders' behavior is the equivalent of the out-of-court statement, "Lerna was the murderer." I also object that the evidence of the dog's behavior is irrelevant.

PROSECUTOR: *How can you respond to these objections?* Assume that the judge summons counsel to the bench and asks you for an "offer of proof" concerning the foundational testimony that you will elicit from Officer Tracy to support the relevance of Cinders's behavior. *What will your offer of proof consist of?*

Problem 10-7: Polly Wants a Conviction

Laurel is charged with murdering Hardy; Laurel's defense is an alibi. To prove Laurel's identity as the murderer, the prosecution calls Police Officer Tracy, who testifies as follows:

PROSECUTOR: When did you arrive at Hardy's apartment?

A: Approximately five minutes after receiving the call reporting that gunshots had been heard coming from the apartment.

PROSECUTOR: What did you see when you entered the apartment?

A: I saw Hardy lying in a pool of blood on the floor, and a parrot in a cage in the same room.

PROSECUTOR: What, if anything, did the parrot do while you were in the room?

A: The parrot repeatedly squawked, "Laurel, why'd you do it? Laurel, why'd you do it?"

DEFENDANT'S ATTORNEY: Objection, hearsay.

PROSECUTOR: No hearsay is involved, Your Honor, because the parrot is not a declarant.

JUDGE: *What is your response to the prosecutor's argument?*

Problem 10-8: News to Me

Ethel is charged with murdering Fred in the apartment they shared. To prove the time of the killing, the prosecution calls next-door neighbor, Lucy, who testifies as follows:

PROSECUTOR: What time did you hear the gunshots?

A: I heard them at 3:00 p.m.

PROSECUTOR: And how do you know that?

A: Because I had been listening to the radio, and I heard the shots right after the announcer said "Here's the 3:00 news." At the same time, I was looking out the window of my apartment, and I saw Quasimodo, the village's long-time bell-ringer, climb the church tower and by pulling the rope he rang the church bells three times.

DEFENDANT'S ATTORNEY: Objection, hearsay.

PROSECUTOR: No hearsay is involved, Your Honor. The radio and the church bells are mechanical devices.

JUDGE: *What is your response to the prosecutor's argument?*

Problem 10-9: Photo Finish

Auto accident case. To prove the extent of the damages to his car, plaintiff Phil offers into evidence a photograph of the car, taken shortly after the accident. Defendant Dean objects that the photo is hearsay because it constitutes an assertion about the car's condition. *Is this a valid argument?*

Plaintiff's counsel: If the hearsay objection is overruled, offer the photograph into evidence after laying a proper foundation through the testimony of Phil.

Problem 10-10: Print — Out?

Auto accident case. To prove the value of her car that was totaled in the accident, plaintiff Paula's attorney makes the following request:

"Your Honor, I ask that Plaintiff's Exhibit #1 be received in evidence. Exhibit #1 is a computer printout taken from the Used Car Dealers Internet Website, indicating the fair market value for plaintiff's make and model of car."

In response to defendant Deena's hearsay objection, plaintiff states that the printout is machine-generated, so no declarant is involved. *How should the judge rule?*

Problem 10-11: My Better Side

Kay Mart is charged with armed robbery of a department store. The prosecution offers into evidence a visual recording taken by the store's security camera, showing Kay in profile pointing a gun at the store clerk and grabbing cash out of the register. In response to Kay's hearsay objection, the prosecution responds that the video camera that is the source of the visual recording is not a hearsay declarant. *How should the judge rule?*

Problem 10-12: Just the Ticket

Romero is on trial for speeding. Officer Ward testifies that at around 2 p.m. on October 12, she was assigned to traffic detail on Cyclone Ave., a residential street with a speed limit of 30 m.p.h. She was standing outside her patrol vehicle when she observed Romero's Camaro coming in her direction. Her testimony continues as follows:

PROSECUTOR: Officer Ward, what happened after you first observed Romero's Camaro?

A: I raised my radar gun and pointed it in the direction of the Camaro. I focused the radar gun on the car until a reading appeared on the screen indicating the speed of the car.

PROSECUTOR: And what was that speed?

A: 53 m.p.h.

DEFENDANT'S ATTORNEY: Objection, hearsay. The radar gun reading is an out-of-court assertion because it resulted from the officer's pointing it in the direction of the Camaro.

PROSECUTOR: *What is your response to defense counsel's argument?*

§ 10.07 WAS THE STATEMENT MADE "OUT-OF COURT?"

[A] General Rule

A statement is made "out-of-court" if it is made any time other than by a witness during the trial in which the statement is offered. Even if a statement has been given under oath and in a courtroom proceeding, for purposes of the hearsay rule it is an out-of-court statement if it was not made during the trial in which it is offered.

[B] "Out-of-Court" Problems

Problem 10-13: On My Word

Pola sues Dana for personal injuries growing out of an auto accident. During the trial, in an effort to prove that Dana ran a stop sign, counsel for Pola makes the following request:

> Your Honor, I ask that Pola's Exhibit # 2 be received in evidence. Exhibit # 2 is an excerpt from the transcript of the testimony that Stan gave when Dana's attorney took Stan's deposition. In this deposition excerpt, Stan testified that Dana's car ran a stop sign before colliding with Pola's car.

Does the deposition excerpt constitute an out-of-court statement?"

Problem 10-14: On My Word Again

In Problem 10-13, counsel for Pola makes the following request:

> Your Honor, I ask that Pola's Exhibit #3 be received in evidence. Exhibit #3 is an excerpt from the transcript of the prior trial of this case, which resulted in a mistrial. In this excerpt from the prior trial, Stan testified that Dana's car ran a stop sign before colliding with Pola's car.

Does the trial excerpt constitute an out-of-court statement?

Problem 10-15: Big Mouth

In Problem 10-13, counsel for defendant Dana cross-examines plaintiff Pola as follows:

DEFENDANT'S ATTORNEY: You had just finished talking on your cellular phone when the collision occurred, correct?

A: I wouldn't say that. I'd finished talking at least three or four minutes before the collision.

DEFENDANT'S ATTORNEY: You talked about this case with a friend in the back of the courtroom during the court's morning recess, didn't you?

A: Just a little bit.

DEFENDANT'S ATTORNEY: Didn't you tell your friend during this recess that you'd finished the call just moments before the collision?

Is defense counsel's last question an attempt to offer evidence of an out-of-court statement?

Problem 10-16: Same Ol', Same Ol'

In Problem 10-13, plaintiff Pola testifies as follows:

PLAINTIFF'S ATTORNEY: What speed were you driving just before the collision occurred?

A: Exactly as I told the police officer who showed up soon after the accident, I was driving no more than 25 m.p.h.

Has the plaintiff testified to an out-of-court statement?

§ 10.08 WHAT IS A "STATEMENT?"

[A] Definition and Examples

With this definitional underbrush behind you, consider Step One of the Five-Step Hearsay Matrix: "Does evidence constitute an out-of-court statement?" No matter what it is offered to prove, an out-of-court utterance can constitute hearsay only if it qualifies as a "statement." This term generally poses no problem under Rule 801(a), as it applies broadly to all intentional or purposeful oral or written assertions.

Example 1

PLAINTIFF'S ATTORNEY: What happened after the collision?

A: A bystander walked over to my car and said that the car that hit me had run a red light.

The bystander's post-collision remark is an assertive statement concerning a past event.

Example 2

PLAINTIFF'S ATTORNEY: What happened next?

A: Ann told me that she was going to go to Joe's office and sign the contract.

Ann's remark is an assertive statement concerning an intended future act.

Example 3

PLAINTIFF'S ATTORNEY: Police Officer Tracy, did you observe the traffic collision?

A: I did.

PLAINTIFF'S ATTORNEY: Prior to the collision, did you observe the defendant's BMW?

A: Yes.

PLAINTIFF'S ATTORNEY: And did you prepare a written accident report afterwards?

A: I did.

PLAINTIFF'S ATTORNEY: And does that accident report refer to the defendant's BMW?

A: Yes. The accident report states that the blue BMW ran the red light.

The statement in the accident report is a written assertion.

Subdivision (a) of the Advisory Committee's Note to Rule 801 states that "The effect of the definition of 'statement' is to exclude from the operation of the hearsay rule all evidence of conduct, verbal or non-verbal, not intended as an assertion." Because the definition equates the term "statement" with "intent to assert," a verbal remark constitutes hearsay only if the speaker intended to make the assertion that the statement is offered to prove.

Example 6

Testimony of plaintiff in a negligence action:

PLAINTIFF'S ATTORNEY: And what happened after you got out of your car following the collision?

A: I grabbed the back of my neck and yelled, "Ouch."

"Ouch" constitutes a non-assertive verbal reflex reaction admissible to prove that the plaintiff was in pain. Because the statement is reflexive, it is not the equivalent of the plaintiff's purposeful assertion, "My neck hurts."

[B] Hidden Statements

Rule 801's formulaic definition of hearsay as a statement offered "to prove the truth of the matter asserted" would produce unjust anomalies were it to be applied mechanically to speakers' literal words. People can express the same thought in a myriad of ways. If the hearsay rule is to be fair and sensible, decisions about whether a statement is hearsay should depend on what people intend to communicate, and not merely on the happenstance of their chosen words. Similarly, people may communicate through behavior instead of or in addition to making statements, and when they do it makes sense to treat behavior as assertions.

The subsections below describe common situations in which statements are hearsay even though the words are not offered for their literal truth.

[1] Sub-Assertions

A party might try to avoid the hearsay rule by offering a statement into evidence for the truth of a sub-assertion. The party might claim that "There's no hearsay problem because since I'm not relying on the truth of the entire statement, but only on the accuracy of a sub-assertion, I'm not offering the statement for its literal truth." However, this argument doesn't work because a declarant's intent extends to sub-assertions.

Example

Jill is charged with a murder that occurred at the top of a hill around 3 p.m. To prove that Jill had the opportunity to commit the murder, the prosecutor calls a witness to testify that at around 4 p.m. on the day of the murder, a friend told the witness, "About an hour ago, I saw Jack and Jill run up the hill to fetch a pail of water." In response to the defense attorney's hearsay objection, the prosecutor argues that "I'm offering the statement only to prove that Jill ran up the hill at around 3 p.m. I'm not offering the portion of the statement referring to the pail of water. Because I'm not offering the entire statement for its literal truth, it's not hearsay." The argument fails because the declarant's intent extends to the sub-assertion about the time of day, and the sub-assertion's relevance depends on its accuracy.

[2] Linked Assertions

You often have to go "outside" the boundaries of a speaker's specific remark to decide whether it constitutes an assertion and if so, what it asserts. That is, you often have to link a speaker's statement to the context in which it is made to determine whether it constitutes an assertion for hearsay purposes. For example, assume that a conversation between Al and Ed includes the following question and answer:

Al: Did Jenni run the red light?

Ed: Yes.

Here, Ed's statement has meaning only if you link it to Al's question. Ed's linked assertion is that "Jenni ran the red light."

The context that demonstrates assertiveness may consist not only of a linked remark, but also of a linked event. For example, assume that after watching a golfer sink a hole-in-one, Monica says with a sigh, "Someday maybe that will finally be me." The context suggests that Monica has asserted that "I have never had a hole-in-one."

[3] Invisible Assertions

An assertion may be implied even though neither the question nor the answer refers to it explicitly. This commonly occurs when information is presented as based on a witness' own perceptions, when in reality the witness is simply a conduit for information supplied by an invisible declarant.

Example 1

PLAINTIFF'S ATTORNEY: Following the accident, did you talk to the plaintiff?

A: I did.

PLAINTIFF'S ATTORNEY: After talking to the plaintiff, what was your belief as to whether the defendant had run a red light?

A: I had the firm impression that the defendant had run a red light.

Here, neither the questions nor the answers explicitly refer to an out-of-court assertion. Yet it's obvious that the witness' "firm impression" is based on the plaintiff's out-of-court assertion that the defendant ran the red light. Since that explicit out-of-court assertion would be hearsay, so is the witness' "firm impression."

Invisible assertions are not always as apparent as in the example above. Consider this next testimonial excerpt.

Example 2

PLAINTIFF'S ATTORNEY: Did your spouse talk to the landlord?

A: Yes.

Here, the dialogue itself furnishes no clue as to whether the answer represents the witness' first-hand knowledge, or information imparted to the witness by the spouse (or by someone else). If the cross-examiner has reason to believe the latter, the cross-examiner may ask the judge for "permission to take the witness on voir dire for the purpose of asking foundational questions." If the judge grants permission and the foundational questioning reveals a previously invisible assertion, the cross-examiner may be able to exclude the testimony on hearsay grounds. The process might unfold as in the following example.

Example 3

PLAINTIFF'S ATTORNEY: Did your spouse talk to the landlord?

DEFENDANT'S ATTORNEY: Excuse me, Your Honor, permission to ask a few voir dire questions?

JUDGE: For what reason, Counsel?

DEFENDANT'S ATTORNEY: For the purpose of showing that the witness' answer is hearsay.

JUDGE: Well, I'll permit just a few questions. The jury may remain in the courtroom.*

DEFENDANT'S ATTORNEY: Were you personally present when your spouse talked to the landlord?

A: No.

DEFENDANT'S ATTORNEY: So is it fair to assume that your awareness of whether your spouse talked to the landlord is based on your spouse having told you that such a conversation took place?

A: Yes, that's right.

DEFENDANT'S ATTORNEY: Based on the witness' testimony, I object based on hearsay grounds to the witness' testifying to whether the spouse talked to the landlord.

JUDGE: I'll sustain that objection. Let's resume direct examination.

In *United States v. Brown*,[5] an income tax preparer was charged with tax fraud for overstating deductions on nearly all the tax returns he prepared. At trial, a government agent testified that she had examined the tax returns prepared by the

---

* Judges have discretion to permit mid-examination interruptions for foundational questioning. Depending on the likely length of the voir dire questioning and the risk that the voir dire questioning will disclose to the jury important information that the judge might later determine is inadmissible, the judge also has discretion to decide whether the voir dire questioning should be conducted out of the jury's hearing. *See* Rule 104 (c).

[5] 548 F.2d 1194 (5th Cir. 1977).

defendant and had found that they consistently overstated deductions. The government agent never referred to out-of-court assertions during her testimony. However, the court concluded that the agent could only have known that deductions were overstated on the tax returns if the agent had talked to the taxpayers for whom the returns were prepared and been told by the taxpayers what information they had supplied to the defendant. Because the government agent's testimony "had to have been based" on out-of-court assertions, the court held that the agent's testimony was improper hearsay and reversed the conviction.

[4] Vicarious Assertions

A vicarious assertion consists of a statement made by a declarant that is treated as though it had been made by a different person, who typically is a party to the lawsuit in which the assertion is offered. Rule 801(d)(2) enumerates four types of vicarious assertions, and Chapter 13 examines each of them.

Example

Butch and Sundance are charged with robbing the Last National Bank. The prosecution offers evidence that Sundance and Butch drove to the bank together, that Sundance waited in the car outside the bank with the motor running while Butch ran into the bank and held it up at gunpoint, and that Butch then ran out of the bank and jumped into the car as Sundance sped off. While inside the bank, Butch told the teller that "We've got guns and we're prepared to shoot if necessary." In Sundance's trial, under Rule 801(d)(2)(e), a judge would treat Butch's assertion as though Sundance had made it because they conspired together to rob the bank and the statement was made in the course of the robbery.

[5] Assertive Conduct

As defined in Rule 801(a), a statement includes "nonverbal conduct of a person, if it is intended by the person as an assertion." When a person uses nonverbal conduct as a substitute for verbal expression, treating the conduct as hearsay makes sense. The hearsay dangers are virtually the same, whether declarants communicate through words or conduct.

Example 1

PROSECUTOR: Police Officer Tracy, what happened after you took the defendant to the police station?

We conducted a lineup.

PROSECUTOR: Was Vic Timm present to observe the lineup?

A: Yes.

PROSECUTOR: And what happened?

A: I asked Vic if he recognized any of the people in the lineup as the person who held up the convenience store. Vic pointed to Number 3.

For hearsay purposes, Vic's act of pointing is a statement, the equivalent of a verbal assertion, "Number 3 is the robber." A conclusion that Number

3 robbed the store depends on Vic's sincerity as well as on the accuracy of his perception and memory. Even a form of the narrative danger remains. For example, did Vic point at the person he meant to identify?

By contrast, nonverbal conduct that does *not* reflect an intent to assert is not hearsay. "Pure conduct" (that is, conduct not intended as an assertion) is not hearsay because it is not communicative and therefore does not invoke the hearsay dangers.

Example 2

Testimony of Bystander in an auto accident case:

PLAINTIFF'S ATTORNEY: What happened before you saw the defendant's car collide with the plaintiff's car?

A: I saw the defendant's car swerving back and forth.

PLAINTIFF'S ATTORNEY: Did anything else happen before the collision?

A: Yes. A pedestrian who had started to cross the street when the light changed to green had to dive back to the corner to avoid being hit by the defendant's car.

Both the car's swerving and the pedestrian's reactions constitute non-assertive (pure) conduct tending to prove that the defendant was driving dangerously. The defendant's driving cannot reasonably be regarded as the defendant's chosen means of communicating the idea that "I am driving dangerously." Nor are the pedestrian's reactions an intended way of asserting that "the defendant is driving dangerously" or "I'm frightened." The defendant is driving and the pedestrian is diving for cover; neither is engaged in communicative conduct.

While non-assertive conduct may not raise *hearsay* concerns, conduct may be ambiguous and, if so, its admission may raise *relevance* concerns. Assume, for example, that a party seeks to prove that a ship was seaworthy. The party's witness is an onlooker standing on a dock who testifies that an experienced ship captain looked over the ship from stem to stern, then set out to sea in it. The captain's behavior appears to be non-assertive conduct from which a judge or juror may infer that the ship was in good condition.

However, because the captain did not verbally explain what he was doing, the relevance of his behavior is uncertain. Perhaps the captain was not conducting a safety inspection, but instead was looking for the piece of chewing gum that he had stuck onto the side of the ship a few days earlier. Or, perhaps the captain was suicidal and sailed off despite recognizing that the ship was likely to sink. The point is that behavior unaccompanied by verbal explanations may be ambiguous. If this fact does not render the evidence of conduct irrelevant, it may reduce its probative value and hence make a judge more likely to exclude it under Rule 403.

[6] Implied Assertions

The concept of "implied assertions" raises issues that Rule 801's definition of hearsay does not conclusively resolve. Implying an assertion presents no difficulty when declarants' words do not literally express their intended meaning. Again, people can express the same thought in many different ways. To prevent unfair outcomes based on insignificant and random variations in declarants' particular word choices, judges need only apply the hearsay rule as though the intended meanings had been expressed explicitly.

For example, assume that Pedro is a plaintiff in an auto accident case. If Pedro were to testify that a bystander told Pedro, "Dan's car ran the stop sign," the bystander's assertion would be hearsay if offered to prove that Dan drove negligently. But assume that Pedro testifies that the bystander had made one of these remarks:

- "I can't believe that Dan didn't notice the stop sign."
- "Dan's car was an accident waiting to happen."
- "Look at how Dan was driving and tell me that we don't need more traffic cops on our streets."
- "Teenage daughter of mine, I don't ever want you driving like Dan."
- "Wow — what driving!"
- "Didn't Dan's car go through a stop sign?"

In each instance, Pedro might argue that the hearsay rule doesn't apply because he is not trying to prove that statements are literally accurate. For example, Pedro might say that "I'm not offering the third statement to prove that more traffic cops are needed on the streets. Therefore, the remark is not hearsay." Similarly, Pedro might argue that "The last two utterances are not assertions — one is an exclamation and the other is a question."

However, a judge could reasonably conclude that in each instance the bystander simply chose different ways of intentionally expressing the same idea: that Dan was driving carelessly. If so, it's fair to apply the hearsay rule to what the bystander intended to assert. Otherwise, hearsay rulings would turn on inconsequential variations in word choices.

When the relevance of a statement depends on the accuracy of a declarant's belief, many commentators continue to argue that the statement should be treated as hearsay regardless of the declarant's intent. The famous (to Evidence aficionados, anyway) English case of *Wright v. Tatham* exemplifies their argument.

Decided by the House of Lords in 1838, the case grew out of a will contest filed by Admiral Tatham (pronounced "Tatum"), the sole surviving heir of his wealthy uncle, the decedent John Marsden. Admiral Tatham's financial expectations were shattered when Uncle John left his entire estate to John's steward, Wright. Seeking what he no doubt considered his proper due, the Admiral sought to have Uncle John's will set aside on the ground that his uncle was mentally incompetent at the time he made the will. The hearsay issue involved a series of letters that Wright sought to offer into evidence to prove that Marsden was sane. Marsden had moved from England to America, and the letters at issue were written to Marsden by various acquaintances and relatives of his in England. The letters were quite ordinary. For example, one described a sea voyage that the letter writer had taken, and another asked Marsden to propose a settlement to help resolve a property dispute back in England. Wright's theory in offering the letters into evidence was that since people would not write such letters to a man who had lost his marbles, the letters constituted evidence that Marsden was competent when he signed his will. Moreover, since Wright was not offering the letters for the truth of what they asserted (for example, Wright was not trying to prove that the account of the sea voyage was accurate), the letters were not hearsay.

The majority of the House of Lords excluded the letters as improper hearsay. The reasoning was that just as the letters would have been hearsay had the letter writers directly asserted that "Marsden was sane," so should they be hearsay when a party asks for an inference of sanity to be drawn from the writers having corresponded with Marsden in a way that suggested that the writers believed him to be sane. In the words of Baron Parke, "The letters which are offered only to prove the competence of the testator, that is the truth of the implied statements therein contained, were properly rejected, as the mere statement or opinion of the writer would certainly have been inadmissible."

From the standpoint of the hearsay dangers, the outcome in *Wright v. Tatham* seems justifiable. The declarants' (letter writers') statements allow an inference that Marsden was sane only if their belief that he was sane was accurate. Thus, Admiral Tatham's lawyer could make a strong argument for needing to test the accuracy of their belief through cross-examination. The Admiral's lawyer might have wanted to probe their *sincerity:* they may have only pretended to think that Marsden was competent, perhaps to curry favor in the hopes of being remembered in an eventual will. Similarly, the lawyer may have wanted to probe their *perception* and *memory:* had the letter writers had a sufficient opportunity to evaluate Marsden's competence in England? What did they know of his competence since he'd moved to America? And as Marsden had moved to America some time before the letters had been written, how accurate were the letter writers' memories of Marsden's competence?

The existence of the hearsay dangers leads many evidence scholars to consider the outcome in *Wright v. Tatham* to be "good" law.[6] But it is probably not "good law" under Rule 801. Remember that under Rule 801, the hearsay rule applies only to verbal or nonverbal language "intended as an assertion." Most judges ruling on the admissibility of the letters today would reason that they are not hearsay unless the letter writers intended to assert that "Marsden was sane." In the absence of such an intent, the letters constitute non-hearsay. Subdivision (a) of the Advisory Committee's Note to Rule 801 acknowledges that the credibility of such assertions is untested, but states that the "Committee is of the view that these dangers are

---

[6] *See, e.g.,* C. Mueller & L. Kirkpatrick, Evidence 717 (3d ed. 2003) ("If *Wright* arose today under Rule 801, how should the case be decided? The question is surprisingly hard, and two answers are both defensible.").

minimal in the absence of an intent to assert and do not justify the loss of the evidence on hearsay grounds."

U.S. v. Zenni (*see* Case Library) exemplifies Rule 801's approach to unintended assertions. In that case, police officers lawfully entered the defendant's residence to look for evidence of illegal bookmaking activity. While they were inside the premises, the officers answered the phone a number of times. The callers asked for bets to be placed on various sporting events, saying such things as "Put $50 on Dipsy Doodle in the fifth race at Hialeah." The prosecution offered the phone callers' statements into evidence to prove that the defendant had been engaged in bookmaking. In other words, just as Wright had offered the contents of letters as circumstantial evidence of the letter writers' beliefs that Marsden was sane, so the prosecutor in *Zenni* offered the contents of the phone calls as circumstantial evidence that the callers believed that they were calling a bookmaker, leading to a further inference that the defendant was a bookmaker.

The *Zenni* court held that the calls were non-hearsay. Because it was "obvious that these persons did not intend to make an assertion" that the defendant was a bookmaker, the calls were not barred by Rules 801–802.

Zenni represents the majority approach to "implied assertions." When a declarant's out-of-court assertion is used as circumstantial evidence that a fact that is not directly asserted is true, the assertion is hearsay only if the judge concludes that the declarant intended to assert the fact. However, by making the outcome turn on judges' assessments of declarants' "intent," the *Zenni* approach to whether implied assertions constitute hearsay requires subjective judicial interpretation and thereby creates uncertainty as to the application of the hearsay rule.

Practice Tip: Developing arguments that implied assertions are hearsay.

The continuing debate over the application of the hearsay rule to implied assertions creates space for you to argue that a judge should consider an unintended assertion to be hearsay and therefore exclude it. The more difficult textual support for such an argument is that *Zenni* and cases like it have simply misinterpreted Rule 801(a)'s definition of what constitutes a "statement." *Zenni* reads the final phrase, "if it is intended by the person as an assertion," as applying both to "oral or written assertions" and to "non-verbal conduct." However, the placement of the comma in Rule 801(a) can give rise to a plausible argument that the phrase "if it is intended by the person as an assertion" applies only to "non-verbal conduct." Under this interpretation, the phrase "oral or written assertion" may encompass not only what a declarant intended to assert, but also the declarant's subjective beliefs that underlie the assertion, regardless of whether or not the declarant intended to assert those beliefs. You may also make a broader policy-based argument asking a judge to rule that an implied assertion is hearsay by stressing that the "hearsay dangers" exist when judges admit implied assertions into evidence as non-hearsay. For example, examine the phone callers' statements in *Zenni*. Statements such as "put $50 on Horse Hide to win the third race at Aqueduct" are relevant to prove that the recipient of the phone call is a bookie *if* the caller was sincere about wanting to place a bet and *if* the caller correctly perceived and remembered that the phone number belonged to a bookie. If your argument persuades a judge that the presence of the hearsay dangers undermines the reliability of an unintended assertion, the judge might exclude an out-of-court statement as hearsay.

A Note on Terminology

The term "implied assertions" is unfortunately subject to the risk of ambiguity described earlier in the chapter. Some lawyers, scholars, and judges who agree with the analysis above may use the label "implied assertion" to mean that a statement is *not* hearsay. You have to be careful to look behind the label to determine whether a judicial opinion or a lawyer or scholar who uses it means that a declarant intended to make an assertion.

[C] "Statement" Problems

The following problems focus on whether offered evidence constitutes a "statement." Remember that evidence might constitute a statement yet ultimately be admissible for a non-hearsay purpose or under a hearsay exception or exemption.

Problem 10-17: Flight

Andy Amo is charged with murdering Smith. Prosecution witness Magoo is prepared to testify that Magoo heard gunshots and saw Amo running away from where the shots came from. Amo argues that as the prosecution will claim that Amo's running away shows that Amo was involved in the killing, evidence of his running constitutes testimony to an out-of-court assertion, "I'm the murderer." *Is this a valid argument?*

Problem 10-18: Knock Knock

Lucy is charged with shooting and killing Schroeder in his apartment on May 1 at around 2 a.m.; Lucy's defense is an alibi. Which if any of the following excerpts of testimony allow the prosecution to establish Lucy's presence at the scene of the shooting without offering evidence of an out-of-court assertion?

1. Charlie will testify that he was talking on the phone to Schroeder on May 1 at around 2 a.m. when he heard what sounded like a knock on a door. Shortly afterward, Charlie heard Schroeder say, "Hi, Lucy, come on in."

2. Charlie will testify that he was talking on the phone to Schroeder on May 1 at around 2 a.m. when he heard what sounded like a knock on a door. Shortly afterward, Charlie heard Schroeder say, "Lucy, you've never looked better."

3. Charlie will testify that he was talking on the phone to Schroeder on May 1 at around 2 a.m. when he heard what sounded like a knock on a door. Shortly afterward, Charlie heard Schroeder murmur, "Hmm, I wonder what Lucy is doing here?"

4. Charlie will testify that he was talking on the phone to Schroeder on May 1 at around 2 a.m. when he heard what sounded like a knock on a door. Charlie will

further testify that Lucy always lets people know she's at the door by knocking in a way that imitates the theme of Beethoven's Fifth Symphony, and that's the sound of the knock that Charlie heard when he was talking to Schroeder.

5. Charlie will testify that "I visited Lucy three days after the shooting. I saw an open wall safe, looked inside and found a locked diary. I broke open the lock and looked through it, and I recognized the handwriting as Lucy's. I took it with me and gave it to the police." The prosecution offers the last entry of the diary into evidence; it reads, "May 1, 2 a.m. Visited Schroeder's apartment."

6. None of the above involves out-of-court assertions.

7. All of the above involve out-of-court assertions.

Problem 10-19: Hard Landing I

Flora Walker sues McBroccoli's for personal injuries after she allegedly slipped and fell on a puddle of mustard that the restaurant had failed to clean up. To prove that the floor was unsafe, Flora testifies that while lying on the restaurant's floor after having slipped, Flora heard one nearby diner say to another, "Why are restaurant personnel so careless these days?" McBroccoli's objects that the diner's remark is hearsay. Flora responds that the utterance is non-hearsay as the diner's remark does not constitute an out-of-court assertion. *Is Flora's response valid?*

Problem 10-20: Hard Landing II

Same case as previous example. To prove that the floor was unsafe, Flora proposes to testify, "I'll say again what I've said all along, that there was a huge blob of mustard on the floor." Does Flora's testimony constitute an out-of-court assertion?

Problem 10-21: Hard Landing III

Same case as previous example. To prove that the floor was unsafe, Flora proposes to testify, "Just before I slipped and fell, I noticed a McBroccoli's employee walking toward the spill holding a pail and a mop." *Is Flora testifying to an out-of-court assertion by the employee that "There's a spill on the restaurant's floor"?*

Problem 10-22: Help!

Caryl is charged with sexually assaulting Lorna in a car parked in a secluded spot. To counter Caryl's claim of consent, the prosecution seeks to have Lorna testify that she repeatedly honked the car's horn in an effort to summon help during the assault. *Is Lorna testifying to her own out-of-court statement?*

Problem 10-23: Take Notes

Breach of contract action filed by Cain against Abel. Never having testified in court before, Cain is very nervous. Therefore, in response to direct examination questions, Cain testifies by looking at the written notes he made before trial and paraphrasing what he had written. *Is Cain testifying to out-of-court statements?*

Problem 10-24: Raise a Glass

In the breach of contract action that Cain filed against Abel, Abel's defense is that the parties never finalized the contract. To prove that the parties reached an agreement during lunch at Denny's on September 22, Cain calls a Denny's server to testify that "I served lunch to Cain and Abel on September 22, and saw them toast each other with wine glasses at the conclusion of the lunch." *Is the server testifying to Cain's or Abel's out-of-court statement?*

Problem 10-25: Cell Phone

Jack Carr is charged with carjacking. Jack's defense is that he was walking down the street when a car pulled over and the driver, a stranger, asked Jack to circle the block once or twice so the stranger could pick up an order in a nearby store. When the car's owner hadn't returned after Jack circled the block once, Jack drove a few blocks away and was arrested. To prove that Jack stole the car, the prosecutor seeks to have the arresting officer testify to searching Jack incident to the arrest and finding a cell phone in his pocket. The phone rang and the officer answered it. The caller said, "The nearest chop shop is on Maple Avenue. Turn left on Maple and go about 10 blocks, then drive up the blue driveway on the right." (A "chop shop" quickly breaks down stolen cars for their parts.) *Is the caller's statement hearsay if offered against Jack? If offered against the caller?*

Problem 10-26: Loot Lips

Jekyll is charged with bank robbery on June 4. To prove Jekyll's guilt, the prosecution calls Louie to testify as follows:

PROSECUTOR: On June 5, who was in the apartment when you arrived?

A: Hekyll and Jekyll.

PROSECUTOR: Were they both in the same room as you?

A: Yes. We were all in the living room.

PROSECUTOR: What happened after you entered the living room?

A: I saw stacks of money on a coffee table. Hekyll said that the money was the take from the bank job that he and Jekyll had pulled off the day before. Jekyll then asked me if I wanted a cup of tea. I said no, and we all left to go to the art museum to see the Impressionists exhibit.

DEFENDANT'S ATTORNEY: Objection and move to strike the last answer as irrelevant because no statement of Jekyll's pertaining to the bank robbery has been offered.

JUDGE: *What ruling?*

Problem 10-27: Slippery Slope I

The parents of Josie, a developmentally disabled eight-year-old child, sue Josie's school after Josie allegedly broke her shoulder on September 22 when using an unreasonably dangerous slide on the schoolyard without adult supervision. Josie lacks the capacity to testify. However, to prove that Josie was injured while playing on the slide, her father Wilfrid seek to testify that a few days after the accident, he walked slowly around the schoolyard with Josie and that Josie suddenly began to cry hysterically as they approached the slide. The school district's attorney objects on the ground that Josie's behavior constitutes evidence of an out-of-court statement. *As the judge, would you sustain the school district's objection?*

Problem 10-28: Slippery Slope II

In the same case, the school district seeks to offer evidence that a few days before Josie was injured, the mother of Jeff, another child with similar developmental problems, examined the slide and then allowed Jeff to play on it.

Student # 1: You are the attorney for Josie's parents. Identify the inference that the school district is likely to ask the jury to draw from the evidence of Jeff's mother's actions. Might you object to this evidence on the grounds of hearsay or lack of relevance? If so, present the argument you would make in support of your objection.

Student # 2: You are the attorney for the school district. Support the admissibility of the evidence of Jeff's mother's actions with an argument that they are relevant and do not constitute out-of-court assertions.

Problem 10-29: Slippery Slope III

During the pre-trial discovery phase of the same case, the attorney for the school district takes the deposition of Josie's mother. During the deposition, Josie's mother testifies as follows:

Q:	(by the school district's attorney): Do you know a father of a child in the school by the name of Max?
A:	Yes, Max Dietrich.
Q:	Did you ever talk to Max about Josie's injury?
A:	Yes.
Q:	And what did Max tell you about how Josie got hurt? Attorney for Josie: Objection, the question calls for hearsay.

What is the effect of this objection on the deponent? Can the plaintiff's attorney instruct the client/deponent not to answer the question? Why might the plaintiff's attorney make this objection?

Problem 10-30: Slippery Slope IV

At the conclusion of pre-trial discovery in the same case, the school district submits a Motion for Summary Judgment. The motion asks for the suit to be dismissed on the ground of lack of evidence that the school was responsible for Josie's injuries. Included in motion is an Affidavit of Leonard Vole. Vole's affidavit states in part that "My son attends the same school as Josie. I saw Josie in the schoolyard on September 22. When Josie left the schoolyard with her caregiver around 3 p.m., Josie was unhurt. On September 23, Max Dietrich, a father whose child attends the same school, told me that he was also in the schoolyard on September 22, and that he saw Josie leave the schoolyard unhurt on that day. Max further told me that as Josie and her caregiver crossed the street, Josie stumbled and fell to the ground. According to Max, Josie immediately grabbed her shoulder and began to cry loudly.

What if any portion of this affidavit constitutes hearsay? If Josie's parents object on the ground of hearsay, should the judge sustain the objection? What are the consequences of the judge sustaining the objection?

Problem 10-31: Beersay

Tommy Ake sues The Microbrewery after he allegedly developed food poisoning as a result of drinking improperly brewed beer on the night of March 12. To prove that its beer was not the source of any symptoms that Tommy may have had, Microbrewery's manager offers to testify that the restaurant served 153 other patrons on the night of March 12 and that the manager received no other complaints about the beer. Tommy makes a hearsay objection on the ground that evidence of the lack of complaints is the equivalent of the other patrons' out-of-court assertion, "The beer was fine on March 12." *Is this a valid argument?*

Problem 10-32: Eye Message

Jerry is charged with armed robbery. Jerry's friend Tom is present when Jerry is arrested in his apartment. The prosecution seeks to have Officer Tracy testify that after the officer told Jerry why he was under arrest and administered the "Miranda" warnings, Jerry winked at Tom and said, "Don't you remember that I was with you at the time of the robbery?"

1. The defense attorney objects to Officer Tracy's characterizing Jerry's eye movement as a wink. *As the judge, respond to this objection.*

2. The defense attorney objects to Officer Tracy's testimony that, "The defendant's wink meant that he wanted Tom to agree to a phony alibi." *As the judge, respond to this objection.*

3. The defense attorney objects to evidence of what Jerry said as hearsay. As the judge, you should rule that:

   a. The evidence is not hearsay because Jerry is asking Tom a question, not making an assertion.

   b. The evidence is not hearsay because Jerry did not make an assertion.

   c. Under the circumstances, the judge should consider Jerry's conduct as the equivalent of the out-of-court statement, "Tom, I want you to make up an alibi for me."

   d. The evidence is not hearsay because Jerry spoke in the presence of a police officer.

Problem 10-33: A Civil Action

Environmental suit by a citizens' action group against a factory owner for allegedly polluting a stream that runs by the factory. The plant manager testifies on the factory owner's behalf as follows:

DEFENDANT'S ATTORNEY: Why did you and the plant's owner walk to the stream?

A: We were giving a tour of the factory and the grounds to a group of foreign manufacturers' representatives.

DEFENDANT'S ATTORNEY: What happened when you got to the stream?

A: The owner dipped a cup into the stream and took a drink of water.

PLAINTIFF'S ATTORNEY: Objection, hearsay. Evidence that the owner drank water from the stream is the equivalent of the owner's assertion that the stream is not polluted.

JUDGE: Defense Counsel, any response?

DEFENDANT'S ATTORNEY: Yes, Your Honor, just briefly. The owner clearly did not intend an assertion. It's not like the owner drank water from the stream during a televised news conference. Drinking the water was simply non-assertive conduct, admissible as evidence that the water is safe.

JUDGE: *Does the owner's conduct constitute the owner's out-of-court assertion?*

Problem 10-34: Need Moe Money

Sally sues Moe Torist for personal injuries resulting from a car accident. To prove that Moe was at fault, Sally offers to testify that after the collision, Sally walked over to Moe and said, "This was all your fault." Moe responded by saying "let's just exchange insurance information and get out of here." *Has Moe made a tacit out-of-court statement that he was at fault?*

Problem 10-35: A Ticket, Attack It

Margarita received a ticket in the mail from City for running a red light. The ticket is accompanied by two photos taken by a camera posted at the intersection that automatically takes photos of cars that run red lights. One photo depicts the car entering the intersection, the other depicts the driver. Margarita decides to fight the ticket in court. *Can she exclude the photos on the ground that they constitute out-of-court statements?*

To show that the camera was functioning properly, City offers an Operating Report that the camera equipment produces when it records a car running the red light. *Can Margarita exclude the Operating Report on the ground that it constitutes an out-of-court statement?*

Problem 10-36: Brief Case I

Hawkeye is charged with possession of illegal drugs that were found in a briefcase. To prove that the briefcase in court is the one in which the illegal drugs were found, the prosecution calls Officer Marple to testify that "I recognize the briefcase as the same one because it has the name 'Hawkeye' embossed on the side." *Is the officer testifying to the briefcase owner's out-of-court statement?*

Problem 10-37: Brief Case II

Same case as Problem 10-36. To prove that the briefcase in which the illegal drugs were found belongs to Hawkeye, the prosecution calls Officer Marple to testify that "The briefcase in which I found the drugs had the name 'Hawkeye' embossed on the side." *Is the officer testifying to the briefcase owner's out-of-court statement?*

Problem 10-38: Alibi-Bye

Rosie Olla is charged with murder; her defense is an alibi. To disprove Rosie's alibi, the prosecution calls Officer Gomez to testify that the officer arrested Rosie in Rosie's mother's apartment on the afternoon of the murder. When informed of the charge, Rosie immediately said that she'd been with her mother all day long. At that point, Rosie's mom fainted. *Does the mother's fainting constitute an out-of-court assertion?*

Problem 10-39: At the Movies: Take Dictation

In the film *The Wrong Man*,[7] Manny goes into a loan office to seek a loan. The employees think that he is the man who robbed them about a month earlier using a note that instructed the employee to hand over the money in the cash drawer, but misspelled the last word as "draw." A loan office employee calls the police, who arrest Manny. At the police station, a police officer twice dictates the handwritten note that the robber used in the course of the robbery, each time asking Manny to write down by hand what he dictates. The second time Manny writes down what the police officer says, Manny leaves the "er" off the final word, "drawer." Assume that Manny is charged with the robbery and the prosecution wants to offer into evidence the copies of the robbery note that Manny wrote from the police officer's dictation. *Do the copies constitute out-of-court statements by Manny?*

§ 10.09 COMMON HEARSAY MISCONCEPTIONS

In an effort to spare you some of the anguish felt by previous generations of law students, the subsections below clarify common hearsay misconceptions.

---

[7] Universal Pictures (1956).

[A] "It's Not Hearsay If You Paraphrase"

One common misconception is that what the hearsay rule prevents is testimony to a declarant's exact words. Paraphrasing, then, seemingly avoids the hearsay problem.

For example, a questioner seeking to introduce evidence that a bystander saw the defendant's car run a red light might try to avoid the hearsay rule by phrasing the question as follows:

Q: Without using the bystander's exact words, can you give us the gist of what the bystander said to you following the collision?

The ploy fails. No matter how loosely paraphrased a declarant's out-of-court assertion, the answer is hearsay if it's offered for the truth of its contents. In other words, the hearsay analysis of these answers would be identical:

a. "The bystander said, 'The Mercedes ran a red light.'"

b. "The bystander indicated that the light for the Mercedes was red."

c. "The bystander indicated that the Mercedes entered the intersection illegally, after the light had changed."

d. "The bystander indicated that the Mercedes driver failed to follow the driving laws."

[B] "It's Not Hearsay If the Witness Is Also the Declarant"

As mentioned earlier, the typical hearsay situation involves two people: the declarant, and the in-court witness who testifies to the declarant's out-of-court assertion. Perhaps a resulting misperception is that the hearsay rule is inapplicable when the declarant and the in-court witness are one and the same person. In reality, when a witness testifies to the witness' own out-of-court assertion, the hearsay analysis is identical. To be admissible, the out-of-court assertion must qualify either for a non-hearsay use or a hearsay exception or exemption. For example, consider this brief testimonial excerpt:

PLAINTIFF'S ATTORNEY: And on that date and time, what happened?

A: I saw two cars collide.

PLAINTIFF'S ATTORNEY: Did you speak to either of the drivers after the collision?

A: I did. I walked over and spoke to the driver of the blue car.

PLAINTIFF'S ATTORNEY: And what did you say to the driver of the blue car?

A: I told the driver that the Mercedes ran the red light.

In this example, if what the witness said to the driver of the blue car is hearsay, it is hearsay regardless of whether the driver or the witness testifies to the statement.[8]

---

[8] Rule 801(d)(1) does provide three categories of hearsay exceptions (though defined by the Federal

This outcome seems to conflict with the earlier notion that hearsay protects a party's opportunity to cross-examine adverse witnesses. If the witness and the hearsay declarant are one and the same person, the adversary does in fact have an opportunity for cross-examination. In the example above, for example, the defense attorney can cross-examine the witness concerning what the witness said to the Mercedes driver. Therefore, you might argue, the hearsay bar should not apply when witnesses testify to their own out-of-court statements.

A technical response to this argument is that the hearsay rule provides the opportunity for *contemporaneous* cross-examination. In other words, the statement is hearsay because the cross-examiner did not have an opportunity to question the declarant *at the time the out-of-court statement was made.* This may not strike you as a compelling counter-argument, since cross-examination is never fully contemporaneous. Perhaps a better one is simply this: if the witness is in court, *the witness should testify to the event, not to the out-of-court statement.* Witnesses are supposed to provide judges and jurors with their best current recollections of past events, and they should testify to what they saw or heard, not to what they said out of court about what they saw or heard.

Thus, no hearsay problem would arise had the testimony above gone as follows:

PLAINTIFF'S ATTORNEY: And on that date and time, what happened?

A: I saw two cars collide, a blue car and a Mercedes.

PLAINTIFF'S ATTORNEY: Did you notice either of the cars prior to the collision?

A: Yes. I saw the Mercedes, and it ran the red light.

[C] "The Statement Isn't Hearsay If It's Circumstantial Evidence"

When an out-of-court statement is offered as the basis of an inference that the offering party wants the factfinder to draw, a common misperception is that the statement isn't offered for its truth because the fact asserted and the conclusion are different. In reality, *if the inference depends on the accuracy of the out-of-court statement*, the statement is hearsay.

Example

In a wrongful termination case, the plaintiff claims that she was illegally fired because of her physical disability. The plaintiff seeks to testify that, "Around the time I was fired, a co-worker told me that she had seen my boss painting over the handicapped parking symbols in the office parking lot." The plaintiff offers the testimony to prove that the boss was antagonistic to people with physical disabilities, from which the factfinder might further infer that the plaintiff's disability was the reason for the firing. The co-worker's statement is hearsay, because the plaintiff's desired inferences

---

Rules of Evidence as "non-hearsay) based on a declarant also testifying in court. Chapter 12 considers these "exceptions." At this point, it is enough that you realize that out-of-court statements are not routinely admissible simply because the people who made them also testify at trial.

[D] "It's Not Hearsay If The Statement Was Made in a Police Officer's Presence"

A fourth misperception (sometimes cynically called the "Philadelphia" or the "Chicago" exception to the hearsay rule) is that anything said in the presence of a police officer is admissible in evidence. As you'll see, a police officer's presence can be a relevant factor in some hearsay situations. However, no general doctrine admits out-of-court statements simply because they were made in a police officer's presence.

Practice Tip: "Who would I need to cross-examine?"

If you are uncertain as to whether something said out-of-court is a statement that is offered for its truth, you might ask yourself the question, "Who would I need to cross-examine at the time a statement is made?" If you cannot conduct meaningful cross-examination in the absence of the person whose words are offered into evidence, that is a signal that the words constitute hearsay.

§ 10.10 HEARSAY REVIEW PROBLEMS

Problem 10-40: Carded

Benny Han is charged with burglary in Denver, Colorado. Benny's defense is mistaken identity, and he testifies that he was in the state of Georgia at the time of the burglary. To substantiate this claim, Benny seeks to introduce into evidence a credit card receipt from Clark's Shoe Shop for the purchase of slippers. The receipt indicates an address for Clark's in Atlanta, Georgia, and is dated September 12, the day of the burglary. Benny's credit card number is on the receipt. *Does the receipt constitute a statement for purposes of the hearsay rule? If your answer is "yes," identify the declarant and the out-of-court assertion.*

Problem 10-41: Loretta

Loretta has been sued by homeowner Dion Tology for fraudulently inducing Dion to sign a home improvement contract. *Which if any of the items of evidence below would constitute out-of-court assertions if offered by Dion to prove that Loretta made false statements to Dion about the terms of the contract?*

1. One of Loretta's business associates told Loretta: "At least I don't go around making false statements to customers."

2. The Better Business Bureau revoked Loretta's membership.

3. Loretta has been sued by three other customers for fraudulently inducing them to sign home improvement contracts.

4. One of Loretta's former customers said, "I'm never going to do business with Loretta again."

5. Loretta was fired by the home improvement company that had employed her as a salesperson.

6. Before Dion signed the contract, a neighbor told Dion to "be careful when dealing with Loretta."

7. Another neighbor asked Dion, "Is Loretta still doing business?"

8. Another neighbor told her husband, "Don't answer the door," when she looked out the window and saw it was Loretta who was ringing the bell.

9. Another neighbor looked out his window, saw it was Loretta ringing the bell, and refused to come to the door.

10. A citizen's action group set a pile of home improvement contracts on fire as part of a silent vigil in front of Loretta's office.

Problem 10-42: Stat!

The plaintiff in a medical malpractice case offers the following testimony of an operating room nurse to prove that the plaintiff had a life-threatening medical condition:

PLAINTIFF'S ATTORNEY: And what did the head nurse say just before the plaintiff's operation got under way?

A: The head nurse told me to order an additional three pints of blood.

DEFENDANT'S ATTORNEY: Objection, hearsay.

PLAINTIFF'S ATTORNEY: It's not hearsay because the head nurse's remark does not constitute an assertion under Rule 801. The head nurse was simply requesting additional blood, not intending an assertion about the plaintiff's medical condition.

JUDGE: *Is this a valid response to the objection?*

PLAINTIFF'S ATTORNEY: It's also not hearsay even if you rule that the nurse intended to assert that the plaintiff needed additional blood. I'd be offering that assertion only as the basis of an inference that the plaintiff had a life-threatening medical condition. Because I'd be offering the remark to prove something other than what it asserts, it's not hearsay.

JUDGE: *Is this a valid response to the objection?*

Problem 10-43: No Parking

Ruth seeks to prove that she paid a parking ticket by offering the items of evidence listed below. *Which if any of the items constitutes an out-of-court assertion that Ruth paid the ticket?*

1. Ruth's testimony that she went to the Department of Motor Vehicles two days after she received the ticket and paid it.

2. A Department of Motor Vehicles visual recording depicting Ruth handing money to a Department employee.

3. A copy of the ticket, stamped "Paid" and dated two days after the ticket was issued.

4. The absence of Ruth's name on a list compiled by a Department of Motor Vehicles employee entitled "List of Vehicle Owners With Unpaid Parking Tickets."

5. None of the above.

6. All of the above.

Problem 10-44: Instant Replay

Walt Mart is charged with stealing a jacket from a department store. The prosecution offers into evidence a visual recording made by the store security guard who observed the theft. The security guard testifies that she made the recording moments after the defendant's arrest by having a store employee play the role of the defendant and re-create the theft. Following the security guard's instructions, the recording depicts the employee walking up to the jackets, looking around, picking up a jacket and putting it on, and quickly walking out of the store. The defense makes a motion to exclude the recording, claiming that it constitutes an out-of-court assertion. *Should the judge sustain the objection?*

Problem 10-45: Bettor Beware

In *Zenni*, the court ruled that phone callers' remarks such as "Put $50 on Ocean Wafer to win the fifth race at Pimlico" were not assertions when offered to prove that the location they were calling was used for bookmaking. The defendant to whom the phone number belonged is charged with illegal bookmaking and has pleaded not guilty.

Student # 1: You are the police officer who arrested the defendant. You answered the phone at least five times during the half-hour period you were at the bookmaking site, and in each case the caller gave an account number and placed bets of varying amounts on such events as horse racing, football, basketball, ice hockey, and tiddlywinks. You responded only with comments such as "OK" or "You're down." (You made notes of what the phone callers said immediately after each call, and the judge has given you permission to refer to those notes during cross-examination if necessary to answer the defense counsel's questions.)

Student # 2: You are the defense attorney, and will cross-examine the arresting officer. You'll try to undermine the probative value of the phone calls as evidence that your client was engaged in bookmaking.

Remainder of Class: You are jurors whose task is to evaluate the probative value of the phone call evidence. In addition, consider whether the defense attorney had a reasonable opportunity to test the callers' sincerity, perceptions, and memories.

§ 10.11 HEARSAY AND THE CONFRONTATION CLAUSE

The "Confrontation Clause" of the Sixth Amendment states that "In all criminal proceedings, the accused shall enjoy the right . . . to be confronted with the witnesses against him." While the Confrontation Clause and the hearsay rule both protect the right to cross-examination, should prosecution evidence that is admissible under a hearsay exception or exemption be barred by the Confrontation Clause? The U.S. Supreme Court has confronted this issue often, and has developed conflicting responses.

In *Ohio* v. Roberts,[10] the Court ruled that the Confrontation Clause was satisfied whenever hearsay was admissible under a "firmly rooted" hearsay exception. Because many hearsay exceptions that prosecutors commonly relied upon were held to be "firmly rooted," the Confrontation Clause normally imposed no greater burdens on prosecutors than those imposed by Rules 803 and 804.

The Confrontation Clause generally yielded even when prosecutors offered hearsay that was admissible under non-firmly rooted exceptions (such as Rule 807, the residual exception). In such situations, hearsay was admissible so long as declarants were unavailable and statements had "indicia of reliability."[11]

Crawford v. Washington (2004) literally yanked out these principles by their roots. *Crawford* (*see* Case Library) re-planted the constitutional soil with a principle that admissibility for Confrontation Clause purposes turns on whether hearsay assertions are *testimonial*. Under *Crawford*, testimonial hearsay made by non-testifying and unavailable declarants is admissible against criminal defendants only if a defendant has had a previous opportunity to cross-examine the declarant. If a defendant has not had an opportunity to cross-examine the hearsay is inadmissible, no matter how reliable it may appear to be and no matter how firmly rooted a hearsay exception.

In *Crawford*, the defendant was prosecuted for attempting to kill his wife Sylvia's assailant as Sylvia looked on. The defendant used a spousal privilege (*see* Chapter 17) to prevent the prosecutor from calling Sylvia as a witness. Instead,, the prosecutor offered into evidence a tape recording of the statement that Sylvia had given to the police shortly after the altercation. The statement was admissible under a hearsay exception, Rule 804(b)(3). But *Crawford* decided that it should have been excluded because it was "testimonial." Protection against the use of testimonial assertions, said the Court, was the core of the Confrontation Clause. Testimonial statements made by non-testifying and unavailable declarants can be admitted against a criminal defendant only if the defendant has had a previous opportunity to cross-examine the declarant. As the defendant in *Crawford* had not had a formal opportunity to question Sylvia (even though his own privilege claim rendered her unavailable), the statement was inadmissible under the Confrontation Clause.

---

[10] 448 U.S. 56, 100 S. Ct. 2531 (1980).

[11] Courts had to evaluate "indicia of reliability" by considering only the circumstances under which hearsay statements were made, and could not point to statements' consistency with other facts to conclude that the statements were reliable.

Crawford did not offer a comprehensive definition of testimonial statements. Grounding the concept on the Framers' presumed understanding of what the right to confrontation encompassed in the late 1700's, the opinion opted for examples. According to the opinion, testimonial statements include affidavits, statements given to police officers in the course of custodial interrogations, depositions, courtroom testimony, and "statements that were made under circumstances which would lead an objective witness reasonably to believe that the statement would be available for use at a later trial."[1]

Two years after *Crawford*, the Supreme Court re-visited the testimonial concept in *Davis v. Washington*. (*See* Case Library.) In *Davis*, the Court resolved confrontation clause issues in two domestic violence prosecutions. In one case, the Court decided that Michelle McCottry's description of abuse to a 911 operator was not testimonial because it was not a result of interrogation concerning a past crime. Since the 911 operator sought to resolve an ongoing emergency, McCottry was not a *witness providing testimony* but instead was seeking police assistance to assure her safety. In the second case, the Court ruled that Amy Hammon's description of abuse to police officers was testimonial because the violence had ended by the time police officers arrived and spoke to her. Summarizing the two situations, the Court explained its reasoning as follows:

> Statements are non-testimonial when made in the course of police interrogation under circumstances objectively indicating that the primary purpose of the interrogation is to enable police assistance to meet an ongoing emergency. They are testimonial when the circumstances objectively indicate that there is no such ongoing emergency, and that the primary purpose of the interrogation is to establish or prove past events potentially relevant to later criminal prosecution.

The Court again applied Confrontation Clause analysis to a claimed "ongoing emergency" in *Michigan v. Bryant*. (*See* Case Library.) In *Bryant*, police officers interviewed Covington, a fatally wounded shooting victim. Shortly before he died, Covington provided the police with a few details about the shooting, including the shooter's identity. The Court ruled that Covington's statements were non-testimonial because the totality of the circumstances (including Covington's medical condition, the unknown whereabouts of the shooter and the informality of the interrogation) demonstrated that from an objective standpoint, the primary purpose of the police interrogation was to deal with an ongoing emergency rather than to gather evidence of a past crime. The decision provoked a bitter dissent from Justice Scalia, *Crawford's* author, who had gotten used to winning Confrontation Clause battles. Justice Scalia charged that the majority had created a *"faux* emergency" and demeaned the Court by leaving Confrontation Clause analysis "in a shambles."

---

[1] A question that *Crawford* did not address is whether courts should apply pre-*Crawford* reasoning to non-testimonial statements. In other words, if a prosecutor offers non-testimonial hearsay into evidence under a hearsay exception, must the exception be either "firmly rooted" or must the statement possess "indicia of reliability" to be admissible under the Confrontation Clause? The most likely answer is "no." The Confrontation Clause is probably not implicated when statements are non-testimonial. However, no definitive answer is possible because the Supreme Court has not yet answered the question.

Justice Scalia was happier with the outcomes of two cases involving reports made by non-testifying forensic laboratory analysts. (*Melendez-Diaz v. Massachusetts* and *Bullcoming v. New Mexico; see* Case Library.) In *Melendez-Diaz*, a defendant charged with drug trafficking was convicted based on affidavits certifying that a powdery substance constituted cocaine. In *Bullcoming*, the prosecutor proved a defendant's blood-alcohol level by offering into evidence a forensic laboratory report. The prosecution did call a forensic analyst to testify, but not the one who had run the test and prepared the report. In each case, a 5-4 majority ruled that admission of the laboratory reports violated the Confrontation Clause. The reports were testimonial, since they had been prepared for use at trial. The dissenters argued vehemently that the rulings misinterpreted history and angrily predicted that the rulings will hamstring the operation of overburdened police crime labs.

By the time this edition is published, the Court may have issued a decision in yet another Confrontation Clause case, *Williams v. Illinois*. In *Williams*, a prosecution DNA expert testified to an opinion linking the defendant to a crime scene. The expert relied in part on a DNA report prepared by a non-testifying laboratory analyst, but the prosecutor did not offer the report into evidence. During oral argument, the government contended that the report was not testimonial because its contents were non-hearsay, serving only as a basis for the expert's opinion. Appellant Williams argued that since the expert's opinion relied on the accuracy of the report, failure to afford him an opportunity to cross examine the analyst who prepared it violates the Confrontation Clause.

In *Crawford*, Justice Scalia suggested that a great benefit of the "testimonial" concept was that outcomes of Confrontation Clause disputes would be far more uniform compared to the inconsistent outcomes that the "indicia of reliability" standard had produced. So far, however, even the Supreme Court itself is bitterly divided about the meaning and application of the Confrontation Clause. *Bullcoming* argued that a testimonial statement is one whose primary purpose is to establish or prove past events. But four dissenters responded that lab reports are too reliable to exclude, possibly breathing life back into the *Ohio v. Roberts* standard. Justice Thomas formed part of the majority in *Bullcoming*, but he would not apply the Court's definition of "testimonial" to non-formalized statements. And Justice Sotomayor, who also voted with the majority in *Bullcoming*, implied that she might rule differently in a case like *Williams* when she stated in her concurring opinion in *Bullcoming* that "this is not a case in which an expert witness was asked for his independent opinion about underlying testimonial reports that were not themselves admitted into evidence."

The scope of the "ongoing emergency" concept is equally uncertain. Justice Scalia developed the concept to distinguish *Davis* from *Hammon*, then fumed when in *Bryant* Justice Sotomayor avoided the Confrontation Clause by using the same factors to create what Scalia considered to be a *faux* emergency.

Uncertainty also surrounds the "primary purpose" portion of the definition of testimonial hearsay. In *Bryant*, Justice Sotomayor suggested that judges should assess both an interrogator's purpose in asking questions (assuming that a hearsay remark isn't volunteered) and a declarant's purpose in speaking to evaluate primary purpose "objectively." Justice Scalia disagreed vehemently in his *Bryant* dissent:

"The declarant's intent is what counts." Justice Ginsburg in *Bullcoming* tried a third tack, referring to a *statement's* primary purpose (as though a "statement" can have a "purpose").

Crawford emerged in 2004 looking like a legal vehicle that was seemingly designed to run forever. A scarce few years later, the decision shows a lot of wear and tear. The classic 1930's-1940's radio series *The Shadow* always ended with hero Lamont Cranston ominously warning listeners that "The weed of crime bears bitter fruit." To paraphrase Cranston, in uprooting *Ohio v. Roberts* the weed of *Crawford* has thus far borne a lot of bitterness.

Practice Tip: The Difficulty of Prosecuting Domestic Violence Cases.

More than coincidence accounts for the fact that the two rulings in *Davis* involved domestic violence. Intimidated domestic violence victims frequently refuse to cooperate with prosecutors and often absent themselves from their abusers' trials. Prior to *Crawford*, prosecutors were often able to secure convictions by offering victims' post-abuse statements to police officers into evidence. In *Davis*, the Court acknowledged that in these situations "the Confrontation Cause gives the criminal a windfall," but refused to "vitiate constitutional guarantees." At the same time, the Court pointed to a possible way out for prosecutors: the forfeiture provision of Rule 804(b)(6). If prosecutors can demonstrate that an abuser intimidated his victim into refusing to testify, the abuser "forfeits the constitutional right to confrontation." See Chapter 15 and the Supreme Court's interpretation of Rule 804(b)(6) in *Giles v. California*.

Practice Tip: Pretrial Depositions to Satisfy Crawford.

Prosecutors might react to *Crawford's* interpretation of the Confrontation Clause by making witnesses who have made out-of-court statements that are admissible under the hearsay rule available for cross-examination prior to trial. Since confrontation either at or before trial satisfies *Crawford*, scheduling depositions at which defense lawyers can question witnesses might allow prosecutors to offer hearsay into evidence at trial should the witnesses later become unavailable. Of course, witnesses who make themselves unavailable for trial might try to make themselves equally unavailable for pre-trial depositions. However, when formal pre-trial questioning is feasible, and the importance of the case and the feared unavailability of the witness at trial combine to outweigh the time and expense, depositions are one way that prosecutors can satisfy *Crawford*.

In jurisdictions in which defendants are bound over for trial based on preliminary hearings rather than grand jury proceedings, prosecutors can satisfy *Crawford* by questioning witnesses at preliminary hearings. The reason is that defendants have an opportunity to question government witnesses at preliminary hearings. However, defendants are not present at grand jury proceedings and, of course, have no opportunity to question witnesses who testify before grand juries. Thus, pre-trial depositions may be of particular value in jurisdictions that rely on grand jury proceedings.

Problem 10-46: Scarred

Ross Marshall is charged with armed robbery of a clothing store. Just after the culprit left the store, a customer ran over to the victimized clerk and said, "I got a good look at the robber. He had a big scar on his right cheek." The prosecutor calls the clerk to testify to the customer's statement to prove that Marshall, who has a facial scar, was the robber. Assume that the customer's statement would be admissible under the "excited utterance" exception to the hearsay rule (*see* Chapter 14). *The effect of the Confrontation Clause is that:*

1. The customer's statement is testimonial, and if the customer is unavailable to testify at trial the customer's statement is inadmissible unless Marshall has had a previous opportunity to cross examine the customer.

2. Even if the customer's statement is testimonial and the customer is unavailable to testify, the statement is admissible if it has "indicia of reliability."

3. Since the customer's statement is non-testimonial, its admissibility is not affected by the Confrontation Clause.

4. The Confrontation Clause allows the prosecution to offer the customer's statement into evidence only if the customer testifies at Marshall's trial.

Problem 10-47: One and Done

Jeff Birns is charged with arson. At Birns' preliminary hearing, store clerk Lowe testified that the day before the fire that Birns is charged with setting took place, Lowe sold Birns a bag of rags, a box of matches and a gallon of gasoline. Birns' lawyer cross examined Lowe at the preliminary hearing. At trial, though Lowe is available to testify, the prosecutor chooses not to call Lowe as a witness, and instead seeks to read the transcript of Lowe's preliminary hearing testimony into the record. *Should the trial judge grant the prosecutor's request?*

Problem 10-48: Tender Years

1. Wilson Narita is charged with sexually molesting his four-year-old stepdaughter, Claire. The judge rules without conducting a hearing that "Four-year-old children are too young to testify. They can't really understand the duty to tell the truth, and the courtroom experience would be psychologically damaging. Therefore, I rule that Claire is unavailable as a witness." *Is the judge's determination proper?*

2. With Claire having been deemed unavailable to testify at Narita's trial, the prosecution calls Antonia, a child protective services worker who works for the county, to testify to a statement that Claire made to her. Antonia testifies at a foundational mini-trial that Claire told her that "My daddy keeps putting his thing on my pee pee." Antonia talked to Claire privately at Claire's preschool, in response to a call from Claire's teacher reporting that Claire had been unusually lethargic and non-responsive for a few days. Antonia further testifies in the mini-trial that after a few minutes of conversation about the preschool, Antonia asked Claire if anything was wrong. Claire then made the statement about her father. The prosecution offers Claire's statement into evidence under the jurisdiction's "tender years" hearsay exception, which applies to statements made by children under the

age of 12 describing acts of sexual abuse or neglect. *Is Claire's statement testimonial? If so, what are the consequences of its being testimonial? Might the answer to question 2 be different if Claire's statement had been made to her babysitter rather than to a child protective services worker?*

Problem 10-49: Tipping Point

Thayer is charged with illegally distributing prescription drugs. At trial, undercover government agent Nark identifies Thayer as the person who he saw engaged in the sale of a large quantity of norcodeine pills at the Third Avenue underpass. Nark testifies further that he staked out the location where the sale took place based on statements made to Nark on the street to the effect that "If you need norcodeine, Thayer is the person you want to see and his office is the Third Avenue underpass." Thayer objects to this portion of Nark's testimony under the Confrontation Clause. *Should the judge sustain the objection?*

Problem 10-50: It's Not What You Say, It's Where You Say It

Devin Michaels is charged with armed robbery. The prosecutor seeks to offer into evidence a hearsay statement made by Edna O'Toole stating that O'Toole saw the defendant with loot taken in the robbery. Assume that O'Toole's statement would be admissible as a matter of hearsay law. If O'Toole is unavailable to testify at Michaels' trial, the prosecution could offer her hearsay statement into evidence under the Confrontation Clause if:

1. O'Toole made the statement while testifying under oath to the grand jury that indicted Michaels.

2. O'Toole made the statement while testifying at Michaels's preliminary hearing. Michaels represented himself at the preliminary hearing, at which time he had a chance to cross-examine O'Toole but did not.

3. After reading a story about the armed robbery in her local newspaper, O'Toole voluntarily called the Police Department "Hot Line" and recorded a message describing what she had seen.

4. O'Toole made the statement while testifying for the prosecution in the trial of Michaels's co-conspirator, Sally Welch. Welch was tried separately prior to Michaels, and Welch's lawyer thoroughly cross-examined O'Toole in the earlier trial.

Problem 10-51: There Goes the Neighbor, Hood

1. Hope is charged with selling illegal drugs. Hope's partner in the illegal business was Benny, and the prosecution seeks to offer into evidence against Hope a conversation that Benny had with Diller. In the conversation Benny described how he and Hope did business because he believed that Diller planned to join the partnership. In fact, Diller was an undercover police officer who recorded the conversation. When Benny refuses to testify against Hope, the prosecution offers into evidence the recording of Benny's conversation with Diller. Assume that Benny's statements would be admissible in evidence against Hope under the co-conspirator exception to the hearsay rule (*see* Chapter 13). *Are Benny's statements to Diller testimonial for purposes of the Confrontation Clause?*

2. Change the forgoing problem as follows: (a) Benny is on trial for selling illegal drugs; (b) Benny's statements to Diller that the prosecution seeks to offer into evidence were made after Diller arrested and interrogated Benny. Assume that as a matter of hearsay law, Benny's statements are admissible as party admissions (see Chapter 13). *How should the judge rule on the following argument of Benny's attorney:*

> *Your Honor, I object to the admission of Benny's statements to Officer Diller. Those statements are clearly testimonial. Moreover, my client intends to exercise the constitutional right to remain silent by not testifying at trial. The statements are thus inadmissible under* Crawford, *because Benny's exercise of the right to remain silent means that the defense has no opportunity to question or cross examine Benny. To admit Benny's statements into evidence would improperly punish Benny for exercising a constitutional privilege.*

Arthur Kirkland (Al Pacino) can't take it any more in . . . *And Justice for All.**

Problem 10-52: Brothers in Lawlessness

The Urban Police Department (UPD) has created a special task force in an effort to cripple a violent street gang, the 17th Street Crisps, headed by the Sam brothers, Flot and Jett. The UPD has distributed fill-in-the-blank witness sheets to residents and merchants in the gang's area. The witness sheets ask people to "join in the Crisps Crackdown" by filling out a sheet as soon as they become aware that

---

* *And Justice for All* copyright © 1979 Columbia Pictures Inc. All Rights Reserved. Courtesy of Columbia Pictures.

a crime is in progress. They are to fax the sheets to a special phone number. When a police dispatcher receives a fax, the dispatcher immediately notifies gang unit officers, who are generally on patrol in the area.

In this case, Flot and Jett are charged with murder. The prosecutor seeks to offer into evidence a witness sheet prepared by Molly McGovern. McGovern wrote: "Flot and Jett — hiding in the neighbor's bushes, loading handguns. Wearing dark clothes. Pointing guns at dark sedan. Shots fired. F. and J. jump into blue sedan, driving away south on 17th." The police dispatcher received the fax at 10:02 a.m., a few moments after the time other witnesses reported hearing shots fired.

With McGovern unavailable as a witness, the prosecutor offers her witness sheet into evidence. *Are the statements on the witness sheet testimonial? Was it prepared in the course of an ongoing emergency? What was the UPD's primary purpose in asking people to fill out witness sheets, and what is the significance of that purpose for admissibility?*

Problem 10-53: About Time

John Ramirez is charged with a murder that took place about two decades earlier. Ramirez was a fugitive from justice during this period. A search incident to Ramirez's arrest produced a knife with a distinctive cutting pattern. Based on the medical examiner's 20-year-old report describing the victim's fatal wounds, prosecution expert witness Lorena Edwards is prepared to testify to an opinion that a high probability exists that the knife found in the defendant's possession when he was arrested is the type of knife that caused the fatal wounds. Having passed away during the period when Ramirez was a fugitive from justice, the medical examiner is not available for cross-examination. *Is Edwards's testimony admissible over a Confrontation Clause objection?*

Problem 10-54: Potpourri

Consider the admissibility of hearsay evidence under the Confrontation Clause in the following circumstances:

1. Joe is charged with driving while intoxicated under a DUI (driving under the influence) statute that makes it a felony for a minor previously convicted of drunk driving to drive while under the influence of alcohol or other drugs. To prove that Joe drove with a blood alcohol level above .08 (and thus was intoxicated), that Joe was a minor at the time of the offense and that Joe had previously been convicted of drunk driving, at trial the prosecution offers the following items into evidence:

   (a) A Court Clerk's Certificate stating that an attached document titled "Abstract of Conviction" is a genuine and accurate copy of a court record indicating that Joe was convicted of drunk driving six months prior to the date he was arrested on the current charge.

   (b) A County Clerk's Certificate stating that an attached Certificate of Birth is a genuine and accurate copy of a county record indicating that Joe was 17 years old at the time of his arrest that is the basis of the current charge.

(c) An Analysis Report prepared and sworn to by Ronald Houston, indicating that Houston is a licensed lab analyst and that he administered a Breathalyzer test to Joe in accordance with standard lab procedures following Joe's arrest on the current charge and obtained a readout on the machine indicating that Joe's blood alcohol level was .12.

(d) A Breathalyzer Test Record prepared and sworn to by Judy Schackelford indicating that as an employee of a Breathalyzer testing company she conducted a routine test of the Breathalyzer machine used to determine Joe's blood alcohol level two days before he was arrested and determined that the machine was in proper working order.

Prior to trial, Joe's lawyer tells Joe that "Even though we don't contest your age or your prior drunk driving conviction, I'm going to make *Melendez-Diaz/Bullcoming* objections anyway" to all the documents above when the D.A. offers them into evidence. The lawyer further advises Joe that "when D.A.s rely on documents rather than live witnesses, the Confrontation Clause can be defendants' best friend."

a. *What is a* Melendez-Diaz/Bullcoming *objection*?

b. Is the attorney's position ethically responsible? Ethically required?

c. Assuming that the D.A. offers the documents above into evidence in lieu of live witnesses, and that Joe has not previously had a chance to cross-examine any of them, how should the judge rule on the defense attorney's Confrontation Clause objections?

2. Milt is charged with assaulting Nguyen with a deadly weapon. Officer Ahmadi finds Nguyen lying dazed and bleeding in an alley. The officer asks Nguyen, "What happened? Are you OK? Should I call an ambulance?" Nguyen then says to the officer, "Thank God! Don't know why, somebody wearing a Star Wars mask ran out of the back door of a store and slugged me with a metal pipe. My head hurts so bad." *Assume that Nguyen's statement would be admissible in evidence as a matter of hearsay law. Is the statement testimonial?*

3. Green is charged with the premeditated murder of Venutti. Supporting Green's defense of insanity is Dr. Loeb, who testifies that Green suffered from schizophrenia and that because Green had not been taking his prescribed antipsychotic medications, Green was incapable of planning or understanding that he could harm another human being. In rebuttal, the prosecutor calls Dr. Leopold. Dr. Leopold's opinion is that Green suffers only from a mild form of schizophrenia, and that Green committed the murder to prove that he is a superior human being who can get away with crime. Dr. Leopold arrived at this opinion after extensively examining Green and interviewing Green's parents. *If Green's parents are unavailable to testify and Green has not previously had an opportunity to cross-examine them, would the Confrontation Clause prevent Dr. Leopold from testifying to their statements?*

4. Marian is called by the prosecutor to testify in a bank robbery prosecution in which the defense is mistaken identity. Marian identifies the defendant as the person who ran past her as she walked toward the bank moments after it was

robbed. Marian further testifies that she paid particularly close attention to the defendant because as she approached the bank she heard an unidentified person call out from the bank's door, "The bank's been robbed! There goes the guy who did it (pointing at the running man)!" Assume that the prosecutor does not offer the unidentified person's shout to prove that the running man robbed the bank, but instead to explain why Marian's identification is credible. *Is Marian's testimony to the statement that she says led her to pay close attention to the defendant admissible over the defense attorney's Confrontation Clause objection?*

5. Sandy Dungo is charged with murder by strangulation. The prosecution contends that Dungo killed the victim Lou Pina as part of a turf war between members of rival gangs. Dungo admits that he killed Pina but claims that Pina's insults about Dungo's girlfriend provoked Dungo into a sudden response that at most constitutes voluntary manslaughter. Consider the admissibility of the following two items of prosecution expert testimony over Dungo's Confrontation Clause objections.

   a. The prosecution calls a pathologist, Dr. Lawrence, to testify that Pina was strangled to death, and that the injuries to Pina's neck muscles indicate that Dungo strangled Pina for at least two minutes. Dr. Lawrence was not involved in the autopsy of Pina, but bases his conclusions on the autopsy report prepared by Dr. Balduc. Dr. Balduc performed the autopsy, but the prosecutor does not call Dr. Balduc to testify. Dr. Lawrence refers to Dr. Balduc's autopsy report while testifying, but the prosecutor argues that no Confrontation Clause violation occurred because the report was not offered into evidence and the statements in the report were not offered into evidence for their truth but only as a basis for Dr. Lawrence's opinions.

   b. The prosecutor also calls police officer Luis Fuentes to support the contention that Dungo killed Pina intentionally as part of a gang turf war. Officer Fuentes qualified as a "gang expert" and testified that Dungo was a gang member who killed Pina for the benefit of Dungo's gang. Officer Fuentes based this opinion in part on casual, unrecorded conversations that he had had with various members of both gangs in the days preceding Pina's death. Dungo objects that the gang members' statements were testimonial and that because none of them testified, Officer Fuentes's conclusions are inadmissible under the Confrontation Clause.

§ 10.12 CHAPTER REVIEW PROBLEMS

Review Problem 10-A

Jones is charged with DUI (driving under the influence). The police officer who arrested Jones administered a blood alcohol test at the police station. The officer seeks to testify that Jones "blew" a reading of .13 on the Breathalyzer machine, well over the legal limit of .08. Jones objects that the reading is hearsay. *The judge should:*

1. Sustain the objection because the machine's readout constitutes the arresting officer's out-of-court statement.

§ 10.12 CHAPTER REVIEW PROBLEMS 457

2. Overrule the objection because machines don't make hearsay assertions.

3. Sustain the objection because the machine's readout constitutes the Breathalyzer machine manufacturer's out-of-court statement.

4. Sustain the objection because Jones's erratic driving is the equivalent of Jones's out-of-court assertion that "I drank too much alcohol."

Review Problem 10-B

Which item(s) of evidence below would be non-hearsay if offered by the plaintiff to prove that the sun was shining brightly at the time that a traffic accident took place?

1. The plaintiff's testimony that "As my spouse and I left the store and walked to our car about five minutes before the accident occurred, I asked my spouse, 'Do you have any of that sunblock lotion that you usually carry?' "

2. The plaintiff's testimony that "As my spouse and I left the store and walked to our car about five minutes before the accident occurred, my spouse said, 'Can you believe that this morning's weather report said it was going to be cool and cloudy today?' "

3. The plaintiff's testimony that "As my spouse and I left the store and walked to our car about five minutes before the accident occurred, I saw a man walk outside the store, stop, apply lotion from a bottle labeled 'World's Best Sunblock,' then continue walking."

4. The plaintiff's testimony that "As my spouse and I left the store and walked to our car about five minutes before the accident occurred, my spouse said to me that 'I just saw a man walk outside the store, stop, apply lotion from a bottle labeled "World's Best Sunblock," then continue walking.' "

Review Problem 10-C

Which item(s) of evidence below would be non-hearsay if offered by the plaintiff to prove that a black-and-white Llasa Apso dog belonged to the defendant?

1. The plaintiff seeks to testify that "I saw the black-and-white Llasa Apso jump up on the defendant's lap and lick the defendant's face.

2. Same as #1, but the plaintiff also offers into evidence a passage from the book "Canine Behavior for Dummies" stating that "Llasa Apsos are extremely owner-loyal and will only lick the faces of their owners."

3. A receipt from the Furry Friends Pet Shop that indicates the date on which a black-and-white Llasa Apso was sold to the defendant, as well as the sale price.

4. A book entitled "How to Raise a Llasa Apso" was found on the nightstand next to the defendant's bed.

Review Problem 10-D

Which item(s) of evidence below would be non-hearsay if offered by the plaintiff to prove that a certain cell phone number belongs to Alex Graham?

1. The plaintiff seeks to testify that she called the phone number and heard a recorded message that said, "You've reached Alex Graham's message center. Please leave a message and I'll call you back if and when I feel like it."

2. A printout of the cell phone company's records indicating that the phone number is assigned to Alex Graham.

3. The plaintiff seeks to testify that "I stood near Alex Graham and dialed the phone number. When it rang, I saw a friend of Alex Graham pick the phone off a table and hand it to him.

4. The plaintiff seeks to testify that "I dialed the phone number, and a voice that I recognized as that of Alex Graham said, 'Alex Graham here.'"

§ 10.13 CASE LIBRARY

UNITED STATES v. ZENNI
United States District Court 492 F. Supp. 464 (E.D. Ky. 1980)

BERTELSMAN, J.

This prosecution for illegal bookmaking activities presents a classic problem in the law of evidence, namely, whether implied assertions are hearsay. The problem was a controversial one at common law, the discussion of which has filled many pages in the treatises and learned journals. Although the answer to the problem is clear under the Federal Rules of Evidence, there has been little judicial treatment of the matter, and many members of the bar are unfamiliar with the marked departure from the common law the Federal Rules have effected on this issue.

Facts

The relevant facts are simply stated. While conducting a search of the premises of the defendant, Ruby Humphrey, pursuant to a lawful search warrant which authorized a search for evidence of bookmaking activity, government agents answered the telephone several times. The unknown callers stated directions for the placing of bets on various sporting events. The government proposes to introduce this evidence to show that the callers believed that the premises were used in betting operations. The existence of such belief tends to prove that they were so used. The defendants object on the ground of hearsay.

Common Law Background

At common law, the hearsay rule applied "only to evidence of out-of-court statements offered for the purpose of proving that the facts are as asserted in the statement."

In the instant case, the utterances of the absent declarants are not offered for the truth of the words, and the mere fact that the words were uttered has no relevance of itself. Rather they are offered to show the declarants' belief in a fact sought to be proved.

At common law this situation occupied a controversial no-man's land. It was argued on the one hand that the out-of-court utterance was not hearsay, because the evidence was not offered for any truth stated in it, but for the truth of some other proposition inferred from it. On the other hand, it was also argued that the reasons for excluding hearsay applied, in that the evidence was being offered to show declarant's belief in the implied proposition, and he was not available to be cross-examined. Thus, the latter argument was that there existed strong policy reasons for ruling that such utterances were hearsay.

The classic case, which is discussed in virtually every textbook on evidence, is *Wright v. Tatham, 112 Eng.Rep. 488 (Exch. Ch.1837*. Described as a "celebrated and hard-fought cause," *Wright v. Tatham* was a will contest, in which the will was sought to be set aside on the grounds of the incompetence of the testator at the time of its execution. The proponents of the will offered to introduce into evidence letters to the testator from certain absent individuals on various business and social matters. The purpose of the offer was to show that the writers of the letters believed the testator was able to make intelligent decisions concerning such matters, and thus was competent.

One of the illustrations advanced in the judicial opinions in *Wright v. Tatham* is perhaps even more famous than the case itself. This is Baron Parke's famous sea captain example. Is it hearsay to offer as proof of the seaworthiness of a vessel that its captain, after thoroughly inspecting it, embarked on an ocean voyage upon it with his family?

The court in *Wright v. Tatham* held that implied assertions of this kind were hearsay. The rationale, as stated by Baron Parke, was as follows:

> The conclusion at which I have arrived is, that proof of a particular fact which is not of itself a matter in issue, but which is relevant only as implying a statement or opinion of a third person on the matter in issue, is inadmissible in all cases where such a statement or opinion not on oath would be of itself inadmissible; and, therefore, in this case the letters which are offered only to prove the competence of the testator, that is the truth of the implied statements therein contained, were properly rejected, as the mere statement or opinion of the writer would certainly have been inadmissible.

This was the prevailing common law view, where the hearsay issue was recognized. But frequently, it was not recognized. Thus, two federal appellate cases involving facts virtually identical to those in the case at bar did not even discuss the hearsay issue, although the evidence admitted in them would have been objectionable hearsay under the common law view.

The Federal Rules of Evidence

By the time the federal rules were drafted, two principal arguments were usually expressed for removing implied assertions from the scope of the hearsay rule. First, when a person acts in a way consistent with a belief but without intending by his act to communicate that belief, one of the principal reasons for the hearsay rule to exclude declarations whose veracity cannot be tested by cross-examination does not apply, because the declarant's sincerity is not then involved. In the second place, the underlying belief is in some cases self-verifying: "There is frequently a guarantee of the trustworthiness of the inference to be drawn . . . because the actor has based his actions on the correctness of his belief, i.e. his actions speak louder than words."

The drafters of the Federal Rules agreed with the criticisms of the common law rule that implied assertions should be treated as hearsay and expressly abolished it. They did this by providing that no oral or written expression was to be considered as hearsay, unless it was an "assertion" concerning the matter sought to be proved and that no nonverbal conduct should be considered as hearsay, unless it was intended to be an "assertion" concerning said matter. The relevant provisions are:

> Rule 801. (a) Statement. A "statement" is (1) an oral or written assertion or (2) nonverbal conduct of a person, if it is intended by him as an assertion.
>
> (c) Hearsay. "Hearsay" is a statement, other than one made by the declarant while testifying at the trial or hearing, offered in evidence to prove the truth of the matter asserted.
>
> Rule 802. Hearsay is not admissible except as provided by these rules or by other rules prescribed by the Supreme Court pursuant to statutory authority or by Act of Congress.

"Assertion" is not defined in the rules, but has the connotation of a forceful or positive declaration.

The Advisory Committee note concerning this problem states: The definition of 'statement' assumes importance because the term is used in the definition of hearsay in subdivision (c). The effect of the definition of "statement' is to exclude from the operation of the hearsay rule all evidence of conduct, verbal or nonverbal, not intended as an assertion. The key to the definition is that nothing is an assertion unless intended to be one. It can scarcely be doubted that an assertion made in words is intended by the declarant to be an assertion. Hence verbal assertions readily fall into the category of 'statement.' Whether nonverbal conduct should be regarded as a statement for purposes of defining hearsay requires further consideration. Some nonverbal conduct, such as the act of pointing to identify a suspect in a lineup, is clearly the equivalent of words, assertive in nature, and to be regarded as a statement. Other nonverbal conduct, however, may be offered as evidence that the person acted as he did because of his belief in the existence of the condition sought to be proved, from which belief the existence of the condition may be inferred. This sequence is, arguably, in effect an assertion of the existence of the condition and hence properly includable within the hearsay concept. Admittedly evidence of this character is untested with respect to the perception, memory, and narration (or their equivalents) of the actor, but the Advisory Committee is of the view that these dangers are minimal in the absence of an intent to assert and do not justify the loss of the evidence on hearsay grounds. No class of evidence is free of the possibility of fabrication, but the likelihood is less with nonverbal than with assertive verbal conduct. The situations giving rise to the nonverbal conduct are such as virtually to eliminate questions of sincerity. Motivation, the nature of the conduct, and the presence or absence of reliance will bear heavily upon the weight to be given the evidence. Similar considerations govern nonassertive verbal conduct and verbal conduct which is assertive but offered as a basis for inferring something other than the matter asserted, also excluded from the definition of hearsay by the language of subdivision (c)."

This court, therefore, holds that, Subdivision (a)(2) of Rule 801 removes implied assertions from the definition of statement and consequently from the operation of the hearsay rule.

Applying the principles discussed above to the case at bar, this court holds that the utterances of the betters telephoning in their bets were nonassertive verbal conduct, offered as relevant for an implied assertion to be inferred from them, namely that bets could be placed at the premises being telephoned. The language is not an assertion on its face, and it is obvious these persons did not intend to make an assertion about the fact sought to be proved or anything else.

As an implied assertion, the proffered evidence is expressly excluded from the operation of the hearsay rule by Rule 801 of the Federal Rules of Evidence, and the objection thereto must be overruled. An order to that effect has previously been entered.

CRAWFORD v. WASHINGTON
United States Supreme Court 541 U.S. 36 (2004)

JUSTICE SCALIA delivered the opinion of the Court.

Petitioner Michael Crawford stabbed a man who allegedly tried to rape his wife, Sylvia. At his trial, the State played for the jury Sylvia's tape-recorded statement to the police describing the stabbing, even though he had no opportunity for cross-examination. The Washington Supreme Court upheld petitioner's conviction after determining that Sylvia's statement was reliable. The question presented is whether this procedure complied with the Sixth Amendment's guarantee that, "in all criminal prosecutions, the accused shall enjoy the right . . . to be confronted with the witnesses against him."

I

On August 5, 1999, Kenneth Lee was stabbed at his apartment. Police arrested petitioner later that night. After giving petitioner and his wife *Miranda* warnings, detectives interrogated each of them twice. Petitioner eventually confessed that he and Sylvia had gone in search of Lee because he was upset over an earlier incident in which Lee had tried to rape her. The two had found Lee at his apartment, and a fight ensued in which Lee was stabbed in the torso and petitioner's hand was cut.

Petitioner gave the following account of the fight:

Q: Okay. Did you ever see anything in [Lee's] hands?
A: I think so, but I'm not positive.
Q: Okay, when you think so, what do you mean by that?

A: I coulda swore I seen him goin' for somethin' before, right before everything happened. He was like reachin', fiddlin' around down here and stuff . . . and I just . . . I don't know, I think, this is just a possibility, but I think, I think that he pulled somethin' out and I grabbed for it and that's how I got cut . . . but I'm not positive. I, I, my mind goes blank when things like this happen. I mean, I just, I remember things wrong, I remember things that just doesn't, don't make sense to me later.

Sylvia generally corroborated petitioner's story about the events leading up to the fight, but her account of the fight itself was arguably different — particularly with respect to whether Lee had drawn a weapon before petitioner assaulted him:

Q: Did Kenny do anything to fight back from this assault?

A: (pausing) I know he reached into his pocket . . . or somethin' . . . I don't know what.

Q: After he was stabbed?

A: He saw Michael coming up. He lifted his hand . . . his chest open, he might [have] went to go strike his hand out or something and then (inaudible).

Q: Okay, you, you gotta speak up.

A: Okay, he lifted his hand over his head maybe to strike Michael's hand down or something and then he put his hands in his . . . put his right hand in his right pocket . . . took a step back . . . Michael proceeded to stab him . . . then his hands were like . . . how do you explain this . . . open arms . . . with his hands open and he fell down . . . and we ran (describing subject holding hands open, palms toward assailant).

Q: Okay, when he's standing there with his open hands, you're talking about Kenny, correct?

A: Yeah, after, after the fact, yes.

Q: Did you see anything in his hands at that point?

A: (pausing) um um (no).

The State charged petitioner with assault and attempted murder. At trial, he claimed self-defense. Sylvia did not testify because of the state marital privilege, which generally bars a spouse from testifying without the other spouse's consent. In Washington, this privilege does not extend to a spouse's out-of-court statements admissible under a hearsay exception, so the State sought to introduce Sylvia's tape-recorded statements to the police as evidence that the stabbing was not in self-defense. Noting that Sylvia had admitted she led petitioner to Lee's apartment and thus had facilitated the assault, the State invoked the hearsay exception for statements against penal interest.

Petitioner countered that, state law notwithstanding, admitting the evidence would violate his federal constitutional right to be "confronted with the witnesses against him." According to our description of that right in *Ohio v. Roberts*, 448 U.S.

56 (1980), it does not bar admission of an unavailable witness's statement against a criminal defendant if the statement bears "adequate 'indicia of reliability.'" To meet that test, evidence must either fall within a "firmly rooted hearsay exception" or bear "particularized guarantees of trustworthiness." The trial court here admitted the statement and gave reasons why it was trustworthy: Sylvia was not shifting blame but rather corroborating her husband's story that he acted in self-defense or "justified reprisal"; she had direct knowledge as an eyewitness; she was describing recent events; and she was being questioned by a "neutral" law enforcement officer. The prosecution played the tape for the jury and relied on it in closing, arguing that it was "damning evidence" that "completely refutes [petitioner's] claim of self-defense." The jury convicted petitioner of assault.

We granted certiorari to determine whether the State's use of Sylvia's statement violated the Confrontation Clause.

II

A

The Constitution's text does not alone resolve this case. One could plausibly read "witnesses against" a defendant to mean those who actually testify at trial, those whose statements are offered at trial, or something in-between. We must therefore turn to the historical background of the Clause to understand its meaning.

The right to confront one's accusers is a concept that dates back to Roman times. The founding generation's immediate source of the concept, however, was the common law. English common law has long differed from continental civil law in regard to the manner in which witnesses give testimony in criminal trials. The common-law tradition is one of live testimony in court subject to adversarial testing, while the civil law condones examination in private by judicial officers. See 3 W. Blackstone, Commentaries on the Laws of England 373–374 (1768).

Nonetheless, England at times adopted elements of the civil-law practice. The most notorious instances of civil-law examination occurred in the great political trials of the 16th and 17th centuries. One such was the 1603 trial of Sir Walter Raleigh for treason. Lord Cobham, Raleigh's alleged accomplice, had implicated him in an examination before the Privy Council and in a letter. At Raleigh's trial, these were read to the jury. Raleigh argued that Cobham had lied to save himself. Suspecting that Cobham would recant, Raleigh demanded that the judges call him to appear, arguing that "the Proof of the Common Law is by witness and jury: let Cobham be here, let him speak it. Call my accuser before my face . . . ." The judges refused, and, despite Raleigh's protestations that he was being tried "by the Spanish Inquisition," the jury convicted, and Raleigh was sentenced to death. One of Raleigh's trial judges later lamented that "'the justice of England has never been so degraded and injured as by the condemnation of Sir Walter Raleigh.'" Through a series of statutory and judicial reforms, English law developed a right of confrontation that limited these abuses.

III

This history supports two inferences about the meaning of the Sixth Amendment.

A

First, the principal evil at which the Confrontation Clause was directed was the civil-law mode of criminal procedure, and particularly its use of *ex parte* examinations as evidence against the accused. It was these practices that the Crown deployed in notorious treason cases like Raleigh's; that the Marian statutes invited; that English law's assertion of a right to confrontation was meant to prohibit; and that the founding-era rhetoric decried. The Sixth Amendment must be interpreted with this focus in mind.

Accordingly, we once again reject the view that the Confrontation Clause applies of its own force only to in-court testimony. Leaving the regulation of out-of-court statements to the law of evidence would render the Confrontation Clause powerless to prevent even the most flagrant inquisitorial practices. Raleigh was, after all, perfectly free to confront those who read Cobham's confession in court.

This focus also suggests that not all hearsay implicates the Sixth Amendment's core concerns. An off-hand, overheard remark might be unreliable evidence and thus a good candidate for exclusion under hearsay rules, but it bears little resemblance to the civil-law abuses the Confrontation Clause targeted. On the other hand, *ex parte* examinations might sometimes be admissible under modern hearsay rules, but the Framers certainly would not have condoned them.

The text of the Confrontation Clause reflects this focus. It applies to "witnesses" against the accused — in other words, those who "bear testimony." "Testimony," in turn, is typically "[a] solemn declaration or affirmation made for the purpose of establishing or proving some fact." An accuser who makes a formal statement to government officers bears testimony in a sense that a person who makes a casual remark to an acquaintance does not. The constitutional text, like the history underlying the common-law right of confrontation, thus reflects an especially acute concern with a specific type of out-of-court statement.

Various formulations of this core class of "testimonial" statements exist: "*ex parte* in-court testimony or its functional equivalent — that is, material such as affidavits, custodial examinations, prior testimony that the defendant was unable to cross-examine, or similar pretrial statements that declarants would reasonably expect to be used prosecutorially," . . . "extrajudicial statements . . . contained in formalized testimonial materials, such as affidavits, depositions, prior testimony, or confessions," . . . "statements that were made under circumstances which would lead an objective witness reasonably to believe that the statement would be available for use at a later trial" . . . . These formulations all share a common nucleus and then define the Clause's coverage at various levels of abstraction around it. Regardless of the precise articulation, some statements qualify under any definition — for example, *ex parte* testimony at a preliminary hearing. Statements taken by police officers in the course of interrogations are also testimonial under even a narrow standard.

In sum, even if the Sixth Amendment is not solely concerned with testimonial hearsay, that is its primary object, and interrogations by law enforcement officers fall squarely within that class.

B

The historical record also supports a second proposition: that the Framers would not have allowed admission of testimonial statements of a witness who did not appear at trial unless he was unavailable to testify, and the defendant had had a prior opportunity for cross-examination. The text of the Sixth Amendment does not suggest any open-ended exceptions from the confrontation requirement to be developed by the courts. Rather, the "right . . . to be confronted with the witnesses against him" is most naturally read as a reference to the right of confrontation at common law, admitting only those exceptions established at the time of the founding. As the English authorities above reveal, the common law in 1791 conditioned admissibility of an absent witness's examination on unavailability and a prior opportunity to cross-examine. The Sixth Amendment therefore incorporates those limitations.

V

Although the results of our decisions have generally been faithful to the original meaning of the Confrontation Clause, the same cannot be said of our rationales. *Roberts* conditions the admissibility of all hearsay evidence on whether it falls under a "firmly rooted hearsay exception;" or bears "particularized guarantees of trustworthiness." This test departs from the historical principles identified above in two respects. First, it is too broad: It applies the same mode of analysis whether or not the hearsay consists of *ex parte* testimony. This often results in close constitutional scrutiny in cases that are far removed from the core concerns of the Clause. At the same time, however, the test is too narrow: It admits statements that *do* consist of *ex parte* testimony upon a mere finding of reliability. This malleable standard often fails to protect against paradigmatic confrontation violations.

Members of this Court and academics have suggested that we revise our doctrine to reflect more accurately the original understanding of the Clause. They offer two proposals: First, that we apply the Confrontation Clause only to testimonial statements, leaving the remainder to regulation by hearsay law — thus eliminating the overbreadth referred to above. Second, that we impose an absolute bar to statements that are testimonial, absent a prior opportunity to cross-examine — thus eliminating the excessive narrowness referred to above.

In *White*, we considered the first proposal and rejected it. Although our analysis in this case casts doubt on that holding, we need not definitively resolve whether it survives our decision today, because Sylvia Crawford's statement is testimonial under any definition. This case does, however, squarely implicate the second proposal.

A

Where testimonial statements are involved, we do not think the Framers meant to leave the Sixth Amendment's protection to the vagaries of the rules of evidence, much less to amorphous notions of "reliability." Certainly none of the authorities discussed above acknowledges any general reliability exception to the common-law rule. Admitting statements deemed reliable by a judge is fundamentally at odds with the right of confrontation. To be sure, the Clause's ultimate goal is to ensure reliability of evidence, but it is a procedural rather than a substantive guarantee. It commands, not that evidence be reliable, but that reliability be assessed in a particular manner: by testing in the crucible of cross-examination. The Clause thus reflects a judgment, not only about the desirability of reliable evidence (a point on which there could be little dissent), but about how reliability can best be determined.

The *Roberts* test allows a jury to hear evidence, untested by the adversary process, based on a mere judicial determination of reliability. It thus replaces the constitutionally prescribed method of assessing reliability with a wholly foreign one.

The Raleigh trial itself involved the very sorts of reliability determinations that *Roberts* authorizes. In the face of Raleigh's repeated demands for confrontation, the prosecution responded with many of the arguments a court applying *Roberts* might invoke today: that Cobham's statements were self-inculpatory, that they were not made in the heat of passion, and that they were not "extracted from [him] upon any hopes or promise of Pardon." It is not plausible that the Framers' only objection to the trial was that Raleigh's judges did not properly weigh these factors before sentencing him to death. Rather, the problem was that the judges refused to allow Raleigh to confront Cobham in court, where he could cross-examine him and try to expose his accusation as a lie.

Dispensing with confrontation because testimony is obviously reliable is akin to dispensing with jury trial because a defendant is obviously guilty. This is not what the Sixth Amendment prescribes.

B

The legacy of *Roberts* in other courts vindicates the Framers' wisdom in rejecting a general reliability exception. The framework is so unpredictable that it fails to provide meaningful protection from even core confrontation violations.

Reliability is an amorphous, if not entirely subjective, concept. There are countless factors bearing on whether a statement is reliable; the nine-factor balancing test applied by the Court of Appeals below is representative. Whether a statement is deemed reliable depends heavily on which factors the judge considers and how much weight he accords each of them. Some courts wind up attaching the same significance to opposite facts. For example, the Colorado Supreme Court held a statement more reliable because its inculpation of the defendant was "detailed," while the Fourth Circuit found a statement more reliable because the portion implicating another was "fleeting." The Virginia Court of Appeals found a statement more reliable because the witness was in custody and charged with a crime (thus making the statement more obviously against her penal interest), while the

Wisconsin Court of Appeals found a statement more reliable because the witness was *not* in custody and *not* a suspect. Finally, the Colorado Supreme Court in one case found a statement more reliable because it was given "immediately after" the events at issue, while that same court, in another case, found a statement more reliable because two years had elapsed.

The unpardonable vice of the *Roberts* test, however, is not its unpredictability, but its demonstrated capacity to admit core testimonial statements that the Confrontation Clause plainly meant to exclude. To add insult to injury, some of the courts that admit untested testimonial statements find reliability in the very factors that *make* the statements testimonial. As noted earlier, one court relied on the fact that the witness's statement was made to police while in custody on pending charges — the theory being that this made the statement more clearly against penal interest and thus more reliable. Other courts routinely rely on the fact that a prior statement is given under oath in judicial proceedings. That inculpating statements are given in a testimonial setting is not an antidote to the confrontation problem, but rather the trigger that makes the Clause's demands most urgent. It is not enough to point out that most of the usual safeguards of the adversary process attend the statement, when the single safeguard missing is the one the Confrontation Clause demands.

C

Roberts' failings were on full display in the proceedings below. Sylvia Crawford made her statement while in police custody, herself a potential suspect in the case. Indeed, she had been told that whether she would be released "depended on how the investigation continues." In response to often leading questions from police detectives, she implicated her husband in Lee's stabbing and at least arguably undermined his self-defense claim. Despite all this, the trial court admitted her statement, listing several reasons why it was reliable. In its opinion reversing, the Court of Appeals listed several *other* reasons why the statement was *not* reliable. Finally, the State Supreme Court relied exclusively on the interlocking character of the statement and disregarded every other factor the lower courts had considered. The case is thus a self-contained demonstration of *Roberts*' unpredictable and inconsistent application.

Each of the courts also made assumptions that cross-examination might well have undermined. The trial court, for example, stated that Sylvia Crawford's statement was reliable because she was an eyewitness with direct knowledge of the events. But Sylvia at one point told the police that she had "shut [her] eyes and . . . didn't really watch" part of the fight, and that she was "in shock." The trial court also buttressed its reliability finding by claiming that Sylvia was "being questioned by law enforcement, and, thus, the [questioner] is . . . neutral to her and not someone who would be inclined to advance her interests and shade her version of the truth unfavorably toward the defendant." The Framers would be astounded to learn that *ex parte* testimony could be admitted against a criminal defendant because it was elicited by "neutral" government officers. But even if the court's assessment of the officer's motives was accurate, it says nothing about Sylvia's perception of her situation. Only cross-examination could reveal that.

We readily concede that we could resolve this case by simply reweighing the "reliability factors" under *Roberts* and finding that Sylvia Crawford's statement falls short. But we view this as one of those rare cases in which the result below is so improbable that it reveals a fundamental failure on our part to interpret the Constitution in a way that secures its intended constraint on judicial discretion. Moreover, to reverse the Washington Supreme Court's decision after conducting our own reliability analysis would perpetuate, not avoid, what the Sixth Amendment condemns. The Constitution prescribes a procedure for determining the reliability of testimony in criminal trials, and we, no less than the state courts, lack authority to replace it with one of our own devising.

We have no doubt that the courts below were acting in utmost good faith when they found reliability. The Framers, however, would not have been content to indulge this assumption. They knew that judges, like other government officers, could not always be trusted to safeguard the rights of the people. They were loath to leave too much discretion in judicial hands. By replacing categorical constitutional guarantees with open-ended balancing tests, we do violence to their design. Vague standards are manipulable, and, while that might be a small concern in run-of-the-mill assault prosecutions like this one, the Framers had an eye toward politically charged cases like Raleigh's — great state trials where the impartiality of even those at the highest levels of the judiciary might not be so clear. It is difficult to imagine *Roberts*' providing any meaningful protection in those circumstances.

Where nontestimonial hearsay is at issue, it is wholly consistent with the Framers' design to afford the States flexibility in their development of hearsay law — as does *Roberts*, and as would an approach that exempted such statements from Confrontation Clause scrutiny altogether. Where testimonial evidence is at issue, however, the Sixth Amendment demands what the common law required: unavailability and a prior opportunity for cross-examination. We leave for another day any effort to spell out a comprehensive definition of "testimonial." Whatever else the term covers, it applies at a minimum to prior testimony at a preliminary hearing, before a grand jury, or at a former trial; and to police interrogations. These are the modern practices with closest kinship to the abuses at which the Confrontation Clause was directed.

In this case, the State admitted Sylvia's testimonial statement against petitioner, despite the fact that he had no opportunity to cross-examine her. That alone is sufficient to make out a violation of the Sixth Amendment. *Roberts* notwithstanding, we decline to mine the record in search of indicia of reliability. Where testimonial statements are at issue, the only indicium of reliability sufficient to satisfy constitutional demands is the one the Constitution actually prescribes: confrontation.

The judgment of the Washington Supreme Court is reversed, and the case is remanded for further proceedings not inconsistent with this opinion.

It is so ordered.

DAVIS v. WASHINGTON
United States Supreme Court 547 U.S. 813, 126 S. Ct. 2266 (2006)

JUSTICE SCALIA delivered the opinion of the Court.

These cases require us to determine when statements made to law enforcement personnel during a 911 call or at a crime scene are "testimonial" and thus subject to the requirements of the Sixth Amendment's Confrontation Clause.

I

A

The relevant statements in *Davis* v. *Washington* were made to a 911 emergency operator on February 1, 2001. When the operator answered the initial call, the connection terminated before anyone spoke. She reversed the call, and Michelle McCottry answered. In the ensuing conversation, the operator ascertained that McCottry was involved in a domestic disturbance with her former boyfriend Adrian Davis, the petitioner in this case:

911 Operator: Hello. What's going on?

Complainant: He's here jumpin' on me again.

911 Operator: Okay. Listen to me carefully. Are you in a house or an apartment?

Complainant: I'm in a house.

911 Operator: Are there any weapons?

Complainant: No. He's usin' his fists.

911 Operator: Okay. Has he been drinking?

Complainant: No.

911 Operator: Okay, sweetie. I've got help started. Stay on the line with me, okay?

Complainant: I'm on the line.

911 Operator: Listen to me carefully. Do you know his last name?

Complainant: It's Davis.

911 Operator: Davis? Okay, what's his first name?

Complainant: Adran

911 Operator: What is it?

Complainant: Adrian.

911 Operator: Adrian?

Complainant: Yeah.

911 Operator: Okay. What's his middle initial?

Complainant: Martell. He's runnin' now."

As the conversation continued, the operator learned that Davis had "just r[un] out the door" after hitting McCottry, and that he was leaving in a car with someone else. McCottry started talking, but the operator cut her off, saying, "Stop talking and answer my questions." She then gathered more information about Davis (including his birthday), and learned that Davis had told McCottry that his purpose in coming to the house was "to get his stuff," since McCottry was moving. McCottry described the context of the assault, after which the operator told her that the police were on their way. "They're gonna check the area for him first," the operator said, "and then they're gonna come talk to you." The police arrived within four minutes of the 911 call and observed McCottry's shaken state, the "fresh injuries on her forearm and her face," and her "frantic efforts to gather her belongings and her children so that they could leave the residence."

The State charged Davis with felony violation of a domestic no-contact order. "The State's only witnesses were the two police officers who responded to the 911 call. Both officers testified that McCottry exhibited injuries that appeared to be recent, but neither officer could testify as to the cause of the injuries." McCottry presumably could have testified as to whether Davis was her assailant, but she did not appear. Over Davis's objection, based on the Confrontation Clause of the Sixth Amendment, the trial court admitted the recording of her exchange with the 911 operator, and the jury convicted him. The Supreme Court of Washington, with one dissenting justice, affirmed, concluding that the portion of the 911 conversation in which McCottry identified Davis was not testimonial, and that if other portions of the conversation were testimonial, admitting them was harmless beyond a reasonable doubt. We granted certiorari.

B

In *Hammon* v. *Indiana*, police responded late on the night of February 26, 2003, to a "reported domestic disturbance" at the home of Hershel and Amy Hammon. They found Amy alone on the front porch, appearing " 'somewhat frightened,' " but she told them that " 'nothing was the matter.' She gave them permission to enter the house, where an officer saw "a gas heating unit in the corner of the living room" that had "flames coming out of the . . . partial glass front. There were pieces of glass on the ground in front of it and there was flame emitting from the front of the heating unit."

Hershel, meanwhile, was in the kitchen. He told the police "that he and his wife had 'been in an argument' but 'everything was fine now' and the argument 'never became physical.' " By this point Amy had come back inside. One of the officers remained with Hershel; the other went to the living room to talk with Amy, and "again asked [her] what had occurred." Hershel made several attempts to participate in Amy's conversation with the police, but was rebuffed. The officer later testified that Hershel "became angry when I insisted that [he] stay separated from Mrs. Hammon so that we can investigate what had happened." After hearing Amy's account, the officer "had her fill out and sign a battery affidavit." Amy handwrote the following: "Broke our Furnace & shoved me down on the floor into the broken glass. Hit me in the chest and threw me down. Broke our lamps & phone. Tore up my van where I couldn't leave the house. Attacked my daughter."

The State charged Hershel with domestic battery and with violating his probation. Amy was subpoenaed, but she did not appear at his subsequent bench trial. The State called the officer who had questioned Amy, and asked him to recount what Amy told him and to authenticate the affidavit. Hershel's counsel repeatedly objected to the admission of this evidence. At one point, after hearing the prosecutor defend the affidavit because it was made "under oath," defense counsel said, "That doesn't give us the opportunity to cross examine [the] person who allegedly drafted it. Makes me mad." Nonetheless, the trial court admitted the affidavit as a "present sense impression," and Amy's statements as "excited utterances" that "are expressly permitted in these kinds of cases even if the declarant is not available to testify." The officer thus testified that Amy informed me that she and Hershel had been in an argument. That he became irrate [sic] over the fact of their daughter going to a boyfriend's house. The argument became . . . physical after being verbal and she informed me that Mr. Hammon, during the verbal part of the argument was breaking things in the living room and I believe she stated he broke the phone, broke the lamp, broke the front of the heater. When it became physical he threw her down into the glass of the heater. She informed me Mr. Hammon had pushed her onto the ground, had shoved her head into the broken glass of the heater and that he had punched her in the chest twice I believe."

The trial judge found Hershel guilty on both charges. The Indiana Supreme Court affirmed, concluding that Amy's statement was admissible for state-law purposes as an excited utterance, that "a 'testimonial' statement is one given or taken in significant part for purposes of preserving it for potential future use in legal proceedings," where "the motivations of the questioner and declarant are the central concerns," and that Amy's oral statement was not "testimonial" under these standards. It also concluded that, although the affidavit was testimonial and thus wrongly admitted, it was harmless beyond a reasonable doubt, largely because the trial was to the bench. We granted certiorari.

II

In *Crawford v. Washington*, we held that [the Confrontation Clause] bars "admission of testimonial statements of a witness who did not appear at trial unless he was unavailable to testify, and the defendant had had a prior opportunity for cross-examination." A critical portion of this holding, and the portion central to resolution of the two cases now before us, is the phrase "testimonial statements." Only statements of this sort cause the declarant to be a "witness" within the meaning of the Confrontation Clause. It is the testimonial character of the statement that separates it from other hearsay that, while subject to traditional limitations upon hearsay evidence, is not subject to the Confrontation Clause.

Our opinion in *Crawford* set forth "[v]arious formulations" of the core class of " 'testimonial' " statements, *ibid.*, but found it unnecessary to endorse any of them, because "some statements qualify under any definition," Among those, we said, were "[s]tatements taken by police officers in the course of interrogations." The questioning that generated the deponent's statement in *Crawford* — which was made and recorded while she was in police custody, after having been given

Miranda warnings as a possible suspect herself — "qualifies under any conceivable definition" of an " 'interrogation.' " We therefore did not define that term, except to say that "[w]e use [it] . . . in its colloquial, rather than any technical legal, sense," and that "one can imagine various definitions. . . , and we need not select among them in this case." The character of the statements in the present cases is not as clear, and these cases require us to determine more precisely which police interrogations produce testimony.

Without attempting to produce an exhaustive classification of all conceivable statements — or even all conceivable statements in response to police interrogation — as either testimonial or nontestimonial, it suffices to decide the present cases to hold as follows: Statements are nontestimonial when made in the course of police interrogation under circumstances objectively indicating that the primary purpose of the interrogation is to enable police assistance to meet an ongoing emergency. They are testimonial when the circumstances objectively indicate that there is no such ongoing emergency, and that the primary purpose of the interrogation is to establish or prove past events potentially relevant to later criminal prosecution.

> (Footnote: Our holding refers to interrogations because the statements in the cases presently before us are the products of interrogations. This is not to imply, however, that statements made in the absence of any interrogation are necessarily nontestimonial. The Framers were no more willing to exempt from cross-examination volunteered testimony or answers to open-ended questions than they were to exempt answers to detailed interrogation . . . And of course even when interrogation exists, it is in the final analysis the declarant's statements, not the interrogator's questions, that the Confrontation Clause requires us to evaluate.)

III

A

In *Crawford*, it sufficed for resolution of the case before us to determine that "even if the Sixth Amendment is not solely concerned with testimonial hearsay, that is its primary object, and interrogations by law enforcement officers fall squarely within that class." Moreover, as we have just described, the facts of that case spared us the need to define what we meant by "interrogations." The *Davis* case today does not permit us this luxury of indecision. The inquiries of a police operator in the course of a 911 call are an interrogation in one sense, but not in a sense that "qualifies under any conceivable definition." We must decide, therefore, whether the Confrontation Clause applies only to testimonial hearsay; and, if so, whether the recording of a 911 call qualifies.

The answer to the first question was suggested in *Crawford*, even if not explicitly held:

> The text of the Confrontation Clause reflects this focus [on testimonial hearsay]. It applies to "witnesses" against the accused — in other words, those who "bear testimony". "Testimony," in turn, is typically "solemn declaration or affirmation made for the purpose of establishing or proving

some fact." An accuser who makes a formal statement to government officers bears testimony in a sense that a person who makes a casual remark to an acquaintance does not.

A limitation so clearly reflected in the text of the constitutional provision must fairly be said to mark out not merely its "core," but its perimeter. The question before us in *Davis*, then, is whether, objectively considered, the interrogation that took place in the course of the 911 call produced testimonial statements.

The difference between the interrogation in *Davis* and the one in *Crawford* is apparent on the face of things. In *Davis*, McCottry was speaking about events *as they were actually happening*, rather than "describ[ing]" past events. Sylvia Crawford's interrogation, on the other hand, took place hours after the events she described had occurred. Moreover, any reasonable listener would recognize that McCottry (unlike Sylvia Crawford) was facing an ongoing emergency. Although one *might* call 911 to provide a narrative report of a crime absent any imminent danger, McCottry's call was plainly a call for help against bona fide physical threat. Third, the nature of what was asked and answered in *Davis*, again viewed objectively, was such that the elicited statements were necessary to be able to *resolve* the present emergency, rather than simply to learn (as in *Crawford*) what had happened in the past. That is true even of the operator's effort to establish the identity of the assailant, so that the dispatched officers might know whether they would be encountering a violent felon. And finally, the difference in the level of formality between the two interviews is striking. Crawford was responding calmly, at the station house, to a series of questions, with the officer-interrogator taping and making notes of her answers; McCottry's frantic answers were provided over the phone, in an environment that was not tranquil, or even (as far as any reasonable 911 operator could make out) safe.

We conclude from all this that the circumstances of McCottry's interrogation objectively indicate its primary purpose was to enable police assistance to meet an ongoing emergency. She simply was not acting as a *witness*; she was not *testifying*. No "witness" goes into court to proclaim an emergency and seek help.

This is not to say that a conversation which begins as an interrogation to determine the need for emergency assistance cannot, as the Indiana Supreme Court put it, "evolve into testimonial statements," once that purpose has been achieved. In this case, for example, after the operator gained the information needed to address the exigency of the moment, the emergency appears to have ended (when Davis drove away from the premises). The operator then told McCottry to be quiet, and proceeded to pose a battery of questions. It could readily be maintained that, from that point on, McCottry's statements were testimonial, not unlike the "structured police questioning" that occurred in *Crawford*. This presents no great problem. Just as, for Fifth Amendment purposes, "police officers can and will distinguish almost instinctively between questions necessary to secure their own safety or the safety of the public and questions designed solely to elicit testimonial evidence from a suspect," trial courts will recognize the point at which, for Sixth Amendment purposes, statements in response to interrogations become testimonial. Davis's jury did not hear the *complete* 911 call, although it may well have heard some testimonial portions. We were asked to classify only McCottry's early statements identifying Davis as her assailant, and we agree with the Washington Supreme Court that they were not testimonial.

B

Determining the testimonial or nontestimonial character of the statements that were the product of the interrogation in *Hammon* is a much easier task, since they were not much different from the statements we found to be testimonial in *Crawford*. It is entirely clear from the circumstances that the interrogation was part of an investigation into possibly criminal past conduct — as, indeed, the testifying officer expressly acknowledged. There was no emergency in progress; the interrogating officer testified that he had heard no arguments or crashing and saw no one throw or break anything. When the officers first arrived, Amy told them that things were fine, and there was no immediate threat to her person. When the officer questioned Amy for the second time, and elicited the challenged statements, he was not seeking to determine (as in *Davis*) "what is happening," but rather "what happened." Objectively viewed, the primary, if not indeed the sole, purpose of the interrogation was to investigate a possible crime — which is, of course, precisely what the officer *should* have done.

It is true that the *Crawford* interrogation was more formal. It followed a *Miranda* warning, was tape-recorded, and took place at the station house. While these features certainly strengthened the statements' testimonial aspect — made it more objectively apparent, that is, that the purpose of the exercise was to nail down the truth about past criminal events — none was essential to the point. It was formal enough that Amy's interrogation was conducted in a separate room, away from her husband (who tried to intervene), with the officer receiving her replies for use in his "investigat[ion]." What we called the "striking resemblance" of the *Crawford* statement to civil-law *ex parte* examinations, is shared by Amy's statement here. Both declarants were actively separated from the defendant — officers forcibly prevented Hershel from participating in the interrogation. Both statements deliberately recounted, in response to police questioning, how potentially criminal past events began and progressed. And both took place some time after the events described were over. Such statements under official interrogation are an obvious substitute for live testimony, because they do precisely *what a witness does* on direct examination; they are inherently testimonial.

Although we necessarily reject the Indiana Supreme Court's implication that virtually any "initial inquiries" at the crime scene will not be testimonial, we do not hold the opposite — that *no* questions at the scene will yield nontestimonial answers. We have already observed of domestic disputes that "[o]fficers called to investigate . . . need to know whom they are dealing with in order to assess the situation, the threat to their own safety, and possible danger to the potential victim." Such exigencies may *often* mean that "initial inquiries" produce nontestimonial statements. But in cases like this one, where Amy's statements were neither a cry for help nor the provision of information enabling officers immediately to end a threatening situation, the fact that they were given at an alleged crime scene and were "initial inquiries" is immaterial.

IV

Respondents in both cases, joined by a number of their *amici*, contend that the nature of the offenses charged in these two cases — domestic violence — requires greater flexibility in the use of testimonial evidence. This particular type of crime is notoriously susceptible to intimidation or coercion of the victim to ensure that she does not testify at trial. When this occurs, the Confrontation Clause gives the criminal a windfall. We may not, however, vitiate constitutional guarantees when they have the effect of allowing the guilty to go free. But when defendants seek to undermine the judicial process by procuring or coercing silence from witnesses and victims, the Sixth Amendment does not require courts to acquiesce. While defendants have no duty to assist the State in proving their guilt, they *do* have the duty to refrain from acting in ways that destroy the integrity of the criminal-trial system. We reiterate what we said in *Crawford:* that "the rule of forfeiture by wrongdoing . . . extinguishes confrontation claims on essentially equitable grounds." That is, one who obtains the absence of a witness by wrongdoing forfeits the constitutional right to confrontation.

We take no position on the standards necessary to demonstrate such forfeiture, but federal courts using Federal Rule of Evidence 804(b)(6), which codifies the forfeiture doctrine, have generally held the Government to the preponderance-of-the-evidence standard. Moreover, if a hearing on forfeiture is required, "hearsay evidence, including the unavailable witness's out-of-court statements, may be considered." *Crawford*, in overruling *Roberts*, did not destroy the ability of courts to protect the integrity of their proceedings.

We affirm the judgment of the Supreme Court of Washington. We reverse the judgment of the Supreme Court of Indiana and remand the case to that Court for proceedings not inconsistent with this opinion.

It is so ordered.

JUSTICE THOMAS, concurring in the judgment in part and dissenting in part.

In *Crawford* v. *Washington*, we abandoned the general reliability inquiry we had long employed to judge the admissibility of hearsay evidence under the Confrontation Clause, describing that inquiry as "*inherently*, and therefore *permanently*, unpredictable." Today, a mere two years after the Court decided *Crawford*, it adopts an equally unpredictable test, under which district courts are charged with divining the "primary purpose" of police interrogations. Besides being difficult for courts to apply, this test characterizes as "testimonial," and therefore inadmissible, evidence that bears little resemblance to what we have recognized as the evidence targeted by the Confrontation Clause. Because neither of the cases before the Court today would implicate the Confrontation Clause under an appropriately targeted standard, I concur only in the judgment in *Davis* v. *Washington*, and dissent from the Court's resolution of *Hammon* v. *Indiana*.

I

A

The history surrounding the right to confrontation supports the conclusion that it was developed to target particular practices that occurred under the English bail and committal statutes passed during the reign of Queen Mary, namely, the "civil-law mode of criminal procedure, and particularly its use of *ex parte* examinations as evidence against the accused."

The plain terms of the "testimony" definition we endorsed necessarily require some degree of solemnity before a statement can be deemed "testimonial." This requirement of solemnity supports my view that the statements regulated by the Confrontation Clause must include "extrajudicial statements . . . contained in formalized testimonial materials, such as affidavits, depositions, prior testimony, or confessions." Affidavits, depositions, and prior testimony are, by their very nature, taken through a formalized process. Likewise, confessions, when extracted by police in a formal manner, carry sufficient indicia of solemnity to constitute formalized statements and, accordingly, bear a "striking resemblance to the examinations of the accused and accusers under the Marian statutes.

The Court's standard is not only disconnected from history and unnecessary to prevent abuse; it also yields no predictable results to police officers and prosecutors attempting to comply with the law. In many, if not most, cases where police respond to a report of a crime, whether pursuant to a 911 call from the victim or otherwise, the purposes of an interrogation, viewed from the perspective of the police, are *both* to respond to the emergency situation *and* to gather evidence. Assigning one of these two "largely unverifiable motives," primacy requires constructing a hierarchy of purpose that will rarely be present — and is not reliably discernible. It will inevitably be, quite simply, an exercise in fiction.

B

Neither the 911 call at issue in *Davis* nor the police questioning at issue in *Hammon* is testimonial under the appropriate framework. Neither the call nor the questioning is itself a formalized dialogue. Nor do any circumstances surrounding the taking of the statements render those statements sufficiently formal to resemble the Marian examinations; the statements were neither Mirandized nor custodial, nor accompanied by any similar indicia of formality. Finally, there is no suggestion that the prosecution attempted to offer the women's hearsay evidence at trial in order to evade confrontation. Accordingly, the statements at issue in both cases are nontestimonial and admissible under the Confrontation Clause.

The Court's determination that the evidence against Hammon must be excluded extends the Confrontation Clause far beyond the abuses it was intended to prevent. When combined with the Court's holding that the evidence against Davis is perfectly admissible, however, the Court's *Hammon* holding also reveals the difficulty of applying the Court's requirement that courts investigate the "primary purpose[s]" of the investigation. The Court draws a line between the two cases based on its explanation that *Hammon* involves "no emergency in progress," but instead, mere questioning as "part of an investigation into possibly criminal past conduct," and its explanation that *Davis* involves questioning for the "primary purpose" of "enabl[ing] police assistance to meet an ongoing emergency."

But the fact that the officer in *Hammon* was investigating Mr. Hammon's past conduct does not foreclose the possibility that the primary purpose of his inquiry was to assess whether Mr. Hammon constituted a continuing danger to his wife, requiring further police presence or action. It is hardly remarkable that Hammon did not act abusively towards his wife in the presence of the officers, and his good judgment to refrain from criminal behavior in the presence of police sheds little, if any, light on whether his violence would have resumed had the police left without further questioning, transforming what the Court dismisses as "past conduct" back into an "ongoing emergency." Nor does the mere fact that McCottry needed emergency aid shed light on whether the "primary purpose" of gathering, for example, the name of her assailant was to protect the police, to protect the victim, or to gather information for prosecution. In both of the cases before the Court, like many similar cases, pronouncement of the "primary" motive behind the interrogation calls for nothing more than a guess by courts.

II

Because the standard adopted by the Court today is neither workable nor a targeted attempt to reach the abuses forbidden by the Clause, I concur only in the judgment in *Davis v. Washington*, and respectfully dissent from the Court's resolution of *Hammon v. Indiana*.

MELENDEZ-DIAZ v. MASSACHUSETTS
United States Supreme Court
557 U.S. 305, 129 S.Ct. 2527 (2009)

JUSTICE SCALIA *delivered the opinion of the Court.*

The Massachusetts courts in this case admitted into evidence affidavits reporting the results of forensic analysis which showed that material seized by the police and connected to the defendant was cocaine. The question presented is whether those affidavits are "testimonial," rendering the affiants "witnesses" subject to the defendant's right of confrontation under the Sixth Amendment . . . the certificates were admitted pursuant to state law as "prima facie evidence of the composition, quality, and the net weight of the narcotic . . . analyzed."

II

There is little doubt that the documents at issue in this case fall within the "core class of testimonial statements." The documents at issue here, while denominated by Massachusetts law "certificates," are quite plainly affidavits: "declaration[s] of facts written down and sworn to by the declarant before an officer authorized to administer oaths." They are incontrovertibly a " 'solemn declaration or affirmation made for the purpose of establishing or proving some fact . . . .' " The "certificates" are functionally identical to live, in-court testimony, doing "precisely what a witness does on direct examination." We can safely assume that the analysts were aware of the affidavits' evidentiary purpose, since that purpose was reprinted on the affidavits themselves.

In short, under our decision in *Crawford* the analysts' affidavits were testimonial statements, and the analysts were "witnesses" for purposes of the Sixth Amendment. Absent a showing that the analysts were unavailable to testify at trial *and* that petitioner had a prior opportunity to cross-examine them, petitioner was entitled to "'be confronted with'" the analysts at trial.

III

Respondent and the dissent advance a potpourri of analytic arguments in an effort to avoid this rather straightforward application of our holding in *Crawford* . . . .

A

Respondent first argues that the analysts are not subject to confrontation because they are not "accusatory" witnesses, in that they do not directly accuse petitioner of wrongdoing; rather, their testimony is inculpatory only when taken together with other evidence linking petitioner to the contraband. This finds no support in the text of the Sixth Amendment or in our case law. . .

C

Respondent claims that there is a difference, for Confrontation Clause purposes, between testimony recounting historical events, which is "prone to distortion or manipulation," and the testimony at issue here, which is the "resul[t] of neutral, scientific testing." Relatedly, respondent and the dissent argue that confrontation of forensic analysts would be of little value because "one would not reasonably expect a laboratory professional . . . to feel quite differently about the results of his scientific test by having to look at the defendant." This argument is little more than an invitation to return to our overruled decision in *Roberts*, which held that evidence with "particularized guarantees of trustworthiness" was admissible notwithstanding the Confrontation Clause . . . . Contrary to respondent's and the dissent's suggestion, there is little reason to believe that confrontation will be useless in testing analysts' honesty, proficiency, and methodology — the features that are commonly the focus in the cross-examination of experts.

D

Respondent argues that the analysts' affidavits are admissible without confrontation because they are "akin to the types of official and business records admissible at common law." But the affidavits do not qualify as traditional official or business records, and even if they did, their authors would be subject to confrontation nonetheless.

The dissent identifies a single class of evidence which, though prepared for use at trial, was traditionally admissible: a clerk's certificate authenticating an official record — or a copy thereof — for use as evidence. But a clerk's authority in that regard was narrowly circumscribed. He was permitted "to certify to the correctness of a copy of a record kept in his office," but had "no authority to furnish, as evidence for the trial of a lawsuit, his interpretation of what the record contains or shows, or to certify to its substance or effect." A clerk could by affidavit *authenticate* or provide a copy of an otherwise admissible record, but could not do what the analysts did here: *create* a record for the sole purpose of providing evidence against a defendant.

Far more probative here are those cases in which the prosecution sought to admit into evidence a clerk's certificate attesting to the fact that the clerk had searched for a particular relevant record and failed to find it. Like the testimony of the analysts in this case, the clerk's statement would serve as substantive evidence against the defendant whose guilt depended on the nonexistence of the record for which the clerk searched. Although the clerk's certificate would qualify as an official record under respondent's definition — it was prepared by a public officer in the regular course of his official duties — and although the clerk was certainly not a "conventional witness" under the dissent's approach, the clerk was nonetheless subject to confrontation.

Respondent also misunderstands the relationship between the business-and-official-records hearsay exceptions and the Confrontation Clause. As we stated in *Crawford:* "Most of the hearsay exceptions covered statements that by their nature were not testimonial — for example, business records or statements in furtherance of a conspiracy." Business and public records are generally admissible absent confrontation not because they qualify under an exception to the hearsay rules, but because — having been created for the administration of an entity's affairs and not for the purpose of establishing or proving some fact at trial — they are not testimonial. Whether or not they qualify as business or official records, the analysts' statements here — prepared specifically for use at petitioner's trial — were testimony against petitioner, and the analysts were subject to confrontation under the Sixth Amendment.

E

Respondent asserts that we should find no Confrontation Clause violation in this case because petitioner had the ability to subpoena the analysts. But that power — whether pursuant to state law or the Compulsory Process Clause — is no substitute for the right of confrontation. Converting the prosecution's duty under the Confrontation Clause into the defendant's privilege under state law or the Compulsory Process Clause shifts the consequences of adverse-witness no-shows from the State to the accused. More fundamentally, the Confrontation Clause imposes a burden on the prosecution to present its witnesses, not on the defendant to bring those adverse witnesses into court.

F

Finally, respondent asks us to relax the requirements of the Confrontation Clause to accommodate the " 'necessities of trial and the adversary process.' " It is not clear whence we would derive the authority to do so. The Confrontation Clause may make the prosecution of criminals more burdensome, but that is equally true of the right to trial by jury and the privilege against self-incrimination. The Confrontation Clause — like those other constitutional provisions — is binding, and we may not disregard it at our convenience.

We also doubt the accuracy of respondent's and the dissent's dire predictions. Perhaps the best indication that the sky will not fall after today's decision is that it has not done so already. Many States have already adopted the constitutional rule we announce today, while many others permit the defendant to assert (or forfeit by silence) his Confrontation Clause right after receiving notice of the prosecution's intent to use a forensic analyst's report. Despite these widespread practices, there is no evidence that the criminal justice system has ground to a halt in the States that, one way or another, empower a defendant to insist upon the analyst's appearance at trial.

The dissent finds this evidence "far less reassuring than promised." But its doubts rest on two flawed premises. First, the dissent believes that those state statutes "requiring the defendant to give early notice of his intent to confront the analyst," are "burden-shifting statutes [that] may be invalidated by the Court's reasoning." That is not so. In their simplest form, notice-and-demand statutes require the prosecution to provide notice to the defendant of its intent to use an analyst's report as evidence at trial, after which the defendant is given a period of time in which he may object to the admission of the evidence absent the analyst's appearance live at trial. Contrary to the dissent's perception, these statutes shift no burden whatever. The defendant *always* has the burden of raising his Confrontation Clause objection; notice-and-demand statutes simply govern the *time* within which he must do so. States are free to adopt procedural rules governing objections. It is common to require a defendant to exercise his rights under the Compulsory Process Clause in advance of trial, announcing his intent to present certain witnesses. There is no conceivable reason why he cannot similarly be compelled to exercise his Confrontation Clause rights before trial. Today's decision will not disrupt criminal prosecutions in the many large States whose practice is already in accord with the Confrontation Clause.

Second, the dissent notes that several of the state-court cases that have already adopted this rule did so pursuant to our decision in *Crawford*, and not "independently . . . as a matter of state law." That may be so. But in assessing the likely practical effects of today's ruling, it is irrelevant *why* those courts adopted this rule; it matters only *that* they did so. It is true that many of these decisions are recent, but if the dissent's dire predictions were accurate, and given the large number of drug prosecutions at the state level, one would have expected immediate and dramatic results. The absence of such evidence is telling.

But it is not surprising. Defense attorneys and their clients will often stipulate to the nature of the substance in the ordinary drug case. It is unlikely that defense counsel will insist on live testimony whose effect will be merely to highlight rather than cast doubt upon the forensic analysis. Nor will defense attorneys want to antagonize the judge or jury by wasting their time with the appearance of a witness whose testimony defense counsel does not intend to rebut in any fashion. The *amicus* brief filed by District Attorneys in Support of the Commonwealth in the Massachusetts Supreme Court case upon which the Appeals Court here relied said that "it is almost always the case that [analysts' certificates] are admitted without objection. Generally, defendants do not object to the admission of drug certificates most likely because there is no benefit to a defendant from such testimony." Given these strategic considerations, and in light of the experience in those States that already provide the same or similar protections to defendants, there is little reason to believe that our decision today will commence the parade of horribles respondent and the dissent predict.

This case involves little more than the application of our holding in *Crawford* v. *Washington*. The Sixth Amendment does not permit the prosecution to prove its case via *ex parte* out-of-court affidavits, and the admission of such evidence against Melendez-Diaz was error. We therefore reverse the judgment of the Appeals Court of Massachusetts and remand the case for further proceedings not inconsistent with this opinion.

It is so ordered.

Justice Thomas, concurring.

I write separately to note that I continue to adhere to my position that "the Confrontation Clause is implicated by extrajudicial statements only insofar as they are contained in formalized testimonial materials, such as affidavits, depositions, prior testimony, or confessions.". . . I join the Court's opinion in this case because the documents at issue in this case "are quite plainly affidavits." As such, they "fall within the core class of testimonial statements" governed by the Confrontation Clause.

JUSTICE KENNEDY, *with whom* THE CHIEF JUSTICE, JUSTICE BREYER, *and* JUSTICE ALITO *join, dissenting.*

The Court sweeps away an accepted rule governing the admission of scientific evidence. Until today, scientific analysis could be introduced into evidence without testimony from the "analyst" who produced it. *Crawford* and *Davis* dealt with ordinary witnesses — women who had seen, and in two cases been the victim of, the crime in question. Those cases stand for the proposition that formal statements made by a conventional witness — one who has personal knowledge of some aspect of the defendant's guilt — may not be admitted without the witness appearing at trial to meet the accused face to face. But *Crawford* and *Davis* do not say — indeed, could not have said, because the facts were not before the Court — that anyone who makes a testimonial statement is a witness for purposes of the Confrontation Clause, even when that person has, in fact, witnessed nothing to give them personal knowledge of the defendant's guilt.

Because *Crawford* and *Davis* concerned typical witnesses, the Court should have done the sensible thing and limited its holding to witnesses as so defined. Indeed, as Justice Thomas warned in his opinion in *Davis*, the Court's approach has become "disconnected from history and unnecessary to prevent abuse." The Court's reliance on the word "testimonial" is of little help, of course, for that word does not appear in the text of the Clause. . . .

The Court's opinion suggests this will be a body of formalistic and wooden rules, divorced from precedent, common sense, and the underlying purpose of the Clause. Its ruling has vast potential to disrupt criminal procedures that already give ample protections against the misuse of scientific evidence. For these reasons, as more fully explained below, the Court's opinion elicits my respectful dissent.

I

A

The Court says that, before the results of a scientific test may be introduced into evidence, the defendant has the right to confront the "analyst." There is no accepted definition of analyst, and there is no established precedent to define that term.

Consider how many people play a role in a routine test for the presence of illegal drugs. One person prepares a sample of the drug, places it in a testing machine, and retrieves the machine's printout — often, a graph showing the frequencies of radiation absorbed by the sample or the masses of the sample's molecular fragments. A second person interprets the graph the machine prints out — perhaps by comparing that printout with published, standardized graphs of known drugs. Meanwhile, a third person — perhaps an independent contractor — has calibrated the machine and, having done so, has certified that the machine is in good working order. Finally, a fourth person — perhaps the laboratory's director — certifies that his subordinates followed established procedures.

It is not at all evident which of these four persons is the analyst to be confronted under the rule the Court announces today. If all are witnesses who must appear for in-court confrontation, then the Court has, for all practical purposes, forbidden the use of scientific tests in criminal trials. As discussed further below, requiring even one of these individuals to testify threatens to disrupt if not end many prosecutions where guilt is clear but a newly found formalism now holds sway. . .

2

It is difficult to confine at this point the damage the Court's holding will do in other contexts. Consider just two — establishing the chain of custody and authenticating a copy of a document.

It is the obligation of the prosecution to establish the chain of custody for evidence sent to testing laboratories — that is, to establish "the identity and integrity of physical evidence by tracing its continuous whereabouts." Meeting this obligation requires representations — that one officer retrieved the evidence from the crime scene, that a second officer checked it into an evidence locker, that a third officer verified the locker's seal was intact, and so forth. The iron logic of which the

Court is so enamored would seem to require in-court testimony from each human link in the chain of custody. That, of course, has never been the law.

It is no answer for the Court to say that "[i]t is up to the prosecution to decide what steps in the chain of custody are so crucial as to require evidence." The case itself determines which links in the chain are crucial — not the prosecution. In any number of cases, the crucial link in the chain will not be available to testify and so the evidence will be excluded for lack of a proper foundation.

Consider another context in which the Court's holding may cause disruption: The long-accepted practice of authenticating copies of documents by means of a certificate from the document's custodian stating that the copy is accurate. See, *e.g.*, Fed. Rule Evid. 902(4) (in order to be self-authenticating, a copy of a public record must be "certified as correct by the custodian"); Rule 902(11) (business record must be "accompanied by a written declaration of its custodian"). Under one possible reading of the Court's opinion, record keepers will be required to testify. So far, courts have not read *Crawford* and *Davis* to impose this largely meaningless requirement. But the breadth of the Court's ruling today, and its undefined scope, may well be such that these courts now must be deemed to have erred. The risk of that consequence ought to tell us that something is very wrong with the Court's analysis.

Because the Court is driven by nothing more than a wooden application of the *Crawford* and *Davis* definition of "testimonial," divorced from any guidance from history, precedent, or common sense, there is no way to predict the future applications of today's holding. Surely part of the justification for the Court's formalism must lie in its predictability. There is nothing predictable here, however, other than the uncertainty and disruption that now must ensue.

C

For the sake of these negligible benefits, the Court threatens to disrupt forensic investigations across the country and to put prosecutions nationwide at risk of dismissal based on erratic, all-too-frequent instances when a particular laboratory technician, now invested by the Court's new constitutional designation as the analyst, simply does not or cannot appear.

An analyst cannot hope to be the trial court's top priority in scheduling. The analyst must instead face the prospect of waiting for days in a hallway outside the courtroom before being called to offer testimony that will consist of little more than a rote recital of the written report.

Setting aside, for a moment, all the other crimes for which scientific evidence is required, consider the costs the Court's ruling will impose on state drug prosecutions alone. In 2004, the most recent year for which data are available, drug possession and trafficking resulted in 362,850 felony convictions in state courts across the country . . . Roughly 95% of those convictions were products of plea bargains, which means that state courts saw more than 18,000 drug trials in a single year.

The analysts responsible for testing the drugs at issue in those cases now bear a crushing burden. For example, the district attorney in Philadelphia prosecuted 25,000 drug crimes in 2007. Assuming that number remains the same, and assuming that 95% of the cases end in a plea bargain, each of the city's 18 drug analysts, will be required to testify in more than 69 trials next year . . .

The Federal Government may face even graver difficulties than the States because its operations are so widespread. For example, the FBI laboratory at Quantico, Virginia, supports federal, state, and local investigations across the country. Its 500 employees conduct over one million scientific tests each year. The Court's decision means that before any of those million tests reaches a jury, at least one of the laboratory's analysts must board a plane, find his or her way to an unfamiliar courthouse, and sit there waiting to read aloud notes made months ago.

The Court purchases its meddling with the Confrontation Clause at a dear price, a price not measured in taxpayer dollars alone. Guilty defendants will go free, on the most technical grounds, as a direct result of today's decision, adding nothing to the truth-finding process. The analyst will not always make it to the courthouse in time. He or she may be ill; may be out of the country; may be unable to travel because of inclement weather; or may at that very moment be waiting outside some other courtroom for another defendant to exercise the right the Court invents today . . .

The Court's holding is a windfall to defendants, one that is unjustified by any demonstrated deficiency in trials, any well-understood historical requirement, or any established constitutional precedent.

III

A

In an unconvincing effort to play down the threat that today's new rule will disrupt or even end criminal prosecutions, the Court professes a hope that defense counsel will decline to raise what will soon be known as the *Melendez-Diaz* objection. The Court bases this expectation on its understanding that defense attorneys surrender constitutional rights because the attorneys do not "want to antagonize the judge or jury by wasting their time."

The Court's reasoning is troubling on at least two levels. First, the Court's speculation rests on the apparent belief that our Nation's trial judges and jurors are unwilling to accept zealous advocacy and that, once "antagonize[d]" by it, will punish such advocates with adverse rulings . . . The Court offers no support for this stunning slur on the integrity of the Nation's courts . . .

Second, even if the Court were right to expect trial judges to feel "antagonize[d]" by *Melendez-Diaz* objections and to then vent their anger by punishing the lawyer in some way, there is no authority to support the Court's suggestion that a lawyer may shirk his or her professional duties just to avoid judicial displeasure. There is good reason why the Court cites no authority for this suggestion — it is contrary to what some of us, at least, have long understood to be defense counsel's duty to be a zealous advocate for every client . . .

In further support of its unlikely hope, the Court relies on the Brief for Law Professors as *Amici Curiae*, which reports that nearly 95% of convictions are obtained via guilty plea and thus do not require in-court testimony from laboratory analysts. What the Court does not consider is how its holding will alter these statistics. The defense bar today gains the formidable power to require the government to transport the analyst to the courtroom at the time of trial. Zealous counsel will insist upon concessions: a plea bargain, or a more lenient sentence in exchange for relinquishing this remarkable power.

B

Laboratory analysts who conduct routine scientific tests are not the kind of conventional witnesses to whom the Confrontation Clause refers. The judgment of the Appeals Court of Massachusetts should be affirmed.

MICHIGAN v. BRYANT
United States Supreme Court
562 U.S. __, 131 S. Ct. 1143 (2011)

SOTOMAYOR, J., delivered the opinion of the Court, in which ROBERTS, C. J., and KENNEDY, BREYER, and ALITO, JJ., joined. THOMAS, J., filed an opinion concurring in the judgment. SCALIA, J., and GINSBURG, J., filed dissenting opinions. KAGAN, J., took no part in the consideration or decision of the case.

At respondent Richard Bryant's trial, the court admitted statements that the victim, Anthony Covington, made to police officers who discovered him mortally wounded in a gas station parking lot. A jury convicted Bryant of second-degree murder. On appeal, the Supreme Court of Michigan held that the Sixth Amendment's Confrontation Clause rendered Covington's statements inadmissible testimonial hearsay, and the court reversed Bryant's conviction. We granted the State's petition for a writ of certiorari to consider whether the Confrontation Clause barred the admission at trial of Covington's statements to the police. We hold that the circumstances of the interaction between Covington and the police objectively indicate that the "primary purpose of the interrogation" was "to enable police assistance to meet an ongoing emergency." Therefore, Covington's identification and description of the shooter and the location of the shooting were not testimonial statements, and their admission at Bryant's trial did not violate the Confrontation Clause. We vacate the judgment of the Supreme Court of Michigan and remand.

I

Around 3:25 a.m. on April 29, 2001, Detroit, Michigan police officers responded to a radio dispatch indicating that a man had been shot. At the scene, they found the victim, Anthony Covington, lying on the ground next to his car in a gas station parking lot. Covington had a gunshot wound to his abdomen, appeared to be in great pain, and spoke with difficulty.

The police asked him "what had happened, who had shot him, and where the shooting had occurred." Covington stated that "Rick" shot him at around 3 a.m. He also indicated that he had a conversation with Bryant, whom he recognized based on his voice, through the back door of Bryant's house. Covington explained that when he turned to leave, he was shot through the door and then drove to the gas station, where police found him.

Covington's conversation with the police ended within 5to 10 minutes when emergency medical services arrived. Covington was transported to a hospital and died within hours. The police left the gas station after speaking with Covington, called for backup, and traveled to Bryant's house. They did not find Bryant there but did find blood and a bullet on the back porch and an apparent bullet hole in the back door. Police also found Covington's wallet and identification outside the house.

At trial, the police officers who spoke with Covington at the gas station testified about what Covington had told them. The jury returned a guilty verdict on charges of second-degree murder, being a felon in possession of a firearm, and possession of a firearm during the commission of a felony.

Bryant appealed. The Supreme Court of Michigan held that the admission of Covington's statements constituted prejudicial plain error warranting reversal and ordered a new trial. We granted certiorari to determine whether the Confrontation Clause barred admission of Covington's statements.

II

Deciding this case requires further explanation of the "ongoing emergency" circumstance addressed in *Davis*. We now face a new context: a nondomestic dispute, involving a victim found in a public location, suffering from a fatal gunshot wound, and a perpetrator whose location was unknown at the time the police located the victim. Thus, we confront for the first time circumstances in which the "ongoing emergency" discussed in *Davis* extends beyond an initial victim to a potential threat to the responding police and the public at large. This new context requires us to provide additional clarification with regard to what *Davis* meant by "the primary purpose of the interrogation is to enable police assistance to meet an ongoing emergency."

III

To determine whether the "primary purpose" of an interrogation is "to enable police assistance to meet an ongoing emergency," which would render the resulting statements nontestimonial, we objectively evaluate the circumstances in which the encounter occurs and the statements and actions of the parties.

An objective analysis of the circumstances of an encounter and the statements and actions of the parties to it provides the most accurate assessment of the "primary purpose of the interrogation." The circumstances in which an encounter occurs — *e.g.*, at or near the scene of the crime versus at a police station, during an ongoing emergency or afterwards — are clearly matters of objective fact. The statements and actions of the parties must also be objectively evaluated. That is, the relevant inquiry is not the subjective or actual purpose of the individuals involved in a particular encounter, but rather the purpose that reasonable participants would have had, as ascertained from the individuals' statements and actions and the circumstances in which the encounter occurred.

The existence of an ongoing emergency is relevant to determining the primary purpose of the interrogation because an emergency focuses the participants on something other than "prov[ing] past events potentially relevant to later criminal prosecution." Rather, it focuses them on "end[ing] a threatening situation." Implicit in *Davis* is the idea that because the prospect of fabrication in statements given for the primary purpose of resolving that emergency is presumably significantly diminished, the Confrontation Clause does not require such statements to be subject to the crucible of cross-examination.

This logic is not unlike that justifying the excited utterance exception in hearsay law. Statements "relating to a startling event or condition made while the declarant was under the stress of excitement caused by the event or condition," Fed. Rule Evid. 803(2); are considered reliable because the declarant, in the excitement, presumably cannot form a falsehood . . . An ongoing emergency has a similar effect of focusing an individual's attention on responding to the emergency.

Domestic violence cases like *Davis* and *Hammon* often have a narrower zone of potential victims than cases involving threats to public safety. An assessment of whether an emergency that threatens the police and public is ongoing cannot narrowly focus on whether the threat solely to the first victim has been neutralized because the threat to the first responders and public may continue.

Davis and *Hammon* did not present medical emergencies, despite some injuries to the victims. The medical condition of the victim is important to the primary purpose inquiry to the extent that it sheds light on the ability of the victim to have any purpose at all in responding to police questions and on the likelihood that any purpose formed would necessarily be a testimonial one. The victim's medical state also provides important context for first responders to judge the existence and magnitude of a continuing threat to the victim, themselves, and the public.

None of this suggests that an emergency is ongoing in every place or even just surrounding the victim for the entire time that the perpetrator of a violent crime is on the loose. As we recognized in *Davis*, "a conversation which begins as an interrogation to determine the need for emergency assistance" can "evolve into testimonial statements." This evolution may occur if, for example, a declarant provides police with information that makes clear that what appeared to be an emergency is not or is no longer an emergency or that what appeared to be a public threat is actually a private dispute. It could also occur if a perpetrator is disarmed, surrenders, is apprehended, or, as in *Davis*, flees with little prospect of posing a threat to the public.

Finally, our discussion should not be taken to imply that the existence of an ongoing emergency is dispositive of the testimonial inquiry. As *Davis* made clear, whether an ongoing emergency exists is simply one factor — albeit an important factor — that informs the ultimate inquiry regarding the "primary purpose" of an interrogation.

Another factor . . . is the importance of *informality* in an encounter between a victim and police. Formality is not the sole touchstone of our primary purpose inquiry because, although formality suggests the absence of an emergency and therefore an increased likelihood that the purpose of the interrogation is to "establish or prove past events potentially relevant to later criminal prosecution," informality does not necessarily indicate the presence of an emergency or the lack of testimonial intent. As we explain further below, the questioning in this case occurred in an exposed, public area, prior to the arrival of emergency medical services, and in a disorganized fashion. All of those facts make this case distinguishable from the formal station-house interrogation in *Crawford.*

C

In addition to the circumstances in which an encounter occurs, the statements and actions of both the declarant and interrogators provide objective evidence of the primary purpose of the interrogation. *Davis* requires a combined inquiry that accounts for both the declarant and the interrogator. In many instances, the primary purpose of the interrogation will be most accurately ascertained by looking to the contents of both the questions and the answers. To give an extreme example, if the police say to a victim, "Tell us who did this to you so that we can arrest and prosecute them," the victim's response that "Rick did it," appears purely accusatory because by virtue of the phrasing of the question, the victim necessarily has prosecution in mind when she answers.

The combined approach also ameliorates problems that could arise from looking solely to one participant. Predominant among these is the problem of mixed motives on the part of both interrogators and declarants. Police officers in our society function as both first responders and criminal investigators. Their dual responsibilities may mean that they act with different motives simultaneously or in quick succession. Victims are also likely to have mixed motives when they make statements to the police. During an ongoing emergency, a victim is most likely to want the threat to her and to other potential victims to end, but that does not necessarily mean that the victim wants or envisions prosecution of the assailant. A victim may want the attacker to be incapacitated temporarily or rehabilitated. Alternatively, a severely injured victim may have no purpose at all in answering questions posed; the answers may be simply reflexive. The victim's injuries could be so debilitating as to prevent her from thinking sufficiently clearly to understand whether her statements are for the purpose of addressing an ongoing emergency or for the purpose of future prosecution.

The dissent suggests, that we intend to give controlling weight to the "intentions of the police." That is a misreading of our opinion. At trial, the declarant's statements, not the interrogator's questions, will be introduced to "establis[h] the truth of the matter asserted," and must therefore pass the Sixth Amendment test. In determining whether a declarant's statements are testimonial, courts should look to all of the relevant circumstances. Even Justice Scalia concedes that the interrogator is relevant to this evaluation, and we agree that "[t]he identity of an interrogator, and the content and tenor of his questions," can illuminate the "primary purpose of the interrogation." The dissent, criticizes the complexity of our approach, but we, at least, are unwilling to sacrifice accuracy for simplicity. Simpler is not always better, and courts making a "primary purpose" assessment should not be unjustifiably restrained from consulting all relevant information, including the statements and actions of interrogators.

IV

As we suggested in *Davis*, when a court must determine whether the Confrontation Clause bars the admission of a statement at trial, it should determine the "primary purpose of the interrogation" by objectively evaluating the statements and actions of the parties to the encounter, in light of the circumstances in which the interrogation occurs.

We first examine the circumstances in which the interrogation occurred. The parties disagree over whether there was an emergency when the police arrived at the gas station. Bryant argues, that there was no ongoing emergency because "there . . . was no criminal conduct occurring. No shots were being fired, no one was seen in possession of a firearm, nor were any witnesses seen cowering in fear or running from the scene." Bryant, while conceding that "a serious or life-threatening injury creates a medical emergency for a victim," further argues that a declarant's medical emergency is not relevant to the ongoing emergency determination.

As explained above, the scope of an emergency in terms of its threat to individuals other than the initial assailant and victim will often depend on the type of dispute involved. Nothing Covington said to the police indicated that the cause of the shooting was a purely private dispute or that the threat from the shooter had ended. The record reveals little about the motive for the shooting. The police officers who spoke with Covington at the gas station testified that Covington did not tell them what words Covington and Rick had exchanged prior to the shooting.

This is also the first of our post-*Crawford* Confrontation Clause cases to involve a gun. The physical separation that was sufficient to end the emergency in *Hammon* was not necessarily sufficient to end the threat in this case; Covington was shot through the back door of Bryant's house. Bryant's argument that there was no ongoing emergency because "[n]o shots were being fired," surely construes ongoing emergency too narrowly. An emergency does not last only for the time between when the assailant pulls the trigger and the bullet hits the victim. If an out-of-sight sniper pauses between shots, no one would say that the emergency ceases during the pause. That is an extreme example and not the situation here, but it serves to highlight the implausibility, at least as to certain weapons, of construing the emergency to last only precisely as long as the violent act itself, as some have construed our opinion in *Davis*.

At no point during the questioning did either Covington or the police know the location of the shooter. In fact, Bryant was not at home by the time the police searched his house at approximately 5:30 a.m. At some point between 3 a.m. and 5:30 a.m., Bryant left his house. At bottom, there was an ongoing emergency here where an armed shooter, whose motive for and location after the shooting were unknown, had mortally wounded Covington within a few blocks and a few minutes of the location where the police found Covington.

This is not to suggest that the emergency continued until Bryant was arrested in

California a year after the shooting. We need not decide precisely when the emergency ended because Covington's encounter with the police and all of the statements he made during that interaction occurred within the first few minutes of the police officers' arrival and well before they secured the scene of the shooting — the shooter's last known location.

We reiterate, moreover, that the existence of an ongoing emergency is not the touchstone of the testimonial inquiry; rather, the ultimate inquiry is whether the "primary purpose of the interrogation [was] to enable police assistance to meet [the] ongoing emergency."

We turn now to that inquiry, as informed by the circumstances of the ongoing emergency just described. The circumstances of the encounter provide important context for understanding Covington's statements to the police. When the police arrived at Covington's side, their first question to him was "What happened?"18 Covington's response was either "Rick shot me" or "I was shot," followed very quickly by an identification of "Rick" as the shooter. In response to further questions, Covington explained that the shooting occurred through the back door of Bryant's house and provided a physical description of the shooter. When he made the statements, Covington was lying in a gas station parking lot bleeding from a mortal gunshot wound to his abdomen. His answers to the police officers' questions were punctuated with questions about when emergency medical services would arrive. He was obviously in considerable pain and had difficulty breathing and talking. From this description of his condition and report of his statements, we cannot say that a person in Covington's situation would have had a "primary purpose" "to establish or prove past events potentially relevant to later criminal prosecution."

For their part, the police responded to a call that a man had been shot. As discussed above, they did not know why, where, or when the shooting had occurred. Nor did they know the location of the shooter or anything else about the circumstances in which the crime occurred.

The questions they asked — "what had happened, who had shot him, and where the shooting occurred," were the exact type of questions necessary to allow the police to "'assess the situation, the threat to their own safety, and possible danger to the potential victim'" and to the public, including to allow them to ascertain "whether they would be encountering a violent felon," In other words, they solicited the information necessary to enable them "to meet an ongoing emergency."

Nothing in Covington's responses indicated to the police that, contrary to their expectation upon responding to a call reporting a shooting, there was no emergency or that a prior emergency had ended. Covington did indicate that he had been shot at another location about 25 minutes earlier, but he did not know the location of the shooter at the time the police arrived and, as far as we can tell from the record, he gave no indication that the shooter, having shot at him twice, would be satisfied that Covington was only wounded. In fact, Covington did not indicate any possible motive for the shooting, and thereby gave no reason to think that the shooter would not shoot again if he arrived on the scene. The initial inquiries in this case resulted in the type of nontestimonial statements we contemplated in *Davis*.

Finally, we consider the informality of the situation and the interrogation. This situation is more similar, though not identical, to the informal, harried 911 call in *Davis* than to the structured, station-house interview in *Crawford*. As the officers' trial testimony reflects, the situation was fluid and somewhat confused: the officers arrived at different times; apparently each, upon arrival, asked Covington "what happened?"; and, contrary to the dissent's portrayal, they did not conduct a structured interrogation. The informality suggests that the interrogators' primary purpose was simply to address what they perceived to be an ongoing emergency, and the circumstances lacked any formality that would have alerted Covington to or focused him on the possible future prosecutorial use of his statements.

Because the circumstances of the encounter as well as the statements and actions of Covington and the police objectively indicate that the "primary purpose of the interrogation" was "to enable police assistance to meet an ongoing emergency," Covington's identification and description of the shooter and the location of the shooting were not testimonial hearsay. The Confrontation Clause did not bar their admission at Bryant's trial.

The judgment of the Supreme Court of Michigan is vacated, and the case is remanded for further proceedings not inconsistent with this opinion.

It is so ordered.

JUSTICE THOMAS, concurring in the judgment.

I agree with the Court that the admission of Covington's out-of-court statements did not violate the Confrontation Clause, but I reach this conclusion because Covington's questioning by police lacked sufficient formality and solemnity for his statements to be considered "testimonial."

In determining whether Covington's statements to police implicate the Confrontation Clause, the Court evaluates the " 'primary purpose' " of the interrogation. The majority's analysis illustrates the uncertainty that this test creates for law enforcement and the lower courts. I have criticized the primary-purpose test as "an exercise in fiction" that is "disconnected from history" and "yields no predictable results."

Rather than attempting to reconstruct the "primary purpose" of the participants, I would consider the extent to which the interrogation resembles those historical practices that the Confrontation Clause addressed. As the majority notes, Covington interacted with the police under highly informal circumstances, while he bled from a fatal gunshot wound. The police questioning was not "a formalized dialogue," did not result in "formalized testimonial materials" such as a deposition or affidavit, and bore no "indicia of solemnity." Nor is there any indication that the statements were offered at trial "in order to evade confrontation." This interrogation bears little if any resemblance to the historical practices that the Confrontation Clause aimed to eliminate. Covington thus did not "bea[r] testimony" against and the introduction of his statements at trial did not implicate the Confrontation Clause. I concur in the judgment.

JUSTICE SCALIA, dissenting.

Today's tale — a story of five officers conducting successive examinations of a dying man with the primary purpose, not of obtaining and preserving his testimony regarding his killer, but of protecting him, them, and others from a murderer somewhere on the loose — is so transparently false that professing to believe it demeans this institution. In its vain attempt to make the incredible plausible, however — or perhaps as an intended second goal — today's opinion distorts our Confrontation Clause jurisprudence and leaves it in a shambles. Instead of clarifying the law, the Court makes itself the obfuscator of last resort. Because I continue to adhere to the Confrontation Clause that the People adopted, as described in *Crawford* v. *Washington*, I dissent.

I

A

In *Davis*, we explained how to identify testimonial hearsay prompted by police questioning in the field. A statement is testimonial "when the circumstances objectively indicate . . . that the primary purpose of the interrogation is to establish or prove past events potentially relevant to later criminal prosecution." When, however, the circumstances objectively indicate that the declarant's statements were "a cry for help [o]r the provision of information enabling officers immediately to end a threatening situation," they bear little resemblance to in court testimony. "No 'witness' goes into court to proclaim an emergency and seek help."

Crawford and *Davis* did not address whose perspective matters — the declarant's, the interrogator's, or both — when assessing "the primary purpose of [an] interrogation." In those cases the statements were testimonial from any perspective. I think the same is true here, but because the Court picks a perspective so will I: The declarant's intent is what counts. In-court testimony is more than a narrative of past events; it is a solemn declaration made in the course of a criminal trial. For an out-of-court statement to qualify as testimonial, the declarant must intend the statement to be a solemn declaration rather than an unconsidered or offhand remark; and he must make the statement with the understanding that it may be used to invoke the coercive machinery of the State against the accused. The hidden purpose of an interrogator cannot substitute for the declarant's intentional solemnity or his understanding of how his words may be used.

A declarant-focused inquiry is also the only inquiry that would work in every fact pattern implicating the Confrontation Clause. The Clause applies to volunteered testimony as well as statements solicited through police interrogation. An inquiry into an officer's purposes would make no sense when a declarant blurts out "Rick shot me" as soon as the officer arrives on the scene. I see no reason to adopt a different test — one that accounts for an officer's intent — when the officer asks "what happened" before the declarant makes his accusation. (This does not mean the interrogator is irrelevant. The identity of an interrogator, and the content and tenor of his questions, can bear upon whether a declarant intends to make a solemn statement, and envisions its use at a criminal trial. But none of this means that the interrogator's purpose matters.)

How to assess whether a declarant with diminished capacity bore testimony is a difficult question, and one I do not need to answer today. But the Court's proposed answer — to substitute the intentions of the police for the missing intentions of the declarant — cannot be the correct one. When the declarant has diminished capacity, focusing on the interrogators make less sense, not more. The inquiry under *Crawford* turns in part on the actions and statements of a declarant's audience only because they shape the declarant's perception of why his audience is listening and therefore influence *his purpose* in making the declaration. But a person who cannot perceive his own purposes certainly cannot perceive why a listener might be interested in what he has to say. As far as I can tell, the Court's substituted-intent theory has nothing to be said for it except that it can sometimes make our job easier.

The Court claims one affirmative virtue for its focus on the purposes of both the declarant and the police: It "ameliorates problems that . . . arise" when declarants have "mixed motives." I am at a loss to know how. Sorting out the primary purpose of a declarant with mixed motives is sometimes difficult. But adding in the mixed motives of the police only compounds the problem. Now courts will have to sort through two sets of mixed motives to determine the primary purpose of an interrogation.

The only virtue of the Court's approach (if it can be misnamed a virtue) is that it leaves judges free to reach the "fairest" result under the totality of the circumstances. If the dastardly police trick a declarant into giving an incriminating statement against a sympathetic defendant, a court can focus on the police's intent and declare the statement testimonial. If the defendant "deserves" to go to jail, then a court can focus on whatever perspective is necessary to declare damning hearsay nontestimonial. And when all else fails, a court can mix-and-match perspectives to reach its desired outcome. Unfortunately, under this malleable approach the guarantee of confrontation is no guarantee at all.

B

Looking to the declarant's purpose (as we should), this is an absurdly easy case. From Covington's perspective, his statements had little value except to ensure the arrest and eventual prosecution of Richard Bryant. He knew the "threatening situation," had ended six blocks away and 25 minutes earlier when he fled from Bryant's back porch. Bryant had not confronted him face-to-face before he was mortally wounded, instead shooting him through a door. Even if Bryant had pursued him (unlikely), and after seeing that Covington had ended up at the gas station was unable to confront him there before the police arrived (doubly unlikely), it was entirely beyond imagination that Bryant would again open fire while Covington was surrounded by five armed police officers. And Covington knew the shooting was the work of a drug dealer, not a spree killer who might randomly threaten others.

Covington's knowledge that he had nothing to fear differs significantly from Michelle McCottry's state of mind during her "frantic" statements to a 911 operator at issue in *Davis*. Her "call was plainly a call for help against a bona fide physical threat" describing" events *as they were actually happening.*" She did not have the luxuries of police protection and of time and space separating her from immediate danger that Covington enjoyed when he made his statements.

Covington's pressing medical needs do not suggest that he was responding to an emergency, but to the contrary reinforce the testimonial character of his statements. He understood the police were focused on investigating a past crime, not his medical needs. None of the officers asked Covington how he was doing, attempted more than superficially to assess the severity of his wounds, or attempted to administer first aid. Neither Covington's statements nor the colloquy between him and the officers would have been out of place at a trial; it would have been a routine direct examination. Like a witness, Covington recounted in detail how a past criminal event began and progressed, and like a prosecutor, the police elicited that account through structured questioning. Preventing the admission of "weaker substitute[s] for live testimony at trial" such as this, is precisely what motivated the Framers to adopt the Confrontation Clause and what motivated our decisions in *Crawford* and in *Hammon* v. *Indiana*, decided with *Davis*. *Ex parte* examinations raise the same constitutional concerns whether they take place in a gas-station parking lot or in a police interrogation room.

C

Worse still for the repute of today's opinion, this is an absurdly easy case even if one (erroneously) takes the interrogating officers' purpose into account. The five officers interrogated Covington primarily to investigate past criminal events. None — absolutely none — of their actions indicated that they perceived an imminent threat. They did not draw their weapons, and indeed did not immediately search the gas station for potential shooters. To the contrary, all five testified that they questioned Covington *before conducting any investigation at the scene*. Would this have made any sense if they feared the presence of a shooter? Most tellingly, none of the officers started his interrogation by asking what would have been the obvious first question if any hint of such a fear existed: Where is the shooter? At the very least, the officers' intentions *turned* investigative during their 10-minute encounter with Covington, and the conversation "evolve[d] into testimonial statements."

D

A final word about the Court's active imagination. The Court invents a world where an ongoing emergency exists whenever "an armed shooter, whose motive for and location after the shooting [are] unknown, . . . mortally wound[s]" one individual "within a few blocks and [25] minutes of the location where the police" ultimately find that victim. Because almost 90 percent of murders involve a single victim, it is much more likely — indeed, I think it certain — that the officers viewed their encounter with Covington for what it was: an investigation into a past crime with no ongoing or immediate consequences. This is a dangerous definition of emergency. Many individuals who testify against a defendant at trial first offer their accounts to police in the hours after a violent act. If the police can plausibly claim that a "potential threat to . . . the public" persisted through those first few hours, and if the claim is plausible here it is always plausible) a defendant will have no constitutionally protected right to exclude the uncross-examined testimony of such witnesses. His conviction could rest (as perhaps it did here) solely on the officers' recollection at trial of the witnesses' accusations. The Framers could not have envisioned such a hollow constitutional guarantee.

II

A

But today's decision is not only a gross distortion of the facts. It is a gross distortion of the law — a revisionist narrative in which reliability continues to guide our Confrontation Clause jurisprudence, at least where emergencies and faux emergencies are concerned.

According to today's opinion, the *Davis* inquiry into whether a declarant spoke to end an ongoing emergency or rather to "prove past events potentially relevant to later criminal prosecution," is *not* aimed at answering whether the declarant acted as a witness. Instead, the *Davis* inquiry probes the *reliability* of a declarant's statements, "[i]mplicit[ly]" importing the excited utterances hearsay exception into the Constitution. A statement during an ongoing emergency is sufficiently reliable, the Court says, "because the prospect of fabrication . . . is presumably significantly diminished," so it "does not [need] to be subject to the crucible of cross examination." Compare that with the holding of *Crawford*: "Where testimonial statements are at issue, the only indicium of reliability sufficient to satisfy constitutional demands is the one the Constitution actually prescribes: confrontation."

The Court attempts to fit its resurrected interest in reliability into the *Crawford* framework, but the result is incoherent. Reliability, the Court tells us, is a good indicator of whether "a statement is . . . an out-of-court substitute for trial testimony." That is patently false. Reliability tells us *nothing* about whether a statement is testimonial. Testimonial and nontestimonial statements alike come in varying degrees of reliability. An eyewitness's statements to the police after a fender bender, for example, are both reliable and testimonial. Statements to the police from one driver attempting to blame the other would be similarly testimonial but rarely reliable.

Is it possible that the Court does not recognize the contradiction between its focus on reliable statements and *Crawford*'s focus on testimonial ones? Does it not realize that the two cannot coexist? Or does it intend, by following today's illogical roadmap, to resurrect *Roberts* by a thousand unprincipled distinctions without ever explicitly overruling *Crawford*? After all, honestly overruling *Crawford* would destroy the illusion of judicial minimalism and restraint. And it would force the Court to explain how the Justices' preference comports with the meaning of the Confrontation Clause that the People adopted — or to confess that only the Justices' preference really matters.

B

The Court recedes from *Crawford* in a second significant way. It requires judges to conduct "open-ended balancing tests" and "amorphous, if not entirely subjective," inquiries into the totality of the circumstances bearing upon reliability. Where the prosecution cries "emergency," the admissibility of a statement now turns on "a highly context-dependent inquiry," into the type of weapon the defendant wielded, the type of crime the defendant committed, the medical condition of the declarant, if the declarant is injured, whether paramedics have arrived on the scene, whether the encounter takes place in an "exposed public area," whether the encounter appears disorganized, whether the declarant is capable of forming a purpose, whether the police have secured the scene of the crime, the formality of the statement, and finally, whether the statement strikes us as reliable. This is no better than the nine-factor balancing test we rejected in *Crawford*. I do not look forward to resolving conflicts in the future over whether knives and poison are more like guns or fists for Confrontation Clause purposes, or whether rape and armed robbery are more like murder or domestic violence.

It can be said, of course, that under *Crawford* analysis of whether a statement is testimonial requires consideration of all the circumstances, and so is also something of a multifactor balancing test. But the "reliability" test does not replace that analysis; it supplements it. As I understand the Court's opinion, even when it is determined that no emergency exists (or perhaps before that determination is made) the statement would be found admissible as far as the Confrontation Clause is concerned if it is not testimonial.

Judicial decisions, like the Constitution itself, are nothing more than "parchment barriers." Both depend on a judicial culture that understands its constitutionally assigned role, has the courage to persist in that role when it means announcing unpopular decisions, and has the modesty to persist when it produces results that go against the judges' policy preferences. Today's opinion falls far short of living up to that obligation — short on the facts, and short on the law. For all I know, Bryant has received his just deserts. But he surely has not received them pursuant to the procedures that our Constitution requires. And what has been taken away from him has been taken away from us all.

Justice Ginsburg, dissenting.

I agree with JUSTICE SCALIA that Covington's statements were testimonial and that "[t]he declarant's intent is what counts." Even if the interrogators' intent were what counts, I further agree, Covington's statements would still be testimonial. It is most likely that "the officers viewed their encounter with Covington [as] an investigation into a past crime with no ongoing or immediate consequences." Today's decision, Justice Scalia rightly notes, "creates an expansive exception to the Confrontation Clause for violent crimes." In so doing, the decision confounds our recent Confrontation Clause jurisprudence, which made it plain that "[r]eliability tells us nothing about whether a statement is testimonial."

I would add, however, this observation. In *Crawford* v. *Washington*, this Court noted that, in the law we inherited from England, there was a well-established exception to the confrontation requirement: The cloak protecting the accused against admission of out-of-court testimonial statements was removed for dying declarations. This historic exception applied to statements made by a person about to die and aware that death was imminent. Were the issue properly tendered here, I would take up the question whether the exception for dying declarations survives our recent Confrontation Clause decisions. The Michigan Supreme Court, however, held, as a matter of state law, that the prosecutor had abandoned the issue. The matter, therefore, is not one the Court can address in this case.

BULLCOMING v. NEW MEXICO
United States Supreme Court
564 U.S. ___, 131 S. Ct. 2705 (2011)

JUSTICE GINSBURG delivered the opinion of the Court, except as to Part IV and footnote 6.

In *Melendez-Diaz v. Massachusetts*, this Court held that a forensic laboratory report stating that a suspect substance was cocaine ranked as testimonial for purposes of the Sixth Amendment's Confrontation Clause. The report had been created specifically to serve as evidence in a criminal proceeding.

In the case before us, petitioner Donald Bullcoming was arrested on charges of driving while intoxicated (DWI). Principal evidence against Bullcoming was a forensic laboratory report certifying that Bullcoming's blood alcohol concentration was well above the threshold for aggravated DWI. At trial, the prosecution did not call as a witness the analyst who signed the certification. Instead, the State called another analyst who was familiar with the laboratory's testing procedures, but had neither participated in nor observed the test on Bullcoming's blood sample.

The question presented is whether the Confrontation Clause permits the prosecution to introduce a forensic laboratory report containing a testimonial certification — made for the purpose of proving a particular fact — through the in-court testimony of a scientist who did not sign the certification or perform or observe the test reported in the certification. We hold that surrogate testimony of that order does not meet the constitutional requirement. The accused's right is to be confronted with the analyst who made the certification, unless that analyst is unavailable at trial, and the accused had an opportunity, pretrial, to cross-examine that particular scientist.

I

A

In August 2005, Bullcoming was arrested for driving a vehicle while "under the influence of intoxicating liquor" (DWI). A sample of Bullcoming's blood was drawn at a local hospital. To determine Bull coming's blood-alcohol concentration (BAC), the police sent the sample to the New Mexico Department of Health, Scientific Laboratory Division (SLD). In a standard SLD form titled "Report of Blood Alcohol

Analysis," participants in the testing were identified, and the forensic analyst certified his finding.

SLD's report contained in the top block "information . . . filled in by [the] arresting officer." This information included the "reason [the] suspect [was] stopped" (the officer checked "Accident"), and the date ("8.14.05") and time ("18:25 PM") the blood sample was drawn. The arresting officer also affirmed that he had arrested Bullcoming and witnessed the blood draw. The next two blocks contained certifications by the nurse who drew Bullcoming's blood and the SLD intake employee who received the blood sample sent to the laboratory.

Following these segments, the report presented the "certificate of analyst," completed and signed by Curtis Caylor, the SLD forensic analyst assigned to test Bullcoming's blood sample. Caylor recorded that the BAC in Bullcoming's sample was 0.21 grams per hundred milliliters, an inordinately high level. Caylor also affirmed that "[t]he seal of th[e] sample was received intact and broken in the laboratory," that "the statements in [the analyst's block of the report] are correct," and that he had "followed the procedures set out on the reverse of th[e] report." Those "procedures" instructed analysts, inter alia, to "re tai[n] the sample container and the raw data from the analysis," and to "not[e] any circumstance or condition which might affect the integrity of the sample or otherwise affect the validity of the analysis." Finally, in a block headed "certificate of reviewer," the SLD examiner who reviewed Caylor's analysis certified that Caylor was qualified to conduct the BAC test, and that the "established procedure" for handling and analyzing Bullcoming's sample "ha[d] been followed."

SLD analysts use gas chromatograph machines to determine BAC levels. Operation of the machines requires specialized knowledge and training. Several steps are involved in the gas chromatograph process, and human error can occur at each step. Caylor's report that Bullcoming's BAC was 0.21 supported a prosecution for aggravated DWI, the threshold for which is a BAC of 0.16 grams per hundred milliliters. The State accordingly charged Bullcoming with this more serious crime.

B

On the day of trial, the State announced that it would not be calling SLD analyst Curtis Caylor as a witness because he had "very recently [been] put on unpaid leave" for a reason not revealed. A startled defense counsel objected. The State, however, proposed to introduce Caylor's finding as a "business record" during the testimony of Gerasimos Razatos, an SLD scientist who had neither observed nor reviewed Caylor's analysis. Bullcoming's counsel opposed the State's proposal. The trial court overruled the objection and admitted the SLD report as a business record. The jury convicted Bullcoming of aggravated DWI.

C

We granted certiorari to address this question: Does the Confrontation Clause permit the prosecution to introduce a forensic laboratory report containing a testimonial certification, made in order to prove a fact at a criminal trial, through the in-court testimony of an analyst who did not sign the certification or personally perform or observe the performance of the test reported in the certification.

Our answer is in line with controlling precedent: As a rule, if an out-of-court statement is testimonial in nature, it may not be introduced against the accused at trial unless the witness who made the statement is unavailable and the accused has had a prior opportunity to confront that witness. Because the New Mexico Supreme Court permitted the testimonial statement of one witness, i.e., Caylor, to enter into evidence through the in-court testimony of a second person, i.e., Razatos, we reverse that court's judgment.

II

The State in the instant case never asserted that the analyst who signed the certification, Curtis Caylor, was unavailable. The record showed only that Caylor was placed on unpaid leave for an undisclosed reason. Nor did Bullcoming have an opportunity to cross-examine Caylor. *Crawford* and *Melendez-Diaz*, therefore, weigh heavily in Bullcoming's favor.

We explain first why Razatos' appearance did not meet the Confrontation Clause requirement. We next address the State's argument that the SLD report ranks as "nontestimonial," and therefore "[was] not subject to the Confrontation Clause" in the first place.

A

Caylor certified that he received Bullcoming's blood sample intact with the seal unbroken, that he checked to make sure that the forensic report number and the sample number "correspond[ed]," and that he performed on Bullcoming's sample a particular test, adhering to a precise protocol. He further represented, by leaving the "[r]emarks" section of the report blank, that no "circumstance or condition . . . affect[ed] the integrity of the sample or . . . the validity of the analysis." These representations, relating to past events and human actions not revealed in raw, machine-produced data, are meet for cross-examination.

In any event, the comparative reliability of an analyst's testimonial report drawn from machine-produced data does not overcome the Sixth Amendment bar. This Court settled in *Crawford* that the "obviou[s] reliab[ility]" of a testimonial statement does not dispense with the Confrontation Clause. Accordingly, the analysts who write reports that the prosecution introduces must be made available for confrontation even if they possess "the scientific acumen of Mme. Curie and the veracity of Mother Teresa."

B

Surrogate testimony of the kind Razatos was equipped to give could not convey what Caylor knew or observed about the events his certification concerned, i.e., the particular test and testing process he employed. Nor could such surrogate testimony expose any lapses or lies on the certifying analyst's part. Significant here, Razatos had no knowledge of the reason why Caylor had been placed on unpaid leave. With Caylor on the stand, Bullcoming's counsel could have asked questions designed to reveal whether incompetence, evasiveness, or dishonesty accounted for Caylor's removal from his work station. In this light, Caylor's live testimony could hardly be typed "a hollow formality."

More fundamentally, as this Court stressed in *Crawford*, "[t]he text of the Sixth Amendment does not suggest any open-ended exceptions from the confrontation requirement to be developed by the courts." Accordingly, the Clause does not tolerate dispensing with confrontation simply because the court believes that questioning one witness about another's testimonial statements provides a fair enough opportunity for cross-examination.

In short, when the State elected to introduce Caylor's certification, Caylor became a witnes Bullcoming had the right to confront. Our precedent cannot sensibly be read any other way.

III

The State maintains that the affirmations made by analyst Caylor were not "adversarial" or "inquisitorial; instead, they were simply observations of an "independent scientis[t]" made "according to a non-adversarial public duty." That argument fares no better here than it did in *Melendez-Diaz*. A document created solely for an "evidentiary purpose," *Melendez-Diaz* clarified, made in aid of a police investigation, ranks as testimonial.

In all material respects, the laboratory report in this case resembles those in *Melendez-Diaz* . . . Here, as in *Melendez-Diaz*, a law-enforcement officer provided seized evidence to a state laboratory required by law to assist in police investigations. Like the analysts in *Melendez-Diaz*, analyst Caylor tested the evidence and prepared a certificate concerning the result of his analysis. Like the *Melendez-Diaz* certificates, Caylor's certificate is "formalized" in a signed document, headed a "report." Noteworthy as well, the SLD report form contains a legend referring to municipal and magistrate courts' rules that provide for the admission of certified blood-alcohol analyses.

In sum, the formalities attending the "report of blood alcohol analysis" are more than adequate to qualify Caylor's assertions as testimonial. The absence of notarization does not remove his certification from Confrontation Clause governance.

IV

The State and its *amici* urge that unbending application of the Confrontation Clause to forensic evidence would impose an undue burden on the prosecution. This argument, also advanced in the dissent, largely repeats a refrain rehearsed and rejected in *Melendez-Diaz*.

New Mexico law, it bears emphasis, requires the laboratory to preserve samples, which can be retested by other analysts. The State had that option here: New Mexico could have avoided any Confrontation Clause problem by asking Razatos to retest the sample, and then testify to the results of his retest rather than to the results of a test he did not conduct or observe.

For the reasons stated, the judgment of the New Mexico Supreme Court is reversed, and the case is remanded for further proceedings not inconsistent with this opinion. It is so ordered.

JUSTICE SOTOMAYOR and JUSTICE KAGAN join all but Part IV of this opinion. JUSTICE THOMAS joins all but Part IV and footnote 6.

JUSTICE SOTOMAYOR, concurring in part.

I agree with the Court that the trial court erred by admitting the blood alcohol concentration (BAC) report. I write separately first to highlight why I view the report at issue to be testimonial — specifically because its "primary purpose" is evidentiary — and second to emphasize the limited reach of the Court's opinion.

I

A

To determine if a statement is testimonial, we must decide whether it has "a primary purpose of creating an out-of-court substitute for trial testimony." In this case, for the reasons the Court sets forth, the BAC report and Caylor's certification on it clearly have a primary purpose of creating an out-of-court substitute for trial testimony.

The formality inherent in the certification further suggests its evidentiary purpose. Although "[f]ormality is not the sole touchstone of our primary purpose inquiry," a statement's formality or informality can shed light on whether a particular statement has a primary purpose of use at trial. I agree with the Court's assessment that the certificate at issue here is a formal statement, despite the absence of notarization. The formality derives from the fact that the analyst is asked to sign his name and "certify" to both the result and the statements on the form.

II

Although this case is materially indistinguishable from the facts we considered in *Melendez-Diaz*, I highlight some of the factual circumstances that this case does not present.

First, this is not a case in which the State suggested an alternate purpose, much less an alternate primary purpose, for the BAC report. For example, the State has not claimed that the report was necessary to provide Bullcoming with medical treatment.

Second, this is not a case in which the person testifying is a supervisor, reviewer, or someone else with a personal, albeit limited, connection to the scientific test at issue. Razatos conceded on cross-examination that he played no role in producing the BAC report and did not observe any portion of Curtis Caylor's conduct of the testing.

Third, this is not a case in which an expert witness was asked for his independent opinion about underlying testimonial reports that were not themselves admitted into evidence. As the Court notes, the State does not assert that Razatos offered an independent, expert opinion about Bullcoming's blood alcohol concentration. We would face a different question if asked to determine the constitutionality of allowing an expert witness to discuss others' testimonial statements if the testimonial statements were not themselves admitted as evidence.

Finally, this is not a case in which the State introduced only machine-generated results, such as a printout from a gas chromatograph. The State here introduced Caylor's statements, which included his transcription of a blood alcohol concentration, apparently copied from a gas chromatograph printout, along with other statements about the procedures used in handling the blood sample. Thus, we do not decide whether a State could introduce (assuming an adequate chain of custody foundation) raw data generated by a machine in conjunction with the testimony of an expert witness.

JUSTICE KENNEDY, with whom THE CHIEF JUSTICE, JUSTICE BREYER, and JUSTICE ALITO JOIN, dissenting.

Whether or not one agrees with the reasoning and the result in *Melendez-Diaz*, the Court today takes the new and serious misstep of extending that holding to instances like this one. Here a knowledgeable representative of the laboratory was present to testify and to explain the lab's processes and the details of the report; but because he was not the analyst who filled out part of the form and transcribed onto it the test result from a machine printout, the Court finds a confrontation violation.

I

Before today, the Court had not held that the Confrontation Clause bars admission of scientific findings when an employee of the testing laboratory authenticates the findings, testifies to the laboratory's methods and practices, and is cross-examined at trial. Far from replacing live testimony with "systematic" and "extrajudicial" examinations, these procedures are fully consistent with the Confrontation Clause and with well-established principles for ensuring that criminal trials are conducted in full accord with requirements of fairness and reliability and with the confrontation guarantee. They do not "resemble Marian proceedings."

The procedures followed here, but now invalidated by the Court, make live testimony rather than the "solemnity" of a document the primary reason to credit the laboratory's scientific results. Unlike *Melendez-Diaz*, where the jury was asked to credit a laboratory's findings based solely on documents that were "quite plainly affidavits," here the signature, heading, or legend on the document were routine authentication elements for a report that would be assessed and explained by in-court testimony subject to full cross-examination. The only sworn statement at issue was that of the witness who was present and who testified.

The record reveals that the certifying analyst's role here was no greater than that of anyone else in the chain of custody. The information contained in the report was the result of a scientific process comprising multiple participants' acts, each with its own evidentiary significance. These acts included receipt of the sample at the laboratory; recording its receipt; storing it; placing the sample into the testing device; transposing the printout of the results of the test onto the report; and review of the results.

In the New Mexico scientific laboratory where the blood sample was processed, analyses are run in batches involving 40–60 samples. Each sample is identified by a computer-generated number that is not linked back to the file containing the name of the person from whom the sample came until after all testing is completed. The analysis is mechanically performed by the gas chromatograph, which may operate — as in this case — after all the laboratory employees leave for the day. And whatever the result, it is reported to both law enforcement and the defense.

The representative of the testing laboratory whom the prosecution called was a scientific analyst named Mr. Razatos. He testified that he "help[ed] in overseeing the administration of these programs throughout the State," and he was qualified to answer questions concerning each of these steps. The Court has held that the government need not produce at trial "everyone who laid hands on the evidence" (*Melendez-Diaz*). Here, the defense used the opportunity in cross-examination to highlight the absence at trial of certain laboratory employees. Under questioning by Bullcoming's attorney, Razatos acknowledged that his name did not appear on the report; that he did not receive the sample, perform the analysis, or complete the review; and that he did not know the reason for some personnel decisions. After weighing arguments from defense counsel concerning these admissions, and after considering the testimony of Mr. Razatos, who knew the laboratory's protocols and processes, the jury found no reasonable doubt as to the defendant's guilt.

II

The protections in the Confrontation Clause, and indeed the Sixth Amendment in general, are designed to ensure a fair trial with reliable evidence. But the *Crawford v. Washington* line of cases has treated the reliability of evidence as a reason to exclude it. Today, for example, the Court bars admission of a lab report because it "is formalized in a signed document." The Court's unconventional and unstated premise is that the State — by acting to ensure a statement's reliability — makes the statement more formal and therefore less likely to be admitted. That is so, the Court insists, because reliability does not animate the Confrontation Clause. Yet just this Term the Court ruled that, in another confrontation context, reliability was an essential part of the constitutional inquiry. *Michigan v. Bryant*.

Like reliability, other principles have weaved in and out of the *Crawford* jurisprudence. Solemnity has sometimes been dispositive, and sometimes not. So, too, with the elusive distinction between utterances aimed at proving past events, and those calculated to help police keep the peace.

It is not even clear which witnesses' testimony could render a scientific report admissible under the Court's approach. *Melendez-Diaz* stated an inflexible rule: Where "analysts' affidavits" included "testimonial statements," defendants were "entitled to be confronted with the analysts" themselves. Now, the Court reveals, this rule is either less clear than it first appeared or too strict to be followed. A report is admissible, today's opinion states, if a "live witness competent to testify to the truth of the statements made in the report" appears. Such witnesses include not just the certifying analyst, but also any "scientist who . . . perform[ed] or observe[d] the test reported in the certification."

Today's majority is not committed in equal shares to a common set of principles in applying the holding of *Crawford*. That the Court in the wake of *Crawford* has had such trouble fashioning a clear vision of that case's meaning is unsettling; for *Crawford* binds every judge in every criminal trial in every local, state, and federal court in the Nation. The persistent ambiguities in the Court's approach are symptomatic of a rule not amenable to sensible applications. Procedures involving multiple participants illustrate the problem. In *Melendez-Diaz* the Court insisted that its opinion did not require everyone in the chain of custody to testify but then qualified that "what testimony is introduced must . . . be introduced live." This could mean that a statement that evidence remained in law-enforcement custody is admissible if the statement's maker appears in court. If so, an intern at police headquarters could review the evidence log, declare that chain of custody was retained, and so testify. The rule could also be that that the intern's statement — which draws on statements in the evidence log — is inadmissible unless every officer who signed the log appears at trial. That rule, if applied to this case, would have conditioned admissibility of the report on the testimony of three or more identified witnesses. In other instances, 7 or even 40 witnesses could be required. The court has thus — in its fidelity to *Melendez-Diaz* — boxed itself into a choice of evils: render the Confrontation Clause pro forma or construe it so that its dictates are unworkable.

III

Today's opinion repeats an assertion from *Melendez-Diaz* that its decision will not "impose an undue burden on the prosecution." But evidence to the contrary already has begun to mount. New and more rigorous empirical studies further detailing the unfortunate effects of *Melendez-Diaz* are sure to be forthcoming.

In the meantime, New Mexico's experience exemplifies the problems ahead. From 2008 to 2010, subpoenas requiring New Mexico analysts to testify in impaired-driving cases rose 71%, to 1,600 — or 8 or 9 every workday. In a State that is the Nation's fifth largest by area and that employs just 10 total analysts, each analyst in blood alcohol cases recently received 200 subpoenas per year. The analysts now must travel great distances on most working days. The result has been, in the laboratory's words, "chaotic." And if the defense raises an objection and the analyst is tied up in another court proceeding; or on leave; or absent; or delayed in transit; or no longer employed; or ill; or no longer living, the defense gets a windfall. As a result, good defense attorneys will object in ever-greater numbers to a prosecution failure or inability to produce laboratory analysts at trial. The concomitant increases in subpoenas will further impede the state laboratory's ability to keep pace with its obligations. Scarce state resources could be committed to other urgent needs in the criminal justice system.

Seven years after its initiation, it bears remembering that the *Crawford* approach was not preordained. This Court's missteps have produced an interpretation of the word "witness" at odds with its meaning elsewhere in the Constitution, including elsewhere in the Sixth Amendment, and at odds with the sound administration of justice. It is time to return to solid ground. A proper place to begin that return is to decline to extend *Melendez-Diaz* to bar the reliable, common sense evidentiary framework the State sought to follow in this case.

Chapter 11

NON-HEARSAY PURPOSES FOR OUT-OF-COURT STATEMENTS

§ 11.01 CHAPTER CHECKLIST

1. Who determines what a statement is offered to prove?

2. What is an "assertion first" approach to case planning?

3. How is admissibility determined when a statement is offered for a non-hearsay use?

4. What are the most common non-hearsay purposes?

§ 11.02 RELEVANT FEDERAL RULES OF EVIDENCE

Rule 801. Definitions That Apply to This Article; Exclusions from Hearsay (partial text)

(c) Hearsay. "Hearsay" means a statement that:

(1) the declarant does not make while testifying at the current trial or hearing; and

(2) a party offers in evidence to prove the truth of the matter asserted in the statement.

Rule 802. The Rule Against Hearsay

Hearsay is not admissible unless any of the following provides otherwise:

- A federal statute;
- These rules; or
- Other rules prescribed by the Supreme Court.

§ 11.03 INTRODUCTION

Chapter 10 reviewed various types of verbal and nonverbal behavior that constitute "statements" within the meaning of Rule 801, and explained that an out-of-court statement is barred by the hearsay rule only if it is offered for "the truth of the matter asserted." This chapter examines a variety of circumstances in which statements can be admissible for purposes that do not rely on the statements' truth, or for what lawyers and judges commonly refer to as "non-hearsay purposes."

Chapter 10 set forth a "Five-Step Hearsay Matrix" and analyzed Steps One and Five of that Matrix. This chapter analyzes Steps Two and Three:

Step Two: What is a statement offered to prove?

Step Three: If the statement is offered for a non-hearsay purpose, is that purpose relevant, and if so, is its probative value substantially outweighed by any of the factors set forth in Rule 403?

§ 11.04 STEP TWO OF THE HEARSAY MATRIX: IDENTIFYING AN ASSERTION'S NON-HEARSAY PURPOSE

In our adversarial system, when a relevance issue arises with respect to an item of evidence, the burden is generally on the offeror to establish the connection between the evidence and the material fact (or credibility concern) that the offeror seeks to prove or disprove. Thus, it's up to the party who seeks to offer an out-of-court statement into evidence as non-hearsay to identify how the statement is relevant without regard to its accuracy.

A legitimate non-hearsay use for a statement may be apparent to an adversary. Nevertheless, to prevent jurors from using an out-of-court statement for its truth, the adversary may ask for a ruling on the record that limits the statement's admissibility to its non-hearsay use.

Example 1

Defendant Phil Abuster is charged with murdering Basil Leaf and calls Sue Asponte to support the self-defense plea. Sue's testimony proceeds in part as follows:

DEFENDANT'S ATTORNEY: What happened when you met up with Mr. Abuster, about an hour before Mr. Leaf was killed?

A: He started talking nervously about Basil Leaf.

DEFENDANT'S ATTORNEY: Do you know Basil Leaf?

A: Yes. He's someone that Phil and I used to play cards with.

DEFENDANT'S ATTORNEY: And what did Mr. Abuster say about Basil Leaf?

A: He said that Basil was a violent and vicious individual who always carried a gun and a knife. PROSECUTOR: Your Honor, for the record I ask that admissibility of the witness' testimony concerning the defendant's statement be limited to the issue of the defendant's state of mind.

DEFENDANT'S ATTORNEY: No objection.

JUDGE: The record will reflect that the statement is admitted solely on the issue of the defendant's belief about Mr. Leaf. I instruct the jury to consider it only for that purpose and not as evidence that what Mr. Abuster said about Mr. Leaf was accurate.

In Example 1 above, the defendant's assertion about Basil Leaf is relevant without regard to its truth. The defendant's assertion that Basil always carried a gun and a knife is circumstantial evidence that the defendant was afraid of Basil. From that fear, the jurors may infer that the defendant would not have attacked Basil, an inference that supports the defendant's self-defense claim. The prosecutor therefore does not object to the statement's admissibility, but also does not want the jurors to use the defendant's out-of-court assertion for its truth, that is, as evidence that Basil was violent and always carried a gun and a knife. Thus, the prosecutor asks for and obtains an instruction that the jury can use the defendant's assertion only for the non-hearsay purpose of reflecting the defendant's claimed belief about Basil.

As this example suggests, out-of-court assertions admitted as non-hearsay resemble the shares of common stock often awarded as bonuses to corporate insiders — they are restricted. In the case of non-hearsay, lawyers and judges call the restriction a "limited purpose," meaning that a judge or juror can properly consider an assertion admitted as non-hearsay only for the limited use for which it was admitted. In jury trials, judges typically try to confine the use of non-hearsay to its limited purpose. On request or *sua sponte*, a judge may give a "limiting instruction" immediately, admonishing jurors to consider an assertion only for its non-hearsay use as soon as a witness testifies to the assertion. And during final summation, a lawyer can refer to the non-hearsay assertion only for the limited purpose for which it's been admitted. For example, the defense attorney in the example above could not say during closing argument that "We know from what Phil Abuster said that Basil Leaf was a violent and vicious individual who always carried a gun and a knife." By contrast, the defense attorney could legitimately argue that "We know from what Phil Abuster said that Abuster was afraid of Basil Leaf and therefore would not have acted aggressively towards him."

A party cannot rely on an assertion admitted for a non-hearsay purpose to prove an element of a claim or defense when proof of that element depends on the statement's accuracy. For example, change the Abuster/Leaf example so that Basil Leaf is charged with unlawfully carrying a weapon. The prosecution could not rely on Abuster's out-of-court assertion to Sue Asponte as proof of this fact.

Practice Tip: Credibility v. Admissibility

Offering an out-of-court statement as evidence of a party's state of mind may produce an objection that the testimony is "unreliable" or "self-serving" and therefore inadmissible under Rule 403 because the statement's probative value is outweighed by the danger of unfair prejudice. For example, the prosecutor in the Abuster/Leaf example may object to Abuster's statement to Sue Asponte on the ground that Abuster might have been "planting a defense." That is, perhaps Abuster intended to kill Leaf all along, and told Sue (and possibly others) that Leaf was always armed in order to support a phony self-defense claim. You should respond to such objections by pointing out that they improperly conflate credibility with admissibility. Judges should not evaluate credibility when determining whether evidence is admissible under Rule 403. That is a jury function. If jurors can rationally conclude that Abuster believed that Leaf was always armed, the judge should admit Sue's testimony and leave the ultimate determination of his testimony's credibility to the jury.

Identifying a legitimate non-hearsay use for an assertion depends on your knowing the elements of the substantive rules that you are trying to prove or disprove. Only by tying a non-hearsay use to a particular element (or to the credibility of a witness) can you establish an assertion's relevance. Typically, trials involve claims and/or defenses with multiple elements, and an out-of-court assertion may constitute hearsay if you offer it to support or disprove one element but admissible non-hearsay if you offer it to support or disprove a different element.

Example 2

Julie is injured when she slips and falls in Aisle 3 of a supermarket, and she sues the market for failing to clean up the wet spot on the floor that allegedly caused her fall. Under applicable substantive law, two of the elements that Julie has to prove are that (1) a wet spot made the floor unreasonably dangerous, and (2) the supermarket knew of the dangerous condition. Julie calls Randy to testify that a few minutes before she fell, Randy had been shopping in the market and had told the store manager that "You've got a very slippery wet spot on the floor in Aisle 3." Randy's statement would be inadmissible hearsay were Julie to offer it to prove Element # 1. However, Randy's statement would be admissible as non-hearsay if Julie offers it to prove Element # 2 (notice to the store). Accurate or not, Randy's statement to the manager provided notice of the possible existence of a dangerous condition. The judge would admit the statement for the limited purpose of notice, and admonish the jurors not to use it as evidence that the floor was dangerously wet. Julie would have to prove that the dangerous condition existed through some means other than Randy's out-of-court statement to the manager.

Practice Tip: "Assertion-first" case planning.

In order to maximize a presentation's persuasiveness, experienced litigators may take an "assertion-first" approach to case planning. That is, a lawyer who is anxious to offer a very helpful out-of-court assertion into evidence may try to develop a legal theory that creates a non-hearsay use for that assertion.

Example 3

You represent a pedestrian who was injured by an allegedly drunk driver who was driving a borrowed car with the owner's permission. You have evidence that before the owner gave permission to the driver, a close friend of the driver had told the owner, "The driver is regularly stewed to the gills." This assertion would be hearsay and probably inadmissible if you offer it as evidence that the driver was drunk when your client was struck. However, the assertion is certainly one that you would want to offer into evidence on your client's behalf. You can create a non-hearsay use for the assertion if you sue not only the driver but also the owner for "negligent entrustment" of the car to a dangerous driver. The friend's assertion would probably then be admissible for the limited purpose of proving that the owner knew that the driver had a propensity to drink.

§ 11.05 STEP THREE OF THE HEARSAY MATRIX: DETERMINING THE RELEVANCE OF A CLAIMED "NON-HEARSAY USE"

In the abstract, there's no magic in being able to identify a non-hearsay use for an out-of-court assertion. Virtually any statement can give rise to a myriad of non-hearsay uses. For example, assume that in a personal injury case growing out of an auto accident, Mary is prepared to testify that "Patrick told me that the blue car ran a red light." You might offer this testimony as non-hearsay to prove such matters as:

Mary is capable of hearing.

Patrick is capable of speaking.

Patrick is capable of distinguishing colors.

Patrick is aware of traffic rules.

Mary is acquainted with Patrick.

The drawback, of course, is that none of these potential non-hearsay uses is likely to have the slightest bearing on who was at fault for the accident. A claimed non-hearsay use for an out-of-court assertion can serve as a ticket to admissibility only if that use is relevant. Under the familiar relevance principle of Rule 401, this means that a non-hearsay use either must bear on a witness' credibility or must have a tendency to make a material fact more or less probable than it would be without the evidence.

Thus, once the offering party has identified a non-hearsay use for an out-of court statement, often the next step is to determine whether that use has any bearing on material facts. As is always true when relevance issues arise, that determination depends not only on abstract legal elements, but on parties' specific factual contentions.

Example

Ginger is charged with murdering Fred. Ginger claims that two days before the alleged murder, her friend Gene told her, "Fred recently told me that you're a goner the next time he sees you." Gene's statement would be relevant as non-hearsay if Ginger's claim was that she killed Fred in self-defense. Whether or not what Gene said was accurate, hearing it might make Ginger afraid of Fred. If Ginger were afraid of Fred, arguably she wouldn't attack him, which lends credence to her self-defense claim. The direct examination of Ginger eliciting Gene's statement in support of her self-defense claim might go something like this:

DEFENDANT'S ATTORNEY: Ginger, when did you next see Gene?

A: It was two days before I saw Fred.

512   NON-HEARSAY PURPOSES FOR OUT-OF-COURT STATEMENTS   CH. 11

DEFENDANT'S ATTORNEY: And at that time, did you and Gene have a conversation?

A: Yes. I was alone outside a café, having coffee. Gene walked up to me and said, "Ginger, I hate to tell you this, but Fred recently told me that you're a goner the next time he sees you."

PROSECUTOR: Objection and move to strike, Your Honor. Hearsay.

[In an actual trial, a prosecutor who anticipates Ginger's answer and thinks it improper would object after the question, before Ginger gave the answer. Delaying an objection until after an improper question is answered may lead a judge to rule that an adversary has waived the objection.]

JUDGE: Defense counsel, any response? What is this statement being offered to prove?

DEFENDANT'S ATTORNEY: The testimony is relevant as non-hearsay to show that Ginger acted in self-defense, Your Honor. Even if Gene was joking or lying or just trying to scare Ginger, what Gene said is relevant to explain why Ginger was fearful of Fred, which in turn made it highly unlikely that she would attack him, leading to the conclusion that if she killed Fred she did so in self-defense. The only issue is whether Gene made the statement to Ginger, and Ginger can be cross-examined as to that claim.

[Of course, a judge or jury might instead conclude that Ginger's fear of Fred led her to "off" Fred at her earliest opportunity. As you know, however, the possibility of conflicting inferences is quite common and does not render evidence irrelevant.]

JUDGE: I'll admit the testimony as non-hearsay.

This non-hearsay argument would not succeed, however, if Ginger's defense were an alibi. For example, assume that Ginger's defense is that she was watching an old musical at the Bijou Theater at the time Fred was killed. In this factual scenario, Ginger's fear of Fred would simply be irrelevant. If the defense attorney nevertheless did try to offer Gene's statement into evidence for this non-hearsay use, Ginger's testimony would probably go something like this:

DEFENDANT'S ATTORNEY: Ginger, when did you next see Gene?

A: It was two days before I saw Fred.

DEFENDANT'S ATTORNEY: And at that time, did you and Gene have a conversation?

A: Yes. I was alone outside a café, having coffee. Gene walked up to me and said, "Ginger, I hate to tell you this, but Fred recently told me that you're a goner the next time he sees you."

PROSECUTOR: Objection and move to strike, Your Honor. Hearsay.

[Again, in an actual trial the prosecutor would object after the question, before Ginger's answer.]

JUDGE: Defense counsel, any response? What is this statement offered to prove?

DEFENDANT'S ATTORNEY: I offer the testimony as non-hearsay to show that hearing Gene's statement made Ginger fearful of Fred.

JUDGE: Counsel, so what? There's no connection between your client's possible fear of Fred and your defense. Your client's fear might be relevant to prove how she might have reacted in the victim's presence, but because your client's claim is that she was nowhere near the victim at the time of his death, her fear is irrelevant. I'll sustain the objection, strike the response and instruct the jury to disregard it.

Again, nothing inherent in the words of an out-of-court assertion determines its relevance as non-hearsay. As with any other item of proffered evidence, you need to establish a connection between your desired non-hearsay use and a material fact or the credibility of a witness.

§ 11.06 PROBATIVE VALUE VERSUS UNFAIR PREJUDICE

Even if an offering party identifies a relevant non-hearsay use, the admissibility of an out-of-court assertion can (like any other type of evidence) be derailed by other evidentiary considerations. The primary evidence rule that comes into play with non-hearsay uses is Rule 403, the flip side of the basic relevance rule set forth in Rule 401. Rule 403, as you recall, authorizes judges to exclude evidence when its probative value is substantially outweighed by such factors as the danger of unfair prejudice or undue consumption of time.[1] This section addresses Rule 403 in the context of out-of-court statements offered for non-hearsay uses.

Offering an out-of-court assertion for a non-hearsay purpose always gives rise to a potential Rule 403 argument that the risk that a jury will improperly use the assertion for the truth of its contents outweighs the probative value of the non-hearsay use. Thus, as the proponent of non-hearsay, you may have to develop an argument not only supporting the probative value of the non-hearsay use but also minimizing the risk of improper use.

Example

Return to the example of Ginger, and assume that her defense to the charge that she murdered Fred is that she killed him in self-defense. Ginger seeks to offer evidence that two days before Fred was killed, Gene said to her, "Fred recently told me that you're a goner the next time he sees you." Once the defense attorney identifies the desired non-hearsay use (to

---

[1] Chapter 4 examines Rule 403 in detail.

show that Ginger had reason to fear Fred), the prosecutor may make a Rule 403 objection. If so, the arguments may go as follows:

PROSECUTOR: Your Honor, the government objects to the defendant's testimony concerning Gene's statement on Rule 403 grounds. The defense offers the statement as non-hearsay, to show that the defendant was fearful of Fred and therefore would be unlikely to attack him. I submit that the evidence has little probative value, because the jury would be justified in making the exact opposite inference, that if the defendant were afraid for her life, she might well attack Fred before he could harm her. And balanced against this minimal probative value is the significant risk that the jury will improperly accept Gene's statement for its truth, and infer that Fred had threatened to kill Ginger. This is exactly the reasoning that the hearsay rule is designed to prevent, so exclusion of the evidence is necessary to avoid unfairly prejudicing the government's case.

JUDGE: Defense counsel, any response?

DEFENDANT'S ATTORNEY: The government is arguing Ginger's credibility concerning her reaction to Gene's statement, and I submit that that's a matter for the jury to decide. This evidence is critical, because the jury can't possibly render a fair verdict unless it knows what was going through Ginger's mind at the time she killed Fred, and Gene's statement is the key to understanding her mental state. As for the possibility of misuse of the statement, the government has not identified any way in which the risk is greater in this case than in any other case in which non-hearsay is offered. Your Honor should admit the statement and admonish the jurors not to use the statement for its truth.

JUDGE: I'll admit the statement and admonish the jury accordingly. Will the bailiff please ask the jurors to return to the courtroom?

With non-hearsay as with any other piece of evidence admitted for a limited purpose, there's no guarantee that jurors will obey a judge's admonishment. Evidence rules are more effective in controlling the information that reaches jurors than they are in controlling how jurors react to evidence once they've heard it. For example, assume that during deliberations in the case of *State v. Ginger*, a couple of jurors argue that, "I can't believe that Gene would have told Ginger that Fred had threatened to kill her unless Fred had really made the threat. And I bet that Fred followed through and did try to kill her." These jurors would be improperly using Gene's statement for its truth.

When such misuse occurs, most of the time the presiding judge and the lawyers don't find out about it at all. Jurors may not talk to them after deciding a case, and even when they do, they may not talk in detail about what was said during deliberations. Moreover, if the presiding judge and the lawyers do find out about misuse of evidence they usually do not do so until after a case has been decided. At that time, as you know, Rule 606 makes it nearly impossible to impeach a verdict on the ground that jurors misused evidence (*see* Chapter 7).

A concern that admonishing jurors not to use non-hearsay assertions for their truth may be asking jurors to perform a nearly impossible mental task is a factor that some judges will consider when deciding whether to exclude non-hearsay under Rule 403.

§ 11.07 COMMON NON-HEARSAY USES

[A] Overview

No matter how thoroughly you pore over the Federal Rules of Evidence, you will not find a rule authorizing the use of out-of-court assertions for non-hearsay purposes. Such rules are unnecessary. The admissibility of a statement as non-hearsay depends on the existence of a logical relationship between a claimed non-hearsay use and the legal, factual, and credibility issues in a particular case, and thus is governed by general relevance principles. However, certain non-hearsay uses appear routinely in trials, and this chapter focuses on those uses. These routine non-hearsay uses include:

Assertion offered as evidence of a speaker's state of mind.

Assertion offered as evidence of a listener's state of mind.

Assertion offered as a "verbal act" or "words of independent legal significance."

Assertion offered to contradict (impeach) in-court testimony.

Assertion offered to provide context and meaning.

> *Practice Tip: Non-Hearsay Uses and "State of Mind."*
>
> Many substantive rules include "state of mind" elements such as "intent," "knowledge," and "willfully." As a result, one of the most common claimed non-hearsay uses for out-of-court statements involves state of mind. While having legal outcomes rest partly on state of mind elements may further important policy goals, the frequency with which they appear in substantive rules greatly expands the range of potential non-hearsay uses for out-of-court statements. If you find yourself searching for an argument for the admissibility of an out-of-court assertion, always consider "state of mind."

[B] Assertion Relevant to Declarant's State of Mind

As in Example 1 above, declarants' assertions often reflect their subjective beliefs (states of mind). Whether or not the assertions are accurate, the subjective beliefs that spawned them may be relevant. Thus, an assertion may be admissible as non-hearsay when offered as circumstantial evidence of a declarant's subjective belief. A declarant's subjective belief can be relevant in two common circumstances:

The declarant's belief is itself a material fact.

The declarant's belief is circumstantial evidence of the declarant's behavior.

Example: Declarant's State of Mind a Material Fact

In a will contest case involving a claim that the testator was mentally incompetent to make a will, the contesting party's attorney is questioning a witness who has testified that she was a close friend of the testator:

PLAINTIFF'S ATTORNEY: How often did you speak with the testator in the weeks before he signed the will?

A: Oh, at least every other day. I'd try to visit with him as often as I could.

PLAINTIFF'S ATTORNEY: Were these conversations in any way unusual?

A: Yes. One thing was that just about every time we'd get together, the testator would say a few times, "I am the walrus."

DEFENDANT'S ATTORNEY: Objection, hearsay.

JUDGE: Response from plaintiff's attorney?

PLAINTIFF'S ATTORNEY: The statement is offered as non-hearsay to prove that the testator was delusional and therefore incompetent to make a will, a material fact in this case. The making of statements claiming to be an animal is evidence of delusion.

JUDGE: Objection overruled. I'll admit the statement as circumstantial evidence of the defendant's mental state.

Example: Declarant's State of Mind as Circumstantial Evidence of Declarant's Behavior

Jill is charged with murdering her live-in boyfriend Barker; the defense is self-defense based on Battered Women's Syndrome. Jill's attorney examines Jill's close friend Madeleine:

DEFENDANT'S ATTORNEY: Do you recall a conversation with Jill that took place the day before Barker's death?

A: Yes, I do.

DEFENDANT'S ATTORNEY: How did you happen to be talking to Jill?

A: She called and asked me to come over to her apartment before Barker got there.

DEFENDANT'S ATTORNEY: How did Jill seem to be when you got to her apartment?

A: She seemed extremely nervous. She kept looking out the window. She kept repeating that Barker would be home any minute.

DEFENDANT'S ATTORNEY: Did Jill say anything else about Barker?

A: Yes. She said that Barker kept a gun hidden somewhere in the apartment, and that if she tried to leave he would find her and kill her.

PROSECUTOR: Objection, hearsay.

JUDGE: Defense attorney, any response?

DEFENDANT'S ATTORNEY: Yes. Jill's statement is non-hearsay to prove that Jill was an abused woman who feared that Barker would kill her. Apart from the accuracy of her statements, what Jill said sheds light on how she experienced her relationship with Barker. Her statements support an inference that Jill suffered from Battered Women's Syndrome and that she felt trapped in the relationship and used deadly force in the belief that her survival depended on it.

JUDGE: Objection overruled.

Important Limitation: A declarant's state of mind CANNOT serve as the basis of an inference about the behavior of someone *other than* the declarant.

Example: Improper Attempt to Use a Declarant's State of Mind as Circumstantial Evidence of the Behavior of a Different Person

Jill is charged with murdering her live-in boyfriend Barker; the defense is self-defense based on Battered Women's Syndrome. Jill's attorney examines Jill's close friend Madeleine:

DEFENDANT'S ATTORNEY: Do you recall a conversation with Jill that took place the day before Barker's death?

A: Yes, I do.

DEFENDANT'S ATTORNEY: How did you happen to be talking to Jill?

A: She called and asked me to come over to her apartment before Barker got there.

DEFENDANT'S ATTORNEY: How did Jill seem to be when you got to her apartment?

A: She seemed extremely nervous. She kept looking out the window. She kept repeating that Barker would be home any minute.

DEFENDANT'S ATTORNEY: Did Jill say anything else about Barker?

A: Yes. She said that Barker kept a gun hidden somewhere in the apartment, and that if she tried to leave he would find her and kill her.

PROSECUTOR: Objection, hearsay.

JUDGE: Defense attorney, any response?

DEFENDANT'S ATTORNEY: Yes. Jill's statement is non-hearsay. We can infer that Jill suffered from Battered Women's Syndrome, from which we can further infer that Barker had subjected her to past abuse.

JUDGE: Objection sustained. An assertion of the defendant's mental state cannot serve as the basis of an inference about Barker's behavior.

Problem 11-1: Up the Creek I

Jones' widow sues Life Insurance Co. to collect the proceeds of Jones's life insurance policy. To prove that the disfigured body found at the bottom of a steep cliff alongside Crooked Creek was Jones's, the widow offers into evidence a letter written by Jones stating, "In a couple of days I'm going to head west to Crooked Creek." *Can the widow offer Jones's letter for a non-hearsay use?*

Problem 11-2: Up the Creek II

Same case as previous problem. To prove that the disfigured body found next to Crooked Creek was Jones's, the widow offers into evidence a second letter written by Jones stating, "Crooked Creek is like heaven on earth." *Can the widow offer Jones's letter for a non-hearsay use?*

Problem 11-3: Mother and Child

Husband and Wife each seek custody of their five-year-old son, Child. To prove that it would be in Child's best interests for Wife to have custody, Wife seeks to testify that "Last week, Child told me that Husband is mean and often hits Child." *Can Wife offer Child's statement for a non-hearsay use?*

Problem 11-4: Mine!

Prosecution of Marconi for assaulting Morse; both of whom work for the same computer company. To prove that Marconi had a motive to attack Morse, the prosecution calls Kevin to testify that a month before the alleged assault, Marconi told Kevin that "I actually wrote the program that Morse got the award for creating." *Can the prosecution offer Kevin's testimony for a non-hearsay use?*

Problem 11-5: Backache

Pedro sues D'Amato for personal injuries growing out of an auto accident. To prove that he was in pain after the accident, Pedro calls Wilton to testify that "I was with Pedro on the night of the accident, and Pedro told me that his back was really stiff and sore." *Can Pedro offer his statement to Wilton for a non-hearsay use?*

Problem 11-6: At the Movies: The Boyfriend

The film *The Good Mother*[2] involves a custody battle between divorced parents. The couple's eight-year-old daughter Molly lives with the mother and her live-in boyfriend, Leo. The father testifies that while Molly was visiting with him, she

---

[2] Warner Bros./Touchstone Pictures/Silver Screen Partners (1988).

walked in on him just after he had finished showering, while he was clad only in a towel tied around his waist. The father further testifies that Molly asked him to "let me see it," and that "Leo always lets me see his penis." The mother's lawyer makes a hearsay objection to the father's testimony to Molly's statements. *Representing the father, for what, if any, non-hearsay use can you offer Molly's statements?*

Problem 11-7: At the Movies: Motive for Murder

In the film *Jagged Edge*,[3] Jack Forrester is on trial for the murder of his wealthy wife Page. The prosecution's theory is that Forrester killed Page to prevent her from obtaining a divorce that would destroy his social and economic status. Virginia Howell, a prosecution witness who was Page's good friend, testifies that shortly before Page was killed, Page told Virginia that "my husband doesn't love me, he's been seeing other women, I'm going to divorce him." *In response to the defendant's hearsay objections to these statements, for what, if any, non-hearsay use can the prosecutor offer them?*

[C] Assertion Relevant to Listener's State of Mind

Just as statements can provide a window into a declarant's state of mind, so can hearing another's statement affect a listener's state of mind. When a listener's state of mind is *relevant*, the out-of-court statement that gave rise to that state of mind can qualify for admission as non-hearsay. As is true for a declarant's state of mind, a listener's state of mind may be relevant either because it is itself a material fact, or because it constitutes circumstantial evidence of behavior.

Example: Listener's State of Mind as a Material Fact

Medical malpractice case in which plaintiff Petra claims that defendant Dr. Phibes gave Petra an overdose of X-rays and severely burned her leg. The substantive law in Petra's jurisdiction allows recovery of damages for "reasonable fear of developing cancer." Petra's attorney is questioning Petra:

PLAINTIFF'S ATTORNEY: Did you seek medical advice about the condition of your leg?

A: Yes, from Dr. Frank Enstein, a dermatologist.

PLAINTIFF'S ATTORNEY: What happened when you went to see Dr. Enstein?

A: Dr. Enstein examined my leg and told me that there's a very high risk that it's going to become cancerous in the future.

DEFENSE ATTORNEY: Objection, hearsay.

PLAINTIFF'S ATTORNEY: Dr. Enstein's statement to Petra is offered as non-hearsay to prove that she reasonably feared developing cancer, a mental state which is itself a material fact on the issue of damages.

JUDGE: Objection overruled.

---

[3] Colombia Pictures (1985).

Example: Listener's State of Mind as Circumstantial Evidence of Behavior

Jill is charged with murdering her live-in boyfriend Barker; the defense is self-defense based on Battered Women's Syndrome. Jill's attorney examines Jill's close friend Madeleine:

DEFENDANT'S ATTORNEY: Do you recall a conversation with Jill that took place the day before Barker's death?

A: Yes, I do.

DEFENDANT'S ATTORNEY: How did you happen to be talking to Jill?

A: She called and asked me to come over to her apartment before Barker got there.

DEFENDANT'S ATTORNEY: How did Jill seem to be when you got to her apartment?

A: She seemed extremely nervous. She kept looking out the window. She kept repeating that Barker would be home any minute.

DEFENDANT'S ATTORNEY: Did you say anything to Jill about Barker?

A: Yes. I told her that about a week earlier, Barker had told me that he kept a gun hidden in the apartment, and that if Jill ever tried to leave him he would find her and kill her.

PROSECUTOR: Objection, hearsay.

JUDGE: Defense attorney, any response?

DEFENDANT'S ATTORNEY: Yes. Madeleine's statement is offered as non-hearsay to support Jill's belief that Barker would kill her if she tried to end the relationship. Apart from the accuracy of what Madeleine said, her statements support an inference that Jill felt trapped in the relationship and was forced to do what she did in order to survive.

JUDGE: Objection overruled.

Problem 11-8: Bagged

Debra is charged with possession of illegal drugs. To prove that Debra knew that the substance in the baggies found in Debra's home was contraband, the prosecution calls Seller to testify that "I assured Debra that the baggies contained Grade A-1 heroin."

1. *Can the prosecution offer Seller's testimony as non-hearsay?*

2. *Is Seller's testimony admissible to prove that the baggies contained heroin?*

Problem 11-9: Medical Mal

Sue Cherr sues Hospital for negligently employing Doctor Mal, who allegedly performed an unnecessary operation on Sue. To prove Hospital's negligence, Sue offers to prove that six months before Hospital hired Dr. Mal, the monthly issue of

§ 11.07   COMMON NON-HEARSAY USES   521

the state's Medical Quality Assurance Board Newsletter had rated the doctor as "unqualified to practice medicine or anything else, for that matter." *Can Sue offer the Newsletter's statement as non-hearsay?*

Problem 11-10: Hold the Dressing

Pei Pei slips and falls in the Cracked Barrel Restaurant on March 31, and sues the restaurant for negligently failing to clean up the spilled liquid that allegedly caused Pei Pei to fall. The restaurant's defense is that the floor was clean. Pei Pei calls Tal, who was eating in the restaurant on the night that Pei Pei fell, to testify to events that occurred prior to the time she fell. The defense (restaurant's) attorney and the judge should respond to the numbered portions of the transcript.

PLAINTIFF'S ATTORNEY: Do you recall where you were on the evening of March 31 last, at around 8 p.m.?

A: Yes, I was eating dinner with a companion in the Cracked Barrel Restaurant.

PLAINTIFF'S ATTORNEY: Do you know about an incident in which a small puddle of liquid in the restaurant caused Pei Pei to fall that night?

DEFENSE ATTORNEY: (*What if any, objection might you make to this question?*)

JUDGE: (*Rule on any objection*)

PLAINTIFF'S ATTORNEY: Well, let me ask you this. Did you notice anything unusual about the floor near where you were dining?

DEFENSE ATTORNEY: Objection, leading question.

JUDGE: Overruled. (*Is this ruling correct?*)

A: Yes. PLAINTIFF'S ATTORNEY: What did you notice?

A: A few feet from where I was sitting, between me and the salad bar, there was a puddle of some kind of clear liquid on the floor. I couldn't tell what it was; it looked like salad oil that had been laying there for some time.

DEFENSE ATTORNEY: Objection, improper opinion.

JUDGE: Overruled. (*Is this ruling correct?*)

PLAINTIFF'S ATTORNEY: Did you discuss this puddle with your dining companion?

A: I did. I told my companion that the spill was a dangerous one and that someone could easily slip and fall in it and get hurt.

DEFENSE ATTORNEY: Objection, hearsay.

PLAINTIFF'S ATTORNEY: Your Honor, I'm offering the statement only to corroborate the witness' testimony that a spill was on the floor, so on that basis it's not hearsay. I'll stipulate that the statement is not offered to prove that the spill was dangerous or that someone could get easily hurt.

JUDGE: (*What ruling on this response to the objection?*)

PLAINTIFF'S ATTORNEY: I also offer the statement for the non-hearsay purpose of its effect on the companion's state of mind. Hearing Tal's assertion gave the companion reason to believe that the spill was a dangerous one.

JUDGE: (*What ruling on this response to the objection?*)

PLAINTIFF'S ATTORNEY: Did you say anything else to your companion?

A: Yes, I said that I was going to notify an employee to clean it up.

DEFENSE ATTORNEY: Objection, hearsay.

PLAINTIFF'S ATTORNEY: Your Honor, I'm offering the statement to show notice to the restaurant, so it's not hearsay.

JUDGE: (*What ruling on the objection?*)

PLAINTIFF'S ATTORNEY: Did your companion respond to your comment?

A: Yes. My companion said, "You don't have to bother. I already mentioned it to the hostess."

DEFENSE ATTORNEY: Objection, hearsay.

PLAINTIFF'S ATTORNEY: Your Honor, I'm offering the statement only to prove notice to the restaurant, so it's not hearsay.

DEFENSE ATTORNEY: (*How would you respond to the plaintiff's argument?*)

JUDGE: (*Rule on the Defense Attorney's response*)

PLAINTIFF'S ATTORNEY: What happened next?

A: Just at that moment the hostess walked past the table. My companion told her, "Don't forget to take care of that spill over there near the salad bar."

DEFENSE ATTORNEY: Objection, hearsay.

PLAINTIFF'S ATTORNEY: The companion's statement is a command, not an assertion that a spill existed, and therefore is not hearsay. (*Is this a valid argument?*)

PLAINTIFF'S ATTORNEY: Also, the companion's statement is non-hearsay for the reason that it's admissible to show notice to the restaurant that a spill existed. (*Is this a valid argument?*)

[D] Assertion Offered as a "Verbal Act" (aka "Words of Independent Legal Significance" or "Legally Operative Conduct")

An assertion is non-hearsay when the assertion itself constitutes direct evidence of a material fact. If this were not so, you'd have the absurdity of a substantive rule creating a legal right negated by an evidence rule preventing proof of a material fact establishing the legal right. As with the other non-hearsay uses, admitting out-of-court statements as "verbal acts" protects an adversary's opportunity for meaningful cross-examination. The issue is whether words constituting direct evidence were spoken or written, and the witness who testifies that they were is in court and subject to cross-examination.

Example 1

Faye sues Ray for defamation, claiming that Ray made a false statement to a group of people that damaged Faye's reputation. Faye's attorney is questioning Faye:

PLAINTIFF'S ATTORNEY: What took place during this meeting of the California Post-Modern Club?

A: I heard Ray tell a group of club members that I like red meat and that when I order a salad I don't ask for the salad dressing on the side.

DEFENSE ATTORNEY: Objection, hearsay.

PLAINTIFF'S ATTORNEY: Ray's statement is non-hearsay because it constitutes words of independent legal significance. Faye's testimony provides direct evidence that Ray spoke the words that we claim are defamatory. That is, Ray's uttering of those words satisfies a material fact that we have to prove to make out a case of defamation. We'll later offer evidence of other material facts, including the falsity of Ray's statement.

JUDGE: Objection overruled.

Example 2

Arnold Schwartz sues Vic Tanney for breach of contract, alleging that Vic refused to honor a written agreement to hire Arnold as a fitness trainer in Vic's gym. Arnold's attorney offers a written exhibit into evidence:

PLAINTIFF'S ATTORNEY: Your Honor, I offer into evidence a written contract that we will show was signed by Arnold and Vic in which Vic agrees to employ Arnold as a fitness trainer in Vic's fitness club.

DEFENSE ATTORNEY: Objection, hearsay.

PLAINTIFF'S ATTORNEY: The contents of the contract constitute non-hearsay words of independent legal significance, as the contents provide direct evidence of the terms of the agreement between Arnold and Vic, and thus satisfy a material fact in this breach of contract case.

JUDGE: Objection overruled.

Example 3

Kathy sues Lee for reneging on a legally enforceable gift. Kathy's attorney is examining Kathy:

PLAINTIFF'S ATTORNEY: And what happened when Lee talked to you at your thirtieth birthday party?

A: Lee handed me an ATM card and a small piece of paper with a PIN written on it, and told me that the money in the account that she had set up for me was mine as thanks for all the kindnesses I'd shown to Lee.

DEFENSE ATTORNEY: Objection, hearsay.

PLAINTIFF'S ATTORNEY: What Lee told Kathy when giving her the ATM card and the PIN constitutes non-hearsay verbal acts, as Lee's words establish that Lee made a gift to Kathy.

JUDGE: Objection overruled.

Similar considerations support the admissibility of "verbal parts of acts" as non-hearsay. When words and deeds are intertwined, and the words establish the legal character of the deed, the words are admissible as "the verbal part of the act."

Example 4

A county supervisor is charged with accepting bribes in exchange for votes. The prosecution offers evidence that the treasurer of a trash collection company handed the supervisor a cash-filled envelope and said, "This should take care of your vote on the trash collection contract." The treasurer's statements are non-hearsay because they establish the legal character of the act as a bribe rather than a loan or a donation to the supervisor's favorite charity.

Problem 11-11: Death and . . .

The Internal Revenue Service sues Dee Duction for failing to report the value of a Lexus automobile as earned income. Dee claims that the Lexus was a gift from Smith and not taxable income. To prove that the Lexus was a gift from Smith, Dee could call Wesson to testify that:

1. Smith told me, "I gave my Lexus as a gift to Dee Duction yesterday."

2. Smith told me, "I'm going to give my Lexus as a gift to Dee Duction tomorrow."

3. I was standing next to Dee and Smith when Smith said, "Dee, here are the keys to my Lexus. Accept it as my gift to you."

§ 11.07   COMMON NON-HEARSAY USES   525

4. I was standing next to Dee and Smith when Dee said, "Smith, I still can't tell you how much I appreciate your giving me the Lexus yesterday."

5. All of the above.

Problem 11-12: Payback Time

George sues Gracie for failing to repay a loan of $5,000. To prove that the loan was repaid, Gracie testifies that "I handed George five $1,000 bills and told him that this was payment in full of the loan." *Is Gracie's statement to George hearsay?*

Problem 11-13: Cellar Dweller

Reggie is charged with being an "accessory after the fact" for helping Archie to evade capture after robbing a bank. The prosecutor calls Doug Head as a witness to testify that "I was visiting Reggie when Archie ran into the house and told us that he'd just robbed a bank and needed help. Reggie told Archie to hide in the cellar, that he'd be safe there. A few minutes after Archie had run into the cellar, a police officer knocked on the door and asked us if we'd seen Archie. Reggie told the officer that he had no idea of Archie's whereabouts." *What if any portions of this testimony constitute inadmissible hearsay?*

Problem 11-14: Protection

Nitti is charged with obtaining money from retailers through means of extortion. The prosecution calls Marcus Nieman, a small jewelry store owner, to testify that "Nitti came into my store and told me that he'd blow up my store if I didn't pay him $1,000 a month." *Does Nitti's statement constitute a verbal act?*

Problem 11-15: Mea Culpa

Whit Lasch sues May Aculpa for injuries growing out of an auto accident. Whit offers to testify that a week after the accident, May called Whit and said, "I'm really sorry. The accident was all my fault." *Does May's statement constitute a verbal act?*

Problem 11-16: Up in Arms

Bonnie is charged with armed bank robbery. To prove that Bonnie was armed at the time of the robbery, the prosecution calls Officer Ness to testify that "I arrested Clyde for robbing the bank along with Bonnie. Clyde then told me that Bonnie had used a gun during the robbery." *Does Clyde's statement to the officer constitute a verbal act?*

[E]   Assertion Offered to Contradict (Impeach) Testimony ("Prior Inconsistent Statement")

Evidence of a witness' out-of-court assertion that is inconsistent with the same witness' in-court testimony is admissible as non-hearsay. A judge or juror may regard a witness who "speaks with a forked tongue" to be lying, mistaken, or a reptile. Thus, regardless of the out-of-court assertion's accuracy, the mere fact that a witness has made inconsistent statements is relevant for its possible impact on the witness' credibility.

Example

Miguel sues Dustin for personal injuries growing out of an auto accident. Miguel's witness Sara testified on direct examination that Dustin's car ran a stop sign. The defense attorney's cross-examination goes as follows:

DEFENSE ATTORNEY: Sara, you saw Dustin's car run the stop sign?

A: I did, that's what I testified to.

DEFENSE ATTORNEY: Yet the day after the accident, you talked about it with Maria, your supervisor at work, correct?

A: I'm sure I did. It was pretty unnerving.

DEFENSE ATTORNEY: And didn't you tell Maria that you thought that the driver of the car that collided with Dustin's car was to blame for the accident?

PLAINTIFF'S ATTORNEY: Objection, hearsay.

DEFENSE ATTORNEY: Sara's statement to Maria is offered as non-hearsay to contradict Sara's direct-examination testimony. Sara's giving contradictory accounts of the same event may lead the jury to disbelieve Sara.

JUDGE: Objection overruled. The witness will answer the question.

Remember that even if Sara admits to making this statement to Maria, the defense attorney can't use the statement for the truth of its contents (i.e., that the plaintiff Miguel was at fault). Sara's out-of-court statement to Maria is admissible only for the limited purpose of impeachment, and the judge is likely to instruct the jurors not to use it as evidence that Miguel was at fault. (As you'll see in Chapter 12, Rule 801 (d)(1)(A) makes contradictory out-of-court assertions admissible for their truth when they are made under oath, perhaps in a deposition. Some jurisdictions, such as California, go even further and admit all self-contradictory statements for their truth. See Cal. Evid. Code § 1235.)

Though a prior inconsistent statement may be non-hearsay, other rules may impact the "time, place, and manner" of impeachment with a prior statement. For a discussion of those rules, please see Chapter 7.

Problem 11-17: Speed Test 1

In a personal injury case growing out of an auto accident, By Stander testifies on direct examination by the plaintiff that "The plaintiff's Mazda was traveling about 25 m.p.h. when it was struck by the defendant's Buick." Which, if any, of the following questions that the defense attorney might put to By on cross-examination constitute prior inconsistent statements?

1. "Didn't you tell the investigating officer that the plaintiff's Mazda wasn't going much faster than 20 m.p.h. just before the accident?"

2. "Didn't you tell the investigating officer that you couldn't remember how fast the plaintiff's Mazda was going just before the accident?"

3. "Isn't it true that Ahn Looker told the investigating officer that the plaintiff's Mazda was going at least 35 m.p.h. just before the accident?"

4. "Didn't you tell the investigating officer that you're not too good at judging the speed of cars?"

5. "Isn't it true that you lied about a year ago when you falsely reported to your insurance company that three laptop computers had been stolen from your car?"

6. "Didn't you tell the investigating officer that the defendant's Buick entered the intersection with the green light just before the accident?"

Problem 11-18: Speed Test 2

Same case as previous example. During the defense attorney's cross-examination of plaintiff's witness By Stander, the following testimony occurs:

DEFENSE ATTORNEY: By the way, how fast was the defendant's car going just before the accident?

A: I'm sorry, I don't remember.

DEFENSE ATTORNEY: Well, didn't you tell the investigating officer that the defendant's car was traveling no more than 30 m.p.h?

Does the defense attorney's last question constitute proper impeachment with a prior inconsistent statement?

[F] Assertions Offered to Provide Context and Meaning

In an effort to convince judges and jurors that testimony is accurate and that legal claims are valid, litigators typically strive to elicit testimony so that it portrays events in a way that makes the events appear real and memorable. Unless a witness is testifying to a performance by a mime, real-world incidents consist both of actions (e.g., "A robber entered the store carrying a gun") and words (e.g., "I heard someone say that we should run out the back door"). Thus, to help witnesses appear credible, attorneys normally ask witnesses to testify to stories that consist of statements that were part and parcel of the events to which they're testifying. Such statements often qualify as non-hearsay for the simple reason that they are not offered for their truth, but to portray a detailed and accurate version of events relevant to a litigated dispute. Of course, trial judges have the power under Rule 403 to exclude contextual assertions if the time necessary to recount them or their unfairly prejudicial impact outweighs their probative value.

Example

Huntz and Leo are charged with conspiring to distribute illegal drugs. The prosecutor is questioning Bobby, a former member of the conspiracy who has agreed to testify for the government concerning the conspirators' operations. Bobby is about to testify to what took place at a meeting in Leo's apartment:

PROSECUTOR: And what happened when you arrived at that location?

A: Huntz opened the door and we went into the living room. Leo was on the phone when I got there, so Huntz and I just talked about stuff for a few minutes until he was off the phone.

PROSECUTOR: Can you remember what you and Huntz talked about?

A: Nothing special. I think he told me that he hadn't been feeling well for the last few days, and that his family was really pressuring him to go back to school or get a job.

PROSECUTOR: Anything else happen before Leo got off the phone?

A: I remember telling Huntz that school wasn't such a bad idea, I was thinking along the same lines for myself. Oh, I told him I was sorry he didn't feel well, and that he looked OK to me, I think that's about it.

PROSECUTOR: Did Leo join you and Huntz at some point?

A: Yeah, he wasn't on the phone more than a few minutes. He said something about his sister having trouble with her kid, and that she hoped that Leo could talk to him.

PROSECUTOR: Then what happened?

A: Leo came over to where we were sitting and said that there was a problem with a meth delivery. . . .

In this example, the alleged conspirators' comments are non-hearsay because their relevance does not depend on their accuracy. The various statements are relevant because they demonstrate that Bobby was personally present and can recall what took place at a real event. Moreover, the testimony is too brief and non-emotive to raise Rule 403 concerns.

§ 11.08 CHAPTER REVIEW PROBLEMS

Problem 11-19: Summation

Darla is charged with murdering Spanky; her defense is self-defense. Darla's attorney offered evidence that a few days before Spanky's death, a friend of Darla's had told Darla that Spanky was usually armed to the teeth with weapons. The defense offered the friend's statement as non-hearsay to show that Darla had reason to fear Spanky. Based on the friend's statement, evaluate the propriety of this portion of the defense attorney's final summation:

> Ladies and gentlemen, the prosecution's argument that Darla attacked Spanky doesn't make any sense. Darla testified that she was afraid of Spanky, and we know that Darla had good reason to fear him since Spanky normally was fully armed with weapons.

Problem 11-20: My Case is Shot

Shot Gunn is a plaintiff in a case growing out of an accident in which Shot was a passenger in a car that collided with the defendant's car. At trial, the driver of the car in which Shot was riding as a passenger testifies on direct examination as follows:

PLAINTIFF'S ATTORNEY: And what happened next?

A: Well, just moments before the collision, I heard Shot say that I had better be careful because the defendant's car was traveling way over the speed limit and was constantly changing lanes.

DEFENSE ATTORNEY: Objection, hearsay, move to strike.

PLAINTIFF'S ATTORNEY: Your Honor, the statement is offered as non-hearsay to help explain why the driver of the car in which Shot was a passenger was driving with particular care.

JUDGE: Objection overruled. I'll admit the statement for that limited purpose.

PLAINTIFF'S ATTORNEY: And what, if any, effect did Shot's remark have on your own driving?

A: I slowed down and made sure that I stayed in my lane.

Assume that at the close of Shot's case, the above testimony is Shot's only evidence as to the defendant's driving. The defendant moves for a directed verdict, asking that the judge dismiss Shot's case. *How should the judge rule on the motion?*

Problem 11-21: Policy Argument

Hy Strung's heirs file suit against Life Insurance Company after the Company refuses to pay the policy proceeds after Hy's death. The Company claims that Hy obtained the policy by lying about his health history, particularly his history of high blood pressure. The Company offers into evidence Hy's written insurance application, in which Hy wrote "none" next to the question, "Do you have any history of elevated blood pressure?" Hy's heirs object to admission of the application on the ground of hearsay. *What result?*

Problem 11-22: Bad Heir Day 1

This is a will contest case in which plaintiff Aggie Tator, Tess Tator's daughter and sole heir, seeks to set aside Tess's will disinheriting Aggie on the ground that the will was a product of Tess's insane delusion that Aggie was a drug addict. The beneficiary of the will, the Friends of Crabgrass Society, seeks to call three witnesses to testify that within three weeks prior to the will's execution, each of the witnesses had independently told Tess that they had seen Aggie buying and injecting heroin. *Can the Friends of Crabgrass Society offer this testimony as non-hearsay?*

Problem 11-23: Bad Heir Day 2

In this will contest case, plaintiff Darth Tator, Tess Tator's son and sole heir, seeks to set aside Tess's will disinheriting him on the ground that the will was a product of Tess's insane delusion that Darth was a drug addict. The beneficiary of the will, the Friends of Bluegrass Society, seeks to call as a witness Tess's friend Bill to testify as follows to a conversation that took place about a week before the will's execution:

DEFENSE ATTORNEY: Bill, do you have a friend by the name of Jim?

A: Yes, I do. Jim, I, and Tess Tator had all been good friends.

DEFENSE ATTORNEY: And did you speak to Jim about Tess in mid-August, about a week before Tess signed her will?

A: Yes, I did.

DEFENSE ATTORNEY: And what did Jim tell you?

A: Jim said that he'd talked to Tess the day before our conversation. He said that he'd told her that he'd recently seen her son Darth buying and injecting heroin.

PLAINTIFF'S ATTORNEY: Objection, hearsay, move to strike.

DEFENSE ATTORNEY: I offer Jim's statement to Tess as non-hearsay to show that Tess had a rational reason to disinherit Darth.

JUDGE: *(What ruling?)*

Problem 11-24: Bad Heir Day 3

In this will contest case, plaintiffs Aggie and Darth, Tess Tator's two children and sole heirs, seek to set aside Tess's will disinheriting them on the ground that the will was a product of Tess's insane delusion that they were drug addicts. The beneficiary of the will, the Friends of Greengrass Society, seeks to call Tess's friend Jim to testify as follows to a conversation that Jim had with Tess about a week before the will's execution:

DEFENSE ATTORNEY: Jim, what happened during your conversation with Tess?

A: Tess talked a little bit about Darth and Aggie, her children.

DEFENSE ATTORNEY: And what did Tess say about Darth and Aggie in this conversation?

A: Tess told me that three of Darth's and Aggie's friends had recently told her that they'd seen Darth and Aggie buying and injecting heroin.

PLAINTIFF'S ATTORNEY: Objection, hearsay, move to strike. The witness is testifying to what Tess said that some other declarants had told her.

DEFENSE ATTORNEY: The testimony is non-hearsay to show that Tess acted rationally in disinheriting her children.

JUDGE: *(What ruling?)*

Problem 11-25: Affordable Hearsay

Pavel sues Afford Motor Cars, his former employer, for wrongful termination. Afford had fired Pavel, an assistant manager, after receiving and investigating complaints from a number of female employees that Pavel had sexually harassed them. Assume that substantive law protects employers against wrongful termination suits if the employers investigate claims of employee wrongdoing and find a reasonable justification for termination. Afford commissioned an investigation, and offers into evidence the investigator's report that it allegedly considered before firing Pavel. The report recites employee accounts of Pavel's acts of sexual harassment, and concludes that Pavel committed numerous acts of sexual harassment. *You represent the employer; for what if any non-hearsay purpose can you offer the report into evidence?*

Problem 11-26: Honeymoon Over

Alice sues Ed for wrongful death, alleging that Ed's negligent driving caused the death of Alice's husband Ralph. In such cases, the monetary value of the husband-wife relationship is itself an element of damages. Ed calls Alice's coworker Trixie to testify, "A couple of weeks before Ralph was killed, Alice told me that Ralph had been cruel and indifferent to her throughout all the years of their marriage, and had repeatedly stuck his fist in her face and threatened to send her to the moon." *Can Ed offer Trixie's testimony into evidence for a legitimate non-hearsay purpose?*

Problem 11-27: Mind the Gap

Otis sues the Sears Tower Management Co. for personal injuries as a result of Otis's tripping when he got out of an elevator car that allegedly had stopped below the level of the floor. Al Urter is prepared to testify that he was riding in the elevator car at the same time as Otis and that when the elevator door opened and before Otis started to walk out, Al said to Otis, "Watch out for the gap between the elevator and the floor."

1. Otis offers Al's statement into evidence to prove that the elevator had stopped below the level of the floor. In response to Sears Tower's hearsay objection, Otis's attorney argues that "It's non-hearsay because Al's statement does not constitute an assertion that a gap existed between the elevator and the floor." *Ruling?*

2. Sears Tower offers Al's statement into evidence to prove that Otis's own carelessness contributed to his injuries. Otis makes a hearsay objection. *Ruling?*

Problem 11-28: Garden Variety Hearsay 1

Rose sues Fern, alleging that Fern failed to make good on a promise to pay Rose $1,000 to remove all the ivy from Fern's front yard. To prove that the parties entered into a contract on March 1, Rose testifies in part as follows:

PLAINTIFF'S ATTORNEY: And what was said in this March 1 conversation with Fern?

A: Fern asked how much I would charge to clear the ivy from her front yard. I said $1,000, and Fern said that we had a deal.

DEFENSE ATTORNEY: Objection, hearsay.

JUDGE: *(What ruling?)*

Problem 11-29: Garden Variety Hearsay 2

Same case. To prove that Rose and Fern entered into a contract on March 1, Rose calls Fern's next-door neighbor Daisy, who testifies as follows:

PLAINTIFF'S ATTORNEY: And did you talk to Fern on February 28?

A: I did.

PLAINTIFF'S ATTORNEY: And what did Fern tell you?

A: Fern said that on the following day, she was going to offer Rose $1,000 to remove all the ivy from her front yard.

DEFENSE ATTORNEY: Objection, hearsay.

JUDGE: *(What ruling?)*

Problem 11-30: Garden Variety Hearsay 3

Same case. To prove that Rose and Fern entered into a contract on March 1, Rose calls Fern's next-door neighbor Daisy, who testifies as follows:

PLAINTIFF'S ATTORNEY: And did you talk to Fern on February 28?

A: I did.

PLAINTIFF'S ATTORNEY: And what did you tell Fern?

A: I told Fern that she had better clear the ivy from her front yard or she would have a terrible rat problem.

DEFENSE ATTORNEY: Objection and move to strike. Hearsay and irrelevant.

PLAINTIFF'S ATTORNEY: *Can you offer the testimony for a relevant non-hearsay use?*

Problem 11-31: Garden Variety Hearsay 4

Same case. To prove that Rose and Fern entered into a contract on March 1, Rose calls Fern's next-door neighbor Daisy, who testifies as follows:

PLAINTIFF'S ATTORNEY: Daisy, did you talk to the plaintiff, Rose, on March 3?

A: I did.

PLAINTIFF'S ATTORNEY: Where did that conversation take place?

A: In Fern's front yard, when Rose was clearing ivy from Fern's yard.

PLAINTIFF'S ATTORNEY: And what was said in this conversation?

A: I asked Rose how much she would charge to clear ivy from my yard. Rose said that Fern had agreed to pay her $1,000 to clear the ivy from Fern's yard, so she'd charge me the same if the yards were about the same size.

DEFENSE ATTORNEY: Objection and move to strike, hearsay.

PLAINTIFF'S ATTORNEY: Rose's statement to Daisy is non-hearsay because it recites the terms of the agreement.

JUDGE: (*What ruling?*)

Problem 11-32: Alternate Defenses

Ojay Simpson is charged with murdering his ex-wife, Nicole Brown. The prosecution seeks to offer evidence from Nicole's friend Sara that three days before Nicole was found stabbed to death, Nicole had told Sara that "My ex has been stalking me day and night, and yesterday he vandalized my car. I'm really scared of him." Assume either that Ojay's defense is an alibi, or that his defense is that he killed his ex-wife in self-defense after she came at him with a hammer. *Discuss the impact of these alternative defenses on the hearsay status of Nicole's statement to Sara.*

Problem 11-33: Security Alert (Role Play)

Prosecution of Walter Denton, a teenage boy, for armed robbery of a convenience store. Walter's defense is an alibi, and the primary issue at trial is the credibility of Sharon, the security guard who was on duty the night of the robbery and who identifies Walter as the robber. A few days before the robbery, the store manager had posted an "Alert" in the employees' lounge that stated in part that "Police reports indicate that convenience stores such as ours are increasingly a target of violent robberies by teenage boys." A hearing will take place out of the jury's presence in which the prosecutor will seek a ruling that the contents of the Alert are admissible, and the defense attorney will seek to have the contents excluded from evidence.

Student # 1: You are the prosecutor, and in the hearing will argue that you should be permitted to offer the contents of the "Alert" into evidence during Sharon's direct examination. Interview Sharon outside of class, and try to develop foundational evidence that Sharon can provide that allows you to offer the Alert's contents into evidence as non-hearsay. During the hearing, support your argument as to the admissibility of the Alert's contents as non-hearsay by making an "offer of proof" as to the foundational evidence that Sharon can provide, based on what you were told during the interview. With the judge's permission, you may also respond to the defense attorney's counter-argument if you think it necessary to do so.

Student # 2: You are Sharon, and will meet with the prosecutor outside of class to discuss the testimony you will give if you are permitted to testify. Like the prosecutor, try to think of what testimony you can give that will make the contents of the Alert admissible as non-hearsay, and then assume that such testimony is consistent with your duty to tell the truth.

Student # 3: You are the defense attorney who represents Walter. Try to anticipate the prosecutor's argument to support admissibility of the Alert's contents as non-hearsay, and argue against admissibility. After hearing the prosecutor's argument, you may argue that the Alert is irrelevant, or that the contents are unduly prejudicial, or both.

Student # 4: As the judge, preside over the hearing and rule on the admissibility of the Alert's contents.

Problem 11-34: Zoo Suit

Annie Malle has sued a zoo for personal injuries that she sustained as a result of being bitten by an iguana. While visiting the zoo, Annie had reported to Osa, a zoo employee, that she'd seen the iguana running loose, and Osa told Annie to "please show me where you last saw it." Annie pointed out a spot on a dirt path on the far side of a sign that read "Danger; Employees Only," and told Osa that "the iguana ran into the bushes over there." Osa asked Annie to walk to where she'd last seen the iguana, saying "don't worry about that sign, it's perfectly safe." When Annie and Osa walked to the point on the path where Annie had last seen the iguana, Annie crouched down, pointed toward a bush, and was bitten. The zoo claims that Annie's own carelessness contributed to her injuries.

The zoo's attorney makes a hearsay objection to Annie's testifying to the statements that she made to Osa and that Osa made to her. *Are any of these statements admissible as non-hearsay?*

Annie's attorney makes a hearsay objection to Osa's testifying to the message on the sign. *Is this message admissible as non-hearsay?*

Problem 11-35: Last Words (Role Play)

Sunny Von is charged with murdering her husband Claus by poisoning his tea. Sunny claims that Claus was depressed and took his own life. The prosecution calls the Von family housekeeper, Alan Dersh, to testify that the day before Claus died, Claus told Alan with his last words that "I think Sunny has been poisoning me." The judge will conduct a hearing (out of the jury's presence) on the admissibility of Claus's statement to Alan. The hearing will go as follows:

Student # 1: As the prosecutor, identify a non-hearsay use for Claus's assertion and develop and present an argument in support of your proposed use. You may with the judge's permission respond to the defense attorney's argument.

Student # 2: As the defense attorney, try to anticipate the prosecutor's likely proposed non-hearsay use for Claus's assertion and develop and present an argument in opposition.

Student # 3: As the judge, preside over the hearing and rule on the assertion's admissibility.

Note: In the case of *Shepard v. United States*, 290 U.S. 96 (1933), Dr. Shepard was charged with murdering his wife. The government argued on appeal that the wife's statement, "Dr. Shepard has poisoned me," was admissible for the limited purpose of showing that the wife wanted to live and was not suicidal. Justice

Cardozo dismissed the argument, for at trial the government offered the wife's statement for its truth, not for the limited purpose it belatedly put forward on appeal. However, Justice Cardozo's memorable words indicate how he would have ruled had the government offered the wife's statement for the limited purpose at trial:

> Discrimination so subtle is a feat beyond the compass of ordinary minds. The reverberating clang of those accusatory words would drown out allweaker sounds. It is for ordinary minds, and not for psychoanalysts, that our rules of evidence are framed.

Justice's Cardozo's conclusion is not, of course, binding on the judge in this problem. His opinion was dictum, and the case pre-dated the Federal Rules of Evidence by decades.

Problem 11-36: Under Cover

To prove that Dana illegally solicited an act of prostitution, Police Officer Millhone offers to testify that Dana walked up to the officer's parked car. The officer said, "I'm feeling lonely tonight." Dana replied, "I'd be glad to help you out, but if you want to have sex with me, it'll cost you $100." *Are any of the statements hearsay?*

Problem 11-37: Rite to Trial

Irv has been sued for intentional infliction of emotional distress by Dinah, whose husband Bill was struck by a car just after he left the restaurant in which he and Dinah had been eating. Irv had walked out of the restaurant just after Bill did. Irv saw a car strike Bill, and then Irv watched as a Catholic priest ran over to Bill and began administering the last rites. At that point, Irv ran back into the restaurant and told Dinah, "I'm sorry to tell you this. The fellow you were eating with was just hit by a car and is going to die at any moment." Bill survived, and Dinah has sued Irv to recover for the emotional shock allegedly caused by his statement.

1. When Dinah seeks to testify to Irv's statement to her, Irv's attorney objects on the basis of hearsay. *Is this a valid objection?*

2. When Irv seeks to testify to the priest administering the last rites, Dinah objects that his actions constitute an out-of-court statement and are hearsay. *Is this a valid objection?*

Problem 11-38: Pre-School

Mack Martin is charged with sexually abusing a four-year-old child who was a student in Mack's preschool class. Mack denies the charges.

1. At trial, the child testifies hesitantly and incompletely. The prosecutor then calls Officer Millhone to testify to the explicit details concerning the sexual act allegedly perpetrated by Mack that the child provided to the officer in a pre-trial interview. *Would the officer's testimony be admissible for a non-hearsay purpose?*

2. At trial, the child testifies to the explicit details concerning the sexual act allegedly perpetrated by Mack. The defense attorney then calls Officer Millhone to

testify that in a pre-trial interview conducted by the officer, the child described the sexual act allegedly perpetrated by Mack hesitantly and incompletely. *Would the officer's testimony be admissible for a non-hearsay purpose?*

3. At trial, the child testifies to the explicit details concerning the sexual act allegedly perpetrated by Mack. Mack's attorney then seeks to offer into evidence a videotape of a children's services worker's pre-trial interviews of the child, which depicts the child initially denying that any sexual misconduct occurred, and after repeated insistence by the children's services worker that sexual abuse had occurred, recanting the denial and agreeing with the worker. *On what non-hearsay basis might the defense attorney seek to offer the videotape into evidence?*

Related Case Note: The "Triangle Shirtwaist Fire" was a watershed event in the U.S. labor movement. The fire occurred in 1911 in a lower Manhattan garment factory, and resulted in the deaths of more than 100 mostly poor, immigrant female garment workers. The deaths were generally attributed to the factory owners' violating labor laws by keeping exit doors locked until quitting time. The owners were criminally charged with causing the death of one of the employees, who according to key prosecution witness Kate Altermann burned to death while trying to escape through a locked exit door. Defense attorney Max Steuer, representing the owners, used an unusual trial tactic when he cross-examined Altermann. Steuer asked Altermann to "describe what happened again," and her narrative response was nearly a verbatim match to the testimony she had given on direct examination. Steuer then asked Altermann to "describe what happened again," and she used the identical words when she again repeated her story. (When Steuer pointed out that she had changed one word, she quickly corrected herself.) Steuer then offered evidence of the very different language Altermann had used when she gave a statement to the prosecutor nine months prior to trial, soon after the fire. The contrast between Altermann's earlier courtroom accounts apparently undermined her credibility with the jurors, because the owners were acquitted. *What non-hearsay use did Steuer make of the out-of-court statement that Altermann gave to the prosecutor?*

Problem 11-39: Self Service

Otto Mobeel sues Van Dorr for personal injuries incurred as a result of Van's alleged physical assault on Otto after a dispute as to which of them had first arrived at a gas station pump. Van contends that if he struck Otto at all he did so only in self-defense.

1. Otto seeks to testify that after Van got out of his car and walked toward Otto brandishing the windshield cleaning tool, Otto said two or three times that "I don't want to fight, let's stop this nonsense." *Are Otto's statements admissible for a non-hearsay purpose?*

2. Otto seeks to testify that as Van was advancing toward him with the windshield cleaning tool, another patron who was pumping gas on the other side of the island said to Otto that, "It looks like that guy is going to attack you." In response to Van's hearsay objection, Otto responds that "I'm offering the statement for the non-hearsay purpose of proving that the patron believed that Van was the aggressor." *How should the judge rule on the objection?*

3. Van seeks to testify that a few minutes after Otto left the gas station, a gas station employee walked over to Van and said, "We'll never let that guy pump gas here again." Otto makes a hearsay objection; Van responds that the employee's statement is admissible because it is relevant to prove that Otto started the fight apart from the assertion's accuracy. *How should the judge rule?*

Problem 11-40: Parole Evidence

Carla and Trevor are charged with jointly planning and carrying out a bank robbery. Carla's defense is that she knew nothing about the robbery until Trevor forced her at gunpoint to enter the bank with him and point a gun at the bank employees while he emptied their cash drawers. The prosecution seeks to offer testimony from David that a week before the bank robbery took place, he and Carla were in their parole officer's waiting room. While they were waiting for their monthly meetings to take place, Carla said to David that "Maybe you can live like this, but this guy Trevor and me are going to score a big hit on a bank soon and get out of here."

PROSECUTOR: *Argue for the admissibility of David's testimony as non-hearsay.*

DEFENSE ATTORNEY: *Argue for the exclusion of all or a portion of David's testimony.*

JUDGE: *Preside over the arguments and rule on the admissibility of David's testimony.*

Problem 11-41: 2-B or Not 2-B

Sherm is charged with possession of illegal drugs that a police officer found stuffed under a shirt in the corner of a closet after legally entering Apt. 2-B. Sherm's defense is that he lives in Apt. 3-B and knows nothing about the drugs in Apt. 2-B. To prove that Sherm lives in Apt. 2 B, the prosecutor calls the police officer who found the drugs to testify that the officer found an envelope and a letter in a pocket of the shirt under which the drugs were stuffed. The envelope was addressed to Sherm in Apt. 2-B; inside was a letter addressed to Sherm at the same address from Knight Law School, denying Sherm's application for admission. The defense attorney objects to the envelope and letter as hearsay. *How should the judge rule?*

Problem 11-42: At the Movies: Self-Defense

In the made-for-TV movie *Final Appeal*,[4] Christine is charged with murdering her husband Ed. Christine claims that she shot Ed when he confronted her and advanced toward her, and she thought that he was going to attack her. Christine seeks to testify to an incident that took place about a week before the shooting, when Ed chased her through their house with a machete and said, "If I catch you spying on me again, you'll die." *Would Christine's testimony to Ed's statement be admissible over the prosecution's hearsay objection?*

---

[4] Republic Television (1993).

Problem 11-43: At the Movies: Addiction

In the same film as in Problem 11-42, the prosecution calls Police Officer Ayers to testify that he investigated Christine's complaint the day after the alleged attack that her husband Ed had assaulted her with a machete. After denying that the incident had taken place, Ed told Officer Ayers that Christine was addicted to amphetamines and that she imagined many incidents that never took place. The judge strikes the testimony concerning Ed's statements as inadmissible hearsay. The judge's ruling is:

1. Improper if the prosecution's theory is that Christine killed Ed to prevent him from destroying her drug cache.

2. Improper if the prosecution's theory is that Christine killed Ed because he was about to file for a divorce that she opposed.

3. Improper if the prosecution's theory is that when Christine killed Ed she was under the influence of amphetamines.

4. Improper because Ed's statements explain why the officer failed to arrest Ed for assault with a deadly weapon.

5. Improper because Ed's statements tend to undermine Christine's claim that Ed would have confronted her and advanced on her on the day of the shooting.

Problem 11-44: Bad Call

Sue Ellen is charged with trafficking in illegal drugs. Officer Liu testifies that she and other police officers raided a warehouse filled with illegal drugs. The officers received a number of phone calls from callers who sought to make drug purchases. Officer Liu testifies that two of the callers asked for "100 pounds of your finest hashish and make sure that Sue Ellen prepares the order, she always includes a little extra in a package." The prosecution offers the callers messages to prove that the warehouse was a place where drugs were being sold and that Sue Ellen was a seller. *How should the judge rule on the defense attorney's hearsay objection?*

Problem 11-45: Sold!

Auction House sues Bidder to enforce an agreement that was allegedly arrived at when its auctioneer accepted the last bid for a rare set of "Great Law Professor Trading Cards." The auctioneer seeks to testify that Bidder made the final and highest bid, after which the auctioneer said, "Sold." Bidder objects that the auctioneer's testimony is inadmissible hearsay. *How should the judge rule?*

Problem 11-46: At the Movies: The Shout

In the film *Let Him Have It*,[5] Derek Bentley and Chris Craig are charged with murdering a police officer who intervened in their attempt to burgle a warehouse. Craig fired the bullet that killed the police officer. Bentley was unarmed, but his

---

[5] Luc Roeg & Robert Warr (1991).

culpability for the killing is based on the proposed testimony of a second police officer that when Craig pointed a weapon at the shooting victim, Bentley shouted, "Let him have it, Chris." *What is the relevance of Bentley's statement to the prosecution's case, and does it constitute hearsay? If Bentley does not testify at trial, should the judge sustain Craig's objection that Bentley's statement is barred by the Confrontation Clause?*

Problem 11-47: Probable Claus

Kris Kringle is on trial for robbery of a toy store. At trial, the store's owner was uncertain whether Kringle was the robber, but did testify that the robber was a heavy-set older white male who had a long white beard and was dressed in a red suit. Officer Nunez pulled Kringle's car over shortly after the robbery took place, after noticing that Kringle matched the description of the robber that was broadcast on her police radio. After finding a white beard and red suit on the floor of Kringle's car, Nunez placed him under arrest. At trial, the prosecutor seeks to have Nunez testify to the information about the robbery and the robber that was broadcast on the police radio. However, the judge has ruled that the broadcast is not admissible for the non-hearsay purpose of demonstrating that Nunez had probable cause arrest Kringle, because probable cause issues are decided prior to trial.

Student # 1: As the prosecutor, identify another non-hearsay use for the information in the broadcast and argue for its admissibility.

Student # 2: As the defense attorney, you may respond to the prosecutor's argument by arguing that the information in the broadcast is inadmissible hearsay and that Nunez's testimony to the information would be unfairly prejudicial under Rule 403.

Student # 3: As the judge, preside over the hearing and make a ruling.

Problem 11-48: Transcript Analysis

Carrie is charged with murdering Fay Tallity; the defense is self-defense. The transcript below consists of the testimony of Robert, a defense witness. Please respond to the italicized portions of the transcript.

DEFENSE ATTORNEY: Robert, were you with Carrie on November 14?

A: Yes, along with another friend, Menky.

DEFENSE ATTORNEY: Did you happen to say anything about Fay Tallity on that date? PROSECUTOR: Objection, leading.

JUDGE: Overruled. (*Is this ruling correct?*)

A: Yes.

DEFENSE ATTORNEY: Where were you when you mentioned Ms. Tallity?

A: The three of us were riding in Menky's car. Menky was driving, I was in the passenger seat in front, and Carrie was in the back seat.

DEFENSE ATTORNEY: And how did you happen to be talking about Ms. Tallity?

A:	Well, Menky was saying that we were going to be graduating soon and that there were lots of different kinds of kids we'd gone to school with.
PROSECUTOR:	Objection to what Menky said and move to strike, hearsay.
JUDGE:	*How should the judge rule? Why?*
DEFENSE ATTORNEY:	Did you respond to Menky's comment?
A:	Yeah. I'd transferred from Main High a couple of months earlier, and I said that Main really had some really nasty students in it.
PROSECUTOR:	Objection, hearsay.
DEFENSE ATTORNEY:	It's not hearsay because Robert is testifying to his own out-of-court statement.
JUDGE:	*(Please respond to this argument.)*
DEFENSE ATTORNEY:	It's also not hearsay because _____. *(Please read the through the remainder of the transcript and identify a non-hearsay use for this testimony.)*
JUDGE:	I'll overrule the objection.
DEFENSE ATTORNEY:	OK, what happened next?
A:	My guess is that Menky asked if I was referring to anyone who Menky might know.
PROSECUTOR:	Objection, speculation.
JUDGE:	Sustained, that testimony is stricken. *(Is this ruling correct?)*
DEFENSE ATTORNEY:	What's the next thing you remember?
PROSECUTOR:	Your Honor, I think we're getting into an area where the defense plans to offer a statement that I'm going to object to as hearsay. I'd ask that the jury be excused so that Your Honor can rule on my objection before the statement is repeated in open court.
JUDGE:	All right, I'll excuse the jury. (The jury exits stage left.) Defense counsel may continue the questioning.
DEFENSE ATTORNEY:	All right, I'll ask you again. What's the next thing that you remember?
A:	Right about then is when I told Menky that Fay, who we'd all seen at a party a couple of nights before, was one of the nasty people I was talking about.
DEFENSE ATTORNEY:	What else if anything do you recall saying about Ms. Tallity?
A:	I remember telling Menky that Fay was a member of a street gang called the South Street Bullies.
PROSECUTOR:	Objection, hearsay.

§ 11.08   CHAPTER REVIEW PROBLEMS   541

DEFENSE ATTORNEY: This is non-hearsay, not offered to prove that Ms. Tallity really was a member of a street gang, but to show that Carrie had reason to be fearful of Ms. Tallity and therefore wouldn't have attacked her.

JUDGE: Counsel, for the statement to be admissible on that basis I'll need to hear foundational evidence convincing me by a preponderance of the evidence that the defendant heard the witness' statement. Please inquire further. (*Is this ruling correct?*)

DEFENSE ATTORNEY: There were four of you in the car, correct?

PROSECUTOR: Objection, leading. (*Is this objection well-founded?*)

A: That's correct.

DEFENSE ATTORNEY: Can you please briefly describe the car?

A: Menky drives a Saturn, a two-door model.

DEFENSE ATTORNEY: About how far away from Carrie were you when the three of you were riding in the car?

A: Gee, it's a small car, no more than four feet I guess. Carrie was sitting behind me on the passenger side.

DEFENSE ATTORNEY: Was the radio on while you were talking to Menky about Ms. Tallity?

A: Yes, we were listening to a talk show host who was saying that the Internet was going to revolutionize the economy. (*Is the talk show host's statement hearsay?*)

DEFENSE ATTORNEY: And do you recall whether Carrie made any comments concerning your remarks about Fay Tallity?

A: I think she did; I'm not absolutely sure.

PROSECUTOR: Objection, speculation.

JUDGE: (*How should the judge rule? Why?*)

DEFENSE ATTORNEY: What tone of voice did you use when you made the statement about Ms. Tallity to Menky?

A: Normal voice, kind of like I'm talking here. I wasn't whispering or anything.

DEFENSE ATTORNEY: That's all on the foundational issue, Your Honor.

JUDGE: Prosecutor, any inquiries?

PROSECUTOR: None on the foundational issue. I submit that the evidence is insufficient as a matter of law to show that the defendant heard the witness' remark. It would be pure speculation to assume that someone sitting in the back seat of a car could hear what the passenger was saying to the driver, especially with the radio on.

JUDGE: In my opinion the defendant's evidence establishes that the defendant heard Robert's remark, so I'm going to overrule the objection as to lack of foundation. But so both counsel will know my thinking on this, be advised that I plan to include in the jury instructions an instruction that it's up to the jurors to decide whether the defendant overheard the witness' remark about Ms. Tallity, and that they may disregard the witness' testimony concerning the remark if they conclude that the defendant didn't hear it. Anything else before I bring back the jury? (*Is this ruling and statement correct?*)

PROSECUTOR: Yes. Might I question the witness briefly as to my hearsay objection?

JUDGE: You may.

PROSECUTOR: Robert, did you say anything more about Ms. Tallity than what you've already testified to?

A: No.

PROSECUTOR: And did the defendant in any way respond specifically to your statement about Ms. Tallity?

A: No, not that I remember.

PROSECUTOR: No further questions at this time. Your Honor, on the hearsay issue, I object to admission of the remark as non-hearsay based on Rule 403. The probative value of the defendant's non-hearsay use is minimal. At most, the defendant overheard a single casual remark, and never asked about it or responded to it in any way. Thus, whether possibly overhearing the remark made the defendant in any way fearful of Ms. Tallity is highly doubtful. Balanced against this is the highly unfair prejudice of the risk that the jury will misuse the evidence to believe that Ms. Tallity was a gangster, who either attacked the defendant or whose life is unworthy of legal protection.

DEFENSE ATTORNEY: (*How might the defense attorney respond to the prosecutor's argument?*)

JUDGE: (*After hearing the defense attorney's response, please rule on the admissibility of Robert's statement as non-hearsay.*)

§ 11.09 MULTIPLE-CHOICE REVIEW PROBLEMS

Review Problem 11-A

Ronald McDonald sues King Corp. for violating age discrimination laws when it terminated his employment as an accountant. McDonald seeks to offer into evidence an e-mail that he sent to his former co-workers in the accounting department stating that "King Corp. terminated my employment today as part of its effort to save money by firing older workers and bringing in new ones at much lower salaries." Assume that McDonald properly authenticates the e-mail. Which statement below is accurate?

1. The portion of the e-mail stating that King Corp. fired McDonald is non-hearsay, admissible as "words of independent legal significance" because termination of employment is a material fact that McDonald has to prove.

2. The entire e-mail is non-hearsay, admissible as "words of independent legal significance" because both termination of employment and age discrimination are material facts that McDonald has to prove.

3. The entire e-mail is admissible as non-hearsay because McDonald, the maker of the statement, testifies and is subject to cross-examination.

4. The entire e-mail is admissible as non-hearsay to show that McDonald's former co-workers' belief that McDonald was improperly terminated is reasonable.

5. The e-mail is inadmissible hearsay.

Review Problem 11-B

In a traffic accident case, to prove that the defendant drove negligently the plaintiff can offer evidence that:

1. Just prior to the accident, the passenger in the defendant's car said, "There's a sharp turn up ahead, you should probably slow down."

2. Shortly after the accident, the passenger in the defendant's car said, "That was a sharp turn back there, you should have slowed down."

3. Just prior to the accident, the passenger in the plaintiff's car said, "There's a sharp turn up ahead, that car coming the other way needs to slow down."

4. Shortly after the accident, the passenger in the plaintiff's car said, "That was a sharp turn back there, that car coming the other way should have slowed down."

Review Problem 11-C

Police Officer Sara O'Hara places Miggins under arrest for burglary. Miggins momentarily manages to break free and run away, but O'Hara recaptures Miggins quickly. At Miggins's trial for burglary, the prosecution seeks to offer evidence of Miggins's escape attempt. The judge should rule that the evidence of the escape attempt is:

1. Irrelevant to the issue of Miggins's guilt, as many people might try to avoid arrest regardless of whether they have committed a crime.

2. Inadmissible character evidence, tending to prove only that Miggins committed the crime of "attempted escape" and therefore has a propensity to violate the law.

3. Admissible to prove Miggins's guilt.

4. Hearsay, since Miggins's escape attempt constitutes an implied assertion, "I am guilty."

Review Problem 11-D

Miggins sues Police Officer Sara O'Hara for false arrest. At trial, Officer O'Hara seeks to offer evidence that she responded to an alarm at the home of Lemieux, who pointed in the direction of Miggins and said, "That's the guy who broke into my house." Evidence of Lemieux's statement is:

1. Admissible to show that the officer reasonably believed that Miggins had committed the burglary.

2. Admissible as non-hearsay to prove that Miggins did commit the burglary, because the statement explains why Lemieux pointed in Miggins's direction.

3. Inadmissible hearsay.

4. Admissible to prove that Lemieux believed that Miggins committed the burglary.

Review Problem 11-E

Kramden is charged with assaulting Norton; Kramden contends that Norton was the aggressor and that Kramden acted in self-defense. Kramden seeks to have Alice testify that the day before the alleged assault, Kramden told her, "That guy Norton is as mean and vicious as they come." Kramden's statement to Alice is:

1. Admissible to prove that Norton is mean and vicious and therefore was the aggressor.

2. Admissible to prove Kramden's fear of Norton, from which it can be inferred that Kramden would not have attacked Norton.

3. Inadmissible evidence of Norton's propensity for violence.

4. Inadmissible unless, pursuant to Rule 104(b), Kramden offers foundational evidence sufficient to support a finding that Norton had previously engaged in violent conduct.

Chapter 12

THE ADMISSIBILITY OF TESTIFYING WITNESSES' HEARSAY STATEMENTS

§ 12.01 CHAPTER CHECKLIST

1. What are the two routes through which an out-of-court assertion may be admitted for the truth of its contents?

2. Why do the Federal Rules of Evidence distinguish between "exemptions" and "exceptions?"

3. Is the use of an out-of-court assertion affected by whether it is admitted under an exemption or an exception?

4. What happens during a foundational "mini-trial?"

5. What foundational requirements are necessary for the following types of out-of-court statements to be admissible for the truth of their contents?

    a. The out-of-court statement conflicts with a witness' courtroom testimony.

    b. The out-of-court statement is consistent with a witness' courtroom testimony.

    c. The out of-court statement constitutes an identification made by a testifying witness.

6. Case Library:

    Tome v. United States

    United States v. Owens

§ 12.02 RELEVANT FEDERAL RULES OF EVIDENCE

Rule 801. Definitions That Apply to This Article; Exclusions from Hearsay (PARTIAL TEXT)

(d) Statements That Are Not Hearsay. A statement that meets the following conditions is not hearsay:

(1) *A Declarant-Witness's Prior Statement.* The declarant testifies and is subject to cross-examination about a prior statement, and the statement:

(A) is inconsistent with the declarant's testimony and was given under penalty of perjury at a trial, hearing, or other proceeding or in a deposition;

(B) is consistent with the declarant's testimony and is offered to rebut an express or implied charge that the declarant recently fabricated it or acted from a recent improper influence or motive in so testifying; or

(C) identifies a person as someone the declarant perceived earlier.

§ 12.03 INTRODUCTION

Chapter 11 reviewed circumstances in which hearsay statements may be admissible for non-truth purposes. In two common circumstances, however, parties seek to offer out-of-court statements for their truth:

1. A relevant non-hearsay purpose may be unavailable. That is, an out-of-court assertion may be relevant only if it is accurate.

Example 1

Auto accident case in which the driver of a silver car sues the driver of a blue car for negligence. The driver of the silver car seeks to offer evidence that Bystander saw the collision and told Companion that "the blue car ran the red light." In all likelihood, a relevant non-hearsay use for this statement is unavailable. For example, the Bystander's and the Companion's states of mind are irrelevant. Thus, the only way the silver car driver could offer Bystander's statement into evidence against the driver of the blue car would be to offer it for its truth.

2. Even if a potential non-hearsay use is available, a party may want an out-of-court statement admitted for the truth of its contents.

Example 2

In the same auto accident case, Bystander testifies at trial on behalf of the blue car driver that "the blue car driver had the green light." The silver car driver could offer Bystander's inconsistent out-of-court statement to Companion into evidence to attack Bystander's credibility. However, the silver car driver would probably prefer that Bystander's statement also be admissible to prove that the blue car driver ran the red light.

The Federal Rules of Evidence establish two routes by which parties can offer hearsay statements for the truth of their contents. Rule 801 is the "exemption" or "exclusion" route. When a party offering a hearsay statement into evidence satisfies the foundational requirements set forth in Rule 801(d)(1), the statement is exempt from (or excluded from) Rule 802's hearsay bar.[1] Rules 803, 804, and 807 constitute the primary "exception route" to admissibility of hearsay. When a party proffering

---

[1] Judges and commentators sometimes refer to statements exempted from the hearsay rule as "statutory non-hearsay."

hearsay satisfies the foundational requirements set forth in any of these provisions, an assertion is excepted from Rule 802's hearsay bar. After providing a brief overview of exemptions and exceptions, this chapter examines "witnesses' prior statements," one of the two major categories of exempt out-of-court statements.

Insofar as the use of statements at trial is concerned, the distinction between "exempt" or "excluded" statements and statements that are admitted into evidence under a hearsay exception is meaningless. The routes lead to the same destination: they make hearsay statements admissible for the truth of their contents. However, some commentators have cynically suggested that the array of exemptions and exceptions set forth in the Federal Rules of Evidence is so great that perhaps Rule 802 ought to be phrased the other way around: "Hearsay is admissible, except on the rare occasions that an attorney can't think of an exemption or exception provided by these rules." In fact, had John Keats's interests run to Evidence law rather than romantic poetry, he might have written "Ode on a Hearsay Assertion," and begun it with the verse, "How can I admit thee? Let me count the ways. . . ."

§ 12.04 WHY DISTINGUISH EXEMPTIONS FROM EXCEPTIONS?

As you know from Chapter 10, one of the hearsay rule's primary purposes is to protect a litigant's opportunity to cross-examine adverse witnesses. If this is so, then a sensible corollary to this policy is to admit hearsay statements into evidence for their truth when hearsay declarants testify at trial, subject to cross-examination. While this justification has not resulted in the complete admissibility of testifying witnesses' hearsay statements, the justification nevertheless underlies many of the exemptions (exclusions) set forth in Rule 801.

As you also know, one of the adversary system's primary purposes is to promote accurate decision-making by providing judges and jurors with reliable evidence. If this is so, then a second sensible corollary is to admit declarants' hearsay statements into evidence for their truth when the statements are made in circumstances suggesting that they are likely to be accurate. In such situations, admitting hearsay promotes accurate decision-making regardless of whether declarants are available for cross-examination. This justification underlies the exceptions established by Rules 803, 804, and 807.

Even though the policies underlying the Rule 801 exemptions are different from those underlying the Rules 803, 804, and 807 exceptions, the drafters of the Federal Rules of Evidence might not have bothered to distinguish one from the other but for the creation of the residual ("catch-all") hearsay exception, now codified as Rule 807. Most of the hearsay statements that Rule 801 classifies as exemptions started out life as common-law exceptions, and in fact are still regarded as exceptions in California and some other jurisdictions. However, Rule 807 makes admissible statements not specifically covered by Rule 803 or 804, so long as statements have "equivalent circumstantial guarantees of trustworthiness." The drafters of the Rules reasoned that judges couldn't sensibly compare the trustworthiness of hearsay offered into evidence under Rule 807 to the trustworthiness of the hearsay lumped together as exemptions in Rule 801, because the Rule 801 exemptions are not based on trustworthiness. Rather, the Rule 801 exemptions rest either on declarants' also testifying at trial subject to cross-examination (the situations grouped together in Rule 801(d)(1)), or on declarants also being parties (the situations grouped together in Rule 801(d)(2)). Thus, the assertions that Rule 801 makes exempt were severed from those listed in Rules 803 and 804 so that judges could compare "apples" with "apples" when ruling on the admissibility of hearsay offered into evidence under Rule 807. In other words, a judge considering the trustworthiness of hearsay offered under Rule 807 can ignore Rule 801 and evaluate the assertion according to the circumstances set forth in Rules 803 and 804, which are thought to produce accuracy. But whatever its logical merit, the distinction between exemptions and exceptions is a long way around the block for labels that make no substantive difference.

§ 12.05 LAYING FOUNDATIONS FOR HEARSAY ADMISSIBILITY THROUGH "MINI-TRIALS"

Every exemption or exception in the Federal Rules of Evidence specifies the factors ("foundational elements") that litigants must satisfy for hearsay to be admissible. To the proponent of hearsay, the need to lay a foundation means that offering hearsay into evidence pursuant to a hearsay exemption or exception often resembles painting a room. What a painter really wants to do is slap a new coat of paint on the walls. But first, the painter typically must prepare the walls by removing wallpaper, cleaning the walls, repairing cracks, and putting on a primer coat.

So too at trial, what a proponent of hearsay really wants to do is put the assertion before a judge or jury. But first, the proponent has to prepare the record by offering evidence satisfying the requisite foundational elements. In setting out different foundational elements for each exemption or exception, the Federal Rules of Evidence are more a recipe book than a collection of exclusionary rules. Just as a recipe book might tell cooks what ingredients must be assembled in order to make a chocolate cake or a Denver omelet, the Federal Rules tell lawyers and judges what foundational elements have to be satisfied for hearsay to be admissible under an exemption or an exception.

Arguments about whether hearsay is admissible under an exemption or an exception typically center on a proponent's ability to satisfy the required foundational elements (or as lawyers and judges often say, "to make the necessary foundational showing"). A proponent's effort to establish foundational elements often gives rise to a "mini-trial." Whereas in the "main" trial the issue might be whether a defendant drove carelessly or committed a crime, in a mini-trial the issue might be whether an assertion was an "excited utterance" (Rule 803(2)) or was made "in furtherance of a conspiracy" (Rule 801(d)(2)(E)).

During mini-trials, proponents offer evidence in support of foundational elements, and adversaries may cross-examine the proponents' witnesses, with questions limited to the foundational issue, and offer evidence of their own. Under Rule 104(c), in most circumstances the judge has discretion to decide whether the jury will be present during the mini-trial. (A party seeking to exclude hearsay often asks a judge to exclude jurors from the courtroom during a mini-trial, so that the jurors don't hear evidence that the judge may ultimately decide is inadmissible.) After listening to the evidence and considering the parties' arguments, under Rule 104(a) the judge decides whether the proponent of hearsay has met the burden of proving (by a preponderance of the evidence) the necessary foundational elements. (If an adversary disputes a hearsay declarant's personal knowledge, the judge resolves the dispute pursuant to Rule 104(b).)

Example

Pamela has sued Amanda for negligence for personal injuries resulting from an auto accident. Pamela seeks to offer into evidence a hearsay assertion made by bystander Ann Teek pursuant to the "excited utterance" exception (Rule 803(2)). Pamela is about to testify to Teek's assertion. If Amanda disputes the adequacy of the foundation, the mini-trial may unfold as follows:

PLAINTIFF'S ATTORNEY: And what happened after you got out of your car following the accident?

A: A woman named Ann Teek walked over to me and asked if she should call an ambulance.

PLAINTIFF'S ATTORNEY: Did Ms. Teek say anything to you about the events leading up to the collision?

DEFENSE ATTORNEY: Objection, hearsay.

PLAINTIFF'S ATTORNEY: Your Honor, I'm offering Ms. Teek's remark as an excited utterance under Rule 803(2). I'm prepared to lay the necessary foundation.

[To lay a proper foundation, Pamela has to convince the judge that

(a) the statement related to a startling event or condition; and that

(b) Teek spoke under the stress of excitement caused by the event.]

JUDGE: Do we need to excuse the jury?

PLAINTIFF'S ATTORNEY: I don't think that will be necessary. I think I can elicit the foundational evidence without referring to the assertion itself.

DEFENSE ATTORNEY: No objection to the jury remaining.

JUDGE: Proceed with the foundation, counsel.

[At this point the "mini-trial" begins, with the issue being the adequacy of the foundation for an excited utterance.]

[If either of the attorneys or the witness will refer to the assertion during foundational questioning, the judge may decide to excuse the jury. If the judge ultimately decides that the assertion is admissible, excusing the jury may waste time. The reason is that after the jury returns the proponent is likely to repeat the foundational questioning because the information both satisfies foundational elements and supports the assertion's credibility. On the other hand, if the jury remains present during the mini-trial and the judge ultimately decides that hearsay referred to during foundational questioning is inadmissible, the less-than-satisfactory solution is for the judge to admonish the jurors to ignore what they've already heard. Rule 104(c) leaves the decision entirely up to the judge's "interests of justice" discretion in civil cases.]

PLAINTIFF'S ATTORNEY: How much time passed between the collision and the time you spoke to Ms. Teek?

A: I can't be sure, of course, maybe a minute.

PLAINTIFF'S ATTORNEY: And what was her general demeanor?

A: She seemed really upset. She kept repeating "Are you OK? Are you OK?" I also remember her saying something like "My God, I can't believe you're able to walk out of your car."

[Under Rule 104(a), evidence rules (other than those relating to privileges) don't apply to foundational questioning. Thus, even if these remarks did constitute hearsay, they would not be excluded.]

PLAINTIFF'S ATTORNEY: Anything else you can remember about her demeanor or behavior?

A: She was out of breath and her face seemed flushed.

PLAINTIFF'S ATTORNEY: Nothing further on the foundation, Your Honor.

JUDGE: Defense counsel, do you wish to cross-examine?

DEFENSE ATTORNEY: One or two questions, Your Honor.

[If the defense attorney thinks that the plaintiff's foundation fails to satisfy the foundational requirements by a preponderance of the evidence, the attorney may forego questioning and submit the matter on the record as it stands.]

[If the defense attorney does cross-examine, the questioning will be limited to the foundational issue. The defense attorney will have a further opportunity to cross-examine the witness on all other issues at the conclusion of the direct examination.]

[When mini-trials involve more complex foundational issues (e.g., pursuant to Rule 803(6), the reliability of a business' record-keeping procedures), the proponent may call additional witnesses, and the opposing attorney may both cross-examine and call witnesses.]

DEFENSE ATTORNEY: The woman who spoke to you was calm enough to tell you that her name was Ann Teek, correct?

A: Yes, she gave me her name.

DEFENSE ATTORNEY: And she also gave you a business address and phone number, right?

A: Yes.

DEFENSE ATTORNEY:	In fact she wrote down this information on a card and handed it to you, right?
A:	Right.
DEFENSE ATTORNEY:	And after talking to you she walked over and spoke to Amanda, right?
A:	She walked in that direction, I was really hurting and I wasn't paying that much attention to what she did.
DEFENSE ATTORNEY:	Nothing further. Your Honor, I renew my objection. While the collision may have been a startling event, I don't think that the record establishes that Ms. Teek spoke under the stress of excitement.
JUDGE:	Plaintiff's counsel, any response?
PLAINTIFF'S ATTORNEY:	The testimony amply shows that Ms. Teek spoke under the stress of excitement. She had just witnessed a head-on collision, she expressed surprise that the plaintiff was able to get out of the car, and she was flushed and out of breath.
JUDGE:	I think the foundation is adequate. The objection is overruled. Counsel, resume the direct examination.
PLAINTIFF'S ATTORNEY:	Pamela, directing your attention to Ms. Teek, did she say anything to you about the events leading up to the collision?
A:	Yes. She said that Amanda had run a red light.
PLAINTIFF'S ATORNEY:	Now, after speaking to Ms. Teek, what happened?

. . . .

Practice Tip: "Offer of Proof" mini-trials.

Whether you are the proponent or the opponent of hearsay, an "offer of proof" is often a speedier, alternative form of mini-trial. This form of mini-trial typically takes place with both counsel at the judge's bench. Instead of foundational testimony unfolding in question-answer format as above, the hearsay proponent summarizes the foundational evidence that supports admissibility. The adversary may respond by pointing out the weaknesses in the foundation. The judge can then rule without having to hear the actual foundational testimony. If you are the proponent of hearsay, an advantage of the "offer of proof" strategy is that you avoid having to elicit the same evidence twice, with its attendant risks that witnesses will appear less credible the second time around or will create conflicts by describing events one way during a mini-trial and a different way when the jury returns and you cover the same ground. If you are the opponent, an "offer of proof" affords you a preview of the proponent's foundational evidence, helping you decide whether to object and giving you additional time to think through cross-examination. No matter which side you find yourself on, of course, it is incumbent on you as an officer of the court to make an offer of proof that accurately summarizes the testimony that witnesses will give.

§ 12.06 TESTIFYING WITNESSES' PRIOR STATEMENTS

[A] Three Categories of Exempt Statements

Rule 801(d)(1) provides that declarants' hearsay statements are "not hearsay" (i.e., are exempt or excluded from the hearsay rule) if the declarant testifies at the trial in which the statement is offered and is subject to cross-examination concerning the statement; *and* (a) the declarant's prior statement is inconsistent with the declarant's in-court testimony and was given under oath; *or* (b) the declarant's prior statement is consistent with the in-court testimony and is offered to rebut a charge of "recent fabrication" or "improper influence or motive;" *or* (c) the declarant's prior statement consists of an identification. The following sections examine each of these types of exemption.

[B] Prior Inconsistent Statements (Rule 801(d)(1)(A))

Statutory Elements:

* The declarant testifies at the trial or hearing;

* The declarant is subject to cross-examination concerning the prior statement;

* The prior statement is inconsistent with the declarant's testimony;

* The prior statement was given under oath subject to the penalty of perjury at a trial, hearing or other proceeding, or in a deposition.

As you know from Chapter 11, a witness' hearsay assertion is admissible for the non-hearsay purpose of impeaching that same witness' conflicting in-court testimony. For instance, if Marcia testifies for the prosecution that "the robber was wearing a blue shirt," the defense may introduce into evidence Marcia's out-of-court statement, "the robber was wearing a green shirt," to cast doubt on Marcia's credibility. Admissibility of hearsay in this situation does not require a hearsay exemption or exception. The prior statement is admissible not for its truth (i.e., to prove that the robber was wearing a green shirt), but as non-hearsay to cast doubt on Marcia's credibility.

When the proponent of a prior inconsistent statement satisfies the foundational elements of Rule 801(d)(1)(A), by contrast, hearsay is admissible not simply to cast doubt on the declarant's credibility, but also for the truth of its contents.

Example 1

Marcia testifies for the prosecution at trial that "the robber was wearing a blue shirt." The defense cross-examination is as follows:

DEFENSE ATTORNEY: You testified on direct that the robber wore a blue shirt?

A: Right.

DEFENSE ATTORNEY: Your Honor, I'd like to read into the record a portion of the witness' grand jury testimony in this case, which, of course, was given under oath. The testimony appears on page 56, lines 12–15, of the transcript of the grand jury proceedings.

JUDGE: Prosecutor, any objection?

PROSECUTOR: None, Your Honor.

JUDGE: Proceed.

DEFENSE ATTORNEY (reading from the grand jury transcript): "Question: How was the robber dressed? Answer: The robber wore a green shirt." Marcia, were you asked that question in front of the grand jury and did you give that answer?

A: Yes.

Because Marcia's prior inconsistent statement was given under oath, Rule 801(d)(1)(A) makes it admissible for its truth — that is, as evidence that the robber wore a green shirt.

When the content of a prior inconsistent statement is not necessarily more helpful to a cross-examiner's case than in-court testimony, the proponent of the prior inconsistent statement is likely to be agnostic as to whether the statement qualifies for a hearsay exemption under Rule 801(d)(1)(A) or is admissible as non-hearsay solely for impeachment. The existence of the inconsistency is what is important, and either way the judge or jury finds out that the witness has given contradictory accounts of the same event. However, the distinction can be important if the content of the prior inconsistent statement supports the cross-examiner's legal claims. Then, Rule 801(d)(1)(A)'s hearsay exemption means that the prior statement constitutes substantive evidence for those claims. Without the exemption, the cross-examiner would be limited to arguing the prior inconsistent statement's effect on the witness' credibility.

Example 2

Marcia testifies for the prosecution at trial that "the robber had a scar on his left cheek." The defense introduces into evidence Marcia's prior inconsistent statement that "the robber had no facial markings." Assume that the defendant in fact has a scar on his left cheek.

If Marcia's prior inconsistent statement was made under oath so as to be admissible under Rule 801(d)(1)A), the defense attorney can argue that "Marcia's prior statement proves the defendant's innocence. Her previous statement, made under oath, is evidence that the robber had no facial markings. Since, as you can plainly see the defendant has a scar on his left cheek, the defendant cannot be the robber."

If Marcia's prior inconsistent statement was not made under oath and so is admissible only as non-hearsay to impeach Marcia, the defense attorney is limited to arguing that "You should not believe Marcia's testimony that the robber had a scar on his left cheek. Marcia stated previously that the robber had no facial markings, so her convenient change of testimony is not trustworthy."

Proponents of prior inconsistent statements can offer them into evidence in a variety of ways. The most common is simply to cross-examine a witness about a prior inconsistent statement.

Example 3

Q: You testified on direct examination that the robber had a scar on his left cheek?

A: That's right.

Q: However, you testified before the grand jury that you couldn't recall which of the robber's cheeks had a scar on it, isn't that right?

A: Yes.

If the witness denies giving this testimony before the grand jury, the cross-examiner can "prove up" the prior inconsistent statement by reading the inconsistent grand jury testimony into the record.

Practice Tip: Reducing the risk of an explanation.

When you confront witnesses with prior inconsistent statements on cross-examination, you run the risk that they will immediately blurt out explanations that bolster the credibility of their in-court testimony. By way of example, assume that an adverse witness in a personal injury case growing out of an auto accident testifies that your client ran a red light. On cross-examination, you elicit the witness' testimony that shortly after the accident the witness told your client, "you had the green light, pal." The witness may add at once that "the reason I said that to your client is that he was hysterical and I was just trying to calm him down." If the judge or jury thinks this a reasonable explanation of the inconsistency, your impeachment has probably lost much of its force. (It is generally a bad idea to ask adverse witnesses to explain why they've made inconsistent statements; the likely result is an answer that is the equivalent to getting a pie in the face, as in this example. But a witness may volunteer an explanation without your asking for one. Judges often allow volunteered explanations to remain in the record so long as the volunteered information is admissible, reasoning that they are part of the give-and-take of cross-examination.)

To minimize the risk of an explanation, you may choose to forgo cross examination about a prior inconsistent statement, and instead read the prior inconsistent statement into the record, or call a witness to testify to the prior inconsistent statement, when it is your turn to present evidence. To use this procedure, you'll obviously need either a written document that contains the statement or a witness who can testify to the prior inconsistent statement. In either situation, however, the witness whose prior statement you offer is not on the stand when you offer it, and so cannot blurt out an immediate explanation.

If you plan to use this alternative impeachment procedure, you'll need to know about a couple of other rules that Chapter 7 covers. One is the "collateral evidence rule," which limits impeachment to cross-examination if an inconsistency relates to a minor point. The second is Rule 613, which provides that "extrinsic evidence of a prior inconsistent statement" (i.e., evidence offered other than during cross-examination) is inadmissible unless the impeached witness has "an opportunity to explain or deny" the inconsistency, or unless "the interests of justice otherwise require." Rule 613 seeks to ensure that the party who called the witness whose prior inconsistent statement has been offered into evidence has an opportunity at a later point in the trial to re-call the witness and ask the witness to explain the inconsistency (if the witness has a satisfactory explanation).

Example 4

Marcia testified for the prosecution that "the robber had a scar on his left cheek." The defense attorney cross-examined Marcia on a number of points, but made no reference to her inconsistent grand jury testimony. During the defense case-in-chief, the defense attorney plans to read into the record Marcia's grand jury testimony, in which she said that she didn't know which of the robber's cheeks had a scar. To comply with Rule 613, the defense attorney would conclude Marcia's cross-examination as follows:

DEFENSE ATTORNEY: No further questions of the witness at this time.

JUDGE: May this witness be excused?

DEFENSE ATTORNEY: No, Your Honor. I ask that she remain subject to subpoena.

JUDGE: Very well. The witness may stand down, but shall remain on call and subject to the previously issued subpoena.

By not excusing Marcia, the defense attorney satisfies Rule 613. The defense attorney could then read Marcia's inconsistent grand jury testimony into the record during the defense case-in-chief:

DEFENSE ATTORNEY: Your Honor, I'd like to open the defendant's case by reading into the record an excerpt from Marcia's grand jury testimony. I'll be reading from page 56, lines 8–11.

JUDGE: Prosecutor, any objection? Hearing none, defense counsel may proceed.

[Defense counsel's precise reference to the transcript testimony gives the prosecutor a chance to determine whether the foundational requirements have been met, in this instance the requirement that the prior statement be "inconsistent" with Marcia's trial testimony.]

DEFENSE ATTORNEY (reading from the grand jury transcript): "Question: Did you notice whether the robber had any facial markings? Answer: Yes, the robber had a scar on his cheek. Question: Do you know which of the robber's cheeks was scarred? Answer: No, I don't." Thank you, Your Honor, I'll now proceed to call the first witness for the defense.

The "Close the Doors" technique may also help cross-examiners reduce the risk of explanations. Close the Doors consists of identifying one or two explanations with which a witness may try to explain away an inconsistency, and eliminate those explanations before offering the inconsistency into evidence. The film *My Cousin Vinny* has a wonderful illustration of this technique. Although the illustration does not arise in the context of impeachment with a prior inconsistent statement, the Close the Doors technique applies whenever a cross-examiner seeks to impeach a witness.

In the film, Vinny cross-examines a witness who testified that only five minutes elapsed between the time that the defendants entered a convenience store and the time the witness heard gunshots and saw them run out of the store. The witness bases his time estimate on how long it took him to cook his breakfast grits. Vinny plans to impeach the witness' time estimate by eliciting the witness' admission that grits require 20 minutes of cooking. Before doing so, however, Vinny closes the doors on possible explanations the witness may give for why his grits were ready in five minutes. The Close the Doors portion of the cross-examination proceeds as follows:

VINNY: How do you like your grits — regular, creamy, or *al dente*?

A: Just regular, I guess.

VINNY: Do you use instant grits?

A: I use regular grits. No self-respecting Southerner uses instant grits.

These questions eliminate two potential explanations the witness might have given for his grits being ready to eat in five minutes: he likes his grits extra-tough, and he uses instant grits. Having closed the doors to these explanations, Vinny elicits the witness' admission that grits need to be cooked for 20 minutes before they are ready to eat.

Practice Tip: Elicit an inconsistent statement during direct examination to "take the sting out" of cross-examination.

You may be the proponent of a witness who has made an inconsistent statement and you are confident that your adversary intends to elicit the inconsistent statement during cross-examination. In this situation, consider eliciting the inconsistent statement yourself, during direct examination. Doing so conveys the idea that you have nothing to hide. And if the witness has a reasonable explanation for the inconsistency, you can elicit the explanation immediately.

Problem 12-1: Try to Remember

(a) Paolo sues Deng for personal injuries suffered in an auto accident. Prior to trial, Paolo deposed Willis, who was riding in Deng's car when the accident occurred. At the deposition, Willis testified as follows:

PLAINTIFF'S ATTORNEY: Willis, was Mr. Deng talking on a cell phone when the collision took place?

A: Sorry, I don't remember.

§ 12.06   TESTIFYING WITNESSES' PRIOR STATEMENTS   557

At trial, Willis testifies on Deng's behalf that Deng was not talking on a cell phone when the collision took place.

Is Willis's deposition testimony inconsistent with his trial testimony?

(b) Assume that you represent Deng. When you meet with Willis prior to his scheduled deposition by the lawyer for plaintiff Paolo, Willis tells you that he and Deng have decided that Willis should not think about the accident at all prior to the deposition. This way, as often as possible, Willis will be able to respond to questions honestly by saying, "I don't remember." Deng and Willis have decided that this is a dandy strategy for providing as little information as possible to Paolo's attorney at the deposition. *Do you agree?*

(c) When Paolo's attorney takes Willis's deposition, Willis testifies as follows:

PLAINTIFF'S ATTORNEY: Willis, was Mr. Deng talking on a cell phone when the collision took place?

A: Yes, I think he was talking on a cell phone.

At trial, while testifying on Deng's behalf, Willis states that he cannot remember whether Deng was talking on a cell phone when the collision took place.

Can Paolo's attorney offer Willis' deposition testimony into the record as a prior inconsistent statement?

(d) When Paolo's attorney takes Willis's deposition, Willis testifies as follows:

PLAINTIFF'S ATTORNEY: Willis, was Mr. Deng talking on a cell phone when the collision took place?

A: Yes, he was on the phone having a big argument with his ex-wife about child custody arrangements.

At trial, Paolo's attorney calls Willis as a witness. Willis testifies as follows:

PLAINTIFF'S ATTORNEY: Willis, what if anything was Deng doing at the time the collision took place?

A: I'm sorry, I can't remember.

[At this point the judge allows Paolo's lawyer to try to stimulate Willis's recollection by showing Willis the portion of the deposition testimony in which Willis testified that Deng was talking on a cell phone to his ex-wife at the time of the collision. For more information about this procedure, see Chapter 14.]

PLAINTIFF'S ATTORNEY: Willis, now that you've had a chance to review your deposition testimony, let me ask you again what, if anything, was Mr. Deng doing at the time the collision took place?

A: I still can't remember. I really don't remember a thing about that day.

PLAINTIFF'S ATTORNEY: Do you recall being a passenger in Mr. Deng's car when a collision occurred?

A: No.

PLAINTIFF'S ATTORNEY: Since the accident, have you been under a doctor's care for any kind of medical problem relating to your mental functioning?

A: No. It's just that I don't remember anything about an accident when I was a passenger in Deng's car.

PLAINTIFF'S ATTORNEY: Are you and Mr. Deng good friends?

A: Of course. We've worked together for a few years and we hang around socially sometimes.

PLAINTIFF'S ATTORNEY: And do you know whether Mr. Deng owns a cell phone?

A: I don't remember whether he does or not.

On this record, can Paolo's attorney offer Willis's deposition testimony into the record as a prior inconsistent statement?

Problem 12-2: Blame Worthy

Alison Anderson sues Mel Atonin for personal injuries suffered in an auto accident. Mel's attorney deposes Worthy, who the police report identifies as a witness to the accident. At the deposition, Worthy testifies that "I saw Mel's car, the blue SUV, run the red light." Between the time of the deposition and the trial, however, Worthy calls both counsel and tells them that his deposition testimony was wrong, and that he didn't see the cars before hearing the crash. Worthy also tells the attorneys that if he is called as a witness at trial, he'll testify that he didn't see what happened prior to the collision. When Alison's attorney nevertheless calls Worthy as a witness at trial, the following ensues:

PLAINTIFF'S ATTORNEY: Plaintiff next calls Worthy to the stand.

DEFENDANT'S ATTORNEY: Your Honor, might the plaintiff make an offer of proof out of the jury's presence as to what information she seeks to elicit from Worthy? I believe that the plaintiff's putting Worthy on the witness stand is simply a ruse to offer hearsay.

JUDGE: Very well, counsel. I've excused the jury. Plaintiff, what evidence do you plan to elicit from this witness?

PLAINTIFF'S ATTORNEY: I'm informed by Worthy that he will testify inconsistently from his deposition that he did not see either of the cars prior to the crash. After he so testifies, I will then impeach Worthy with his deposition testimony that the defendant's blue SUV ran the red light.

DEFENDANT'S ATTORNEY: In that case, I renew the hearsay objection and ask that Your Honor not permit the plaintiff to call Worthy as a witness.

JUDGE: I'll rule based on the assumption that Worthy will testify that he didn't see what happened prior to the collision. On that basis, I'll hear argument from both counsel before ruling on the objection. You might address the impact on my ruling of Rule 607.

Student # 1: You are the defense attorney. Argue that because the plaintiff seeks to call Worthy only for the purpose of offering his deposition testimony into evidence, the judge should not permit the plaintiff to call Worthy as a witness.

Student # 2: You are the plaintiff's attorney. Argue that you can call Worthy as a witness and, if his testimony conflicts with his deposition testimony, you can offer Worthy's deposition testimony into evidence.

Student # 3: You are the judge. Preside over the arguments and rule on whether the plaintiff can call Worthy as a witness and offer Worthy's deposition testimony into evidence should Worthy testify that he did not see the cars prior to the collision.

Problem 12-3: Bar Exam 1

Donahue is on trial for assault with a deadly weapon. The prosecution claims that Donahue and Meeker exchanged heated words in a bar, and that as Meeker walked out Donahue threw a beer bottle at him, striking Meeker on the head and shoulder. Prosecution witness Friedman testifies on direct examination that after Donahue and Meeker got into an argument, Meeker picked up a pool cue and advanced on Donahue with it. At that point, according to Friedman, Donahue threw the beer bottle at Meeker. After Friedman concludes testifying, the prosecutor seeks to call Police Officer Ono to testify that on the evening of the bar fight, Friedman told Ono that "Meeker was walking away when Donahue threw the beer bottle at him."

Is Officer Ono's testimony admissible against Donahue under the Confrontation Clause?

Problem 12-4: Bar Exam 2

Same case as previous problem. Assume that Friedman's hearsay statement that Meeker was walking away when Donahue threw the beer bottle at him was not made to a police officer on the night of the bar fight, but rather under oath during a grand jury hearing. When Friedman testifies during direct examination that Donahue threw the bottle at Meeker after Meeker picked up a pool cue and advanced on Donahue with it, the prosecution seeks to read Friedman's inconsistent grand jury testimony into the record for the truth of its contents.

Is Friedman's grand jury testimony admissible against Donahue under the Confrontation Clause?

Problem 12-5: Computer Caper

In Palmer's lawsuit against his former employer for wrongful termination, Erica testifies on the employer's behalf that she was Palmer's co-worker and that she saw him steal company property. Palmer's attorney cross-examines Erica in part as follows:

PLAINTIFF'S ATTORNEY:	You testified on direct examination that you saw Palmer take computer equipment that was still packed in its original cartons from a company storage closet and put it in his car, correct?
A:	That's right.
PLAINTIFF'S ATTORNEY:	And you testified that you saw him take monitors, printers, keyboards, and software, right?
A:	Yes.
PLAINTIFF'S ATTORNEY:	At your deposition, I asked you to identify what property you had seen Palmer take, right?
A:	Yes, you did.
PLAINTIFF'S ATTORNEY:	Yet you did not mention at that time that you had seen him take software, isn't that right?
A:	No, I didn't, I must have forgotten that.
DEFENDANT'S ATTORNEY:	Objection and move to strike. Counsel's question does not refer to anything that witness said at deposition that is inconsistent with the testimony she's given today at trial.
PLAINTIFF'S ATTORNEY:	*What is your response to the objection?*
PLAINTIFF'S ATTORNEY:	And isn't it also true that Ballam, another employee of the company, testified at her deposition that the computer equipment that Palmer took was used and marked with labels saying "To Be Trashed?"
DEFENDANT'S ATTORNEY:	*What if any objection might you make to this question?*

Problem 12-6: Baby Ruth

Duncan is charged with murdering "Baby Ruth" Jackson, an elderly woman who was admired in her neighborhood for providing candy and telling stories to little children. Duncan was charged with the murder based primarily on information provided by McCarthy. McCarthy told police officers that he heard a scream coming from Baby Ruth's home and saw Duncan jump over her fence carrying a purse and a knife. McCarthy also told the officers that shortly afterwards he heard Duncan tell his mother that he'd stabbed Baby Ruth. Called as a prosecution witness at trial, however, McCarthy testifies that "I never saw Duncan on the night Baby Ruth was killed, and I didn't hear him confess to nobody." The prosecution offers McCarthy's statements to the police officers into evidence as prior inconsistent statements. McCarthy testifies that he made the statements, but that they were not true and he made them "because I was mad at Duncan for trying to steal my woman."

1. Assume that the information above constitutes the entirety of the prosecution's case linking Duncan to the murder of Baby Ruth. *Under the Federal Rules of*

Evidence, how should the judge rule in response to the defense attorney's Motion to Dismiss the case against Duncan?

2. In contrast to Rule 801(d)(1)(A), **California Evidence Code Section 1235** makes all prior inconsistent statements admissible for their truth, regardless of whether they were given under oath. *Under the California Evidence Code, how should the judge rule in response to the defense attorney's Motion to Dismiss the case against Duncan?*

3. Assume that McCarthy's statements implicating Duncan in the murder of Baby Ruth were made not to police officers, but under oath during federal grand jury proceedings.

Student # 1: As the prosecutor, make a brief closing argument based on the summary of evidence above in an effort to convince the jury to believe McCarthy's grand jury testimony.

Student # 2: As the defense attorney, make a brief closing argument based on the summary of evidence above in an effort to raise a reasonable doubt about Duncan's guilt.

Problem 12-7: Ask the Expert

Your local representative to the U.S. Congress seeks your advice with respect to changing Rule 801(d)(1)(A) to make all prior inconsistent statements admissible for the truth of their contents (as the California Evidence Code provides). When deciding how to respond to the Congressperson's request, consider the following questions:

(a) In adopting the rule that all prior inconsistent statements are admissible for their truth, the California Law Revision Commission stated that "the inconsistent statement is more likely to be true than the testimony of the witness at the trial because it was made nearer in time to the matter to which it relates and is less likely to be influenced by the controversy that gave rise to the litigation." Do you agree with this generalization?

(b) Do you agree with the Federal Rules drafters' position that prior statements are more likely to be truthful if they are made under oath?

(c) When judges instruct jurors to consider a prior inconsistent statement only for its effect on a witness' credibility and not for the truth of its contents, how likely are jurors to follow the admonition?

(d) In criminal cases, would the proposed change be more likely to benefit prosecutors or defense lawyers? To the extent one group is likely to benefit more than the other, is this a relevant or legitimate consideration?

(e) Would you favor an alternative amendment providing that prior inconsistent statements are admissible for their truth only if the party offering it shows that the adversary turned the witness into a "turncoat" by bribing or intimidating the witness into a changed story?

Problem 12-8: Excuse Me

David is charged with bank robbery; the defense is an alibi. Beth testifies that David was with her at the movies at the time of the robbery. After cross-examining Beth and agreeing to excuse Beth as a witness, the prosecutor learns that two months before the trial, a different prosecutor had instituted proceedings seeking to revoke Beth's probation. In the probation revocation hearing, Beth had testified that "I haven't been in David's company for over a year." The prosecutor seeks to read this portion of Beth's testimony during the probation revocation hearing into the record during David's trial. Defense counsel objects, arguing that because Beth had already been excused as a witness, granting the prosecutor's request would leave the defense with no opportunity to offer evidence to explain or deny the probation revocation testimony. *How should the judge rule on the prosecutor's request?*

Problem 12-9: The Woodshed

Paul Biegler is an Assistant U.S. Attorney who is prosecuting Laura for armed robbery. Prior to trial, Biegler meets with Fred Manion, an eyewitness who will identify Laura as the robber. When he talked to the police shortly after the robbery, Manion said that he didn't really get a good look at the robber, and that beyond thinking that the robber was female he thought he'd have a hard time identifying the person who did it. Biegler expects the defense to impeach Manion with his statements to the police. Biegler hopes that his meeting with Manion will produce a satisfactory explanation for those statements that Biegler can elicit on redirect examination of Manion. Below is a partial transcript of Biegler's pre-trial meeting with Manion. *Consider whether Biegler complies with ABA Model Rule of Professional Conduct 3.4-(b), which provides that "A lawyer shall not . . . counsel or assist a witness to testify falsely."*

BIEGLER: So just to review, you're prepared to testify that Laura was the robber?

MANION: That's right. There's no doubt in my mind about that.

BIEGLER: Do you remember that when you talked to the police right after the robbery, you said you didn't get a good look at the robber, and that you thought you'd have a hard time recognizing her if you saw her again?

MANION: Yes, I do. I'm really sorry, I hope that doesn't mess you up.

BIEGLER: Well, on cross-examination you can certainly expect Laura's attorney to bring out those statements and later argue that your identification isn't worth diddly.

MANION: Is there anything we can do?

BIEGLER: Well, I can bring out what you said to the police during direct examination, and ask you to explain why you made those statements. Or, I can let the defense attorney bring the statements out during cross-examination and ask you for an explanation during my redirect. Either way, the key is giving the jury a satisfactory explana-

	tion. Can you tell me why you told the police that you didn't get a good look at the robber?
MANION:	I wish I could. That whole period is kind of a blur — the robbery, seeing a gun, being questioned by the cops, it was really unnerving.
BIEGLER:	Are you saying that you were frightened, maybe of retaliation by Laura or her friends, and saying that to the police was your way of not getting involved?
MANION:	Yes, I'd say that's correct.
BIEGLER:	That's fine. When your statements to the police are brought up, either by me or the defense, you can give that explanation. I think it's a reasonable one that the jury will accept.

Problem 12-10: Gimme Shelter

Wes Quire, Esq., is the defendant in an attorney malpractice action. The complainant alleges that Quire provided incompetent advice as to the legitimacy of a Tibetan Winery Trust as a tax shelter, causing the complainant to incur tax penalties of more than $200,000. At trial, Kirk Stark, Esq., testifies as an expert on Quire's behalf. Stark testifies that he is a tax specialist and that Quire had a reasonable basis for believing that the investment was a legitimate tax shelter. On cross-examination, Stark admits that six months earlier, he signed an affidavit under penalty of perjury stating that "Among the topics I will cover is that no competent tax professional would consider Tibetan Winery Trusts to be legitimate tax shelters." Stark submitted this affidavit to a law school when seeking an appointment to teach Tax 1 six months earlier. *Is the affidavit admissible for the truth of its contents?*

[C] Prior Consistent Statements (Rule 801(d)(1)(B))

Statutory Elements:

* The declarant testifies at the trial or hearing;

* The declarant is subject to cross-examination concerning the prior statement;

* The prior statement is consistent with the declarant's testimony;

* The statement is offered to rebut an adversary's express or implied charge that the declarant's testimony is recently fabricated or the result of improper influence or motive.

A prior consistent statement consists of a witness' hearsay statement that agrees with or corroborates the same witness' courtroom testimony. While prior *inconsistent* statements are tools for *discrediting* witnesses, prior *consistent* statements are tools for *accrediting or rehabilitating* witnesses.

Example

Millie is testifying against the defendant in a sexual assault case.

PROSECUTOR: Millie, what happened after the defendant offered to give you a ride home?

A: The defendant drove into a basement garage about a mile from the club.

PROSECUTOR: Did you speak to the police after escaping from the defendant's car?

A: I did. I phoned 911 as soon as I could.

PROSECUTOR: And what did you tell the 911 operator?

A: I said that the defendant had offered to drive me home from a club but instead had driven to an underground parking lot.

The last answer constitutes a "prior consistent statement," as Millie offers evidence that in essence asserts that "I said the same thing before trial that I'm saying now."

You might reasonably expect the admissibility of prior consistent statements to be parallel to that of prior inconsistent statements. If it were, prior consistent statements would be generally admissible as non-hearsay to support a witness' credibility, and admissible for their truth under a hearsay exemption if made under oath. However, the common-law treatment of prior consistent and inconsistent statements was not parallel, and the Federal Rules of Evidence continue the non-parallel common-law tradition.

While it is not always consistently applied, the general rule is that in the absence of an attack of the type provided for by Rule 801(d)(1)(B), prior consistent statements are not admissible as non-hearsay to bolster witnesses' credibility. A rationale for this policy is that Rule 403 factors are likely to outweigh the probative value of such statements. For one thing, undue delays would no doubt occur if hearsay rules permitted attorneys to parade in the people to whom witnesses had spoken with before trial, to testify in essence that "what do you know, the witness told me the very same thing." (And if prior consistent statements were generally admissible as non-hearsay, you can bet that lawyers would encourage important witnesses to tell their stories to as many highly credible people as possible.) Thus, the policy generally barring the use of prior consistent statements as non-hearsay to bolster witnesses' credibility is a specialized application of Rule 403. However, in a particular case, the Rule 403 factors may tip in favor of admissibility to bolster credibility when witnesses' out-of-court statements are consistent with their in-court testimony and the Rule 801(d)(1)(B) factors are not present.

Rule 801(d)(1)(B), as interpreted by *Tome v. United States* (*see* Case Library) makes prior consistent statements admissible only if hearsay statements "rebut an express or implied charge . . . that the declarant recently fabricated it or acted from a recent improper influence or motive" when testifying. Rebuttal occurs when the hearsay statements have been made before the time that the improper influence or motive arose. Rule 801(d)(1)(B) does *not* however require that the out-of court consistent statement also be made under oath.

Under Rule 801(d)(1)(B), admission of prior consistent statements normally involves a three-step process:

Step One: A witness (Jones) testifies on behalf of Party A.

Step Two: While cross-examining Jones or through offering extrinsic evidence, Party B charges or implies that Jones has been influenced by an external event, condition, or person to give false or incorrect testimony.

Step Three: Party A offers evidence (either through Jones or extrinsic evidence, usually a witness to whom Jones made the consistent statement) that Jones made a consistent statement at a time before the influence of the external event, condition or person existed.

Thus, as in so much of life, timing is everything under Rule 801(d)(1)(B). The importance of timing is evident in the 5-4 decision of the U.S. Supreme Court in *Tome v. United States*. The defendant in that case was charged with sexually abusing his four-year-old daughter. Tome denied the charges, claiming that his former wife (the girl's mother) had convinced her daughter to make up the sexual abuse stories as a way to gain custody of her. The daughter, only six years old at the time of the trial, testified to the acts of sexual abuse hesitantly and reluctantly. To strengthen its case, the prosecutor called six additional witnesses to testify to statements the daughter had made to them describing Tome's sexual assaults.

The Supreme Court held that the daughter's prior statements were not admissible under Rule 801(d)(1)(B) because her possible motive to testify falsely at trial was no different than at the time she spoke to the other six witnesses. (The Court remanded the case to the lower court for consideration of whether some or all of the girl's pre-trial statements were admissible under the "catch-all" hearsay exception, now Rule 807, or the hearsay exception for "statements for purposes of medical diagnosis," Rule 803(4). To read the lower court's decision upon remand, please see Chapter 14.)

Practice Tip: Check for specialized hearsay exceptions.

A number of states have created "tender years" hearsay exceptions for out-of-court statements such as the daughter's in *Tome* admissible. For example, under **California Evidence Code Section 1360**, a child's hearsay statement is admissible if all of the following foundational elements are shown to exist:

- The statement is offered in a criminal case.

- The child was under 12 years old when the statement was made.

- The statement describes an act or acts of sexual abuse.

- The judge concludes that the statement is reliable.

Problem 12-11: The Howling

Susan Bee sues Elizabeth Cady for personal injuries resulting from an auto accident that occurred two years prior to trial. During direct examination on the issue of damages, Susan testified that, "Ever since the accident, I howl every time there's a full moon." The cross-examination of Susan included the following excerpt:

DEFENSE ATTORNEY: Isn't it true that you decided to claim that you howl at the full moon only after you found out that our

Supreme Court ruled last month that uncontrollable howling was an element of damages in personal injury cases?

A: That's not true.

Under Rule 801(d)(1)(B), can Susan call Harriett Beecher to testify that "Twelve months ago, Susan told me that ever since the auto accident, she howls at every full moon"?

Problem 12-12: Sun Burned

In the same case, Susan calls William Jennings to testify to the speed of Susan's car just prior to the accident. On direct examination, William testified that, "Susan's car was traveling no more than 25 m.p.h. just before the crash." The cross-examination of William included the following excerpt:

DEFENSE ATTORNEY: Didn't you testify at your deposition that the sun was in your eyes and that you couldn't really tell how fast Susan's car was traveling just before the crash?

A: Yes, I did say that.

Under Rule 801(d)(1)(B), can Susan call William's neighbor Harry to testify that in a conversation that Harry had with William a month before William's deposition was taken, William told Harry, "It looked to me that Susan's car was traveling less than 25 m.p.h. at the time of the crash"?

Problem 12-13: Park Place

Defendant Pancho Kramer is charged with sexual assault. Martina Budge testifies on behalf of the prosecution that while taking a walk in the park in which the attack occurred, Budge noticed a gray jacket on the ground underneath a bench near the park's tennis courts. (Assume that this testimony links the defendant to the assault.) A portion of the defense attorney's cross-examination of Budge goes as follows:

DEFENSE ATTORNEY: You walk in the park regularly, correct?

A: Yes, I do.

DEFENSE ATTORNEY: In fact, you've been taking evening walks in the park pretty regularly for the last four to five years, correct?

A: That's true.

DEFENSE ATTORNEY: And you often see articles of clothing lying around the park when you take your walks, don't you?

A: Yes.

DEFENSE ATTORNEY: So it would not be unusual for a gray jacket to be underneath a park bench?

A: No.

DEFENSE ATTORNEY:	You didn't stop walking to go over and take a look at the jacket, did you?
A:	No.
DEFENSE ATTORNEY:	And you can't describe any other articles of clothing that had been left in the park that night, can you?
A:	No, I suppose not.
DEFENSE ATTORNEY:	About five months have gone by since that evening, correct?
A:	That's about right.
DEFENSE ATTORNEY:	Yet you claim that you remember specifically seeing a gray jacket underneath a bench near the tennis courts?
A:	That's what I remember.

Following this questioning, under Rule 801(d)(1)(B), can the prosecution call police officer Nastase to testify that a few days after the assault, Budge voluntarily came into the police station to tell Nastase that Budge had seen a gray jacket lying underneath a bench near the park's tennis courts on the night of the attack? If not, might the police officer's testimony be admitted on any other rationale?

Problem 12-14: Just One More Thing

Dmitri is charged with armed sexual assault of Sean. Armed sexual assault is punishable more heavily than the crime of unarmed sexual assault. During direct examination by the prosecutor, Sean testified that, "On March 1, Dmitri offered me a ride home from the club, drove to a dark basement parking lot instead, and tried to pull my clothes off. I got out of the car and ran away before anything else happened." Defense counsel's cross-examination of Sean included the following excerpt:

DEFENSE ATTORNEY:	Isn't it true that you decided to make up this story only after Dmitri fired you on March 15?
A:	That's not true.

To prove that Dmitri was armed at the time of the assault, the prosecutor seeks to call Police Officer Sakamoto to testify as follows: "On March 3, Sean came into the police station and told me that Dmitri had offered him a ride home but instead had driven to an underground parking lot. Sean told me that Dmitri pulled a knife, pointed it at him with one hand and tried to tear his clothes off with the other. Sean said that he managed to get out of the car and run away before anything else happened."

Would Officer Sakamoto's testimony be admissible as a prior consistent statement under Rule 801(d)(1)(B)?

Problem 12-15: Emot ("Tome" Reversed)

The four dissenters in *Tome v. United States* argued that Rule 801(d)(1)(B) does not contain an explicit timing requirement, and that a prior consistent statement might be relevant to rebut a charge of "recent fabrication" or "improper motive" even if it was made at a time when the same motive existed as at trial. Under their view, the admissibility of a prior consistent statement would be based on general relevance principles, with a judge having the power to exclude a prior consistent statement under Rule 403 if its unfair prejudice outweighed its probative value.

Assume that the Supreme Court overrules *Tome*, or that Congress amends Rule 801(d)(1)(B) so as to adopt the dissenters' approach.

As the prosecutor faced with the facts in Tome, *what argument would you make in an effort to persuade the trial judge to admit the daughter's prior consistent statements on relevance principles?*

As the defense attorney faced with the facts in Tome, *what argument would you make in an effort to persuade the trial judge to exclude the daughter's prior consistent statements under Rule 403?*

[D] Pretrial Identifications (Rule 801(d)(1)(C))

Statutory Elements:

* The declarant testifies at the trial or hearing;

* The declarant is subject to cross-examination concerning the prior statement;

* The prior statement identifies a person;

* The statement was made after the declarant perceived the person.

   This element generally refers to post-crime identifications, such as when a crime victim tells the police than the person pictured in a mug shot was the attacker.

The hearsay exemption for pre-trial identifications is a powerful prosecutorial tool in criminal cases. "Identity" is often the crux of a criminal trial. Yet, weeks or even months may pass between the time that witnesses observe criminal activity and the time that trials occur. The delay can provide defendants with a strong argument that witnesses' in-court identifications are mistaken or worthless. ("Witnesses will identify whoever is seated next to the defense attorney as the perpetrator.") This hearsay exemption allows prosecutors to offer evidence of identifications that are made closer in time to actual events, and therefore perhaps of greater probative value to jurors than in-court identifications.

Witnesses whose prior identifications are admitted in evidence almost always repeat their identifications at trial. Thus, a hearsay statement admitted as a "prior identification" is almost always also a "prior consistent statement," but of a type that is admissible without the intermediate attack on the witness' credibility. However, this is not invariably true. In *United States v. Owens* (*see* Case Library), defendant Owens was a prisoner who was charged with beating a correctional counselor named John Foster with a lead pipe. Foster suffered such severe memory loss that at trial he could remember very little about the attack and could not identify the attacker. However, while in the hospital, Foster told an FBI agent that Owens had attacked him, and Foster also picked out a photo of Owens as his attacker. The Court held that Foster's identification of Owens in the hospital was admissible under Rule 801(d)(1)(C). Though Owens claimed that Foster's mental condition prevented thorough cross-examination, Foster was "subject to cross-examination concerning the statement" and the rule requires nothing more. (In this pre-*Crawford* case, the Court also decided that Owens' opportunity for cross-examination satisfied the Confrontation Clause.)

Example

In the made-for-TV movie *Criminal Justice*,[2] an assailant slashes Denise Moore's face and takes the small amount of cash that she was carrying. Moore describes her attacker to the police as follows: "Male, Black, mid-20s, 6' 1," 220 pounds, dark skin, short hair." Moore then looks though mug shots, holds up a photograph of Jessie Williams, and tells the police officers: "This is him . . . this is the guy, except he had sort of a rough beard . . . I'm sure this is him." The police officers arrest Williams the next day and put him in a lineup. Viewing the lineup, Moore says that "It's Number 4 (Williams) . . . he's the one that cut me. I'm sure." Sometime later, Moore testifies during grand jury indictment proceedings that Williams is the person who slashed her face and robbed her. Each of these out-of-court statements by Moore constitutes a prior identification that is potentially admissible under Rule 801(d)(1)(C).

Practice Tip: A judge may exclude one or more "prior identifications."

When a prosecutor seeks to offer several "prior identifications" into evidence in the same case, a defense attorney may argue that the judge should exclude one or more of the out-of-court identifications under Rule 403. For example, because an identification of a mug shot suggests that a defendant has a criminal record, a judge may exclude evidence of a mug shot identification as unfairly prejudicial. Moreover, multiple prior identifications may consume an unwarranted amount of time. Thus, prior identifications may be exempt from the hearsay rule but be excluded for other reasons.

Should it matter how much time elapses between an event and an out-of-court identification? Cf. California's version of Rule 801(d)(1)(C), Cal. Evid. Code § 1238. Section 1238 includes a foundational requirement that the out-of-court identification be made "at a time when the crime or other occurrence was fresh in the witness' memory."

---

[2] Home Box Office 1990.

Problem 12-16: Bagged

Reina, who is blind, grabs the arm of a thief who had just wrenched her purse off her arm. Reina yells for help, and holds on to the thief until a police officer arrives. Reina tells the officer that the person she is holding onto is the one who tried to steal her purse. The thief is charged with robbery. At trial, Reina describes the attempted theft of her purse but cannot identify the defendant as the robber. The police officer identifies the defendant as the person who was in Reina's grasp. The police officer also seeks to testify that when the officer handed Reina the purse that the suspect had been holding, Reina stated, "Yes, this is my purse." *Under Rule 801(d)(1)(C), can the police officer testify that (a) "Reina told me that the person whose arm she was holding onto was the person who had grabbed her purse;" and that (b) "Reina told me that the purse that I took out of the suspect's hands and placed in her hand was her purse?"*

Problem 12-17: Hitting a Brick Wall

Edna Cleary testifies for the prosecution in a case in which McCormick is charged with grand theft of bricks that were sufficient in number to build a wall. After eliciting testimony from Cleary that she watched the theft unfold from an office window, the prosecutor elicits the following testimony from Cleary:

PROSECUTOR: Do you see the individual who loaded the bricks into the bed of his truck here in the courtroom?

A: No.

PROSECUTOR: Calling your attention to the defendant McCormick, seated next to defense counsel, can you tell us whether the defendant is the person you saw loading the bricks into the truck bed?

A: He is definitely not the person who took the bricks.

Following this testimony, the prosecutor calls Chad Bourne as a witness. Bourne's testimony goes as follows:

PROSECUTOR: Mr. Bourne, do you know Edna Cleary, the witness who just testified?

A: I do. We work together.

PROSECUTOR: And calling your attention to Dec. 2, a week after the charged theft, were you and Ms. Cleary at work that day?

A: We were.

PROSECUTOR: Please tell us what took place between Ms. Cleary and you at approximately 10 AM on that date.

A: Sure. Our desks are just a few feet apart. Ms. Cleary called me over and pointed to her computer screen and said, "Look at this- there's a photo of the guy who stole the bricks last week."

PROSECUTOR: Did you look at the photo she pointed to?

A: I did.

PROSECUTOR: And do you recognize anyone here in court as the person depicted in that photo?

A: Yes, it was the defendant, seated over there (pointing to McCormick).

Defense attorney objects on the ground that Cleary's in-court denial that McCormick was the person who committed the theft means that the pre-trial identification of McCormick is inadmissible. Defense counsel further objects that as Cleary's statement to Bourne is hearsay, Bourne's testimony is improper. *How should the judge rule on these objections? Would the prosecutor be better off offering Cleary's statement to Bourne into evidence as a prior inconsistent statement under Rule 801(d)(1)(A) rather than as a prior identification under Rule 801(d)(1)(C)?*

Problem 12-18: Lengthy Rivalry

Capulet is charged with attempted murder. The charges result from a savage beating that Capulet allegedly administered to Montague, a member of a rival street gang. Montague suffered severe and permanent memory loss. Asked to describe what happened at trial, Montague testifies that he remembers two men hitting him and that it was dark. He cannot recall other details of the attack nor can he identify either attacker. He recalls being in a hospital room for many days, but doesn't remember speaking to anyone while he was there. The prosecutor then makes an offer of proof that Dr. Ophelia Tybalt will testify that she provided medical care for Montague while he was in the hospital. When Montague was well enough to talk a few days after the attack, Dr. Tybalt spoke to him for a few minutes about where he was and why he was there. At one point Dr. Tybalt asked Montague how he had gotten hurt, and he answered, "It was Capulet and someone else." Dr. Tybalt asked him about the attack on a few other occasions, but Montague could say nothing more about it than he testified to in court. *Can Dr. Tybalt testify to the above information under Rule 801(d)(1)(C)? Would allowing Dr. Tybalt to testify be consistent with the principles underlying the Confrontation Clause as interpreted by* Crawford *(see Chapter 10)?*

Problem 12-19: The Lineup

Arnold Kim is charged with armed robbery of a jewelry store; the defense is an alibi. Wigmore, the store owner, later identifies the defendant in a lineup as the person who robbed her at gunpoint.

1. On the morning of trial, Wigmore calls the prosecutor and says, "I'm calling you from Bermuda. I'm not coming to court, I got an email message from someone stating that he was a friend of Kim and that if I identify Kim as the robber in court I'm a goner. I've heard too many stories of government witnesses suddenly going missing." *Can the prosecutor offer Wigmore's lineup identification into evidence under Rule 801(d)(1)(C)?*

2. Assume that Wigmore is prepared to identify Kim at trial as the robber. Prior to trial, Kim's attorney submits a motion *in limine* asking the trial judge to rule that because the police employed improper lineup procedures, Wigmore should not be allowed to identify the defendant in court and her lineup identification of the

defendant should not be admitted. The defense bases the motion on the case of *Neil v. Biggers*,³ in which the U.S. Supreme Court ruled that a defendant can suppress both a witness' in-court and pre-trial identifications if police procedures were so suggestive as to create a substantial likelihood of misidentification. The judge schedules a foundational hearing ("mini-trial") on the issue of the propriety of the lineup procedures. A partial transcript of that hearing reads as follows:

PROSECUTOR: And after viewing the lineup, Wigmore, were you able to identify the person who robbed you at gunpoint?

A: Yes, I did make an identification.

PROSECUTOR: And who did you point out as the robber?

A: That man over there (pointing to the defendant).

PROSECUTOR: And is it your testimony here today that the defendant is the person who robbed you in the jewelry store at gunpoint?

A: Yes.

PROSECUTOR: No further foundational questions, Your Honor. I ask that you rule that Wigmore can testify to the lineup identification and also that he be allowed to testify to the defendant's identity at trial if possible.

JUDGE: Defense may inquire.

DEFENSE ATTORNEY: Thank you, Your Honor. Wigmore, when you viewed the six people in the lineup, you initially told the police officer that you weren't sure that you recognized any of them as the robber, is that right?

A: That's true.

DEFENSE ATTORNEY: The officer then asked you to look very carefully, and told you that it was important that you identify someone if you could?

A: Yes, the officer did say that.

DEFENSE ATTORNEY: And after again studying everyone in the lineup, you again told the officer that you couldn't be sure if the robber was amongst them?

A: That's right.

DEFENSE ATTORNEY: And the police officer then asked you to look very carefully at Suspect # 3?

A: Yes.

DEFENSE ATTORNEY: The officer further mentioned that Suspect # 3 closely matched the description you gave of the robber just moments after the robbery?

A: The officer did say something like that.

---

³ 409 U.S. 188, 93 S. Ct. 375, 34 L. Ed. 2d 401 (1972).

DEFENSE ATTORNEY:	And after this you said that the officer was right, that Suspect # 3 was the robber?
A:	Yes.
DEFENSE ATTORNEY:	And Suspect # 3 is the defendant, the person you're prepared to identify here today as the robber?
A:	Yes.
DEFENSE ATTORNEY:	Isn't it true that your recollection of Mr. Kim today is based entirely on having seen him at the lineup?
A:	No. I recognize him from the robbery.
DEFENSE ATTORNEY:	Yet when you first saw Mr. Kim in the lineup, just a week after the robbery, you told the officer that you weren't sure if the robber was in the lineup?
A:	That's true, I was nervous.
DEFENSE ATTORNEY:	Yet now you're certain that Mr. Kim was the robber?
A:	Yes, quite certain.
DEFENSE ATTORNEY:	No further questions.
JUDGE:	Prosecution, anything further?
PROSECUTOR:	Thank you, Your Honor, just briefly. Wigmore, did you identify the defendant as the robber because the police officer told you to?
A:	No.
PROSECUTOR:	As you sit in this courtroom now, do have in your mind a clear picture of the person who robbed your store?
A:	Yes.
PROSECUTOR:	And do you see that person here in the courtroom?
A:	Yes, it's him, seated over there (indicating the defendant).
PROSECUTOR:	No further foundational questions, Your Honor.
JUDGE:	If that concludes the foundational evidence, I'll hear briefly from counsel before ruling on the defense motion.

Student # 1: As the defense attorney, argue in support of the motion *in limine.* Be sure to mention which side has the burden of proof on the foundational issue, and what that burden consists of.

Student # 2: As the prosecutor, argue in support of the admissibility of the pre-trial and in-court identifications.

Student # 3: As the judge, rule on the admissibility of the pre-trial and in-court identifications.

Problem 12-20: At the Movies: Turncoat

In the film *Knock on Any Door*,[4] Nick Romano is charged with murdering a policeman while attempting to escape after robbing a bar. The defense is an alibi. The prosecutor calls Juan Rodriguez, Romano's friend, expecting Rodriguez to testify that he saw Romano shoot the officer. However, Rodriguez testifies that he is unable to remember anything that happened on the night of the robbery/murder. The prosecutor then reads a statement that Rodriguez admits that he gave to the police, in which Rodriguez states that he saw Romano kill the policeman. *Is Rodriguez's out-of-court statement to the police admissible as a prior inconsistent statement? As a prior identification?*

Problem 12-21: At the Movies: Better Late Than Never

In the film *Destination Murder*,[5] Laura Mansfield witnesses her father's murder. She views a lineup, but tells the police that she can't identify any of the lineup participants (one of whom is Jackie Wales) as the murderer. Assume that Laura eventually testifies at Wales's trial that she saw him kill her father. *Can the defense offer the statement that Laura made to the police at the lineup into evidence under Rule 801(d)(1)(C)?*

Problem 12-22: Statutory Interpretation Process

ASSIGNMENT: Please prepare outside of class a brief (3-5 single-spaced pages, double-spacing between paragraphs) set of answers to the questions below concerning the *Tome* case. (The case is in the Case Library for this chapter.)

Questions to consider:

1. *Text:* How did the Court use the text of Rule 801(d)(1)(B) in reaching its decision? How did it use what was missing from the text, that is, the text's silence about certain things, and why would such silence matter? Why was text (or its absence) relevant, and what weight did the Court give to the text? Was the Court able to assign meaning to text in isolation from other data sources, or was text given meaning only in conjunction with other data sources? If the latter, what other data sources and why?

2. *Audience:* Whom does the Court assume are the readers of the Rules' text, that is, who constitutes the interpretive community? What are the characteristics of this community's members? Is the community a real one or an idealized one? Why did the Court choose to assume this particular interpretive community, and what is its significance concerning the case's outcome and reasoning?

3. *"Precedent":* What use did the Court make of common law precedent and why? Of academic commentary at the time that the Rules were adopted? Did the commentary serve the same role as did common law precedent or some other function?

4. *Advisory Committee Notes:* What use or uses did the Court make of the

---

[4] Columbia Pictures, 1949.
[5] RKO Radio Pictures, 1950.

Advisory Committee Notes? Was the Court using the Notes to divine legislative "intent" or legislative "purpose" (and what is the difference?) or to serve some other or additional function? Does legislative intent (or purpose) settle the interpretive question before the Court or is it but one data source among others? What weight does the Court give legislative intent (or purpose) and why? Why does the Court rely on the Advisory Committee Notes without even considering the more detailed legislative history in the Bailey and Trelles treatise?

5. *Judicial Discretion:* What is the significance of judicial discretion to the Court's task? Is the Court concerned about legislative intent (or purpose) and, if so, in what way, if any, is the concern here different from that in its discussion of the Advisory Committee Notes? Is the Court concerned about the future impact on the truth-finding or other evidentiary processes of its attitude toward judicial discretion?

6. *Other Opinions:* Ask yourselves the same questions above but concerning Justice Scalia's partial concurrence and Justice Breyer's dissent. How and why do these opinions answer any or all of the above questions differently from the majority? Are each of the Justices being completely candid about what it is they are doing and why? Is candor a desirable goal in opinions interpreting statutes or codes? Are there any data sources in addition to the ones above that either Scalia, Breyer, or both rely on but the majority does not? Do Scalia and Breyer, respectively, give different weight to the above data sources than does the majority? What weight and why?

7. *Narrative:* What narrative does the Court tell about the Rule? The circumstances bringing it about? Congress?

8. *Candor:* Is there a difference between what each opinion claims to be using as its approach to statutory interpretation and what it is in fact doing?

Problem 12-23: Transcript Exercise

Will Lee Sutton is charged with armed bank robbery; robbery is the taking of property by means of force or fear. The defense is an alibi. The transcript excerpt below consists of the testimony of prosecution witness Hank Teller. Please respond to the italicized portions of the transcript.

PROSECUTOR: And then what happened?

A: The next thing I knew this guy had handed me a note. The note said "Don't look up. I've got a gub — I took it to mean gun — give me all your money."

DEFENSE ATTORNEY: Objection to the contents of the note as hearsay.

JUDGE: Overruled. (*Is this ruling correct?*)

PROSECUTOR: After handing you the note, did he say anything to you?

DEFENSE ATTORNEY: Objection, leading.

JUDGE: (*What ruling?*)

A: Yes. He said to hurry it up and if I didn't he'd blow my head off.

DEFENSE ATTORNEY: Objection, hearsay.

PROSECUTOR: Not offered for the truth, Your Honor. (*What non-hearsay purpose might the prosecutor identify?*)

PROSECUTOR: Then what happened?

A: I did what he said: took money out of my cash drawer and gave it to him. I also pushed a hidden emergency button with my knee.

PROSECUTOR: This button activates an alarm of some sort?

DEFENSE ATTORNEY: (*Can you legitimately object to this leading question?*)

A: Yes, a silent alarm in the bank's security office.

PROSECUTOR: Did you have a pretty good opportunity to observe the robber's face?

DEFENSE ATTORNEY: (*What objection, if any?*)

A: Yes. Even though he said not to, I looked up just as he grabbed the bills and turned to run away.

PROSECUTOR: Please describe what you saw of the robber's face.

A: He had bushy eyebrows, dark eyes, a longish nose, and kind of a sallow complexion.

PROSECUTOR: Is that person the defendant, seated at counsel table?

DEFENSE ATTORNEY: (*What objection, if any?*)

A: Yes.

PROSECUTOR: What happened when the security guard returned from her break?

DEFENSE ATTORNEY: (*What objection, if any?*)

A: Wendy Friedman, our chief security officer, got there about a minute after the robbery. I gave her a description of the robber.

PROSECUTOR: And was the description you gave to Ms. Friedman essentially what you've just testified to?

A: Yes.

DEFENSE ATTORNEY: Objection and move to strike, hearsay.

JUDGE: (*What ruling?*)

DEFENSE ATTORNEY: Also object and move to strike, improper conclusion.

JUDGE: (*What ruling?*)

PROSECUTOR: What happened next?

A: I closed my teller window and went downstairs to the employee's lounge, and talked to a couple of police officers about the robbery. Then one of them got a phone call and asked me to accompany him to the security office, because a suspect had been apprehended and they wanted to know if I could identify him.

§ 12.06   TESTIFYING WITNESSES' PRIOR STATEMENTS   577

DEFENSE ATTORNEY: Objection to what the phone caller said to the police officer, hearsay.

JUDGE: (*What ruling?*)

PROSECUTOR: Did you go to the security office?

A: I did.

PROSECUTOR: And what happened when you arrived there?

A: As soon as I saw him, I said, "that's him, that's the robber." *Is this testimony admissible?* PROSECUTOR: Besides Ms. Friedman, the police officers and the suspect, was anyone else in the security office?

A: Yes, Ann Teeyem, who was the teller at the next window at the time of the robbery, was also there. I noticed that she was looking at the defendant as he ran out of the bank.

PROSECUTOR: And what if anything did you hear Ms. Teeyem say in the security office?

A: She said that I was correct, that the suspect was the robber.

DEFENSE ATTORNEY: *What if any objection?*

PROSECUTOR: No further questions of this witness at this time.

JUDGE: Defense counsel may inquire.

DEFENSE ATTORNEY: Mr. Teller, isn't it true that just after the robbery, you told Ms. Teeyem that you wished that you had gotten a longer look at the robber's face?

PROSECUTOR: Objection on two grounds. The question is leading, and constitutes improper impeachment because the witness' statement to Ms. Teeyem was not made under oath and does not directly contradict the witness' testimony.

JUDGE: Overruled as to all grounds. (*Is this ruling correct?*)

A: I did say that.

DEFENSE ATTORNEY: Mr. Teller, when you spoke to Ms. Friedman after the robbery, you didn't say anything about the robber having bushy eyebrows, did you?

A: It's possible that I didn't mention that; I was pretty nervous.

DEFENSE ATTORNEY: You decided to say that only after the police officers brought the defendant to the bank and you saw that he had bushy eyebrows, isn't that right?

A: No, I realized from the outset that he had bushy eyebrows.

DEFENSE ATTORNEY: You were robbed a couple of years ago while working as a teller in a different bank, correct?

A: Yes.

DEFENSE ATTORNEY: And isn't it true that the jury acquitted the defendant who was charged with committing that bank robbery even though you testified that the defendant was the robber?

PROSECUTOR: (*What if any objection might you make to this question?*)

A: Yes.

DEFENSE ATTORNEY: Mr. Teller, the bank conducted a training exercise about three months before the robbery in which bank employees were shown videotapes of bank robberies and were later asked to pick the robbers out of lineups, correct?

A: Yes, that's true.

DEFENSE ATTORNEY: Isn't it also true that you misidentified the robber 40% of the time, which was reported to you as one of the highest incidences of misidentification amongst all the employees?

PROSECUTOR: Objection, irrelevant and misleading under Rule 403. Also object as hearsay.

JUDGE: (*What ruling on these objections?*)

A: That's true. But I'm correct now.

DEFENSE ATTORNEY: You expect the jury to believe that you're more likely to be accurate when you're facing the wrong end of a gun than when you're in a comfortable employees' lounge watching videotapes?

PROSECUTOR: (*What if any objection?*)

A: I can only tell you what I saw.

DEFENSE ATTORNEY: Mr. Teller, isn't it true that over the last 10 years you've used illegal drugs heavily and have been in and out of drug rehabilitation programs?

PROSECUTOR: (*What if any objection?*)

A: That's correct.

DEFENSE ATTORNEY: And finally, you were convicted of spousal abuse six months ago, isn't that right?

PROSECUTOR: Objection, improper character evidence.

JUDGE: (*Assuming that the defense attorney can demonstrate that the conviction occurred, will you allow the question?*)

DEFENSE ATTORNEY: No further questions.

JUDGE: Prosecutor, any further questions of this witness?

PROSECUTOR: Just briefly, Your Honor, thank you. Mr. Teller, did you speak to Ms. Teeyem before the police arrived?

A: I did.

PROSECUTOR: And did you describe the robber to her?

A: Yes I did.

PROSECUTOR: And what did you tell her?

A: I know I told her that the robber had bushy eyebrows.

DEFENSE ATTORNEY: Objection, hearsay.

JUDGE: Overruled, on the ground that it's admissible both as a prior identification and as a prior consistent statement. (*Is this ruling correct?*)

§ 12.07 MULTIPLE-CHOICE REVIEW PROBLEMS

Review Problem 12-A

Sara Jane, who had been a fugitive from justice for 25 years, is arrested and tried for attempted murder for planting a car bomb under a police car. Three days after the bombing, Lee identified Jane as the bomber after looking through photos and selecting the photo depicting Jane. At Jane's trial 25 years later, Lee testifies that "I'm sorry, it's been so long ago that I just can't remember whether Jane is the person who I saw plant the bomb." *Which of the following statements is accurate?*

1. The prosecution can offer evidence of Lee's photo identification to prove that Jane was the bomber.

2. The prosecution can offer evidence of Lee's photo identification as a prior inconsistent statement to prove that Jane was the bomber.

3. The prosecution can offer evidence of Lee's photo identification as a prior consistent statement to prove that Jane was the bomber.

4. The prosecution cannot offer evidence of Lee's photo identification.

Review Problem 12-B

In a slip-and-fall case filed by plaintiffs Ben and Anna Peel against a department store for damages including loss of consortium, Ben testifies that he tripped on loose carpeting in the store's sportswear department. Ben seeks to testify that "While I was being treated in the emergency room, I told a nurse that I had tripped on loose carpeting." Ben's statement to the nurse is:

1. Admissible as a prior consistent statement not for its truth, but for the non-hearsay purpose of corroborating Ben's credibility.

2. Inadmissible as a prior consistent statement because the statement to the nurse was not made under oath.

3. Admissible as a prior consistent statement after Ben admits during cross-examination that he lost his job a month after the accident and needs money to pay family bills.

4. Admissible as a prior consistent statement after the defense attorney asks Ben on cross-examination, "Isn't it true that you falsified your personal statement when you applied to law schools?" (Ben denied having done this.)

5. Admissible as a prior consistent statement after Ben admits during cross-examination that after being treated in the emergency room, he told the friend who drove him home that "I'm not really sure why I fell."

Review Problem 12-C

Josh is charged with distribution of cocaine. At trial, Jenni testifies for the government under a grant of immunity that she bought a package of what was later determined to be cocaine from Josh. On cross-examination, Josh's attorney asks Jenni, "Didn't you previously say that Jerry and not Josh was the person from whom you bought the cocaine?" Which of the following statements is accurate?

1. Jenni's prior statement is admissible to prove that Jerry was the cocaine seller if it was made under oath during grand jury proceedings.

2. Jenni's prior statement is admissible only for its truth and not to impeach her credibility as a witness if it was made under oath during grand jury proceedings.

3. Jenni's prior statement is inadmissible unless it was made under oath.

4. Jenni's prior statement is admissible as a prior inconsistent statement to prove that Jerry was the cocaine seller if it was made to the police shortly after they arrested her for possession of cocaine.

Review Problem 12-D

At trial, government witness Sarah points to the defendant Robertson as the person she saw take money at gunpoint. During cross-examination, the defense attorney seeks to elicit testimony from Sarah that when she attended a lineup that included Robertson a few days after the robbery, she told a police officer that "I don't think that any of these people are the robber." Sarah's statement to the police officer is:

1. Inadmissible because Sarah was uncertain as to whether the robber was in the lineup.

2. Admissible under Rule 801(d)(1)(C) for the purpose of proving that the person she saw commit the robbery was not in the lineup.

3. Inadmissible because Sarah was not under oath at the time she spoke to the police officer.

4. Admissible as non-hearsay for the purpose of casting doubt on Sarah's in-court identification.

§ 12.08 CASE LIBRARY

TOME v. UNITED STATES

United States Supreme Court 513 U.S. 150, 115 S. Ct. 696, 130 L. Ed. 2d 574
(1995)

JUDGES: KENNEDY, J., announced the judgment of the Court and delivered the opinion of the Court with respect to Parts I, II-A, II-C, and III, in which STEVENS, SCALIA, SOUTER, AND GINSBURG, JJ., joined, and an opinion with respect to Part II-B, in which STEVENS, SOUTER, AND GINSBURG, JJ., joined. SCALIA, J., filed an opinion concurring in part and concurring in the judgment. BREYER, J., filed a dissenting opinion, in which REHNQUIST, C. J., and O'CONNOR AND THOMAS, JJ., joined.

JUSTICE KENNEDY delivered the opinion of the Court, except as to Section II-B.

Various Federal Courts of Appeals are divided over the evidence question presented by this case. At issue is the interpretation of a provision in the Federal Rules of Evidence bearing upon the admissibility of statements, made by a declarant who testifies as a witness, that are consistent with the testimony and are offered to rebut a charge of a "recent fabrication or improper influence or motive." Fed. Rule Evid. 801(d)(1)(B). The question is whether out-of-court consistent statements made after the alleged fabrication, or after the alleged improper influence or motive arose, are admissible under the Rule.

I.

Petitioner Tome was charged in a one-count indictment with the felony of sexual abuse of a child, his own daughter, aged four at the time of the alleged crime. The case having arisen on the Navajo Indian Reservation, Tome was tried by a jury in the United States District Court for the District of New Mexico, where he was found guilty of violating 18 U.S.C. §§ 1153, 2241(c), and 2245(2)(A) and (B).

Tome and the child's mother had been divorced in 1988. A tribal court awarded joint custody of the daughter, A.T., to both parents, but Tome had primary physical custody. In 1989 the mother was unsuccessful in petitioning the tribal court for primary custody of A.T., but was awarded custody for the summer of 1990. Neither parent attended a further custody hearing in August 1990. On August 27, 1990, the mother contacted Colorado authorities with allegations that Tome had committed sexual abuse against A.T.

The prosecution's theory was that Tome committed sexual assaults upon the child while she was in his custody and that the crime was disclosed when the child was spending vacation time with her mother. The defense argued that the allegations were concocted so the child would not be returned to her father. At trial A.T., then 6 1/2 years old, was the Government's first witness. For the most part, her direct testimony consisted of one-and two-word answers to a series of leading questions. Cross-examination took place over two trial days. The defense asked A.T. 348

questions. On the first day A.T. answered all the questions posed to her on general, background subjects.

The next day there was no testimony, and the prosecutor met with A.T. When cross-examination of A.T. resumed, she was questioned about those conversations but was reluctant to discuss them. Defense counsel then began questioning her about the allegations of abuse, and it appears she was reluctant at many points to answer. As the trial judge noted, however, some of the defense questions were imprecise or unclear. The judge expressed his concerns with the examination of A.T., observing there were lapses of as much as 40–55 seconds between some questions and the answers and that on the second day of examination the witness seemed to be losing concentration. The trial judge stated, "We have a very difficult situation here."

After A.T. testified, the Government produced six witnesses who testified about a total of seven statements made by A.T. describing the alleged sexual assaults: A.T.'s babysitter recited A.T.'s statement to her on August 22, 1990, that she did not want to return to her father because he "gets drunk and he thinks I'm his wife"; the babysitter related further details given by A.T. on August 27, 1990, while A.T.'s mother stood outside the room and listened after the mother had been unsuccessful in questioning A.T. herself; the mother recounted what she had heard A.T. tell the babysitter; a social worker recounted details A.T. told her on August 29, 1990, about the assaults; and three pediatricians, Drs. Kuper, Reich, and Spiegel, related A.T.'s statements to them describing how and where she had been touched by Tome. All but A.T.'s statement to Dr. Spiegel implicated Tome. (The physicians also testified that their clinical examinations of the child indicated that she had been subjected to vaginal penetrations. That part of the testimony is not at issue here.)

A.T.'s out-of-court statements, recounted by the six witnesses, were offered by the Government under Rule 801(d)(1)(B). The trial court admitted all of the statements over defense counsel's objection, accepting the Government's argument that they rebutted the implicit charge that A.T.'s testimony was motivated by a desire to live with her mother. The court also admitted A.T.'s August 22d statement to her babysitter under Rule 803(24), and the statements to Dr. Kuper (and apparently also to Dr. Reich) under Rule 803(4) (statements for purposes of medical diagnosis). The Government offered the testimony of the social worker under both Rules 801(d)(1)(B) and 803(24), but the record does not indicate whether the court ruled on the latter ground. No objection was made to Dr. Spiegel's testimony. Following trial, Tome was convicted and sentenced to 12 years' imprisonment.

On appeal, the Court of Appeals for the Tenth Circuit affirmed, adopting the Government's argument that all of A.T.'s out-of-court statements were admissible under Rule 801(d)(1)(B) even though they had been made after A.T.'s alleged motive to fabricate arose . . .

We granted certiorari, and now reverse.

II

The prevailing common-law rule for more than a century before adoption of the Federal Rules of Evidence was that a prior consistent statement introduced to rebut a charge of recent fabrication or improper influence or motive was admissible if the statement had been made before the alleged fabrication, influence, or motive came into being, but it was inadmissible if made afterwards . . . McCormick and Wigmore stated the rule in a more categorical manner: "The applicable principle is that the prior consistent statement has no relevancy to refute the charge unless the consistent statement was made before the source of the bias, interest, influence or incapacity originated." . . . The question is whether Rule 801(d)(1)(B) embodies this temporal requirement. We hold that it does.

A

Rule 801 defines prior consistent statements as nonhearsay only if they are offered to rebut a charge of "recent fabrication or improper influence or motive." Noting the "troublesome" logic of treating a witness' prior consistent statements as hearsay at all (because the declarant is present in court and subject to cross-examination), the Advisory Committee decided to treat those consistent statements, once the preconditions of the Rule were satisfied, as nonhearsay and admissible as substantive evidence, not just to rebut an attack on the witness' credibility. A prior consistent statement meeting the requirements of the Rule is thus placed in the same category as a declarant's inconsistent statement made under oath in another proceeding, or prior identification testimony, or admissions by a party opponent.

The Rules do not accord this weighty, nonhearsay status to all prior consistent statements. To the contrary, admissibility under the Rules is confined to those statements offered to rebut a charge of "recent fabrication or improper influence or motive," the same phrase used by the Advisory Committee in its description of the "traditional" common law of evidence, which was the background against which the Rules were drafted. Prior consistent statements may not be admitted to counter all forms of impeachment or to bolster the witness merely because she has been discredited. In the present context, the question is whether A.T.'s out-of-court statements rebutted the alleged link between her desire to be with her mother and her testimony, not whether they suggested that A.T.'s in-court testimony was true. The Rule speaks of a party rebutting an alleged motive, not bolstering the veracity of the story told.

This limitation is instructive, not only to establish the preconditions of admissibility but also to reinforce the significance of the requirement that the consistent statements must have been made before the alleged influence, or motive to fabricate, arose. That is to say, the forms of impeachment within the Rule's coverage are the ones in which the temporal requirement makes the most sense. Impeachment by charging that the testimony is a recent fabrication or results from an improper influence or motive is, as a general matter, capable of direct and forceful refutation through introduction of out-of-court consistent statements that predate the alleged fabrication, influence, or motive. A consistent statement that predates the motive is a square rebuttal of the charge that the testimony was contrived as a consequence of that motive. By contrast, prior consistent statements carry little rebuttal force when most other types of impeachment are involved.

There may arise instances when out-of-court statements that postdate the alleged fabrication have some probative force in rebutting a charge of fabrication or improper influence or motive, but those statements refute the charged fabrication in a less direct and forceful way. Evidence that a witness made consistent statements after the alleged motive to fabricate arose may suggest in some degree that the in-court testimony is truthful, and thus suggest in some degree that that testimony did not result from some improper influence; but if the drafters of Rule 801(d)(1)(B) intended to countenance rebuttal along that indirect inferential chain, the purpose of confining the types of impeachment that open the door to rebuttal by introducing consistent statements becomes unclear. If consistent statements are admissible without reference to the timeframe we find imbedded in the Rule, there appears no sound reason not to admit consistent statements to rebut other forms of impeachment as well. Whatever objections can be leveled against limiting the Rule to this designated form of impeachment and confining the rebuttal to those statements made before the fabrication or improper influence or motive arose, it is clear to us that the drafters of Rule 801(d)(1)(B) were relying upon the common-law temporal requirement.

The underlying theory of the Government's position is that an out-of-court consistent statement, whenever it was made, tends to bolster the testimony of a witness and so tends also to rebut an express or implied charge that the testimony has been the product of an improper influence. Congress could have adopted that rule with ease, providing, for instance, that "a witness' prior consistent statements are admissible whenever relevant to assess the witness' truthfulness or accuracy." The theory would be that, in a broad sense, any prior statement by a witness concerning the disputed issues at trial would have some relevance in assessing the accuracy or truthfulness of the witness' in-court testimony on the same subject. The narrow Rule enacted by Congress, however, cannot be understood to incorporate the Government's theory.

The language of the Rule, in its concentration on rebutting charges of recent fabrication or improper influence or motive to the exclusion of other forms of impeachment, as well as in its use of wording that follows the language of the common-law cases, suggests that it was intended to carry over the common-law pre-motive rule.

C.

The Government's final argument in favor of affirmance is that the common-law pre-motive rule advocated by petitioner is inconsistent with the Federal Rules' liberal approach to relevancy and with strong academic criticism, beginning in the 1940's, directed at the exclusion of out-of-court statements made by a declarant who is present in court and subject to cross-examination. This argument misconceives the design of the Rules' hearsay provisions.

Hearsay evidence is often relevant. "The only way in which the probative force of hearsay differs from the probative force of other testimony is in the absence of oath, demeanor, and cross-examination as aids in determining credibility." That does not resolve the matter, however. Relevance is not the sole criterion of admissibility. Otherwise, it would be difficult to account for the Rules' general proscription of hearsay testimony (absent a specific exception), let alone the traditional analysis of hearsay that the Rules, for the most part, reflect. ("The approach to hearsay in these rules is that of the common law . . . . The traditional hearsay exceptions are drawn upon for the exceptions . . ."). That certain out-of-court statements may be relevant does not dispose of the question whether they are admissible.

The Government's reliance on academic commentators critical of excluding out-of-court statements by a witness is subject to like criticism. To be sure, certain commentators in the years preceding the adoption of the Rules had been critical of the common-law approach to hearsay, particularly its categorical exclusion of out-of-court statements offered for substantive purposes. General criticism was directed to the exclusion of a declarant's out-of-court statements where the declarant testified at trial. As an alternative, they suggested moving away from the categorical exclusion of hearsay and toward a case-by-case balancing of the probative value of particular statements against their likely prejudicial effect. The Advisory Committee, however, was explicit in rejecting this balancing approach to hearsay: "The Advisory Committee has rejected this approach to hearsay as involving too great a measure of judicial discretion, minimizing the predictability of rulings, [and] enhancing the difficulties of preparation for trial." Given the Advisory Committee's rejection of both the general balancing approach to hearsay and of Uniform Rule 63(1) the Government's reliance on the views of those who advocated these positions is misplaced.

D

The case before us illustrates some of the important considerations supporting the Rule as we interpret it, especially in criminal cases. If the Rule were to permit the introduction of prior statements as substantive evidence to rebut every implicit charge that a witness' in-court testimony results from recent fabrication or improper influence or motive, the whole emphasis of the trial could shift to the out-of-court statements, not the in-court ones. The present case illustrates the point. In response to a rather weak charge that A.T.'s testimony was a fabrication created so the child could remain with her mother, the Government was permitted to present a parade of sympathetic and credible witnesses who did no more than recount A.T.'s detailed out-of-court statements to them. Although those statements might have been probative on the question whether the alleged conduct had occurred, they shed but minimal light on whether A.T. had the charged motive to fabricate. At closing argument before the jury, the Government placed great reliance on the prior statements for substantive purposes but did not once seek to use them to rebut the impact of the alleged motive.

We are aware that in some cases it may be difficult to ascertain when a particular fabrication, influence, or motive arose. Yet, as the Government concedes, a majority of common-law courts were performing this task for well over a century, and the Government has presented us with no evidence that those courts, or the judicial circuits that adhere to the rule today, have been unable to make the determination. Even under the Government's hypothesis, moreover, the thing to be rebutted must be identified, so the date of its origin cannot be that much more difficult to ascertain. By contrast, as the Advisory Committee commented, see the Government's approach, which would require the trial court to weigh all of the circumstances surrounding a statement that suggest its probativeness against the court's assessment of the strength of the alleged motive, would entail more of a burden, with no guidance to attorneys in preparing a case or to appellate courts in reviewing a judgment.

III

Courts must be sensitive to the difficulties attendant upon the prosecution of alleged child abusers. In almost all cases a youth is the prosecution's only eye witness. But "this Court cannot alter evidentiary rules merely because litigants might prefer different rules in a particular class of cases." When a party seeks to introduce out-of-court statements that contain strong circumstantial indicia of reliability, that are highly probative on the material questions at trial, and that are better than other evidence otherwise available, there is no need to distort the requirements of Rule 801(d)(1)(B). If its requirements are met, Rule 803(24) exists for that eventuality. We intimate no view, however, concerning the admissibility of any of A.T.'s out-of-court statements under that section, or any other evidentiary principle. These matters, and others, are for the Court of Appeals to decide in the first instance.

Our holding is confined to the requirements for admission under Rule 801(d)(1)(B). The Rule permits the introduction of a declarant's consistent out-of-court statements to rebut a charge of recent fabrication or improper influence or motive only when those statements were made before the charged recent fabrication or improper influence or motive. These conditions of admissibility were not established here.

The judgment of the Court of Appeals for the Tenth Circuit is reversed, and the case is remanded for further proceedings consistent with this opinion.

It is so ordered.

JUSTICE SCALIA, concurring in part and concurring in the judgment.

I concur in the judgment of the Court, and join its opinion except for Part II-B. That Part, which is devoted entirely to a discussion of the Advisory Committee's Notes pertinent to Rule 801(d)(1)(B), gives effect to those Notes not only because they are "a respected source of scholarly commentary," but also because they display the "purpose," or "intent" of the draftsmen.

I have previously acquiesced in, and indeed myself engaged in, similar use of the Advisory Committee Notes. More mature consideration has persuaded me that is wrong. Having been prepared by a body of experts, the Notes are assuredly persuasive scholarly commentaries — ordinarily *the* most persuasive — concerning the meaning of the Rules. But they bear no special authoritativeness as the work of the draftsmen, any more than the views of Alexander Hamilton (a draftsman) bear more authority than the views of Thomas Jefferson (not a draftsman) with regard to the meaning of the Constitution. It is the words of the Rules that have been authoritatively adopted — by this Court, or by Congress if it makes a statutory change. In my view even the adopting Justices' thoughts, unpromulgated as Rules, have no authoritative (as opposed to persuasive) effect, any more than their thoughts regarding an opinion (reflected in exchanges of memoranda before the opinion issues) authoritatively demonstrate the meaning of that opinion. And the same for the thoughts of congressional draftsmen who prepare statutory amendments to the Rules. Like a judicial opinion and like a statute, the promulgated Rule says what it says, regardless of the intent of its drafters.

JUSTICE BREYER, with whom THE CHIEF JUSTICE, JUSTICE O'CONNOR, and JUSTICE THOMAS join, dissenting.

The basic issue in this case concerns not hearsay, but relevance. As the majority points out, the common law permitted a lawyer to rehabilitate a witness (after a charge of improper motive) by pointing to the fact that the witness had said the same thing earlier — but only if the witness made the earlier statement *before* the motive to lie arose. The reason for the time limitation was that, otherwise, the prior consistent statement had no *relevance* to rebut the charge that the in-court testimony was the product of the motive to lie.

The majority believes that a hearsay-related rule codifies this absolute timing requirement. I do not. Rule 801(d)(1)(B) has nothing to do with relevance. Rather, that Rule carves out a subset of prior consistent statements that were formerly admissible only to rehabilitate a witness (a nonhearsay use that relies upon the fact that the statement was made). It then says that members of that subset are "not hearsay." This means that, *if* such a statement is admissible for a particular rehabilitative purpose (to rebut a charge of recent fabrication or improper influence or motive), its proponent now may use it substantively, for a hearsay purpose (*i.e.*, as evidence of its truth), as well.

The majority is correct in saying that there are different kinds of categories of prior consistent statements that can rehabilitate a witness in different ways, including statements (a) placing a claimed inconsistent statement in context; (b) showing that an inconsistent statement was not made; (c) indicating that the witness' memory is not as faulty as a cross-examiner has claimed; and (d) showing that the witness did not recently fabricate his testimony as a result of an improper influence or motive. But, I do not see where, in the existence of several categories, the majority can find the premise, which it seems to think is important, that the reason the drafters singled out one category (category (d)) was that category's special probative force in respect to rehabilitating a witness. Nor, in any event, do I understand how that premise can help the majority reach its conclusion about the common-law timing rule.

I doubt the premise because, as McCormick points out, other categories of prior consistent statements (used for rehabilitation) also, on occasion, seem likely to have strong probative force. What, for example, about such statements introduced to rebut a charge of faulty memory (category (c) above)? McCormick says about such statements: "If the witness's accuracy of memory is challenged, it seems *clear common sense* that a consistent statement made shortly after the event and before he had time to forget, should be received in support." Would not such statements (received in evidence to rehabilitate) often turn out to be highly probative as well?

More important, the majority's conclusion about timing seems not to follow from its "especially probative force" premise. That is because probative force has little to do with the concerns underlying hearsay law. Hearsay law basically turns on an out-of-court declarant's reliability, as tested through cross-examination; it does not normally turn on the probative force (if true) of that declarant's statement. The "timing" circumstance (the fact that a prior consistent statement was made after a motive to lie arose) may diminish probative force, but it does not diminish reliability. Thus, from a hearsay perspective, the timing of a prior consistent statement is basically beside the point.

At the same time, one can find a *hearsay*-related reason why the drafters might have decided to restrict the Rule to a particular category of prior consistent statements. Juries have trouble distinguishing between the rehabilitative and substantive use of the kind of prior consistent statements listed in Rule 801(d)(1)(B). Judges may give instructions limiting the use of such prior consistent statements to a rehabilitative purpose, but, in practice, juries nonetheless tend to consider them for their substantive value. It is possible that the Advisory Committee made them "nonhearsay" for that reason, *i.e.*, as a concession "more of experience than of logic." If there was a reason why the drafters excluded from Rule 801(d)(1)(B)'s scope other kinds of prior consistent statements (used for rehabilitation), perhaps it was that the drafters concluded that those other statements caused jury confusion to a lesser degree. On this rationale, however, there is no basis for distinguishing between *pre* motive and *post*-motive statements, for the confusion with respect to each would very likely be the same.

In sum, because the Rule addresses a hearsay problem and one can find a reason, unrelated to the pre-motive rule, for why it does so, I would read the Rule's plain words to mean exactly what they say: If a trial court properly admits a statement that is "consistent with the declarant's testimony" for the purpose of "rebutting an express or implied charge . . . of recent fabrication or improper influence or motive," then that statement is "not hearsay," and the jury may also consider it for the truth of what it says.

Assuming Rule 801(d)(1)(B) does not codify the absolute timing requirement, I must still answer the question whether, as a *relevance* matter, the common-law statement of the pre-motive rule stands as an absolute bar to a trial court's admission of a post-motive prior consistent statement for the purpose of rebutting a charge of recent fabrication or improper influence or motive. The majority points to statements of the timing rule that do suggest that, for reasons of relevance, the law of evidence *never* permits their admission. Yet, absolute-sounding rules often allow exceptions. And, there are sound reasons here for permitting an exception to the timing rule where circumstances warrant.

For one thing, one can find examples where the timing rule's claim of "no relevancy" is simply untrue. A post-motive statement *is* relevant to rebut, for example, a charge of recent fabrication based on improper motive, say, when the speaker made the prior statement while affected by a far more powerful motive to tell the truth. A speaker might be moved to lie to help an acquaintance. But, suppose the circumstances *also* make clear to the speaker that only the truth will save his child's life. Or, suppose the post-motive statement was made spontaneously, or when the speaker's motive to lie was much weaker than it was at trial. In these and similar situations, special circumstances may indicate that the prior statement was made for some reason other than the alleged improper motivation; it may have been made not *because of*, but *despite*, the improper motivation. Hence, post-motive statements can, *in appropriate circumstances*, directly refute the charge of fabrication based on improper motive, not because they bolster in a general way the witness' trial testimony, but because the circumstances indicate that the statements are not causally connected to the alleged motive to lie.

For another thing, the common-law pre-motive rule was not as uniform as the majority suggests. A minority of courts recognized that postmotive statements could be relevant to rebut a charge of recent fabrication or improper influence or motive under the right circumstances. I concede that the majority of courts took the rule of thumb as absolute. But, I have searched the cases (and the commentators) in vain for an explanation of why that should be so.

One can imagine a possible explanation: Trial judges may find it easier to administer an absolute rule. Yet, there is no indication in any of the cases that trial judges would, or do, find it particularly difficult to administer a more flexible rule in this context. And, there is something to be said for the greater authority that flexibility grants the trial judge to tie rulings on the admissibility of rehabilitative evidence more closely to the needs and circumstances of the particular case. Furthermore, the majority concedes that the pre-motive rule, while seemingly bright line, poses its own administrative difficulties.

This Court has acknowledged that the Federal Rules of Evidence worked a change in common-law relevancy rules in the direction of flexibility. Article IV of the Federal Rules, which concerns relevance, liberalizes the rules for admission of relevant evidence. The Rules direct the trial judge generally to admit all evidence having "any tendency" to make the existence of a material fact "more probable or less probable than it would be without the evidence." The judge may reject the evidence (assuming compliance with other rules) only if the probative value of the evidence is substantially outweighed by its tendency to prejudice a party or delay a trial. Rule 403. The codification, as a general matter, relies upon the trial judge's administration of Rules 401, 402, and 403 to keep the barely relevant, the time wasting, and the prejudicial from the jury.

It is difficult to find any strong practical or logical considerations for making the premotive rule an absolute condition of admissibility here. Perhaps there are other circumstances in which categorical common-law rules serve the purposes of Rules 401, 402, and 403, and should, accordingly, remain absolute in the law. But, for the reasons stated above, this case does not present such a circumstance. Thus, considered purely as a matter of relevancy law (and as though Rule 801(d)(1)(B) had not been written), I would conclude that the pre-motive rule did not survive the adoption of the Rules.

Accordingly, I would hold that the Federal Rules authorize a district court to allow (where probative in respect to rehabilitation) the use of post-motive prior consistent statements to rebut a charge of recent fabrication or improper influence or motive (subject of course to, for example, Rule 403). Where such statements are admissible for this rehabilitative purpose, Rule 801(d)(1)(B), as stated above, makes them admissible as substantive evidence as well (provided, of course, that the Rule's other requirements, such as the witness' availability for cross-examination, are satisfied). In most cases, this approach will not yield a different result from a strict adherence to the pre-motive rule for, in most cases, post-motive statements will not be significantly probative. And, even in cases where the statement is admitted as significantly probative (in respect to rehabilitation), the effect of admission on the trial will be minimal because the prior consistent statements will (by their nature) do no more than repeat in-court testimony.

In this case, the Court of Appeals, applying an approach consistent with what I have described above, decided that A.T.'s prior consistent statements were probative on the question of whether her story as a witness reflected a motive to lie. There is no reason to reevaluate this factbound conclusion. Accordingly, I would affirm the judgment of the Court of Appeals.

UNITED STATES v. OWENS
United States Supreme Court 484 U.S. 554, 108 S. Ct. 838, 98 L. Ed. 2d 951 (1988)

SCALIA, J., delivered the opinion of the Court, in which REHNQUIST, C. J., and WHITE, BLACKMUN, STEVENS, and O'CONNOR, JJ., joined. BRENNAN, J., filed a dissenting opinion, in which MARSHALL, J., joined. KENNEDY, J., took no part in the consideration or decision of the case.

JUSTICE SCALIA delivered the opinion of the Court.

This case requires us to determine whether either the Confrontation Clause of the Sixth Amendment or Rule 802 of the Federal Rules of Evidence bars testimony concerning a prior, out-of-court identification when the identifying witness is unable, because of memory loss, to explain the basis for the identification.

I

On April 12, 1982, John Foster, a correctional counselor at the federal prison in Lompoc, California, was attacked and brutally beaten with a metal pipe. His skull was fractured, and he remained hospitalized for almost a month. As a result of his injuries, Foster's memory was severely impaired. When Thomas Mansfield, an FBI agent investigating the assault, first attempted to interview Foster, on April 19, he found Foster lethargic and unable to remember his attacker's name. On May 5, Mansfield again spoke to Foster, who was much improved and able to describe the attack. Foster named respondent as his attacker and identified respondent from an array of photographs.

Respondent was tried in Federal District Court for assault with intent to commit murder. At trial, Foster recounted his activities just before the attack, and described feeling the blows to his head and seeing blood on the floor. He testified that he clearly remembered identifying respondent as his assailant during his May 5th interview with Mansfield. On cross-examination, he admitted that he could not remember seeing his assailant. He also admitted that, although there was evidence that he had received numerous visitors in the hospital, he was unable to remember any of them except Mansfield, and could not remember whether any of these visitors had suggested that respondent was the assailant. Defense counsel unsuccessfully sought to refresh his recollection with hospital records, including one indicating that Foster had attributed the assault to someone other than respondent. Respondent was convicted and sentenced to 20 years' imprisonment to be served consecutively to a previous sentence.

We granted certiorari to resolve the conflict on the significance of a hearsay declarant's memory loss both with respect to the Confrontation Clause and with respect to Rule 802.

II

[Discussion of Confrontation Clause omitted]

III

Respondent urges as an alternative basis for affirmance a violation of Federal Rule of Evidence 802, which generally excludes hearsay. Rule 801(d)(1)(C) defines as not hearsay a prior statement "of identification of a person made after perceiving the person," if the declarant "testifies at the trial or hearing and is subject to cross-examination concerning the statement." The Court of Appeals found that Foster's identification statement did not come within this exclusion because his memory loss prevented his being "subject to cross-examination concerning the statement." Although the Court of Appeals concluded that the violation of the Rules of Evidence was harmless (applying for purposes of that determination a "more-probable-than-not" standard, rather than the "beyond-a-reasonable-doubt" standard applicable to the Confrontation Clause violation, respondent argues to the contrary.

It seems to us that the more natural reading of "subject to cross-examination concerning the statement" includes what was available here. Ordinarily a witness is regarded as "subject to cross-examination" when he is placed on the stand, under oath, and responds willingly to questions. Just as with the constitutional prohibition, limitations on the scope of examination by the trial court or assertions of privilege by the witness may undermine the process to such a degree that meaningful cross-examination within the intent of the Rule no longer exists. But that effect is not produced by the witness' assertion of memory loss — which, as discussed earlier, is often the very result sought to be produced by cross-examination, and can be effective in destroying the force of the prior statement. Rule 801(d)(1)(C), which specifies that the cross-examination need only "concer[n] the statement," does not on its face require more.

This reading seems even more compelling when the Rule is compared with Rule 804(a)(3), which defines "[u]navailability as a witness" to include situations in which a declarant "testifies to a lack of memory of the subject matter of the declarant's statement." Congress plainly was aware of the recurrent evidentiary problem at issue here — witness forgetfulness of an underlying event — but chose not to make it an exception to Rule 801(d)(1)(C).

The reasons for that choice are apparent from the Advisory Committee's Notes on Rule 801 and its legislative history. The premise for Rule 801(d)(1)(C) was that, given adequate safeguards against suggestiveness, out-of-court identifications were generally preferable to courtroom identifications. Thus, despite the traditional view that such statements were hearsay, the Advisory Committee believed that their use was to be fostered rather than discouraged. Similarly, the House Report on the Rule noted that since, "[a]s time goes by, a witness' memory will fade and his identification will become less reliable," minimizing the barriers to admission of more contemporaneous identification is fairer to defendants and prevents "cases falling through because the witness can no longer recall the identity of the person he saw commit the crime." To judge from the House and Senate Reports, Rule 801(d)(1)(C) was in part directed to the very problem here at issue: a memory loss that makes it impossible for the witness to provide an in-court identification or testify about details of the events underlying an earlier identification. Respondent argues that this reading is impermissible because it creates an internal inconsistency in the Rules, since the forgetful witness who is deemed "subject to cross-examination" under 801(d)(1)(C) is simultaneously deemed "unavailable" under 804(a)(3). It seems to us, however, that this is not a substantive inconsistency, but only a semantic oddity resulting from the fact that Rule 804(a) has for convenience of reference in Rule 804(b) chosen to describe the circumstances necessary in order to admit certain categories of hearsay testimony under the rubric "Unavailability as a witness." These circumstances include not only absence from the hearing, but also claims of privilege, refusals to obey a court's order to testify, and inability to testify based on physical or mental illness or memory loss. Had the rubric instead been "unavailability as a witness, memory loss, and other special circumstances" there would be no apparent inconsistency with Rule 801, which is a definition section excluding certain statements entirely from the category of "hearsay." Quite obviously, the two characterizations are made for two entirely different purposes and there is no requirement or expectation that they should coincide.

For the reasons stated, we hold that neither the Confrontation Clause nor Federal Rule of Evidence 802 is violated by admission of an identification statement of a witness who is unable, because of a memory loss, to testify concerning the basis for the identification. The decision of the Court of Appeals is reversed, and the case is remanded for proceedings consistent with this opinion.

So ordered.

Chapter 13

THE ADMISSIBILITY OF OPPOSING PARTIES' HEARSAY STATEMENTS

§ 13.01 CHAPTER CHECKLIST

1. Must an opposing party's hearsay statement admit to wrongdoing to be admissible under Rule 801(d)(2)?

2. Can parties offer their own hearsay into evidence under Rule 801(d)(2)?

3. Can a non-party's hearsay statement be admissible under Rule 801(d)(2)?

4. Can the contents of a hearsay assertion alone support admissibility under Rule 801(d)(2)?

6. By what standard does a judge decide whether Rule 801(d)(2)'s foundational requirements have been satisfied?

7. Case Library: *Bourjaily v. United States*.

§ 13.02 RELEVANT FEDERAL RULES OF EVIDENCE

Rule 801. Definitions That Apply to This Article; Exclusions from Hearsay (partial text)

. . . .

(d) Statements That Are Not Hearsay. A statement that meets the following conditions is not hearsay:

. . . .

(2) *An Opposing Party's Statement.* The statement is offered against an opposing party and:

(A) was made by the party in an individual or representative capacity;

(B) is one the party manifested that it adopted or believed to be true;

(C) was made by a person whom the party authorized to make a statement on the subject;

(D) was made by the party's agent or employee on a matter within the scope of that relationship and while it existed; or

(E) was made by the party's coconspirator during and in furtherance of the conspiracy.

The statement must be considered but does not by itself establish the declarant's authority under (C); the existence or scope of the relationship under (D); or the existence of the conspiracy or participation in it under (E).

Rule 802. The Rule Against Hearsay

Hearsay is not admissible unless any of the following provides otherwise:

- a federal statute;
- these rules; or
- other rules prescribed by the Supreme Court.

§ 13.03 INTRODUCTION

Rule 801(d)(2) exempts an "opposing party's statement" from Rule 802's hearsay bar. As a result, hearsay statements that satisfy the foundational requirements of Rule 801(d)(2) are received for the truth of their contents.

This chapter analyzes each of the five circumstances in which an "opposing party's statement" is admissible under Rule 801(d)(2). However, no matter the individual circumstances, the admissibility of opposing parties' statements under Rule 801(d)(2) is governed by the following three basic principles.

1. *Parties cannot offer their own hearsay statements into evidence under Rule 801(d)(2).* Hearsay is admissible under Rule 801(d)(2) only if an *adversary* offers an opposing party's statement into evidence.

Example 1

Plaintiff Samantha is testifying against defendant Steve in an auto accident case:

PLAINTIFF'S ATTORNEY: Samantha, did you say anything to the defendant after the police officer left the scene of the accident?

A: Yes. I walked over to him and said, "You knucklehead, this was all your fault."

DEFENSE ATTORNEY: Objection, hearsay.

PLAINTIFF'S ATTORNEY: Rule 801(d)(2) Your Honor. It's Samantha's own statement, and she's a party.

JUDGE: Objection sustained. Back to Evidence class for you, counsel. You can't offer your client's own statement into evidence under that rule. (Of course, defendant Steve could offer Samantha's statement into evidence under Rule 801(d)(2), should Steve believe it in his interest to do so.)

2. *An opposing party's hearsay statement is admissible under Rule 801(d)(2) regardless of whether it confesses wrongdoing or was in any way against a party's interests at the time it was made.*

Example 2

A police officer is testifying against a defendant who is charged with robbing a jewelry store:

PROSECUTOR: And after the defendant agreed to talk to you, Officer, what happened?

A: I asked the defendant where he was at 10 a.m., the time of the robbery.

PROSECUTOR: And how did the defendant reply?

A: He said that he didn't commit the robbery, and that he was at the movies watching *The John Dillinger Story* at that time.

Example 3

Plaintiff Samantha is testifying against defendant Steve in an auto accident case:

PLAINTIFF'S ATTORNEY: And what happened after you and the defendant got out of your cars after the accident?

A: We checked out the damage to the cars.

PLAINTIFF'S ATTORNEY: Did the defendant say anything to you while you were both looking at the cars?

A: Yes. He said that he'd been temporarily blinded by the sun glaring off my cell phone.

In Examples 2 and 3, the defendants' hearsay statements are admissible under Rule 801(d)(2) even though they may have been self-serving at the time they were made. Of course, in an adversary system of justice, parties do not usually offer opposing parties' statements into evidence if they support an opposing party's claims. However, a hearsay statement that was not seemingly against a speaker's interests at the time it was made can turn out to be antithetical to the speaker's interests by the time of trial. When this situation arises, Rule 801(d)(2) allows a party to offer a speaker's hearsay statement into evidence if the speaker is the opposing party.

Example 4

Plaintiff Gale Winns sues Mommin Popp for injuries suffered when she allegedly slipped on a wet spot in Popp's convenience market. Popp's defense at trial is that the fall was due entirely to Winns' carelessness because the floor was bone-dry at the time of the fall. Gale testifies as follows:

PLAINTIFF'S ATTORNEY: And what happened when you were lying on the floor?

A: Mr. Popp walked over and said that it was my own fault that I had fallen. He said that he'd warned me to watch out for the big wet spot.

In Example 4, Popp's statement seemed self-serving (favorable to Popp) at the time Popp spoke to Winns. Nevertheless, Winns might offer Popp's statement into evidence at trial to undermine Popp's defense that the floor was bone-dry.

3. Rule 801(d)(2) can make admissible an opposing party's hearsay statement regardless of when it was made. Admissibility does not depend on a declarant being a party to a lawsuit at the time a hearsay statement is made. As a result, anything that any of us has ever said (personally or vicariously) is a potential ticking time bomb, just waiting for our becoming a party to the right lawsuit to light the fuse.

Example 5

When they are both in high school, Al Gebra tells Cal Culus that "No matter how long it takes, I'm going to get back at you someday for copying my geometry homework." Some years later, Al is charged with murdering Cal. Subject to judicial discretion under the general relevance provisions of Rules 401, 402, and 403, a judge might admit Al's high school threat as an opposing party's statement under Rule 801(d)(2) to prove that Al murdered Cal.

Practice Tip: Rule 801(d)(2) and Party Admissions.

Up until the 2011 revision of the Federal Rules of Evidence, the hearsay statements made admissible by Rule 801(d)(2) were known as "party admissions." The FRE revisers expurgated the term "party admissions" from the text of the rules. One reason was the word "admissions" wrongly implied that statements had to be admit to wrongdoing in order to be admissible. Also, even judges sometimes confused Rule 801(d)(2)'s "party admissions exemption" with Rule 804(b)(3)'s very different hearsay exception for "declarations against interest," referring to the former as "admissions against interest."[1] Recognize however that despite the change in the text of Rule 801(d)(2), judges, lawyers, state rules and some law professors may continue to refer to it as the "party admissions exemption."

§ 13.04 OPPOSING PARTIES' STATEMENTS AND THE ADVERSARY SYSTEM

Unlike the hearsay exceptions collected in Rules 803 and 804, the hearsay exemption for opposing parties' statements set forth in Rule 801(d)(2) is not based on trustworthiness. That is, the exemption does not reflect a belief that hearsay assertions made by opposing parties (or their vicarious representatives) are any more likely to be accurate or reliable than hearsay assertions made by anyone else. Rather, the exemption is rooted in an adversary system in which parties are responsible for advancing and protecting their legal rights. The considerations underlying the exemption for opposing parties' statements include the following:

- A "gotcha" attitude of "you said it, you explain it." The exemption holds people accountable for their out-of-court statements, and increases the likelihood that parties' courtroom positions will be consistent with their pre-trial statements.

- The "hearsay dangers" (see Chapter 10) are minimized:

---

[1] For a case employing this confused terminology, see *Bill v. Farm Bureau Life Insurance Co.*, 119 N.W.2d 768 (Iowa 1963).

An opposing party can't readily complain about being unable to probe the party's (or vicarious agent's) own sincerity, perception, memory, or use of language.

The opposing party will almost certainly be in court and available to testify and can, if warranted, explain the assertion or deny making it, consistent with the oath.

- When the exemption admits a hearsay statement made by a party's agent, the party will often have an ongoing relationship with the declarant. If so, the party can normally produce the declarant as a witness to explain or deny the statement, consistent with the oath.

The policy of allowing parties to tar adversaries with their out-of-court statements is so strong that judges typically admit opposing parties' statements into evidence even when the statements are subject to evidentiary infirmities that would result in exclusion under other rule of evidence. For example, perhaps a party spoke about an event though lacking personal knowledge of what actually happened. Or, the party's statement may consist of little more than a conclusory legal opinion. Though "defects" such as these generally result in exclusion of evidence, both statements will probably be admitted under Rule 801(d)(2). The rationale is that "if a party had a good enough basis for saying it, that's a good enough basis for admitting it into evidence." On the other hand, the exemption does not invariably run roughshod over every other rule of evidence. For example, judges can exclude opposing parties' statements if their contents are irrelevant, or if their probative value is outweighed by the danger of unfair prejudice.

Example

Jon sues Barbara on a "negligent entrustment" theory for personal injuries incurred in an auto accident. Jon alleges that Barbara carelessly loaned her car to Jennifer, a driver who Barbara knew or should have known to be the town drunk. Jon calls Barbara's neighbor as a witness to testify that when the neighbor told Barbara that her car had been involved in an accident, Barbara said, "Jennifer must have been drunk." Despite the conclusory form of Barbara's statement and her lack of personal knowledge as to how the accident occurred, a judge would in all likelihood receive Barbara's statement under Rule 801(d)(2) if Jon offers it into evidence to prove both that Barbara knew of Jennifer's drinking problem and that her drinking caused the accident. However, if instead Barbara had responded to the neighbor by saying that, "I hope that after the accident, the cops didn't find the mask I used in my last bank robbery," her assertion would probably be excluded as irrelevant to the issue of negligent entrustment.

§ 13.05 DECLARANT IS THE OPPOSING PARTY (RULE 801(d)(2)(A))

Statutory Elements:

* The declarant is a party to the lawsuit in which the hearsay is offered;
* The declarant's adversary offers the party's statement into evidence.

Under Rule 801(d)(2)(A), a hearsay statement is admissible if offered against the party who made it, whether "in an individual or a representative capacity." The proviso prevents a party sued in one capacity from weaseling out of an assertion by claiming that "I made it in a different capacity." For example, a defendant charged with defrauding a bank cannot prevent the prosecution from offering into evidence a hearsay statement made by the defendant to a bank officer by claiming that "I was speaking to the bank officer not as an individual, but in my capacity as trustee of my parent's trust."

Problem 13-1: Multiple Choys

Mr. and Mrs. Choy sue Rhoda for personal injuries resulting from an auto accident. To prove that Rhoda was speeding just prior to the accident, *which if any of the following items of evidence would be admissible under Rule 801(d)(2) if the Choys' lawyer offers them?*

1. The Choys' lawyer calls a bystander to testify that after the accident, Dad Choy told the bystander, "Rhoda was speeding just before she ploughed into my car."

2. Rhoda testified at her deposition that "I might have been going over the speed limit just before the accident."

3. The Choys' lawyer calls Mom Choy to testify that, "A couple of days after the accident, Rhoda's neighbor Katie told me that Rhoda had admitted to her that Rhoda had been speeding just before the collision."

4. The Choys' lawyer calls a bystander to testify that after the collision, the bystander heard Rhoda mutter to herself, "Must have been the darn brakes."

Problem 13-2: Who's a Party?

Maso Menos is charged with armed robbery of Des Pacio. Maso denies being the robber, and on direct examination by defense counsel Maso testifies as follows:

DEFENSE ATTORNEY: And what happened next?

A: The officer placed me under arrest and drove me back to the place where the robbery had supposedly taken place.

DEFENSE ATTORNEY: And then what happened?

A: The officer left me in the back seat and walked over to a man who was standing about 10 feet away, who I later learned was Des Pacio. I'd never seen Mr. Pacio before.

DEFENSE ATTORNEY: OK. What happened next?

A: The officer talked to Mr. Pacio for a few minutes, then walked back over to me.

DEFENSE ATTORNEY: Did you overhear any of the conversation between the officer and Mr. Pacio?

A: Yes. I heard the officer say that she was concerned about some differences between me and the description that Mr. Pacio had given of the robber.

PROSECUTOR: Objection, hearsay.

DEFENSE ATTORNEY: the police officer constitutes the opposing party in a criminal case, so the statement is admissible under Rule 801(d)(2)(A).

JUDGE: *What ruling?*

Problem 13-3: Oh Canida

In *Mahlandt v. Wild Canid Survival and Research Center*, 588 F.2d 626 (8th Cir. 1978), the Center and its Director of Education were sued for civil damages after "Sophie," a wolf kept in the front yard of the home of the Center's Education Director, allegedly bit a three-year-old girl in the face. Their defense was that the girl's facial injuries were a result of her having crawled into the yard under a wire fence, not a wolf bite. (The name "Wild Canid" may not have made a good impression on the jury. Perhaps organizations ought to consult with lawyers before choosing names. "*Mahlandt v. Cuddly Critter Center*" wouldn't have sounded nearly as intimidating.)

1. When informed by telephone of the child's injuries, the Education Director wrote the Center's President a note stating that "Sophie bit a child who came into my backyard." The plaintiff offers the note into evidence against the Director under Rule 801(d)(2)(A). *Is this note admissible over the Director's "lack of personal knowledge" objection?*

2. Assume that you represent the plaintiff (the child who was allegedly bitten and her parents). *How might you have used the tools of formal discovery to uncover the Director's note prior to trial? Assume that the note was either (a) handwritten by the Director (b) was an email message that the Director sent to the Center's President.*

3. Assume that the Education Director's note to the President reads as follows: "It's been reported to me that Sophie bit a child that came into my backyard." The plaintiff offers the note into evidence against the Director under Rule 801(d)(2)(A). *Is this note admissible over the Director's "lack of personal knowledge" objection?*

4. Assume that you are the Defense Attorney representing the Education Director, and are discussing the note with the Director on the eve of trial. That discussion goes as follows:

DEFENSE ATTORNEY: I may not be able to prevent the plaintiff from introducing this note into evidence. If it is admitted, of course, you'll have a chance to explain that you didn't know what had actually happened when you wrote the note. It might be helpful if you could offer the jury a good reason for writing the note anyway. Can you recall what your thinking was at the time you wrote it?

A: I was pretty shocked. I never thought Sophie capable of harming a child, and I still don't. But I'm not sure how to answer your question.

DEFENSE ATTORNEY: Well, one possibility is that you wrote the note to make sure that the President would order an immediate and thorough investigation. Thinking back, might that have been in the back of your mind?

A: Well, certainly we were all concerned about what had happened. So, yes, I'd agree with that.

DEFENSE ATTORNEY: OK. If we're in court and the note is admitted into evidence, I'll ask you why you wrote the note and you can say that you wanted to make sure that the President ordered an immediate and thorough investigation. That's the truth, right?

A: Yes.

Does this portion of the meeting satisfy ethical guidelines forbidding lawyers from "making up" testimony for their clients to give?

5. At trial, in lieu of offering a written note into evidence, the plaintiff calls Sara to testify that she heard the Education Director say that Sophie had bitten a child. Sara begins by testifying that at the time of the alleged biting incident, she was working as a computer technician at the Wild Canid Center. About half an hour after the incident took place, Sara heard the Education Director talking with a small group of people. When the plaintiff's attorney asks Sara to testify to the Director's hearsay statement, the trial continues as follows:

DEFENSE ATTORNEY: Objection to this testimony, based on lack of foundation.

JUDGE: Counsel for plaintiff, on what basis are you offering this statement?

PLAINTIFF'S ATTORNEY: Opposing party statement, Your Honor.

DEFENSE ATTORNEY: And my objection goes to foundation as an admission. Our position is that the Director did not make the statement that this witness attributes to him. I'd ask that the jury be excused for a hearing as to the adequacy of the foundation.

JUDGE: All right, the jury has been excused, counsel for plaintiff may proceed.

[At this point a "mini-trial" begins with the plaintiff trying to lay the foundation for a straight admission, which entails offering evidence that the Director made the out-of-court assertion.]

PLAINTIFF'S ATTORNEY: Sara, what is it that you heard the Director say?

A: The Director said, "It sounds like Sophie bit a child who came into my backyard."

PLAINTIFF'S ATTORNEY: And how do you know it was the Director who said this?

A:	I'd worked in the Center for over a year, I've heard the Director's voice many times and recognized it.
PLAINTIFF'S ATTORNEY:	Were there any background noises that might have caused you to mishear what the Director said?
A:	No, it was pretty quiet. We'd all heard about the accident and everyone was pretty subdued.
PLAINTIFF'S ATTORNEY:	Nothing further.
JUDGE:	Defense counsel, any questions for this witness?
DEFENSE ATTORNEY:	Thank you, just a couple. Your employment at Wild Canid was terminated about a month after the biting incident, correct?
A:	That's right.
DEFENSE ATTORNEY:	And you blame the Director for your termination, don't you?
A:	I didn't think the Director's evaluation of my performance was accurate, but that's all in the past.
DEFENSE ATTORNEY:	At this point I'd like to excuse this witness for a moment and call the defendant briefly to testify as to the foundation.
JUDGE:	You may do so.
DEFENSE ATTORNEY:	Director, did you make the statement just attributed to you?
A:	I did not.
DEFENSE ATTORNEY:	Did you say anything at all to indicate that you believed that Sophie bit the child?
A:	No, I had no idea what had happened.
DEFENSE ATTORNEY:	Did anyone to your knowledge make such a statement?
A:	No. I was just briefly talking to a few staffers in my office before leaving to check on the child's condition. I remember that somebody, I think it was Jean, asked if I thought that Sophie could have bitten the child. I said it didn't sound like Sophie at all, and that we shouldn't jump to any conclusions before we knew more facts. Then I left.
DEFENSE ATTORNEY:	Was there any other conversation at all about whether Sophie bit the child?
A:	No, not that I heard, at least.
DEFENSE ATTORNEY:	No further questions.
JUDGE:	Plaintiff, any questions of this witness?
PLAINTIFF'S ATTORNEY:	Not as to the foundation, Your Honor.

JUDGE: Director, you may stand down. Under Rule 104, the Director's statement is admissible once the plaintiff offers evidence sufficient to support a jury finding that the Director made the statement. Having listened to the foundational evidence, I find the evidence equally balanced on both sides but believe that the jury could reasonably conclude that the Director made the statement. Therefore, I'll admit it. Defense, you'll have a chance to have the Director testify in front of the jury that the statement was never made, and the jury can believe who it chooses. OK, recall the jury and let's get started.

Is the judge's statement of the foundational burden correct? After ruling that the plaintiff has offered sufficient evidence that the Director made the statement for it to be received in evidence, is the judge correct in saying that the Director will be able to deny making the statement in front of the jury? Based on the evidence that the attorneys elicited during the mini-trial, what ruling would you have made as to the statement's admissibility?

Problem 13-4: Wrenching an Admission

Amy sues Beth for injuries incurred when Beth allegedly struck Amy with a monkey wrench that Beth pulled out of her desk drawer:

1. During pre-trial discovery, Beth responded to Amy's Request for Admission as follows:

> Amy's Request # 5: Admit that the following fact is true: You always keep a monkey wrench in your desk drawer at work. Beth's response: Admitted.

After the judge admits Beth's response to Request # 5 into evidence, can Beth testify that "I have never kept a monkey wrench in my desk drawer at work"?

2. Linda will testify when called by Amy as a witness that she works with Beth and that a week after the quarrel, Beth told Linda that "I always keep a monkey wrench in my desk drawer here at work."

After Linda testifies to Beth's statement, can Beth testify trial that "I have never kept a monkey wrench in my desk drawer at work"?

3. After she was fired for allegedly striking Amy, Beth sued her employer for wrongful termination. Beth's complaint in that lawsuit alleged in part that "Plaintiff Beth never struck Amy with the monkey wrench that she keeps in her desk drawer at work or with any other object."

Can Amy offer this allegation into evidence as an opposing party's statement made by Beth in the trial of her personal injury case?

4. Assume that Amy initially named both Beth and Jacob as defendants in her personal injury lawsuit, and that she later dismissed Jacob from the case and proceeded to trial against only Beth. Amy's initial complaint included the following allegation: "Defendant Beth or defendant Jacob, or both defendants Beth and Jacob, intentionally struck me with a monkey wrench."

Can Beth offer this allegation into evidence as an opposing party statement made by Amy (to prove that Jacob and not Beth was the cause of any injuries that

Amy incurred)? When responding to this question, consider that Rule 8(e)(2) of the Federal Rules of Civil Procedure includes the following language: "A party may set forth two or more statements of a claim or defense alternatively or hypothetically . . . . All statements shall be made subject to the obligations set forth in Rule 11." (Rule 11 requires in essence a good-faith basis for claims and defenses.)

Problem 13-5: Pleading Ticket

You represent Jill, who's been sued civilly for damages by Gustavo following an auto accident in which her car collided with Gustavo's car. Gustavo's complaint alleges that the accident was caused by Jill's negligent failure to keep her car in good repair. After the accident, a police officer inspected Jill's car and wrote her a ticket for driving with bald tires. Jill tells you that "I'm planning to dispose of the traffic ticket quickly by going down to traffic court and pleading guilty. Do you think that's what I should do?" *How would you respond to Jill's question?*

Problem 13-6: Brag Art

Art is charged with armed robbery of a convenience market; the defense is an alibi. The prosecutor calls the convenience store clerk to testify that after the clerk had handed over money at gunpoint to Art, Art said "I'm having a good week. I knocked over two liquor stores the day before yesterday, and now I'm making a haul today." *As the defense attorney, what argument might you make against the admissibility of the statement?*

Problem 13-7: Nocturnal Admission?

Dion Tology is charged with armed robbery of the Belmont Bar & Grill. Dmitri will testify when called as a prosecution witness that "I was camping with Dion two weeks ago. One night after we'd each had a few beers, I was awakened by his talking in his sleep. I shined my flashlight at him, and he looked like he was sound asleep. But he was saying all sorts of things, including that he had robbed the Belmont." *As the defense attorney, what argument might you make against the admissibility of Dion's statement?*

§ 13.06 ADOPTIVE STATEMENTS (RULE 801(d)(2)(B))

Statutory Elements:

* A party adopted or by words or deeds manifested belief in the truth of a non-party declarant's hearsay statement;

* The party's adversary offers the hearsay statement into evidence.

Rule 801(d)(2)(B) makes a non-party declarant's hearsay statement admissible if the party against whom the statement is offered adopts the statement or by words or actions demonstrates that the party believed it to be true.

Example

Ruby Pearl is charged with robbing a jewelry store. Opal is testifying as a witness for the prosecution:

PROSECUTOR: Opal, what happened when you entered Ruby's apartment?

A: I told Ruby that I'd heard that she'd pulled off the jewelry store caper, and that she must have come away with some great stuff.

PROSECUTOR: And how did Ruby respond?

A: She just smiled at me and showed me a handful of gold rings and bracelets.

Opal's testimony lays a foundation for the prosecutor to offer her statement ("Ruby pulled off the jewelry store caper and got great stuff") into evidence against Ruby under Rule 801(d)(2)(B). Ruby's conduct adopted and manifested belief in the truth of Opal's statement.

Often, as in the example of Ruby above, a party makes an affirmative response that provides a basis for concluding that the party intended to adopt or manifested a belief in the accuracy of another person's statement. However, a party's silence can on occasion be enough for a judge to conclude that the party adopted another person's statement. If a party remains silent in circumstances when a reasonable person would have denied a statement had it not been true, an "adoption by silence" can result.

The potential scope of this exemption is extremely broad. If the foundational elements for "adoption by silence" were loosely interpreted, anything said by anyone within a party's earshot could become admissible under Rule 801(d)(2)(B). To insure that people don't have to run around shaking their heads "no" or yelling "no way" every time they overhear a statement they disagree with on pain of it being admitted as an opposing party's statement should litigation occur, judges tend to apply the foundational elements rigorously. *McCormick on Evidence* notes that a party seeking to offer a declarant's statement as an adversary's adopted statement must usually satisfy the following foundational elements:

- The circumstances must show that the party heard the statement.

- The party must have understood the statement.

- The subject matter of the statement must have been within the party's personal knowledge. (This is an exception to the general rule that personal knowledge is unnecessary under Rule 801(d)(2)).

- Under the circumstances, a reasonable person would have denied the statement had it not been true.

Should a judge determine whether the offering party has satisfied these foundational factors pursuant to Rule 104(a) or 104(b)? Disagreement on this issue exists among courts and commentators alike. A compromise position that some favor calls for the judge to decide whether a reasonable person would have denied the statement had it not been true pursuant to Rule 104(a), and decide the other foundational factors pursuant to Rule 104(b). Under this position, the offering party has to convince the judge by a preponderance of evidence that a reasonable person would have denied the statement had it not been true, and must offer evidence sufficient to support a finding that the remaining factors are true.

Problem 13-8: On the Tube: "Barb-Accuse"

On an episode of the former television soap opera *Melrose Place*, 20-year-old Alison unexpectedly shows up at a barbecue in her parents' backyard. Many of her parents' close friends, including at least one judge, are present. Her father and mother both angrily ask her to leave, saying "you don't belong here." Alison says in a loud voice, "You going to do what you used to do to Meredith and me?" Her father says, "Alison, this is neither the time nor the place for this." Alison then shouts in a voice loud enough for everyone to hear, "Daddy, why don't you tell them all our dirty little secret, about how you used to take me and Meredith down to the basement and do things to us." Daddy stands silent for a few moments, and Alison walks away. Assume that Daddy is now charged with doing illegal things to Alison and Meredith in the basement.

Student # 1: As the Prosecutor, make a brief argument to support your position that the trial judge should admit Alison's statement as Daddy's adopted statement.

Student # 2: As the Defense Attorney, argue in response to the prosecutor's argument that the judge should not admit Alison's statement into evidence as your client's adopted statement.

Student # 3: As the Judge, preside over the argument and rule on the prosecutor's request, and state for the record the following:

1. Under Rule 104, which party has the burden of proof with respect to the foundational elements and what does the burden consist of?

2. When announcing your ruling, explain the factors that incline you to admit or exclude the statement.

Problem 13-9: I Wanna Hold Your Hand (of Cards)

John is charged with armed robbery of the Abbey Road Bank on June 4. To prove John's identity as the robber, the prosecutor calls Paul as a witness, whose testimony goes in part as follows:

PROSECUTOR: Paul, where were you on the evening of June 6th?

DEFENSE ATTORNEY: Your Honor, pursuant to our previous discussion, I object and ask that the jury be excused.

[From pre-trial discovery and conferences, the defense attorney knows that the prosecution now intends to lay the foundation for a party admission, and both sides and the judge may well have planned in advance to excuse the jury when the "mini-trial" begins.]

JUDGE: OK, the jury has been excused. Witness, do you remember the question?

A: Yes. I was at John's place for our regular poker game. As usual, George and Ringo were also in the game that night.

PROSECUTOR: How long had you been meeting regularly to play cards?

A: Oh, about a year and a half I guess. We miss some weeks, and sometimes one of us has to miss a game and someone else will join in instead.

PROSECUTOR: Would you say that you're all good friends?

A: Yes.

PROSECUTOR: Is it common for the players to talk about things other than the betting during the game?

A: I guess. We talk about stuff that's going on, like at work, what we've been doing, that sort of stuff.

PROSECUTOR: Did you say anything to John on June 6 about the Abbey Road Bank?

A: Yes. I told him that I was hoping to win some of the loot he'd just taken off the Abbey Road Bank.

PROSECUTOR: Were Ringo and George present at the card table at this time?

A: Yes, I said this while Ringo was shuffling a deck of cards.

PROSECUTOR: Did John respond to this remark?

A: Yes. He smiled and said something like "what do you mean?"

PROSECUTOR: And then what happened?

A: I told him it's me he's talking to, and that I'd heard that he'd stuck up the bank a couple of days earlier and gotten away with about $20,000.

PROSECUTOR: Did John respond to this comment?

A: No, he just asked Ringo to finish shuffling and deal the next hand.

PROSECUTOR: Nothing further on the foundation at this time.

JUDGE: Defense, any questions for the witness?

DEFENSE ATTORNEY: Do you all commonly tease each other and tell jokes during your poker games?

A: Sure.

DEFENSE ATTORNEY: And I take it that you don't respond every time somebody teases you or needles you?

A: That's right.

Student # 1: You are the Defense Counsel. Are there any other foundational facts you would try to establish by questioning Paul? If so, you may question the witness. After all the evidence has been elicited, make a brief argument in support of your objection to the admissibility of this portion of Paul's testimony.

Student # 2: You are the Prosecutor. Are there any other foundational facts you would try to establish during redirect questioning of Paul? If so, you may question the witness. After all the evidence has been elicited, make a brief argument in support of the admissibility of this portion of Paul's testimony.

Student # 3: You are the Judge. After considering the testimony above, any other foundational evidence that the parties might elicit, and the arguments of counsel, rule as to whether this portion of Paul's testimony is admissible as John's adopted statement.

Student # 4: You are the witness, John. Be prepared to answer questions concerning the card game; your answers should be consistent with the information provided in the transcript.

Problem 13-10: Silent Right

Beverly is arrested in her apartment for selling illegal drugs. The prosecutor calls the arresting officer to testify that after the officer arrested Beverly, Beverly claimed said that the drugs didn't belong to her. Beverly's partner, Danny, who was present in the apartment when the arrest occurred, then told Beverly, "Tell the truth for a change. You know that the drugs are yours." Beverly responded by hanging her head and saying nothing. *Does Beverly's silence establish a sufficient foundation for an adoption of Danny's statement?*

Problem 13-11: Car Jack

Jill sues Jack for damages resulting from an auto accident. Jill offers to testify that after the collision, both drivers got out of their cars. Jill then said, "You never even slowed down at the red light. This is all your fault."

1. Assume that Jack says nothing in response to Jill's remark. *Does his response constitute an adoption of Jill's accusation?*

2. Assume that Jack responded to Jill's remark by saying, "I'm really sorry about what happened. Let's just exchange information and let the insurance companies worry about it." *Does Jack's response amount to an adoption of Jill's accusation?*

3. Assume that Jack responded to Jill's remark by immediately jumping back into his car and driving away. *Does Jack's conduct amount to an adoption of Jill's accusation?*

4. Jill also says to Jack, "Luckily, my passenger took a picture of your car going through the red light on this cell phone." Jack then grabbed the cell phone out of Jill's hand, threw it to the ground, and stomped it to bits. *Does Jack's conduct amount to an adoption of Jill's accusation?*

Problem 13-12: Keeping Up Appearances

Willie has sued Mickey for breach of contract, alleging that Mickey reneged on an agreement to make personal appearances at a series of motivational seminars that Willie developed and conducts. Mickey denies agreeing to appear at the seminars. After Mickey fails to appear at the initial seminar, the two exchange electronic mail ("email") messages as follows:

1. Willie sends Mickey a message stating in part that "we had a deal for you to attend each seminar, and your missing the first one has cost me big time."

2. Mickey's response states in part that "we have very different views about my supposed agreement to appear at your seminars, and I won't be appearing at future ones either."

3. Willie's response to this message states in part that "you can't just walk away from deals you've made. You know what our deal was as well as I do, and unless I hear from you I'll assume that you will do the right thing and show up at future seminars as you agreed to do."

Mickey does not respond to this last e-mail. *Is Mickey's failure to respond tantamount to adopting Willie's assertion that the parties had a deal?*

§ 13.07 AUTHORIZED STATEMENTS (RULE 801(d)(2)(C))

Statutory Elements:

* A non-party hearsay declarant was expressly or impliedly a party's authorized agent;

* The party's adversary offers the hearsay statement into evidence.

Rule 801(d)(2)(C) makes a declarant's hearsay statement admissible if the party against whom the statement is offered authorized the declarant to speak on the adversary's behalf about the statement's subject matter. Thus, a party seeking to offer an "authorized statement" must offer foundational evidence showing that the declarant had "speaking authority," and that the declarant's statement was within the scope of that authority.

A declarant may have *express* authority to speak for a party. For example, before leaving for a day at the races, Harpo might prepare a document stating that "I hereby authorize Groucho to speak on my behalf about what happened during the night at the opera." More often, a declarant's authority to speak is a by-product of agency law principles, which *imply* both authority and the scope of the authority from the declarant's relationship to a party.

Example 1

Jay and Bob are partners in a dry-cleaning business. Under agency law, partners have the power to bind each other in business dealings. Hence, a letter written by Jay and sent to a bank in the course of arranging for a business loan would probably be admissible against Bob as an authorized statement in a collection action brought by the bank against Bob. However, agency law principles would not give Jay the implied authority to speak about Bob's personal marital situation. Therefore, a statement that Jay makes about Bob's plans with respect to his children would not constitute an authorized statement by Bob that his wife Oprah could offer into evidence against him in a dissolution of marriage action.

Example 2

In the *Mahlandt* case (*see* Problem 13-3 above), assume that a member of the Board of Directors stated that "Sophie the wolf bit a young child." The statement would qualify as the organization's authorized statement, because under agency law Board members have the implied authority to speak for corporations on matters concerning corporate activities.

A foundational issue that has arisen often is the extent to which a judge can consider a declarant's claim of authority to speak when determining whether a declarant in fact had authority to speak for a party. Some courts have disregarded the agent's claim entirely and have looked only to the surrounding circumstances to determine whether authority existed. Other courts have treated a declarant's claim of authority with varying degrees of respect. Rule 801(d)(2) resolves the uncertainty by providing that on the foundational issue of a declarant's authority, a statement's contents must be considered but are not alone sufficient to establish a declarant's authority. Thus, a party seeking to offer an out-of-court statement as an authorized statement must offer evidence independent of the statement that authority existed.

Example 3

Anne is fired from her place of employment. A few days later, Anne's former colleague Vy Karious contacts Anne's former employer and states that "Anne is really upset by her firing and she asked me to talk to you to see if she can somehow get her job back. Anne admits that she showed up to work drunk a few times, but that was because of a personal problem that's now been resolved, and you can be sure that it will never happen again."

Anne doesn't get her job back, and sues her ex-employer for wrongful termination. The employer wants to offer Vy's statement into evidence to prove that Anne had come to work drunk, and relies on Vy's statement to prove that Anne had authorized Vy to speak for her. Anne however testifies during a mini-trial that "I never authorized Vy to talk about my work experiences. I just asked her to talk to the employer and make an appointment for me." Under Rule 801(d)(2), the trial judge considers Vy's statement as evidence that Anne authorized Vy to speak. However, the employer would have to offer independent evidence of Vy's authority before her statement could be admitted into evidence as Anne's authorized statement.

Problem 13-13: Lawyer Lee

Juan Lee, Esq., represents Jackson in a case involving Jackson's tripping on a toy truck on the sidewalk in front of Binder's home. After his initial interview of Jackson, Lee sends Binder a letter seeking the name of Binder's home insurance carrier. In that letter Lee outlines how Jackson's mishap occurred and describes Jackson's injuries. The letter states that "perhaps Mr. Jackson was a bit intoxicated, but that doesn't excuse your carelessness." *Can Binder offer Lee's letter into evidence against Jackson to prove that Jackson was under the influence of alcohol at the time of the mishap?*

Problem 13-14: Scoop

Eppy Demic sues Toxicity Inc. for polluting her town's drinking water. After the suit is filed, Toxicity's press secretary Bill tells a journalist that "We've never actually tested the sludge we dump into the river. How do you expect us to know whether it's safe?" *Would the press secretary's statement qualify as Toxicity's authorized statement? What if Bill is Toxicity's bookkeeper, whose job is to take care of payroll and insurance matters for the company's employees?*

Problem 13-15: Gilligan's Island

You represent Blairwood Construction, a development company that is planning to build a luxury resort complex on the island of Knott Atoll. Gilligan, who heads a local environmental group opposed to the project, claims that construction would destroy the habitat of an endangered species of bird known as the "yellow twitbill." Blairwood's President wants to send out a conciliatory press release, but doesn't want to say anything that might be used against the company should Gilligan go to court and try to stop the project. Which one of the following remarks will you recommend to the President, and why?

1. "As a good corporate citizen, Blairwood wants to minimize harm to the yellow twitbill."

2. "The yellow twitbill may be an endangered species, though the ornithological community is deeply divided over the issue."

3. "We at Blairwood are aware of and take very seriously Gilligan's claim that the yellow twitbill's habitat may be affected by the building of the resort."

4. "Blairwood has hired a local ornithologist who will suggest ways to minimize harm to the yellow twitbill."

Problem 13-16: Way Out

John L. Way, former star quarterback for the Denver Buncos, has sued the team for breach of contract for kicking Way off the team for violating the "public appearance" provision of the standard player agreement incorporated into Way's contract. The team contends that Way violated the provision by secretly demanding money for making appearances that the team arranged for and that Way was contractually obligated to attend for free. To support its claim that Way demanded payments, the team seeks to offer into evidence a statement made by players' union representative Les Strike to a newspaper reporter. Strike stated to the reporter: "I've talked to Mr. Way about the matter, and he's asked me to convey to you that he sees nothing wrong with asking for appearance money. Almost all players do the same thing." The team claims that Way authorized Strike to make this statement; Way denies that Strike had any authority to speak for him.

The team calls the reporter as a witness to testify to Strike's statement. When Way objects that the statement is inadmissible hearsay, the following mini-trial ensues:

JUDGE: Counsel for the Buncos, do you have any evidence other than the statement itself that Mr. Strike was authorized by Mr. Way to speak for him on this matter?

DEFENSE ATTORNEY: I do, Your Honor.

Student # 1: You are conducting the mini-trial as the attorney for the Buncos, and seek to admit Strike's statement into evidence as Way's authorized admission. You will elicit the following foundational information from the reporter: Before speaking with Strike, the reporter saw Strike and Way conversing quietly with each other in a corner of the team's locker room for about five minutes. On a couple of occasions, Strike pointed in the reporter's direction and Way nodded his head up and down. In addition, when Strike made the statement quoted above, the reporter asked Strike for the names of other players who took money for charitable appearances. Strike excused himself, talked to Way quietly for a few moments, then returned and said that the previous statement was the only information he would provide.

Student # 2: You are conducting the mini-trial as the attorney for Way, and seek to prevent Strike's statement from being admitted as your client's admission. You may cross-examine the reporter. You may then also call Way as an opposition foundational witness. Way will testify that he did talk to Strike on the occasion in question, but that he never authorized Strike to speak to the reporter on his behalf about appearance money or anything else. According to Way, he and Strike talked generally about the issue of appearance money, but Way said that he needed time to think about the issue and wasn't ready to discuss the matter publicly. Way also claims that Strike is out to "get" Way for Way's making public statements that the standard player agreement agreed to by the union the previous year was a "sweetheart deal" that sold out the players to benefit the union executives.

Student # 3: You are the judge and will preside over the mini-trial and rule on the admissibility of Strike's statement to the reporter as an authorized statement.

§ 13.08 EMPLOYEE STATEMENTS (RULE 801(d)(2)(D))

Statutory Elements:

* A non-party declarant is a party's agent or employee;

* The declarant's hearsay statement concerns a matter within the scope of the agency or employment.

* The declarant's hearsay statement was made during the existence of the agent/servant relationship;

* The party's adversary offers the hearsay statement into evidence.

Example

In the *Mahlandt* case (*see* Problem 13-3 above), the Survival Center's Education Director wrote a note stating that "Sophie the wolf bit a child in my backyard." The Director's statement would be admissible both against the Director personally and against the Center (as a statement by an employee), since the Director was the Center's employee, the note talks about a matter within the scope of the Director's employment, and the Director wrote the note while a Center employee.

Rule 801(d)(2)(D) greatly liberalizes employer-friendly common law principles. This issue of employee statements often becomes important when an injured plaintiff sues an employer on a "respondent superior" theory for damages caused by an employee's alleged carelessness. In such situations, the plaintiff frequently seeks to offer into evidence against the employer a hearsay statement made by the employee following the mishap. For instance, in a civil negligence case in which the employer is a defendant, a plaintiff might seek to testify that following the collision, the employee said, "I never should have drunk those last two martinis." Prior to the adoption of the Federal Rules of Evidence, judges typically ruled that such hearsay statements of employees were not admissible against employers. The judges' reasoning tended to regard employees as little more than dog meat, paid to carry out their daily tasks but certainly not authorized to speak on behalf of their employers.

The restrictive common law approach is typified by the case of *Big Mack Trucking Co. Inc. v. Dickerson.*[2] In *Big Mack*, Leday and Dickerson were employed as truck drivers by Big Mack. They parked their loaded trucks one behind the other, Leday's truck on higher ground. As Dickerson stood between the trucks, Leday's truck rolled forward and crushed him between the two trucks, killing him. Dickerson's family sued Big Mack for wrongful death, alleging that the brakes on Leday's truck were defective. To prove that the brakes were defective, the plaintiffs called as witnesses a Big Mack vice-president and a police offer who had investigated the accident. Both these witnesses testified that Leday had told them that he'd been having brake trouble and that he hadn't been maintaining his brakes properly. The court decided that Leday's statements should have been excluded as inadmissible hearsay as against Leday's employer, Big Mack. In the judges' view, Leday was neither expressly nor impliedly authorized by Big Mack to explain how the accident happened. (The court also held that Leday's statements did not qualify as "spontaneous utterances," see Rule 803 (2), discussed in Chapter 14, because too much time had elapsed between the accident and the making of the statements.)

Rule 801(d)(2)(D) produces a dramatically different result in cases such as *Big Mack*. Leday's statements satisfies the foundational requirements of Rule 801(d)(2)(D) because:

- Leday was an employee of Big Mack.

- Leday's statements concerned a matter within the scope of his employment. His job was to drive trucks, and his statements concerned a truck driving accident.

- At the time he spoke, Leday was a Big Mack employee.

Under Rule 801(d)(2)(D), then, the plaintiffs in *Big Mack* could have offered Leday's statement into evidence against the trucking company.

As with authorized statements, Rule 801(d)(2) states that judges must consider the contents of an employee's statement when determining whether an adequate foundation has been established for its admission into evidence. For example, assume that a declarant says, "I'm in charge of explosions for my employer, Detonator Inc. I want to apologize for setting off that last explosion so close to your house. What's that? Yes, I'll speak a bit louder in the future." Under 801(d)(2), the

---

[2] 497 S.W.2d 283 (Texas 1973).

statement itself is some evidence that the declarant was employed by Detonator Inc., and of the scope of the declarant's employment. However, the statement does not by itself by itself "establish . . . the agency or employment relationship and scope thereof." Thus, a party seeking to offer the assertion into evidence as Detonator's employee statement would need to offer evidence independent of the assertion of the declarant's employment status and job responsibilities.

Problem 13-17: Late for Class

A typical foundational dispute under Rule 801(d)(2)(D) is whether a matter about which an employee spoke is within the employee's scope of employment. Assume that one of your law school classmates slips and falls on a banana peel while rushing into a classroom so as not to be late for Evidence. The injured student sues the law school for negligence, and wants to offer into evidence the statement, "That banana peel should have been picked up yesterday." This statement would qualify as a statement by a law school employee statement if it were made by (select as many declarants as you think appropriate):

1. Your Evidence instructor, who spoke after the law student hobbled into the classroom and explained what happened.

2. A law school janitor whose duties include cleaning the hallway in which the mishap occurred.

3. A law school janitor whose duties do not include the hallway in which the mishap occurred.

4. The law school's supervising janitor, whose oversees law school janitorial services but does not have clean-up duties.

5. The university's supervising janitor, who generally oversees campus janitorial services but has no direct law school responsibilities.

6. The law school's Dean.

7. The law school's Director of Admissions.

8. The University's Chancellor or President.

9. Another student enrolled in Evidence.

Problem 13-18: Pickup Line

A pedestrian is hit by a small delivery van owned by Federal Parcel Service. Lori, the van's driver, tells the pedestrian after the accident that "I didn't see you, I was checking on my next pickup." Lori's statement constitutes an employee statement by Federal Parcel:

1. If Lori made it while she was working for Federal Parcel, even if she'd been fired by the time the case came to trial.

2. If Lori made it while she was working for Federal Parcel, but only if she is still a Federal Parcel employee when the case comes to trial.

3. Only if Federal Parcel expressly or impliedly adopts Lori's statement.

4. Only if Lori has express authority to speak for Federal Parcel.

Problem 13-19: No Brakes

Rachel is injured when the car she is driving is struck by a car driven by Jeff. Rachel sues Jeff and also Sue, the car's owner, for failing to maintain the car properly. Rachel testifies that after the accident, Jeff told her that "I stepped on the brakes in plenty of time to stop before hitting you, but the car never slowed down." Rachel's attorney is conducting Jeff's direct examination, and seeks to offer Jeff's hearsay statement into evidence as Sue's statement. *Based on the foundation set forth below, how would you rule on Rachel's offer?*

PLAINTIFF'S ATTORNEY: Jeff, how did you happen to be driving Sue's car?

A: She called me from the airport, saying that she had forgotten her passport and asking me to bring it to her ASAP. She told me to use her car, since I was supposed to start it up a couple of times while she was away.

PLAINTIFF'S ATTORNEY: What happened after you received the call from Sue?

A: I went into her apartment, found the passport where she said it would be, and drove to the airport. It's when I was driving the car back to Sue's place that I collided with Rachel.

Would your answer be different if Jeff also testified that, "As she promised, Sue paid me $100 for retrieving her passport"?

Problem 13-20: Acid Remark

Seeking to rehabilitate two dilapidated inner-city apartment buildings that it owns so that they can be rented out to low- and middle-income families, City hires Get the Lead Out to remove all vestiges of lead paint from both premises. During the lead removal process, a Get the Lead Out employee spills acid on a passerby and says, "I'm sorry. I thought that was a container of juice. My bad for not sobering up before coming to work." The passerby sues City for personal injuries. *Is the Get the Lead Out employee's statement admissible against City under Rule 801(d)(2)(D)?*

Problem 13-21: Rumor Mill

In the *Mahlandt* case (see Problem 13-3 above), the parents of a young girl sued the Wild Canid Survival Center after Sophie, a wolf who was in the yard of the Center's Education Director, allegedly bit the girl. The parents seek to offer evidence that the day following the incident, a Wild Canid employee who cares for injured animals on the grounds of the Center itself told another employee that "I heard some talk that Sophie snapped at another kid a few weeks ago." *Is the employee's statement admissible against the Center under Rule 801(d)(2)(D)?*

§ 13.09 CO-CONSPIRATOR STATEMENTS (RULE 801(d)(2)(E))

Statutory Elements:

* The hearsay declarant is a party's co-conspirator;

  Co-conspirators are two or more people who knowingly join together to commit an illegal act.

* The statement was made in the course of the conspiracy;

* The declarant's statement was made in furtherance of the conspiracy;

* The party's adversary offers the hearsay statement into evidence.

When two or more partners engage in a common enterprise, each has implicit authority to speak for the enterprise so that an enterprise-related hearsay statement made by any one partner is admissible against any of the others. Rule 801(d)(2)(E) extends this general principle of agency law to illegal enterprises.

Example

Ralph is charged with selling illegal drugs. Ralph's confederate, Alice, tells the undercover police officer who pretends to be purchasing the drugs that "Ralph just got these in — our finest quality goods ever." If the Rule 801(d)(2)(E) foundational requirements are met, the government could offer Alice's statement into evidence against Ralph to prove that the drugs that Alice tried to sell to the police officer belonged to Ralph.

The exemption for co-conspirator statements is a major prosecutorial weapon. Co-conspirator statements are potentially admissible whenever two or more persons have joined together in illegal activity, even if only one of the persons is a defendant and even if a defendant isn't charged with a crime of conspiracy. For example, assume again that the government offers evidence that Alice and Ralph joined together to sell illegal drugs. Alice's statement to the undercover police officer may be admitted against Ralph under the coconspirator exemption even if only Ralph is a defendant in the case, or Ralph is charged only with selling illegal drugs, not with the crime of conspiracy to sell illegal drugs. (As you probably recall if you've studied criminal law, "conspiracy" is itself a crime, independent of the crime that conspirators try to commit or succeed in committing.)

The United States Supreme Court clarified the foundational requirements for co-conspirator statements (and by implication for the other exemptions for opposing parties' statements) in *Bourjaily v. United States* (*see* Case Library). (The case name is vaguely reminiscent of a fine red wine. If so, the vintage probably left a bitter aftertaste in many defendants' mouths.) In *Bourjaily*, the defendant was charged with conspiring with Angelo Lonardo to distribute cocaine and with possession of cocaine for sale. The Court held that what Lonardo said about the drug deal to an undercover FBI informant was admissible against the defendant as admissions of a co-conspirator. In the course of its opinion, the Court ruled that judges were to determine the admissibility of vicarious statements pursuant to Rule 104(a), meaning that the government had to convince the trial judge of the sufficiency of the foundation by a "preponderance of the evidence." And because

Rule 104(a) states that courts need not adhere to evidentiary rules (except privilege) when determining whether foundations are sufficient, the trial judge could consider Lonardo's statements themselves as evidence that Lonardo and the defendant were co-conspirators.

Left open by *Bourjaily* was the question of whether a co-conspirator's hearsay statements alone could be sufficient to prove that a conspiracy existed. The *Bourjaily* court did not have to decide this issue because the government in that case offered evidence independent of Lonardo's statements that Lonardo and the defendant were co-conspirators. The defendant showed up at the pre-arranged time in the parking lot, put the cocaine in his car, and at the time of his arrest had more than $20,000 in cash in his car. After *Bourjaily* was decided, Congress amended Rule 801 to ensure that a hearsay statement alone was not sufficient to establish the foundation for any type of vicarious statement. Thus, Rule 801(d)(2) currently provides that "The statement must be considered but does not by itself establish the declarant's authority under (C); the existence or scope of the relationship under (D); or the existence of the conspiracy or participation in it under (E)."

Practice Tip: Rule 801(d)(2)(E) and prosecutorial discretion.

The hearsay exemption for co-conspirator statements helps to explain why prosecutors often forego filing conspiracy charges even when they have evidence that two or more defendants joined together to commit a crime. Prosecutors can offer co-conspirators' statements into evidence regardless of whether a defendant is charged with conspiracy. To satisfy the foundational elements for offering co-conspirator statements into evidence, prosecutors need only convince judges by a preponderance of the evidence that a declarant and a defendant were co-conspirators. By contrast, charging a defendant with conspiracy requires prosecutors to prove beyond a reasonable doubt that a conspiracy existed. Because judges may not punish a defendant convicted of, say, "conspiracy to rob a bank" and "bank robbery" any more severely than a defendant convicted simply of "bank robbery," prosecutors often choose to lighten their burden by foregoing conspiracy charges while putting co-conspirators' statements before judges and juries under Rule 801(d)(2)(E).

When defendants are charged with conspiracy and the government seeks to offer co-conspirator statements into evidence, the foundational issue that the judge has to decide by a preponderance of the evidence ("Was there a conspiracy?") is identical to the ultimate fact that the jury has to decide beyond a reasonable doubt ("Is the defendant guilty of conspiracy?") Thus, when a judge admits a statement into evidence under Rule 801(d)(2)(E), the jury is not informed that the judge has decided that a conspiracy existed.

Problem 13-22: Et tu Ilona?

Ilona is charged with killing Armando. At Ilona's trial, the government offers evidence that Justin committed the murder by putting rat poison in Armando's tea. To prove that Ilona conspired with Justin to kill Armando, the government calls Melissa as a witness to testify to a conversation she had with Justin. Ilona's attorney makes a hearsay objection. The prosecutor conducts a foundational mini-trial out of the jury's presence, during which Melissa testifies as follows:

PROSECUTOR: Do you know Justin?

A: Yes, we went to school together and we've stayed friends.

PROSECUTOR: When's the last time you saw him?

A: He was going up the walkway toward Armando's house.

PROSECUTOR: And did you speak with him?

A: Yes. I asked Justin what he was doing, and he said that he was finally going to get rid of Armando by poisoning his tea. He said that Ilona knew all about it and wanted to get rid of Armando, too, and that she had given him the rat poison that he was going to put in Armando's tea. He asked whether I wanted to help him out by distracting Armando's attention while he laced his tea with poison. I said no thanks, and walked away.

PROSECUTOR: I offer Justin's statement to Melissa into evidence against Ilona as the statement of a co-conspirator under Rule 801(d)(2)(E).

JUDGE: To prove what, counsel?

PROSECUTOR: To prove that Ilona knew that Justin planned to kill Armando and that she actively and intentionally participated in the killing by securing the rat poison.

DEFENSE ATTORNEY: I renew my hearsay objection. The foundation is inadequate.

JUDGE: (*How should the judge rule? Why?*)

Problem 13-23: Loot Out

Tom and Dick rob a bank, and Dick is now on trial for the robbery. To prove that Dick was armed with a weapon during the robbery, the prosecutor calls Tom's friend Harry, who testifies during a mini-trial out of the jury's presence to the following events that took place on the day following the bank robbery:

PROSECUTOR: And what happened when you arrived at Tom's apartment?

A: As soon as I walked in, I saw bundles of money on the coffee table. I asked him how he'd gotten so much cash.

PROSECUTOR: Did Tom reply to this?

A: Yes. He said that he and Dick had had some luck robbing a bank, and that this was his share of the take.

PROSECUTOR: Did you respond to this remark?

A: Yes. I said, "Sorry, Tom, we've been friends for a long time, but I might have to tell the cops about this."

PROSECUTOR: And what, if anything, did Tom say in response?

A: He told me to do what I like, and then said that Dick had an itchy trigger finger. He said that Dick had used a gun in the bank and probably wouldn't hesitate to use it on me. He said that I'd been a good friend over the years, but that he and Dick had done enough time in their lives and they had decided in advance that they would do whatever it took not to go back to prison.

PROSECUTOR: That's the foundation, Your Honor. I offer Tom's statements as co-conspirator statements by Dick under Rule 801(d)(2)(E).

JUDGE: *Assume that sufficient evidence independent of this statement exists to establish as a foundational matter that Tom and Dick were co-conspirators. Would you admit what Tom said against Dick under the hearsay exemption for co-conspirators' statements?*

Problem 13-24: Handoff

Sol is charged with conspiring with his sister Pearl to distribute cocaine. The prosecutor offers evidence from Ben, a government informant, that on three occasions Ben bought cocaine from Pearl. According to Ben, he and Pearl would fly in a small private plane to a local airport, Pearl would go to a phone and make a call, and a short time later a cab from the Blue Cab Co. would pull up and a man would reach out and hand Pearl a package, which later turned out to contain cocaine; the cab would then drive away. When Ben asked, "Who are you calling," Pearl said, "Sol." Ben asked, "Sol isn't a government informant, is he?" Pearl said, "No, silly, Sol is my brother." After the third drug transaction, the informant arrested Pearl. Other police officers then went to Sol's house and arrested him. The government also offers records of the Blue Cab Co. showing that on two of the three dates that drug transactions took place, one of its cabs picked up a passenger on a corner two blocks away from Sol's address, took the passenger to the airport, and dropped the passenger off at the same corner. Elana, a Blue Cab Co. cabdriver, testifies at the foundational hearing that "It's possible that Sol is the person I picked up on the corner, drove to the airport, and then returned to the corner, but I can't be sure."

1. Assuming that the foundational requirements of Rule 801(d)(2)(E) are satisfied, if Pearl does not testify, is the prosecutor barred from offering Pearl's statements to Ben (a government agent) into evidence against Sol under the Confrontation Clause as interpreted by *Crawford v. Washington* (*see* Chapter 10)?

2. Foundational Argument

Student # 1: You are the prosecutor, and will argue that you've offered a sufficient foundation to admit Pearl's statements against Sol as the statements of a co-conspirator.

Student # 2: You are the defense attorney, and will argue that the foundation is insufficient for Pearl's statements to be admitted against Sol.

Student # 3: You are the judge; preside over the arguments and rule on the admissibility of Pearl's statements against Sol.

Problem 13-25: The Latecomer

Patricia is charged with armed bank robbery. The prosecutor has offered evidence that Thelma and Louise robbed a bank using weapons and then escaped in a getaway car driven by Patricia. The prosecutor also offers evidence that Thelma and Louise asked Patricia to drive the getaway car one day before the robbery took place, when they pulled out a book, "Bank Robbery in a Nutshell," and read that "The successful robber needs a getaway car." To prove that Patricia is guilty of the more severe charge of an "armed" robbery, the government offers evidence that one week before the robbery, Thelma told Louise, "Be sure to bring your gun. We'll shoot our way out of the bank if necessary." Patricia objects to the admission of this statement as hearsay. *The court should:*

1. Sustain the objection because the passage from the *Nutshell* is inadmissible hearsay.

2. Sustain the objection because Thelma's statement was not made in the course of Patricia's membership in the conspiracy.

3. Sustain the objection because the statement was not made in Patricia's presence.

4. Overrule the objection.

Problem 13-26: At the Movies: Change of Emphasis

In the comic courtroom film *My Cousin Vinny*,[3] Bill and Stan stop at a convenience store while driving cross country to attend college at UCLA. They buy a few items and leave, and are shocked when the police soon pull their car over and place them under arrest for killing the store's clerk in the course of committing a robbery. At the police station, Bill and Stan are interviewed separately. After waiving his right to talk to an attorney and agreeing to talk, Bill says in wonderment to a police officer, "I shot the clerk? I shot the clerk?" At Bill and Stan's trial on a charge of murder, the police officer repeats Bill's statements as an assertion, "I shot the clerk."

True or False: Bill's statement is admissible against Stan under the coconspirator exemption.

Problem 13-27: Unfilled Offer

Rasheed is charged with murdering Patel, a drug dealer. The prosecution claims that Rasheed and Pierre jointly planned and carried out the killing so as to take control of Patel's drug business. A police informant who had posed as a drug buyer will testify on the prosecution's behalf that when he arrested Rasheed in a quiet nighttime raid, Pierre was still at large. Pierre was apparently unaware of Rasheed's arrest because the next day, Pierre contacted the same informant and said, "I'll sell you some of the drugs that Rasheed and I took after we got rid of Patel; I'm expecting Rasheed to bring it by my place later today."

---

[3] 20th Century Fox, 1992.

True or False: Pierre's offer to sell drugs to the informant is admissible against Rasheed under the co-conspirator exemption.

Comparative Note: *California Foundational Requirements.* California departs from the federal rules with respect to the foundational requirements for vicarious statements in two ways. First, California judges decide these issues under Evidence Code Section 403, California's equivalent of Federal Rule of Evidence 104(b). Some commentators are particularly critical of the California rule in the context of co-conspirator statements, believing that jurors are particularly likely to "bootstrap" in this context. In other words, use of the lower foundational threshold of admissibility means that co-conspirator statements are more likely to be heard by jurors in California than in federal court trials, giving California jurors the opportunity to use the statements themselves to determine the adequacy of the proof of the other foundational requirements. At the same time, as a result of a second conflict between the California and the FRE, in California the foundation for vicarious statements has to be established entirely independently of the statements' contents. Thus, the California rules with respect to foundational requirements for vicarious statements appear to be just a bit schizoid.

Problem 13-28: Transcript Exercise

Bob Roberts is charged with possession of illegal drugs (cocaine) for sale. The government contends that Roberts and Sam Samuels received a shipment of cocaine with a street value of about $500,000 with the intent to sell it off in pieces to a network of local distributors. The police found the drugs in the trunk of Samuels's car, during a search pursuant to a valid search warrant. Roberts claims that he had no knowledge of Samuels's involvement with illegal drugs, and that he thought that Samuels was in the business of importing and distributing legal dietary supplements and vitamins. Assume that all of the events referred to below took place prior to Roberts's arrest. The transcript below includes the direct, cross and redirect examination of Bill Williams and the direct examination of Jim James, both of whom are called to testify on behalf of the government. *Please respond to the italicized questions.*

PROSECUTOR: Mr. Williams, are you acquainted with the defendant Bob Roberts?

A: Yes. We work out at the same gym, so we talk to each other once in a while.

PROSECUTOR: Do you recall a conversation you had with the defendant sometime in early July?

A: I do. Bob told me that he'd met some guy who had an import business and that he was thinking of going in with him on some deals.

DEFENSE ATTORNEY: Objection, hearsay, move to strike.

PROSECUTOR: Opposing party statement, Your Honor.

DEFENSE ATTORNEY: The statement admits nothing.

JUDGE: Objection overruled. (*Is this ruling correct?*)

§ 13.09   CO-CONSPIRATOR STATEMENTS (RULE 801(d)(2)(E))   621

PROSECUTOR: Did you respond?

A: Yes, I asked Bob what he'd be importing, and he said that he wasn't exactly sure but that he hoped he'd someday be making a pot of money.

DEFENSE ATTORNEY: Objection to that portion of the answer that consists of speculation by Mr. Roberts.

JUDGE: Overruled. (*Is this ruling correct?*)

Q: Did he mention that the guy he'd be doing business with was Sam Samuels?

DEFENSE ATTORNEY: Objection, leading.

JUDGE: Overruled. (*Is this ruling correct?*)

A: I don't really remember.

PROSECUTOR: All right, then what happened?

A: A woman walked over to us, I'm not sure of her name, but I'd often seen her at the gym. We nodded hello to her. She said hi, and asked Bob if the rumors were true that he'd soon be getting his hands on some top-quality cocaine.

PROSECUTOR: Would the defendant have been able to hear what she said?

DEFENSE ATTORNEY: Objection, calls for speculation.

JUDGE: Overruled. (*Is this ruling correct?*)

A: I'm sure he did. We were all standing right next to each other.

PROSECUTOR: Had the defendant ever spoken with this woman previously?

DEFENSE ATTORNEY: (*What objection if any might you raise with respect to this question?*)

A: I'm sure he had. We all often happen to work out around the same time, so I'm sure he's spoken to her.

PROSECUTOR: What, if anything, did the defendant do in response?

A: He just said that he had to finish his workout, and walked over to a stair-climbing machine.

DEFENSE ATTORNEY: Objection to the woman's remark and move to strike, hearsay.

PROSECUTOR: (*How would you respond to the defendant's objection?*)

JUDGE: (*After hearing the prosecutor's response, how would you rule on the defendant's objection?*)

PROSECUTOR: Nothing further at this time.

JUDGE: Defense may cross-examine.

DEFENSE ATORNEY: Mr. Williams, do you recall talking with Paula Dreck, who identified herself as my investigator?

A: I do.

DEFENSE ATTORNEY: And didn't you tell Ms. Dreck that you couldn't remember whether the woman who talked to you and Mr. Roberts at the gym said anything about cocaine?

PROSECUTOR: Objection, improper hearsay, what the witness said to Ms. Dreck was not under oath.

JUDGE: Overruled. (*Is this ruling correct?*)

DEFENSE ATTORNEY: But now after meeting a few times with the prosecutor you can miraculously remember that she used the word "cocaine"?

PROSECUTOR: (*What objection if any could you raise with respect to this question?*)

A: Well, I've thought about it more since then.

DEFENSE ATTORNEY: Isn't it true that a month ago the restaurant that you're a part owner of was cited for serving alcohol to underage minors?

A: That's true.

DEFENSE ATTORNEY: And that citation was later cancelled?

A: Yes, it was all a mistake.

DEFENSE ATTORNEY: Wasn't it cancelled only after you agreed to testify that this woman at the gym used the word "cocaine"?

A: That's not true — there's absolutely no connection.

DEFENSE ATTORNEY: Mr. Williams, didn't you also tell Ms. Dreck that you had never observed Mr. Roberts using drugs?

PROSECUTOR: (*What objection if any could you raise with respect to this question?*)

A: I did.

DEFENSE ATTORNEY: And you've been arrested twice, once for spousal abuse and once for making false statements in an application for a liquor license, isn't that right?

PROSECUTOR: (*What objection if any could you raise with respect to this question?*)

A: That's true.

DEFENSE ATTORNEY: Nothing further.

JUDGE: Anything further from the prosecutor on redirect examination?

PROSECUTOR: Just one matter, Your Honor. Mr. Williams, did you talk to the police about this conversation in the gym before or after your restaurant was cited for serving alcohol to underage minors?

A: I talked to the police before getting the citation.

§ 13.09   CO-CONSPIRATOR STATEMENTS (RULE 801(d)(2)(E))   623

PROSECUTOR: And when you spoke to the police about this conversation, was it before or after you spoke to Ms. Dreck, the defense investigator?

A: It was after I talked to her.

PROSECUTOR: And what did you tell the police about what the woman had said in this conversation?

A: I told them what I testified to today — that she mentioned that she'd heard that he'd be getting his hands on some cocaine.

DEFENSE ATTORNEY: Objection, hearsay.

PROSECUTOR: Your Honor, I offer this as a prior consistent statement under Rule 801(d)(1)(B) to rebut the charge that the witness' testimony was motivated by the cancellation of the citation.

JUDGE: *(What ruling on the objection?)*

JUDGE: Any further prosecution witnesses?

PROSECUTOR: I call Jim James as a witness. Mr. James, are you acquainted with the defendant Mr. Roberts as well as with Sam Samuels?

A: Yes, I am.

PROSECUTOR: I'd like to ask you about a conversation you had with the defendant, Mr. Roberts, on August 1. Where were you on that evening?

A: I was in the Lizard Lounge, just relaxing.

PROSECUTOR: And did you see the defendant on that evening?

A: Yeah — Bob came in a little while after I did.

PROSECUTOR: And what happened?

A: He walked over to the table where I was sitting with Ed Edwards. We started talking. Bob said something about getting into a deal with Sam Samuels. Ed said that he should be careful — that Samuels was a big drug dealer who the cops probably had their eyes on.

DEFENSE ATTORNEY: Objection, hearsay.

PROSECUTOR: Not offered for the truth, Your Honor.

JUDGE: *(What ruling?)*

PROSECUTOR: Did the defendant respond to Mr. Edwards' comment?

A: Yes. Bob said that the deal was a lock, that there was no way that the cops could trace the goods that he was about to get hold of.

PROSECUTOR: And what do you think the defendant meant by the term "goods?"

DEFENSE ATTORNEY: *(What objection if any could you raise with respect to this question?)*

A: He was referring to illegal drugs.

PROSECUTOR: Then what happened?

A: I was getting tired, so I got up to go home.

PROSECUTOR: Did you speak to anyone before you got home?

A: Yes, as I got to my car, Sam Samuels walked over to me.

PROSECUTOR: What happened then?

A: We just talked about a couple of things, and then he asked whether I still had a space in a storage facility over on 3rd Street. I said that I did. He asked did I mind storing some drugs for him and Bob Roberts for a couple of weeks. I said that I was done with that sort of thing, and drove home.

DEFENSE ATTORNEY: Objection, hearsay.

PROSECUTOR: Statement of a co-conspirator under Rule 801(d)(2)(E), Your Honor.

Student # 1: As the prosecutor, argue that the government has satisfied the foundational elements for the co-conspirator exemption.

Student # 2: As the defense attorney, argue that the government has not satisfied the foundational elements for the co-conspirator exemption.

Student # 3: As the Judge, preside over the arguments and rule on the admissibility of the statement.

§ 13.10 MULTIPLE-CHOICE REVIEW QUESTIONS

Review Problem 13-A

Jyoti Williamson is charged with attempting to blow up a federal building. Jyoti's first statement to the arresting officer was "Rats! All that McGregor and I needed was one more day to finish making the bomb." The government seeks to offer Jyoti's statement into evidence against McGregor. *The judge should rule that:*

1. The statement is inadmissible unless McGregor is charged with conspiring with Jyoti to blow up a federal building.

2. The statement is inadmissible unless McGregor is charged with conspiring with Jyoti to blow up a federal building and they are tried together.

3. The statement is inadmissible hearsay.

4. The statement is admissible against McGregor so long as the government also offers evidence independent of the statement that Jyoti and McGregor jointly attempted to blow up a federal building, regardless of whether McGregor is charged with conspiracy.

Review Problem 13-B

In a civil suit for personal injuries, plaintiff Jackson testifies that defendant Carter was the driver of a car that struck and injured Jackson as Jackson attempted to cross a road. Carter denies any involvement in the accident. During direct examination, Jackson seeks to testify that "When I saw Carter's photo in the newspaper about a week after the accident, I said to my spouse, "Can you believe that the paper has a photo of the driver who hit me last week?" *Jackson's testimony would be:*

1. Admissible under Rule 801(d)(2) to prove that Carter was the driver of the car that struck Jackson.

2. Admissible as a prior identification to prove that Carter was the driver of the car that struck Jackson.

3. Admissible as non-hearsay to support Jackson's credibility because Jackson's words don't directly assert that Carter was the driver of the car.

4. Inadmissible hearsay.

Review Problem 13-C

Poppy sues the Hi Carb Bagel Co. for damages resulting from a collision involving Poppy's car and Hi Carb delivery van # 2. Poppy seeks to offer evidence that when the driver of the van reported the accident to Arturo, Hi Carb's chief mechanic, Arturo, stated, "We should have taken care of the brakes on that van months ago." Arturo's statement is:

1. Admissible as Hi Carb's employee statement to prove that van # 2 was not properly maintained.

2. Inadmissible hearsay because Arturo lacked personal knowledge of whether failure to maintain the brakes was in any way responsible for the collision.

3. Admissible as non-hearsay to show that the van's driver knew or should have known that the van was unsafe to drive.

4. Inadmissible hearsay in the absence of foundational evidence indicating that Arturo's job duties include driving delivery vans.

Review Problem 13-D

Breach of contract case brought by Pierre against de la Torre; de la Torre contends that the parties never entered into an agreement. Prior to trial, de la Torre's lawyer sends an e-mail to Pierre's attorney stating in part that "my client may have violated the contract, but it'll cost you lots of time and money to prove it, so we'll give you half of what you're asking for, take it or leave it." Pierre leaves it, and the case goes to trial. Pierre seeks to offer the above portion of the e-mail into evidence to prove that a valid contract existed. The judge should rule that:

1. The e-mail is inadmissible under Rule 408 because the statement was made in an effort to resolve the claim prior to trial.

2. The e-mail is inadmissible in the absence of foundational evidence showing

that de la Torre authorized the lawyer to send the email to Pierre's lawyer.

3. The e-mail is admissible to prove that a contract existed and that de la Torre breached it.

4. Based on the e-mail, the judge should rule that as a matter of law a valid contract existed and de la Torre breached it.

§ 13.11 CASE LIBRARY

BOURJAILY v. UNITED STATES
United States Supreme Court 483 U.S. 171, 107 S. Ct. 2775, 97 L. Ed. 2d 144 (1987)

REHNQUIST, C. J., delivered the opinion of the Court, in which WHITE, POWELL, STEVENS, O'CONNOR, and SCALIA, JJ., joined. STEVENS, J., filed a concurring opinion. BLACKMUN, J., filed a dissenting opinion, in which BRENNAN and MARSHALL, JJ., joined.

CHIEF JUSTICE REHNQUIST delivered the opinion of the Court.

Federal Rule of Evidence 801(d)(2)(E) provides: "A statement is not hearsay if . . . the statement is offered against a party and is . . . a statement by a coconspirator of a party during the course and in furtherance of the conspiracy." We granted certiorari to answer three questions regarding the admission of statements under Rule 801(d)(2)(E): (1) whether the court must determine by independent evidence that the conspiracy existed and that the defendant and the declarant were members of this conspiracy; (2) the quantum of proof on which such determinations must be based; and (3) whether a court must in each case examine the circumstances of such a statement to determine its reliability.

In May 1984, Clarence Greathouse, an informant working for the Federal Bureau of Investigation (FBI), arranged to sell a kilogram of cocaine to Angelo Lonardo. Lonardo agreed that he would find individuals to distribute the drug. When the sale became imminent, Lonardo stated in a tape-recorded telephone conversation that he had a "gentleman friend" who had some questions to ask about the cocaine. In a subsequent telephone call, Greathouse spoke to the "friend" about the quality of the drug and the price. Greathouse then spoke again with Lonardo, and the two arranged the details of the purchase. They agreed that the sale would take place in a designated hotel parking lot, and Lonardo would transfer the drug from Greathouse's car to the "friend," who would be waiting in the parking lot in his own car. Greathouse proceeded with the transaction as planned, and FBI agents arrested Lonardo and petitioner immediately after Lonardo placed a kilogram of cocaine into petitioner's car in the hotel parking lot. In petitioner's car, the agents found over $ 20,000 in cash.

Petitioner was charged with conspiring to distribute cocaine and possession of cocaine with intent to distribute. The Government introduced, over petitioner's objection, Angelo Lonardo's telephone statements regarding the participation of the "friend" in the transaction. The District Court found that, considering the events in the parking lot and Lonardo's statements over the telephone, the Government had established by a preponderance of the evidence that a conspiracy involving Lonardo and petitioner existed, and that Lonardo's statements over the telephone had been made in the course of and in furtherance of the conspiracy. Accordingly, the trial court held that Lonardo's out-of-court statements satisfied Rule 801(d)(2)(E) and were not hearsay. Petitioner was convicted on both counts and sentenced to 15 years. We affirm.

Before admitting a co-conspirator's statement over an objection that it does not qualify under Rule 801(d)(2)(E), a court must be satisfied that the statement actually falls within the definition of the Rule. There must be evidence that there was a conspiracy involving the declarant and the nonoffering party, and that the statement was made "during the course and in furtherance of the conspiracy." Federal Rule of Evidence 104(a) provides: "Preliminary questions concerning . . . the admissibility of evidence shall be determined by the court." Petitioner and the Government agree that the existence of a conspiracy and petitioner's involvement in it are preliminary questions of fact that, under Rule 104, must be resolved by the court. The Federal Rules, however, nowhere define the standard of proof the court must observe in resolving these questions.

We are therefore guided by our prior decisions regarding admissibility determinations that hinge on preliminary factual questions. We have traditionally required that these matters be established by a preponderance of proof. Evidence is placed before the jury when it satisfies the technical requirements of the evidentiary Rules, which embody certain legal and policy determinations. The inquiry made by a court concerned with these matters is not whether the proponent of the evidence wins or loses his case on the merits, but whether the evidentiary Rules have been satisfied. Thus, the evidentiary standard is unrelated to the burden of proof on the substantive issues, be it a criminal case, or a civil case. The preponderance standard ensures that before admitting evidence, the court will have found it more likely than not that the technical issues and policy concerns addressed by the Federal Rules of Evidence have been afforded due consideration. Therefore, we hold that when the preliminary facts relevant to Rule 801(d)(2)(E) are disputed, the offering party must prove them by a preponderance of the evidence.

Even though petitioner agrees that the courts below applied the proper standard of proof with regard to the preliminary facts relevant to Rule 801(d)(2)(E), he nevertheless challenges the admission of Lonardo's statements. Petitioner argues that in determining whether a conspiracy exists and whether the defendant was a member of it, the court must look only to independent evidence — that is, evidence other than the statements sought to be admitted.

The Federal Rules of Evidence now govern the treatment of evidentiary questions in federal courts. Rule 104(a) provides: "Preliminary questions concerning . . . the admissibility of evidence shall be determined by the court . . . . In making its determination it is not bound by the rules of evidence except those with respect to privileges." Similarly, Rule 1101(d)(1) states that the Rules of Evidence (other than with respect to privileges) shall not apply to "the determination of questions of fact preliminary to admissibility of evidence when the issue is to be determined by the court under rule 104."

Petitioner concedes that Rule 104, on its face, appears to allow the court to make the preliminary factual determinations relevant to Rule 801(d)(2)(E) by considering any evidence it wishes, unhindered by considerations of admissibility. That would seem to many to be the end of the matter. Congress has decided that courts may consider hearsay in making these factual determinations. Out-of-court statements made by anyone, including putative co-conspirators, are often hearsay. Even if they are, they may be considered. But petitioner nevertheless argues that the bootstrapping rule, as most Courts of Appeals have construed it, survived this apparently unequivocal change in the law unscathed and that Rule 104, as applied to the admission of co-conspirator's statements, does not mean what it says. We disagree.

Petitioner claims that Congress evidenced no intent to disturb the bootstrapping rule, which was embedded in the previous approach, and we should not find that Congress altered the rule without affirmative evidence so indicating. It would be extraordinary to require legislative history to *confirm* the plain meaning of Rule 104. The Rule on its face allows the trial judge to consider any evidence whatsoever, bound only by the rules of privilege. We think that the Rule is sufficiently clear that to the extent that it is inconsistent with petitioner's interpretation of *Glasser* and *Nixon*, the Rule prevails.

We think that there is little doubt that a co-conspirator's statements could themselves be probative of the existence of a conspiracy and the participation of both the defendant and the declarant in the conspiracy. Petitioner's case presents a paradigm. The out-of-court statements of Lonardo indicated that Lonardo was involved in a conspiracy with a "friend." The statements indicated that the friend had agreed with Lonardo to buy a kilogram of cocaine and to distribute it. The statements also revealed that the friend would be at the hotel parking lot, in his car, and would accept the cocaine from Greathouse's car after Greathouse gave Lonardo the keys. Each one of Lonardo's statements may itself be unreliable, but taken as a whole, the entire conversation between Lonardo and Greathouse was corroborated by independent evidence. The friend, who turned out to be petitioner, showed up at the prearranged spot at the prearranged time. He picked up the cocaine, and a significant sum of money was found in his car. On these facts, the trial court concluded, in our view correctly, that the Government had established the existence of a conspiracy and petitioner's participation in it.

We need not decide in this case whether the courts below could have relied solely upon Lonardo's hearsay statements to determine that a conspiracy had been established by a preponderance of the evidence. To the extent that *Glasser* meant that courts could not look to the hearsay statements themselves for any purpose, it has clearly been superseded by Rule 104(a). It is sufficient for today to hold that a court, in making a preliminary factual determination under Rule 801(d)(2)(E), may examine the hearsay statements sought to be admitted. As we have held in other cases concerning admissibility determinations, "the judge should receive the evidence and give it such weight as his judgment and experience counsel." The courts below properly considered the statements of Lonardo and the subsequent events in finding that the Government had established by a preponderance of the evidence that Lonardo was involved in a conspiracy with petitioner. We have no reason to believe that the District Court's factfinding of this point was clearly erroneous. We hold that Lonardo's out-of-court statements were properly admitted.

Chapter 14

THE ADMISSIBILITY OF HEARSAY STATEMENTS UNDER RULE 803

§ 14.01 CHAPTER CHECKLIST

1. Does admissibility of hearsay under Rule 803 depend on a declarant's availability to testify?

2. Are the trustworthiness considerations underlying each Rule 803 hearsay exception the same?

3. How does the permitted gap between event and statement differ among the exceptions for present sense impressions, excited utterances, and past recollection recorded?

4. For an excited utterance to be admissible, does it have to have been made spontaneously?

5. If a hearsay statement satisfies any one of the Rule 803 foundational requirements, is it admissible as a matter of law?

6. Does the admissibility of an excited utterance require that an event be both objectively and subjectively startling?

7. For a statement to qualify under the medical hearsay exception, must it be made to a treating physician? Can it qualify for admission if it is made to non-physicians?

8. When might a statement be admissible under the medical hearsay exception, but not under the "state of mind" exception?

9. How does the "state of mind" hearsay exception compare to non-hearsay uses of statements as circumstantial evidence of state of mind?

10. Does the "state of mind" exception make admissible an assertion of the fact giving rise to the state of mind?

11. What are three common ways of obtaining evidence from a forgetful witness? Which of these depend on use of a document prepared or adopted by the forgetful witness?

12. Does the business records exception apply only to the records of for-profit entities?

13. What is the role of a "sponsoring witness" when a party seeks to offer a business or official record into evidence?

14. Do the business record and public record exceptions both require that a document be prepared in the regular course of operations?

15. Are police reports admissible against criminal defendants under the public records exception?

16. Case Library:

Hillmon v. Mutual Life Insurance

United States v. Pheaster

United States v. Tome

Palmer v. Hoffman

Beech Aircraft Corporation v. Rainey

§ 14.02 RELEVANT FEDERAL RULES OF EVIDENCE

Rule 612. Writing Used to Refresh a Witness's Memory

    (a) Scope. This rule gives an adverse party certain options when a witness uses a writing to refresh memory:

        (1) while testifying; or

        (2) before testifying, if the court decides that justice requires the party to have those options.

    (b) Adverse Party's Options; Deleting Unrelated Matter. Unless 18 U.S.C. § 3500 provides otherwise in a criminal case, an adverse party is entitled to have the writing produced at the hearing, to inspect it, to cross-examine the witness about it, and to introduce in evidence any portion that relates to the witness's testimony. If the producing party claims that the writing includes unrelated matter, the court must examine the writing in camera, delete any unrelated portion, and order that the rest be delivered to the adverse party. Any portion deleted over objection must be preserved for the record.

    (c) Failure to Produce or Deliver the Writing. If a writing is not produced or is not delivered as ordered, the court may issue any appropriate order. But if the prosecution does not comply in a criminal case, the court must strike the witness's testimony or — if justice so requires — declare a mistrial.

Rule 803. Exceptions to the Rule Against Hearsay — Regardless of Whether the Declarant Is Available as a Witness (partial text)

The following are not excluded by the rule against hearsay, regardless of whether the declarant is available as a witness:

    (1) *Present Sense Impression.* A statement describing or explaining an event or condition, made while or immediately after the declarant perceived it.

(2) *Excited Utterance.* A statement relating to a startling event or condition, made while the declarant was under the stress of excitement that it caused.

(3) *Then-Existing Mental, Emotional, or Physical Condition.* A statement of the declarant's then-existing state of mind (such as motive, intent, or plan) or emotional, sensory, or physical condition (such as mental feeling, pain, or bodily health), but not including a statement of memory or belief to prove the fact remembered or believed unless it relates to the validity or terms of the declarant's will.

(4) *Statement Made for Medical Diagnosis or Treatment. A statement that:*

    (A) is made for — and is reasonably pertinent to — medical diagnosis or treatment; and

    (B) describes medical history; past or present symptoms or sensations; their inception; or their general cause.

(5) *Recorded Recollection* A record that:

    (A) is on a matter the witness once knew about but now cannot recall well enough to testify fully and accurately;

    (B) was made or adopted by the witness when the matter was fresh in the witness's memory; and

    (C) accurately reflects the witness's knowledge.

If admitted, the record may be read into evidence but may be received as an exhibit only if offered by an adverse party.

(6) *Records of a Regularly Conducted Activity.* A record of an act, event, condition, opinion, or diagnosis if:

    (A) the record was made at or near the time by — or from information transmitted by — someone with knowledge;

    (B) the record was kept in the course of a regularly conducted activity of a business, organization, occupation, or calling, whether or not for profit;

    (C) making the record was a regular practice of that activity;

    (D) all these conditions are shown by the testimony of the custodian or another qualified witness, or by a certification that complies with Rule 902(11) or (12) or with a statute permitting certification;

    And

    (E) neither the source of information nor the method or circumstances of preparation indicate a lack of trustworthiness.

(7) *Absence of a Record of a Regularly Conducted Activity.* Evidence that a matter is not included in a record described in paragraph (6) if:

    (A) the evidence is admitted to prove that the matter did not occur or exist;

(B) a record was regularly kept for a matter of that kind; and

(C) neither the possible source of the information nor other circumstances indicate a lack of trustworthiness.

(8) *Public Records.* A record or statement of a public office if:

(A) it sets out:

(i) the office's activities;

(ii) a matter observed while under a legal duty to report, but not including, in a criminal case, a matter observed by law-enforcement personnel; or

(iii) in a civil case or against the government in a criminal case, factual findings from a legally authorized investigation; and

(B) neither the source of information nor other circumstances indicate a lack of trustworthiness.

(10) *Absence of a Public Record.* Testimony — or a certification under Rule 902 — that a diligent search failed to disclose a public record or statement if the testimony or certification is admitted to prove that:

(A) the record or statement does not exist; or

(B) a matter did not occur or exist, if a public office regularly kept a record or statement for a matter of that kind.

§ 14.03 INTRODUCTION

This chapter examines the major categories of hearsay statements that satisfy foundational requirements set forth in Rule 803 and thus may be admitted into evidence as exceptions to the hearsay rule. Like the Rule 801 hearsay exemptions reviewed in Chapters 12 and 13, Rule 803 exceptions make out-of-court statements admissible for the truth of their contents. However, the Rule 801 hearsay exemptions apply to situations where the maker of the out-of-court statement is present in court either as a witness or a party. By contrast, Rule 803 admits out-of-court assertions from declarants whose presence in court is immaterial. That is, under Rule 803 a party offering the hearsay statement of a declarant who is absent from the trial does not have to explain or justify the declarant's absence for the statement to be admissible.[1]

Practice Tip: Substituting hearsay for in-court testimony.

As a tactical matter, attorneys generally prefer to offer live testimony rather than hearsay because the former is more likely to impress judges and jurors. However, attorneys can take advantage of Rule 803 to get

---

[1] A hearsay declarant's absence from trial may result in exclusion of hearsay under the Confrontation Clause as interpreted by *Crawford v. Washington* (see Chapter 10) if a prosecutor offers the hearsay into evidence against a criminal defendant.

helpful evidence into the record when hearsay declarants are "problem witnesses" whose live appearance may be damaging. For example, assume that a bystander's "present sense impression" supports a plaintiff's version of how a traffic accident took place. However, the bystander is unlikely to be a convincing witness, perhaps because of poor demeanor or because the witness is likely to testify to a version of events that is less helpful to the plaintiff than the hearsay. In either event, the plaintiff's attorney may prefer to present the hearsay through the testimony of a percipient witness who heard the bystander's remark rather than call the bystander as a witness.

Rule 803 has 23 subparts, each one identifying the foundational elements of a different hearsay exception. Under Rule 104(a), the party offering a hearsay assertion into evidence pursuant to one of these exceptions generally has the burden of convincing a judge by a preponderance of the evidence that the required foundational elements exist.[2]

Rule 803's introductory phrase ("*The following are not excluded by the hearsay rule . . .*") serves as a reminder that satisfying the foundational requirements for a hearsay exception is not an automatic ticket to admissibility because judges may exclude statements for other evidentiary failings. For example, hearsay may satisfy an exception but be barred by the Confrontation Clause. Similarly, under Rule 403, hearsay's potential for unfair prejudice may substantially outweigh its probative value, or hearsay satisfying a Rule 803 exception may be excluded because an assertion is unduly vague or speculative.

A number of important Rule 803 hearsay exceptions tie directly to topics examined in other chapters, and are therefore covered in those other chapters rather than this one. For example, Rule 803(18) provides a hearsay exception for "learned treatises." Treatises are hearsay when parties offer them for the truth of what they assert because they embody the written statements of the author. Because this exception allows parties to introduce expert testimony in the form of statements made in treatises that have been shown to be reliable, you will find a discussion of this exception in Chapter 9. Because they address forms of character evidence, the hearsay exceptions provided for by Rule 803(21) for reputation evidence and by Rule 803(22) for certain judgments of conviction are addressed in Chapter 5. Reputation evidence involves hearsay because the declarants are the people who make the assertions from which reputations are derived (e.g., "Sara is as honest as the day is long.") With convictions, the hearsay declarants are the convicting judges and jurors whose out-of-court statements ("the defendant is guilty") are offered for their truth (that the defendant committed the charged crime).

---

[2] While judges decide most Rule 803 foundational issues under Rule 104(a), declarants' personal knowledge is a foundational element in many of the 803 exceptions and judges determine personal knowledge pursuant to Rule 104(b). Typically, judges also resolve authenticity disputes (did the claimed declarant make the statement?) under Rule 104(b).

§ 14.04 TRUSTWORTHINESS

Trustworthiness is the common thread that ties together Rule 803 hearsay exceptions. Each exception's foundational elements define circumstances that the drafters of the Federal Rules of Evidence (who for the most part followed the lead of their common law forebears) considered likely to produce accurate assertions. The Rules regard the likelihood of assertions' accuracy as an acceptable trade-off for a party's possible inability to cross-examine a hearsay declarant.

Despite the lengthy common-law pedigree of most of the Rule 803 hearsay exceptions, their soundness is debatable for a number of reasons:

- The situations defined by the exceptions grouped together in Rule 803 are wildly disparate, so that one's confidence level that an exception's foundational elements correctly identify trustworthy assertions must vary from one exception to the next. Compare, for example, the likely accuracy of an assertion by a startled declarant (Rule 803(2)) with the likely accuracy of a routinely-prepared business record (Rule 803(6)).

- Even inside the fence posts of a single hearsay exception, the circumstances in which assertions are made may be very different yet still satisfy foundational requirements. For example, business records (Rule 803(6)) are likely to be admissible whether the record is that of a small, local not-for-profit organization or of a multinational corporation.

- Some of the exceptions are probably at least as much a product of folklore and tradition as empirical reality. For example, Rule 803(2) reflects the common wisdom that a startled declarant who immediately makes a statement regarding an exciting event is likely to be truthful and accurate. However, the common wisdom has not been borne out by empirical research, which often shows that startling events tend to distort observers' memory and perceptions.[3]

At the end of the day, the Rule 803 exceptions resolve these doubts in favor of admissibility, trusting to the ability of judges and jurors to recognize weaknesses and devalue even supposedly reliable hearsay to the extent warranted. Moreover, judges do have the authority to avoid the mischief that a set of pre-defined hearsay exceptions of varying degrees of reliability can create. On the one hand, though judges are not generally supposed to evaluate credibility when making admissibility determinations, at least some of the 803 exceptions incorporate trustworthiness into their foundational requirements (see, e.g., Rule 803 (6)). As a result, judges may have room to exclude hearsay of questionable trustworthiness. On the other, judges have the power under Rule 807 to admit a hearsay assertion even though it does not fit within any of the pre-ordained Rule 803 exceptions, so long as it has "equivalent circumstantial guarantees of trustworthiness."

---

[3] The classic essay suggesting the weakness of the reasoning underlying "excited utterances" is Hutchins & Schlesinger, *Some Observations on the Law of Evidence*, 28 Colum. L. Rev. 432 (1928). *See also* Moorehead, *Compromising the Hearsay Rule: The Fallacy of Res Gestae Reliability*, 29 Loy. L.A. L. Rev. 203 (1995); Stewart, *Perception, Memory and Hearsay: A Criticism of Present Law and the Proposed Federal Rules of Evidence*, 1970 Utah L. Rev. 1.

Practice Tip: "Objection, the statement is self-serving."

Though presumed trustworthiness is the common thread binding together the Rule 803 hearsay exceptions, most of them do not include an explicit foundational requirement that a hearsay statement be trustworthy. Nevertheless, and especially when parties testify to or otherwise offer into evidence their own hearsay statements, adversaries sometimes object on the ground that the evidence is "self-serving" and therefore untrustworthy. However, the "self-serving" objection does not exist and is improper. The admissibility of hearsay depends on whether it satisfies the foundational requirements of an exception, and presumably parties do not offer their own statements into evidence unless they are self-serving. A "self-serving" objection may be the equivalent of a claim that a party's own hearsay statement is motivated by self-interest and therefore is unworthy of belief. But it's up to jurors and not judges to determine the probative value of hearsay.

Problem 14-1: Redraft

The plaintiff in an auto accident case seeks to offer a bystander's statement into evidence as an "excited utterance" under Rule 803(2). The defense attorney objects and makes the following request:

> Your Honor, in support of my hearsay objection, I request that you conduct a foundational hearing out of the jury's presence so that I can make a record as to the general lack of trustworthiness of excited utterances. I am prepared to call three University researchers, who I will establish are regarded as the best experts in the field, to present the results of their independent research projects indicating that assertions made at a time when people are excited or under stress are much less likely to be accurate than statements made when people are calm and in full possession of their faculties. Based on their testimony and their research, the defense urges that the excited utterance exception is not grounded on empirical reality and that therefore you should exclude the bystander's hearsay statement.

Which, if any, of the rulings below might the judge properly make in response to the attorney's request?

1. The judge should grant the request and exclude the bystander's statement if the judge concludes that the excited utterance exception is not grounded in empirical reality.

2. The judge should deny the request and rule that because the experts' testimony would contradict Congress' findings in approving Rule 803(2), the experts' testimony is irrelevant and therefore inadmissible.

3. The judge should deny the request but allow the defense attorney to offer evidence concerning the effect of stress on accuracy for whatever weight the jury gives it.

4. The judge should deny the request and rule that expert testimony about the effect of stress on accuracy is irrelevant if the plaintiff offers evidence that

establishes by a preponderance of evidence that stress tends to improve accuracy.

§ 14.05 CONTEMPORANEOUS AND EXCITED UTTERANCES (RULES 803(1) AND (2))

Statutory Elements (803(1)):

- The declarant made a statement while or immediately after perceiving an event or condition;
- The statement describes or explains the event or condition.

Statutory Elements (803(2)):

- The declarant made a statement relating to a startling event or condition;
- The declarant was under the stress of excitement caused by the event or condition at the time the declarant made the statement.

Rules 803(1) and (2) authorize the admission of hearsay statements that declarants make roughly contemporaneously with the events or conditions that the statements describe. The narrow time frame between an event and a hearsay assertion relating to that event tends to obviate memory problems and to minimize a declarant's chance to reflect and make up a lie.[4]

Moreover, the admission of essentially contemporaneous statements usually furnishes an adversary with a reasonable opportunity to cross-examine. Either a declarant will testify to the declarant's own hearsay assertion, or a witness who personally heard the declarant make the assertion will testify to it. In the latter situation, the witness will almost certainly have witnessed the same event that the declarant did. Thus, a party will normally have an opportunity to cross-examine a percipient observer, even if not the declarant whose hearsay statement is received in evidence.

Admissibility under both of these exceptions requires that a declarant have first-hand knowledge. The personal knowledge element isn't stated explicitly in the rule, but the Advisory Committee Note to Rule 803 states that personal knowledge is an implicit requirement of these and virtually all hearsay exceptions.

Example 1

The plaintiff is a Chicago resident who has sued the owner of an apartment on the twentieth floor of a high-rise for damages for carelessly allowing a window air conditioner to fall out the window and injure the plaintiff, who at the time was walking under the window. The defendant denies that the air conditioner fell from his window. The plaintiff calls a passerby whose testimony is in part as follows:

PLAINTIFF'S ATTORNEY: And what happened as you walked along Wacker Drive?

---

[4] Examined from a more cynical perspective, of course, the effect of the hearsay exception is to reward really fast liars.

A: Just after I turned the corner I heard a loud noise coming from somewhere over my head. I looked up and saw what looked like a window air conditioner falling off a window ledge.

PLAINTIFF'S ATTORNEY: Were you alone when this happened?

A: No, I was on my way to lunch with a colleague from work.

PLAINTIFF'S ATTORNEY: What, if anything, did you say to the colleague when you saw the air conditioner begin to fall.

A: As soon as I saw it, I turned to my companion and said, "Oh my God, an air conditioner just fell out of that window, the one with the 'Let's Go Cubs!' sign in the window." [The defendant's window had such a sign in it.]

Here, the declarant observes an event that most people would find startling. The statement describes the event, and the declarant made the statement while under the stress of the excitement that the event created. Thus, it is a classic excited utterance. (When trying to establish that declarants spoke under the stress of excitement, you'll find it helpful, though not absolutely necessary, if the declarants were considerate enough to preface whatever they said with "Oh my God.")

The foundational requirement that an event be startling has both objective and subjective components. The subjective aspect is that a declarant has to be personally startled. It is possible, therefore, that an assertion might be excluded for the reason that though most people would have found an event startling, the declarant in question did not. For example, a Los Angeles driver might have a hard time convincing a judge that "I was startled by the sight of three drivers completing left turns after a traffic light in their direction turned red." The objective aspect is that an event must be one that most reasonable people would find unusual and startling. Thus, an assertion such as, "Oh my God, what a terrible hangnail that man has," is unlikely to qualify as an excited utterance.

Rule 803(2) eliminates the common-law foundational requirement that a startled utterance had to be "spontaneous." A few older decisions excluded assertions that were preceded by questions such as, "What happened to you?" on the ground that they weren't made spontaneously. Rule 803(2) saves lawyers who wander past the scenes of traffic accidents from the need to rush up to ambulance attendants and bystanders and instruct them, "Don't say a thing to the injured driver. Let's see what she has to say about what happened on her own." Nevertheless, if a proffered statement was preceded by other conversation, a judge may conclude that the declarant was not under the "stress of excitement" at the time the statement was made.

Example 2

Defendant Leticia is charged with murder; her defense is an alibi. The prosecution calls a witness who can place Leticia at the murder scene around the time of the killing:

PROSECUTOR: And at that time, what were you doing?

A: I was looking out my front window, waiting for a taxi.

PROSECUTOR: And then what happened?

A: I saw Leticia walk past and go into the house next door.

PROSECUTOR: Is Leticia someone you knew?

A: Oh, yes. She used to live in the neighborhood, but she'd moved away a few months earlier.

PROSECUTOR: Did you mention to anyone that you had seen Leticia?

A: Yes. As she was walking past my window I called out to my roommate that "Leticia just walked past our house."

Here, what the witness said to the roommate constitutes a present sense impression. The statement describes an event and the witness made it while perceiving the event.

The present sense impression exception is broader in scope than the exception for excited utterances in that the former does not require that an event or condition described by a statement be startling or in any way unusual. On the other hand, the excited utterance exception is broader in that it seems to permit a greater lapse of time between the time that an event occurs and a declarant makes a statement describing the event. A present sense impression must be made during or "immediately after" an event, which the Advisory Committee Note to Rule 803(1) describes as requiring "substantial contemporaneity." By contrast, the allowable time lapse between event and statement for an excited utterance is measured not merely by the clock, but also by judges' conclusions about how startling an event was and the duration of a declarant's state of excitement. If a judge concludes that the stress of excitement caused by an event continued for hours or even longer, a statement relating to that event might qualify as an excited utterance long after it would cease to qualify as a present sense impression.

Rule 803(2) is also potentially broader than Rule 803(1) in that the latter requires that a statement *describe or explain* an act or condition, while for the former to apply a statement need only *relate to* an event or condition.

Problem 14-2: Red or Blue

Denise, a pedestrian, sues Steve for injuries resulting from being struck in a hit-and-run, allegedly by Steve's red car. Steve's defense is that Denise was actually struck by a blue car that passed Steve's car shortly before the mishap. Marisa, an ambulance driver, arrived at the accident scene 10 minutes after Denise was struck. To prove that Denise was struck by a red car, her attorney calls Marisa, whose testimony is as follows:

PLAINTIFF'S ATTORNEY: Marisa, what did you see when you arrived at the scene of the accident?

A: Denise was laying on the ground, a few people were standing around her.

PLAINTIFF'S ATTORNEY: What did you notice about Denise?

A: She appeared to be in great pain. She was writhing around, yelling out, and crying.

§ 14.05   CONTEMPORANEOUS AND EXCITED UTTERANCES   639

PLAINTIFF'S ATTORNEY: Then what happened?

A: I knelt down to do a quick check on her condition. I tried to comfort her, telling her, "You'll be OK, you'll be OK." Then I asked her where she was feeling pain.

PLAINTIFF'S ATTORNEY: Did Denise respond to you?

A: Yes. Right after I started saying this she said, "I hurt so bad, especially my legs and my back. That red car hit me right after I stepped into the street."

DEFENSE ATTORNEY: Objection. Hearsay.

JUDGE: From the plaintiff's description of how she was hit, I'm dubious about her claim that she saw the color of the car that hit her. I'm leaning toward excluding the last sentence on that ground. (*Is this a legitimate basis for a ruling?*)

JUDGE: (*Assuming that the judge ignores the credibility of Denise's testimony, what ruling on the objection?*)

PLAINTIFF'S ATTORNEY: What happened next?

A: My partner and I got Denise stabilized. Then we put her in the ambulance to take her to the emergency room.

PLAINTIFF'S ATTORNEY: Were there other people nearby at the time you were stabilizing Denise?

A: Yes, maybe five or six people.

PLAINTIFF'S ATTORNEY: Did you hear any conversation between any of these people?

A: Yes, I heard one person ask what happened. Another person said that a pedestrian was hit by a red car, and that the driver of the red car drove off without stopping.

PLAINTIFF'S ATTORNEY: Do you know which two individuals had this conversation?

A: I don't, I was focused on helping Denise.

DEFENSE ATTORNEY: I object and move to strike the unknown onlooker's remark, hearsay. I also ask that Your Honor instruct the jury to disregard that testimony.

JUDGE: (*What ruling on the objection?*)

Problem 14-3: Excited Acceptance

Assume the same factual circumstances as in Problem 14-2, except that Denise has filed a separate lawsuit against Bob for breaching a verbal agreement to buy Denise's car for $25,000. Bob denies that he agreed to buy the car. In the breach of contract suit, Denise calls Marisa, the ambulance driver, to testify that when Denise was in the ambulance still writhing in pain, Denise said, "Oh my God, even though I'm in agony, I remember that Bob agreed to buy my car for $25,000." *Is*

Denise's statement to Marisa admissible in Denise's breach of contract suit against Bob to prove that he agreed to buy her car for $25,000?

Problem 14-4: Stepdaddy

Max is charged with physical abuse of his five-year-old stepson, Larry. The prosecution makes an offer of proof that a police officer will testify to entering into an apartment at 10 a.m., and finding Larry alone in the apartment and crying. The officer will also testify that Larry was standing lethargically, had numerous bruises on his face, had swollen and reddened hands, and an open cut on one of his hands. Larry did not respond to the officer's questions about what had happened. The officer took Larry to the hospital. Larry received medical treatment and was questioned further by the doctor and the officer about what had happened, but didn't answer.

The prosecutor also offers to prove that a nurse was with Larry in a hospital room when Larry's natural father, Joe, arrived at about 4 p.m. When Larry saw him, Larry said at once, "Oh Dad, stepdaddy keeps whipping me. You don't whip me, Dad." Finally, the parties stipulate that the doctor's examination revealed that some of Larry's injuries were new, other were a few weeks old.

Student # 1: As the Prosecutor, argue for the admissibility of Larry's statement to his father as an excited utterance, to prove that Larry's stepfather beat him.

Student # 2: As the Defense Attorney, argue that Larry's statement to his father is inadmissible hearsay.

Student # 3: As the Judge, preside over the hearing and rule on the admissibility of Larry's statement to his father.

Problem 14-5: Mach Trial 1

Julio sues Hyun for injuries resulting from a collision between their two cars that occurred on Arrow Road. Julio's witness Amanda testifies that she was a passenger in a car that was passed by Hyun's car, a two-year-old black Saab convertible, at about 3:00 p.m. on March 31, about 10 minutes prior to the collision. Please answer the italicized questions embedded in the following partial transcript of Amanda's testimony:

PLAINTIFF'S ATTORNEY: What did you notice about the defendant's car when it passed the one in which you were riding?

A: I noticed that he was going a lot faster than we were. When he passed us, I looked over at the speedometer in our car and saw that we were going at the speed limit on Arrow, 55 m.p.h. I know that was the speed limit because we had just passed a speed limit sign.

DEFENSE ATTORNEY: Objection to the testimony concerning the speedometer reading and the statement on the speed limit sign, hearsay. Move to strike.

JUDGE: *(Ruling?)*

§ 14.05   CONTEMPORANEOUS AND EXCITED UTTERANCES   641

PLAINTIFF'S ATTORNEY: Since the defendant's car passed yours and yours was traveling at the speed limit, would it be fair to say that the defendant was exceeding the speed limit?

DEFENSE ATTORNEY: Objection, leading question and calls for a conclusion.

JUDGE: Overruled. The witness may answer. (*Is this ruling correct?*)

A: Yes.

PLAINTIFF'S ATTORNEY: Amanda, are you a licensed driver?

A: Yes, for about 12 years.

PLAINTIFF'S ATTORNEY: Do you drive regularly on Arrow and similar roads?

A: Sure, I drive all the time.

PLAINTIFF'S ATTORNEY: Based on that experience, can you estimate how much faster than your car the defendant's black Saab was going when it passed you?

A: I'd say at least 10 m.p.h. faster, but I can't be sure.

DEFENSE ATTORNEY: Objection, lack of foundation, speculation. Move to strike.

JUDGE: Sustained. (*Is this ruling correct?*)

PLAINTIFF'S ATTORNEY: And what happened after the defendant's car passed yours?

A: I watched him for a while, maybe half a minute, until he was out of sight.

PLAINTIFF'S ATTORNEY: Then what happened?

A: I turned to the driver and said, "I think that car is an accident waiting to happen."

DEFENSE ATTORNEY: Objection, hearsay. Move to strike.

PLAINTIFF'S ATTORNEY: Present sense impression, Your Honor.

JUDGE: On the ground of hearsay, the objection is overruled. (*Is this ruling correct?*)

DEFENSE ATTORNEY: I also object that the statement should be excluded because it's speculative.

JUDGE: (*How should the judge rule on this objection?*)

DEFENSE ATTORNEY: I also object based on relevance. Even if Hyun was exceeding the speed limit at the point he passed Amanda, which we contest, that point was 10 minutes before the accident, and about 10 miles from the location of the accident. Thus, any evidence as to how Hyun might have been driving when Amanda observed him is irrelevant, and any relevance is substantially outweighed by the likelihood of unfair prejudice.

JUDGE: (*What ruling on the relevance objection? Would your ruling be affected by whether Arrow Road is a main highway without traffic lights or an urban street with occasional traffic lights?*)

PLAINTIFF'S ATTORNEY: Finally, Amanda, did you say anything else to the driver of the car in which you were a passenger?

A: This is a hearsay chapter, so you know I did. Just after the black Saab passed us, I said that the way the car was being driven, its driver must be drunk.

DEFENSE ATTORNEY: (*What objection if any would you make to this testimony?*)

Problem 14-6: Mach Trial 2

Same case as previous problem. Assume that Amanda testifies that the car she saw pass the one in which she was riding was a black Saab convertible and that she thinks that it had a "Go Packers" sticker on the right rear bumper. (This matches the description of the defendant's car, except that the bumper sticker on the defendant's car says only "Packers.") The defense attorney then approaches the bench and asks for a mini-trial on the foundational issue of whether the car that Amanda saw was that of Hyun, the defendant. When the judge grants permission, the testimony proceeds as follows:

DEFENSE ATTORNEY: You noticed that a black Saab passed you, right?

A: Yes.

DEFENSE ATTORNEY: You didn't find that extremely unusual, did you?

A: No. These days you get passed all the time even though you're going the speed limit.

DEFENSE ATTORNEY: So you didn't notice the license plate number of the car that passed you?

A: That's right.

DEFENSE ATTORNEY: All you noticed was that the car that passed you was a black Saab?

PLAINTIFF'S ATTORNEY: (*What if any objection might you make to this question?*)

A: Also that it was a late-model convertible, and the bumper sticker.

DEFENSE ATTORNEY: As you look at Hyun here in court, you can't testify that he personally was driving the car that passed you, right?

A: That's true.

DEFENSE ATTORNEY: And did this car pass you on the left or the right?

A: On the right. That's one reason I noticed it.

DEFENSE ATTORNEY: And what make and model of car were you in?

A: A blue Prius.

DEFENSE ATTORNEY:	Nothing further. If plaintiff has no foundational questions, I'd like to call the defendant Hyun as a foundational witness.
JUDGE:	Plaintiff indicates no questions, so defense counsel you may call your client for foundational questioning only.
DEFENSE ATTORNEY:	Thank you, Your Honor. Hyun, I want to call your attention to approximately 3:00 p.m. on March 31. Were you driving on Arrow Road at that time?
A:	Yes, I was.
DEFENSE ATTORNEY:	Were you exceeding the speed limit at any time prior to the accident?
A:	No.
DEFENSE ATTORNEY:	Did you pass a blue Prius on the right?
A:	No. I was in the far left lane, and, of course, I might have passed some Priuses while I was driving, but none on the right. I never pass on the right.
DEFENSE ATTORNEY:	Around 3:00 on that date, did you see any other black Saab convertibles on the road?
A:	I did. I saw one other car, I noticed it because it was the same make and model as mine.
DEFENSE ATTORNEY:	Did you notice whether it had any kind of bumper sticker on it?
A:	No, I didn't.
DEFENSE ATTORNEY:	What did you observe about how this other black Saab was being driven?
A:	Very fast — it passed me, and the driver was weaving in and out of lanes.
DEFENSE ATTORNEY:	No further questions.
JUDGE:	Plaintiff's attorney, any questions? OK, if none, I'll hear brief argument.
DEFENSE ATTORNEY:	Your Honor, I move to strike Amanda's testimony on the ground that if the car that passed hers was not my client's car, her testimony is irrelevant. And it's speculative as to whether it was my client's car that she saw. She didn't see him personally behind the wheel, she testified that there's nothing unusual about being passed, there was at least one other black Saab in the vicinity, and she was inaccurate about the bumper sticker.
JUDGE:	Under Rule 104, it's up to the plaintiff to convince me by a preponderance of the evidence that Amanda's testimony pertains to

the defendant's car. (*Is this a proper statement of the foundational burden?*)

JUDGE: I conclude that the plaintiff has satisfied the requisite foundational standard, so the motion to strike Amanda's testimony is denied. (*Is this a proper ruling?*)

PLAINTIFF'S ATTORNEY: No further questions of Amanda, Your Honor. I have one additional witness to call and make an offer of proof that this witness will testify to having seen the defendant speeding and driving erratically on the same portion of Arrow Road 10 days before the March 31 collision that gave rise to this lawsuit.

DEFENSE ATTORNEY: Objection, improper character evidence.

JUDGE: (*What ruling on the defendant's objection?*)

Problem 14-7: Nine One Mum

Warren Peace is charged with murdering Diane, his former fianc'ee, on the evening of September 22. Peace's defense is self-defense. The police found Diane about 11:00 p.m., shot to death in her bedroom. To prove Peace's identity and intent, the prosecution calls Diane's mother to testify that Diane telephoned her around 10:30 p.m. on the evening that she died. Diane was sobbing and asking her mother for help. She told her mother, "Warren's here. He's been drinking' he's got a gun, and he's planning to use it." Diane's mother then called the police. *Please rule on the following defense objections to the mother's testimony:*

1. The defense objects to the testimony in its entirety as hearsay. The defense attorney argues that the excited utterance and present sense impression exceptions are not available because they both rest on the likelihood that the adverse party will have an opportunity to cross-examine a percipient observer, either the declarant or the witness who heard the declarant's statement. As Diane's statement was made over the phone and her mother was not at the scene of the shooting, the statement should be excluded because the defense has no opportunity to cross-examine a percipient observer.

2. The defense objects that Diane's statement is hearsay, and argues that the excited utterance and present sense impression exceptions are unavailable because there is no way to ascertain whether Diane had personal knowledge.

3. The defense objects to the portion of Diane's statement, "he's planning to use it" as speculative and not based on personal knowledge.

4. Assume that Diane called 911 instead of her mother, and made the same statement to the 911 operator. Assume that the 911 operator who took the call is not available to testify. However, all calls to 911 are automatically recorded, and those recordings are time-and date-stamped. Can the prosecution offer the recording of Diane's phone call into evidence?

Problem 14-8: Eek Mail

Bill is charged with threatening Jim. The prosecution calls Jim to testify that when he saw an e-mail message from an unidentified sender telling him to "prepare to die," Jim immediately told his roommate, "Oh my God, this must be another threat from Bill!" *Is Jim's statement admissible in evidence to prove that Bill sent the message?*

Problem 14-9: Mind the Gap

Jean Yuss sues The Gap, alleging that she hurt her knee when she tripped and fell in a Gap store when getting out of an elevator that stopped two inches below the level of the fourth floor. To prove that the elevator did not stop at floor level, Jean's attorney calls a Gap customer service representative as an adverse witness to testify that about 30 minutes after Jean fell, a customer told the customer service representative that "You need to check your elevators. I just saw a woman trip getting out of an elevator on the fourth floor a little while earlier because the elevator didn't stop evenly with the floor." Gap's attorney makes a hearsay objection. *How should the judge rule on the objection?*

Problem 14-10: Second Opinion

Ruth Kanal sues Dr. Oral Scrivello for dental malpractice, alleging that Dr. Scrivello improperly fitted her with a bridge. When two visits to Dr. Scrivello failed to stop the pain caused by the allegedly improperly fitted bridge, Ruth went to another dentist. To prove that Dr. Scrivello's work was substandard, Ruth seeks to testify that when the second dentist examined the bridge for the first time, the second dentist immediately said, "Oh my God, who performed this shoddy work on you?" Dr. Scrivello objects that Rhonda's testimony is inadmissible hearsay. *How should the judge rule on the objection?*

Problem 14-11: When the Bough Breaks

Phil Bert sues his neighbor Mary Birch for injuries after a limb from a eucalyptus tree on Birch's property allegedly broke off suddenly and struck Bert, who at the time was asleep in a hammock in his front yard. Bert calls Hazel to testify that while she and Kilmer were walking past Bert's and Birch's properties, Kilmer suddenly shouted, "Oh my God, did you see that, Hazel? A limb from that big tree just fell onto that man lying in the hammock in the next yard!" Kilmer is unavailable to testify, and except for Kilmer's hearsay statement, Bert has no evidence that a falling limb caused his injuries. *Is Kilmer's hearsay statement admissible to prove that Bert was struck by a limb that fell from a tree on Birch's property?*

Problem 14-12: First Words

John Jones is charged with sexually assaulting a college student, Kay Stevens. To prove that Jones assaulted Stevens, the prosecution calls Stevens's friend Todd Wilson to testify that the day after the assault, Stevens came to his dorm room around 4 a.m. and told him that Jones, her ex-boyfriend, had sexually assaulted her a few hours earlier. Stevens also told Wilson that he was the first person she had told. She hadn't said anything earlier because she felt shameful and guilty and was too embarrassed to go to the police or her family. Stevens finally decided to tell Wilson because she trusted him, and she wanted to protect future potential victims. *Is Wilson's testimony to Stevens' statement that Jones sexually assaulted her admissible?*

§ 14.06 STATEMENT OF PRESENTLY-EXISTING STATE OF MIND, FEELING OR BELIEF (RULE 803(3))

Statutory Elements:

- The declarant's statement identifies his or her concurrently existing state of mind, emotion, sensation, or physical condition;

- A statement identifying a concurrently existing state of mind, emotion, sensation, or physical condition is admissible to prove the fact that produced the state of mind only if it is relevant to issues surrounding the declarant's will.

As you may recall (*see* Chapter 11), a routine non-hearsay use for out-of-court assertions is to offer them as circumstantial evidence of either the declarant's or a listener's state of mind. When offered as circumstantial evidence of state of mind, an assertion skirts the hearsay rule. For example, a declarant's assertion that "Gene always carries a gun" would normally be admissible as non-hearsay if the declarant were charged with murdering Gene and claimed that the killing was done in self-defense. Without regard to the statement's truth, a judge or juror might infer from the declarant's having made the statement that the declarant was fearful of Gene, from that infer that the declarant would be unlikely to act aggressively toward Gene, and from that conclude that any killing would have been done in self-defense.

Rule 803(3)'s hearsay exception for statements of presently existing internal conditions or beliefs is the "other shoe," the counterpart to using out-of-court assertions as circumstantial evidence of state of mind. When declarants directly assert their beliefs, feelings, emotions, physical conditions, and the like, non-hearsay analysis doesn't work. Rather, judges and jurors must rely on the accuracy of out-of-court statements in order to conclude that those feelings and beliefs existed.

For example, assume that the declarant pleading self-defense to a charge of murdering Gene had said before the killing occurred that, "I'm really afraid of Gene." This statement proves that the declarant feared Gene only if the statement was accurate. Hence, a hearsay exception is necessary for this statement to be admissible to prove the declarant's fear of Gene, and one is provided by Rule 803(3), commonly known as the "state of mind" exception.

Rule 803(3) distinguishes assertions of fact about the world outside a declarant (e.g., "Gene always carries a gun") from assertions describing a declarant's "inner world" (e.g., "I'm afraid of Gene"), and establishes a hearsay exception for the latter. Statements regarding a declarant's then-existing "state of mind, emotion, sensation or physical condition (such as intent, plan, motive, design, mental feeling and bodily health)" are regarded as generally trustworthy. Memory problems are nonexistent, because the condition or belief exists simultaneously with the statement. Perceptual problems are also largely absent, on the theory that declarants are more reliable observers and reporters of their inner selves than of the outside world.

On the other hand, admitting "state of mind" hearsay does not obviate the other two hearsay dangers. Ambiguity remains a risk. In fact, emotions, feelings, and beliefs tend to be complex, and statements about them may be, if anything, more prone to ambiguity dangers than statements about whether a person carries a gun, the color of a light, or many other aspects of the outside world. Sincerity problems also remain; mendacious declarants may conceal or misrepresent their states of mind. However, the risk of insincerity is likely to be obvious to judges and jurors, and out-of-court assertions of then-existing state of mind are likely to be at least as trustworthy as in-court testimony. Finally, the need for state of mind evidence is often great, because so many legal issues turn on the state of mind with which an act was performed. For all of these reasons, this hearsay exception is of long standing.

Rule 803(3) has its roots in the case of *Mutual Life Ins. Co. v. Hillmon* (*see* Case Library), one of the most colorful cases ever decided by the U.S. Supreme Court. The case was tried to a jury six different times over the span of nearly 25 years. In this case, Hillmon's alleged widow, Sally, sued to collect the proceeds of life insurance policies that her husband had taken out with three different life insurance companies shortly before heading west from their home in Kansas, supposedly hoping to buy a ranch. Mrs. Hillmon claimed that her husband had died, and presented as proof a badly burned corpse found by the side of a campfire in Crooked Creek, Kansas. The insurance companies disagreed, claiming that the corpse was Walters, a man who disappeared around the same time as Hillmon. The companies argued that Hillmon had asked Walters to accompany him west in order to bump him off, pass the corpse off as Hillmon, and collect the insurance proceeds. (The events took place late in the 19th century, remember; perhaps "D" had been discovered, but "N" and "A" were still unknown.) As evidence that Walters had accompanied Hillmon, the life insurance companies offered into evidence letters written by Walters to relatives shortly before he disappeared. In a portion of one letter, written to his "sweetheart," Alvina Kasten, in 1879, Walters stated that he "will leave here to see part of the country which I never expected to see when I left home, as I am going with a man by the name of Hillmon, who intends to start a sheep ranch."

The U.S. Supreme Court's 1892 opinion reversed the jury verdict in favor of Mrs. Hillmon in Trial No. 3. The Court held that the letters were admissible to prove that Walters accompanied Hillmon to Crooked Creek. Identifying the policy now incorporated into Rule 803(3), the Court held that "whenever the intention is of itself a distinct and material fact in a chain of circumstances, it may be proved by contemporaneous oral or written declarations of the party . . . . Wherever the bodily or mental feelings of an individual are material to be proved, the usual expressions of such feelings are original and competent evidence." Under *Hillmon* and now under Rule 803(3), an assertion of a declarant's concurrently existing intention to perform a future act is admissible to prove that the declarant followed through and did it.[5]

Practice Tip:

For a detailed description of the conflicting evidence in *Hillmon* in the form of a transcript of hypothetical closing arguments, see Bergman and Wesson, *I Am Going With a Man by the Name of Hillmon* in Trial Stories (Tigar and Davis, eds., 2008).

That Rule 803(3) admits contemporaneous assertions relating only to a declarant's inner world explains the reason for its very important limitation. Rule 803(3) specifically excludes from its scope "a statement of memory or belief to prove the fact remembered or believed." This limitation is necessary because every assertion about the outside world reflects a declarant's then-existing inner belief. Without the limitation, therefore, the state of mind exception would swallow the hearsay rule. ("Good riddance," you might be thinking.)

For example, assume that Sandy, who'd been involved in a traffic accident, tells a friend a few days after the accident that, "I had the green light." If Sandy's lawyer offers the statement to the friend into evidence to prove that Sandy had the green light, the assertion is garden-variety hearsay, inadmissible unless an exception applies. Now consider the Rule 803(3) argument that Sandy's lawyer might make if the exclusion of the "fact remembered or believed" did not exist:

> Your Honor, the statement, "I had the green light," was really an assertion of Sandy's then-existing state of mind. That is, what Sandy was really saying to the friend was, "My presently-existing belief is that the light in my direction was green." As the assertion reflected Sandy's contemporaneous inner belief as to the light's color, it's admissible under the state of mind exception.

If Rule 803(3) did not bar the use of a "statement of memory or belief to prove the fact remembered or believed," this argument would succeed in this and perhaps every other instance in which hearsay is offered. The limitation ensures that state of mind hearsay statements are admitted only to prove a declarant's state of mind, not to prove a fact about the outside world that gave rise to that state of mind.

A hearsay assertion that qualifies for admission under Rule 803(3) may be relevant because the declarant's state of mind is itself a material fact.

Example 1

Danny sues Melissa for personal injuries growing out of an auto accident. Danny calls Amy, who testifies that she spoke with Danny about six months after the accident:

---

[5] The *Hillmon* case became a huge political "cause céelèebre," seen by many Populists of the day as pitting a poor grieving widow against rapacious business interests. The case produced a second Supreme Court decision in 1903, which reversed another verdict in favor of Mrs. Hillmon in Trial No. 6 and resulted in an order that the case be retried a seventh time. Eventually, all the insurance companies settled with Mrs. Hillmon. Neither Hillmon nor Walters were officially seen or heard from again.

PLAINTIFF'S ATTORNEY: Where were you and Danny when this conversation took place?

A: In a mall. We were shopping for a present for a colleague's baby shower.

PLAINTIFF'S ATTORNEY: And what happened?

A: Danny bent down to check on the price of a car seat. All of a sudden he winced and grabbed his back. He said that his back was killing him, and that he was in terrible pain.

Danny's statement reflects his then-existing physical condition: back pain. His back pain is itself a material fact on the issue of damages in the personal injury case.

A hearsay assertion that qualifies for admission under Rule 803(3) may also be relevant because it sheds light on the declarant's conduct.

Example 2

Melissa is charged with murdering Danny; the alleged motive was Danny's failure to contribute to the cost of a car seat that Melissa and Danny gave to a colleague at a baby shower. The prosecution calls Amy to testify to a conversation that Amy had with Danny the day before he was killed:

PROSECUTOR: Where did this conversation with Danny take place?

A: In the employees' lounge. It was after work hours, and Melissa had just left the lounge. So Danny and I were alone.

PROSECUTOR: And what did Danny say to you at that time?

A: Danny said that he was going to tell Melissa that he was no longer interested in contributing to the cost of the car seat.

Danny's statement to Amy reflects his then-existing state of mind: his intention to tell Melissa that he would not contribute to the car seat's cost. Danny's intention is relevant to his conduct and Melissa's alleged motive: The trier of fact can infer from Danny's statement to Amy that he followed through and told Melissa that he would not contribute to the car seat's cost.

Most declarants are unschooled in the niceties of the state of mind exception, and can therefore be forgiven for often failing to confine assertions exclusively either to facts in the outside world or to their inner world beliefs and emotions. For example, Han may say that, "I'm really angry that the stockbroker didn't tell me that a big lawsuit was about to be filed against the company she recommended that I invest in." Here, Han combines an assertion about the outside world (the stockbroker failed to provide important information) with an inner-world assertion (Han is angry).

Rule 803(3) makes the inner-world portion of the statement admissible at trial, assuming that Han's anger toward the stockbroker pertains to a material fact. However, Rule 803(3) does not make Han's statement admissible to prove that the stockbroker failed to provide important information about a stock purchase. After all, had Han said only that "the stockbroker didn't tell me that a big lawsuit was about to be filed against the company she recommended that I invest in," the assertion's status as inadmissible hearsay is apparent. The inadmissibility of that portion of Han's assertion should not change merely because Han happens to utter a related remark that qualifies under the state of mind exception.[6]

The seeming incongruity of having to differentiate between assertions of state of mind (admissible) and assertions about the outside world giving rise to those states of mind (inadmissible) sometimes induces judges to fudge the distinction. For example, consider the case of *United States v. Annunziato*.[7] In that case, Annunziato and other union officials were charged with unlawfully asking for and receiving kickbacks in connection with a bridge construction project. As proof that Annunziato had taken kickbacks, the government called an employee of the construction company to testify that the company's president had told the employee that, in substance, "I'm going to send some money to Annunziato because he's asked for some money on the bridge project." Judge Friendly's opinion recognized that the statement of intention to send money to Annunziato was admissible under the state of mind hearsay exception. The statement that Annunziato had previously asked for the payment was not, but in colorful language the court ruled that it was nonetheless admissible: "True also, the statement of the past event would not be admitted if it stood alone; but this would not be the only hearsay exception where the pure metal may carry some alloy along with it."

Annunziato's logic is troubling, because declarants so commonly join assertions of state of mind with assertions about the past events that produced them. Rather than twist the state of mind hearsay exception, *Annunziato* might better have regarded the company president's statement that he intended to send money to Annunziato because Annunziato had asked for a payment as a *verbal part of an act*. That is, the president's statement established the legal character of the payment: it was a bribe, not a holiday present or a loan. (*See* Chapter 11.)

Practice Tip: Trustworthiness and the state of mind exception.

Does the foundation for the state of mind exception include a statement's trustworthiness? Compare Rule 803(3) with California Evidence Code Section 1252, which provides that an assertion of state of mind "is inadmissible . . . if the statement was made under circumstances such as to indicate its lack of trustworthiness." While Rule 803(3) does not explicitly mention trustworthiness, some federal court judges read an element of trustworthiness into the exception. As a result, a judge might exclude an assertion that otherwise satisfies Rule 803(3) because of a declarant's apparent contemporaneous motive to fabricate. For example, assume that the day before allegedly committing a murder, the defendant tells a friend, "I'll be going out of town for a few days." A judge who believes that the statement was part of the defendant's attempt to set up a phony alibi might

---

[6] The analysis here might remind you of the psychological experiment involving three white dots arranged in the shape of a triangle on a dark background. When you look at the dots, your mind connects them together so that you "see" a triangle. But the triangle is an illusion; it disappears when any of the white dots are removed. Similarly, the state of mind portion of a statement may seem to make the entire assertion admissible. But take that portion away, and the hearsay exception disappears.

[7] 293 F.2d 373 (2d Cir. 1961).

exclude the statement although it otherwise satisfies the foundational requirements of Rule 803(3). A judge who does so might say that the statement is "too self-serving," or that "the defendant had an obvious motive to fabricate," or that "the statement lacks probative value and I'm excluding it under Rule 403." Pronouncements such as these conflict with the text of Rule 803(3), and judges are supposed to leave credibility determinations to jurors. However, if you object to the admissibility of hearsay offered pursuant to Rule 803(3), you might ground your objection partly on the statement's lack of trustworthiness. And if you are the proponent of Rule 803(3) hearsay that a judge excludes for lack of trustworthiness, make the best record that you can that the statement satisfies the explicit foundational requirements of the rule, and hope that if the verdict is unfavorable, an appellate court will conclude that the ruling was erroneous and prejudicial.

Problem 14-13: Before and After

Spin is charged with murdering Marty. Consider the following two potential items of evidence:

1. The prosecution calls Marty's friend Darlene to testify that "I talked to Marty on the morning of the day that he was killed. During that conversation, Marty told me that Spin had visited him the day before and said that he was going to kill him." Under Rule 803 (3), the judge sustains Spin's objection that Darlene's testimony is inadmissible hearsay.

2. The prosecution calls Marty's friend Darlene to testify that "I talked to Marty on the morning of the day that he was killed. During that conversation, Marty told me that after I left he was going to pay a visit to Spin." Under Rule 803 (3), the judge overrules Spin's objection that Darlene's testimony is inadmissible hearsay.

Assume that both of these rulings are correct. Can you justify the opposite outcomes based on the statements' likely trustworthiness?

Problem 14-14: Driver's Ed

Mary sues William for personal injuries growing out of an automobile accident. Which of the following potential items of evidence should the judge receive in evidence?

1. To prove that she was driving carefully, Mary testifies that minutes before the accident she told Ed, the passenger in her car, that "I'm always afraid of getting a speeding ticket on this stretch of road."

2. To prove that she was driving carefully, Mary testifies that minutes before the accident she told Ed, the passenger in her car, that "Traffic cops like to hide in driveways along this stretch of road."

3. To prove that William was speeding, Mary testifies that minutes before the accident she told Ed, the passenger in her car, that "I'm really afraid that one of these speed demons is going to hit us."

4. To prove that the injuries caused by the accident were still bothering her one month later, Mary calls Henry to testify that when he visited Mary a month after the accident, Mary told him that "My back is really killing me. It's hurt me every day since the accident."

5. To prove that William was speeding, Mary calls Henry to testify that when he visited Mary a month after the accident, Mary told him that "My back still really hurts from when that guy William was speeding and ran into my car."

Problem 14-15: At the Movies: Last Page

Re-examine Problem 11-7 in the context of Rule 803(3). Recall that in the film *Jagged Edge*,[8] Jack Forrester is charged with murdering his wealthy wife Page. To prove that Jack's motive for killing Page was to prevent a divorce that would leave him with few assets, the prosecution calls Page's friend Virginia Howell to testify that "I spoke to Page a couple of weeks before she was killed. She told me that Jack had been seeing other women, that he didn't love her anymore, and that she wanted a divorce." *Is Ms. Howell's testimony admissible over the defendant's hearsay objection?*

Problem 14-16: Fearsay 1

Abe Yusir is charged with abusing three stepchildren. The stepchildren have been placed temporarily in the same foster home. On a day scheduled for Yusir to have a monitored visit with each stepchild, the following events take place:

A. When told that Yusir is about to visit with him, Yusir's eight-year-old stepson Hakeem immediately tells the foster mother that "I'm really afraid of my stepdad." The prosecution offer's Hakeem's statement into evidence pursuant to the state of mind exception to prove that Yusir abused Hakeem. *How should the judge rule on defense counsel's hearsay objection?*

B. When the foster mother tells Yusir's seven-year-old stepdaughter Patty that Yusir is about to visit with her, Patty screams and runs from the room. The prosecution offers Patty's reaction to prove that Yusir abused her. *How should the judge rule on defense counsel's hearsay and irrelevance objections?*

C. When the foster mother tells Yusir's six-year-old stepson Anthony that Yusir is about to visit him, Anthony says, "My stepdaddy was always beating me." The prosecution offers the statement as non-hearsay to prove that Anthony feared Yusir. *How should the judge rule on defense counsel's irrelevance objection?*

Problem 14-17: Fearsay 2

Attila is charged with the murder of Genghis; Attila's defense is an alibi. The prosecution calls Nero to testify that the day before Genghis's death, Genghis told Nero that "I'm afraid that one day, Attila is going to try to kill me." The court

---

[8] Columbia Pictures, 1985.

§ 14.06   PRESENT STATE OF MIND, FEELING OR BELIEF   653

should rule that:

1. The testimony is admissible to prove that Genghis was not the aggressor.

2. The testimony is admissible under the state of mind exception to prove that Attila killed Genghis.

3. The testimony is inadmissible hearsay.

4. The testimony is non-hearsay to prove that Attila had a motive to attack Genghis.

Problem 14-18: Fearsay 3

Attila is charged with the murder of Genghis. During the defense case-in-chief, Attila testifies that, "What happened was that Genghis asked me to take out my new gun so that he could look at it. When I handed it to him, he cocked it and took his own life." The prosecution calls Nero to testify that the day before Genghis' death, Genghis told Nero that "I'm afraid that one day, Attila is going to try to kill me." *True or False: Genghis' statement to Nero is admissible to rebut Attila's testimony.*

Problem 14-19: Proof Possibles

Jerry is charged with robbery of a small convenience store. Robbery consists of "taking the property of another through means of force or fear." Which of the following out-of-court statements could the prosecution offer to prove that the robber used force or fear? (Choose as many would be admissible.)

1. Tom's testimony that "I saw the robbery and heard the clerk say, 'Please, please don't shoot me.'"

2. Tom's testimony that "As soon as the robber ran off I went to check on the clerk, who told me that 'I was really terrified that I was going to get shot.'"

3. Tom's testimony that "As soon as the robber ran off, another person and I ran over to check on the clerk. The other person said, 'Oh my God, the victim must have been terrified!'"

4. Tom's testimony that "The day after the robbery, the clerk said to me that 'I was really afraid that I was going to get shot during the robbery.'"

5. Tom's testimony that "I saw the robbery and heard the clerk call out to me, 'Stay away, he's got a gun and he's going to use it.'"

6. Sylvester's testimony that "The day after the robbery, the defendant Jerry told me that 'The clerk I stuck up yesterday was really terrified.'"

Problem 14-20: Tea Party

Earl Grey is charged with killing his wife Jasmine by poisoning her tea. Grey's defense is that Jasmine had been depressed for weeks and finally took her own life. Consider the admissibility of the following potential items of evidence.

1. To prove that Grey committed the murder, the prosecution calls Jasmine's friend Green to testify that the day before she died, Jasmine told him that "I'm afraid that my husband has been trying to poison me."

2. To rebut the defense claim that Jasmine committed suicide, the prosecution calls Jasmine's friend Green to testify that the day before she died, Jasmine told him that "I'm afraid that my husband has been trying to poison me."

3. To rebut the defense claim that Jasmine committed suicide, the prosecution calls Jasmine's friend Green to testify that the day before she died, Jasmine told him that "I want to live."

4. To prove that Jasmine was depressed, the defense calls Jasmine's friend Green to testify that two weeks before she died, Jasmine told him that "I just can't seem to stop crying these days."

5. To prove that Jasmine took her own life, the defense calls Jasmine's friend Green to testify that the day before she died, Jasmine told him that "Soon, I might just end it all."

6. To prove that Jasmine took her own life, the defense calls Jasmine's friend Green to testify that the day before she died, Jasmine's sister told Green that "I'm really sad because I just left Jasmine's house and she told me that soon she might just end it all.

7. To prove that Jasmine took her own life, the defense calls Jasmine's friend Green to testify that the day she died, Green rushed in, saw Jasmine lying on her bedroom floor and said, "Oh my God, she's taken her own life!"

Problem 14-21: Chat Room

James Naiden is on trial for using the Internet to attempt to induce a minor to have sex with him. The prosecutor offers into evidence transcripts of sexual chat room communications between Naiden and the police officer who posed as a 14-year-old girl. Naiden's defense is that he didn't believe that the person he was corresponding with was a minor. As proof of his belief, Naiden calls a friend, Louise, to testify pursuant to Rule 803(3) that during the time that Naiden was corresponding with the police officer, Naiden told Louise that he (Naiden) did not believe that the person he had recently met on the Internet was a minor. The prosecutor objects on the ground that Naiden's statement to Louise is inadmissible hearsay.

Student # 1: As the defense attorney, argue briefly that Louise's testimony is admissible under Rule 803(3).

Student # 2: As the prosecutor, argue briefly that Louise's testimony is inadmissible hearsay.

Student # 3: As the judge, preside over the arguments and rule on the objection.

The issue of whether an assertion describing a declarant's inner world should make admissible a closely related assertion about the outside world has arisen in a number of cases in which a declarant has announced an intention to meet another person. In these cases, the courts have often admitted the entire statement not merely to prove what the declarant did, but also to prove that the other person attended the meeting. A dramatic example is the case of *United States v. Pheaster* (*see* Case Library).

In *Pheaster*, defendant Angelo and others were charged with kidnapping Larry Adell, the teenage son of a Palm Springs multimillionaire. The prosecution offered evidence that shortly before he disappeared, Larry had told a friend that "I'm going to meet Angelo at Sambo's North at 9:30 p.m. to pick up the free pound of marijuana he promised me." The court upheld the prosecution's contention that Larry's statement was admissible to prove that Angelo had met with Larry. At the same time, in an unusual display of judicial humility, the court stated that it "recognized the force of the (defense) objection to the application of the *Hillmon* doctrine in the instant case." The court noted: "When hearsay evidence concerns the declarant's statement of his intention to do something with another person, the *Hillmon* doctrine requires that the trier of fact infer from the state of mind of the declarant the probability of a particular act not only by the declarant but also by the other person . . . . A much more significant and troubling objection is based on the inconsistency of such an inference with the state of mind exception." Moreover, the court quoted from the Notes of the House Committee on the Judiciary commenting on then-proposed Rule 803(3), which stated that "the Committee intends that the Rule be construed to limit (the *Hillmon* doctrine) so as to render statements of intent by a declarant admissible only to prove his future conduct, not the future conduct of another person." However, while the *Pheaster* court acknowledged that "the matter is certainly not free from doubt," a prior California decision helped to persuade the court that Rule 803(3) left the *Hillmon* decision "undisturbed." In *Hillmon* the Supreme Court had said that Walters's letters were admissible to prove that Walters went west "and that he went with Hillmon." Thus, under the *Hillmon* reasoning, Larry's comment was admissible to prove that he met with Angelo. The following poem may help you recall the *Pheaster* doctrine:

A Pheaster Sonnet

> In chichi Palm Springs on one evening hot,
> Larry said he was going out to a parking lot.
> Angelo was the man he said he was going to see,
> About some pot that could be his with no fee.
> Only to find himself kidnapped and then never set free.
> Resulting in Angelo's arrest before he could flee.
> Now Larry's last words being heard by the jury,
> Raised in defendant Angelo a terrible fury.
> He knew all about the exception for state of mind,
> Years ago in *Hillmon* by the Supreme Court opined.
> But surely here the prosecution was in a bind,
> The foundation for this hearsay the judge couldn't find.
> For Larry's assertion about his own intent
> Is trustworthy only as to where he went.
> And not as to the whereabouts of a different gent.
> How can an assertion *Hillmon* possibly cover
> When a declarant refers to the conduct of another?

The court noted that the issue was not free from doubt.
But said that it would be wrong to keep it out.
To a California case the *Pheaster* court did cling,
And said it's too late to spoil a good thing.
So the state of mind exception may allow you to cheat,
When declarants refer to people they are going to meet.
The next three problems are based on the *Pheaster* case.

Problem 14-22: Pheaster 1

Angelo is charged with drug dealing. As evidence that Angelo was selling drugs, the prosecution offers evidence that Larry told a friend, "I'm going to meet my drug dealer Angelo in the parking lot in order to stock up on my supply of illegal drugs." The friend called the cops, who came to the parking lot and arrested Angelo. Larry's statement to his friend is admissible to prove that:

1. The friend reasonably believed Angelo to be a drug dealer and therefore had probable cause to call the police.

2. Larry met Angelo in the parking lot, but it is not admissible to prove that Angelo was a dealer who was selling drugs.

3. Larry met Angelo in the parking lot and that Angelo was selling drugs.

4. Larry was in the parking lot, but it is not admissible to prove either that Angelo was in the parking lot or that he was selling drugs.

Problem 14-23: Pheaster 2

Angelo is charged with killing Larry in the parking lot of Sambo's North restaurant; Angelo's defense is an alibi. *True or False: To prove that Angelo was in the parking lot, the prosecution could offer evidence from Larry's friend Bonnie that "On the morning he died, Larry told me that Angelo was going to be in the Sambo's North parking lot later in the day."*

Problem 14-24: Pheaster 3

Angelo is charged with killing Larry in the parking lot of Sambo's North restaurant. *True or False: To prove that Larry was in the parking lot, the prosecution could offer evidence from Angelo's friend Carla that "On the morning that Angelo was arrested, Angelo told me that Larry was going to be in the Sambo's North parking lot later in the day."*

§ 14.07 STATEMENTS MADE FOR PURPOSES OF MEDICAL DIAGNOSIS OR TREATMENT (RULE 803(4))

Statutory Elements:

- The declarant made a statement for the purpose of obtaining medical treatment or seeking a diagnosis;

§ 14.07 STATEMENTS MADE FOR MEDICAL DIAGNOSIS OR TREATMENT

- The information in the statement is reasonably pertinent to diagnosis or treatment;

- The statement concerns the declarant's medical history, past or present symptoms, pain or sensations, or the inception or general character of the cause or external source of the declarant's medical condition.

Example

Indy sues Stocker for personal injuries growing out of an auto accident. Indy is in physical therapy for many weeks following the accident. Indy's treating physician testifies to a conversation that she had with Indy about three months after the accident:

PLAINTIFF'S LAWYER: What did Indy tell you about her right arm?

A: She said that it was still very sore, and that she couldn't lift it above her shoulder.

PLAINTIFF'S LAWYER: Did she say anything else about her physical condition?

A: Yes, as I recall she mentioned that her right wrist had been sore for a long time after the accident, but that now it was feeling better.

Indy's statements to her physician are admissible under Rule 803(4) to prove the extent and duration of the injuries allegedly caused by the accident, and to support any expert opinions the doctor may give regarding Indy's prognosis. To the extent that Indy described her then-existing physical condition to the physician, the statements would also be admissible under Rule 803(3). However, Indy's statements regarding past symptoms ("my right wrist had been sore") are admissible only under Rule 803(4).

The likely trustworthiness of statements made to treating medical personnel is transparent. Declarants are likely to be careful and accurate when describing their present and past physical condition to someone who will treat them medically. ("You did what with my spleen??? I meant to say that I was interested in *gene* therapy!!!")

However, statements made for purposes of diagnosis rather than treatment do not necessarily carry the same aura of trustworthiness. For example, consider a plaintiff in a personal injury case who describes his physical condition to a forensic medical expert who has been retained to testify at the plaintiff's trial to the extent of the plaintiff's injuries. The expert isn't going to treat or remove any body parts of the plaintiff, and the plaintiff certainly has a motive to exaggerate his pain and suffering. Nevertheless, Rule 803(4) extends the common law "medical hearsay" exception to include statements made for purposes of "diagnosis or treatment."

In part, the liberalization of the common law rule is based on the belief that a declarant's motive to gild the lily when speaking to a diagnosing physician is likely to be apparent to judges and jurors. In addition, even before the rule was liberalized, such statements generally were admitted anyway, when medical experts testified to the bases for their opinions. The statements were typically admitted as non-hearsay; jurors were instructed to consider them only as to the weight they gave an expert's opinions. Extending Rule 803(4) to admit statements made for purposes of diagnosis avoids the previous fiction that jurors are capable of making such fine distinctions.

To be admissible under Rule 803(4), a hearsay statement needn't necessarily be made to a doctor. Nearly any type of medical personnel will do (e.g., an ambulance attendant, a nurse, a physical therapist, perhaps even a family member), so long as the judge concludes that the statement was "reasonably pertinent to diagnosis or treatment."

United States v. Tome (*see* Case Library) suggests how judges may interpret the "reasonably pertinent" foundational requirement. The defendant in *Tome* was charged with sexual abuse of his young daughter. The Court held that the daughter's statement to a pediatrician that "my father put his thing in me" was admissible under Rule 803(4). Her statement was reasonably pertinent to treatment even though it was made during a "get acquainted" conversation, because making patients comfortable was part of the pediatrician's examination process. On the other hand, similar statements that the daughter made to a children's services caseworker were not admissible under the rule because the caseworker's role was limited to referring the daughter to other medical professionals for treatment.[9] The court's reasoning suggests that admissibility requires both a patient's subjective belief that information is pertinent to diagnosis or treatment and the objective reasonableness of that belief.

Problem 14-25: Blue Skye

Lucy is charged with the attempted murder of Skye, her former fianc'e. Lucy claims that she acted in self-defense, in part as a result of months of physical abuse by Skye. Skye denies abusing Lucy. To prove that she had been abused by Skye, Lucy calls Dr. Diamond, a psychiatrist, to testify that before the incident took place, Dr. Diamond had treated Lucy for a variety of symptoms associated with "battered spouse syndrome." Dr. Diamond's testimony was in part as follows:

DEFENSE ATTORNEY: Dr. Diamond, when was your first appointment with Lucy?

A: It was on the 17th of October.

DEFENSE ATTORNEY: And what did she tell you on that occasion regarding her physical condition?

A: She told me that she'd been suffering from terrible headaches, was not able to sleep more than an hour or two at a time, had lost her appetite, and often started crying for no apparent reason.

DEFENSE ATTORNEY: Did she tell you when these symptoms had started?

A: Yes. She said they had begun in May, after her fianc'e Skye started physically abusing her when he had had too much to drink.

---

[9] The *Tome* case had been remanded to the Court of Appeal by the U.S. Supreme Court after it had held that the daughter's statements were inadmissible as prior consistent statements under Rule 801(d)(1)(B). For a discussion of the Supreme Court's *Tome* opinion, see Chapter 12.

§ 14.07 STATEMENTS MADE FOR MEDICAL DIAGNOSIS OR TREATMENT   659

PROSECUTOR: Objection, hearsay. The statement is inadmissible under the medical hearsay exception because neither identifying the alleged source of past abuse nor tying the abuse to drinking was reasonably pertinent to the doctor's treatment of Lucy.

JUDGE: (*How should the judge rule on the prosecutor's objection?*)

Problem 14-26: Child Abuse Expert

Ralph Waldo is charged with sexually assaulting seven-year-old Debra, the daughter of a woman he had been dating. The prosecutor retained pediatrician Dr. Joyce Weathers to examine Debra and to diagnose the cause of Debra's physical injuries. At trial, Dr. Weathers testifies that in her opinion, the physical injuries that she observed on Debra are consistent with abusive sexual contact. Pursuant to Rule 803(4), the prosecutor also seeks to have Dr. Weathers testify that while she was examining Debra, Debra told her that "My mom's friend Ralph tried to stick something down there (pointing to her vagina) and it really hurt, and he put his hand over my mouth so I couldn't scream. I couldn't breathe." *Can Dr. Weathers testify to Debra's statement under the exception for medical hearsay? If Debra doesn't testify, what is the impact of* Crawford v. Washington *(see Chapter 10) on the admissibility of her statement to Dr. Weathers?*

Problem 14-27: Bitten

John sues Vicki on behalf of his three-year-old daughter Lyndon for injuries suffered by Lyndon allegedly as a result of being bitten by Vicki's dog, a breed of big dog called a "pitweiler." Vicki claims that a neighbor's small Yorkie caused the injuries. John took Lyndon to an emergency room. John calls the emergency room physician to testify that "When he brought his daughter in, John told me that she had scratches and a deep gash on her right leg, and that she seemed to be having lots of pain in the neck area. He also told me that she'd been bitten by a large dog." Vicki's attorney makes the following objections:

1. John was not the patient so his statement is inadmissible under Rule 803(4).

2. John concededly wasn't present when Lyndon was bitten. Because he lacks personal knowledge of how the injuries occurred, his statement is inadmissible under Rule 803(4).

3. Identifying the source of the injuries as a "large dog" was not reasonably pertinent to Lyndon's treatment, so that portion of his statement is inadmissible under Rule 803(4).

How should the judge rule on the objections?

Problem 14-28: At the Movies: Sister

In the film *The Verdict*,[10] the sister of a comatose patient files a medical malpractice lawsuit on her behalf against two anesthesiologists and the hospital that employed them. The suit alleges that the patient went to the hospital's

---

[10] 20th Century Fox (1982).

emergency room in distress to give birth and ended up comatose because of the use of an improper anesthetic. To prove that the patient had eaten a full meal one hour before arriving at the hospital (and that therefore the defendants used an improper anesthetic), the plaintiff seeks to offer evidence that the sister, who had accompanied the patient to the hospital, told the hospital's admitting nurse that "My sister ate a full meal an hour ago."

Is the sister's statement to the admitting room nurse admissible under Rule 803(4)?

Problem 14-29: Back Talk

Jeff sues Arlene for injuries suffered in an auto accident allegedly caused by Arlene's careless driving of her sports utility vehicle ("SUV"). Arlene claims that the accident could not have caused Jeff's injuries, and that any injuries he had were the result of an earlier water skiing mishap. *Which of the following statements that Jeff might have made after the accident to his treating physician would be admissible by him under Rule 803(4)?*

1. My back really hurts.

2. My back has been hurting me ever since the accident.

3. My back has been hurting me ever since I was hit by that SUV.

4. My back has been hurting me ever since I was hit by that SUV that was going at least 30 m.p.h.

5. My back has been hurting me ever since I was hit by that SUV that was going at least 30 m.p.h., and I've never hurt my back before.

6. My back has been hurting me ever since I was hit by that SUV that was going at least 30 m.p.h. and ran the red light.

7. My back has been hurting me ever since I was hit by that SUV that a woman who must have been boozing it up was driving at least 30 m.p.h. and ran the red light.

Problem 14-30: Friendly Advice

Hedda Furst attends a dinner party and sees an old friend, Dr. Liz Ishen. Hedda has never been a patient of Dr. Ishen, an internist. However, from time to time when they have been together on social occasions, Hedda has talked to Dr. Ishen about personal medical concerns. At the dinner party, Hedda tells Dr. Ishen that "I've been getting really bad headaches for a few weeks now; they started when that auto paint shop opened up next to where I live. Do you think I should wait to see if they go away, or should I make an appointment with my doctor?" Sometime later, Hedda files suit against the auto paint shop. *Is Hedda's statement to Dr. Ishen at the dinner party admissible under the medical hearsay exception?*

§ 14.07 STATEMENTS MADE FOR MEDICAL DIAGNOSIS OR TREATMENT   661

Problem 14-31: Medi-Cal

Matt sues Randy for personal injuries stemming from Randy's allegedly intentionally running into Matt with the intent to injure him during an adult league ice hockey game. To prove that his injuries resulted from the collision with Randy, Matt calls Cal, the coach of his ice hockey team, as a witness to testify to what happened. Cal's testimony goes as follows:

PLAINTIFF'S ATTORNEY: And what happened after you saw Randy collide with Matt?

A: Matt skated off the ice immediately and went to the far end of the bench. When the period was over, I asked him whether he could play and he said that he couldn't, that his shoulder and his back were killing him from when Randy ran into him on purpose. He also asked me to put an ice pack on his shoulder.

DEFENSE ATTORNEY: Objection, hearsay.

PLAINTIFF'S ATTORNEY: Medical hearsay exception, Rule 803(4).

JUDGE: I'll sustain the objection, subject to the plaintiff's eliciting further foundational evidence.

PLAINTIFF'S ATTORNEY: Thank you, Your Honor. Cal, does the league have any policy with respect to injuries that players suffer during league games?

A: Yes. A first-aid official is supposed to attend all games. That official's job is to check on any player who is hurt during a game. If the first-aid official thinks that an injury needs more attention than just the usual first-aid procedures, he or she is supposed to refer a player to a hospital emergency room.

PLAINTIFF'S ATTORNEY: As a coach, what is your role with respect to injured players?

A: Because coaches often have a better chance to observe how an injury occurred than players, the league encourages us to describe how an injury occurred to the first-aid official. Also, coaches are to pass along any information that players give them to the official. And of course as a coach I bring a first aid kit to every game. So if a player isn't hurt too seriously, I often provide ice packs, bandages, aspirin, and other basics.

PLAINTIFF'S ATTORNEY: Do you tell the players about your role in case of injury to a player?

A: Yes, I go over the processes in a team meeting before the start of each season.

PLAINTIFF'S ATTORNEY: Nothing further by way of foundation, Your Honor.

JUDGE: Does the defense want to make any foundational inquiries?

DEFENSE ATTORNEY: Just a couple. Coach, does it happen that games are played even though a first-aid official might not be in attendance?

A: That's happened, yes. I don't like it.

DEFENSE ATTORNEY: And on this occasion, did either you or Matt talk to a first-aid official after the collision with Randy?

A: I don't remember. I know Matt stayed on the bench until the end of the game.

DEFENSE ATTORNEY: And so far as you remember, Matt didn't ask you to call over the first-aid official, right?

A: That's right.

DEFENSE ATTORNEY: That concludes my foundational questioning.

Student # 1: As the plaintiff's attorney, argue briefly that the foundation is sufficient to admit Matt's statement to the Coach under Rule 803(4).

Student # 2: As the defense attorney, argue briefly that the foundation is insufficient to admit Matt's statement to the Coach under Rule 803(4).

Student # 3: As the judge, preside over the arguments and rule on the objection, indicating which party has the burden of establishing its position, what that burden consists of, and the reasons for your ruling.

§ 14.08 PAST RECOLLECTION RECORDED (RULE 803(5)); REFRESHING RECOLLECTION (RULE 612)

Statutory Elements (Rule 803(5)):

- The declarant has personal knowledge of a matter;

- The declarant has insufficient recollection to testify about the matter fully and accurately;

Unlike the other Rule 803 exceptions, Rule 803(5) makes a declarant's presence on the witness stand quite material: the declarant has to testify for the declarant's out-of-court statement to be admissible under Rule 803(5).

- The declarant made a memorandum or record concerning the matter, or adopted a memorandum or record prepared by someone else:

- The matter was fresh in the declarant's memory at the time the memorandum or record was made or adopted;

- The declarant testifies that the memorandum or record is accurate.

- Even if the information in the memorandum or record is admissible, only an adverse party may offer the memorandum or record itself into evidence as an exhibit.

Statutory Elements (Rule 612):

- If a testifying declarant uses a writing to refresh the declarant's recollection either while or (in the judge's discretion) before testifying, the adverse party may examine the writing and offer pertinent portions of it into evidence.

Despite what may be ample pretrial preparation, witnesses sometimes lose their train of thought while testifying and omit information that their questioners know that the witnesses can provide. Given this common human frailty, evidence rules give attorneys two ready ways to refresh a forgetful witness' recollection. First, questioners can use leading questions to remind witnesses of the forgotten information. While under Rule 611 leading questions are not ordinarily allowed during direct examination, an exception that most judges recognize occurs when an attorney is refreshing the memory of a witness who apparently can provide the information the attorney is seeking but has momentarily forgotten it.

Example 1

The witness is to testify to a meeting in which the purchase of new computers was discussed:

PLAINTIFF'S ATTORNEY: And who attended this meeting?

A: It was me, Shelley, Jerry, Luke and . . . I'm sorry, I know one other person was there, her name has slipped my mind momentarily.

PLAINTIFF'S ATTORNEY: Was it Corey?

A: Yes, thank you. Corey attended the meeting also.

The leading question is permissible in this situation because the lawyer is not putting words in the witness' mouth. It is apparent that the witness has personal knowledge that another person attended the meeting but has momentarily forgotten her name.

An attorney can also refresh the recollection of a forgetful witness under Rule 612 by showing the witness a document that refers to the forgotten information. If the document enables the witness to recall the forgotten information, the attorney re-asks the question and the examination proceeds. Under Rule 612 as at common-law, an attorney may use any document to refresh recollection. The document needn't be admissible in evidence nor authored by the testifying witness.[11]

Under Rule 612 the adversary can demand "to have the writing produced at the hearing, to inspect it, to cross-examine the witness thereon, and to introduce in evidence those portions which relate to the testimony of the witness," even if the witness used the document to refresh the witness' memory prior to testifying, perhaps during a pre-trial preparation meeting. Thus, a questioner using a document to refresh a witness' recollection, either before or during trial, must be careful not to use a document that contains harmful or embarrassing information.

---

[11] One colorful opinion noted that if for some reason it refreshed a witness' memory, an attorney might even refresh recollection with "the dolorous refrain of 'The Tennessee Waltz' " or "the sweet carbonation of a chocolate soda." *See Baker v. State*, 371 A.2d 699 (Md. Ct. Spec. App. 1977). Don't be too quick to bring music or a picnic basket into the courtroom, however. In practice, attorneys invariably refresh recollection with documents.

Example 2

The witness is to testify to a meeting in which the purchase of new computers was discussed:

PLAINTIFF'S ATTORNEY: And who attended this meeting?

A: It was me, Shelley, Jerry, Luke and . . . I'm sorry, I know one other person was there, her name has slipped my mind momentarily.

PLAINTIFF'S ATTORNEY: If I were to show you the minutes of the meeting, might they enable you to recall the name of the other person who attended it?

A: I'm sure they would.

Many judges regard this question and answer as foundational to allowing an attorney to attempt to refresh a witness' recollection.

The questioner hands the minutes to the witness and allows the witness some time to review them. The questioner should then remove the minutes from the witness before continuing the questioning.

PLAINTIFF'S ATTORNEY: Are you now able to recall the name of the other person who attended the meeting?

A: Yes.

PLAINTIFF'S ATTORNEY: And who was this other person?

A: It was Corey.

The memory-refreshing techniques described above do not raise hearsay issues because they do not involve offering out-of-court statements into evidence. Even when an attorney refreshes recollection with a document under Rule 612, the witness testifies from present memory, not to the contents of the document (in theory, at least). When a witness genuinely lacks present recall, however, the "refreshing" rubric is unavailable. In such situations, Rule 803(5) can make a declarant's hearsay statement admissible. If the rule's foundational requirements are satisfied, the offering party reads a document's contents into evidence. The *written memorandum or record itself is not received* in evidence unless offered by the adversary. The purpose of this restriction is to avoid giving an unfair advantage to a party whose witness lacks sufficient memory to testify from present recollection. If the memorandum or record were physically admitted into evidence, the jury could examine it during deliberations. Thus, it might have undue influence compared to other evidence in the case, most of which will be oral.

The trustworthiness rationale for Rule 803(5)'s "recorded recollection" exception is similar to that for present sense impressions (Rule 803(1)), which is the lack of time to fabricate or forget. In each case, the statement that is admitted must have been made soon after the event to which the statement refers. Rule 803(1) requires that the statement be made during the event or "immediately thereafter." Rule 803(5) has a somewhat looser standard, but requires that the statement have been made "when the matter was fresh." In both situations, the short time frame perhaps obviates memory problems, and reduces a declarant's chance to reflect and make up a lie.

§ 14.08 PAST RECOLLECTION RECORDED; REFRESHING RECOLLECTION

Rule 803(5) contains an additional trustworthiness requirement: the declarant has to testify that the written statement was correct at the time the declarant made it. This makes sense, because when hearsay is admitted under Rule 803(1), the adversary generally has an opportunity to cross-examine either the declarant or a witness who personally heard the out-of-court assertion, and who therefore will usually have witnessed the same event as the declarant. Under Rule 803(5), by contrast, an opportunity for cross-examination is likely to be lacking. Typically, the only witness is the declarant, who by definition can no longer remember much about what happened.

Example 3

A witness in a bank robbery prosecution testifies that she saw the robbers leap into the getaway car. The witness wrote down the car's license plate number on the back of an envelope, but can no longer remember the number. The prosecutor lays the foundation to qualify the statement on the envelope as the witness' "recorded recollection" as follows:

PROSECUTOR: And what happened after you heard the noise and shouting coming from the bank?

A: Two men ran out of the bank, jumped into a car and drove off at high speed.

PROSECUTOR: Can you describe this car?

A: I can't remember much. It was a few years' old, dark color, sedan-type.

PROSECUTOR: Did you notice the car's license plate number?

A: Yes. I looked at it as the car drove off. I knew something was wrong, and I wanted to at least get the license plate number.

PROSECUTOR: Do you now recall the car's license plate number?

A: Not really. I remember it started with the letter "N," that's about all I really remember now.

The recorded recollection exception doesn't require that a witness be entirely devoid of memory. All that's required is that the witness have "insufficient recollection . . . to testify fully and accurately."

PROSECUTOR: After you watched the car drive off, what did you do?

A: I kept whispering the license plate number to myself. As I did that, I pulled an envelope and a pen out of my jacket pocket and wrote down the license plate number.

PROSECUTOR: How long after the car drove off did you write down the license plate number?

A: It couldn't have been more than a minute.

PROSECUTOR: So would you say that the license plate number was fresh in your mind when you wrote it down on the envelope?

> Although leading, the question is permissible under Rule 611(c), because it refers to testimony the witness has already given. Moreover, the question pertains to a foundational issue, and under Rule 104(a), when deciding foundational issues courts are not "bound by the rules of evidence except those with respect to privileges." As a result, counsel often have considerable leeway regarding the use of leading questions during foundational questioning.

A: Yes.

PROSECUTOR: Your Honor, I have here an envelope marked Government's No. 8 for Identification, which I've already shown to defense counsel. May it be shown to the witness? (The bailiff hands the envelope to the witness.) Please look at Exhibit 8 and tell us if you recognize what that is.

A: This is the envelope with the license plate number on it.

PROSECUTOR: How do you recognize it?

A: Well, it's my handwriting, and I also recognize the envelope because it has my dentist's return address on it.

PROSECUTOR: At the time, did you write down accurately the license plate number of the car you saw the two men drive off in?

A: I did.

PROSECUTOR: At this time, Your Honor, I ask permission to read into the record the license plate number as recorded on Exhibit 8.

JUDGE: You may do so.

PROSECUTOR: What's written on the envelope is NOM 1234. OK, now after you wrote down the license plate number, what happened next?

Problem 14-32: Forget It

Kris is a witness for the prosecution in an armed robbery case. Please answer the italicized questions in the transcript below.

PROSECUTOR: Kris, how many people were working behind the counter when you heard the defendant yell for them to hand over all the money in the register?

A: I know more than one, but I'm sorry, I don't remember exactly.

PROSECUTOR: Might it refresh your recollection if I show you the police report?

A: Possibly.

PROSECUTOR: Permission to show the witness the police report prepared by the investigating officer, Your Honor?

DEFENSE ATTORNEY: Excuse me. Might I first ask a foundational question?

JUDGE: Go ahead.

§ 14.08 PAST RECOLLECTION RECORDED; REFRESHING RECOLLECTION 667

DEFENSE ATTORNEY: Did you personally speak to a police officer after the robbery?

A: No, I was too upset. I gave a police officer my name and phone number and went home.

DEFENSE ATTORNEY: In that case I object to the witness being shown the police report, Your Honor. Nothing in the report is based on information from this witness.

JUDGE: That objection is overruled. The witness may be shown the report.

(Is this ruling correct?)

PROSECUTOR: Kris, you've had a chance to look over the report. Are you now able to recall how many employees were working behind the counter when the defendant yelled for them to hand over the money?

A: According to the report, three employees were working behind the counter.

DEFENSE ATTORNEY: Objection, hearsay, move to strike.

JUDGE: *(How would you rule on the objection?)*

PROSECUTOR: When the defendant yelled for them to hand over money, did you notice anything unusual about his manner of speaking?

A: It's possible. Again, I'm just not sure.

PROSECUTOR: Well, he slurred a number of his words, right?

DEFENSE ATTORNEY: Objection, leading.

JUDGE: *(How would you rule on the objection?)*

A: That's right, he did.

PROSECUTOR: Did the robber have any facial marks?

A: No.

PROSECUTOR: Permission to show the police report to the witness again, Your Honor?

JUDGE: Both counsel please approach the bench. (At the bench) Why do you want to show the police report to the witness?

PROSECUTOR: To refresh the witness' recollection that the robber had a scar on his right cheek.

JUDGE: No foundation for refreshing recollection exists, so the request is denied. Both counsel may return to counsel table. *(Is the judge's ruling proper?)*

PROSECUTOR: Just one more thing I'd like to ask you about. Following the robbery, did you speak to any of the other customers who were in the store at the time of the robbery?

A: Yes, I talked to Cynthia Greene, one of the other witnesses, about a week after the robbery. She must have gotten my phone number from the police, I said it would be OK for other witnesses to call me.

PROSECUTOR: In this conversation, what if anything did Cynthia say about the defendant?

A: I know she said something about him, but I'm sorry, I've forgotten what she said.

PROSECUTOR: May I approach the bench, Your Honor? (At the bench, both counsel present) I'd like to show the witness the notes that Ms. Greene made following her conversation with the witness. By way of an offer of proof, I expect that the witness' memory will be refreshed that Ms. Greene, who testified earlier in the trial that she was unable to identify the defendant as the robber, told this witness that a few days after the robbery she attended a police lineup and identified Suspect # 4 as the robber. Other evidence will show that Suspect # 4 was the defendant.

DEFENSE ATTORNEY: Object on the ground that even if the witness' memory is refreshed as to what Ms. Greene told her, the answer would constitute inadmissible hearsay.

JUDGE: Objection sustained. Counsel, the refreshing recollection technique doesn't enable you to offer evidence that is otherwise inadmissible. (*Is the judge's ruling correct?*)

Problem 14-33: Forget Me Not

Same case as previous problem. Abbott and Costello happened to be walking past the store just after the robbery took place. The prosecutor seeks to have Abbott testify that he saw the defendant jump into a waiting car, which immediately sped down the street and around the corner. Thinking that trouble was afoot, Abbott ran after the car and chased it around the corner and down the next block, but soon lost sight of it. While chasing the car, Abbott had a chance to observe its license plate. After resting for about a minute, Abbott walked back to Costello and told him how the license plate number read. At trial, Abbott is unable to recall anything other than that the license plate started with the letter "M." The prosecutor then seeks to have Costello testify that he didn't see the car's license plate, but that he took a pen and a tissue out of his jacket pocket and accurately wrote down the information about the license plate that Abbott gave him. The tissue has written on it the words "Me Not." (*If the prosecutor were to elicit this evidence, are the words on the tissue admissible as Abbott's recollection recorded?*)

Assume that at the time Abbott told him the car's license plate number, neither pen nor tissue was available to Costello. However, Costello has an excellent memory, and is prepared to testify that Abbott told him that the license plate number of the getaway car was "Me Not." *Can Costello verbally testify to Abbott's statement regarding the license plate number of the getaway car under the exception for recollection recorded?*

Problem 14-34: Lasting Freshness

Sherrill is charged with selling illegal drugs. The primary government witness is Al, who was employed as an undercover informant. At trial, Al identifies Sherrill as a dealer from whom he bought drugs. Asked by the prosecutor to testify to the quantity of drugs he purchased from Sherrill and their price, Al replies, "I don't remember." The prosecutor then seeks to read into evidence pursuant to Rule 803(5) the following memorandum that Al wrote:

> Dealer # 4: Sherrill. Asked for a lid of cocaine. Sherrill said she could sell me a lid of nearly pure cocaine; price $500. Gave her five marked $100 bills; she went into the alley and returned with a lid of cocaine, which she gave to me.

Evidence offered by both parties during the foundational mini-trial established the following: At the time he bought drugs from Sherrill, Al had been employed as an undercover police officer for three months. During that time, he'd been involved in about 100 purchases of illegal drugs. Al wrote the memorandum approximately one hour after the transaction with Sherrill. In the 20 minutes or so prior to the transaction with Sherrill, Al had bought drugs from three other dealers, and before writing the memorandum he purchased drugs from two more dealers. These other transactions involved from one-half to two lids of cocaine, and prices ranging from $300 to $1,200. All the drug transactions took place within a two-block radius. After completing six drug transactions, Al radioed for police backup, pointed out the individuals who were to be arrested, and then wrote out six memoranda of the type given above, in the order in which the transactions took place.

Student # 1: You are the prosecutor. Make a brief argument that the drug transaction was fresh in Al's mind at the time he wrote the memorandum and that therefore it is admissible as Al's recollection recorded.

Student # 2: You are the defense attorney. Make a brief argument that the drug transaction was not fresh in Al's mind at the time he wrote the memorandum and that therefore it is inadmissible as Al's recollection recorded.

Student # 3: You are the judge. Preside over the arguments and rule on the admissibility of the memorandum as Al's recollection recorded.

Problem 14-35: Preppie-ration

A defense attorney is about to cross-examine Sheldon Bottomhew IV, an Ivy League college student who is a government witness in a murder case. The defense attorney's first two questions to Sheldon are:

1. "Did you meet with anyone from the prosecutor's office prior to trial to go over the information that you have testified to today?"

2. After receiving an affirmative response to the prior question, the next question is, "When you met with someone from the prosecutor's office to go over that information, did you look at any documents?"

What is the potential significance of Sheldon's answer for the defense attorney's ability to gain access to documents in the prosecutor's possession?

Best Memory Ever? If there were a *Guinness Book of World Records* for evidence rulings, the case of *United States v. Senak*[12] might qualify in the category of "strangest foundation for recollection recorded." *Senak* upheld a trial court's ruling that a written statement given by a declarant to an FBI agent, describing a conversation that had occurred three years earlier, was made at a time when the event was still fresh in the declarant's memory, and so qualified as the declarant's recollection recorded.

Practice Tip: How the use of "past recollection recorded" presents problems for cross-examiners.

Witnesses whose out-of-court statements are admitted under the hearsay exception for past recollection recorded are generally very difficult to cross-examine. They have already admitted on direct examination that they no longer remember much about the events in question, and are likely to respond to cross-examination questions with answers that consist of little more than, "Sorry, I don't remember." The lack of recollection can make it very difficult for a cross-examiner to undermine the version of events as set forth in the writing that constituted the witness' past recollection recorded. By contrast, the opportunity for meaningful cross-examination is likely to be far greater when witnesses say that a writing has refreshed their recollection. As such witnesses purport to testify from present memory, a cross-examiner can fully explore the extent and accuracy of their testimony.

§ 14.09 BUSINESS RECORDS (RULES 803(6), (7))

Statutory Elements:

- A business entity (as broadly defined) produces a memorandum, report, record, or data compilation in any form of acts, events, conditions, opinions, or diagnoses concerning the entity's business practices;

- Entity representatives with personal knowledge contributed the information contained in the memorandum, etc.;

- The representatives recorded the information at or near the time that business-related activity occurred;

- The entity's regular business practice was to prepare the memorandum, report, record, or data compilation;

- The acts, events, conditions, opinions, or diagnoses relate to a regularly conducted business activity.

The business records exception (Rule 803(6)) is a bedrock of modern commercial litigation. An extremely broad exception, Rule 803(6) allows organizations to prove facts by introducing their records into evidence, whether those records consist of traditional paper documents or data stored in computers.

---

[12] 527 F.2d 129 (7th Cir. 1975).

For purposes of Rule 803(6), a covered entity includes a "business, institution, association, profession, occupation, and calling of every kind, whether or not conducted for profit." For example, a sole proprietorship, a church or synagogue, a PTA group, a labor union, and a charitable environmental organization are entities whose records would qualify for admission into evidence as business records.

Evidence satisfying these foundational requirements must be "shown by the testimony of the custodian or other qualified witness, or by certification that complies with Rule 902(11), Rule 902(12) or a statute permitting certification." As parties, entities may seek to offer their own records into evidence under Rule 803(6). Or, "outside" parties may seek to offer entities' records into evidence as business records. For example, a plaintiff in a personal injury case may offer the records of the hospital that treated the plaintiff's injuries following a mishap. In either event, the "sponsoring" witness whose testimony supports the foundational factors listed in Rule 803(6) is often a "custodian of records." A custodian of records testifies to an entity's practices and procedures regarding the preparation and maintenance of records. Of course, custodians typically have no firsthand knowledge of the events described in any particular set of records. However, their testimony describing an entity's usual record-keeping procedures and the conformity of the records produced in court to those procedures, assures a judge that the records are trustworthy.

A requirement that custodians of records testify personally can be a nuisance for "repeat litigation player" entities such as hospitals, whose records are routinely subpoenaed in personal injury cases to which the hospitals are not parties. Thus, Rule 803(6) allows a business whose records are subpoenaed to send the records to court along with a certification from a custodian or other qualified person declaring that the records meet the foundational requirements of Rule 803(6).

Business records are inadmissible if "the source of information or the method or circumstances of preparation indicate lack of trustworthiness." This phrasing puts the onus on a party seeking to exclude a business record from evidence to convince a judge that an otherwise qualified business record is untrustworthy.

The business records exception is a product of both necessity and trustworthiness. The exception is necessary because in most modern entities, numerous employees are likely to contribute to business records. A simple wholesale transaction may begin with a salesperson "in the field" who submits an order via e-mail to another employee who transmits the order to a central order desk. From there, the order may pass through several employees, each of whom makes entries related to the transaction. Eventually a record may be transmitted to the shipping department, which sends out the goods that were ordered. An evidence rule requiring foundational testimony from all employees with personal knowledge of transaction-related events would be at best tremendously burdensome and at worst (especially given employee turnover) impossible to satisfy.

Trustworthiness results from regularity of record keeping and commercial reality. Records are likely to be accurate when they are prepared according to regular business practices by employees whose continued employment rests on knowing and following those practices. Moreover, entities need to establish and follow regular and reliable procedures for reasons that have nothing to do with litigation. Entities that do not have or do not follow regular procedures often do not survive long enough to become parties to anything other than bankruptcy proceedings.

Clearly admissible under the business records exception are documents memorializing "objective" business details, such as what goods were bought, how much was paid, when they were shipped, and the like. However, the modern scope of the exception is far broader than this. As a written report made admissible by Rule 803(6) may include "opinions or diagnoses," the rule may admit a doctor's notation in a hospital record concerning a patient's prognosis. An admissible record may also consist of a "report" pertaining to "events or conditions." As a result, the report of an entity's investigation into an accident in which it was involved may also qualify as a business record.

During the common-law period of the business record exception's history, courts were likely to exclude reports resulting from companies' internal investigations, on the ground that they were likely to be "self-serving" and untrustworthy. The paradigm case was *Palmer v. Hoffman*.[13] There, a railroad was sued for the wrongful death of person struck by a train because of the engineer's alleged failure to warn of the train's approach to a crossing. The railroad offered into evidence the engineer's written statement, made two days after the accident when the railroad, as it regularly did, investigated the cause of the accident. Justice Douglas, writing for the Court, held that the statement did not qualify for admission as a business record. Justice Douglas's reasoning was that while the statement may have affected the railroad's business, it was not made "in the regular course of business" within the meaning of the hearsay exception, because "the business of the (railroad) is the railroad business," not litigating. (Actually, a count of the number of cases in which railroads appear as parties might prove Justice Douglas wrong about this.) Justice Douglas thought such statements generally untrustworthy, and he worried that businesses could bootstrap self-serving reports into evidence simply by establishing regular procedures for making them: "Any business by installing a regular system for recording and preserving its version of accidents for which it was potentially liable could qualify those reports" as business records. Reports like the engineer's statement lack trustworthiness because "these reports are calculated for use essentially in the court, not in the business. Their primary utility is in litigating, not in railroading."

Modern courts, however, tend to interpret Rule 803(6) so as to make organizations' internal investigative reports admissible. Judges' attitudes tends to be that almost all business records, even receipts from grocery stores, are produced partly to protect an entity should a dispute arise. Thus, so long as a judge is convinced that an entity established and followed routine procedures, and those procedures are generally trustworthy, the resulting record is very likely to be admitted into evidence. Judges trust juries to recognize that reports stemming from internal investigations may be slanted in an entity's favor and to discount their contents appropriately.

---

[13] 318 U.S. 109, 63 S. Ct. 477, 87 L. Ed. 645 (1943).

Example 1

Mike Rohard has sued Abee See Co. for damages for breach of contract, alleging that Abee See breached a written agreement to deliver 10,000 computer hard drives to Rohard by May 1. Abee See claims that the hard drives were delivered to Rohard's place of business as set forth in the agreement on April 30. To prove delivery, Abee See calls Les See, its custodian of records, to lay the foundation for records proving that delivery was made. Les's foundational testimony may proceed along these lines:

DEFENDANT'S ATTORNEY: And what are your duties as the custodian of records?

A: I'm responsible for setting up the company's record-keeping procedures, communicating them to all employees, and ensuring that they are followed. I also supervise the employees who maintain and file the records.

DEFENDANT'S ATTORNEY: Have you set up procedures for establishing that the company has shipped goods and that those goods have been received by its customers?

A: Certainly. We maintain both paper and computer records for all shipments. The shipping supervisor and the delivery driver both initial a shipping invoice as soon as goods have been moved from our warehouse to a truck. At the other end, both the driver and the customer rep sign the same invoice as soon as delivery is made. Computer records are also updated whenever an entry is made on an invoice.

DEFENDANT'S ATTORNEY: Showing you what has been previously marked as Defense Exhibit C for Identification, do you recognize what this is?

A: I do. It's an Abee See shipping invoice. It's the form I set up, we have hundreds like it in our records.

DEFENDANT'S ATTORNEY: Calling your attention to what appear to be signatures, do you recognize any of them?

A: Just the one of Baltic See, our shipping supervisor. I don't recognize the others, but this one appears to be that of our delivery driver, because it's signed twice, once when it was loaded onto the truck by us and once when it was delivered. You'll notice there's a company time stamp next to the signatures; that's also standard company practice.

DEFENDANT'S ATTORNEY: What happens to a document such as Exhibit C after the goods are delivered?

A: The driver brings it to the records office, where it's stamped as you see here in the upper left-hand corner. We then update the computer records and store the original invoice in an Invoice File. A file contains all the invoices for each year, arranged chronologically by date of delivery.

DEFENDANT'S ATTORNEY: And where did you find the invoice that is Exhibit C?

A: In this year's Invoice File.

DEFENDANT'S ATTORNEY: I ask that Exhibit C be received in evidence.

JUDGE: Exhibit C in evidence. Here, the witness' testimony establishes that Exhibit C was prepared according to regular and timely practices. Moreover, no evidence suggests that it lacks trustworthiness.

While in complex cases the foundational testimony can be far more extensive, the custodian's testimony is probably sufficient to lay the foundation for a simple shipping document.

The admissibility of a business record is not necessarily an "all or nothing" proposition.

Arguments about the admissibility of a business record may concede that while some portions of a record qualify for admission, other portions should be excluded. The usual arguments that attorneys make in an effort to exclude portions of a business record are that particular assertions lack trustworthiness or constitute "double hearsay" (sometimes called "hearsay upon hearsay," or in the heat of trial, "garbage").

With regard to trustworthiness, the less that a statement in a business record relates to a matter that a judge considers to be routine and objectively verifiable, the more likely a judge is to exclude it as falling outside the scope of the business records exception. Because trustworthiness partly depends on routine, judges may conclude that statements that are the product of subjective judgment lack trustworthiness. For example, consider two hospital records. One contains an orthopedist's opinion that a patient's left arm was broken. The other contains a psychiatrist's opinion that a patient suffers from "undifferentiated schizophrenia that is likely to produce grand mal seizures." A judge is more likely to admit the former statement than the latter. A judge is likely to consider diagnosing a broken arm a matter of objective routine, whereas psychiatric diagnoses are often considered subjective and non-routine.

The "double hearsay" limitation on business records originates with the case of *Johnson v. Lutz*.[14] In this wrongful death case, a motorcyclist collided with a truck, with the usual outcome. To prove that the truck had been operated carefully, the truck driver offered a police officer's accident investigation report into evidence. The court concluded that the officer's report did not qualify as a business record because the police officer did not personally observe what happened. Rather, the report was "made from the hearsay statements of third persons who happened to be present at the scene of the accident when he arrived." The business records exception "was not intended to permit the receipt in evidence of entries based on voluntary hearsay statements by third parties not engaged in the business or under any duty in relation thereto." Judges continue to exclude statements by "outsiders" (those without a business duty to be accurate) under the business records exception. Of

---

[14] 170 N.E. 517 (N.Y. 1930).

course, if outsiders' statements qualify under a separate hearsay exception, their statements may be admissible.

Example 2

Shore Worker sues his employer for injuries suffered when a load crashed on him, allegedly because the employer neglected to maintain a winch properly. Shore is taken to an emergency room for treatment.

1. Shore offers the records of his emergency room treatment into evidence as a business record. The physician's notes indicate in part that "Patient stated that he was hurt when the winch failed to operate properly." Even if the hospital records qualify generally as a business record, Shore's statement to the physician would probably be excluded as inadmissible hearsay, because Shore is an "outsider" to the hospital entity and not under a business duty to be accurate. (Nor would a judge be likely to admit Shore's statement under the exception for "medical hearsay," because whether or not the winch was operating properly is probably not reasonably pertinent to treatment.)

2. Shore's employer offers the records of Shore's emergency room treatment into evidence as a business record. The physician's notes indicate in part that "Patient stated that he was hurt when he was unable to hold onto the rope and a beer bottle with the same hand." If the report qualifies as a business record, Shore's statement to the physician would probably also be admissible, under two different hearsay exceptions. The physician had a business duty to accurately report what Shore said about how he got hurt, and Shore's statement is a party admission under Rule 801(d)(2)(A) if offered into evidence against Shore by the employer.

The Business Records Exception in the News: Professional basketball player Chris Webber was indicted in September 2002 and charged in federal court with obstructing justice by committing perjury when he denied in grand jury testimony that he had received and paid back money from gambler Ed Martin while Webber was playing basketball at the University of Michigan. The government's evidence that Martin had had financial dealings with Webber and other Michigan basketball players consisted in large part of Martin's written business records consisting of the names of players to whom he had given gifts and made loans, any amounts repaid by the players, and the dates of those transactions. However, Martin died of natural causes in February 2003, before the government was able to bring the case to trial. Martin's death deprived the government of the only witness whose testimony could support the foundational elements of Rule 803(6). As a result, the government had to make a deal, and so dismissed the obstruction of justice charge in exchange for Webber's pleading guilty to a much lesser offense, criminal contempt.[15]

---

[15] *See* Webber Avoids Jail, Pleading Guilty on a Contempt Charge, N.Y. Times, July 15, 2003, at D5.

Problem 14-36: Floor-ida

Ida has been sued by We'll Floor You Inc. for failure to pay the $4,500 balance due the company for refinishing the wood floors in Ida's home. To prove payment, Ida offers a portion of her check register into evidence under Rule 803(6). The check register is a small account booklet that Ida's bank sends to her whenever she orders blank checks. Ida is prepared to testify that for years, it has been her regular and routine practice to make an entry in her check register every time and as soon as she writes a check. In the register, she records each check's number, the date she wrote it, the name of the payee, and the amount of the check. Ida seeks to offer into evidence the portion of her check register indicating that on March 12, she wrote Check # 2004 to We'll Floor You in the amount of $4,500. *How should the judge rule on We'll Floor You's objection that the check register is inadmissible hearsay?*

Assume that instead of recording her checking records in a check register, Ida does so on a computer, using a software program called Budget Builder. Ida seeks to offer into evidence a printout of an entry she made on March 12, indicating that she wrote Check # 2004 to "We'll Floor You" in the amount of $4,500. *How should the judge rule on "We'll Floor You's" objection that the printout is inadmissible hearsay?*

To prove that Ida owes $4,500 as the balance due for floor refinishing, "We'll Floor You" offers into evidence its computer record of the work it performed in Ida's home. The record includes the contract specifying a total cost of $9,000 and a partial payment by Ida of $4,500. We'll Floor You's manager testifies to the company's method of regularly preparing such records in the usual course of business. The manager also proposes to testify that the company's bookkeeper regularly enters the words "Final Payment Received" into a record as soon as final payment is received, and that no such notation has been made on Ida's record. *Are the record and the manager's testimony admissible under Rules 803(6) and 803(7)?*

Problem 14-37: On the Tube: Dear Diary

In an episode of the television show "Murder One," Wilson is charged with murdering Kim, a prostitute. The defense seeks to show that Kim had been blackmailing a number of her clients, to show that others had a motive to kill her. As evidence that Kim had been blackmailing clients, the defense seeks to offer into evidence her diary in which she identified clients by name, and recorded the amounts of money she had demanded that the clients pay her, the dates of the demands, and any payments made by the clients. The prosecutor objects that the diary is inadmissible hearsay, on the grounds that (1) prostitution is illegal, (2) a prostitute is not engaged in a business activity within the meaning of Rule 803(6), and (3) the defense has failed to satisfy other foundational requirements in Rule 803(6). *How should the judge rule on these objections?*

Problem 14-38: Hotel California Alibi

Arthur A. Chester is charged with murdering Stanley Morgan in Broomall, PA; the defense is an alibi. To prove that he was in California on the night Morgan was killed, the defendant offers into evidence a hotel registration card from the Fresno Hilton Hotel. The registration card is dated the night of the killing, and contains handwritten information consisting of the defendant's name, home and business addresses and phone numbers, and the number and expiration date of a credit card belonging to the defendant. The card is not signed. The defendant offers evidence that the hotel regularly asks guests to fill out registration forms upon check-in. *How should the judge rule on the government's objection that the registration card is inadmissible hearsay?*

Problem 14-39: Track Record 1

Oscar Ramirez, a freight train brakeman, sues his employer, the B & Uh-O Railroad, alleging that he was injured when the brakes on the train car on which he was riding malfunctioned, causing it to slam into a train car ahead of it. The Railroad claims that the cause of the accident was Ramirez's failure to set the brake properly. To prove that the brake was operating properly at the time of the accident, the Railroad offers into evidence an "inspection report" prepared by its Safety Supervisor. According to the report, the Supervisor inspected the train car on which Ramirez was riding about four hours after the accident occurred, and found that the brake was working properly. The Railroad offers further foundational evidence indicating that it regularly asks for inspection reports following accidents resulting in injuries.

Student # 1: You are the attorney for Ramirez, and have objected that the inspection report is hearsay and inadmissible under Rule 803(6). Make a brief argument in support of your objection.

Student # 2: You are the attorney for the Railroad. Make a brief argument that the report is trustworthy and should be admitted to prove that the brake was operating properly.

Student # 3: As the judge, preside over the hearing and rule on the report's admissibility under Rule 803(6).

Problem 14-40: Track Record 2

Same case as previous problem. Assume that the judge has concluded that the Safety Supervisor's inspection report is sufficiently trustworthy to qualify as a business record. *Consider which of the following statements in the report the plaintiff might be able to exclude.*

1. "A check of company maintenance records indicate that the brake had passed a complete safety inspection one month before the accident."

2. "Harry Chu, yard maintenance worker, states that Ramirez indicated to Chu that Ramirez had forgotten to pressurize the brake before moving the car."

3. "Pepper Roni, who runs a nearby diner, states that Ramirez had drunk a few beers shortly before starting work on the night of the accident."

4. "Ramirez previously worked for a trucking company. I am informed by the trucking company's personnel officer that according to that company's records, Ramirez had failed to set a brake properly on three different occasions in the six months prior to his leaving there and coming to work for our company."

5. "My conclusion is that the accident was due to Ramirez's own carelessness in neglecting to set the brake properly."

Problem 14-41: Building the Foundation

Martina sues Lewis for personal injuries arising out of an auto accident, and seeks damages for pain and suffering caused by a separated shoulder, an injury that Martina alleges was due to the accident. To support Lewis's claim that Martina's separated shoulder is unrelated to the auto accident, Lewis wants to offer into evidence the records of Martina's emergency room treatment following the accident. The records make no reference to shoulder problems. You are defendant Lewis's attorney. Under Rule 803(7), indicate who you would call as a witness and the foundational evidence you would seek to elicit to convince the trial judge to admit the records as evidence that Martina did not suffer a separated shoulder in the accident.

Problem 14-42: Truss-worthiness

Same case as previous problem. Assume that it is plaintiff Martina who wants to offer the records of her emergency treatment into evidence, and that the judge has ruled that they qualify as business records. The records include the emergency room physician's opinion that "X-rays reveal damage to three of the patient's vertebrae. Likely prognosis: patient will have permanent back pain, will have to wear a truss to support her back when standing for lengthy periods, and is at increased risk for early onset of rheumatoid arthritis."

If you represent Lewis, what objection and argument might you make under Rule 803(6) in an effort to exclude all or part of the opinion? As the judge, how would you rule on the objection?

Problem 14-43: Report In?

Same case as previous problem. To prove the extent of her injuries, plaintiff Martina offers into evidence a "Medical Report and Evaluation," prepared by Dr. Forensic. Dr. Forensic evaluated Martina for the purpose of testifying as an expert at trial, and it is Dr. Forensic's regular practice to prepare such reports when preparing to give expert testimony. When Martina offers the report into evidence while questioning Dr. Forensic, defendant Lewis objects that the report is inadmissible hearsay under Rule 803(6). *How should the judge rule on the objection?*

Assume that when she meets with Dr. Forensic the day before Dr. Forensic is to testify, Martina tells him that "I've been doing everything the doctors said to do, but my back pain is as bad as ever." *Can Dr. Forensic testify to Martina's statement at trial?*

Problem 14-44: Nail File

Cindy Rellah sues the Silver Slipper Dance Club after a nail allegedly sticking out of the dance floor penetrated her shoe and gashed her foot. To prove that the dance floor was safe, the club offers into evidence under Rule 803(6) a written report prepared by its floor manager the day following the plaintiff's alleged injury. The report indicates that the manager made a complete visual inspection of the dance floor and did not see a nail in the dance floor or find any indication that a nail had ever been sticking out of the floor. Foundational evidence elicited by the plaintiff indicates that the manager prepared the report after getting a phone call from the owner of the club telling the manager that "I just got off the phone with one of the customers who was at the club last night. She claimed that her foot was cut open by a nail on the dance floor. She sounded like trouble. Better check it out fast and get something down on paper." *How should the judge rule on Cindy's hearsay objection to the club's offer of the floor manager's report?*

Problem 14-45: Safety Record

The parents of three-year-old Todd Lerr sue Hasbroken Toy Co. for injuries Todd suffered as the result of swallowing a button on a toy truck manufactured by Hasbroken. The lawsuit alleges design defects on one of Hasbroken's "Nuke 'Em" series of "Toy Trucks for Healthy Children." To prove that the truck's bomb release feature was safe, Hasbroken offers into evidence a computer-generated report prepared for purposes of the litigation. The report, based on company records, recites (a) all the sales of "Nuke 'Em" model trucks since Hasbroken started manufacturing them three years earlier; and (b) a statement by Hasbroken's Vice President for Safety that Hasbroken logs consumer complaints for each line of its toys, and that a check of the records revealed that Hasbroken has never received a complaint concerning the bomb release button on "Nuke 'Em" trucks. *The judge should make which of the following rulings under Rules 803(6) and 803(7)?*

1. The report is inadmissible because it was prepared specifically for use in the lawsuit in which it is offered.

2. The report is inadmissible unless Hasbroken presents foundational evidence from an expert on computers about the reliability of computers.

3. The report is inadmissible because consumers are under no business duty to report problems with the bomb release button.

4. The report is admissible if Hasbroken convinces the judge that the sales records and complaint logs upon which the computer printout was based were kept as a part of Hasbroken's regularly conducted business.

5. None of the above answers is accurate.

Problem 14-46: Testimonial Custodian?

Dr. Hermione Yu, a radiologist, is charged with theft for billing a county hospital for hours that she did not actually work. To prove the hours for which Yu claimed and received compensation, the prosecutor offers into evidence under Rule 803(6) the relevant portions of the hospital's accounting records. The records are accompanied by a certificate of a hospital custodian of records certifying under Rule 902(11) that the accounting records satisfy the foundational factors set forth in Rule 803(6). The defense objects that the certificate is inadmissible under the Confrontation Clause as interpreted by *Crawford v. Washington* (see Chapter 10), because the certificate is testimonial and the defense has not had an opportunity to cross-examine the custodian who prepared it. *Should the judge sustain the objection?*

Problem 14-47: Lay A Foundation

The purpose of this role-play exercise is for students to understand how translate the foundational elements of the business records exception into trial testimony. Two students will select a familiar business record (e.g., a monthly bill for wireless telephone services or credit card charges). The students will meet outside of class and plan the foundational testimony that they think would establish the foundational factors set forth in Rule 803(6). Complete accuracy is not required. Student # 1 (Attorney) will conduct foundational questioning of Student # 2 (Custodian of Records).

§ 14.10 PUBLIC RECORDS (RULE 803(8))

Statutory Elements:

- Records, reports, statements, or data compilations in any form are those of a public office or agency;

- The records etc. set forth:

    (A) the activities of the agency or office;

    (B) matters that an agency or office has a legal duty to report (except for law enforcement reports in criminal cases); or

    (C) in civil cases and against the government in criminal cases, factual findings resulting from an investigation carried out pursuant to legal authority.

Just as the trustworthiness of business records emanates from an entity's "business duty" to prepare and maintain accurate records, so Rule 803(8) is based on public employees' duty to accurately report and record information in the course of carrying out government duties.

Necessity is also a common basis of both exceptions. Requiring parties to bring to court the numerous public employees who typically contribute to the information stored in public records would be at best highly burdensome to parties and public agencies alike, and in many cases would be impossible.

Perhaps out of a belief that procedures vary less from one public agency to another than from one private entity to another, the foundational requirements for public records are in general less onerous than for business records. The most notable distinction is that while the business records exception requires that a record be prepared pursuant to an entity's "regular practice," and that the record pertain to a "regularly conducted business activity," Rule 803(8) omits any mention of regularity.

Rule 803(8) describes three types of public records. While the foundational requirements are different for each, many public records are admissible under at least two of the subsections. In general, Rule 803(8) broadly applies to "records, reports, statements or data compilations, in any form, of public offices or agencies." This language encompasses public agencies at all levels of government, federal, state and municipal. (For example, a public state law school's student records constitute public records for purposes of the rule.)

Rule 803(8)(A) applies to written records of the activities of a public office or agency. This subsection makes admissible records that pertain to a public agency's internal affairs, such as a purchasing office's receipts and disbursements or a sheriff office's "return of service" on a subpoena. Similarly, an IRS record of sending a taxpayer a refund would be admissible under subsection A.

Rule 803(8)(B) applies to records of matters observed by public servants pursuant to their official duty to observe and report. The phrase "matters observed" indicates that public employees must have personal knowledge of the information in their reports. This subsection makes admissible reports pertaining to the infinite variety of tasks that public employees carry on in the outside world as part of their duties. For example, it would make admissible the record of a health inspector's observations of conditions in a restaurant, a housing inspector's report about the condition of heaters in an apartment house, and a police officer's report indicating the lengths of the skid marks behind two vehicles that collided in an intersection.

An important limitation in Rule 803(8)(B) is that reports pertaining to "matters observed by police officers and other law enforcement personnel" are inadmissible in criminal cases. The obvious concern here is to protect criminal defendants' constitutional right to confront the witnesses against them. Thus, the Rule does not authorize admission of reports that police officers typically prepare in the course of criminal investigations, such as reports that summarize witness interviews and describe other investigative information. The language of the statute has no provision allowing criminal defendants to offer police agency reports into evidence against the government, but most courts allow them to do so.[16]

Rule 803(8)(C) applies to records setting forth factual findings resulting from an authorized investigation. Such reports are admissible in civil cases and, if offered by a defendant against the government, in criminal cases. The absence of a "regularity" foundational requirement means that even "one-shot" investigations, such as the report of the Warren Commission's investigation into the death of President John F. Kennedy, might be admissible under this subsection.

Public records are admissible unless circumstances indicate a lack of trustworthiness. Again, this phrasing puts the burden on a party seeking to exclude otherwise admissible public records to convince a judge that they are unreliable.

Parties offering public records into evidence usually don't need to call "sponsoring" or "foundational" witnesses. In response to a subpoena, a public agency can

---

[16] *See, e.g.*, U.S. v. DePeri, 778 F.2d 963 (3d Cir. 1985).

mail a certified copy of a requested public record to the court. Under Rule 902, the certification stamp or seal establishes the public record's genuineness. Under Rule 1005, the copy is admissible to prove the contents of the original public record.

Example

Anne Athema sues Len Krocher, alleging that Len built a fence on her property. To prove that she owns the land on which Len built the fence, Anne subpoenas her Title Deed from the Office of the County Recorder. The County Recorder mails a copy of Anne's Title Deed to the court in which Anne has filed the case. The Deed bears a County Recorder's purple stamp, and a statement by an employee of the County Recorder's office certifying that the document is a copy of the original Deed on file in the County Recorder's office. The Deed is admissible without Anne having to call a sponsoring witness.

The broad language of subsection (C) was liberally interpreted by *Beech Aircraft Corp. v. Rainey* (*see* Case Library). After the crash of a Navy training airplane, the flight instructor's husband sued the aircraft's manufacturer, claiming that equipment malfunction had caused the crash; the manufacturer claimed that pilot error was responsible. The Navy appointed a Naval officer to investigate and prepare a report on the cause of the crash. The manufacturer offered the report into evidence, and the Court held that it was admissible under Rule 803(8)(C).

One issue concerned the meaning of the phrase "factual findings." The plaintiff asked the court to distinguish "factual findings" from "opinions," and contended that Rule 803(8)(C) made only former admissible. Under the plaintiff's desired interpretation, the investigator's statement that "the aircraft's engine was operating at the time of impact" might constitute an admissible "factual finding." By contrast, the investigator's statement that "the most probable cause of the accident was the pilot's failure to maintain proper interval" would constitute an inadmissible opinion.

The Court rejected the plaintiff's position based on the generally "liberal thrust" of the Federal Rules of Evidence, the legislative history of Rule 803(8)(C) and the linguistic difficulties inherent in trying to distinguish a "fact" from an "opinion."[17] The Court stated that "as long as the conclusion is based on a factual investigation and satisfies the Rule's trustworthiness requirement, it should be admissible along with other portions of the report." Thus, a judge may exclude an opinion in an investigatory report on the ground that it is unreliable, but not on the ground that it constitutes an opinion as opposed to a fact.

Most investigative reports have a "double hearsay" aspect. An investigator's observations and factual findings constitute one layer of hearsay, and information provided by "outsiders" on which the investigator bases those factual findings are another. For example, the Naval investigator in *Beech Aircraft* undoubtedly talked to non-public employees in the course of his investigation, and in his report undoubtedly referred to their statements as part of the justification for his findings.

---

[17] Despite the Court's reliance on legislative history, the opinion recognized that some of that history was flatly contradictory. The House favored a narrow interpretation of the term "factual findings," whereas the Senate favored a broad interpretation. As is so often the case, Congress was able to pass the rule only by passing the buck to judges to figure out the meaning of legislation.

The usual result is that such "outsider" statements are not themselves admissible for the truth of their contents, unless of course they are independently admissible under some other hearsay exception. For example, if the investigator in *Beech Aircraft* had attached transcripts of his interviews with non-public employees to his report, those transcripts would not have been admissible for the truth of their contents. In effect, investigator's opinions under Rule 803(8)(C) are treated the same as experts' opinions under Rules 702 and 703. Both authorized investigators and experts may consider hearsay in the course of arriving at their opinions, but the hearsay does not thereby become admissible.

Problem 14-48: Reporting for Duty

1. Red Handed is charged with burglary. The prosecution offers into evidence under Rule 803(8)(B) a written report from the fingerprint expert of the Police Forensics Lab, which indicates that the expert compared the fingerprints found at the crime scene with those on file in police agencies for Red and concluded that they match. *How should the judge rule on Red's objections that the report is inadmissible hearsay and that it is inadmissible under the Confrontation Clause?*

2. Assume that the fingerprint report was prepared by an employee of Whorls Inc., a private company that contracts with police agencies to do fingerprint analyses. The prosecutor offers the Whorls Inc. report into evidence as a business record under Rule 803(6) rather than a public record under Rule 803(8)(B). *Should the judge determine the report's admissibility pursuant to Rule 803(6) rather than pursuant to Rule 803(8)(B)?*

3. When the police arrest Red, they find a plastic baggie in his pants pocket. A Forensics Lab criminalist prepares a report indicating that the baggie contains five rocks of methamphetamine. As a result, Red is also charged with illegal possession of methamphetamine. To prove that the rocks were methamphetamine, the prosecutor offers the lab report into evidence through the testimony of Greg Laskowski, the lab's supervising criminalist. Laskowski didn't personally prepare the report, but he provides foundational testimony that the trial judge determines qualifies the report for admission under Rule 803(8). Red objects that the report is inadmissible under the Confrontation Clause, because it is testimonial and he has not had an opportunity to cross-examine the criminalist who tested the baggie's contents and prepared the report. *How should the judge rule on Red's objection?*

Problem 14-49: Weather Report

Millie Barr sues Hugh Middity for personal injuries arising out of an auto accident. Millie offers the National Weather Bureau's rainfall records for the area in which the accident occurred to prove that there was no precipitation on the day of the accident. *Are the records admissible under Rule 803(8) over Hugh's hearsay objection? If so, under which subsection of Rule 803(8) would Millie offer the records into evidence?*

Problem 14-50: Bad Breath

Sal Lune is involved in an automobile accident. The results of a Breathalyzer test administered to Sal by the police following the accident show that his blood alcohol level at the time of the accident was .12, above the jurisdiction's legal limit of .08. *Determine the admissibility of the Breathalyzer test record under Rule 803(8) in the following situations:*

1. The heirs of the other driver involved in the accident offer the record into evidence against Sal in a wrongful death case growing out of the accident.

2. The government offers the report against Sal in a vehicular manslaughter prosecution growing out of the accident.

3. Sal's attorney offers the report into evidence as part of Sal's defense to the vehicular manslaughter charges. Sal's defense is that the criminal charge is the result of police officer bias against him, and that inconsistencies and erasures in the report show that the police doctored it to support their claim that Sal was inebriated at the time of the accident.

Problem 14-51: Confrontation

Joe is charged in federal court with robbing the Last Federal Bank. *Determine the admissibility under Rule 803(8) and the Confrontation Clause of the following items of evidence:*

1. To prove that the bank was federally chartered (and therefore that the federal court has jurisdiction over the case), the prosecutor offers into evidence a certified copy of a record from the U.S. government bank chartering agency indicating that the Last Federal is a federally chartered bank.

2. To prove that the bills found in Joe's possession came from the Last Federal Bank, the prosecutor offers into evidence an FBI report that lists the serial numbers of the specially marked bills that have been allocated to each U.S. bank. The bills taken from Joe have the serial numbers identified in the report as having been allocated to the Last Federal.

3. As proof of Joe's identity as the robber, the prosecutor offers into evidence a certified copy of a record from the state's Department of Motor Vehicles indicating that the car that witnesses identified as the one that the robber sped away in after the bank robbery is registered to Joe.

4. As proof that a bullet that was fired during the robbery came from the gun taken from Joe pursuant to his arrest, the prosecutor offers into evidence a report from a police ballistics expert indicating that markings on the bullet show that it was fired by Joe's gun.

Problem 14-52: Guarded Remarks

Noah Bayle has sued Jay Lehr, a guard, and his employer, the County Sheriff, for damages in federal court, alleging that when Noah was a County Jail inmate, Lehr violated Noah's civil rights by knowingly permitting Bluto, another prisoner, to assault Noah. After Noah reported the assault, the Sheriff, whose office operates the County Jail, appointed a lawyer, Anna Turney, to investigate and prepare a report concerning the alleged incident. At trial, Noah seeks to offer Turney's report into evidence under Rule 803(8). *How should the judge rule on the following objections which the defendants might make?*

1. Objection; the report is inadmissible as a public record because the investigation was not authorized by a federal official.

2. Objection; the report is inadmissible as a public record because the investigator was a private individual and not a public employee.

3. Objection; the report is untrustworthy because the findings are based on information supplied by declarants who are not public employees.

4. Included in the report is a statement made to the investigator by Mark Time. The report indicates that Mark Time was a County Jail inmate at the time of the assault on Noah Bayle. Time told the investigator that he did not personally see the assault, but that on the day before it took place, Jay Lehr told him that he (Lehr) was going to see to it that Noah was beaten up for reporting that guards were selling drugs inside the jail. The defendants object to admission of the statement on the grounds of hearsay. Noah responds that it is admissible under a combination of the public records exception and hearsay exemptions for admissions (as to Lehr), and work-related statements by a party's employee (as to the Sheriff).

5. Assume that the judge sustains the objection in # 4 and rules that Mark Time's statement is hearsay and therefore not admissible for the truth of its contents. One of the findings in the report is as follows: "Based in part on the information provided by Mark Time, the investigator concludes that Jay Lehr knowingly permitted the attack on Noah Bayle to occur as revenge for Mr. Bayle's having reported that guards were selling drugs inside the jail." The defendants object that this finding be excluded because it relies on inadmissible hearsay.

6. One of the findings in the report is as follows: "Jay Lehr and the Sheriff violated Noah Bayle's rights under **42 U.S.C. 1983**, the federal civil rights law." The defendants object that this portion of the report is inadmissible.

7. Another one of the findings in the report is as follows: "Jay Lehr knew when he left Mr. Bayle alone with Bluto that Bluto would attack Mr. Bayle." The defendants object that this portion of the report is an inadmissible opinion regarding a matter as to which the investigator lacks personal knowledge.

8. When Noah offers a certified copy of Turney's report into evidence, the trial continues according to the transcript below. Please respond to the italicized questions. As you do so, consider that the Advisory Committee Note to Rule 803(8) states that in evaluating a report's trustworthiness, a judge may consider (1) the timeliness of the investigation, (2) the special skill or experience of the investigator, (3) whether a hearing was held, and (4) the motivations of the individuals who contributed to the report.

DEFENDANT'S ATTORNEY: (at the bench): We object to the report's admissibility, Your Honor. The report is untrustworthy and therefore should be excluded. We ask you to

	excuse the jury and hold a foundational hearing as to the report's trustworthiness.
JUDGE:	Counsel, I have the authority not to excuse the jury, and I will not do so at this time. I will reconsider the matter if it looks like we'll be getting into the contents of the report during the hearing. (*Is this statement correct?*)
JUDGE:	Also, I'll state for the record that the burden is on the defense to convince me that the report is untrustworthy. (*Is this statement correct?*)
DEFENDANT'S ATTORNEY:	The defense calls Anna Turney, the investigator who prepared the report. Ms. Turney, how did you come to be named as the investigator in this matter?
A:	The Sheriff phoned me about three weeks after the alleged assault took place.
DEFENDANT'S ATTORNEY:	Had you ever been involved in an investigation on behalf of the Sheriff previously?
A:	No.
DEFENDANT'S ATTORNEY:	How about on behalf of any other law enforcement agency?
A:	No.
PLAINTIFF'S ATTORNEY:	Objection, irrelevant as to experience with other aspects of law enforcement.
JUDGE:	Overruled. (*Is this ruling correct?*)
DEFENDANT'S ATTORNEY:	In fact, didn't you give a speech about a year earlier in which you said that you thought that the County Jail was rife with corruption?
PLAINTIFF'S ATTORNEY:	Objection, hearsay.
DEFENDANT'S ATTORNEY:	Party admission, Your Honor. (*Is this response correct?*)
DEFENDANT'S ATTORNEY:	Also, admissible as non-hearsay as to state of mind. (*Is this response correct?*)
JUDGE:	I'll overrule the objection. The witness may answer.
A:	No, I said that I'd read some articles in the local paper about jail conditions, and suggested that a general review take place.
DEFENDANT'S ATTORNEY:	Does your practice ever bring you into contact with defendants charged with crimes or incarcerated prisoners?
A:	No. I'm sure that's one reason the Sheriff appointed me — the Sheriff would have wanted an unbiased investigator with no previous dealings with the criminal justice system.

DEFENDANT'S ATTORNEY: Objection, speculation as to the Sheriff's reasons. Move to strike.

JUDGE: Overruled. Evidence rules don't apply to foundational evidence. (*Is this ruling correct?*)

DEFENDANT'S ATTORNEY: What did you do after you became investigator?

A: I asked the Sheriff to send me any written material he had pertaining to the alleged assault.

DEFENDANT'S ATTORNEY: And were you sent any materials?

A: Yes. I received a file consisting of Mr. Bayle's original statement and Mr. Lehr's written response, the records of Mr. Bayle's medical treatment following the alleged assault, a roster of jail personnel and the names of the alleged assailant as well as other inmates who were potential witnesses.

DEFENDANT'S ATTORNEY: And then what happened?

A: Well, it took three or four weeks before this material was sent to me and I had a chance to review it. Then I had to be out of town on an unrelated trial for about a week. When I got back to my office, I went to County Jail a day or two later to interview Mr. Bayle.

DEFENDANT'S ATTORNEY: Who else did you talk to?

A: Mr. Lehr; an inmate named Mark Time; Bluto, the alleged assailant; and another inmate who was in the vicinity at the time of the alleged assault. I also talked to two guards.

DEFENDANT'S ATTORNEY: Is it true that Mr. Lehr asked you to talk to Pa Rolee, an inmate who'd been released after the date of the alleged assault, and that Mr. Lehr told you that Mr. Rolee had information about previous fights between Mr. Bayle and Bluto?

PLAINTIFF'S ATTORNEY: Objection, hearsay as to what Mr. Lehr said that Mr. Rolee might say.

JUDGE: Overruled. You may answer. (*Is this ruling correct?*)

A: Yes.

DEFENDANT'S ATTORNEY: Did you talk to Mr. Rolee?

A: No. He was not at the address listed in the County's release record.

DEFENDANT'S ATTORNEY: Did you try to locate him in other ways?

A: No.

DEFENDANT'S ATTORNEY: None of the people you talked to were placed under oath, correct?

A: Of course not. I didn't have the power to swear witnesses.

DEFENDANT'S ATTORNEY: And were Mr. Lehr or the Sheriff present when you spoke to Mr. Bayle?

A: No.

DEFENDANT'S ATTORNEY: You relied for your findings on information given to you by Mark Time, correct?

A: Well, along with a lot of other information.

DEFENDANT'S ATTORNEY: And Mr. Time admitted to you, did he not, that Mr. Lehr had previously cited him for misconduct, which caused Mr. Time to lose his good-time credits?

A: Yes, he said that.

DEFENDANT'S ATTORNEY: Nothing further. Your Honor, the defendants object to admission of the report on the grounds that the circumstances render it untrustworthy.

Student # 1: You are the defense counsel. Make a brief argument in support of your objection.

Student # 2: You are the plaintiff's attorney. Make a brief argument in support of admissibility of the report.

Student # 3: You are the judge. Preside over the arguments and rule on the report's admissibility.

§ 14.11 OTHER RULE 803 HEARSAY EXCEPTIONS

The Rule 803 hearsay exceptions reviewed above, along with those examined in other chapters, are by far the ones most often used in actual trials. Among the remaining Rule 803 exceptions are the following:

[A] Records of Vital Statistics (Rules 803(9), (11))

A variety of public agencies collect data from hospitals, clergy, and individuals regarding births, deaths, and marriages. This hearsay exception makes such records admissible for the truth of their contents. For example, to prove the date and place of a person's birth, an executor can offer into evidence a certified copy of a birth certificate Rule 803(11) creates a similar exception for regularly kept records of religious organizations containing information about personal or family history, such as births, deaths, and ancestry. For both subsections, trustworthiness emanates from the usual desire of family members to report this information accurately, and the official (subsection 9) or religious (subsection 11) duty to record the information accurately.

[B] Family Records (Rule 803(13))

One of the mustier hearsay exceptions admits statements of fact concerning personal or family history written in family Bibles; inscribed on rings; engraved on urns, crypts, or tombstones; or found in other similar locations. As a rule, people do not inscribe family history in such meaningful and even sacred locations unless it is accurate. Dracula could rely on this exception to defend against a claim of unauthorized collection of blood by offering a tombstone into evidence to prove that he died centuries earlier. On the other hand, "P.B." could not prove that he loves "A.S." by offering evidence that this information was carved into the bark of a tree or sprayed on a building wall; those are not sufficiently respectful locales.

[C] Statements in Dispositive Documents (Rule 803(15))

This hearsay exception admits statements in property-affecting documents such as deeds, mortgages, wills, security agreements, and the like. Such statements are likely to be reliable because the statements reflect important matters, and the documents are usually drawn with care. For example, a testator's statement in a will that "John is my only son" would be admissible for its truth. Similarly, a statement in a deed that property is owned by "Rhoda and Bernard, as community property" would be admissible for its truth.

[D] Statements in Ancient Documents (Rule 803(16))

This exception admits statements in documents that are more than 20 years old. Sorry, if you are reading this book, you (like the authors) are almost certainly older than an ancient document. The exception's main justification is need. Age may be no guarantor of trustworthiness, but if a statement made many years earlier is relevant to a dispute, the fact that it was written down means that it may be superior to any other form of available proof. Thus, an entry in Noah's diary would (if properly authenticated, meaning established as genuine) be admissible to prove that "the animals, they came on, they came on by twosies twosies;" and a story in an old newspaper would be admissible to prove that "City Hall's clock tower was destroyed by a bolt of lightning" the day before the story was written.

[E] Market Reports and Commercial Publications (Rule 803(17))

This hearsay exception admits statements in commercially-prepared publications in general use by the public and people in various occupations. For example, the price of a share of Disney stock on a certain day could be proved by a website's stock market quotations. And an entry in the *Martindale-Hubbell Lawyer's Directory* could be used to prove that Marx & Engels were partners in a law firm specializing in mergers and acquisitions.

§ 14.12 MULTIPLE-CHOICE REVIEW QUESTIONS

Review Problem 14-A

Edy Dreyer sells ice cream novelties door to door from her small truck. At the end of each day, Edy enters data into a computer file consisting of each day's gross receipts and how many units of each variety of ice cream she sold. She prints out the data for each day and stores it in a notebook. Edy's printout for November 17 contains this handwritten addition: "Today I observed a collision between a Saab and a BMW while I was selling ice cream on Elm Drive. A few minutes later, the drivers came over to buy ice cream. I heard one driver tell the other, 'Sorry, I blew the stop sign and hit your BMW with my Saab.'" None of the other printouts contain information beyond that relating to ice cream sales. The BMW driver sues the Saab driver for negligence and seeks to offer Edy's November 17 printout into evidence to prove that the Saab driver was negligent. *The judge should rule that:*

1. The printout is inadmissible hearsay because Edy's handwritten addition is not admissible under the business records exception.

2. The printout is inadmissible because the Saab driver's statement constitutes an offer to compromise that is barred under Rule 408.

3. The printout is admissible under Rules 801(d)(2) and 803(6) because the Saab driver's statement constitutes a party admission and the admission is incorporated into a business record.

4. The printout is inadmissible because Edy lacks personal knowledge of which driver caused the collision.

Review Problem 14-B

A defendant is charged with committing arson to a residence by pouring kerosene around the outside of the house and igniting it. The defendant seeks to offer evidence that moments before the fire broke out, one resident of the house said to the other, "Harry, is that gas that I smell?" *Which statement below is correct?*

1. The judge should sustain the prosecutor's "lack of personal knowledge" objection.

2. The judge should admit the statement as an excited utterance.

3. The judge should admit the statement because it does not constitute an assertion.

4. The judge should admit the statement as a present sense impression.

Review Problem 14-C

Samantha, a newspaper food critic, sues Lars's Taco Bar for intentionally serving her contaminated food that caused Samantha to become seriously ill with food poisoning. The alleged incident occurred when Samantha returned to the restaurant for lunch about two weeks after her scathing attack on the quality of Lars's food appeared in the paper. Lars's defense is that Samantha's illness was unrelated to the lunch meal. Samantha collapsed at work a couple of hours after she returned from lunch. She seeks to testify that she told the paramedic who attended to her in the ambulance on the way to the hospital that "I think I have food poisoning. I started feeling dizzy and nauseous as soon as I started eating Lars's Eel Special." *In response to Lars's objection, the judge should rule that:*

1. Samantha's statement to the ambulance attendant is inadmissible because as a lay witness she does not have the expertise to identify her illness as caused by food poisoning.

2. Samantha's statement to the ambulance attendant is admissible in its entirety under the state of mind and medical diagnosis hearsay exceptions.

3. Samantha's statement that "I think I have food poisoning" is admissible under the hearsay exception for then-existing state of mind or physical condition. However, the remainder is inadmissible because it is a statement of memory as to what Samantha did and how she felt prior to making the statement.

4. Samantha's statement to the ambulance attendant is inadmissible in its entirety because Samantha's motive to blame Lars's Taco Bar for her illness means that her statement lacks trustworthiness.

Review Problem 14-D

One Saturday night, six-year-old Joey's parents tell him that "Marty will be babysitting for you again tonight." Joey then told his parents that "I don't want Marty to babysit because the last time he babysat he took off his pants and made me play with his privates." Marty is charged with child sexual abuse; his defense is that no sexual abuse whatsoever took place when he babysat for Joey. The prosecution seeks to offer Joey's statement to his parents into evidence. *In response to Marty's objection, the judge should rule that:*

1. The statement is admissible as a present sense impression if no more than a few days had gone by since Marty had previously babysat for Joey.

2. The statement is admissible as "medical hearsay."

3. The statement is inadmissible hearsay.

4. The statement is admissible under the state of mind hearsay exception.

Review Problem 14-E

Patrol Officer Ritzik is parked when she hears the sound of a collision in the intersection about 50 yards away from her patrol vehicle. She immediately ran to the intersection to investigate. She later prepared a report stating in part that "I did not observe any skid marks behind the blue Acura, which was in the middle of the intersection facing south when I arrived at the intersection, which is controlled by traffic signals. Upon my arrival, bystander Finnegan told me that the driver of the Acura ran the red light. Finnegan also reported hearing the driver of the Acura say upon exiting the vehicle that "I shouldn't have had those last few martinis." Assume that the driver of the Acura is a defendant in a personal injury case brought by the driver of the other car, and that the plaintiff seeks to offer the quoted portion of the report into evidence. *Which of the statements below is accurate?*

1. The report is inadmissible hearsay in its entirety.

2. The portion of the report indicating the location of the Acura and the lack of skid marks is admissible, but the remainder of the report is inadmissible hearsay.

3. The portion of the report indicating the location of the Acura and the lack of skid marks, as well as Finnegan's statement that the Acura ran the red light, is

admissible, but Finnegan's reference to the Acura driver's statement is inadmissible hearsay.

4. The report is admissible in its entirety.

§ 14.13 CASE LIBRARY

MUTUAL LIFE INSURANCE COMPANY v. HILLMON
United States Supreme Court 145 U.S. 285, 12 S. Ct. 909, 36 L. Ed. 706
(1892)

On July 13, 1880, Sallie E. Hillmon, a citizen of Kansas, brought an action against the Mutual Life Insurance Company, a corporation of New York, on a policy of insurance, dated December 10, 1878, on the life of her husband, John W. Hillmon, in the sum of $10,000, payable to her within sixty days after notice and proof of his death. On the same day the plaintiff brought three other actions on similar policies of life insurance for the sum of $5000 each.

In each case, the declaration alleged that Hillmon died on March 17, 1879, during the continuance of the policy, but that the defendant, though duly notified of the fact, had refused to pay the amount of the policy. The answer denied the death of Hillmon, and alleged that he, together with John H. Brown and other, conspired to defraud the defendant by falsely pretending that Hillmon was dead and substituting a dead body which they had procured for his.

At the trial the plaintiff introduced evidence tending to show that on or about March 5, 1879, Hillmon and Brown left Wichita in the State of Kansas, and traveled together through Southern Kansas in search of a site for a cattle ranch; that on the night of March 18, while they were in camp at a place called Crooked Creek, Hillmon was killed by the accidental discharge of a gun; that Brown at once notified persons living in the neighborhood; and that the body was thereupon taken to a neighboring town, where, after an inquest, it was buried. The defendants introduced evidence tending to show that the body found in the camp at Crooked Creek on the night of March 18 was not the body of Hillmon, but was the body of one Frederick Adolph Walters. Upon the question whose body this was, there was much conflicting evidence, including photographs and descriptions of the corpse, and of the marks and scars upon it, and testimony to its likeness to Hillmon and to Walters.

The defendants introduced testimony that Walters left his home at Fort Madison in the State of Iowa in March, 1878, and was afterwards in Kansas; that during that time his family frequently received letters from him, the last of which was written from Wichita; and that he had not been heard from since March, 1879. The defendants also offered the following evidence:

Elizabeth Rieffenach testified that she was a sister of Frederick Adolph Walters and that she received the following letter in her brother's handwriting in March 1879:

> Dear sister and all: I now in my usual style drop you a few lines to let you know that I expect to leave Wichita on or about March the 5th, with a certain Mr. Hillmon, a sheep trader, for Colorado or parts unknown to me.

I expect to see the country now. News are of no interest to you, as you are not acquainted here. I will close with compliments to all inquiring friends. Love to all. I am truly your brother, FRED. ADOLPH WALTERS.

Alvina D. Kasten testified that she was twenty-one years of age and resided in Fort Madison; that she was engaged to be married to Frederick Adolph Walters; and that the last time she received a letter from him was dated at Wichita, March 1, 1879, and was signed by Walters. The letter began as follows:

> Dearest Alvina: Your kind and ever welcome letter was received yesterday afternoon about an hour before I left Emporia. I will stay here until the fore part of next week, and then will leave here to see a part of the country that I never expected to see when I left home, as I am going with a man by the name of Hillmon, who intends to start a sheep ranch, and as he promised me more wages than I could make at anything else I concluded to take it, for a while at least, until I strike something better. There is so many folks in this country that have got the Leadville fever, and if I could not of got the situation that I have now I would have went there myself; but as it is at present I get to see the best portion of Kansas, Indian Territory, Colorado, and Mexico. The route that we intend to take would cost a man to travel from $150 to $200, but it will not cost me a cent; besides, I get good wages. I will drop you a letter occasionally until I get settled down; then I want you to answer it.

MR. JUSTICE GRAY delivered the opinion of the court.

There is, however, one question of evidence so important, so fully argued at the bar, and so likely to arise upon another trial, that it is proper to express an opinion upon it.

This question is of the admissibility of the letters written by Walters on the first days of March, 1879, which were offered in evidence by the defendants, and excluded by the court. In order to determine the competency of these letters, it is important to consider the state of the case when they were offered to be read.

The matter chiefly contested at the trial was the death of John W. Hillmon, the insured; and that depended upon the question whether the body found at Crooked Creek on the night of March 18, 1879, was his body, or the body of one Walters.

The evidence that Walters was at Wichita on or before March 5, and had not been heard from since, together with the evidence to identify as his the body found at Crooked Creek on March 18, tended to show that he went from Wichita to Crooked Creek between those dates. Evidence that just before March 5 he had the intention of leaving Wichita with Hillmon would tend to corroborate the evidence already admitted, and to show that he went from Wichita to Crooked Creek with Hillmon. Letters from him to his family and his betrothed were the natural, if not the only attainable, evidence of his intention.

The position, taken at the bar, that the letters were competent evidence as memoranda made in the ordinary course of business, cannot be maintained, for they were clearly not such.

But upon another ground suggested they should have been admitted. A man's state of mind or feeling can only be manifested to others by countenance, attitude or gesture, or by sounds or words, spoken or written. The nature of the fact to be proved is the same, and evidence of its proper tokens is equally competent to prove it, whether expressed by aspect or conduct, by voice or pen. When the intention to be proved is important only as qualifying an act, its connection with that act must be shown, in order to warrant the admission of declarations of the intention. But whenever the intention is of itself a distinct and material fact in a chain of circumstances, it may be proved by contemporaneous oral or written declarations of the party.

The existence of a particular intention in a certain person at a certain time being a material fact to be proved, evidence that he expressed that intention at that time is as direct evidence of the fact, as his own testimony that he then had that intention would be. After his death there can hardly be any other way of proving it; and while he is still alive, his own memory of his state of mind at a former time is no more likely to be clear and true than a bystander's recollection of what he then said, and is less trustworthy than letters written by him at the very time and under circumstances precluding a suspicion of misrepresentation.

The letters in question were competent, not as narratives of facts communicated to the writer by others, nor yet as proof that he actually went away from Wichita, but as evidence that, shortly before the time when other evidence tended to show that he went away, he had the intention of going, and of going with Hillmon, which made it more probable both that he did go and that he went with Hillmon, than if there had been no proof of such intention. In view of the mass of conflicting testimony introduced upon the question whether it was the body of Walters that was found in Hillmon's camp, this evidence might properly influence the jury in determining that question.

The rule applicable to this case has been thus stated by this court: "Wherever the bodily or mental feelings of an individual are material to be proved, the usual expressions of such feelings are original and competent evidence. Those expressions are the natural reflexes of what it might be impossible to show by other testimony. If there be such other testimony, this may be necessary to set the facts thus developed in their true light, and to give them their proper effect. As independent explanatory or corroborative evidence, it is often indispensable to the due administration of justice. Such declarations are regarded as verbal acts, and are as competent as any other testimony, when relevant to the issue. Their truth or falsity is an inquiry for the jury."

Upon principle and authority, therefore, we are of opinion that the two letters were competent evidence of the intention of Walters at the time of writing them, which was a material fact bearing upon the question in controversy; and that for the exclusion of these letters, as well as for the undue restriction of the defendants' challenges, the verdicts must be set aside, and a new trial had.

Judgment reversed, and case remanded to the Circuit Court, with directions to set aside the verdict and to order a new trial.

UNITED STATES v. PHEASTER
United States Court of Appeals 544 F.2d 353 (9th Cir. 1976)

Renfrew, District Judge:

Appellants Pheaster and Inciso were tried before a jury in the United States District Court for the Central District of California and were convicted on all counts of a 12-count criminal indictment. Count One charged appellants, together with other unindicted co-conspirators whose names were unknown to the grand jury, with a conspiracy to kidnap and hold Larry Adell for ransom. The remaining eleven counts charged Pheaster with depositing letters in the mail containing both requests for ransom for the release of Larry Adell and extortionate threats to injure Larry Adell. Inciso was charged with having aided and abetted the offenses charged in Counts Two through Twelve. Pheaster and Inciso were each sentenced to seventy years' imprisonment on Counts Two through Twelve of the indictment and to life imprisonment on Count One, with the sentences on Count One to run concurrently with the 70-year terms imposed on Counts Two through Twelve.

We have considered all of the arguments advanced by appellants and have found no reversible error. Accordingly, we affirm.

I. FACTS

This case arises from the disappearance of Larry Adell, the 16-year-old son of Palm Springs multi-millionaire Robert Adell. At approximately 9:30 p.m. on June 1, 1974, Larry Adell left a group of his high school friends in a Palm Springs restaurant known as Sambo's North. He walked into the parking lot of the restaurant with the expressed intention of meeting a man named Angelo who was supposed to deliver a pound of free marijuana. Larry never returned to his friends in the restaurant that evening, and his family never saw him thereafter.

Admissibility of Hearsay Testimony Concerning Statements of Larry Adell

Appellant Inciso argues that the district court erred in admitting hearsay testimony by two teenaged friends of Larry Adell concerning statements made by Larry on June 1, 1974, the day that he disappeared. Timely objections were made to the questions which elicited the testimony on the ground that the questions called for hearsay. In response, the Government attorney stated that the testimony was offered for the limited purpose of showing the "state of mind of Larry." After instructing the jury that it could only consider the testimony for that limited purpose and not for "the truth or falsity of what [Larry] said", the district court allowed the witnesses to answer the questions. Francine Gomes, Larry's date on the evening that he disappeared, testified that when Larry picked her up that evening, he told her that he was going to meet Angelo at Sambo's North at 9:30 p.m. to "pick up a pound of marijuana which Angelo had promised him for free". She also testified that she had been with Larry on another occasion when he met a man named Angelo, and she identified the defendant as that man. Miss Gomes stated that it was approximately 9:15 p.m. when Larry went into the parking lot. Doug Sendejas, one of Larry's friends who was with him at Sambo's North just prior to his disappearance, testified that Larry had made similar statements to him in the afternoon and early evening of June 1st regarding a meeting that evening with Angelo. Mr. Sendejas also testified that when Larry left the table at Sambo's North to go into the parking lot, Larry stated that "he was going to meet Angelo and he'd be right back."

Inciso's contention that the district court erred in admitting the hearsay testimony of Larry's friends is premised on the view that the statements could not properly be used by the jury to conclude that Larry did in fact meet Inciso in the parking lot of Sambo's North at approximately 9:30 p.m. on June 1, 1974. The correctness of that assumption is, in our view, the key to the analysis of this contention of error.

The Government argues that Larry's statements were relevant to two issues in the case. First, the statements are said to be relevant to an issue created by the defense when Inciso's attorney attempted to show that Larry had not been kidnapped but had disappeared voluntarily as part of a simulated kidnapping designed to extort money from his wealthy father from whom he was allegedly estranged. In his brief on appeal, Inciso concedes the relevance and, presumably, the admissibility of the statements to "show that Larry did not voluntarily disappear". However, Inciso argues that for this limited purpose, there was no need to name the person with whom Larry intended to meet, and that the district court's limiting instruction was insufficient to overcome the prejudice to which he was exposed by the testimony.

Second, the Government argues that the statements are relevant and admissible to show that, as intended, Larry did meet Inciso in the parking lot at Sambo's North on the evening of June 1, 1974. If the Government's second theory of admissibility is successful, Inciso's arguments regarding the excision of his name from the statements admitted under the first theory is obviously mooted.

The Government's position that Larry Adell's statements can be used to prove that the meeting with Inciso did occur raises a difficult and important question concerning the scope of the so-called "*Hillmon* doctrine", a particular species of the "state of mind" exception to the general rule that hearsay evidence is inadmissible. The doctrine takes its name from the famous Supreme Court decision in *Mutual Life Insurance Co. v. Hillmon*, 145 U.S. 285, 12 S. Ct. 909, 36 L. Ed. 706 (1892). That the *Hillmon* doctrine should create controversy and confusion is not surprising, for it is an extraordinary doctrine. Under the state of mind exception, hearsay evidence is admissible if it bears on the state of mind of the declarant and if that state of mind is an issue in the case. For example, statements by a testator which demonstrate that he had the necessary testamentary intent are admissible to show that intent when it is in issue. The exception embodied in the *Hillmon* doctrine is fundamentally different, because it does not require that the state of mind of the declarant be an actual issue in the case. Instead, under the *Hillmon* doctrine the state of mind of the declarant is used inferentially to prove other matters which are in issue. Stated simply, the doctrine provides that when the performance of a particular act by an individual is an issue in a case, his intention (state of mind) to perform that act may be shown. From that intention, the trier of fact may draw the inference that the person carried out his intention and performed the act. Within this conceptual framework, hearsay evidence of statements by the person which tend to show his intention is deemed admissible under the state of mind exception. Inciso's objection to the doctrine concerns its application in situations in which the declarant has stated his intention to do something *with another person*, and the issue is whether he did so.

There can be no doubt that the theory of the *Hillmon* doctrine is different when the declarant's statement of intention necessarily requires the action of one or more others if it is to be fulfilled.

When hearsay evidence concerns the declarant's statement of his intention to do something with another person, the *Hillmon* doctrine requires that the trier of fact infer from the state of mind of the declarant the probability of a particular act not only by the declarant but also by the other person. Several objections can be raised against a doctrine that would allow such an inference to be made. One such objection is based on the unreliability of the inference but is not, in our view, compelling. A much more significant and troubling objection is based on the inconsistency of such an inference with the state of mind exception. This problem is more easily perceived when one divides what is really a compound statement into its component parts. In the instant case, the statement by Larry Adell, "I am going to meet Angelo in the parking lot to get a pound of grass," is really two statements. The first is the obvious statement of Larry's intention. The second is an implicit statement of Angelo's intention. Surely, if the meeting is to take place in a location which Angelo does not habitually frequent, one must assume that Angelo intended to meet Larry there if one is to make the inference that Angelo was in the parking lot and the meeting occurred. The important point is that the second, implicit statement has nothing to do with Larry's state of mind. For example, if Larry's friends had testified that Larry had said, "Angelo is going to be in the parking lot of Sambo's North tonight with a pound of grass", no state of mind exception or any other exception to the hearsay rule would be available. Yet, this is in effect at least half of what the testimony did attribute to Larry.

Despite the theoretical awkwardness associated with the application of the *Hillmon* doctrine to facts such as those now before us, the authority in favor of such an application is impressive. The *Hillmon* doctrine has been applied by the California Supreme Court in *People v. Alcalde (1944)*. In *Alcalde* the defendant was tried and convicted of first degree murder for the brutal slaying of a woman whom he had been seeing socially. One of the issues before the California Supreme Court was the asserted error by the trial court in allowing the introduction of certain hearsay testimony concerning statements made by the victim on the day of her murder. As in the instant case, the testimony was highly incriminating, because the victim reportedly said that she was going out with Frank, the defendant, on the evening she was murdered. On appeal, a majority of the California Supreme Court affirmed the defendant's conviction, holding that *Hillmon* was "the leading case on the admissibility of declarations of intent to do an act as proof that the act thereafter was accomplished." The court found no error in the trial court's admission of the disputed hearsay testimony. "Unquestionably the deceased's statement of her intent and the logical inference to be drawn therefrom, namely, that she was with the defendant that night, were relevant to the issue of the guilt of the defendant."

In addition to the decisions in *Hillmon* and *Alcalde*, support for the Government's position can be found in the California Evidence Code and the new Federal Rules of Evidence, although in each instance resort must be made to the comments to the relevant provisions.

Section 1250 of the California Evidence Code carves out an exception to the general hearsay rule for statements of a declarant's "then existing mental or physical state". The *Hillmon* doctrine is codified in Section 1250(2) which allows the use of such hearsay evidence when it "is offered to prove or explain acts or conduct of the declarant." The comment to Section 1250(2) states that, "Thus, a statement of the declarant's intent to do certain acts is admissible to prove that he did those acts." Although neither the language of the statute nor that of the comment specifically addresses the particular issue now before us, the comment does cite the *Alcalde* decision and, therefore, indirectly rejects the limitation urged by Inciso.

Although the new Federal Rules of Evidence were not in force at the time of the trial below, we refer to them for any light that they might shed on the status of the common law at the time of the trial. The codification of the state of mind exception in Rule 803(3) does not provide a direct statement of the *Hillmon* doctrine. Although Rule 803(3) is silent regarding the *Hillmon* doctrine, both the Advisory Committee on the Proposed Rules and the House Committee on the Judiciary specifically addressed the doctrine. After noting that Rule 803(3) would not allow the admission of statements of memory, the Advisory Committee stated broadly that

> The rule of *Mutual Life Ins. Co. v. Hillmon* [citation omitted] allowing evidence of intention as tending to prove the doing of the act intended, is, of course, left undisturbed.

Significantly, the Notes of the House Committee on the Judiciary regarding Rule 803(3) are far more specific and revealing:

> However, the Committee intends that the Rule be construed to limit the doctrine of *Mutual Life Insurance Co. v. Hillmon* so as to render statements of intent by a declarant admissible *only to prove his future conduct, not the future conduct of another person.*

Although the matter is certainly not free from doubt, we read the note of the Advisory Committee as presuming that the *Hillmon* doctrine would be incorporated in full force, including necessarily the application in *Hillmon* itself. The language suggests that the Advisory Committee presumed that such a broad interpretation was the prevailing common law position. The notes of the House Committee on the Judiciary are significantly different. The language used there suggests a legislative intention to cut back on what that body also perceived to be the prevailing common law view, namely, that the *Hillmon* doctrine could be applied to facts such as those now before us.

Although we recognize the force of the objection to the application of the *Hillmon* doctrine in the instant case, we cannot conclude that the district court erred in allowing the testimony concerning Larry Adell's statements to be introduced.

For the reasons set out above, we affirm the convictions.

UNITED STATES v. TOME
United States Court of Appeals 61 F.3d 1446 (10th Cir. 1995)

TACHA, CIRCUIT JUDGE.

I. BACKGROUND

A jury convicted defendant Matthew Wayne Tome of aggravated sexual abuse. In his appeal to this court, defendant challenged the admissibility of the hearsay statements relayed by six witnesses. Each witness related out-of-court statements made by the child victim (A.T.). We held that, even though A.T. made the statements after her alleged motive to fabricate had arisen, the statements were prior consistent statements admissible under Rule 801(d)(1)(B).

The United States Supreme Court reversed our decision. Specifically, the Court held that Rule 801(d)(1)(B) "permits the introduction of a declarant's consistent out-of-court statements to rebut a charge of recent fabrication or improper influence or motive only when those statements were made before the charged recent fabrication or improper influence or motive."

The case is now before us on remand. Pursuant to our order, the parties have submitted supplemental briefs addressing the remaining issues. On remand, we must first determine whether the challenged evidence could have been admitted under another rule of evidence. If we find that any of the statements were inadmissible, we must then assess whether the district court's error in admitting them was nevertheless harmless.

III. DISCUSSION

A. Testimony of Karen Kuper, Laura Reich, and Jean Spiegel

We first address the testimony of three pediatricians who examined A.T. In their testimony, the three doctors relayed statements made by A.T. either before or during the doctors' physical examinations of the child. At trial, the district court admitted the doctors' hearsay testimony under both Rules 801(d)(1)(B) and 803(4).

Although hearsay testimony is generally inadmissible, Rule 802, the Federal Rules of Evidence contain a number of exceptions to the hearsay prohibition. One of these exceptions, Rule 803(4), makes admissible "statements made for purposes of medical diagnosis or treatment and describing medical history, or past or present symptoms, pain, or sensations, or the inception or general character of the cause or external source thereof insofar as reasonably pertinent to diagnosis or treatment." Rule 803(4). This exception is premised on the theory that a patient's statements to her physician are likely to be particularly reliable because the patient has a self-interested motive to be truthful: She knows that the efficacy of her medical treatment depends upon the accuracy of the information she provides to the doctor. Stated differently, "a statement made in the course of procuring medical services, where the declarant knows that a false statement may cause misdiagnosis or mistreatment, carries special guarantees of credibility."

A declarant's statement to a physician that identifies the person responsible for the declarant's injuries is ordinarily inadmissible under Rule 803(4) because the assailant's identity is usually unnecessary either for accurate diagnosis or effective treatment. This court held in Joe, however, that a hearsay statement revealing the identity of a sexual abuser who is a member of the victim's family or household "is admissible under Rule 803(4) where the abuser has such an intimate relationship with the victim that the abuser's identity becomes 'reasonably pertinent' to the victim's proper treatment." In so holding, we reasoned that all victims of domestic sexual abuse suffer emotional and psychological injuries, the exact nature and extent of which depend on the identity of the abuser. The physician generally must know who the abuser was in order to render proper treatment because the physician's treatment will necessarily differ when the abuser is a member of the victim's family or household. In the domestic sexual abuse case, for example, the treating physician may recommend special therapy or counseling and instruct the victim to remove herself from the dangerous environment by leaving the home and seeking shelter elsewhere.

Although the victim in Joe was an adult, we stated that "the identity of the abuser is reasonably pertinent in virtually every domestic sexual assault case," including those in which the victim is a child. Thus, when a victim of domestic sexual abuse identifies her assailant to her physician, the physician's recounting of the identification is admissible under Rule 803(4) when it is "reasonably pertinent" to the victim's treatment or diagnosis. After reviewing the testimony of each pediatrician, we conclude that A.T.'s statements to those doctors were reasonably pertinent to her diagnosis or treatment.

1. Testimony of Karen Kuper

Kae Ecklebarger of Child Protection Services referred A.T. to Dr. Karen Kuper, a board certified pediatrician, for a physical examination. Kuper testified that she examined A.T. on two occasions, in September and October 1990. Prior to the first examination, Kuper interviewed A.T. Kuper testified that the purpose of the interview was "to ascertain exactly what injuries had occurred." In response to Kuper's questions, A.T. told Kuper about the sexual abuse, at times pointing to the appropriate areas of dolls to answer Kuper's questions. A.T. also identified defendant as her abuser. After the interview, Kuper performed a complete physical examination of A.T.

We find it clear that A.T.'s statement to Kuper was reasonably pertinent to Kuper's proper diagnosis and treatment of A.T. The information contained in the statement was important to Kuper's determination of A.T.'s condition. This statement was therefore admissible under Rule 803(4).

2. Testimony of Laura Reich

A.T. saw Dr. Laura Reich on September 21, 1990, for treatment of a skin rash in the vaginal area that was unrelated to any sexual abuse. At the time of Reich's examination of A.T., Reich was aware of the allegations of sexual abuse. Reich testified that, prior to conducting the physical examination, she asked A.T. several personal questions. One of these questions was whether "anybody had ever touched her in her private area." According to Reich's testimony, A.T. replied "that her father had put his thing in her." The remainder of Reich's testimony concerned her findings and conclusions from the physical examination.

Reich testified that the reason she had conducted a preexamination interview with A.T was "that the child needs to be comfortable with me before I examine her." Because the adequacy of Reich's examination in part depended on the child's comfort with her, we find that A.T.'s statement was reasonably pertinent to Reich's diagnosis or treatment. It consequently was admissible under Rule 803(4).

3. Testimony of Jean Spiegel

Dr. Jean Spiegel, an assistant professor of pediatrics at the University of New Mexico, testified that she examined A.T. for the purpose of offering a second opinion as to whether the child had been sexually abused. Spiegel had extensive training in the area of child sexual abuse, and teaches other doctors how to examine children to detect molestation. Most of Spiegel's testimony focused on the technical aspects of her examination of A.T. and her conclusion that A.T. had experienced chronic vaginal penetration.

On redirect examination, Spiegel testified that A.T. told her where on her body she had been touched during the abuse. Spiegel did not ask, nor did A.T. volunteer, who had touched her. Clearly, A.T.'s statement regarding where she had been touched was pertinent to Spiegel's diagnosis of A.T. The district court therefore properly admitted the statement under Rule 803(4).

B. Testimony of Kae Ecklebarger

Kae Ecklebarger, a caseworker for Colorado Springs Child Protection Services, interviewed A.T. on August 29, 1990. Ecklebarger testified that during the interview, A.T. gave Ecklebarger a detailed account of the alleged abuse, at times using anatomically correct dolls to demonstrate what had occurred. Ecklebarger also testified that A.T. claimed she had told her grandmother and aunt of the abuse. The government argues that Ecklebarger's testimony is admissible under either Rule 803(4) or Rule 803(24), the residual hearsay exception. We discuss the applicability of these two exceptions in order.

For a hearsay statement to be admissible under Rule 803(4), the declarant need not have necessarily made the statement to a physician. As the advisory committee's note to the rule explains, "statements to hospital attendants, ambulance drivers, or even members of the family might be included." Rule 803(4) advisory committee's note. Accordingly, the government argues that A.T.'s statement to Ecklebarger is admissible because the job of a Child Protection Services caseworker "was equivalent to that of a doctor under Rule 803(4)," and because A.T. understood that Ecklebarger's role was to "help kids."

As stated previously, however, the test for admissibility under Rule 803(4) is "whether the subject matter of the statements is reasonably pertinent to diagnosis or treatment." Ecklebarger neither diagnosed nor treated A.T. She described her role as "the initial short-term investigator." Ecklebarger spoke to A.T. two times, after which "the case was sent on to an ongoing protection worker." Clearly, Ecklebarger did not treat A.T. in any way.

Nor did Ecklebarger diagnose A.T. Indeed, Ecklebarger referred the child to Dr. Kuper for a medical opinion regarding the allegations of abuse. Moreover, Ecklebarger testified that she interviewed A.T. only to the extent necessary to make a decision whether a protective order was appropriate. Because Ecklebarger did not diagnose or treat A.T., the child's statement to Ecklebarger could not have been for the "purpose[] of medical diagnosis or treatment," and thus was not properly admitted under Rule 803(4). (The Court also held that A.T.'s statement to Ecklebarger and similar statements to other witnesses was not admissible as "residual hearsay" under what is now Rule 807.)

IV. CONCLUSION

A.T.'s statements related by Kuper, Reich, and Spiegel were admissible hearsay pursuant to Rule 803(4). But the statements of A.T. included in the testimony of Ecklebarger, Rocha, and Padilla were inadmissible hearsay. Because the erroneous admission of this evidence was not harmless, the judgment of the district court is REVERSED, and the case is REMANDED for further proceedings consistent with this opinion.

PALMER v. HOFFMAN
United States Supreme Court 318 U.S. 109, 63 S. Ct. 477, 87 L. Ed. 645 (1943)

Mr. Justice Douglas delivered the opinion of the Court.

This case arose out of a grade crossing accident which occurred in Massachusetts. Diversity of citizenship brought it to the federal District Court in New York.

The accident occurred on the night of December 25, 1940. On December 27, 1940, the engineer of the train, who died before the trial, made a statement at a freight office of petitioners where he was interviewed by an assistant superintendent of the road and by a representative of the Massachusetts Public Utilities Commission. This statement was offered in evidence by petitioners under 28 U. S. C. § 695. They offered to prove (in the language of the Act) that the statement was signed in the regular course of business, it being the regular course of such business to make such a statement. Respondent's objection to its introduction was sustained.

We agree with the majority view below that it was properly excluded.

We may assume that if the statement was made "in the regular course" of business, it would satisfy the other provisions of the Act. But we do not think that it was made "in the regular course" of business within the meaning of the Act. The business of the petitioners is the railroad business. That business like other enterprises entails the keeping of numerous books and records essential to its conduct or useful in its efficient operation. Though such books and records were considered reliable and trustworthy for major decisions in the industrial and business world, their use in litigation was greatly circumscribed or hedged about by the hearsay rule — restrictions which greatly increased the time and cost of making the proof where those who made the records were numerous. It was that problem which started the movement towards adoption of legislation embodying the principles of the present Act.

The engineer's statement which was held inadmissible in this case falls into quite a different category. It is not a record made for the systematic conduct of the business as a business. An accident report may affect that business in the sense that it affords information on which the management may act. It is not, however, typical of entries made systematically or as a matter of routine to record events or occurrences, to reflect transactions with others, or to provide internal controls. The conduct of a business commonly entails the payment of tort claims incurred by the negligence of its employees. But the fact that a company makes a business out of recording its employees' versions of their accidents does not put those statements in the class of records made "in the regular course" of the business within the meaning of the Act. If it did, then any law office in the land could follow the same course, since business as defined in the Act includes the professions. We would then have a real perversion of a rule designed to facilitate admission of records which experience has shown to be quite trustworthy. Any business by installing a regular system for recording and preserving its version of accidents for which it was potentially liable could qualify those reports under the Act. The result would be that the Act would cover any system of recording events or occurrences provided it was "regular" and though it had little or nothing to do with the management or operation of the business as such. Preparation of cases for trial by virtue of being a "business" or incidental thereto would obtain the benefits of this liberalized version of the early shop book rule. The probability of trustworthiness of records because they were routine reflections of the day to day operations of a business would be forgotten as the basis of the rule. Regularity of preparation would become the test rather than the character of the records and their earmarks of reliability acquired from their source and origin and the nature of their compilation. We cannot so completely empty the words of the Act of their historic meaning. If the Act is to be extended to apply not only to a "regular course" of a business but also to any "regular course" of conduct which may have some relationship to business, Congress not this Court must extend it. Such a major change which opens wide the door to avoidance of cross-examination should not be left to implication. Nor is it any answer to say that Congress has provided in the Act that the various circumstances of the making of the record should affect its weight, not its admissibility. That provision comes into play only in case the other requirements of the Act are met.

In short, it is manifest that in this case those reports are not for the systematic conduct of the enterprise as a railroad business. Unlike payrolls, accounts receivable, accounts payable, bills of lading and the like, these reports are calculated for use essentially in the court, not in the business. Their primary utility is in litigating, not in railroading.

It is, of course, not for us to take these reports out of the Act if Congress has put them in. But there is nothing in the background of the law on which this Act was built or in its legislative history which suggests for a moment that the business of preparing cases for trial should be included. In this connection it should be noted that 45 U. S. C. § 38 requires officers of common carriers by rail to make under oath monthly reports of railroad accidents to the Interstate Commerce Commission, setting forth the nature and causes of the accidents and the circumstances connected therewith. And 45 U. S. C. § 40 gives the Commission authority to investigate and to make reports upon such accidents. It is provided, however, that "Neither the report required by section 38 of this title nor any report of the investigation provided for in section 40 of this title nor any part thereof shall be admitted as evidence or used for any purpose in any suit or action for damages growing out of any matter mentioned in said report or investigation." A similar provision bars the use in litigation of reports concerning accidents resulting from the failure of a locomotive boiler or its appurtenances. That legislation reveals an explicit Congressional policy to rule out reports of accidents which certainly have as great a claim to objectivity as the statement sought to be admitted in the present case. We can hardly suppose that Congress modified or qualified by implication these long standing statutes when it permitted records made "in the regular course" of business to be introduced. Nor can we assume that Congress having expressly prohibited the use of the company's reports on its accidents impliedly altered that policy when it came to reports by its employees to their superiors. The inference is wholly the other way. The several hundred years of history behind the Act indicate the nature of the reforms which it was designed to effect. It should of course be liberally interpreted so as to do away with the anachronistic rules which gave rise to its need and at which it was aimed. But "regular course" of business must find its meaning in the inherent nature of the business in question and in the methods systematically employed for the conduct of the business as a business.

Affirmed.

BEECH AIRCRAFT CORPORATION v. RAINEY
United States Supreme Court 488 U.S. 153, 109 S. Ct. 439, 102 L. Ed. 2d 445
(1988)

JUSTICE BRENNAN delivered the opinion of the Court.

In this action we address a longstanding conflict among the Federal Courts of Appeals over whether Federal Rule of Evidence 803(8)(C), which provides an exception to the hearsay rule for public investigatory reports containing "factual findings," extends to conclusions and opinions contained in such reports.

I

This litigation stems from the crash of a Navy training aircraft at Middleton Field, Alabama, on July 13, 1982, which took the lives of both pilots on board, Lieutenant Commander Barbara Ann Rainey and Ensign Donald Bruce Knowlton. The accident took place while Rainey, a Navy flight instructor, and Knowlton, her student, were flying "touch-and-go" exercises in a T-34C Turbo-Mentor aircraft, number 3E955. Their aircraft and several others flew in an oval pattern, each plane making successive landing/takeoff maneuvers on the runway. Following its fourth pass at the runway, 3E955 appeared to make a left turn prematurely, cutting out the aircraft ahead of it in the pattern and threatening a collision. After radio warnings from two other pilots, the plane banked sharply to the right in order to avoid the other aircraft. At that point it lost altitude rapidly, crashed, and burned.

Because of the damage to the plane and the lack of any survivors, the cause of the accident could not be determined with certainty. The two pilots' surviving spouses brought a product liability suit against petitioners Beech Aircraft Corporation, the plane's manufacturer, and Beech Aerospace Services, which serviced the plane under contract with the Navy. The plaintiffs alleged that the crash had been caused by a loss of engine power, known as "rollback," due to some defect in the aircraft's fuel control system. The defendants, on the other hand, advanced the theory of pilot error, suggesting that the plane had stalled during the abrupt avoidance maneuver.

At trial, the only seriously disputed question was whether pilot error or equipment malfunction had caused the crash. Both sides relied primarily on expert testimony. One piece of evidence presented by the defense was an investigative report prepared by Lieutenant Commander William Morgan on order of the training squadron's commanding officer and pursuant to authority granted in the Manual of the Judge Advocate General. This "JAG Report," completed during the six weeks following the accident, was organized into sections labeled "finding of fact," "opinions," and "recommendations," and was supported by some 60 attachments. The "finding of fact" included statements like the following:

> 13. At approximately 1020, while turning crosswind without proper interval, 3E955 crashed, immediately caught fire and burned.
>
> . . . .
>
> 27. At the time of impact, the engine of 3E955 was operating but was operating at reduced power." "

Among his "opinions" Lieutenant Commander Morgan stated, in paragraph 5, that due to the deaths of the two pilots and the destruction of the aircraft "it is almost impossible to determine exactly what happened to Navy 3E955 from the time it left the runway on its last touch and go until it impacted the ground." He nonetheless continued with a detailed reconstruction of a possible set of events, based on pilot error, that could have caused the accident. The next two paragraphs stated a caveat and a conclusion:

> 1. Although the above sequence of events is the most likely to have occurred, it does not change the possibility that a "rollback" did occur.

2. The most probable cause of the accident was the pilots [sic] failure to maintain proper interval.

The trial judge initially determined, at a pretrial conference, that the JAG Report was sufficiently trustworthy to be admissible, but that it "would be admissible only on its factual findings and would not be admissible insofar as any opinions or conclusions are concerned." The day before trial, however, the court reversed itself and ruled, over the plaintiffs' objection, that certain of the conclusions would be admitted. Accordingly, the court admitted most of the report's "opinions," including the first sentence of paragraph 5 about the impossibility of determining exactly what happened, and paragraph 7, which opined about failure to maintain proper interval as "[t]he most probable cause of the accident." On the other hand, the remainder of paragraph 5 was barred as "nothing but a possible scenario," and paragraph 6, in which investigator Morgan refused to rule out rollback, was deleted as well.

II

Federal Rule of Evidence 803 provides that certain types of hearsay statements are not made excludable by the hearsay rule, whether or not the declarant is available to testify.

Because the Federal Rules of Evidence are a legislative enactment, we turn to the "traditional tools of statutory construction," in order to construe their provisions. We begin with the language of the Rule itself. Proponents of the narrow view have generally relied heavily on a perceived dichotomy between "fact" and "opinion" in arguing for the limited scope of the phrase "factual findings."

For several reasons, we do not agree. In the first place, it is not apparent that the term "factual findings" should be read to mean simply "facts" (as opposed to "opinions" or "conclusions"). A common definition of "finding of fact" is, for example, "[a] conclusion by way of reasonable inference from the evidence." To say the least, the language of the Rule does not compel us to reject the interpretation that "factual findings" includes conclusions or opinions that flow from a factual investigation. Second, we note that, contrary to what is often assumed, the language of the Rule does not state that "factual findings" are admissible, but that "*reports . . . setting forth . . . factual findings*" (emphasis added) are admissible. On this reading, the language of the Rule does not create a distinction between "fact" and "opinion" contained in such reports.

Turning next to the legislative history of Rule 803(8)(C), we find no clear answer to the question of how the Rule's language should be interpreted. Indeed, in this litigation the legislative history may well be at the origin of the dispute. Rather than the more usual situation where a court must attempt to glean meaning from ambiguous comments of legislators who did not focus directly on the problem at hand, here the Committees in both Houses of Congress clearly recognized and expressed their opinions on the precise question at issue. Unfortunately, however, they took diametrically opposite positions. Moreover, the two Houses made no effort to reconcile their views, either through changes in the Rule's language or through a statement in the Report of the Conference Committee. The House

Judiciary Committee, which dealt first with the proposed rules after they had been transmitted to Congress by this Court, included in its Report but one brief paragraph on Rule 803(8):

> The Committee approved Rule 803(8) without substantive change from the form in which it was submitted by the Court. The Committee intends that the phrase "factual findings" be strictly construed and that evaluations or opinions contained in public reports shall not be admissible under this Rule.

The Senate Committee responded at somewhat greater length, but equally emphatically:

> The House Judiciary Committee report contained a statement of intent that "the phrase 'factual findings' in subdivision (c) be strictly construed and that evaluations or opinions contained in public reports shall not be admissible under this rule." The committee takes strong exception to this limiting understanding of the application of the rule. We do not think it reflects an understanding of the intended operation of the rule as explained in the Advisory Committee notes to this subsection . . . . We think the restrictive interpretation of the House overlooks the fact that while the Advisory Committee assumes admissibility in the first instance of evaluative reports, they are not admissible if, as the rule states, "the sources of information or other circumstances indicate lack of trustworthiness."
>
> . . . .
>
> The committee concludes that the language of the rule together with the explanation provided by the Advisory Committee furnish sufficient guidance on the admissibility of evaluative reports.

Clearly this legislative history reveals a difference of view between the Senate and the House that affords no definitive guide to the congressional understanding. It seems clear however that the Senate understanding is more in accord with the wording of the Rule and with the comments of the Advisory Committee.

Our conclusion that neither the language of the Rule nor the intent of its framers calls for a distinction between "fact" and "opinion" is strengthened by the analytical difficulty of drawing such a line. It has frequently been remarked that the distinction between statements of fact and opinion is, at best, one of degree:

> All statements in language are statements of opinion, i.e., statements of mental processes or perceptions. So-called "statements of fact" are only more specific statements of opinion. What the judge means to say, when he asks the witness to state the facts, is: 'The nature of this case requires that you be more specific, if you can, in your description of what you saw.

In the present action, the trial court had no difficulty in admitting as a factual finding the statement in the JAG Report that "[a]t the time of impact, the engine of 3E955 was operating but was operating at reduced power." Surely this "factual finding" could also be characterized as an opinion, which the investigator presumably arrived at on the basis of clues contained in the airplane wreckage. Rather than requiring that we draw some inevitably arbitrary line between the various shades of fact/opinion that invariably will be present in investigatory reports, we believe the

Rule instructs us — as its plain language states — to admit "reports . . . setting forth . . . factual findings." The Rule's limitations and safeguards lie elsewhere: First, the requirement that reports contain factual findings bars the admission of statements not based on factual investigation. Second, the trustworthiness provision requires the court to make a determination as to whether the report, or any portion thereof, is sufficiently trustworthy to be admitted.

A broad approach to admissibility under Rule 803(8)(C), as we have outlined it, is also consistent with the Federal Rules' general approach of relaxing the traditional barriers to "opinion" testimony. Rules 702–705 permit experts to testify in the form of an opinion, and without any exclusion of opinions on "ultimate issues." And Rule 701 permits even a lay witness to testify in the form of opinions or inferences drawn from her observations when testimony in that form will be helpful to the trier of fact. We see no reason to strain to reach an interpretation of Rule 803(8)(C) that is contrary to the liberal thrust of the Federal Rules.

We hold, therefore, that portions of investigatory reports otherwise admissible under Rule 803(8)(C) are not inadmissible merely because they state a conclusion or opinion. As long as the conclusion is based on a factual investigation and satisfies the Rule's trustworthiness requirement, it should be admissible along with other portions of the report. As the trial judge in this action determined that certain of the JAG Report's conclusions were trustworthy, he rightly allowed them to be admitted into evidence. We therefore reverse the judgment of the Court of Appeals in respect of the Rule 803(8)(C) issue.

Chapter 15

ADMISSIBILITY OF HEARSAY STATEMENTS UNDER RULES 804 AND 807

§ 15.01 CHAPTER CHECKLIST

1. Why are the Rule 804 hearsay exceptions considered to be "second tier" exceptions?

2. Can a person be physically present in court, yet be considered unavailable under Rule 804?

3. Can a witness who improperly refuses to testify be considered unavailable under Rule 804?

4. Can failure of recollection render a witness unavailable under Rule 804?

5. Is a person who breaks a promise to show up for trial unavailable under Rule 804?

6. Does deposition testimony qualify as former testimony? What if the deposition testimony is given in one case and offered into evidence in another?

7. Can testimony that a witness has previously given be admissible against a party who neither offered the testimony initially nor had an opportunity to cross-examine the witness who provided it?

8. In what types of cases are dying declarations admissible?

9. Can a dying declaration be admissible even if the declarant is alive?

10. Can a statement qualify as against interest if it was initially self-serving but later turns out to be against the declarant's interest?

11. Does a self-serving statement qualify as against a declarant's interest if it is part of a larger set of statements that taken as a whole are against the declarant's interest?

12. In what way do the foundational requirements for statements against a declarant's penal interests differ from the requirements for statements against other interests?

13. When ruling on the admissibility of a hearsay statement under Rule 807, how does a judge decide whether it has "equivalent circumstantial guarantees of trustworthiness" as compared to statements admitted under Rules 803 and 804?

14. What is the "near miss" argument?

15. What is the effect of a declarant's failure to testify at trial on the admissibility of hearsay under Rule 807?

16. How does the *Crawford* case (*see* Case Library for Chapter 10) affect the admissibility of hearsay offered into evidence under Rules 804 and 807?

17. Case Library:

Williamson v. United States

Giles v. California

§ 15.02 RELEVANT FEDERAL RULES OF EVIDENCE

Rule 804. Exceptions to the Rule Against Hearsay — When the Declarant Is Unavailable as a Witness (partial text)

(a) Criteria for Being Unavailable. A declarant is considered to be unavailable as a witness if the declarant:

(1) is exempted from testifying about the subject matter of the declarant's statement because the court rules that a privilege applies;

(2) refuses to testify about the subject matter despite a court order to do so;

(3) testifies to not remembering the subject matter;

(4) cannot be present or testify at the trial or hearing because of death or a then-existing infirmity, physical illness, or mental illness; or

(5) is absent from the trial or hearing and the statement's proponent has not been able, by process or other reasonable means, to procure:

(A) the declarant's attendance, in the case of a hearsay exception under Rule 804(b)(1) or (6); or

(B) the declarant's attendance or testimony, in the case of a hearsay exception under Rule 804(b)(2), (3), or (4).

But this subdivision (a) does not apply if the statement's proponent procured or wrongfully caused the declarant's unavailability as a witness in order to prevent the declarant from attending or testifying.

(b) The Exceptions. The following are not excluded by the rule against hearsay if the declarant is unavailable as a witness:

(1) *Former Testimony.* Testimony that:(A) was given as a witness at a trial, hearing, or lawful deposition, whether given during the current proceeding or a different one; and

(B) is now offered against a party who had — or, in a civil case, whose predecessor in interest had an opportunity and similar motive to develop it by direct, cross-, or redirect examination.

(2) *Statement Under the Belief of Imminent Death.* In a prosecution for homicide or in a civil case, a statement that the declarant, while believing the declarant's death to be imminent, made about its cause or circumstances.

(3) *Statement Against Interest.* A statement that: (A) a reasonable person in the declarant's position would have made only if the person believed it to be true because, when made, it was so contrary to the declarant's proprietary or pecuniary interest or had so great a tendency to invalidate the declarant's claim against someone else or to expose

the declarant to civil or criminal liability; and (B) is supported by corroborating circumstances that clearly indicate its trustworthiness, if it is offered in a criminal case as one that tends to expose the declarant to criminal liability.

(4) *Statement of Personal or Family History.* A statement about: (A) the declarant's own birth, adoption, legitimacy, ancestry, marriage, divorce, relationship by blood, adoption, or marriage, or similar facts of personal or family history, even though the declarant had no way of acquiring personal knowledge about that fact; or (B) another person concerning any of these facts, as well as death, if the declarant was related to the person by blood, adoption, or marriage or was so intimately associated with the person's family that the declarant's information is likely to be accurate.

(5) [*Other Exceptions.*] [Transferred to Rule 807.]

(6) *Statement Offered Against a Party That Wrongfully Caused the Declarant's Unavailability.* A statement offered against a party that wrongfully caused — or acquiesced in wrongfully causing — the declarant's unavailability as a witness, and did so intending that result.

Rule 807. Residual Exception

(a) In General. Under the following circumstances, a hearsay statement is not excluded by the rule against hearsay even if the statement is not specifically covered by a hearsay exception in Rule 803 or 804:

(1) the statement has equivalent circumstantial guarantees of trustworthiness;

(2) it is offered as evidence of a material fact;

(3) it is more probative on the point for which it is offered than any other evidence that the proponent can obtain through reasonable efforts; and

(4) admitting it will best serve the purposes of these rules and the interests of justice.

(b) Notice. The statement is admissible only if, before the trial or hearing, the proponent gives an adverse party reasonable notice of the intent to offer the statement and its particulars, including the declarant's name and address, so that the party has a fair opportunity to meet it.

§ 15.03 INTRODUCTION

Rule 804 consists of a small number of hearsay exceptions for which "unavailability of the declarant" is a common foundational element. In other words, whatever other foundational elements are necessary to prove, a party seeking to offer a declarant's hearsay assertion into evidence under Rule 804 must also prove that the declarant is unavailable to testify at trial.

Compared to the hearsay exceptions established by Rule 803, those of Rule 804 constitute "second tier" exceptions. On the one hand, their existence demonstrates that the drafters of the Federal Rules are at least somewhat confident that statements made under the circumstances described in Rule 804 are likely to be trustworthy. On the other, the requirement that the proponent of hearsay prove a declarant's unavailability demonstrates a reluctance to admit the types of hearsay statements described in Rule 804 unless the only alternative is to do without the evidence altogether. Thus, a combination of trustworthiness and need underlies the Rule 804 exceptions.[1]

The chapter concludes by examining Rule 807, the "catch-all" or "residual" exception to the hearsay rule. Rule 807 fits nicely into this chapter because the language of Rule 807(B) ("the statement is more probative . . . than any other evidence that the proponent can obtain through reasonable efforts") creates a "soft" unavailability requirement.

§ 15.04 UNAVAILABILITY

Establishing a witness' unavailability under Rule 804 requires more than showing that a hearsay declarant is not present in court when called to testify. For example, an attorney cannot prove unavailability by saying something like, "The bailiff and I have shouted the declarant's name three times now, Your Honor. We even wandered into the cafeteria. We had no response. How about we go with the hearsay?" Paradoxically, a declarant may actually have to be present in court for the declarant's unavailability to be established. The reason is that even if a declarant is *personally* present in court and testifying, the declarant's *testimony about the subject matter of a prior statement* may be unavailable.

Rule 804(a) allows a party to establish a declarant's unavailability in the following ways. Remember, however, that unavailability alone does not permit introduction of hearsay. Even if a declarant is unavailable within the meaning of Rule 804(a), a hearsay proponent also has to satisfy other foundational elements.

---

[1] Ironically, the more suspect a hearsay assertion's accuracy, the greater the need for cross examination of a declarant. Yet Rule 804 premises admissibility on the declarant being unavailable, thus assuring that no cross examination will occur.

1. Under Rule 804(a)(1), a declarant is unavailable if a judge upholds the declarant's claim of privilege with respect to the subject matter of the declarant's prior statement. (See Chapter 17 for a discussion of common privileges.) In this situation, it's possible that a declarant will testify in person on some matters, yet be "unavailable" with regard to the subject matter of the prior statement.

Example 1

Abe is charged with burglarizing a computer parts warehouse. The police learn that Abe sold many of the computer parts to Cesar, and that Cesar had bragged to Tara about purchasing computer parts from Abe at a ridiculously low price. When the prosecutor calls Cesar as a witness, the testimony goes as follows:

PROSECUTOR: Cesar, I'd now like to ask you about a purchase you made from Abe on November 15. Did you meet with him on that date?

A: I refuse to answer that question on the ground that the answer might tend to incriminate me.

[After discussion out of the jury's hearing, the judge decides that by answering the questions Cesar might provide information that could be used against him in a criminal prosecution, and upholds his claim of privilege with respect to all questions concerning his purchasing allegedly stolen items from Abe.]

PROSECUTOR: In view of Your Honor's ruling, I submit that Cesar is unavailable with respect to the subject matter of purchasing computer parts from Abe.

JUDGE: I agree, and rule that Cesar is unavailable with respect to the subject matter of purchasing computer parts from Abe.

PROSECUTOR: In view of this ruling, we have no more questions for Cesar. Defense may cross-examine.

JUDGE: Defense counsel, any questions?

DEFENSE ATTORNEY: None.

PROSECUTOR: I now call Tara to testify to what Cesar told her about purchasing computer parts from Abe.

[If Cesar's statements to Tara qualify for admission under one of the Rule 804 exceptions, the unavailability of Cesar's testimony means that Tara could testify to them.]

[The prosecutor would also think about any other hearsay exceptions that might make Cesar's prior statement to Tara admissible. For example, if the statement qualified as a "co-conspirator statement," the prosecutor could offer it under Rule 801(d)(2)(E), and if so would not have to establish Cesar's unavailability.]

2. Under Rule 804(a)(2), a declarant who improperly yet persistently refuses a judge's order to testify concerning the subject matter of the declarant's prior statement is unavailable. This basis of unavailability is similar to subsection (1), the difference here being that the declarant's refusal to testify is improper.

Example 2

Same case as the previous example. However, the prosecutor knew before trial that Cesar would claim his privilege against self-incrimination when asked about purchasing computer parts from Abe. To overcome the privilege claim, the prosecution granted Cesar "use immunity." As a result, nothing that Cesar testifies to in Abe's trial could be used against him in a future criminal case. When Cesar is asked to testify about his purchasing computer parts from Abe, the testimony goes as follows:

PROSECUTOR: Cesar, I'd now like to ask you about a purchase you made from Abe on November 15. Did you meet with him on that date?

A: I refuse to answer that question on the ground that the answer might tend to incriminate me.

[After discussion out of the jury's hearing, the judge decides that since Cesar was granted "use immunity," he no longer has a privilege to refuse to answer concerning his purchasing allegedly stolen items from Abe.]

JUDGE: The claim of privilege is invalid; the witness will answer the question.

PROSECUTOR: Cesar, do you remember the question?

A: Yes, and I will not answer it or any other questions about anything having to do with Abe.

JUDGE: Cesar, you have no choice. I have ordered you to answer the question.

A: I know, but I will not answer.

JUDGE: You understand that your refusal to answer is legally improper, and will result in my holding you in contempt of court and possibly ordering that you be taken to jail?

A: I understand, but I will not answer these questions.

PROSECUTOR: In view of the witness' persistent refusal, Your Honor, I submit that Cesar is unavailable with respect to the subject matter of purchasing computer parts from Abe.

JUDGE: I agree, and rule that Cesar is unavailable with respect to the subject matter of purchasing computer parts from Abe.

PROSECUTOR: In view of this ruling, we have no more questions for Cesar. Defense may cross-examine.

JUDGE: Defense counsel, any questions?

DEFENSE ATTORNEY: None.

PROSECUTOR: I now call Tara to testify to what Cesar told her about purchasing computer parts from Abe.

[If Cesar's statements to Tara qualify for admission under one of the Rule 804 exceptions, Tara could testify to them. And because his refusal to testify was improper, Cesar might well end up in jail.]

3. Rule 804(a)(3) provides that a declarant who is unable to remember the subject matter of the declarant's prior statement is unavailable.

Example 3

Same case as previous example. When Cesar is asked to testify about his purchasing computer parts from Abe, the testimony goes as follows:

PROSECUTOR: Cesar, I'd now like to ask you about a purchase you made from Abe on November 15. Did you meet with him on that date?

A: I'm sorry, I don't remember.

PROSECUTOR: Do you remember any dealings with Abe concerning computer parts in November?

A: No, I don't.

At this point the prosecutor tries to refresh Cesar's memory by showing him the police officer's notes regarding Cesar's conversation with Tara. (*See* Chapter 14 for additional information about refreshing recollection.)

PROSECUTOR: Cesar, is your memory now refreshed as to a meeting you had with Abe on November 15?

A: I'm sorry, I still don't remember it.

Cesar may well be feigning his inability to remember. It's often been said that "Failure of recollection is the last refuge of a scoundrel." As a foundational factor for unavailability, however, it matters little whether the failure of recollection is real or feigned. If the latter, inability to remember is essentially a refusal to testify, which constitutes unavailability under Rule 804(a)(2).

PROSECUTOR: In view of the witness' answers, Your Honor, I submit that Cesar is unavailable with respect to the subject matter of purchasing computer parts from Abe.

JUDGE: I agree, and rule that Cesar is unavailable with respect to the subject matter of purchasing computer parts from Abe.

PROSECUTOR: In view of this ruling, we have no more questions for Cesar. Defense may cross-examine.

JUDGE: Defense counsel, any questions?

DEFENSE ATTORNEY: Still can't think of any for Cesar. But somehow I'm beginning to feel that I know him.

PROSECUTOR: I now call Tara to testify to what Cesar told her about purchasing computer parts from Abe.

If Cesar's statements to Tara qualify for admission under one of the Rule 804 exceptions, Tara could testify to them.

4. Rule 804(a)(4) sensibly provides that a deceased declarant is unavailable. In addition, a declarant is unavailable if a physical or mental infirmity prevents the declarant from attending the trial or testifying. A party can offer a certified copy of a death certificate to establish with certainty that a declarant is deceased.

> While the death certificate would be admissible as a public record under Rule 803(6), remember that Rule 104(a) provides that the rules of evidence (other than those relating to privilege) do not apply to foundational issues.) When a party claims that unavailability is due to physical or mental infirmity, however, judges often demand foundational testimony as to the extent of the infirmity from medical experts or others with knowledge of a declarant's condition.

The foundational testimony may allow a judge to tailor proceedings according to an infirmity's effects, rather than rule that a declarant is unavailable. If an infirmity is likely to be of short duration, the judge may continue a trial until the declarant is able to testify. For instance, if Cesar is unavailable to testify because of an adverse reaction to bee sting medication, and the prosecutor represents to the judge that Cesar will fully recover in a day or two, the judge may continue the case until Cesar is available. Similarly, if a declarant is physically unable to come to court, a judge may travel a short distance and hold court at the declarant's location. For example, assume that Cesar's bad reaction to the bee sting medication means that he'll have to remain in a hospital for a week, though he is fully able to communicate. The judge may decide to obtain Cesar's testimony at his bedside. In criminal cases, a defendant's constitutional right to confront and cross-examine adverse witnesses may force a judge to take such steps to secure an infirm declarant's testimony rather than to simply declare the declarant unavailable.

5. Finally, Rule 804(a)(5) provides that a declarant is unavailable if the declarant "is absent from the hearing and the proponent of a statement has been unable to procure the declarant's attendance or testimony . . . by process or other reasonable means." One way to satisfy subsection (5) is to demonstrate that a witness is beyond a court's subpoena power and has refused to attend trial voluntarily. A second way is to demonstrate that efforts to locate a declarant have been futile. However, judges tend to require by way of foundation that a party claiming inability to secure a declarant's attendance offer evidence of genuine and timely efforts to locate and subpoena the declarant. In addition, by requiring that a proponent of hearsay procure either a "declarant's attendance or testimony," Rule 804(a)(5) expresses a preference for deposition testimony over unsworn hearsay. Thus, if a party has an opportunity to depose but chooses not to depose a declarant who is unavailable at trial, a judge might rule that the party has not shown an inability to procure the declarant's testimony.

The opinion in *Gordon v. D & G Escrow Corp.*[2] suggests the type of effort that parties may have to make to convince a judge that they have been unable to secure a declarant's attendance. In *Gordon*, an ex-husband sued an escrow company for wrongfully paying all the proceeds from the sale of the family home to his ex-wife.

---

[2] 48 Cal. App. 3d 616 (1975).

To prove that the house was community property, and that therefore he was entitled to half the sale proceeds, the ex-husband sought to enter his ex-wife's hearsay statement into evidence. (If the ex-wife were shown to be unavailable, the statement would have been admissible under California's equivalent of Rule 804(b)(3).) To prove that his ex-wife was unavailable, the ex-husband offered the following foundational evidence:

- He hadn't seen or spoken to his ex-wife in three years.

- Two years before trial, he sent his ex-wife a letter at the address where he was told she was living. The letter was returned as undeliverable, and it turned out that a creditor of the ex-wife had foreclosed on the house.

- A number of the ex-wife's creditors had contacted the ex-husband's attorney, asking for information on his ex-wife's whereabouts.

- He was unable to find a listing for his ex-wife in any local phone directory.

- He submitted an affidavit by his ex-wife's former attorney stating that the attorney did not know of her whereabouts. The court ruled that this foundational showing was insufficient to establish the ex-wife's unavailability. The ex-husband hadn't demonstrated sufficient "persevering and untiring efforts" to secure her attendance.

Even in criminal cases, judges should not insist that parties throw away time and money on obviously futile efforts to locate a declarant. *See Ohio v. Roberts.* As *Gordon* suggests, however, a claim that "I've done some checking and I have no idea where the declarant is" probably will not suffice. "Inability to secure a witness' attendance" requires a reasonable effort to locate a hearsay declarant. The investigatory steps that parties can take include checking hospital records and information from government motor vehicle agencies; contacting utility companies, Social Security, and welfare agencies; contacting a declarant's last known employer; and contacting any labor union or other employee organization of which the declarant was a member. Attorneys often hire professional investigators, and then call those investigators as foundational witnesses to testify to the efforts they made to locate a declarant whose attendance they have been unable to procure.

In some situations, it can be to a party's advantage for a hearsay declarant to be unavailable. For example, a party may prefer to offer a declarant's favorable hearsay into evidence rather than have the declarant show up and offer unconvincing or even downright harmful testimony. To prevent parties from convincing declarants to take sudden holidays or suffer mysterious failures of recollection while testifying, Rule 804(a) provides that a declarant is not unavailable if the hearsay statement's proponent "procured or wrongfully caused the declarant's unavailability as a witness in order to prevent the declarant from attending or testifying."

Example 4

Ma Barker is a plaintiff in a personal injury case. Ma deposed Elly Utness prior to trial. Elly's deposition testimony was quite favorable to Ma. Elly testified that the defendant Don Corleone was speeding and weaving in and out of lanes just prior to the accident. At trial, Ma claims that Elly is deceased (while hunting, she was accidentally shot by her hunting companion), and seeks to offer her deposition testimony into evidence. Corleone's attorney objects that the deposition testimony is inadmissible hearsay, and calls Ma in an effort to show that Ma procured Elly's unavailability. The foundational testimony goes as follows:

DEFENDANT'S ATTORNEY: Ma, am I correct that prior to her death you and Elly got together socially on a number of occasions?

A: That's true.

DEFENDANT'S ATTORNEY: And during one of these social occasions, Elly told you that she needed a vacation, correct?

A: That's right.

DEFENDANT'S ATTORNEY: And you suggested that she go hunting?

A: Well, she had told me previously that she'd gone once and enjoyed it. I reminded her of that and mentioned that Bonnie Clyde, a friend of mine, had talked about going hunting and that maybe they could go together.

DEFENDANT'S ATTORNEY: So it was you who convinced her to go hunting?

A: No. I just made the suggestion to Elly and gave her Bonnie's phone number. I had nothing more to do with it.

DEFENDANT'S ATTORNEY: And you knew that Bonnie's hunting license had been suspended twice previously for carelessness?

A: She'd told me something about that, but she said that she'd gotten it back.

DEFENDANT'S ATTORNEY: Did you talk to Bonnie before they left on the trip?

A: Just the night before they left, just to wish her good hunting. Nothing else.

DEFENDANT'S ATTORNEY: Nothing further. Your Honor, I submit that the timing leads to an inference that the plaintiff procured Elly's unavailability by sending her on a hunting trip from which the plaintiff was reasonably certain that Elly would never return.

JUDGE: Counsel, under Rule 104(a) the burden is on you to convince me that the plaintiff knowingly procured the witness' unavailability. The record does emit a faint aroma of planning, but I'm unable to say that you've convinced me. I conclude that Elly is unavailable, and that the plaintiff may read her deposition testimony into evidence.

Federal Rule of Civil Procedure 32(a)(3) is in effect an evidence rule providing alternative bases for establishing unavailability when a party to a civil lawsuit seeks to offer deposition testimony into evidence on the ground that the deponent is unavailable to testify at trial. Under Federal Rule of Civil Procedure 32(a), a deponent is unavailable (and deposition testimony is therefore admissible) in any of the following situations:

- The deponent is deceased.

- The deponent is located more than 100 miles from the place of trial.

- The deponent is unable to attend trial or testify because of age, illness, infirmity, or imprisonment.

- The party offering the deposition has been unable to procure the deponent's attendance with a subpoena.

- Such exceptional circumstances exist that the interests of justice allow use of the deposition.

Perhaps because deposition testimony is given under oath and all parties have a right to attend depositions and question the deponents, the Federal Rule of Civil Procedure 32(a) grounds of unavailability are in general more relaxed than those listed in Rule 804(a). For example, under Rule 804(a), a declarant's distance from the place of trial is irrelevant. A party normally has to try to locate and subpoena a declarant anywhere within the court's jurisdiction, even if the declarant is in prison. (Interstate compacts sometimes allow a prisoner to be brought to another jurisdiction for the purpose of testifying.) Under Federal Rule of Civil Procedure 32(a), by contrast, unavailability is established by showing that a deponent is more than 100 miles from the place of trial.

Problem 15-1: Fair-Weather Friend

Dana is a plaintiff in a personal injury case. Jeff is Dana's close friend. He was with her when she was injured by an allegedly defective hedge cutter, and can provide evidence that supports Dana's claims. Jeff orally assures Dana on many occasions that he will testify on her behalf. However, Jeff calls Dana on the morning of trial and tells her that he can't come to court because he had gone away for the weekend on a ski trip and is snowed in. *Is Jeff unavailable as a witness under Rule 804(a)? Is Jeff unavailable as a witness under Federal Rule of Civil Procedure 32(a)?*

15-2: Wherefore Art Thou, Waldo?

Consuela is charged with burglary of a home. Waldo identifies Consuela at her preliminary hearing as the person he saw running out the back door of the home when an alarm went off. Consuela is held for trial on the burglary charge, and the prosecution serves Waldo with a subpoena for the trial, set for five weeks later. A week before trial, the prosecutor calls Waldo at home to clarify a portion of his testimony, and is told that "Waldo is no longer at this phone number. I don't know where he went." When Waldo doesn't appear for the trial, the prosecutor asks that the judge rule that Waldo is unavailable and that his preliminary hearing testimony can be read into the record as "former testimony" under Rule 804(b)(1). The defense objects and argues that the prosecution's failure to keep tabs on Waldo's whereabouts means that unavailability has not been shown.

You are the trial judge. *Has the prosecutor established Waldo's unavailability under Rule 804(a)(5)? How will you respond to the defense attorney's request that the trial be continued and the prosecution ordered to take steps to try to locate Waldo and bring him to court? Apart from Rule 804(b)(1), what is the effect of the Confrontation Clause on the prosecutor's request to read Waldo's deposition testimony into evidence?*

Problem 15-3: Doctor's Orders

Lester Sherr sues Devon Warwick for personal injuries, and wants to offer into evidence a hearsay statement from Elizabeth. To prove that Elizabeth is unavailable as a witness, Lester's attorney hands the judge a letter written under the letterhead of "Anne Atomy, M.D," and dated the day prior to trial. The letter reads as follows:

> To Whom It May Concern. I am a physician licensed to practice in this state and Board-Certified in obstetrics. Elizabeth is currently an obstetrical patient of mine in her fifth month of pregnancy. My medical opinion is that Elizabeth should not attend the trial because, due to complications of pregnancy, she needs complete bed rest and cannot participate in ordinary daily activities, including testifying as a witness. To do so would endanger both her health and that of her child. I expect this condition to continue indefinitely, possibly until she delivers the child. Anne Atomy, M.D.

The letter constitutes Dr. Atomy's out-of-court statement. *Is it admissible to prove that Elizabeth is unavailable? If so, does the letter establish that Elizabeth is unavailable within the meaning of Rule 804(a)?*

Problem 15-4: Try to Remember

Maisie Kreskin is a witness for the homeowner in a breach of warranty case against a builder based on construction defects in a new home. Maisie testifies to defects that she observed in the living room and one of the bathrooms when she visited the home just prior to the homeowner's moving in. When the homeowner's attorney asks her about problems that she observed in the kitchen, however, Maisie testifies only to seeing uneven countertops. At trial, Maisie is unable to recall problems with the kitchen floor that she testified to at her deposition, even after the homeowner's attorney tries to refresh her recollection with the deposition transcript. *Is Maisie unavailable as a witness under Rule 804(a) with respect to problems with the kitchen floor?*

Problem 15-5: Fear of Testifying

Basil is charged with sexually abusing his two stepchildren, A and B. A is eight years old at the time of trial; B is five. Both A and B have previously made statements that are non-testimonial and therefore would not be barred by the Confrontation Clause as interpreted by *Crawford v. Washington* (see Chapter 10), and would be admissible against Basil at trial if the judge rules under Rule 804(a) that they are unavailable. Consider A's and B's unavailability under each of the scenarios below.

1. The prosecutor tells the judge that "I've spoken to A and B. Neither of them is willing to testify. Frankly, they are both scared to death by the courtroom atmosphere, and also scared that the defendant will punish them if they testify. They are both crying. Your Honor; it would be psychologically devastating to require them to testify, so I ask that they be declared unavailable under Rule 804(a)(4)." *How should the judge rule on the prosecutor's request?*

2. The mother of A and B testifies that both children have told her that they are afraid of going to court. They both have had nightmares every night for the past two weeks, cry often, and have become withdrawn as the trial date approached. The judge then meets with A and B informally in chambers. The judge tells them that "I understand how you feel and will not let anything happen to you. I'm ordering you to testify, but anytime you want to stop for a timeout just let me know." However, A and B continue to say that they are scared of being in court and don't want to testify. *Should the judge rule that A and B are unavailable under Rule 804(a)(2), in that they have persistently refused to testify despite the judge's order that they do so? Should the judge rule that A and B are unavailable under Rule 804(a)(4), in that the emotional trauma of testifying constitutes a mental infirmity? Should the judge be allowed to talk to the children informally? Should both counsel be present? Should the judge ask A and B to testify via closed circuit TV?*[3]

3. The judge appoints a psychiatrist who specializes in child abuse to examine A. The psychiatrist testifies during a foundational mini-trial that testifying is stressful for young victims of abuse, that testifying would be harmful to A because it would trigger the memory of the abuse, that A expressed to the psychiatrist a strong desire not to testify, and that in the long run it would be best for A's mental health not to testify. *Should the judge rule that A is unavailable under Rule 804(a)(4), in that the emotional trauma of testifying constitutes a mental infirmity?*

4. The same psychiatrist examines B, and testifies during a foundational hearing that B indicated a strong desire not to testify. The psychiatrist also testifies that especially because of B's age, B is extremely vulnerable to stress, that B is anxious and depressed, and spoke of suicide. In the psychiatrist's opinion, testifying could cause B to become psychotic. *Should the judge rule that B is unavailable under Rule 804(a)(4), in that the emotional trauma of testifying constitutes a mental infirmity?*

Problem 15-6: Building a Foundation

Polly Sigh sues a bus company for $60,000 for personal injuries she sustained when the bus in which she was a passenger collided with a car driven by Eben Flow. The bus company denies liability and seeks to offer Eben's hearsay statement into evidence under one of the subsections of Rule 804(b). The judge has granted the bus company attorney's request for a foundational mini-trial, during

---

[3] For a statute authorizing testimony via closed-circuit television, see **18 U.S.C. § 3509.**

which the attorney will try to establish that Eben is unavailable as a witness under Rule 804(a)(5).

Student # 1: You are the attorney for the bus company. Meet outside of class with Student # 2, the investigator who you retained to locate and subpoena Eben. Plan the foundational testimony you will present through the investigator's testimony in an effort to convince the judge that Eben is unavailable. (Be careful not to overly gild the lily. The judge is aware of the amount that Polly seeks as damages, and may disbelieve testimony suggesting that the investigator went to extraordinary lengths to try to locate Eben.)

Student # 2: You are a professional investigator and were retained by Student # 1 to locate and subpoena Eben Flow. You met with Eben at his apartment about a week after the accident and took his statement. However, you were informed by Student # 1 that Eben was no longer at that address, and that he had quit his job, so could not be subpoenaed. Review the activities you engaged in to try to locate Eben with Student # 1 prior to class, and be prepared to testify to those activities during a foundational hearing.

Student # 3: You represent Polly Sigh. You may cross-examine the bus company's investigator in an effort to establish reasonable steps to locate Eben that the investigator neglected to take. (Insist on a pre-hearing meeting with the investigator so that you know what testimony to expect.) If reasonable to do so, make a brief argument to support a position that the investigator's testimony has not established Eben's unavailability.

Student # 4: You are the judge. Preside over the foundational hearing and rule on Eben Flow's unavailability.

§ 15.05 FORMER TESTIMONY (RULE 804(b)(1))

Statutory Elements:

* The declarant is unavailable as a witness;

* The declarant has previously testified under oath in a hearing or deposition in the same or a different case;

* The party against whom the testimony is offered (or in civil cases, a predecessor in interest):

    * previously offered the testimony; or

    * previously had an opportunity to cross examine the declarant.

* The party against whom the former testimony is offered has the same motive as when the party either offered it previously or had an opportunity to cross examine the declarant.

Rule 804(b)(1) establishes a hearsay exception for unavailable declarants' "former testimony." The exception consists of two elements. The hearsay statement must have been made during a qualifying hearing or deposition. And the party against whom the testimony is offered (or in civil cases also a predecessor in interest) must have had an opportunity and similar motive to "develop" the testimony at the time the hearsay statement was made.

Former testimony seems almost the ideal hearsay exception: the prior statement is made under oath, in a formal setting, with the opportunity for cross-examination. On the other hand, prior testimony is typically given long after the occurrence of the events to which the testimony relates. Moreover, judges and juries lose the opportunity to observe a declarant's demeanor when testimony is read to them under the former testimony exception. The result is that former testimony is relegated to the second tier of hearsay exceptions.

The first element broadly defines former testimony as testimony given by a witness in a "hearing" or a "deposition," whether in the "same or a different proceeding." The term "hearing" incorporates almost any formalized legal proceeding in which a witness is placed under oath. For example, testimony given before a grand jury or in an administrative hearing may constitute "former testimony."

Example 1

Moe sues Larry for injuries that Moe sustained in a fall in Larry's store. Called as a witness by Moe, Shemp testifies to the slippery condition of the floor where Moe fell. Moe wins, but the judgment is reversed on appeal and a new trial is ordered. If Shemp is unavailable for the retrial, Shemp's testimony in the original trial qualifies as "former testimony" within the meaning of Rule 804(b)(1).

Example 2

Moe sues Larry for injuries sustained in a fall in Larry's store. Larry deposes Shemp, who testifies to the slippery condition of the floor where Moe fell. Shemp also signs an affidavit attesting to the floor's slipperiness, which Moe submits as part of a pre-trial summary judgment motion. However, the case is settled prior to trial, and Shemp never testifies in court. In a separate case, Curly sues Larry for injuries that Curly sustained in a different fall on the same date in the same store. If Shemp is unavailable to testify in the trial of *Curly v. Larry*, Shemp's deposition testimony in the case of *Moe v. Larry* qualifies as "former testimony" within the meaning of Rule 804(b)(1). However, the statements in the affidavit do not constitute former testimony, as they were not made during a proceeding.

The second element requires a proponent of former testimony to show that the party against whom the testimony is offered (or in a civil case, that party's predecessor in interest) had a valid "opportunity and similar motive to develop the testimony" at the prior hearing "by direct, cross or redirect examination."

The "similar motive" foundational requirement promotes fairness by assuring that the party against whom former testimony is offered had an incentive to thoroughly probe the same topic on the earlier occasion when that party elicited (or had an opportunity to elicit) the testimony. When evaluating the similarity of a party's motivations in different proceedings, courts consider such factors as the amount of money in dispute and the purposes of the proceedings. For example,

United States v. DiNapoli[4] involved a racketeering prosecution that was preceded by an extensive grand jury investigation. Hoping to elicit incriminating evidence of bid rigging in the construction industry against some of the "bigger fish" defendants, the government granted immunity to two of the alleged "smaller fish" and questioned them before the grand jury. The "smaller fish" testified that no bid rigging had occurred. Nevertheless, the defendants were indicted for racketeering based on other evidence. At trial, the defendants called the "smaller fish" as witnesses. When the "smaller fish" invoked the Fifth Amendment and refused to testify (thereby becoming unavailable), the defendants offered the "smaller fish's" grand jury testimony into evidence as former testimony. The defendants' argument was that the government's motivation in eliciting the testimony of the smaller fish before the grand jury was the same as it would have been at trial: to link the defendants to the bid rigging scheme.

The *DiNapoli* court disagreed, holding that the defense could not offer the "smaller fish's" grand jury testimony as former testimony. The court stated that "the proper approach . . . in assessing similarity of motive under Rule 804(b)(1) must consider whether the party resisting the offered testimony at a pending proceeding had at a prior proceeding an interest of substantially similar intensity to prove (or disprove) the same side of a substantially similar issue. The nature of the two proceedings — both what is at stake and the applicable burden of proof . . . will be relevant though not necessarily conclusive on the ultimate issue of similarity of motive." The court concluded that similarity of motive did not exist in this case because it was "beyond reasonable dispute that the prosecutor had no interest at the grand jury in proving the falsity of the witnesses' assertions." The court noted that the defendants had already been indicted at the time the smaller fish testified. Moreover, the grand jury record indicated that the grand jurors didn't believe the smaller fish's denials. According to the court, "a prosecutor has no interest in showing the falsity of testimony that a grand jury already disbelieves." However, the court refused to announce a bright line rule that the government's motive when eliciting grand jury testimony is always different than at trial. The court concluded that the similar motive inquiry must be "fact specific, and the grand jury context will sometimes, but not invariably, present circumstances that demonstrate the prosecutor's lack of a similar motive." (Can you alter the facts of *DiNapoli* so as to strengthen the defendant's argument that the government had similar motives before the grand jury and at trial with respect to the "smaller fish's" testimony?)

Notwithstanding cases such as *DiNapoli*, the second element of Rule 804(b)(1) is generally satisfied when a declarant's former testimony is *offered against a party who previously offered the testimony*. Accordingly, a litigant who conducts a deposition or presents testimony at a trial or other formal hearing runs a risk that if the deponent or the witness becomes unavailable, some other party will be able to offer the deponent's or witness' testimony into evidence against the litigant in a future proceeding. But Rule 804(b)(1) offers some protection against unfair use of former testimony.

---

[4] 8 F.3d 909 (2d Cir. 1993).

Example 3

Passenger # 1 sued Bus Co. for injuries sustained when one of its buses struck a lamppost. During the trial of *Passenger # 1 v. Bus Co.*, Bus Co. called Bystander as a witness. Bystander, however, testified that the bus was speeding at the time it struck the lamppost. Passenger # 2 also sued Bus Co. for injuries sustained in the same incident. Bystander is unavailable by the time the case of *Passenger # 2 v. Bus Co.* goes to trial. Passenger # 2 can offer Bystander's former testimony against Bus Co., as follows:

PLAINTIFF'S ATTORNEY: At this time, Your Honor, I'd like to read into the record under Rule 804(b)(1) Bystander's testimony from the earlier trial of Passenger # 1 v. Bus Co. As Your Honor can see from the transcript, Bus Co. offered Bystander's testimony in that case.

JUDGE: Counsel for Bus Co., is that correct?

DEFENDANT'S ATTORNEY: That's correct.

JUDGE: Counsel for Bus Co., is there an issue as to whether your client had a full opportunity to elicit testimony from Bystander during the earlier trial?

DEFENDANT'S ATTORNEY: No.

JUDGE: Counsel for Passenger # 2, did Bus Co. have a similar motive for questioning Bystander in both cases?

PLAINTIFF'S ATTORNEY: Clearly yes, Your Honor. Both cases involve personal injury claims made by passengers injured in the same accident, and in both cases Bus Co. would have wanted to elicit testimony from Bystander that the bus was being driven safely.

[Rule 607 allows parties to impeach their own witnesses. Thus, when Bystander testified unfavorably to the bus company in Passenger # 1 v. Bus Co., the bus company had an opportunity and motive to attack Bystander's credibility and elicit evidence that the bus was being driven carefully.]

JUDGE: Counsel for Bus Co., any argument as to similarity of motive?

DEFENDANT'S ATTORNEY: No, Your Honor, though I would ask of course that Bystander's entire testimony from the earlier trial be read, including Bus Co.'s redirect examination.

JUDGE: So ordered. I find that Bystander's testimony offered by Bus Co. in *Passenger # 1 v. Bus Co.* is admissible under Rule 804(b)(1) as former testimony in this case. Counsel for Passenger # 2 can now commence reading of Bystander's testimony.

[Bystander's testimony would normally be read into the record orally. If the written transcript of the testimony were admitted into evidence, jurors might give it undue weight. If the former testimony is at all lengthy, the offering attorney is likely to try to keep the judge's or jury's attention by asking a colleague or even the court clerk to serve as the witness and read the answers as the attorney reads the questions.]

Perhaps the most common use of former testimony under Rule 804(b)(1) arises when a declarant's former testimony is *offered against a party who previously had an opportunity to cross-examine the declarant.* Thus, a litigant who has an opportunity to or does cross-examine a witness at a deposition, trial or similar formal proceeding runs a risk that if the witness becomes unavailable, some other party can offer the witness' testimony into evidence against the litigant in a future proceeding. (Because this portion of the rule requires a previous opportunity to cross-examine, prosecutors who offer former testimony against criminal defendants under this provision also comply with the Confrontation Clause as interpreted by *Crawford v. Washington.*)

Example 4

Passenger # 1 sued Bus Co. for injuries sustained when one of its buses struck a lamppost. During pre-trial discovery, Passenger # 1 deposed Bystander. At the deposition, Bystander testifies that the bus was speeding at the time it struck the lamppost. Passenger # 1 and Bus Co. settled the case prior to trial. Passenger # 2 also sues Bus Co. for injuries sustained in the same incident. Bystander is unavailable by the time the case of *Passenger # 2 v. Bus Co.* goes to trial. Passenger # 2 can offer Bystander's deposition testimony from *Passenger # 1 v. Bus Co.* into evidence, as follows:

PLAINTIFF'S ATTORNEY: At this time, Your Honor, I'd like to read into the record pursuant to Rule 804(b)(1) Bystander's deposition testimony given in connection with the case of *Passenger # 1 v. Bus Co.* Bystander was deposed by Passenger # 1, and Bus. Co. had an opportunity to attend the deposition and question Bystander.

JUDGE: Counsel for Bus Co., is that correct?

DEFENDANT'S ATTORNEY: That's correct, Your Honor. However, as you can see from the transcript, counsel for Bus Co. did not in fact attend Bystander's deposition, so I would ask that the testimony not be used.

JUDGE: Counsel for Bus Co., is there any argument that Passenger # 1's deposition notice was in any way deficient, or that your client would not have had a full opportunity to question Bystander at the deposition?

DEFENDANT'S ATTORNEY: No, Your Honor.

JUDGE: Counsel for Passenger # 2, would Bus Co. have a similar motive for questioning Bystander in both cases?

PLAINTIFF'S ATTORNEY: Yes, Your Honor. Both cases involve personal injury claims made by passengers injured in the same accident, and in both cases Bus Co. would have wanted to elicit testimony from Bystander that the bus was being driven safely.

JUDGE: Counsel for Bus Co., any argument as to similarity of motive?

DEFENDANT'S ATTORNEY: None, Your Honor.

JUDGE: In that case, I find that Bystander's deposition testimony given in connection with the case of *Passenger # 1 v. Bus Co.* is admissible under Rule 804(b)(1) as former testimony in this case. Bus Co. had an opportunity to attend the deposition and question Bystander, and under Rule 804(b)(1) it's irrelevant that Bus Co. failed to take advantage of that opportunity. Bus Co.'s motive was similar in both cases. Counsel for Passenger # 2 can now commence reading of Bystander's testimony.

[As the judge indicates, all that Rule 804(b)(1) requires is that the party against whom testimony is offered had the *opportunity* to question the declarant. In essence, the party against whom testimony is offered is locked into its earlier cross-examination if a deponent or witness becomes unavailable, even if the party conducted no cross-examination at all.]

A third and final situation that satisfies the second element of Rule 804(b)(1) arises in *civil cases only*. A witness' former testimony is admissible in a civil case if it is *offered against a party whose "predecessor in interest" had an opportunity and similar motive to cross-examine the declarant.* Under this somewhat extraordinary provision, former testimony can be offered against a party if a *different party* earlier had a chance to cross-examine a now-unavailable witness with a similar motive to that of the party against whom the former testimony is offered. As criminal defendants have a constitutional right to confront and cross-examine adverse witnesses, the statute sensibly provides that former testimony is admissible based on a different party's opportunity to cross-examine only in civil cases.

Rule 804(b)(1) offers the same protection against unfair use of former testimony in this situation as in the earlier ones. Before admitting former testimony, the judge must be satisfied that the cross-examiner had a valid "opportunity" and a "similar motive" to question the declarant. Because one party is in essence stuck with whatever cross-examination a different party conducted, the statute also offers an additional protection: the cross-examiner must be the "predecessor in interest" of the party against whom the former testimony is offered. The meaning of "predecessor in interest," however, is cloudy. According to most legal definitions, a predecessor in interest is a person who precedes another in an office or position. A strict, mechanistic interpretation of the term "predecessor in interest" would require the cross-examiner and the party against whom former testimony is offered to have a "mutuality of interest" in the same property. For example, the cross-examiner might have been a landowner who later deeded the property to the party against whom the former testimony is offered. While this situation probably won't arise often, perhaps it is the only fair reading if one party is to be stuck with testimony from an unavailable declarant based on some other party's opportunity to cross-examine. Many judges and commentators prefer a broader reading that regards "similar motive and opportunity" as sufficient to admit former testimony against a party who hasn't had an opportunity to cross-examine a declarant, thereby disregarding the "predecessor in interest" language entirely. Other judges pay lip service to the "predecessor in interest" requirement, but regard any connection between two parties as sufficient to constitute "predecessor in interest" status. The legislative history of Rule 804(b)(1) is silent with respect to the meaning of "predecessor in interest," and the cases do not reach consistent outcomes.

How broadly or narrowly a judge chooses to interpret the meaning of "predecessor in interest" can be determinative as to whether hearsay is admitted as former testimony. For example, assume again that Passenger # 1 sues Bus Co. for injuries sustained when one of its buses struck a lamppost. At trial, Bus Co. calls Bystander as a witness, and Bystander testifies favorably for Bus Co. that the bus hit the lamppost because the bus driver swerved to avoid a child who had suddenly darted into the bus' path. Passenger # 1 cross-examines Bystander. Passenger # 2 also sues Bus Co. for injuries sustained in the same incident. Bystander is unavailable by the time the case of *Passenger # 2 v. Bus Co.* goes to trial. Can Bus Co. offer Bystander's testimony from *Passenger # 1 v. Bus Co.* into evidence against Passenger # 2? Under the strict interpretation of "predecessor in interest," the answer is probably "no." Passengers # 1 and 2 do not have a mutuality of interest in common property. Under a broader interpretation emphasizing their common motive to attack Bystander's credibility, the testimony might be admissible as former testimony.

Once a judge has determined that former testimony is admissible, can the adversary ask the judge to exclude specific portions of a transcript? For example, can the adversary object to an answer on the ground that it is inadmissible hearsay, or that it is improperly speculative? Should the outcome depend on whether an objection was made at the time the testimony was first given? Neither Rule 804(b)(1) nor the Advisory Committee notes address these questions. The California version of the former testimony exception, **Cal. Evid. Code §§ 1291–1292**, does address it, and its provisions identify the majority approach. If former testimony is admitted against the party who earlier offered it in evidence or who had the opportunity to cross-examine the witness who provided the testimony, the former testimony is admitted subject to "substantive" objections (e.g., "improper hearsay") but is not subject to "form" objections (e.g., "leading") unless those objections were made when the former testimony was first given. If former testimony is admitted against a party based on a different party's opportunity to cross-examine, the former testimony is admitted subject to both types of objections. In all cases, objections based on competency or privilege cannot be made unless those infirmities existed at the time the former testimony was first given.

Practice Tip: Keep your audience in mind.

Former testimony admitted into evidence is read to the jurors. The jurors do not read the transcripts themselves, out of fear that jurors may pore over the written testimony and give it greater weight than the oral testimony they've heard from the witness stand. But if the former testimony is at all lengthy, reading it to the jury may take hours or even days. If you are the proponent of lengthy former testimony, try to avoid lulling the jurors to sleep. A common and generally acceptable method is to use two readers; you may read the questions, for example, and ask an associate to read the answers. If your associate has previously received an Academy Award for Best Actor, so much the better.

Problem 15-7: You Go First

Alphonse and Gaston are indicted for jointly robbing a bank, and are tried separately. In the trial of Alphonse, the government calls Hank Teller as a witness. Teller identifies Alphonse and Gaston as the robbers. By the time Gaston's case goes to trial, Teller is unavailable. *Can the government offer Teller's testimony from Alphonse's trial into evidence against Gaston?*

Problem 15-8: Play It Against Sam

After Sam allegedly holds up a fast food restaurant at gunpoint, the victimized cashier sues Sam for civil damages. As soon as the lawsuit is filed, the cashier's lawyer videotapes the deposition of an elderly patron who was in the restaurant at the time of the robbery, to perpetuate the patron's testimony for trial, pursuant to Federal Rule of Civil Procedure 27. In that deposition, which takes place in jail so that Sam can attend, the patron identifies Sam as the robber and describes how Sam committed the robbery. In separate criminal proceedings, the government charges Sam with armed robbery. The patron passes away before either the criminal or the civil case can go to trial.

Is the videotaped deposition admissible if offered into evidence by the cashier against Sam in the civil case?

What if it is offered into evidence by the government against Sam in the criminal case?

Problem 15-9: Blazing Objections

Kara Seene sues Insurance Co. to recover the proceeds of a fire insurance policy on her house. Kara had previously been charged with arson for setting the fire that burned the house down. In the criminal trial, Yvonne testified for the prosecution that she saw Kara set the fire. Kara was found not guilty. With Yvonne now unavailable, Insurance Co. seeks to offer Yvonne's testimony from the criminal trial into evidence against Kara. *How should the court rule on the following objections that Kara might make?*

1. "Objection; testimony given in a criminal trial cannot be used as former testimony."

2. "Objection; Yvonne's criminal trial testimony is inadmissible as former testimony because Kara represented herself in the criminal trial."

3. "Objection; Yvonne's criminal trial testimony is inadmissible as former testimony because Kara's attorney did not cross-examine her in the criminal trial."

4. "Objection; Yvonne's criminal trial testimony is inadmissible as former

testimony because as she testified in a criminal trial and the testimony is offered against Kara in a civil trial, Kara's motives are too dissimilar."

5. "Objection, hearsay, to that portion of Yvonne's testimony in the criminal trial in which she testified that Kara's next-door neighbor told Yvonne that the neighbor had also seen Kara set the fire." (Consider whether your answer depends on Kara having made this objection during the criminal trial.)

6. "Objection to that portion of Yvonne's testimony in the criminal trial in which the prosecutor used a leading question to elicit Yvonne's testimony that it was Kara rather than Kara's sister Ethel who she saw setting the fire." (Consider whether your answer depends on Kara having made this objection during the criminal trial.)

7. "Objection under Rule 403. Because one jury has already found Yvonne's testimony unconvincing by finding Kara not guilty, its prejudicial impact outweighs its probative value."

Problem 15-10: Bus Stop

Passenger # 1 sued Bus Co. for injuries sustained when a bus hit a lamppost. At the ensuing trial, Bystander testified on behalf of Passenger # 1 that the bus was speeding just before hitting the lamppost. When Bus Co.'s lawyer begins to cross-examine him, Bystander becomes ill and has to be hospitalized. To expedite the trial, counsel for Bus Co. waives the right to cross-examine Bystander after stipulating with counsel for Passenger # 1 that "Bystander had drunk three beers in the hour preceding the accident and had previously been fired from Bystander's job as a Bus Co. maintenance worker due to excessive absence."

Later on, Passenger # 2 sued Bus Co. for injuries sustained in the same accident. Bystander is now unavailable, and Passenger # 2 seeks to offer Bystander's testimony from *Passenger # 1 v. Bus Co.* (including the stipulations) into evidence. Bus Co. makes a hearsay objection. *Is Bystander's testimony from Action # 1 admissible as former testimony?*

Problem 15-11: Fire Escape Clause

Bob has sued Tonedeaf Concert Promotions for personal injuries he sustained, allegedly due to Tonedeaf's failure to provide proper concert security. Bob was injured when a fire broke out mid-concert and members of the audience rushed to the exits. He contends that most of the exits were locked, and Tonedeaf disagrees. Bob was knocked down and trampled while trying to reach an open exit, sustaining two cracked ribs and a broken cheekbone. Bob's complaint asks for actual damages in the amount of $250,000 and punitive damages. Under Rule 804(b)(1), Bob seeks to offer into evidence against Tonedeaf testimony given by Ray in Ray's case against Tonedeaf for personal injuries that Ray sustained during the same concert. In the trial of that case, Ray testified that after the fire broke out, he tried to exit through four different doors, all of which were locked. Ray sustained only minor injuries, and asked for $25,000 in damages. Ray is now unavailable. Tonedeaf objects to the admissibility of Ray's testimony, and in a hearing out of the jury's presence the arguments of counsel proceed as follows:

DEFENDANT'S ATTORNEY: Your Honor, our objection is that Ray's testimony is hearsay that does not qualify for admission under Rule 804(b)(1). The statute requires similarity of motive, and clearly Tonedeaf did not have a similar motive in the two cases. Ray's suit asked for $25,000, so our motive to cross-examine to show that he was mistaken about the doors can't be compared to our motive to do so in a suit asking for $250,000 plus punitives.

PLAINTIFF'S ATTORNEY: Your Honor, the law doesn't require that the motives be exact, only that they be similar. Tonedeaf was the party in each case. This isn't a case where we're trying to hold Tonedeaf to the cross-examination conducted by an entirely different party. And in each case Tonedeaf had a similar motive-to try to show that the doors were open. Ray's testimony is clearly admissible under Rule 804(b)(1).

DEFENDANT'S ATTORNEY: Counsel's argument flies in the face of the economics of law practice. As Your Honor well knows, a lawyer can't invest a large amount of time and effort in a case worth at most $25,000, compared to one in which the plaintiff asks for $250,000 plus punitives. I'd also point out that my firm, with Tonedeaf's full cooperation, assigned a junior associate to handle the defense in Ray's case. We think that allowing new associates to handle small cases is important for their training and for the good of the profession as a whole. But if our clients are to be bound by their trial strategies, the policy is one that we and other firms would have to rethink.

PLAINTIFF'S ATTORNEY: Your Honor, $25,000 wasn't exactly chump change. Tonedeaf had a genuine motive in Ray's case to defend its security operations.

JUDGE: *Is an argument based on the economics of law practice one that you should consider? Would you be concerned about basing evidentiary rulings on lawyers' financial status and ability to finance cases? What ruling on the admissibility of Ray's testimony? Remember to indicate for the record which party has the burden of proof, and what that burden consists of.*

Problem 15-12: No Questions Asked 1

Lew Manion is charged with the attempted murder of Barney Quill. Manion's defense is that he stabbed Quill in self-defense. Eve Brooks testified for the prosecution at Manion's preliminary hearing that Manion attacked Quill. At the preliminary hearing, Manion was represented by a deputy public defender who had only a few minutes to meet with Manion and prepare for the hearing. The defense lawyer did not cross-examine Brooks even though Manion told the lawyer that Brooks was drunk at the time of the incident. Brooks is unavailable at the time of trial, and the prosecutor offers her preliminary examination testimony into evidence as former testimony under Rule 804(b)(1). The defense lawyer objects to the testimony's admissibility. The defense lawyer argues that Manion did not have a realistic opportunity to cross-examine Brooks at the preliminary hearing. Moreover, with Brooks unavailable to testify, the defense has no way of showing that she was drunk at the time of the incident other than through the testimony of Manion, who has a constitutional right not to testify. Thus, it would be unfair under the circumstances to admit Brooks' testimony into evidence. *Should the judge admit Brooks's preliminary examination testimony into evidence at trial?*

Problem 15-13: No Questions Asked 2

Mutt is on trial a second time on a charge of murdering Jeff. Mutt was convicted of murder after a first trial, but that conviction was reversed by the appellate court based on defense counsel's incompetent representation. One primary reason for the reversal was the defense counsel's failure to cross-examine Magoo, the prosecution's key eyewitness. Magoo is unavailable for the second trial, so the prosecution seeks to offer into evidence Magoo's testimony from the first trial under Rule 804(b)(1). Without Magoo's evidence, the case will have to be dismissed.

Student # 1: As the defense attorney, make a brief argument to support your position that Magoo's testimony is inadmissible.

Student # 2: As the prosecutor, respond to the defense objection with a brief argument supporting the admission of Magoo's testimony.

Student # 3: As the judge, preside over the arguments and rule on the admissibility of Magoo's testimony.

> *Practice Tip: Preliminary hearings and grand jury proceedings:*
>
> Preliminary hearings and grand jury proceedings are key components of the criminal justice process when defendants are charged with felonies. In a preliminary hearing, a prosecutor has to present evidence sufficient to convince a judge that probable cause exists that a felony was committed and that the defendant committed it. The defendant has a right to appear with counsel at a preliminary hearing, to cross-examine witnesses, and to present exculpatory evidence. If the judge concludes that probable cause exists, the defendant is held or "bound over" for trial. In a grand jury proceeding, a prosecutor presents evidence supporting probable cause to a group of citizens sitting as a grand jury. A defendant has no right to appear at grand jury proceedings, either in person or through counsel. Indeed, grand jury proceedings are usually secret. Prosecutors typically seek indictments as defendants go about their daily lives, unaware that they are the subject of grand jury proceedings.

Whether prosecutors proceed via preliminary hearing or grand jury (and in some jurisdictions, prosecutors can choose one or the other) entails consequences under Rule 804(b)(1). Because defendants have the opportunity to question government witnesses at preliminary hearings, their testimony is likely to be admissible as former testimony (and not barred by the Confrontation Clause) should the witnesses be unavailable at the time of trial. As a result, defense attorneys may have to make difficult strategic decisions. They may not want to cross-examine government witnesses too aggressively, to avoid revealing information that they would rather save for trial. The risk of that strategy is that if the defense attorney has no means of offering evidence other than through cross-examination of an unavailable witness whose preliminary hearing testimony is read into the record by the prosecutor at trial, the defense has to do without the evidence entirely.

For prosecutors who conduct preliminary hearings, Rule 804(b)(1) may affect decisions as to what witnesses to call. Rules in many jurisdictions allow prosecutors to offer hearsay at preliminary hearings. Thus, rather than force a crime victim to testify at a preliminary hearing, a prosecutor can present the victim's story through the testimony of a police officer who talked to the victim as part of the investigation. The risk for the prosecutor is that if the victim is unavailable for trial, the prosecutor has no preliminary hearing testimony to offer as the victim's former testimony.

Grand jury testimony is not admissible against defendants under Rule 804(b)(1), as well as under the Confrontation Clause, as defendants have no opportunity to cross-examine the witnesses.

§ 15.06 DYING DECLARATIONS (RULE 804(b)(2))

Statutory Elements:

* The declarant is unavailable as a witness;

  The declarant needn't be deceased. This is a big break to declarants compared to the common-law rule, which conditioned admissibility on their demise.

* The statement is offered in either a homicide prosecution or a civil proceeding;

  Dying declarations are inadmissible in non-homicide criminal cases. *Is this sensible doctrine? If dying declarations are reliable enough for homicide cases, aren't they reliable enough for less serious crimes?*

* The declarant believed that death was imminent at the time the statement was made:

* The statement concerns the cause or circumstances of what the declarant believed to be imminent death.

Aided by scores of films and television shows, probably all of us can visualize one person comforting another who is facing certain death, with the latter uttering a final thought with his or her last breath.[1] The assumed trustworthiness of that final thought reflects the traditional belief of a "God-fearing" populace that "people would not want to meet their Maker with a lie on their lips." That belief was the foundation of the common law dying declaration exception to the hearsay rule. Whatever its current currency in more secular times, the belief continues to be reflected in Rule 804(b)(2), which refers to the exception as one for a "statement under belief of imminent death."

Despite its longevity, the rationale for the dying declaration exception is shaky. Granting that declarants' last words may be sincere, the ability of a person who is near death to perceive, recall, and communicate accurately may be uncertain. However, even sincerity cannot be assumed. Declarants may use their last words as an opportunity to get revenge on and vilify long-time enemies. Concerns such as these may explain why dying declarations are in the second tier of exceptions, and we must trust judges and jurors to discount their probative value appropriately according to circumstances.

Example 1

A badly wounded Sangeeta tells a passerby that "Jones just shot me," at a time when Sangeeta believed that death was imminent. Sangeeta survived, but at her civil trial against Jones for damages, cannot remember that Jones was the person who shot her. Sangeeta is unavailable within the meaning of Rule 804(a)(3), and the statement is likely to admitted as a dying declaration because the other foundational elements are satisfied.

A declarant's subjective belief as to death's imminence can be shown directly, by the declarant's own statements ("I think I'm dying"). A declarant's subjective belief can also be inferred from statements made to the declarant ("I think you're dying"). Both types of statements are admissible despite the hearsay rule, which under Rule 104(a) does not apply to foundational issues. At any rate, such assertions would be admissible even in the absence of Rule 104(a). Declarants' assertions of their own belief ("I'm not going to make it") are admissible under the "state of mind" exception, Rule 803(3). And an outsider's statement affecting a declarant's subjective belief as to death's imminence ("Sorry, it doesn't look like you're going to make it") is admissible as non-hearsay for its "effect on the hearer."

A judge's foundational ruling will also be affected by a declarant's objective physical condition. A judge is unlikely to believe that a toothache caused a declarant to believe that death was imminent, no matter how distraught the declarant seemed to be at the time. This is not an exception that favors hypochondriacs.

Problem 15-14: *Famous's Last Words*

Ben Famous is walking along a street with Freddie Billity when he is grazed by a bullet fired from a passing car. Famous received only a slight flesh wound and immediately told Freddie, "That must have been Kwon who shot me; she made a threat against me last week. I'm lucky I got off so cheaply." Nevertheless, Famous

---

[1] For a classic example, see Alfred Hitchcock's suspense masterpiece, *The Man Who Knew Too Much* (Paramount Pictures 1956).

decided to go to a hospital emergency room, where he was treated for the wound. Before he could leave the hospital, the wound became seriously infected and Famous lapsed into a coma. He died the next day, never having uttered another word. As a result, Kwon is charged with murder, and the prosecution calls Freddie to testify to Famous's statement. *Is the statement admissible under Rule 804(b)(2)?*

Problem 15-15: Safe Passage

Jose and Alice were walking along the side of a multi-story building when a voice from high above yelled, "Watch out below." They both looked up and saw a large safe falling directly toward them. The safe missed Alice, but it crushed Jose. According to Alice, Jose's last words after he was hit by the safe were, "I couldn't get out of the way. I'm done for. Now I'll never see that $50,000 that my company loaned Sean." Jose's company sues Sean for repayment of the loan, and offers the deceased Jose's statement to prove that the money was a loan and not a gift. *Is Jose's statement to Alice admissible under Rule 804(b)(2)?*

Problem 15-16: Jesse and Billy

Jesse is close to death from a gunshot wound. With his last breath Jesse tells Wyatt, "Ike shot me." At Ike's trial for murdering Jesse, the prosecutor calls Wyatt to testify to Jesse's last words. Ike objects that because he did not have an opportunity to cross-examine Jesse, what Jesse told Wyatt is inadmissible under the Confrontation Clause regardless of whether the statement constitutes a dying declaration. *How should the judge rule on the objection?*

Assume that despite what Jesse said, the government charges Frank with Jesse's murder. *Assuming all foundational requirements are met, can Frank offer Jesse's last words into evidence as a dying declaration?*

Problem 15-17: Capital Letter

Edwards is charged with the capital murder of Vic Timm. The prosecution contends that Edwards is subject to the death penalty because before killing Vic, Edwards robbed and kidnapped him. The prosecution calls a deputy sheriff to testify that "Following a lead, I found Timm in a remote mountain cabin. He was dead. Lying next to him I found a blood-stained letter, which reads as follows: "I don't have long to live. Two days ago, Edwards kidnapped me at gunpoint and robbed me, then drove me to this cabin and left me tied up without food or water. Then Edwards returned and shot me." The parties stipulate that Timm died of the gunshot wound, and that the letter was written by Timm. The prosecution offers the entire letter as Timm's dying declaration under Rule 804(b)(2). The defense objects that the remarks about kidnapping and robbery must be stricken as they do not concern the cause and circumstances of Timm's death. The defense also objects on the ground that Timm was a lifelong atheist who spoke often against the existence of a Supreme Being. *How should the judge rule on these objections?*

Problem 15-18: On the Tube: Tight Squeeze

On the former television courtroom drama "The Practice," a wife is charged with the attempted murder of her husband. The prosecution contends that the wife intentionally drove her car into her husband after he got out of the passenger-side door to open the garage door. The husband is hospitalized both because of the injuries he suffered when hit by the car, and because he had a previously existing serious heart condition. The trial takes place in the husband's hospital room. The defense attorney's vigorous cross-examination attacks the husband's testimony that he could tell that his wife meant to hit him from her facial expression and the way the car sprang at him. The cross-examiner also angrily and repeatedly accuses the husband of committing perjury. The husband becomes so agitated that he goes into cardiac arrest. With emergency personnel rushing toward the husband, the prosecutor asks the husband to "squeeze the doctor's hand if your wife intended to kill you." The husband squeezes the doctor's hand, and then dies. The prosecutor offers the husband's squeezing of the doctor's hand as his dying declaration, meaning "my wife intended to kill me." *On what bases might the defense attorney object to the admissibility of the evidence? Should the judge admit the evidence as a dying declaration?*

Practice Tip: The Confrontation Clause and adverse witnesses who testify at trial.

The Confrontation Clause has a broader reach than situations involving the admission of hearsay as discussed in *Crawford v. Washington* and its progeny. The Confrontation Clause also ensures that criminal defendants have an adequate opportunity to cross examine prosecution witnesses who testify at trial. If following a prosecution witness' direct examine the witness should die, disappear, or otherwise become unavailable before the defense has a legitimate opportunity to complete its cross-examination of the witness, upon defense motion the judge should strike the witness' direct examination testimony from the record and instruct the jurors to disregard it. In some circumstances, the judge may have to declare a mistrial.

Problem 15-19: Dying Declaration Mini-Trial

Smith is charged with murdering Wesson in a drive-by gang shooting. The prosecution offers Wesson's statement to a hospital nurse into evidence under Rule 804(b)(2); the defense objects that it is inadmissible hearsay. The judge has excused the jury and will conduct a mini-trial as to the statement's admissibility. The parties have stipulated that Wesson underwent emergency surgery at the hospital after he was shot and lived for a week, though he was comatose for most of that time.

Student # 1: You are the prosecutor. Elicit the foundational evidence below and make a brief argument supporting the statement's admissibility under Rule 804(b)(2).

Student # 2: You represent the defendant Wesson. Cross-examine the prosecution's witnesses and make a brief argument that all or a portion of Wesson's statement is inadmissible.

Student # 3: You are the judge. Preside over the mini-trial and rule on the admissibility of all or part of the statement. As part of your ruling, indicate what the foundational burdens are with respect to the foundational elements such as personal knowledge and belief in imminent death.

Student # 4: You are witness Franklin, who can testify as follows: You, Wesson, and Barretta were walking down 3rd Street at about 11 p.m. on the night of the shooting. You were all walking home after playing some pool. You heard a car pull up behind you, and heard a voice from the direction of the car say, "Get off our street." You instinctively ducked down, and saw your friends do the same. You heard three gunshots come from the direction of the car, and heard the car drive off quickly. You didn't recognize any of the occupants of the car, but you were farthest from the street. You think there were three people in the car. Wesson was closest to the street. When you and Baretta realized that Wesson had been shot, Baretta ran to call 911.

Student # 5: You are Metcalf, an ambulance attendant. You and your partner picked up Wesson at the scene of a shooting. Wesson was bleeding heavily from the chest and his left arm. After stabilizing him as best you could, you took him in the ambulance to the hospital. To give him the best chance of survival, you kept telling him, "You'll be all right, buddy. You'll be just fine." Most of the time, Wesson was fading in and out of consciousness and screaming in pain.

Student # 6: You are Nurse Hoolihan, employed at General Hospital. You first saw Wesson when he was wheeled into the emergency room. He was bleeding heavily from his chest and left arm, and was going in and out of consciousness. On the way to the surgical room, he asked you if he was going to make it, and you said, "It looks pretty serious, but we've got great doctors here and we'll do everything we can." About a minute later, Wesson said to you, "When is a doctor going to see me? I'm really in a lot of pain. I may not make it. Smith did this to me with a rifle. He's part of the 3rd Street Visigoths. He tried before, and this time he got me." Wesson then lapsed into unconsciousness again and one week later was pronounced dead, without having uttered another word.

§ 15.07 STATEMENTS AGAINST INTEREST (RULE 804(b)(3))

Statutory Elements:

* The declarant is unavailable as a witness;

* The statement is sufficiently contrary to the declarant's interests (which may be pecuniary, proprietary, or penal in nature) that a reasonable person in the declarant's position would not have made the statement unless it was believed to be accurate.

* If a statement against penal interest is offered by either the prosecution or the defense in a criminal case, the offering party must also offer evidence of corroborating circumstances that clearly indicate that the statement is

trustworthy.

Under Rule 804(b)(3), an unavailable declarant's out-of-court assertion constitutes a declaration against interest if "a reasonable person in the declarant's position would not have made the statement unless believing it to be true," because *at the time the statement was made* the statement: (1) was contrary to the declarant's "pecuniary or proprietary interest," (2) tended to subject the declarant to civil or criminal liability, or (3) tended to render invalid a claim by the declarant against another. The trustworthiness of statements against interest grows out of the belief that most people are self-interested. Therefore, people are unlikely to make statements harming their pecuniary or penal interests, so when they do so, the statements are likely to be accurate.

Determining whether statements were against declarants' interests at the time they were made often requires more than simply looking at statements' "four corners." Foundational evidence offered to oppose admissibility of a hearsay assertion may indicate either that a statement that on the surface appears to be against interest really is not. By the same token, foundational evidence offered to support admissibility of a hearsay assertion may indicate that a statement that on the surface appears not to be against interest really is. Thus, the admissibility of a declaration against interest often depends on surrounding circumstances as well as "what a declarant knew and when the declarant knew it."

Example 1

Mei-lan seeks to offer evidence of Quintos's out-of-court assertion, "I am the owner of Pesticide Playthings International." On its surface, a claim to own a business does not appear harmful to Quintos's pecuniary or proprietary interest. However, Mei-lan may be able to convince the judge that the statement was against Quintos's interest by offering foundational evidence showing that at the time Quintos spoke, Quintos was aware that government attorneys had begun criminal proceedings against the company and its officers for manufacturing dangerous children's toys.

A declarant whose assertion is offered as a declaration against interest will almost never be a party to the action in which the assertion is offered.[5] As a result, when a party seeks to offer an assertion into evidence as a declaration against interest, typically the party's reason for offering it grows out of what the declarant said about the party (or the adversary). Often, the result is uncertainty about whether the portions of out-of-court assertions that refer to other people are against the declarants' interests and therefore admissible under Rule 804(b)(3).

Example 2

Hamilton is charged with participating in the robbery of the Conglomerate Bank on October 9. Hamilton seeks to offer evidence that Burr, an unavailable declarant, said that "I single-handedly robbed the Conglomerate Bank on October 9. Hamilton had nothing to do with it." Hamilton seeks to offer Burr's statement into evidence as a declaration against interest. The judge would have to decide whether the portion of the statement

---

[5] Were it otherwise, the declarant's assertion would normally be admissible as a party admission.

exculpating Hamilton was against Burr's interest.

Example 3

Hamilton is charged with participating in the robbery of the Conglomerate Bank on October 9. The prosecutor seeks to offer evidence that Burr, an unavailable declarant, said that "Hamilton and I robbed the Conglomerate Bank on October 9." The prosecutor seeks to offer Burr's statement into evidence as a declaration against interest. The judge would have to decide whether the portion of the statement inculpating Hamilton was against Burr's interest.

A badly divided United States Supreme Court provided an approach for analyzing statements in which declarants refer to themselves as well as others in *Williamson v. United States* (*see* Case Library). In *Williamson*, a drug courier confessed to an arresting officer that he was transporting cocaine on behalf of Williamson, its owner. The prosecution offered the courier's statement into evidence against Williamson under Rule 804(b)(3). The majority opinion stated that Rule 804(b)(3) did not necessarily make the courier's confession admissible against Williamson. The Court took a line-by-line, "weeding the garden" approach and held that Rule 804(b)(3) makes admissible "only those declarations or remarks within the confession that are individually self-inculpatory . . . it does not allow admission of non-self-inculpatory statements, even if they are made within a broader narrative that is generally self-inculpatory."[6]

As interpreted by *Crawford v. Washington* (*see* Chapter 10), the Confrontation Clause prevents prosecutors from offering the evidence that was offered in *Williamson*. The drug courier's confession to the police was clearly "testimonial" as that term is used in *Crawford*. Because Williamson had no opportunity to cross-examine the courier, the Confrontation Clause bars introduction of the courier's confession. However, *Williamson's* strict interpretation of Rule 804(b)(3) probably continues to operate in situations in which a declaration against interest might be admissible over a Confrontation Clause challenge.

When the Federal Rules of Evidence were first enacted, vestiges of the common hostility to admitting "declarations against penal interests" were evident in a foundational requirement that applied only to criminal defendants who offered statements exposing declarants to criminal liability into evidence for exculpatory purposes. In such situations, a statement was not admissible unless corroborating circumstances clearly indicated the trustworthiness of the statement. This foundational requirement reflected a fear that criminal defendants were likely to call nefarious cronies to swear falsely that conveniently unavailable declarants had confessed to committing the exact crimes with which the defendants were charged. One way that a criminal defendant was able to corroborate a statement asserting that someone other than the defendant committed the charged crime was to offer additional foundational evidence linking the supposed perpetrator to the crime. A second form of corroboration consisted of foundational evidence pertaining to the circumstances under which the assertion was made.

---

[6] *Williamson* controls only the interpretation of Rule 804(b)(3) in federal courts. States that have an evidence rule identical to Rule 804(b)(3) are free to interpret their rule differently.

As a result of a 2009 amendment, Rule 804(b)(3) requires any party to a criminal case who offers a statement against penal interest into evidence to corroborate it. This was not as significant a change as it may appear to be, because, as the Committee note indicates, "A number of courts have applied the corroborating circumstances requirement to declarations against penal interest offered by the prosecution, even though the text of the Rule did not so provide."

The Committee also added a comment reminding judges that they are not to consider the credibility of the in-court witness who testifies to a declarant's statement against penal interest when determining whether corroborating circumstances exist. The Committee pointed out that "to base admission or exclusion of a hearsay statement on the witness' credibility would usurp the jury's role of determining the credibility of testifying witnesses."

Example 4

Hamilton is charged with participating in the robbery of the Conglomerate Bank on October 9. Pursuant to Rule 804(b)(3), the prosecutor seeks to offer evidence of a statement made by Adams, an unavailable declarant, in which Adams said that "I need to brush up on my getaway driver skills. I was a minute late picking up Hamilton after he robbed the bank; we're lucky we got away before the cops showed up." Pursuant to the same rule, Hamilton seeks to offer evidence that Burr, an unavailable declarant, said that "I single-handedly robbed the Conglomerate Bank on October 9." Both parties would have to convince the judge that the assertions were against the declarants' penal interests when they were spoken and that the foundational evidence clearly indicates that the statements are trustworthy. For example, the prosecutor might support trustworthiness with foundational evidence showing that Adams made the statement very shortly after the robbery took place while he was displaying the wad of bills that Adams said was his share of the robbery proceeds. Hamilton might support trustworthiness with foundational evidence consisting of testimony from an eyewitness saying that: "Based on a picture of Burr that I have seen, I can tell you that Burr is the person I saw running out of the bank carrying a gun and a brown bag."

California's version of the declaration against interest exception, **Cal. Evid. Code § 1230**, includes a hearsay statement that creates "a risk of making [a declarant] an object of hatred, ridicule, or social disgrace in the community." A similar provision was deleted from a draft of the Federal Rules of Evidence during the legislative process. Perhaps Congress was wise. In an era when people seemingly compete to see who can air the most sordid details of their lives via international media, perhaps the California expansion no longer makes sense. Can we have any confidence that a statement that creates a risk of making a declarant an object of social disgrace is trustworthy?

Problem 15-20: Spoke Too Soon

Sailing away from a cheering throng at the dock on the *Titanic*'s maiden voyage, John walks up to one of the passengers and says proudly, "I designed this ship." Later in the voyage, the ship strikes an iceberg and sinks, taking John with it. The passenger survives and sues John's estate, claiming that he negligently designed the *Titanic*. *Is John's statement admissible under Rule 804(b)(3) as a declaration against interest?*

Problem 15-21: Deep-Pocket Defendant

Lorinda is charged with possession of the cocaine that a police officer found in the pocket of the red jacket she was wearing. Lorinda's defense is that she had borrowed the jacket from Natasha and didn't know that the cocaine was in the pocket. Lorinda calls Carlos to testify that the night before Lorinda was arrested, Natasha told him that "I loaned my red jacket to Lorinda yesterday." *Natasha's statement is admissible:*

1. As a declaration against interest if Natasha is unavailable as a witness.

2. As a declaration against interest if Natasha is unavailable as a witness and if Carlos testifies that when he called Natasha to tell her that Lorinda had been arrested, Natasha said, "I hope it wasn't because of the cocaine I left in the pocket of the jacket that I loaned her."

3. As a prior inconsistent statement to prove that it was Natasha's jacket, if Natasha testifies and denies that the red jacket that Lorinda was wearing belonged to her.

4. As Natasha's present sense impression.

5. Under none of the above.

Problem 15-22: I Owe You?

Benny Fishiary (the executor of his late uncle's estate) sues Ellis Atey to enforce a promissory note for $50,000. Ellis had executed the note when he borrowed that amount of money from the uncle three years earlier.

1. Ellis calls Elle Satt, a friend of the uncle, to testify that about a year after Ellis signed the promissory note, the uncle told Satt that, "I told Ellis that he doesn't have to pay back the money I loaned to him; he should consider it a gift." *Is the uncle's statement to Satt admissible as his declaration against interest?*

2. Same situation as in # 1, except assume that the uncle and Satt are husband and wife. *Is the uncle's statement to Satt admissible as his declaration against interest?*

3. Ellis calls Elle Satt, a friend of the uncle, to testify that about a year after Ellis signed the promissory note, the uncle told Satt that, "Ellis still owes me $20,000 of the money that I loaned him." *Is the uncle's statement to Satt admissible as his declaration against interest?*

4. Assume that the uncle died from a self-inflicted gunshot wound. Ellis seeks to offer into evidence the portion of the uncle's suicide note that states, "Ellis paid off the note and owes nothing to me." *Is this portion of the suicide note admissible as the uncle's declaration against interest?*

Problem 15-23: Stool Pigeon 1

Jess Mist is on trial for the attempted murder of Hank O'Hare. The government claims that the attempt was carried out by Jess along with Robin Steele, who drove the car from which Jess shot at Hank. Yves Dropper, promised a recommendation of leniency by the government in Yves' upcoming sentencing hearing, is prepared to testify on behalf of the prosecution that "When I was in the cell next to Robin's in County Jail, I heard Robin tell his cellmate that Hank was lucky that Jess missed him, and that Jess wouldn't miss the next time." *Yves' testimony is:*

1. Admissible as a co-conspirator's admission under Rule 801(d)(2)(E), regardless of whether Robin is unavailable as a witness.

2. Inadmissible hearsay.

3. Admissible as Robin's declaration against interest if Robin exercises his Fifth Amendment privilege and refuses to testify.

4. Potentially admissible as Robin's declaration against interest if Robin exercises his Fifth Amendment privilege and refuses to testify, but barred by the Confrontation Clause.

5. Inadmissible if the judge concludes that Yves Dropper is an unreliable witness.

Problem 15-24: Stool Pigeon 2

Same case as the previous problem. Assume that Yves is prepared to testify for the government that "When I was in the cell next to Robin's in County Jail, I heard Robin tell his cellmate that Hank was lucky that Robin had to swerve to avoid hitting a gnatcatcher because it is an endangered species just as Jess shot at Hank, and that Hank won't be so lucky the next time." *Yves' testimony is:*

1. Admissible as a co-conspirator's admission under Rule 801(d)(2)(E), regardless of whether Robin is unavailable as a witness.

2. Admissible as Robin's declaration against interest if Robin exercises his Fifth Amendment privilege and refuses to testify, if the judge concludes that "Dropper's testimony is credible, and therefore the government has corroborated the trustworthiness of Robin's statement."

3. Potentially admissible as Robin's declaration against interest if Robin exercises his Fifth Amendment privilege and refuses to testify, but barred by the Confrontation Clause.

4. None of the above answers is accurate.

Problem 15-25: Defense Pigeon 1

Same case as the previous problem. Assume that Yves is prepared to testify for Jess, the defendant, that "When I was in the cell next to Robin's in County Jail, I heard Robin tell his cellmate that he and Joe tried to kill Hank as a way of getting into a gang, that Hank was lucky that Robin had to swerve to avoid an endangered gnatcatcher just as Joe shot at Hank, and that he and Joe wouldn't miss the next time." *Yves' testimony is:*

1. Admissible as a co-conspirator's admission under Rule 801(d)(2)(E), regardless of whether Robin is unavailable as a witness.

2. Inadmissible hearsay.

3. Admissible as Robin's declaration against interest if Robin exercises his Fifth Amendment privilege and refuses to testify.

4. Admissible as Robin's declaration against interest if Robin exercises his Fifth Amendment privilege and refuses to testify, and if Jess' attorney produces testimony from the person who was walking next to Hank at the time of the shooting that "I think that Robin and Joe were the occupants of the car from which the shots were fired."

Problem 15-26: Defense Pigeon 2

Same case as the previous problem, except that this time Hank O'Hare is the plaintiff in a civil suit that he filed against Jess Mist. Hank seeks damages from Jess resulting from Jess's alleged attempt to shoot Hank. Yves Dropper is prepared to testify for Jess that "When I was in the cell next to Robin's in County Jail, I heard Robin tell his cellmate that he and Joe tried to kill Hank as a way of getting into a gang, that Hank was lucky that Robin had to swerve to avoid an endangered gnatcatcher just as Joe shot at Hank, and that he and Joe wouldn't miss the next time." *Yves' testimony is:*

1. Admissible as a co-conspirator's admission under Rule 801(d)(2)(E), regardless of whether Robin is unavailable as a witness.

2. Inadmissible hearsay.

3. Admissible as Robin's declaration against interest if Robin exercises his Fifth Amendment privilege and refuses to testify.

4. Admissible as Robin's declaration against interest if Robin exercises his Fifth Amendment privilege and refuses to testify, and if Jess' attorney produces testimony from the person who was walking next to Hank at the time of the shooting that "I think that Robin and Joe were the occupants of the car from which the shots were fired."

Problem 15-27: At the Movies: Cell Talk

In the film *The Shawshank Redemption*,[7] Andy Dufresne is imprisoned after having been wrongly convicted of murder. Tommy Williams, another inmate, tells Dufresne that a former cellmate had confessed to Williams that he committed the murder for which Dufresne was convicted. The whereabouts of the confessor are unknown. Assume that Dufresne might be granted a new trial if the cellmate's confession is admissible in evidence. *What foundational elements do you have to satisfy for the confession to be admissible?*

---

[7] Columbia Pictures, 1994. Thanks to Prof. David Schwartz for calling this example to our attention.

After talking to Williams, Dufresne excitedly repeats Williams's statement to the warden. The warden, however, does not want Dufresne released because Dufresne might reveal that the warden has been ripping off the prison system. When the warden realizes that Williams is ready to testify in court to his former cellmate's confession, the warden arranges for Williams to be killed. *After Williams's death, does Dufresne have admissible evidence of the confession?*

Problem 15-28: Fishing Expedition

Jim Teacher and Ward Robey are charged with burgling a warehouse filled with sports equipment on August 1. Jim is tried first; he testifies that he had nothing to do with the burglary, and that he was shooting pool with Ed Fisical at the time it occurred. Ed testifies and corroborates Jim's alibi. Jim and the prosecutor stipulate that Ward is unavailable to testify, and Jim then calls Jose to testify to a statement that Ward made to Jose a few days after the burglary. Jim offers Ward's statement to Jose as Ward's declaration against interest under Rule 804(b)(3). The judge conducts a foundational mini-trial, which produces the evidence set forth in the transcript below.

DEFENSE ATTORNEY: Jose, where were you on the afternoon of August 4?

A: I was fishing out at the lake, with Dil Capote and Ward Robey.

DEFENSE ATTORNEY: Was this the first time the three of you had gone fishing together?

A: Oh, no. We've been going fishing together for a few years now. We go maybe 10–12 times a year in Dil's boat.

DEFENSE ATTORNEY: Do you know Jim Teacher?

A: I know him. Ward's brought him along on a few of the fishing trips, but I don't know him too well.

DEFENSE ATTORNEY: Was Jim with you on the August 4 fishing trip?

A: No.

DEFENSE ATTORNEY: While you were fishing on August 4, did Ward say anything about his fishing gear?

A: Yes. I said that I really liked the rod and reel he was using, that it looked brand new. Ward said he'd picked it up at a warehouse, and kind of smiled and winked at me. I asked him what was up with that, and he said, "Between the three of us, I got talked into doing something stupid. Me and this other guy took some stuff from a warehouse."

DEFENSE ATTORNEY: Did you respond in any way?

A: I said that was pretty dumb because he'd been clean for a long time, and that I hoped he wouldn't get in trouble. Dil asked him who the other guy was, was it that guy, Jim, he brings on the fishing trips sometimes. He said no, that the other guy suggested Jim, but that Jim had nothing to do with it.

DEFENSE ATTORNEY: Did Ward say anything else about Jim?

§ 15.08   FORFEITURE BY WRONGDOING (RULE 804(b)(6))   745

A: I don't know if I should say this, but Ward said that Jim had taken some masonry work away from him and that he realized that Jim was a jerk.

DEFENSE ATTORNEY: Was there any further discussion of taking stuff from the warehouse?

A: No, that was about it.

DEFENSE ATTORNEY: Nothing further.

JUDGE: Prosecutor, any questions as to foundation?

PROSECUTOR: Just a few, thank you. Jose, you would describe the three of you as good friends, correct?

A: Yes.

PROSECUTOR: If you mentioned to Dil or Ward that you had done something illegal, you wouldn't expect them to run to the police with the information, right?

A: I suppose that's true, depending on what it was.

PROSECUTOR: And when Ward talked to you about the warehouse, he undoubtedly had the same expectation about you and Dil, right?

A: I wouldn't know.

PROSECUTOR: When Ward made this statement about the warehouse, no other boats were in the area, correct?

A: That's right.

PROSECUTOR: Nothing further at this time.

JUDGE: If there's no additional evidence, I'll hear brief argument before ruling.

Student # 1: You represent Jim. Make a brief argument as to the admissibility of Ward's statement as a declaration against interest.

Student # 2: You are the prosecutor. Make a brief argument as to the inadmissibility of Ward's statement as a declaration against interest.

Student # 3: You are the judge. Preside over the arguments and rule on the admissibility of Ward's statement as a declaration against interest.

§ 15.08   FORFEITURE BY WRONGDOING (RULE 804(b)(6))

Statutory Elements:

* The declarant is unavailable as a witness;

* The party against whom the statement is offered engaged or acquiesced in wrongdoing that was intended to and did result in the declarant's unavailability.

Rule 804(b)(6) codified the rulings of many cases that hearsay from an unavailable declarant is admissible in evidence if the party procured the unavailability through wrongdoing that was intended to and did result in the declarant's unavailability. The rule typically applies to post-event conduct that is intended to and does prevent a witness from testifying or induce a witness not to testify. The wrongdoing need not constitute a crime. A party seeking to offer an unavailable declarant's hearsay statement into evidence under Rule 804(b)(6) has to convince a judge by a preponderance of the evidence under Rule 104(a) that the adversary's wrongdoing is responsible for the declarant's unavailability. A party claiming that forfeiture has occurred can also satisfy Rule 804(b)(6) with foundational evidence showing that the adversary acquiesced in another's wrongdoing that was intended to and did procure a declarant's unavailability.

Example 1

Following a automobile collision in which she was involved, celebrity Katie notices a bystander talking to a police officer and repeatedly and angrily pointing in Katie's direction. Sometime thereafter, Katie agrees to go along with an arrangement made by her personal manager for the bystander to have the free use of Katie's overseas villa in exchange for the bystander's promise to remain in the villa until after any litigation related to the collision concludes. Katie has acquiesced in conduct that interferes with the system of justice. If Katie is a defendant in either a civil or criminal case growing out of the collision and the bystander is unavailable to testify, the bystander's statement to the police officer is admissible under Rule 804(b)(6).

The U.S. Supreme Court decision in *Davis v. Washington* (*see* Chapter 10) suggests that Rule 804(b)(6) may be of particular importance in domestic violence cases. Domestic violence victims frequently call the police for help during or soon after an attack, but later refuse to testify against their attackers. In *Davis*, the Court ruled that the account of an attack that a domestic violence victim gave to a police officer was testimonial, and that since the victim did not appear for the trial, the Confrontation Clause prevented the prosecutor from offering her account into evidence against her abuser.

The Court in *Davis* acknowledged that domestic violence is a "type of crime notoriously susceptible to intimidation or coercion of the victim to ensure that she does not testify at trial. When this occurs, the Confrontation Clause gives the criminal a windfall." The opinion referred prosecutors of domestic violence cases to Rule 804(b)(6), noting that "one who obtains the absence of a witness by wrongdoing forfeits the constitutional right to confrontation." Leaving proof problems to lower courts, *Davis* took "no position on the standards necessary to demonstrate such forfeiture."

Two years after *Davis*, the Court did take a position on the forfeiture question in *Giles v. California* (see Case Library). In *Giles*, the defendant was charged with murdering Brenda Avie, his ex-girlfriend. To rebut the defendant's testimony that he was acting in self-defense when he shot Brenda, the prosecutor was allowed to call a police officer to testify to statements that Brenda had made to the officer about three weeks earlier when the officer responded to a domestic violence call. Brenda told the officer that the defendant had choked her, punched her in the face and head, and threatened to kill her. The California state courts ruled that the statements were admissible because the defendant had forfeited his right to confrontation by killing the declarant, Brenda.

In *Giles*, the U.S. Supreme Court ruled that the defendant's killing of Brenda resulted in a forfeiture only if he killed her *for the purpose of preventing her from testifying*. The Court acknowledged that it had often invoked the maxim that "a defendant should not be permitted to benefit from his own wrong," but concluded that to constitute forfeiture by wrongdoing, the "wrong" must consist of conduct designed to prevent a witness from testifying. The Court vacated Giles's conviction. Brenda Avie's hearsay might yet be admissible, if following remand the prosecution establishes by a preponderance of the evidence that Giles killed her for the purpose of preventing her from testifying against him. If so, Brenda's hearsay would be admissible to prove that Giles murdered her.

Though *Giles* reads an "intent to prevent from testifying" requirement into the jurisprudence of the Sixth Amendment and forfeiture doctrine, it also establishes that the prosecution can invoke the forfeiture doctrine when a defendant is prosecuted for the very act that causes the declarant's absence. That is, Brenda's hearsay account of Giles's prior attack could be admissible to prove that Giles murdered her, so long as the state can make a foundational showing that Giles killed her to prevent her from testifying against him. (Of course, the jury would not find out that in order for the hearsay statements to be admissible in evidence, the judge had to make a foundational finding that the defendant committed the very crime for which he or she is on trial.)

Problem 15-29: Owens' Flip Side

Johnny Angel, a prison inmate, is charged with attempting to kill Bob Owens, a correctional counselor. Angel admits striking Owens, but claims that he did so in self-defense after Owens dragged him into an empty cell and began to hit and kick him. Owens was so badly injured that he has remained hospitalized ever since the alleged attack, and is sometimes comatose. When police officers went to the hospital to interview Owens and gather information about what happened, he was unresponsive except for one occasion when he told Police Officer Shelley Faber that Angel "pulled me into an empty cell and beat me until other prisoners and correctional officers pulled him off me." After listening to the prosecution's foundational evidence, the judge rules that Owens is unavailable as a witness under Rule 804(a)(4). The prosecution then calls Officer Faber to testify to Owens's description of the incident in the hospital. In response to Angel's Confrontation Clause objection, the prosecutor argues that the statement is admissible under Rule 804(b)(6), because Angel forfeited his right to cross-examine Owens by attacking him so viciously that he remains hospitalized. *Is Faber's testimony admissible against Angel?*

Problem 15-30: Five-feiture

Pat Barron is charged with domestic violence. Two days after the alleged attack, Barron's wife Alita called the police and gave them a complete description of Barron's attack. Assume that the trial judge has correctly ruled that Alita is unavailable as a witness under one or more of the provisions of Rule 804(a)(5), and that the prosecutor offers Alita's statement to the police into evidence under the forfeiture provision, Rule 804(b)(6). *Which, if any, of the five circumstances below would support a judge's conclusion under Rule 104(a) that Barron forfeited his right to claim that Alita's statement is inadmissible under the Confrontation Clause? If you conclude that the foundational information provided in a sub-part is inadequate to support a finding of forfeiture, establish a sufficient foundation through the testimony of a new witness (who must be someone other than the defendant or Alita) who you will question in class. You and your witness should meet before class to develop the information that you will elicit.*

1. The prosecutor has no evidence of post-attack contact between Barron and Alita. However, the prosecutor calls a police officer to testify that when Alita contacted the police after a similar attack by Barron a few weeks earlier, Alita reported that Barron had said after striking her, "If you show up in court, you're a dead woman."

2. The prosecutor has no evidence of post-attack contact between Barron and Alita. Alita appears for Barron's trial, but refuses to testify to anything that Barron did to her despite the trial judge's repeatedly warning Alita of the consequences of wrongfully refusing to testify. All that Alita will say on the stand is: "I just can't testify. I'm scared. I came down here with good intentions, but I know my husband and his friends and you don't. I know that if I testify they'll do something terrible to me or my son."

3. The prosecutor has no evidence of post-attack contact between Barron and Alita. Despite having been subpoenaed, Alita fails to appear for trial and the prosecutor does not know her whereabouts. The prosecutor calls Alita's friend Marta to testify that two weeks before the trial, Alita phoned Marta and told her that "Oh my God, I just got off the phone with Joe, my husband's brother. Joe said he'd just come back from talking with Pat in jail, and Pat asked him to tell me that if I show up in court and testify about the argument, he's going to see to it that I'm killed. I know he means it. No way I'm showing up in court."

4. While out on bail awaiting trial on the domestic violence charges, Barron decides to raise money for his legal defense by burning down his house and fraudulently collecting the insurance proceeds. Alita was sleeping inside the house at the time and perished in the flames.

5. Assume now that Barron is charged with murdering Alita. After taking Alita's domestic violence report, the police searched for but were unable to arrest Barron. Two weeks later, Barron showed up at Alita's home and shot and killed her. At trial, Barron testifies that he shot Alita in self-defense, thinking that she was advancing on him with a knife. To rebut the self-defense claim, the prosecution seeks to offer Alita's statement to the police following the domestic violence incident into evidence. In response to Barron's Confrontation Clause objection, the prosecutor argues that by killing Alita, Barron forfeited his right to confrontation. *How should the judge rule?*

When evaluating the admissibility of Alita's statements in the sub-parts above, consider this language from Justice Souter's concurring opinion in *Giles* (which Justice Breyer's dissent quotes):

Examining the early cases and commentary, however, reveals two things that count in favor of the Court's understanding of forfeiture when the evidence shows domestic abuse . . . The second is the absence from the early material of any reason to doubt that the element of intention would normally be satisfied by the intent inferred on the part of the domestic abuser in the classic abusive relationship, which is meant to isolate the victim from outside help, including the aid of law enforcement and the judicial process. If the evidence for admissibility shows a continuing relationship of this sort, it would make no sense to suggest that the oppressing defendant miraculously abandoned the dynamics of abuse the instant before he killed his victim, say in a fit of anger.

§ 15.09 RESIDUAL HEARSAY (RULE 807)

Statutory Elements:

* A statement has equivalent circumstantial guarantees or trustworthiness compared to statements made admissible by Rules 803 and 804, but not specifically covered by those rules;

As you have probably realized by now, the exceptions grouped together in Rules 803 and 804 vary in the degree to which they promote trustworthiness. The official comments of the drafters of the Rules are silent on the question of how judges are supposed to determine trustworthiness when making the comparison required by Rule 807.

* The statement pertains to a material fact;

This foundational element does little more than restate the relevance rule, as all evidence must bear on a "material" or "ultimate" fact. The drafters may have intended the term "material" as a signal to judges to limit admissibility of residual hearsay to important issues, and to be especially concerned to balance probative value against the risk of unfair prejudice under Rule 403.

* The statement is more probative than any other evidence that the party offering the statement can reasonably procure;

This foundational element permits a judge to exclude residual hearsay on the ground that a reasonable effort by the proponent might have produced either the declarant or more trustworthy hearsay. Thus, as suggested earlier the element imposes a soft unavailability requirement.

* Admission of the statement serves the interests of justice;

* The offering party gives the adversary adequate notice in advance of trial of the party's intent to offer the statement into evidence.

The notice must include contact information about the declarant, and must be given sufficiently in advance of trial to give the adversary "a fair opportunity to meet" the hearsay. An adversary who has a fair chance to investigate both the hearsay declarant and the circumstances under which the hearsay statement was made may be able to argue successfully that it lacks trustworthiness and so should either be not admitted or not believed.

The adoption of the Federal Rules of Evidence in the late 1970s generally moved evidence law in the direction of greater admissibility as compared to common law evidence principles. Increasing the discretion of trial judges when making evidentiary rulings was one of the tools that the Rules drafters used to promote admissibility, and this approach is perhaps nowhere more apparent than in Rule 807, the residual hearsay exception.[8]

A cartoon in a 1966 issue of the magazine *Saturday Review* depicts two judges on the bench in mid-hearing. Ignoring a lawyer's impassioned argument, one judge slyly whispers to the other: "Sure it's hearsay, but it's great hearsay." What seemed humorous in 1966 is now good law under Rule 807. Rule 807 gives judges the discretion to admit hearsay that they consider trustworthy and more probative than other evidence that might reasonably be procured, even if the statement doesn't qualify for admission under any other hearsay exception.

The residual exception was quite controversial when it was first introduced. A number of commentators and legislators argued that a residual exception was unnecessary and would inject too much uncertainty into trials. Advocates of the residual exception argued that it was consistent with the general philosophy of the Federal Rules of Evidence as enunciated in Rule 102, to promote the "growth and development of the law of evidence." Advocates also tried to reassure the doubters that in practice, the residual exception's impact would be minimal. The Report of the Senate Committee on the Judiciary stated:

> It is intended that the residual hearsay exception will be used very rarely, and only in exceptional circumstances. The committee does not intend to establish a broad license for trial judges to admit hearsay statements that do not fall within one of the other exceptions . . . the residual exceptions are not meant to authorize major judicial revisions of the hearsay rule.

Whether this statement reflected the Judiciary Committee's true expectations, a claim that judges have in practice used the catch-all sparingly is at least open to doubt.[9] Moreover, judges have excused parties' obligations to provide pre-trial notice that they will offer hearsay under Rule 807, especially when the need for the hearsay is not apparent prior to trial and a short continuance provides an adversary with sufficient opportunity to prepare to counter it.[10]

---

[8] The "catch-all" exception actually started life as two virtually identical exceptions, one a part of Rule 803 and the other part of Rule 804. They were combined as Rule 807 in 1997.

[9] Perhaps the first case to do so was *United States v. Carlson*, 547 F.2d 1346 (8th Cir. 1976), *cert. denied*, 431 U.S. 914 (1977).

[10] Professor Raeder's study of appellate court decisions from 1975 (the date the Federal Rules of Evidence were enacted) through mid-1991 indicated that more than 400 opinions had considered the admissibility of hearsay offered under the residual exceptions. Obviously, residual hearsay was offered and no doubt received in many more cases that were not appealed or did not result in published opinions. The study revealed that prosecutors were the most frequent residual hearsay offerors, and they were successful 81% of the time. Defense attorneys, by contrast, had only a 15% success rate. *See* Myrna Raeder, *The Hearsay Rule at Work: Has It Been Abolished De Facto by Judicial Discretion?*, 76 Minn. L. Rev. 507 (1992).

§ 15.09   RESIDUAL HEARSAY (RULE 807)   751

Example

Ella Mentry, a third-grade teacher, sues Pete Teeyay, a parent of one of the children in Ella's class, for intentional infliction of emotional distress. Ella claims that Pete made verbal threats against her during an after-school conference. To prove that Pete made threats, Ella seeks to offer into evidence a note given to her by Bill Jones. The parties stipulate that Ella could not reasonably produce Bill Jones to testify, and that Ella's attorney notified Pete's attorney well before trial that Ella would seek to offer the contents of the note into evidence.

PLAINTIFF'S ATTORNEY: And what happened after Pete left the classroom?

A: I took a walk to try to calm my nerves. What he said really shook me up.

PLAINTIFF'S ATTORNEY: Did you talk to anyone?

A: No, I just walked around the campus by myself for about 15 or 20 minutes.

PLAINTIFF'S ATTORNEY: Then what did you do?

A: I went back to my classroom. That's when Bill Jones, who at that time taught fourth grade across the hall, came in. He said he'd heard someone yelling at me and asked if I was OK.

Bill's statement to Ella that he'd heard someone yelling may itself be hearsay, but if so is admissible under Rule 104(a) because it is foundational to show that he had personal knowledge.

PLAINTIFF'S ATTORNEY: What then happened?

A: I told him that I wasn't hurt, but that I had to get away. He said that he'd write down what he'd heard, in case I ever needed proof of what happened. I thanked him, gave him that piece of paper over there off my desk, and he wrote down what's on the paper.

Ella's attorney marks the document to which Ella referred as Exhibit #1 and asks her to identify it as the one that she saw Bill prepare.

PLAINTIFF'S ATTORNEY: Nothing further at this time.

JUDGE: The defense may inquire.

DEFENDANT'S ATTORNEY: Ms. Mentry, I assume that you close the doors to your room during parent conferences?

A: Yes.

DEFENDANT'S ATTORNEY: Was Bill Jones also holding parent conferences that afternoon?

A: Probably. The whole school was that afternoon.

DEFENDANT'S ATTORNEY: And is it the principal's policy that teachers close their doors during parent conferences?

A: Yes.

DEFENDANT'S ATTORNEY:	So if Bill Jones followed this policy, any sounds from your classroom would have had to travel through two sets of closed doors and a hallway?
A:	I guess so.
DEFENDANT'S ATTORNEY:	And you were walking for at least 15 or 20 minutes before you returned to your classroom and Bill Jones walked in?
A:	No more than that.
DEFENDANT'S ATTORNEY:	You weren't looking at your watch though, correct?
A:	That's true.
DEFENDANT'S ATTORNEY:	Nothing further.
PLAINTIFF'S ATTORNEY:	Your Honor, I'd now like to read the contents of Exhibit # 1 into evidence under Rule 807.
JUDGE:	I'll hear argument from counsel.
PLAINTIFF'S ATTORNEY:	I submit that Mr. Jones's note clearly has equivalent circumstantial guarantees of trustworthiness compared to the Rules 803 and 804 hearsay exceptions. Mr. Jones had personal knowledge of what took place, and he wrote the note shortly after the event. While the note may not have been prepared immediately after the shouting so as to qualify as a present sense impression under Rule 803(1) or pursuant to an excited state of mind so as to be admissible under Rule 803(2), it was made so soon after the events that Bill Jones's memory problems were nonexistent. Moreover, Bill was a neutral witness — he taught fourth grade and hadn't had any contact yet with the child or the parent. And given Ella's testimony as to the loudness of the defendant's voice, I don't believe that Mr. Jones's ability to hear is in serious question.
DEFENDANT'S ATTORNEY:	To the contrary, Your Honor, the evidence suggests that Mr. Jones's ability to hear what happened in Ms. Mentry's classroom is in serious question. He didn't come in to check on the plaintiff until after she returned from her walk, so we can't be confident about what he heard or how accurately he heard it. Also, the plaintiff testified that she was very shaken by what had happened and was not looking at her watch, so we can't be sure that it wasn't more than 20 minutes between the incident and the time Mr.

Jones wrote the note. The note is not trustworthy and should be excluded.

JUDGE: I'm satisfied that the note has equivalent reliability to statements admitted under other hearsay exceptions, so I'll admit its contents into evidence. Counsel may read it to the jury.

In this example, as is typically the case when parties offer hearsay pursuant to Rule 807, the attorneys' arguments center on the "hearsay dangers" that gave rise to the general rule proscribing hearsay in the first place: the declarant's sincerity, perception and memory, and the risk of communication problems, such as ambiguity. As is also common, the judge's ruling doesn't specify precisely how the judge made the trustworthiness comparison called for by Rule 807. The judge might, for example, have compared the trustworthiness of Jones's statement to a particular Rule 803 or 804 hearsay exception, or might have compared it to what the judge considers the "average trustworthiness" of hearsay statements admissible under Rules 803 and 804.

In the example above, Pete's attorney might also have tried to make what has been called a "near miss" argument. A "near miss" argument is that the residual exception should apply only to situations not contemplated by any of the specific exceptions listed in Rules 803 and 804. That is, if an out-of-court statement is of a type provided for by an existing hearsay exception and fails to meet that exception's foundational requirements, it should be inadmissible. For example, Pete's attorney's "near miss" argument might have gone as follows:

> Under Rule 803(1), a hearsay statement is admissible if it was made during or immediately after the event which it describes. Bill Jones's statement is of a type contemplated by Rule 803(1), but as Your Honor has correctly ruled, the statement does not qualify for admission under that exception. Nor does his statement qualify as an excited utterance under Rule 803(2). Thus, you should not admit the statement under Rule 807. To admit it would be to flout the drafters' purpose in enacting Rules 803(1) and (2).

Some commentators would support such an argument.[11] However, judges have generally not accepted the "near miss" argument. A major problem with the "near miss" argument is that probably every hearsay statement can be analogized to at least one of the Rule 803 and 804 exceptions. For example, every out-of-court statement in which a declarant mentions a medical condition might be argued to be "admissible under the Rule 803(4) medical hearsay exception or not at all." Carried to its logical extent, therefore, the "near miss" argument would wipe out the residual exception altogether. Thus, the majority of court rulings implicitly recognize that if the residual exception is to admit any hearsay at all, admissibility can not turn on whether a statement offered under Rule 807 is completely dissimilar to the types of statements admitted under Rules 803 or 804. Perhaps "the most that can usefully be retrieved from the 'near miss' theory is that courts should consider the question whether failing to satisfy requirements of a categorical exception that

---

[11] *See, e.g.*, Glen Weissenberger & James Duane, Federal Rules of Evidence: Rules, Legislative History, Commentary and Authority § 807.3 (2001).

almost covers the statement indicates a reason to be wary of it in applying the catchall."[12]

Problem 15-31: Hospital Hearsay

Florence Nighten, a nurse, has been civilly sued for battery by Maria Moore, a hospital patient; Florence denies striking Maria. To prove that Florence attacked her, Maria calls Dr. Killdear to testify to a statement made to the doctor by Dee Clarant, who at the time of the incident was a patient who shared Maria's hospital room. Dr. Killdear will testify that she spoke to Dee about 15 minutes after the attack on Maria. At the time Dr. Killdear spoke to Dee, Dee was semi-conscious, coming out of general anesthetic administered in connection with knee surgery for a torn meniscus. Dee told Dr. Killdear, "Heard yelling and hitting . . . next bed . . . thought imagining . . . saw nurse leaving room . . . scar right cheek." Other foundational evidence will show that:

- Florence has a scar on her right cheek, and is the only nurse who was on the floor at the time of the attack with such a mark.

- Because Maria's bed was closer to the door than Dee's, Dee at best could have seen Florence in profile and from behind.

- Dee had only a single previous contact with Florence, when Florence came into the room to check on Dee's blood pressure following the surgery and about 15 minutes before the time of the attack on Maria. Dee looked at Florence momentarily and raised her arm in response to Florence's request, then lapsed back to sleep.

- The day before the attack, Florence had told another nurse on the floor that "I've had all I can take of Maria Moore. She demands everything and then has the gall to file a complaint because I'm late with her dinner."

- A thin bracelet, of a type Florence usually wears, was found in Maria's bed following the attack.

Defense counsel objects to admission of Dee's statement to Dr. Killdear under Rule 403, stating: "Regardless of whether the statement meets the foundational requirements of a Rule 803 hearsay exception, the circumstances under which it was made indicate that it lacks trustworthiness. Its probative value is therefore substantially outweighed by its unfair prejudice."

The judge then asks you, a law clerk, for advice: "In considering the statement's trustworthiness, should I look only to the circumstances under which Dee spoke to Dr. Killdear? If so, I'm inclined to exclude the statement because Dee was barely conscious. Or can I also look to corroborating information, such as the bracelet and the defendant's statement to the nurse the day before the attack? If I can, I'd be inclined to admit the statement because it's corroborated by this information. What do you think makes the most sense under the Federal Rules?" *What advice will you give the judge?*

---

[12] Christopher Mueller & Laird Kirkpatrick, Evidence § 8.81 (3d ed. 2003).

Problem 15-32: Home Work

Rip Toff has sued Bill Kem Construction Co. to set aside Kem's foreclosure on Rip's house, claiming that Kem fraudulently induced Rip to sign an agreement to pay for unnecessary home repairs and improvements that Rip could not afford. Rip contends, and Kem denies, that Kem told Rip that "the piece of paper you're signing is just my standard agreement under which you can never lose your house." To corroborate Rip's testimony that Kem did make this representation, Rip's attorney seeks to offer into evidence a signed out-of-court statement given under penalty of perjury to the attorney's investigator by Sue Porter. At the time she met with the investigator, Sue lived a block away from Rip. Sue's statement includes the assertion that "Two days ago, Kem knocked on my door and tried to talk me into doing some home repairs. Kem told me that under the standard home repair contract I would sign with Kem, I could never lose my house. I was planning to move, so I did not agree to have any work done." Sue moved out of state within weeks of talking to the investigator, and is unavailable to testify.

1. You are Rip's attorney. Assume that Sue's statement is admissible, if at all, under Rule 807. *(As Sue is unavailable as a witness, why wouldn't her statement be admissible under Rule 804?)* Identify three factors that in your opinion suggest that Sue's statement is trustworthy. *To what extent are these factors similar to foundational requirements mentioned in any of the Rule 803 and 804 hearsay exceptions? Incorporate the three factors into a brief argument to the judge in support of the statement's admissibility under Rule 807.* (Kem's lawyer has stipulated to receiving proper notice of the intent to offer the statement under Rule 807, so that requirement needn't be argued.)

2. You are Rip's attorney. Assume that Kem's lawyer has offered to settle the case for about one-third of what you have demanded. In your opinion, Kem's settlement offer is worth Rip's consideration if the judge excludes Sue's statement, but unacceptably low if Sue's statement is admitted into evidence. You have no information about the judge who will preside over the trial. *How might you explain to Rip the likelihood of the admissibility of Sue's statement and its impact on whether Rip should accept Kem's settlement offer?*

Problem 15-33: Cartune

Minnie Vann has sued Lex Sussman for injuries sustained in an auto accident. To prove that Lex's careless driving caused the accident, Minnie calls Ron to testify that a few hours after the accident, Ron's wife Pam told him that "I was lucky I wasn't hurt when I was in Lex Sussman's car today. Lex hit another car when he took his eyes off the road to change the radio station when a country and western song came on." *Under Rule 807, Ron's testimony is:*

1. Inadmissible because Pam's statement is of a type made admissible by Rules 803(1) and (2), and was not made soon enough after the accident to qualify as a present sense impression or an excited utterance.

2. Inadmissible if Minnie called Ron instead of Pam to testify because Ron has testified in court previously and would probably be more believable.

3. Admissible unless Lex can convince the judge that Pam's statement is untrustworthy.

4. Admissible if Minnie offers it for the non-hearsay purpose of showing why Ron believes that Lex was at fault.

Problem 15-34: Fireside Chat

You are a newly appointed federal judge, and have erased the sands of time in order to convene a group of more experienced colleagues to help you decide how to interpret Rule 807. After considering their views, you'll have a chance to state yours. Please indicate which, if any, of their statements captures your view as to how best to interpret Rule 807, and why. Because you have a lifetime appointment, you are, of course, free to put forth a differing opinion.

Judge Baron Parke: I wrote the key opinion in *Wright v. Tatham* nearly 200 years ago, and I'm still really upset that judges have interpreted the hearsay rule so that statements are not hearsay when they are offered for points that declarants did not intend to assert. (*See* Chapter 10.) You should be suspicious of all hearsay. To promote accurate factfinding, reduce uncertainty about admissibility and give effect to the drafters' intention that Rule 807 should be used sparingly, you should admit a hearsay statement offered under Rule 807 only if it is as trustworthy as the most trustworthy type of hearsay offered pursuant to Rules 803 and 804. I'll leave that determination to you, but for my money that's Rule 803(6); I've found business records to be pretty darn reliable. But my basic point is that you should admit residual hearsay only if it is at least as trustworthy as whatever kind of hearsay you think most reliable. Doesn't that make sense?

Judge Jeremy Bentham: I've been around at least as long as Baron Parke. I think that Rule 102 best captures the general movement of modern evidence law in the direction of greater discretion and admissibility, shifting what in the past were technical arguments about admissibility to a jury's evaluation of the weight of evidence. Hearsay is presumptively admissible under Rule 807 if it is as trustworthy as the least trustworthy type of hearsay that may be offered pursuant to Rules 803 and 804. For my money that's Rule 803 (2); I've found that people often make mistakes when they speak under conditions of great stress, but I'll leave that determination to you. For purposes of Rule 807, I'd place the admissibility bar as low as the legislation permits, and look to Rule 403 if I think probative value is low and the risk of unfair prejudice is high. Doesn't this approach make sense to you?

Judge Solomon: With due respect to my learned friends, I think that the only sensible way to interpret Rule 807 is to split the difference. That is, by directing us to look generally at Rules 803 and 804, the drafters of the Federal Rules had in mind that as we accumulate experience first as lawyers and then as judges, we develop a general sense of the trustworthiness of statements that are commonly admissible under those statutes. Thus, we should make trustworthiness determinations under Rule 807 without regard to any of the specific subsections of Rules 803 and 804. Instead, we should admit any hearsay statements that are as trustworthy as those that we on average admit. That makes sense, doesn't it?

You: I'm really grateful to you all for traveling so far to consult with me. My present thinking is this: . . . . *How would you complete the thought? What policy arguments would you rely on: efficiency of trials, consistent interpretation of Rule 807 from one judge to another, ease of administering the rule, fairness to parties, some other argument?*

Problem 15-35: Voicemail

Rhoda Runner sues Wiley for personal injuries resulting from Wiley's allegedly unprovoked attack on Rhoda. Wiley has plead self-defense. Rhoda's attorney offers into evidence under Rule 807 a message left on Rhoda's home phone two days after the alleged attack. The message is as follows: "Rhoda, this is Ray Jacks. You don't know me, but I saw the notice in the local newspaper with your name and number asking for information from anyone who saw Wiley attack you. I was waiting to cross the street and I heard you honking your horn at Wiley, who was crossing the street really slowly. Then Wiley suddenly exploded, running over to your side of the car and hitting you a couple of times through the open window. Then Wiley ran off. At no time did you strike Wiley. I hope this is helpful, what I've said is the truth." *Is the voicemail message admissible under Rule 807?*

Problem 15-36: Building a Foundation

Shirin sues Kim's Auto Care for severe burns that Shirin sustained when having her car worked on at Kim's. Shirin claims that she was injured by an explosion that occurred on March 31 when Juan, a Kim's mechanic, poured gasoline directly into her car's carburetor when the engine was running. Kim's defense is that Shirin herself poured the gasoline into the carburetor despite Juan's warning her not to so do. To prove that Shirin's own carelessness was the cause of her injuries, Kim's seeks to offer into evidence under Rule 807 a note written by Guillermo, a customer who was waiting to pick up his car when the explosion occurred. After talking to Guillermo, Juan asked him to write down what happened. As Juan watched, Guillermo wrote the following: "March 31. I was at Kim's Auto Care waiting for my car when I saw a lady pour gasoline into her car's carburetor. I heard the mechanic, who was sitting in the car revving the engine, tell her not to, but she did anyway. Then there was an explosion and a fire, and the lady was burned. The mechanic and I put the fire out and called an ambulance. Guillermo. 823 Bolas Street, La Ronda Heights. E-mail: Guill@yabadabadoo.com. Tel: 438-555-1234." Kim's has been unable to locate Guillermo and so plans to offer the note into evidence pursuant to Rule 807.

Student # 1: You represent Kim's Auto Care and seek to offer Guillermo's handwritten note into evidence under Rule 807. Meet with Juan (Student # 2) before class and prepare foundational testimony that you will offer to make the contents of the note admissible in evidence. (Prior to class, notify Student # 3, who represents Shirin, of the testimony you plan to elicit.) You will call Juan as a witness at a foundational mini-trial during class, and after eliciting his testimony briefly argue for the admissibility of the note.

Student # 2: You are Juan, a mechanic employed by Kim's. Meet with Kim's lawyer before class and prepare the testimony you will provide during class.

Student # 3: You represent Shirin. Cross-examine Juan in an effort to undermine the note's trustworthiness, and at the conclusion of the testimony briefly argue against the note's admissibility if such an argument is warranted.

Student # 4: You are the judge. Preside at the foundational mini-trial, indicating which party has the burden of proving that the note is admissible under Rule 807 and what that burden consists of. After listening to brief arguments of counsel, rule on the note's admissibility.

All Students: As counsel for Kim's Auto Care, refer to the text of Rule 807 and draft a Notice that satisfies that section concerning your intention to offer Guillermo's note into evidence. Assume that you tried to contact Guillermo by phone and by regular and electronic mail. The phone number did not work, e-mails bounced back, and letters delivered by regular mail were returned marked "Addressee Unknown."

Problem 15-37: Transcript Analysis I

Datamark Manufacturing Co. has sued Fidelity Insurance Co. for $100,000 pursuant to an insurance policy that provides coverage up to that amount for employee theft. Datamark claims that a former assistant accountant, Lem Bezzler, stole that much from the company by reimbursing himself for phony expenditures. The insurance company's defense is that Datamark has not produced adequate proof of loss. *Answer the italicized questions embedded in the transcript below.*

PLAINTIFF'S ATTORNEY: Your Honor, at this time I'd like to read into the record portions of the testimony given by Cookie Booker in the case of *State v. Bezzler*, in which Bezzler was charged with embezzlement.

JUDGE: Is Ms. Booker available to testify?

PLAINTIFF'S ATTORNEY: No. Ms. Booker retired from Datamark six months ago. She then moved across the country and has indicated that she is unwilling to return for this trial. I have a written copy of her e-mail response indicating her refusal to return for trial right here if Your Honor wishes to see it. As Your Honor is well aware, I am not able to subpoena witnesses who live out of state.

DEFENDANT'S ATTORNEY: Objection to the contents of the e-mail message, hearsay.

JUDGE: Overruled. (*Is this ruling correct?*)

JUDGE: Counsel for Datamark, was Ms. Booker retired at the time of Bezzler's criminal trial?

PLAINTIFF'S ATTORNEY: No. She had announced her retirement, but that trial took place about two months before she formally retired and moved out of the state.

§ 15.09 RESIDUAL HEARSAY (RULE 807) 759

JUDGE: At the time of the criminal trial, I take it that your client had already submitted a claim to the insurance company under the policy, and that the insurer had rejected the claim?

PLAINTIFF'S ATTORNEY: That's correct.

JUDGE: By the time of the criminal trial, you had spoken with Ms. Booker and learned that she had information linking Bezzler to the disappearance of the $100,000?

PLAINTIFF'S ATTORNEY: Yes, we had.

JUDGE: And even though you knew that she planned to move out of the state and a trial date in this case had been set, you didn't serve her with a subpoena?

PLAINTIFF'S ATTORNEY: It's true that we did not serve Ms. Booker with a subpoena. There were some miscommunications within the company. We thought she was going to retire a year later than she actually did. And she had been fully cooperative both with the prosecutor's office and my office. (Assume that Datamark's attorney provides evidentiary support for each of the representations above.)

JUDGE: I find that Ms. Booker is unavailable as a witness within the meaning of Rule 804(a)(5). (*Is this ruling correct?*)

PLAINTIFF'S ATTORNEY: In view of the ruling that Ms. Booker is unavailable as a witness, I'd first like to read into the record a portion of the written statement that Ms. Booker prepared at the request of the company president, Patty Oh, when Ms. Oh first learned that $100,000 had gone missing. In the portion of the statement I seek to offer, Ms. Booker states that she saw Bezzler altering company records on his computer.

JUDGE: (*Is this portion of the written statement admissible in evidence?*)

PLAINTIFF'S ATTORNEY: I'd now like to read into the record the portion of Ms. Booker's testimony before the grand jury that indicted Bezzler in which Booker testified that she overheard Bezzler talking on the phone and heard him say, "Make out a bill for $5,000, and say it's for parts. Nobody here will be any the wiser."

DEFENDANT'S ATTORNEY: Objection, double hearsay. Apart from whether Ms. Booker's grand jury testimony is admissible, she testified to Bezzler's out-of-court statement, and Bezzler's statement is inadmissible hearsay.

JUDGE: Objection sustained. (*Is this ruling correct?*)

DEFENSE ATTORNEY: I also object based on hearsay to the admission in this case of any testimony that Ms. Booker gave to the grand jury.

JUDGE: That objection is also sustained.

PLAINTIFF'S ATTORNEY: I'd also like to read into the record a portion of Ms. Booker's testimony that she gave during the preliminary hearing in Bezzler's criminal case.

DEFENDANT'S ATTORNEY: Objection, hearsay. My client was, of course, not a party to the criminal case, and it is improper to use testimony given in a criminal case against a different party who's had no chance to cross-examine the declarant.

JUDGE: Overruled. (*Is this a correct ruling?*)

PLAINTIFF'S ATTORNEY: The portions of Ms. Booker's preliminary hearing testimony that I'd now like to read into the record are as follows:

Page 16, lines 11–14. "Question by District Attorney: What is the next thing that you recall? Answer: When I was in the employees' lounge, I overheard Mr. Bezzler say to an employee named Hy Lighter, 'I've been stealing cash from the company a few thousand dollars at a time for months now.'"

DEFENDANT'S ATTORNEY: Objection, hearsay.

JUDGE: Counsel for plaintiff, any response?

PLAINTIFF'S ATTORNEY: Yes. Mr. Bezzler's remark is both an admission under Rule 803 and a declaration against interest by him under Rule 804. Anyway, it's not even hearsay. It's a verbal act because it refers directly to theft of company property.

JUDGE: (*What ruling on the objection?*)

PLAINTIFF'S ATTORNEY: I'd also like to read into the record the following portion of Ms. Booker's preliminary hearing transcript.

Also on page 16, lines 20–24: "Question by District Attorney: What happened after Mr. Lighter left the room? Answer: I walked over to Mr. Bezzler and told him that I was really upset and angry, and I said that at least I had never stolen company property."

JUDGE: (*Is this portion of the transcript admissible in evidence?*)

PLAINTIFF'S ATTORNEY: I'd next like to read into the record the following portion of Ms. Booker's preliminary hearing transcript.

On page 23, lines 4–9: Question by District Attorney: What did you notice when you walked by Mr. Bezzler's desk? Answer: I asked him what he was working on. He said that he was working on an invoice from one of our ink suppliers, and that since the supplier had sent a blank invoice by mistake he was filling it in. I can tell you that our suppliers never send blank

§ 15.09   RESIDUAL HEARSAY (RULE 807)   761

invoices, so he obviously was going to pocket whatever amount he wrote on the invoice.

JUDGE: *(Is this portion of the transcript admissible in evidence?)*

PLAINTIFF'S ATTORNEY: That concludes the evidence that I seek to offer from Ms. Booker's preliminary hearing testimony. I next offer into evidence under Rule 804(b)(3) a signed statement from Lem Bezzler. In this statement, Bezzler admits that he used phony invoices to steal $100,000 of company money over a two-year period. Counsel for the insurance company stipulates that Mr. Bezzler is unavailable as a witness, and that he prepared the statement three days after attending a meeting for all employees conducted by the company's President, Patty Oh.

JUDGE: Counsel for the insurance company, any objection to my receiving Mr. Bezzler's statement in evidence?

DEFENDANT'S ATTORNEY: Yes indeed. The statement is hearsay, and foundational evidence will demonstrate that it is not admissible under Rule 804(b)(3) because it was not against Bezzler's interest to admit to taking company assets. As I understand it, the plaintiff's contention that the foundation is sufficient to carry its burden of proving that the statement was against Mr. Bezzler's interest rests on the content of the statement itself.

JUDGE: Is that correct?

PLAINTIFF'S ATTORNEY: That's correct. I have nothing additional to offer by way of foundation.

DEFENDANT'S ATTORNEY: In that event, I'd like to call William Bord, a Datamark employee, to testify as a foundational witness.

JUDGE: Proceed, and please get right to the point. I like truly mini mini-trials.

DEFENDANT'S ATTORNEY: Mr. Bord, do you know about the all-employee meeting that Ms. Oh conducted on June 6?

A: I do.

DEFENDANT'S ATTORNEY: Do you know whether Lem Bezzler attended that meeting?

A: He did.

PLAINTIFF'S ATTORNEY: Objection, lack of foundation, no personal knowledge.

JUDGE: Overruled. The witness' testimony establishes that he has personal knowledge. Also, this is a foundational hearing. Evidence rules don't apply except for those pertaining to privilege. So on both grounds, I overrule that objection. *Is the judge's statement accurate?*

DEFENDANT'S ATTORNEY: Mr. Bord, please tell us what you heard Ms. Oh say at the meeting.

A: She said that based on an auditor's report, the company had been billed for and paid at least $65,000 for supplies that it had not actually received.

PLAINTIFF'S ATTORNEY: Objection, double hearsay. The witness is testifying to what Ms. Oh said that an auditor's report said. Moreover, Ms. Oh had no personal knowledge of the information referred to in the report.

DEFENDANT'S ATTORNEY: No hearsay is involved; Ms. Oh's statement is foundational for showing why Lem Bezzler might have falsely admitted to stealing from the company. Also, the statement is admissible as a party admission.

JUDGE: I'll overrule the objection. *(Is the ruling correct?)*

DEFENDANT'S ATTORNEY: Mr. Bord, what else did Ms. Oh say at the meeting?

A: She said that she was going to report the matter to the police, but that if an employee came forward privately and admitted to stealing from the company, she would not go to the police as long as the company's insurance policy, which provided coverage up to $100,000, paid the company for the amount that was taken.

DEFENDANT'S ATTORNEY: What, if anything, happened after Ms. Oh said this?

A: Mary Sindon, who works in the shipping department, shouted, "Oh my God, Patty Oh is just trying to cover the company's losses by scaring one of us into admitting to a theft and collecting the insurance!" *(Does Ms. Sindon's statement constitute an "excited utterance?")*

DEFENDANT'S ATTORNEY: Did you talk to Mr. Bezzler anytime after the meeting?

A: Yes, the next day. Lem said that maybe an employee could scratch the company's back as well as his own by admitting to taking more than Patty Oh wanted, and splitting the extra insurance money with the company.

PLAINTIFF'S ATTORNEY: Objection, hearsay.

DEFENDANT'S ATTORNEY: Admissible under Rule 803(3) as Mr. Bezzler's state of mind, Your Honor. It's the equivalent of a statement of plan or intent. *(Is the defense attorney's argument correct?)*

DEFENDANT'S ATTORNEY: Did you ever hear from Mr. Bezzler again?

§ 15.09 RESIDUAL HEARSAY (RULE 807) 763

A: He never came to work again. He telephoned me at home a few weeks later. His voice was barely audible. He said that he'd taken some bad drugs, that he wasn't going to make it, and that he wanted me to know that he hadn't really stolen any money.

PLAINTIFF'S ATTORNEY: Objection to the remark about the money, hearsay.

DEFENDANT'S ATTORNEY: Mr. Bezzler's remark is admissible as a dying declaration. (*Is the defense attorney's response correct?*)

DEFENDANT'S ATTORNEY: Also, what Mr. Bezzler told this witness conflicts with the signed statement that plaintiff Datamark has offered, so it's also an inconsistent statement, admissible to prove that Mr. Bezzler had not stolen any money. (*Is this response accurate?*)

DEFENDANT'S ATTORNEY: No further questions.

JUDGE: Counsel for Oh, any questions for this witness?

PLAINTIFF'S ATTORNEY: Just one. Mr. Bord, when you spoke to Mr. Bezzler the day after the meeting, did he say anything about Patty Oh?

A: Yes. He said that a former employee had once told him that a promise by Patty Oh wasn't worth the time of day.

PLAINTIFF'S ATTORNEY: (*Can you think of a valid non-hearsay use for this testimony?*)

JUDGE: If that concludes the foundational evidence, I'll hear brief argument from counsel concerning the admissibility of Mr. Bezzler's statement as a declaration against interest.

PLAINTIFF'S ATTORNEY: (*Argue based on the foundational record above that the written confession qualifies as Lem Bezzler's statement against interest.*)

DEFENDANT'S ATTORNEY: (*Argue based on the foundational record above that the written confession does not qualify as Lem Bezzler's statement against interest.*)

JUDGE: (*Rule on the admissibility of Lem Bezzler's written confession under Rule 804(b)(3).*)

Problem 15-38: Transcript Analysis II

Bjorn Freed was fired from his job as a financial aid counselor at State University. When Bjorn was fired, his boss sent an e-mail message to the other financial aid counselors stating that Bjorn was fired for repeatedly coming to work late and intoxicated to such an extent that he was unable to fulfill his job responsibilities, and reminding the counselors that the University had "zero tolerance" for intoxication on the job. Claiming that the e-mail statement was false, Bjorn sued the University for defamation; the University's defense is that the statement was true. *Please indicate the evidentiary propriety of the numbered portions of the transcript below.*

PLAINTIFF'S ATTORNEY: Your Honor, I'd like to begin the plaintiff's case by offering into evidence a printout of the allegedly defamatory electronic mail message that includes the statement that "Mr. Freed repeatedly came to work late and intoxicated to such an extent that he was unable to fulfill his job responsibilities." It has been stipulated that this message was sent by my client's boss to the other financial aid counselors in the department.

JUDGE: Counsel, any hearsay problems with the message that I should be concerned about?

PLAINTIFF'S ATTORNEY: *(How would you respond to the judge's question?)*

PLAINTIFF'S ATTORNEY: We now call Elsa Lyon as a witness.

Preliminary questioning establishes that Elsa was the assistant manager of the financial aid office during the time that Bjorn worked there.

PLAINTIFF'S ATTORNEY: Ms. Lyon, you and Mr. Freed were responsible for working on the financial aid problems of newly admitted students, correct?

DEFENDANT'S ATTORNEY: Objection, leading.

JUDGE: *(What ruling on the objection?)*

A: That's correct.

PLAINTIFF'S ATTORNEY: How many employees worked in the financial aid office during the time that Mr. Freed was an employee?

A: Usually there were about 10 of us.

PLAINTIFF'S ATTORNEY: Did any of these employees ever mention to you that they had noticed Mr. Freed come to work late or intoxicated?

A: No.

DEFENDANT'S ATTORNEY: Objection and move to strike, hearsay.

JUDGE: Overruled, the witness may answer. *Is this a correct ruling?*

DEFENDANT'S ATTORNEY: I also object based on lack of foundation. Without additional evidence explaining why other employees would complain about the plaintiff to this witness, the lack of complaints is irrelevant.

PLAINTIFF'S ATTORNEY: *(Please indicate whether you believe that the record as it stands is sufficient to establish the relevance of the previous answer. If you think that additional foundational evidence is needed, please make an*

§ 15.09   RESIDUAL HEARSAY (RULE 807)   765

offer of proof as to what additional evidence you would offer.)

PLAINTIFF'S ATTORNEY: Ms. Lyon, did you ever personally notice that Bjorn was intoxicated at work?

A: I remember a couple of times I saw him stumbling. I asked him what the problem was, and he told me that his hip was bothering him.

DEFENDANT'S ATTORNEY: Objection and move to strike what Mr. Freed said, hearsay.

PLAINTIFF'S ATTORNEY: It's a party admission, and also admissible under the state of mind exception, Rule 803(3) and the exception for a medical condition, Rule 803(4).

JUDGE: *(How would you rule on the objection?)*

PLAINTIFF'S ATTORNEY: Ms. Lyon, I'd like to take you back to the Wednesday before Mr. Freed was fired. Do you remember that day?

A: I do.

PLAINTIFF'S ATTORNEY: And what happened that day?

A: Joy Adams, another financial aid counselor, told me that she'd been on a coffee break with Mr. Freed. Joy said that while they were in the employee's coffee room, Jan Attor, a maintenance worker, pulled out a bottle of whiskey and started to take a drink. According to Joy, Mr. Freed went over to Jan, said that drinking on the job was against University rules, and told Jan to put the bottle away or he'd have to file a report.

DEFENDANT'S ATTORNEY: Objection as to what Mr. Freed said to the maintenance worker, irrelevant and hearsay.

JUDGE: Overruled. *(Is this a correct ruling?)*

DEFENDANT'S ATTORNEY: I also object that Ms. Adams' statement to Ms. Lyons is hearsay.

JUDGE: Counsel for Mr. Freed, any response?

PLAINTIFF'S ATTORNEY: Yes. Ms. Adams's statement is offered under the residual hearsay exception, Rule 807. As counsel for the University will concede, I gave counsel written notice of my intention to offer Ms. Adams's statement into evidence under Rule 807 more than a month ago. The notice also referred to the contents of Ms. Adams' statement and gave her work address and telephone number.

DEFENDANT'S ATTORNEY: Counsel is correct with regard to the notice, but my hearsay objection still stands.

JUDGE: Counsel for Mr. Freed, is there any additional foundational evidence you want me to consider before making my ruling under Rule 807?

PLAINTIFF'S ATTORNEY: Just a few more questions, thank you. Do you know how much time passed between the time that Mr. Freed allegedly spoke to Jan Attor and Ms. Adams told you what Mr. Freed had said?

A: It couldn't have been more than 20 minutes. Coffee breaks are limited to 15 minutes, and Ms. Adams told me that she'd made a quick stop at the publications office upstairs to pick up some pamphlets after she finished her coffee break.

DEFENSE ATTORNEY: Objection, speculation as to the length of time.

JUDGE: *(What ruling?)*

PLAINTIFF'S ATTORNEY: In your opinion, is Ms. Adams honest and trustworthy?

DEFENDANT'S ATTORNEY: *(What if any objection might you make to this question?)*

A: Yes.

PLAINTIFF'S ATTORNEY: To your knowledge, were Mr. Freed and Ms. Adams anything more than work colleagues to each other?

A: No. Their relationship was strictly professional.

PLAINTIFF'S ATTORNEY: Did you ever receive independent corroboration of Joy's statement?

A: Actually, yes. I know Jan, and a few minutes after I talked to Joy, Jan came over to my desk. Jan handed me a whiskey bottle and ask me to put it away for her for the day, and said that some "hard ass" — pardon my French, those were Jan's words — had gotten on her for having a bit of liquid refreshment.

DEFENDANT'S ATTORNEY: Objection. Evidence independent of the statement is inadmissible on the issue of trustworthiness when hearsay is offered pursuant to Rule 807.

JUDGE: *(What ruling on the objection?)*

JUDGE: Counsel for Mr. Freed, let me ask you this. What effort, if any, did you make to produce Ms. Adams as a witness?

PLAINTIFF'S ATTORNEY: My process server went to serve her with a subpoena. She told him that the date of the trial made it impossible for her to attend. She said that the trial was set during the week that entering students' financial aid requests had to be processed, and that because of a recent resignation she was the only available employee who could do it and that hundreds of students depended on her for their tuition. When the process server told me this, I said not to subpoena Ms. Adams, that we'd go the

Rule 807 route instead. That's when I served the Rule 807 notice on defense counsel.

DEFENDANT'S ATTORNEY: I'll accept counsel's representations as to the reasons why Ms. Adams was not subpoenaed. However, as those circumstances do not constitute unavailability, I object to the admission of the statement.

JUDGE: Overruled. Admissibility does not depend on a showing that the witness is unavailable. (*Is this an accurate response to the objection?*)

DEFENDANT'S ATTORNEY: I also object on the basis that Rule 807(B) requires counsel to make a reasonable effort to procure more probative evidence. Because counsel's representation establishes that Ms. Adams was available for subpoena and that counsel intentionally declined to subpoena her, counsel has not satisfied Rule 807(B). I will also point out that counsel had an opportunity to but did not depose Ms. Adams.

JUDGE: In making my ruling, I can properly consider the fact that after receiving the notice the University knew exactly where Ms. Adams worked and could have subpoenaed her as a witness or deposed her if it so desired. *Is the judge's statement accurate?*

JUDGE: (*How would you rule on the objection that the plaintiff did not make a reasonable effort to procure more probative evidence?*)

DEFENDANT'S ATTORNEY: I also object under Rule 807(A) that the foundation is inadequate in that Ms. Adams's testimony does not relate to a material fact. That language is a signal that hearsay is admissible under Rule 807 only if it pertains to a significant issue. Here, Ms. Adams statement pertains to a peripheral issue, what the plaintiff may have said that may reflect on his state of mind. Your Honor ought not to admit hearsay under Rule 807 for such a marginal purpose.

JUDGE: (*How would you rule on the admissibility of Ms. Adams' statement?*)

PLAINTIFF'S ATTORNEY: Nothing further from this witness at this time.

JUDGE: Defense counsel, any additional questions?

DEFENDANT'S ATTORNEY: Just a few. Ms. Lyon, you've been testifying about something that happened on the Wednesday before Mr. Freed was fired. Let me call your attention to Thursday, the very next day. You were at work that day, correct?

A: I was.

DEFENDANT'S ATTORNEY: And Mr. Freed was working that day as well?

A: Yes, he was.

DEFENDANT'S ATTORNEY: And after lunch, you saw Ms. Adams walk over to Mr. Freed's desk and heard her tell him that she had noticed him at lunchtime belting down the sauce pretty good at the Salty Dog Tavern?

A: Yes.

DEFENDANT'S ATTORNEY: And Ms. Adams was using a normal tone of voice?

A: Well, she didn't shout but she wasn't whispering, if that's what you mean.

DEFENDANT'S ATTORNEY: Were there other financial aid employees in the office at this time?

A: Yes, about five to six other people.

DEFENDANT'S ATTORNEY: And is it fair to say that most of them were in at least as good a position to hear what Ms. Adams said to Mr. Freed as you were?

PLAINTIFF'S ATTORNEY: Objection, speculation.

JUDGE: Overruled, the witness may answer. (*Is this a proper ruling?*)

A: Yes, I'd say so.

DEFENDANT'S ATTORNEY: Mr. Freed said nothing in response to Ms. Adams's accusation, did he?

PLAINTIFF'S ATTORNEY: (*What if any objection might you make to the form of this question?*)

A: No, he just sat there and then started shuffling through some papers. Ms. Adams just walked away.

PLAINTIFF'S ATTORNEY: Objection, move to strike this entire line of questioning as hearsay by Ms. Adams.

DEFENDANT'S ATTORNEY: Party admission, Your Honor.

JUDGE: (*How would you rule on the objection?*)

§ 15.10 MULTIPLE-CHOICE REVIEW PROBLEMS

Review Problem 15-A

O'Brien, the defendant in an automobile accident case, seeks to offer into evidence deposition testimony from Biscailuz stating that "I saw O'Brien's car make a full stop before entering the intersection where the collision took place." O'Brien can establish a foundation for reading this deposition testimony into the record at trial by offering evidence that:

1. Biscailuz is not present in the courtroom, and O'Brien sent Biscailuz at least three e-mail messages and left 4–5 telephone messages on Biscailuz's answering machine during the two weeks prior to trial informing Biscailuz of the trial date and the exact place and time of the trial.

2. Biscailuz is not present in the courtroom, and O'Brien produces a letter from Biscailuz's employer stating: "We have a deadline on a big project and since our place of business is 20 miles from the courthouse we simply can't allow Biscailuz to take the time to go to court."

3. Biscailuz appears at trial and testifies that "I have no recollection of anything leading up to or concerning the collision."

4. Biscailuz appears at trial and testifies as to the events leading up to the collision, but also testifies that "I have no recollection whatsoever of the testimony I gave at deposition."

Review Problem 15-B

Testifying on Rich's behalf in a lawsuit against a ski resort for personal injuries, Eileen testifies that "I know that it was 9 a.m. when the ski lift broke down because I looked at Rich's watch that was inside the pork pie-style hat that Rich always wears when he skis and that was lying on the lift chair between us." A year later, Rich is charged with armed robbery of a skier. The skier testifies that the robber wore a pork pie-style hat. The prosecution then offers evidence that Eileen is unavailable as a witness and seeks to offer her "former testimony" from the personal injury trial as evidence that Rich was the robber. *The judge should rule that:*

1. Eileen's testimony from the personal injury trial is inadmissible because Rich did not have a chance to cross-examine her in that trial.

2. Eileen's testimony from the personal injury trial is inadmissible because Rich's motives with respect to the pork pie hat testimony in the criminal trial are too dissimilar.

3. Eileen's testimony from the personal injury trial is inadmissible because former testimony from civil proceedings is inadmissible in criminal proceedings.

4. Eileen's testimony from the personal injury trial is admissible as former testimony because Rich had himself offered that testimony into evidence.

Review Problem 15-C

As Jelani is waiting for a traffic light to change to green, someone rips open the driver's side door, shoves Jelani to the side, and drives off. While the car is traveling at high speed, the driver opens the passenger side door and shoves Jelani out of the car. By the time Marie, another driver, sees Jelani and stops to help him, he is barely breathing and is bleeding profusely from multiple wounds. Jelani whispers to Marie, "I know I'm done for. Please just tell them that it was Eddie Malone who did this to me." Jelani then becomes unconscious. Eddie Malone is arrested, and when Jelani survives, Malone is charged with attempted murder and carjacking. However, by the time of trial Jelani has vanished and the judge rules that he is unavailable as a witness. The prosecution then offers Jelani's statement into evidence as a "dying declaration" by calling Marie as a witness. *In response to Malone's objection, the judge should rule that:*

1. The statement is inadmissible hearsay because it does not concern the cause and circumstances of Jelani's injuries.

2. The statement is inadmissible hearsay because dying declarations are not admissible in attempted murder and carjacking prosecutions.

3. The statement is inadmissible hearsay because Jelani survived the attack.

4. The statement is admissible under the dying declarations hearsay exception.

5. Jelani's statement is inadmissible under the Confrontation Clause.

Review Problem 15-D

Walt Whitman is arrested for cultivating a large quantity of marijuana in a national wilderness area. Whitman tells the arresting officer that "I didn't have any choice. The person you really want is John Barth, these are all his plants and he told me he'd have me killed if I didn't look after them." The government eventually charges Barth with illegally cultivating marijuana, and the judge rules that Whitman is unavailable as a witness after Whitman repeatedly refuses to testify though the government has granted him "use immunity." The government then seeks to offer Whitman's statement to the arresting officer implicating Barth into evidence. *In response to Barth's objection, the judge should rule that:*

1. The statement is inadmissible hearsay.

2. The statement is admissible as a declaration against interest.

3. The statement is admissible as a "co-conspirator party admission."

4. The statement is admissible under the state of mind hearsay exception.

5. The statement is inadmissible under the Confrontation Clause.

Review Problem 15-E

Lilly Calla is charged with receiving stolen property after police officers responding to a 911 call found a cache of stolen electronic equipment in her garage. Calla's defense is that she was unaware of the equipment's presence. Calla seeks to offer evidence that on the morning of the day that he was attacked by another prisoner and killed, Bob Newton told his cellmate, "Some associate of that weasel Lilly Calla may have me killed for doing this, but at least I got back at her a few days ago, just before they put me in the slammer. I stole some fancy electronic equipment and hid it in Calla's garage, then made sure the cops found it before she did." Calla seeks to offer evidence of Newton's statement into evidence by calling the cellmate as a witness. *Upon objection by the government, the judge should rule that:*

1. Newton's statement is admissible as a present sense impression.

2. Newton's statement is admissible as a declaration against interest.

3. Newton's statement is inadmissible hearsay.

4. Newton's statement is admissible as a dying declaration.

5. The statement is inadmissible under the Confrontation Clause.

Review Problem 15-F

Kobashian sues Dour Chemical Co. for personal injuries allegedly caused by a chemical leak. Kobashian calls Lewis, a next-door neighbor, to testify to an out-of-court statement made to Lewis by Kobashian about 24 hours after the leak occurred. In response to Dour's hearsay objection, Kobashian makes an offer of proof that Lewis will testify that when Lewis stopped by and asked how Kobashian was feeling, Kobashian said that "I'm really feeling nauseous and I've got ringing in my ears." Dour's counsel then makes a further offer of proof that "If Lewis is allowed to testify, I intend to call Clark to testify to an opinion that Kobashian is a dishonest scoundrel." *The judge should respond to these offers of proof by ruling that:*

1. Lewis' testimony is inadmissible in the absence of foundational evidence that Lewis has medical training and that Kobashian made the statement in order to obtain a medical diagnosis or receive treatment.

2. Lewis' testimony is admissible but Clark's testimony is inadmissible unless and until Kobashian testifies under oath at trial.

3. Lewis' testimony is admissible but Clark's testimony is not because character evidence is not admissible in civil cases.

4. Lewis's testimony is admissible, and after Lewis testifies, Clark's testimony is also admissible.

Review Problem 15-G

After returning to the office after eating lunch at Penny's Always Open Diner, Maysie tells a co-worker that "I slipped on some wet noodles near the salad bar." Maysie sues Penny's for personal injuries and calls the co-worker to testify to the statement she made when she came back from lunch. *In response to Penny's objection, the court should rule that:*

1. If the statement fails to meet the foundational requirements for a present sense impression, it is inadmissible under Rule 807.

2. Since Maysie is a party, her statement is admissible as a party admission.

3. The statement is admissible under Rule 807 if the judge is convinced that it was made under circumstances demonstrating that it is trustworthy.

4. The statement is admissible as non-hearsay "words of independent legal significance."

5. The statement is admissible under Rule 807 if Maysie offers evidence sufficient to support a jury finding that it was made under circumstances demonstrating that it is trustworthy.

Review Problem 15-H

In a murder prosecution, the prosecutor seeks to offer a hearsay statement into evidence against the defendant under Rule 807. *Which statement below is correct?*

1. The statement is admissible only if the declarant is unavailable as a witness under Rule 804(a).

2. The prosecutor has to offer evidence showing that the statement has "indicia of reliability."

3. The statement is inadmissible if it was made during grand jury proceedings and the defendant has no opportunity to question the declarant.

4. If the statement is "testimonial," it is inadmissible regardless of whether the defendant has an opportunity to question the declarant.

§ 15.11 CASE LIBRARY

WILLIAMSON v. UNITED STATES

United States Supreme Court 512 U.S. 594, 114 S. Ct. 2431, 129 L. Ed. 2d 476 (1994)

O'CONNOR, J., announced the judgment of the Court and delivered the opinion of the Court with respect to Parts I, II-A, and II-B, in which BLACKMUN, STEVENS SCALIA, SOUTER, and GINSBURG, JJ., joined, and an opinion with respect to Part II-C, in which SCALIA, J., joined. SCALIA, J., filed a concurring opinion. GINSBURG, J., filed an opinion concurring in part and concurring in the judgment, in which BLACKMUN, STEVENS, and SOUTER, JJ., joined. KENNEDY, J., filed an opinion concurring in the judgment, in which REHNQUIST, C. J., and THOMAS, J., joined. JUSTICE O'CONNOR delivered the opinion of the Court, except as to Part II-C. In this case we clarify the scope of the hearsay exception for statements against penal interest. Fed. Rule Evid. 804(b)(3).

I

A deputy sheriff stopped the rental car driven by Reginald Harris for weaving on the highway. Harris consented to a search of the car, which revealed 19 kilograms of cocaine in two suitcases in the trunk. Harris was promptly arrested.

Shortly after Harris' arrest, Special Agent Donald Walton of the Drug Enforcement Administration (DEA) interviewed him by telephone. During that conversation, Harris said that he got the cocaine from an unidentified Cuban in Fort Lauderdale; that the cocaine belonged to petitioner Williamson; and that it was to be delivered that night to a particular dumpster. Williamson was also connected to Harris by physical evidence: The luggage bore the initials of Williamson's sister, Williamson was listed as an additional driver on the car rental agreement, and an envelope addressed to Williamson and a receipt with Williamson's girlfriend's address were found in the glove compartment.

Several hours later, Agent Walton spoke to Harris in person. During that interview, Harris said he had rented the car a few days earlier and had driven it to Fort Lauderdale to meet Williamson. According to Harris, he had gotten the cocaine from a Cuban who was Williamson's acquaintance, and the Cuban had put the cocaine in the car with a note telling Harris how to deliver the drugs. Harris repeated that he had been instructed to leave the drugs in a certain dumpster, to return to his car, and to leave without waiting for anyone to pick up the drugs.

Agent Walton then took steps to arrange a controlled delivery of the cocaine. But as Walton was preparing to leave the interview room, Harris "got out of [his] chair . . . and . . . took a half step toward [Walton] . . . and . . . said, . . . 'I can't let you do that,' threw his hands up and said 'that's not true, I can't let you go up there for no reason.'" Harris told Walton he had lied about the Cuban, the note, and the dumpster. The real story, Harris said, was that he was transporting the cocaine to Atlanta for Williamson, and that Williamson was traveling in front of him in another rental car. Harris added that after his car was stopped, Williamson turned around and drove past the location of the stop, where he could see Harris' car with its trunk open. Because Williamson had apparently seen the police searching the car, Harris explained that it would be impossible to make a controlled delivery.

Harris told Walton that he had lied about the source of the drugs because he was afraid of Williamson. Though Harris freely implicated himself, he did not want his story to be recorded, and he refused to sign a written version of the statement. Walton testified that he had promised to report any cooperation by Harris to the Assistant United States Attorney. Walton said Harris was not promised any reward or other benefit for cooperating.

Williamson was eventually convicted of possessing cocaine with intent to distribute, conspiring to possess cocaine with intent to distribute, and traveling interstate to promote the distribution of cocaine. When called to testify at Williamson's trial, Harris refused, even though the prosecution gave him use immunity and the court ordered him to testify and eventually held him in contempt. The District Court then ruled that, under Rule 804(b)(3), Agent Walton could relate what Harris had said to him:

Williamson appealed his conviction, claiming that the admission of Harris' statements violated Rule 804(b)(3) and the Confrontation Clause of the Sixth Amendment. The Court of Appeals for the Eleventh Circuit affirmed without opinion, and we granted certiorari.

II

A

To decide whether Harris' confession is made admissible by Rule 804(b)(3), we must first determine what the Rule means by "statement," which Federal Rule of Evidence 801(a)(1) defines as "an oral or written assertion." One possible meaning, "a report or narrative," Webster's Third New International Dictionary connotes an extended declaration. Under this reading, Harris' entire confession — even if it contains both self-inculpatory and non-self-inculpatory parts — would be admissible so long as in the aggregate the confession sufficiently inculpates him. Another meaning of "statement," "a single declaration or remark," would make Rule 804(b)(3) cover only those declarations or remarks within the confession that are individually self-inculpatory.

Although the text of the Rule does not directly resolve the matter, the principle behind the Rule, so far as it is discernible from the text, points clearly to the narrower reading. Rule 804(b)(3) is founded on the commonsense notion that reasonable people, even reasonable people who are not especially honest, tend not to make self-inculpatory statements unless they believe them to be true. This notion simply does not extend to the broader definition of "statement." The fact that a person is making a broadly self-inculpatory confession does not make more credible the confession's non-self-inculpatory parts. One of the most effective ways to lie is to mix falsehood with truth, especially truth that seems particularly persuasive because of its self-inculpatory nature.

In this respect, it is telling that the non-self-inculpatory things Harris said in his first statement actually proved to be false, as Harris himself admitted during the second interrogation. And when part of the confession is actually self-exculpatory, the generalization on which Rule 804(b)(3) is founded becomes even less applicable. Self-exculpatory statements are exactly the ones which people are most likely to make even when they are false; and mere proximity to other, self-inculpatory, statements does not increase the plausibility of the self-exculpatory statements.

We therefore cannot agree with Justice Kennedy's suggestion that the Rule can be read as expressing a policy that collateral statements — even ones that are not in any way against the declarant's interest — are admissible. Nothing in the text of Rule 804(b)(3) or the general theory of the hearsay Rules suggests that admissibility should turn on whether a statement is collateral to a self-inculpatory statement. The fact that a statement is self-inculpatory does make it more reliable; but the fact that a statement is collateral to a self-inculpatory statement says nothing at all about the collateral statement's reliability. We see no reason why collateral statements, even ones that are neutral as to interest, should be treated any differently from other hearsay statements that are generally excluded.

Congress certainly could, subject to the constraints of the Confrontation Clause, make statements admissible based on their proximity to self-inculpatory statements. But we will not lightly assume that the ambiguous language means anything so inconsistent with the Rule's underlying theory. In our view, the most faithful reading of Rule 804(b)(3) is that it does not allow admission of non-self-inculpatory statements, even if they are made within a broader narrative that is generally self-inculpatory. The district court may not just assume for purposes of Rule 804(b)(3) that a statement is self-inculpatory because it is part of a fuller confession, and this is especially true when the statement implicates someone else. "The arrest statements of a codefendant have traditionally been viewed with special suspicion. Due to his strong motivation to implicate the defendant and to exonerate himself, a codefendant's statements about what the defendant said or did are less credible than ordinary hearsay evidence."

B

We also do not share Justice Kennedy's fears that our reading of the Rule "eviscerates the against penal interest exception," or makes it lack "meaningful effect." There are many circumstances in which Rule 804(b)(3) does allow the admission of statements that inculpate a criminal defendant. Even the confessions of arrested accomplices may be admissible if they are truly self-inculpatory, rather than merely attempts to shift blame or curry favor.

For instance, a declarant's squarely self-inculpatory confession — "yes, I killed X" — will likely be admissible under Rule 804(b)(3) against accomplices of his who are being tried under a co-conspirator liability theory. Likewise, by showing that the declarant knew something, a self-inculpatory statement can in some situations help the jury infer that his confederates knew it as well. And when seen with other evidence, an accomplice's self-inculpatory statement can inculpate the defendant directly: "I was robbing the bank on Friday morning," coupled with someone's testimony that the declarant and the defendant drove off together Friday morning, is evidence that the defendant also participated in the robbery.

Moreover, whether a statement is self-inculpatory or not can only be determined by viewing it in context. Even statements that are on their face neutral may actually be against the declarant's interest. "I hid the gun in Joe's apartment" may not be a confession of a crime; but if it is likely to help the police find the murder weapon, then it is certainly self-inculpatory. "Sam and I went to Joe's house" might be against the declarant's interest if a reasonable person in the declarant's shoes would realize that being linked to Joe and Sam would implicate the declarant in Joe and Sam's conspiracy. And other statements that give the police significant details about the crime may also, depending on the situation, be against the declarant's interest. The question under Rule 804(b)(3) is always whether the statement was sufficiently against the declarant's penal interest "that a reasonable person in the declarant's position would not have made the statement unless believing it to be true," and this question can only be answered in light of all the surrounding circumstances.

C

In this case, however, we cannot conclude that all that Harris said was properly admitted. Some of Harris' confession would clearly have been admissible under Rule 804(b)(3); for instance, when he said he knew there was cocaine in the suitcase, he essentially forfeited his only possible defense to a charge of cocaine possession, lack of knowledge. But other parts of his confession, especially the parts that implicated Williamson, did little to subject Harris himself to criminal liability. A reasonable person in Harris' position might even think that implicating someone else would decrease his practical exposure to criminal liability, at least so far as sentencing goes. Small fish in a big conspiracy often get shorter sentences than people who are running the whole show, especially if the small fish are willing to help the authorities catch the big ones.

Nothing in the record shows that the District Court or the Court of Appeals inquired whether each of the statements in Harris' confession was truly self-inculpatory. As we explained above, this can be a fact-intensive inquiry, which would require careful examination of all the circumstances surrounding the criminal activity involved; we therefore remand to the Court of Appeals to conduct this inquiry in the first instance.

In light of this disposition, we need not address Williamson's claim that the statements were also made inadmissible by the Confrontation Clause, and in particular we need not decide whether the hearsay exception for declarations against interest is "firmly rooted" for Confrontation Clause purposes. We note, however, that the very fact that a statement is genuinely self-inculpatory — which our reading of Rule 804(b)(3) requires — is itself one of the "particularized guarantees of trustworthiness" that makes a statement admissible under the Confrontation Clause. We also need not decide whether the second sentence of Rule 804(b)(3) — "A statement tending to expose the declarant to criminal liability *and offered to exculpate the accused* is not admissible unless corroborating circumstances clearly indicate the trustworthiness of the statement" (emphasis added) — also requires that statements inculpating the accused be supported by corroborating circumstances. The judgment of the Court of Appeals is vacated, and the case is remanded for further proceedings.

So ordered.

JUSTICE GINSBURG, with whom JUSTICE BLACKMUN, JUSTICE STEVENS, and JUSTICE SOUTER join, concurring in part and concurring in the judgment.

The Court recognizes the untrustworthiness of statements implicating another person. A person arrested in incriminating circumstances has a strong incentive to shift blame or downplay his own role in comparison with that of others, in hopes of receiving a shorter sentence and leniency in exchange for cooperation.

Unlike Justice O'Connor, however, I conclude that Reginald Harris' statements, as recounted by Drug Enforcement Administration (DEA) Special Agent Donald E. Walton, do not fit, even in part, within the exception described in Rule 804(b)(3), for Harris' arguably inculpatory statements are too closely intertwined with his self-serving declarations to be ranked as trustworthy. Harris was caught red-handed with 19 kilos of cocaine — enough to subject even a first-time offender to a minimum of 12 1/2 years' imprisonment. He could have denied knowing the drugs were in the car's trunk, but that strategy would have brought little prospect of thwarting a criminal prosecution. He therefore admitted involvement, but did so in a way that minimized his own role and shifted blame to petitioner Williamson (and a Cuban man named Shawn).

To the extent some statements tended to incriminate Harris, they provided only marginal or cumulative evidence of his guilt. They project an image of a person acting not against his penal interest, but striving mightily to shift principal responsibility to someone else. For these reasons, I would hold that none of Harris' hearsay statements were admissible under Rule 804(b)(3). I concur in the Court's decision to vacate the Court of Appeals' judgment, however, because I have not examined the entire trial court record; I therefore cannot say the Government should be denied an opportunity to argue that the erroneous admission of the hearsay statements, in light of the other evidence introduced at trial, constituted harmless error.

Justice Kennedy, with whom The Chief Justice and Justice Thomas join, concurring in the judgment.

I

The rationale of the hearsay exception for statements against interest is that people seldom "make statements which are damaging to themselves unless satisfied for good reason that they are true." Advisory Committee's Notes on Fed. Rule Evid. 804. Of course, the declarant may make his statement against interest (such as "I shot the bank teller") together with collateral but related declarations (such as "John Doe drove the getaway car"). The admissibility of those collateral statements under Rule 804(b)(3) is the issue we must decide here.

The Court resolves the issue, as I understand its opinion, by adopting the extreme position that no collateral statements are admissible under Rule 804(b)(3). The Court reaches that conclusion by relying on the "principle behind the Rule" that reasonable people do not make statements against their interest unless they are telling the truth, and reasons that this policy "expressed in the Rule's text," "simply does not extend" to collateral statements. Though conceding that Congress can "make statements admissible based on their proximity to self-inculpatory statements," the Court says that it cannot "lightly assume that the ambiguous language means anything so inconsistent with the Rule's underlying theory."

With respect, I must disagree with this analysis. All agree that the justification for admission of hearsay statements against interest was, as it still is, that reasonable people do not make those statements unless believing them to be true, but that has not resolved the long-running debate over the admissibility of collateral statements, as to which there is no clear consensus in the authorities. Indeed, to the extent the authorities come close to any consensus, they support admission of some collateral statements. Given that the underlying principle for the hearsay exception has not resolved the debate over collateral statements one way or the other, I submit that we should not assume that the text of Rule 804(b)(3), which is silent about collateral statements, in fact incorporates one of the competing positions. The Rule's silence no more incorporates Jefferson's position respecting collateral statements than it does McCormick's or Wigmore's.

II

Because the text of Rule 804(b)(3) expresses no position regarding the admissibility of collateral statements, we must determine whether there are other authoritative guides on the question. In my view, three sources demonstrate that Rule 804(b)(3) allows the admission of some collateral statements: the Advisory Committee's Note, the common law of the hearsay exception for statements against interest, and the general presumption that Congress does not enact statutes that have almost no effect.

First, the Advisory Committee's Note establishes that some collateral statements are admissible. In fact, it refers in specific terms to the issue we here confront: "Ordinarily the third-party confession is thought of in terms of exculpating the accused, but this is by no means always or necessarily the case: it may include statements implicating him, and under the general theory of declarations against interest they would be admissible as related statements."

Second, even if the Advisory Committee's Note were silent about collateral statements, I would not adopt a rule excluding all statements collateral or related to the specific words against penal interest. Absent contrary indications, we can presume that Congress intended the principles and terms used in the Federal Rules of Evidence to be applied as they were at common law. "From the very beginning of this exception, it has been held that a declaration against interest is admissible, not only to prove the disserving fact stated, but also to prove other facts contained in collateral statements connected with the disserving statement."

There is yet a third reason weighing against the Court's interpretation, one specific to statements against penal interest that inculpate the accused. There is no dispute that the text of Rule 804(b)(3) contemplates the admission of those particular statements. Absent a textual direction to the contrary, therefore, we should assume that Congress intended the penal interest exception for inculpatory statements to have some meaningful effect. That counsels against adopting a rule excluding collateral statements.

To be sure, under the approach adopted by the Court, there are some situations where the Rule would still apply. For example, if the declarant said that he stole certain goods, the statement could be admitted in a prosecution of the accused for receipt of stolen goods in order to show that the goods were stolen. But as the commentators have recognized, it is likely to be the rare case where the precise self-inculpatory words of the declarant, without more, also inculpate the defendant. I would not presume that Congress intended the penal interest exception to the Rule to have so little effect with respect to statements that inculpate the accused.

I note finally that the Court's decision applies to statements against penal interest that exculpate the accused as well as to those that inculpate the accused. Thus, if the declarant said, "I robbed the store alone," only the portion of the statement in which the declarant said "I robbed the store" could be introduced by a criminal defendant on trial for the robbery. The Court gives no justification for such a rule and no explanation that Congress intended the exception for exculpatory statements to have this limited effect.

III

Though I would conclude that Rule 804(b)(3) allows admission of statements collateral to the precise words against interest, that conclusion of course does not answer the remaining question whether all collateral statements related to the statement against interest are admissible; and if not, what limiting principles should apply.

It appears that the Advisory Committee's Note contemplates exclusion of a collateral self-serving statement, but admission of a collateral neutral statement. In the criminal context, a self-serving statement is one that tends to reduce the charges or mitigate the punishment for which the declarant might be liable. For example, if two masked gunmen robbed a bank and one of them shot and killed the bank teller, a statement by one robber that the other robber was the triggerman may be the kind of self-serving statement that should be inadmissible. By contrast, when two or more people are capable of committing a crime and the declarant simply names the involved parties, that statement often is considered neutral, not self-serving.

In sum, I would adhere to the following approach with respect to statements against penal interest that inculpate the accused. A court first should determine whether the declarant made a statement that contained a fact against penal interest. If so, the court should admit all statements related to the precise statement against penal interest, subject to two limits. Consistent with the Advisory Committee's Note, the court should exclude a collateral statement that is so self-serving as to render it unreliable (if, for example, it shifts blame to someone else for a crime the defendant could have committed). In addition, in cases where the statement was made under circumstances where it is likely that the declarant had a significant motivation to obtain favorable treatment, as when the government made an explicit offer of leniency in exchange for the declarant's admission of guilt, the entire statement should be inadmissible.

GILES v. CALIFORNIA
United States Supreme Court
554 U.S. 353, 128 S.Ct. 2678 (2008)

JUSTICE SCALIA delivered the opinion of the Court, except as to Part II-D-2.

We consider whether a defendant forfeits his Sixth Amendment right to confront a witness against him when a judge determines that a wrongful act by the defendant made the witness unavailable to testify at trial.

I

On September 29, 2002, petitioner Dwayne Giles shot his ex-girlfriend, Brenda Avie, outside the garage of his grandmother's house. No witness saw the shooting, but Giles' niece heard what transpired from inside the house. She heard Giles and Avie speaking in conversational tones. Avie then yelled "Granny" several times and a series of gunshots sounded. Giles' niece and grandmother ran outside and saw Giles standing near Avie with a gun in his hand. Avie, who had not been carrying a weapon, had been shot six times. Giles fled the scene after the shooting. He was apprehended by police about two weeks later and charged with murder.

At trial, Giles testified that he had acted in self-defense. Giles described Avie as jealous, and said he knew that she had once shot a man, that he had seen her threaten people with a knife, and that she had vandalized his home and car on prior occasions. He said that on the day of the shooting, Avie came to his grandmother's house and threatened to kill him and his new girlfriend, who had been at the house earlier. Giles testified that after Avie threatened him at the house, he went into the garage and retrieved a gun, took the safety off, and started walking toward the back door of the house. He said that Avie charged at him, and that he was afraid she had something in her hand. According to Giles, he closed his eyes and fired several shots, but did not intend to kill Avie.

Prosecutors sought to introduce statements that Avie had made to a police officer responding to a domestic-violence report about three weeks before the shooting. Avie, who was crying when she spoke, told the officer that Giles had accused her of having an affair, and that after the two began to argue, Giles grabbed her by the shirt, lifted her off the floor, and began to choke her. According to Avie, when she broke free and fell to the floor, Giles punched her in the face and head, and after she broke free again, he opened a folding knife, held it about three feet away from her, and threatened to kill her if he found her cheating on him. Over Giles' objection, the trial court admitted these statements into evidence under a provision of California law that permits admission of out-of-court statements describing the infliction or threat of physical injury on a declarant when the declarant is unavailable to testify at trial and the prior statements are deemed trustworthy. Cal. Evid. Code § 1370.

A jury convicted Giles of first-degree murder. He appealed. While his appeal was pending, this Court decided in *Crawford* v. *Washington*, that the Confrontation Clause requires that a defendant have the opportunity to confront the witnesses who give testimony against him, except in cases where an exception to the confrontation right was recognized at the time of the founding. The California Court of Appeal held that the admission of Avie's unconfronted statements at Giles' trial did not violate the Confrontation Clause as construed by *Crawford* because *Crawford* recognized a doctrine of forfeiture by wrongdoing. It concluded that Giles had forfeited his right to confront Avie because he had committed the murder for which he was on trial, and because his intentional criminal act made Avie unavailable to testify. The California Supreme Court affirmed on the same ground. We granted certiorari.

II

The Sixth Amendment . . . contemplates that a witness who makes testimonial statements admitted against a defendant will ordinarily be present at trial for cross-examination, and that if the witness is unavailable, his prior testimony will be introduced only if the defendant had a prior opportunity to cross-examine him. *Crawford*. The State does not dispute here, and we accept without deciding, that Avie's statements accusing Giles of assault were testimonial. But it maintains that the Sixth Amendment did not prohibit prosecutors from introducing the statements because an exception to the confrontation guarantee permits the use of a witness's unconfronted testimony if a judge finds, as the judge did in this case, that the defendant committed a wrongful act that rendered the witness unavailable to testify at trial. We held in *Crawford* that the Confrontation Clause is "most naturally read as a reference to the right of confrontation at common law, admitting only those exceptions established at the time of the founding." We therefore ask whether the theory of forfeiture by wrongdoing accepted by the California Supreme Court is a founding-era exception to the confrontation right.

A

We have previously acknowledged that two forms of testimonial statements were admitted at common law even though they were unconfronted. The first of these were declarations made by a speaker who was both on the brink of death and aware that he was dying. Avie did not make the unconfronted statements admitted at Giles' trial when she was dying, so her statements do not fall within this historic exception.

A second common-law doctrine, which we will refer to as forfeiture by wrongdoing, permitted the introduction of statements of a witness who was "detained" or "kept away" by the "means or procurement" of the defendant. The doctrine has roots in the 1666 decision in *Lord Morley's Case*, at which judges concluded that a witness's having been "detained by the means or procurement of the prisoner," provided a basis to read testimony previously given at a coroner's inquest. Courts and commentators also concluded that wrongful procurement of a witness's absence was among the grounds for admission of statements made at bail and committal hearings conducted under the Marian statutes, which directed justices of the peace to take the statements of felony suspects and the persons bringing the suspects before the magistrate, and to certify those statements to the court. This class of confronted statements was also admissible if the witness who made them was dead or unable to travel.

The terms used to define the scope of the forfeiture rule suggest that the exception applied only when the defendant engaged in conduct *designed* to prevent the witness from testifying. We are aware of no case in which the exception was invoked although the defendant had not engaged in conduct designed to prevent a witness from testifying, such as offering a bribe.

B

The manner in which the rule was applied makes plain that unconfronted testimony would *not* be admitted without a showing that the defendant intended to prevent a witness from testifying. In cases where the evidence suggested that the defendant had caused a person to be absent, but had not done so to prevent the person from testifying — as in the typical murder case involving accusatorial statements by the victim — the testimony was excluded unless it was confronted or fell within the dying-declaration exception. Prosecutors do not appear to have even *argued* that the judge could admit the unconfronted statements because the defendant committed the murder for which he was on trial.

The State and the dissent note that common-law authorities justified the wrongful-procurement rule by invoking the maxim that a defendant should not be permitted to benefit from his own wrong. But as the evidence amply shows, the "wrong" and the "evil Practices" to which these statements referred was conduct *designed* to prevent a witness from testifying. The absence of a forfeiture rule covering this sort of conduct would create an intolerable incentive for defendants to bribe, intimidate, or even kill witnesses against them. There is nothing mysterious about courts' refusal to carry the rationale further. The notion that judges may strip the defendant of a right that the Constitution deems essential to a fair trial, on the basis of a prior *judicial* assessment that the defendant is guilty as charged, does not sit well with the right to trial by jury. It is akin, one might say, to "dispensing with jury trial because a defendant is obviously guilty." *Crawford.*

In 1997, this Court approved a Federal Rule of Evidence, entitled "Forfeiture by Wrongdoing," which applies only when the defendant "engaged or acquiesced in wrongdoing that was intended to, and did, procure the unavailability of the declarant as a witness." Fed. Rule of Evid. 804(b)(6). We have described this as a rule "which codifies the forfeiture doctrine." *Davis* v. *Washington.* Every commentator we are aware of has concluded the requirement of intent "means that the exception applies only if the defendant has in mind the particular purpose of making the witness unavailable." The commentators come out this way because the dissent's claim that knowledge is sufficient to show intent is emphatically *not* the modern view.

In sum, our interpretation of the common-law forfeiture rule is supported by (1) the most natural reading of the language used at common law; (2) the absence of common-law cases *admitting* prior statements on a forfeiture theory when the defendant had not engaged in conduct designed to prevent a witness from testifying; (3) the common law's uniform exclusion of unconfronted inculpatory testimony by murder victims (except testimony given with awareness of impending death) in the innumerable cases in which the defendant was on trial for killing the victim, but was not shown to have done so for the purpose of preventing testimony; (4) a subsequent history in which the dissent's broad forfeiture theory has not been applied. The first two and the last are highly persuasive; the third is in our view conclusive.

D

2.

Having destroyed its own case, the dissent issues a thinly veiled invitation to overrule *Crawford* and adopt an approach not much different from the regime of *Ohio* v. *Roberts*, under which the Court would create the exceptions that it thinks consistent with the policies underlying the confrontation guarantee, regardless of how that guarantee was historically understood. The "basic purposes and objectives" of forfeiture doctrine, it says, require that a defendant who wrongfully caused the absence of a witness be deprived of his confrontation rights, whether or not there was any such rule applicable at common law.

If we were to reason from the "basic purposes and objectives" of the forfeiture doctrine, we are not at all sure we would come to the dissent's favored result. The common-law forfeiture rule was aimed at removing the otherwise powerful incentive for defendants to intimidate, bribe, and kill the witnesses against them — in other words, it is grounded in "the ability of courts to protect the integrity of their proceedings." *Davis.* The boundaries of the doctrine seem to us intelligently fixed so as to avoid a principle repugnant to our constitutional system of trial by jury: that those murder defendants whom the judge considers guilty (after less than a full trial, mind you, and of course before the jury has pronounced guilt) should be deprived of fair-trial rights, lest they benefit from their judge-determined wrong.

The larger problem with the dissent's argument, however, is that the guarantee of confrontation is no guarantee at all if it is subject to whatever exceptions courts from time to time consider "fair." It is not the role of courts to extrapolate from the words of the Sixth Amendment to the values behind it, and then to enforce its guarantees only to the extent they serve (in the courts' views) those underlying values. The Sixth Amendment seeks fairness indeed — but seeks it through very specific means (one of which is confrontation) that were the trial rights of Englishmen. It "does not suggest any open-ended exceptions from the confrontation requirement to be developed by the courts." *Crawford.*

E

The dissent closes by pointing out that a forfeiture rule which ignores *Crawford* would be particularly helpful to women in abusive relationships — or at least particularly helpful in punishing their abusers. Not as helpful as the dissent suggests, since only *testimonial* statements are excluded by the Confrontation Clause. Statements to friends and neighbors about abuse and intimidation, and statements to physicians in the course of receiving treatment would be excluded, if at all, only by hearsay rules, which are free to adopt the dissent's version of forfeiture by wrongdoing. In any event, we are puzzled by the dissent's decision to devote its peroration to domestic abuse cases. Is the suggestion that we should have one Confrontation Clause for all other crimes, but a special, improvised, Confrontation Clause for those crimes that are frequently directed against women? Domestic violence is an intolerable offense that legislatures may choose to combat through many means — from increasing criminal penalties to adding resources for investigation and prosecution to funding awareness and prevention campaigns. But for that serious crime, as for others, abridging the constitutional rights of criminal defendants is not in the State's arsenal.

The domestic-violence context is, however, relevant for a separate reason. Acts of domestic violence often are intended to dissuade a victim from resorting to outside help, and include conduct designed to prevent testimony to police officers or cooperation in criminal prosecutions. Where such an abusive relationship culminates in murder, the evidence may support a finding that the crime expressed the intent to isolate the victim and to stop her from reporting abuse to the authorities or cooperating with a criminal prosecution — rendering her prior statements admissible under the forfeiture doctrine. Earlier abuse, or threats of abuse, intended to dissuade the victim from resorting to outside help would be highly relevant to this inquiry, as would evidence of ongoing criminal proceedings at which the victim would have been expected to testify. This is not, as the dissent charges, nothing more than "knowledge-based intent." (Emphasis deleted.)

The state courts in this case did not consider the intent of the defendant because they found that irrelevant to application of the forfeiture doctrine. This view of the law was error, but the court is free to consider evidence of the defendant's intent on remand.

We decline to approve an exception to the Confrontation Clause unheard of at the time of the founding or for 200 years thereafter. The judgment of the California Supreme Court is vacated, and the case is remanded for further proceedings not inconsistent with this opinion.

It is so ordered.

JUSTICE THOMAS, concurring.

I write separately to note that I adhere to my view that statements like those made by the victim in this case do not implicate the Confrontation Clause. The contested evidence is indistinguishable from the statements made during police questioning in response to the report of domestic violence in *Hammon* v. *Indiana*, decided with *Davis* v. *Washington*. There, as here, the police questioning was not "a formalized dialogue"; it was not "sufficiently formal to resemble the Marian examinations" because "the statements were neither Mirandized nor custodial, nor accompanied by any similar indicia of formality"; and "there is no suggestion that the prosecution attempted to offer [Ms. Avie's] hearsay evidence at trial in order to evade confrontation."

Nonetheless, in this case respondent does not argue that the contested evidence is nontestimonial; the court below noted "no dispute" on the issue, and it is outside the scope of the question presented. Because the Court's opinion accurately reflects our Confrontation Clause jurisprudence where the applicability of that Clause is not at issue, I join the Court in vacating the decision below.

JUSTICE ALITO, concurring.

I join the Court's opinion, but I write separately to make clear that, like *Justice Thomas*, I am not convinced that the out-of-court statement at issue here fell within the Confrontation Clause in the first place. The dissent's displeasure with the result in this case is understandable, but I suggest that the real problem concerns the scope of the confrontation right. The Confrontation Clause does not apply to out-of-court statements unless it can be said that they are the equivalent of statements made at trial by "witnesses." It is not at all clear that Ms. Avie's statement falls within that category. But the question whether Ms. Avie's statement falls within the scope of the Clause is not before us, and assuming for the sake of argument that the statement falls within the Clause, I agree with the Court's analysis of the doctrine of forfeiture by wrongdoing.

JUSTICE SOUTER, with whom JUSTICE GINSBURG joins, concurring in part.

I am convinced that the Court's historical analysis is sound and I join all but Part II-D-2 of the opinion. As the Court demonstrates, the confrontation right as understood at the Framing and ratification of the Sixth Amendment was subject to exception on equitable grounds for an absent witness's prior relevant, testimonial statement, when the defendant brought about the absence with intent to prevent testimony. It was, and is, reasonable to place the risk of untruth in an unconfronted, out-of-court statement on a defendant who meant to preclude the testing that confrontation provides. The importance of that intent in assessing the fairness of placing the risk on the defendant is most obvious when a defendant is prosecuted for the very act that causes the witness's absence, homicide being the extreme example. If the victim's prior statement were admissible solely because the defendant kept the witness out of court by committing homicide, admissibility of the victim's statement to prove guilt would turn on finding the defendant guilty of the homicidal act causing the absence; evidence that the defendant killed would come in because the defendant probably killed. The only thing saving admissibility and liability determinations from question begging would be (in a jury case) the distinct functions of judge and jury: judges would find by a preponderance of evidence that the defendant killed (and so would admit the testimonial statement), while the jury could so find only on proof beyond a reasonable doubt. Equity demands something more than this near circularity before the right to confrontation is forfeited, and more is supplied by showing intent to prevent the witness from testifying.

It is this rationale for the limit on the forfeiture exception rather than a dispositive example from the historical record that persuades me that the Court's conclusion is the right one in this case. The contrast between the Court's and *Justice Breyer*'s careful examinations of the historical record tells me that the early cases on the exception were not calibrated finely enough to answer the narrow question here. The historical record as revealed by the exchange simply does not focus on what should be required for forfeiture when the crime charged occurred in an abusive relationship or was its culminating act; today's understanding of domestic abuse had no apparent significance at the time of the Framing, and there is no early example of the forfeiture rule operating in that circumstance.

Examining the early cases and commentary, however, reveals two things that count in favor of the Court's understanding of forfeiture when the evidence shows domestic abuse. The first is the substantial indication that the Sixth Amendment was meant to require some degree of intent to thwart the judicial process before thinking it reasonable to hold the confrontation right forfeited; otherwise the right would in practical terms boil down to a measure of reliable hearsay, a view rejected in *Crawford* v. *Washington*. The second is the absence from the early material of any reason to doubt that the element of intention would normally be satisfied by the intent inferred on the part of the domestic abuser in the classic abusive relationship, which is meant to isolate the victim from outside help, including the aid of law enforcement and the judicial process. If the evidence for admissibility shows a continuing relationship of this sort, it would make no sense to suggest that the oppressing defendant miraculously abandoned the dynamics of abuse the instant before he killed his victim, say in a fit of anger. The Court's conclusion in Part II-E thus fits the rationale that equity requires and the historical record supports.

JUSTICE BREYER, with whom *Justice Stevens* and *Justice Kennedy* join, dissenting.

In *Crawford* v. *Washington*, we held that the Sixth Amendment's Confrontation Clause bars admission against a criminal defendant of an un-cross-examined "testimonial" statement that an unavailable witness previously made out of court. We simultaneously recognized an exception: that the defendant, by his own "wrongdoing," can forfeit "on essentially equitable grounds" his Confrontation

Clause right. In *Davis* v. *Washington*, we again recognized this exception, stating that "one who obtains the absence of a witness by wrongdoing forfeits the constitutional right to confrontation."

This case involves a witness who, crying as she spoke, told a police officer how her former boyfriend (now, the defendant) had choked her, "opened a folding knife," and "threatened to kill her." Three weeks later, the defendant did kill her. At his murder trial, the defendant testified that he had acted in self-defense. To support that assertion, he described the victim as jealous, vindictive, aggressive, and violent. To rebut the defendant's claim of self-defense and impeach his testimony, the State introduced into evidence the witness' earlier uncross-examined statements (as state hearsay law permits it to do) to help rebut the defendant's claim of self-defense. It is important to underscore that this case is premised on the assumption, not challenged here, that the witness' statements are testimonial for purposes of the Confrontation Clause. With that understanding, we ask whether the defendant, through his wrongdoing, has forfeited his Confrontation Clause right. The Court concludes that he may not have forfeited that right. In my view, however, he has.

II

There are several strong reasons for concluding that the forfeiture by wrongdoing exception applies here — reasons rooted in common-law history, established principles of criminal law and evidence, and the need for a rule that can be applied without creating great practical difficulties and evidentiary anomalies.

First, the language that courts have used in setting forth the exception is broad enough to cover the wrongdoing at issue in the present case (murder) and much else besides.

Second, an examination of the forfeiture rule's basic purposes and objectives indicates that the rule applies here. At the time of the founding, a leading treatise writer described the forfeiture rule as designed to assure that the prisoner "shall never be admitted to shelter himself by such evil Practices on the Witness, that being to give him Advantage of his own Wrong." This Court's own leading case explained the exception as finding its "foundation in the maxim that no one shall be permitted to take advantage of his own wrong." *Reynolds*. What more "evil practice," what greater "wrong," than to murder the witness? And what greater evidentiary "advantage" could one derive from that wrong than thereby to prevent the witness from testifying, *e.g.*, preventing the witness from describing a history of physical abuse that is not consistent with the defendant's claim that he killed her in self-defense?

Third, related areas of the law motivated by similar equitable principles treat forfeiture or its equivalent similarly. The common law, for example, prohibits a life insurance beneficiary who murders an insured from recovering under the policy. Similarly, a beneficiary of a will who murders the testator cannot inherit under the will.

Fourth, under the circumstances presented by this case, there is no difficulty demonstrating the defendant's intent. This is because the defendant here knew that murdering his ex-girlfriend would keep her from testifying; and that knowledge is sufficient to show the *intent* that law ordinarily demands. As this Court put the matter more than a century ago: A " 'man who performs an act which it is known will produce a particular result is from our common experience presumed to have anticipated that result and to have intended it.' " With a few criminal law exceptions not here relevant, the law holds an individual responsible for consequences known likely to follow just as if that individual had intended to achieve them.

The majority tries to overcome this elementary legal logic by claiming that the "forfeiture rule" applies, not where the defendant *intends* to prevent the witness from testifying, but only where that is the defendant's *purpose, i.e.*, that the rule applies only where the defendant acts from a particular *motive*, a *desire* to keep the witness from trial. But the law does not often turn matters of responsibility upon *motive*, rather than *intent.* And there is no reason to believe that application of the rule of forfeiture constitutes an exception to this general legal principle.

Indeed, to turn application of the forfeiture rule upon proof of the defendant's *purpose* (rather than *intent*), as the majority does, creates serious practical evidentiary problems. Consider H who assaults W, knows she has complained to the police, and then murders her. H *knows* that W will be unable to testify against him at any future trial. But who knows whether H's knowledge played a major role, a middling role, a minor role, or no role at all, in H's decision to kill W? Who knows precisely what passed through H's mind at the critical moment?

Moreover, the majority's insistence upon a showing of *purpose* or *motive* cannot be squared with the exception's basically ethical objective. If H, by killing W, is able to keep W's testimony out of court, then he has successfully "take[n] advantage of his own wrong." And he does so whether he killed her *for the purpose of* keeping her from testifying, with *certain knowledge* that she will not be able to testify, or with *a belief* that rises to a *reasonable level of probability.* The inequity consists of his being able to *use* the killing to keep out of court her statements against him. That inequity exists whether the defendant's state of mind is purposeful, intentional (*i.e.*, with knowledge), or simply probabilistic.

Fifth, the majority's approach both creates evidentiary anomalies and aggravates existing evidentiary incongruities. Contrast (a) the defendant who assaults his wife and subsequently threatens her with harm if she testifies, with (b) the defendant who assaults his wife and subsequently murders her in a fit of rage. Under the majority's interpretation, the former (whose threats make clear that his purpose was to prevent his wife from testifying) cannot benefit from his wrong, but the latter (who has committed what is undoubtedly the greater wrong) can. This is anomalous, particularly in this context where an equitable rule applies.

Sixth, to deny the majority's interpretation is not to deny defendants evidentiary safeguards. It does, of course, in this particular area, deny defendants the right *always* to cross-examine. But the hearsay rule has always contained exceptions that permit the admission of evidence where the need is significant and where alternative safeguards of reliability exist. Those exceptions have evolved over time.

More importantly, to apply the forfeiture exception here simply lowers a constitutional barrier to admission of earlier testimonial statements; it does not *require* their admission. State hearsay rules remain in place; and those rules will determine when, whether, and how evidence of the kind at issue here will come into evidence. A State, for example, may enact a forfeiture rule as one of its hearsay exceptions, while simultaneously reading into that rule requirements limiting its application. To lower the constitutional barrier to admission is to allow the States to do just that, *i.e.*, to apply their evidentiary rules with flexibility and to revise their rules as experience suggests would be advisable. The majority's rule, which requires exclusion, would deprive the States of this freedom and flexibility.

III

B

Given the absence of any evidence squarely requiring purpose rather than intent, what is the majority to say? The majority first tries to draw support from the *absence* of any *murder* case in which the victim's Marian statement was read to the jury on the ground that the defendant had killed the victim. I know of no instance in which this Court has drawn a conclusion about the meaning of a common-law rule *solely* from the absence of cases showing the contrary — at least not where there are other plausible explanations for that absence. And there are such explanations here.

The most obvious reason why the majority cannot find an instance where a court applied the rule of forfeiture at a murder trial is that many (perhaps all) common-law courts thought the rule of forfeiture irrelevant in such cases. In a murder case, the relevant witness, the murder victim, was dead; and historical legal authorities tell us that, when a witness was dead, the common law admitted a Marian statement. Because the Marian statements of a deceased witness were admissible simply by virtue of the witness' death, there would have been no need to argue for their admission pursuant to a forfeiture rule.

Historical authorities also tell us that a Marian statement could not be admitted unless it was a *proper* Marian deposition, meaning that the statement was given in the presence of the defendant thereby providing an opportunity to cross-examine the witness. And this was the case whether the witness' unavailability was due to death or the "means or procurement" of the defendant. Thus, in a murder trial, where the witness was dead, either the Marian statement was proper and it came into evidence *without* the forfeiture exception; or it was improper and the forfeiture exception *could not have helped it come in.*

The upshot is that the majority fails to achieve its basic objective. It cannot show that the common law insisted upon a showing that a defendant's purpose or motive in killing a victim was to prevent the victim from testifying. At the least its authority is consistent with my own view, that the prosecution in such a case need show no more than intent (based on knowledge) to do so. And the most the majority might show is that the common law was not clear on the point.

IV

A

The majority, describing its next argument as "conclusive," points to "innumerable cases" where courts did not admit "unconfronted inculpatory testimony by murder victims" against a defendant. The majority is referring to those dying declaration cases in which unconfronted statements were not admitted because the witness was not sufficiently aware of his impending death when he made them. But as I have explained, the forfeiture rule would have been unhelpful under these circumstances.

Finally, the majority points to a "subsequent history" in the United States where questions about the defendant's state of mind did not begin to arise until the 1980's. I have explained why that history does not support its view. Having only begun to swallow the elephant in the late 1970's and early 1980's, it makes sense that courts would not have previously considered the gnat.

While I have set forth what I believe is the better reading of the common-law cases, I recognize that different modern judges might read that handful of cases differently. All the more reason then *not* to reach firm conclusions about the precise metes and bounds of a contemporary forfeiture exception by trying to guess the state of mind of 18th century lawyers when they decided *not* to make a particular argument, *i.e.*, forfeiture, in a reported case. That is why, in Part II, *supra*, I have set forth other, more conclusive reasons in support of the way I would read the exception.

Second, the majority objects to that aspect of the forfeiture rule that requires a judge to make a preliminary assessment of the defendant's wrongful act in order to determine whether the relevant statements should be admitted. But *any* forfeiture rule requires a judge to determine as a preliminary matter that the defendant's own wrongdoing caused the witness to be absent. Regardless, preliminary judicial determinations are not, as the majority puts it "akin . . . to 'dispensing with jury trial.'" We have previously said that courts may make preliminary findings of this kind. For example, where a defendant is charged with conspiracy, the judge is permitted to make an initial finding that the conspiracy existed so as to determine whether a statement can be admitted under the co-conspirator exception to the hearsay rule. See *Bourjaily* v. *United States*. And even the plurality is forced to admit that it is "sometimes" necessary for "judge . . . to inquire into guilt of the charged offense in order to make a preliminary evidentiary ruling."

Third, the plurality seems to believe that an ordinary intent requirement, rather than a purpose or motive requirement, would let in too much out-of-court testimonial evidence. Ordinarily a murderer would know that his victim would not be able to testify at a murder trial. Hence all of the victim's prior testimonial statements would come in at trial for use against a defendant. To insist upon a showing of purpose rather than plain (knowledge-based) intent would limit the amount of unconfronted evidence that the jury might hear.

This argument fails to account for the fact that overcoming a constitutional objection does not guarantee admissibility of the testimonial evidence at issue. The

States will still control admissibility through hearsay rules and exceptions. And why not? What important constitutional interest is served, say, where a prior testimonial statement of a victim of abuse is at issue, by a constitutional rule that lets that evidence in if the defendant killed a victim *purposely* to stop her from testifying, but keeps it out if the defendant killed her *knowing* she could no longer testify while acting out of anger or revenge?

B

Even the majority appears to recognize the problem with its "purpose" requirement, for it ends its opinion by creating a kind of presumption that will transform *purpose* into *knowledge-based intent* — at least where domestic violence is at issue; and that is the area where the problem is most likely to arise.

JUSTICE SOUTER, concurring in part, says:

> "[The requisite] element of intention would normally be satisfied by the intent inferred on the part of the domestic abuser in the classic abusive relationship, which is meant to isolate the victim from outside help, including the aid of law enforcement and the judicial process. If the evidence for admissibility shows a continuing relationship of this sort, it would make no sense to suggest that the oppressing defendant miraculously abandoned the dynamics of abuse the instant before he killed his victim, say in a fit of anger."

This seems to say that a showing of domestic abuse is sufficient to call into play the protection of the forfeiture rule in a trial for murder of the domestic abuse victim. Doing so when, in fact, the abuser may have had other matters in mind apart from preventing the witness from testifying, is in effect not to insist upon a showing of "purpose." Consequently, I agree with this formulation, though I would apply a simple intent requirement across the board.

V

Regardless of a defendant's purpose, threats, further violence, and ultimately murder, can stop victims from testifying. A *constitutional* evidentiary requirement that insists upon a showing of purpose (rather than simply intent or probabilistic knowledge) may permit the domestic partner who made the threats, caused the violence, or even murdered the victim to avoid conviction for earlier crimes by taking advantage of later ones. In *Davis*, we recognized that "domestic violence" cases are "notoriously susceptible to intimidation or coercion of the victim to ensure that she does not testify at trial." We noted the concern that "[w]hen this occurs, the Confrontation Clause gives the criminal a windfall." And we replied to that concern by stating that "one who obtains the absence of a witness by wrongdoing forfeits the constitutional right to confrontation." To the extent that it insists upon an additional showing of purpose, the Court breaks the promise implicit in those words and, in doing so, grants the defendant not fair treatment, but a windfall. I can find no history, no underlying purpose, no administrative consideration, and no constitutional principle that requires this result.

Insofar as Justice Souter's rule in effect presumes "purpose" based on no more than evidence of a history of domestic violence, I agree with it. In all other respects, however, I must respectfully dissent.

Chapter 16

SHAPING OUTCOMES: BURDENS OF PROOF, PRESUMPTIONS, AND JUDICIAL NOTICE

§ 16.01 CHAPTER CHECKLIST

1. Do the Federal Rules of Evidence allocate burdens of proof or determine their content?

2. What is the difference between the "burden of producing evidence" and the "burden of persuasion"?

3. What is a "prima facie case"?

4. If a plaintiff makes out a prima facie case, does either the burden of producing evidence or the burden of persuasion then shift to the defendant?

5. How is a "presumption" different from a "permissive inference"?

6. How does a "social policy presumption" differ from a "common practice presumption"?

7. What does it mean to say that a presumption is "rebuttable"?

8. What is the effect of a "bursting bubble" presumption?

9. Does Rule 301 create any presumptions? If not, what are their sources?

10. What is the distinction between a presumption's "basic facts" and its "presumed fact?"

11. How does the impact of presumptions differ in criminal versus civil cases?

12. What are the bases upon which judges can take judicial notice?

13. What is the distinction between "adjudicative facts" and "legislative facts," and why does the distinction matter?

14. Can a party offer evidence to contradict a judicially-noticed fact?

15. Case Library: *County Court of Ulster County v. Allen*

§ 16.02 RELEVANT FEDERAL RULES OF EVIDENCE

Rule 201. Judicial Notice of Adjudicative Facts

(a) Scope. This rule governs judicial notice of an adjudicative fact only, not a legislative fact.

(b) Kinds of Facts That May Be Judicially Noticed. The court may judicially notice a fact that is not subject to reasonable dispute because it:

(1) is generally known within the trial court's territorial jurisdiction;

or

(2) can be accurately and readily determined from sources whose accuracy cannot reasonably be questioned.

(c) Taking Notice. The court:

(1) may take judicial notice on its own; or

(2) must take judicial notice if a party requests it and the court is supplied with the necessary information.

(d) Timing. The court may take judicial notice at any stage of the proceeding.

(e) Opportunity to Be Heard. On timely request, a party is entitled to be heard on the propriety of taking judicial notice and the nature of the fact to be noticed. If the court takes judicial notice before notifying a party, the party, on request, is still entitled to be heard.

(f) Instructing the Jury. In a civil case, the court must instruct the jury to accept the noticed fact as conclusive. In a criminal case, the court must instruct the jury that it may or may not accept the noticed fact as conclusive.

Rule 301. Presumptions in Civil Actions Generally

In a civil case, unless a federal statute or these rules provide otherwise, the party against whom a presumption is directed has the burden of producing evidence to rebut the presumption. But this rule does not shift the burden of persuasion, which remains on the party who had it originally.

Rule 302. Applying State Law to Presumptions in Civil Cases

In a civil case, state law governs the effect of a presumption regarding a claim or defense for which state law supplies the rule of decision.

§ 16.03 INTRODUCTION

For the most part, evidence rules regulate only the information that judges and jurors are legally allowed to consider. If you think of a juror's mind as the proverbial "black box," evidence rules determine what case-specific information can enter the box. Through "admonishments" or "limiting instructions," judges can instruct jurors not to use evidence for forbidden purposes.[1]

---

[1] For example, a judge may admonish jurors not to use an out-of-court statement admitted for a non-hearsay purpose for the truth of its contents. Similarly, a judge may admonish jurors not to use a past act admitted against a party for a non-character use under Rule 404(b) as evidence of the party's character.

However, once a case is turned over to jurors for decision, evidence rules largely cease to operate. How jurors analyze and evaluate what ends up inside the box is for the most part beyond legislative and judicial control. For example, assume that the defendant in a criminal case introduces evidence that the key prosecution witness is biased against the defendant. Jurors may choose to ignore the bias evidence, may decide that the witness is biased but truthful, may decide that the witness is truthful but mistaken, or may decide that the witness is lying. The policy of allowing judges' and jurors' factual conclusions to be a product of their own experiences and reasoning processes rather than of legal strictures is confirmed by the general rule that those factual conclusions are for the most part binding on appellate court judges.

Within this broad terrain of factfinder freedom exist three important pockets of principles through which rule makers attempt to shape decision-making. These pockets represent legislative and judicial efforts to produce trial outcomes that are consistent with what they regard as rational principles and desirable social policies.

[A] Burdens of Proof

One outcome-shaping principle is that the risk of uncertainty about which party is in the right should fall on the party seeking to change the status quo. This social policy is reflected in the allocation of burdens of proof. Burdens of proof shape outcomes by instructing judges and jurors not to rule in a burdened party's favor unless that party discharges its predetermined quantum of proof. For example, in criminal cases judges instruct jurors not to reach guilty verdicts unless the government proves defendants guilty beyond a reasonable doubt. (Of course, one social policy can trump another. No matter how strong the government's proof, criminal juries retain the power to "nullify" the law by acquitting a defendant.) In civil cases, judges instruct jurors not to hold defendants liable unless plaintiffs prove liability either by a preponderance of the evidence or by clear and convincing evidence, depending on applicable substantive law principles. A similar social policy explains why defendants often have the burden of proof when they rely on affirmative defenses, such as the defense of "accord and satisfaction" in breach of contract cases or "insanity" in criminal cases.

[B] Presumptions (Rule 301)

Presumptions, a second outcome-shaping tool, reflect rule makers' desires that verdicts conform to their conceptions of accuracy and rationality. Presumptions are an attempt to ensure that particular foundational facts always produce the same conclusions. As you know, most inferences are "permissive," meaning that judges and jurors are normally free to draw or not draw inferences from circumstantial evidence as they see fit. For example, a judge or juror who hears evidence that Kelly was standing inside an office wearing a wet raincoat and carrying a wet umbrella may infer that Kelly was outside in the rain, that the office has a serious leaky roof problem, that Kelly was rehearsing for a revival of "Singing in the Rain," or draw a different inference altogether.

If circumstantial evidence is subject to a presumption, however, a judge or juror *must* draw the inference created by the presumption unless the party burdened by the presumption adequately rebuts it. Thus, assume the unlikely existence of a presumption that, "A person wearing a wet raincoat and carrying a wet umbrella is presumed to have been out in the rain." In that event, a judge or juror who believes that Kelly was wearing a wet raincoat and carrying a wet umbrella must conclude that Kelly was out in the rain, unless the adversary produces evidence that overcomes the presumption.

[C] Judicial Notice (Rule 201)

Judicial notice also represents a tool for producing accurate and rational outcomes. When a judge concludes that a fact cannot be reasonably disputed, the judge may instruct jurors that they must accept that the fact is true. In addition to fostering rationality, judicial notice is a labor-saving device. Judges can instruct jurors to accept facts as true even in the absence of formal proof, thereby saving parties the trouble of having to "prove the obvious."

§ 16.04 BURDENS OF PROOF

The Federal Rules of Evidence neither allocate burdens of proof nor set forth the degrees of proof required to prevail on a legal claim. (If you've been feverishly searching the Rules for provisions defining and allocating burdens of proof, you can stop now.) Rather, burdens of proof emanate from other sources.

For example, the so-called "Hinckley rule" was enacted after John Hinckley was found not guilty by reason of insanity of shooting then-President Reagan. At the time of Hinckley's trial in 1982, the prosecution had the burden of proving beyond a reasonable doubt that Hinckley was sane. Following the trial, Congress changed the law to provide that criminal defendants relying on the insanity defense in federal court bear the burden of proving insanity by clear and convincing evidence. This burden of proof is set forth in **18 U.S.C. § 17(b)**, not in the Federal Rules of Evidence.

Thus, a detailed examination of the social policies and processes underlying the allocation and degrees of burdens of proof is largely beyond the scope of an evidence course.[2]

The primary evidentiary issue concerning burdens of proof involves the sufficiency of a burdened party's evidence to discharge its burden. In this respect, a burdened party actually has to discharge two burdens, the burden of production and the burden of persuasion. Initially, a burdened party bears the "burden of production," sometimes also called the "burden of producing evidence" or the "burden of going forward with evidence." This means that the burdened party will lose its claim or defense as a matter of law unless the party produces evidence that, if believed, is sufficient to sustain a verdict in the party's favor (i.e., evidence sufficient to constitute a "prima facie case"). Whether a burdened party has made out a prima facie case is a question of law for the trial judge. If the judge decides that the burdened party's evidence, even if believed, is not sufficient to constitute a

---

[2] For a useful overview of the subject, see the classic article by Edward Cleary, *Presuming and Pleading: An Essay on Juristic Immaturity*, 12 Stan. L. Rev. 5 (1959).

prima facie case, the judge should enter judgment against that party before the case reaches the jury. *See* Federal Rule of Civil Procedure 50(a), authorizing "motions for judgment" when "there is no legally sufficient evidentiary basis for a reasonable jury to find for" the burdened party on an issue. *See also* Federal Rule of Criminal Procedure 29(a), providing for a defense "motion for judgment of acquittal" when "the evidence is insufficient to sustain a conviction" of an offense.

As you would imagine, in almost all the cases that survive to trial, a burdened party does offer sufficient evidence to sustain the burden of producing evidence.[3] The typical result is that the adversary then offers conflicting evidence, and the judge or jurors consider both parties' evidence when deciding whether the burdened party has carried its second burden, the more familiar burden of persuasion. Whereas a judge decides as a matter of law whether a party has sustained the burden of producing evidence, the issue of whether a burdened party has carried the burden of persuasion is a question of fact.

Example 1

Meg O'Bight sues Chip, a computer technician, for malpractice. Meg alleges that instead of increasing the memory capacity of her computer, Chip carelessly erased all the programs and files on her computer's hard drive. During her case-in-chief, Meg neglects to offer evidence that any programs or files were on her computer before Chip began working on it. The judge should grant Chip's motion for judgment at the close of Meg's case, because there is no legally sufficient basis for the judge or jurors to conclude that Chip erased anything from Meg's computer.

Example 2

Same case as previous example. As part of her case-in-chief, Meg elicits the following testimony from Mike Rohard: "I'm a computer dealer, and I personally installed [particular software programs and files] on Meg's computer before she left it with Chip for additional memory installation." Cross-examined by Chip, Mike admits that he's previously been convicted of perjury. Together with other evidence establishing Chip's negligence, Mike's testimony would probably be sufficient for Meg to establish a prima facie case. Whether Mike is telling the truth is a question of fact that the judge or jurors can consider when deciding whether the totality of the evidence establishes Chip's liability by a preponderance of the evidence.

Example 3

Cat Berger is charged with first-degree burglary for burglarizing a detached building near a lake on her next-door neighbor's property. Under the jurisdiction's law, to prove that a defendant committed first-degree burglary, the prosecution is required to prove that the building was being used as a residence. However, the prosecutor fails to offer evidence of such use. The judge should grant Cat's motion for judgment of acquittal of

---

[3] A case in which a burdened party's evidence is too weak to sustain the burden of going forward is likely to be derailed before trial gets under way. For example, in civil cases, weak cases are often disposed of through the summary judgment process.

first-degree burglary at the close of the government's case, because the evidence is insufficient as a matter of law to sustain a conviction for that offense.

Example 4

Same case as previous example. Before concluding its case-in-chief, the prosecution elicits evidence from the building's owner that "members of my family often stay overnight in that building when we work down by the lake." Together with evidence satisfying the other elements of first-degree burglary, the prosecution has now made out a prima facie case and it's up to the judge or jurors to evaluate the prosecution's evidence along with any defense evidence and determine whether Cat's guilt has been proved beyond a reasonable doubt.

Once a burdened party makes out a prima facie case, does the burden of producing evidence then shift to the adversary, with the result that failure to produce evidence would result in judgment as a matter of law in the burdened party's favor? For example, if in a personal injury case the plaintiff makes out a prima facie case of the defendant's negligence, does the defendant have to counter the plaintiff's evidence to avoid judgment being automatically entered in the plaintiff's favor?

The general answer to this is "no." Of course, especially in civil cases, burdened parties' adversaries do typically offer evidence in support of their own versions of events. For example, a personal injury plaintiff's evidence that a defendant was driving carelessly is apt to be countered by defense evidence of the defendant's careful driving and the plaintiff's own carelessness. Nevertheless, the burden of producing evidence does not shift to the defendant; judgment will not be automatically entered against a defendant who fails to counter a plaintiff's evidence. Rather, the judge or jurors decide whether the burdened party's evidence, even in the unusual case in which it is unchallenged, is sufficiently persuasive to merit a favorable verdict.

The general rule that evidence that an adversary fails to contest does not automatically satisfy the burden of persuasion is subject to two common "exceptions":

Exception 1. When the burdened party establishes the basic facts that give rise to a presumption (*see* § 16.05), the judge or jury must find that the presumed fact is true. If the presumed fact is itself a material fact, the burdened party's uncontested evidence automatically satisfies the burden of persuasion as to that fact. In such a situation, a presumption does more than shape a trial's outcome, it controls the outcome.

Example 5

A common presumption provides: "One who possesses an object is presumed to own it." (Perhaps you used to sneer at your little sibling who tried to grab a toy over which you claimed dominion that "possession is nine-tenths of the law." If so, you'll find comfort in this presumption, though the fact that the presumption is rebuttable means that your childhood estimate may have been a bit high.) Vincent sues Fire Insurance Co., seeking compensation for a valuable painting that hung in Vincent's house when it burned down. The insurance company denies that the picture belonged to Vincent. If the jury believes Vincent's evidence that the painting was in his house before the fire, and the insurance company fails to contest ownership, the existence of the presumption means that Vincent has carried the burden of persuasion on the issue of whether he owned the painting.

Exception 2. If the burdened party's evidence in a civil case is exceedingly compelling and the adversary fails to offer contrary evidence rationally worthy of belief, a judge may conclude that as a matter of law the burdened party has satisfied the burden of persuasion. Relatively few cases are decided under this exception, both because most civil parties contest the evidence offered against them and because most judges take parties' rights to jury trial very seriously. (This doctrine cannot of course be used at all in criminal cases, where defendants have a constitutional right to remain mute. No matter how strong a judge considers a prosecutor's case to be, a criminal defendant is entitled to have a case go to a jury.)

Problem 16-1: Allocating Burdens

You have been retained as Evidence Guru by the Civil Justice Council of the newly formed Republic of Xanadid. The Council has sent you an electronic message asking for your thoughts on the following issue: "In personal injury cases based on negligence, should we require plaintiffs to have to prove that they were not contributorily negligent in order to make out a prima facie case? Or should a plaintiff's contributory negligence be an affirmative defense as to which defendants have the burden of producing evidence? Thank you — have a nice day." When you reply by suggesting that the burden of responding be allocated to the republic's Civil Procedure Guru, the Council gently reminds you that it has not yet been able to totally eradicate the populace's ancient cannibalistic practices. *What recommendation as to allocation would you give to the Council and why?*

Problem 16-2: Into the Breach

Elgin Marbles sues Rose Ettastone for breach of contract; trial is to a jury. Elgin testifies that Rose agreed to publish his book on ancient hieroglyphics and then refused to go ahead with the project after Elgin turned down other offers of publication. *At this stage of the case, which of the statements below is correct?*

1. If the judge doesn't believe Elgin's testimony, the judge should enter a judgment in Rose's favor.

2. Even if Rose fails to offer additional evidence, Elgin has the burden of persuading the jury by a preponderance of the evidence that Rose breached the contract.

3. Rose now has the burden of producing evidence that she did not breach the contract.

4. If Elgin's evidence is sufficient to make out a prima facie case and Rose fails to offer additional evidence, the judge should enter judgment in Elgin's favor.

Problem 16-3: Don't Believe It

Ray sues Vivian for personal injuries that Ray sustained in an auto accident, allegedly due to Vivian's negligence. To prove that Vivian was negligent, Ray calls Derek as a witness and elicits the following testimony on direct examination:

PLAINTIFF'S ATTORNEY: Derek, did you see the collision involving Ray's and Vivian's cars last August 1?

A: Yes, I did.

PLAINTIFF'S ATTORNEY: Did you observe Vivian's car prior to the collision?

A: Yes. I was walking west on Piedmont, and I saw her make a right turn and go east on Piedmont, driving in my direction.

PLAINTIFF'S ATTORNEY: What, if anything, did you notice about Vivian's driving after she made the right turn?

A: Nothing in particular. She was driving slowly in the right-hand lane.

PLAINTIFF'S ATTORNEY: In your opinion, was she driving carefully?

A: Yes.

PLAINTIFF'S ATTORNEY: Derek, isn't it true that you told your friend Kent the next day that you thought Vivian ran into Ray's car because she was driving too fast?

A: I did say that. But I've thought more about it since then.

PLAINTIFF'S ATTORNEY: And what is your relationship with Vivian?

A: We're currently engaged to be married. I actually met her as a result of this accident.

PLAINTIFF'S ATTORNEY: What were you doing at the time you observed the collision?

A: I had just left a restaurant after eating lunch. Maybe drinking lunch is more accurate — I'd just been fired so I'd been drowning my sorrows in a few martinis.

PLAINTIFF'S ATTORNEY: No further questions. Plaintiff rests.

DEFENDANT'S ATTORNEY: (At sidebar): Your Honor, the defense makes a motion for judgment as a matter of law, based on the plaintiff's failure to establish a prima facie case of Vivian's negligence through Derek's testimony.

PLAINTIFF'S ATTORNEY: I submit that Derek's testimony does make out a prima facie case that Vivian was negligent. Sure, he testified that Vivian was driving carefully. But he was thoroughly impeached. He had been drinking heavily just before the collision, so his ability to have observed her driving carefully is highly doubtful. He's engaged to the defendant, so he's obviously biased in her favor. Moreover, consider his contradictory statement to his friend Kent the very next day. I realize that under Rule 801 the contradictory statement to Kent is not admissible for its truth, but it does cast extreme doubt on Derek's credibility. All in all, Derek's testimony supports an inference that exactly the opposite of what he testified to is true, and thus is sufficient to make out a prima facie case that Vivian was negligent.

JUDGE: *What ruling on the defense attorney's motion for judgment?*

Problem 16-4: Got the Blues

As Luke Outt crosses a dark Rocky Road late one night, a large vehicle strikes him and continues on its way. Luke sues the Blue Bus Co. to recover for his personal injuries. The Blue Bus Co. denies that one of its buses struck Luke. At trial, Luke testifies that the vehicle that struck him was a bus, but he does not remember any of its distinguishing features.

1. Luke also offers evidence that only two bus companies operate on Rocky Road, the Blue Bus Co. and the Brown Bus Co. The Blue Bus Co. operates 75% of the buses on Rocky Road while the Brown Bus Co. operates 25% of the buses. *If Luke presents no additional evidence, is his evidence (if believed) sufficient to demonstrate by a preponderance of the evidence that the Blue Bus Co. operated the bus that hit him?*

2. Assume that instead of the evidence described in question 1, Luke offers evidence that the Blue Bus Co. operates 90% of the buses that run along Rocky Road, and the Brown Bus Co. operates the other 10%. *If Luke presents no additional evidence, is his evidence (if believed) sufficient to demonstrate by a preponderance of the evidence that the Blue Bus Co. operated the bus that hit him?*

3. As in question 1, Luke offers evidence that the Blue Bus Co. operates 75% of the buses on Rocky Road while the Brown Bus Co. operates 25% of the buses. In addition, Luke offers into evidence a copy of the "Blue Bus Co. Schedule." According to the schedule for the Rocky Road Route, a Blue Bus Co. bus traveling in Luke's direction should have departed from a bus stop about five blocks away from where Luke was hit about five minutes before he was struck. *Is Luke's evidence (if believed) sufficient to demonstrate by a preponderance of the evidence that the Blue Bus Co. operated the bus that hit him?*

Problem 16-5: High Witness Testimony

As Luke Outt crosses a dark Rocky Road late one night, a large vehicle strikes him and continues on its way. Luke sues the Blue Bus Co. to recover for his personal injuries. The Blue Bus Co. denies that one of its buses struck Luke. At trial, Luke testifies that the vehicle that struck him was a bus, but he does not remember any of its distinguishing features. Luke also offers evidence that only two bus companies operate on Rocky Road, the Blue Bus Co. and the Brown Bus Co.

Luke elicits testimony from Han Looker that Looker is a homeless individual who was asleep in a doorway about 20 yards away from where Luke was struck by what he testified was a bus. Looker awakened upon hearing the impact, and testifies on direct examination by Luke's attorney that "I saw what looked to me like a bus driving away. I think I saw the words, 'Blue Bus Co.' on the back of the bus." On cross-examination by the Blue Bus Co.'s lawyer, Looker testifies that he had drunk a bottle of Old Rotgut earlier in the evening and felt dizzy when he woke up, that the bus was at least 50 yards from him when he saw it, and that it was just barely light enough for him to make out that the vehicle was a bus. The cross-examiner also elicits testimony that Looker was angry upon learning shortly after the accident that the Blue Bus Co. had discontinued its policy of allowing homeless individuals to ride on its buses for free. Finally, the Blue Bus. Co. offers evidence that it operates only 25% of the buses on Rocky Road, whereas the Brown Bus Co. operates 75% of the buses. *Based on this evidence, should the judge grant the Blue Bus Co.'s motion for judgment based on Luke's failure to establish a prima facie case?*

Problem 16-6: Note Worthy?

Gotham Bank has sued Bruce Wayne for failure to pay any of the principal and interest of a Note. During its case-in-chief, the Bank introduced testimony and documentary evidence showing that the Bank was the holder of a Note in the principal amount of $50,000 signed by Wayne. The Bank's evidence further showed that the Note was in default, that Wayne had made no payments on the Note, and that Wayne owed the Bank $68,000 in unpaid principal and interest. Wayne had asked for a jury trial, but rested without presenting evidence. The Bank moves for judgment, asking the judge to enter judgment in its favor in the amount of $68,000 plus costs and reasonable attorneys' fee (as the Note provides for). *Should the judge grant the motion?*

Problem 16-7: Cold Case

Jesse Eaton was brutally bludgeoned to death more than 25 years ago, but after trying unsuccessfully to find Eaton's killer, the police department closed the file. However, as the result of a "cold DNA hit," Evan Oaks was charged with killing Eaton. Oaks was charged with the murder on the basis of a DNA test indicating that Oaks's DNA matched the DNA left by Eaton's killer on crime scene evidence that was preserved in the police files. Other than showing that Oaks lived in the same general vicinity as Eaton at the time of the murder, the only evidence that the prosecutor can offer of Oaks's guilt consists of the testimony of a DNA expert analyst that "the chance that a random person in the population would match Oaks's DNA is one in a million, and given the match evidence the chance that Oaks is not the source of the DNA found at the crime scene is one in 1,000." *If the jurors believe the DNA expert's testimony, is it sufficient to prove Oaks guilty of the murder beyond a reasonable doubt?*

§ 16.05 PRESUMPTIONS IN CIVIL CASES (RULE 301)

Rule 301 creates a general rule for civil cases that presumptions shift the burden of producing evidence to rebut the presumption but do not shift the burden of persuasion.

Presumptions, or mandatory inferences, represent legislators' and judges' desire for specified types of circumstantial evidence to produce pre-determined conclusions, at least in the absence of contrary evidence. Every presumption consists of two parts. One part is the "basic" or "foundational" facts, which are the facts that activate a presumption. The second part is the "presumed fact," the mandatory inference that follows from proof of the basic facts.

The party seeking the benefit of a presumption has the burden of offering evidence sufficient to establish (by a preponderance of evidence) that the basic facts are true.[4]

For example, a common presumption is that "a letter correctly addressed and properly mailed is presumed to have been received in the ordinary course of mail." The basic or foundational facts of this presumption are that (1) a letter was correctly addressed, and (2) the letter was properly mailed. The presumed fact — the mandatory inference — is that the letter was received in the ordinary course of mail. To be entitled to the benefit of the presumption, the party seeking to prove that a letter was received must establish by a preponderance of evidence that the letter was correctly addressed and properly mailed.

Presumptions exist to produce trial outcomes that either further desirable social policies or comport with objective reality.[5] These goals may be in conflict. For example, a traditional "social policy presumption" is that "a child conceived during the time that a married couple is cohabiting is presumed to be a child of the marriage." The presumption's effect is that a child must be found to be "of the marriage" if the party seeking to activate it proves that a husband and a wife were cohabiting at the time a child was conceived. This mandatory inference may not reflect objective reality. Perhaps the husband and wife were not having sexual intercourse with each other around the time of conception. However, the presumption is a way of legitimating children and providing them with sources of financial support. Accomplishing those ends outweighs the risk of burdening a biological non-parent with support obligations.

A second common "social policy presumption" is that "A person not heard from in five years is presumed dead." (Seven years was the traditional common-law period of time needed to activate this presumption. Modern living has thus produced not only a quicker pace of life, but apparently of presumed death as well.) This presumption furthers social policies favoring the marketability of property and allowing the relatives of long-absent people to move on with their lives. Does it in your opinion comport with likely objective reality?

---

[4] By contrast, as you will shortly see, the burden of proof with respect to presumed facts can shift from one party to the other.

[5] At least, desirable or realistic in the eyes of presumptions' creators.

"Common practice presumptions" generally exist to conserve trial time while fostering outcomes that are consistent with "what really happened." For example, the ubiquitous "mailed letter" presumption is a common practice presumption. It does not owe its existence to a social policy favoring the receipt of mail. Rather, the presumption recognizes the objective reality that mail almost always reaches addressees according to predictable schedules. The presumption seeks to ensure that unless a genuine dispute exists as to whether a letter was received, a judge or jury must conclude that it was.

While none of this may seem astonishing, rest assured that major intellectual wars have been fought on the battleground of presumptions. Everyone in the pantheon of Great Evidence Scholars, including such giants as Wigmore, Thayer, and Morgan, has weighed in with a position. All have agreed that when the evidence giving rise to a presumption is uncontested, the presumed fact must be accepted. All have also agreed that almost all presumptions should be "rebuttable." That is, the party on the wrong end of a presumption should normally have an opportunity to offer evidence contesting both the basic facts and its presumed fact. The bickering has involved how much "staying power" presumptions should have when parties contest them.

For example, return to the common practice presumption that "a letter correctly addressed and properly mailed is presumed to have been received in the ordinary course of mail." Assume that in a breach of contract case, Joe testifies that "I sent a written offer to Frank in a correctly addressed and properly mailed envelope." Frank then contests the presumption's mandatory inference by testifying that "I never received Joe's offer." At this point, what role should the "mailed letter" presumption play in the decisional process? The three primary competing positions have been these:

One strong view of presumptions. A presumption is itself evidence that judges and juries can consider when deciding whether to draw the inference that a presumption prescribes. Under this long-abandoned view, the judge in our hypothetical case might instruct jurors along these lines: "In deciding whether Frank received Joe's offer, you may consider that a presumption exists that a letter that is properly addressed and mailed was received by the addressee."

A second strong view of presumptions. Presumptions reflect important values of our system of justice, and thus should continue to influence outcomes even if parties contest them. The best way to achieve this goal is to shift the burden of persuasion to the contesting party. Under this view, the judge in our hypothetical case might instruct jurors along these lines: "You are to conclude that Frank received Joe's offer, unless Frank convinces you by a preponderance of the evidence that he didn't receive it."

A weak view of presumptions. Presumptions are simply convenient procedural devices, mandating outcomes only in the absence of evidence to the contrary. Once contested, they should disappear. Advocates for this position have used colorful phrases (by evidence scholar standards, anyway), analogizing presumptions to "bursting bubbles" and "bats of the law, flitting in the twilight but disappearing in the sunshine of actual facts."[6] Under this view, Frank's testimony that he never received Joe's offer eliminates the presumption. Thus, the judge in our hypothetical case would say nothing to the jurors about whether Frank received Joe's letter. Of course, the jurors' own experiences as senders and recipients of letters may lead them to conclude that Frank received Joe's offer. However, once Frank denies receiving the letter, the fact that Joe was at one time sailing with the wind of a presumption at his back is under this view irrelevant.[7]

Aware of these and other possible approaches, the drafters of Rule 301 opted for the weak view of presumptions identified above (though they unfortunately left out the colorful language about bubbles and bats). Under Rule 301, a presumption "imposes on the party against whom it is directed the burden of going forward with evidence to rebut or meet the presumption, but does not shift to such party the burden of proof in the sense of the risk of nonpersuasion, which remains throughout the trial upon the party on whom it was originally cast."

Applying Rule 301's language to the example involving Joe's testimony that he mailed an offer to Frank yields the following results:

- "A presumption imposes on the party against whom it is directed . . ." In the example above, Frank is the party against whom the presumption is directed; because of the presumption, he will be found to have received the offer unless he contests Joe's testimony.

- the burden of going forward with evidence to rebut or meet the presumption . . ." Frank went forward with evidence to rebut the presumed fact by testifying that he didn't get Joe's letter. Because he has satisfied the burden that Rule 301 imposed on him, it has burst and has no further force or effect.

- but does not shift to such party the burden of proof in the sense of the risk of nonpersuasion . . ." With the presumption gone, Joe retains the burden of persuading the judge or jury that Frank received the letter.

Even the weaker form of presumption provided for by Rule 301 can survive an evidentiary challenge if the opposing party's evidence contests only the basic fact. In such a situation, the response fails to "rebut or meet the presumption." As a result, the only issue for the judge or jury to decide is which party's version of the basic fact is accurate. If the judge or jury concludes that the basic fact exists, it must find the presumed fact. In other words, under Rule 301 the party opposing a presumption has to contest the *presumed* fact to cause the presumption to disappear. Consider the possibilities in the context of Joe's testimony that he mailed an offer to Frank.

---

[6] The "bats" analogy is from *Mackowick v. Kansas City, St. Joseph & Council Bluffs R.R. Co.*, 196 Mo. 550, 94 S.W. 256, 262 (1906).

[7] When a presumption is of the "bursting bubble" type, some jurisdictions authorize judges to pay homage to the remnants of a vanished presumption by informing jurors that they "can but don't have to" draw the inference that a presumption identifies. Thus, in the hypothetical in the text, a judge might instruct jurors that they "can but do not have to" conclude that Frank received Joe's letter. Of course, this is simply "permissive inference" language, and the same is true for any other item of circumstantial evidence.

- Frank contests only the basic facts. For example, assume that following Joe's testimony Frank calls Chet as a witness to testify that "I was with Joe when he mailed the offer to Frank. Just as Joe was putting the envelope in the mail slot, I noticed that he had put the wrong zip code on it." If this is the only evidence that Frank offers to refute Joe's testimony, a judge would instruct a jury that "if you find that Joe properly mailed a correctly addressed offer to Frank, you are to find that Frank received the offer."[8] (Reminder: the party seeking the benefit of a presumption — Joe, in this example — has the burden of persuasion with regard to the basic facts.)

- Frank contests only the presumed fact that he received the letter. Frank can do so by testifying that "I never received a letter from Joe." Frank has now satisfied the burden of going forward with evidence to "rebut or meet the presumed fact." The presumption disappears, and the judge or jury will decide whether Frank received Joe's letter without reference to a presumption.

- Frank contests both the basic and presumed facts. That is, Frank calls Chet to testify that the zip code was incorrect, and Frank testifies that he never received Joe's letter. Again, Frank has satisfied the burden of going forward so the presumption disappears.

Three-Step Civil Presumptions Matrix

Asking yourself the three questions below can help you analyze the effect of presumptions. (BPE = Burden of Producing Evidence; BP = Burden of Proof)

1. Does the language of a statute or court opinion create a presumption?

2. Does the presumption affect the BPE or the BP? Alternatively, is a person a BFP? (Sorry, this last question pertains to the Contracts course. You don't have to ask yourself this question in Evidence.)

3. Does the evidence offered by the party seeking the benefit of the presumption pertain to the basic fact or to the presumed fact? Example: Jones's spouse testifies, "Jones went to the market six years ago and I've neither seen nor heard from Jones since." This testimony pertains to the basic fact of the presumption, "A person missing for five years is presumed dead." (Sad fact: poor Jones.)

State laws on presumptions may differ from Rule 301. In California, for example, the consequences of presumptions differ depending on whether a presumption is of the "social policy" or of the "common practice" variety. In California, social policy presumptions shift the burden of proof to the other party.[9] Common practice presumptions, like presumptions under Rule 301, reflect the weak view of presumptions and burst when contested.[10] Thus, if the California scheme is a bit more complicated than Rule 301, at least California honors the contributions of almost every evidence scholar who ever wrote about presumptions.

---

[8] In a bench trial, the judge would of course adhere to the same principles.

[9] See **Cal. Evid. Code § 605**.

[10] See **Cal. Evid. Code § 603**.

However, federal presumption practices are closer to California's than the language of Rule 301 suggests. Just as in California, federal court judges too often use presumptions to shift burdens of proof. A primary reason for this is that the Federal Rules of Evidence do not themselves create any presumptions. (As was true for rules allocating burdens of proof, if you've been flipping through the Rules looking for a list of presumptions, you can stop.) And Rule 301 provides that presumptions do not shift the burden of proof unless "otherwise provided for by Act of Congress." And in fact, many presumptions, perhaps numbering into the hundreds, are scattered through federal statutes. For example:

- 30 U.S.C. § 921: It is presumed that a person who's worked in a coal mine for at least 10 years and developed black lung disease developed the disease from working in the mine.

- 35 U.S.C. § 282: A patent is presumed to be valid.

- 18 U.S.C. § 343: A person with a blood alcohol content in excess of .10 is presumed to be under the influence of alcohol.

When construing such statutes, judges often decide that presumptions are entitled to greater weight than that established by Rule 301. And in accord with the California scheme, federal judges generally treat a presumption as shifting the burden of persuasion when they believe that its purpose is to further social policies rather than simply to reflect common practices.

While statutes are the most common sources of presumptions, judges may also create presumptions through the common-law appellate court process. For example, the case of *Kaminsky v. Hertz Corp.*,[11] concerned a motorist who was hurt when a sheet of ice came loose from a truck bearing a Hertz logo that was traveling in front of the motorist and smashed into the windshield of the motorist's car. The motorist sued Hertz for negligence; Hertz denied that it owned the truck. The motorist's only proof that the truck was owned by Hertz was that it bore the Hertz logo. The court created a presumption that commercial logos on objects establish ownership. The presumption meant that Hertz had to produce evidence of non-ownership or lose on that issue.

Practice Tip: The sometimes confusing vocabulary of presumptions: Legislators and judges aren't always thoughtful enough to use the word "presumptions" when they create these outcome-shaping devices. *Prima facie evidence* is an alternative term that may signal a presumption. For example, assume that a judicial opinion states that "performing open heart surgery without first anesthetizing the patient is prima facie evidence of negligence." You may take this to mean that the evidence creates a presumption of medical malpractice that shifts either the burden of producing evidence of non-negligence or the burden of proof of non-negligence to the doctor. On the other hand, judicial opinions may use the term "presumption" in a misleading way. For example, an opinion may refer to "a permissive presumption that the person wearing a white coat and a stethoscope was a doctor." You may take this to mean merely that the

---

[11] 94 Mich. App. 356, 288 N.W.2d 426 (1979).

judge or jury could reasonably *infer* that the person was a doctor, not that a formal burden-shifting presumption exists. Finally, a statute or judge may use the term "presumption" as meaning a *conclusive* or *mandatory* presumption rather than a *rebuttable* (or "evidentiary") presumption. While few conclusive presumptions exist, they are substantive principles clothed in the language of presumption. For example, a formerly common substantive rule provided that a child conceived during the time a married couple was cohabiting was conclusively presumed to be the husband's child. This was a conclusive and not an evidentiary presumption, because its presumed fact was irrebuttable.

Under Rule 302, when federal judges apply a state's substantive laws (as is common when federal court jurisdiction is based on diversity of citizenship), they also apply the state's rules with regard to the effect of presumptions governing material facts. Thus, if under a state's evidence rules the effect of a presumption governing a material fact is to shift the burden of persuasion, a federal judge would give that presumption the same effect in a diversity case. For example, **California Evidence Code Sections 660–670** establish presumptions whose effect is to shift the burden of persuasion to the party against whom the presumption is directed. If any of those presumptions govern material facts in a diversity case, a federal judge in California will also use that presumption to shift the burden of proof.

Example 1

Following an insured's death, a Maryland resident who is the beneficiary of a life insurance policy sues the Illinois insurance company that issued the policy. The insurance company claims that the insured committed suicide a few weeks after the policy was taken out, voiding the policy. Suit is in Illinois federal court based on diversity, but Illinois state law governs the case. The federal judge would be bound by an Illinois state law providing that a "presumption against suicide" is a burden-shifting presumption.

Example 2

Assume that the following presumption affects the Burden of Producing Evidence: "People are presumed to be the owners of the things they possess." Party A, locked in a property battle with ex-spouse Party B, testifies in support of the basic fact that, "The diamond ring that I claim is mine was in my safe deposit box."

1. Party B offers no evidence at all. Party A's testimony shifted the burden of producing evidence countering the presumed fact to Party B, who didn't meet the burden. Result: If Party A's testimony is believed, Party A has conclusively proved ownership of the ring. In a jury trial, the judge would instruct a jury that, "If Party A convinces you by a preponderance of the evidence that the ring was in Party A's safe deposit box, you are to find that Party A owns the ring."

2. Party B contests the basic fact only, calling a friend to testify that "Months ago, A and B gave the diamond ring to me for safe-keeping." Party A's testimony shifted the burden of producing evidence countering the presumed fact to Party B, who didn't meet the burden. Result: If Party A's testimony is believed, Party A has conclusively proved ownership of the ring. In a jury trial, the judge would instruct

a jury that, "If Party A convinces you by a preponderance of the evidence that the ring was in Party A's safe deposit box, you are to find that Party A owns the ring."[12]

3. Party B contests the presumed fact by testifying that "The diamond ring is mine; Party A gave it to me as a present." Whether or not Party B contests the basic fact, Party B has met the burden of producing evidence countering the presumed fact. Result: The presumption vanishes. Gone. Nada. Pffft. Nichts. Arrivederci. In a bench trial, the judge will decide which party owns the ring apart from any presumption. In a jury trial, the judge would not refer to the presumption.[13]

Example 3

Assume that the following presumption affects the Burden of Proof: "A person who is missing for five years is presumed dead." Party A, seeking to prove that his spouse Amelia Cooper is deceased, offers evidence from various family members and friends that they have not heard from or seen Amelia in more than five years.

1. Party B offers no evidence at all. Party A's evidence shifted the burden of producing evidence countering the presumed fact to Party B, who didn't meet the burden. Result: A judge who believes Party A's evidence must conclude that Amelia Cooper is dead. In a jury trial, the judge would instruct a jury that, "If Party A convinces you by a preponderance of the evidence that Amelia Cooper has not been heard from in five years, you are to find that Amelia Cooper is dead."

2. Party B contests the basic fact only, calling a friend of Amelia to testify that "Amelia phoned me about three years ago. We had a nice chat." Party A's testimony shifted the burden of producing evidence countering the presumed fact to Party B, who didn't meet the burden. However, Party B did contest the basic fact. Result: If Party A's testimony is believed, Party A has conclusively proved that Amelia is dead. In a jury trial, the judge would instruct a jury that, "If Party A convinces you by a preponderance of the evidence that Amelia Cooper has been missing for over five years, you are to find that she is dead."

3. Party B contests the presumed fact only, calling a witness to testify that "My name is Amelia Cooper." Party A's testimony shifted the burden of producing evidence countering the presumed fact to Party B, who has met the burden. However, Party B did not contest the basic fact. Result: The burden of proof switches to Party B to convince the judge or jury that the presumed fact is not true. In a jury trial, the judge would instruct a jury that, "You are to find that Amelia Cooper is dead, unless Party B convinces you by a preponderance of the evidence that she is alive."[14]

---

[12] If Party A fails to establish the presumption's basic facts by a preponderance of evidence, a judge or jury would simply decide which party owns the ring in the absence of any presumption.

[13] When bubbles burst, some jurisdictions give judges the discretion to honor their former existence by telling jurors that they "may but are under no obligation to infer from Party A's testimony that the ring belongs to Party A." Of course, this is the language of a permissive inference, not a presumption.

[14] As in this and the other examples in this chapter, an instruction can refer to the *effect* of a presumption without using the term "presumption" itself. Rules in many jurisdictions forbid use of the term "presumption" for the reason that the term may unfairly influence jurors.

4. Party B contests both the basic fact and the presumed fact. Party B calls a friend of Amelia to testify that "Amelia phoned me about three years ago. We had a nice chat." Party B also calls a witness to testify that "My name is Amelia Cooper." Result: If Party A convinces the judge or jury that Amelia has been missing for more than five years, the burden of proving that Amelia is alive shifts to Party B. In a jury trial, the judge would instruct the jury that, "If Party A convinces you by a preponderance of evidence that Amelia Cooper has been missing for more than five years, you are to find that she is dead unless Party B convinces you by a preponderance of the evidence that she is alive."

Problem 16-8: Party Smarty

Enjoying a veggie dip at a party, Law Professor Evy Denss is sought out by an anguished friend who tells her the following:

> "I'm the plaintiff in a case that goes to trial next week. The other side is claiming that I received an important letter that I never got. A few minutes ago one of your law students told me something about a presumption that I got the letter. I'm really upset — what can I do about the presumption?"

Evy replies, "Don't worry. Your lawyer will be able to eliminate that nasty old presumption with just one simple question."

What is that question?

Problem 16-9: Pick Your Own

Appellate court judges sometimes create new presumptions to reflect what they consider to be social policies or everyday truths not reflected in existing presumptions. For example, in a case involving Jones's alleged legal malpractice, a judge may decide to create a presumption that "A lawyer who has taken the course in Evidence is presumed to understand the declarations against interest exception to the hearsay rule." (Whether such a presumption would reflect social policy or common practice we leave to you!) *With that in mind, create a presumption that you might apply in an appropriate case concerning one of the following topics and state "for the record" whether you think that it reflects social policy or common practice:*

1. Law School
2. The Internet
3. Domestic Relations
4. Electronic Mail
5. Your Favorite Pet Peeve

Problem 16-10: Make-Up Case

Distinguish the basic facts from the presumed facts in the following presumptions, and develop a factual scenario that might give rise to the presumption:

1. "An obligation delivered up to the debtor is presumed to have been paid." ((Cal. Evid. Code § 633)

2. "An employee who is involved in an accident while driving a vehicle owned by his or her employer is presumed to have been acting within the scope of employment."

3. "When an injury or accident occurs which ordinarily does not occur in the absence of negligence, which was caused by an agency or instrumentality in the defendant's exclusive control and was not due to any voluntary action or contribution on the part of the plaintiff, the injury or accident is presumed to have been caused by the defendant's negligence."

Problem 16-11: The Classifieds

Laws that create presumptions often neglect to classify them as either a bursting-bubble presumption or one shifting the burden of persuasion. Judges may then have to decide into which category to place a presumption. *Make an argument as to how a judge should classify the following presumptions using the everyday experience/policy-based dichotomy described above.*

1. "A person who has worked in a coal mine for at least 10 years and develops black lung disease is presumed to have developed the disease from working in the mine."

2. "The driver of a car is presumed to be driving it with the owner's permission."

3. "A transaction between a trustee and a beneficiary by which the trustee gains an advantage is presumed to be the product of undue influence."

4. "If a will is shown to have been in the possession of a competent decedent prior to the decedent's death and cannot be found after death, it is presumed that the decedent revoked the will."

5. "A violent death caused by external means is presumed to have been the result of accident rather than suicide."

6. "A transfer of property without consideration made within three years of a person's death is presumed to have been made in contemplation of death." (A gift made in contemplation of death may be included in a taxpayer's estate, which could have estate tax consequences.)

7. "When goods are damaged during transit provided by more than one carrier, it is presumed that the last carrier caused the damage."

Problem 16-12: Donna For

Bella sues Donna to recover for personal injuries resulting from an automobile accident; trial is to a jury. Bella testifies that, "I had slowed down for a pedestrian when Donna's car rear-ended mine." A judicially created presumption in the jurisdiction where the trial takes place is that the driver of a car that rear-ends another car is presumed to have been negligent. Donna presents no evidence in her own behalf. In these circumstances, which of the following statements is correct?

1. If the jurors believe Bella's testimony that Donna's car rear-ended Bella's, they must conclude that Donna was negligent.

2. Bella has satisfied the burden of producing evidence of Donna's negligence, and it's up to the jury to decide whether Bella has carried the burden of persuasion on the issue of Donna's negligence.

3. The jury must conclude that Donna was negligent only if the presumption is one that shifts the burden of persuasion.

4. Bella has to offer evidence that the collision was the result of Donna's negligence in order to satisfy her burden of producing evidence.

5. The judge must take the case from the jury and rule that as a matter of law that Donna was negligent.

Problem 16-13: Basic Training

Same case as previous problem. As before, Donna presents no evidence as to her own driving. However, after Bella testified that Donna's car ran into hers, Donna's attorney cross-examined Bella as follows:

DEFENDANT'S ATTORNEY: Bella, up until the time of the collision you weren't aware that a car was behind yours, correct?

A: That's true.

DEFENDANT'S ATTORNEY: And after the collision, the driver of the car that hit yours drove off without stopping, correct?

A: Yes.

DEFENDANT'S ATTORNEY: So you can't be sure that my client, Donna, was driving the car the rear-ended you, right?

A: No. I know the driver was a woman. Also, I saw the car go by me, and the make and model match Donna's car. Also, I got a quick look at the license plate and the first two letters match Donna's license plate number.

DEFENDANT'S ATTORNEY: But as you've also admitted, the sun was directly in your eyes at the time of the collision, which made it more difficult for you to see, right?

A: Yes.

In the light of Bella's direct and cross-examination, which of the following statements is correct?

1. The judge must take the case from the jury and rule that as a matter of law Donna was negligent.

2. If the presumption is a bursting-bubble presumption, it has vanished as a result of Donna's cross-examination and the jury will decide the issue of Donna's negligence without regard to a presumption.

3. The judge should instruct the jury that if Bella proves by a preponderance

of the evidence that Donna was driving the car that collided with Bella's, it must find that Donna was negligent.

4. If the presumption is one that shifts the burden of persuasion, the judge should instruct the jury that Donna has the burden of persuasion on the issues of whether she was driving the car that collided with Bella's car and whether she was negligent.

Problem 16-14: Donna Speaks

Same case as previous problem, except assume that the presumption is one affecting the burden of producing evidence. Donna's attorney does not cross-examine Bella. Instead, Donna testifies on her own behalf as follows:

DEFENDANT'S ATTORNEY: Donna, were you driving your car on the afternoon that Bella was rear-ended?

A: I was.

DEFENDANT'S ATTORNEY: And did your cars come into contact?

A: Yes. I was completely stopped for a red light a couple of feet behind Bella's car. Then a pick-up truck hit me from the rear so hard that it pushed my car into Bella's.

DEFENDANT'S ATTORNEY: Did you have any chance to avoid being hit by the pick-up truck?

A: None whatsoever. I never saw or heard it coming, and didn't know what happened until after I was hit.

DEFENDANT'S ATTORNEY: No further questions.

JUDGE: Plaintiff's counsel, any cross-examination?

PLAINTIFF'S ATTORNEY: Thank you, just one question. Donna, you were convicted of perjury last year, correct?

A: That's true.

PLAINTIFF'S ATTORNEY: That's all, Your Honor.

True or False: On this state of the record, the judge should instruct the jury that if they believe that Donna's car rear-ended Bella's, the jury must find that Donna was negligent.

Problem 16-15: Dueling Wills

Real estate tycoon Armand Giddy dies, leaving an estate of $3 billion. Two wills are found in his desk drawer. Will A is dated one year earlier than Will B. Will A leaves Giddy's entire estate to the Society for the Development of Marshmallows That Don't Melt in Hot Chocolate. Will B states that it revokes Will A and leaves Giddy's entire estate to family members. However, Will B also has a large red "X" drawn across the first page. The Society claims that Will A is valid; Giddy's family members file suit to establish the validity of Will B. A presumption exists that "a will that is made but mutilated is presumed revoked."

As the attorney for the Society, what evidence or arguments might you offer in order to get the benefit of this presumption?

As the attorney for Giddy's family members, you are about to begin factual investigation. *Identify evidence that you will look for to rebut the presumption. In addition, what difference does it make whether the presumption is a bursting-bubble presumption or one that shifts the burden of persuasion?*

Problem 16-16: Conclusive Presumption

Star Lett brings a paternity action against her estranged husband Stu Deeyo to establish that he is the father of her newborn child. Assume that a relevant statute enacted more than 50 years ago provides that, "A child conceived while a non-impotent husband and wife are cohabiting is conclusively presumed to be the child of the husband."

As the attorney for Star, what evidence will you offer to trigger the presumption?

You are the attorney for Stu. Stu emphatically denies that he is the child's father, and shows you the results of a DNA test eliminating him as the child's father. Stu is extremely upset when you tell him that the DNA test results are irrelevant under the statute because of the conclusive presumption. *Assuming that you can't contest the basic facts giving rise to the presumption, do you have any avenue for giving your client a chance to contest the presumed fact?*

Problem 16-17: A Night at the Opera

Lem Ozine has sued Val's Parking Service for damage to his car; trial is to a jury. A presumption states that "Goods damaged or lost while in a bailee's possession are presumed to have been damaged or lost as a result of the bailee's negligence." The presumption has been construed as one shifting the burden of proof.

Lem testifies that he parked his brand new Megamobile with Val's Parking Service when he went to opening night at the opera. He offers into evidence a "Val's Claim Check" to substantiate his claim. He further testifies that when the car was brought to him after the opera concluded five long hours later, dents and scratches were all over it. Lem offers into evidence a photo of the car's appearance to substantiate this claim. He further testifies that none of this damage was present when he dropped the car off with Val's before the opera.

Val testifies and denies that Lem parked his car with her parking service. She knows that because she and her employees always stamp a distinctive "V" on a claim check before they give it to a customer, and the one offered into evidence by Lem doesn't have a "V" on it. Val further testifies that Lem could easily have picked up the claim check he offered into evidence without anyone noticing, as they are stacked on a table and it was a very busy night. Finally, Val calls John to testify that he is Lem's work colleague, and that in a conversation a week before opera opening night, Lem complained to John that "some vandals ruined my new Megamobile."

On rebuttal, Lem denies making the statement to John, and testifies that John is angry at him because Lem and not John got an important promotion.

Assume that trial is to the jury. Based on the information set forth above, should the judge instruct the jury with respect to the presumption? If so, prepare the instruction that the judge should give.

Problem 16-18: Dueling Presumptions

When Bobby is 10 years old, his mother Susan brings a paternity action against Phil seeking to prove that Phil is Bobby's father and asking for child support from Phil. The judge orders Phil to take a blood test. The results of the blood test show a very strong likelihood of at least 98% that Phil is Bobby's father, and give rise to a presumption of paternity that shifts to Phil the burden of proving that he is not Bobby's father. This presumption is based on the belief that blood test results are highly reliable and determine paternity with a high degree of certainty.

Phil offers evidence that at the time Bobby was conceived, Susan was lawfully married to and cohabiting with Jonah. This evidence gives rise to a presumption that Jonah is the father, a presumption that would shift the burden of proof to Jonah to prove that he is not Bobby's father. This presumption is based on a desire to legitimize children and provide them with a source of financial support.

Given these conflicting presumptions, should Susan have the burden of proving that Phil is the father, or should Phil have the burden of proving that he is not? What role should the presumptions play in the outcome of this case?

§ 16.06 PRESUMPTIONS IN CRIMINAL CASES

Like civil statutes, criminal laws sometimes create presumptions. However, presumptions cannot operate against criminal defendants in the same way that they do against civil parties. To see why, assume that one element of a statute making it a crime to "receive stolen goods" is that the defendant acquired the goods with actual or constructive knowledge that they were stolen. The statute further provides that when a dealer in secondhand goods acquires stolen goods, "knowledge that the goods were stolen shall be presumed from evidence that the dealer acquired the goods in circumstances that should have caused the dealer to make a reasonable inquiry to determine whether the person from whom the goods were bought had legal title to them."

This statute would clearly be unconstitutional if it shifted the burden of proof to a defendant charged with violating this statute to prove lack of knowledge that secondhand goods were stolen. In criminal cases the government has to prove each and every element of a crime beyond a reasonable doubt. Criminal defendants may permissibly be assigned the burden of proof with respect to affirmative defenses, such as insanity. However, criminal defendants cannot be found guilty unless the government proves their guilt beyond a reasonable doubt. Thus, statutes cannot assign to criminal defendants the burden of disproving facts that constitute elements of crimes.

The statute would be similarly unconstitutional if it shifted the burden of producing evidence of lack of knowledge that secondhand goods were stolen to a defendant charged with violating this statute. Defendants in criminal cases have a Fifth Amendment right to remain silent in response to criminal charges. A presumption that required defendants to produce evidence on pain of having an element of a crime established as a matter of law, would conflict with the right of silence. Thus, defendants cannot be burdened by mandatory presumptions in criminal cases.

However, statutes can legitimately refer to presumptions if the presumptions are interpreted so as only to give rise to permissive inferences. For example, consider the case of *County Court of Ulster v. Allen* (*see* Case Library). In that case, four occupants of a car (three males and one female) were charged with possession of illegal weapons and drugs. The police found some of the contraband in the handbag of the 16-year-old female occupant; other items were in the trunk. All the occupants of the car were convicted with the aid of a statutory "presumption" that the presence of a firearm in a car is presumptive evidence of its illegal possession by all of the car's occupants. The U.S. Supreme Court upheld the convictions, ruling that the statute created only a "permissive statutory presumption" rather than a "mandatory presumption." The statute's presumption would have been "a far more troublesome evidentiary device" if it could "affect not only the strength of the 'no reasonable doubt' burden, but also the placement of that burden." This statute however created only a permissive presumption that "allows, but does not require, the trier of fact to infer the elemental fact from proof by the prosecutor of the basic one and which places no burden of any kind on the defendant." In other words, all that the "presumption" did was to inform the jurors that they could if they chose infer from the presence of the contraband in the car that all four of the car's occupants possessed it. Unlike the civil presumptions examined in § 16.05 above, which provide for mandatory inferences if uncontroverted, the Court's construction of the presumption in *Ulster County* left the jurors free to reject the inference even if the defendants offered no evidence at all.

The *Ulster County* decision emphasized that to sustain a conviction, the inference identified by a "permissive statutory presumption" must be rational when applied to the facts of a case. A permissive statutory presumption would be improper "only if, under the facts of the case, there is no rational way the trier could make the connection permitted by the inference. For only in that situation is there any risk that an explanation of the permissible inference to a jury, or its use by a jury, has caused the presumptively rational fact finder to make an erroneous factual determination." Under the *Ulster County* facts, concluded the Court, the inference of possession by all occupants was entirely rational. None of the occupants were "hitchhikers or other casual passengers;" the guns partially in the girl's handbag were car were plainly visible to all occupants; and "a 16 year old girl in the company of three adult men . . . was the least likely of the four to be carrying one, let alone two, heavy handguns."

With these principles in mind, return to the presumption that a secondhand dealer's "knowledge that goods were stolen" is presumed from "evidence that the dealer acquired the goods in circumstances that should have caused the dealer to make a reasonable inquiry to determine whether the person from whom the goods were bought had legal title to them." Under the *Ulster County* reasoning, the statute's "presumption" would be valid only if (1) the judge instructed the jurors that they might, but did not have to, infer knowledge from a dealer's acquisition of goods in suspicious circumstances; and (2) the inference was rational under the facts of the case.

Problem 16-19: Pet(ty) Offense

Al Falfa, a 12-year-old boy, is charged with criminal trespass. The owner of a pet store claims that a small group of boys who appeared to be between the ages of 11 and 13 ran into his shop, opened the cages of numerous dogs and cats, and ran out. The pet store owner's testimony with respect to Al was as follows:

PROSECUTOR: Did you see the defendant in the shop before the cages were opened?

A: I did. Moments before the other boys ran in, he was looking at various animals, including the birds and the fish.

PROSECUTOR: Was the defendant among the group of boys who you saw opening the cages?

A: I really couldn't say.

PROSECUTOR: Did the defendant run out along with the others?

A: No, he was laughing but he stayed in the store. Before the jurors began deliberating, the judge instructed them pursuant to a statutory presumption that they "might, but were not required to, infer from the defendant's presence in the store moments before the attack that the defendant was acting as a lookout and was a participant in the unlawful activities." *Is this instruction valid under the principles of the "Ulster County" case?*

Problem 16-20: Fire Escape

Penny Tenshery is charged with first degree murder. The prosecution contends that shortly before the killing, Penny had escaped from prison and was carrying a prison guard's gun. According to the prosecution, Penny came to the victim's house and demanded the victim's car keys. Penny shot and killed the victim when the victim started to slam the front door in Penny's face. Penny's defense is lack of intent to kill; Penny asserts that the gun fired accidentally when the door came into contact with it. *Which if any of the following jury instructions would be valid?*

1. "A person of sound mind is presumed to intend the acts that he or she performs."

2. "You may but are not required to infer from the fact that the defendant was in the process of escaping from prison at the time of the killing that the killing was intentional."

3. "All homicides are presumed intentional in the absence of evidence that would rebut the presumption. Thus, if the State has proved beyond a reasonable doubt that a killing has occurred it is presumed that the killing was done

intentionally, but the defendant may rebut this presumption either with direct or circumstantial evidence."

4. "The defendant is presumed innocent."

Assume that Penny was charged with first-degree murder under the following statute: "A killing that occurs in the course of escaping from prison is first-degree murder, unless the killing is the result of accident in which case the killing is murder in the second degree. The defendant shall have the burden of proving by clear and convincing evidence that a killing that occurred in the course of escaping from prison was the result of accident." The judge instructs the jurors in accordance with the statute that Penny has the burden of proof on the issue of whether the killing was accidental. *Is this a valid instruction?*

§ 16.07 JUDICIAL NOTICE (RULE 201)

Rule 201 allows (and sometimes compels) judges to rule that adjudicative facts have been established. Subject to notice provisions and the right to a hearing, judges may judicially notice facts that are "generally known within the trial court's general jurisdiction" or facts that "can be accurately and readily determined from sources whose accuracy cannot reasonably be questioned."

Judicial notice is a mechanism by which parties can conclusively establish the accuracy of factual information while bypassing the usual proof process. For example, a judge supplied during a pre-trial conference with reliable supporting information may take judicial notice that "The Florida Marlins won the baseball World Series for the second time in 2003." Once the judge judicially notices this fact, it need not be proved (and indeed cannot be proved) by witnesses or other evidence and is binding on the jury.

Like presumptions, judicial notice is both a shortcut to proof and an effort to further the rationality of trial outcomes. It is a shortcut to proof in that parties can establish the accuracy of factual information without having to call witnesses or otherwise go through the formal proof process. Judicial notice also furthers rationality by making information that is unquestionably accurate binding on judges and jurors.

Example 1

A judge sitting in Cook County (Chicago) could take judicial notice that "Michigan Avenue north of the Chicago River is a busy commercial thoroughfare." While this information might not be generally known throughout the country, it would certainly be generally known within the territorial jurisdiction of a judge sitting in Chicago.

Example 2

After referring to a smart phone's calendar, a judge could take judicial notice that "June 14 of last year was a Sunday." Few people would carry this information around in their heads, but it is readily established by reference to a reliable source. Similarly, a judge could rely on a physics textbook as a basis for taking judicial notice of the atomic number of krypton, if the judge ever cared to do so.

Rule 201 further provides as follows:

- If judicial notice is appropriate, a judge has the power to take judicial notice whether or not one of the parties asks the judge to do so.

- If judicial notice is appropriate, a judge *must* take judicial notice if requested by a party and supplied with the necessary supporting information.

- Whether a judge is about to take judicial notice on the judge's own motion or at the behest of a party, any party has a right to a hearing on the propriety of taking judicial notice.

- A judge may take judicial notice at any stage of a proceeding, even on appeal.

Example 3

A plaintiff suing for infringement of a trademark forgets to offer the legally necessary evidence that the trademark was registered with the federal government. The defendant fails to notice the omission until the case is on appeal, at which time the defendant asks the appellate court to dismiss the case. After the plaintiff provides the necessary documentation and the defendant has a chance to dispute it, the appellate court might take judicial notice that the trademark had been registered with the government.

- In civil jury trials, judges must instruct jurors to accept judicially noticed information as conclusive. In criminal jury trials, jurors are told that they "may but are not required to" accept judicially noticed information as conclusive.

- Rule 201 govern only judicial notice of "adjudicative facts." Rule 201 nowhere defines what constitutes an "adjudicative fact," an omission that may unjustly unnerve you if you think that this is the sort of information you should have already known when you entered law school. One possible reason for the omission is that the term is imprecise. You can perhaps best understand it to signify the case-specific factual information that constitutes parties' versions of "what happened." For instance, at trial you can elicit stories through a combination of oral testimony, documents, party admissions in discovery papers and judicially-noticed facts. Thus, representing the plaintiff in an ordinary negligence case growing out of an automobile accident, two adjudicative facts in your story might consist of:

1. A witness' testimony that the defendant was driving at least 55 m.p.h. just prior to the accident; and

2. The judicially noticed adjudicative fact that it was raining at the time of the accident, as established by official Weather Bureau records.

The primary significance of Rule 201's adjudicative facts limitation is that it allows judges and jurors to make decisions based in part on factual information that is neither offered into evidence during the trial nor judicially noticed. Reference to such "outside the record" factual information occurs when judges and jurors use experience and common sense to make factual determinations. They evaluate stories through the use of heuristics drawn from daily life. For example, a judge or juror might conclude that a defendant who was late for an appointment was speeding at the time of an accident, based in part on a heuristic that "people who are late for appointments often speed to get to the appointments as soon as possible." Information about the general behavior of people who are late to appointments will be neither offered into evidence during trial nor judicially noticed. Such information is the sort that we expect judges and jurors to "bring to the table." The information does not constitute an adjudicative fact, and it is not subject to the strictures of Rule 201.

Judges, primarily appellate court judges, commonly also rely on "outside the record" information in the course of common law rule-making. Professor Kenneth Davis has labeled such factual information "legislative facts," because like legislators considering new legislation, appellate court judges rely on generalizations drawn from everyday experience when making decisions. For example, when the U.S. Supreme Court in the famous case of *Miranda v. Arizona*,[15] decided that statements resulting from police interrogations of prisoners were inadmissible in the absence of "Miranda warnings," the Court relied in part on an assertion that "the compulsion to speak in the isolated setting of the police station may well be greater than in courts." That assertion was probably not based on evidence in the record. Rather, the assertion reflected the majority justices' beliefs about the effect of arrest and confinement on arrestees. Judges commonly rely on such beliefs when making common-law decisions, and their ability to do so is not limited by Rule 201.

"Foreign law" is sometimes relevant to the outcome of a federal court case. For example, a federal court sitting in Florida might have to interpret a contract according to New York or German law. In such situations, the federal court judge has the power to take judicial notice of foreign law, whether contained in statutes or judicial opinions. Rule 201 does not govern the process, since laws are not adjudicative facts. Traditionally, foreign law was no different than any other item of evidence; it had to be proved and submitted to the factfinder as a question of fact. Modern rules in most jurisdictions authorize judges to take judicial notice of foreign law, usually after being furnished with the relevant law by one of the parties. See, for example, Federal Rules of Civil Procedure 44.1, providing in part that a "court, in determining foreign law, may consider any relevant material or source, including testimony, whether or not submitted by a party or admissible under the Federal Rules of Evidence. The court's determination shall be treated as a ruling on a question of law." This broad language allows a federal judge seeking foreign law to phone a knowledgeable friend in a foreign jurisdiction and obtain information as to the jurisdiction's law. Of course, all parties would be able to weigh in on the friend's information.

---

[15] 384 U.S. 436 (1966).

Problem 16-21: The Knowledgeable Judge

Personal injury case growing out of an automobile collision. When plaintiff's counsel asks the plaintiff to describe the intersection where the collision took place, the judge states that "I drive past that intersection every day. I take judicial notice that there was a four-way stop sign at that intersection at the time of the collision, and instruct the jury to accept that fact as conclusively established." *Has the judge properly taken judicial notice?*

After the plaintiff introduces evidence that the defendant was late for an important business meeting at the time of the collision, the judge states that "I take judicial notice that people who are late for important business meetings are likely to drive too fast, and instruct the jury to accept that fact as conclusively established." *Has the judge properly taken judicial notice?*

Problem 16-22: The Expert Judge

Cole Motose sues Dr. Frank Galvin, an anesthesiologist, for brain damage allegedly resulting from the doctor's use of an improper anesthetic during surgery. Cole claims that Dr. Galvin gave him the wrong anesthetic because Galvin misread the time of her last meal on her medical chart. The judge states that "I was an anesthesiologist before going to law school, and specialized in medical malpractice cases before going on the bench. It's hornbook medicine that the anesthetic administered by Dr. Galvin should not have been given to a patient who had eaten within an hour of surgery. I'll take judicial notice of that fact and instruct the jury to find that the anesthetic was improper if the jury concludes that Cole's medical chart accurately indicated that she had eaten within an hour of surgery. *Has the judge properly taken judicial notice?*

Problem 16-23: Consider the Source

Dustin Miojo is charged with a murder that took place on March 8 at 9 p.m., and testifies that he was at home watching "Cooking With Pearl Edna Gates" on Channel 5 at the time of the murder. To attack this alibi, the prosecutor wants the trial judge to take judicial notice that "Cooking With Pearl Edna Gates" was not showing on Channel 5 at the time of the murder. Indicate which if any of the following sources would provide adequate support for this request (more than one may be adequate):

1. A copy of the local area "TV Guide" for the week of the murder, indicating that "Barney Goes Undercover" was the program scheduled to be shown on Channel 5 at 9 p.m. on March 8.

2. The telephone number of Channel 5's program manager, who will orally inform the judge that the cooking show did not begin airing on Channel 5 until March 15.

3. An affidavit of Pearl Edna Gates stating that "My cooking show did not begin airing in any market until March 15."

4. A story in the local newspaper for the date of March 15 downloaded off the paper's web site, headlined "Pearl Edna Gates Cooking Show to Debut Tonight."

5. Testimony of a friend who accompanied Dustin's mother when she visited Dustin in jail that the mother fainted when Dustin told her that he'd been at home watching the "Pearl Edna Gates Cooking Show" at the time of the murder."

Problem 16-24: Source Spot

Same case as previous problem. In support of Dustin's alibi defense, Dustin's lawyer tries to discredit the identification by the prosecution's principal eyewitness. The defense lawyer's cross-examination emphasizes that Dustin and the eyewitness are of different ethnicities, and that the eyewitness feared being shot in the same incident. Defense counsel then furnishes the judge with the book *Eyewitness Identification* by Dr. Elizabeth Loftus, who the prosecutor stipulates is an authority in the field of eyewitness identification. Based on the results of experiments described in the book and the opinions of Dr. Loftus, defense counsel asks the judge to take judicial notice that the accuracy of identifications is diminished when people are of different ethnicities and the person making the identification is scared and nervous. *Should the judge accede to the defense counsel's request?*

Problem 16-25: Read My Clips

In a suit by City seeking to enjoin the holding of a rally by the Marching Tuba Players Asso. (MTPA), City furnishes the court with newspaper clippings reporting on recent MTPA rallies in other communities and asks the court to take judicial notice that the previous rallies have been extremely loud and disorganized and have led to violence. *Should the judge grant the request?*

Problem 16-26: Hear No Evil

In a child custody dispute, the son's father asks the judge to order that the son not be present while the parents testify. To support the request, which the mother opposes, the father asks the judge to take judicial notice that listening to each of the parents testify to the other's misdeeds would be harmful to the son.

1. Is the request for judicial notice proper?

2. Is the answer to the previous question different if the father furnishes the judge with a copy of *Child Development in a Nutshell* by Dr. Yung Sigmund, in which the author states that listening to parents accuse each other of misdeeds can cause irreparable damage to children's superegos?

3. Can the judge refuse to take judicial notice yet order that the child not be present during the parents' testimony on the ground that hearing their testimony might be harmful to the son?

4. To support his petition for custody of his son, the father cites an appellate court case decided in the same jurisdiction about 45 years earlier in which the court stated in a child custody case that "the court takes judicial notice that all other things being equal it's better for a father to have custody of a son because as is generally known, they can then develop their mutual interests in such masculine activities as athletics, fishing, and working with mechanical devices." As the mother's attorney, what argument would you make in opposition to the father's

request that the judge take judicial notice that it is generally in the best interests of a son to be in his father's custody?

Problem 16-27: Power Play

Wayne sues Katerina for intentionally injuring Wayne while they were playing in an adult league ice hockey game. Katerina asks the judge to take judicial notice and instruct the jurors that ice hockey is a rough physical contact sport.

1. Is Katerina's request proper?

2. If the request is proper, what if any supporting information would Katerina have to furnish to the judge?

Problem 16-28: Attorney's Fees

Anna Turney sues the *Local Gazette* for libel after the Gazette publishes an article stating that Turney was "the subject of numerous disciplinary complaints pending before the State Bar." Based on State Bar records furnished to the judge, the *Gazette* asks the judge to take judicial notice that six complaints against Turney for fee gouging are currently pending before the State Bar.

1. Is the *Gazette*'s request proper?

2. What is the propriety of these further requests for judicial notice by the *Gazette:*

   a. "Your Honor, we ask that you take judicial notice that six complaints constitute "numerous complaints."

   b. "Your Honor, we ask that you take judicial notice that complaints for fee gouging constitute disciplinary complaints."

3. Assume that the *Gazette* article also stated that "a review of the complaints indicates that Turney routinely misleads clients as to the amount of fees they'll have to pay." The *Gazette* asks the judge to examine the complaints and take judicial notice that Turney misleads clients as to the amount of her fees. *Is the request proper? What if the article stated that "all of the complaints involve claims that Turney routinely misleads clients as to the amount of fees they'll have to pay," and the* Gazette *asks the judge to examine the complaints and take judicial notice that they involve claims about improper fees?*

4. Assume that the judge takes judicial notice that six complaints against Turney for fee gouging are currently pending before the State Bar. *May Turney then offer evidence that she was not the attorney named in those complaints?*

Problem 16-29: Fellin Down

Rex Fellin is charged with armed robbery and with being an ex-felon in possession of a firearm. Rex's defense to the armed robbery charge is mistaken identity; his defense to the possession of a firearm charge is that he knew nothing about the gun that the police found in his car at the time of his arrest and that the gun did not belong to him.

1. The prosecutor asks the judge to take judicial notice that Rex is an ex-felon, and gives the judge a certified "Record of Judgment of Conviction" indicating that Rex had been convicted of armed robbery five years ago. *Can the judge take judicial notice as requested? If so, what instruction should the judge give the jury with respect to judicial notice?*

2. The prosecutor seeks to prove that Fellin committed both a previous armed robbery and the armed robbery for which he is now on trial by posing as a wedding guest, stealing the wedding presents at gunpoint and later writing thank you notes. Assume that such evidence would be admissible to prove identity as a "signature crime" under Rule 404 (b). The prosecutor asks the judge to take judicial notice that Fellin carried out the prior crime in this manner, and supports the request by offering a Certified Transcript of the sentencing hearing in Fellin's prior trial, during which the judge stated that "I find that Rex Fellin committed the crime by posing as a wedding guest, stealing the wedding presents at gunpoint and later writing thank you notes." *Is the prosecutor's request proper?*

3. Fellin is convicted of being an ex-felon in possession of a firearm, and appeals the conviction. The appellate court indicates its intention to reverse the conviction on the ground that the prosecutor's only evidence that Fellin was an ex-felon consisted of inadmissible hearsay. The prosecutor then submits to the appellate court a certified "Record of Judgment of Conviction" indicating that Rex had been convicted of armed robbery five years ago, and asks the appellate court to affirm the conviction by taking judicial notice that Fellin is an ex-felon. *Is the prosecutor's request proper?*

Problem 16-30: Pane and Simple

You are prosecuting Larry Burg for nighttime residential burglary. You claim that Larry broke into the burgled residence at midnight. Identification of Larry as the burglar rests in part on the results of fingerprint analysis, which according to the report of a police fingerprint analyst shows that fingerprints found on a windowsill of the burgled house are Larry's.

1. Proving that the burglary took place at night elevates the crime to a more serious felony. The next-door neighbor testifies that "It was midnight when I heard smashing glass and saw someone crawl through a broken window, and called the police." *Following this testimony, can the judge properly instruct the jurors that "If you conclude that a burglary took place at midnight, you are instructed to find that it took place at nighttime?"*

2. To establish the reliability of fingerprint analysis, can you properly ask the judge to take judicial notice of the general reliability of fingerprint analysis, or do you have to lay a foundation as to its reliability through expert testimony or by submitting relevant scientific studies to the judge?

3. You may properly offer into evidence a police fingerprint analyst's report indicating that the fingerprints found on a windowsill of the burgled house are Larry's by which of the following methods?

   a. Asking the judge to take judicial notice that the results of the fingerprint analysis are accurate.

b. Calling the police fingerprint analyst as a witness to testify to how the analysis was performed and what results were obtained.

c. Offering the report into evidence as an Official Record under Rule 803(8).

d. All of the above.

Problem 16-31: Dicta

You are an Associate Justice of your state's Supreme Court (congratulations on your rapid ascent through the ranks). An 18-year-old male convicted of statutory rape, defined as "sexual intercourse with a female under the age of 16," has challenged the constitutionality of the statutory rape law on equal protection grounds because only males and not females can be convicted of statutory rape. Assume that the record from the courts below is silent as to the following statements. *Which could your opinion properly refer to either because you took judicial notice or because they constitute legislative facts not subject to judicial notice requirements? Which could you not properly refer to?*

1. "A recent study by the National Institute of Health found that more than half of the teenage girls who become pregnant fail to graduate from high school."

2. "Teenage females often seek the company of older males, and males often seek the company of younger females."

3. "The defendant accomplished the intercourse through subtle means of force and intimidation."

4. "Gender-neutral statutory rape laws are in force in 38 other states."

Problem 16-32: Transcript Analysis

Emma Lee is the beneficiary of a $1 million life insurance policy taken out by her late husband Phil three years before he died as the result of a self-inflicted gunshot wound. Emma claims that Phil shot himself accidentally in the course of cleaning his revolver, which under the terms of the policy obligates the life insurance company to pay double the face amount of the policy. The life insurance company claims that Phil committed suicide, which means that it only has to pay Emma the face value of the policy, which it has already done. Thus, Emma has filed this suit to recover the other $1 million that she believes the insurance company is obligated to pay. *Please answer the italicized questions embedded in the transcript below.*

PLAINTIFF'S ATTORNEY: Emma, do you recall what happened the day that your husband died?

A: I'll never forget it. We'd been watching TV at night, and were about to go upstairs to bed when he said that he'd be up in a minute, that he was going to the kitchen to clean his gun.

DEFENDANT'S ATTORNEY: Objection, move to strike what the husband said, hearsay.

JUDGE: *What ruling?*

PLAINTIFF'S ATTORNEY: And then what happened?

A: Well, I went upstairs and about five minutes later I heard a loud noise that sounded to me like a gunshot.

DEFENDANT'S ATTORNEY: Objection, move to strike, improper opinion, speculation.

JUDGE: Overruled. *Is this ruling correct?*

PLAINTIFF'S ATTORNEY: From the sound of the shot, could you tell what kind of gun it came from?

DEFENDANT'S ATTORNEY: *What if any objection might defense counsel make to this question?*

A: Yes, it came from a revolver.

PLAINTIFF'S ATTORNEY: What did you do then?

A: I screamed, "Oh my God, Phil has accidentally fired the gun!"

DEFENDANT'S ATTORNEY: Objection, hearsay.

PLAINTIFF'S ATTORNEY: The statement is admissible as an excited utterance.

JUDGE: *What ruling?*

PLAINTIFF'S ATTORNEY: Please continue.

A: I didn't hear Phil say anything in response, so I ran down the stairs and into the kitchen. I saw Phil sitting in a chair at the table with his head and the top part of his body slumped over onto the table, and I saw some blood on the table. It was awful.

PLAINTIFF'S ATTORNEY: Your Honor, it has been stipulated between the parties that Mr. Lee died of a gunshot wound to his left temple.

DEFENDANT'S ATTORNEY: That's correct, Your Honor. So stipulated.

JUDGE: Very well, I accept the stipulation.

PLAINTIFF'S ATTORNEY: No further questions at this time.

DEFENDANT'S ATTORNEY: Just a couple of questions, Your Honor. Ms. Lee, from the date of your husband's death until the date you filed this lawsuit, you lost over half a million dollars in the stock market, correct?

A: That's true.

DEFENDANT'S ATTORNEY: And two days after your husband died, you told a neighbor that you didn't remember a thing about the events leading up to his death, correct?

A: That's true.

DEFENDANT'S ATTORNEY: No further questions.

PLAINTIFF'S ATTORNEY: No questions. Plaintiff rests.

§ 16.07   JUDICIAL NOTICE (RULE 201)   827

DEFENDANT'S ATTORNEY: I move to dismiss. The plaintiff has the burden of producing evidence sufficient to establish a prima facie case that Mr. Lee's death was an accident. Here, the evidence is at least as consistent with suicide as it is with accident, and Ms. Lee's account of the events leading up to her husband's death was called seriously into question on cross-examination.

JUDGE: In ruling on that motion, I'll not consider the evidence elicited on cross-exam because I'm limited to deciding whether the plaintiff's evidence if believed is sufficient to establish a prima facie case. *Is this an accurate statement?*

JUDGE: Nevertheless, I conclude that the plaintiff's evidence, even were it not contradicted, is insufficient as a matter of law to support a finding that death was accidental, so I'll sustain the motion. *Is this ruling accurate?*

PLAINTIFF'S ATTORNEY: While I disagree with Your Honor's ruling, I am prepared to offer additional evidence, so do I have permission to reopen the plaintiff's case-in — chief? Thank you, Your Honor. Ms. Lee, what if anything did you and your husband talk about while you and he were watching TV on the night he died?

A: One thing he said was that his job as an accountant was getting boring and that middle-school teachers had much more satisfying lives.

DEFENDANT'S ATTORNEY: Objection and move to strike, hearsay.

JUDGE: Overruled. *Is this ruling correct?*

PLAINTIFF'S ATTORNEY: And did your husband seem depressed in the days prior to his death?

A: Not at all.

DEFENDANT'S ATTORNEY: Objection and move to strike, speculation, lack of foundation.

JUDGE: Overruled. *Is this ruling correct?*

PLAINTIFF'S ATTORNEY: Now, you've described seeing your husband slumped on the kitchen table after you heard the gunshot. What else did you notice about the table?

A: I saw a small pile of rags that Phil used to use for cleaning his gun and an open can of gun cleaning fluid.

PLAINTIFF'S ATTORNEY: I'd ask that the court take judicial notice that the presence of cleaning rags and cleaning fluid indicates that Mr. Lee was in the process of cleaning

	his gun rather than committing suicide when the gun fired. *Is this request proper?*
PLAINTIFF'S ATTORNEY:	I'd also ask the court to take judicial notice of the rule in our jurisdiction that a violent death is presumed not to have been the result of suicide.
JUDGE:	I will apply that rule to this case.
DEFENDANT'S ATTORNEY:	Objection. Under Rule 201(e), I'm entitled to be heard as to the propriety of Your Honor's taking judicial notice.
JUDGE:	The request is denied. Rule 201(e) is inapplicable in this situation. *Is this statement correct?*
PLAINTIFF'S ATTORNEY:	Plaintiff rests.
DEFENDANT'S ATTORNEY:	Renew the motion to dismiss for lack of a prima facie case.
JUDGE:	That motion is denied; the plaintiff's evidence together with the presumption is sufficient to establish a prima facie case that Mr. Lee died as the result of an accidentally self-inflicted gunshot wound. *Is this ruling correct?*
PLAINTIFF'S ATTORNEY:	Your Honor, it has never been determined in our jurisdiction whether the presumption is one affecting the burden of proof or the burden of producing evidence. Evidence rules in our jurisdiction give Your Honor the power to construe it as one or the other, and I ask that Your Honor take judicial notice that in our jurisdiction there exists a strong social policy disfavoring suicide and based on this social policy should construe the presumption as one affecting the burden of proof.
JUDGE:	Based on the existence of a strong social policy against concluding that people have died as the result of suicide, I rule that the presumption is one that affects the burden of proof.
DEFENDANT'S ATTORNEY:	Objection under Rule 201. The policy to which Your Honor refers is vague and neither generally known within this court's territorial jurisdiction nor capable of accurate and ready determination.
JUDGE:	I'm not limited by Rule 201 in making this ruling, Counsel. *Is this statement correct?*
JUDGE:	Based on my ruling that the presumption against suicide is one affecting the burden of proof, if the defendant fails to present evidence to rebut the presumed fact of non-suicide, I'll enter judgment as a matter of law in the plaintiff's favor. *Is this ruling correct?*

JUDGE: Also as a result of my ruling, I'll indicate for the record that if the defendant offers evidence from which the jury can rationally conclude that death occurred as the result of suicide, I'll instruct the jurors that the defendant has the burden of proving that Mr. Lee did not die of violent means and of proving that his death was the result of suicide. *Would this instruction be correct?*

§ 16.08 MULTIPLE-CHOICE REVIEW PROBLEMS

Review Problem 16-A

Suit for personal injuries growing out of an automobile accident. *Which if any of the following items of evidence could not be properly proved through the mechanism of judicial notice?*

1. That small children frequently play in the residential alleyway in which the collision occurred.

2. That the alleyway in which the collision occurred is located within the city limits of the city of Phoenix, Arizona.

3. That at 5 p.m. on October 3, when the collision took place, the sun had not yet set.

4. That skid marks will be produced if the brakes are suddenly applied to a car going at least 40 m.p.h.

5. All of the above may be proper subjects for judicial notice.

Review Problem 16-B

Tom Paine sues Dr. Billie Burke for dental malpractice, alleging that Dr. Burke's negligence in extracting a dead tooth caused Paine to lose two additional teeth, one on either side of the extracted tooth. The jurisdiction in which the case is brought has a "*res ipsa loquitur*" presumption that negligence is presumed if, among other things, an injury is one that does not normally occur in the absence of negligence. (The other elements of the *res ipsa loquitur* presumption are not in dispute.) This presumption has been construed in accord with Rule 301, as one shifting the burden of producing evidence. During his case-in-chief, plaintiff Paine presents testimony from expert witness Dr. Don Dentin D.D.S. that Dr. Burke used improper extraction techniques, and that loss of additional teeth does not occur in the absence of negligence. The defense's case consists of testimony from expert witness Dr. Beth Moeller D.D.S. that "loss of surrounding teeth is a common side effect of dead tooth extractions, no matter how carefully they are performed." *As a result of the presumption and the testimony, the judge should:*

1. Ignore the presumption and instruct the jurors that the burden is on Paine to prove that Dr. Burke was negligent.

2. Instruct the jurors that if they conclude that loss of additional teeth does not occur in the absence of negligence, they must find that Dr. Burke was negligent

unless they are convinced by a preponderance of the evidence that Dr. Burke was not negligent.

3. Instruct the jurors that if they conclude that loss of additional teeth does not occur in the absence of negligence, they must find that Dr. Burke was negligent.

4. Take judicial notice that loss of additional teeth is a common side effect of dead tooth extractions.

Review Problem 16-C

Alison Garvey is charged with uttering a bad check with intent to defraud. The prosecution offers evidence that Garvey paid by check for a variety of small electronic items at Sears. The check was in the amount of $83, and was returned unpaid, marked "not sufficient funds." The law under which Garvey is prosecuted provides that "intent to defraud shall be presumed from the utterance of a check in the amount of $50 or more when the maker of the check does not have sufficient funds in the account on which the check is drawn to cover the full amount of the check." *Based on the evidence and the presumption, the judge should:*

1. Instruct the jurors that Garvey is presumed to have uttered the check with the intent to defraud.

2. Instruct the jurors that the burden of proof is on Garvey to raise a reasonable doubt as to whether she uttered the check with intent to defraud.

3. Instruct the jurors that they may infer intent to defraud from the utterance of the bad check if they choose to do so.

4. Sustain Garvey's motion for judgment of acquittal if the prosecution is unable to offer additional evidence of Garvey's guilt.

Review Problem 16-D

A group of parents sues a school district in an effort to obtain a court order requiring the district to give children from lower-income areas a fair chance to gain entry into top colleges by offering additional Advanced Placement courses in inner-city high schools. *Which, if any, of the following trial court conclusions must have been either testified to at trial or have been properly judicially noticed?*

1. "Attending a top university is an important way of making connections that can open doors in later life."

2. "The competition to get into the country's top colleges and universities is fierce."

3. "Students admitted last year into a group of 25 universities typically ranked as among the top universities in the country took an average of nine Advanced Placement courses."

4. "A college education is as important for the maturation process that it stimulates as for the knowledge and skills that students obtain."

5. All of these conclusions must have been either testified to at trial or have been properly judicially noticed.

§ 16.09 CASE LIBRARY

COUNTY COURT OF ULSTER COUNTY v. ALLEN
United States Supreme Court 442 U.S. 140, 99 S. Ct. 2213, 60 L. Ed. 2d 777 (1979)

Mr. Justice Stevens delivered the opinion of the Court.

A New York statute provides that, with certain exceptions, the presence of a firearm in an automobile is presumptive evidence of its illegal possession by all persons then occupying the vehicle. The United States Court of Appeals for the Second Circuit held that respondents may challenge the constitutionality of this statute in a federal habeas corpus proceeding and that the statute is "unconstitutional on its face." We granted certiorari to review these holdings and also to consider whether the statute is constitutional in its application to respondents.

Four persons, three adult males (respondents) and a 16-year-old girl (Jane Doe, who is not a respondent here), were jointly tried on charges that they possessed two loaded handguns, a loaded machinegun, and over a pound of heroin found in a Chevrolet in which they were riding when it was stopped for speeding on the New York Thruway shortly after noon on March 28, 1973. The two large-caliber handguns, which together with their ammunition weighed approximately six pounds, were seen through the window of the car by the investigating police officer. They were positioned crosswise in an open handbag on either the front floor or the front seat of the car on the passenger side where Jane Doe was sitting. Jane Doe admitted that the handbag was hers. The machinegun and the heroin were discovered in the trunk after the police pried it open. The car had been borrowed from the driver's brother earlier that day; the key to the trunk could not be found in the car or on the person of any of its occupants, although there was testimony that two of the occupants had placed something in the trunk before embarking in the borrowed car. The jury convicted all four of possession of the handguns and acquitted them of possession of the contents of the trunk.

Counsel for all four defendants objected to the introduction into evidence of the two handguns, the machinegun, and the drugs, arguing that the State had not adequately demonstrated a connection between their clients and the contraband. The trial court overruled the objection, relying on the presumption of possession created by the New York statute. At the close of the trial, the judge instructed the jurors that they were entitled to infer possession from the defendants' presence in the car.

II

Inferences and presumptions are a staple of our adversary system of factfinding. It is often necessary for the trier of fact to determine the existence of an element of the crime — that is, an "ultimate" or "elemental" fact — from the existence of one or more "evidentiary" or "basic" facts. The value of these evidentiary devices, and their validity under the Due Process Clause, vary from case to case, however, depending on the strength of the connection between the particular basic and elemental facts involved and on the degree to which the device curtails the fact finder's freedom to assess the evidence independently. Nonetheless, in criminal cases, the ultimate test of any device's constitutional validity in a given case remains constant: the device must not undermine the fact finder's responsibility at trial, based on evidence adduced by the State, to find the ultimate facts beyond a reasonable doubt.

The most common evidentiary device is the entirely permissive inference or presumption, which allows — but does not require — the trier of fact to infer the elemental fact from proof by the prosecutor of the basic one and which places no burden of any kind on the defendant. In that situation the basic fact may constitute prima facie evidence of the elemental fact. When reviewing this type of device, the Court has required the party challenging it to demonstrate its invalidity as applied to him. Because this permissive presumption leaves the trier of fact free to credit or reject the inference and does not shift the burden of proof, it affects the application of the "beyond a reasonable doubt" standard only if, under the facts of the case, there is no rational way the trier could make the connection permitted by the inference. For only in that situation is there any risk that an explanation of the permissible inference to a jury, or its use by a jury, has caused the presumptively rational fact finder to make an erroneous factual determination.

The trial judge's instructions make it clear that the presumption was merely a part of the prosecution's case, that it gave rise to a permissive inference available only in certain circumstances, rather than a mandatory conclusion of possession, and that it could be ignored by the jury even if there was no affirmative proof offered by defendants in rebuttal. The judge explained that possession could be actual or constructive, but that constructive possession could not exist without the intent and ability to exercise control or dominion over the weapons. He also carefully instructed the jury that there is a mandatory presumption of innocence in favor of the defendants that controls unless it, as the exclusive trier of fact, is satisfied beyond a reasonable doubt that the defendants possessed the handguns in the manner described by the judge. In short, the instructions plainly directed the jury to consider all the circumstances tending to support or contradict the inference that all four occupants of the car had possession of the two loaded handguns and to decide the matter for itself without regard to how much evidence the defendants introduced.

III

As applied to the facts of this case, the presumption of possession is entirely rational. [R]espondents were not "hitchhikers or other casual passengers," and the guns were neither "a few inches in length" nor "out of [respondents'] sight." The argument against possession by any of the respondents was predicated solely on the fact that the guns were in Jane Doe's pocketbook. But several circumstances made it highly improbable that she was the sole custodian of those weapons.

Even if it was reasonable to conclude that she had placed the guns in her purse before the car was stopped by police, the facts strongly suggest that Jane Doe was not the only person able to exercise dominion over them. The two guns were too large to be concealed in her handbag. The bag was consequently open, and part of one of the guns was in plain view, within easy access of the driver of the car and even, perhaps, of the other two respondents who were riding in the rear seat.

Moreover, it is highly improbable that the loaded guns belonged to Jane Doe or that she was solely responsible for their being in her purse. As a 16year-old girl in the company of three adult men she was the least likely of the four to be carrying one, let alone two, heavy handguns. It is far more probable that she relied on the pocketknife found in her brassiere for any necessary self-protection. Under these circumstances, it was not unreasonable for her counsel to argue and for the jury to infer that when the car was halted for speeding, the other passengers in the car anticipated the risk of a search and attempted to conceal their weapons in a pocketbook in the front seat. The inference is surely more likely than the notion that these weapons were the sole property of the 16-year-old girl.

Under these circumstances, the jury would have been entirely reasonable in rejecting the suggestion — which, incidentally, defense counsel did not even advance in their closing arguments to the jury — that the handguns were in the sole possession of Jane Doe. Assuming that the jury did reject it, the case is tantamount to one in which the guns were lying on the floor or the seat of the car in the plain view of the three other occupants of the automobile. In such a case, it is surely rational to infer that each of the respondents was fully aware of the presence of the guns and had both the ability and the intent to exercise dominion and control over the weapons.

Mr. Justice Powell, with whom Mr. Justice Brennan, Mr. Justice Stewart, and Mr. Justice Marshall join, dissenting.

I am not in agreement with the Court's conclusion that the presumption as charged to the jury in this case meets the constitutional requirements of due process. On the contrary, an individual's mere presence in an automobile where there is a handgun does not even make it "more likely than not" that the individual possesses the weapon.

I

In the criminal law, presumptions are used to encourage the jury to find certain facts, with respect to which no direct evidence is presented, solely because other facts have been proved. The purpose of such presumptions is plain: Like certain other jury instructions, they provide guidance for jurors' thinking in considering the evidence laid before them. Once in the jury room, jurors necessarily draw inferences from the evidence — both direct and circumstantial. Through the use of presumptions, certain inferences are commended to the attention of jurors by legislatures or courts.

Legitimate guidance of a jury's deliberations is an indispensable part of our criminal justice system. Nonetheless, the use of presumptions in criminal cases poses at least two distinct perils for defendants' constitutional rights. The Court accurately identifies the first of these as being the danger of interference with "the fact finder's responsibility at trial, based on evidence adduced by the State, to find the ultimate facts beyond a reasonable doubt." If the jury is instructed that it must infer some ultimate fact (that is, some element of the offense) from proof of other facts unless the defendant disproves the ultimate fact by a preponderance of the evidence, then the presumption shifts the burden of proof to the defendant concerning the element thus inferred.

But [e]volving from our decisions is a second standard for judging the constitutionality of criminal presumptions which is based on the due process rule that when the jury is encouraged to make factual inferences, those inferences must reflect some valid general observation about the natural connection between events as they occur in our society.

This due process rule was first articulated by the Court in *Tot v. United States,* in which the Court reviewed the constitutionality of § 2 (f) of the Federal Firearms Act. That statute provided in part that "possession of a firearm or ammunition by any . . . person [who has been convicted of a crime of violence] shall be presumptive evidence that such firearm or ammunition was shipped or transported [in interstate or foreign commerce]." As the Court interpreted the presumption, it placed upon a defendant only the obligation of presenting some exculpatory evidence concerning the origins of a firearm or ammunition, once the Government proved that the defendant had possessed the weapon and had been convicted of a crime of violence. Noting that juries must be permitted to infer from one fact the existence of another essential to guilt, "if reason and experience support the inference," the Court concluded that under some circumstances juries may be guided in making these inferences by legislative or common-law presumptions, even though they may be based "upon a view of relation broader than that a jury might take in a specific case." To provide due process, however, there must be at least a "rational connection between the fact proved and the ultimate fact presumed" — a connection grounded in "common experience." In *Tot,* the Court found that connection to be lacking.

In sum, our decisions uniformly have recognized that due process requires more than merely that the prosecution be put to its proof. In addition, the Constitution restricts the court in its charge to the jury by requiring that, when particular factual inferences are recommended to the jury, those factual inferences be accurate reflections of what history, common sense, and experience tell us about the relations between events in our society. Generally, this due process rule has been articulated as requiring that the truth of the inferred fact be more likely than not whenever the premise for the inference is true. Thus, to be constitutional a presumption must be at least more likely than not true.

II

Undeniably, the presumption charged in this case encouraged the jury to draw a particular factual inference regardless of any other evidence presented: to infer that respondents possessed the weapons found in the automobile "upon proof of the presence of the machine gun and the hand weapon" and proof that respondents "occupied the automobile at the time such instruments were found." I believe that the presumption thus charged was unconstitutional because it did not fairly reflect what common sense and experience tell us about passengers in automobiles and the possession of handguns. People present in automobiles where there are weapons simply are not "more likely than not" the possessors of those weapons.

Plainly, the mere presence of an individual in an automobile — without more — does not indicate that he exercises "dominion or control over" everything within it. [T]here are countless situations in which individuals are invited as guests into vehicles the contents of which they know nothing about, much less have control over. Similarly, those who invite others into their automobile do not generally search them to determine what they may have on their person; nor do they insist that any handguns be identified and placed within reach of the occupants of the automobile. Indeed, handguns are particularly susceptible to concealment and therefore are less likely than are other objects to be observed by those in an automobile.

Because the specific factual inference recommended to the jury in this case is not one that is supported by the general experience of our society. I cannot say that the presumption charged is "more likely than not" to be true. Accordingly, respondents' due process rights were violated by the presumption's use. I dissent.

Chapter 17

PRIVILEGES

§ 17.01 CHAPTER CHECKLIST

1. What is the applicable privilege law in federal courts, the federal common law or the pertinent state law?

2. Is information privileged because it is a confidential communication associated with a special relationship, otherwise based on an important public policy or protected from disclosure by the Constitution?

3. If information is potentially privileged, has the privilege been expressly or impliedly waived?

4. If information is privileged, is there an exception that requires disclosure by the professional who received the information because of a competing public policy?

5. What do *Upjohn Co. v. United States*, 449 U.S. 383, 101 S. Ct. 677, 66 L. Ed. 2d 584 (1981), *Nix v. Whiteside*, 475 U.S. 157, 106 S. Ct. 988, 89 L. Ed. 2d 123 (1986), and *Jaffee v. Redmond*, 518 U.S. 1, 116 S. Ct. 1923, 135 L. Ed. 2d 337 (1996), add to the body and scope of privilege law? These cases are found in the Case Library at the end of the chapter.

§ 17.02 RELEVANT FEDERAL RULES OF EVIDENCE AND PROPOSED (BUT REJECTED) RULES

Rule 501. General Rule

Except as otherwise required by the Constitution of the United States or provided by Act of Congress or in rules prescribed by the Supreme Court pursuant to statutory authority, the privilege of a witness, person, government, State or political subdivision thereof shall be governed by the principles of the common law as they may be interpreted by the courts of the United States in the light of reason and experience. However, in civil actions and proceedings, with respect to an element of a claim or defense as to which State law supplies the rule of decision, the privilege of a witness, person, government, State, or political subdivision thereof shall be determined in accordance with State law.

Rule 502. Attorney-Client Privilege and Work Product; Limitations on Waiver

The following provisions apply, in the circumstances set out, to disclosure of a communication or information covered by the attorney-client privilege or work-product protection.

- a. **Disclosure Made in a Federal proceeding or to a Federal Office or Agency; Scope of a Waiver** — When the disclosure is made in a Federal proceeding or to a Federal office or agency and waives the attorney-client privilege or work-product protection, the waiver extends to an undisclosed communication or information in a Federal or State proceeding only if:

    1. the waiver is intentional;
    2. the disclosed and undisclosed communications or information concern the same subject matter; and
    3. they ought in fairness to be considered together.

- b. **Inadvertent Disclosure** — When made in a Federal proceeding or to a Federal office or agency, the disclosure does not operate as a waiver in a Federal or State proceeding if:

    1. the disclosure is inadvertent;
    2. the holder of the privilege or protection took reasonable steps to prevent disclosure; and
    3. the holder promptly took reasonable steps to rectify the error, including (if applicable) following Federal Rule of Civil Procedure 26(b)(5)(B).

- c. **Disclosure Made in a State Proceeding** — When the disclosure is made in a State proceeding and is not the subject of a State-court order concerning waiver, the disclosure does not operate as a waiver in a Federal proceeding if the disclosure:

    1. Would not be a waiver under this rule if it had been made in a Federal proceeding; or
    2. Is not a waiver under the law of the State where the disclosure occurred.

- d. **Controlling Effect of a Court Order** — A Federal court may order that the privilege or protection is not waived by disclosure connected with the litigation pending before the court — in which event the disclosure is also not a waiver in any other Federal or State proceeding.

- e. **Controlling Effect of a Party Agreement** — An agreement on the effect of disclosure in a Federal proceeding is binding only on the parties to the agreement, unless it is incorporated into a court order.

- f. **Controlling Effect of This Rule** — Notwithstanding Rules 101 and 1101, this rule applies to State proceedings and to Federal court-annexed and Federal court-mandated arbitration proceedings, in the circumstances set out in the rule. And notwithstanding Rule 501, this rule applies even if State law provides the rule of decision.

g. **Definitions** — In this rule:

1. 1."Attorney-Client privilege" means the protection that applicable law provides for confidential attorney-client communications; and

2. "Work-product protection" means the protection that applicable law provides for tangible material (or its intangible equivalent) prepared in anticipation of litigation or for trial."

Rule 1101. Applicability of Rules

. . . .

(c) Rule of privilege. The rule with respect to privileges applies at all stages of all actions, cases and proceedings.

* * * *

(The following rules were proposed but not adopted.)

Proposed Rule 502. Required Reports Privileged By Statute [Not Enacted]

A person, corporation, association, or other organization or entity, either public or private, making a return or report required by law to be made has a privilege to refuse to disclose and to prevent any other person from disclosing the return or report, if the law requiring it to be made so provides. A public officer or agency to whom a return or report is required by law to be made has a privilege to refuse to disclose the return or report if the law requiring it to be made so provides. No privilege exists under this rule in actions involving perjury, false statements, fraud in the return or report, or other failure to comply with the law in question.

Proposed Rule 503. Lawyer-Client Privilege [Not Enacted]

(a) **Definitions.** As used in this rule:

(1) A "client" is a person, public officer, or corporation, association, or other organization or entity, either public or private, who is rendered professional legal services by a lawyer, or who consults a lawyer with a view to obtaining professional legal services from him.

(2) A "lawyer" is a person authorized, or reasonably believed by the client to be authorized, to practice law in any state or nation.

(3) A "representative of the lawyer" is one employed to assist the lawyer in the rendition of professional legal services.

(4) A communication is "confidential" if not intended to be disclosed to third persons other than those to whom disclosure is in furtherance of the rendition of professional legal services to the client or those reasonably necessary for the transmission of the communication.

(b) General rule of privilege. A client has a privilege to refuse to disclose and to prevent any other person from disclosing confidential communications made for the purpose of facilitating the rendition of professional legal services to the client, (1) between himself or his representative and his lawyer or his lawyer's representative, or (2) between his lawyer and the lawyer's representative, or (3) by him or his lawyer to a lawyer representing another in a matter of common interest, or (4) between representatives of the client or between the client and a representative of the client, or (5) between lawyers representing the client.

(c) Who may claim the privilege. The privilege may be claimed by the client, his guardian or conservator, the personal representative of a deceased client, or the successor, trustee, or similar representative of a corporation, association, or other organization, whether or not in existence. The person who was the lawyer at the time of the communication may claim the privilege but only on behalf of the client . . .

(d) Exceptions. There is no privilege under this rule:

(1) **Furtherance of crime or fraud.** If the services of the lawyer were sought or obtained to enable or aid anyone to commit or plan to commit what the client knew or reasonably should have known to be a crime or fraud; or

(2) **Claimants through same deceased client.** As to a communication relevant to an issue between parties who claim through the same deceased client, regardless of whether the claims are by testate or intestate succession or by inter vivos transaction; or

(3) **Breach of duty by lawyer or client.** As to a communication relevant to an issue of breach of duty by the lawyer to his client or by the client to his lawyer; or

(4) **Document attested by lawyer.** As to a communication relevant to an issue concerning an attested document to which the lawyer is an attesting witness; or

(5) **Joint clients.** As to a communication relevant to a matter of common interest between two or more clients if the communication was made by any of them to a lawyer retained or consulted in common, when offered in an action between any of the clients.

Proposed Rule 504. Psychotherapist-Patient Privilege [Not Enacted]

(a) Definitions

(1) A "patient" is a person who consults or is examined or interviewed by a psychotherapist.

(2) A "psychotherapist" is (A) a person authorized to practice medicine in any state or nation, or reasonably believed by the patient so to be, while engaged in the diagnosis or treatment of a mental or emotional condition, including drug addiction, or (B) a person licensed or

certified as a psychologist under the laws of any state or nation, while similarly engaged.

(3) A communication is "confidential" if not intended to be disclosed to third persons other than those present to further the interest of the patient in the consultation, examination, or interview, or persons reasonably necessary for the transmission of the communication, or persons who are participating in the diagnosis and treatment under the direction of the psychotherapist, including members of the patient's family.

(b) **General rule of privilege.** A patient has a privilege to refuse to disclose and to prevent any other person from disclosing confidential communications, made for the purposes of diagnosis or treatment of his mental or emotional condition, including drug addiction, among himself, his psychotherapist, or persons who are participating in the diagnosis or treatment under the direction of the psychotherapist, including members of the patient's family.

(c) **Who may claim the privilege.** The privilege may be claimed by the patient, by his guardian or conservator, or by the personal representative of a deceased patient . . .

(d) **Exceptions.**

(1) **Proceedings for hospitalization.** There is no privilege under this rule for communications relevant to an issue in proceedings to hospitalize the patient for mental illness, if the psychotherapist in the course of diagnosis or treatment has determined that the patient is in need of hospitalization.

(2) **Examination by order of judge.** If the judge orders an examination of the mental or emotional condition of the patient, communications made in the course thereof are not privileged. . . .

(3) **(3) Condition an element of claim or defense.** There is no privilege under this rule as to communications relevant to an issue of the mental or emotional condition of the patient in any proceeding in which he relies upon the condition as an element of his claim or defense, or, after the patient's death, in any proceeding in which any party relies upon the condition as an element of his claim or defense.

Proposed Rule 505. Husband-Wife [Not Enacted]

(a) **(a) General rule of privilege.** An accused in a criminal proceeding has a privilege to prevent his spouse from testifying against him.

(b) **Who may claim the privilege.** The privilege may be claimed by the accused or by the spouse on his behalf. The authority of the spouse to do so is presumed in the absence of evidence to the contrary.

(c) **Exceptions.** There is no privilege under this rule (1) in proceedings in which one spouse is charged with a crime against the person or property of the other or of a child of either, or with a crime against the person or property of a third person committed in the course of committing a crime against the other, or (2) as to matters occurring prior to the marriage, or (3) in proceedings in which a spouse is charged with importing an alien for prostitution or other immoral purposes. . . .

Proposed Rule 506. Communications to Clergymen [Not Enacted]

(a) **(a) Definitions.** As used in this rule:

(1) A "clergyman" is a minister, priest, rabbi, or other similar functionary of a religious organization, or an individual reasonably believed so to be by the person consulting him.

(2) A communication is "confidential" if made privately and not intended for further disclosure except to other persons present in furtherance of the purpose of the communication.

(b) **(b) General rule of privilege.** A person has a privilege to refuse to disclose and to prevent another from disclosing a confidential communication by the person to a clergyman in his professional character as spiritual advisor.

(c) **Who may claim the privilege.** The privilege may be claimed by the person, by his guardian or conservator, or by his personal representative if he is deceased. The clergyman may claim the privilege on behalf of the person. . . .

Proposed Rule 507. Political Vote [Not Enacted]

Every person has a privilege to refuse to disclose the tenor of his vote at a political election conducted by secret ballot unless the vote was cast illegally.

Proposed Rule 508. Trade Secrets. [Not Enacted]

A person has a privilege, which may be claimed by him or his agent or employee, to refuse to disclose and to prevent other persons from disclosing a trade secret owned by him, if the allowance of the privilege will not tend to conceal fraud or otherwise work injustice. When disclosure is directed, the judge shall take such protective measure as the interests of the holder of the privilege and of the parties and the furtherance of justice may require.

Proposed Rule 509. Secrets of State and Other Official Information. [Not Enacted]

(a) **Definitions**

(1) **Secret of state.** A "secret of state" is a governmental secret relating to the national defense or the international relations of the United States.

(2) **Official information.** "Official information" is information within the custody or control of a department or agency of the government the disclosure of which is shown to be contrary to the public interest . . .

(b) **General rule of privilege.** The government has a privilege to refuse to give evidence and to prevent any person from giving evidence upon a showing of reasonable likelihood of danger that the evidence will disclose a secret of state or official information, as defined in this rule.

Proposed Rule 510. Identity of Informer. [Not enacted]

(a) **Rule of privilege.** The government or a state or subdivision thereof has a privilege to refuse to disclose the identity of a person who has furnished information relating to or assisting in an investigation of a possible violation of law to a law enforcement officer or member of a legislative committee or its staff conducting an investigation.

(b) **Who may claim.** The privilege may be claimed by an appropriate representative of the government, regardless of whether the information was furnished to an officer of the government . . . except that in a criminal case the privilege shall not be allowed if the government objects.

(c) **Exceptions.**

(1) **Voluntary disclosure; informer a witness.** No privilege exists under this rule if the identity of the informer or his interest in the subject matter of his communication has been disclosed to those who would have cause to resent the communication . . . or if the informer appears as a witness for the government.

(2) **Testimony on merits.** If it appears from the evidence in the case or from other showing by a party that an informer may be able to give testimony necessary to a fair determination of the issue of guilt or innocence in a criminal case or of a material issue on the merits in a civil case . . . the judge shall give the government an opportunity to show in camera facts relevant to determining whether the informer can, in fact, supply that testimony. . . .

(3) **Legality of obtaining evidence.** If information from an informer is relied upon to establish the legality of the means by which evidence was obtained and the judge is not satisfied that the information was received from an informer reasonably believed to be reliable or credible, he may require the identity of the informer to be disclosed. . . .

Proposed Rule 511. Waiver of Privilege by Voluntary Disclosure. [Not Enacted]

A person upon whom these rules confer a privilege against disclosure of the confidential matter or communication waives the privilege if he or his predecessor while holder of the privilege voluntarily discloses or consents to disclosure of any significant part of the matter or communication. This rule does not apply if the disclosure is itself a privileged communication.

§ 17.03 INTRODUCTION TO PRIVILEGES

Privileges are based on a "public good transcending the normally predominant principle of utilizing all rational means for ascertaining the truth." *Elkins v. United States*, 364 U.S. 206, 234, 80 S. Ct. 1437, 1454, 4 L. Ed. 2d 1669 (1960) (Frankfurter, J., dissenting). In effect, the existence of a privilege signifies a balancing of interests favoring the exclusion of relevant information. The protected interests are variously described as privacy and the promotion of a greater external good. Privacy is illustrated by the confidential communications privilege between husband and wife and the greater good by the adverse spousal testimony privilege.

[A] The Definition of Privileged Evidence

A privilege authorizes the non-disclosure of information. It can be framed as both a right and a power — a right to refuse the dissemination of information and the power to control that information, even after one's death. In effect, a privilege wraps potential evidence in a "cone of silence," much like the shield used to ensure private communications in a popular television show of the 1970s, and subsequent film of the same name, *Get Smart*.

Privileges can operate outside of the courtroom, as well as at trial. A privilege may be invoked in response to pre-trial discovery requests, coerced interrogation, or an attempt to compel testimony. Thus, a deponent in a pre-trial deposition may assert one privilege, a person being interrogated by the police may claim another privilege, and a person's estate may advance still another privilege on the decedent's behalf.

Significantly, a privilege continues to operate regardless of the relevance or importance of the information it shields from disclosure. Even if the information is crucial to the outcome of a case, such as the location of a murder victim's body, the privilege rules maintain the "cone of silence." This limitation on the search for truth is deemed warranted because of public policy considerations. In effect, privileges advance values thought to outweigh the need for a fair and accurate trial process. These values, such as the ability to speak in confidence to an attorney, therapist, spouse, or priest, are arguably essential to core relationships that should not be compromised.

As illustrated by the rejection of specific codified privileges by the drafters of the Federal Rules of Evidence, the decision as to what values to recognize through the law of privileges is a difficult one. Why, for example, should a patient's discussions with a psychotherapist be protected, but not an alleged sexual assault victim's conversation with a licensed sexual assault counselor? Why should the spousal relationship be protected by two privileges, the confidential communications and adverse testimony privileges, when there is absolutely no protection for conversations between parent and child?

Much of the demarcation between what is privileged and what is not owes its existence to the historical development of the law. The fact that some privileges, such as attorney-client and husband-wife, are historically embedded in the common law has not stopped the debate. Some observers have argued that the relationship between parent and child needs as much fostering as spousal and attorney-client relationships.

The exclusion of useful information based on privilege is unusual but not unique. The law of privilege parallels the rules relating to several other evidentiary exclusions, including "relevant but inadmissible" evidence such as subsequent remedial measures, offers to compromise and completed compromises, offers to pay medical expenses, and plea negotiations. *See* Rules 407–410. Those exclusions are sometimes labeled "quasi-privileges," and also are based — at least in part — on public policy considerations designed to encourage certain conduct by the parties. (*See* Chapters 4 and 6, above.)

[B] Federal and State Privileges

Privileges operate in both federal and state courts. The type of evidence that is considered privileged may vary from state to state, from federal to state courts, and within the same court over time. Yet, whether a privilege applies in federal or state court, it generally operates in the same way — to exclude information.

Significantly, state privilege rules sometimes operate in federal court proceedings, effectively replacing the federal common law at these times. Under Rule 501, state privileges apply when state law provides the rule of decision in a civil action or proceeding, which most often occurs in a case where federal jurisdiction is based on diversity of citizenship. *See Erie R. Co. v. Tompkins*, 304 U.S. 64, 58 S. Ct. 817, 82 L. Ed. 1188 (1938).

[C] Sources of Privilege

Privileges are created by courts through the common law, by legislatures through statutory enactments and by the Constitution. All three sources of privilege may be invoked at a single trial or hearing. An example of a privilege firmly entrenched within the common law is the attorney-client privilege. An example of a privilege essentially constructed by statute is the physician-patient privilege. An illustration of a constitutional privilege is the Fifth Amendment privilege against self-incrimination.

While privileges used to be created primarily through the common law, the law of privilege in most states is currently based on statute. The codified privileges often reflect the established common law, such as the attorney-client privilege. Sometimes, however, states have expanded the number of privileges through statutory enactments, adding such privileges as an accident report privilege, an accountant-client privilege, a sexual assault counselor-victim privilege and a domestic violence counselor-victim privilege. Some of these privileges are designed to encourage the free flow of information for public policy reasons. An apt illustration is the accident report privilege. Some states require a person who has been in an automobile accident to cooperate with a police officer who is writing a report about the accident. To promote cooperation, the privilege generally "immunizes" statements made by such persons involved in auto accidents from disclosure.

The third source of privilege, the United States Constitution, includes important express and implied privileges. The Fifth Amendment, as noted above, contains the privilege against self-incrimination. This privilege, often described as "taking the Fifth," is an important protection against coerced testimony. *See, e.g., United States v. Hubbell*, 167 F.3d 552 (D.C. Cir. 1999). Another important constitutional privilege is executive privilege, an implied privilege derived from the principle of the separation of powers. This privilege protects the interests of the United States government by exempting some presidential communications from disclosure in a trial or hearing. (*See United States v. Nixon*, 418 U.S. 683, 94 S. Ct. 3090, 41 L. Ed. 2d 1039 (1974), in which the Supreme Court held that there was a constitutional basis for executive privilege, but that it was only a qualified privilege, depending on the subject matter.)

Example

In the early 1970s, the Committee to Reelect the President (C.R.E.E.P.), engaged in various surveillance and spying activities against political opponents. This group, whose mission was to re-elect President Richard M. Nixon, burglarized the office of the psychiatrist of Daniel Ellsberg, hoping to find incriminating information. (Ellsberg had leaked "The Pentagon Papers," government documents concerning the Vietnam War, to *The New York Times*.) The burglary, at an apartment complex called The Watergate, led to news reports about a cover-up of the relationship between the burglars and C.R.E.E.P.

The authors of most of the news reports were two reporters for *The Washington Post*, Robert Woodward and Carl Bernstein. The reporters refused to disclose their sources, particularly the main one, whom they called "Deep Throat." What is the basis for their refusal?

Answer: The basis for refusing to disclose sources, even in the face of a subpoena, is often called "the newsperson's privilege" or "journalist's privilege," and is traced to the First Amendment of the Constitution. The freedom of the press has been interpreted to include a qualified privilege for journalists that allows them to refuse to disclose their sources. The privilege is qualified, however, and not absolute. A judge might find the privilege outweighed by a particular interest in national security. Over the years, many reporters have voiced a preference for jail over disclosure, warning that forced disclosure would negatively impact the freedom of sources to provide information.

An additional illustration of the scope of the constitutionally based executive privilege resulted from the investigation of President William Jefferson Clinton and others in his administration by special prosecutor Kenneth Starr. In one case, the question arose as to whether Secret Service agents assigned to guard the President in the White House could invoke executive privilege. The Courts held that there was no such ancillary privilege, and that the agents would have to disclose what they saw and heard. Thus, Secret Service agents could be called to testify before a grand jury about the President. *See In re Sealed Case*, 148 F.3d 1073 (D.C. Cir.), *cert. denied*, 525 U.S. 990 (1998).

[D] The Operation of Privileges

Privileges do not operate automatically. A privilege will operate only upon a timely refusal to disclose information or to testify, usually occurring through an objection by counsel at trial or a motion *in limine* (in advance). When a privilege is asserted, the proponent of the privilege is generally assigned the burden of establishing the elements underlying a privilege. Without such action by counsel, an otherwise valid privilege may be waived. Waiver is a complicated concept. It can occur by implication as well as expressly. An implied waiver might occur under widely disparate circumstances, such as if a party reveals confidential communications to a third party or raises a claim at trial that creates a need for the privileged information (e.g., raising an insanity defense may result in waiver of the physician-patient privilege).

Even if counsel objects to disclosure, the objection must be timely. Once a timely objection is made, the court usually considers the merits of the claim *in camera*, outside the hearing of the jury. The need for secrecy is clear. Once jurors have heard information, it is extremely difficult for them to "unhear" it. Thus, judges have to determine whether information is privileged before the information can be disclosed to jurors.

Not all privileges exclude evidence in the same way. Some privileges extend only to confidential communications, such as the clergy-penitent privilege. For privileges based on communications, the witness must still testify and provide all relevant, non-privileged information. The witness may refuse to answer all questions whose answers come within the domain of the privilege.

Other privileges permit a witness to completely refuse to testify. An example of a privilege that offers the option of refusing to testify is the adverse spousal testimony privilege, which allows one spouse to refuse to testify against the other.

[E] Confidential Communication Privileges Generally

Confidential communication privileges, such as attorney-client and clergy-penitent, are based on the following principles:

- A legally recognized *relationship* between the holder of the privilege and the person being consulted (i.e., husband-wife, attorney-client, priest-penitent) exists.

- A *communication* — written, oral, or nonverbal — took place between the holder and the person consulted.

- The communication is *confidential*.

- The *holder* of the privilege, generally the client, patient, or supplicant, can assert it, or the person consulted may assert it on the holder's behalf.

- The privilege does not operate if it has been expressly or impliedly *waived*.

- An *exception* to the privilege, such as using the privilege to commit a future crime, removes its protective cloak.

Waiver of a privilege generally does not result from an unknown eavesdropper overhearing a confidential communication. If a communication is intended to be confidential and the circumstances lead to a reasonable expectation of confidentiality, the law views the communication in the same way. For example, it is likely more reasonable to expect confidentiality in the privacy of one's own home than in a crowded rush-hour subway train.

As indicated above, not every important relationship is protected under the confidential communications privileges. While some relationships, such as marriage, are given extensive protection by allowing the spouses to refuse to testify at all, even to things other than confidential communications, other relationships, such as that of parent and child, receive no protection. *See In re Grand Jury*, 103 F.3d 1140, 1146 (3d Cir. 1997) ("Although legal academicians appear to favor adoption of a parent-child testimonial privilege, no federal Court of Appeals and no state supreme court has recognized such a privilege.").

[F] Public Policy-Based Privileges Generally

Many states create privileges based on public policy. These states want to encourage certain types of behavior and conclude that without the privilege, the desired behavior will not be advanced. One example of a privilege generated by public policy is the domestic violence counselor-domestic violence victim privilege, which applies to confidential communications between the two parties for the purpose of counseling. Several states have made such communications privileged to promote disclosure and the free flow of information.

§ 17.04 THE FEDERAL RULES OF EVIDENCE APPROACH TO PRIVILEGE

Privileges in federal court are generally derived from the federal common law, with one glaring exception. When state law supplies the rule of decision, such as in cases based on the diversity of citizenship, the pertinent state privilege law applies. *See Erie R. Co. v. Tompkins*, 304 U.S. 64, 58 S. Ct. 817, 82 L. Ed. 1188 (1938). In this regard, privilege rules are considered "substantive" law and not simply "procedural rules relating to trial governance." The Senate Committee charged with reviewing the proposed rules concluded:

> The [Senate Committee on the Judiciary] agrees . . . federal developed common law based on modern reason and experience shall apply except where the State nature of the issues renders deference to State privilege law the wiser course, as in the usual diversity case.[1]

At first glance, it is unclear why Congress decided to retain the traditional but evolving federal common law instead of enacting specific privilege rules, especially in light of the fairly specific codification in the other areas of the Federal Rules of

---

[1] Rule 501, Report of Senate Committee on the Judiciary.

§ 17.04 THE FEDERAL RULES OF EVIDENCE APPROACH TO PRIVILEGE   849

Evidence. The reason may be due to the fact that privileges provided Congress with a particularly controversial and enigmatic subject, one firmly rooted in public policy. If any evidence area generated sparks of excitement in the general public as well as with trial lawyers and legal scholars, this was it. The controversial nature of the subject and thorniness of negotiating a consensus on what to include in the realm of exclusions provides some insight into why Congress might have decided to leave this area virtually untouched.

Under the common law process, demands by lawyers for new privileges regularly challenge the status quo. The demands offer judges the opportunity to adopt new directions, while at the same time force judges to face up to the limits of existing precedent. For the most part, judges dismiss the proposals, rejecting such additions as a parole officer-parolee privilege, a sexual assault counselor-victim privilege, a legislative privilege, and an academic peer-review privilege.

The drafters of the Federal Rules of Evidence had suggested adopting thirteen distinct privilege rules (*see* § 17.02). The proposed rules included a wide variety of privileges, many of which had been well established in the states and in the federal common law. Instead of adopting any or all of these specific privileges, Congress chose to adopt a single governing rule on privilege. Federal Rule of Evidence 501 perpetuates the use of the privileges previously recognized in the federal common law. Interestingly, the rejected proposed privileges have received different treatment by the courts. In some cases, the courts turn to the proposals for assistance in determining the parameters of federal common-law privilege. *See, e.g., United States v. McPartlin*, 595 F.2d 1321, 1335–1337 (7th Cir. 1979). In other cases, the courts do not give the proposals any weight at all. *See, e.g., United States v. Bizzard*, 674 F.2d 1382, 1387 (11th Cir. 1982).

The unease caused by leaving only the area of privilege tied to the common law, while subjecting the remaining rules of evidence to codification, led the Advisory Committee toward the end of 2003 to reconsider leaving privileges as the only significant area of evidence law governed by the common law. The lack of action by the Advisory Committee suggests its acceptance of the current framework.

Debate continues as to whether this approach to the law of privileges is appropriate. On the one hand, a single general rule casting a backward glance to established precedent incorporates the wisdom of the federal judiciary, which is already responsible for applying the doctrine of privilege, while also permitting flexibility and responsiveness to changing times. On the other hand, the domain of privilege is the one area where Congress failed to codify bright-line rules and where historical precedent trumps modern ideas about what should be privileged, such as the statements made by victims of sexual abuse or domestic violence to respective counselors.

§ 17.05 SOME SPECIFIC PRIVILEGES

[A] The Husband-Wife Privileges — Adverse Spousal Testimony and Confidential Communications

Two well-recognized privileges in both federal and state law concern husbands and wives. Each husband-wife privilege, adverse spousal testimony and confidential communications, has markedly different characteristics and must be distinguished from the other. The important distinctions include what triggers the privileges, their scope of application, the types of cases in which they apply, and who holds the privilege.

[1] The Adverse Spousal Testimony Privilege

The adverse spousal testimony privilege is triggered at the time a spouse is called to testify against his or her spouse in a criminal case. As the word "spouse" suggests, a valid marriage is a prerequisite to asserting this privilege, specifically at the time of trial. The marriage requirement is met even if the spouses were separated at the time of trial, depending on the length and nature of the separation.

If the privilege is triggered, the testifying spouse is afforded considerable protection. The adverse spousal testimony privilege allows the accused's spouse to avoid testifying by choosing not to take the witness stand. While the scope of the privilege is broad, the privilege is available only in criminal cases. In addition, the privilege is held only by the testifying spouse, not by the defendant spouse. This means that if the testifying spouse wishes to testify, the defendant spouse cannot stand in the witness spouse's way.

The privilege was not always held by the testifying spouse. Under earlier common law, it was the defendant spouse who held the key to opposing spousal testimony. This earlier rule was abandoned in *Trammel v. United States*, 445 U.S. 40, 53, 100 S. Ct. 906, 63 L. Ed. 2d 186 (1980), in which the Supreme Court held that the prevailing rule, enunciated in *Hawkins v. United States*, 358 U.S. 74, 78–79, 79 S. Ct. 136, 3 L. Ed. 2d 125 (1958), should be changed. *Hawkins* had perpetuated the common-law rule, barring testimony by one spouse against the other unless both consented. The court in *Trammel* found that the justification for the *Hawkins* rule no longer existed, and overruled it. The Court stated:

> Our consideration of the foundations for the privilege and its history satisfy us that "reason and experience" no longer justify so sweeping a rule as that found acceptable by the Court in Hawkins. Accordingly, we conclude that the existing rule should be modified so that the witness spouse alone has a privilege to refuse to testify adversely; the witness may be neither compelled to testify nor foreclosed from testifying. This modification — vesting the privilege in the witness spouse — furthers the important public interest in marital harmony without unduly burdening legitimate law enforcement needs. 445 U.S. at 53.

What the justices appear to be saying here is that if a person wishes to testify against that person's spouse, the public policy of saving the marriage is not worth

[2] The Husband-Wife Confidential Communications Privilege

Unlike the adverse spousal testimony privilege, the confidential communications privilege also is triggered by a valid marriage, but the marriage need only have existed *at the time of the communication*, not at the time of trial. Thus, a communication that occurred years prior to a trial still might be privileged, so long as it was made during the marriage, even if the husband and wife had been long-divorced by the time of trial.

The scope of the confidential communications privilege is narrower than that of the adverse spousal testimony privilege. The confidential communications privilege merely prohibits the disclosure by the spouse-witness of any confidential communications with the other spouse that occur during the marriage. This means that a spouse can be called to the witness stand and asked to testify against the defendant spouse, including observations about the other spouse or non-confidential communications with the spouse.

The confidential communications privilege may apply in both criminal and civil cases and either spouse may assert the privilege. Thus, in a civil case, a spouse-defendant can prevent an adverse spouse-witness from testifying about confidential communications.

There are several important exceptions to the privilege. These exceptions include proceedings in which one spouse has been charged with crimes against the other spouse or against one or more of the spouse's children.

[3] Problems

Problem 17-1: Bonnie and Clyde — Scenarios

1. Bonnie and Clyde lived together for two years. During that time, Clyde told Bonnie that he robbed banks for a living. The two subsequently were married. Clyde was then charged with several bank robberies. *Is Clyde's statement to Bonnie about robbing banks privileged?*

2. The prosecution calls Bonnie to testify that Clyde was wearing a red sweater and matching suede shoes on the day of one of the robberies.

   a. Can Clyde prevent Bonnie from testifying to those facts if the husband-wife confidential communications privilege applies?

   b. Can Clyde prevent Bonnie from testifying to those facts if the adverse spousal testimony privilege applies?

3. Clyde tells his secretary to take down the following letter, to be delivered to Bonnie: "Bonnie, meet me at the southeast corner of the bank right before closing time. Bring all of the 'stuff' for the bank; you know what I mean. Love and Kisses, Clyde." The government wishes to introduce this letter at the bank robbery trial in

which Clyde is the defendant. *Is this letter admissible? Explain.*

4. Bonnie dies of a chronic illness during the trial. *Does Bonnie's death terminate the husband-wife confidential communications privilege?*

5. Based on bruises found on Bonnie, Clyde also is charged with aggravated spousal battery, a felony. At trial, Bonnie is called to testify by the prosecution. *Can Clyde assert one of the marital privileges? Can Bonnie claim privilege and refuse to testify?*

6. Suppose that after Clyde's death, Clyde's estate is sued by a third party claiming that Clyde had robbed her, buried the jewelry that he had taken, and informed Bonnie of the location of the jewelry before he had died. *If Bonnie had been told by Clyde that he had stolen the jewelry and had buried it in a certain place, must Bonnie disclose this information at trial?* Explain.

[B] The Attorney-Client Privilege

[1] Elements of Privilege

The attorney-client privilege extends to confidential communications between attorney and client. To promote the attorney-client relationship, even introductory confidential conversations are protected, as are communications that occur with necessary third parties, such as a paralegal, in attendance.

What is not protected, however, is material evidence. If a client gives the attorney potential evidence to hold or control, that evidence is not shielded by the privilege. In *State ex rel. Sowers v. Olwell*, 64 Wash. 2d 828, 829, 394 P.2d 681, 682 (1964), an attorney was served with a subpoena asking him to produce "all knives in [his] possession and under [his] control relating to Henry LeRoy Gray, Gloria Pugh or John W. Warren." The attorney refused to comply, asserting the attorney-client privilege on behalf of his client. The Supreme Court of Washington held that the attorney's refusal was improper, stating:

> Here we must consider the balancing process between the attorney/client privilege and the public interest in criminal investigation. We are in agreement that the attorney/client privilege is applicable to the knife held by appellant, but do not agree that the privilege warrants the attorney, as an officer of the court, from withholding it after being properly requested to produce the same. The attorney should not be a depository for criminal evidence (such as a knife, other weapons, stolen property, etc.), which in itself has little, if any, material value for the purposes of aiding counsel in the preparation of the defense of his client's case. 64 Wash. 2d at 833, 394 P.2d at 684.

Problem 17-2: Free Toaster Oven

Amy worries that she may have committed a crime, so she seeks legal advice. After going food shopping, she stops and speaks to a person named Mazzen, who is seated in a booth outside of the supermarket. The booth is decorated with a large sign stating, "Lawyer — reasonable fees. First consultation free." Amy discusses her situation with Mazzen, but decides not to hire him.

1. If Amy is later charged with a crime concerning the same situation she discussed with Mazzen, can the prosecutor call Mazzen to testify about what Amy had told him? What is the significance of Amy's decision not to hire Mazzen?

2. Suppose it turns out that Mazzen had passed the bar examination, but had never completed his bar application and thus was not a qualified lawyer at the time he offered his advice. Can the prosecutor now call Mazzen to testify?

3. If, during the same conversation, Amy sought business advice from Mazzen (who had earned an M.B.A. as well as a law degree) about a particular real estate investment that was quite successful, would the conversation be privileged?

4. If Amy's brother, Lenny, said to Amy, "Don't worry, I'll pay for your attorney," and as a result, Amy hires Mazzen, is there an attorney-client relationship between Amy and Mazzen? Is there an attorney-client relationship between Lenny and Mazzen? (*See, e.g., United States v. Edwards*, 39 F. Supp. 2d 716 (M.D. La. 1999).)

5. Suppose Amy hires Mazzen and there is immediate friction between them. After just one month of representation, Amy fired Mazzen, but not before providing him with incriminating information that could easily lead to her criminal conviction. Two months later, Amy is charged with a crime, and Mazzen is called to testify by the prosecution. Mazzen would love nothing better than to tell everyone what Amy had told him. Can Mazzen disclose all? Does it matter whether Amy had given Mazzen specific instructions regarding any subsequent disclosure of their conversations?

Problem 17-3: No Name

A defense lawyer, Paula, is subpoenaed by a grand jury investigating a stabbing leading to a person's death.

1. Paula is asked about a knife allegedly given to Paula by her client. If, in fact, her client did give her a knife, can Paula refuse to acknowledge or disclose information about the knife? Does Paula have to turn the knife over to the prosecution?

2. Paula is asked by the grand jury about the name of the person who is paying her attorney's fees and the amount of those fees. Paula refuses to answer, claiming that the answer is privileged information. Is it? *See Baird v. Koerner*, 279 F.2d 623 (9th Cir. 1960).

3. The prosecutor issues a subpoena for Paula's personal notes about the case. Must she disclose them?

4. Assuming that the name of Paula's client is disclosed, can her client be subpoenaed to provide a handwriting sample?

5. Can Paula's client be required to provide a hair sample, to see if hairs found at the crime scene match those of her client?

6. Paula's client asks Paula how best to lie before the grand jury. Does the attorney-client privilege apply?

Problem 17-4: Waiver?

Jimmy is charged with receiving stolen property after he purchased new televisions from a friend for a fraction of their cost. Jimmy decides to testify on his own behalf. During the course of his testimony, the following exchange occurs.

DEFENSE COUNSEL: Jimmy, what happened that led you to receive those television sets?

A: You know, my good friend Bernie said his friend George, who owned an electronics store, was going out of business.

PROSECUTOR: Objection. Hearsay.

JUDGE: Overruled. Please continue, counsel.

DEFENSE COUNSEL: Jimmy, what did you do in response to Bernie telling you about the television sets?

A: I wanted to buy them, naturally, and I did, for a fair price.

DEFENSE COUNSEL: I have no further questions, Your Honor.

JUDGE: Prosecutor, you may proceed with cross-examination.

PROSECUTOR: Thank you, Your Honor. Now Jimmy, you told your lawyer, did you not, that you knew those televisions were being sold for way under their fair price?

A: Yeah, I did, but only because I worked at a Great Buy Electronics store for a couple of years.

DEFENSE COUNSEL: Objection, your honor. May we approach the bench?

If defense counsel argues at the bench that any statements made by defendant to counsel are privileged and that the defendant was effectively tricked into revealing confidential communications, how should the judge rule?

[2] The Attorney-Client Privilege and the Corporate Client

At common law, the paradigm for the attorney-client privilege involved a lawyer offering advice to an individual client. As businesses and corporate entities began to consult regularly with attorneys, issues relating to the scope of the attorney-client privilege arose — who in a corporation possessed the privilege? The early law granted a privilege only to the "control group" — those persons who had controlling power over the corporation.

The traditional rule proved to be less than satisfactory, however, given modern business practices. Often, many members of a corporation outside the control group consulted attorneys on legal matters for the company. These consultations were awkward at best, given the potential risk of disclosure. The apparent inconsistency was rectified in the case of *Upjohn Co. v. United States*, 449 U.S. 383, 392–393, 101 S. Ct. 677, 66 L. Ed. 2d 584 (1981). *Upjohn Co.* addressed the issue of the scope of the attorney-client privilege within the corporate setting. The Supreme Court adopted a more flexible test instead of the bright-line control group requirement. The Court stated:

> The narrow scope given the attorney client privilege [in the control group test] not only makes it difficult for corporate attorneys to formulate sound advice when their client is faced with a specific legal problem but also threatens to limit the valuable efforts of corporate counsel to ensure their client's compliance with the law. . . . The very terms of the [control group] test adopted by the court below suggest the unpredictability of its application. The test restricts the availability of the privilege to those

officers who play a "substantial role" in deciding and directing a corporation's legal response. 449 U.S. at 392–393.

In light of this position, the Supreme Court held that middle-level and lower-level employees also could claim the attorney-client privilege, so long as they were acting in the course of their duties including legal advice about a subject relevant to the corporation. *See also Harper & Row Publishers, Inc. v. Decker*, 423 F.2d 487, 491–492 (7th Cir. 1970).

Problem 17-5: I.B.S.

The I.B.S. Corporation consults with its attorney, Bingem, Dingem, and Wingem, about pending litigation against the company. A technician employed by I.B.S. is subpoenaed to provide information about his communications with the attorneys for I.B.S. *Can the technician assert the attorney-client privilege?*

Problem 17-6: L.A. Cooke

A company named L.A. Cooke is charged with fraudulently violating security laws relating to a stock redemption. *Can the shareholders obtain the communications between the corporation's managers and its attorneys relating to the stock redemption? See Ward v. Succession of Freeman*, 854 F.2d 780 (5th Cir. 1988).

[C] Other Privileges

There are several other well-established privileges worth reviewing, including the "work product" privilege, the psychotherapist-patient privilege and the Fifth Amendment privilege against self-incrimination.

[1] "Work Product" Privilege

The so-called "work product" privilege is really an appendage of the litigation process. It prevents the discovery of mental impressions, conclusions, opinions, or legal theories of attorneys (or representatives of those attorneys) involved in, or preparing for, litigation. *See* Fed.R. Civ. P. 26(b)(3); *Hickman v. Taylor*, 329 U.S. 495, 67 S. Ct. 385, 91 L. Ed. 451 (1947). This protection of litigation strategy allows attorneys to try their own cases, and permits some secrecy in how evidence is offered, approached, and evaluated by the parties. Significantly, the work product privilege applies only to materials that are "otherwise discoverable." Thus, if materials are protected by another privilege, such as the attorney-client privilege, the issue of work product protection need never arise. *See, e.g., Miller v. Federal Express Corp.*, 186 F.R.D. 376 (W.D. Tenn. 1999).

Problem 17-7: The Union

James was the president of the largest union in New York City. During a difficult period, in which the Union threatened to strike, James met with several union representatives about their strategy regarding a potential strike. Before a strike could occur, the employer sued the union in federal court, claiming it violated several federal labor laws. James met with the Union's lawyer, Emily, who wrote down her thoughts about the situation, including the strategies and tactics that were legally available. During pre-trial discovery, the employer sought disclosure of the meeting James had with his representatives and of Emily's notes of her meeting with James. *What must be disclosed, if anything?*

[2] Psychotherapist-Patient Privilege

A psychotherapist-patient privilege is recognized under the common law of many states and under the federal common law. *See Jaffee v. Redmond*, 518 U.S. 1, 116 S. Ct. 1923, 135 L. Ed. 2d 337 (1996). In *Jaffee*, a police officer who killed a man while on duty was sued for violating that person's civil rights. The defendant officer received counseling following the incident from a licensed clinical social worker. The plaintiff sought the disclosure of the substance of that counseling, and the therapist was ordered to do so by the judge. The defendant and therapist refused, claiming they were protected by a psychotherapist-patient privilege. The Supreme Court agreed, finding that the federal law should reflect the states' enthusiastic endorsement of the privilege. The Court found that the privilege extended not only to psychiatrists and psychologists, but also to licensed clinical social workers who are administering psychotherapy.

Significantly, the privilege applies only to confidential communications made during the course of diagnosis or treatment of the patient. Statements made outside of diagnosis or treatment, such as those involving business matters or other unrelated subjects, are not privileged. Further, this privilege, like others, may be expressly or impliedly waived. An implied waiver may occur when litigants place their mental state at issue or sue the professional, necessitating the use of the psychotherapy records. In *Jaffee*, the officer refused to expressly waive the privilege and did not impliedly waive the privilege by raising an insanity defense.

Example

Mark David Chapman shot and killed John Lennon, a former member of the Beatles, outside of Lennon's apartment building in New York City in 1980. Instead of pleading guilty to the crime, Chapman could have sought a trial. If Chapman had asked for a trial and raised an insanity defense, his prior visits to a psychotherapist would have been subject to discovery by the prosecution because his assertion of insanity created an implied waiver of his psychotherapist-patient privilege — under either New York or federal law.

Problem 17-8: Crazy for You

Alex is charged with murder. Alex has been in therapy for nine years to treat his excessive and repetitive outbursts of anger against others.

If Alex raises an insanity defense at trial, can the prosecution call Alex's therapist, Marcy, to the witness stand to testify about what Alex told her in their therapy sessions? Why?

Problem 17-9: Bundy

The defendant, Bundy, is charged with a series of rapes. The prosecution attempts to discover what Bundy told his psychiatrist prior to the date charges were filed.

1. Are the conversations between Bundy and his psychiatrist privileged?

2. Would the conversations be privileged if the psychiatrist's secretary was present during them?

Problem 17-10: Still Crazy, After All These . . .

Paul, the defendant, objects to the admission of statements he made to his doctor, Dr. Simon, claiming that he believed Dr. Simon was also a psychotherapist. At a sidebar, the plaintiff's attorney makes the following proffer:

PLAINTIFF'S ATTORNEY: Your Honor, the evidence will show that Dr. Simon has been a practicing podiatrist for 21 years and planned on doing bunion surgery on the defendant. Paul knew Dr. Simon was a podiatrist and not a psychotherapist. Paul's statements to Dr. Simon are not part of the psychotherapist-patient relationship.

DEFENDANT'S ATTORNEY: Your honor, with all due respect, Dr. Simon discussed James Redfield's book, *The Tenth Insight*, with Paul, as well as the Dali Lama's book, *The Art of Happiness*. Everybody knows those books are within the realm of psychology.

How should the judge rule? See Henry v. Kernan, 177 F.3d 1152, 1159 (9th Cir. 1999).

[3] The Physician-Patient Privilege

Under the federal common law, there was no privilege to avoid the compelled disclosure of confidential information shared in a physician-patient relationship. A majority of state jurisdictions have altered this rule, however, protecting confidential communications between a physician and her patient. *See, e.g.*, N.Y. Rev. Stat. 1828, 406 (pt. 3, ch. 7, Tit. 3, Art. 9, Section 73). Some of these states provide only limited protection to the doctor-patient relationship, requiring disclosure under a court subpoena or extending protection only during the course of litigation. *See, e.g.*, Florida Evidence Code, Fla. Stat., ch. 90 *et seq.* Thus, the physician-patient rule of confidentiality is stronger outside of a court proceeding than in it.

Like most professional confidential communications privileges that belong to the layperson, the doctor-patient privilege, when it exists, is generally held by the patient. The privilege does not protect the fact that the doctor has treated the patient or peripheral facts about the treatment (such as how many times treatment has occurred). In addition, the privilege may be abrogated for equally important public policy purposes, such as the disclosure of the existence of communicable or deadly diseases, like tuberculosis or AIDS. On the other hand, if the privilege attaches, it generally prevails even after the patient has died.

Problem 17-11: Booth

J.W. Booth woke up his family physician, claiming he was shot while hunting in Washington, D.C. The doctor examined the wound and saw that Booth was losing blood. Booth was taken to the doctor's adjoining office, where the doctor treated Booth. Booth then hurried away, despite remaining in a medically unstable condition.

If the treatment occurred in a state where the physician-patient privilege is recognized, and the state law supplies the rule of decision in a case where Booth's injury and its cause are relevant, can the doctor be required to testify about his treatment of Booth and the statements Booth made to him?

Problem 17-12: Booth II

Assume the same facts as in the previous problem. Suppose that J.W. Booth's brother, Bob Booth, helped to carry Booth to the doctor's office and assisted during the treatment. *Can J.W.'s brother be required to testify about what he saw and heard in J.W.'s office?*

[4] The Fifth Amendment Privilege Against Self-Incrimination

While it is amorphous in scope and heavily litigated, the privilege against self-incrimination is readily defined. It prohibits any compelled testimony that constitutes self-incrimination. *See, e.g., United States v. Hubbell*, 167 F.3d 552 (D.C. Cir. 1999). To invoke the privilege, the incrimination must result from the compelled testimony — and be "substantial and real." Thus, the modern interpretation is not tied so much to privacy, which focuses on the freedom from government snooping, as it is to autonomy and the freedom from governmental compulsion. *Id.* at 572. It is not a violation of the privilege to compel a defendant to provide a hair sample, voice exemplar or even blood, for example, because while the defendant is being compelled, it is not compelled testimony. On the other hand, it is a violation to force communications that implicate the defendant in a crime, such as confessions.

Problem 17-13: Lowering the Bar

Lynn filed a bar complaint against her attorney, Sam, alleging that he acted unethically in disclosing to her opponent certain confidential information that she gave him in the course of their attorney-client relationship. The Bar Disciplinary

Commission wrote Sam, asking for his understanding of the facts. Sam claimed that his Fifth Amendment right against self-incrimination protected him from providing any information. *Is Sam correct?*

Problem 17-14: Illegal Gambling

To stop the proliferation of unlawful gambling in the United States, Congress enacts a law requiring "all proceeds from gambling, legal or otherwise, to be declared as income for tax purposes." *Is this law constitutional? Why?*

[D] Additional Privilege Problems

Problem 17-15: Father and Son

John Sr. tells John Jr., "Look, I want you to keep a secret. Just between us, I cheated a bit on my taxes between 1995 and 2002 to help the family through hard times. Now the Internal Revenue Service is after me. Even if what I did was criminal, I never wanted to hurt you, got that? One more thing, if you would, try to minimize the expenses at college this semester; this fight is going to be a costly one."

If John Sr. is charged with tax evasion, can the prosecution call John Jr. as a witness to testify to the above conversation? Must John Jr. testify? What would you argue on John Sr.'s behalf?

Problem 17-16: Deep Throat

The identity of Deep Throat, the mysterious informant in the Watergate scandal who supposedly leaked information to journalists Woodward and Bernstein, becomes an issue in a subsequent trial. The media defendant in the trial subpoenas the Watergate reporters, Woodward and Bernstein. Can the reporters refuse to disclose the name of their informant? *See United States v. Caporale*, 806 F.2d 1487 (11th Cir. 1986). *Does it matter whether it is a criminal or civil case?* [Note: After 30 years of silence, Mr. W. Mark Felt, former Deputy Director of the FBI, disclosed publicly in 2005 that he was the "Deep Throat" who had provided Woodward and Bernstein with information.]

Problem 17-17: Confession

Joanne is charged with kidnapping. The prosecution attempts to introduce inculpatory statements Joanne made to her priest during a confession immediately prior to the kidnapping.

Are the statements Joanne made to her priest admissible? If Joanne had mentioned the substance of the confession to her mother, can the priest be subpoenaed to testify?

Problem 17-18: Accidental Discovery Disclosure

In a copyright and trademark infringement action by Burger King against McDonalds, discovery requests for documents and e-mails numbered in the tens of thousands. When Burger King realized it had turned over 20 documents it believed were privileged under the attorney-client privilege, it filed a motion to classify those documents as privileged and to have them returned. If the disclosure was indeed inadvertent, did Burger King waive its privilege?

§ 17.06 EXAMPLES OF STATE LAW PRIVILEGES

Georgia Chapter 24-9-21. Confidentiality of certain communications.

There are certain admissions and communications excluded on grounds of public policy. Among these are:

(1) Communications between husband and wife;

(2) Communications between attorney and client;

(3) Communications among grand jurors;

(4) Secrets of state; and

(5) Communications between psychiatrist and patient.

Florida Statute § 90.5035. Sexual assault counselor-victim privilege.

(1) For purposes of this section:

    (a) a "rape crisis center" is any public or private agency that offers assistance to victims of sexual assault or sexual battery and their families.

    (b) a "sexual counselor" is any employee of a rape crisis center whose primary purpose is the rendering of advice, counseling, or assistance to victims of sexual assault or sexual battery.

(2) A victim has a privilege to refuse to disclose and to prevent any other person from disclosing, a confidential communication made by the victim to a sexual assault counselor or any record made in the course of advising, counseling, or assisting the victim. Such confidential communication or record may be disclosed only with the prior written consent of the victim. This privilege includes any advice given by the sexual assault counselor in the course of that relationship.

Florida Statute § 90.5055. Accountant-client privilege.

(2) A client has a privilege to refuse to disclose, and to prevent any other person from disclosing, the contents of confidential communications with an accountant when such other person learned of the communications because they were made in the rendition of accounting services to the client. This privilege includes other confidential information obtained by the accountant from the client for the purpose of rendering accounting advice.

Nebraska § 27-504. Physician-patient privilege.

(2) A patient has a privilege to refuse to disclose and to prevent any other person from disclosing confidential communications made for the purposes of diagnosis or treatment of his or her physical, mental, or emotional condition among himself or herself, his or her physician, or persons who are participating in the diagnosis or treatment under the direction of the physician, including members of the patient's family.

Hawaii Rule 506. Communications to clergyman.

(a) **Definitions.** As used in this rule:

  (1) A "clergyman" is a minister, priest, rabbi, Christian Science practitioner, or other similar functionary of a religious organization, or an individual reasonably believed so to be by the person consulting him.

  (2) A communication is "confidential" if made privately and not intended for further disclosure except to other persons present in furtherance of the purpose of the communication.

(b) **General rule of privilege.** A person has a privilege to refuse to disclose and to prevent another from disclosing a confidential communication by the person to a clergyman in his professional character as spiritual advisor.

New Jersey § 2A:84A-21. Newspaperman's privilege.

Subject to Rule 37, a person engaged on, engaged in, connected with, or employed by a news media for the purpose of gathering, procuring, transmitting, compiling, editing or disseminating news for the general public or on whose behalf news is so gathered, procured, transmitted, compiled, edited or disseminated has a privilege to refuse to disclose, in any legal or quasi-legal proceeding or before any investigative body, including, but not limited to, any court, grand jury, petit jury, administrative agency, the Legislature or legislative committee, or elsewhere.

  a. The source, author, means, agency or person from or through whom any information was procured, obtained, supplied, furnished, gathered, transmitted, compiled, edited, disseminated, or delivered; and

  b. Any news or information obtained in the course of pursuing his professional activities whether or not it is disseminated.

§ 17.07 SUMMARY AND REVIEW

1. How many privileges do the Federal Rules of Evidence expressly recognize?

2. How many marital privileges exist? Why?

3. Who should hold the adverse spousal privilege, the accused or the spouse who is called to testify? Why?

4. What are the various sources of federal privileges?

5. When does state privilege law apply in federal court?

6. Why have a privilege for the political vote?

7. Why have a privilege for the identity of an informer?

8. How can a privilege be waived?

9. Why don't the states and federal common law recognize a parent-child privilege?

§ 17.08 CHAPTER REVIEW PROBLEMS

Problem 17-A

Barlie Thompson is called to testify against her husband, Artis Thompson, in a fraud action brought against Artis by a local bank, First National City Bank. Artis allegedly told Barlie he was cashing a check he knew to be fraudulent and was hiding the stolen money in his sock drawer. Artis asserts the spousal immunity privilege and attempts to keep Barlie off of the witness stand. *How should the judge rule?*

1. The judge should exclude Barlie from testifying, but only if Barlie asserts the privilege.

2. The judge should exclude Barlie from testifying because the privilege extends to the entire testimony about the events in question, before, during, and after the alleged fraud took place.

3. The judge should not exclude Barlie from testifying if she has competent and relevant information.

4. The judge should not exclude Barlie from testifying, but should prohibit any questions about her husband, Artis.

Problem 17-B

Biloxi Barnes was married to Harold Hines, an alleged member of a large crime syndicate in Chicago, Illinois. After Harold had passed away, Biloxi was called to testify in a criminal case involving her husband's business associates. The associates had been charged with mail fraud and conspiracy. Harold had allegedly told Biloxi, "Yeah, me and the boys had to take charge of our business and minimize the opportunities of our competitors, if you know what I mean." This statement:

1. Is not admissible as a co-conspirator admission if it was made in privacy by Harold to his wife.

2. Is not admissible as a statement against interest, because, now that Harold has passed away, it is not against his interest.

3. Is admissible as a co-conspirator admission, because Harold concedes he was working in concert with his business partners, those individuals on trial.

4. Is admissible as a statement against interest, because it was against Harold's interest when he made it.

Problem 17-C

Alice went to her massage therapist to work out the pain in her back after her car was rear-ended by another car. During the massage, Alice told her therapist, Adin, whom she had known for many years, "In the strictest of confidence, the pain in my lower back resulted from straining my back years ago at the supermarket, not from this accident." If, during a subsequent trial, the therapist is called to testify by the defendant against Alice, this testimony should be:

1. Admitted, because Alice's statement is relevant and not hearsay.

2. Admitted, because it falls into an exception to the therapist's privilege.

3. Excluded, because the statement is privileged under the broad interpretation given the therapist privilege.

4. Excluded, because the promise to keep the information confidential binds the therapist in the face of the law.

Problem 17-D

The Cinderella Cruise Line routinely reviews accidents on its ships after they occur. As part of the routine, an investigator is appointed, a file is created, and a confidential meeting is held to determine if safety standards have been met. After an accident in the dining room of one of the Cinderella ships and after a report has been prepared by Cinderella, a lawsuit is filed. The plaintiff seeks access to the report prepared by the cruise line, and the cruise line claims privilege. *How should the court rule?*

1. The document is privileged because it was intended to be confidential and was reviewed only by certain company employees.

2. The document is privileged under the attorney-client privilege.

3. The document is not privileged because there is only a qualified self-analysis privilege, at best, and this was a routine, habitual act by the company.

4. The document is not privileged because it is an admission of a party-opponent.

§ 17.09 CASE LIBRARY

UPJOHN CO. v. UNITED STATES
United States Supreme Court
449 U.S. 383, 101 S. Ct. 677, 66 L. Ed. 2d 584 (1981)

JUSTICE REHNQUIST delivered the opinion of the Court:

We granted certiorari in this case to address important questions concerning the scope of the attorney-client privilege in the corporate context and the applicability of the work-product doctrine in proceedings to enforce tax summonses. 445 U.S. 925. With respect to the privilege question the parties and various *amici* have described our task as one of choosing between two "tests" which have gained adherents in the courts of appeals. We are acutely aware, however, that we sit to decide concrete cases and not abstract propositions of law. We decline to lay down a broad rule or series of rules to govern all conceivable future questions in this area, even were we able to do so. We can and do, however, conclude that the attorney-client privilege protects the communications involved in this case from compelled disclosure and that the work-product doctrine does apply in tax summons enforcement proceedings.

Petitioner Upjohn Co. manufactures and sells pharmaceuticals here and abroad. In January 1976 independent accountants conducting an audit of one of Upjohn's foreign subsidiaries discovered that the subsidiary made payments to or for the benefit of foreign government officials in order to secure government business. The accountants so informed petitioner Mr. Gerard Thomas, Upjohn's Vice President, Secretary, and General Counsel . . . . It was decided that the company would conduct an internal investigation of what were termed "questionable payments." As part of this investigation the attorneys prepared a letter containing a questionnaire which was sent to "All Foreign General and Area Managers" over the Chairman's signature . . . . Managers were instructed to treat the investigation as "highly confidential" and not to discuss it with anyone other than Upjohn employees who might be helpful in providing the requested information. The responses were to be sent directly to Thomas. Thomas and outside counsel also interviewed the recipients of the questionnaire and some 33 other Upjohn officers or employees as part of the investigation.

. . . .

. . . . On November 23, 1976, the [Internal Revenue] Service issued a summons . . . demanding production of:

> "All files relative to the investigation conducted under the supervision of Gerard Thomas to identify payments to employees of foreign governments . . . .

> "The records should include but not be limited to written questionnaires sent to managers of the Upjohn Company's foreign affiliates, and memorandums or notes of the interviews conducted . . . with officers and employees of the Upjohn Company and its subsidiaries." . . .

The company declined to produce the documents specified . . . on the grounds that they were protected from disclosure by the attorney-client privilege. . . .

II.

Federal Rule of Evidence 501 provides that "the privilege of a witness . . . shall be governed by the principles of the common law as they may be interpreted by the courts of the United States in light of reason and experience." The attorney-client privilege is the oldest of the privileges for confidential communications known to the common law . . . . Its purpose is to encourage full and frank communication between attorneys and their clients and thereby promote broader public interests in the observance of law and administration of justice. The privilege recognizes that sound legal advice or advocacy serves public ends and that such advice or advocacy depends upon the lawyer's being fully informed by the client. As we stated last Term in *Trammel v. United States*, 445 U. S. 40, 51 (1980): "The lawyer-client privilege rests on the need for the advocate and counselor to know all that relates to the client's reasons for seeking representation if the professional mission is to be carried out." And in *Fisher v. United States*, 425 U. S. 391, 403 (1976), we recognized the purpose of the privilege to be "to encourage clients to make full disclosure to their attorneys." . . . Admittedly complications in the application of the privilege arise when the client is a corporation, which in theory is an artificial creature of the law, and not an individual; but this Court has assumed that the privilege applies when the client is a corporation. . . .

The Court of Appeals, however, considered the application of the privilege in the corporate context to present a "different problem," since the client was an inanimate entity and "only the senior management, guiding and integrating the several operations, . . . can be said to possess an identity analogous to the corporation as a whole." 600 F. 2d at 1226. The first case to articulate the so-called "control group test" adopted by the court below . . . reflected a similar approach:

. . . "[T]he most satisfactory solution . . . is that if the employee making the communication, of whatever rank he may be, is in a position to control or even to take a substantial part in a decision about any action which the corporation may take upon the advice of the attorney, . . . then, in effect, *he is (or personifies) the corporation* when he makes his disclosure to the lawyer and the privilege would apply." (Emphasis supplied.)

Such a view, we think, overlooks the fact that the privilege exists to protect not only the giving of professional advice to those who can act on it but also the giving of information to the lawyer to enable him to give sound and informed advice. . . .

. . . Middle-level — and indeed lower-level — employees can, by actions within the scope of their employment, embroil the corporation in serious legal difficulties, and it is only natural that these employees would have the relevant information needed by corporate counsel if he is adequately to advise the client with respect to such actual or potential difficulties. . . .

The control group test adopted by the court below thus frustrates the very purpose of the privilege by discouraging the communication of relevant information by employees of the client to attorneys seeking to render legal advice to the client corporation. The attorney's advice will also frequently be more significant to noncontrol group members than to those who officially sanction the advice, and the control group test makes it more difficult to convey full and frank legal advice to the employees who will put into effect the client corporation's policy. . . .

The narrow scope given the attorney-client privilege by the court below not only makes it difficult for corporate attorneys to formulate sound advice when their client is faced with a specific legal problem but also threatens to limit the valuable efforts of corporate counsel to ensure their client's compliance with the law. In light of the vast and complicated array of regulatory legislation confronting the modern corporation, corporations, unlike most individuals, "constantly go to lawyers to find out how to obey the law," Burnham, The Attorney-Client Privilege in the Corporate Arena, 24 Bus. Law. 901, 913 (1969), particularly since compliance with the law in this area is hardly an instinctive matter . . . . The test adopted by the court below is difficult to apply in practice, though no abstractly formulated and unvarying "test" will necessarily enable courts to decide questions such as this with mathematical precision. But if the purpose of the attorney-client privilege is to be served, the attorney and client must be able to predict with some degree of certainty whether particular discussions will be protected. An uncertain privilege, or one which purports to be certain but results in widely varying applications by the courts, is little better than no privilege at all. The very terms of the test adopted by the court below suggest the unpredictability of its application. The test restricts the availability of the privilege to those officers who play a "substantial role" in deciding and directing a corporation's legal response. Disparate decisions in cases applying this test illustrate its unpredictability. . . .

The communications at issue were made by Upjohn employees to counsel for Upjohn acting as such, at the direction of the corporate superiors in order to secure legal advice from counsel . . . . The communications concerned matters within the scope of the employees' corporate duties, and the employees themselves were sufficiently aware that they were being questioned in order that the corporation could obtain legal advice . . . . Pursuant to explicit instructions from the Chairman of the Board, the communications were considered "highly confidential" when made . . . and have been kept confidential by the company. Consistent with the underlying purposes of the attorney-client privilege, these communications must be protected against compelled disclosure.

. . . .

. . . [W]e conclude that the narrow "control group test" . . . cannot, consistent with "the principles of common law as . . . interpreted . . . in light of reason and experience," Fed. Rule Evid. 501, govern the development of the law in this area.

. . . .

NIX v. WHITESIDE
United States Supreme Court
475 U.S. 157, 106 S. Ct. 988, 89 L. Ed. 2d 123 (1986)

CHIEF JUSTICE BURGER delivered the opinion of the Court:

We granted certiorari to decide whether the Sixth Amendment right of a criminal defendant to assistance of counsel is violated when an attorney refuses to cooperate with the defendant in presenting perjured testimony at his trial.

I

A

Whiteside was convicted of second-degree murder by a jury verdict which was affirmed by the Iowa courts. The killing took place on February 8, 1977, in Cedar Rapids, Iowa. Whiteside and two others went to one Calvin Love's apartment late that night, seeking marihuana. Love was in bed when White-side and his companions arrived; an argument between Whiteside and Love over the marihuana ensued. At one point, Love directed his girlfriend to get his "piece," and at another point got up, then returned to his bed. According to Whiteside's testimony, Love then started to reach under his pillow and moved toward Whiteside. Whiteside stabbed Love in the chest, inflicting a fatal wound.

Whiteside was charged with murder, and when counsel was appointed he objected to the lawyer initially appointed, claiming that he felt uncomfortable with a lawyer who had formerly been a prosecutor. Gary L. Robinson was then appointed and immediately began an investigation. Whiteside gave him a statement that he had stabbed Love as the latter "was pulling a pistol from underneath the pillow on the bed." Upon questioning by Robinson, however, Whiteside indicated that he had not actually seen a gun, but that he was convinced that Love had a gun. . . .

. . . . About a week before trial, during preparation for direct examination, Whiteside for the first time told Robinson and his associate Donna Paulsen that he had seen something "metallic" in Love's hand. When asked about this, Whiteside responded:

> "[I]n Howard Cook's case there was a gun. If I don't say I saw a gun, I'm dead."

Robinson told Whiteside that such testimony would be perjury and repeated that it was not necessary to prove that a gun was available but only that Whiteside reasonably believed that he was in danger. On Whiteside's insisting that he would testify that he saw "something metallic" Robinson told him, according to Robinson's testimony:

> "[W]e could not allow him to [testify falsely] because that would be perjury, and as officers of the court we would be suborning perjury if we allowed him to do it; . . . I advised him that if he did do that it would be my duty to advise the Court of what he was doing and that I felt he was committing

perjury; also, that I probably would be allowed to attempt to impeach that particular testimony." App. to Pet. for Cert. A-85.

Robinson also indicated he would seek to withdraw from the representation if Whiteside insisted on committing perjury. (Footnote omitted.)

Whiteside testified in his own defense at trial and stated that he "knew" that Love had a gun and that he believed Love was reaching for a gun and he had acted swiftly in self-defense. On cross-examination, he admitted that he had not actually seen a gun in Love's hand. . . .

. . . .

II

A

The right of an accused to testify in his defense is of relatively recent origin. Until the latter part of the preceding century, criminal defendants in this country, as at common law, were considered to be disqualified from giving sworn testimony at their own trial by reason of their interest as a party to the case. . . .

By the end of the 19th century, however, the disqualification was finally abolished by statute in most states and in the federal courts. . . .

B

In *Strickland v. Washington*, we held that to obtain relief by way of federal habeas corpus on a claim of a deprivation of effective assistance of counsel under the Sixth Amendment, the movant must establish both serious attorney error and prejudice. To show such error, it must be established that the assistance rendered by counsel was constitutionally deficient in that "counsel made errors so serious that counsel was not functioning as 'counsel' guaranteed the defendant by the Sixth Amendment." . . .

. . . .

In *Strickland*, we recognized counsel's duty of loyalty and his "overarching duty to advocate the defendant's cause." *Ibid.* Plainly, that duty is limited to legitimate, lawful conduct compatible with the very nature of a trial as a search for truth. Although counsel must take all reasonable lawful means to attain the objectives of the client, counsel is precluded from taking steps or in any way assisting the client in presenting false evidence or otherwise violating the law. This principle has consistently been recognized in most unequivocal terms by expositors of the norms of professional conduct since the first Canons of Professional Ethics were adopted by the American Bar Association in 1908 . . . .

These principles have been carried through to contemporary codifications of an attorney's professional responsibility. Disciplinary Rule 7-102 of the Model Code of Professional Responsibility (1980), entitled "Representing a Client Within the Bounds of the Law," provides:

"(A) In his representation of a client, a lawyer shall not:

. . .

"(4) Knowingly use perjured testimony or false evidence.

. . . .

"(7) Counsel or assist his client in conduct that the lawyer knows to be illegal or fraudulent."

This provision has been adopted by Iowa, and is binding on all lawyers who appear in its courts. *See* Iowa Code of Professional Responsibility for Lawyers (1985). The more recent Model Rules of Professional Conduct (1983) similarly admonish attorneys to obey all laws in the course of representing a client. . . .

. . . .

It is universally agreed that at a minimum the attorney's first duty when confronted with a proposal for perjurious testimony is to attempt to dissuade the client from the unlawful course of conduct . . . .

The commentary thus also suggests that an attorney's revelation of his client's perjury to the court is a professionally responsible and acceptable response to the conduct of a client who has actually given perjured testimony. . . .

D

. . . .

On this record, the accused enjoyed continued representation within the bounds of reasonable professional conduct, and did in fact exercise his right to testify; at most he was denied the right to have the assistance of counsel in the presentation of false testimony . . . . A defendant who informed his counsel that he was arranging to bribe or threaten witnesses or members of the jury would have no "right" to insist on counsel's assistance or silence. Counsel would not be limited to advising against that conduct. An attorney's duty of confidentiality, which totally covers the client's admission of guilt, does not extend to a client's announced plans to engage in future criminal conduct . . . . In short, the responsibility of an ethical lawyer, as an officer of the court and a key component of a system of justice, dedicated to a search for truth, is essentially the same whether the client announces an intention to bribe or threaten witnesses or jurors or to commit or procure perjury. No system of justice worthy of the name can tolerate a lesser standard.

. . . .

E

We hold that, as a matter of law, counsel's conduct complained of here cannot establish the prejudice required for relief under the second strand of the *Strickland* inquiry. . . .

. . . .

Whiteside's attorney treated Whiteside's proposed perjury in accord with professional standards, and since Whiteside's truthful testimony could not have prejudiced the result of his trial, the Court of Appeals was in error to direct the issuance of a writ of habeas corpus and must be reversed.

. . . .

JAFFEE v. REDMOND
United States Supreme Court
518 U.S. 1, 116 S. Ct. 1923, 135 L. Ed. 2d 337 (1996)

STEVENS, J.

After a traumatic incident in which she shot and killed a man, a police officer received extensive counseling from a licensed clinical social worker. The question we address is whether statements the officer made to her therapist during the counseling sessions are protected from compelled disclosure in a federal civil action brought by the family of the deceased. Stated otherwise, the question is whether it is appropriate for federal courts to recognize a "psychotherapist privilege" under Rule 501 of the Federal Rules of Evidence.

I

. . . .

On June 27, 1991, Redmond was the first officer to respond to a "fight in progress" call at an apartment complex . . . . [During the fracas], Redmond drew her service revolver. Two other men then burst out of the building, one, Ricky Allen, chasing the other . . . . Redmond shot Allen when she believed he was about to stab the man he was chasing.

Petitioner [administrator of the estate of Ricky Allen] filed suit in Federal District Court alleging that [police officer] Redmond had violated Allen's constitutional rights by using excessive force during the encounter at the apartment complex.

. . . [A]fter the shooting, Redmond had participated in about 50 counseling sessions with Karen Beyer, a clinical social worker . . . . Petitioner sought access to Beyer's notes concerning the sessions for use in cross-examining Redmond. Respondents vigorously resisted . . . [and refused to comply with the district judge's] order to disclose the contents of Beyer's notes.

II

. . . "[T]he common law is not immutable but flexible, and by its own principles adapts itself to varying conditions." *Funk v. United States*, 290 U.S. 371, 383 (1933)
. . . .

. . . .

III

Like the spousal and attorney-client privileges, the psychotherapist-patient privilege is "rooted in the imperative need for confidence and trust." *Trammel v. United States*, 445 U.S. 40, 51 (1980) . . . . Because of the sensitive nature of the problems for which individuals consult psychotherapists, disclosure of confidential communications made during counseling sessions may cause embarrassment or disgrace.

. . . .

. . . The psychotherapist privilege serves the public interest by facilitating the provision of appropriate treatment for individuals suffering the effects of a mental or emotional problem.

. . . .

. . . That it is appropriate for the federal courts to recognize a psychotherapist privilege under Rule 501 is confirmed by the fact that all 50 States and the District of Columbia have enacted into law some form of psychotherapist privilege.

. . . .

V

The conversations between Officer Redmond and Karen Beyer and the notes taken during their counseling sessions are protected from compelled disclosure under Rule 501 of the Federal Rules of Evidence.

Chapter 18

AUTHENTICATION, IDENTIFICATION, AND THE "BEST EVIDENCE" RULE

§ 18.01 CHAPTER CHECKLIST

1. Is the thing to be admitted into evidence what it purports to be?

2. Have all of the "magic" foundation questions for authentication been asked of the witness in a recognizable form?

3. Does the so-called best evidence rule apply to the case?

4. To determine the applicability of the best evidence rule, is a party proving the contents of a writing that is important to the case?

5. If the best evidence rule applies, is there an adequate alternative to the original writing that can serve as a substitute?

6. How is *Seiler v. Lucasfilm, Ltd.*, 808 F.2d 1316 (9th Cir. 1986), in the Case Library at the end of the chapter, a good illustration of the rationale underlying the "best evidence rule"?

§ 18.02 RELEVANT FEDERAL RULES OF EVIDENCE

ARTICLE IX. AUTHENTICATION AND IDENTIFICATION

Rule 901. Requirement of Authentication or Identification

(a) **General provision.** The requirement of authentication or identification as a condition precedent to admissibility is satisfied by evidence sufficient to support a finding that the matter in question is what its proponent claims.

(b) **Illustrations.** By way of illustration only, and not by way of limitation, the following are examples of authentication or identification conforming with the requirements of this rule:

(1) **Testimony of witness with knowledge.** Testimony that a matter is what it is claimed to be.

(2) **Nonexpert opinion on handwriting.** Nonexpert opinion as to the genuineness of handwriting, based upon familiarity not acquired for purposes of the litigation.

(3) **Comparison by trier or expert witness.** Comparison by the trier of fact or by expert witnesses with specimens which have been authenticated.

(4) **Distinctive characteristics and the like.** Appearance, contents substance, internal patterns, or other distinctive characteristics, taken in conjunction with circumstances.

(5) **Voice Identification.** Identification of a voice, whether heard firsthand or through mechanical or electronic transmission or recording, by opinion based upon hearing the voice at any time under circumstances connecting it with the alleged speaker.

(6) **Telephone conversations.** Telephone conversations, by evidence that a call was made to the number assigned at the time by the telephone company to a particular person or business, if (a) in the case of a person, circumstances, including self-identification, show the person answering to be the one called, or (b) in the case of a business, the call was made to a place of business and the conversation related to business reasonably transacted over the telephone.

. . . .

Rule 902. Self-Authentication

Extrinsic evidence of authenticity as a condition precedent to admissibility is not required with respect to the following:

(1) **Domestic public documents under seal.** A document bearing a seal purporting to be that of the United States, or of any State, district, Commonwealth, territory, or insular possession thereof,
. . . .

(2) **Domestic public documents not under seal.** A document purporting to bear the signature in the official capacity of an officer or employee of any entity included in paragraph (1) hereof, having no seal, if a public officer having a seal and having official duties in the district or political subdivision of the officer or employee certifies under seal that the signer has the official capacity and that the signature is genuine.

(3) **Foreign public documents.** A document purporting to be executed or attested in an official capacity by a person authorized by the laws of a foreign country to make the execution or attestation.
. . . .

(4) **Certified copies of public records.** A copy of an official record or report or entry therein . . . certified as correct by the custodian or other person authorized to make the certification, ...

(5) **Official publications.** Books, pamphlets, or other publications purporting to be issued by public authority.

(6) **Newspapers and periodicals.** Printed materials purporting to be newspapers or periodicals.

(7) **Trade inscriptions and the like.** Inscriptions, signs, tags, or labels purporting to have been affixed in the course of business and indicating ownership, control, or origin.

(8) **Acknowledged documents.** Documents accompanied by a certificate of acknowledgment executed in the manner provided by law by a notary public or other officer authorized by law to take acknowledgments.

(9) **Commercial paper and related documents.** Commercial paper, signatures thereon, and documents relating thereto to the extent provided by general commercial law.

(10) **Presumptions under Acts of Congress.** Any signature, document, or other matter declared by Act of Congress to be presumptively or prima facie genuine or authentic.

(11) **Certified domestic records of regularly conducted activity.** The original or a duplicate of a domestic record of regularly conducted activity that would be admissible under Rule 803(6) if accompanied by a written declaration of its custodian or other qualified person, in a manner complying with any Act of Congress or rule prescribed by the Supreme Court pursuant to statutory authority, certifying that the record —

   (A) was made at or near the time of the occurrence of the matters set forth by, or from information transmitted by, a person with knowledge of those matters;

   (B) was kept in the course of the regularly conducted activity; and

   (C) was made by the regularly conducted activity as a regular practice.

   A party intending to offer a record into evidence under this paragraph must provide written notice of that intention to all adverse parties, and must make the record and declaration available for inspection sufficiently in advance of their offer into evidence to provide an adverse party with a fair opportunity to challenge them.

(12) **Certified foreign records of regularly conducted activity.** In a civil case, the original or a duplicate of a foreign record of regularly conducted activity that would be admissible under Rule 803(6) if accompanied by a written declaration by its custodian or other qualified person certifying that the record —

   (A) was made at or near the time of the occurrence of the matters set forth by, or from information transmitted by, a person with knowledge of those matters;

(B) was kept in the course of the regularly conducted activity; and

(C) was made by the regularly conducted activity as a regular practice.

The declaration must be signed in a manner that, if falsely made, would subject the maker to criminal penalty under the laws of the country where the declaration is signed. A party intending to offer a record into evidence under this paragraph must provide written notice of that intention to all adverse parties, and must make the record and declaration available for inspection sufficiently in advance of their offer into evidence to provide an adverse party with a fair opportunity to challenge them.

Rule 903. Subscribing Witness' Testimony Unnecessary

The testimony of a subscribing witness is not necessary to authenticate a writing unless required by the laws of the jurisdiction whose laws govern the validity of the writing.

ARTICLE X. CONTENTS OF WRITINGS, RECORDINGS, AND PHOTOGRAPHS

Rule 1001. Definitions

For purposes of this article the following definitions are applicable:

(1) **Writings and recordings.** "Writings" and "recordings" consist of letters, words, or numbers, or their equivalent, set down by handwriting, typewriting, printing, photostating, photographing, magnetic impulse, mechanical or electronic recording, or other form of data compilation.

(2) **Photographs.** "Photographs" include still photographs, X-ray films, video tapes and motion pictures.

(3) **Original.** An "original" of a writing or recording is the writing or recording itself or any counterpart intended to have the same effect by a person executing or issuing it. An "original" of a photograph includes the negative or any print therefrom. If data are stored in a computer or similar device, any printout or other output readable by sight, shown to reflect the data accurately, is an "original."

(4) **Duplicate.** A "duplicate" is a counterpart produced by the same impression as the original, or from the same matrix, or by means of photography, including enlargements and miniatures, or by mechanical or electronic re-recording, or by chemical reproduction, or by other equivalent technique which accurately reproduces the original.

Rule 1002. Requirement of Original

To prove the content of a writing, recording, or photograph, the original writing, recording or photograph is required, except as otherwise provided in these rules or by Act of Congress.

Rule 1003. Admissibility of Duplicates

A duplicate is admissible to the same extent as an original unless (1) a genuine question is raised as to the authenticity of the original or (2) in the circumstances it would be unfair to admit the duplicate in lieu of the original.

Rule 1004. Admissibility of Other Evidence of Contents

The original is not required, and other evidence of the contents of a writing, recording, or photograph is admissible if —

(1) **Originals lost or destroyed.** All originals are lost or have been destroyed, unless the proponent lost or destroyed them in bad faith; or

(2) **Original not obtainable.** No original can be obtained by any available judicial process or procedure; or

(3) **Original in possession of opponent.** At a time when an original was under the control of the party against whom offered, that party was put on notice, by the pleadings or otherwise, that the contents would be a subject of proof at the hearing, and that party does not produce the original at the hearing; or

(4) **Collateral matters.** The writing, recording, or photograph is not closely related to a controlling issue.

Rule 1005. Public Records

The contents of an official record . . . may be proved by copy. . . .

Rule 1006. Summaries

The contents of voluminous writings, recordings, or photographs . . . may be presented in the form of a chart, summary, or calculation. . . . .

Rule 1007. Testimony or Written Admission of Party

Contents of writings, recordings, or photographs may be proved by the testimony or deposition of the party against whom offered or by that party's written admission, without accounting for the nonproduction of the original.

Rule 1008. Functions of Court and Jury

> When the admissibility of other evidence of contents of writings, recordings, or photographs under these rules depends upon the fulfillment of a condition of fact, the question . . . is ordinarily for the court . . . . However, when an issue is raised (a) whether the asserted writing ever existed, or (b) whether another writing, recording, or photograph produced at the trial is the original, . . . the issue is for the trier of fact . . . .

§ 18.03 AUTHENTICATION AND IDENTIFICATION

[A] Requirement of Authentication

"Authentication and identification represent a special aspect of relevancy . . . . Wigmore describes the need for authentication as 'an inherent logical necessity.'" Advisory Committee Note, Rule 901.

In a sense, all evidence admitted at trial must first be authenticated. Authentication requires a basic showing that evidence is relevant to the case and, at least to a certain minimum extent, reliable — that the evidence is what it purports to be. For example, eyewitnesses to an event must show they have personal knowledge of the event, and the possessor of a radar gun must show the gun accurately assesses the speed of vehicles. Authentication, therefore, can be viewed as a special type of relevancy requirement that applies to a wide variety of evidence. Authentication is like requiring a list of ingredients on the side of a product sold in a supermarket. It is truth in advertising, showing how the evidence connects to the issues in the case.

Authentication also addresses another type of relevancy problem. If the evidence is not authentic, it likely will be irrelevant or misleading in the attempt to prove the case. To illustrate, a knife produced at trial in a murder case will be helpful only if it is relevant to resolving the issues in the case (e.g., it is the knife used in the killing at issue or it is sufficiently similar to the alleged knife to be used for demonstrative purposes). Similarly, a photograph must be a fair and accurate representation of whatever it depicts, or else it will be misleading. Even witnesses must be authenticated, by showing that they have relevant evidence to contribute. The admission of unauthenticated evidence would waste time and distract jurors from their fact-finding responsibilities.

The Federal Evidence Rules on the subject, 901 and 902, focus on specific authentication problems. A recurring authentication issue is determining what method will be sufficient to authenticate different kinds of evidence. Rule 901 provides some assistance in this endeavor. It lists some methods of authentication that are used in common situations. For example, it discusses ways to authenticate voices, handwriting, and telephone conversations.

Rule 902 provides help with a different issue — forms of evidence that everyone knows are authentic, but would require considerable expenditures of time and effort to formally lay a foundation. In these instances, the rule spares a party the trouble of formally offering foundational evidence and calling a stream of witnesses. Instead, like judicially noticed evidence, this category of evidence simply bypasses the formalities of laying the foundation. The party offers the evidence as self-authenticating under Rule 902. Rule 902, however, does not ensure automatic admissibility of the evidence. Other objections to the admissibility of the evidence can still be raised, just not one based on a lack of foundation.

The category of self-authenticating evidence provides a laundry list of examples. These include certified copies of public records (such as convictions of crimes), newspapers, periodicals, trade inscriptions, and commercial paper. *See* Rule 902.

[B] Procedures for Authentication

The authentication and introduction of evidence generally proceed in the following fashion. After evidence is marked, identified, and shown to opposing counsel, there are three traditional questions to ask a witness for authentication purposes:

Basic Question #1: Do you recognize prosecution/plaintiff/defendant's Exhibit #1 for identification purposes?

Basic Question #2: What is Exhibit #1 for identification purposes?

Basic Question #3: How do you recognize it?

Real or documentary evidence can be modified or altered. For example, a shotgun can be sawed off, a document can be erased or changed, and metal can rust or erode. Consequently, a fourth question is usually required to ensure that the real or documentary evidence has not changed in such a way as to make it unfairly prejudicial:

Basic Question #4: (Real Evidence): Witness, is Exhibit # 1 for identification purposes in substantially the same condition as it was when you last saw it?

If the witness responds by saying that the condition of the evidence has been altered, the next question asked by counsel could probe the differences. For example, counsel could inquire, "What are the three markings that have been added to the document?"

For representative evidence, the inquiry focuses on the accuracy of the evidence, not on the likelihood of tampering. Photographs, for example, can distort and not simply reproduce pertinent information. A photograph of an intersection on a bright, sunny day may be substantially different than a photograph of the same intersection during stormy conditions, which may have existed at the time in question. Further, the physical characteristics of an intersection can change dramatically over time. Thus, a fourth question is required to authenticate representative evidence.

Basic Question #5: (Representative Evidence): Is Exhibit # 1 for identification purposes a fair and accurate representation of what it depicts as of a particular time and date [when the incident in question occurred]?

An additional foundational requirement may arise when evidence is susceptible to changes in its condition between the time the evidence is gathered and the time it is presented in court. The fungibility of the evidence makes it susceptible to fraud. In such cases, authentication is not complete with the asking of the four "magic" questions. Instead, a *chain of custody* for the evidence must be shown as well.

A chain of custody means that the evidence is traced from its source, such as the crime scene in a criminal case or the accident scene in a personal injury action, all the way to the courtroom. The trace is intended to show that no custodian of the evidence has permitted alteration or tampering that would impugn the evidence's authenticity. For example, narcotics or an ordinary kitchen knife must be traced to the crime scene to ensure that the evidence has not been the subject of tampering.

Proof of a chain of custody is not always necessary. An item that is unique, nonfungible or readily identifiable does not require such a foundation. To illustrate, a specially designed pearl-handled, neon green knife with the word "Mom" inlaid in jade on the handle will likely be considered unique, which would abrogate the need to establish a chain of custody. Further, non-unique real evidence sometimes can be made unique. A plain, ordinary kitchen knife, for example, will become unique if a witness' initials and the date are etched into it.

If evidence is authenticated, it may then be offered by a party "into evidence" at any time during the party's case. The offer need not occur when the authenticating witness is on the witness stand, although that is the most common and most appropriate time. Offering the evidence while the witness is on the stand affords the party the opportunity to repair any problems that might arise with the offer. The court usually will ask for objections prior to admitting the evidence. It also may permit a brief *voir dire* by the opposing party concerning authentication. A *voir dire* on an exhibit is essentially a miniature cross-examination restricted to the question of whether a proper foundation has been laid for admissibility.

If evidence is admitted, it is the offering party's responsibility to request that it be "published" (i.e., shown) to the jury. Generally, the court will allow admitted evidence to be published to the jury, subject to exceptions such as easily lost or fragile items. When publication is occurring, the questioning of a witness usually ceases, so the jury's attention can remain solely on the admitted evidence.

As noted above, the Rules categorize some evidence as self-authenticating. Self-authentication saves precious jury time and, like judicial notice, permits the jury to focus on disputed issues of fact. *See* Rule 902. Self-authenticating evidence, such as domestic public documents, both under seal and not under seal, official publications, newspapers and periodicals, and trade inscriptions, also can be published to the jury.

> *Practice Tip* — *Make sure the jury has an unobstructed view:* When laying a foundation for an exhibit, be careful about where you stand. An attorney authenticating evidence should not block the jurors' ability to observe the witness or provide the jury with a view of the attorney's back. (This principle applies to presenting witness testimony generally.) If standing near a witness while questioning the witness about a document, stand out of the way. The jury will appreciate it.

Problem 18-1: Yeah, That's the Ticket

In a complex commercial litigation case, the plaintiff offers various items in evidence. *What would the plaintiff have to do, if anything, to authenticate the following evidence? Briefly explain.*

1. A telephone conversation.
2. A business associate's handwriting.
3. A *Newsweek* magazine.
4. A Diet Coke label.
5. A photograph of the defendant.
6. A blueprint of a house.

Problem 18-2: Authenticate This . . .

After picking up his daughter from school in their green Town & Country van, Jean turned onto busy Commercial Boulevard. When he looked down to put a Raffi tape into the cassette player, he drifted into the left lane of the road. The driver in the left lane, Dirk, was speeding and not paying attention. In the ensuing crash, Dirk broke his leg, but everyone else was fine. Jean was sued by Dirk. *In this lawsuit, how would you authenticate the following evidence? Briefly explain.*

1. A photograph of the scene of the auto accident.
2. The statement of a bystander, who happened to be a C.P.A.
3. The report of the emergency room physician who treated Dirk.
4. The police officer's accident report.
5. A can of Budweiser beer recovered from the backseat of Dirk's car.

Problem 18-3: Not So Sweet

Rick and Associates, an advertising firm, sued Sarah's Pastries for breach of contract. Rick claimed that Sarah's owed him $4,000 for their performance under an agreement to create an advertising campaign. Rick's associate, Pam, had agreed on Rick's behalf to create a print advertising campaign for Sarah's products in several newspapers and trade publications. Sarah's associate, Ben, and Pam had signed the agreement after three telephone calls between them. Further, Ben sent back the agreement with a separate piece of paper indicating that Sarah always reserved the right to review any advertising proposal "to her personal satisfaction." Three advertisements were created. The ads ran in various papers after Pam had sent them to Ben via Bay State Messenger Service. Rick requested payment from Sarah, and had not heard any reply after four days.

You represent Sarah's Pastries at trial.

1. What evidence will you offer on her behalf? How will you authenticate that evidence?

2. What evidence will Rick offer? How will you oppose that evidence?

Problem 18-4: Making Money the Old-Fashioned Way

Sarah Gooding was an executive at Ortuna Web Systems, a business-to-business e-commerce company. During a highly contentious meeting, she observed a heated argument between Paul, the Chief Executive Officer, and Lisette, the Chief Financial Officer. Lisette subsequently sued Paul and the company, claiming she had been fired at the meeting. Paul rebutted her claims by alleging that Lisette had quit during the meeting. Sarah is questioned at trial:

PLAINTIFF'S ATTORNEY: Sarah, what did you see at the meeting that occurred in the company boardroom at 3:00 p.m. on the 4th?

A: I saw a ferocious argument between Paul and Lisette over the company's direction. It was a real power struggle that I thought would come to blows.

PLAINTIFF'S ATTORNEY: Sarah, what, if anything, did you hear while you were at that meeting?

A: Bits and pieces of things. I heard Lisette say something like "we used to make money the old-fashioned way, by earning it," or something like that.

PLAINTIFF'S ATTORNEY: I show you what has been marked Plaintiff's Exhibit A for Identification Purposes. Do you recognize it?

A: It is a cassette tape.

PLAINTIFF'S ATTORNEY: How do you recognize it?

A: I've seen cassettes before; I own several, for that matter. I believe I have heard this one as well.

PLAINTIFF'S ATTORNEY: (playing it outside of the hearing of the jury) Do you recognize the contents of this cassette tape?

A: Parts. It sounded like the meeting on the 4th.

PLAINTIFF'S ATTORNEY: How do you recognize that it was the meeting on the 4th?

A: I was at the meeting and caught a lot of what they were saying.

PLAINTIFF'S ATTORNEY: Your Honor, I offer in evidence Plaintiff's Exhibit A for Identification Purposes.

JUDGE: Any objections?

DEFENDANT'S ATTORNEY: May I *voir dire* on the exhibit, Your Honor?

JUDGE: Certainly.

DEFENDANT'S ATTORNEY: You did not record this audiotape, did you, Sarah?

A: No, sir.

DEFENDANT'S ATTORNEY: You don't remember all of what was said on it, only parts, right?

A: True, but significant parts of it.

DEFENDANT'S ATTORNEY: You don't know who handled this tape prior to it being produced in court or whether it has been the subject of tampering?

A: True.

DEFENDANT'S ATTORNEY: I object, Your Honor, to the admission of the tape. There may be a break in the chain of custody, and Sarah cannot recollect all of the conversation.

If you were the judge, how would you rule on the admissibility of the audiotape? See United States v. Brown, 136 F.3d 1176 (7th Cir. 1998).

§ 18.04 THE BEST EVIDENCE RULE

[A] The Production of Original Documents

"In an earlier day, when discovery and other related procedures were strictly limited, the misleading[ly] named 'best evidence rule' afforded substantial guarantees against inaccuracies and fraud by its insistence upon production of original documents." Rule 1001, Advisory Committee's Note.

The best evidence rule imposes a special type of authentication requirement on some writings, which is why it is grouped with authentication in this chapter. As the Advisory Committee's Note to Rule 1001 indicates, writings can be susceptible to fraud and distortion. Consequently, the Federal Rules of Evidence continued the tradition of the common law, seeking to minimize potential problems by requiring the originals of writings that play a significant role at trial.

Objections based on the best evidence rule can cause quite a stir, if only because the rule's intricacies appear to be inscrutable. Because of its mystique, the rule often creates a formidable obstacle, much more formidable than the situation warrants.

As noted above, the so-called best evidence rule is actually a misnomer. While appearing to require the "best evidence," the rule really has a much more circumscribed application. It is more accurately described as "the original writings rule" or, as it is sometimes called, the "original documents rule." The rule applies only when a witness is testifying solely based on the contents of a writing or when a party attempts to prove the contents of a writing related to an issue in a case. For example, the rule would apply to a witness testifying about a written confession, the written contract in a breach of contract action, or a motion picture in an obscenity action. The rule would not apply to an eyewitness to an automobile accident who took notes about the accident but left them at home, as the testimony is being offered to prove the circumstances of the accident, not the contents of the witness's notes.

Even in situations where the rule applies, it is perforated with exceptions. For example, a duplicate generally will suffice instead of the original. *See* Rules 1001(4),

1003.

While the rule may have limited applicability and is "fraught with exceptions," there is good reason to have it. One apt illustration of its value can be found in *Seiler v. Lucasfilm, Ltd.*, 808 F.2d 1316 (9th Cir. 1986), *cert. denied*, 484 U.S. 826 (1987), included at the end of the chapter in the Case Library. In *Seiler*, a graphic artist alleged that filmmaker George Lucas and others infringed the copyright on creatures the artist had created, called "Garthian Striders." Plaintiff contended that Lucas had used similar creatures, which Lucas called "Imperial Walkers," in the science fiction film, *The Empire Strikes Back*. At trial, the plaintiff intended to offer enlargements of the Garthian Striders. After a pre-trial evidentiary hearing

on the matter, the trial court held that the best evidence rule prevented the plaintiff from offering the enlargements and granted summary judgment for the defendants.

The trial court's ruling was based on the fact that the plaintiff could not produce the original drawings of the Garthian Striders, or in the alternative, any evidence of their existence prior to 1980, when *The Empire Strikes Back*, was released. Because of the danger of fraud, secondary evidence was excluded.

On appeal, the Ninth Circuit affirmed. The Court stated, "We hold that Seiler's drawings were 'writings' within the meaning of [the best evidence rule]; . . . . The contents of Seiler's work are at issue . . . . Since the contents are material and must be proved, Seiler must either produce the original or show that it is unavailable through no fault of his own . . . . This he could not do." 808 F.2d at 1318–1319. In fact, the Ninth Circuit noted that this case supported the very reason for the "best evidence" rule. Seiler's evidence consisted of reconstructions that apparently were made after the film was released, without any proof that his creations existed prior to the film. (The text of this opinion is reprinted in the Case Library at the end of this chapter.)

The best evidence rule applies to "writings," "recordings," and "photographs," which can include documents, x-rays, motion pictures, and videotapes. *See* Rules 1001(1), (2), 1002. Sometimes, it is unclear what constitutes a "writing" for the purposes of the rule. In *United States v. Duffy*, 454 F.2d 809 (5th Cir. 1972), for example, the defendant was convicted of transporting a stolen motor vehicle in interstate commerce. The car contained a suitcase that included a white shirt that had a laundry label reading, "D-U-F." The government offered testimony about the shirt at trial without producing it. In a decision handed down prior to the adoption of the Federal Rules of Evidence, the Fifth Circuit affirmed the trial court's decision to permit the testimony. The Court of Appeals stated:[1]

> The [best evidence rule] is not, by its terms or because of the policies underlying it, applicable to the instant case. The shirt with a laundry mark would not, under ordinary understanding, be considered a writing, and would not, therefore, be covered by the "Best Evidence Rule." When the disputed evidence, such as the shirt in this case, is an object bearing a mark or inscription, and is therefore a chattel and a writing, the trial judge has

---

[1] 454 F.2d at 812.

discretion to treat the evidence as a chattel or as a writing. The shirt was collateral evidence of the crime. Furthermore, it was only one piece of evidence in a substantial case against Duffy.

Under the best evidence rule, disputes about whether a writing ever existed, whether a different writing is the original, or whether other evidence correctly reflects the writing's contents are considered questions of fact to be determined by the trier of fact. *See* Rule 1008. These are not admissibility questions to be decided by the judge pursuant to Rule 104(a).

Example

Princess Genevieve files an invasion of privacy action against *The Star Mail* tabloid for publishing a photograph of her at a secluded Caribbean hideaway with her new boyfriend, Count Zigfried von Jonk. Does the best evidence rule apply to the production of the photograph at trial?

Answer: The best evidence rule likely applies to the photograph. The photograph is not collateral to the case, but rather is the basis of the cause of action. A photograph also is considered to be a writing pursuant to Federal Rule of Evidence 1001. Thus, *The Daily Star Mail* must produce the original photograph unless one of the numerous statutory exceptions governs.

[B] Exceptions to the Requirement of an Original

The flexibility of the "original writing" rule is a prevailing characteristic. As the Advisory Committee stated, "[b]asically the rule requiring the production of the original as proof of contents has developed as a rule of preference: if failure to produce the original is satisfactorily explained, secondary evidence is admissible." Rule 1004, Advisory Committee's Note. The Advisory Committee's rationale is based on common sense: if a writing is at issue, the writing should be produced for a firsthand review. Production of the writing should not be required, however, if it would not be helpful to resolving the issues of the trial and would involve extra time and expense.

Even when the rule applies, the non-production of the original writing is allowed when:

- A duplicate is offered in lieu of the original. A "duplicate" is a counterpart produced from the original by a technique, such as photography or re-recording, that accurately reproduces the original. (Rule 1001(4).)

- The original has been lost or destroyed and no bad faith exists. (Rule 1004.)

- The original is not obtainable. For example, it is locked away in a safe in a foreign country and cannot be retrieved. (Rule 1004.)

- The original is in the possession of the opposing party. This exception prevents the rule from being used as both a sword and a shield, which would occur if a party possessing the original asks that the opposing party be penalized for not producing the original. (Rule 1004.)

- The writing whose contents are in question is collateral to the issues at trial. (Rule 1004.)

Other limitations on the requirement of providing the original are as follows:

- Copies of public records are permitted to promote judicial economy and avoid "serious inconvenience." (Rule 1005, Advisory Committee's Note.)

- Summaries of voluminous writings are allowed to promote judicial economy. (Rule 1006.)

- The testimony, deposition, or written admission of a party opponent about the contents of the writing may be used as proof of the contents without the production of the original. (Rule 1007.)

Despite the rule permitting the non-production of the original under a variety of circumstances, foundational limits to secondary evidence exist. Rule 1003 provides that a duplicate is allowed in all situations when proving the contents of a writing, except: (1) when there exists a genuine question as to the authenticity of the original writing, such as a dispute over which of the parties possesses the real contract in question; or (2) when the admission of a duplicate would be unfair under the circumstances. Thus, if a party challenges a document central to the case as a forgery, the document's authenticity is at issue and the original might be required. In addition, on fairness grounds, the original may be required if only a partial duplicate of a record is provided at trial. Under such circumstances, the opposing counsel would be at a disadvantage in countering the evidence and examining witnesses about it.

Destroying documents through bad faith also prohibits the proponent's admission of secondary evidence about the documents. Bad faith generally means more than the negligent loss or destruction of evidence and is usually the result of an intentional culpable act. Yet, not all intentional destruction of evidence qualifies as bad faith. For example, if a business routinely destroyed records after saving them for a certain period of time, such conduct might not satisfy the bad faith requirement.

Practice Tip: "If you haven't got a Ha'Penny . . ." The introduction to Federal Rule of Evidence 1004 states that if an original is not required, "other secondary evidence" of a writing's contents is admissible. This language means that if you're excused from having to offer the original of a writing, whether you prove its contents with a tangible copy (if one exists) or oral testimony is up to you. However, assuming that you have a choice, better practice is to follow the lyrics of an old English Christmas tune: "If you haven't got a penny, then a ha'penny will do; if you haven't got a ha'penny, then God bless you." As a general practice, prove the contents of an unavailable original writing through a tangible copy, if one is available. If a tangible copy is not available, then resort to oral testimony to the original's contents. (For more information about the Christmas tune, visit the web address *http://en.wikipedia.org/wiki/Christmas_Is_Coming.*)

Problem 18-5: Hagar

Harold Hagar was hired to build a porch on Paulette Pogo's house. Hagar claimed he was not paid for the job after completing it, so he brought suit. At trial, the only issue was whether Hagar completed the work. Hagar testified in his case-in-chief:

PLAINTIFF'S ATTORNEY: Hagar, are you employed?

A: Yes, I am a licensed building contractor.

DEFENDANT'S ATTORNEY: Objection. Since Hagar is testifying about a written license, he is violating the best evidence rule. He must bring the license in for proper examination.

Is the defense counsel correct? Why?

PLAINTIFF'S ATTORNEY: Who did the work on the infrastructure of the deck?

A: Johnny Walker.

DEFENDANT'S ATTORNEY: Objection. Johnny Walker is the best witness to testify about who did the work on the deck. This testimony violates the best evidence rule.

Is the defense counsel correct? Why?

PLAINTIFF'S ATTORNEY: What was your role in the project?

A: I supervised construction, and kept copious records on a daily basis of who did what.

DEFENDANT'S ATTORNEY: Objection. Again, Your Honor, Hagar's testimony is in violation of the best evidence rule. Hagar must bring in the records and then properly authenticate them as business records.

Is the defense counsel correct? Why?

Problem 18-6: Sweet Suit

The plaintiff, Ethel, sued the defendant, Rose, for breach of contract involving the sale of chocolate bars on March 12. The sole issue at trial was whether the number of bars stated in the contract was 3,800 or 38,000. The defendant offers a duplicate of the contract at trial.

Will a duplicate suffice? Explain.

Problem 18-7: More Breach

In the same breach of contract action as in the previous problem, the defendant Rose contends that the original contract was washed away in a huge rainstorm that destroyed her office. She only was able to save a copy of it.

Will the defendant be able to offer a copy of the contract in lieu of the original? Explain.

Problem 18-8: Meet the Jetsons

Plaintiff, the Jetson Motor Credit Company, sued the defendant for allegedly failing to make a $5,500 payment on defendant's new Astro electric car. At trial, the defendant, Elroy, offers a duplicate of his payment receipt.

Will the duplicate receipt violate the best evidence rule? Explain.

Problem 18-9: Elroy Was Here

Elroy subsequently brings suit for an alleged overpayment to Jetson. Jetson defends by claiming that no overpayment occurred and that he had a receipt to prove it. At trial, Jetson forgets to bring in the receipt, but still testifies about the payment. Elroy objects to the testimony, claiming that any testimony about the payment without the receipt violates the best evidence rule.

How should the judge rule on this objection?

Problem 18-10: All Business

To prove that a famous person had been present on the San Diego boat, *All Business*, the plaintiff offers the duplicate of a photograph taken of the famous individual on the boat.

Is the duplicate admissible? Why?

Problem 18-11: I Confess!

Defendant Magoo is charged with a crime. After orally confessing to the police, the defendant signs a verbatim written version of his confession. At trial, the police forget to bring the written confession, but attempt to testify about the oral confession anyway.

Can a police officer who heard the confession testify to it? Why?

Can a police officer who read the confession testify to it? Explain.

Problem 18-12: Dat's Da Guy

Hillerich is charged with bank robbery of the National Bank. Bradley, the teller who was robbed, testifies for the prosecution. He is shown a copy of a photograph of the robbery taken by the bank surveillance camera. Bradley verifies that the people and their locations were as depicted in the photograph. Bradley also indicates that the photograph shows the robber carrying a gun in his belt. (Bradley does not independently remember seeing the gun on the assailant during the robbery because of Bradley's fear at the time.)

1. Does this testimony violate the best evidence rule? Why?

2. What is the significance, if any, of the defendant contesting the authenticity of the photograph?

Problem 18-13: Roll the Videotape, Please

Barnaby sues NBS Television for distributing a videotape in which NBS made allegedly libelous statements about him. At trial, Barnaby testifies about the tape but does not bring it with him.

1. Does Barnaby's testimony violate the best evidence rule? Explain.

2. If Barnaby brings a copy of the videotape, does this satisfy the best evidence rule? Explain.

3. The president of NBS was overheard two weeks prior to trial at a cocktail party saying, "Our employee said in that videotape that Barnaby was a slippery snake. So what?" Does Barnaby still have to offer the original videotape? Why?

4. If Barnaby has accidentally destroyed the videotape, what recourse does he have, if any, at trial? Explain.

Problem 18-14: Damages

In a workers' compensation action, the primary issue at trial was the plaintiff's earning capacity. Plaintiff testified on direct examination:

PLAINTIFF'S ATTORNEY: How much did you earn in 2005?

A: I earned the amount of —

DEFENDANT'S ATTORNEY: Objection. This testimony violates the best evidence rule, Your Honor.

1. Why does the defense counsel claim that this testimony violates the "best evidence" rule?

2. What ruling and why?

§ 18.05 SUMMARY AND REVIEW

1. What kinds of evidence must be authenticated? Why?

2. What is the difference between the authentication of real evidence and the authentication of representative evidence?

3. Why is some evidence self-authenticating?

4. Why is the term "best evidence rule" a misnomer?

5. Describe two situations in which the best evidence rule applies.

6. Name three substitutes that may be offered in lieu of the original writing when the best evidence rule applies.

§ 18.06 CHAPTER REVIEW PROBLEMS

CHAPTER REVIEW PROBLEMS

Problem 18-A

Ann Larimore purchased a "Balancing" nutrition bar from the local supermarket, Everyday's Market. Shortly after eating the bar, Larimore became very ill. Upon recovering, she sued the maker of the bar. At trial, Larimore offered a bar in the identical wrapper to the one she purchased. While testifying, her own attorney asked her, "Ann, do you recognize plaintiff's Exhibit #11 for identification purposes?" Ann responded, "Yes, it is exactly the type of Balancing Bar I purchased that made me sick." The attorney then offered the bar in evidence. The defendant objected on several grounds, including lack of authentication. *As to the objection relating to authentication, how should the court rule?* Explain.

1. The exhibit should be excluded because the attorney failed to satisfy authentication requirements.

2. The exhibit should be excluded because it is unfairly prejudicial and will mislead the jury.

3. The exhibit should not be excluded based on a lack of authentication because under the circumstances, there is sufficient authentication.

4. The exhibit should not be excluded because the importance of the document outweighs the minor omissions by counsel in laying the foundation.

Problem 18-B

In a negligence action resulting from a collision between a sports utility vehicle and a truck, the plaintiff called an expert in accident reconstruction to describe what exactly occurred during the accident. The expert was admitted by the court and, after laying a foundation of how she constructed her demonstrative computer graphics, the expert attempted to use a computer reenactment of the accident to illustrate her testimony. The defense objects. *How should the court rule?*

1. Admit, if it is reasonably accurate and will aid in the witness' testimony.

2. Admit, if counsel shows the reenactment constitutes business records under the applicable hearsay exception.

3. Exclude, because such a reenactment is highly prejudicial.

4. Exclude, because the reenactment is not probative of a fact of consequence.

Problem 18-C

Johnny Epstein and Melissa Matsui were charged with wire fraud for allegedly selling millions of dollars of fraudulent bonds to retirees by telephone. At trial, the prosecutor offered transcripts of several wiretapped phone conversations on Melissa's phone between the defendants pursuant to a properly obtained warrant. The defense objects to the admission of the transcripts. *Which of the following statements is the most accurate?*

1. The best evidence rule applies, and the tape or a copy of the tape must be produced.

2. The tape is hearsay and inadmissible.

3. The phone conversations between the co-defendants are privileged.

4. The Rule of Completeness does not allow the conversations unless all of the conversations between the defendants were taped.

Problem 18-D

Serena Shelley was prosecuted for theft of social security checks from the United States mail. At trial, after laying the necessary foundation and authenticating its evidence, the prosecution offered four original checks and a partial photocopy of a fifth check. *If there is an objection to the admissibility of these five checks, how should the judge rule?*

1. The five checks should be admitted, so long as they were properly authenticated.

2. The partial photocopy should be admitted because the rule requiring the production of the remainder of a document does not apply to checks.

3. The partial photocopy should be admitted because the best evidence rule does not apply.

4. The partial photocopy should not be admitted, unless the remainder of the check is irrelevant or not useful to the opponent of the evidence.

§ 18.07 CASE LIBRARY

SEILER v. LUCASFILM, LTD.
United States Court of Appeals, 808 F.2d 1316 (9th Cir. 1986)

FARRIS, CIRCUIT JUDGE:

Lee Seiler, a graphic artist and creator of science fiction creatures, alleged copyright infringement by George Lucas and others who created and produced the science fiction movie "The Empire Strikes Back." Seiler claimed that creatures known as "Imperial Walkers" which appeared in The Empire Strikes Back infringed Seiler's copyright on his own creatures called "Garthian Striders." The Empire Strikes Back appeared in 1980; Seiler did not obtain his copyright until 1981.

Because Seiler wished to show blown-up comparisons of his creatures and Lucas' Imperial Walkers to the jury at opening statement, the district judge held a pre-trial evidentiary hearing. At the hearing, Seiler could produce no originals of his Garthian Striders nor any documentary evidence that they existed before The Empire Strikes Back appeared in 1980. The district judge, applying the best evidence rule, found that Seiler had lost or destroyed the originals in bad faith under Fed. R. Evid. 1004(1) and denied admissibility of any secondary evidence, even the copies that Seiler had deposited with the Copyright Office. With no admissible evidence, Seiler then lost at summary judgment.

Facts

Seiler contends that he created and published in 1976 and 1977 science fiction creatures called Garthian Striders. In 1980, George Lucas released The Empire Strikes Back, a motion picture that contains a battle sequence depicting giant machines called Imperial Walkers. In 1981 Seiler obtained a copyright on his Striders, depositing with the Copyright Office "reconstructions" of the originals as they had appeared in 1976 and 1977.

Seiler contends that Lucas' Walkers were copied from Seiler's Striders which were allegedly published in 1976 and 1977. Lucas responds that Seiler did not obtain his copyright until one year after the release of The Empire Strikes Back and that Seiler can produce no documents that antedate The Empire Strikes Back.

. . . .

Discussion

1. Application of the best evidence rule

The best evidence rule embodied in Rules 1001–1008 represented a codification of longstanding common law doctrine. Dating back to 1700, the rule requires not, as its common name implies, the best evidence in every case but rather the production of an original document instead of a copy. Many commentators refer to the rule not as the best evidence rule but as the original document rule.

We hold that Seiler's drawings were "writings" within the meaning of Rule 1001(1); they consist not of "letters, words, or numbers" but of "their equivalent." To hold otherwise would frustrate the policies underlying the rule and introduce undesirable inconsistencies into the application of the rule.

The modern justification for the rule has expanded from prevention of fraud to a recognition that writings occupy a central position in the law. When the contents of a writing are at issue, oral testimony as to the terms of the writing is subject to a greater risk of error than oral testimony as to events or other situations. The human memory is not often capable of reciting the precise terms of a writing, and when the terms are in dispute only the writing itself, or a true copy, provides reliable evidence. To summarize then, we observe that the importance of the precise terms of writings in the world of legal relations, the fallibility of the human memory as reliable evidence of the terms, and the hazards of inaccurate or incomplete duplication are the concerns addressed by the best evidence rule.

Viewing the dispute in the context of the concerns underlying the best evidence rule, we conclude that the rule applies. McCormick summarizes the rule as follows:

[I]n proving the terms of a writing, where the terms are material, the original writing must be produced unless it is shown to be unavailable for some reason other than the serious fault of the proponent.

McCormick on Evidence § 230, at 704.

The contents of Seiler's work are at issue. There can be no proof of "substantial similarity" and thus of copyright infringement unless Seiler's works are juxtaposed with Lucas' and their contents compared. Since the contents are material and must be proved, Seiler must either produce the original or show that it is unavailable through no fault of his own. Rule 1004(1). This he could not do.

The facts of this case implicate the very concerns that justify the best evidence rule. Seiler alleges infringement by The Empire Strikes Back, but he can produce no documentary evidence of any originals existing before the release of the movie. His secondary evidence does not consist of true copies or exact duplicates but of "reconstructions" made after The Empire Strikes Back. In short, Seiler claims that the movie infringed his originals, yet he has no proof of those originals.

The dangers of fraud in this situation are clear. The rule would ensure that proof of the infringement claim consists of the works alleged to be infringed. Otherwise, "reconstructions" which might have no resemblance to the purported original would suffice as proof for infringement of the original. Furthermore, application of the rule here defers to the rule's special concern for the contents of writings. Seiler's claim depends on the content of the originals, and the rule would exclude reconstituted proof of the originals' content. Under the circumstances here, no "reconstruction" can substitute for the original.

Seiler argues that the best evidence rule does not apply to his work, in that it is artwork rather than "writings, recordings, or photographs." He contends that the rule both historically and currently embraces only words or numbers. Neither party has referred us to cases which discuss the applicability of the rule to drawings.

To recognize **Seiler's** works as writings does not, as **Seiler** argues, run counter to the rule's preoccupation with the centrality of the written word in the world of legal relations. Just as a contract objectively manifests the subjective intent of the makers, so **Seiler's** drawings are objective manifestations of the creative mind. The copyright laws give legal protection to the objective manifestations of an artist's ideas, just as the law of contract protects through its multifarious principles the meeting of minds evidenced in the contract. Comparing **Seiler's** drawings with Lucas' drawings is no different in principle than evaluating a contract and the intent behind it. **Seiler's** "reconstructions" are "writings" that affect legal relations; their copyrightability attests to that.

A creative literary work, which is artwork, and a photograph whose contents are sought to be proved, as in copyright, defamation, or invasion of privacy, are both covered by the best evidence rule. *See* McCormick, § 232 at 706 n. 9; Advisory Committee's Note to Rule 1002; 5 Louisell & Mueller, § 550 at 285 n. 27. We would be inconsistent to apply the rule to artwork which is literary or photographic but not to artwork of other forms. Furthermore, blueprints, engineering drawings, architectural designs may all lack words or numbers yet still be capable of copyright and susceptible to fraudulent alteration. In short, **Seiler's** argument would have us restrict the definitions of Rule 1001(1) to "words" and "numbers" but ignore "or their equivalent." We will not do so in the circumstances of this case.

Our holding is also supported by the policy served by the best evidence rule in protecting against faulty memory. **Seiler's** reconstructions were made four to seven years after the alleged originals; his memory as to specifications and dimensions may have dimmed significantly. Furthermore, reconstructions made after the release of the Empire Strikes Back may be tainted, even if unintentionally, by exposure to the movie. Our holding guards against these problems.

2. Rule 1008.

As we hold that the district court correctly concluded that the best evidence rule applies to **Seiler's** drawings, **Seiler** was required to produce his original drawings unless excused by the exceptions set forth in Rule 1004. The pertinent subsection is 1004(1), which provides:

> The original is not required, and other evidence of the contents of a writing, recording, or photograph is admissible if —
>
> (1) Originals lost or destroyed. All originals are lost or have been destroyed, unless the proponent lost or destroyed them in bad faith. . .

In the instant case, prior to opening statement, **Seiler** indicated that he planned to show to the jury reconstructions of his "Garthian Striders" during the opening statement. The trial judge would not allow items to be shown to the jury until they were admitted in evidence. **Seiler's** counsel reiterated that he needed to show the reconstructions to the jury during his opening statement. Hence, the court excused the jury and held a seven-day hearing on their admissibility. At the conclusion of the hearing, the trial judge found that the reconstructions were inadmissible under the best evidence rule as the originals were lost or destroyed in bad faith. This finding is amply supported by the record.

Seiler argues on appeal that regardless of Rule 1004(1), Rule 1008 requires a trial because a key issue would be whether the reconstructions correctly reflect the content of the originals. Rule 1008 provides:

> When the admissibility of other evidence of contents of writings, recordings, or photographs under these rules depends upon the fulfillment of a condition of fact, the question whether the condition has been fulfilled is ordinarily for the court to determine in accordance with the provisions of rule 104. However, when an issue is raised (a) whether the asserted writing ever existed, or (b) whether another writing, recording, or photograph produced at the trial is the original, or (c) whether other evidence of contents correctly reflects the contents, the issue is for the trier of facts to determine as in the case of other issues of fact.

Seiler's position confuses admissibility of the reconstructions with the weight, if any, the trier of fact should give them, after the judge has ruled that they are admissible. Rule 1008 states, in essence, that when the *admissibility* of evidence other than the original depends upon the fulfillment of a condition of fact, the trial judge generally makes the determination of that condition of fact. The notes of the Advisory Committee are consistent with this interpretation in stating: "Most preliminary questions of fact in connection with applying the rule preferring the original as evidence of contents are for the judge . . . [t]hus the question of . . . fulfillment of other conditions specified in Rule 1004 . . . is for the judge." In the instant case, the condition of fact which **Seiler** needed to prove was that the originals were not lost or destroyed in bad faith. Had he been able to prove this, his reconstructions would have been admissible and then their accuracy would have been a question for the jury. In sum, since admissibility of the reconstructions was dependent upon a finding that the originals were not lost or destroyed in bad faith, the trial judge properly held the hearing to determine their admissibility.

Affirmed.

Chapter 19

REVIEW PROBLEMS

§ 19.01 PROBLEMS

Answers to Problems 19-9 through 19-80 appear below, in § 19.02.

Problem 19-1: United States v. O'Ruben

This review problem is presented in the form of a mock trial which can be acted out by the participants. It involves the robbery of a convenience store, with one witness for the prosecution and one for the defense. The sworn statements of the store clerk, Sally Smith, and the defendant, Rick O'Ruben, provide the basis for each witness' testimony.

The problem is designed as a review of evidence law, touching on many subject areas of the course. Unlike previous problems where the subject matter is expressly labeled, this review is intended to promote issue-spotting skills as well as legal analysis.

The Prosecution's Case

1. The robbery note.
2. The gun.
3. A note written by Sally after the robbery containing the purported getaway car's license plate number.
4. The testimony of Sally Smith. (This testimony should be consistent with Sally Smith's statement below.)
5. The sworn statement of Sally Smith.

The following is the true signed and sworn statement of Sally Smith, made on January 25, within one month of the alleged robbery:

> "My name is Sally Smith. I am 29 years old and I had been working on the night shift at Magruder's Convenience Store on Main Street for the past six months. I was fired from Magruder's last Thursday for allegedly taking money from the cash register. They can't prove it, however, and that's because I did not do it.
>
> I flunked out of high school and have had a few problems with the law. I was convicted of possessing marijuana, a misdemeanor, two years ago; of aggravated assault on my ex-husband, a felony, ten years ago; of embezzle-

ment from my prior employer (although I was framed), a misdemeanor, last year; and of the unlawful possession of a firearm, a misdemeanor, twelve years ago. Also, I was arrested for the attempted murder of my ex-husband three years ago, but the charges was dropped.

I am now working as a receptionist in the Body Boutique, a nails and hair salon. I've been there for a week or so, and I like it a lot.

On January 6th of this year, a Wednesday, I was working the night shift at Magruder's. Magruder's is like any other convenience store — big on the beer, potato chips, muffins, and things like that. There is only one entrance into the store, and the clerk's counter is about ten yards or so from the front entrance. There are six aisles perpendicular to my counter, and mirrors near the ceiling so I can see the entire store. There is a surveillance camera as well, but it wasn't working on January 6th. The lighting is pretty good, since the whole store has fluorescent lights.

I started that evening around 8:00 p.m. It was pretty quiet that night, only about fifteen customers each hour. I even had time to do inventory work. At 9:00 p.m., I was the only person in the store. When this guy walked into the store, he seemed nervous; he looked around some.

He then came right up to me at the checkout counter, and put this note on the counter that said, "Your money or your life." I told my sister last week that when he first walked in, he seemed like a nice guy, not the monster he turned out to be.

Anyway, he really was a creep. I guess I was going too slow for him, because he hit me on the shoulder real hard with his fist and said, "Faster, faster, sister, I mean it!" I thought I saw a gun in his hand, but I wasn't sure. After I gave him all of the money in the register, he started humming a song, I think it was Springsteen's "Tunnel of Love" or something like that. He then walked quickly out of the store. The whole thing lasted no more than five or ten minutes. I felt nauseous, and my knees buckled, but I took a deep breath and ran after him. I saw him get in his car and drive away. I wrote down his license plate number, but I can't remember what I wrote down — I was very nervous at the time. In looking at the paper I wrote it on, it says "license plate number: DDP 514."

I then ran back into the store and called the police. I told them I had just been robbed by a guy who was about 5 feet, 9 inches tall, and 140 pounds, white male, beard, shoulder length dark hair, with fingerless black gloves and an earring in his right ear. I told them the robbery probably took about a minute.

Several days after the robbery, the police showed me some photographs of people. I looked over all of them and pointed out the person who I thought was the robber. As sure as I am sitting here, it was that guy, Rick O'Ruben.

I had never seen him before, although I did see someone who looked just like him in the nearby supermarket about two months prior to the robbery.

This was one of the scariest things to ever happen to me. I will remember the robber's face as long as I live. I don't ever want to get robbed again; it still causes me nightmares.

As I ran out after the robber, I saw a gun lying on the floor just inside the store entrance. The robber must have dropped it. I had never seen the gun before. I picked up the gun, put my initials in the barrel along with the date, and turned it over to the police, along with the robbery note and the paper on which I wrote down the license plate number. I put my initials and the date on the robbery note as well.

I swear that this statement is true and accurate to the best of my knowledge.

(Signed) Sally Smith"

The Defense Case

1. One of the defendant's blue fingerless gloves.

2. A letter from Rick O'Ruben's friend, Tim, a sailor in the Navy, which reads, "I look forward to playing tennis with you each Wednesday in January, at 8:00 p.m. at Holiday Park." The letter was dated December 1.

3. The testimony of Rick O'Ruben. (This testimony will be consistent with Rick O'Ruben's statement, below.)

4. The Statement of Rick O'Ruben

The following is the signed and sworn statement of the defendant, Rick O'Ruben, taken on January 30th of the same year.

"My name is Rick O'Ruben. I am 27 years old and I live on Talbot Street, right off of Main Street. I shop in the stores, restaurants and bars in the area, including the Magruder's that they say had been robbed. I think Magruder's is overpriced so I don't go there often.

I am a white male, approximately 6 feet, 1 inch, 190 pounds, with dark shoulder-length hair, no beard or mustache, and I wear an earring in my left ear.

I have attended the local community college for one semester and am a licensed automobile mechanic. I work at the Shell Station over on 17th Street and own many blue fingerless gloves, which I often wear at work to protect my hands.

I have had a few problems with the law. Seven years ago, I was convicted as an adult of a felony robbery of a Magruder's convenience store. I admit to committing that crime, but not to this one! I was just a kid then, and did not know better. I was found guilty of misdemeanor shoplifting three years ago; of a heroin sale as a juvenile; and aggravated mayhem, a felony two years ago. The mayhem conviction resulted from a bar fight where I was just defending myself.

I've had some tough times. I've been arrested eight times for fighting, three times for vandalism, and twice for suspicion of robbery, but they couldn't make any of the charges stick.

On that Wednesday night, I was playing tennis at Holiday Park from 8:00 to 9:00 p.m. with my buddy, Tim Lovell, who's in the Navy and presently at sea in the Indian Ocean. Every time Tim is in town, we play tennis on Wednesday evenings at Holiday Park, unless it rains. I don't have a reserved court, but it is not too difficult to get a court at that time. Tim and I are pretty even, although he almost always wins. Actually, that Wednesday night I recall beating him.

When the police arrested me at the Shell station where I work, I didn't say anything to them. I am innocent though. I have done some bad things in the past, but there is one thing I did not do — and that's rob the Magruder's like they claim.

I have a wife and a four-year-old child named Sherri. I am trying to save some money so Sherri can go to a good school. My wife Becky used to be a bookkeeper, but had to quit because she has bad migraine headaches and has to lie down a lot. I wouldn't do anything to jeopardize my relationship with either of them. That is why I often work overtime at the Shell station. I want us to be able to afford a decent car. Right now I'm driving a junker with the license plate number, "PDD 514."

I was in the Magruder's once or twice in the month prior to January 6th to buy some beer and chips. It's on my way home from work.

I owned a gun at one time just like the handgun they told me they found at Magruder's. My gun was stolen from my car about two months ago along with some other stuff. I used it for protection; I often have to drive through some bad neighborhoods.

I swear the aforementioned is true and accurate to the best of my knowledge.

(Signed), Rick O'Ruben"

Stipulations

1. The government tested the gun and the counter area for fingerprints. Four prints were found on the gun. One matched the defendant, two were of unknown persons, and one was too smudged to make an identification.

2. The alleged robbery note was smudged, which prevented any form of comparison with the defendant's handwriting.

3. The statements of Sally Smith and Rick O'Ruben were taken in depositions. After each deposition, the person making the statement was given an opportunity to review it for any inaccuracies.

4. The defendant was given his *Miranda* warnings upon his arrest.

5. The defendant is being charged with one count of armed robbery. The judge will instruct the jury on the lesser included charge of robbery as well.

6. The letter from Tim Lovell is authentic.

Brief Jury Instructions

Members of the jury, the defendant, Rick O'Ruben, stands charged by information of armed robbery, alleged to have been committed in the Magruder's convenience store on January 6th of this year at approximately 9:00 p.m. The defendant has pleaded not guilty.

A defendant is presumed to be innocent until each and every element of the case is proven by the prosecution beyond a reasonable doubt. That means a doubt for which you can give a reason. If a reasonable doubt as to one or more of the elements of the crime charged exists in your mind, you must find the defendant not guilty.

In the present case, the defendant is charged with armed robbery. Robbery is the trespassory taking and carrying away of money or other personal property that may be the subject of a larceny from the person or custody of another person and, in the course of the taking, there is the use of force, violence, assault, or putting in fear.

If, in the course of committing the robbery, the offender possesses a firearm or other deadly weapon, then the robbery is considered to be an armed robbery.

An act shall be deemed "in the course of committing the robbery" if it occurs in an attempt to commit robbery or in flight after the attempt or commission.

If, based on the evidence presented at trial, you find beyond and to the exclusion of every reasonable doubt that on the 6th day of January, the defendant, Rick O'Ruben, did rob the Magruder's store, then you must find the defendant guilty as charged.

Please select a jury foreperson when you first begin to deliberate. You will be permitted to take with you all of the admitted evidence, a verdict form, and a copy of the charging document, the information, which is not evidence. You may now go to the jury room to deliberate.

Assignment

1. Prepare closing arguments for the prosecution and for the defense. What is the theory of each case? What is the most significant evidence for each side?

2. Which evidence offered by the prosecution likely will be admitted? Which evidence likely will not be admitted? Explain, describing the likely objections to each piece of evidence and the probable ruling on those objections.

3. Which evidence offered by the defense likely will be admitted? Which evidence likely will not be admitted? Explain, describing the likely objections to each piece of evidence and the probable rulings on those objections.

4. Prepare direct and cross-examinations of Sally Smith and Rick O'Ruben. Do your examinations comply with the applicable rules of evidence?

Problem 19-2: Crash Davis

An automobile accident occurred between cars driven by Davis and Lenny during a busy rush hour morning. Neither driver was seriously injured. As they waited for the police to arrive, Lenny muttered just within Davis' hearing, "You're going to pay for this!" In response, Davis said to Lenny, "Look, I must admit it, I'm not really sure what happened here because I was daydreaming, but it may well be I'm at fault and I did not look where I was going. I'll pay your medical expenses; actually, my insurance company will pay, if you agree not to sue me." Lenny does not accept Davis' proposal and brings suit against Davis.

1. Are Davis' statements to Lenny admissible in a subsequent trial?

2. If Davis takes the witness stand at trial and states, "I was driving with my full attention on the road when that guy, Lenny, went right through a red light," can Davis' previous statements at the scene be offered to impeach him? Why?

Problem 19-3: Benni and Hannah

Benni and Hannah owned a 1987 Shakami truck. Three months after they bought it, the vehicle rolled over, injuring both owners. The truck was being properly and non-negligently driven when it crashed. Benni and Hannah brought suit against Shakami, Inc., on a strict products liability theory. The plaintiffs would like to introduce the following evidence at their trial. *Will the evidence be admitted? Explain.*

1. A *Consumer Reports* magazine article, published after the crash, claiming that the Shakami truck is not safe, particularly with respect to its susceptibility to rollover.

2. A modification made by Shakami in 1989 that minimizes the potential for roll-over.

Problem 19-4: United States v. Bowie

The defendant, state court judge Allen Bowie, is alleged to have conspired with a friend, Johnny Bart, to accept a bribe. The object of the conspiracy was to trade a lenient sentence in a serious criminal case for money. The government attempted to catch the judge and his friend by having a retired FBI agent pose as a representative of the soon-to-be sentenced criminal defendant. As a signal that the judge would participate in the conspiracy, he was to have breakfast at the famous Grand Hotel on June 1, 1993. The judge appeared at the hotel as expected.

The government's case is based on the judge's appearance at the hotel, on taped conversations between Bart and the judge that appear to be in some sort of mysterious code, and on the judge's behavior in the criminal case. The judge's defense is that his appearance at the hotel was coincidence — he often ate there — and that his conversations with Bart were not in code, but merely two friends chatting. Bart is maintaining his silence and refuses to testify for the government.

Decide which of the following potential items of evidence will be admissible at the judge's trial (note that the cases against Bart and the judge are severed for trial):

1. An FBI report, stating that an anonymous source indicated, "The judge is willing to trade his office for money."

2. The FBI agent called the defendant at his hotel in Washington, D.C., for questioning after Bart was arrested. The defendant did not return the call, but instead checked out of the hotel and flew back to his home jurisdiction the same day (two days prior to his scheduled departure).

3. The FBI agent overheard Bart say to an unidentified third party: "I'm going to meet with the judge tonight; I'll tell him that I've made contact with the pilgrim."

4. The FBI had evidence that the judge was involved in two previous bribery schemes in 1989. No charges were ever filed.

5. The defendant's law clerk wrote a memorandum to the judge stating, "I'm working as fast as I can on this sentencing, your honor; I worked the past twelve hours on it and have pushed all other work aside as per your order." (The memorandum was brought to court and testified to by an FBI agent; the clerk was not called as a witness).

6. A former business associate of Bart claims his reputation in the community is that of a liar.

7. A photograph of the Grand Hotel's Restaurant.

8. A photograph of Bart.

9. A diagram of the Grand Hotel's Restaurant.

10. The primary FBI witness was convicted of shoplifting three years earlier.

11. The fact that the undercover FBI agent in the case hated judges.

Problem 19-5: Not Again!

The defendant Loni is charged with shoplifting. Upon apprehending her, Diane, the store manager, exclaimed, "I can't believe you just put those cosmetics in your pocket, Ma'am. That is at least the third time this past month you have done something similar to that!" At trial, the prosecution wishes to offer the testimony of the assistant manager, who heard Diane's statement. *Is Diane's statement admissible? Explain.*

Problem 19-6: One Tough Hombre

In the early morning hours of June 1, 1993, Jorge Gonzales, a longshoreman, was struck on the back of the head with what appeared to be a large baseball bat as he left the Façade Nightclub. There were no eyewitnesses. Jorge suffered head injuries from the blow and fractured a wrist as a result of his fall. Another longshoreman with whom Gonzales had worked, Robert Epstein, is charged with attempted murder.

Which of the following evidence is admissible at trial? Explain your answers.

A. For the prosecution:

1. Doug King, Jorge's friend, will testify that:

a. He was with Gonzales at the Façade Disco on the evening of May 31 and the morning of June 1, 1993.

b. He saw Epstein leave the disco furtively, like a guilty man, at approximately 1:00 a.m.

c. He heard a sound, saw Gonzales fall to the ground "like a lump of coal," and saw someone large, "like another longshoreman," running away. "It sounded just like Epstein," said King.

d. King and Epstein had a fistfight in May of 1987. Charges were brought against Epstein, but were later dropped.

e. King was drinking Coca-Cola on May 31st, with nothing added.

f. "Epstein is real violent person — real dangerous to others if you know what I mean. He'll steal you blind, too."

2. On cross-examination, King is asked the following questions. Which, if any, call for admissible responses?

   a. "Weren't you indicted for tax evasion in 1990?"

   b. (1) "You were convicted of grand theft auto in 1987, right?" (2) "You were convicted of aggravated assault in 1986?" (3) "You were adjudicated a juvenile delinquent for murder in 1986?"

   c. "You stated in a deposition taken after the incident: 'I left the nightclub with Gonzales and the next thing I knew, Gonzales was lying unconscious on the ground. I don't remember anything else, except for a watch and a baseball bat lying on the ground nearby.' The watch, by the way, was later shown to be Epstein's."

   d. "You hate Epstein as a result of your prior fight with him, correct?"

   e. "Two waitresses each served you a rum and Coke that night, didn't they?"

   f. "Epstein stole a pen from you several years earlier, correct?"

3. Dr. Dent, an expert witness, will testify for the prosecution.

   a. Dent is offered as an expert on the cause of death, medical diagnosis, and treatment. He states that he had been a pediatric surgeon for five years. Prior to that, he was an emergency room physician for eight years.

   b. In Dr. Dent's opinion, the head injuries suffered by Gonzales were a result of being forcefully struck with a blunt object by a large man. Such a blow could easily have killed Gonzales.

   c. Dent also believes that, given Epstein's psychological profile as a borderline sociopathic personality (a mental illness, but not a psychosis),

   Epstein "beyond a doubt" hit Gonzales, and had the "legal intent" to kill him.

B. For the defendant:

1. The defendant, Epstein, will testify on direct examination as follows:

    a. "I was in the Façade nightclub on the night of May 31st. I left around 11:30 p.m. Earlier in the evening, a customer I did not know challenged me to a fight. I didn't want to fight; I never do. So I walked away as I always do when challenged to a fight, which seems to be about every time I go to a nightclub."

    b. "I lost my watch somewhere inside of the disco."

    c. "I go to Façade often, and always leave at 11:30 p.m."

    d. "I do not remember seeing Jorge at the disco."

2. On cross-examination, Epstein is asked the following questions. Which, if any, call for admissible responses?

    a. "Weren't you convicted of aggravated assault of your girlfriend in June of 1988?"

    b. "You were convicted of disorderly conduct in 1987 and 1988, right?"

    c. "Mr. Epstein, you wrote on a job application that you were certified as a longshoreman in 1981 when, in fact, you had been certified in 1988?"

    d. "You stated to a friend prior to trial that you'd gone to the club that night and left around 2:00 a.m. because it was boring."

Problem 19-7: Transcript

The defendant is charged with selling stolen watches on the streets of San Antonio. At trial, the prosecution offers the testimony of Sam Spark, private eye, who will testify on direct examination as follows. *Answer the italicized questions embedded in the transcript below.*

PROSECUTOR: What happened on June 10, 1993, at approximately 3:00 p.m.?

A: The defendant walked up to me and said, "I will sell you this Cartier watch cheap; today only, $100. What do you say?"

DEFENSE COUNSEL: *What objection, if any, is appropriate?*

JUDGE: *What ruling?*

PROSECUTOR: What occurred after he made you that offer?

A: A police car arrived with its siren blaring, and the defendant ran away.

DEFENSE COUNSEL: *What objection, if any, is appropriate?*

JUDGE: *What ruling?*

PROSECUTOR: Where did he go?

A: I'm not sure; I guess he hopped the fence and ran to the porch where he couldn't be found.

DEFENSE COUNSEL: *What objection, if any, is appropriate?*

JUDGE: *What ruling?*

PROSECUTOR: Did you ever see him again?

DEFENSE COUNSEL: *What objection, if any, is appropriate?*

JUDGE: *What ruling?*

A: Yeah. I saw him come around the other side of the building, and I pointed to the guy and said, "Look officer, there is the guy who tried to sell me the watch! That's him."

DEFENSE COUNSEL: *What objection, if any, is appropriate?*

JUDGE: *What ruling?*

PROSECUTOR: After pointing at him, what did you do?

A: I backed away a couple of feet because the defendant looked like he was going to have a fit; I could see "guilty" written all over his face.

On cross-examination, Sam testifies as follows:

DEFENSE COUNSEL: Last week, during a job interview, you told the owner of the Blue Parrot restaurant that you had prior experience working in restaurants, when you had none, isn't that right?

PROSECUTOR: *What objection, if any, is appropriate?*

JUDGE: *What ruling?*

A: Well, uh, yes.

DEFENSE COUNSEL: You were convicted in 1991 of the possession of cocaine, weren't you?

PROSECUTOR: *What objection, if any, is appropriate?*

JUDGE: *What ruling?*

A: Yes, That is correct.

DEFENSE COUNSEL: You have a pending charge against you for the misdemeanor, destruction of property, isn't that right?

PROSECUTOR: *What objection, if any, is appropriate?*

JUDGE: *What ruling?*

A: Yes.

DEFENSE COUNSEL: You have 30% hearing loss in your right ear, correct?

PROSECUTOR: *What objection, if any, is appropriate?*

JUDGE: *What ruling?*

A: Yes.

DEFENSE COUNSEL: The defendant's brother beat you up in a fight two years ago, right?

PROSECUTOR: *What objection, if any, is appropriate?*

JUDGE: *What ruling?*

A: No, it was about even.

DEFENSE COUNSEL: You don't leave tips any time you eat at restaurants, do you?

PROSECUTOR: *What objection, if any, is appropriate?*

JUDGE: *What ruling?*

A: No sir, I don't believe in it.

Problem 19-8: "The Sheriff"

Sheriff Sal, of a small Midwestern town, is sued for negligently running over and injuring the plaintiff, Penny, at a busy intersection. *Which of the following evidence is admissible, if any? Explain your answers.*

1. The defendant sheriff testifies on his own behalf. The sheriff states, "Why I told my deputy, Martin, soon after the accident that a woman darted out into the intersection suddenly, before I had a chance to hit the brakes."

2. The defendant, Sal, calls his friend, Marcy, to the stand to testify that Sal has a reputation for peacefulness in the community.

3. The plaintiff, Penny, then calls Wally Witness in her rebuttal case to testify that sheriff Sal once had another person fraudulently take a history exam for him in college.

4. The plaintiff also calls Shirley in her rebuttal case to testify that Sheriff Sal has a reputation in the community for being a violent person.

5. After losing the above negligence action, a distraught Sheriff Sal drives home. His mind wanders and he is involved in a serious accident. The sheriff panics and leaves the scene to drive home. He lies down to take a nap. When he awakens, he reads a note left him by his wife: "I'm taking the car to the shop to fix the dents caused by the 'seagull.' No one will ever know what really happened. Love, W." The sheriff is subsequently charged with reckless driving and leaving the scene of the accident. The prosecution offers the note against the sheriff. Is it admissible?

Problem 19-9

D is charged with shooting a victim to death; the killing occurred on a busy sidewalk. Cop races over to scene and picks up the gun that turns out to have fired the fatal bullet. D was standing 10 feet away from where the cop picked up the gun; two other people were standing 5 feet away. D objects "irrelevant" when the prosecutor offers the gun into evidence, on the ground that it's more likely that one of the other two people was the killer. *Ruling?*

Problem 19-10

Same case as previous problem. To show that D didn't do it, D offers evidence that, after the cop arrested D, D stayed at the scene and didn't try to run away even though the cop was too busy talking to witnesses to handcuff or restrain D. The prosecution objects that D's evidence is irrelevant, because it's at least as likely that D stayed at the scene simply to avoid committing the crime of "escape," or so as not to get shot trying to escape. *Ruling?*

Problem 19-11

Same case as previous problem. The prosecution offers evidence that D is a heroin addict. *Relevant? What about evidence that D was under the influence of heroin at the time of D's arrest at the crime scene?*

Problem 19-12

D is charged with stalking V. W testifies, for the defense, that on a number of occasions it was V who tried to contact W's good friend D. As evidence that W is testifying falsely, the prosecutor offers evidence that W knew that D had been arrested for and charged with stalking, yet didn't pass along this information to the cops or the prosecutor before trial. *Relevant?*

Problem 19-13

D is charged with sexually molesting V, D's 8-year-old stepdaughter. V testifies to the details of the sexual assaults. In order to prove that V acquired her knowledge of sexual behavior other than by being assaulted by D, D offers evidence that V told her mother that another man had also sexually assaulted her. *Ruling?*

Problem 19-14

D is charged with committing a murder in L.A. on June 1. D is arrested on the murder charge in L.A. on September 1. At D's trial, the prosecutor offers evidence from A and B, two women who live in Hawaii. The women will testify that D is the person who raped them in Hawaii on June 4 and June 6, respectively. *Upon D's objection to the testimony of A and B, which of the following should be the judge's ruling:*

1. Their testimony is irrelevant.

2. Their testimony is relevant, if it is "sanitized" so as to omit reference to the rapes.

3. Their testimony is fully admissible.

Problem 19-15

A convenience store clerk is held up at gunpoint; D is charged with the crime. D's defense is alibi. At trial, the clerk identifies D as the robber and proposes to testify, "I recognized D's face because I'd seen a photo of him committing a robbery of one of our other stores a week earlier." *Is this testimony admissible?*

Problem 19-16

D is charged with ADW (assault with a deadly weapon) for a stabbing incident outside a bar. W testifies for D that D acted in self-defense. To show W's bias in favor of D, the prosecution offers evidence that D and W are members of "Da Bomb Squad," a street gang. *Admissible? Would your answer be any different if the bartender were prepared to testify that "D and W often come into the bar and have drinks together?"*

Problem 19-17

D is charged with assault and battery on V. D claims self-defense, claiming that he struck V only after V advanced on him and made threats. V proposes to testify that V saw D wearing a black leather biker jacket that had an insignia on the front saying, "Go Ahead Sucker — Make My Day," and that seeing this made V afraid of D and want to avoid D. *Is V's testimony admissible?*

Problem 19-18

D is charged with murder on June 1. The prosecutor offers the following testimony from an eyewitness, "On June 1, I saw D pull the trigger." D objects to the testimony as improper character evidence as it supports an inference that D has a propensity to be violent. *Ruling?*

Problem 19-19

D is charged with robbery of the Wells Far To Go Bank; defense is an alibi. Teller testifies for the prosecution that D handed Teller a note reading, "I have a gub. Give me all your money." The prosecution then calls Teller-2, who will testify that a month earlier, Teller-2 was held up by D at the Bank of Americash; on that occasion, D handed Teller-2 a note reading, "I have a gub. Give me all your money." D objects to Teller-2's testimony as improper character evidence. *Ruling?*

Problem 19-20

D is charged with armed bank robbery on June 1. The prosecutor offers evidence that, after D's arrest, D was given *Miranda* warnings, denied committing the June 1 robbery, but confessed to committing three other bank robberies. Prosecutor offers the statement as D's party statement. D objects that the evidence is improper character evidence. *Ruling?*

Problem 19-21

Medical malpractice action, in which P claims that D negligently prescribed medicine, causing P to become asthmatic. D's defense is that P's reaction to the medication could not reasonably have been anticipated. P offers evidence that two other patients of D's had previously developed asthma after D prescribed the same drug. D objects that this is improper character evidence. *Ruling?*

Problem 19-22

Negligence action; P claims that D's speeding was the cause of the accident. D denies speeding. P offers evidence that D ran a red light, a few moments before the accident, at an intersection about two blocks away from the site of the accident. D objects that this is improper character evidence. *Ruling?*

Problem 19-23

D was charged with a robbery that occurred on May 1. D's defense is alibi, that D was out of town all day on May 1. W testifies for the prosecution, "I know that the robbery took place about 3:00 p.m., because when I heard the robber yell, 'This is the 4th robbery I've pulled this month, sucker,' I looked at my watch and saw that was the time." D objects that this is improper character evidence. The prosecutor responds that it's non-character evidence, as it's offered only to fix the time of the robbery. *Ruling?*

Problem 19-24

D is charged with passing a bad check; D claims it was accidental because of a miscalculation of her checking account balance. The prosecution offers evidence that D had passed a bad check a month earlier. D objects that this is improper character evidence. *Ruling?*

Problem 19-25

D has been sued for damages resulting from a car crash. P claims that D's speeding was the cause of an accident. D calls a witness to testify that, in her opinion, D is a safe and careful driver. *Admissible?*

Problem 19-26

Abbott is charged with the murder of Costello. The prosecutor offers evidence that, one week before Abbott killed Costello, Costello was present when Abbott killed Jones. Abbott objects to evidence of murder of Jones as inadmissible character evidence. *What say you?*

Problem 19-27

D is charged with physical abuse of his 5-year-old son. D claims that his son was accidentally injured during a fun wrestling match. The prosecution offers evidence that, 3 years earlier, D had physically abused his daughter, who was 7 years old at the time. *Improper character evidence?*

Problem 19-28

D is charged with "date rape" of V on June 1; the defense is consent. As evidence that V consented to sexual intercourse on June 1, D offers evidence that he and V had been sexually intimate on 5 or 6 earlier occasions. *Is D's evidence admissible?*

Problem 19-29

D is charged with attempted rape of V, a babysitter, while driving V back home after she'd been babysitting at D's house. V claims that D's attack caused scratches and vaginal contusions. D offers evidence that V's injuries resulted from sexual byplay between V and V's boyfriend before D took V home. In addition, D offers evidence that V's father had recently warned V that she'd be "grounded for 3 months" if she continued to be sexually active with boyfriends. *Are these pieces of evidence admissible?*

Problem 19-30

D is charged with raping V in D's car in the car park of the Bar Revue. V claims that they met in the bar, and danced and had a couple of drinks. D offered to give her a ride home, and she accepted. When V got into D's car, D raped her. Assume that D's story is essentially the same, except that he claims that he and V had consensual sex in the car. *Can D offer evidence that V had consensual intercourse with ten other men she had met in a bar during the previous year?*

Problem 19-31

Same case as previous problem, except this time D offers to prove that, three times in the week before he met her, V had picked up men in a bar, danced with them, and then had consensual sex with them in a car in the car park. *Admissible?*

Problem 19-32

Same case as previous problem, except that D calls B to testify that B had met V in a bar a month earlier and had consensual sex with him in a car in the bar's car park. Afterwards, V falsely accused B of raping her. *Admissible?*

Problem 19-33

Same case as previous problem, except that D offers to prove that V takes birth control pills. *Admissible?*

Problem 19-34

Same case as previous problem, except that D offers to prove that V is a prostitute. *Admissible?*

Problem 19-35

Same case as previous problem, except that D offers to prove that V often comes into the bar wearing low cut mini-dresses and uses crude language. *Admissible? What if D offers to prove that V was dressed like this on the night of the alleged rape?*

Problem 19-36

Same case as previous problem. Assume that D's defense is that he agreed to pay V for her sexual services, that they had consensual intercourse in his car in the parking lot, and that V falsely accused him of rape when he refused to pay more than the agreed-to price. *Can D offer evidence that V is a prostitute?*

Problem 19-37

Civil suit brought by A against D. A claims that D raped her, and seeks damages for emotional distress and pain and suffering. On the issue of damages, D offers evidence that A had been sexually active with 3 other men during the 2-year period preceding the rape. *Is this evidence barred by the rape shield statute?*

Problem 19-38

Even if a criminal defendant doesn't testify, the prosecutor can offer the defendant's prior conviction into evidence for purposes of impeachment. *True or False?*

Problem 19-39

D is charged with sexually molesting a 4-year-old child; D's defense is a denial. To counter the jury's reaction that the child could have described the details of the molestation only if D had molested the child, D offers evidence that the child had previously been sexually molested by another person. *Admissible?*

Problem 19-40

D is charged with raping V; defense is consent. As evidence of non-consent, V testifies, "I'm a lesbian and would not have consensual sex with a man." *Barred by the rape shield law?*

Problem 19-41

D is charged with bank robbery. During its case-in-chief, the prosecution tries to impeach D's credibility by calling J, who's lived next door to D for 2 years. The prosecutor seeks to elicit J's opinion, "When I heard about the film 'Liar Liar,' I thought that a film had been made about D's life." *Admissible?*

Problem 19-42

Same case as previous problem. D testifies and denies robbing the bank. D then calls L to testify, "D has an excellent reputation in the community for honesty." *Admissible?*

Problem 19-43

Same case as previous problem. During cross-examination of D, the prosecutor impeached D with evidence of three prior inconsistent statements that D had given to police officers. *After this impeachment, is L's testimony in the previous problem admissible?*

Problem 19-44

Same case as previous problem. D calls W to testify to an alibi. On cross of W, the prosecutor asks, "Isn't it true that 6 months ago you stole $100 from the church homeless fund?" *Proper? If the court allows the question and W says "No," can the prosecutor call the minister to testify that W did commit the theft?*

Problem 19-45

Same case as previous problem. *Instead of the question in the previous problem, which if any of these questions can the prosecutor ask?*

1. Isn't it true that 6 months ago you were arrested for stealing $100 from the church homeless fund?"

2. Isn't it true that 6 months ago you were indicted for stealing $100 from the church homeless fund?

3. Isn't it true that 6 months ago you were fired by your employer, the church, for stealing $100 from its homeless fund?

Problem 19-46

Same case as previous problem, except that this is a civil case in which the bank has sued D to recover the stolen money. On cross-examination, D's witness W is asked, "Isn't it true that 6 months ago you stole $100 from the church homeless fund?" *Is the question proper?*

Problem 19-47

Same case as Problem 19-45. On cross, W is asked, "Isn't it true that a week before the trial D agreed to pay you $5000 if you'd make the prosecution witness disappear?" *If W denies, could the government offer extrinsic evidence of the agreement, by e.g., calling the jail trustee who overheard the conversation?*

Problem 19-48

A national celebrity is charged with making fraudulent misrepresentations in connection with a land development project. The celebrity testifies and denies making any misrepresentations. On cross, the prosecutor wants to ask the questions below. *Are they permissible under Rule 608(b)?*

1. "Isn't it true that you had extra-marital sexual relations with an intern in your office?"

2. "Isn't it true that you lied to a Grand Jury when you denied having sexual relations with an intern in your office?"

Problem 19-49

D is charged with murder. B, a prosecution witness, identifies D as the killer. On cross of B, D's attorney asks, based on good faith belief, "Isn't it true that you embezzled $150,000 from the bank in which you used to work?" B admits that this is true. *Can the prosecutor now call C to testify that B has an excellent reputation for truth and honesty?*

Problem 19-50

D, a prison inmate, is charged with ADW (assault with a deadly weapon) and possession of a "shank" (a homemade weapon resembling a knife). D claims self-defense. The prosecutor indicates that, if D testifies, the prosecutor intends to impeach D with prior convictions for assault (a misdemeanor), possession of drugs for sale (a felony), and possession of a shank by a prison inmate (a felony). D files a motion in limine, requesting a pre-trial ruling that the prior convictions are inadmissible. *What ruling?*

Problem 19-51

D is charged with bank robbery. The prosecutor intends to impeach D with a prior conviction for armed robbery. The judge indicates reluctance to admit the prior, in the belief that it has little bearing on D's character for truth and veracity. *True or false:* the prosecutor can argue for admissibility based on the defendant's having lured the victim of the armed robbery to the scene of the crime by falsely telling the victim that there was a family emergency.

Problem 19-52

D is charged with murder. D testifies, and is impeached by the prosecutor with a prior felony conviction for perjury. On redirect, D hopes to minimize the impact of the prior conviction by testifying that it was based on D's falsifying a driver's license application. *Is D's testimony on redirect admissible?*

Problem 19-53

P, a movie patron, sues D Theater for personal injuries. P went to get popcorn (no-oil variety) in a darkened theater and tripped on an uneven surface where the end of the row of seats joined the aisle. W, P's date, testifies to condition of surface, e.g., that the floor on the aisle side was about a half inch higher than the floor of the row joining it. W also states that it was "dangerous" to have such a condition in a dark theater. *Valid opinion?*

Problem 19-54

P sues D for injuries resulting from an auto accident. P claims that D's excessive speed while making a turn caused D to lose control of the car; D claims that the accident was an unavoidable result of D having to swerve suddenly when a child ran into the street. W testifies on P's behalf that, just before the accident, D made a left hand turn at a speed of about 20 m.p.h. W's opinion is that D was going "too fast" to make the turn safely. *Valid opinion?*

Problem 19-55

Murder case. W was jogging, and saw the bloody remains of a person in the bushes, and a long, sharp knife lying a few feet away. W's opinion is that "the knife could have been the murder weapon." *Valid opinion?*

Problem 19-56

D is charged with murder. Before arresting D, the cops question D and D's friend W as to D's whereabouts at the time of the murder. D says, "I was watching TV with my friend W." The prosecution seeks to offer testimony from one of the arresting cops that, when D said this, D winked at W and that the wink sent a message to W, "Play along with my story." *Valid testimony?*

Problem 19-57

P sues Huffy Puffy Bike Co. for injuries caused when the front of the one-year-old Huffy bike that P was riding suddenly collapsed. P has commuted to work by bike for 30 years, and has worked on numerous bikes that P has owned over the years. P inspected the bike after it collapsed, and is of the opinion that the bike collapsed because of metal fatigue in the front wheel fork, which caused the quick release mechanism to come loose without warning and the wheel to fall off. *Valid opinion?*

Problem 19-58

D is charged with armed robbery of a fast food restaurant. A police officer who arrived at the scene saw a muddy shoe print on the countertop. Witnesses have testified that D climbed over the counter during the robbery. Cop later goes to D's home, arrests D and seizes the shoes that D is wearing at the time of the arrest. The cop's opinion is that the shoe print that the cop found at the robbery scene matches the bottom of the right shoe. *Valid opinion?*

Problem 19-59

P sues D, Port O'Bello Mushroom Co., for illness allegedly caused by eating D's poisoned mushrooms. D claims P's illness was caused by eating tainted coconut. P calls Dr. Fun Guy as an expert in the diagnosis of mushroom-related illness. Dr. Guy has won three Nobel Prizes for work on mushroom chemistry, is President of the Royal Mushroom Society, has published five books on mushrooms, has testified in scads of mushroom poisoning cases, and won a third grade Penmanship Certificate. D offers to stipulate to Dr. Guy's expertise. *Should P accept the stipulation? Can P refuse it?*

Problem 19-60

P sues the Aryan Nation for damages for burning P's church to the ground. To prove that the fire was purposely set, P calls E, who qualifies as an expert in the cause of fires.

1. E proposes to testify that her opinion that the fire was intentionally set rests in part on the fact that the church's roof vent was blocked. E relies for this information on a statement of a bystander who told a fireman, "There's no smoke at all coming out of the roof vent." *Can E properly use this information in arriving at her opinion?*

2. If your answer to the previous question is "yes," can P's attorney argue during final argument, "We know from E's testimony that no smoke was coming out of the church's roof vent"?

3. E also proposes to testify, "I checked my opinion with L, an internationally recognized arson expert. L told me that he agreed with my opinion 100%." *Is this testimony proper?*

Problem 19-61

D is charged with robbery. D's defense is that he committed the offense under duress, in that a gang had threatened to kill him if he didn't pay them $1000 by nightfall. D calls Perry Mason, a lawyer who is an expert in criminal defense, to testify that duress is established when people commit crimes in order to save their own lives. *Assuming that this accurately characterizes the defense of duress, is Mason's testimony proper?*

Problem 19-62

D is charged with assault with intent to rape V. D's defense is that, at the time of the act, D was under the influence of alcohol to such an extent that D was incapable of forming an intent to rape. *Which of the following opinions, if presented by D's qualified expert witness, would be admissible?*

1. D lacked the intent to rape at the time of the attack.

2. D should at most be found guilty of simple assault.

3. Excessive use of alcohol is a defense to a criminal charge requiring specific intent.

4. D suffers from Adult Onset Fetal Alcohol Syndrome. People who suffer from this syndrome and become intoxicated typically are unable to control their behavior.

Problem 19-63

D is charged with bombing a frog-filled pond, an act of "toad rage." The prosecution's properly-qualified expert testifies: "From the size of the crater, I determined that the bomb contained 200 pounds of explosives." D's attorney has a copy of a book by Neils Bohr, *Blast Analysis in a Nutshell*, which states, "There's no way to determine from the size of a crater the amount of explosives in a bomb." D's attorney can read this statement into the record under which of the following circumstances:

1. The expert testifies, "I am familiar with that book."

2. The expert testifies, "I consider the book to be a reliable authority."

3. Bohr testifies and is subject to cross examination.

4. In all of these circumstances.

Problem 19-64

Jennifer, an Evidence student, is asked to testify orally to what her instructor said in class about presumptions. When Jennifer admits that she has class notes reflecting what her instructor said, the opponent objects under the Best Evidence Rule, arguing that Jennifer's oral testimony is inadmissible because the notes would be the best evidence of the content of the class. *Valid objection?*

Problem 19-65

P sues D for striking P with a carelessly thrown boomerang. At trial, P testifies about the shape and general appearance of the boomerang, but makes no attempt to offer the boomerang itself into evidence or account for its absence. *Best evidence rule violation?*

Problem 19-66

Same case, except that P also testifies that the words, "Property of D" were painted on the side of the boomerang. *Best evidence rule violation?*

Problem 19-67

P sues D for libel, based on the contents of a letter written by D to P. P seeks to testify orally to the letter's contents, after testifying to having burned it in a rage immediately after reading it. *Oral testimony OK? What if P sent the letter to P's relative in another state, who refuses to return it?*

Problem 19-68

Title dispute between P and D. P proposes to testify that D executed a deed to P conveying title of Tara to P. *Best evidence rule violation?*

Problem 19-69

P, an auto dealer, sues D for libel, claiming that D placed a giant photo of a lemon on a billboard next to P's dealership. On the photo, D drew a big arrow pointing to the dealership. At trial, P orally describes what the billboard looked like. *OK?*

Problem 19-70

D is being prosecuted for knowingly possessing a stolen car. D testifies that D bought the car from Fast Eddie's Completely Used Cars in Bakersfield. The prosecution then calls Officer L to testify, "I searched the Bakersfield telephone directory for any dealers by that or similar names and found none." *Does L's testimony concerning the phone directory violate the best evidence rule?*

Problem 19-71

D is charged with murder committed in Gotham City. To prove that L had the opportunity to commit the murder, D calls W to testify that "A week before the murder, L told me that he was going to head for Gotham City shortly." *Is W's testimony inadmissible hearsay?*

Problem 19-72

To prove that D has acquired a prescriptive easement to use a road on P's land, D calls W to testify that "D frequently told people that D had a right to use the road on P's land." *Is W's testimony inadmissible hearsay?*

Problem 19-73

To prove that P authorized L to speak on P's behalf, D testifies that "L told me that P had authorized L to tell me that I was welcome to use P's beach house whenever I wanted to." *Does D's testimony establish that L's statement constitutes P's party statement?*

Problem 19-74

To prove that D did not like L, L offers evidence that D's web blog included a section recounting acts of child molestation that L had committed. *Are the blog statements hearsay?*

Problem 19-75

P, L's adult child, sues L for having molested P when P was a young child. To prove that L is a molester, P offers into evidence the section of D's web blog referring to P as one of the children that L had molested. *Are the blog statements hearsay?*

Problem 19-76

To prove that D operated an illegal drug cartel out of D's house, the prosecution offers evidence that numerous known drug dealers were seen coming and going from the house day and night. *Do the drug dealers' activities constitute hearsay?*

Problem 19-77

D is charged with theft of a small electronic device. To prove that D had purchased the device, D offers into evidence a sales receipt identifying D as the purchaser of the device. *Does the sales receipt constitute hearsay?*

Problem 19-78

D is charged with knowingly possessing stolen electronic devices. D's defense is that D believed that A, from whom D had acquired the devices, had purchased them legally. To support this defense, D offers into evidence the sales receipt that A showed D, identifying A as the purchaser of the devices. *Does the sales receipt constitute hearsay?*

Problem 19-79

Auto accident case. To prove that the brakes on D's car were bad, P calls L to testify that a few days before the accident, L heard a mechanic tell D, "Your brakes are shot, you need to replace them." *Does L's testimony constitute hearsay?*

Problem 19-80

Same case as the previous problem. To prove that D knowingly drove a car that had a dangerous defect, P calls L to testify to the mechanic's statement. *Does L's testimony constitute hearsay?*

Problem 19-81: The Breckenridge Bandit

The accused, Thelma, is charged with robbing a federally insured bank in Fargo, North Dakota on September 6th. During the robbery, the accused supposedly wore a "Breckenridge, Colorado" ski hat with a partial face mask attached. At trial, the prosecution wishes to offer evidence of a prior robbery allegedly committed by the accused in July of the same year. The prosecution calls a witness to the stand, Anville Moody.

PROSECUTOR: Would you state your name for the record, please?

A: My name is Anville Moody, and I live in Fargo.

PROSECUTOR: Where were you, Anville, on July 9th at approximately 7:00 p.m.?

A: I was in my living room.

PROSECUTOR: What happened then?

A: The defendant, Thelma, I would never forget her, even if she was wearing that Breckenridge ski hat . . .

DEFENSE COUNSEL: Objection. Irrelevant.

If a sidebar occurred, and the prosecutor proffered that Anville will testify that Thelma broke into Anville's house and robbed him while wearing a "Breckenridge, Colorado" ski hat, should the judge sustain the objection? Explain. See Dowling v. United States, 493 U.S. 342 (1990).

Problem 19-82: Megan's Law

The defendant, Buddy Castleman, was charged with sexual battery. At trial, evidence of his prior sexual misconduct on three separate occasions was offered by the prosecution. The following exchange occurred at trial:

DEFENSE ATTORNEY: Your Honor, I object to the proposed evidence and ask to approach the bench.

JUDGE: You may.

DEFENSE ATTORNEY: (at sidebar) Your Honor, this evidence is highly and unfairly prejudicial, given its close similarity to the current alleged offense. It should be excluded pursuant to Rule 403 as unfairly prejudicial evidence.

PROSECUTOR: Your Honor, the evidence is very relevant to determining whether the defendant committed the crime in this case, and is admissible pursuant to Rule 414.

You are the judge. *Does Rule 403 apply? See* Chapter 4. *How does it relate to Rule 414? See* Chapter 5. *How do you rule? See, e.g.,* United States v. Castillo, 140 F.3d 874 (10th Cir. N.M. 1998).

§ 19.02 ANSWERS

Problem 19-9

Relevant; it shows D's access to murder weapon; other evidence will have to further link D to crime.

Problem 19-10

Relevant; innocence is one possible inference of the evidence.

Problem 19-11

Mere fact of being "addict" is not relevant. There is no link between "status" of being an addict and committing a murder. Maybe different if victim was heroin dealer, etc.

Being under the influence is relevant; it rebuts the inference of innocence resulting from the evidence in the previous problem, because maybe D didn't flee because D was too out of it to do so. Also, being under the influence casts doubt on D's ability to be aware of and recall events.

Problem 19-12

Relevant. Based on generalization that "People who know that close friends are wrongly accused are likely to step forward as soon as possible."

Problem 19-13

Relevant. Based on generalization that "8-year-old girls would be unable to describe sexual acts in detail unless they'd been sexually molested." The problem is based on the case of *People v. Salas*, 30 Cal. App. 4th 417, 36 Cal. Rptr. 2d 374 (1994), in which the complainant was 10 years old. Seem dubious? Maybe true of a child 3-4 years old but not an 8-year-old?

Problem 19-14

The most likely correct response is No. 2. Evidence that D was in Hawaii a few days after a murder occurred in L.A. is relevant as the basis of a possible inference that D fled to Hawaii to evade arrest for murder.

As for the evidence that D raped 2 women, A and B, in Hawaii, the prosecution might try to offer this under Rule 413. However, that theory does not work because D is not charged with a crime of sexual assault. Therefore the prosecutor might offer evidence of the rapes to bolster A's and B's ability to observe D and recall that D was in Hawaii on the dates that they were raped. Under Rule 403, the judge would have to balance the probative value of the evidence to bolster the credibility of A and B against the possible unfair prejudice of the jury learning that D might be a rapist in addition to a murderer. So the judge should probably try to "sanitize" the evidence in a way that allows A and B to testify to their ability to observe D without referring to the rapes.

Problem 19-15

Important evidence, since alibi defense makes clerk's ability to perceive very important. But potentially lots of unfair prejudice. Options: let it in, keep it out, let it in and instruct jurors not to infer that D committed the earlier crime, try to "sanitize," e.g., let clerk say only that clerk "saw photo of D," but that sounds hokey, not giving prosecution the benefit of a believable story.

Problem 19-16

Could sanitize the evidence, e.g., not refer to the name of the gang, maybe not even refer to it as a gang, just show that D and W are members of the same group. *Does that give a potentially misleading impression, e.g., jurors think they belong to the Elks?*

Would it matter if the prosecutor has a witness who can testify that W and D are good friends? (Then maybe not admissible, because the evidence isn't as probative if it's cumulative.) *See People v. Maestas*, 20 Cal. App. 4th 1482, 25 Cal. Rptr.2d 644 (1993).

Problem 19-17

Good probative value, but also potential for prejudice. Court is likely to admit with admonition.

Problem 19-18

Admitted. Relevance of evidence doesn't depend on D's propensity to violence. It establishes what happened without reference to D's character.

Problem 19-19

Admitted. Unusual and similar circumstances show that whoever committed first robbery probably committed the second one, without regard to propensity. OK for "identity."

Problem 19-20

Excluded. Even if in the form of an admission, it's still character evidence.

Problem 19-21

Not character evidence. Purpose is to negate D's claim that he couldn't have reasonably anticipated a bad medical reaction.

Problem 19-22

Not character evidence, because part of the same conduct. Apart from propensity, we can infer that on this one occasion, D's going through a red light makes it more likely that D was speeding two blocks later. (But if red light was the day before, then it is character evidence)

Problem 19-23

Evidence is being offered on non-character theory, but relevance is so minimal for that use (especially since D has alibi for the entire day) and propensity inference so prejudicial that court should exclude under Federal Rule of Evidence 403 (**Cal. Evid. Code 352**).

Problem 19-24

Admitted. Prior act tends to negate D's claim of accident.

Problem 19-25

No. Under Federal Rule of Evidence 404(a)(1), defendants can offer "mercy evidence" only in criminal and not in civil cases.

Problem 19-26

Admit. Costello's presence at earlier killing suggests a motive.

Problem 19-27

A judge could rule that the earlier act suggests D's intent to harm, since situations are somewhat similar. Close issue.

Problem 19-28

Yes; there is a specific exception for such evidence in Federal Rule of Evidence 412.

Problem 19-29

Both pieces of evidence are admissible. The first is admissible under Federal Rule of Evidence 412 to show that someone other than D was responsible for V's injuries. The second part shows V's prior sexual conduct, but is admissible because it gives V a motive to blame D for the injuries (subject to Rule 403 weighing, but it's hard to imagine a judge excluding this evidence).

Problem 19-30

No; this would be propensity evidence, it is clearly barred.

Problem 19-31

Close. D could argue that the evidence shows a "pattern" of conduct (and therefore is not propensity evidence) because of the similarity to D's version. Most important difference is that there was no false claim of rape, so perhaps not a pattern.

Problem 19-32

Probably admissible. False accusation is relevant, and not barred because not offered to prove V has a propensity to consent.

Problem 19-33

No; prohibition in Rule 412 covers wide array of "sexual behavior"; it's not limited to overt sexual behavior.

Problem 19-34

No; it's just a form of character evidence ("propensity for pay").

Problem 19-35

No, just propensity evidence.

Problem 19-36

Yes. Evidence admissible to establish the conditions under which they had sex, not to show that V consented this time since V has often consented in the past.

Problem 19-37

D might argue admissible on the issue of damages. If she's sexually active, arguably less emotional damage and pain and suffering. But probably would be excluded.

Problem 19-38

False.

Problem 19-39

Okay; goes to child's "knowledge." *See People v. Daggett,* 225 Cal. App. 3d 751, 275 Cal. Rptr. 287 (1990). Note that prior sexual conduct may potentially be covered by rape shield statute even though child was victim of other conduct; conduct needn't be consensual to be covered.

Problem 19-40

The lesbian testimony may be admissible on the ground that it's not character evidence at all. Rather it's a characteristic of the person, like whether she's left-handed or tall. Of course once it's in the record, her prior intercourse with a man is admissible to contradict. Purpose would be to disprove S's claim, not to show S's sexual behavior.

If judge regards "I'm a lesbian" as evidence of sexual predisposition, maybe inadmissible under Federal Rule of Evidence 412 because it has no exception for evidence offered by a victim instead of a defendant. That is, Rule 412 applies to evidence offered to prove that "any alleged victim engaged in other sexual behavior." Argument to admit: the purpose of Rule 412 is to protect victims, so victims should be able to "waive" protection by testifying to their own sexual predispositions.

Problem 19-41

No. Improper to impeach D since D has not yet testified.

Problem 19-42

L's character testimony is not admissible to support D's credibility as a witness, since the prosecution has not yet attacked D's character for truth-telling. However, L's testimony is probably admissible as substantive evidence of innocence under the "mercy rule," Rule 404(a)(1), to show that D has a trait of character that is inconsistent with committing robbery.

Problem 19-43

L's character testimony is still not admissible to bolster D's credibility as a witness, because impeachment by means of prior inconsistent statements does not constitute an attack on character for truth-telling. As in the prior problem, however, L's testimony is probably admissible as substantive evidence of innocence under the "mercy rule," Rule 404(a)(1).

Problem 19-44

The question is okay, subject to the judge's discretion under Rule 608(b), but it's not permitted to call the minister to rebut a denial.

Problem 19-45

None of the questions are proper; can just ask about the act, not about arrests or other consequences of the act — other than convictions.

Problem 19-46

Same as the answer to Problem 19-44.

Problem 19-47

Admissible because it's not character evidence. Evidence that D was willing to pay money to bump off the prosecution witness is evidence of D's consciousness of guilt. Extrinsic evidence is OK because this is important, not collateral.

Problem 19-48

First question is not proper, because that behavior doesn't involve truth and honesty; second question is OK because it involves lying. So note, even if what you did wouldn't be admissible to impeach, evidence that you lied about it can be!

Problem 19-49

Yes; this evidence is OK because B's character for honesty has been attacked.

Problem 19-50

Assault conviction: not admissible under Federal Rules, because it's a misdemeanor not involving dishonesty. Drug possession: not an "honesty" offense, so admissible subject to judge's discretion. (Because the question involves impeachment of a criminal D, the usual Rule 403 presumption is reversed — probative value has to outweigh presumed prejudice.) Shank OK subject to discretion, though similarity cuts against admission. So possible that judge would exclude all three.

In arguing the motion, D should point out that the charged incident took place in a prison, so even without impeachment jury will know that D was a convict.

Problem 19-51

False. Admissibility of a prior conviction is based only on the elements of an offense, not the method in which it was carried out.

Problem 19-52

No. Circumstances of conviction are irrelevant and inadmissible.

Problem 19-53

Maybe. "Dangerous" adds an element that details alone couldn't provide: degree of darkness, exact angle of floor, etc. Chances of admission and exclusion are about 50-50. Opinion clearly wouldn't be OK if W had said "negligent," because that adds an element of community judgment that's outside common experience.

Problem 19-54

OK, because it would be hard to give underlying details like exact speed, sharpness of turn, etc., and from everyday life people have a sense of what's a safe speed for making a turn.

Problem 19-55

No; the jury can figure this out as easily as W. W acquired no special knowledge from being at the scene.

Problem 19-56

Testimony presents two opinions: that blinking of eye was a wink, and what D intended by the wink. First opinion is OK, because winking is within common experience. Second opinion is questionable. Something subtle about the way people wink that allows us to draw inferences that we can't provide detailed support for?

Problem 19-57

P is giving a technical opinion, and the issue is whether just having worked on bikes gives sufficient expertise for opinion. In the shadowy area between lay and expert opinion. Some judges would admit, others would exclude.

Problem 19-58

A cop was allowed to testify to this opinion in *People v. Lucero*, 64 Cal. App. 4th 1107, 75 Cal. Rptr. 2d 806 (1998), even though cop was not an expert.

Problem 19-59

P can refuse to accept stipulation, would want to parade expert's honors before jury.

Problem 19-60

1. E might be able to rely on the bystander's information if arson experts typically and reasonably rely on information of this sort. However, judges tend to be wary of hearsay from anonymous sources and so may rule that E cannot rely on the bystander's information. Moreover, even if the judge were to allow E to rely on the information, the judge may preclude E from referring to it.

2. P's counsel's argument is improper. Even if the judge allowed E to rely on and refer to information from the bystander, the bystander's statement would not be admissible for the truth of its contents. Rather, P's counsel would only be able to refer to the statement as part of the basis for E's opinion.

3. Not OK. L's opinion is not a basis of E's opinion; it is simply a hearsay statement that another expert agrees.

Problem 19-61

Not proper; the judge informs the jury of the applicable law, not an expert W.

Problem 19-62

Correct answer is "4."

Old common-law rule that "expert can't testify to ultimate issue" has been repealed (Fed. R. Evid. 704). However, Rule 704(b) bars opinions about whether a criminal defendant had or did not have a mental state that's an element of the crime or a defense. This addition is known as the "Hinckley rule" because it was enacted as a result of Hinckley's trial for shooting Pres. Reagan. In his trial, D's shrinks testified that Hinckley was insane and had no intent to kill Reagan. He was convicted of lesser crime that didn't require showing of "intent to kill."

What the law has basically done is prevent experts from using the ultimate legal label of the mental state or condition. But they can testify to the opinion from which the legal label almost automatically follows. Law rewards a bit of subtlety! E.g., a government drug expert can testify that quantity of drugs that D had shows that D possessed drugs for sale. But couldn't say, "D is guilty."

Problem 19-63

Correct answers are "2" and "3."

Problem 19-64

No. Jennifer is not testifying to a writing's contents.

Problem 19-65

No; boomerang is a physical object, not a writing.

Problem 19-66

Possibly; this raises the problem of "inscribed chattels." W can refer to written matter if it's incidental or just a way of identifying an object, like a blue streak of paint. But if using this to prove that the boomerang belongs to D, that's a communicative use and best evidence rule probably applies.

Problem 19-67

Oral testimony probably OK in both examples: original destroyed without fraudulent intent; original beyond reach of court process.

Problem 19-68

Yes; best evidence rule violation. P would be testifying to deed's contents.

Problem 19-69

The billboard is a writing. P could probably successfully argue that the original isn't obtainable by judicial process.

Problem 19-70

No violation; the best evidence rule doesn't apply when W testifies to what's not in a writing.

Problem 19-71

Admissible under the state of mind hearsay exception.

Problem 19-72

W's testimony is admissible because D's statements are "words of independent legal significance." Establishing a prescriptive easement depends in part on using property under a claim of right.

Problem 19-73

No. A judge could consider L's statement as evidence of authority, but the statement is not alone sufficient to establish authority to speak.

Problem 19-74

Not hearsay. D's making statements accusing P of being a molester suggest that D does not like P without considering their accuracy.

Problem 19-75

Yes. D's blog statement that L molested P is relevant for its offered use only if it is accurate.

Problem 19-76

No. The dealers' activities are non-assertive conduct.

Problem 19-77

Yes, the sales receipt is hearsay because it proves that P purchased the device only if its contents are accurate.

Problem 19-78

Not hearsay. The sales receipt supports D's claim that D believed that A had acquired the devices legitimately, even if the contents of the receipt are false.

Problem 19-79

Yes, the mechanic's statement proves that the brakes were bad only if it is accurate.

Problem 19-80

No, the mechanic's statement is relevant to D's awareness of the risk of driving regardless of its accuracy.

Appendix

EXISTING AND PROPOSED FEDERAL RULES OF EVIDENCE

The Federal Judiciary has proposed substituting the set of proposed "Restyled Federal Rules of Evidence" below for the presently existing Federal Rules of Evidence. Barring delays, the new set of evidence rules will probably become effective in 2011.

The proposed set of Restyled Federal Rules of Evidence includes the following introductory language:

Formatting Changes

Many of the changes in the restyled Evidence Rules result from using format to achieve clearer presentations. The rules are broken down into constituent parts, using progressively indented subparagraphs with headings and substituting vertical for horizontal lists. "Hanging indents" are used throughout. These formatting changes make the structure of the rules graphic and make the restyled rules easier to read and understand even when the words are not changed. Rules 103, 404(b), 606(b), and 612 illustrate the benefits of formatting changes.

Changes to Reduce Inconsistent, Ambiguous, Redundant, Repetitive, or Archaic Words

The restyled rules reduce the use of inconsistent terms that say the same thing in different ways. Because different words are presumed to have different meanings, such inconsistencies can result in confusion. The restyled rules reduce inconsistencies by using the same words to express the same meaning. For example, consistent expression is achieved by not switching between "accused" and "defendant" or between "party opponent" and "opposing party" or between the various formulations of civil and criminal action/case/proceeding.

The restyled rules minimize the use of inherently ambiguous words. For example, the word "shall" can mean "must," "may," or something else, depending on context. The potential for confusion is exacerbated by the fact the word "shall" is no longer generally used in spoken or clearly written English. The restyled rules replace "shall" with "must," "may," or "should," depending on which one the context and established interpretation make correct in each rule.

The restyled rules minimize the use of redundant "intensifiers." These are expressions that attempt to add emphasis, but instead state the obvious and create negative implications for other rules. The absence of intensifiers in the restyled rules does not change their substantive meaning. *See, e.g.*, Rule 104(c) (omitting "in all cases"); Rule 602 (omitting "but need not"); Rule 611(b) (omitting "in the exercise of discretion").

The restyled rules also remove words and concepts that are outdated or redundant.

Rule Numbers

The restyled rules keep the same numbers to minimize the effect on research. Subdivisions have been rearranged within some rules to achieve greater clarity and simplicity.

No Substantive Change

The Committee made special efforts to reject any purported style improvement that might result in a substantive change in the application of a rule. The Committee considered a change to be "substantive" if any of the following conditions were met:

> a. Under the existing practice in any circuit, the change could lead to a different result on a question of admissibility (e.g., a change that requires a court to provide either a less or more stringent standard in evaluating the admissibility of particular evidence);
>
> b. Under the existing practice in any circuit, it could lead to a change in the procedure by which an admissibility decision is made (e.g., a change in the time in which an objection must be made, or a change in whether a court must hold a hearing on an admissibility question);
>
> c. It alters the structure of a rule in a way that may alter the approach that courts and litigants have used to think about, and argue about, questions of admissibility (e.g., merging Rules 104(a) and 104(b) into a single subdivision); or
>
> d. It changes a "sacred phrase" — phrases that have become so familiar in practice that to alter them would be unduly disruptive. Examples in the Evidence Rules include "unfair prejudice" and "truth of the matter asserted."

In the text below, the now-existing rules of evidence are on the left-hand column; the proposed rules are in the right-hand column.

Committee Notes remain when they do more than mention that changes are stylistic only.

ARTICLE I. GENERAL PROVISIONS Rule 101. Scope	ARTICLE I. GENERAL PROVISIONS Rule 101. Scope; Definitions
These rules govern proceedings in the courts of the United States and before the United States bankruptcy judges and United States magistrate judges, to the extent and with the exceptions stated in rule 1101.	(a) **Scope.** These rules apply to proceedings before United States courts. The specific courts and proceedings to which the rules apply, along with exceptions, are set out in Rule 1101. (b) **Definitions.** In these rules: 　(1) "civil case" means a civil action or proceeding; 　(2) "criminal case" includes a criminal proceeding; 　(3) "public office" includes a public agency; 　(4) "record" [in Rules 803, 901, 902, and 1005] includes a memorandum, report, or data compilation; 　(5) a "rule prescribed by the Supreme Court" means a rule adopted by the Supreme Court under statutory authority; and 　(6) a reference to any kind of written material includes electronically stored information.

Rule 102. Purpose and Construction	Rule 102. Purpose
These rules shall be construed to secure fairness in administration, elimination of unjustifiable expense and delay, and promotion of growth and development of the law of evidence to the end that the truth may be ascertained and proceedings justly determined.	These rules should be construed so as to administer every proceeding fairly, eliminate unjustifiable expense and delay, and promote the development of evidence law, to the end of ascertaining the truth and securing a just determination.

Rule 103. Rulings on Evidence	Rule 103. Rulings on Evidence
(a) Effect of erroneous ruling. Error may not be predicated upon a ruling which admits or excludes evidence unless a substantial right of the party is affected, and 　(1) Objection. In case the ruling is one admitting evidence, a timely objection or motion to strike appears of record, stating the specific ground of objection, if the specific ground was not apparent from the context; or 　(2) Offer of proof. In case the ruling is one excluding evidence, the substance of the evidence was made known to the court by offer or was apparent from the context within which questions were asked. 　Once the court makes a definitive ruling on the record admitting or excluding evidence, either at or before trial, a party need not renew an objection or offer of proof to preserve a claim of error for appeal.	**(a) Preserving a Claim of Error.** A party may claim error in a ruling to admit or exclude evidence only if the error affects a substantial right of the party and: 　**(1)** if the ruling admits evidence, the party, on the record: 　　**(A)** timely objects or moves to strike; and 　　**(B)** states the specific ground, unless it was apparent from the context; or 　**(2)** if the ruling excludes evidence, the party informs the court of its substance by an offer of proof, unless the substance was apparent from the context. **(b) Not Needing to Renew an Objection or Offer of Proof.** Once the court rules definitively on the record — either before or at trial — a party need not renew an objection or offer of proof to preserve a claim of error for appeal.
(b) Record of offer and ruling. The court may add any other or further statement which shows the character of the evidence, the form in which it was offered, the objection made, and the ruling thereon. It may direct the making of an offer in question and answer form.	**(c) Court's Statement About the Ruling; Directing an Offer of Proof.** The court may make any statement about the character or form of the evidence, the objection made, and the ruling. The court may direct that an offer of proof be made in question-and-answer form.

(c) Hearing of jury. In jury cases, proceedings shall be conducted, to the extent practicable, so as to prevent inadmissible evidence from being suggested to the jury by any means, such as making statements or offers of proof or asking questions in the hearing of the jury.	**(d) Preventing the Jury from Hearing Inadmissible Evidence.** To the extent practicable, the court must conduct a jury trial so that inadmissible evidence is not suggested to the jury by any means.
(d) Plain error. Nothing in this rule precludes taking notice of plain errors affecting substantial rights although they were not brought to the attention of the court.	**(e) Taking Notice of Plain Error.** A court may take notice of a plain error affecting a substantial right, even if the claim of error was not properly preserved.

Rule 104. Preliminary Questions	Rule 104. Preliminary Questions
(a) Questions of admissibility generally. Preliminary questions concerning the qualification of a person to be a witness, the existence of a privilege, or the admissibility of evidence shall be determined by the court, subject to the provisions of subdivision (b). In making its determination it is not bound by the rules of evidence except those with respect to privileges.	**(a) In General.** The court must decide any preliminary question about whether a witness is qualified, a privilege exists, or evidence is admissible. In so deciding, the court is not bound by evidence rules, except those on privilege.
(b) Relevancy conditioned on fact. When the relevancy of evidence depends upon the fulfillment of a condition of fact, the court shall admit it upon, or subject to, the introduction of evidence sufficient to support a finding of the fulfillment of the condition.	**(b) Relevancy That Depends on a Fact.** When the relevancy of evidence depends on fulfilling a factual condition, the court may admit it on, or subject to, the introduction of evidence sufficient to support a finding that the condition is fulfilled.
(c) Hearing of jury. Hearings on the admissibility of confessions shall in all cases be conducted out of the hearing of the jury. Hearings on other preliminary matters shall be so conducted when the interests of justice require, or when an accused is a witness and so requests.	**(c) Matters That the Jury Must Not Hear.** A hearing on a preliminary question must be conducted outside the jury's hearing if: (1) the hearing involves the admissibility of a confession; (2) a defendant in a criminal case is a witness and requests that the jury not be present; or (3) justice so requires.
(d) Testimony by accused. The accused does not, by testifying upon a preliminary matter, become subject to cross-	**(d) Testimony by a Defendant in a Criminal Case.** By testifying on a preliminary question, a defendant in a criminal case does not become

examination as to other issues in the case.	subject to cross-examination on other issues in the case.
(e) Weight and credibility. This rule does not limit the right of a party to introduce before the jury evidence relevant to weight or credibility.	(e) **Evidence Relevant to Weight and Credibility.** This rule does not limit a party's right to introduce before the jury evidence that is relevant to the weight or credibility of other evidence.

Rule 105. Limited Admissibility	Rule 105. Limiting Evidence That Is Not Admissible Against Other Parties or for Other Purposes
When evidence which is admissible as to one party or for one purpose but not admissible as to another party or for another purpose is admitted, the court, upon request, shall restrict the evidence to its proper scope and instruct the jury accordingly.	If the court admits evidence that is admissible against a party or for a purpose — but not against another party or for another purpose — the court, on request, must restrict the evidence to its proper scope and instruct the jury accordingly.

Rule 106. Remainder of or Related Writings or Recorded Statements	Rule 106. Rest of or Related Writings or Recorded Statements
When a writing or recorded statement or part thereof is introduced by a party, an adverse party may require the introduction at that time of any other part or any other writing or recorded statement which ought in fairness to be considered contemporaneously with it.	If a party introduces all or part of a writing or recorded statement, an adverse party may require the introduction, at that time, of any other part — or any other writing or recorded statement — that in fairness ought to be considered at the same time.

ARTICLE II. JUDICIAL NOTICE Rule 201. Judicial Notice of Adjudicative Facts	ARTICLE II. JUDICIAL NOTICE Rule 201. Judicial Notice of Adjudicative Facts
(a) Scope of rule. This rule governs only judicial notice of adjudicative facts.	**(a) Scope.** This rule governs judicial notice of an adjudicative fact only, not a legislative fact.
(b) Kinds of facts. A judicially noticed fact must be one not subject to reasonable dispute in that it is either (1) generally known within the territorial jurisdiction of the trial court or (2) capable of accurate and ready determination by resort to sources whose accuracy cannot reasonably be questioned.	**(b) Kinds of Facts That May Be Judicially Noticed.** The court may judicially notice a fact that is not subject to reasonable dispute because it: (1) is generally known within the court's territorial jurisdiction; or (2) can be accurately and readily determined from sources whose accuracy cannot reasonably be questioned.
(c) When discretionary. A court may take judicial notice, whether requested or not. **(d) When mandatory.** A court shall take judicial notice if requested by a party and supplied with the necessary information.	**(c) Taking Notice.** At any stage of the proceeding, the court: (1) may take judicial notice on its own; or (2) must take judicial notice if a party requests it and the court is supplied with the necessary information.

(e) Opportunity to be heard. A party is entitled upon timely request to an opportunity to be heard as to the propriety of taking judicial notice and the tenor of the matter noticed. In the absence of prior notification, the request may be made after judicial notice has been taken.	**(d) Opportunity to Be Heard.** On timely request, a party is entitled to be heard on the propriety of taking judicial notice and the nature of the noticed fact. If the court takes judicial notice before notifying a party, the party, on request, is still entitled to be heard.
(f) Time of taking notice. Judicial notice may be taken at any stage of the proceeding.	
(g) Instructing jury. In a civil action or proceeding, the court shall instruct the jury to accept as conclusive any fact judicially noticed. In a criminal case, the court shall instruct the jury that it may, but is not required to, accept as conclusive any fact judicially noticed.	**(e) Instructing the Jury.** In a civil case, the court must instruct the jury to accept the noticed fact as conclusive. In a criminal case, the court must instruct the jury that it may or may not accept the noticed fact as conclusive.

ARTICLE III. PRESUMPTIONS IN CIVIL ACTIONS AND PROCEEDINGS	ARTICLE III. PRESUMPTIONS IN CIVIL CASES
Rule 301. Presumptions in General in Civil Actions and Proceedings	**Rule 301. Presumptions in a Civil Case Generally**
In all civil actions and proceedings not otherwise provided for by Act of Congress or by these rules, a presumption imposes on the party against whom it is directed the burden of going forward with evidence to rebut or meet the presumption, but does not shift to such party the burden of proof in the sense of the risk of nonpersuasion, which remains throughout the trial upon the party on whom it was originally cast.	In a civil case, unless a federal statute or these rules provide otherwise, the party against whom a presumption is directed has the burden of going forward with evidence to rebut the presumption. But this rule does not shift the burden of proof in the sense of the risk of nonpersuasion; the burden of proof remains on the party who had it originally.

Rule 302. Applicability of State Law in Civil Actions and Proceedings	Rule 302. Effect of State Law on Presumptions in a Civil Case
In civil actions and proceedings, the effect of a presumption respecting a fact which is an element of a claim or defense as to which State law supplies the rule of decision is determined in accordance with State law.	In a civil case, state law governs the effect of a presumption regarding a claim or defense for which state law supplies the rule of decision.

ARTICLE IV. RELEVANCY AND ITS LIMITS Rule 401. Definition of "Relevant Evidence"	ARTICLE IV. RELEVANCY AND ITS LIMITS Rule 401. Test for Relevant Evidence
"Relevant evidence" means evidence having any tendency to make the existence of any fact that is of consequence to the determination of the action more probable or less probable than it would be without the evidence.	Evidence is relevant if it has any tendency to make more or less probable the existence of a fact that is of consequence in determining the action.

Rule 402. Relevant Evidence Generally Admissible; Irrelevant Evidence Inadmissible	Rule 402. General Admissibility of Relevant Evidence
All relevant evidence is admissible, except as otherwise provided by the Constitution of the United States, by Act of Congress, by these rules, or by other rules prescribed by the Supreme Court pursuant to statutory authority. Evidence which is not relevant is not admissible.	Relevant evidence is admissible unless any of the following provides otherwise: - the United States Constitution; - a federal statute; - these rules; or - other rules prescribed by the Supreme Court. Irrelevant evidence is not admissible.

Rule 403. Exclusion of Relevant Evidence on Grounds of Prejudice, Confusion, or Waste of Time	Rule 403. Excluding Relevant Evidence for Prejudice, Confusion, Waste of Time, or Other Reasons
Although relevant, evidence may be excluded if its probative value is substantially outweighed by the danger of unfair prejudice, confusion of the issues, or misleading the jury, or by considerations of undue delay, waste of time, or needless presentation of cumulative evidence.	The court may exclude relevant evidence if its probative value is substantially outweighed by a danger of one or more of the following: unfair prejudice, confusing the issues, misleading the jury, undue delay, wasting time, or needlessly presenting cumulative evidence.

Rule 404. Character Evidence Not Admissible to Prove Conduct; Exceptions; Other Crimes	Rule 404. Character Evidence; Crimes or Other Acts

(a) Character evidence generally. Evidence of a person's character or a trait of character is not admissible for the purpose of proving action in conformity therewith on a particular occasion, except:
 	
(1) Character of accused. In a criminal case, evidence of a pertinent trait of character offered by an accused, or by the prosecution to rebut the same, or if evidence of a trait of character of the alleged victim of the crime is offered by an accused and admitted under Rule 404(a)(2), evidence of the same trait of character of the accused offered by the prosecution;
 	
(2) Character of alleged victim. In a criminal case, and subject to the limitations imposed by Rule 412, evidence of a pertinent trait of character of the alleged victim of the crime offered by an accused, or by the prosecution to rebut the same, or evidence of a character trait of peacefulness of the alleged victim offered by the prosecution in a homicide case to rebut evidence that the alleged victim was the first aggressor;
 	
(3) Character of witness. Evidence of the character of a witness, as provided in Rules 607, 608, and 609.
	(a) Character Evidence.
	
	(1) Prohibited Uses. Evidence of a person's character or character trait is not admissible to prove that on a particular occasion the person acted in accordance with the character or trait.
	
	(2) Exceptions in a Criminal Case. The following exceptions apply in a criminal case:
	
	(A) a defendant may offer evidence of the defendant's pertinent trait, and if the evidence is admitted, the prosecutor may offer evidence to rebut it;
	
	(B) subject to the limitations in Rule 412, a defendant may offer evidence of an alleged crime victim's pertinent trait, and if the evidence is admitted, the prosecutor may:
	
	    (i) offer evidence to rebut it; and
	
	    (ii) offer evidence of the defendant's same trait; and
	
	(C) in a homicide case, the

	prosecutor may offer evidence of the alleged victim's trait of peacefulness to rebut evidence that the victim was the first aggressor.
	(3) **Exceptions for a Witness.** Evidence of a witness's character may be admitted under Rules 607, 608, and 609.
(b) Other crimes, wrongs, or acts. Evidence of other crimes, wrongs, or acts is not admissible to prove the character of a person in order to show action in conformity therewith. It may, however, be admissible for other purposes, such as proof of motive, opportunity, intent, preparation, plan, knowledge, identity, or absence of mistake or accident, provided that upon request by the accused, the prosecution in a criminal case shall provide reasonable notice in advance of trial, or during trial if the court excuses pretrial notice on good cause shown, of the general nature of any such evidence it intends to introduce at trial.	**(b)** **Crimes or Other Acts.** **(1)** **Prohibited Uses.** Evidence of a crime or other act is not admissible to prove a person's character in order to show that on a particular occasion the person acted in accordance with the character. **(2)** **Permitted Uses; Notice.** This evidence may be admissible for another purpose, such as proving motive, opportunity, intent, preparation, plan, knowledge, identity, absence of mistake, or lack of accident. On request by a defendant in a criminal case, the prosecutor must: **(A)** provide reasonable notice of the general nature of any such evidence that the prosecutor intends to offer at trial; and **(B)** do so before trial — or during trial if the court, for good cause, excuses lack of pretrial notice.

Rule 405. Methods of Proving Character	Rule 405. Methods of Proving Character
(a) Reputation or opinion. In all cases in which evidence of character or a trait of character of a person is admissible, proof may be made by testimony as to reputation or by testimony in the form of an opinion. On cross-examination, inquiry is allowable into relevant specific instances of conduct.	**(a) By Reputation or Opinion.** When evidence of a person's character or character trait is admissible, it may be proved by testimony about the person's reputation or by testimony in the form of an opinion. On cross-examination, the court may allow an inquiry into relevant specific instances of the person's conduct.
(b) Specific instances of conduct. In cases in which character or a trait of character of a person is an essential element of a charge, claim, or defense, proof may also be made of specific instances of that person's conduct.	**(b) By Specific Instances of Conduct.** When a person's character or character trait is an essential element of a charge, claim, or defense, the character or trait may also be proved by relevant specific instances of the person's conduct.

Rule 406. Habit; Routine Practice	Rule 406. Habit; Routine Practice
Evidence of the habit of a person or of the routine practice of an organization, whether corroborated or not and regardless of the presence of eyewitnesses, is relevant to prove that the conduct of the person or organization on a particular occasion was in conformity with the habit or routine practice.	Evidence of a person's habit or an organization's routine practice may be admitted to prove that on a particular occasion the person or organization acted in accordance with the habit or routine practice. The court may admit this evidence regardless of whether it is corroborated or whether there was an eyewitness.

Rule 407. Subsequent Remedial Measures	Rule 407. Subsequent Remedial Measures
When, after an injury or harm allegedly caused by an event, measures are taken that, if taken previously, would have made the injury or harm less likely to occur, evidence of the subsequent measures is not admissible to prove negligence, culpable conduct, a defect in a product, a defect in a product's design, or a need for a warning or instruction. This rule does not require the exclusion of evidence of subsequent measures when offered for another purpose, such as proving ownership, control, or feasibility of precautionary measures, if controverted, or impeachment.	When measures are taken that would have made an earlier injury or harm less likely to occur, evidence of the subsequent measures is not admissible to prove: • negligence; • culpable conduct; • a defect in a product or its design; or • a need for a warning or instruction. But the court may admit this evidence for another purpose, such as impeachment or — if disputed — proving ownership, control, or the feasibility of precautionary measures.

Committee Note

The language of Rule 407 has been amended as part of the general restyling of the Evidence Rules to make them more easily understood and to make style and terminology consistent throughout the rules. These changes are intended to be stylistic only. There is no intent to change any result in any ruling on evidence admissibility.

Rule 407 previously provided that evidence was not excluded if offered for a purpose not explicitly prohibited by the Rule. To improve the language of the Rule, it now provides that the court may admit evidence if offered for a permissible purpose. There is no intent to change the process for admitting evidence covered by the Rule. It remains the case that if offered for an impermissible purpose, it must be excluded, and if offered for a purpose not barred by the Rule, its admissibility remains governed by the general principles of Rules 402, 403, 801, etc.

Rule 408. Compromise and Offers to Compromise	Rule 408. Compromise Offers and Negotiations
(a) Prohibited uses. Evidence of the following is not admissible on behalf of any party, when offered to prove liability for, invalidity of, or amount of a claim that was disputed as to validity or amount, or to impeach through a prior inconsistent statement or contradiction: **(1)** furnishing or offering or promising to furnish—or accepting or offering or promising to accept—a valuable consideration in compromising or attempting to compromise the claim; and **(2)** conduct or statements made in compromise negotiations regarding the claim, except when offered in a criminal case and the negotiations related to a claim by a public office or agency in the exercise of regulatory, investigative, or enforcement authority.	**(a) Prohibited Uses.** Evidence of the following is not admissible — on behalf of any party — either to prove or disprove the validity or amount of a disputed claim or to impeach by a prior inconsistent statement or a contradiction: **(1)** furnishing, promising, or offering — or accepting, promising to accept, or offering to accept — a valuable consideration in order to compromise the claim; and **(2)** conduct or a statement made during compromise negotiations about the claim — except when offered in a criminal case and when the negotiations related to a claim by a public office in the exercise of its regulatory, investigative, or enforcement authority.
(b) Permitted uses. This rule does not require exclusion if the evidence is offered for purposes not prohibited by subdivision (a). Examples of permissible purposes include proving a witness's bias or prejudice; negating a contention of undue delay; and proving an effort to obstruct a criminal investigation or prosecution.	**(b) Exceptions.** The court may admit this evidence for another purpose, such as proving a witness's bias or prejudice, negating a contention of undue delay, or proving an effort to obstruct a criminal investigation or prosecution.

Committee Note

The language of Rule 408 has been amended as part of the general restyling of the Evidence Rules to make them more easily understood and to make style and terminology consistent throughout the rules. These changes are intended to be stylistic only. There is no intent to change any result in any ruling on evidence admissibility.

Rule 408 previously provided that evidence was not excluded if offered for a purpose not explicitly prohibited by the Rule. To improve the language of the Rule, it now provides that the court may admit evidence if offered for a permissible purpose. There is no intent to change the process for admitting evidence covered by the Rule. It remains the case that if offered for an impermissible purpose, it must be excluded, and if offered for a purpose not barred by the Rule, its admissibility remains governed by the general principles of Rules 402, 403, 801, etc.

Rule 409. Payment of Medical and Similar Expenses	Rule 409. Offers to Pay Medical and Similar Expenses
Evidence of furnishing or offering or promising to pay medical, hospital, or similar expenses occasioned by an injury is not admissible to prove liability for the injury.	Evidence of furnishing, promising to pay, or offering to pay medical, hospital, or similar expenses resulting from an injury is not admissible to prove liability for the injury.

EXISTING AND PROPOSED FEDERAL RULES OF EVIDENCE

Rule 410. Inadmissibility of Pleas, Plea Discussions, and Related Statements	Rule 410. Pleas, Plea Discussions, and Related Statements
Except as otherwise provided in this rule, evidence of the following is not, in any civil or criminal proceeding, admissible against the defendant who made the plea or was a participant in the plea discussions: **(1)** a plea of guilty which was later withdrawn; **(2)** a plea of nolo contendere; **(3)** any statement made in the course of any proceedings under Rule 11 of the Federal Rules of Criminal Procedure or comparable state procedure regarding either of the foregoing pleas; or **(4)** any statement made in the course of plea discussions with an attorney for the prosecuting authority which do not result in a plea of guilty or which result in a plea of guilty later withdrawn. However, such a statement is admissible (i) in any proceeding wherein another statement made in the course of the same plea or plea discussions has been introduced and the statement ought in fairness be considered contemporaneously with it, or (ii) in a criminal proceeding for perjury or false statement if the statement was made by the defendant under oath, on the record and in the presence of counsel.	**(a) Prohibited Uses.** In a civil or criminal case, evidence of the following is not admissible against the defendant who made the plea or participated in the plea discussions: **(1)** a guilty plea that was later withdrawn; **(2)** a nolo contendere plea; **(3)** a statement about either of those pleas made during a proceeding under Federal Rule of Criminal Procedure 11 or a comparable state procedure; or **(4)** a statement made during plea discussions with an attorney for the prosecuting authority if the discussions did not result in a guilty plea or they resulted in a later-withdrawn guilty plea. **(b) Exceptions.** The court may admit a statement described in Rule 410(a)(3) or (4): **(1)** in any proceeding in which another statement made during the same plea or plea discussions has been introduced, if in fairness both statements ought to be considered together; or **(2)** in a criminal proceeding for perjury or false statement, if the defendant made the statement under oath, on the record, and

Rule 411. Liability Insurance	Rule 411. Liability Insurance
Evidence that a person was or was not insured against liability is not admissible upon the issue whether the person acted negligently or otherwise wrongfully. This rule does not require the exclusion of evidence of insurance against liability when offered for another purpose, such as proof of agency, ownership, or control, or bias or prejudice of a witness.	Evidence that a person did or did not have liability insurance is not admissible to prove that the person acted negligently or otherwise wrongfully. But the court may admit this evidence for another purpose, such as proving a witness's bias or prejudice or — if disputed — proving agency, ownership, or control.

Committee Note

The language of Rule 411 has been amended as part of the general restyling of the Evidence Rules to make them more easily understood and to make style and terminology consistent throughout the rules. These changes are intended to be stylistic only. There is no intent to change any result in any ruling on evidence admissibility.

Rule 411 previously provided that evidence was not excluded if offered for a purpose not explicitly prohibited by the Rule. To improve the language of the Rule, it now provides that the court may admit evidence if offered for a permissible purpose. There is no intent to change the process for admitting evidence covered by the Rule. It remains the case that if offered for an impermissible purpose, it must be excluded, and if offered for a purpose not barred by the Rule, its admissibility remains governed by the general principles of Rules 402, 403, 801, etc.

Rule 412. Sex Offense Cases; Relevance of Alleged Victim's Past Sexual Behavior or Alleged Sexual Predisposition	Rule 412. Sex-Offense Cases: The Victim's Sexual Behavior or Predisposition
(a) Evidence Generally Inadmissible. The following evidence is not admissible in any civil or criminal proceeding involving alleged sexual misconduct except as provided in subdivisions (b) and (c): **(1)** Evidence offered to prove that any alleged victim engaged in other sexual behavior. **(2)** Evidence offered to prove any alleged victim's sexual predisposition.	**(a) Prohibited Uses.** The following evidence is not admissible in a civil or criminal proceeding involving alleged sexual misconduct: **(1)** evidence offered to prove that a victim engaged in other sexual behavior; or **(2)** evidence offered to prove a victim's sexual predisposition.

(b) Exceptions.	**(b) Exceptions.**
(1) In a criminal case, the following evidence is admissible, if otherwise admissible under these rules:	(1) **Criminal Cases.** The court may admit the following evidence in a criminal case:
(A) evidence of specific instances of sexual behavior by the alleged victim offered to prove that a person other than the accused was the source of semen, injury or other physical evidence;	(A) evidence of specific instances of a victim's sexual behavior, if offered to prove that someone other than the defendant was the source of semen, injury, or other physical evidence;
(B) evidence of specific instances of sexual behavior by the alleged victim with respect to the person accused of the sexual misconduct offered by the accused to prove consent or by the prosecution; and	(B) evidence of specific instances of a victim's sexual behavior toward the defendant, if offered by the prosecutor or if offered by the defendant to prove consent; and
(C) evidence the exclusion of which would violate the constitutional rights of the defendant.	(C) evidence whose exclusion would violate the defendant's constitutional rights.
(2) In a civil case, evidence offered to prove the sexual behavior or sexual predisposition of any alleged victim is admissible if it is otherwise admissible under these rules and its probative value substantially outweighs the danger of harm to any victim and of unfair prejudice to any party. Evidence of an alleged victim's reputation is admissible only if it has been placed in controversy by the alleged victim.	(2) **Civil Cases.** In a civil case, the court may admit evidence offered to prove a victim's sexual behavior or sexual predisposition if its probative value substantially outweighs the danger of harm to any victim and of unfair prejudice to any party. The court may admit evidence of a victim's reputation only if the victim has placed it in controversy.

EXISTING AND PROPOSED FEDERAL RULES OF EVIDENCE 953

(c) Procedure To Determine Admissibility.
 	
(1) A party intending to offer evidence under subdivision (b) must—
 	
    (A) file a written motion at least 14 days before trial specifically describing the evidence and stating the purpose for which it is offered unless the court, for good cause requires a different time for filing or permits filing during trial; and
 	
    (B) serve the motion on all parties and notify the alleged victim or, when appropriate, the alleged victim's guardian or representative.
 	
(2) Before admitting evidence under this rule the court must conduct a hearing in camera and afford the victim and parties a right to attend and be heard. The motion, related papers, and the record of the hearing must be sealed and remain under seal unless the court orders otherwise.
	(c) Procedure to Determine Admissibility.
	
	(1) **Motion.** If a party intends to offer evidence under Rule 412(b), the party must:
	
	    (A) file a motion that specifically describes the evidence and states the purpose for which it is to be offered;
	
	    (B) do so at least 14 days before trial unless the court, for good cause, sets a different time;
	
	    (C) serve the motion on all parties; and
	
	    (D) notify the victim or, when appropriate, the victim's guardian or representative.
	
	(2) **Hearing.** Before admitting evidence under this rule, the court must conduct an in-camera hearing and give the victim and parties a right to attend and be heard. Unless the court orders otherwise, the motion, related materials, and the record of the hearing must be and remain sealed.

	(d) Definition of "Victim." In this rule, "victim" includes an alleged victim.

Rule 413. Evidence of Similar Crimes in Sexual Assault Cases	Rule 413. Similar Crimes in Sexual-Assault Cases
(a) In a criminal case in which the defendant is accused of an offense of sexual assault, evidence of the defendant's commission of another offense or offenses of sexual assault is admissible, and may be considered for its bearing on any matter to which it is relevant.	**(a) Permitted Uses.** In a criminal case in which a defendant is accused of a sexual assault, the court may admit evidence that the defendant committed any other sexual assault. The evidence may be considered on any matter to which it is relevant.
(b) In a case in which the Government intends to offer evidence under this rule, the attorney for the Government shall disclose the evidence to the defendant, including statements of witnesses or a summary of the substance of any testimony that is expected to be offered, at least fifteen days before the scheduled date of trial or at such later time as the court may allow for good cause.	**(b) Disclosure.** If the prosecutor intends to offer this evidence, the prosecutor must disclose it to the defendant, including witnesses' statements or a summary of the expected testimony. The prosecutor must do so at least 15 days before trial or at a later time that the court allows for good cause.
(c) This rule shall not be construed to limit the admission or consideration of evidence under any other rule.	**(c) Effect on Other Rules.** This rule does not limit the admission or consideration of evidence under any other rule.

EXISTING AND PROPOSED FEDERAL RULES OF EVIDENCE 955

(d) For purposes of this rule and Rule 415, "offense of sexual assault" means a crime under Federal law or the law of a State (as defined in section 513 of title 18, United States Code) that nvolved—	**(d) Definition of "Sexual Assault."** In this rule and Rule 415, "sexual assault" means a crime under federal law or under state law (as "state" is defined in 18 U.S.C. § 513) involving:
(1) any conduct proscribed by chapter 109A of title 18, United States Code;	(1) any conduct prohibited by 18 U.S.C. chapter 109A;
(2) contact, without consent, between any part of the defendant's body or an object and the genitals or anus of another person;	(2) contact, without consent, between any part of the defendant's body — or an object — and another person's genitals or anus;
(3) contact, without consent, between the genitals or anus of the defendant and any part of another person's body;	(3) contact, without consent, between the defendant's genitals or anus and any part of another person's body;
(4) deriving sexual pleasure or gratification from the infliction of death, bodily injury, or physical pain on another person; or	(4) deriving sexual pleasure or gratification from inflicting death, bodily injury, or physical pain on another person; or
(5) an attempt or conspiracy to engage in conduct described in paragraphs (1)–(4).	(5) an attempt or conspiracy to engage in conduct described in paragraphs (1)–(4).

Rule 414. Evidence of Similar Crimes in Child Molestation Cases	Rule 414. Similar Crimes in Child-Molestation Cases
(a) In a criminal case in which the defendant is accused of an offense of child molestation, evidence of the defendant's commission of another offense or offenses of child molestation is admissible, and may be considered for its bearing on any matter to which it is relevant.	(a) **Permitted Uses.** In a criminal case in which a defendant is accused of child molestation, the court may admit evidence that the defendant committed any other act of child molestation. The evidence may be considered on any matter to which it is relevant.
(b) In a case in which the Government intends to offer evidence under this rule, the attorney for the Government shall disclose the evidence to the defendant, including statements of witnesses or a summary of the substance of any testimony that is expected to be offered, at least fifteen days before the scheduled date of trial or at such later time as the court may allow for good cause.	(b) **Disclosure.** If the prosecutor intends to offer this evidence, the prosecutor must disclose it to the defendant, including witnesses' statements or a summary of the expected testimony. The prosecutor must do so at least 15 days before trial or at a later time that the court allows for good cause.
(c) This rule shall not be construed to limit the admission or consideration of evidence under any other rule.	(c) **Effect on Other Rules.** This rule does not limit the admission or consideration of evidence under any other rule.

(d) For purposes of this rule and Rule 415, "child" means a person below the age of fourteen, and "offense of child molestation" means a crime under Federal law or the law of a State (as defined in section 513 of title 18, United States Code) that involved—	**(d) Definition of "Child" and "Child Molestation."** In this rule and Rule 415:
(1) any conduct proscribed by chapter 109A of title 18, United States Code, that was committed in relation to a child;	**(1)** "child" means a person below the age of 14; and
(2) any conduct proscribed by chapter 110 of title 18, United States Code;	**(2)** "child molestation" means a crime under federal law or under state law (as "state" is defined in 18 U.S.C. § 513) involving:
	(A) any conduct prohibited by 18 U.S.C. chapter 109A and committed with a child;
	(B) any conduct prohibited by 18 U.S.C. chapter 110;
(3) contact between any part of the defendant's body or an object and the genitals or anus of a child;	**(C)** contact between any part of the defendant's body — or an object — and a child's genitals or anus;
(4) contact between the genitals or anus of the defendant and any part of the body of a child;	**(D)** contact between the defendant's genitals or anus and any part of a child's body;
(5) deriving sexual pleasure or gratification from the infliction of death, bodily injury, or physical pain on a child; or	**(E)** deriving sexual pleasure or gratification from inflicting death, bodily injury, or physical pain on a child; or
(6) an attempt or conspiracy to engage in conduct described in paragraphs (1)–(5).	**(F)** an attempt or conspiracy to engage in conduct described in paragraphs (A)–(E).

Rule 415. Evidence of Similar Acts in Civil Cases Concerning Sexual Assault or Child Molestation	Rule 415. Similar Acts in Civil Cases Involving Sexual Assault or Child Molestation
(a) In a civil case in which a claim for damages or other relief is predicated on a party's alleged commission of conduct constituting an offense of sexual assault or child molestation, evidence of that party's commission of another offense or offenses of sexual assault or child molestation is admissible and may be considered as provided in Rule 413 and Rule 414 of these rules.	**(a) Permitted Uses.** In a civil case involving a claim for relief based on a party's alleged sexual assault or child molestation, the court may admit evidence that the party committed any other sexual assault or act of child molestation. The evidence may be considered as provided in Rules 413 and 414.
(b) A party who intends to offer evidence under this Rule shall disclose the evidence to the party against whom it will be offered, including statements of witnesses or a summary of the substance of any testimony that is expected to be offered, at least fifteen days before the scheduled date of trial or at such later time as the court may allow for good cause.	**(b) Disclosure.** If a party intends to offer this evidence, the party must disclose it to the party against whom it will be offered, including witnesses' statements or a summary of the expected testimony. The party must do so at least 15 days before trial or at a later time that the court allows for good cause.
(c) This rule shall not be construed to limit the admission or consideration of evidence under any other rule.	**(c) Effect on Other Rules.** This rule does not limit the admission or consideration of evidence under any other rule.

ARTICLE V. PRIVILEGES	ARTICLE V. PRIVILEGES
Rule 501. General Rule	**Rule 501. Privilege in General**
Except as otherwise required by the Constitution of the United States or provided by Act of Congress or in rules prescribed by the Supreme Court pursuant to statutory authority, the privilege of a witness, person, government, State, or political subdivision thereof shall be governed by the principles of the common law as they may be interpreted by the courts of the United States in the light of reason and experience. However, in civil actions and proceedings, with respect to an element of a claim or defense as to which State law supplies the rule of decision, the privilege of a witness, person, government, State, or political subdivision thereof shall be determined in accordance with State law.	The common law — as interpreted by United States courts in the light of reason and experience — governs a claim of privilege unless any of the following provides otherwise: • the United States Constitution; • a federal statute; or • other rules prescribed by the Supreme Court. But in a civil case, state law governs privilege regarding a claim or defense for which state law supplies the rule of decision.

Rule 502. Attorney-Client Privilege and Work Product; Limitations on Waiver	Rule 502. Attorney-Client Privilege and Work Product; Limitations on Waiver
The following provisions apply, in the circumstances set out, to disclosure of a communication or information covered by the attorney-client privilege or work-product protection.	The following provisions apply, in the circumstances set out, to disclosure of a communication or information covered by the attorney-client privilege or work-product protection.
(a) Disclosure made in a Federal proceeding or to a Federal office or agency; scope of a waiver. When the disclosure is made in a Federal proceeding or to a Federal office or agency and waives the attorney-client privilege or work-product protection, the waiver extends to an undisclosed communication or information in a Federal or State proceeding only if: **(1)** the waiver is intentional; **(2)** the disclosed and undisclosed communications or information concern the same subject matter; and **(3)** they ought in fairness to be considered together.	**(a) Disclosure Made in a Federal Proceeding or to a Federal Office or Agency; Scope of a Waiver.** When the disclosure is made in a federal proceeding or to a federal office or agency and waives the attorney-client privilege or work-product protection, the waiver extends to an undisclosed communication or information in a federal or state proceeding only if: **(1)** the waiver is intentional; **(2)** the disclosed and undisclosed communications or information concern the same subject matter; and **(3)** they ought in fairness to be considered together.

(b) Inadvertent disclosure. When made in a Federal proceeding or to a Federal office or agency, the disclosure does not operate as a waiver in a Federal or State proceeding if: **(1)** the disclosure is inadvertent; **(2)** the holder of the privilege or protection took reasonable steps to prevent disclosure; and **(3)** the holder promptly took reasonable steps to rectify the error, including (if applicable) following Federal Rule of Civil Procedure 26(b)(5)(B).	**(b) Inadvertent Disclosure.** When made in a federal proceeding or to a federal office or agency, the disclosure does not operate as a waiver in a federal or state proceeding if: **(1)** the disclosure is inadvertent; **(2)** the holder of the privilege or protection took reasonable steps to prevent disclosure; and **(3)** the holder promptly took reasonable steps to rectify the error, including (if applicable) following Federal Rule of Civil Procedure 26(b)(5)(B).
(d) Controlling effect of a court order. A Federal court may order that the privilege or protection is not waived by disclosure connected with the litigation pending before the court—in which event the disclosure is also not a waiver in any other Federal or State proceeding.	**(d) Controlling Effect of a Court Order.** A federal court may order that the privilege or protection is not waived by disclosure connected with the litigation pending before the court — in which event the disclosure is also not a waiver in any other federal or state proceeding.
(f) Controlling effect of this rule. Notwithstanding Rules 101 and 1101, this rule applies to State proceedings and to Federal court-annexed and Federal court-mandated arbitration proceedings, in the circumstances set out in the rule. And notwithstanding Rule 501, this rule applies even if State	**(f) Controlling Effect of this Rule.** Notwithstanding Rules 101 and 1101, this rule applies to state proceedings and to federal court-annexed and federal court-mandated arbitration proceedings, in the circumstances set out in the rule.

law provides the rule of decision.	And notwithstanding Rule 501, this rule applies even if state law provides the rule of decision.
(g) Definitions. In this rule: (1) "attorney-client privilege" means the protection that applicable law provides for confidential attorney-client communications; and (2) "work-product protection" means the protection that applicable law provides for tangible material (or its intangible equivalent) prepared in anticipation of litigation or for trial.	**(g)** **Definitions.** In this rule: (1) "attorney-client privilege" means the protection that applicable law provides for confidential attorney-client communications; and (2) "work-product protection" means the protection that applicable law provides for tangible material (or its intangible equivalent) prepared in anticipation of litigation or for trial.

ARTICLE VI. WITNESSES

Rule 601. General Rule of Competency	Rule 601. Competency to Testify in General
Every person is competent to be a witness except as otherwise provided in these rules. However, in civil actions and proceedings, with respect to an element of a claim or defense as to which State law supplies the rule of decision, the competency of a witness shall be determined in accordance with State law.	Every person is competent to be a witness unless these rules provide otherwise. But in a civil case, state law governs the witness's competency regarding a claim or defense for which state law supplies the rule of decision.

Rule 602. Lack of Personal Knowledge	Rule 602. Need for Personal Knowledge
A witness may not testify to a matter unless evidence is introduced sufficient to support a finding that the witness has personal knowledge of the matter. Evidence to prove personal knowledge may, but need not, consist of the witness' own testimony. This rule is subject to the provisions of rule 703, relating to opinion testimony by expert witnesses.	A witness may testify to a matter only if evidence is introduced sufficient to support a finding that the witness has personal knowledge of the matter. Evidence to prove personal knowledge may consist of the witness's own testimony. This rule does not apply to testimony by an expert witness under Rule 703.

Rule 603. Oath or Affirmation	Rule 603. Oath or Affirmation to Testify Truthfully
Before testifying, every witness shall be required to declare that the witness will testify truthfully, by oath or affirmation administered in a form calculated to awaken the witness' conscience and impress the witness' mind with the duty to do so.	Before testifying, a witness must give an oath or affirmation to testify truthfully. It must be in a form designed to impress that duty on the witness's conscience.

Rule 604. Interpreters	Rule 604. Interpreter
An interpreter is subject to the provisions of these rules relating to qualification as an expert and the administration of an oath or affirmation	An interpreter must be qualified and must give an oath or affirmation to make a true translation.

Rule 605. Competency of Judge as Witness	Rule 605. Judge's Competency as a Witness
The judge presiding at the trial may not testify in that trial as a witness. No objection need be made in order to preserve the point.	The presiding judge may not testify as a witness at the trial. A party need not object to preserve the issue.

Rule 606. Competency of Juror as Witness	Rule 606. Juror's Competency as a Witness
(a) At the trial. A member of the jury may not testify as a witness before that jury in the trial of the case in which the juror is sitting. If the juror is called so to testify, the opposing party shall be afforded an opportunity to object out of the presence of the jury.	**(a) At the Trial.** A juror may not testify as a witness before the other jurors at the trial. If a juror is called to testify, the court must give an adverse party an opportunity to object outside the jury's presence.
(b) Inquiry into validity of verdict or indictment. Upon an inquiry into the validity of a verdict or indictment, a juror may not testify as to any matter or statement occurring during the course of the jury's deliberations or to the effect of anything upon that or any other juror's mind or emotions as influencing the juror to assent to or dissent from the verdict or indictment or concerning the juror's mental processes in connection therewith. But a juror may testify about (1) whether extraneous prejudicial information was improperly brought to the jury's attention, (2) whether any outside influence was improperly brought to bear upon any juror, or (3) whether there was a mistake in entering the verdict onto the verdict form. A juror's affidavit or evidence of any statement by the juror may not be received on a matter about which the juror would be precluded from testifying.	**(b) During an Inquiry into the Validity of a Verdict or Indictment.** **(1) Prohibited Testimony or Other Evidence.** During an inquiry into the validity of a verdict or indictment, a juror may not testify about any statement made or incident that occurred during the jury's deliberations; the effect of anything on that juror's or another juror's vote; or any juror's mental processes concerning the verdict or indictment. The court may not receive a juror's affidavit or evidence of a juror's statement on these matters. **(2) Exceptions.** A juror may testify about whether: **(A)** extraneous prejudicial information was improperly brought to the jury's attention;

Rule 607. Who May Impeach	Rule 607. Who May Impeach a Witness
The credibility of a witness may be attacked by any party, including the party calling the witness.	Any party, including the party that called the witness, may attack the witness's credibility.

Rule 608. Evidence of Character and Conduct of Witness	Rule 608. A Witness's Character for Truthfulness or Untruthfulness
(a) Opinion and reputation evidence of character. The credibility of a witness may be attacked or supported by evidence in the form of opinion or reputation, but subject to these limitations: (1) the evidence may refer only to character for truthfulness or untruthfulness, and (2) evidence of truthful character is admissible only after the character of the witness for truthfulness has been attacked by opinion or reputation evidence or otherwise.	**(a) Reputation or Opinion Evidence.** A witness's credibility may be attacked or supported by testimony about the witness's reputation for having a character for truthfulness or untruthfulness, or by testimony in the form of an opinion about that character. But evidence of truthful character is admissible only after the witness's character for truthfulness has been attacked.

(b) Specific instances of conduct. Specific instances of the conduct of a witness, for the purpose of attacking or supporting the witness' character for truthfulness, other than conviction of crime as provided in rule 609, may not be proved by extrinsic evidence. They may, however, in the discretion of the court, if probative of truthfulness or untruthfulness, be inquired into on cross-examination of the witness (1) concerning the witness' character for truthfulness or untruthfulness, or (2) concerning the character for truthfulness or untruthfulness of another witness as to which character the witness being cross-examined has testified.
 	
The giving of testimony, whether by an accused or by any other witness, does not operate as a waiver of the accused's or the witness' privilege against self-incrimination when examined with respect to matters that relate only to character for truthfulness.
	(b) Specific Instances of Conduct. Except for a criminal conviction under Rule 609, extrinsic evidence is not admissible to prove specific instances of a witness's conduct in order to attack or support the witness's character for truthfulness. But the court may, on cross-examination, allow them to be inquired into if they are probative of the character for truthfulness or untruthfulness of:
	
	  (1) the witness; or
	
	  (2) another witness whose character the witness being cross-examined has testified about.
	
	(c) Privilege Against Self-Incrimination. A witness does not waive the privilege against self-incrimination by testifying about a matter that relates only to a character for truthfulness.

Committee Note

The language of Rule 608 has been amended as part of the general restyling of the Evidence Rules to make them more easily understood and to make style and terminology consistent throughout the rules. These changes are intended to be stylistic only. There is no intent to change any result in any ruling on evidence admissibility.

The Committee is aware that the Rule's limitation of bad-act impeachment to "cross-examination" is trumped by Rule 607, which allows a party to impeach witnesses on direct examination. Courts have not relied on the term "on cross-examination" to limit impeachment that would otherwise be permissible under Rules 607 and 608. The Committee therefore concluded that no change to the language of the Rule was necessary in the context of a restyling project.

Rule 609. Impeachment by Evidence of Conviction of Crime	Rule 609. Impeachment by Evidence of a Criminal Conviction

(a) General rule. For the purpose of attacking the character for truthfulness of a witness,
 	
(1) evidence that a witness other than an accused has been convicted of a crime shall be admitted, subject to Rule 403, if the crime was punishable by death or imprisonment in excess of one year under the law under which the witness was convicted, and evidence that an accused has been convicted of such a crime shall be admitted if the court determines that the probative value of admitting this evidence outweighs its prejudicial effect to the accused; and
 	
(2) evidence that any witness has been convicted of a crime shall be admitted regardless of the punishment, if it readily can be determined that establishing the elements of the crime required proof or admission of an act of dishonesty or false statement by the witness.
	(a) **In General.** The following rules apply to attacking a witness's character for truthfulness by evidence of a criminal conviction:
	
	(1) for a crime that, in the convicting jurisdiction, was punishable by death or by imprisonment for more than one year, the evidence:
	
	    (A) must be admitted, subject to Rule 403, if the witness is not a defendant in a criminal case; and
	
	    (B) must be admitted if the witness is a defendant in a criminal case and the probative value of the evidence outweighs its prejudicial effect; and
	
	(2) for any crime regardless of the punishment, the evidence must be admitted if the court can readily determine that establishing the elements of the crime required proving — or the witness's admitting — a dishonest act or false statement.

(b) Time limit. Evidence of a conviction under this rule is not admissible if a period of more than ten years has elapsed since the date of the conviction or of the release of the witness from the confinement imposed for that conviction, whichever is the later date, unless the court determines, in the interests of justice, that the probative value of the conviction supported by specific facts and circumstances substantially outweighs its prejudicial effect. However, evidence of a conviction more than 10 years old as calculated herein, is not admissible unless the proponent gives to the adverse party sufficient advance written notice of intent to use such evidence to provide the adverse party with a fair opportunity to contest the use of such evidence.	**(b) Limit on Using the Evidence After 10 Years.** This subdivision (b) applies if more than 10 years have passed since the witness's conviction or release from confinement for the conviction, whichever is later. Evidence of the conviction is admissible only if: (1) its probative value, supported by specific facts and circumstances, substantially outweighs its prejudicial effect; and (2) the proponent gives an adverse party reasonable written notice of the intent to use it so that the party has a fair opportunity to contest its use.
(c) Effect of pardon, annulment, or certificate of rehabilitation. Evidence of a conviction is not admissible under this rule if (1) the conviction has been the subject of a pardon, annulment, certificate of rehabilitation, or other equivalent procedure based on a finding of the rehabilitation of the person convicted, and that person has not been convicted of a subsequent crime that was punishable by death or imprisonment in excess of one year, or (2) the conviction has been the subject of a pardon, annulment, or other equivalent procedure based on a finding of innocence.	**(c) Effect of a Pardon, Annulment, or Certificate of Rehabilitation.** Evidence of a conviction is not admissible if: (1) the conviction has been the subject of a pardon, annulment, certificate of rehabilitation, or other equivalent procedure based on a finding that the person has been rehabilitated, and the person has not been convicted of a later crime punishable by death or by imprisonment for more than one year; or (2) the conviction has been the subject of a pardon, annulment, or other equivalent procedure

	based on a finding of innocence.
(d) Juvenile adjudications. Evidence of juvenile adjudications is generally not admissible under this rule. The court may, however, in a criminal case allow evidence of a juvenile adjudication of a witness other than the accused if conviction of the offense would be admissible to attack the credibility of an adult and the court is satisfied that admission in evidence is necessary for a fair determination of the issue of guilt or innocence.	**(d) Juvenile Adjudications.** Evidence of a juvenile adjudication is admissible under this rule only if: **(1)** it is offered in a criminal case; **(2)** the adjudication was of a witness other than the defendant; **(3)** a conviction of an adult for that offense would be admissible to attack the adult's credibility; and **(4)** admitting the evidence is necessary to fairly determine guilt or innocence.
(e) Pendency of appeal. The pendency of an appeal therefrom does not render evidence of a conviction inadmissible. Evidence of the pendency of an appeal is admissible.	**(e) Pendency of an Appeal.** A conviction that satisfies this rule is admissible even if an appeal is pending. Evidence of the pendency is also admissible.

Rule 610. Religious Beliefs or Opinions	Rule 610. Religious Beliefs or Opinions
Evidence of the beliefs or opinions of a witness on matters of religion is not admissible for the purpose of showing that by reason of their nature the witness' credibility is impaired or enhanced.	Evidence of a witness's religious beliefs or opinions is not admissible to attack or support the witness's credibility.

EXISTING AND PROPOSED FEDERAL RULES OF EVIDENCE

Rule 611. Mode and Order of Interrogation and Presentation	Rule 611. Mode and Order of Questioning Witnesses and Presenting Evidence
(a) Control by court. The court shall exercise reasonable control over the mode and order of interrogating witnesses and presenting evidence so as to (1) make the interrogation and presentation effective for the ascertainment of the truth, (2) avoid needless consumption of time, and (3) protect witnesses from harassment or undue embarrassment.	(a) **Control by the Court; Purposes.** The court should exercise reasonable control over the mode and order of questioning witnesses and presenting evidence so as to: (1) make those procedures effective for determining the truth; (2) avoid wasting time; and (3) protect witnesses from harassment or undue embarrassment.
(b) Scope of cross-examination. Cross-examination should be limited to the subject matter of the direct examination and matters affecting the credibility of the witness. The court may, in the exercise of discretion, permit inquiry into additional matters as if on direct examination.	(b) **Scope of Cross-Examination.** Cross-examination should not go beyond the subject matter of the direct examination and matters affecting a witness's credibility. The court may allow inquiry into additional matters as if on direct examination.
(c) Leading questions. Leading questions should not be used on the direct examination of a witness except as may be necessary to develop the witness' testimony. Ordinarily leading	(c) **Leading Questions.** Leading questions should not be used on direct examination except as necessary to develop the witness's testimony. Ordinarily,

questions should be permitted on cross-examination. When a party calls a hostile witness, an adverse party, or a witness identified with an adverse party, interrogation may be by leading questions.	the court should allow leading questions on cross-examination. And the court should allow leading questions when a party calls a hostile witness, an adverse party, or a witness identified with an adverse party.

Rule 612. Writing Used To Refresh Memory	Rule 612. Writing Used to Refresh a Witness's Memory
Except as otherwise provided in criminal proceedings by section 3500 of title 18, United States Code, if a witness uses a writing to refresh memory for the purpose of testifying, either— (1) while testifying, or (2) before testifying, if the court in its discretion determines it is necessary in the interests of justice, an adverse party is entitled to have the writing produced at the hearing, to inspect it, to cross-examine the witness thereon, and to introduce in evidence those portions which relate to the testimony of the witness. If it is claimed that the writing contains matters not related to the subject matter of the testimony the court shall examine the writing in camera, excise any portions not so related, and order delivery of the remainder to the party entitled thereto. Any portion withheld over objections shall be preserved and made available to the appellate court in the event of an appeal. If a writing is not produced or delivered pursuant to order under this rule, the court shall make any order justice requires, except that in criminal cases when the prosecution elects not to comply, the order shall be one striking the testimony or, if the court in its discretion determines that the interests of justice so require, declaring a mistrial.	**(a) Scope.** This rule gives an adverse party certain options when a witness uses a writing to refresh memory: (1) while testifying; or (2) before testifying, if the court decides that justice requires a party to have those options. **(b) Adverse Party's Options; Deleting Unrelated Matter.** Unless 18 U.S.C. § 3500 provides otherwise in a criminal case, an adverse party is entitled to have the writing produced at the hearing, to inspect it, to cross-examine the witness about it, and to introduce in evidence any portion that relates to the witness's testimony. If the producing party claims that the writing includes unrelated matter, the court must examine the writing in camera, delete any unrelated portion, and order that the rest be delivered to the adverse party. Any portion deleted over objection must be preserved for the record. **(c) Failure to Produce or Deliver.** If a writing is not produced or is not delivered as ordered, the court may issue any appropriate order. But if the prosecution does not comply in a criminal case, the court must strike the witness's testimony or — if justice so requires — declare a mistrial.

Rule 613. Prior Statements of Witnesses	Rule 613. Witness's Prior Statement
(a) Examining witness concerning prior statement. In examining a witness concerning a prior statement made by the witness, whether written or not, the statement need not be shown nor its contents disclosed to the witness at that time, but on request the same shall be shown or disclosed to opposing counsel.	**(a) Showing or Disclosing the Statement During Questioning.** When questioning a witness about the witness's prior statement, the party need not show it or disclose its contents to the witness. But the party must, on request, show it or disclose its contents to an adverse party's attorney.
(b) Extrinsic evidence of prior inconsistent statement of witness. Extrinsic evidence of a prior inconsistent statement by a witness is not admissible unless the witness is afforded an opportunity to explain or deny the same and the opposite party is afforded an opportunity to interrogate the witness thereon, or the interests of justice otherwise require. This provision does not apply to admissions of a party-opponent as defined in rule 801(d)(2).	**(b) Extrinsic Evidence of a Prior Inconsistent Statement.** Extrinsic evidence of a witness's prior inconsistent statement is admissible only if the witness is given an opportunity to explain or deny the statement and an adverse party is given an opportunity to question the witness about it, or if justice so requires. This subdivision (b) does not apply to an opposing party's statement under Rule 801(d)(2).

Rule 614. Calling and Interrogation of Witnesses by Court	Rule 614. Court's Calling or Questioning a Witness
(a) Calling by court. The court may, on its own motion or at the suggestion of a party, call witnesses, and all parties are entitled to cross-examine witnesses thus called.	**(a) Calling.** The court may call a witness on its own or at a party's suggestion. Each party is entitled to cross-examine the witness.
(b) Interrogation by court. The court may interrogate witnesses, whether called by itself or by a party.	**(b) Questioning.** The court may question a witness regardless of who calls the witness.
(c) Objections. Objections to the calling of witnesses by the court or to interrogation by it may be made at the time or at the next available opportunity when the jury is not present.	**(c) Objections.** A party may object to the court's calling or questioning a witness either at that time or at the next opportunity when the jury is not present.

Rule 615. Exclusion of Witnesses	Rule 615. Excluding Witnesses
At the request of a party the court shall order witnesses excluded so that they cannot hear the testimony of other witnesses, and it may make the order of its own motion. This rule does not authorize exclusion of (1) a party who is a natural person, or (2) an officer or employee of a party which is not a natural person designated as its representative by its attorney, or (3) a person whose presence is shown by a party to be essential to the presentation of the party's cause, or (4) a person authorized by statute to be present.	At a party's request, the court must order witnesses excluded so that they cannot hear other witnesses' testimony. Or the court may do so on its own. But this rule does not authorize excluding: **(a)** a party who is a natural person; **(b)** an officer or employee of a party that is not a natural person, after being designated as the party's representative by its attorney; **(c)** a person whose presence a party shows to be essential to presenting the party's claim or defense; or **(d)** a person authorized by statute to be present.

ARTICLE VII. OPINIONS AND EXPERT TESTIMONY	ARTICLE VII. OPINIONS AND EXPERT TESTIMONY
Rule 701. Opinion Testimony by Lay Witnesses	Rule 701. Opinion Testimony by Lay Witnesses
If the witness is not testifying as an expert, the witness' testimony in the form of opinions or inferences is limited to those opinions or inferences which are (a) rationally based on the perception of the witness, and (b) helpful to a clear understanding of the witness' testimony or the determination of a fact in issue, and (c) not based on scientific, technical, or other specialized knowledge within the scope of Rule 702.	If a witness is not testifying as an expert, testimony in the form of an opinion is limited to one that is: **(a)** rationally based on the witness's perception; **(b)** helpful to clearly understanding the witness's testimony or to determining a fact in issue; and **(c)** not based on scientific, technical, or other specialized knowledge within the scope of Rule 702.

Committee Note

The language of Rule 701 has been amended as part of the general restyling of the Evidence Rules to make them more easily understood and to make style and terminology consistent throughout the rules. These changes are intended to be stylistic only. There is no intent to change any result in any ruling on evidence admissibility.

The Committee deleted all reference to an "inference" on the grounds that the deletion made the Rule flow better and easier to read, and because any "inference" is covered by the broader term "opinion." Courts have not made substantive decisions on the basis of any distinction between an opinion and an inference. No change in current practice is intended.

Rule 702. Testimony by Experts	Rule 702. Testimony by Expert Witnesses
If scientific, technical, or other specialized knowledge will assist the trier of fact to understand the evidence or to determine a fact in issue, a witness qualified as an expert by knowledge, skill, experience, training, or education, may testify thereto in the form of an opinion or otherwise, if (1) the testimony is based upon sufficient facts or data, (2) the testimony is the product of reliable principles and methods, and (3) the witness has applied the principles and methods reliably to the facts of the case.	A witness who is qualified as an expert by knowledge, skill, experience, training, or education may testify in the form of an opinion or otherwise if: **(a)** the expert's scientific, technical, or other specialized knowledge will help the trier of fact to understand the evidence or to determine a fact in issue; **(b)** the testimony is based on sufficient facts or data; **(c)** the testimony is the product of reliable principles and methods; and **(d)** the expert has reliably applied the principles and methods to the facts of the case.

Rule 703. Bases of Opinion Testimony by Experts	Rule 703. Bases of an Expert's Opinion Testimony
The facts or data in the particular case upon which an expert bases an opinion or inference may be those perceived by or made known to the expert at or before the hearing. If of a type reasonably relied upon by experts in the particular field in forming opinions or inferences upon the subject, the facts or data need not be admissible in evidence in order for the opinion or inference to be admitted. Facts or data that are otherwise inadmissible shall not be disclosed to the jury by the proponent of the opinion or inference unless the court determines that their probative value in assisting the jury to evaluate the expert's opinion substantially outweighs their prejudicial effect.	An expert may base an opinion on facts or data in the case that the expert has been made aware of or personally observed. If experts in the particular field would reasonably rely on those kinds of facts or data in forming an opinion on the subject, they need not be admissible for the opinion to be admitted. But if the facts or data would otherwise be inadmissible, the proponent of the opinion may disclose them to the jury only if their probative value in helping the jury evaluate the opinion substantially outweighs their prejudicial effect.

Committee Note

The language of Rule 703 has been amended as part of the general restyling of the Evidence Rules to make them more easily understood and to make style and terminology consistent throughout the rules. These changes are intended to be stylistic only. There is no intent to change any result in any ruling on evidence admissibility.

The Committee deleted all reference to an "inference" on the grounds that the deletion made the Rule flow better and easier to read, and because any "inference" is covered by the broader term "opinion." Courts have not made substantive decisions on the basis of any distinction between an opinion and an inference. No change in current practice is intended.

Rule 704. Opinion on Ultimate Issue	Rule 704. Opinion on an Ultimate Issue
(a) Except as provided in subdivision (b), testimony in the form of an opinion or inference otherwise admissible is not objectionable because it embraces an ultimate issue to be decided by the trier of fact.	**(a) In General — Not Automatically Objectionable.** An opinion is not objectionable just because it embraces an ultimate issue.
(b) No expert witness testifying with respect to the mental state or condition of a defendant in a criminal case may state an opinion or inference as to whether the defendant did or did not have the mental state or condition constituting an element of the crime charged or of a defense thereto. Such ultimate issues are matters for the trier of fact alone.	**(b) Exception.** In a criminal case, an expert witness must not state an opinion about whether the defendant did or did not have a mental state or condition that constitutes an element of the crime charged or of a defense.

Committee Note

The language of Rule 704 has been amended as part of the general restyling of the Evidence Rules to make them more easily understood and to make style and terminology consistent throughout the rules. These changes are intended to be stylistic only. There is no intent to change any result in any ruling on evidence admissibility.

The Committee deleted all reference to an "inference" on the grounds that the deletion made the Rule flow better and easier to read, and because any "inference" is covered by the broader term "opinion." Courts have not made substantive decisions on the basis of any distinction between an opinion and an inference. No change in current practice is intended.

Rule 705. Disclosure of Facts or Data Underlying Expert Opinion	Rule 705. Disclosing the Facts or Data Underlying an Expert's Opinion
The expert may testify in terms of opinion or inference and give reasons therefor without first testifying to the underlying facts or data, unless the court requires otherwise. The expert may in any event be required to disclose the underlying facts or data on cross-examination.	Unless the court orders otherwise, an expert may state an opinion — and give the reasons for it — without first testifying to the underlying facts or data. But the expert may be required to disclose those facts or data on cross-examination.

Committee Note

The language of Rule 705 has been amended as part of the general restyling of the Evidence Rules to make them more easily understood and to make style and terminology consistent throughout the rules. These changes are intended to be stylistic only. There is no intent to change any result in any ruling on evidence admissibility.

The Committee deleted all reference to an "inference" on the grounds that the deletion made the Rule flow better and easier to read, and because any "inference" is covered by the broader term "opinion." Courts have not made substantive decisions on the basis of any distinction between an opinion and an inference. No change in current practice is intended.

Rule 706. Court Appointed Experts	Rule 706. Court-Appointed Expert Witnesses
(a) Appointment. The court may on its own motion or on the motion of any party enter an order to show cause why expert witnesses should not be appointed, and may request the parties to submit nominations. The court may appoint any expert witnesses agreed upon by the parties, and may appoint expert witnesses of its own selection. An expert witness shall not be appointed by the court unless the witness consents to act. A witness so appointed shall be informed of the witness' duties by the court in writing, a copy of which shall be filed with the clerk, or at a conference in which the parties shall have opportunity to participate. A witness so appointed shall advise the parties of the witness' findings, if any; the witness' deposition may be taken by any party; and the witness may be called to testify by the court or any party. The witness shall be subject to cross-examination by each party, including a party calling the witness.	**(a) Appointment Process.** On a party's motion or on its own, the court may order the parties to show cause why expert witnesses should not be appointed and may ask the parties to submit nominations. The court may appoint any expert witness that the parties agree on and any of its own choosing. But the court may only appoint someone who consents to act. **(b) Expert's Role.** The court must inform the expert in writing of the expert's duties and have a copy filed with the clerk. Or the court may so inform the expert at a conference in which the parties have an opportunity to participate. The expert: **(1)** must advise the parties of any findings the expert makes; **(2)** may be deposed by any party; **(3)** may be called to testify by the court or any party; and **(4)** may be cross-examined by any party, including the party that called the expert.

(b) Compensation. Expert witnesses so appointed are entitled to reasonable compensation in whatever sum the court may allow. The compensation thus fixed is payable from funds which may be provided by law in criminal cases and civil actions and proceedings involving just compensation under the fifth amendment. In other civil actions and proceedings the compensation shall be paid by the parties in such proportion and at such time as the court directs, and thereafter charged in like manner as other costs.	**(c) Compensation.** The expert is entitled to whatever reasonable compensation the court allows. The compensation is payable as follows: **(1)** in a criminal case or in a civil case involving just compensation under the Fifth Amendment, from any funds that are provided by law; and **(2)** in any other civil case, by the parties in the proportion and at the time that the court directs — and the compensation is then charged like other costs.
(c) Disclosure of appointment. In the exercise of its discretion, the court may authorize disclosure to the jury of the fact that the court appointed the expert witness.	**(d) Disclosing the Appointment.** The court may authorize disclosure to the jury that the court appointed the expert.
(d) Parties' experts of own selection. Nothing in this rule limits the parties in calling expert witnesses of their own selection.	**(e) Parties' Choice of Their Own Experts.** This rule does not limit a party in calling its own experts.

ARTICLE VIII. HEARSAY Rule 801. Definitions	ARTICLE VIII. HEARSAY Rule 801. Definitions That Apply to This Article; Exclusions from Hearsay
The following definitions apply under this article: **(a) Statement.** A "statement" is (1) an oral or written assertion or (2) nonverbal conduct of a person, if it is intended by the person as an assertion.	**(a) Statement.** "Statement" means: (1) a person's oral or written assertion; or (2) a person's nonverbal conduct, if the person intended it as an assertion.
(b) Declarant. A "declarant" is a person who makes a statement.	**(b) Declarant.** "Declarant" means the person who made the statement.
(c) Hearsay. "Hearsay" is a statement, other than one made by the declarant while testifying at the trial or hearing, offered in evidence to prove the truth of the matter asserted.	**(c) Hearsay.** "Hearsay" means a prior statement — one the declarant does not make while testifying at the current trial or hearing — that a party offers in evidence to prove the truth of the matter asserted by the declarant.

(d) Statements which are not hearsay. A statement is not hearsay if—	**(d) Statements That Are Not Hearsay.** A statement that meets the following conditions is not hearsay:
(1) Prior statement by witness. The declarant testifies at the trial or hearing and is subject to cross-examination concerning the statement, and the statement is (A) inconsistent with the declarant's testimony, and was given under oath subject to the penalty of perjury at a trial, hearing, or other proceeding, or in a deposition, or (B) consistent with the declarant's testimony and is offered to rebut an express or implied charge against the declarant of recent fabrication or improper influence or motive, or (C) one of identification of a person made after perceiving the person; or	**(1)** ***A Declarant-Witness's Prior Statement.*** The declarant testifies and is subject to cross-examination about the prior statement, and the statement: **(A)** is inconsistent with the declarant's testimony and was given under penalty of perjury at a trial, hearing, or other proceeding or in a deposition; **(B)** is consistent with the declarant's testimony and is offered to rebut an express or implied charge that the declarant recently fabricated it or acted from a recent improper influence or motive in so testifying; or **(C)** identifies a person as someone the declarant perceived earlier.

(2) Admission by party-opponent. The statement is offered against a party and is (A) the party's own statement, in either an individual or a representative capacity or (B) a statement of which the party has manifested an adoption or belief in its truth, or (C) a statement by a person authorized by the party to make a statement concerning the subject, or (D) a statement by the party's agent or servant concerning a matter within the scope of the agency or employment, made during the existence of the relationship, or (E) a statement by a coconspirator of a party during the course and in furtherance of the conspiracy. The contents of the statement shall be considered but are not alone sufficient to establish the declarant's authority under subdivision (C), the agency or employment relationship and scope thereof under subdivision (D), or the existence of the conspiracy and the participation therein of the declarant and the party against whom the statement is offered under subdivision (E).	**(2)** *An Opposing Party's Statement.* The statement is offered against an opposing party and: **(A)** was made by the party in an individual or representative capacity; **(B)** is one that the party appeared to adopt or accept as true; **(C)** was made by a person whom the party authorized to make a statement on the subject; **(D)** was made by the party's agent or employee on a matter within the scope of that relationship and while it existed; or **(E)** was made by the party's co-conspirator during and in furtherance of the conspiracy. The statement must be considered but does not by itself establish the declarant's authority under (C); the existence or scope of the relationship under (D); or the existence of the conspiracy or participation in it under (E).

Committee Note

The language of Rule 801 has been amended as part of the general restyling of the Evidence Rules to make them more easily understood and to make style and terminology consistent throughout the rules. These changes are intended to be stylistic only. There is no intent to change any result in any ruling on evidence admissibility.

Statements falling under the hearsay exclusion provided by Rule 801(d)(2) are no longer referred to as "admissions" in the title to the subdivision. The term "admissions" is confusing because not all statements covered by the exclusion are admissions in the colloquial sense — a statement can be within the exclusion even if it "admitted" nothing and was not against the party's interest when made. The term "admissions" also raises confusion in comparison with the Rule 804(b)(3) exception for declarations against interest. No change in application of the exclusion is intended.

Rule 802. Hearsay Rule	Rule 802. The Rule Against Hearsay
Hearsay is not admissible except as provided by these rules or by other rules prescribed by the Supreme Court pursuant to statutory authority or by Act of Congress.	Hearsay is not admissible unless any of the following provides otherwise: • a federal statute; • these rules; or • other rules prescribed by the Supreme Court.

Rule 803. Hearsay Exceptions; Availability of Declarant Immaterial	Rule 803. Exceptions to the Rule Against Hearsay — Regardless of Whether the Declarant Is Available as a Witness
The following are not excluded by the hearsay rule, even though the declarant is available as a witness:	The following are not excluded by the rule against hearsay, regardless of whether the declarant is available as a witness:
(1) Present sense impression. A statement describing or explaining an event or condition made while the declarant was perceiving the event or condition, or immediately thereafter.	(1) *Present Sense Impression.* A statement describing or explaining an event or condition, made while or immediately after the declarant perceived it.
(2) Excited utterance. A statement relating to a startling event or condition made while the declarant was under the stress of excitement caused by the event or condition.	(2) *Excited Utterance.* A statement relating to a startling event or condition, made while the declarant was under the stress or excitement that it caused.
(3) Then existing mental, emotional, or physical condition. A statement of the declarant's then existing state of mind, emotion, sensation, or physical condition (such as intent, plan, motive, design, mental feeling, pain, and bodily health), but not including a statement of memory or belief to prove the fact remembered or believed unless it relates to the execution, revocation, identification, or terms	(3) *Then-Existing Mental, Emotional, or Physical Condition.* A statement of the declarant's then-existing state of mind (such as motive, intent, or plan) or emotional, sensory, or physical condition (such as mental feeling, pain, or bodily health), but not including a statement of memory or belief to prove the fact remembered or believed unless it relates to the validity

of declarant's will.	or terms of the declarant's will.
(4) Statements for purposes of medical diagnosis or treatment. Statements made for purposes of medical diagnosis or treatment and describing medical history, or past or present symptoms, pain, or sensations, or the inception or general character of the cause or external source thereof insofar as reasonably pertinent to diagnosis or treatment.	(4) *Statement Made for Medical Diagnosis or Treatment.* A statement that: (A) is made for — and is reasonably pertinent to — medical diagnosis or treatment; and (B) describes medical history; past or present symptoms or sensations; their inception; or their general cause.
(5) Recorded recollection. A memorandum or record concerning a matter about which a witness once had knowledge but now has insufficient recollection to enable the witness to testify fully and accurately, shown to have been made or adopted by the witness when the matter was fresh in the witness' memory and to reflect that knowledge correctly. If admitted, the memorandum or record may be read into evidence but may not itself be received as an exhibit unless offered by an adverse party.	(5) *Recorded Recollection.* A record that: (A) is on a matter the witness once knew about but now cannot recall well enough to testify fully and accurately; (B) was made or adopted by the witness when the matter was fresh in the witness's memory; and (C) accurately reflects the witness's knowledge.

	If admitted, the record may be read into evidence but may be received as an exhibit only if offered by an adverse party.
(6) Records of regularly conducted activity. A memorandum, report, record, or data compilation, in any form, of acts, events, conditions, opinions, or diagnoses, made at or near the time by, or from information transmitted by, a person with knowledge, if kept in the course of a regularly conducted business activity, and if it was the regular practice of that business activity to make the memorandum, report, record or data compilation, all as shown by the testimony of the custodian or other qualified witness, or by certification that complies with Rule 902(11), Rule 902(12), or a statute permitting certification, unless the source of information or the method or circumstances of preparation indicate lack of trustworthiness. The term "business" as used in this paragraph includes business, institution, association, profession, occupation, and calling of every kind, whether or not conducted for profit.	**(6) Records of a Regularly Conducted Activity.** A record of an act, event, condition, opinion, or diagnosis if: **(A)** the record was made at or near the time by — or from information transmitted by — someone with knowledge; **(B)** the record was kept in the course of a regularly conducted activity of a business, organization, occupation, or calling, whether or not for profit; **(C)** making the record was a regular practice of that activity; and **(D)** all these conditions are shown by the testimony of the custodian or another qualified witness, or by a certification that complies with Rule 902(b)(11) or (12) or with a statute permitting certification.

	But this exception does not apply if the source of information or the method or circumstances of preparation indicate a lack of trustworthiness.
(7) Absence of entry in records kept in accordance with the provisions of paragraph (6). Evidence that a matter is not included in the memoranda reports, records, or data compilations, in any form, kept in accordance with the provisions of paragraph (6), to prove the nonoccurrence or nonexistence of the matter, if the matter was of a kind of which a memorandum, report, record, or data compilation was regularly made and preserved, unless the sources of information or other circumstances indicate lack of trustworthiness.	**(7)** *Absence of a Record of a Regularly Conducted Activity.* Evidence that a matter is not included in a record described in paragraph (6) if: **(A)** the evidence is admitted to prove that the matter did not occur or exist; and **(B)** a record was regularly kept for a matter of that kind. But this exception does not apply if the possible source of the information or other circumstances indicate a lack of trustworthiness.

(8) Public records and reports. Records, reports, statements, or data compilations, in any form, of public offices or agencies, setting forth (A) the activities of the office or agency, or (B) matters observed pursuant to duty imposed by law as to which matters there was a duty to report, excluding, however, in criminal cases matters observed by police officers and other law enforcement personnel, or (C) in civil actions and proceedings and against the Government in criminal cases, factual findings resulting from an investigation made pursuant to authority granted by law, unless the sources of information or other circumstances indicate lack of trustworthiness.	(8) ***Public Records.*** A record of a public office setting out: **(A)** the office's activities; **(B)** a matter observed while under a legal duty to report, but not including, in a criminal case, a matter observed by law-enforcement personnel; or **(C)** in a civil case or against the government in a criminal case, factual findings from a legally authorized investigation. But this exception does not apply if the source of information or other circumstances indicate a lack of trustworthiness.
(9) Records of vital statistics. Records or data compilations, in any form, of births, fetal deaths, deaths, or marriages, if the report thereof was made to a public office pursuant to requirements of law.	(9) ***Public Records of Vital Statistics.*** A record of a birth, death, or marriage, if reported to a public office in accordance with a legal duty.
(10) Absence of public record or entry. To prove the absence of a record, report, statement, or data compilation, in any form, or	(10) ***Absence of a Public Record.*** Testimony — or a certification under Rule 902 — that a diligent search failed to

the nonoccurrence or nonexistence of a matter of which a record, report, statement, or data compilation, in any form, was regularly made and preserved by a public office or agency, evidence in the form of a certification in accordance with rule 902, or testimony, that diligent search failed to disclose the record, report, statement, or data compilation, or entry.	disclose a public record if the testimony or certification is admitted to prove that: **(A)** the record does not exist; or **(B)** a matter did not occur or exist, even though a public office regularly kept a record for a matter of that kind.
(11) Records of religious organizations. Statements of births, marriages, divorces, deaths, legitimacy, ancestry, relationship by blood or marriage, or other similar facts of personal or family history, contained in a regularly kept record of a religious organization.	**(11) *Records of Religious Organizations Concerning Personal or Family History.*** A statement of birth, legitimacy, ancestry, marriage, divorce, death, relationship by blood or marriage, or similar facts of personal or family history, contained in a regularly kept record of a religious organization.
(12) Marriage, baptismal, and similar certificates. Statements of fact contained in a certificate that the maker performed a marriage or other ceremony or administered a sacrament, made by a clergyman, public official, or other person authorized by the rules or practices of a religious organization or by law to perform the act certified, and purporting to have been issued at the time of the act or within a reasonable time thereafter.	**(12) *Certificates of Marriage, Baptism, and Similar Ceremonies.*** A statement of fact contained in a certificate: **(A)** made by a person who is authorized by a religious organization or by law to perform the act certified; **(B)** attesting that the person performed a marriage or similar ceremony or

	administered a sacrament; and **(C)** purporting to have been issued at the time of the act or within a reasonable time after it.
(13) Family records. Statements of fact concerning personal or family history contained in family Bibles, genealogies, charts, engravings on rings, inscriptions on family portraits, engravings on urns, crypts, or tombstones, or the like.	**(13)** *Family Records.* A statement of fact about personal or family history contained in a family record, such as a Bible, genealogy, chart, engraving on a ring, inscription on a portrait, or engraving on an urn or burial marker.
(14) Records of documents affecting an interest in property. The record of a document purporting to establish or affect an interest in property, as proof of the content of the original recorded document and its execution and delivery by each person by whom it purports to have been executed, if the record is a record of a public office and an applicable statute authorizes the recording of documents of that kind in that office.	**(14)** *Records of Documents That Affect an Interest in Property.* The record of a document that purports to establish or affect an interest in property if: **(A)** the record is admitted to prove the content of the original recorded document, along with its signing and its delivery by each person who purports to have signed it; **(B)** the record is kept in a public office; and **(C)** a statute authorizes recording documents of

	that kind in that office.
(15) Statements in documents affecting an interest in property. A statement contained in a document purporting to establish or affect an interest in property if the matter stated was relevant to the purpose of the document, unless dealings with the property since the document was made have been inconsistent with the truth of the statement or the purport of the document.	*(15) **Statements in Documents That Affect an Interest in Property.*** A statement contained in a document that purports to establish or affect an interest in property if the matter stated was relevant to the document's purpose — unless later dealings with the property are inconsistent with the truth of the statement or the purport of the document.
(16) Statements in ancient documents. Statements in a document in existence twenty years or more the authenticity of which is established.	*(16) **Statements in Ancient Documents.*** A statement in a document that is at least 20 years old and whose authenticity is established.
(17) Market reports, commercial publications. Market quotations, tabulations, lists, directories, or other published compilations, generally used and relied upon by the public or by persons in particular occupations.	*(17) **Market Reports and Similar Commercial Publications.*** Market quotations, lists, directories, or other compilations that are generally relied on by the public or by persons in particular occupations.

(18) Learned treatises. To the extent called to the attention of an expert witness upon cross-examination or relied upon by the expert witness in direct examination, statements contained in published treatises, periodicals, or pamphlets on a subject of history, medicine, or other science or art, established as a reliable authority by the testimony or admission of the witness or by other expert testimony or by judicial notice. If admitted, the statements may be read into evidence but may not be received as exhibits.	**(18) *Statements in Learned Treatises, Periodicals, or Pamphlets.*** A statement contained in a treatise, periodical, or pamphlet if: **(A)** the statement is called to the attention of an expert witness on cross-examination or relied on by the expert on direct examination; and **(B)** the publication is established as a reliable authority by the expert's admission or testimony, by another expert's testimony, or by judicial notice. If admitted, the statement may be read into evidence but not received as an exhibit.
(19) Reputation concerning personal or family history. Reputation among members of a person's family by blood, adoption, or marriage, or among a person's associates, or in the community, concerning a person's birth, adoption, marriage, divorce, death, legitimacy, relationship by blood, adoption, or marriage, ancestry, or other similar fact of personal or family history.	**(19) *Reputation Concerning Personal or Family History.*** A reputation among a person's family by blood, adoption, or marriage — or among a person's associates or in the community — concerning the person's birth, adoption, legitimacy, ancestry, marriage, divorce, death, relationship by blood, adoption, or marriage, or similar facts of personal or family history.

(20) Reputation concerning boundaries or general history. Reputation in a community, arising before the controversy, as to boundaries of or customs affecting lands in the community, and reputation as to events of general history important to the community or State or nation in which located.	**(20) *Reputation Concerning Boundaries or General History.*** A reputation in a community — arising before the controversy — concerning boundaries of land in the community or customs that affect the land, or concerning general historical events important to that community, state, or nation.
(21) Reputation as to character. Reputation of a person's character among associates or in the community.	**(21) *Reputation Concerning Character.*** A reputation among a person's associates or in the community concerning the person's character.
(22) Judgment of previous conviction. Evidence of a final judgment, entered after a trial or upon a plea of guilty (but not upon a plea of nolo contendere), adjudging a person guilty of a crime punishable by death or imprisonment in excess of one year, to prove any fact essential to sustain the judgment, but not including, when offered by the Government in a criminal prosecution for purposes other than impeachment, judgments against persons other than the accused. The pendency of an appeal may be shown but does not affect admissibility.	**(22) *Judgment of a Previous Conviction.*** Evidence of a final judgment of conviction if: **(A)** the judgment was entered after a trial or guilty plea, but not a nolo contendere plea; **(B)** the judgment was for a crime punishable by death or by imprisonment for more than a year; **(C)** the evidence is admitted to prove any fact essential to the judgment; and

	(D) when offered by the prosecutor in a criminal case for a purpose other than impeachment, the judgment was against the defendant. The pendency of an appeal may be shown but does not affect admissibility.
(23) Judgment as to personal, family, or general history, or boundaries. Judgments as proof of matters of personal, family or general history, or boundaries, essential to the judgment, if the same would be provable by evidence of reputation.	**(23) Judgments Involving Personal, Family, or General History or a Boundary.** A judgment that is admitted to prove a matter of personal, family, or general history, or boundaries, if the matter: **(A)** was essential to the judgment; and **(B)** could be proved by evidence of reputation.
(24) [Other exceptions.] [Transferred to Rule 807]	**(24) [Other exceptions.]** [Transferred to Rule 807]

Rule 804. Hearsay Exceptions; Declarant Unavailable	Rule 804. Exceptions to the Rule Against Hearsay — When the Declarant Is Unavailable as a Witness
(a) Definition of unavailability. "Unavailability as a witness" includes situations in which the declarant—	**(a) Criteria for Being Unavailable.** A declarant is considered to be unavailable as a witness if the declarant:
(1) is exempted by ruling of the court on the ground of privilege from testifying concerning the subject matter of the declarant's statement; or	**(1)** is exempted by a court ruling on the ground of having a privilege to not testify about the subject matter of the declarant's statement;
(2) persists in refusing to testify concerning the subject matter of the declarant's statement despite an order of the court to do so; or	**(2)** refuses to testify about the subject matter despite a court order to do so;
(3) testifies to a lack of memory of the subject matter of the declarant's statement; or	**(3)** testifies to not remembering the subject matter;
(4) is unable to be present or to testify at the hearing because of death or then existing physical or mental illness or infirmity; or	**(4)** cannot be present or testify at the trial or hearing because of death or a then-existing infirmity, physical illness, or mental illness; or
(5) is absent from the hearing and the proponent of a statement has been unable to procure the declarant's attendance (or in the case of a hearsay exception under subdivision (b)(2), (3), or (4), the declarant's attendance or testimony) by process or other	**(5)** is absent from the trial or hearing and the statement's proponent has not been able, by process or other reasonable means, to procure:

reasonable means. A declarant is not unavailable as a witness if exemption, refusal, claim of lack of memory, inability, or absence is due to the procurement or wrongdoing of the proponent of a statement for the purpose of preventing the witness from attending or testifying.	**(A)** the declarant's attendance, in the case of a hearsay exception under Rule 804(b)(1) or (5); or **(B)** the declarant's attendance or testimony, in the case of a hearsay exception under Rule 804(b)(2), (3), or (4). But this subdivision (a) does not apply if the statement's proponent procured or wrongfully caused the declarant's unavailability in order to prevent the declarant from attending or testifying.
(b) Hearsay exceptions. The following are not excluded by the hearsay rule if the declarant is unavailable as a witness: **(1) Former testimony.** Testimony given as a witness at another hearing of the same or a different proceeding, or in a deposition taken in compliance with law in the course of the same or another proceeding, if the party against whom the testimony is now offered, or, in a civil action or proceeding, a predecessor in interest, had an opportunity and similar motive to develop the testimony by direct, cross, or	**(b) The Exceptions.** The following are not excluded by the rule against hearsay if the declarant is unavailable as a witness: **(1)** *Former Testimony.* Testimony that: **(A)** was given as a witness at a trial, hearing, or lawful deposition, whether given during the current proceeding or a different one; and

redirect examination.	**(B)** is now offered against a party who had — or, in a civil case, whose predecessor in interest had — an opportunity and similar motive to develop it by direct, cross-, or redirect examination.
(2) Statement under belief of impending death. In a prosecution for homicide or in a civil action or proceeding, a statement made by a declarant while believing that the declarant's death was imminent, concerning the cause or circumstances of what the declarant believed to be impending death.	**(2) *Statement Under the Belief of Imminent Death.*** In a prosecution for homicide or in a civil case, a statement that the declarant, while believing the declarant's death to be imminent, made about its cause or circumstances.
(3) Statement against interest. A statement that: **(A)** a reasonable person in the declarant's position would have made only if the person believed it to be true because, when made, it was so contrary to the declarant's proprietary or pecuniary interest or had so great a tendency to invalidate the declarant's claim against someone else or to expose the declarant to civil or criminal liability; and (B) is supported **by** corroborating circumstances that clearly indicate its trustworthiness, if it is offered in a criminal case as one that tends to expose the declarant to criminal liability.	(3) Statement against interest. A statement that: **(A)** a reasonable person in the declarant's position would have made only if the person believed it to be true because, when made, it was so contrary to the declarant's proprietary or pecuniary interest or had so great a tendency to invalidate the declarant's claim against someone else or to expose the declarant to civil or criminal liability; and (B) is supported **by** corroborating circumstances that clearly indicate its trustworthiness, if it is offered in a criminal case as one that tends to expose the declarant to criminal liability.

(4) Statement of personal or family history. (A) A statement concerning the declarant's own birth, adoption, marriage, divorce, legitimacy, relationship by blood, adoption, or marriage, ancestry, or other similar fact of personal or family history, even though declarant had no means of acquiring personal knowledge of the matter stated; or (B) a statement concerning the foregoing matters, and death also, of another person, if the declarant was related to the other by blood, adoption, or marriage or was so intimately associated with the other's family as to be likely to have accurate information concerning the matter declared.	**(4)** *Statement of Personal or Family History.* A statement about: **(A)** the declarant's own birth, adoption, legitimacy, ancestry, marriage, divorce, relationship by blood or marriage, or similar facts of personal or family history, even though the declarant had no way of acquiring personal knowledge about that fact; or **(B)** another person concerning any of these facts, as well as death, if the declarant was related to the person by blood, adoption, or marriage or was so intimately associated with the person's family that the declarant's information is likely to be accurate.
(5) [Other exceptions.] [Transferred to Rule 807] **(6) Forfeiture by wrongdoing.** A statement offered against a party that has engaged or acquiesced in wrongdoing that was intended to, and did, procure the unavailability of the declarant as a witness.	**(5)** *Statement Offered Against a Party Who Wrongfully Caused the Declarant's Unavailability.* A statement offered against the party that wrongfully caused — or acquiesced in wrongfully causing — the declarant's unavailability in order to prevent the declarant from attending or testifying.

Committee Note

The language of Rule 804 has been amended as part of the general restyling of the Evidence Rules to make them more easily understood and to make style and terminology consistent throughout the rules. These changes are intended to be stylistic only. There is no intent to change any result in any ruling on evidence admissibility.

The amendment to Rule 804(b)(3) provides that the corroborating circumstances requirement applies not only to declarations against penal interest offered by the defendant in a criminal case, but also to such statements offered by the government. The language in the original rule does not so provide, but a proposed amendment to Rule 804(b)(3) — released for public comment in 2008 and scheduled to be enacted before the restyled rules — explicitly extends the corroborating circumstances requirement to statements offered by the government . . . .

No comment opposed requiring the government to show corroborating circumstances. Two comments suggested that although the government should **be** required to show corroborating circumstances, the defendant should not.

The Advisory Committee rejected that suggestion. One comment suggested the rule should be amended further to overturn a controlling Supreme Court decision on another aspect of the rule. The Advisory Committee rejected that suggestion.

Rule 804(b)(6) has been renumbered to fill a gap left when the original Rule 804(b)(5) was transferred to Rule 807.

Rule 805. Hearsay Within Hearsay	Rule 805. Hearsay Within Hearsay
Hearsay included within hearsay is not excluded under the hearsay rule if each part of the combined statements conforms with an exception to the hearsay rule provided in these rules.	Hearsay within hearsay is not excluded by the rule against hearsay if each part of the combined statements conforms with an exception to the rule.

Rule 806. Attacking and Supporting Credibility of Declarant	Rule 806. Attacking and Supporting the Declarant's Credibility
When a hearsay statement, or a statement defined in Rule 801(d)(2)(C), (D), or (E), has been admitted in evidence, the credibility of the declarant may be attacked, and if attacked may be supported, by any evidence which would be admissible for those purposes if declarant had testified as a witness. Evidence of a statement or conduct by the declarant at any time, inconsistent with the declarant's hearsay statement, is not subject to any requirement that the declarant may have been afforded an opportunity to deny or explain. If the party against whom a hearsay statement has been admitted calls the declarant as a witness, the party is entitled to examine the declarant on the statement as if under cross-examination.	When a hearsay statement — or a statement described in Rule 801(d)(2)(C), (D), or (E) — has been admitted in evidence, the declarant's credibility may be attacked, and then supported, by any evidence that would be admissible for those purposes if the declarant had testified as a witness. The court may admit evidence of the declarant's inconsistent statement or conduct, regardless of when it occurred or whether the declarant had an opportunity to explain or deny it. If the party against whom the statement was admitted calls the declarant as a witness, the party may examine the declarant on the statement as if on cross-examination.

EXISTING AND PROPOSED FEDERAL RULES OF EVIDENCE

Rule 807. Residual Exception	Rule 807. Residual Exception
A statement not specifically covered by Rule 803 or 804 but having equivalent circumstantial guarantees of trustworthiness, is not excluded by the hearsay rule, if the court determines that (A) the statement is offered as evidence of a material fact; (B) the statement is more probative on the point for which it is offered than any other evidence which the proponent can procure through reasonable efforts; and (C) the general purposes of these rules and the interests of justice will best be served by admission of the statement into evidence. However, a statement may not be admitted under this exception unless the proponent of it makes known to the adverse party sufficiently in advance of the trial or hearing to provide the adverse party with a fair opportunity to prepare to meet it, the proponent's intention to offer the statement and the particulars of it, including the name and address of the declarant.	**(a) In General.** Under the following circumstances, a hearsay statement is not excluded by the rule against hearsay even if the statement is not specifically covered by a hearsay exception in Rule 803 or 804: **(1)** the statement has equivalent circumstantial guarantees of trustworthiness; **(2)** it is offered as evidence of a material fact; **(3)** it is more probative on the point for which it is offered than any other evidence that the proponent can obtain through reasonable efforts; and **(4)** admitting it will best serve the purposes of these rules and the interests of justice. **(b) Notice.** The statement is admissible only if, before the trial or hearing, the proponent gives an adverse party reasonable notice of the intent to offer the statement and its particulars, including the declarant's name and address, so that the party has a fair opportunity to meet it.

ARTICLE IX. AUTHENTICATION AND IDENTIFICATION	ARTICLE IX. AUTHENTICATION AND IDENTIFICATION
Rule 901. Requirement of Authentication or Identification	**Rule 901. Authenticating or Identifying Evidence**
(a) General provision. The requirement of authentication or identification as a condition precedent to admissibility is satisfied by evidence sufficient to support a finding that the matter in question is what its proponent claims.	**(a) In General.** To authenticate or identify an item of evidence in order to have it admitted, the proponent must produce evidence sufficient to support a finding that the item is what the proponent claims it is.
(b) Illustrations. By way of illustration only, and not by way of limitation, the following are examples of authentication or identification conforming with the requirements of this rule:	**(b) Examples.** The following are examples only — not a complete list — of evidence that satisfies the requirement:
(1) Testimony of witness with knowledge. Testimony that a matter is what it is claimed to be.	**(1) Testimony of a Witness with Knowledge.** Testimony that an item is what it is claimed to be.
(2) Nonexpert opinion on handwriting. Nonexpert opinion as to the genuineness of handwriting, based upon familiarity not acquired for purposes of the litigation.	**(2) Nonexpert Opinion About Handwriting.** A nonexpert's opinion that handwriting is genuine, based on a familiarity with it that was not acquired for the current litigation.

EXISTING AND PROPOSED FEDERAL RULES OF EVIDENCE 1009

(3) Comparison by trier or expert witness. Comparison by the trier of fact or by expert witnesses with specimens which have been authenticated.	**(3) *Comparison by an Expert Witness or the Trier of Fact.*** A comparison with an authenticated specimen by an expert witness or the trier of fact.
(4) Distinctive characteristics and the like. Appearance, contents, substance, internal patterns, or other distinctive characteristics, taken in conjunction with circumstances.	**(4) *Distinctive Characteristics and the Like.*** The appearance, contents, substance, internal patterns, or other distinctive characteristics of the item, taken together with all the circumstances.
(5) Voice identification. Identification of a voice, whether heard firsthand or through mechanical or electronic transmission or recording, by opinion based upon hearing the voice at any time under circumstances connecting it with the alleged speaker.	**(5) *Opinion About a Voice.*** An opinion identifying a person's voice — whether heard firsthand or through mechanical or electronic transmission or recording — based on hearing the voice at any time under circumstances that connect it with the alleged speaker.
(6) Telephone conversations. Telephone conversations, by evidence that a call was made to the number assigned at the time by the telephone company to a particular person or business, if (A) in the case of a person, circumstances, including self-identification, show the person answering to be the one called, or (B) in the case of a business, the call was made to a place of business and the conversation related to business reasonably transacted over the telephone.	**(6) *Evidence About a Telephone Conversation.*** For a telephone conversation, evidence that a call was made to the number assigned at the time to: **(A)** a particular person, if circumstances, including self-identification, show that the person answering was the one called; or **(B)** a particular business, if the call was made to a business

	and the call related to business reasonably transacted over the telephone.
(7) Public records or reports. Evidence that a writing authorized by law to be recorded or filed and in fact recorded or filed in a public office, or a purported public record, report, statement, or data compilation, in any form, is from the public office where items of this nature are kept.	**(7) Evidence About Public Records.** Evidence that: **(A)** a record is from the public office where items of this kind are kept; or **(B)** a document was lawfully recorded or filed in a public office.
(8) Ancient documents or data compilation. Evidence that a document or data compilation, in any form, (A) is in such condition as to create no suspicion concerning its authenticity, (B) was in a place where it, if authentic, would likely be, and (C) has been in existence 20 years or more at the time it is offered.	**(8) Evidence About Ancient Documents or Data Compilations.** For a document or data compilation, evidence that it: **(A)** is in a condition that creates no suspicion about its authenticity; **(B)** was in a place where, if authentic, it would likely be; and **(C)** is at least 20 years old when offered.

(9) Process or system. Evidence describing a process or system used to produce a result and showing that the process or system produces an accurate result.	**(9) Evidence About a Process or System.** Evidence describing a process or system and showing that it produces an accurate result.
(10) Methods provided by statute or rule. Any method of authentication or identification provided by Act of Congress or by other rules prescribed by the Supreme Court pursuant to statutory authority.	**(10) Methods Provided by a Statute or Rule.** Any method of authentication or identification allowed by a federal statute or a rule prescribed by the Supreme Court.

Rule 902. Self-authentication	Rule 902. Evidence That Is Self-Authenticating
Extrinsic evidence of authenticity as a condition precedent to admissibility is not required with respect to the following:	The following items of evidence are self-authenticating; they require no extrinsic evidence of authenticity in order to be admitted:
(1) Domestic public documents under seal. A document bearing a seal purporting to be that of the United States, or of any State, district, Commonwealth, territory, or insular possession thereof, or the Panama Canal Zone, or the Trust Territory of the Pacific Islands, or of a political subdivision, department, officer, or agency thereof, and a signature purporting to be an attestation or execution.	(1) *Domestic Public Documents That Are Signed and Sealed.* A document that bears: **(A)** a signature purporting to be an execution or attestation; and **(B)** a seal purporting to be that of the United States; any state, district, commonwealth, territory, or insular possession of the United States; the former Panama Canal Zone; the Trust Territory of the Pacific Islands; a political subdivision of any of these entities; or a department, agency, or officer of any entity named above.

EXISTING AND PROPOSED FEDERAL RULES OF EVIDENCE

(2) Domestic public documents not under seal. A document purporting to bear the signature in the official capacity of an officer or employee of any entity included in paragraph (1) hereof, having no seal, if a public officer having a seal and having official duties in the district or political subdivision of the officer or employee certifies under seal that the signer has the official capacity and that the signature is genuine.	**(2) Domestic Public Documents That Are Signed But Not Sealed.** A document that bears no seal if: **(A)** it bears the signature of an officer or employee of an entity named in Rule 902(1)(B); and **(B)** another public officer who has a seal and official duties within that same entity certifies under seal — or its equivalent — that the signer has the official capacity and that the signature is genuine.
(3) Foreign public documents. A document purporting to be executed or attested in an official capacity by a person authorized by the laws of a foreign country to make the execution or attestation, and accompanied by a final certification as to the genuineness of the signature and official position (A) of the executing or attesting person, or (B) of any foreign official whose certificate of genuineness of signature and official position relates to the execution or attestation or is in a chain of certificates of genuineness of signature and official position relating to the execution or attestation. A final certification may be made by a secretary of an embassy or legation, consul	**(3) Foreign Public Documents.** A document that purports to be signed or attested by a person who is authorized by a foreign country's law to do so. The document must be accompanied by a final certification that certifies the genuineness of the signature and official position of the signer or attester — or of any foreign official whose certificate of genuineness relates to the signature or attestation or is in a chain of certificates of genuineness relating to the signature or attestation. The certification may be made by a secretary of a United States embassy or

general, consul, vice consul, or consular agent of the United States, or a diplomatic or consular official of the foreign country assigned or accredited to the United States. If reasonable opportunity has been given to all parties to investigate the authenticity and accuracy of official documents, the court may, for good cause shown, order that they be treated as presumptively authentic without final certification or permit them to be evidenced by an attested summary with or without final certification.	legation; by a consul general, vice consul, or consular agent of the United States; or by a diplomatic or consular official of the foreign country assigned or accredited to the United States. If all parties have been given a reasonable opportunity to investigate the document's authenticity and accuracy, the court may, for good cause, either: **(A)** order that it be treated as presumptively authentic without final certification; or **(B)** allow it to be evidenced by an attested summary with or without final certification.
(4) Certified copies of public records. A copy of an official record or report or entry therein, or of a document authorized by law to be recorded or filed and actually recorded or filed in a public office, including data compilations in any form, certified as correct by the custodian or other person authorized to make the certification, by certificate complying with paragraph (1), (2), or (3) of this rule or complying with any Act of Congress or rule prescribed by the Supreme Court pursuant to statutory authority.	**(4) *Certified Copies of Public Records.*** A copy of an official record — or a copy of a document that was lawfully recorded or filed in a public office — if the copy is certified as correct by: **(A)** the custodian or another person authorized to make the certification; or **(B)** a certificate that complies with Rule

	902(1), (2), or (3), a federal statute, or a rule prescribed by the Supreme Court.
(5) Official publications. Books, pamphlets, or other publications purporting to be issued by public authority.	(5) *Official Publications.* A book, pamphlet, or other publication purporting to be issued by a public authority.
(6) Newspapers and periodicals. Printed materials purporting to be newspapers or periodicals.	(6) *Newspapers and Periodicals.* Printed material purporting to be a newspaper or periodical.
(7) Trade inscriptions and the like. Inscriptions, signs, tags, or labels purporting to have been affixed in the course of business and indicating ownership, control, or origin.	(7) *Trade Inscriptions and the Like.* An inscription, sign, tag, or label purporting to have been affixed in the course of business and indicating origin, ownership, or control.
(8) Acknowledged documents. Documents accompanied by a certificate of acknowledgment executed in the manner provided by law by a notary public or other officer authorized by law to take acknowledgments.	(8) *Acknowledged Documents.* A document accompanied by a certificate of acknowledgment that is lawfully signed by a notary public or another officer who is authorized to take acknowledgments.

(9) Commercial paper and related documents. Commercial paper, signatures thereon, and documents relating thereto to the extent provided by general commercial law.	**(9) *Commercial Paper and Related Documents.*** Commercial paper, a signature on it, and related documents, to the extent allowed by general commercial law.
(10) Presumptions under Acts of Congress. Any signature, document, or other matter declared by Act of Congress to be presumptively or prima facie genuine or authentic.	**(10) *Presumptions Under a Federal Statute.*** A signature, document, or anything else that a federal statute declares to be presumptively or prima facie genuine or authentic.
(11) Certified domestic records of regularly conducted activity. The original or a duplicate of a domestic record of regularly conducted activity that would be admissible under Rule 803(6) if accompanied by a written declaration of its custodian or other qualified person, in a manner complying with any Act of Congress or rule prescribed by the Supreme Court pursuant to statutory authority, certifying that the record— **(A)** was made at or near the time of the occurrence of the matters set forth by, or from information transmitted by, a person with knowledge of those matters; **(B)** was kept in the course of the regularly conducted	**(11) *Certified Domestic Records of a Regularly Conducted Activity.*** The original or a copy of a domestic record that meets the requirements of Rule 803(6), modified as follows: the conditions referred to in 803(6)(D) must be shown by a certification of the custodian or another qualified person that complies with a federal statute or a rule prescribed by the Supreme Court. Before the trial or hearing, the proponent must give an adverse party reasonable written notice of the intent to offer the record — and must make the record and certification available for inspection — so that the party has a fair opportunity to challenge them.

activity; and **(C)** was made by the regularly conducted activity as a regular practice. A party intending to offer a record into evidence under this paragraph must provide written notice of that intention to all adverse parties, and must make the record and declaration available for inspection sufficiently in advance of their offer into evidence to provide an adverse party with a fair opportunity to challenge them.	
(12) Certified foreign records of regularly conducted activity. In a civil case, the original or a duplicate of a foreign record of regularly conducted activity that would be admissible under Rule 803(6) if accompanied by a written declaration by its custodian or other qualified person certifying that the record— **(A)** was made at or near the time of the occurrence of the matters set forth by, or from information transmitted by, a person with knowledge of those matters; **(B)** was kept in the course of the regularly conducted activity; and	**(12)** *Certified Foreign Records of a Regularly Conducted Activity.* In a civil case, the original or a copy of a foreign record that meets the requirements of Rule 902(11), modified as follows: the certification, rather than complying with a federal statute or Supreme Court rule, must be signed in a manner that, if falsely made, would subject the maker to a criminal penalty in the country where the certification is signed. The proponent must also meet the notice requirements of Rule 902(11).

(C) was made by the regularly conducted activity as a regular practice. The declaration must be signed in a manner that, if falsely made, would subject the maker to criminal penalty under the laws of the country where the declaration is signed. A party intending to offer a record into evidence under this paragraph must provide written notice of that intention to all adverse parties, and must make the record and declaration available for inspection sufficiently in advance of their offer into evidence to provide an adverse party with a fair opportunity to challenge them.	

Rule 903. Subscribing Witness' Testimony Unnecessary	**Rule 903. Subscribing Witness's Testimony**
The testimony of a subscribing witness is not necessary to authenticate a writing unless required by the laws of the jurisdiction whose laws govern the validity of the writing.	A subscribing witness's testimony is necessary to authenticate a writing only if required by the law of the jurisdiction that governs its validity.

ARTICLE X. CONTENTS OF WRITINGS, RECORDINGS, AND PHOTOGRAPHS **Rule 1001. Definitions**	**ARTICLE X. CONTENTS OF WRITINGS, RECORDINGS, AND PHOTOGRAPHS** **Rule 1001. Definitions That Apply to This Article**
For purposes of this article the following definitions are applicable: **(1) Writings and recordings.** "Writings" and "recordings" consist of letters, words, or numbers, or their equivalent, set down by handwriting, typewriting, printing, photostating, photographing, magnetic impulse, mechanical or electronic recording, or other form of data compilation. **(2) Photographs.** "Photographs" include still photographs, X-ray films, video tapes, and motion pictures. **(3) Original.** An "original" of a writing or recording is the writing or recording itself or any counterpart intended to have the same effect by a person executing or issuing it. An "original" of a photograph includes the negative or any print therefrom. If data are stored in a computer or similar device, any printout or other output readable by sight, shown to reflect the data	In this article, the following definitions apply: **(a) Writing.** A "writing" consists of letters, words, numbers, or their equivalent set down in any form. **(b) Recording.** A "recording" consists of letters, words, numbers, or their equivalent recorded in any manner. **(c) Photograph.** "Photograph" means a photographic image or its equivalent stored in any form. **(d) Original.** An "original" of a writing or recording means the writing or recording itself or any counterpart intended to have the same effect by the person who executed or issued it. For electronically stored information, "original" means any printout — or other output readable by sight — if it accurately reflects the information. An "original" of a photograph includes the

accurately, is an "original".	negative or a print from it.
(4) Duplicate. A "duplicate" is a counterpart produced by the same impression as the original, or from the same matrix, or by means of photography, including enlargements and miniatures, or by mechanical or electronic re-recording, or by chemical reproduction, or by other equivalent techniques which accurately reproduces the original.	**(e) Duplicate.** "Duplicate" means a counterpart produced by a mechanical, photographic, chemical, electronic, or other equivalent process or technique that accurately reproduces the original.

Rule 1002. Requirement of Original	Rule 1002. Requirement of the Original
To prove the content of a writing, recording, or photograph, the original writing, recording, or photograph is required, except as otherwise provided in these rules or by Act of Congress.	An original writing, recording, or photograph is required in order to prove its content unless these rules or a federal statute provides otherwise.

Rule 1003. Admissibility of Duplicates	Rule 1003. Admissibility of Duplicates
A duplicate is admissible to the same extent as an original unless (1) a genuine question is raised as to the authenticity of the original or (2) in the circumstances it would be unfair to admit the duplicate in lieu of the original.	A duplicate is admissible to the same extent as the original unless a genuine question is raised about the original's authenticity or the circumstances make it unfair to admit the duplicate.

Rule 1004. Admissibility of Other Evidence of Contents	Rule 1004. Admissibility of Other Evidence of Content
The original is not required, and other evidence of the contents of a writing, recording, or photograph is admissible if—	An original is not required and other evidence of the content of a writing, recording, or photograph is admissible if:
(1) Originals lost or destroyed. All originals are lost or have been destroyed, unless the proponent lost or destroyed them in bad faith; or	**(a)** all the originals are lost or destroyed, and not by the proponent acting in bad faith;
(2) Original not obtainable. No original can be obtained by any available judicial process or procedure; or	**(b)** an original cannot be obtained by any available judicial process;
(3) Original in possession of opponent. At a time when an original was under the control of the party against whom offered, that party was put on notice, by the pleadings or otherwise, that the contents would be a subject of proof at the hearing, and that party does not produce the original at the hearing; or	**(c)** the party against whom the original would be offered had control of the original; was at that time put on notice, by pleadings or otherwise, that the original would be a subject of proof at the trial or hearing; and fails to produce it at the trial or hearing; or
(4) Collateral matters. The writing, recording, or photograph is not closely related to a controlling issue.	**(d)** the writing, recording, or photograph is not closely related to a controlling issue.

Rule 1005. Public Records	Rule 1005. Copies of Public Records to Prove Content
The contents of an official record, or of a document authorized to be recorded or filed and actually recorded or filed, including data compilations in any form, if otherwise admissible, may be proved by copy, certified as correct in accordance with rule 902 or testified to be correct by a witness who has compared it with the original. If a copy which complies with the foregoing cannot be obtained by the exercise of reasonable diligence, then other evidence of the contents may be given.	The proponent may use a copy to prove the content of an official record — or of a document that was lawfully recorded or filed in a public office — if these conditions are met: the record or document is otherwise admissible; and the copy is certified as correct in accordance with Rule 902(4) or is testified to be correct by a witness who has compared it with the original. If no such copy can be obtained by reasonable diligence, then the proponent may use other evidence to prove the content.

Rule 1006. Summaries	Rule 1006. Summaries to Prove Content
The contents of voluminous writings, recordings, or photographs which cannot conveniently be examined in court may be presented in the form of a chart, summary, or calculation. The originals, or duplicates, shall be made available for examination or copying, or both, by other parties at reasonable time and place. The court may order that they be produced in court.	The proponent may use a summary, chart, or calculation to prove the content of voluminous writings, recordings, or photographs that cannot be conveniently examined in court. The proponent must make the originals or duplicates available for examination or copying, or both, by other parties at a reasonable time or place. And the court may order the proponent to produce them in court.

Rule 1007. Testimony or Written Admission of Party	Rule 1007. Testimony or Admission of a Party to Prove Content
Contents of writings, recordings, or photographs may be proved by the testimony or deposition of the party against whom offered or by that party's written admission, without accounting for the nonproduction of the original.	The proponent may prove the content of a writing, recording, or photograph by the testimony, deposition, or written admission of the party against whom the evidence is offered. The proponent need not account for the original.

Rule 1008. Functions of Court and Jury	Rule 1008. Functions of the Court and Jury
When the admissibility of other evidence of contents of writings, recordings, or photographs under these rules depends upon the fulfillment of a condition of fact, the question whether the condition has been fulfilled is ordinarily for the court to determine in accordance with the provisions of rule 104. However, when an issue is raised (a) whether the asserted writing ever existed, or (b) whether another writing, recording, or photograph produced at the trial is the original, or (c) whether other evidence of contents correctly reflects the contents, the issue is for the trier of fact to determine as in the case of other issues of fact.	Ordinarily, the court determines whether the proponent has fulfilled the factual conditions for admitting other evidence of the content of a writing, recording, or photograph under Rule 1004 or 1005. But in a jury trial, the jury determines — in accordance with Rule 104(b) — any issue about whether: **(a)** an asserted writing, recording, or photograph ever existed; **(b)** another one produced at the trial or hearing is the original; or **(c)** other evidence of content accurately reflects the content.

ARTICLE XI. MISCELLANEOUS RULES **Rule 1101. Applicability of Rules**	**ARTICLE XI. MISCELLANEOUS RULES** **Rule 1101. Applicability of the Rules**
(a) Courts and judges. These rules apply to the United States district courts, the District Court of Guam, the District Court of the Virgin Islands, the District Court for the Northern Mariana Islands, the United States courts of appeals, the United States Claims Court, and to United States bankruptcy judges and United States magistrate judges, in the actions, cases, and proceedings and to the extent hereinafter set forth. The terms ''judge'' and ''court'' in these rules include United States bankruptcy judges and United States magistrate judges.	**(a) To Courts and Judges.** These rules apply to proceedings before: - United States district courts; - United States bankruptcy and magistrate judges; - United States courts of appeals; - the United States Court of Federal Claims; and - the district courts of Guam, the Virgin Islands, and the Northern Mariana Islands.
(b) Proceedings generally. These rules apply generally to civil actions and proceedings, including admiralty and maritime cases, to criminal cases and proceedings, to contempt proceedings except those in which the court may act summarily, and to proceedings and cases under title 11, United States Code.	**(b) To Proceedings.** These rules apply in: - civil cases and proceedings, including admiralty and maritime cases; - criminal cases and proceedings; - contempt proceedings, except those in which the court may act summarily; and - cases and proceedings under 11 U.S.C.
(c) Rule of privilege. The rule with respect to privileges applies at all stages of all actions, cases, and	**(c) Rules on Privilege.** The rules on privilege apply to all stages of a case or proceeding.

proceedings.	
(d) Rules inapplicable. The rules (other than with respect to privileges) do not apply in the following situations: **(1) Preliminary questions of fact.** The determination of questions of fact preliminary to admissibility of evidence when the issue is to be determined by the court under rule 104. **(2) Grand jury.** Proceedings before grand juries. **(3) Miscellaneous proceedings.** Proceedings for extradition or rendition; preliminary examinations in criminal cases; sentencing, or granting or revoking probation; issuance of warrants for arrest, criminal summonses, and search warrants; and proceedings with respect to release on bail or otherwise.	**(d) Exceptions.** These rules — except for those on privilege — do not apply to the following: (1) the court's determination, under Rule 104(a), on a preliminary question of fact governing admissibility; (2) grand-jury proceedings; and (3) miscellaneous proceedings such as: - extradition or rendition; - issuing an arrest warrant, criminal summons, or search warrant; - a preliminary examination in a criminal case; - sentencing; - granting or revoking probation or supervised release; and - considering whether to release on bail or otherwise.

(e) Rules applicable in part. In the following proceedings these rules apply to the extent that matters of evidence are not provided for in the statutes which govern procedure therein or in other rules prescribed by the Supreme Court pursuant to statutory authority: the trial of misdemeanors and other petty offenses before United States magistrate judges; review of agency actions when the facts are subject to trial de novo under section 706(2)(F) of title 5, United States Code; review of orders of the Secretary of Agriculture under section 2 of the Act entitled "An Act to authorize association of producers of agricultural products" approved February 18, 1922 (7 U.S.C. 292), and under sections 6 and 7(c) of the Perishable Agricultural Commodities Act, 1930 (7 U.S.C. 499f, 499g(c)); naturalization and revocation of naturalization under sections 310–318 of the Immigration and Nationality Act (8 U.S.C. 1421–1429); prize proceedings in admiralty under sections 7651–7681 of title 10, United States Code; review of orders of the Secretary of the Interior under section 2 of the Act entitled "An Act authorizing associations of producers of aquatic products" approved June 25, 1934 (15 U.S.C. 522); review of orders of petroleum control boards under section 5 of the Act entitled "An Act to regulate interstate and foreign commerce in petroleum and its products by prohibiting the shipment in such commerce of petroleum and its products produced in violation of State law, and for other purposes", approved February 22, 1935 (15 U.S.C. 715d); actions for fines, penalties, or forfeitures under part V of title IV of the Tariff Act of 1930 (19 U.S.C. 1581–1624), or under the Anti-Smuggling Act (19 U.S.C. 1701–1711); criminal libel for condemnation, exclusion of imports, or other	**(e) Other Statutes and Rules.** A federal statute or a rule prescribed by the Supreme Court may provide for admitting or excluding evidence independently from these rules.

proceedings under the Federal Food, Drug, and Cosmetic Act (21 U.S.C. 301–392); disputes between seamen under sections 4079, 4080, and 4081 of the Revised Statutes (22 U.S.C. 256–258); habeas corpus under sections 2241–2254 of title 28, United States Code; motions to vacate, set aside or correct sentence under section 2255 of title 28, United States Code; actions for penalties for refusal to transport destitute seamen under section 4578 of the Revised Statutes (46 U.S.C. 679); actions against the United States under the Act entitled ''An Act authorizing suits against the United States in admiralty for damage caused by and salvage service rendered to public vessels belonging to the United States, and for other purposes'', approved March 3, 1925 (46 U.S.C. 781–790), as implemented by section 7730 of title 10, United States Code.	

Rule 1102. Amendments	Rule 1102. Amendments
Amendments to the Federal Rules of Evidence may be made as provided in section 2072 of title 28 of the United States Code.	These rules may be amended as provided in 28 U.S.C. § 2072.

Rule 1103. Title	Rule 1103. Title
These rules may be known and cited as the Federal Rules of Evidence.	These rules may be cited as the Federal Rules of Evidence.

(Effective 7-9-95)

Rule 414. Evidence of Similar Crimes in Child Molestation Cases

(a) In a criminal case in which the defendant is accused of an offense of child molestation, evidence of the defendant's commission of another offense or offenses of child molestation is admissible, and may be considered for its bearing on any matter to which it is relevant.

(b) In a case in which the Government intends to offer evidence under this rule, the attorney for the Government shall disclose the evidence to the defendant, including statements of witnesses or a summary of the substance of any testimony that is expected to be offered, at least fifteen days before the scheduled date of trial or at such later time as the court may allow for good cause.

(c) This rule shall not be construed to limit the admission or consideration of evidence under any other rule.

(d) For purposes of this rule and Rule 415, "child" means a person below the age of fourteen, and "offense of child molestation" means a crime under Federal law or the law of a State (as defined in section 513 of title 18, United States Code) that involved — (1) any conduct proscribed by chapter 109A of title 18, United States Code, that was committed in relation to a child;

(2) any conduct proscribed by chapter 110 of title 18, United States Code;

(3) contact between any part of the defendant's body or an object and the genitals or anus of a child;

(4) contact between the genitals or anus of the defendant and any part of the body of a child;

(5) deriving sexual pleasure or gratification from the infliction of death, bodily injury, or physical pain on a child; or

(6) an attempt or conspiracy to engage in conduct described in paragraphs (1)–(5).

(Effective 7-9-95)

Rule 415. Evidence of Similar Acts in Civil Cases Concerning Sexual Assault or Child Molestation

(a) In a civil case in which a claim for damages or other relief is predicated on a party's alleged commission of conduct constituting an offense of sexual assault or child molestation, evidence of that party's commission of another offense or offenses of sexual assault or child molestation is admissible and may be considered as provided in Rule 413 and Rule 414 of these rules.

(b) A party who intends to offer evidence under this Rule shall disclose the evidence to the party against whom it will be offered, including statements of witnesses or a summary of the substance of any testimony that is expected to be offered, at least fifteen days before the scheduled date of trial or at such later time as the court may allow for good cause.

(c) This rule shall not be construed to limit the admission or consideration of evidence under any other rule.

(Effective 7-9-95)

ARTICLE V   PRIVILEGES

Rule 501.   General Rule

Except as otherwise required by the Constitution of the United States or provided by Act of Congress or in rules prescribed by the Supreme Court pursuant to statutory authority, the privilege of a witness, person, government, State, or political subdivision thereof shall be governed by the principles of the common law as they may be interpreted by the courts of the United States in the light of reason and experience. However, in civil actions and proceedings, with respect to an element of a claim or defense as to which State law supplies the rule of decision, the privilege of a witness, person, government, State, or political subdivision thereof shall be determined in accordance with State law.

ARTICLE VI   WITNESSES

Rule 601.   General Rule of Competency

Every person is competent to be a witness except as otherwise provided in these rules. However, in civil actions and proceedings, with respect to an element of a claim or defense as to which State law supplies the rule of decision, the competency of a witness shall be determined in accordance with State law.

Rule 602. Lack of Personal Knowledge

A witness may not testify to a matter unless evidence is introduced sufficient to support a finding that the witness has personal knowledge of the matter. Evidence to prove personal knowledge may, but need not, consist of the witness' own testimony. This rule is subject to the provisions of Rule 703, relating to opinion testimony by expert witnesses.

(Amended, eff 10-1-87; 11-1-88)

Rule 603. Oath or Affirmation

Before testifying, every witness shall be required to declare that the witness will testify truthfully, by oath or affirmation administered in a form calculated to awaken the witness' conscience and impress the witness' mind with the duty to do so.

(Amended, eff 10-1-87)

Rule 604. Interpreters

An interpreter is subject to the provisions of these rules relating to qualification as an expert and the administration of an oath or affirmation to make a true translation.

(Amended, eff 10-1-87)

Rule 605. Competency of Judge as Witness

The judge presiding at the trial may not testify in that trial as a witness. No objection need be made in order to preserve the point.

Rule 606. Competency of Juror as Witness

(a) At the trial. — A member of the jury may not testify as a witness before that jury in the trial of the case in which the juror is sitting. If the juror is called so to testify, the opposing party shall be afforded an opportunity to object out of the presence of the jury.

(b) Inquiry into validity of verdict or indictment. — Upon an inquiry into the validity of a verdict or indictment, a juror may not testify as to any matter or statement occurring during the course of the jury's deliberations or to the effect of anything upon that or any other juror's mind or emotions as influencing the juror to assent to or dissent from the verdict or indictment or concerning the juror's mental processes in connection therewith. But a juror may testify about (1) whether extraneous prejudicial information was improperly brought to the jury's attention, (2) whether any outside influence was improperly brought to bear upon any juror, or (3) whether there was a mistake in entering the verdict onto the verdict form. A juror's affidavit or evidence of any statement by the juror may no be received on a matter about which the juror would be precluded from testifying.

(Amended, eff 12-1-06)

Rule 607. Who May Impeach

The credibility of a witness may be attacked by any party, including the party calling the witness.

(Amended, eff 10-1-87)

Rule 608. Evidence of Character and Conduct of Witness

(a) **Opinion and reputation evidence of character.** The credibility of a witness may be attacked or supported by evidence in the form of opinion or reputation, but subject to these limitations: (1) the evidence may refer only to character for truthfulness or untruthfulness, and (2) evidence of truthful character is admissible only after the character of the witness for truthfulness has been attacked by opinion or reputation evidence or otherwise.

(b) **Specific instances of conduct.** Specific instances of the conduct of a witness, for the purpose of attacking or supporting the witness' character for truthfulness, other than conviction of crime as provided in rule 609, may not be proved by extrinsic evidence. They may, however, in the discretion of the court, if probative of truthfulness or untruthfulness, be inquired into on cross-examination of the witness (1) concerning the witness' character for truthfulness or untruthfulness, or (2) concerning the character for truthfulness or untruthfulness of another witness as to which character the witness being cross-examined has testified.

The giving of testimony, whether by an accused or by any other witness, does not operate as a waiver of the accused's or the witness' privilege against self-incrimination when examined with respect to matters that relate only to character for truthfulness.

(Amended, eff 1-2-75; 10-1-87; 11-1-88; 12-1-03)

Rule 609. Impeachment by Evidence of Conviction of Crime

(a) **General rule.** — For the purpose of attacking the character for truthfulness of a witness,

(1) evidence that a witness other than the accused has been convicted of a crime shall be admitted, subject to Rule 403, if the crime was punishable by death or imprisonment in excess of one year under the law under which the witness was convicted, and evidence that an accused has been convicted of such a crime shall be admitted if the court determines that the probative value of admitting this evidence outweighs its prejudicial effect to the accused; and

(2) evidence that any witness has been convicted of a crime shall be admitted regardless of the punishment, if it readily can be determined that establishing the elements of the crime required proof or admission of an act of dishonesty or false statement by the witness.

(b) **Time limit.** — Evidence of a conviction under this rule is not admissible if a period of more than ten years has elapsed since the date of the conviction or of the release of the witness from the confinement imposed for that conviction, whichever is the later date, unless the court determines, in the interests of justice, that the probative value of the conviction supported by specific facts and circumstances substantially outweighs its prejudicial effect. However, evidence of a conviction more than 10 years old as calculated herein, is not admissible unless the proponent gives to the adverse party sufficient advance written notice of intent to use such evidence to provide the adverse party with a fair opportunity to contest the use of such evidence.

(c) **Effect of pardon, annulment, or certificate of rehabilitation.** — Evidence of a conviction is not admissible under this rule if (1) the conviction has been the subject of a pardon, annulment, certificate of rehabilitation of the person convicted, and that person has not been convicted of a subsequent crime that was punishable by death or imprisonment in excess of one year, or (2) the conviction has been the subject of a pardon, annulment, or other equivalent procedure based on a finding of innocence.

(d) **Juvenile adjudications.** — Evidence of juvenile adjudications is generally not admissible under this rule. The court may, however, in a criminal case allow evidence of a juvenile adjudication of a witness other than the accused if conviction of the offense would be admissible to attack the credibility of an adult and the court is satisfied that admission in evidence is necessary for a fair determination of the issue of guilt or innocence.

(e) **Pendency of appeal.** — The pendency of an appeal therefrom does not render evidence of a conviction inadmissible. Evidence of the pendency of an appeal is admissible.

(Amended, eff 12-1-06)

Rule 610. Religious Beliefs or Opinions

Evidence of the beliefs or opinions of a witness on matters of religion is not admissible for the purpose of showing that by reason of their nature the witness' credibility is impaired or enhanced.

(Amended, eff 10-1-87)

Rule 611. Mode and Order of Interrogation and Presentation

(a) **Control by court.** The Court shall exercise reasonable control over the mode and order of interrogating witnesses and presenting evidence so as to (1) make the interrogation and presentation effective for the ascertainment of the truth, (2) avoid needless consumption of time, and (3) protect witnesses from harassment or undue embarrassment.

(b) **Scope of cross-examination.** Cross-examination should be limited to the subject matter of the direct examination and matters affecting the credibility of the witness. The court may, in the exercise of discretion, permit inquiry into additional matters as if on direct examination.

(c) **Leading questions.** Leading questions should not be used on the direct examination of a witness except as may be necessary to develop the witness' testimony. Ordinarily leading questions should be permitted on cross-examination. When a party calls a hostile witness, an adverse party, or a witness identified with an adverse party, interrogation may be by leading questions.

(Amended, eff 10-1-87)

Rule 612. Writing Used to Refresh Memory

Except as otherwise provided in criminal proceedings by section 3500 of title 18, United States Code, if a witness uses a writing to refresh memory for the purpose of testifying, either —

(1) while testifying, or

(2) before testifying, if the court in its discretion determines it is necessary in the interests of justice, an adverse party is entitled to have the writing produced at the hearing, to inspect it, to cross-examine the witness thereon, and to introduce in evidence those portions which relate to the testimony of the witness.

If it is claimed that the writing contains matters not related to the subject matter of the testimony the court shall examine the writing in camera, excise any portions not so related, and order delivery of the remainder to the party entitled thereto. Any portion withheld over objections shall be preserved and made available to the appellate court in the event of an appeal. If a writing is not produced or delivered pursuant to order under this rule, the court shall make any order justice requires, except that in criminal cases when the prosecution elects not to comply, the order shall be one striking the testimony or, if the court in its discretion determines that the interests of justice so require, declaring a mistrial.

(Amended, eff 10-1-87)

Rule 613. Prior Statements of Witnesses

(a) **Examining witness concerning prior statement.** In examining a witness concerning a prior statement made by the witness, whether written or not, the statement need not be shown nor its contents disclosed to the witness at that time, but on request the same shall be shown or disclosed to opposing counsel.

(b) **Extrinsic evidence of prior inconsistent statement of witness.** Extrinsic evidence of a prior inconsistent statement by a witness is not admissible unless the witness is afforded an opportunity to explain or deny the same and the opposite party is afforded an opportunity to interrogate the witness thereon, or the interests of justice otherwise require. This provision does not apply to admissions of a party-opponent as defined in Rule 801(d)(2).

(Amended, eff 10-1-87; 11-1-88)

Rule 614. Calling and Interrogation of Witnesses by Court

(a) **Calling by court.** The court may, on its own motion or at the suggestion of a party, call witnesses, and all parties are entitled to cross-examine witnesses thus called.

(b) **Interrogation by court.** The court may interrogate witnesses, whether called by itself or by a party.

(c) **Objections.** Objections to the calling of witnesses by the court or to interrogation by it may be made at the time or at the next available opportunity when the jury is not present.

Rule 615. Exclusion of Witnesses

At the request of a party the court shall order witnesses excluded so that they cannot hear the testimony of other witnesses, and it may make the order of its own motion. This rule does not authorize exclusion of (1) a party who is a natural person, or (2) an officer or employee of a party which is not a natural person designated as its representative by its attorney, or (3) a person whose presence is shown by a party to be essential to the presentation of the parry's cause, or (4) a person authorized by statute to be present.

(Amended, eff 10-1-87; 11-1-88; 11-18-88; 12-1-98)

ARTICLE VII   OPINIONS AND EXPERT TESTIMONY

Rule 701. Opinion Testimony by Lay Witnesses

If the witness is not testifying as an expert, the witness' testimony in the form of opinions or inferences is limited to those opinions or inferences which are (a) rationally based on the perception of the witness, and (b) helpful to a clear understanding of the witness' testimony or the determination of a fact in issue, and (c) not based on scientific, technical or other specialized knowledge within the scope of Rule 702.

(Amended, eff 10-1-87; 12-1-00)

Rule 702. Testimony by Experts

If scientific, technical, or other specialized knowledge will assist the trier of fact to understand the evidence or to determine a fact in issue, a witness qualified as an expert by knowledge, skill, experience, training, or education, may testify thereto in the form of an opinion or otherwise, if (1) the testimony is based upon sufficient facts or data, (2) the testimony is the product of reliable principles and methods, and (3) the witness has applied the principles and methods reliably to the facts of the case.

(Amended, eff 12-1-00)

Rule 703. Bases of Opinion Testimony by Experts

The facts or data in the particular case upon which an expert bases an opinion or inference may be those perceived by or made known to the expert at or before the hearing. If of a type reasonably relied upon by experts in the particular field in forming opinions or inferences upon the subject, the facts or data need not be admissible in evidence in order for the opinion or inference to be admitted. Facts or data that are otherwise inadmissible shall not be disclosed to the jury by the proponent of the opinion or inference unless the court determines that their probative value in assisting the jury to evaluate the expert's opinion substantially outweighs their prejudicial effect.

(Amended, eff 10-1-87; 12-1-00)

Rule 704. Opinion on Ultimate Issue

(a) Except as provided in subdivision (b), testimony in the form of an opinion or inference otherwise admissible is not objectionable because it embraces an ultimate issue to be decided by the trier of fact.

(b) No expert witness testifying with respect to the mental state or condition of a defendant in a criminal case may state an opinion or inference as to whether the defendant did or did not have the mental state or condition constituting an element of the crime charged or of a defense thereto. Such ultimate issues are matters for the trier of fact alone.

(Amended, eff 10-12-84)

Rule 705. Disclosure of Facts or Data Underlying Expert Opinion

The expert may testify in terms of opinion or inference and give reasons therefor without first testifying to the underlying facts or data, unless the court requires otherwise. The expert may in any event be required to disclose the underlying facts or data on cross-examination.

(Amended, eff 10-1-87; 12-1-93)

Rule 706. Court Appointed Experts

(a) **Appointment.** The court may on its own motion or on the motion of any party enter an order to show cause why expert witnesses should not be appointed, and may request the parties to submit nominations. The court may appoint any expert witnesses agreed upon by the parties, and may appoint expert witnesses of its own selection. An expert witness shall not be appointed by the court unless the witness consents to act. A witness so appointed shall be informed of the witness' duties by the court in writing, a copy of which shall be filed with the clerk, or at a conference in which the parties shall have opportunity to participate. A witness so appointed shall advise the parties of the witness' findings, if any; the witness' deposition may be taken by any party; and the witness may be called to testify by the court or any party. The witness shall be subject to cross-examination by each party, including a party calling the witness.

(b) **Compensation.** Expert witnesses so appointed are entitled to reasonable compensation in whatever sum the court may allow. The compensation thus fixed is payable from funds which may be provided by law in criminal cases and civil actions and proceedings involving just compensation under the fifth amendment. In other civil actions and proceedings the compensation shall be paid by the parties in such proportion and at such time as the court directs, and thereafter charged in like manner as other costs.

(c) **Disclosure of appointment.** In the exercise of its discretion, the court may authorize disclosure to the jury of the fact that the court appointed the expert witness.

(d) **Parties' experts of own selection.** Nothing in this rule limits the parties in calling expert witnesses of their own selection.

(Amended, eff 10-1-87)

ARTICLE VIII   HEARSAY

Rule 801.   Definitions

The following definitions apply under this article:

(a) **Statement.** A "statement" is (1) an oral or written assertion or (2) nonverbal conduct of a person, if it is intended by the person as an assertion.

(b) **Declarant.** A "declarant" is a person who makes a statement.

(c) **Hearsay.** "Hearsay" is a statement, other than one made by the declarant while testifying at the trial or hearing, offered in evidence to prove the truth of the matter asserted.

(d) **Statements which are not hearsay.** A statement is not hearsay if —

(1) *Prior statement by witness.* The declarant testifies at the trial or hearing and is subject to cross-examination concerning the statement, and the statement is (A) inconsistent with the declarant's testimony, and was given under oath subject to the penalty of perjury at a trial, hearing, or other proceeding, or in a deposition, or (B) consistent with the declarant's testimony and is offered to rebut an express or implied charge against the declarant of recent fabrication or improper influence or motive, or (C) one of identification of a person made after perceiving the person; or (2) *Admission by party-opponent.* The statement is offered against a party and is (A) the party's own statement, in either an individual or a representative capacity or (B) a statement of which the party has manifested an adoption or belief in its truth, or (C) a statement by a person authorized by the party to make a statement concerning the subject, or (D) a statement by the party's agent or servant concerning a matter within the scope of the agency or employment, made during the existence of the relationship, or (E) a statement by a coconspirator of a party during the course and in furtherance of the conspiracy. The contents of the statement shall be considered but are not alone sufficient to establish the declarant's authority under subdivision (C), the agency or employment relationship and scope thereof under subdivision (D), or the existence of the conspiracy and the participation therein of the declarant and the party against whom the statement is offered under subdivision (E).

(Amended, eff 10-31-75; 10-1-87; 12-1-97)

Rule 802.   Hearsay Rule

Hearsay is not admissible except as provided by these rules or by other rules prescribed by the Supreme Court pursuant to statutory authority or by Act of Congress.

Rule 803.   Hearsay Exceptions; Availability of Declarant Immaterial

The following are not excluded by the hearsay rule, even though the declarant is available as a witness:

(1) *Present sense impression.* A statement describing or explaining an event or condition made while the declarant was perceiving the event or condition, or

immediately thereafter.

(2) *Excited utterance.* A statement relating to a startling event or condition made while the declarant was under the stress of excitement caused by the event or condition.

(3) *Then existing mental, emotional, or physical condition.* Statement of the declarant's then existing state of mind, emotion, sensation, or physical condition (such as intent, plan, motive, design, mental feeling, pain, and bodily health), but not including a statement of memory or belief to prove the fact remembered or believed unless it relates to the execution, revocation, identification, or terms of declarant's will.

(4) *Statements for purposes of medical diagnosis or treatment.* Statements made for purposes of medical diagnosis or treatment and describing medical history, or past or present symptoms, pain, or sensations, or the inception or general character of the cause or external source thereof insofar as reasonably pertinent to diagnosis or treatment.

(5) *Recorded recollection.* A memorandum or record concerning a matter about which a witness once had knowledge but now has insufficient recollection to enable the witness to testify fully and accurately, shown to have been made or adopted by the witness when the matter was fresh in the witness' memory and to reflect that knowledge correctly. If admitted, the memorandum or record may be read into evidence but may not itself be received as an exhibit unless offered by an adverse party.

(6) *Records of regularly conducted activity.* A memorandum, report, record, or data compilation, in any form, of acts, events, conditions, opinions, or diagnoses, made at or near the time by, or from information transmitted by, a person with knowledge, if kept in the course of a regularly conducted business activity, and if it was the regular practice of that business activity to make the memorandum, report, record or data compilation, all as shown by the testimony of the custodian or other qualified witness, or by certification that complies with Rule 902(11), Rule 902(12), or a statute permitting certification, unless the source of information or the method or circumstances of preparation indicate lack of trustworthiness. The term "business" as used in this paragraph includes business, institution, association, profession, occupation, and calling of every land, whether or not conducted for profit.

(7) *Absence of entry in records kept in accordance with the provisions of paragraph (6).* Evidence that a matter is not included in the memoranda reports, records, or data compilations, in any form, kept in accordance with the provisions of paragraph (6), to prove the nonoccurrence or nonexistence of the matter, if the matter was of a kind of which a memorandum, report, record, or data compilation was regularly made and preserved, unless the sources of information or other circumstances indicate lack of trustworthiness.

(8) *Public records and reports.* Records, reports, statements, or data compilations, in any form, of public offices or agencies, setting forth (A) the activities of the office or agency, or (B) matters observed pursuant to duty imposed by law as to which matters there was a duty to report, excluding, however, in criminal

cases matters observed by police officers and other law enforcement personnel, or (C) in civil actions and proceedings and against the government in criminal cases, factual findings resulting from an investigation made pursuant to authority granted by law, unless the sources of information or other circumstances indicate lack of trustworthiness.

(9) *Records of vital statistics.* Records or data compilations, in any form, of births, fetal deaths, deaths, or marriages, if the report thereof was made to a public office pursuant to requirements of law.

(10) *Absence of public record or entry.* To prove the absence of a record, report, statement, or data compilation, in any form, or the nonoccurrence or nonexistence. of a matter of which a record, report, statement, or data compilation, in any form, was regularly made and preserved by a public office or agency, evidence in the form of a certification in accordance with Rule 902, or testimony, that diligent search failed to disclose the record, report, statement, or data compilation, or entry.

(11) *Records of religious organizations.* Statements of births, marriages, divorces, deaths, legitimacy, ancestry, relationship by blood or marriage, or other similar facts of personal or family history, contained in a regularly kept record of a religious organization.

(12) *Marriage, baptismal, and similar certificates.* Statements of fact contained in a certificate that the maker performed a marriage or other ceremony or administered a sacrament, made by a clergyman, public official, or other person authorized by the rules or practices of a religious organization or by law to perform the act certified, and purporting to have been issued at the time of the act or within a reasonable time thereafter.

(13) *Family records.* Statements of fact concerning personal or family history contained in family Bibles, genealogies, charts, engravings on rings, inscriptions on family portraits, engravings on urns, crypts, or tombstones, or the like.

(14) *Records of documents affecting an interest in property.* The record of a document purporting to establish or affect an interest in property, as proof of the content of the original recorded document and its execution and delivery by each person by whom it purports to have been executed, if the record is a record of a public office and an applicable statute authorizes the recording of documents of that kind in that office.

(15) *Statements in documents affecting an interest in property.* A statement contained in a document purporting to establish or affect an interest in property if the matter stated was relevant to the purpose of the document, unless dealings with the property since the document was made have been inconsistent with the truth of the statement or the purport of the document.

(16) *Statements in ancient documents.* Statements in a document in existence twenty years or more the authenticity of which is established.

(17) *Market reports, commercial publications.* Market quotations, tabulations, lists, directories, or other published compilations, generally used and relied upon by the public or by persons in particular occupations.

(18) *Learned Treatises.* To the extent called to the attention of an expert witness upon cross-examination or relied upon by the expert witness in direct examination, statements contained in published treatises, periodicals, or pamphlets on a subject of history, medicine, or other science or art, established as a reliable authority by the testimony or admission of the witness or by other expert testimony or by judicial notice. If admitted, the statements may be read into evidence but may not be received as exhibits.

(19) *Reputation concerning personal or family history.* Reputation among members of a person's family by blood, adoption, or marriage or among a person's associates, or in the community, concerning a person's birth, adoption, marriage, divorce, death, legitimacy, relationship by blood, adoption, or marriage, ancestry, or other similar fact of personal or family history.

(20) *Reputation concerning boundaries or general history.* Reputation in a community, arising before the controversy, as to boundaries of or customs affecting lands in the community, and reputation as to events of general history important to the community or State or nation in which located.

(21) *Reputation as to character.* Reputation of a person's character among associates or in the community.

(22) *Judgment of previous conviction.* Evidence of a final judgment, entered after a trial or upon a plea of guilty (but not upon a plea of nolo contendere), adjudging a person guilty of a crime punishable by death or imprisonment in excess of one year, to prove any fact essential to sustain the judgment, but not including, when offered by the Government in a criminal prosecution for purposes other than impeachment, judgments against persons other than the accused. The pendency of an appeal may be shown but does not affect admissibility.

(23) *Judgment as to personal, family, or general history, or boundaries.* Judgments as proof of matters of personal, family, or general history, or boundaries, essential to the judgment, if the same would be provable by evidence of reputation.

(24) [Transferred to Rule 807] (Amended, eff 12-12-75; 10-1-87; 12-1-97; 12-1-00)

Rule 804. Hearsay Exceptions: Declarant Unavailable

(a) **Definition of unavailability.** "Unavailability as a witness" includes situations in which the declarant —

(1) is exempted by ruling of the court on the ground of privilege from testifying concerning the subject matter of the declarant's statement; or

(2) persists in refusing to testify concerning the subject matter of the declarant's statement despite an order of the court to do so; or

(3) testifies to a lack of memory of the subject matter of the declarant's statement; or

(4) is unable to be present or to testify at the hearing because of death or then

existing physical or mental illness or infirmity; or

(5) is absent from the hearing and the proponent of a statement has been unable to procure the declarant's attendance (or in the case of a hearsay exception under subdivision (b)(2), (3), or (4), the declarant's attendance or testimony) by process or other reasonable means. A declarant is not unavailable as a witness if his exemption, refusal, claim of lack of memory, inability, or absence is due to the procurement or wrongdoing of the proponent of a statement for the purpose of preventing the witness from attending or testifying.

(b) Hearsay exceptions. The following are not excluded by the hearsay rule if the declarant is unavailable as a witness:

(1) *Former testimony.* Testimony given as a witness at another hearing of the same or a different proceeding, or in a deposition taken in compliance with law in the course of the same or another proceeding, if the party against whom the testimony is now offered, or, in a civil action or proceeding, a predecessor in interest, had an opportunity and similar motive to develop the testimony by direct, cross, or redirect examination.

(2) *Statement under belief of impending death.* In a prosecution for homicide or in a civil action or proceeding, a statement made by a declarant while believing that the declarant's death was imminent, concerning the cause or circumstances of what the declarant believed to be impending death.

(3) *Statement against interest.* A statement which was at the time of its making so far contrary to the declarant's pecuniary or proprietary interest, or so far tended to subject the declarant to civil or criminal liability, or to render invalid a claim by the declarant against another, that a reasonable person in the declarant's position would not have made the statement unless believing it to be true. A statement tending to expose the declarant to criminal liability and offered to exculpate the accused, is not admissible unless corroborating circumstances clearly indicate the trustworthiness of the statement.

(4) *Statement of personal or family history.* (A) A statement concerning the declarant's own birth, adoption, marriage, divorce, legitimacy, relationship by blood, adoption, or marriage, ancestry, or other similar fact of personal or family history, even though declarant had no means of acquiring personal knowledge of the matter stated; or (B) a statement concerning the foregoing matters, and death also, of another person, if the declarant was related to the other by blood, adoption, or marriage or was so intimately associated with the other's family as to be likely to have accurate information concerning the matter declared.

(5) [Transferred to Rule 807]

(6) *Forfeiture by wrongdoing.* A statement offered against a party that has engaged or acquiesced in wrongdoing that was intended to, and did, procure the unavailability of the declarant as a witness. (Amended, eff 12-12-75; 10-1-87; 11-18-88; 12-1-97)

Rule 805. Hearsay Within Hearsay

Hearsay included within hearsay is not excluded under the hearsay rule if each part or the combined statements conforms with an exception to the hearsay rule provided in these rules.

Rule 806. Attacking and Supporting Credibility of Declarant

When a hearsay statement, or a statement defined in Rule 801(d)(2)(C), (D), or (E), has been admitted in evidence, the credibility of the declarant may be attacked, and if attacked may be supported, by any evidence which would be admissible for those purposes if declarant had testified as a witness. Evidence of a statement or conduct by the declarant at any time, inconsistent with the declarant's hearsay statement, is not subject to any requirement that the declarant may have been afforded an opportunity to deny or explain. If the party against whom a hearsay statement has been admitted calls the declarant as a witness, the party is entitled to examine the declarant on the statement as if under cross-examination.

(Amended, eff 10-1-87; 12-1-97)

Rule 807. Residual Exception

A statement not specifically covered by Rule 803 or 804 but having equivalent circumstantial guarantees of trustworthiness, is not excluded by the hearsay rule, if the court determines that (A) the statement is offered as evidence of a material fact; (B) the statement is more probative on the point for which it is offered than any other evidence which the proponent can procure through reasonable efforts; and (C) the general purposes of these rules and the interests of justice will best be served by admission of the statement into evidence. However, a statement may not be admitted under this exception unless the proponent of it makes known to the adverse party sufficiently in advance of the trial or hearing to provide the adverse party with a fair opportunity to prepare to meet it, the proponent's intention to offer the statement and the particulars of it, including the name and address of the declarant.

(Effective 12-1-97)

ARTICLE IX   AUTHENTICATION AND IDENTIFICATION

Rule 901. Requirement of Authentication or Identification

(a) **General provision.** The requirement of authentication or identification as a condition precedent to admissibility is satisfied by evidence sufficient to support a finding that the matter in question is what its proponent claims.

(b) **Illustrations.** By way of illustration only, and not by way of limitation, the following are examples of authentication or identification conforming with the requirements of this rule:

(1) *Testimony of witness with knowledge.* Testimony that a matter is what it is claimed to be.

(2) *Nonexpert opinion on handwriting.* Nonexpert opinion as to the genuineness of handwriting, based upon familiarity not acquired for purposes of the

litigation.

(3) *Comparison by trier or expert witness.* Comparison by the trier of fact or by expert witnesses with specimens which have been authenticated.

(4) *Distinctive characteristics and the like.* Appearance, contents, substance, internal patterns, or other distinctive characteristics, taken in conjunction with circumstances.

(5) *Voice Identification.* Identification of a voice, whether heard firsthand or through mechanical or electronic transmission or recording, by opinion based upon hearing the voice at any time under circumstances connecting it with the alleged speaker.

(6) *Telephone conversations.* Telephone conversations, by evidence that a call was made to the number assigned at the time by the telephone company to a particular person or business, if (A) in the case of a person, circumstances, including self-identification, show the person answering to be the one called, or (B) in the case of a business, the call was made to a place of business and the conversation related to business reasonably transacted over the telephone.

(7) *Public records or reports.* Evidence that a writing authorized by law to be recorded or filed and in fact recorded or filed in a public office, or a purported public record, report, statement, or data compilation, in any form, is from the public office where items of this nature are kept.

(8) *Ancient documents or data compilation.* Evidence that a document or data compilation, in any form, (A) is in such condition as to create no suspicion concerning its authenticity, (B) was in a place where it, if authentic, would likely be, and (C) has been in existence 20 years or more at the time it is offered.

(9) *Process or system.* Evidence describing a process or system used to produce a result and showing that the process or system produces an accurate result.

(10) *Methods provided by statute or rule.* Any method of authentication or identification provided by Act of Congress or by other rules prescribed by the Supreme Court pursuant to statutory authority.

Rule 902. Self-authentication

Extrinsic evidence of authenticity as a condition precedent to admissibility is not required with respect to the following:

(1) *Domestic public documents under seal.* A document bearing a seal purporting to be that of the United States, or of any State, district, Commonwealth, territory, or insular possession thereof, or the Panama Canal Zone, or the Trust Territory of the Pacific Islands, or of a political subdivision, department, officer or agency thereof, and a signature purporting to be an attestation or execution.

(2) *Domestic public documents not under seal.* A document purporting to bear the signature in the official capacity of an officer or employee of any entity included in paragraph (1) hereof, having no seal, if a public officer having a seal

and having official duties in the district or political subdivision of the officer or employee certifies under seal that the signer has the official capacity and that the signature is genuine.

(3) *Foreign public documents.* A document purporting to be executed or attested in an official capacity by a person authorized by the laws of a foreign country to make the execution or attestation, and accompanied by a final certification as to the genuineness of the signature and official position (A) of the executing or attesting person, or (B) of any foreign official whose certificate of genuineness of signature and official position relates to the execution or attestation or is in a chain of certificates of genuineness of signature and official position relating to the execution or attestation. A final certification may be made by a secretary of an embassy or legation, consul general, consul, vice consul, or consular agent of the United States, or a diplomatic or consular official of the foreign country assigned or accredited to the United States. If reasonable opportunity has been given to all parties to investigate the authenticity and accuracy of official documents, the court may, for good cause shown, order that they be treated as presumptively authentic without final certification or permit them to be evidenced by an attested summary with or without final certification.

(4) *Certified copies of public records.* A copy of an official record or report or entry therein, or of a document authorized by law to be recorded or filed and actually recorded or filed in a public office, including data compilations in any form, certified as correct by the custodian or other person authorized to make the certification, by certificate complying with paragraph (1), (2), or (3) of this rule or complying with any Act of Congress or rule prescribed by the Supreme Court pursuant to statutory authority.

(5) *Official publications.* Books, pamphlets, or other publications purporting to be issued by public authority.

(6) *Newspapers and periodicals.* Printed materials purporting to be newspapers or periodicals.

(7) *Trade inscriptions and the like.* Inscriptions, signs, tags, or labels purporting to have been affixed in the course of business and indicating ownership, control, or origin.

(8) *Acknowledged documents.* Documents accompanied by a certificate of acknowledgment executed in the manner provided by law by a notary public or other officer authorized by law to take acknowledgments.

(9) *Commercial paper and related documents.* Commercial paper, signatures thereon, and documents relating thereto to the extent provided by general commercial law.

(10) *Presumptions under Acts of Congress.* Any signature, document, or other matter declared by Act of Congress to be presumptively or prima facie genuine or authentic.

(11) *Certified domestic records of regularly conducted activity.* The original or a duplicate of a domestic record of regularly conducted activity that would be admissible under Rule 803(6) if accompanied by a written declaration of its

custodian or other qualified person, in a manner complying with any Act of Congress or rule prescribed by the Supreme Court pursuant to statutory authority, certifying that the record —

(A) was made at or near the time of the occurrence of the matters set forth by, or from information transmitted by, a person with knowledge of those matters;

(B) was kept in the course of the regularly conducted activity; and

(C) was made by the regularly conducted activity as a regular practice. A party intending to offer a record into evidence under this paragraph must provide written notice of that intention to all adverse parties, and must make the record and declaration available for inspection sufficiently in advance of their offer into evidence to provide an adverse party with a fair opportunity to challenge them.

(12) *Certified foreign records of regularly conducted activity.* In a civil case, the original or a duplicate of a foreign record of regularly conducted activity that would be admissible under Rule 803(6) if accompanied by a written declaration by its custodian or other qualified person certifying that the record —

(A) was made at or near the time of the occurrence of the matters set forth by, or from information transmitted by, a person with knowledge of those matters;

(B) was kept in the course of the regularly conducted activity; and

(C) was made by the regularly conducted activity as a regular practice.

The declaration must be signed in a manner that, if falsely made, would subject the maker to criminal penalty under the laws of the country where the declaration is signed. A party intending to offer a record into evidence under this paragraph must provide written notice of that intention to all adverse parties, and must make the record and declaration available for inspection sufficiently in advance of their offer into evidence to provide an adverse party with a fair opportunity to challenge them.

(Amended, eff 10-1-87; 11-1-88; 12-1-00)

Rule 903. Subscribing Witness' Testimony Unnecessary

The testimony of a subscribing witness is not necessary to authenticate a writing unless required by the laws of the jurisdiction whose laws govern the validity of the writing.

ARTICLE X   CONTENTS OF WRITINGS, RECORDINGS, AND PHOTOGRAPHS

Rule 1001. Definitions

For purposes of this article the following definitions are applicable:

(1) **Writings and recordings.** "Writings" and "recordings" consist of letters, words, or numbers, or their equivalent, set down by handwriting, typewriting,

printing, photostating, photographing, magnetic impulse, mechanical or electronic recording, or other form of data compilation.

(2) **Photographs.** "Photographs" include still photographs, X-ray films, video tapes, and motion pictures.

(3) **Original.** An "original" of a writing or recording is the writing or recording itself or any counterpart intended to have the same effect by a person executing or issuing it. An "original" of a photograph includes the negative or any print therefrom. If data are stored in a computer or similar device, any printout or other output readable by sight, shown to reflect the data accurately, is an "original."

(4) **Duplicate.** A "duplicate" is a counterpart produced by the same impression as the original, or from the same matrix, or by means of photography, including enlargements and miniatures, or by mechanical or electronic rerecording, or by chemical reproduction, or by other equivalent techniques which accurately reproduces the original.

Rule 1002. Requirement of Original

To prove the content of a writing, recording or photograph, the original writing, recording, or photograph is required, except as otherwise provided in these rules or by Act of Congress.

Rule 1003. Admissibility of Duplicates

A duplicate is admissible to the same extent as an original unless (1) a genuine question is raised as to the authenticity of the original or (2) in the circumstances it would be unfair to admit the duplicate in lieu of the original.

Rule 1004. Admissibility of Other Evidence of Contents

The original is not required, and other evidence of the contents of a writing, recording, or photograph is admissible if —

(1) **Originals lost or destroyed.** All originals are lost or have been destroyed, unless the proponent lost or destroyed them in bad faith; or

(2) **Original not obtainable.** No original can be obtained by any available judicial process or procedure; or

(3) **Original in possession of opponent.** At a time when an original was under the control of the party against whom offered, that party was put on notice, by the pleadings or otherwise, that the contents would be a subject of proof at the hearing, and that party does not produce the original at the hearing; or

(4) **Collateral matters.** The writing, recording, or photograph is not closely related to a controlling issue.

(Amended, eff 10-1-87)

Rule 1005. Public Records

The contents of an official record, or of a document authorized to be recorded or filed and actually recorded or filed, including data compilations in any form, if otherwise admissible, may be proved by copy, certified as correct in accordance with Rule 902 or testified to be correct by a witness who has compared it with the original. If a copy which complies with the foregoing cannot be obtained by the exercise of reasonable diligence, then other evidence of the contents may be given.

Rule 1006. Summaries

The contents of voluminous writings, recordings, or photographs which cannot conveniently be examined in court may be presented in the form of a chart, summary, or calculation. The originals, or duplicates, shall be made available for examination or copying, or both, by other parties at reasonable time and place. The court may order that they be produced in court.

Rule 1007. Testimony or Written Admission of Party

Contents of writings, recordings, or photographs may be proved by the testimony or deposition of the party against whom offered or by that party's written admission, without accounting for the nonproduction of the original.

(Amended, eff 10-1-87)

Rule 1008. Functions of Court and Jury

When the admissibility of other evidence of contents of writings, recordings, or photographs under these rules depends upon the fulfillment of a condition of fact, the question whether the condition has been fulfilled is ordinarily for the court to determine in accordance with the provisions of Rule 104. However, when an issue is raised (a) whether the asserted writing ever existed, or (b) whether another writing, recording, or photograph produced at the trial is the original, or (c) whether other evidence of contents correctly reflects the contents, the issue is for the trier of fact to determine as in the case of other issues of fact.

ARTICLE XI MISCELLANEOUS RULES

Rule 1101. Applicability of Rules

(a) **Courts and judges.** These rules apply to the United States district courts, the District Court of Guam, the District Court of the Virgin Islands, the District Court for the Northern Mariana Islands, the United States courts of appeals, the United States Claims Court, and to United States bankruptcy judges and United States magistrate judges, in the actions, cases, and proceedings and to the extent hereinafter set forth. The terms "judge" and "court" in these rules include United States bankruptcy judges and United States magistrate judges.

(b) **Proceedings generally.** These rules apply generally to civil actions and proceedings, including admiralty and maritime cases, to criminal cases and proceedings, to contempt proceedings except those in which the court may act summarily, and to proceedings and cases under title 11, United States Code.

(c) **Rule of privilege.** The rule with respect to privileges applies at all stages of all actions, cases, and proceedings.

(d) **Rules inapplicable.** The rules (other than with respect to privileges) do not apply in the following situations:

(1) *Preliminary question of fact.* The determination of questions of fact preliminary to admissibility of evidence when the issue is to be determined by the court under Rule 104.

(2) *Grand jury.* Proceedings before grand juries.

(3) *Miscellaneous proceedings.* Proceedings for extradition or rendition; preliminary examinations in criminal cases; sentencing, or granting or revoking probation; issuance of warrants for arrest, criminal summonses, and search warrants; and proceedings with respect to release on bail or otherwise.

(e) Rules applicable in part. In the following proceedings these rules apply to the extent that matters of evidence are not provided for in the statutes which govern procedure therein or in other rules prescribed by the Supreme Court pursuant to statutory authority: the trial of misdemeanors and other petty offenses before United States magistrate judges; review of agency actions when the facts are subject to trial de novo under section 706(2)(F) of title 5, United States Code; review of orders of the Secretary of Agriculture under section 2 of the Act entitled "An Act to authorize association of producers of agricultural products" approved February 18, 1922 (7 U.S.C. 292), and under sections 6 and 7(c) of the Perishable Agricultural Commodities Act, 1930 (7 U.S.C. 499f, 499g(c)); naturalization and revocation of naturalization under sections 310–318 of the Immigration and Nationality Act (8 U.S.C. 1421–1429); prize proceedings in admiralty under sections 7651–7681 of title 10, United States Code; review of orders of the Secretary of the Interior under section 2 of the Act entitled "An Act authorizing associations of producers of aquatic products" approved June 25, 1934 (15 U.S.C. 522); review of orders of petroleum control boards under section 5 of the Act entitled "An Act to regulate interstate and foreign commerce in petroleum and its products by prohibiting the shipment in such commerce of petroleum and its products produced in violation of State law, and for other purposes", approved February 22, 1935 (15 U.S.C. 715d); actions for fines, penalties, or forfeitures under part V of title IV of the Tariff Act of 1930 (19 U.S.C. 1581–1624), or under the Anti-Smuggling Act (19 U.S.C. 1701–1711); criminal libel for condemnation, exclusion of imports, or other proceedings under the Federal Food, Drug, and Cosmetic Act (21 U.S.C. 301–392); disputes between seamen under sections 4079, 4080, and 4081 of the Revised Statutes (22 U.S.C. 256–258); habeas corpus under sections 2241–2254 of title 28, United States Code; motions to vacate, set aside or correct sentence under section 2255 of title 28, United States Code; actions for penalties for refusal to transport destitute seamen under section 4578 of the Revised Statutes (46 U.S.C. 679); actions against the United States under the Act entitled "An Act authorizing suits against the United States in admiralty for damage caused by and salvage service rendered to public vessels belonging to the United States, and for other purposes", approved March 3, 1925 (46 U.S.C. 781–790), as implemented by section 7730 of title 10, United States Code. (Amended, eff 12-12-75; 10-179; 10-1-82; 101-87; 11-1-88; 11-18-88; 12-1-93)

Rule 1102. Amendments

Amendments to the Federal Rules of Evidence may be made as provided in section 2072 of title 28 of the United States Code.

(Amended, eff 12-1-91)

Rule 1103. Title

These rules may be known and cited as the Federal Rules of Evidence.

TABLE OF CASES

[References are to pages]

A

Aiken v. People. 211; 223
Allis v. United States. 212
Annunziato; United States v.. 650

B

Badger v. Badger. 213
Baird v. Koerner. 853
Baker v. State. 663
Ballou v. Henri Studios, Inc. 70
Beech Aircraft Corp. v. Rainey 705
Big Mack Trucking Co. v. Dickerson. 612
Bill v. Farm Bureau Life Insurance Co.. 596
Bizzard; United States v.. 849
Bonnett; United States v.. 260
Bordenkircher v. Hayes 264
Bourjaily v. United States. 33; 626
Boykin v. Alabama. 259
Brackeen; United States v.. 298
Brooklyn Savings Bank v. O'Neil. 262; 268
Brown v. United States 261
Brown; United States v. 429; 883
Bullcoming v. New Mexico. 497

C

Caporale; United States v. 859
Carlson; United States v.. 750
Castillo; United States v.. 920
Chaffin v. Stynchcombe 265
Chambers; People v. 194
Chemical Foundation, Inc.; United States v. . . .265
City of (see name of city). . . . .
Collins; People v. 72; 82
Commonwealth v. (see name of defendant). . . .
Coonan; United States v. 260
Cooper v. Firestone Tire and Rubber Co. 58
Corbitt v. New Jersey 264
County Court of Ulster County v. Allen 831
Court; Commonwealth v. 217
Crawford v. Washington. 461
Cree v. Hatcher. 300
Crosby v. United States 259; 266

D

Daggett; People v. 923
Daubert v. Merrell Dow Pharmaceuticals, Inc. . .74; 380
Davis; United States v.. 153

Davis v. Washington. 469
DePeri; U.S. v.. 681
DiNapoli; United States v.. 724
Dortch; United States v. 258; 269
Dowling v. United States. 179; 919
Duffy; United States v.. 884

E

Edgington v. United States. 213; 220
Edwards; United States v.. 853
EEOC v. Gear Petroleum, Inc.. 239
Elkins v. United States. 844
Elliott; People v.. 214
Erie R. Co. v. Tompkins 845; 848
Evans v. Jeff D. 259

F

Fall v. United States. 212
Filippelli v. United States 215, 216
Fisher v. United States. 865
Fox; State v.. 245
Francis v. State 54
Frye v. United States. 74; 372
Funk v. United States 871

G

General Electric Co. v. Joiner 75; 390; 401
Giles v. California. 779
Gilley; United States v. 57
Glenn; U.S. v. 298
Goetz; People v. 55
Gomez; People v. 61
Gordon v. D & G Escrow Corp.. 716
Grand Jury, In re 848
Green v. Bock Laundry Machine Co. 299
Green v. United States. 264
Greer v. United States 212; 217
Guidry v. Sheet Metal Workers Nat. Pension Fund. .268

H

Hannigan; United States v.. . . . . .48, 49
Hannon; People v.. . . . . .211; 216; 223
Harper & Row Publishers, Inc. v. Decker. . . .855
Haslip; United States v. 299

Hatem v. United States. 212
Hawkins v. United States 850
Hearst; United States v.. 194
Henry v. Kernan 857
Hickman v. Taylor. 855
Holly; State v. 223
Hubbell; United States v.. . . . . .846; 858
Huddleston v. United States 33; 179; 191

I

In re (see name of party) . . . .

J

Jaffee v. Redmond 837; 856; 870
Jenkins v. Anderson 261
Johnson v. Lutz. 674
Johnson v. Zerbst. 259; 266
Josefik; United States v.. 261
Josey v. United States 216

K

Kaminsky v. Hertz Corp. 807
Keith; People v.. 133
Knapp v. State. 45; 64
Kumho Tire Co., Ltd. v. Carmichael . . 75; 390; 392

L

Laudiero; People v.. 214
Leon Guerrero; United States v.. 245
Levin v. United States. 203
Little v. United States 215, 216
Lopez; United States v. 159
Lucero; People v.. 926

M

Mackowick v. Kansas City, St. Joseph & Council Bluffs R.R. Co.. 805
Maestas; People v.. 921
Mahlandt v. Wild Canid Survival and Research Center. 599
Mannix v. United States 215, 216
Marendi; People v.. 215
Martinez; United States v.. 311
McPartlin; United States v. 849
McWhorter v. City of Birmingham 205
Melendez-Diaz v. Massachusetts 477
Mezzanatto; United States v.. . . .246; 253; 257; 259; 263

Michelson v. United States. 209; 211; 221
Michigan v. Bryant. 485
Miller v. Federal Express Corp 856
Miranda v. Arizona. 820
Mutual Life Ins. Co. v. Hillmon. 692; 696

N

Nash v. United States 212
Neil v. Biggers. 572
Newman; United States v.. 281
Newton v. Rumery. 265
Nix v. Whiteside 837; 867
Nixon; United States v.. 846

O

Ohio v. Roberts. 447; 463
Ohler v. United States 158
Olano; United States v.. 262
Old Chief v. United States 69; 87; 180
Owens; United States v.. 590

P

Page; People v.. 223
Palmer v. Hoffman 672; 702
Payton; United States v.. 301
People v. (see name of defendant). . . . .
Peretz v. United States. 259
Pheaster; United States v.. 695
Pierce v. Tripler & Co.. 240
Pittman v. United States 215
Ponder v. Warren Tool Corp. 78
Powell; United States v.. 269
Prewitt; United States v.. 238

R

Ricketts v. Adamson. 259
Robinson; United States v.. 179

S

Sac and Fox Indians of Miss. in Iowa v. Sac and Fox Indians of Miss. in Okl. 260
Salas; People v.. 920
Santobello v. New York. 267
Sealed Case, In re 847
Seiler v. Lucasfilm, Ltd. 873; 884; 891
Senak; United States v. 670
Senra v. Cunningham 176

TABLE OF CASES

[References are to pages]

Shepard v. United States............534
Shepherd; State v..................223
Shull; State v.....................216
Shutte v. Thompson.................259
Sloan v. United States.............215
Sloman; United States v............299
Smith v. State.....................223
Smith v. United States........259; 266
Sowers, State ex rel. v. Olwell....852
Spalitto v. United States..........216
St. Mary's Honor Ctr. v. Hicks.....401
State v. (see name of defendant)......
State ex rel. (see name of relator)...
Stevens; United States v...........268
Stewart v. United States...........216
Succession of (see name of party).....

T

Tanner v. United States............282
Tennessee Valley Auth. v. Hill.....268
Tome v. United States..............581
Tome; United States v..............699
Touche Ross & Co. v. Redington.....268

Trammel v. United States....850; 865; 871
Tupman Thurlow Co. v. S.S. Cap Castillo....260

U

U.S. v. (see name of defendant)........
United States v. (see name of defendant)....
Upjohn Co. v. United States...837; 854; 864; 865

V

Van Gaasbeck; People v..........213, 214
Viliborghi v. State................223

W

Ward v. Succession of Freeman......855
Washington St. Physicians Ins. v. Fisons Corp...204
Wheat v. United States.............261
Williams; State v..................131
Williams v. United States..........215
Williamson v. United States....212; 267; 772
Wing; United States v..............260
Wood v. United States..............212

INDEX

[References are to page numbers.]

A

ACCUSED
Character of, under Rule 404(a)(2)(A) . . . 5.06[B]

ADMISSIBILITY OF HEARSAY STATEMENTS
Rule 803, under
    Generally . . . 14.03
    Beech Aircraft Corporation v. Rainey . . . 14.13[E]
    Business records under Rules 803(6), (7) . . . 14.09
    Contemporaneous utterance under Rule 803(1) . . . 14.05
    Excited utterance under Rule 803(1) . . . 14.05
    Federal Rules, relevant . . . 14.02
    Hearsay exceptions
        Generally . . . 14.11
        Commercial publications under Rule 803(17) . . . 14.11[E]
        Family records under Rules 803(13) . . . 14.11[B]
        Market reports under Rule 803(17) . . . 14.11[E]
        Vital statistics under Rules 803(9), (11), records of . . . 14.11[A]
    Medical diagnosis or treatment under Rule 803(4), statements for . . . 14.07
    Mutual Life Insurance Company v. Hillmon . . . 14.13[A]
    Palmer v. Hoffman . . . 14.13[D]
    Past recollection recorded, Rule 803(5) . . . 14.08
    Presently-existing state of mind, feeling or belief under Rule 803(3) . . . 14.06
    Public records under Rule 803(8) . . . 14.10
    Refreshing recollection, Rule 612 . . . 14.08
    Statements in, hearsay exceptions
        Ancient documents under Rule 803(16) . . . 14.11[D]
        Dispositive documents under Rule 803(15) . . . 14.11[C]
    Trustworthiness . . . 14.04
    United States v. Pheaster . . . 14.13[B]
    United States v. Tome . . . 14.13[C]
Rules 804 and 807, under
    Generally . . . 15.03
    Dying declarations under Rule 804(b)(2) . . . 15.06
    Federal Rules, relevant . . . 15.02
    Former testimony under Rule 804(b)(1) . . . 15.05
    Giles v. California . . . 15.11[B]
    Residual hearsay under Rule 807 . . . 15.09
    Statements against interest under Rule 804(b)(3) . . . 15.07
    Unavailability . . . 15.04

ADMISSIBILITY OF HEARSAY STATEMENTS—Cont.
Rules 804 and 807, under—Cont.
    Williamson v. United States . . . 15.11[A]
    Wrongdoing under Rule 804(b)(6), forfeiture by . . . 15.08

ADVERSARY SYSTEM
Opposing parties statements and . . . 13.04

ADVERSE SPOUSAL TESTIMONY (See PRIVILEGES, subhead: Husband-wife)

ANCIENT DOCUMENTS
Hearsay exceptions under Rule 803(16) . . . 14.11[D]

ATTORNEYS
Competency as witnesses under Rule 605 . . . 7.03[D]
Role at trial
    Generally . . . 2.03; 2.06; 2.07
    Federal Rules, relevant . . . 2.02

AUTHENTICATION AND IDENTIFICATION
Generally . . . 18.05
Federal Rules, relevant . . . 18.02
Procedures for . . . 18.03[B]
Requirement of . . . 18.03[A]
Seiler v. Lucasfilm, Ltd. . . . 18.07

B

BEST EVIDENCE RULE
Generally . . . 18.05
Authentication and identification (See AUTHENTICATION AND IDENTIFICATION)
Federal Rules, relevant . . . 18.02
Original documents
    Production of . . . 18.04[A]
    Requirement of, exceptions to . . . 18.04[B]
Seiler v. Lucasfilm, Ltd. . . . 18.07

BURDENS OF PROOF
Generally . . . 16.03; 16.03[A]; 16.04
County Court of Ulster County v. Allen . . . 16.09
Federal Rules, relevant . . . 16.02

BUSINESS RECORDS
Hearsay exception under Rule 803(6),(7) . . . 14.09

C

CHARACTER AND HABIT EVIDENCE
Generally . . . 5.09
Accused character under Rule 404(a)(2)(A) . . . 5.06[B]
Admissible instances of propensity evidence . . . 5.06[A]

[References are to page numbers.]

CHARACTER AND HABIT EVIDENCE—Cont.
Basics
    Act versus mental propensity evidence under Rules 404(a) and 405(b) . . . 5.03[B]
    Defining character evidence . . . 5.03[A]
Character of accused under Rule 404(a)(2)(A) . . . 5.06[B]
Criminal defendant, prosecutor attack on . . . 5.06[D]
Defendant's character in criminal or civil sexual assault or child molestation case under Rules 413, 414, 415 . . . 5.07[B]
Diagrammatic approach
    Generally . . . 5.09[B]
    Categorizing character . . . 5.09[B][1]
Evidence, propensity
    Act versus mental, under Rules 404(a) and 405(b) . . . 5.03[B]
    Admissible instances of . . . 5.06[A]
Exceptions to Rule 404(a) propensity ban
    Admissible instances of propensity evidence . . . 5.06[A]
    Character of accused under Rule 404(a)(2)(A) . . . 5.06[B]
    Homicide cases, victim's character under Rule 404(a)(2)(C) . . . 5.06[E]
    Victim's character in cases other than homicide and sexual misconduct under Rule 404(a)(2)(B) . . . 5.06[C]
Federal Rules, relevant . . . 5.02
Forms of
    Generally . . . 5.04[B]
    Admissibility of reputation, opinion, and specific acts evidence under Rule 404(b), 1st Sentence, Rule 405(a)–(b) . . . 5.04[A]
Habit . . . 5.11[B]
Impeachment under Rules 404(a)(3), 608, and 609
    Distinction between impeachment and substantive evidence . . . 5.08[A]
    Prior convictions impeachment under Rule 609
        Generally . . . 5.08[C]
        Crimen Falsi convictions under Rule 609(a)(2) . . . 5.08[C][2]
        Eliciting details . . . 5.08[C][5]
        Extrinsic evidence . . . 5.08[C][4]
        Felony convictions under Rule 609(a)(1) . . . 5.08[C][1]
        Misdemeanor convictions under Rule 609(a)(2) . . . 5.08[C][2]
        Special qualifications to Rule 609 . . . 5.08[C][3]
    Rule 608
        Generally . . . 5.08[B]
        Opinion under Rule 608(a) . . . 5.08[B][1]
        Reputation under Rule 608(a) . . . 5.08[B][1]
        Specific acts under Rule 608(b) . . . 5.08[B][2]
Laying foundation for
    Generally . . . 5.05
    Opinion . . . 5.05[B]
    Reputation . . . 5.05[A]

CHARACTER AND HABIT EVIDENCE—Cont.
Mental propensity uses (See subhead: Specific acts offered for non-character uses under Rule 404(b))
Michelson v. United States . . . 5.13
Non-propensity uses under Rules 401, 404(a), 405(b) . . . 5.10
Propensity evidence
    Act versus mental, under Rules 404(a) and 405(b) . . . 5.03[B]
    Admissible instances of . . . 5.06[A]
Prosecutor attack on criminal defendant . . . 5.06[D]
Rape shield law
    Admissibility procedure determination under Rule 412(c) . . . 5.07[A][4]
    Civil cases exceptions under Rule 412(b)(2) . . . 5.07[A][3]
    Criminal cases exceptions under Rule 412(b)(1) . . . 5.07[A][2]
    Rule 412(a) . . . 5.07[A][1]
Schematic . . . 5.09[A]
Sexual offenses and misconduct
    Defendant's character in criminal or civil sexual assault or child molestation case under Rule 413, 414, 415 . . . 5.07[B]
    Rape Shield Law (See subhead: Rape shield law)
Specific acts offered for non-character uses under Rule 404(b)
    Balancing, Rule 403 . . . 5.11[A][1][c]
    Common plan . . . 5.11[A][6]
    Design . . . 5.11[A][6]
    Identity . . . 5.11[A][4]
    Intent . . . 5.11[A][5]
    Knowledge . . . 5.11[A][5]
    Motive . . . 5.11[A][2]
    Opportunity . . . 5.11[A][3]
    Proof of specific acts . . . 5.11[A][1][b]
    Purposes other than character . . . 5.11[A][1][a]
    Scheme . . . 5.11[A][6]

CHILD MOLESTATION
Defendant's character under Rule 413, 414, 415 . . . 5.07[B]

CIRCUMSTANTIAL EVIDENCE
Distinguishing from direct evidence . . . 1.06

CIVIL SETTLEMENT AGREEMENTS AND NEGOTIATIONS EVIDENCE UNDER RULE 408
Quasi-privileges . . . 6.05[B]

COMMERCIAL PUBLICATIONS
Hearsay exceptions under Rule 803(17) . . . 14.11[E]

COMMON PLAN
Specific acts evidence . . . 5.11[A][6]

[References are to page numbers.]

COMPROMISE, OFFERS TO (See QUASI-PRIVILEGES, subhead: Offers to compromise under Rules 408 and 410)

CONFIDENTIAL COMMUNICATION PRIVILEGES
Generally . . . 17.03[E]
Husband-wife privilege . . . 17.05[A][2]

CONFRONTATION CLAUSE (See HEARSAY RULE)

CONTRADICTION
Impeachment of witnesses . . . 7.04[C][2]

CONVICTIONS OF CRIME (See IMPEACHMENT OF WITNESSES, subhead: Convictions of crime)

CRIMINAL CASE
Probability evidence of identity in . . . 4.04

CROSS-EXAMINATION
Generally . . . 7.03[G][3]
Expert testimony . . . 9.04[C]

D

DEFENDANT
Character of, in criminal or civil sexual assault or child molestation case under Rule 413, 414, 415 . . . 5.07[B]
Criminal, prosecutor attack on . . . 5.06[D]

DESIGN
Specific acts evidence . . . 5.11[A][6]

DIRECT EVIDENCE
Distinguishing from circumstantial evidence . . . 1.06

DIRECT EXAMINATION
Generally . . . 7.03[G][2]

DYING DECLARATIONS
Hearsay exception under Rule 804(b)(2) . . . 15.06

E

EVIDENCE
Best evidence rule (See BEST EVIDENCE RULE)
Categories of . . . 1.05
Character and habit (See CHARACTER AND HABIT EVIDENCE)
Circumstantial . . . 1.06
Different meanings of . . . 1.04
Direct . . . 1.06
Distinction, another helpful . . . 1.06
Exclusions of relevant (See QUASI-PRIVILEGES)
Expert opinion (See EXPERT OPINION EVIDENCE)
Federal Rules, relevant . . . 1.02
Lawsuits of . . . 1.03
Lay opinion (See LAY OPINION EVIDENCE)
Peers, jury of . . . 1.08
Prejudicial (See PREJUDICIAL EVIDENCE)

EVIDENCE—Cont.
Real . . . 1.05
Representative . . . 1.05
Rules of . . . 1.03
Scientific (See SCIENTIFIC EVIDENCE)
Testimonial . . . 1.05
Trial courts, in . . . 1.07

EXAMINATION OF WITNESSES
Generally . . . 7.03; 7.03[A]; 7.05
Attorney's competency as witnesses under Rule 605 . . . 7.03[D]
Competency
   Generally . . . 7.03[B]
   Attorney's as witnesses under Rule 605 . . . 7.03[D]
   Judge's as witnesses under Rule 605 . . . 7.03[D]
   Jurors' as witnesses under Rule 606 . . . 7.03[D]
Eligibility to testify . . . 7.03[B]
Federal Rules, relevant . . . 7.02
Judge's competency as witnesses under Rule 605 . . . 7.03[D]
Jurors' competency as witnesses under Rule 606 . . . 7.03[D]
Personal knowledge, requirement of . . . 7.03[C]
Strategy, witness
   Generally . . . 7.03[G][1]
   Cross-examination . . . 7.03[G][3]
   Direct examination . . . 7.03[G][2]
Testify, eligibility to . . . 7.03[B]
Testimony, sequential order and objections to . . . 7.03[F]

EXPERT OPINION EVIDENCE
Daubert test
   Factors . . . 9.05[B][2][b][i]
   Federal Rules of evidence, interpretation of . . . 9.05[B][2][a]
   Gatekeeping function . . . 9.05[B][2][b][iii]
   Procedural concerns . . . 9.05[B][2][b][iv]
   Testability, defining . . . 9.05[B][2][b][ii]
Expert testimony (See EXPERT TESTIMONY)
Federal Rules, relevant . . . 9.02
Frye test
   Generally . . . 9.05[B][1][a]
   Forensic evidence, developmental stages of . . . 9.05[B][1][d]
   Relevant field, defining . . . 9.05[B][1][c]
   Validity versus reliability . . . 9.05[B][1][b]
Major premises
   Scientific evidence (See subhead: Scientific evidence)
   Technical and other specialized knowledge, evidence based on . . . 9.05[C]
   Terms, definition of . . . 9.05[A]
Minor premises . . . 9.06
Review problems . . . 9.07
Scientific evidence
   Daubert test (See subhead: *Daubert* test)
   Frye test (See subhead: *Frye* test)
Social sciences, evidence based on . . . 9.05[C]

[References are to page numbers.]

EXPERT TESTIMONY
Direct examination of
    Generally . . . 9.04[B][3]
    Federal Rules of evidence, liberalization under
        Rule 703 . . . 9.04[B][2][a]
        Rule 705 . . . 9.04[B][2][b]
    Hypothetical question and four data sources
        . . . 9.04[B][1]
    Opinion rule . . . 9.04[B][6]
    Out-of-court statements . . . 9.04[B][6]
    Professional certainty, reasonable degree of
        . . . 9.04[B][5]
    Ultimate issue rule . . . 9.04[B][4]
Nature of
    Necessity of . . . 9.03[A]
    Special expert admissibility rules, necessity of
        . . . 9.03[C]
    Syllogistic nature of . . . 9.03[B]
Presentation of
    Cross-examination . . . 9.04[C]
    Direct examination (See subhead: Direct examination of)
    Helpfulness of expert opinion . . . 9.04[A]
    Qualifications of expert . . . 9.04[A]

EXTRINSIC IMPEACHMENT
Impeachment of witnesses . . . 7.04[C][8]
Intrinsic impeachment, compared with . . . 7.04[B]

F

FAMILY RECORDS
Hearsay exceptions under Rules 803(13)
    . . . 14.11[B]

FIFTH AMENDMENT
Privilege against self-incrimination . . . 17.05[C][4]

H

HABIT EVIDENCE (See CHARACTER AND HABIT EVIDENCE)

HEARSAY RULE
Generally . . . 10.03
Adversary system and
    Admitting hearsay "for what it's worth," argument for . . . 10.05[C]
    Cross-examine, protects right to . . . 10.05[A]
    Dangers, hearsay . . . 10.05[B]
    Problems, hearsay policy . . . 10.05[D]
Assertions
    Implied . . . 10.08[B][6]
    Invisible . . . 10.08[B][3]
    Linked . . . 10.08[B][2]
    Sub-assertions . . . 10.08[B][1]
Bullcoming v. New Mexico . . . 10.13[F]
Circumstantial evidence, statement as . . . 10.09[C]
Conduct, assertive . . . 10.08[B][5]
Confrontation clause and . . . 10.11
Crawford v. Washington . . . 10.13[B]
Davis v. Washington . . . 10.13[C]
Declarants
    Definition . . . 10.06[A]

HEARSAY RULE—Cont.
Declarants—Cont.
    Problems . . . 10.06[B]
Definition : . . . 10.04
Federal Rules, relevant . . . 10.02
Melendez-Diaz v. Massachusetts . . . 10.13[D]
Michigan v. Bryant . . . 10.13[E]
Misconceptions
    Generally . . . 10.09
    Circumstantial evidence, statement as
        . . . 10.09[C]
    Paraphrase as hearsay . . . 10.09[A]
    Police officer's presence, statement made in
        . . . 10.09[D]
    Witness as declarant . . . 10.09[B]
Non-hearsay purposes (See NON-HEARSAY PURPOSES FOR OUT-OF-COURT STATEMENTS)
Opposing parties statements, admissibility of (See OPPOSING PARTIES STATEMENTS, ADMISSIBILITY OF)
Out-of-court statements
    General rule . . . 10.07[A]
    Problems . . . 10.07[B]
Paraphrase as hearsay . . . 10.09[A]
Police officer's presence, statement made in
    . . . 10.09[D]
Rule 803, admissibility of hearsay statements under (See ADMISSIBILITY OF HEARSAY STATEMENTS, subhead: Rule 803, under)
Rules 804 and 807, admissibility of hearsay statements under (See ADMISSIBILITY OF HEARSAY STATEMENTS, subhead: Rules 804 and 807, under)
Statement
    Definition . . . 10.08[A]
    Hidden statements
        Generally . . . 10.08[B]
        Assertive conduct . . . 10.08[B][5]
        Implied assertions . . . 10.08[B][6]
        Invisible assertions . . . 10.08[B][3]
        Linked assertions . . . 10.08[B][2]
        Sub-assertions . . . 10.08[B][1]
        Vicarious assertions . . . 10.08[B][4]
    Problems . . . 10.08[C]
Testifying witnesses, admissibility of (See TESTIFYING WITNESSES, ADMISSIBILITY OF)
United States v. Zenni . . . 10.13[A]
Vicarious . . . 10.08[B][4]
Witness as declarant . . . 10.09[B]

HOMICIDE CASES
Victim's character under Rule 404(a)(2)(C)
    . . . 5.06[E]

HUSBAND-WIFE PRIVILEGE (See PRIVILEGES, subhead: Husband-wife)

I

IDENTITY
Probability evidence of . . . 4.04
Specific acts evidence . . . 5.11[A][4]

[References are to page numbers.]

IMPEACHMENT OF WITNESSES
Generally . . . 7.04[A]; 7.05
Bias . . . 7.04[C][3]
Contradiction . . . 7.04[C][2]
Convictions of crime
    Generally . . . 7.04[C][4]
    Crimes of dishonesty . . . 7.04[C][4][a]
    False statement . . . 7.04[C][4][a]
    Felony convictions . . . 7.04[C][4][b]
Extrinsic impeachment
    Generally . . . 7.04[C][8]
    Intrinsic impeachment, compared with . . . 7.04[B]
Federal Rules of evidence . . . 7.02
Intrinsic and extrinsic, compared . . . 7.04[B]
Memory, refreshing witness's . . . 7.04[G]
Prior inconsistent statements
    Generally . . . 7.04[C][7]
    Admissibility of, two-way . . . 7.04[D]
Rehabilitation of witnesses . . . 7.04[F]
Statutes . . . 7.04[H]
Testimonial capacities . . . 7.04[C][6]
Truthfulness, poor character for . . . 7.04[C][8]
Types of
    Generally . . . 7.04[C][1]
    Bias . . . 7.04[C][3]
    Contradiction . . . 7.04[C][2]
    Convictions of crime (See subhead: Convictions of crime)
    Extrinsic impeachment only . . . 7.04[C][8]
    Inconsistent statements, prior . . . 7.04[C][7]
    Prior untruthful acts . . . 7.04[C][5]
    Testimonial capacities . . . 7.04[C][6]
    Truthfulness, poor character for . . . 7.04[C][8]
Untruthful acts, prior . . . 7.04[C][5]

INCONSISTENT STATEMENTS, PRIOR
Generally . . . 7.04[C][7]
Two-way admissibility of some . . . 7.04[D]

INTENT
Specific acts evidence . . . 5.11[A][5]

INTRINSIC IMPEACHMENT
Extrinsic impeachment, compared with . . . 7.04[B]

J

JUDGES
Competency as witnesses under Rule 605 . . . 7.03[D]
Role of
    Generally . . . 2.03; 2.04; 2.07
    Admissibility, questions of . . . 2.04[A]
    Appellate judges . . . 2.04[B]
    Federal Rules, relevant . . . 2.02

JUDICIAL NOTICE
Generally . . . 16.03; 16.03[C]; 16.07
County Court of Ulster County v. Allen . . . 16.09
Federal Rules, relevant . . . 16.02

JURORS
Competency as witnesses under Rule 606 . . . 7.03[D]

JURY
Peers, jury of . . . 1.08
Role of
    Generally . . . 2.03; 2.05; 2.07
    Federal Rules, relevant . . . 2.02

K

KNOWLEDGE
Examination of witnesses . . . 7.03[C]
Specific acts evidence . . . 5.11[A][5]

L

LAY OPINION EVIDENCE
Expert testimony, distinguishing between lay and
    Generally . . . 8.03[A]
    Conditional relevance, connection to . . . 8.03[B]
    Laypersons offering opinions
        Caveats . . . 8.03[C][4]
        Collective facts . . . 8.03[C][2]
        Perceptions of witness, rationally based on . . . 8.03[C][1]
        Skilled lay observers . . . 8.03[C][3]
Federal Rules, relevant . . . 8.02
Testimony, distinguishing between lay and expert (See LAY OPINION EVIDENCE, subhead: Expert testimony, distinguishing between lay and)

LIABILITY INSURANCE
Quasi-privileges . . . 6.07

M

MARKET REPORTS
Hearsay exceptions under Rule 803(17) . . . 14.11[E]

MEDICAL DIAGNOSIS OR TREATMENT
Hearsay statements under Rule 803(4) . . . 14.07

MEDICAL EXPENSES
Quasi-privileges . . . 6.06

MEMORY
Refreshing witness's . . . 7.04[G]

MINI-TRIALS
Hearsay admissibility through, laying foundations for . . . 12.05

MOTIVE
Specific acts evidence . . . 5.11[A][2]

N

NON-HEARSAY PURPOSES FOR OUT-OF-COURT STATEMENTS
Generally . . . 11.03

[References are to page numbers.]

NON-HEARSAY PURPOSES FOR OUT-OF-COURT STATEMENTS—Cont.
Contradict (impeach) testimony, assertion offered to . . . 11.07[E]
Determination relevance of claimed . . . 11.05
Federal Rules, relevant . . . 11.02
Identifying purpose . . . 11.04
Probative value versus unfair prejudice . . . 11.06
Uses, common
    Generally . . . 11.07[A]
    Contradict (impeach) testimony . . . 11.07[E]
    Declarant's state of mind . . . 11.07[B]
    Listener's state of mind . . . 11.07[C]
    Provide context and meaning . . . 11.07[F]
    Verbal act . . . 11.07[D]
Verbal act, assertion offered to . . . 11.07[D]

O

OPINION EVIDENCE
Foundation for . . . 5.05[B]
Impeachment . . . 5.08[B][1]
Lay (See LAY OPINION EVIDENCE)
Specific acts evidence . . . 5.04[A]

OPPORTUNITY
Specific acts evidence . . . 5.11[A][3]

OPPOSING PARTIES STATEMENTS, ADMISSIBILITY OF
Generally . . . 13.03
Adoptive statements, Rule 801(d)(2)(B) . . . 13.06
Adversary system and . . . 13.04
Authorized statements, Rule 801(d)(2)(C) . . . 13.07
Bourjaily V. United States . . . 13.11
Co-conspirator statements, Rule 801(d)(2)(E) . . . 13.09
Declarant as . . . 13.05
Employee statements, Rule 801(d)(2)(D) . . . 13.08
Federal Rules, relevant . . . 13.02

P

PAST RECOLLECTION RECORDED
Hearsay statements under Rule 803(5) . . . 14.08

PHYSICIAN-PATIENT PRIVILEGES
Generally . . . 17.05[C][3]

POLICE OFFICERS
Hearsay when statement made in presence of officer . . . 10.09[D]

PREJUDICIAL EVIDENCE
Generally . . . 4.03; 4.08
Events, similar . . . 4.07
Evidence of excessive violence . . . 4.05
Federal Rules, relevant . . . 4.02
Happenings, similar . . . 4.07
Identity in criminal case, probability evidence of . . . 4.04
Occurrences, similar . . . 4.07
Old Chief v. United States . . . 4.10[B]

PREJUDICIAL EVIDENCE—Cont.
People v. Collins . . . 4.10[A]
Probability evidence of identity in criminal case . . . 4.04
Scientific evidence . . . 4.06

PRESUMPTIONS
Generally . . . 16.03; 16.03[B]
Civil cases, in . . . 16.05
County Court of Ulster County v. Allen . . . 16.09
Criminal cases, in . . . 16.06
Federal Rules, relevant . . . 16.02

PRIVILEGES
Generally . . . 17.03; 17.05[C]; 17.07
Adverse spousal testimony and confidential communications (See subhead: Husband-wife)
Attorney-client privilege
    Corporate client and . . . 17.05[B][2]
    Elements of . . . 17.05[B][1]
Confidential communication . . . 17.03[E]
Evidence, definition of . . . 17.03[A]
Federal Rules, relevant
    Generally . . . 17.02
    Approach to . . . 17.04
Fifth amendment privilege against self-incrimination . . . 17.05[C][4]
Husband-wife
    Generally . . . 17.05[A]
    Adverse spousal testimony privilege . . . 17.05[A][1]
    Confidential communications . . . 17.05[A][2]
Jaffee v. Redmond . . . 17.09[C]
Nix v. Whiteside . . . 17.09[B]
Operation of . . . 17.03[D]
Physician-patient . . . 17.05[C][3]
Proposed (rejected) rules . . . 17.02
Psychotherapist-patient . . . 17.05[C][2]
Public policy-based . . . 17.03[F]
Quasi-privileges (See QUASI-PRIVILEGES)
Sources of . . . 17.03[C]
State law privileges
    Generally . . . 17.06
    Federal and state privileges . . . 17.03[B]
Upjohn Co. v. United States . . . 17.09[A]
Work product . . . 17.05[C][1]

PROPENSITY
Ban, exceptions to Rule 404(a) (See CHARACTER AND HABIT EVIDENCE, subhead: Exceptions to Rule 404(a) propensity ban)
Evidence
    Act versus mental, under Rules 404(a) and 405(b) . . . 5.03[B]
    Admissible instances of . . . 5.06[A]

PSYCHOTHERAPIST-PATIENT PRIVILEGE
Generally . . . 17.05[C][2]

PUBLIC POLICY-BASED PRIVILEGES
Generally . . . 17.03[F]

[References are to page numbers.]

Q

QUASI-PRIVILEGES
Generally . . . 6.03
Federal Rules, relevant . . . 6.02
Liability insurance under Rule 411 . . . 6.07
Offers to compromise under Rules 408 and 410
    Civil settlement agreements and negotiations evidence under Rule 408 . . . 6.05[B]
    Compromise in civil and criminal cases, importance of . . . 6.05[A]
    Plea bargains and related statements in criminal cases under Rule 410 . . . 6.05[C]
Payment of medical and similar expenses . . . 6.06
Subsequent remedial measures under Rule 407 . . . 6.04
United States v. Mezzanatto . . . 6.09

R

RAPE SHIELD LAW (See CHARACTER AND HABIT EVIDENCE, subhead: Rape shield law)

REAL EVIDENCE
Generally . . . 1.05

REHABILITATION
Witnesses . . . 7.04[F]

RELEVANCE
Generally . . . 3.07
Comparing rules . . . 3.06
Conditional . . . 3.05
Defining . . . 3.04
Federal Rules, relevant . . . 3.02
Importance of . . . 3.03
Inadmissible, relevant but (See PREJUDICIAL EVIDENCE)
Knapp v. State . . . 3.09
Non-hearsay purposes, statements offered for . . . 11.05

REMEDIAL MEASURES
Quasi-privileges . . . 6.04

REPRESENTATIVE EVIDENCE
Generally . . . 1.05

REPUTATION
Impeachment . . . 5.08[B][1]
Laying foundation for . . . 5.05[A]
Specific acts evidence . . . 5.04[A]

S

SCIENTIFIC EVIDENCE
Generally . . . 4.06
Daubert test (See EXPERT OPINION EVIDENCE, subhead: *Daubert* test)
Frye test (See EXPERT OPINION EVIDENCE, subhead: *Frye* test)

SEXUAL ASSAULT
Defendant's character under Rule 413, 414, 415 . . . 5.07[B]

SIMILAR OCCURENCES
Prejudicial evidence . . . 4.07

SOCIAL SCIENCE
Expert testimony based on specialized knowledge . . . 9.05[C]

SPECIFIC ACTS
Evidence, admissibility of reputation, opinion under Rule 404(b), 1st Sentence, Rule 405(a)–(b) . . . 5.04[A]
Impeachment under Rule 608(b) . . . 5.08[B][2]
Offered for non-character uses (See CHARACTER AND HABIT EVIDENCE, subhead: Specific acts offered for non-character uses under Rule 404(b))

STATEMENTS
Prior inconsistent . . . 7.04[C][7]
Two-way admissibility of some prior inconsistent . . . 7.04[D]

STATE OF MIND
Presently-existing state of mind, feeling or belief under Rule 803(3) . . . 14.06

T

TESTIFYING WITNESSES, ADMISSIBILITY OF
Generally . . . 12.03
Exemptions versus exceptions . . . 12.04
Federal Rules, relevant . . . 12.02
Mini-trials, establishing foundation through . . . 12.05
Prior statements
    Consistent statements under Rule 801(d)(1)(B) . . . 12.06[C]
    Exempt statements, three categories of . . . 12.06[A]
    Identifications under Rule 801(d)(1)(C) . . . 12.06[D]
    Inconsistent statements under Rule 801(d)(1)(A) . . . 12.06[B]
Tome v. United States . . . 12.08[A]
United States v. Owens . . . 12.08[B]

TESTIMONY
Evidence . . . 1.05
Examination of witnesses . . . 7.03[F]
Lay and expert, distinguished (See subhead: Expert testimony, distinguishing between lay and)

TRIAL COURTS
Evidence, in . . . 1.07

TRUSTWORTHINESS
Generally . . . 14.04

V

VICTIM'S CHARACTER
Cases other than homicide and sexual misconduct, in . . . 5.06[C]
Homicide cases, under Rule 404(a)(2)(C) . . . 5.06[E]

[References are to page numbers.]

VIOLENCE
Evidence of excessive . . . 4.05

VITAL STATISTICS
Hearsay exceptions under Rules 803(9), (11) . . . 14.11[A]

W

WITNESSES
Admissibility of testifying (See TESTIFYING WITNESSES, ADMISSIBILITY OF)

WITNESSES—Cont.
Examination of (See EXAMINATION OF WITNESSES)
Impeachment of (See IMPEACHMENT OF WITNESSES)

WORK PRODUCT PRIVILEGE
Generally . . . 17.05[C][1]

WRONGDOING, FORFEITURE BY
Exceptions to hearsay rule . . . 15.08